Literature
A Portable Anthology

Literature
A Portable Anthology

Edited by

JANET E. GARDNER
University of Massachusetts at Dartmouth

BEVERLY LAWN
Adelphi University

JACK RIDL
Hope College

PETER SCHAKEL
Hope College

Bedford/St. Martin's   BOSTON   ◆   NEW YORK

For Bedford/St. Martin's
Executive Editor: Stephen A. Scipione
Production Editor: Deborah Baker
Production Supervisor: Yexenia Markland
Marketing Manager: Jenna Bookin Barry
Editorial Assistant: Anne Noyes
Copyeditor: Melissa Cook
Text Design: Sandra Rigney
Cover Design: Donna Lee Dennison
Cover Art: © Kamil Vojnar/Photonica
Composition: Stratford Publishing Services, Inc.
Printing and Binding: Haddon Craftsmen, Inc., an R.R. Donnelley & Sons Company

President: Joan E. Feinberg
Editorial Director: Denise B. Wydra
Editor in Chief: Karen S. Henry
Director of Marketing: Karen Melton Soeltz
Director of Editing, Design, and Production: Marcia Cohen
Managing Editor: Elizabeth M. Schaaf

Library of Congress Control Number: 2003107457

Manufactured in the United States of America.

8 7 6 5 4
f e d

For information, write: Bedford/St. Martin's, 75 Arlington Street, Boston, MA 02116 (617-399-4000)

ISBN: 0–312–41279–7

Acknowledgments
Chinua Achebe, "Civil Peace" from *Girls at War and Other Stories.* Copyright © 1972, 1973 by Chinua Achebe. Reprinted by permission of Harold Ober Associates, Incorporated and Doubleday, a division of Random House, Inc.
Ai, "Why Can't I Leave You?" from *Vice: New and Selected Poems.* Copyright © 1999 by Ai. Used by permission of W. W. Norton & Company, Inc.
Sherman Alexie, "Postcards to Columbus" from *Old Shirts and New Skins.* Copyright © 1993 by Sherman Alexie. Reprinted by permission of the author.

Acknowledgments and copyrights are listed at the back of the book on pages 1457–66, which constitute an extension of the copyright page. It is a violation of the law to reproduce these selections by any means whatsoever without the written permission of the copyright holder.

Preface for Instructors

Literature: A Portable Anthology presents, in a compact and highly afford-able format, an ample and flexible choice of fiction, poetry, and drama for introductory literature courses. Adapted from other volumes in the Bedford Portable Anthology series—*40 Short Stories, 250 Poems,* and *12 Plays*—*Literature: A Portable Anthology* features a well-balanced and teachable selection of classic and contemporary works, arranged chrono-logically and by genre. The stories, poems, and plays are complemented by editorial matter that offers enough help for students learning to think, read, and write about literature, without the copiousness that might interfere with their enjoyment of the literary works.

In these pages students will discover:

- 35 engaging and significant stories from classic authors like Edgar Allan Poe and William Faulkner and current writers such as Alice Walker and Sandra Cisneros;

- A judicious and varied selection of 250 poems—not only an abun-dant selection of many classic and frequently assigned works by canonical writers such as William Blake, Emily Dickinson, Lang-ston Hughes, and Elizabeth Bishop, but also the most diverse sel-ection of contemporary American poetry in an anthology of this scope—poems by Alberto Ríos, Li-Young Lee, Naomi Shihab Nye, Thylias Moss, Sherman Alexie, and many others.

- A teaching canon of 9 plays—from Sophocles' classical tragedy *Oedipus Rex* to August Wilson's profound and recent *The Piano Les-son,* the selection represents important works in the Western dra-matic tradition as well as a core of plays most frequently assigned and popular in the classroom.

At the back of the book students will find biographical notes on every author, a glossary of literary terms, and an index of authors, titles, and first lines to help them quickly find the literature they are looking for.

To help students read and write more effectively about literature, an appendix (written by Janet E. Gardner and also available as a separate supplementary volume, *Writing about Literature: A Portable Guide*) explains how to think critically, read analytically, and write a variety of commonly assigned papers about literature, from summaries to research papers, with several sample student papers included as models.

A companion Web site (<www.bedfordstmartins.com/portablelit>) presents access to the suite of Bedford/St. Martin's Online Literature Resources, with specific instructor and student resources for *Literature: A Portable Anthology*. Book-specific resources include a discussion of how to read poetry, various pedagogical groupings of poems, an annotated list of video resources, and a brief history of Western theater.

ACKNOWLEDGMENTS

At Bedford/St. Martin's, the editors would like to thank retired publisher Charles H. Christensen, who inaugurated the Portable Anthology series; Bedford/St. Martin's president Joan E. Feinberg; managing editor Elizabeth Schaaf; executive editor Steve Scipione; editorial assistant Anne Noyes; production editor Deborah Baker; and permissions manager Sandy Schechter.

Beverly Lawn prepared the materials for the fiction section, Jack Ridl and Peter Schakel for the poetry section, and Janet E. Gardner for the drama section. Beverly Lawn particularly thanks her husband, Robert Lawn, and her daughters, Hilary Cantilina and Pamela Lawn-Williams, for their help. Jack Ridl and Peter Schakel are grateful to their Hope College colleagues, Susan Atefat Peckham, Marla Lunderberg, Jesse Montaño, and William Pannapacker; to Charles Huttar; and to Myra Kohsel, office manager for the Department of English at Hope College. Janet Gardner deeply thanks Stephanie Tucker, Parmita Kapadia, Sarah Johnson, and Patrick McCorkle for their contributions and support.

Contents

PART TWO. 250 POEMS   369

Contents

PART TWO. 250 POEMS   369

PART THREE. 9 PLAYS 717

PART ONE

35 Stories

NATHANIEL HAWTHORNE [1804–1864]

Young Goodman Brown

Young Goodman Brown came forth at sunset into the street at Salem village; but put his head back, after crossing the threshold, to exchange a parting kiss with his young wife. And Faith, as the wife was aptly named, thrust her own pretty head into the street, letting the wind play with the pink ribbons of her cap while she called to Goodman Brown.

"Dearest heart," whispered she, softly and rather sadly, when her lips were close to his ear, "prithee put off your journey until sunrise and sleep in your own bed to-night. A lone woman is troubled with such dreams and such thoughts that she's afeared of herself sometimes. Pray tarry with me this night, dear husband, of all nights in the year."

"My love and my Faith," replied young Goodman Brown, "of all nights in the year, this one night must I tarry away from thee. My journey, as thou callest it, forth and back again, must needs be done 'twixt now and sunrise. What, my sweet, pretty wife, dost thou doubt me already, and we but three months married?"

"Then God bless you!" said Faith, with the pink ribbons, "and may you find all well when you come back."

"Amen!" cried Goodman Brown. "Say thy prayers, dear Faith, and go to bed at dusk, and no harm will come to thee."

So they parted; and the young man pursued his way until, being about to turn the corner by the meeting-house, he looked back and saw the head of Faith still peeping after him with a melancholy air, in spite of her pink ribbons.

"Poor little Faith!" thought he, for his heart smote him. "What a wretch am I to leave her on such an errand! She talks of dreams, too. Methought as she spoke there was trouble in her face, as if a dream had warned her what work is to be done to-night. But no, no; 't would kill her to think it. Well, she's a blessed angel on earth, and after this one night I'll cling to her skirts and follow her to heaven."

With this excellent resolve for the future, Goodman Brown felt himself justified in making more haste on his present evil purpose. He had taken a dreary road, darkened by all the gloomiest trees of the forest, which barely stood aside to let the narrow path creep through, and closed immediately behind. It was all as lonely as could be; and there is this peculiarity in such a solitude, that the traveller knows not who may be concealed by the innumerable trunks and the thick boughs overhead; so that with lonely footsteps he may yet be passing through an unseen multitude.

"There may be a devilish Indian behind every tree," said Goodman Brown to himself; and he glanced fearfully behind him as he added, "What if the devil himself should be at my very elbow!"

His head being turned back, he passed a crook of the road, and, looking forward again, beheld the figure of a man, in grave and decent attire, seated at the foot of an old tree. He arose at Goodman Brown's approach and walked onward side by side with him.

"You are late, Goodman Brown," said he. "The clock of the Old South was striking as I came through Boston, and that is full fifteen minutes agone."

"Faith kept me back a while," replied the young man, with a tremor in his voice, caused by the sudden appearance of his companion, though not wholly unexpected.

It was now deep dusk in the forest, and deepest in that part of it where these two were journeying. As nearly as could be discerned, the second traveller was about fifty years old, apparently in the same rank of life as Goodman Brown, and bearing a considerable resemblance to him, though perhaps more in expression than features. Still they might have been taken for father and son. And yet, though the elder person was as simply clad as the younger, and as simple in manner too, he had an indescribable air of one who knew the world, and who would not have felt abashed at the governor's dinner table or in King William's court, were it possible that his affairs should call him thither. But the only thing about him that could be fixed upon as remarkable was his staff, which bore the likeness of a great black snake, so curiously wrought that it might almost be seen to twist and wriggle itself like a living serpent. This, of course, must have been an ocular deception, assisted by the uncertain light.

"Come, Goodman Brown," cried his fellow-traveller, "this is a dull pace for the beginning of a journey. Take my staff, if you are so soon weary."

"Friend," said the other, exchanging his slow pace for a full stop, "having kept covenant by meeting thee here, it is my purpose now to return whence I came. I have scruples touching the matter thou wot'st of."

"Sayest thou so?" replied he of the serpent, smiling apart. "Let us walk on, nevertheless, reasoning as we go; and if I convince thee not thou shalt turn back. We are but a little way in the forest yet."

"Too far! too far!" exclaimed the goodman, unconsciously resuming his walk. "My father never went into the woods on such an errand, nor his father before him. We have been a race of honest men and good

Christians since the days of the martyrs; and shall I be the first of the name of Brown that ever took this path and kept"—

"Such company, thou wouldst say," observed the elder person, interpreting his pause. "Well said, Goodman Brown! I have been as well acquainted with your family as with ever a one among the Puritans; and that's no trifle to say. I helped your grandfather, the constable, when he lashed the Quaker woman so smartly through the streets of Salem; and it was I that brought your father a pitch-pine knot, kindled at my own hearth, to set fire to an Indian village, in King Philip's war.° They were my good friends, both; and many a pleasant walk have we had along this path, and returned merrily after midnight. I would fain be friends with you for their sake."

"If it be as thou sayest," replied Goodman Brown, "I marvel they never spoke of these matters; or, verily, I marvel not, seeing that the least rumor of the sort would have driven them from New England. We are a people of prayer, and good works to boot, and abide no such wickedness."

"Wickedness or not," said the traveller with the twisted staff, "I have a very general acquaintance here in New England. The deacons of many a church have drunk the communion wine with me; the selectmen of divers towns make me their chairman; and a majority of the Great and General Court are firm supporters of my interest. The governor and I, too—But these are state secrets."

"Can this be so?" cried Goodman Brown, with a stare of amazement at his undisturbed companion. "Howbeit, I have nothing to do with the governor and council; they have their own ways, and are no rule for a simple husbandman like me. But, were I to go on with thee, how should I meet the eye of that good old man, our minister, at Salem village? Oh, his voice would make me tremble both Sabbath day and lecture day."

Thus far the elder traveller had listened with due gravity; but now burst into a fit of irrepressible mirth, shaking himself so violently that his snake-like staff actually seemed to wriggle in sympathy.

"Ha! ha! ha!" shouted he again and again; then composing himself, "Well, go on, Goodman Brown, go on; but, prithee, don't kill me with laughing."

"Well, then, to end the matter at once," said Goodman Brown, considerably nettled, "there is my wife, Faith. It would break her dear little heart; and I'd rather break my own."

"Nay, if that be the case," answered the other, "e'en go thy ways, Goodman Brown. I would not for twenty old women like the one hobbling before us that Faith should come to any harm."

King Philip: Wampanoag chief who waged war against the New England colonists (1675–76).

As he spoke he pointed his staff at a female figure on the path, in whom Goodman Brown recognized a very pious and exemplary dame, who had taught him his catechism in youth, and was still his moral and spiritual adviser, jointly with the minister and Deacon Gookin.

"A marvel, truly that Goody Cloyse should be so far in the wilderness at nightfall," said he. "But with your leave, friend, I shall take a cut through the woods until we have left this Christian woman behind. Being a stranger to you, she might ask whom I was consorting with and whither I was going."

"Be it so," said his fellow-traveller. "Betake you to the woods, and let me keep the path."

Accordingly the young man turned aside, but took care to watch his companion, who advanced softly along the road until he had come within a staff's length of the old dame. She, meanwhile, was making the best of her way, with singular speed for so aged a woman, and mumbling some indistinct words—a prayer, doubtless—as she went. The traveller put forth his staff and touched her withered neck with what seemed the serpent's tail.

"The devil!" screamed the pious old lady.

"Then Goody Cloyse knows her old friend?" observed the traveller, confronting her and leaning on his writhing stick.

"Ah, forsooth, and is it your worship indeed?" cried the good dame. "Yea, truly is it, and in the very image of my old gossip, Goodman Brown, the grandfather of the silly fellow that now is. But—would your worship believe it?—my broomstick hath strangely disappeared, stolen, as I suspect, by that unhanged witch, Goody Cory, and that, too, when I was all anointed with the juice of smallage, and cinquefoil, and wolf's bane"—

"Mingled with fine wheat and the fat of a new-born babe," said the shape of old Goodman Brown.

"Ah, your worship knows the recipe," cried the old lady, cackling aloud. "So, as I was saying, being all ready for the meeting, and no horse to ride on, I made up my mind to foot it; for they tell me there is a nice young man to be taken into communion to-night. But now your good worship will lend me your arm, and we shall be there in a twinkling."

"That can hardly be," answered her friend. "I may not spare you my arm, Goody Cloyse; but here is my staff, if you will."

So saying, he threw it down at her feet, where, perhaps, it assumed life, being one of the rods which its owner had formerly lent to the Egyptian magi. Of this fact, however, Goodman Brown could not take cognizance. He had cast up his eyes in astonishment, and, looking down again, beheld neither Goody Cloyse nor the serpentine staff, but his fellow-traveller alone, who waited for him as calmly as if nothing had happened.

"That old woman taught me my catechism," said the young man; and there was a world of meaning in this simple comment.

They continued to walk onward, while the elder traveller exhorted his companion to make good speed and persevere in the path, discoursing so aptly that his arguments seemed rather to spring up in the bosom of his auditor than to be suggested by himself. As they went, he plucked a branch of maple to serve for a walking stick, and began to strip it of the twigs and little boughs, which were wet with evening dew. The moment his fingers touched them they became strangely withered and dried up as with a week's sunshine. Thus the pair proceeded, at a good free pace, until suddenly, in a gloomy hollow of the road, Goodman Brown sat himself down on the stump of a tree and refused to go any farther.

"Friend," he said, stubbornly, "my mind is made up. Not another step will I budge on this errand. What if a wretched old woman do choose to go to the devil when I thought she was going to heaven: is that any reason why I should quit my dear Faith and go after her?"

"You will think better of this by and by," said his acquaintance, composedly. "Sit here and rest yourself a while; and when you feel like moving again, there is my staff to help you along."

Without more words, he threw his companion the maple stick, and was as speedily out of sight as if he had vanished into the deepening gloom. The young man sat a few moments by the roadside, applauding himself greatly, and thinking with how clear a conscience he should meet the minister in his morning walk, nor shrink from the eye of good old Deacon Gookin. And what calm sleep would be his that very night, which was to have been spent so wickedly, but so purely and sweetly now, in the arms of Faith! Amidst these pleasant and praiseworthy meditations, Goodman Brown heard the tramp of horses along the road, and deemed it advisable to conceal himself within the verge of the forest, conscious of the guilty purpose that had brought him thither, though now so happily turned from it.

On came the hoof tramps and the voices of the riders, two grave old voices, conversing soberly as they drew near. These mingled sounds appeared to pass along the road, within a few yards of the young man's hiding-place; but, owing doubtless to the depth of the gloom at that particular spot, neither the travellers nor their steeds were visible. Though their figures brushed the small boughs by the wayside, it could not be seen that they intercepted, even for a moment, the faint gleam from the strip of bright sky athwart which they must have passed. Goodman Brown alternately crouched and stood on tiptoe, pulling aside the branches and thrusting forth his head as far as he durst without discerning so much as a shadow. It vexed him the more, because he could have sworn, were such a thing possible, that he recognized the voices of the minister and Deacon Gookin, jogging along quietly, as they were wont to do, when bound to some ordination or ecclesiastical council. While yet within hearing, one of the riders stopped to pluck a switch.

"Of the two, reverend sir," said the voice like the deacon's, "I had rather miss an ordination dinner than to-night's meeting. They tell me that some of our community are to be here from Falmouth and beyond, and others from Connecticut and Rhode Island, besides several of the Indian powwows, who, after their fashion, know almost as much deviltry as the best of us. Moreover, there is a goodly young woman to be taken into communion."

"Mighty well, Deacon Gookin!" replied the solemn old tones of the minister. "Spur up, or we shall be late. Nothing can be done, you know, until I get on the ground."

The hoofs clattered again; and the voices, talking so strangely in the empty air, passed on through the forest, where no church had ever been gathered or solitary Christian prayed. Whither, then, could these holy men be journeying so deep into the heathen wilderness? Young Goodman Brown caught hold of a tree for support, being ready to sink down on the ground, faint and overburdened with the heavy sickness of his heart. He looked up to the sky, doubting whether there really was a heaven above him. Yet there was the blue arch, and the stars brightening in it.

"With heaven above and Faith below, I will yet stand firm against the devil!" cried Goodman Brown.

While he still gazed upward into the deep arch of the firmament and had lifted his hands to pray, a cloud, though no wind was stirring, hurried across the zenith and hid the brightening stars. The blue sky was still visible, except directly overhead, where this black mass of cloud was sweeping swiftly northward. Aloft in the air, as if from the depths of the cloud, came a confused and doubtful sound of voices. Once the listener fancied that he could distinguish the accents of towns-people of his own, men and women, both pious and ungodly, many of whom he had met at the communion table, and had seen others rioting at the tavern. The next moment, so indistinct were the sounds, he doubted whether he had heard aught but the murmur of the old forest, whispering without a wind. Then came a stronger swell of those familiar tones, heard daily in the sunshine at Salem village, but never until now from a cloud of night. There was one voice, of a young woman, uttering lamentations, yet with an uncertain sorrow, and entreating for some favor, which, perhaps, it would grieve her to obtain; and all the unseen multitude, both saints and sinners, seemed to encourage her onward.

"Faith!" shouted Goodman Brown, in a voice of agony and desperation; and the echoes of the forest mocked him, crying, "Faith! Faith!" as if bewildered wretches were seeking her all through the wilderness.

The cry of grief, rage, and terror was yet piercing the night, when the unhappy husband held his breath for a response. There was a scream, drowned immediately in a louder murmur of voices, fading into far-off laughter, as the dark cloud swept away, leaving the clear and silent sky above Goodman Brown. But something fluttered lightly down through the air and caught on the branch of a tree. The young man seized it, and beheld a pink ribbon.

"My Faith is gone!" cried he after one stupefied moment. "There is no good on earth; and sin is but a name. Come, devil; for to thee is this world given."

And, maddened with despair, so that he laughed loud and long, did Goodman Brown grasp his staff and set forth again, at such a rate that he seemed to fly along the forest path rather than to walk or run. The road grew wilder and drearier and more faintly traced, and vanished at length, leaving him in the heart of the dark wilderness, still rushing onward with the instinct that guides mortal man to evil. The whole forest was peopled with frightful sounds—the creaking of the trees, the howling of wild beasts, and the yell of Indians; while sometimes the wind tolled like a distant church bell, and sometimes gave a broad roar around the traveller, as if all Nature were laughing him to scorn. But he was himself the chief horror of the scene, and shrank not from its other horrors.

"Ha! ha! ha!" roared Goodman Brown when the wind laughed at him. "Let us hear which will laugh loudest. Think not to frighten me with your deviltry. Come witch, come wizard, come Indian powwow, come devil himself, and here comes Goodman Brown. You may as well fear him as he fear you."

In truth, all through the haunted forest there could be nothing more frightful than the figure of Goodman Brown. On he flew among the black pines, brandishing his staff with frenzied gestures, now giving vent to an inspiration of horrid blasphemy, and now shouting forth such laughter as set all the echoes of the forest laughing like demons around him. The fiend in his own shape is less hideous than when he rages in the breast of man. Thus sped the demoniac on his course, until, quivering among the trees, he saw a red light before him, as when the felled trunks and branches of a clearing have been set on fire, and throw up their lurid blaze against the sky, at the hour of midnight. He paused, in a lull of the tempest that had driven him onward, and heard the swell of what seemed a hymn, rolling solemnly from a distance with the weight of many voices. He knew the tune; it was a familiar one in the choir of the village meeting-house. The verse died heavily away, and was length-ened by a chorus, not of human voices, but of all the sounds of the benighted wilderness pealing in awful harmony together. Goodman Brown cried out, and his cry was lost to his own ear by its unison with the cry of the desert.

In the interval of silence he stole forward until the light glared full upon his eyes. At one extremity of an open space, hemmed in by the dark wall of the forest, arose a rock, bearing some rude, natural resemblance either to an altar or a pulpit, and surrounded by four blazing pines, their tops aflame, their stems untouched, like candles at an evening meeting. The mass of foliage that had overgrown the summit of the rock was all on fire, blazing high into the night and fitfully illuminating the whole field. Each pendent twig and leafy festoon was in a blaze. As the red light arose and fell, a numerous congregation alternately shone forth, then disappeared in shadow, and again grew, as it were, out of the darkness, peopling the heart of the solitary woods at once.

"A grave and dark-clad company," quoth Goodman Brown.

In truth they were such. Among them, quivering to and fro between gloom and splendor, appeared faces that would be seen next day at the council board of the province, and others which, Sabbath after Sabbath, looked devoutly heavenward, and benignantly over the crowded pews, from the holiest pulpits in the land. Some affirm that the lady of the gov-ernor was there. At least there were high dames well known to her, and wives of honored husbands, and widows, a great multitude, and ancient maidens, all of excellent repute, and fair young girls, who trembled lest their mothers should espy them. Either the sudden gleams of light flash-ing over the obscure field bedazzled Goodman Brown, or he recognized a score of the church members of Salem village famous for their especial sanctity. Good old Deacon Gookin had arrived, and waited at the skirts of that venerable saint, his revered pastor. But, irreverently consorting with these grave, reputable, and pious people, these elders of the church, these chaste dames and dewy virgins, there were men of dissolute lives and women of spotted fame, wretches given over to all mean and filthy vice, and suspected even of horrid crimes. It was strange to see that the good shrank not from the wicked, nor were the sinners abashed by the saints. Scattered also among their pale-faced enemies were the Indian priests, or powwows, who had often scared their native forest with more hideous incantations than any known to English witchcraft.

"But where is Faith?" thought Goodman Brown; and, as hope came into his heart, he trembled.

Another verse of the hymn arose, a slow and mournful strain, such as the pious love, but joined to words which expressed all that our nature can conceive of sin, and darkly hinted at far more. Unfathomable to mere mortals is the lore of fiends. Verse after verse was sung; and still the chorus of the desert swelled between like the deepest tone of a mighty organ; and with the final peal of that dreadful anthem there came a sound, as if the roaring wind, the rushing streams, the howling beasts, and every other voice of the unconcerted wilderness were mingling and according with the voice of guilty man in homage to the prince of all. The four blazing pines threw up a loftier flame, and obscurely discovered shapes and visages of horror on the smoke wreaths above the impious assembly. At the same moment the fire on the rock shot redly forth and formed a flowing arch above its base, where now appeared a figure. With reverence be it spoken, the figure bore no slight similitude, both in garb and manner, to some grave divine of the New England churches.

"Bring forth the converts!" cried a voice that echoed through the field and rolled into the forest.

At the word, Goodman Brown stepped forth from the shadow of the trees and approached the congregation, with whom he felt a loathful brotherhood by the sympathy of all that was wicked in his heart. He could have well-nigh sworn that the shape of his own dead father beckoned him to advance, looking downward from a smoke wreath, while a woman, with dim features of despair, threw out her hand to warn him back. Was it his mother? But he had no power to retreat one step, nor to resist, even in thought, when the minister and good old Deacon Gookin seized his arms and led him to the blazing rock. Thither came also the slender form of a veiled female, led between Goody Cloyse, that pious teacher of the catechism, and Martha Carrier, who had received the devil's promise to be queen of hell. A rampant hag was she. And there stood the proselytes beneath the canopy of fire.

"Welcome, my children," said the dark figure, "to the communion of your race. Ye have found thus young your nature and your destiny. My children, look behind you!"

They turned; and flashing forth, as it were, in a sheet of flame, the fiend worshippers were seen; the smile of welcome gleamed darkly on every visage.

"There," resumed the sable form, "are all whom ye have reverenced from youth. Ye deemed them holier than yourselves and shrank from your own sin, contrasting it with their lives of righteousness and prayerful aspirations heavenward. Yet here are they all in my worshipping assembly. This night it shall be granted you to know their secret deeds: how hoary-bearded elders of the church have whispered wanton words to the young maids of their households; how many a woman, eager for widows' weeds, has given her husband a drink at bedtime and let him sleep his last sleep in her bosom; how beardless youths have made haste to inherit their fathers' wealth; and how fair damsels—blush not, sweet ones—have dug little graves in the garden, and bidden me, the sole guest, to an infant's funeral. By the sympathy of your human hearts for sin ye shall scent out all the places—whether in church, bedchamber, street, field, or forest—where crime has been committed, and shall exult to behold the whole earth one stain of guilt, one mighty blood spot. Far more than this. It shall be yours to penetrate, in every bosom, the deep mystery of sin, the fountain of all wicked arts, and which inexhaustibly supplies more evil impulses than human power—than my power at its utmost—can make manifest in deeds. And now, my children, look upon each other."

They did so; and, by the blaze of the hell-kindled torches, the wretched man beheld his Faith, and the wife her husband, trembling before that unhallowed altar.

"Lo, there ye stand, my children," said the figure, in a deep and solemn tone, almost sad with its despairing awfulness, as if his once angelic nature could yet mourn for our miserable race. "Depending upon one another's hearts, ye had still hoped that virtue were not all a dream. Now are ye undeceived. Evil is the nature of mankind. Evil must be your only happiness. Welcome again, my children, to the communion of your race."

"Welcome," repeated the fiend worshippers, in one cry of despair and triumph.

And there they stood, the only pair, as it seemed, who were yet hesitating on the verge of wickedness in this dark world. A basin was hallowed, naturally, in the rock. Did it contain water, reddened by the lurid light? or was it blood? or, perchance, a liquid flame? Herein did the shape of evil dip his hand and prepare to lay the mark of baptism upon their foreheads, that they might be partakers of the mystery of sin, more conscious of the secret guilt of others, both in deed and thought, than they could now be of their own. The husband cast one look at his pale wife, and Faith at him. What polluted wretches would the next glance show them to each other, shuddering alike at what they disclosed and what they saw!

"Faith! Faith!" cried the husband, "look up to heaven, and resist the wicked one."

Whether Faith obeyed he knew not. Hardly had he spoken when he found himself amid calm night and solitude, listening to a roar of the wind which died heavily away through the forest. He staggered against the rock, and felt it chill and damp; while a hanging twig, that had been all on fire, besprinkled his cheek with the coldest dew.

The next morning young Goodman Brown came slowly into the street of Salem village, staring around him like a bewildered man. The good old minister was taking a walk along the graveyard to get an appetite for breakfast and meditate his sermon, and bestowed a blessing, as he passed, on Goodman Brown. He shrank from the venerable saint as if to avoid an anathema. Old Deacon Gookin was at domestic worship, and the holy words of his prayer were heard through the open window. "What God doth the wizard pray to?" quoth Goodman Brown. Goody Cloyse, that excellent old Christian, stood in the early sunshine at her own lattice, catechizing a little girl who had brought her a pint of morning's milk. Goodman Brown snatched away the child as from the grasp of the fiend himself. Turning the corner by the meeting-house, he spied the head of Faith, with the pink ribbons, gazing anxiously forth, and bursting into such joy at sight of him that she skipped along the street and almost kissed her husband before the whole village. But Goodman Brown looked sternly and sadly into her face, and passed on without a greeting.

Had Goodman Brown fallen asleep in the forest and only dreamed a wild dream of a witch-meeting?

Be it so if you will; but, alas! it was a dream of evil omen for young Goodman Brown. A stern, a sad, a darkly meditative, a distrustful, if not a desperate man did he become from the night of that fearful dream. On the Sabbath day, when the congregation were singing a holy psalm, he could not listen because an anthem of sin rushed loudly upon his ear and drowned all the blessed strain. When the minister spoke from the pulpit with power and fervid eloquence, and, with his hand on the open Bible, of the sacred truths of our religion, and of saint-like lives and triumphant deaths, and of future bliss or misery unutterable, then did Goodman Brown turn pale, dreading lest the roof should thunder down upon the gray blasphemer and his hearers. Often, awaking suddenly at midnight, he shrank from the bosom of Faith; and at morning or eventide, when the family knelt down at prayer, he scowled and muttered to himself, and gazed sternly at his wife, and turned away. And when he had lived long, and was borne to his grave a hoary corpse, followed by Faith, an aged woman, and children and grandchildren, a goodly procession, besides neighbors not a few, they carved no hopeful verse upon his tombstone, for his dying hour was gloom.

[1835]

EDGAR ALLAN POE [1809–1849]

The Cask of Amontillado

The thousand injuries of Fortunato I had borne as I best could; but when he ventured upon insult, I vowed revenge. You, who so well know the nature of my soul, will not suppose, however, that I gave utterance to a threat. *At length* I would be avenged; this was a point definitely settled— but the very definitiveness with which it was resolved precluded the idea of risk. I must not only punish, but punish with impunity. A wrong is unredressed when retribution overtakes its redresser. It is equally unredressed when the avenger fails to make himself felt as such to him who has done the wrong.

It must be understood, that neither by word nor deed had I given Fortunato cause to doubt my good-will. I continued, as was my wont, to smile in his face, and he did not perceive that my smile *now* was at the thought of his immolation.

He had a weak point—this Fortunato—although in other regards he was a man to be respected and even feared. He prided himself on his connoisseurship in wine. Few Italians have the true virtuoso spirit. For the most part their enthusiasm is adopted to suit the time and opportunity—to practise imposture upon the British and Austrian *millionaires*. In painting and gemmary Fortunato, like his countrymen, was a quack—but in the matter of old wines he was sincere. In this respect I did not differ from him materially: I was skilful in the Italian vintages myself, and bought largely whenever I could.

It was about dusk, one evening during the supreme madness of the carnival season, that I encountered my friend. He accosted me with excessive warmth, for he had been drinking much. The man wore motley. He had on a tight-fitting parti-striped dress, and his head was surmounted by the conical cap and bells. I was so pleased to see him, that I thought I should never have done wringing his hand.

I said to him: "My dear Fortunato, you are luckily met. How remarkably well you are looking to-day! But I have received a pipe° of what passes for Amontillado, and I have my doubts."

Pipe: A large cask.

"How?" said he. "Amontillado? A pipe? Impossible! And in the middle of the carnival!"

"I have my doubts," I replied; "and I was silly enough to pay the full Amontillado price without consulting you in the matter. You were not to be found, and I was fearful of losing a bargain."

"Amontillado!"

"I have my doubts."

"Amontillado!"

"And I must satisfy them."

"Amontillado!"

"As you are engaged, I am on my way to Luchesi. If any one has a critical turn, it is he. He will tell me——"

"Luchesi cannot tell Amontillado from Sherry."

"And yet some fools will have it that his taste is a match for your own."

"Come, let us go."

"Whither?"

"To your vaults."

"My friend, no; I will not impose upon your good nature. I perceive you have an engagement. Luchesi——"

"I have no engagement;—come."

"My friend, no. It is not the engagement, but the severe cold with which I perceive you are afflicted. The vaults are insufferably damp. They are encrusted with nitre."

"Let us go, nevertheless. The cold is merely nothing. Amontillado! You have been imposed upon. And as for Luchesi, he cannot distinguish Sherry from Amontillado."

Thus speaking, Fortunato possessed himself of my arm. Putting on a mask of black silk, and drawing a *roquelaire*° closely about my person, I suffered him to hurry me to my palazzo.

There were no attendants at home; they had absconded to make merry in honor of the time. I had told them that I should not return until the morning, and had given them explicit orders not to stir from the house. These orders were sufficient, I well knew, to insure their immediate disappearance, one and all, as soon as my back was turned.

I took from their sconces two flambeaux, and giving one to Fortunato, bowed him through several suites of rooms to the archway that led into the vaults. I passed down a long and winding staircase, requesting him to be cautious as he followed. We came at length to the foot of the descent, and stood together on the damp ground of the catacombs of the Montresors.

Roquelaire: A cloak.

The gait of my friend was unsteady, and the bells upon his cap jingled as he strode.

"The pipe?" said he.

"It is farther on," said I; "but observe the white web-work which gleams from these cavern walls."

He turned toward me, and looked into my eyes with two filmy orbs that distilled the rheum of intoxication.

"Nitre?" he asked, at length.

"Nitre," I replied. "How long have you had that cough?"

"Ugh! ugh! ugh!—ugh! ugh! ugh!—ugh! ugh! ugh!—ugh! ugh! ugh!—ugh! ugh! ugh!"

My poor friend found it impossible to reply for many minutes.

"It is nothing," he said, at last.

"Come," I said, with decision, "we will go back; your health is precious. You are rich, respected, admired, beloved; you are happy, as once I was. You are a man to be missed. For me it is no matter. We will go back; you will be ill, and I cannot be responsible. Besides, there is Luchesi—"

"Enough," he said; "the cough is a mere nothing; it will not kill me. I shall not die of a cough."

"True—true," I replied; "and, indeed, I had no intention of alarming you unnecessarily; but you should use all proper caution. A draught of this Medoc will defend us from the damps."

Here I knocked off the neck of a bottle which I drew from a long row of its fellows that lay upon the mould.

"Drink," I said, presenting him the wine.

He raised it to his lips with a leer. He paused and nodded to me familiarly, while his bells jingled.

"I drink," he said, "to the buried that repose around us."

"And I to your long life."

He again took my arm, and we proceeded.

"These vaults," he said, "are extensive."

"The Montresors," I replied, "were a great and numerous family."

"I forget your arms."

"A huge human foot d'or,° in a field azure; the foot crushes a serpent rampant whose fangs are imbedded in the heel."

"And the motto?"

"*Nemo me impune lacessit.*"°

"Good!" he said.

D'or: Of gold.
Nemo me impune lacessit: "No one wounds me with impunity"; the motto of the Scottish royal arms.

THE CASK OF AMONTILLADO 17

The wine sparkled in his eyes and the bells jingled. My own fancy grew warm with the Medoc. We had passed through walls of piled bones, with casks and puncheons intermingling into the inmost recesses of the catacombs. I paused again, and this time I made bold to seize Fortunato by an arm above the elbow.

"The nitre!" I said; "see, it increases. It hangs like moss upon the vaults. We are below the river's bed. The drops of moisture trickle among the bones. Come, we will go back ere it is too late. Your cough——"

"It is nothing," he said; "let us go on. But first, another draught of the Medoc."

I broke and reached him a flagon of De Grâve. He emptied it at a breath. His eyes flashed with a fierce light. He laughed and threw the bottle upward with a gesticulation I did not understand.

I looked at him in surprise. He repeated the movement—a grotesque one.

"You do not comprehend?" he said.

"Not I," I replied.

"Then you are not of the brotherhood."

"How?"

"You are not of the masons."

"Yes, yes," I said; "yes, yes."

"You? Impossible! A mason?"

"A mason," I replied.

"A sign," he said.

"It is this," I answered, producing a trowel from beneath the folds of my *roquelaire*.

"You jest," he exclaimed, recoiling a few paces. "But let us proceed to the Amontillado."

"Be it so," I said, replacing the tool beneath the cloak, and again offering him my arm. He leaned upon it heavily. We continued our route in search of the Amontillado. We passed through a range of low arches, descended, passed on, and descending again, arrived at a deep crypt, in which the foulness of the air caused our flambeaux rather to glow than flame.

At the most remote end of the crypt there appeared another less spacious. Its walls had been lined with human remains, piled to the vault overhead, in the fashion of the great catacombs of Paris. Three sides of this interior crypt were still ornamented in this manner. From the fourth the bones had been thrown down, and lay promiscuously upon the earth, forming at one point a mound of some size. Within the wall thus exposed by the displacing of the bones, we perceived a still interior recess, in depth about four feet, in width three, in height six or seven. It seemed to have been constructed for no especial use within itself, but formed merely the interval between two of the colossal supports of the roof of the catacombs, and was backed by one of their circumscribing walls of solid granite.

It was in vain that Fortunato, uplifting his dull torch, endeavored to pry into the depth of the recess. Its termination the feeble light did not enable us to see.

"Proceed," I said; "herein is the Amontillado. As for Luchesi——"

"He is an ignoramus," interrupted my friend, as he stepped unsteadily forward, while I followed immediately at his heels. In an instant he had reached the extremity of the niche, and finding his progress arrested by the rock, stood stupidly bewildered. A moment more and I had fettered him to the granite. In its surface were two iron staples, distant from each other about two feet, horizontally. From one of these depended a short chain, from the other a padlock. Throwing the links about his waist, it was but the work of a few seconds to secure it. He was too much astounded to resist. Withdrawing the key I stepped back from the recess.

"Pass your hand," I said, "over the wall; you cannot help feeling the nitre. Indeed it is *very* damp. Once more let me *implore* you to return. No? Then I must positively leave you. But I must first render you all the little attentions in my power."

"The Amontillado!" ejaculated my friend, not yet recovered from his astonishment.

"True," I replied; "the Amontillado."

As I said these words I busied myself among the pile of bones of which I have before spoken. Throwing them aside, I soon uncovered a quantity of building stone and mortar. With these materials and with the aid of my trowel, I began vigorously to wall up the entrance of the niche.

I had scarcely laid the first tier of the masonry when I discovered that the intoxication of Fortunato had in a great measure worn off. The earliest indication I had of this was a low moaning cry from the depth of the recess. It was *not* the cry of a drunken man. There was then a long and obstinate silence. I laid the second tier, and the third, and the fourth; and then I heard the furious vibrations of the chain. The noise lasted for several minutes, during which, that I might hearken to it with the more satisfaction, I ceased my labors and sat down upon the bones. When at last the clanking subsided, I resumed the trowel, and finished without interruption the fifth, the sixth, and the seventh tier. The wall was now nearly upon a level with my breast. I again paused, and holding the flambeaux over the masonwork, threw a few feeble rays upon the figure within.

A succession of loud and shrill screams, bursting suddenly from the throat of the chained form, seemed to thrust me violently back. For a brief moment I hesitated—I trembled. Unsheathing my rapier, I began to grope with it about the recess; but the thought of an instant reassured me. I placed my hand upon the solid fabric of the catacombs, and felt satisfied. I reapproached the wall. I replied to the yells of him who clamored. I reechoed—I aided—I surpassed them in volume and in strength. I did this, and the clamorer grew still.

It was now midnight, and my task was drawing to a close. I had completed the eighth, the ninth, and the tenth tier. I had finished a portion of the last and the eleventh; there remained but a single stone to be fitted and plastered in. I struggled with its weight; I placed it partially in its destined position. But now there came from out the niche a low laugh that erected the hairs upon my head. It was succeeded by a sad voice, which I had difficulty in recognizing as that of the noble Fortunato. The voice said—

"Ha! ha! ha!—he! he!—a very good joke indeed—an excellent jest. We will have many a rich laugh about it at the palazzo—he! he! he!—over our wine—he! he! he!"

"The Amontillado!" I said.

"He! he! he!—he! he! he!—yes, the Amontillado. But is it not getting late? Will not they be awaiting us at the palazzo, the Lady Fortunato and the rest? Let us be gone."

"Yes," I said, "let us be gone."

"For the love of God, Montresor!"

"Yes," I said, "for the love of God!"

But to these words I hearkened in vain for a reply. I grew impatient. I called aloud:

"Fortunato!"

No answer. I called again:

"Fortunato!"

No answer still. I thrust a torch through the remaining aperture and let it fall within. There came forth in return only a jingling of the bells. My heart grew sick—on account of the dampness of the catacombs. I hastened to make an end of my labor. I forced the last stone into its position; I plastered it up. Against the new masonry I re-erected the old rampart of bones. For the half of a century no mortal has disturbed them. *In pace requiescat!*°

[1846]

In pace requiescat: May he rest in peace (Latin).

HERMAN MELVILLE [1819–1891]

Bartleby, the Scrivener

A Story of Wall Street

I am a rather elderly man. The nature of my avocations, for the last thirty years, has brought me into more than ordinary contact with what would seem an interesting and somewhat singular set of men, of whom, as yet, nothing, that I know of, has ever been written—I mean, the law-copyists, or scriveners. I have known very many of them, professionally and privately, and, if I pleased, could relate divers histories, at which good-natured gentlemen might smile, and sentimental souls might weep. But I waive the biographies of all other scriveners, for a few passages in the life of Bartleby, who was a scrivener, the strangest I ever saw, or heard of. While, of other law-copyists, I might write the complete life, of Bartleby nothing of that sort can be done. I believe that no materials exist, for a full and satisfactory biography of this man. It is an irreparable loss to literature. Bartleby was one of those beings of whom nothing is ascertainable, except from the original sources, and, in his case, those are very small. What my own astonished eyes saw of Bartleby, *that* is all I know of him, except, indeed, one vague report, which will appear in the sequel.

Ere introducing the scrivener, as he first appeared to me, it is fit I make some mention of myself, my *employés,* my business, my chambers, and general surroundings, because some such description is indispensable to an adequate understanding of the chief character about to be presented. Imprimis:° I am a man who, from his youth upwards, has been filled with a profound conviction that the easiest way of life is the best. Hence, though I belong to a profession proverbially energetic and nervous, even to turbulence, at times, yet nothing of that sort have I ever suffered to invade my peace. I am one of those unambitious lawyers who never address a jury, or in any way draw down public applause; but, in the cool tranquillity of a snug retreat, do a snug business among rich men's bonds, and mortgages, and title-deeds. All who know me, consider me an eminently *safe* man. The late John Jacob Astor, a personage little

Imprimis: In the first place (Latin).

20

given to poetic enthusiasm, had no hesitation in pronouncing my first grand point to be prudence; my next, method. I do not speak it in vanity, but simply record the fact, that I was not unemployed in my profession by the late John Jacob Astor; a name which, I admit, I love to repeat; for it hath a rounded and orbicular sound to it, and rings like unto bullion. I will freely add, that I was not insensible to the late John Jacob Astor's good opinion.

Some time prior to the period at which this little history begins, my avocations had been largely increased. The good old office, now extinct in the State of New York, of a Master in Chancery, had been conferred upon me. It was not a very arduous office, but very pleasantly remunerative. I seldom lose my temper; much more seldom indulge in dangerous indignation at wrongs and outrages; but I must be permitted to be rash here and declare, that I consider the sudden and violent abrogation of the office of Master in Chancery, by the new Constitution, as a——premature act; inasmuch as I had counted upon a life-lease of the profits, whereas I only received those of a few short years. But this is by the way.

My chambers were up stairs, at No.—Wall Street. At one end, they looked upon the white wall of the interior of a spacious skylight shaft, penetrating the building from top to bottom.

This view might have been considered rather tame than otherwise, deficient in what landscape painters call "life." But, if so, the view from the other end of my chambers offered, at least, a contrast, if nothing more. In that direction, my windows commanded an unobstructed view of a lofty brick wall, black by age and everlasting shade; which wall required no spy-glass to bring out its lurking beauties, but, for the benefit of all near-sighted spectators, was pushed up to within ten feet of my window-panes. Owing to the great height of the surrounding buildings, and my chambers being on the second floor, the interval between this wall and mine not a little resembled a huge square cistern.

At the period just preceding the advent of Bartleby, I had two persons as copyists in my employment, and a promising lad as an office-boy. First, Turkey; second, Nippers; third, Ginger Nut. These may seem names, the like of which are not usually found in the Directory. In truth, they were nicknames, mutually conferred upon each other by my three clerks, and were deemed expressive of their respective persons or characters. Turkey was a short, pursy Englishman, of about my own age—that is, somewhere not far from sixty. In the morning, one might say, his face was of a fine florid hue, but after twelve o'clock, meridian—his dinner hour—it blazed like a grate full of Christmas coals; and continued blazing—but, as it were, with a gradual wane—till six o'clock, P.M., or thereabouts; after which, I saw no more of the proprietor of the face, which, gaining its meridian with the sun, seemed to set with it, to rise, culminate, and decline the following day, with the like regularity and undiminished glory. There are many singular coincidences I have known in the course of my life, not the least among which was the fact, that, exactly when Turkey displayed his fullest beams from his red and radiant countenance, just then, too, at that critical moment, began the daily period when I considered his business capacities as seriously disturbed for the remainder of the twenty-four hours. Not that he was absolutely idle, or averse to business then; far from it. The difficulty was, he was apt to be altogether too energetic. There was a strange, inflamed, flurried, flighty recklessness of activity about him. He would be incautious in dipping his pen into his inkstand. All his blots upon my documents were dropped there after twelve o'clock, meridian. Indeed, not only would he be reckless, and sadly given to making blots in the afternoon, but, some days, he went further, and was rather noisy. At such times, too, his face flamed with augmented blazonry, as if cannel coal had been heaped on anthracite. He made an unpleasant racket with his chair; spilled his sand-box; in mending his pens, impatiently split them all to pieces, and threw them on the floor in a sudden passion; stood up, and leaned over his table, boxing his papers about in a most indecorous manner, very sad to behold in an elderly man like him. Nevertheless, as he was in many ways a most valuable person to me, and all the time before twelve o'clock, meridian, was the quickest, steadiest creature, too, accomplishing a great deal of work in a style not easily to be matched—for these reasons, I was willing to overlook his eccentricities, though, indeed, occasionally, I remonstrated with him. I did this very gently, however, because, though the civilest, nay, the blandest and most reverential of men in the morning, yet, in the afternoon, he was disposed, upon provocation, to be slightly rash with his tongue—in fact, insolent. Now, valuing his morning services as I did, and resolved not to lose them—yet, at the same time, made uncomfortable by his inflamed ways after twelve o'clock—and being a man of peace, unwilling by my admonitions to call forth unseemly retorts from him, I took upon me, one Saturday noon (he was always worse on Saturdays) to hint to him, very kindly, that, perhaps, now that he was growing old, it might be well to abridge his labors; in short, he need not come to my chambers after twelve o'clock, but, dinner over, had best go home to his lodgings, and rest himself till tea-time. But no; he insisted upon his afternoon devotions. His countenance became intolerably fervid, as he oratorically assured me—gesticulating with a long ruler at the other end of the room—that if his services in the morning were useful, how indispensable, then, in the afternoon?

"With submission, sir," said Turkey, on this occasion, "I consider myself your right-hand man. In the morning I but marshal and deploy my columns; but in the afternoon I put myself at their head, and gallantly charge the foe, thus"—and he made a violent thrust with the ruler.

"But the blots, Turkey," intimated I.

"True; but, with submission, sir, behold these hairs! I am getting old. Surely, sir, a blot or two of a warm afternoon is not to be severely urged against gray hairs. Old age—even if it blot the page—is honorable. With submission, sir, we *both* are getting old."

This appeal to my fellow-feeling was hardly to be resisted. At all events, I saw that go he would not. So, I made up my mind to let him stay, resolving, nevertheless, to see to it that, during the afternoon, he had to do with my less important papers.

Nippers, the second on my list, was a whiskered, sallow, and, upon the whole, rather piratical-looking young man, of about five-and-twenty. I always deemed him the victim of two evil powers—ambition and indigestion. The ambition was evinced by a certain impatience of the duties of a mere copyist, an unwarrantable usurpation of strictly professional affairs such as the original drawing up of legal documents. The indigestion seemed betokened in an occasional nervous testiness and grinning irritability, causing the teeth to audibly grind together over mistakes committed in copying; unnecessary maledictions, hissed, rather than spoken, in the heat of business; and especially by a continual discontent with the height of the table where he worked. Though of a very ingenious mechanical turn, Nippers could never get this table to suit him. He put chips under it, blocks of various sorts, bits of pasteboard, and at last went so far as to attempt an exquisite adjustment, by final pieces of folded blotting paper. But no invention would answer. If, for the sake of easing his back, he brought the table-lid at a sharp angle well up towards his chin, and wrote there like a man using the steep roof of a Dutch house for his desk, then he declared that it stopped the circulation in his arms. If now he lowered the table to his waistbands, and stooped over it in writing, then there was a sore aching in his back. In short, the truth of the matter was, Nippers knew not what he wanted. Or, if he wanted anything, it was to be rid of a scrivener's table altogether. Among the manifestations of his diseased ambition was a fondness he had for receiving visits from certain ambiguous-looking fellows in seedy coats, whom he called his clients. Indeed, I was aware that not only was he, at times, considerable of a ward-politician, but he occasionally did a little business at the justices' courts, and was not unknown on the steps of the Tombs.° I have good reason to believe, however, that one individual who called upon him at my chambers, and who, with a grand air, he insisted was his client, was no other than a dun, and the alleged title-deed, a bill.

The Tombs: Nickname of the Manhattan House of Detention.

But, with all his failings, and the annoyances he caused me, Nippers, like his compatriot Turkey, was a very useful man to me; wrote a neat, swift hand; and, when he chose, was not deficient in a gentlemanly sort of deportment. Added to this, he always dressed in a gentlemanly sort of way; and so, incidentally, reflected credit upon my chambers. Whereas, with respect to Turkey, I had much ado to keep him from being a reproach to me. His clothes were apt to look oily, and smell of eating-houses. He wore his pantaloons very loose and baggy in summer. His coats were execrable, his hat not to be handled. But while the hat was a thing of indifference to me, inasmuch as his natural civility and deference, as a dependent Englishman, always led him to doff it the moment he entered the room, yet his coat was another matter. Concerning his coats, I reasoned with him; but with no effect. The truth was, I suppose, that a man with so small an income could not afford to sport such a lustrous face and a lustrous coat at one and the same time. As Nippers once observed, Turkey's money went chiefly for red ink. One winter day, I presented Turkey with a highly respectable-looking coat of my own—a padded gray coat, of a most comfortable warmth, and which buttoned straight up from the knee to the neck. I thought Turkey would appreciate the favor, and abate his rashness and obstreperousness of afternoons. But no; I verily believe that buttoning himself up in so downy and blanket-like a coat had a pernicious effect upon him upon the same principle that too much oats are bad for horses. In fact, precisely as a rash, restive horse is said to feel his oats, so Turkey felt his coat. It made him insolent. He was a man whom prosperity harmed.

Though, concerning the self-indulgent habits of Turkey, I had my own private surmises, yet, touching Nippers, I was well persuaded that, whatever might be his faults in other respects, he was, at least, a temperate young man. But, indeed, nature herself seemed to have been his vintner, and, at his birth, charged him so thoroughly with an irritable, brandy-like disposition, that all subsequent potations were needless. When I consider how, amid the stillness of my chambers, Nippers would sometimes impatiently rise from his seat, and stooping over his table, spread his arms wide apart, seize the whole desk, and move it, and jerk it, with a grim, grinding motion on the floor, as if the table were a perverse voluntary agent, intent on thwarting and vexing him, I plainly perceive that, for Nippers, brandy-and-water were altogether superfluous.

It was fortunate for me that, owing to its peculiar cause—indigestion—the irritability and consequent nervousness of Nippers were mainly observable in the morning, while in the afternoon he was comparatively mild. So that, Turkey's paroxysms only coming on about twelve o'clock, I never had to do with their eccentricities at one time. Their fits relieved each other, like guards. When Nippers' was on, Turkey's was off; and *vice versa*. This was a good natural arrangement, under the circumstances.

Ginger Nut, the third on my list, was a lad, some twelve years old. His father was a carman, ambitious of seeing his son on the bench instead of a cart, before he died. So he sent him to my office, as student at law, errand-boy, cleaner, and sweeper, at the rate of one dollar a week. He had a little desk to himself, but he did not use it much. Upon inspection, the drawer exhibited a great array of the shells of various sorts of nuts. Indeed, to this quick-witted youth, the whole noble science of the law was contained in a nutshell. Not the least among the employments of Ginger Nut, as well as one which he discharged with the most alacrity, was his duty as cake and apple purveyor for Turkey and Nippers. Copying lawpapers being proverbially a dry, husky sort of business, my two scriveners were fain to moisten their mouths very often with Spitzenbergs, to be had at the numerous stalls nigh the Custom House and Post Office. Also, they sent Ginger Nut very frequently for that peculiar cake—small, flat, round, and very spicy—after which he had been named by them. Of a cold morning, when business was but dull, Turkey would gobble up scores of these cakes, as if they were mere wafers—indeed, they sell them at the rate of six or eight for a penny—the scrape of his pen blending with the crunching of the crisp particles in his mouth. Of all the fiery afternoon blunders and flurried rashness of Turkey, was his once moistening a ginger-cake between his lips, and clapping it on to a mortgage, for a seal. I came within an ace of dismissing him then. But he mollified me by making an oriental bow, and saying—

"With submission, sir, it was generous of me to find you in stationery on my own account."

Now my original business—that of a conveyancer and title hunter, and drawer-up of recondite documents of all sorts—was considerably increased by receiving the Master's office. There was now great work for scriveners. Not only must I push the clerks already with me, but I must have additional help.

In answer to my advertisement, a motionless young man one morning stood upon my office threshold, the door being open, for it was summer. I can see that figure now—pallidly neat, pitiably respectable, incurably forlorn! It was Bartleby.

After a few words touching his qualifications, I engaged him, glad to have among my corps of copyists a man of so singularly sedate an aspect, which I thought might operate beneficially upon the flighty temper of Turkey, and the fiery one of Nippers.

I should have stated before that ground-glass folding-doors divided my premises into two parts, one of which was occupied by my scriveners, the other by myself. According to my humor, I threw open these doors, or closed them. I resolved to assign Bartleby a corner by the folding-doors, but on my side of them, so as to have this quiet man within easy call, in case any trifling thing was to be done. I placed his desk close up to a small side-window in that part of the room, a window which originally had afforded a lateral view of certain grimy brickyards and bricks, but which, owing to subsequent erections, commanded at present no view at all, though it gave some light. Within three feet of the panes was a wall, and the light came down from far above, between two lofty buildings, as from a very small opening in a dome. Still further to a satisfactory arrangement, I procured a high green folding screen, which might entirely isolate Bartleby from my sight, though not remove him from my voice. And thus, in a manner, privacy and society were conjoined.

At first, Bartleby did an extraordinary quantity of writing. As if long famishing for something to copy, he seemed to gorge himself on my documents. There was no pause for digestion. He ran a day and night line, copying by sun-light and by candle-light. I should have been quite delighted with his application, had he been cheerfully industrious. But he wrote on silently, palely, mechanically.

It is, of course, an indispensable part of a scrivener's business to verify the accuracy of his copy, word by word. Where there are two or more scriveners in an office, they assist each other in this examination, one reading from the copy, the other holding the original. It is a very dull, wearisome, and lethargic affair. I can readily imagine that, to some sanguine temperaments, it would be altogether intolerable. For example, I cannot credit that the mettlesome poet, Byron, would have contentedly sat down with Bartleby to examine a law document of, say five hundred pages, closely written in a crimpy hand.

Now and then, in the haste of business, it had been my habit to assist in comparing some brief document myself, calling Turkey or Nippers for this purpose. One object I had, in placing Bartleby so handy to me behind the screen, was, to avail myself of his services on such trivial occasions. It was on the third day, I think, of his being with me, and before any necessity had arisen for having his own writing examined, that, being much hurried to complete a small affair I had in hand, I abruptly called to Bartleby. In my haste and natural expectancy of instant compliance, I sat with my head bent over the original on my desk, and my right hand sideways, and somewhat nervously extended with the copy, so that, immediately upon emerging from his retreat, Bartleby might snatch it and proceed to business without the least delay.

In this very attitude did I sit when I called to him, rapidly stating what it was I wanted him to do—namely, to examine a small paper with me. Imagine my surprise, nay, my consternation, when, without moving from his privacy, Bartleby, in a singularly mild, firm voice, replied, "I would prefer not to."

I sat awhile in perfect silence, rallying my stunned faculties. Immediately it occurred to me that my ears had deceived me, or Bartleby had entirely misunderstood my meaning. I repeated my request in the clearest tone I could assume; but in quite as clear a one came the previous reply, "I would prefer not to."

"Prefer not to," echoed I, rising in high excitement, and crossing the room with a stride. "What do you mean? Are you moonstruck? I want you to help me compare this sheet here—take it," and I thrust it towards him.

"I would prefer not to," said he.

I looked at him steadfastly. His face was leanly composed; his gray eye dimly calm. Not a wrinkle of agitation rippled him. Had there been the least uneasiness, anger, impatience, or impertinence in his manner; in other words, had there been anything ordinarily human about him, doubtless I should have violently dismissed him from the premises. But as it was, I should have as soon thought of turning my pale plaster-of-paris bust of Cicero out of doors. I stood gazing at him awhile, as he went on with his own writing, and then reseated myself at my desk. This is very strange, thought I. What had one best do? But my business hurried me. I concluded to forget the matter for the present, reserving it for my future leisure. So, calling Nippers from the other room, the paper was speedily examined.

A few days after this, Bartleby concluded four lengthy documents, being quadruplicates of a week's testimony taken before me in my High Court of Chancery. It became necessary to examine them. It was an important suit, and great accuracy was imperative. Having all things arranged, I called Turkey, Nippers, and Ginger Nut, from the next room, meaning to place the four copies in the hands of my four clerks, while I should read from the original. Accordingly, Turkey, Nippers, and Ginger Nut had taken their seats in a row, each with his document in his hand, when I called to Bartleby to join this interesting group.

"Bartleby! quick, I am waiting."

I heard a slow scrape of his chair legs on the uncarpeted floor, and soon he appeared standing at the entrance of his hermitage.

"What is wanted?" said he, mildly.

"The copies, the copies," said I, hurriedly. "We are going to examine them. There"—and I held towards him the fourth quadruplicate.

"I would prefer not to," he said, and gently disappeared behind the screen.

For a few moments I was turned into a pillar of salt, standing at the head of my seated column of clerks. Recovering myself, I advanced towards the screen, and demanded the reason for such extraordinary conduct.

"*Why* do you refuse?"

"I would prefer not to."

With any other man I should have flown outright into a dreadful passion, scorned all further words, and thrust him ignominiously from my presence. But there was something about Bartleby that not only strangely disarmed me, but, in a wonderful manner, touched and disconcerted me. I began to reason with him.

"These are your own copies we are about to examine. It is labor saving to you, because one examination will answer for your four papers. It is common usage. Every copyist is bound to help examine his copy. Is it not so? Will you not speak? Answer!"

"I prefer not to," he replied in a flute-like tone. It seemed to me that, while I had been addressing him, he carefully revolved every statement that I made; fully comprehended the meaning; could not gainsay the irresistible conclusion; but, at the same time, some paramount consideration prevailed with him to reply as he did.

"You are decided, then, not to comply with my request—a request made according to common usage and common sense?"

He briefly gave me to understand, that on that point my judgment was sound. Yes: his decision was irreversible.

It is not seldom the case that, when a man is browbeaten in some unprecedented and violently unreasonable way, he begins to stagger in his own plainest faith. He begins, as it were, vaguely to surmise that, wonderful as it may be, all the justice and all the reason is on the other side. Accordingly, if any disinterested persons are present, he turns to them for some reinforcement for his own faltering mind.

"Turkey," said I, "what do you think of this? Am I not right?"

"With submission, sir," said Turkey, in his blandest tone, "I think that you are."

"Nippers," said I, "what do *you* think of it?"

"I think I should kick him out of the office."

(The reader of nice perceptions will have perceived that, it being morning, Turkey's answer is couched in polite and tranquil terms, but Nippers replies in ill-tempered ones. Or, to repeat a previous sentence, Nippers' ugly mood was on duty, and Turkey's off.)

"Ginger Nut," said I, willing to enlist the smallest suffrage in my behalf, "what do *you* think of it?"

"I think, sir, he's a little *luny*," replied Ginger Nut, with a grin.

"You hear what they say," said I, turning towards the screen, "come forth and do your duty."

But he vouchsafed no reply. I pondered a moment in sore perplexity. But once more business hurried me. I determined again to postpone the *would is a hypothetical, but we don't know what it would take*

consideration of this dilemma to my future leisure. With a little trouble
we made out to examine the papers without Bartleby, though at every
page or two Turkey deferentially dropped his opinion, that this proceeding was quite out of the common; while Nippers, twitching in his chair
with a dyspeptic nervousness, ground out, between his set teeth, occasional hissing maledictions against the stubborn oaf behind the screen.
And for his (Nippers') part, this was the first and the last time he would   *he*
do another man's business without pay.   *perfor*

Meanwhile Bartleby sat in his hermitage, oblivious to everything but   *absence*
his own peculiar business there.   *(nothing)*

Some days passed, the scrivener being employed upon another
lengthy work. His late remarkable conduct led me to regard his ways
narrowly. I observed that he never went to dinner; indeed, that he never
went anywhere. As yet I had never, of my personal knowledge, known
him to be outside of my office. He was a perpetual sentry in the corner.
At about eleven o'clock though, in the morning, I noticed that Ginger
Nut would advance towards the opening in Bartleby's screen, as if
silently beckoned thither by a gesture invisible to me where I sat. The
boy would then leave the office, jingling a few pence, and reappear with
a handful of ginger-nuts, which he delivered in the hermitage, receiving
two of the cakes for his trouble.

He lives, then, on ginger-nuts, thought I; never eats a dinner, properly
speaking; he must be a vegetarian, then, but no; he never eats even vegetables, he eats nothing but ginger-nuts. My mind then ran on in reveries
concerning the probable effects upon the human constitution of living
entirely on ginger-nuts. Ginger-nuts are so called, because they contain
ginger as one of their peculiar constituents, and the final flavoring one.
Now, what was ginger? A hot, spicy thing. Was Bartleby hot and spicy?
Not at all. Ginger, then, had no effect upon Bartleby. Probably he preferred it should have none.

Nothing so aggravates an earnest person as a passive resistance. If the
individual so resisted be of a not inhumane temper, and the resisting one
perfectly harmless in his passivity, then, in the better moods of the former, he will endeavor charitably to construe to his imagination what
proves impossible to be solved by his judgment. Even so, for the most
part, I regarded Bartleby and his ways. Poor fellow! thought I, he means
no mischief; it is plain he intends no insolence; his aspect sufficiently
evinces that his eccentricities are involuntary. He is useful to me. I can
get along with him. If I turn him away, the chances are he will fall in
with some less indulgent employer, and then he will be rudely treated,
and perhaps driven forth miserably to starve. Yes. Here I can cheaply
purchase a delicious self-approval. To befriend Bartleby; to humor him
in his strange wilfulness, will cost me little or nothing, while I lay up in
my soul what will eventually prove a sweet morsel for my conscience.

not no or refusal

Just barely that

But this mood was not invariable with me. The passiveness of Bartleby sometimes irritated me. I felt strangely goaded on to encounter him in new opposition — to elicit some angry spark from him answerable to my own. But, indeed, I might as well have essayed to strike fire with my knuckles against a bit of Windsor soap. But one afternoon the evil impulse in me mastered me, and the following little scene ensued:

"Bartleby," said I, "when those papers are all copied, I will compare them with you."

"I would prefer not to."

"How? Surely you do not mean to persist in that mulish vagary?"

No answer.

I threw open the folding-doors nearby, and turning upon Turkey and Nippers, exclaimed:

"Bartleby a second time says, he won't examine his papers. What do you think of it, Turkey?"

It was afternoon, be it remembered. Turkey sat glowing like a brass boiler; his bald head steaming; his hands reeling among his blotted papers.

"Think of it?" roared Turkey. "I think I'll just step behind his screen, and black his eyes for him!"

So saying, Turkey rose to his feet and threw his arms into a pugilistic position. He was hurrying away to make good his promise, when I detained him, alarmed at the effect of incautiously rousing Turkey's combativeness after dinner.

"Sit down, Turkey," said I, "and hear what Nippers has to say. What do you think of it, Nippers? Would I not be justified in immediately dismissing Bartleby?"

"Excuse me, that is for you to decide, sir. I think his conduct quite unusual, and, indeed, unjust, as regards Turkey and myself. But it may only be a passing whim."

"Ah," exclaimed I, "you have strangely changed your mind, then — you speak very gently of him now."

"All beer," cried Turkey; "gentleness is effects of beer — Nippers and I dined together to-day. You see how gentle I am, sir. Shall I go and black his eyes?"

"You refer to Bartleby, I suppose. No, not to-day, Turkey," I replied; "pray, put up your fists."

I closed the doors, and again advanced towards Bartleby. I felt additional incentives tempting me to my fate. I burned to be rebelled against again. I remembered that Bartleby never left the office.

"Bartleby," said I, "Ginger Nut is away; just step around to the Post Office, won't you?" (it was but a three minutes' walk) "and see if there is anything for me."

"I would prefer not to."

"You *will* not?"

"I *prefer* not."

I staggered to my desk, and sat there in a deep study. My blind inveteracy returned. Was there any other thing in which I could procure myself to be ignominiously repulsed by this lean, penniless wight? my hired clerk? What added thing is there, perfectly reasonable, that he will be sure to refuse to do?

"Bartleby!"

No answer.

"Bartleby," in a louder tone.

No answer.

"Bartleby," I roared.

Like a very ghost, agreeably to the laws of magical invocation, at the third summons, he appeared at the entrance of his hermitage.

"Go to the next room, and tell Nippers to come to me."

"I would prefer not to," he respectfully and slowly said, and mildly disappeared.

"Very good, Bartleby," said I, in a quiet sort of serenely-severe self-possessed tone, intimating the unalterable purpose of some terrible retribution very close at hand. At the moment I half intended something of the kind. But upon the whole, as it was drawing towards my dinner-hour, I thought it best to put on my hat and walk home for the day, suffering much from perplexity and distress of mind.

Shall I acknowledge it? The conclusion of this whole business was, that it soon became a fixed fact of my chambers, that a pale young scrivener, by the name of Bartleby, had a desk there; that he copied for me at the usual rate of four cents a folio (one hundred words); but he was permanently exempt from examining the work done by him, that duty being transferred to Turkey and Nippers, out of compliment, doubtless, to their superior acuteness; moreover, said Bartleby was never, on any account, to be dispatched on the most trivial errand of any sort; and that even if entreated to take upon him such a matter, it was generally understood that he would "prefer not to"—in other words, that he would refuse point blank.

As days passed on, I became considerably reconciled to Bartleby. His steadiness, his freedom from all dissipation, his incessant industry (except when he chose to throw himself into a standing revery behind his screen), his great stillness, his unalterableness of demeanor under all circumstances, made him a valuable acquisition. One prime thing was this—*he was always there*—first in the morning, continually through the day, and the last at night. I had a singular confidence in his honesty. I felt my most precious papers perfectly safe in his hands. Sometimes, to be sure, I could not, for the very soul of me, avoid falling into sudden spasmodic passions with him. For it was exceeding difficult to bear in mind all the time those strange peculiarities, privileges, and unheard-of exemptions, forming the tacit stipulations on Bartleby's part under which he remained in my office. Now and then, in the eagerness of dispatching pressing business, I would inadvertently summon Bartleby, in a short, rapid tone, to put his finger, say, on the incipient tie of a bit of red tape with which I was about compressing some papers. Of course, from behind the screen the usual answer, "I prefer not to," was sure to come; and then, how could a human creature, with the common infirmities of our nature, refrain from bitterly exclaiming upon such perverseness—such unreasonableness? However, every added repulse of this sort which I received only tended to lessen the probability of my repeating the inadvertence.

Here it must be said, that, according to the custom of most legal gentlemen occupying chambers in densely populated law buildings, there were several keys to my door. One was kept by a woman residing in the attic, which person weekly scrubbed and daily swept and dusted my apartments. Another was kept by Turkey for convenience sake. The third I sometimes carried in my own pocket. The fourth I knew not who had.

Now, one Sunday morning I happened to go to Trinity Church, to hear a celebrated preacher, and finding myself rather early on the ground I thought I would walk round to my chambers for a while. Luckily I had my key with me; but upon applying it to the lock, I found it resisted by something inserted from the inside. Quite surprised, I called out; when to my consternation a key was turned from within; and thrusting his lean visage at me, and holding the door ajar, the apparition of Bartleby appeared, in his shirt-sleeves, and otherwise in a strangely tattered *deshabille*, saying quietly that he was sorry, but he was deeply engaged just then, and preferred not admitting me at present. In a brief word or two, he moreover added, that perhaps I had better walk round the block two or three times, and by that time he would probably have concluded his affairs.

Now, the utterly unsurmised appearance of Bartleby, tenanting my law-chambers of a Sunday morning, with his cadaverously gentlemanly *nonchalance*, yet withal firm and self-possessed, had such a strange effect upon me, that incontinently I slunk away from my own door, and did as desired. But not without sundry twinges of impotent rebellion against the mild effrontery of this unaccountable scrivener. Indeed, it was his wonderful mildness chiefly, which not only disarmed me, but unmanned me, as it were. For I consider that one, for the time, is sort of unmanned when he tranquilly permits his hired clerk to dictate to him, and order him away from his own premises. Furthermore, I was full of uneasiness as to what Bartleby could possibly be doing in my office in his shirt-sleeves, and in an otherwise dismantled condition on a Sunday morning. Was anything amiss going on? Nay, that was out of the question. It was not to be thought of for a moment that Bartleby was an immoral person. But what could he be doing there?—copying? Nay again, whatever might be his eccentricities, Bartleby was an eminently decorous person. He would be the last man to sit down to his desk in any state approaching to nudity. Besides, it was Sunday; and there was something about Bartleby that forbade the supposition that he would by any secular occupation violate the proprieties of the day.

Nevertheless, my mind was not pacified; and full of a restless curiosity, at last I returned to the door. Without hindrance I inserted my key, opened it, and entered. Bartleby was not to be seen. I looked round anxiously, peeped behind his screen; but it was very plain that he was gone. Upon more closely examining the place, I surmised that for an indefinite period Bartleby must have ate, dressed, and slept in my office, and that too without plate, mirror, or bed. The cushioned seat of a rickety old sofa in one corner bore the faint impress of a lean, reclining form. Rolled away under his desk, I found a blanket; under the empty grate, a blacking box and brush; on a chair, a tin basin, with soap and a ragged towel; in a newspaper a few crumbs of ginger-nuts and a morsel of cheese. Yes, thought I, it is evident enough that Bartleby has been making his home here, keeping bachelor's hall all by himself. Immediately then the thought came sweeping across me, what miserable friendlessness and loneliness are here revealed! His poverty is great; but his solitude, how horrible! Think of it. Of a Sunday, Wall Street is deserted as Petra;° and every night of every day it is an emptiness. This building, too, which of week-days hums with industry and life, at nightfall echoes with sheer vacancy, and all through Sunday is forlorn. And here Bartleby makes his home; sole spectator of a solitude which he has seen all populous—a sort of innocent and transformed Marius° brooding among the ruins of Carthage!

For the first time in my life a feeling of overpowering stinging melancholy seized me. Before, I had never experienced aught but a not unpleasing sadness. The bond of a common humanity now drew me irresistibly to gloom. A fraternal melancholy! For both I and Bartleby were sons of Adam. I remembered the bright silks and sparkling faces I had seen that day, in gala trim, swan-like sailing down the Mississippi of Broadway; and I contrasted them with the pallid copyist, and thought to myself, Ah, happiness courts the light, so we deem the world is gay; but

Petra: A Middle Eastern city, deserted for more than ten centuries until its rediscovery by explorers in 1812.
Marius: Gaius Marius (157?–86 B.C.E.), Roman general and consul who was banished and fled to Africa, scene of his greatest military triumphs.

misery hides aloof, so we deem that misery there is none. These sad fancyings—chimeras, doubtless, of a sick and silly brain—led on to other and more special thoughts, concerning the eccentricities of Bartleby. Presentiments of strange discoveries hovered round me. The scrivener's pale form appeared to me laid out, among uncaring strangers, in its shivering winding-sheet.

Suddenly I was attracted by Bartleby's closed desk, the key in open sight left in the lock.

I mean no mischief, seek the gratification of no heartless curiosity, thought I; besides, the desk is mine, and its contents, too, so I will make bold to look within. Everything was methodically arranged, the papers smoothly placed. The pigeon-holes were deep, and removing the files of documents, I groped into their recesses. Presently I felt something there, and dragged it out. It was an old bandanna handkerchief, heavy and knotted. I opened it, and saw it was a saving's bank.

I now recalled all the quiet mysteries which I had noted in the man. I remembered that he never spoke but to answer; that, though at intervals he had considerable time to himself, yet I had never seen him reading— no, not even a newspaper; that for long periods he would stand looking out, at his pale window behind the screen, upon the dead brick wall; I was quite sure he never visited any refectory or eating-house; while his pale face clearly indicated that he never drank beer like Turkey; or tea and coffee even, like other men; that he never went anywhere in particular that I could learn; never went out for a walk, unless, indeed, that was the case at present; that he had declined telling who he was, or whence he came, or whether he had any relatives in the world; that though so thin and pale, he never complained of ill-health. And more than all, I remembered a certain unconscious air of pallid—how shall I call it?— of pallid haughtiness, say, or rather an austere reserve about him, which has positively awed me into my tame compliance with his eccentricities, when I had feared to ask him to do the slightest incidental thing for me, even though I might know, from his long-continued motionlessness, that behind his screen he must be standing in one of those dead-wall reveries of his.

Revolving all these things, and coupling them with the recently discovered fact, that he made my office his constant abiding place and home, and not forgetful of his morbid moodiness; revolving all these things, a prudential feeling began to steal over me. My first emotions had been those of pure melancholy and sincerest pity; but just in proportion as the forlornness of Bartleby grew and grew to my imagination, did that same melancholy merge into fear, that pity into repulsion. So true it is, and so terrible, too, that up to a certain point the thought or sight of misery enlists our best affections; but, in certain special cases, beyond that point it does not. They err who would assert that invariably this is owing to the inherent selfishness of the human heart. It rather proceeds from a certain hopelessness of remedying excessive and organic ill. To a sensitive being, pity is not seldom pain. And when at last it is perceived that such pity cannot lead to effectual succor, common sense bids the soul be rid of it. What I saw that morning persuaded me that the scrivener was the victim of innate and incurable disorder. I might give alms to his body; but his body did not pain him; it was his soul that suffered, and his soul I could not reach.

I did not accomplish the purpose of going to Trinity Church that morning. Somehow, the things I had seen disqualified me for the time from church-going. I walked homeward, thinking what I would do with Bartleby. Finally, I resolved upon this—I would put certain calm questions to him the next morning, touching his history, etc., and if he declined to answer them openly and unreservedly (and I supposed he would prefer not), then to give him a twenty dollar bill over and above whatever I might owe him, and tell him his services were no longer required; but that if in any other way I could assist him, I would be happy to do so, especially if he desired to return to his native place, wherever that might be, I would willingly help to defray the expenses. Moreover, if, after reaching home, he found himself at any time in want of aid, a letter from him would be sure of a reply.

The next morning came.

"Bartleby," said I, gently calling to him behind his screen.

No reply.

"Bartleby," said I, in a still gentler tone, "come here; I am not going to ask you to do anything you would prefer not to do—I simply wish to speak to you."

Upon this he noiselessly slid into view.

"Will you tell me, Bartleby, where you were born?"

"I would prefer not to."

"Will you tell me *anything* about yourself?"

"I would prefer not to."

"But what reasonable objection can you have to speak to me? I feel friendly towards you."

He did not look at me while I spoke, but kept his glance fixed upon my bust of Cicero, which, as I then sat, was directly behind me, some six inches above my head.

"What is your answer, Bartleby?" said I, after waiting a considerable time for a reply, during which his countenance remained immovable, only there was the faintest conceivable tremor of the white attenuated mouth.

"At present I prefer to give no answer," he said, and retired into his hermitage.

It was rather weak in me I confess, but his manner, on this occasion, nettled me. Not only did there seem to lurk in it a certain calm disdain, but his perverseness seemed ungrateful, considering the undeniable good usage and indulgence he had received from me.

Again I sat ruminating what I should do. Mortified as I was at his behavior, and resolved as I had been to dismiss him when I entered my office, nevertheless I strangely felt something superstitious knocking at my heart, and forbidding me to carry out my purpose, and denouncing me for a villain if I dared to breathe one bitter word against this forlornest of mankind. At last, familiarly drawing my chair behind his screen, I sat down and said: "Bartleby, never mind, then, about revealing your history; but let me entreat you, as a friend, to comply as far as may be with the usages of this office. Say now, you will help to examine papers tomorrow or next day: in short, say now, that in a day or two you will begin to be a little reasonable: — say so, Bartleby."

"At present I would prefer not to be a little reasonable," was his mildly cadaverous reply.

Just then the folding-doors opened, and Nippers approached. He seemed suffering from an unusually bad night's rest, induced by severer indigestion than common. He overheard those final words of Bartleby.

"*Prefer not*, eh?" gritted Nippers — "I'd *prefer* him, if I were you, sir," addressing me — "I'd *prefer* him; I'd give him preferences, the stubborn mule! What is it, sir, pray, that he *prefers* not to do now?"

Bartleby moved not a limb.

"Mr. Nippers," said I, "I'd prefer that you would withdraw for the present."

Somehow, of late, I had got into the way of involuntarily using this word "prefer" upon all sorts of not exactly suitable occasions. And I trembled to think that my contact with the scrivener had already and seriously affected me in a mental way. And what further and deeper aberration might it not yet produce? This apprehension had not been without efficacy in determining me to summary measures.

As Nippers, looking very sour and sulky, was departing, Turkey blandly and deferentially approached.

"With submission, sir," said he, "yesterday I was thinking about Bartleby here, and I think that if he would but prefer to take a quart of good ale every day, it would do much towards mending him, and enabling him to assist in examining his papers."

"So you have got the word, too," said I, slightly excited.

"With submission, what word, sir?" asked Turkey, respectfully crowding himself into the contracted space behind the screen, and by so doing, making me jostle the scrivener. "What word, sir?"

"I would prefer to be left alone here," said Bartleby, as if offended at being mobbed in his privacy.

"*That's* the word, Turkey," said I—"*that's* it."

"Oh, *prefer?* oh yes—queer word. I never use it myself. But, sir, as I was saying, if he would but prefer—"

"Turkey," interrupted I, "you will please withdraw."

"Oh certainly, sir, if you prefer that I should."

As he opened the folding-door to retire, Nippers at his desk caught a glimpse of me, and asked whether I would prefer to have a certain paper copied on blue paper or white. He did not in the least roguishly accent the word "prefer." It was plain that it involuntarily rolled from his tongue. I thought to myself, surely I must get rid of a demented man, who already has in some degree turned the tongues, if not the heads of myself and clerks. But I thought it prudent not to break the dismission at once.

The next day I noticed that Bartleby did nothing but stand at his window in his dead-wall revery. Upon asking him why he did not write, he said that he had decided upon doing no more writing.

"Why, how now? what next?" exclaimed I, "do no more writing?"

"No more."

"And what is the reason?"

"Do you not see the reason for yourself?" he indifferently replied.

I looked steadfastly at him, and perceived that his eyes looked dull and glazed. Instantly it occurred to me, that his unexampled diligence in copying by his dim window for the first few weeks of his stay with me might have temporarily impaired his vision.

I was touched. I said something in condolence with him. I hinted that of course he did wisely in abstaining from writing for a while; and urged him to embrace that opportunity of taking wholesome exercise in the open air. This, however, he did not do. A few days after this, my other clerks being absent, and being in a great hurry to dispatch certain letters by the mail, I thought that, having nothing else earthly to do, Bartleby would surely be less inflexible than usual, and carry these letters to the Post Office. But he blankly declined. So, much to my inconvenience, I went myself.

Still added days went by. Whether Bartleby's eyes improved or not, I could not say. To all appearance, I thought they did. But when I asked him if they did he vouchsafed no answer. At all events, he would do no copying. At last, in replying to my urgings, he informed me that he had permanently given up copying.

"What!" exclaimed I; "suppose your eyes should get entirely well— better than ever before—would you not copy then?"

"I have given up copying," he answered, and slid aside.

He remained as ever, a fixture in my chamber. Nay—if that were possible—he became still more of a fixture than before. What was to be done? He would do nothing in the office; why should he stay there? In plain fact, he had now become a millstone to me, not only useless as a necklace, but afflictive to bear. Yet I was sorry for him. I speak less than truth when I say that, on his own account, he occasioned me uneasiness. If he would but have named a single relative or friend, I would instantly have written, and urged their taking the poor fellow away to some convenient retreat. But he seemed alone, absolutely alone in the universe. A bit of wreck in the mid-Atlantic. At length, necessities connected with my business tyrannized over all other considerations. Decently as I could, I told Bartleby that in six days' time he must unconditionally leave the office. I warned him to take measures, in the interval, for procuring some other abode. I offered to assist him in this endeavor, if he himself would but take the first step towards a removal. "And when you finally quit me, Bartleby," added I, "I shall see that you go not away entirely unprovided. Six days from this hour, remember."

At the expiration of that period, I peeped behind the screen, and lo! Bartleby was there.

I buttoned up my coat, balanced myself; advanced slowly towards him, touched his shoulder, and said, "The time has come; you must quit this place; I am sorry for you; here is money; but you must go."

"I would prefer not," he replied, with his back still towards me.

"You *must*."

He remained silent.

Now I had an unbounded confidence in this man's common honesty. He had frequently restored to me sixpences and shillings carelessly dropped upon the floor, for I am apt to be very reckless in such shirt-button affairs. The proceeding, then, which followed will not be deemed extraordinary.

"Bartleby," said I, "I owe you twelve dollars on account; here are thirty-two; the odd twenty are yours—Will you take it?" and I handed the bills towards him.

But he made no motion.

"I will leave them here, then," putting them under a weight on the table. Then taking my hat and cane and going to the door, I tranquilly turned and added—"After you have removed your things from these offices, Bartleby, you will of course lock the door—since every one is now gone for the day but you—and if you please, slip your key underneath the mat, so that I may have it in the morning. I shall not see you again; so good-bye to you. If, hereafter, in your new place of abode, I can be of any service to you, do not fail to advise me by letter. Good-bye, Bartleby, and fare you well."

But he answered not a word; like the last column of some ruined temple, he remained standing mute and solitary in the middle of the otherwise deserted room.

As I walked home in a pensive mood, my vanity got the better of my pity. I could not but highly plume myself on my masterly management in getting rid of Bartleby. Masterly I call it, and such it must appear to any dispassionate thinker. The beauty of my procedure seemed to consist in its perfect quietness. There was no vulgar bullying, no bravado of any sort, no choleric hectoring, and striding to and fro across the apartment, jerking out vehement commands for Bartleby to bundle himself off with his beggarly traps. Nothing of the kind. Without loudly bidding Bartleby depart—as an inferior genius might have done—I *assumed* the ground that depart he must; and upon that assumption built all I had to say. The more I thought over my procedure, the more I was charmed with it. Nevertheless, next morning, upon awakening, I had my doubts—I had somehow slept off the fumes of vanity. One of the coolest and wisest hours a man has, is just after he awakes in the morning. My procedure seemed as sagacious as ever—but only in theory. How it would prove in practice—there was the rub. It was truly a beautiful thought to have assumed Bartleby's departure; but, after all, that assumption was simply my own, and none of Bartleby's. The great point was, not whether I had assumed that he would quit me, but whether he would prefer to do so. He was more a man of preferences than assumptions.

After breakfast, I walked down town, arguing the probabilities *pro* and *con*. One moment I thought it would prove a miserable failure, and Bartleby would be found all alive at my office as usual; the next moment it seemed certain that I should find his chair empty. And so I kept veering about. At the corner of Broadway and Canal Street, I saw quite an excited group of people standing in earnest conversation.

"I'll take odds he doesn't," said a voice as I passed.

"Doesn't go?—done!" said I, "put up your money."

I was instinctively putting my hand in my pocket to produce my own, when I remembered that this was an election day. The words I had overheard bore no reference to Bartleby, but to the success or non-success of some candidate for the mayoralty. In my intent frame of mind, I had, as it were, imagined that all Broadway shared in my excitement, and were debating the same question with me. I passed on, very thankful that the uproar of the street screened my momentary absent-mindedness.

As I had intended, I was earlier than usual at my office door. I stood listening for a moment. All was still. He must be gone. I tried the knob. The door was locked. Yes, my procedure had worked to a charm; he indeed must be vanished. Yet a certain melancholy mixed with this: I was almost sorry for my brilliant success. I was fumbling under the door mat for the key, which Bartleby was to have left there for me, when accidentally my knee knocked against a panel, producing a summoning sound, and in response a voice came to me from within—"Not yet; I am occupied."

It was Bartleby.

I was thunderstruck. For an instant I stood like the man who, pipe in mouth, was killed one cloudless afternoon long ago in Virginia, by summer lightning; at his own warm open window he was killed, and remained leaning out there upon the dreamy afternoon, till someone touched him, when he fell.

"Not gone!" I murmured at last. But again obeying that wondrous ascendancy which the inscrutable scrivener had over me, and from which ascendancy, for all my chafing, I could not completely escape, I slowly went down stairs and out into the street, and while walking round the block, considered what I should next do in this unheard-of perplexity. Turn the man out by an actual thrusting I could not; to drive him away by calling him hard names would not do; calling in the police was an unpleasant idea; and yet, permit him to enjoy his cadaverous triumph over me—this, too, I could not think of. What was to be done? or, if nothing could be done, was there anything further that I could *assume* in the matter? Yes, as before I had prospectively assumed that Bartleby would depart, so now I might retrospectively assume that departed he was. In the legitimate carrying out of this assumption, I might enter my office in a great hurry, and pretending not to see Bartleby at all, walk straight against him as if he were air. Such a proceeding would in a singular degree have the appearance of a home-thrust. It was hardly possible that Bartleby could withstand such an application of the doctrine of assumption. But upon second thoughts the success of the plan seemed rather dubious. I resolved to argue the matter over with him again.

"Bartleby," said I, entering the office, with a quietly severe expression, "I am seriously displeased. I am pained, Bartleby. I had thought better of you. I had imagined you of such a gentlemanly organization, that in any delicate dilemma a slight hint would suffice—in short, an assumption. But it appears I am deceived. Why," I added, unaffectedly starting, "you have not even touched that money yet," pointing to it, just where I had left it the evening previous.

He answered nothing.

"Will you, or will you not, quit me?" I now demanded in a sudden passion, advancing close to him.

"I would prefer *not* to quit you," he replied, gently emphasizing the *not*.

"What earthly right have you to stay here? Do you pay any rent? Do you pay my taxes? Or is this property yours?"

He answered nothing.

"Are you ready to go on and write now? Are your eyes recovered? Could you copy a small paper for me this morning? or help examine a few lines? or step round to the Post Office? In a word, will you do anything at all, to give a coloring to your refusal to depart the premises?"

He silently retired into his hermitage.

I was now in such a state of nervous resentment that I thought it but prudent to check myself at present from further demonstrations. Bartleby and I were alone. I remembered the tragedy of the unfortunate Adams and the still more unfortunate Colt in the solitary office of the latter; and how poor Colt,° being dreadfully incensed by Adams, and imprudently permitting himself to get wildly excited, was at unawares hurried into his fatal act—an act which certainly no man could possibly deplore more than the actor himself. Often it had occurred to me in my ponderings upon the subject that had that altercation taken place in the public street, or at a private residence, it would not have terminated as it did. It was the circumstance of being alone in a solitary office, up stairs, of a building entirely unhallowed by humanizing domestic associations— an uncarpeted office, doubtless, of a dusty, haggard sort of appearance— this it must have been, which greatly helped to enhance the irritable desperation of the hapless Colt.

But when this old Adam of resentment rose in me and tempted me concerning Bartleby, I grappled him and threw him. How? Why, simply by recalling the divine injunction: "A new commandment give I unto you, that ye love one another." Yes, this it was that saved me. Aside from higher considerations, charity often operates as a vastly wise and prudent principle—a great safeguard to its possessor. Men have committed murder for jealousy's sake, and anger's sake, and hatred's sake, and selfishness' sake, and spiritual pride's sake; but no man, that ever I heard of, ever committed a diabolical murder for sweet charity's sake. Mere selfinterest, then, if no better motive can be enlisted, should, especially with high-tempered men, prompt all beings to charity and philanthropy. At any rate, upon the occasion in question, I strove to drown my exasperated feelings towards the scrivener by benevolently construing his conduct. Poor fellow, poor fellow! thought I, he don't mean anything; and besides, he has seen hard times, and ought to be indulged.

I endeavored, also, immediately to occupy myself, and at the same time to comfort my despondency. I tried to fancy, that in the course of the morning, at such time as might prove agreeable to him, Bartleby, of

Colt: John C. Colt, who murdered the printer Samuel Adams in a fit of rage in January 1842, committed suicide a half-hour before he was to be hanged for the crime.

his own free accord, would emerge from his hermitage and take up some decided line of march in the direction of the door. But no. Half-past twelve o'clock came; Turkey began to glow in the face, overturn his ink-stand, and become generally obstreperous; Nippers abated down into quietude and courtesy; Ginger Nut munched his noon apple; and Bartleby remained standing at his window in one of his profoundest dead-wall reveries. Will it be credited? Ought I to acknowledge it? That afternoon I left the office without saying one further word to him.

Some days now passed, during which, at leisure intervals I looked a little into "Edwards on the Will," and "Priestley° on Necessity." Under the circumstances, those books induced a salutary feeling. Gradually I slid into the persuasion that these troubles of mine, touching the scrivener, had been all predestined from eternity, and Bartleby was billeted upon me for some mysterious purpose of an all-wise Providence, which it was not for a mere mortal like me to fathom. Yes, Bartleby, stay there behind your screen, thought I; I shall persecute you no more; you are harmless and noiseless as any of these old chairs; in short, I never feel so private as when I know you are here. At last I see it, I feel it; I penetrate to the predestined purpose of my life. I am content. Others may have loftier parts to enact; but my mission in this world, Bartleby, is to furnish you with office-room for such period as you may see fit to remain.

I believe that this wise and blessed frame of mind would have continued with me, had it not been for the unsolicited and uncharitable remarks obtruded upon me by my professional friends who visited the rooms. But thus it often is, that the constant friction of illiberal minds wears out at last the best resolves of the more generous. Though to be sure, when I reflected upon it, it was not strange that people entering my office should be struck by the peculiar aspect of the unaccountable Bartleby, and so be tempted to throw out some sinister observations concerning him. Sometimes an attorney, having business with me, and calling at my office, and finding no one but the scrivener there, would undertake to obtain some sort of precise information from him touching my whereabouts; but without heeding his idle talk, Bartleby would remain standing immovable in the middle of the room. So after contemplating him in that position for a time, the attorney would depart, no wiser than he came.

Also, when a reference was going on, and the room full of lawyers and witnesses, and business driving fast, some deeply-occupied legal gentle-

---

Edwards . . . Priestley: Jonathan Edwards (1703–1758), American theologian and author of the Calvinist *Freedom of the Will* (1754), and Joseph Priestley (1733–1804), English scientist, clergyman, and author of *The Doctrine of Philosophical Necessity* (1777).

man present, seeing Bartleby wholly unemployed, would request him to run round to his (the legal gentleman's) office and fetch some papers for him. Thereupon, Bartleby would tranquilly decline, and yet remain idle as before. Then the lawyer would give a great stare, and turn to me. And what could I say? At last I was made aware that all through the circle of my professional acquaintance, a whisper of wonder was running round, having reference to the strange creature I kept at my office. This worried me very much. And as the idea came upon me of his possibly turning out a long-lived man, and keeping occupying my chambers, and denying my authority; and perplexing my visitors; and scandalizing my professional reputation; and casting a general gloom over the premises; keeping soul and body together to the last upon his savings (for doubtless he spent but half a dime a day), and in the end perhaps outlive me, and claim possession of my office by right of his perpetual occupancy: as all these dark anticipations crowded upon me more and more, and my friends continually intruded their relentless remarks upon the apparition in my room, a great change was wrought in me. I resolved to gather all my faculties together, and forever rid me of this intolerable incubus.

Ere revolving any complicated project, however, adapted to this end, I first simply suggested to Bartleby the propriety of his permanent departure. In a calm and serious tone, I commended the idea to his careful and mature consideration. But, having taken three days to meditate upon it, he apprised me, that his original determination remained the same; in short, that he still preferred to abide with me.

What shall I do? I now said to myself, buttoning up my coat to the last button. What shall I do? what ought I to do? what does conscience say I *should* do with this man, or, rather, ghost. Rid myself of him, I must; go, he shall. But how? You will not thrust him, the poor, pale, passive mortal—you will not thrust such a helpless creature out of your door? you will not dishonor yourself by such cruelty? No, I will not, I cannot do that. Rather would I let him live and die here, and then mason up his remains in the wall. What, then, will you do? For all your coaxing, he will not budge. Bribes he leaves under your own paper-weight on your table; in short, it is quite plain that he prefers to cling to you.

Then something severe, something unusual must be done. What! surely you will not have him collared by a constable, and commit his innocent pallor to the common jail? And upon what ground could you procure such a thing to be done?—a vagrant, is he? What! he a vagrant, a wanderer, who refuses to budge? It is because he will not be a vagrant, then, that you seek to count him *as* a vagrant. That is too absurd. No visible means of support: there I have him. Wrong again: for indubitably he *does* support himself, and that is the only unanswerable proof that any man can show of his possessing the means so to do. No more, then.

Since he will not quit me, I must quit him. I will change my offices; I will move elsewhere, and give him fair notice, that if I find him on my new premises I will then proceed against him as a common trespasser.

Acting accordingly, next day I thus addressed him: "I find these chambers too far from the City Hall; the air is unwholesome. In a word, I propose to remove my offices next week, and shall no longer require your services. I tell you this now, in order that you may seek another place."

He made no reply, and nothing more was said.

On the appointed day I engaged carts and men, proceeded to my chambers, and, having but little furniture, everything was removed in a few hours. Throughout, the scrivener remained standing behind the screen, which I directed to be removed the last thing. It was withdrawn; and, being folded up like a huge folio, left him the motionless occupant of a naked room. I stood in the entry watching him a moment, while something from within me upbraided me.

I re-entered, with my hand in my pocket—and—and my heart in my mouth.

"Good-bye, Bartleby; I am going—good-bye, and God some way bless you; and take that," slipping something in his hand. But it dropped upon the floor, and then—strange to say—I tore myself from him whom I had so longed to be rid of.

Established in my new quarters, for a day or two I kept the door locked, and started at every footfall in the passages. When I returned to my rooms, after any little absence, I would pause at the threshold for an instant, and attentively listen, ere applying my key. But these fears were needless. Bartleby never came nigh me.

I thought all was going well, when a perturbed-looking stranger visited me, inquiring whether I was the person who had recently occupied rooms at No.—Wall Street.

Full of forebodings, I replied that I was.

"Then, sir," said the stranger, who proved a lawyer, "you are responsible for the man you left there. He refuses to do any copying; he refuses to do anything; he says he prefers not to; and he refuses to quit the premises."

"I am very sorry, sir," said I, with assumed tranquillity, but an inward tremor, "but, really, the man you allude to is nothing to me—he is no relation or apprentice of mine, that you should hold me responsible for him."

"In mercy's name, who is he?"

"I certainly cannot inform you. I know nothing about him. Formerly I employed him as a copyist; but he has done nothing for me now for some time past."

"I shall settle him, then—good morning, sir."

Several days passed, and I heard nothing more; and, though I often felt a charitable prompting to call at the place and see poor Bartleby, yet a certain squeamishness, of I know not what, withheld me.

All is over with him, by this time, thought I, at last, when, through another week, no further intelligence reached me. But, coming to my room the day after, I found several persons waiting at my door in a high state of nervous excitement.

"That's the man—here he comes," cried the foremost one, whom I recognized as the lawyer who had previously called upon me alone.

"You must take him away, sir, at once," cried a portly person among them, advancing upon me, and whom I knew to be the landlord of No.— Wall Street. "These gentlemen, my tenants, cannot stand it any longer; Mr. B——" pointing to the lawyer, "has turned him out of his room, and he now persists in haunting the building generally, sitting upon the banisters of the stairs by day, and sleeping in the entry by night. Everybody is concerned; clients are leaving the offices; some fears are entertained of a mob; something you must do, and that without delay."

Aghast at this torrent, I fell back before it, and would fain have locked myself in my new quarters. In vain I persisted that Bartleby was nothing to me—no more than to any one else. In vain—I was the last person known to have anything to do with him, and they held me to the terrible account. Fearful, then, of being exposed in the papers (as one person present obscurely threatened), I considered the matter, and, at length, said, that if the lawyer would give me a confidential interview with the scrivener, in his (the lawyer's) own room, I would, that afternoon, strive my best to rid them of the nuisance they complained of.

Going up stairs to my old haunt, there was Bartleby silently sitting upon the banister at the landing.

"What are you doing here, Bartleby?" said I.

"Sitting upon the banister," he mildly replied.

I motioned him into the lawyer's room, who then left us.

"Bartleby," said I, "are you aware that you are the cause of great tribulation to me, by persisting in occupying the entry after being dismissed from the office?"

No answer.

"Now one of two things must take place. Either you must do something, or something must be done to you. Now what sort of business would you like to engage in? Would you like to re-engage in copying for some one?"

"No; I would prefer not to make any change."

"Would you like a clerkship in a dry-goods store?"

"There is too much confinement about that. No, I would not like a clerkship; but I am not particular."

"Too much confinement," I cried, "why, you keep yourself confined all the time!"

"I would prefer not to take a clerkship," he rejoined, as if to settle that little item at once.

"How would a bar-tender's business suit you? There is no trying of the eye-sight in that."

"I would not like it at all; though, as I said before, I am not particular."

His unwonted wordiness inspirited me. I returned to the charge.

"Well, then, would you like to travel through the country collecting bills for the merchants? That would improve your health."

"No, I would prefer to be doing something else."

"How, then, would going as a companion to Europe, to entertain some young gentleman with your conversation — how would that suit you?"

"Not at all. It does not strike me that there is anything definite about that. I like to be stationary. But I am not particular."

"Stationary you shall be, then," I cried, now losing all patience, and, for the first time in all my exasperating connections with him, fairly flying into a passion. "If you do not go away from these premises before night, I shall feel bound — indeed, I *am* bound — to — to — to quit the premises myself!" I rather absurdly concluded, knowing not with what possible threat to try to frighten his immobility into compliance. Despairing of all further efforts, I was precipitately leaving him, when a final thought occurred to me — one which had not been wholly unindulged before.

"Bartleby," said I, in the kindest tone I could assume under such exciting circumstances, "will you go home with me now not to my office, but my dwelling — and remain there till we can conclude upon some convenient arrangement for you at our leisure? Come, let us start now, right away."

"No: at present I would prefer not to make any change at all."

I answered nothing; but, effectually dodging every one by the suddenness and rapidity of my flight, rushed from the building, ran up Wall Street towards Broadway, and, jumping into the first omnibus, was soon removed from pursuit. As soon as tranquillity returned, I distinctly perceived that I had now done all that I possibly could, both in respect to the demands of the landlord and his tenants, and with regard to my own desire and sense of duty, to benefit Bartleby, and shield him from rude persecution. I now strove to be entirely care-free and quiescent; and my conscience justified me in the attempt; though, indeed, it was not so successful as I could have wished. So fearful was I of being again hunted out by the incensed landlord and his exasperated tenants, that, surrendering my business to Nippers, for a few days, I drove about the upper part of the town and through the suburbs, in my rockaway; crossed over to Jersey City and Hoboken, and paid fugitive visits to Manhattanville and Astoria. In fact, I almost lived in my rockaway for the time.

When again I entered my office, lo, a note from the landlord lay upon the desk. I opened it with trembling hands. It informed me that the writer had sent to the police, and had Bartleby removed to the Tombs as a vagrant. Moreover, since I knew more about him than any one else, he wished me to appear at that place, and make a suitable statement of the facts. These tidings had a conflicting effect upon me. At first I was indignant; but, at last, almost approved. The landlord's energetic, summary disposition, had led him to adopt a procedure which I do not think I would have decided upon myself; and yet, as a last resort, under such peculiar circumstances, it seemed the only plan.

As I afterwards learned, the poor scrivener, when told that he must be conducted to the Tombs, offered not the slightest obstacle, but, in his pale, unmoving way, silently acquiesced.

Some of the compassionate and curious bystanders joined the party; and headed by one of the constables arm-in-arm with Bartleby, the silent procession filed its way through all the noise, and heat, and joy of the roaring thoroughfares at noon.

The same day I received the note, I went to the Tombs, or, to speak more properly, the Halls of Justice. Seeking the right officer, I stated the purpose of my call, and was informed that the individual I described was, indeed, within. I then assured the functionary that Bartleby was a perfectly honest man, and greatly to be compassionated, however unaccountably eccentric. I narrated all I knew, and closed by suggesting the idea of letting him remain in as indulgent confinement as possible, till something less harsh might be done — though, indeed, I hardly knew what. At all events, if nothing else could be decided upon, the almshouse must receive him. I then begged to have an interview.

Being under no disgraceful charge, and quite serene and harmless in all his ways, they had permitted him freely to wander about the prison, and, especially, in the inclosed grass-platted yards thereof. And so I found him there, standing all alone in the quietest of the yards, his face towards a high wall, while all around, from the narrow slits of the jail windows, I thought I saw peering out upon him the eyes of murderers and thieves.

"Bartleby!"

"I know you," he said, without looking round — "and I want nothing to say to you."

"It was not I that brought you here, Bartleby," said I, keenly pained at his implied suspicion. "And to you, this should not be so vile a place. Nothing reproachful attaches to you by being here. And see, it is not so sad a place as one might think. Look, there is the sky, and here is the grass."

"I know where I am," he replied, but would say nothing more, and so I left him.

As I entered the corridor again, a broad meat-like man, in an apron, accosted me, and, jerking his thumb over my shoulder, said "Is that your friend?"

"Yes."

"Does he want to starve? If he does, let him live on the prison fare, that's all."

"Who are you?" asked I, not knowing what to make of such an unofficially speaking person in such a place.

"I am the grub-man. Such gentlemen as have friends here, hire me to provide them with something good to eat."

"Is this so?" said I, turning to the turnkey.

He said it was.

"Well, then," said I, slipping some silver into the grub-man's hands (for so they called him), "I want you to give particular attention to my friend there; let him have the best dinner you can get. And you must be as polite to him as possible."

"Introduce me, will you?" said the grub-man, looking at me with an expression which seemed to say he was all impatience for an opportunity to give a specimen of his breeding.

Thinking it would prove of benefit to the scrivener, I acquiesced; and, asking the grub-man his name, went up with him to Bartleby.

"Bartleby, this is a friend; you will find him very useful to you."

"Your sarvant, sir, your sarvant," said the grub-man, making a low salutation behind his apron. "Hope you find it pleasant here, sir; nice grounds—cool apartments—hope you'll stay with us some time—try to make it agreeable. What will you have for dinner to-day?"

"I prefer not to dine to-day," said Bartleby, turning away. "It would disagree with me; I am unused to dinners." So saying, he slowly moved to the other side of the inclosure, and took up a position fronting the dead-wall.

"How's this?" said the grub-man, addressing me with a stare of astonishment. "He's odd, ain't he?"

"I think he is a little deranged," said I, sadly.

"Deranged? deranged is it? Well, now, upon my word, I thought that friend of yourn was a gentleman forger; they are always pale and genteel-like, them forgers. I can't help pity 'em—can't help it, sir. Did you know Monroe Edwards?" he added, touchingly, and paused. Then, laying his hand piteously on my shoulder, sighed, "he died of consumption at Sing-Sing. So you weren't acquainted with Monroe?"

"No, I was never socially acquainted with any forgers. But I cannot stop longer. Look to my friend yonder. You will not lose by it. I will see you again."

Some few days after this, I again obtained admission to the Tombs, and went through the corridors in quest of Bartleby; but without finding him.

"I saw him coming from his cell not long ago," said a turnkey, "may be he's gone to loiter in the yards."

So I went in that direction.

"Are you looking for the silent man?" said another turnkey, passing me. "Yonder he lies—sleeping in the yard there. 'Tis not twenty minutes since I saw him lie down."

The yard was entirely quiet. It was not accessible to the common prisoners. The surrounding walls, of amazing thickness, kept off all sounds behind them. The Egyptian character of the masonry weighed upon me with its gloom. But a soft imprisoned turf grew under foot. The heart of the eternal pyramids, it seemed, wherein, by some strange magic, through the clefts, grass-seed, dropped by birds, had sprung.

Strangely huddled at the base of the wall, his knees drawn up, and lying on his side, his head touching the cold stones, I saw the wasted Bartleby. But nothing stirred. I paused; then went close up to him; stooped over, and saw that his dim eyes were open; otherwise he seemed profoundly sleeping. Something prompted me to touch him. I felt his hand, when a tingling shiver ran up my arm and down my spine to my feet.

The round face of the grub-man peered upon me now. "His dinner is ready. Won't he dine to-day, either? Or does he live without dining?"

"Lives without dining," said I, and closed the eyes.

"Eh!—He's asleep, ain't he?"

"With kings and counselors,"° murmured I.

There would seem little need for proceeding further in this history. Imagination will readily supply the meagre recital of poor Bartleby's interment. But, ere parting with the reader, let me say, that if this little narrative has sufficiently interested him, to awaken curiosity as to who Bartleby was, and what manner of life he led prior to the present narrator's making his acquaintance, I can only reply, that in such curiosity I fully share, but am wholly unable to gratify it. Yet here I hardly know whether I should divulge one little item of rumor, which came to my ear a few months after the scrivener's decease. Upon what basis it rested, I could never ascertain; and hence, how true it is I cannot now tell. But, inasmuch as this vague report has not been without a certain suggestive interest to me, however sad, it may prove the same with some others;

With kings and counselors: A reference to the biblical book of Job, 3:13–14: "then had I been at rest with kings and counselors of the earth, which built desolate places for themselves."

and so I will briefly mention it. The report was this: that Bartleby had been a subordinate clerk in the Dead Letter Office at Washington, from which he had been suddenly removed by a change in the administration. When I think over this rumor, hardly can I express the emotions which seize me. Dead letters! does it not sound like dead men? Conceive a man by nature and misfortune prone to a pallid hopelessness, can any business seem more fitted to heighten it than that of continually handling these dead letters, and assorting them for the flames? For by the cartload they are annually burned. Sometimes from out the folded paper the pale clerk takes a ring—the finger it was meant for, perhaps, moulders in the grave; a bank-note sent in swiftest charity—he whom it would relieve, nor eats nor hungers any more; pardon for those who died despairing; hope for those who died unhoping; good tidings for those who died stifled by unrelieved calamities. On errands of life, these letters speed to death.

Ah, Bartleby! Ah, humanity!

[1853]

SARAH ORNE JEWETT   [1849–1909]

A White Heron

I

The woods were already filled with shadows one June evening, just before eight o'clock, though a bright sunset still glimmered faintly among the trunks of the trees. A little girl was driving home her cow, a plodding, dilatory, provoking creature in her behavior, but a valued companion for all that. They were going away from the western light, and striking deep into the dark woods, but their feet were familiar with the path, and it was no matter whether their eyes could see it or not.

There was hardly a night the summer through when the old cow could be found waiting at the pasture bars; on the contrary, it was her greatest pleasure to hide herself away among the high huckleberry bushes, and though she wore a loud bell she had made the discovery that if one stood perfectly still it would not ring. So Sylvia had to hunt for her until she found her and call Co'! Co'! with never an answering Moo, until her childish patience was quite spent. If the creature had not given good milk and plenty of it, the case would have seemed very different to her owners. Besides, Sylvia had all the time there was, and very little use to make of it. Sometimes in pleasant weather it was a consolation to look upon the cow's pranks as an intelligent attempt to play hide and seek, and as the child had no playmates she lent herself to this amusement with a good deal of zest. Though this chase had been so long that the wary animal herself had given an unusual signal of her whereabouts, Sylvia had only laughed when she came upon Mistress Moolly at the swampside, and urged her affectionately homeward with a twig of birch leaves. The old cow was not inclined to wander farther, she even turned in the right direction for once as they left the pasture, and stepped along the road at a good pace. She was quite ready to be milked now, and seldom stopped to browse. Sylvia wondered what her grandmother would say because they were so late. It was a great while since she had left home at half past five o'clock, but everybody knew the difficulty of making this errand a short one. Mrs. Tilley had chased the horned torment too many summer evenings herself to blame any one else for lingering, and was only thankful as she waited that she had Sylvia, nowadays, to give such valuable assistance. The good woman suspected that Sylvia loitered occasionally on her own account; there never was such a child for straying about out-of-doors since the world was made! Everybody said that it was a good change for a little maid who had tried to grow for eight years in a crowded manufacturing town, but, as for Sylvia herself, it seemed as if she never had been alive at all before she came to live at the farm. She thought often with wistful compassion of a wretched dry geranium that belonged to a town neighbor.

"'Afraid of folks,'" old Mrs. Tilley said to herself, with a smile, after she had made the unlikely choice of Sylvia from her daughter's houseful of children, and was returning to the farm. "'Afraid of folks,' they said! I guess she won't be troubled no great with 'em up to the old place!" When they reached the door of the lonely house and stopped to unlock it, and the cat came to purr loudly, and rub against them, a deserted pussy, indeed, but fat with young robins, Sylvia whispered that this was a beautiful place to live in, and she never should wish to go home.

The companions followed the shady wood-road, the cow taking slow steps, and the child very fast ones. The cow stopped long at the brook to drink, as if the pasture were not half a swamp, and Sylvia stood still and waited, letting her bare feet cool themselves in the shoal water, while the great twilight moths struck softly against her. She waded on through the brook as the cow moved away, and listened to the thrushes with a heart that beat fast with pleasure. There was a stirring in the great boughs overhead. They were full of little birds and beasts that seemed to be wide-awake, and going about their world, or else saying good-night to each other in sleepy twitters. Sylvia herself felt sleepy as she walked along. However, it was not much farther to the house, and the air was soft and sweet. She was not often in the woods so late as this, and it made her feel as if she were a part of the gray shadows and the moving leaves. She was just thinking how long it seemed since she first came to the farm a year ago, and wondering if everything went on in the noisy town just the same as when she was there; the thought of the great red-faced boy who used to chase and frighten her made her hurry along the path to escape from the shadow of the trees.

Suddenly this little woods-girl is horror-stricken to hear a clear whistle not very far away. Not a bird's whistle, which would have a sort of friend-liness, but a boy's whistle, determined, and somewhat aggressive. Sylvia left the cow to whatever sad fate might await her, and stepped discreetly aside into the bushes, but she was just too late. The enemy had discovered her, and called out in a very cheerful and persuasive tone, "Halloa, little girl, how far is it to the road?" and trembling Sylvia answered almost inaudibly, "A good ways."

She did not dare to look boldly at the tall young man, who carried a gun over his shoulder, but she came out of her bush and again followed the cow, while he walked alongside.

"I have been hunting for some birds," the stranger said kindly, "and I have lost my way, and need a friend very much. Don't be afraid," he added gallantly. "Speak up and tell me what your name is, and whether you think I can spend the night at your house, and go out gunning early in the morning."

Sylvia was more alarmed than before. Would not her grandmother consider her much to blame? But who could have foreseen such an accident as this? It did not appear to be her fault, and she hung her head as if the stem of it were broken, but managed to answer, "Sylvy," with much effort when her companion again asked her name.

Mrs. Tilley was standing in the doorway when the trio came into view. The cow gave a loud moo by way of explanation.

"Yes, you'd better speak up for yourself, you old trial! Where'd she tucked herself away this time, Sylvy?" Sylvia kept an awed silence; she knew by instinct that her grandmother did not comprehend the gravity of the situation. She must be mistaking the stranger for one of the farmer-lads of the region.

The young man stood his gun beside the door, and dropped a heavy game-bag beside it; then he bade Mrs. Tilley good-evening, and repeated his wayfarer's story, and asked if he could have a night's lodging.

"Put me anywhere you like," he said. "I must be off early in the morning, before day; but I am very hungry, indeed. You can give me some milk at any rate, that's plain."

"Dear sakes, yes," responded the hostess, whose long slumbering hospitality seemed to be easily awakened. "You might fare better if you went out on the main road a mile or so, but you're welcome to what we've got. I'll milk right off, and you make yourself at home. You can sleep on husks or feathers," she proffered graciously. "I raised them all myself. There's good pasturing for geese just below here towards the ma'sh. Now step round and set a plate for the gentleman, Sylvy!" And Sylvia promptly stepped. She was glad to have something to do, and she was hungry herself.

It was a surprise to find so clean and comfortable a little dwelling in this New England wilderness. The young man had known the horrors of its most primitive housekeeping, and the dreary squalor of that level of society which does not rebel at the companionship of hens. This was the best thrift of an old-fashioned farmstead, though on such a small scale that it seemed like a hermitage. He listened eagerly to the old woman's quaint talk, he watched Sylvia's pale face and shining gray eyes with ever growing enthusiasm, and insisted that this was the best supper he had eaten for a month; then, afterward, the new-made friends sat down in the doorway together while the moon came up.

Soon it would be berry-time, and Sylvia was a great help at picking. The cow was a good milker, though a plaguy thing to keep track of, the hostess gossiped frankly, adding presently that she had buried four children, so that Sylvia's mother, and a son (who might be dead) in California were all the children she had left. "Dan, my boy, was a great hand to go gunning," she explained sadly. "I never wanted for pa'tridges or gray squer'ls while he was to home. He's been a great wand'rer, I expect, and he's no hand to write letters. There, I don't blame him, I'd ha' seen the world myself if it had been so I could.

"Sylvia takes after him," the grandmother continued affectionately, after a minute's pause. "There ain't a foot o' ground she don't know her way over, and the wild creatur's counts her one o' themselves. Squer'ls she'll tame to come an' feed right out o' her hands, and all sorts o' birds. Last winter she got the jay-birds to bangeing here, and I believe she'd 'a' scanted herself of her own meals to have plenty to throw out amongst 'em, if I hadn't kep' watch. Anything but crows, I tell her, I'm willin' to help support,—though Dan he went an' tamed one o' them that did seem to have reason same as folks. It was round here a good spell after he went away. Dan an' his father they didn't hitch, — but he never held up his head ag'in after Dan had dared him an' gone off."

The guest did not notice this hint of family sorrows in his eager interest in something else.

"So Sylvy knows all about birds, does she?" he exclaimed, as he looked round at the little girl who sat, very demure but increasingly sleepy, in the moonlight. "I am making a collection of birds myself. I have been at it ever since I was a boy." (Mrs. Tilley smiled.) "There are two or three very rare ones I have been hunting for these five years. I mean to get them on my own ground if they can be found."

"Do you cage 'em up?" asked Mrs. Tilley doubtfully, in response to this enthusiastic announcement.

"Oh, no, they're stuffed and preserved, dozens and dozens of them," said the ornithologist, "and I have shot or snared every one myself. I caught a glimpse of a white heron three miles from here on Saturday, and I have followed it in this direction. They have never been found in this district at all. The little white heron, it is," and he turned again to look at Sylvia with the hope of discovering that the rare bird was one of her acquaintances.

But Sylvia was watching a hop-toad in the narrow footpath.

"You would know the heron if you saw it," the stranger continued eagerly. "A queer tall white bird with soft feathers and long thin legs. And it would have a nest perhaps in the top of a high tree, made of sticks, something like a hawk's nest."

Sylvia's heart gave a wild beat; she knew that strange white bird, and had once stolen softly near where it stood in some bright green swamp grass, away over at the other side of the woods. There was an open place where the sunshine always seemed strangely yellow and hot, where tall, nodding rushes grew, and her grandmother had warned her that she might sink in the soft black mud underneath and never be heard of more. Not far beyond were the salt marshes and beyond those was the sea, the sea which Sylvia wondered and dreamed about, but never had looked upon, though its great voice could often be heard above the noise of the woods on stormy nights.

"I can't think of anything I should like so much as to find that heron's nest," the handsome stranger was saying. "I would give ten dollars to anybody who could show it to me," he added desperately, "and I mean to spend my whole vacation hunting for it if need be. Perhaps it was only migrating, or had been chased out of its own region by some bird of prey."

Mrs. Tilley gave amazed attention to all this, but Sylvia still watched the toad, not divining, as she might have done at some calmer time, that the creature wished to get to its hole under the doorstep, and was much hindered by the unusual spectators at that hour of the evening. No amount of thought, that night, could decide how many wished-for treasures the ten dollars, so lightly spoken of, would buy.

The next day the young sportsman hovered about the woods, and Sylvia kept him company, having lost her first fear of the friendly lad, who proved to be most kind and sympathetic. He told her many things about the birds and what they knew and where they lived and what they did with themselves. And he gave her a jack-knife, which she thought as great a treasure as if she were a desert-islander. All day long he did not once make her troubled or afraid except when he brought down some unsuspecting singing creature from its bough. Sylvia would have liked him vastly better without his gun; she could not understand why he killed the very birds he seemed to like so much. But as the day waned, Sylvia still watched the young man with loving admiration. She had never seen anybody so charming and delightful; the woman's heart, asleep in the child, was vaguely thrilled by a dream of love. Some premonition of that great power stirred and swayed these young foresters who traversed the solemn woodlands with soft-footed silent care. They stopped to listen to a bird's song; they pressed forward again eagerly, parting the branches—speaking to each other rarely and in whispers; the young man going first and Sylvia following, fascinated, a few steps behind, with her gray eyes dark with excitement.

She grieved because the longed-for white heron was elusive, but she did not lead the guest, she only followed, and there was no such thing as speaking first. The sound of her own unquestioned voice would have terrified her—it was hard enough to answer yes or no when there was need of that. At last evening began to fall, and they drove the cow home together, and Sylvia smiled with pleasure when they came to the place where she heard the whistle and was afraid only the night before.

II

Half a mile from home, at the farther edge of the woods, where the land was highest, a great pine-tree stood, the last of its generation. Whether it was left for a boundary mark, or for what reason, no one could say; the woodchoppers who had felled its mates were dead and gone long ago, and a whole forest of sturdy trees, pines and oaks and maples, had grown again. But the stately head of this old pine towered above them all and made a landmark for sea and shore miles and miles away. Sylvia knew it well. She had always believed that whoever climbed to the top of it could see the ocean; and the little girl had often laid her hand on the great rough trunk and looked up wistfully at those dark boughs that the wind always stirred, no matter how hot and still the air might be below. Now she thought of the tree with a new excitement, for why, if one climbed it at break of day, could not one see all the world, and easily discover whence the white heron flew, and mark the place, and find the hidden nest?

What a spirit of adventure, what wild ambition! What fancied triumph and delight and glory for the later morning when she could make known the secret! It was almost too real and too great for the childish heart to bear.

All night the door of the little house stood open, and the whippoorwills came and sang upon the very step. The young sportsman and his old hostess were sound asleep, but Sylvia's great design kept her broad awake and watching. She forgot to think of sleep. The short summer night seemed as long as the winter darkness, and at last when the whippoorwills ceased, and she was afraid the morning would after all come too soon, she stole out of the house and followed the pasture path through the woods, hastening toward the open ground beyond, listening with a sense of comfort and companionship to the drowsy twitter of a half-awakened bird, whose perch she had jarred in passing. Alas, if the great wave of human interest which flooded for the first time this dull little life should sweep away the satisfactions of an existence heart to heart with nature and the dumb life of the forest!

There was the huge tree asleep yet in the paling moonlight, and small and hopeful Sylvia began with utmost bravery to mount to the top of it, with tingling, eager blood coursing the channels of her whole frame, with her bare feet and fingers, that pinched and held like bird's claws to the monstrous ladder reaching up, up, almost to the sky itself. First she must mount the white oak tree that grew alongside, where she was almost lost among the dark branches and the green leaves heavy and wet with dew; a bird fluttered off its nest, and a red squirrel ran to and fro and scolded pettishly at the harmless housebreaker. Sylvia felt her way easily. She had often climbed there, and knew that higher still one of the oak's upper branches chafed against the pine trunk, just where its lower boughs were set close together. There, when she made the dangerous pass from one tree to the other, the great enterprise would really begin.

She crept out along the swaying oak limb at last, and took the daring step across into the old pine-tree. The way was harder than she thought; she must reach far and hold fast, the sharp dry twigs caught and held her and scratched her like angry talons, the pitch made her thin little fingers clumsy and stiff as she went round and round the tree's great stem, higher and higher upward. The sparrows and robins in the woods below were beginning to wake and twitter to the dawn, yet it seemed much lighter there aloft in the pine-tree, and the child knew that she must hurry if her project were to be of any use.

The tree seemed to lengthen itself out as she went up, and to reach farther and farther upward. It was like a great main-mast to the voyaging earth; it must truly have been amazed that morning through all its ponderous frame as it felt this determined spark of human spirit creeping and climbing from higher branch to branch. Who knows how steadily the least twigs held themselves to advantage this light, weak creature on her way! The old pine must have loved his new dependent. More than all the hawks, and bats, and moths, and even the sweet-voiced thrushes, was the brave, beating heart of the solitary gray-eyed child. And the tree stood still and held away the winds that June morning while the dawn grew bright in the east.

Sylvia's face was like a pale star, if one had seen it from the ground, when the last thorny bough was past, and she stood trembling and tired but wholly triumphant, high in the tree-top. Yes, there was the sea with the dawning sun making a golden dazzle over it, and toward that glorious east flew two hawks with slow-moving pinions. How low they looked in the air from that height when before one had only seen them far up, and dark against the blue sky. Their gray feathers were as soft as moths; they seemed only a little way from the tree, and Sylvia felt as if she too could go flying away among the clouds. Westward, the woodlands and farms reached miles and miles into the distance; here and there were church steeples, and white villages; truly it was a vast and awesome world.

The birds sang louder and louder. At last the sun came up bewilderingly bright. Sylvia could see the white sails of ships out at sea, and the clouds that were purple and rose-colored and yellow at first began to fade away. Where was the white heron's nest in the sea of green branches, and was this wonderful sight and pageant of the world the only reward for having climbed to such a giddy height? Now look down again, Sylvia, where the green marsh is set among the shining birches and dark hemlocks; there where you saw the white heron once you will see him again; look, look! a white spot of him like a single floating feather comes up from the dead hemlock and grows larger, and rises, and comes close at last, and goes by the landmark pine with steady sweep of wing and outstretched slender neck and crested head. And wait! wait! do not move a foot or a finger, little girl, do not send an arrow of light and consciousness from your two eager eyes, for the heron has perched on a pine bough not far beyond yours, and cries back to his mate on the nest, and plumes his feathers for the new day!

The child gives a long sigh a minute later when a company of shouting cat-birds comes also to the tree, and vexed by their fluttering and lawlessness the solemn heron goes away. She knows his secret now, the wild, light, slender bird that floats and wavers, and goes back like an arrow presently to his home in the green world beneath. Then Sylvia, well satisfied, makes her perilous way down again, not daring to look far below the branch she stands on, ready to cry sometimes because her fingers ache and her lamed feet slip. Wondering over and over again what the stranger would say to her, and what he would think when she told him how to find his way straight to the heron's nest.

"Sylvy, Sylvy!" called the busy old grandmother again and again, but nobody answered, and the small husk bed was empty, and Sylvia had disappeared.

The guest waked from a dream, and remembering his day's pleasure hurried to dress himself that it might sooner begin. He was sure from the way the shy little girl looked once or twice yesterday that she had at least seen the white heron, and now she must really be persuaded to tell. Here she comes now, paler than ever, and her worn old frock is torn and tattered, and smeared with pine pitch. The grandmother and the sportsman stand in the door together and question her, and the splendid moment had come to speak of the dead hemlock-tree by the green marsh.

But Sylvia does not speak after all, though the old grandmother fretfully rebukes her, and the young man's kind appealing eyes are looking straight in her own. He can make them rich with money; he has promised it, and they are poor now. He is so well worth making happy, and he waits to hear the story she can tell.

No, she must keep silence! What is it that suddenly forbids her and makes her dumb? Has she been nine years growing, and now, when the great world for the first time puts out a hand to her, must she thrust it aside for a bird's sake? The murmur of the pine's green branches is in her ears, she remembers how the white heron came flying through the golden air and how they watched the sea and the morning together, and Sylvia cannot speak; she cannot tell the heron's secret and give its life away.

Dear loyalty, that suffered a sharp pang as the guest went away disappointed later in the day, that could have served and followed him and loved him as a dog loves! Many a night Sylvia heard the echo of his whistle haunting the pasture path as she came home with the loitering cow. She forgot even her sorrow at the sharp report of his gun and the piteous sight of thrushes and sparrows dropping silent to the ground, their songs hushed and their pretty feathers stained and wet with blood. Were the birds better friends than their hunter might have been, — who can tell? Whatever treasures were lost to her, woodlands and summertime, remember! Bring your gifts and graces and tell your secrets to this lonely country child!

[1886]

GUY DE MAUPASSANT [1850–1893]

The Necklace

TRANSLATED BY MARJORIE LAURIE, 1934

She was one of those pretty and charming girls who are sometimes, as if by a mistake of destiny, born in a family of clerks. She had no dowry, no expectations, no means of being known, understood, loved, wedded by any rich and distinguished man; and she let herself be married to a little clerk at the Ministry of Public Instructions.

She dressed plainly because she could not dress well, but she was as unhappy as though she had really fallen from her proper station, since with women there is neither caste nor rank: and beauty, grace, and charm act instead of family and birth. Natural fineness, instinct for what is elegant, suppleness of wit, are the sole hierarchy, and make from women of the people the equals of the very greatest ladies.

She suffered ceaselessly, feeling herself born for all the delicacies and all the luxuries. She suffered from the poverty of her dwelling, from the wretched look of the walls, from the worn-out chairs, from the ugliness of the curtains. All those things, of which another woman of her rank would never even have been conscious, tortured her and made her angry. The sight of the little Breton peasant, who did her humble housework aroused in her regrets which were despairing, and distracted dreams. She thought of the silent antechambers hung with Oriental tapestry, lit by tall bronze candelabra, and of the two great footmen in knee breeches who sleep in the big armchairs, made drowsy by the heavy warmth of the hot-air stove. She thought of the long *salons* fitted up with ancient silk, of the delicate furniture carrying priceless curiosities, and of the coquettish perfumed boudoirs made for talks at five o'clock with intimate friends, with men famous and sought after, whom all women envy and whose attention they all desire.

When she sat down to dinner, before the round table covered with a tablecloth three days old, opposite her husband, who uncovered the soup tureen and declared with an enchanted air, "Ah, the good *pot-au-feu*! I don't know anything better than that," she thought of dainty dinners, of shining silverware, of tapestry which peopled the walls with ancient personages and with strange birds flying in the midst of a fairy forest; and she thought of delicious dishes served on marvelous plates, and of the whispered gallantries which you listen to with a sphinxlike smile, while you are eating the pink flesh of a trout or the wings of a quail.

She had no dresses, no jewels, nothing. And she loved nothing but that; she felt made for that. She would so have liked to please, to be envied, to be charming, to be sought after.

She had a friend, a former schoolmate at the convent, who was rich, and whom she did not like to go and see any more, because she suffered so much when she came back.

But one evening, her husband returned home with a triumphant air, and holding a large envelope in his hand.

"There," said he. "Here is something for you."

She tore the paper sharply, and drew out a printed card which bore these words:

"The Minister of Public Instruction and Mme. Georges Ramponneau request the honor of M. and Mme. Loisel's company at the palace of the Ministry on Monday evening, January eighteenth."

Instead of being delighted, as her husband hoped, she threw the invitation on the table with disdain, murmuring:

"What do you want me to do with that?"

"But, my dear, I thought you would be glad. You never go out, and this is such a fine opportunity. I had awful trouble to get it. Everyone wants to go; it is very select, and they are not giving many invitations to clerks. The whole official world will be there."

She looked at him with an irritated glance, and said, impatiently:

"And what do you want me to put on my back?"

He had not thought of that; he stammered:

"Why, the dress you go to the theater in. It looks very well, to me."

He stopped, distracted, seeing his wife was crying. Two great tears descended slowly from the corners of her eyes toward the corners of her mouth. He stuttered:

"What's the matter? What's the matter?"

But, by violent effort, she had conquered her grief, and she replied, with a calm voice, while she wiped her wet cheeks:

"Nothing. Only I have no dress and therefore I can't go to this ball. Give your card to some colleague whose wife is better equipped than I."

He was in despair. He resumed:

"Come, let us see, Mathilde. How much would it cost, a suitable dress, which you could use on other occasions. Something very simple?"

She reflected several seconds, making her calculations and wondering also what sum she could ask without drawing on herself an immediate refusal and a frightened exclamation from the economical clerk.

Finally, she replied, hesitatingly:

"I don't know exactly, but I think I could manage it with four hundred francs."

He had grown a little pale, because he was laying aside just that amount to buy a gun and treat himself to a little shooting next summer on the plain of Nanterre, with several friends who went to shoot larks down there, of a Sunday.

But he said:

"All right. I will give you four hundred francs. And try to have a pretty dress."

The day of the ball drew near, and Mme. Loisel seemed sad, uneasy, anxious. Her dress was ready, however. Her husband said to her one evening:

"What is the matter? Come, you've been so queer these last three days."

And she answered:

"It annoys me not to have a single jewel, not a single stone, nothing to put on. I shall look like distress. I should almost rather not go at all."

He resumed:

"You might wear natural flowers. It's very stylish at this time of the year. For ten francs you can get two or three magnificent roses."

She was not convinced.

"No; there's nothing more humiliating than to look poor among other women who are rich."

But her husband cried:

"How stupid you are! Go look up your friend Mme. Forestier, and ask her to lend you some jewels. You're quite thick enough with her to do that."

She uttered a cry of joy:

"It's true. I never thought of it."

The next day she went to her friend and told of her distress.

Mme. Forestier went to a wardrobe with a glass door, took out a large jewelbox, brought it back, opened it, and said to Mme. Loisel:

"Choose, choose, my dear."

She saw first of all some bracelets, then a pearl necklace, then a Venetian cross, gold and precious stones of admirable workmanship. She tried on the ornaments before the glass, hesitated, could not make up her mind to part with them, to give them back. She kept asking:

"Haven't you any more?"

"Why, yes. Look. I don't know what you like."

All of a sudden she discovered, in a black satin box, a superb necklace of diamonds, and her heart began to beat with an immoderate desire. Her hands trembled as she took it. She fastened it around her throat, outside her high necked dress, and remained lost in ecstasy at the sight of herself.

Then she asked, hesitating, filled with anguish:

"Can you lend me that, only that?"

"Why, yes, certainly."

She sprang upon the neck of her friend, kissed her passionately, then fled with her treasure.

The day of the ball arrived. Mme. Loisel made a great success. She was prettier than them all, elegant, gracious, smiling, and crazy with joy. All the men looked at her, asked her name, endeavored to be introduced. All the attachés of the Cabinet wanted to waltz with her. She was remarked by the minister himself.

She danced with intoxication, with passion, made drunk by pleasure, forgetting all, in the triumph of her beauty, in the glory of her success, in a sort of cloud of happiness composed of all this homage, of all this admiration, of all these awakened desires, and of that sense of complete victory which is so sweet to a woman's heart.

She went away about four o'clock in the morning. Her husband had been sleeping since midnight, in a little deserted anteroom, with three other gentlemen whose wives were having a good time. He threw over her shoulders the wraps which he had brought, modest wraps of common life, whose poverty contrasted with the elegance of the ball dress. She felt this, and wanted to escape so as not to be remarked by the other women, who were enveloping themselves in costly furs.

Loisel held her back.

"Wait a bit. You will catch cold outside. I will go and call a cab."

But she did not listen to him, and rapidly descended the stairs. When they were in the street they did not find a carriage; and they began to look for one, shouting after the cabmen whom they saw passing by at a distance.

They went down toward the Seine, in despair, shivering with cold. At last they found on the quay one of those ancient noctambulant coupés° which, exactly as if they were ashamed to show their misery during the day, are never seen round Paris until after nightfall.

It took them to their door in the Rue des Martyrs, and once more, sadly, they climbed up homeward. All was ended, for her. And as to him, he reflected that he must be at the Ministry at ten o'clock.

She removed the wraps which covered her shoulders before the glass, so as once more to see herself in all her glory. But suddenly she uttered a cry. She no longer had the necklace around her neck!

Her husband, already half undressed, demanded:

"What is the matter with you?"

Coupé: An enclosed carriage.

She turned madly toward him:

"I have—I have—I've lost Mme. Forestier's necklace."

He stood up, distracted.

"What!—how?—impossible!"

And they looked in the folds of her dress, in the folds of her cloak, in her pockets, everywhere. They did not find it.

He asked:

"You're sure you had it on when you left the ball?"

"Yes, I felt it in the vestibule of the palace."

"But if you had lost it in the street we should have heard it fall. It must be in the cab."

"Yes. Probably. Did you take his number?"

"No. And you, didn't you notice it?"

"No."

They looked, thunderstruck, at one another. At last Loisel put on his clothes.

"I shall go back on foot," said he, "over the whole route which we have taken to see if I can find it."

And he went out. She sat waiting on a chair in her ball dress, without strength to go to bed, overwhelmed, without fire, without a thought.

Her husband came back about seven o'clock. He had found nothing.

He went to Police Headquarters, to the newspaper offices, to offer a reward; he went to the cab companies—everywhere, in fact, whither he was urged by the least suspicion of hope.

She waited all day, in the same condition of mad fear before this terrible calamity.

Loisel returned at night with a hollow, pale face; he had discovered nothing.

"You must write to your friend," said he, "that you have broken the clasp of her necklace and that you are having it mended. That will give us time to turn round."

She wrote at his dictation.

At the end of a week they had lost all hope.

And Loisel, who had aged five years, declared:

"We must consider how to replace that ornament."

The next day they took the box which had contained it, and they went to the jeweler whose name was found within. He consulted his books.

"It was not I, madame, who sold that necklace; I must simply have furnished the case."

Then they went from jeweler to jeweler, searching for a necklace like the other, consulting their memories, sick both of them with chagrin and anguish.

They found, in a shop at the Palais Royal, a string of diamonds which seemed to them exactly like the one they looked for. It was worth forty thousand francs. They could have it for thirty-six.

So they begged the jeweler not to sell it for three days yet. And they made a bargain that he should buy it back for thirty-four thousand francs, in case they found the other one before the end of February.

Loisel possessed eighteen thousand francs which his father had left him. He would borrow the rest.

He did borrow, asking a thousand francs of one, five hundred of another, five louis here, three louis there. He gave notes, took up ruinous obligations, dealt with usurers and all the race of lenders. He compromised all the rest of his life, risked his signature without even knowing if he could meet it; and, frightened by the pains yet to come, by the black misery which was about to fall upon him, by the prospect of all the physical privation and of all the moral tortures which he was to suffer, he went to get the new necklace, putting down upon the merchant's counter thirty-six thousand francs.

When Mme. Loisel took back the necklace, Mme. Forestier said to her, with a chilly manner:

"You should have returned it sooner; I might have needed it."

She did not open the case, as her friend had so much feared. If she had detected the substitution, what would she have thought, what would she have said? Would she not have taken Mme. Loisel for a thief?

Mme. Loisel now knew the horrible existence of the needy. She took her part, moreover, all of a sudden, with heroism. That dreadful debt must be paid. She would pay it. They dismissed their servant; they changed their lodgings; they rented a garret under the roof.

She came to know what heavy housework meant and the odious cares of the kitchen. She washed the dishes, using her rosy nails on the greasy pots and pans. She washed the dirty linen, the shirts, and the dishcloths, which she dried upon a line; she carried the slops down to the street every morning, and carried up the water, stopping for breath at every landing. And, dressed like a woman of the people, she went to the fruiterer, the grocer, the butcher, her basket on her arm, bargaining, insulted, defending her miserable money sou by sou.

Each month they had to meet some notes, renew others, obtain more time.

Her husband worked in the evening making a fair copy of some tradesman's accounts, and late at night he often copied manuscript for five sous a page.

And this life lasted for ten years.

At the end of ten years, they had paid everything, everything, with the rates of usury, and the accumulations of the compound interest.

Mme. Loisel looked old now. She had become the woman of impoverished households—strong and hard and rough. With frowsy hair, skirts askew, and red hands, she talked loud while washing the floor with great swishes of water. But sometimes, when her husband was at the office, she sat down near the window, and she thought of that gay evening of long ago, of that ball where she had been so beautiful and so fêted.

What would have happened if she had not lost that necklace? Who knows? Who knows? How life is strange and changeful! How little a thing is needed for us to be lost or to be saved!

But, one Sunday, having gone to take a walk in the Champs Elysées to refresh herself from the labor of the week, she suddenly perceived a woman who was leading a child. It was Mme. Forestier, still young, still beautiful, still charming.

Mme. Loisel felt moved. Was she going to speak to her? Yes, certainly. And now that she had paid, she was going to tell her all about it. Why not?

She went up.

"Good-day, Jeanne."

The other, astonished to be familiarly addressed by this plain goodwife, did not recognize her at all, and stammered.

"But—madam!—I do not know—you must be mistaken."

"No. I am Mathilde Loisel."

Her friend uttered a cry.

"Oh, my poor Mathilde! How you are changed!"

"Yes, I have had days hard enough, since I have seen you, days wretched enough—and that because of you!"

"Of me! How so?"

"Do you remember that diamond necklace which you lent me to wear at the ministerial ball?"

"Yes. Well?"

"Well, I lost it."

"What do you mean? You brought it back."

"I brought you back another just like it. And for this we have been ten years paying. You can understand that it was not easy for us, who had nothing. At last it is ended, and I am very glad."

Mme. Forestier had stopped.

"You say that you bought a necklace of diamonds to replace mine?"

"Yes. You never noticed it, then! They were very like."

And she smiled with a joy which was proud and naïve at once.

Mme. Forestier, strongly moved, took her two hands.

"Oh, my poor Mathilde! Why, my necklace was paste. It was worth at most five hundred francs!"

[1884]

KATE CHOPIN [1851–1904]

The Story of an Hour

Knowing that Mrs. Mallard was afflicted with a heart trouble, great care was taken to break to her as gently as possible the news of her husband's death.

It was her sister Josephine who told her, in broken sentences; veiled hints that revealed in half concealing. Her husband's friend Richards was there, too, near her. It was he who had been in the newspaper office when intelligence of the railroad disaster was received, with Brently Mallard's name leading the list of "killed." He had only taken the time to assure himself of its truth by a second telegram, and had hastened to forestall any less careful, less tender friend in bearing the sad message.

She did not hear the story as many women have heard the same, with a paralyzed inability to accept its significance. She wept at once, with sudden, wild abandonment, in her sister's arms. When the storm of grief had spent itself she went away to her room alone. She would have no one follow her.

There stood, facing the open window, a comfortable, roomy armchair. Into this she sank, pressed down by a physical exhaustion that haunted her body and seemed to reach into her soul.

She could see in the open square before her house the tops of trees that were all aquiver with the new spring life. The delicious breath of rain was in the air. In the street below a peddler was crying his wares. The notes of a distant song which some one was singing reached her faintly, and countless sparrows were twittering in the eaves.

There were patches of blue sky showing here and there through the clouds that had met and piled one above the other in the west facing her window.

She sat with her head thrown back upon the cushion of the chair, quite motionless, except when a sob came up into her throat and shook her, as a child who had cried itself to sleep continues to sob in its dreams.

She was young, with a fair, calm face, whose lines bespoke repression and even a certain strength. But now there was a dull stare in her eyes, whose gaze was fixed away off yonder on one of those patches of blue sky. It was not a glance of reflection, but rather indicated a suspension of intelligent thought.

There was something coming to her and she was waiting for it, fearfully. What was it? She did not know; it was too subtle and elusive to name. But she felt it, creeping out of the sky, reaching toward her through the sounds, the scents, the color that filled the air.

Now her bosom rose and fell tumultuously. She was beginning to recognize this thing that was approaching to possess her, and she was striving to beat it back with her will—as powerless as her two white slender hands would have been.

When she abandoned herself a little whispered word escaped her slightly parted lips. She said it over and over under her breath: "free, free, free!" The vacant stare and the look of terror that had followed it went from her eyes. They stayed keen and bright. Her pulses beat fast, and the coursing blood warmed and relaxed every inch of her body.

She did not stop to ask if it were or were not a monstrous joy that held her. A clear and exalted perception enabled her to dismiss the suggestion as trivial.

She knew that she would weep again when she saw the kind, tender hands folded in death; the face that had never looked save with love upon her, fixed and gray and dead. But she saw beyond that bitter moment a long procession of years to come that would belong to her absolutely. And she opened and spread her arms out to them in welcome.

There would be no one to live for her during those coming years: she would live for herself. There would be no powerful will bending hers in that blind persistence with which men and women believe they have a right to impose a private will upon a fellow-creature. A kind intention or a cruel intention made the act seem no less a crime as she looked upon it in that brief moment of illumination.

And yet she had loved him—sometimes. Often she had not. What did it matter! What could love, the unsolved mystery, count for in face of this possession of self-assertion which she suddenly recognized as the strongest impulse of her being!

"Free! Body and soul free!" she kept whispering.

Josephine was kneeling before the closed door with her lips to the keyhole, imploring for admission. "Louise, open the door! I beg; open the door—you will make yourself ill. What are you doing, Louise? For heaven's sake open the door."

"Go away. I am not making myself ill." No; she was drinking in a very elixir of life through that open window.

Her fancy was running riot along those days ahead of her. Spring days, and summer days, and all sorts of days that would be her own. She breathed a quick prayer that life might be long. It was only yesterday she had thought with a shudder that life might be long.

She arose at length and opened the door to her sister's importunities.

There was a feverish triumph in her eyes, and she carried herself unwittingly like a goddess of Victory. She clasped her sister's waist, and
together they descended the stairs. Richards stood waiting for them at
the bottom.

Some one was opening the front door with a latchkey. It was Brently
Mallard who entered, a little travel-stained, composedly carrying his
gripsack and umbrella. He had been far from the scene of accident, and
did not even know there had been one. He stood amazed at Josephine's
piercing cry; at Richards' quick motion to screen him from the view of
his wife.

But Richards was too late.

When the doctors came they said she had died of heart disease—of
joy that kills.

[1894]

ANTON CHEKHOV [1860–1904]

The Lady with the Dog

TRANSLATED BY IVY LITVINOV, N.D.

I

People were telling one another that a newcomer had been seen on the
promenade—a lady with a dog. Dmitri Dmitrich Gurov had been a fortnight in Yalta, and was accustomed to its ways, and he, too, had begun
to take an interest in fresh arrivals. From his seat in Vernet's outdoor
café, he caught sight of a young woman in a toque, passing along the
promenade; she was fair and not very tall; after her trotted a white
pomeranian.

Later he encountered her in the municipal park, and in the square,
several times a day. She was always alone, wearing the same toque, and
the pomeranian always trotted at her side. Nobody knew who she was,
and people referred to her simply as "the lady with the dog."

"If she's here without her husband, and without any friends," thought Gurov, "it wouldn't be a bad idea to make her acquaintance."

He was not yet forty, but had a twelve-year-old daughter and two schoolboy sons. He had been talked into marrying in his second year at college, and his wife now looked nearly twice as old as he was. She was a tall, black-browed woman, erect, dignified, imposing, and, as she said of herself, a "thinker." She was a great reader, omitted the "hard sign" at the end of words in her letters, and called her husband "Dimitri" instead of Dmitrí; and though he secretly considered her shallow, narrowminded, and dowdy, he stood in awe of her, and disliked being at home. It was long since he had first begun deceiving her and he was now constantly unfaithful to her, and this was no doubt why he spoke slightingly of women, to whom he referred as *the lower race*.

He considered that the ample lessons he had received from bitter experience entitled him to call them whatever he liked, but without this "lower race" he could not have existed a single day. He was bored and ill-at-ease in the company of men, with whom he was always cold and reserved, but felt quite at home among women, and knew exactly what to say to them, and how to behave; he could even be silent in their company without feeling the slightest awkwardness. There was an elusive charm in his appearance and disposition which attracted women and caught their sympathies. He knew this and was himself attracted to them by some invisible force.

Repeated and bitter experience had taught him that every fresh intimacy, while at first introducing such pleasant variety into everyday life, and offering itself as a charming, light adventure, inevitably developed, among decent people (especially in Moscow, where they are so irresolute and slow to move), into a problem of excessive complication leading to an intolerably irksome situation. But every time he encountered an attractive woman he forgot all about this experience, the desire for life surged up in him, and everything suddenly seemed simple and amusing.

One evening, then, while he was dining at the restaurant in the park, the lady in the toque came strolling up and took a seat at a neighbouring table. Her expression, gait, dress, coiffure, all told him that she was from the upper classes, that she was married, that she was in Yalta for the first time, alone and bored. . . . The accounts of the laxity of morals among visitors to Yalta are greatly exaggerated, and he paid no heed to them, knowing that for the most part they were invented by people who would gladly have transgressed themselves, had they known how to set about it. But when the lady sat down at a neighbouring table a few yards away from him, these stories of easy conquests, of excursions to the mountains, came back to him, and the seductive idea of a brisk transitory liaison, an affair with a woman whose very name he did not know, suddenly took possession of his mind.

He snapped his fingers at the pomeranian, and when it trotted up to him, shook his forefinger at it. The pomeranian growled. Gurov shook his finger again.

The lady glanced at him and instantly lowered her eyes.

"He doesn't bite," she said, and blushed.

"May I give him a bone?" he asked, and on her nod of consent added in friendly tones: "Have you been long in Yalta?"

"About five days."

"And I am dragging out my second week here."

Neither spoke for a few minutes.

"The days pass quickly, and yet one is so bored here," she said, not looking at him.

"It's the thing to say it's boring here. People never complain of boredom in God-forsaken holes like Belyev or Zhizdra, but when they get here it's: 'Oh, the dullness! Oh, the dust!' You'd think they'd come from Grenada to say the least of it."

She laughed. Then they both went on eating in silence, like complete strangers. But after dinner they left the restaurant together, and embarked upon the light, jesting talk of people free and contented, for whom it is all the same where they go, or what they talk about. They strolled along, remarking on the strange light over the sea. The water was a warm, tender purple, the moonlight lay on its surface in a golden strip. They said how close it was, after the hot day. Gurov told her he was from Moscow, that he was really a philologist, but worked in a bank; that he had at one time trained himself to sing in a private opera company, but had given up the idea; that he owned two houses in Moscow. . . . And from her he learned that she had grown up in Petersburg, but had got married in the town of S., where she had been living two years, that she would stay another month in Yalta, and that perhaps her husband, who also needed a rest, would join her. She was quite unable to explain whether her husband was a member of the gubernia council, or on the board of the Zemstvo, and was greatly amused at herself for this. Further, Gurov learned that her name was Anna Sergeyevna.

Back in his own room he thought about her, and felt sure he would meet her the next day. It was inevitable. As he went to bed he reminded himself that only a very short time ago she had been a schoolgirl, like his own daughter, learning her lessons; he remembered how much there was of shyness and constraint in her laughter, in her way of conversing with a stranger — it was probably the first time in her life that she found herself alone, and in a situation in which men could follow her and watch her, and speak to her, all the time with a secret aim she could not fail to divine. He recalled her slender, delicate neck, her fine grey eyes.

"And yet there's something pathetic about her," he thought to himself as he fell asleep.

II

A week had passed since the beginning of their acquaintance. It was a holiday. Indoors it was stuffy, but the dust rose in clouds out of doors, and people's hats blew off. It was a thirsty day and Gurov kept going to the outdoor café for fruit-drinks and ices to offer Anna Sergeyevna. The heat was overpowering.

In the evening, when the wind had dropped, they walked to the pier to see the steamer in. There were a great many people strolling about the landing-place; some, bunches of flowers in their hands, were meeting friends. Two peculiarities of the smart Yalta crowd stood out distinctly—the elderly ladies all tried to dress very young, and there seemed to be an inordinate number of generals about.

Owing to the roughness of the sea the steamer arrived late, after the sun had gone down, and it had to manoeuvre for some time before it could get alongside the pier. Anna Sergeyevna scanned the steamer and passengers through her lorgnette, as if looking for someone she knew, and when she turned to Gurov her eyes were glistening. She talked a great deal, firing off abrupt questions and forgetting immediately what it was she had wanted to know. Then she lost her lorgnette in the crush.

The smart crowd began dispersing, features could no longer be made out, the wind had quite dropped, and Gurov and Anna Sergeyevna stood there as if waiting for someone else to come off the steamer. Anna Sergeyevna had fallen silent, every now and then smelling her flowers, but not looking at Gurov.

"It's turning out a fine evening," he said. "What shall we do? We might go for a drive."

She made no reply.

He looked steadily at her and suddenly took her in his arms and kissed her lips, and the fragrance and dampness of the flowers closed round him, but the next moment he looked behind him in alarm—had anyone seen them?

"Let's go to your room," he murmured.

And they walked off together, very quickly.

Her room was stuffy and smelt of some scent she had bought in the Japanese shop. Gurov looked at her, thinking to himself: "How full of strange encounters life is!" He could remember carefree, good-natured women who were exhilarated by love-making and grateful to him for the happiness he gave them, however shortlived; and there had been others—his wife among them—whose caresses were insincere, affected, hysterical, mixed up with a great deal of quite unnecessary talk, and whose expression seemed to say that all this was not just love-making or passion, but something much more significant; then there had been two or three beautiful, cold women, over whose features flitted a predatory expression, betraying a determination to wring from life more than it could give, women no longer in their first youth, capricious, irrational, despotic, brainless, and when Gurov had cooled to these, their beauty aroused in him nothing but repulsion, and the lace trimming on their underclothes reminded him of fish-scales.

But here the timidity and awkwardness of youth and inexperience were still apparent; and there was a feeling of embarrassment in the atmosphere, as if someone had just knocked at the door. Anna Sergeyevna, "the lady with the dog," seemed to regard the affair as something very special, very serious, as if she had become a fallen woman, an attitude he found odd and disconcerting. Her features lengthened and drooped, and her long hair hung mournfully on either side of her face. She assumed a pose of dismal meditation, like a repentant sinner in some classical painting.

"It isn't right," she said. "You will never respect me any more."

On the table was a water-melon. Gurov cut himself a slice from it and began slowly eating it. At least half an hour passed in silence.

Anna Sergeyevna was very touching, revealing the purity of a decent, naive woman who had seen very little of life. The solitary candle burning on the table scarcely lit up her face, but it was obvious that her heart was heavy.

"Why should I stop respecting you?" asked Gurov. "You don't know what you're saying."

"May God forgive me!" she exclaimed, and her eyes filled with tears. "It's terrible."

"No need to seek to justify yourself."

"How can I justify myself? I'm a wicked, fallen woman, I despise myself and have not the least thought of self-justification. It isn't my husband I have deceived, it's myself. And not only now, I have been deceiving myself for ever so long. My husband is no doubt an honest, worthy man, but he's a flunkey. I don't know what it is he does at his office, but I know he's a flunkey. I was only twenty when I married him, and I was devoured by curiosity, I wanted something higher. I told myself that there must be a different kind of life. I wanted to live, to live. . . . I was burning with curiosity . . . you'll never understand that, but I swear to God I could no longer control myself, nothing could hold me back, I told my husband I was ill, and I came here. . . . And I started going about like one possessed, like a madwoman . . . and now I have become an ordinary, worthless woman, and everyone has the right to despise me."

Gurov listened to her, bored to death. The naive accents, the remorse, all was so unexpected, so out of place. But for the tears in her eyes, she might have been jesting or play-acting.

"I don't understand," he said gently. "What is it you want?"

She hid her face against his breast and pressed closer to him.

"Do believe me, I implore you to believe me," she said. "I love all that is honest and pure in life, vice is revolting to me. I don't know what I'm doing. The common people say they are snared by the devil. And now I can say that I have been snared by the devil, too."

"Come, come," he murmured.

He gazed into her fixed, terrified eyes, kissed her, and soothed her with gentle affectionate words, and gradually she calmed down and regained her cheerfulness. Soon they were laughing together again.

When, a little later, they went out, there was not a soul on the promenade, the town and its cypresses looked dead, but the sea was still roaring as it dashed against the beach. A solitary fishing-boat tossed on the waves, its lamp blinking sleepily.

They found a droshky and drove to Oreanda.

"I discovered your name in the hall, just now," said Gurov, "written up on the board. Von Diederitz. Is your husband a German?"

"No. His grandfather was, I think, but he belongs to the Orthodox church himself."

When they got out of the droshky at Oreanda they sat down on a bench not far from the church, and looked down at the sea, without talking. Yalta could be dimly discerned through the morning mist, and white clouds rested motionless on the summits of the mountains. Not a leaf stirred, the grasshoppers chirruped, and the monotonous hollow roar of the sea came up to them, speaking of peace, of the eternal sleep lying in wait for us all. The sea had roared like this long before there was any Yalta or Oreanda, it was roaring now, and it would go on roaring, just as indifferently and hollowly, when we had passed away. And it may be that in this continuity, this utter indifference to life and death, lies the secret of our ultimate salvation, of the stream of life on our planet, and of its never-ceasing movement towards perfection.

Side by side with a young woman, who looked so exquisite in the early light, soothed and enchanted by the sight of all this magical beauty — sea, mountains, clouds and the vast expanse of the sky — Gurov told himself that, when you came to think of it, everything in the world is beautiful really, everything but our own thoughts and actions, when we lose sight of the higher aims of life, and of our dignity as human beings.

Someone approached them — a watchman, probably — looked at them and went away. And there was something mysterious and beautiful even in this. The steamer from Feodosia could be seen coming towards the pier, lit up by the dawn, its lamps out.

"There's dew on the grass," said Anna Sergeyevna, breaking the silence.

"Yes. Time to go home."

They went back to the town.

After this they met every day at noon on the promenade, lunching and dining together, going for walks, and admiring the sea. She complained of sleeplessness, of palpitations, asked the same questions over and over again, alternately surrendering to jealousy and the fear that he did not really respect her. And often, when there was nobody in sight in the square or the park, he would draw her to him and kiss her passionately. The utter idleness, these kisses in broad daylight, accompanied by furtive glances and the fear of discovery, the heat, the smell of the sea, and the idle, smart, well-fed people continually crossing their field of vision, seemed to have given him a new lease on life. He told Anna Sergeyevna she was beautiful and seductive, made love to her with impetuous passion, and never left her side, while she was always pensive, always trying to force from him the admission that he did not respect her, that he did not love her a bit, and considered her just an ordinary woman. Almost every night they drove out of town, to Oreanda, the waterfall, or some other beauty-spot. And these excursions were invariably a success, each contributing fresh impressions of majestic beauty.

All this time they kept expecting her husband to arrive. But a letter came in which he told his wife that he was having trouble with his eyes, and implored her to come home as soon as possible. Anna Sergeyevna made hasty preparations for leaving.

"It's a good thing I'm going," she said to Gurov. "It's the intervention of fate."

She left Yalta in a carriage, and he went with her as far as the railway station. The drive took nearly a whole day. When she got into the express train, after the second bell had been rung, she said:

"Let me have one more look at you. . . . One last look. That's right."

She did not weep, but was mournful, and seemed ill, the muscles of her cheeks twitching.

"I shall think of you . . . I shall think of you all the time," she said. "God bless you! Think kindly of me. We are parting for ever, it must be so, because we ought never to have met. Good-bye—God bless you."

The train steamed rapidly out of the station, its lights soon disappearing, and a minute later even the sound it made was silenced, as if everything were conspiring to bring this sweet oblivion, this madness, to an end as quickly as possible. And Gurov, standing alone on the platform and gazing into the dark distance, listened to the shrilling of the grasshoppers and the humming of the telegraph wires, with a feeling that he had only just waked up. And he told himself that this had been just one more of the many adventures in his life, and that it, too, was over, leaving nothing but a memory. . . . He was moved and sad, and felt a slight remorse. After all, this young woman whom he would never again see had not been really happy with him. He had been friendly and affectionate with her, but in his whole behaviour, in the tones of his voice, in his very caresses, there had been a shade of irony, the insulting indulgence of the fortunate male, who was, moreover, almost twice her age. She had insisted in calling him good, remarkable, high-minded. Evidently he had appeared to her different from his real self, in a word he had involuntarily deceived her. . . .

There was an autumnal feeling in the air, and the evening was chilly.

"It's time for me to be going north, too," thought Gurov, as he walked away from the platform. "High time!"

III

When he got back to Moscow it was beginning to look like winter, the stoves were heated every day, and it was still dark when the children got up to go to school and drank their tea, so that the nurse had to light the lamp for a short time. Frost had set in. When the first snow falls, and one goes for one's first sleigh-ride, it is pleasant to see the white ground, the white roofs; one breathes freely and lightly, and remembers the days of one's youth. The ancient lime-trees and birches, white with rime, have a good-natured look, they are closer to the heart than cypresses and palms, and beneath their branches one is no longer haunted by the memory of mountains and the sea.

Gurov had always lived in Moscow, and he returned to Moscow on a fine frosty day, and when he put on his fur-lined overcoat and thick gloves, and sauntered down Petrovka Street, and when, on Saturday evening, he heard the church bells ringing, his recent journey and the places he had visited lost their charm for him. He became gradually immersed in Moscow life, reading with avidity three newspapers a day, while declaring he never read Moscow newspapers on principle. Once more he was caught up in a whirl of restaurants, clubs, banquets, and celebrations, once more glowed with the flattering consciousness that well-known lawyers and actors came to his house, that he played cards in the Medical Club opposite a professor.

He had believed that in a month's time Anna Sergeyevna would be nothing but a wistful memory, and that hereafter, with her wistful smile, she would only occasionally appear to him in dreams, like others before her. But the month was now well over and winter was in full swing, and all was as clear in his memory as if he had only parted with Anna Sergeyevna the day before. And his recollections grew ever more insistent. When the voices of his children at their lessons reached him in his study through the evening stillness, when he heard a song, or the sounds of a musical-box in a restaurant, when the wind howled in the chimney, it all came back to him: early morning on the pier, the misty mountains, the steamer from Feodosia, the kisses. He would pace up and down his room for a long time, smiling at his memories, and then memory turned into dreaming, and what had happened mingled in his imagination with what was going to happen. Anna Sergeyevna did not come to him in his dreams, she accompanied him everywhere, like his shadow, following him everywhere he went. When he closed his eyes, she seemed to stand before him in the flesh, still lovelier, younger, tenderer than she had really been, and looking back, he saw himself, too, as better than he had been in Yalta. In the evenings she looked out at him from the bookshelves, the fire-place, the corner, he could hear her breathing, the sweet rustle of her skirts. In the streets he followed women with his eyes, to see if there were any like her. . . .

He began to feel an overwhelming desire to share his memories with someone. But he could not speak of his love at home, and outside his home who was there for him to confide in? Not the tenants living in his house, and certainly not his colleagues at the bank. And what was there to tell? Was it love that he had felt? Had there been anything exquisite, poetic, anything instructive or even amusing about his relations with Anna Sergeyevna? He had to content himself with uttering vague generalizations about love and women, and nobody guessed what he meant, though his wife's dark eyebrows twitched as she said:

"The role of a coxcomb doesn't suit you a bit, Dimitri."

One evening, leaving the Medical Club with one of his card-partners, a government official, he could not refrain from remarking:

"If you only knew what a charming woman I met in Yalta!"

The official got into his sleigh, and just before driving off turned and called out:

"Dmitri Dmitrich!"

"Yes?"

"You were quite right, you know—the sturgeon was just a *leetle* off."

These words, in themselves so commonplace, for some reason infuriated Gurov, seemed to him humiliating, gross. What savage manners, what people! What wasted evenings, what tedious, empty days! Frantic card-playing, gluttony, drunkenness, perpetual talk always about the same thing. The greater part of one's time and energy went on business that was no use to anyone, and on discussing the same thing over and over again, and there was nothing to show for it all but a stunted, earth-bound existence and a round of trivialities, and there was nowhere to escape to, you might as well be in a mad-house or a convict settlement.

Gurov lay awake all night, raging, and went about the whole of the next day with a headache. He slept badly on the succeeding nights, too, sitting up in bed, thinking, or pacing the floor of his room. He was sick of his children, sick of the bank, felt not the slightest desire to go anywhere or talk about anything.

When the Christmas holidays came, he packed his things, telling his wife he had to go to Petersburg in the interests of a certain young man, and set off for the town of S. To what end? He hardly knew himself. He only knew that he must see Anna Sergeyevna, must speak to her, arrange a meeting, if possible.

He arrived at S. in the morning and engaged the best room in the hotel, which had a carpet of grey military frieze, and a dusty ink-pot on the table, surmounted by a headless rider, holding his hat in his raised hand. The hall porter told him what he wanted to know: von Diederitz had a house of his own in Staro-Goncharnaya Street. It wasn't far from the hotel, he lived on a grand scale, luxuriously, kept carriage-horses, the whole town knew him. The hall porter pronounced the name "Drideritz."

Gurov strolled over to Staro-Goncharnaya Street and discovered the house. In front of it was a long grey fence with inverted nails hammered into the tops of the palings.

"A fence like that is enough to make anyone want to run away," thought Gurov, looking at the windows of the house and the fence.

He reasoned that since it was a holiday, her husband would probably be at home. In any case it would be tactless to embarrass her by calling at the house. And a note might fall into the hands of the husband, and bring about catastrophe. The best thing would be to wait about on the chance of seeing her. And he walked up and down the street, hovering in the vicinity of the fence, watching for his chance. A beggar entered the gate, only to be attacked by dogs, then, an hour later, the faint, vague sounds of a piano reached his ears. That would be Anna Sergeyevna playing. Suddenly the front door opened and an old woman came out, followed by a familiar white pomeranian. Gurov tried to call to it, but his heart beat violently, and in his agitation he could not remember its name.

He walked on, hating the grey fence more and more, and now ready to tell himself irately that Anna Sergeyevna had forgotten him, had already, perhaps, found distraction in another—what could be more natural in a young woman who had to look at this accursed fence from morning to night? He went back to his hotel and sat on the sofa in his room for some time, not knowing what to do, then he ordered dinner, and after dinner, had a long sleep.

"What a foolish, restless business," he thought, waking up and looking towards the dark window-panes. It was evening by now. "Well, I've had my sleep out. And what am I to do in the night?"

He sat up in bed, covered by the cheap grey quilt, which reminded him of a hospital blanket, and in his vexation he fell to taunting himself.

"You and your lady with a dog . . . there's adventure for you! See what you get for your pains."

On his arrival at the station that morning he had noticed a poster announcing in enormous letters the first performance at the local theatre of *The Geisha*. Remembering this, he got up and made for the theatre.

"It's highly probable that she goes to first-nights," he told himself.

The theatre was full. It was a typical provincial theatre, with a mist collecting over the chandeliers, and the crowd in the gallery fidgeting noisily. In the first row of the stalls the local dandies stood waiting for the curtain to go up, their hands clasped behind them. There, in the front seat of the Governor's box, sat the Governor's daughter, wearing a boa, the Governor himself hiding modestly behind the drapes, so that only his hands were visible. The curtain stirred, the orchestra took a long time tuning up their instruments. Gurov's eyes roamed eagerly over the audience as they filed in and occupied their seats.

Anna Sergeyevna came in, too. She seated herself in the third row of the stalls, and when Gurov's glance fell on her, his heart seemed to stop, and he knew in a flash that the whole world contained no one nearer or dearer to him, no one more important to his happiness. This little woman, lost in the provincial crowd, in no way remarkable, holding a silly lorgnette in her hand, now filled his whole life, was his grief, his joy, all that he desired. Lulled by the sounds coming from the wretched orchestra, with its feeble, amateurish violinists, he thought how beautiful she was . . . thought and dreamed. . . .

Anna Sergeyevna was accompanied by a tall, round-shouldered young man with small whiskers, who nodded at every step before taking the seat beside her and seemed to be continually bowing to someone. This must be her husband, whom, in a fit of bitterness, at Yalta, she had called a "flunkey." And there really was something of the lackey's servility in his lanky figure, his side-whiskers, and the little bald spot on the top of his head. And he smiled sweetly, and the badge of some scientific society gleaming in his buttonhole was like the number on a footman's livery.

The husband went out to smoke in the first interval, and she was left alone in her seat. Gurov, who had taken a seat in the stalls, went up to her and said in a trembling voice, with a forced smile: "How d'you do?"

She glanced up at him and turned pale, then looked at him again in alarm, unable to believe her eyes, squeezing her fan and lorgnette in one hand, evidently struggling to overcome a feeling of faintness. Neither of them said a word. She sat there, and he stood beside her, disconcerted by her embarrassment, and not daring to sit down. The violins and flutes sang out as they were tuned, and there was a tense sensation in the atmosphere, as if they were being watched from all the boxes. At last she got up and moved rapidly towards one of the exits. He followed her and they wandered aimlessly along corridors, up and down stairs; figures flashed by in the uniforms of legal officials, high-school teachers and civil servants, all wearing badges; ladies, coats hanging from pegs flashed by; there was a sharp draught, bringing with it an odour of cigarette-stubs. And Gurov, whose heart was beating violently, thought: "What on earth are all these people, this orchestra for? . . ."

The next minute he suddenly remembered how, after seeing Anna Sergeyevna off that evening at the station, he had told himself that all was over, and they would never meet again. And how far away the end seemed to be now!

She stopped on a dark narrow staircase over which was a notice bearing the inscription "To the upper circle."

"How you frightened me!" she said, breathing heavily, still pale and half-stunned. "Oh, how you frightened me! I'm almost dead! Why did you come? Oh, why?"

"But, Anna," he said, in low, hasty tones. "But, Anna. . . . Try to understand . . . do try. . . ."

She cast him a glance of fear, entreaty, love, and then gazed at him steadily, as if to fix his features firmly in her memory.

"I've been so unhappy," she continued, taking no notice of his words. "I could think of nothing but you the whole time, I lived on the thoughts of you. I tried to forget—why, oh, why did you come?"

On the landing above them were two schoolboys, smoking and looking down, but Gurov did not care, and, drawing Anna Sergeyevna towards him, began kissing her face, her lips, her hands.

"What are you doing, oh, what are you doing?" she said in horror, drawing back. "We have both gone mad. Go away this very night, this moment. . . . By all that is sacred, I implore you. . . . Somebody is coming."

Someone was ascending the stairs.

"You must go away," went on Anna Sergeyevna in a whisper. "D'you hear me, Dmitri Dmitrich? I'll come to you in Moscow. I have never been happy, I am unhappy now, and I shall never be happy—never! Do not make me suffer still more! I will come to you in Moscow, I swear it! And now we must part! My dear one, my kind one, my darling, we must part."

She pressed his hand and hurried down the stairs, looking back at him continually, and her eyes showed that she was in truth unhappy.

Gurov stood where he was for a short time, listening, and when all was quiet went to look for his coat, and left the theatre.

IV

And Anna Sergeyevna began going to Moscow to see him. Every two or three months she left the town of S., telling her husband that she was going to consult a specialist on female diseases, and her husband believed her and did not believe her. In Moscow she always stayed at the "Slavyanski Bazaar," sending a man in a red cap to Gurov the moment she arrived. Gurov went to her, and no one in Moscow knew anything about it.

One winter morning he went to see her as usual (the messenger had been to him the evening before, but had not found him at home). His daughter was with him for her school was on the way, and he thought he might as well see her to it.

"It is three degrees above zero," said Gurov to his daughter, "and yet it is snowing. You see it is only above zero close to the ground, the temperature in the upper layers of the atmosphere is quite different."

"Why doesn't it ever thunder in winter, Papa?"

He explained this, too. As he was speaking, he kept reminding himself that he was going to a rendezvous and that not a living soul knew about it, or, probably, ever would. He led a double life—one in public, in the sight of all whom it concerned, full of conventional truth and conventional deception, exactly like the lives of his friends and acquaintances, and another which flowed in secret. And, owing to some strange, possibly quite accidental chain of circumstances, everything that was important, interesting, essential, everything about which he was sincere and never deceived himself, everything that composed the kernel of his life, went on in secret, while everything that was false in him, everything that composed the husk in which he hid himself and the truth which was in him—his work at the bank, discussions at the club, his "lower race," his attendance at anniversary celebrations with his wife—was on the surface. He began to judge others by himself, no longer believing what he saw, and always assuming that the real, the only interesting life of every individual goes on as under cover of night, secretly. Every individual existence revolves around mystery, and perhaps that is the chief reason that all cultivated individuals insisted so strongly on the respect due to personal secrets.

After leaving his daughter at the door of her school Gurov set off for the "Slavyanski Bazaar." Taking off his overcoat in the lobby, he went upstairs and knocked softly on the door. Anna Sergeyevna, wearing the grey dress he liked most, exhausted by her journey and by suspense, had been expecting him since the evening before. She was pale and looked at him without smiling, but was in his arms almost before he was fairly in the room. Their kiss was lingering, prolonged, as if they had not met for years.

"Well, how are you?" he asked. "Anything new?"

"Wait, I'll tell you in a minute. . . . I can't. . . ."

She could not speak, because she was crying. Turning away, she held her handkerchief to her eyes.

"I'll wait till she's had her cry out," he thought, and sank into a chair.

He rang for tea, and a little later, while he was drinking it, she was still standing there, her face to the window. She wept from emotion, from her bitter consciousness of the sadness of their life; they could only see one another in secret, hiding from people, as if they were thieves. Was not their life a broken one?

"Don't cry," he said.

It was quite obvious to him that this love of theirs would not soon come to an end, and that no one could say when this end would be. Anna Sergeyevna loved him ever more fondly, worshipped him, and there would have been no point in telling her that one day it must end. Indeed, she would not have believed him.

He moved over and took her by the shoulders, intending to fondle her with light words, but suddenly he caught sight of himself in the looking-glass.

His hair was already beginning to turn grey. It struck him as strange that he should have aged so much in the last few years. The shoulders on which his hands lay were warm and quivering. He felt a pity for this life, still so warm and exquisite, but probably soon to fade and droop like his own. Why did she love him so? Women had always believed him different from what he really was, had loved in him not himself but the man their imagination pictured him, a man they had sought for eagerly all their lives. And afterwards when they discovered their mistake, they went on loving him just the same. And not one of them had ever been happy with him. Time had passed, he had met one woman after another, become intimate with each, parted with each, but had never loved. There had been all sorts of things between them, but never love.

And only now, when he was grey-haired, had he fallen in love properly, thoroughly, for the first time in his life.

He and Anna Sergeyevna loved one another as people who are very close and intimate, as husband and wife, as dear friends love one another. It seemed to them that fate had intended them for one another, and they could not understand why she should have a husband, and he a wife. They were like two migrating birds, the male and the female, who had been caught and put into separate cages. They forgave one another all that they were ashamed of in the past, in their present, and felt that this love of theirs had changed them both.

Formerly, in moments of melancholy, he had consoled himself by the first argument that came into his head, but now arguments were nothing to him, he felt profound pity, desired to be sincere, tender.

"Stop crying, my dearest," he said. "You've had your cry, now stop. . . . Now let us have a talk, let us try and think what we are to do."

Then they discussed their situation for a long time, trying to think how they could get rid of the necessity for hiding, deception, living in different towns, being so long without meeting. How were they to shake off these intolerable fetters?

"How? How?" he repeated, clutching his head. "How?"

And it seemed to them that they were within an inch of arriving at a decision, and that then a new, beautiful life would begin. And they both realized that the end was still far, far away, and that the hardest, the most complicated part was only just beginning.

[1899]

CHARLOTTE PERKINS GILMAN [1860–1935]
The Yellow Wallpaper

It is very seldom that mere ordinary people like John and myself secure ancestral halls for the summer.

A colonial mansion, a hereditary estate, I would say a haunted house and reach the height of romantic felicity—but that would be asking too much of fate!

Still I will proudly declare that there is something queer about it.

Else, why should it be let so cheaply? And why have stood so long untenanted?

John laughs at me, of course, but one expects that in marriage.

John is practical in the extreme. He has no patience with faith, an intense horror of superstition, and he scoffs openly at any talk of things not to be felt and seen and put down in figures.

John is a physician, and *perhaps*—(I would not say it to a living soul, of course, but this is dead paper and a great relief to my mind)—*perhaps* that is one reason I do not get well faster.

You see, he does not believe I am sick!

And what can one do?

If a physician of high standing, and one's own husband, assures friends and relatives that there is really nothing the matter with one but temporary nervous depression—a slight hysterical tendency—what is one to do?

My brother is also a physician, and also of high standing, and he says the same thing.

So I take phosphates or phosphites—whichever it is, and tonics, and journeys, and air, and exercise, and am absolutely forbidden to "work" until I am well again.

Personally, I disagree with their ideas.

Personally, I believe that congenial work, with excitement and change, would do me good.

But what is one to do?

I did write for a while in spite of them; but it *does* exhaust me a good deal—having to be so sly about it, or else meet with heavy opposition.

I sometimes fancy that in my condition if I had less opposition and more society and stimulus—but John says the very worst thing I can do is to think about my condition, and I confess it always makes me feel bad.

So I will let it alone and talk about the house.

The most beautiful place! It is quite alone, standing well back from the road, quite three miles from the village. It makes me think of English places that you read about, for there are hedges and walls and gates that lock, and lots of separate little houses for the gardeners and people.

There is a *delicious* garden! I never saw such a garden—large and shady, full of box-bordered paths, and lined with long grape-covered arbors with seats under them.

There were greenhouses, too, but they are all broken now.

There was some legal trouble, I believe, something about the heirs and co-heirs; anyhow, the place has been empty for years.

That spoils my ghostliness, I am afraid, but I don't care—there is something strange about the house—I can feel it.

I even said so to John one moonlight evening, but he said what I felt was a *draught*, and shut the window.

I get unreasonably angry with John sometimes. I'm sure I never used to be so sensitive. I think it is due to this nervous condition.

But John says if I feel so, I shall neglect proper self-control; so I take pains to control myself—before him, at least, and that makes me very tired.

I don't like our room a bit. I wanted one downstairs that opened on the piazza and had roses all over the window, and such pretty old-fashioned chintz hangings! but John would not hear of it.

He said there was only one window and not room for two beds, and no near room for him if he took another.

He is very careful and loving, and hardly lets me stir without special direction.

I have a schedule prescription for each hour in the day; he takes all care from me, and so I feel basely ungrateful not to value it more.

He said we came here solely on my account, that I was to have perfect rest and all the air I could get. "Your exercise depends on your strength, my dear," said he, "and your food somewhat on your appetite; but air you can absorb all the time." So we took the nursery at the top of the house.

It is a big, airy room, the whole floor nearly, with windows that look all ways, and air and sunshine galore. It was nursery first and then play-room and gymnasium, I should judge; for the windows are barred for little children, and there are rings and things in the walls.

The paint and paper look as if a boys' school had used it. It is stripped off—the paper—in great patches all around the head of my bed, about as far as I can reach, and in a great place on the other side of the room low down. I never saw a worse paper in my life.

One of those sprawling flamboyant patterns committing every artistic sin.

It is dull enough to confuse the eye in following, pronounced enough to constantly irritate and provoke study, and when you follow the lame uncertain curves for a little distance they suddenly commit suicide—plunge off at outrageous angles, destroy themselves in unheard of contradictions.

The color is repellant, almost revolting; a smouldering unclean yellow, strangely faded by the slow-turning sunlight.

It is a dull yet lurid orange in some places, a sickly sulphur tint in others.

No wonder the children hated it! I should hate it myself if I had to live in this room long.

There comes John, and I must put this away,—he hates to have me write a word.

We have been here two weeks, and I haven't felt like writing before, since that first day.

I am sitting by the window now, up in this atrocious nursery, and there is nothing to hinder my writing as much as I please, save lack of strength.

John is away all day, and even some nights when his cases are serious.

I am glad my case is not serious!

But these nervous troubles are dreadfully depressing.

John does not know how much I really suffer. He knows there is no *reason* to suffer, and that satisfies him.

Of course it is only nervousness. It does weigh on me so not to do my duty in any way!

I meant to be such a help to John, such a real rest and comfort, and here I am a comparative burden already!

Nobody would believe what an effort it is to do what little I am able, — to dress and entertain, and order things.

It is fortunate Mary is so good with the baby. Such a dear baby!

And yet I *cannot* be with him, it makes me so nervous.

I suppose John never was nervous in his life. He laughs at me so about this wallpaper!

At first he meant to repaper the room, but afterward he said that I was letting it get the better of me, and that nothing was worse for a nervous patient than to give way to such fancies.

He said that after the wallpaper was changed it would be the heavy bedstead, and then the barred windows, and then that gate at the head of the stairs, and so on.

"You know the place is doing you good," he said, "and really, dear, I don't care to renovate the house just for a three months' rental."

"Then do let us go downstairs," I said, "there are such pretty rooms there."

Then he took me in his arms and called me a blessed little goose, and said he would go down cellar, if I wished, and have it whitewashed into the bargain.

But he is right enough about the beds and windows and things.

It is an airy and comfortable room as anyone need wish, and, of course, I would not be so silly as to make him uncomfortable just for a whim.

I'm really getting quite fond of the big room, all but that horrid paper.

Out of one window I can see the garden, those mysterious deep-shaded arbors, the riotous old-fashioned flowers, and bushes and gnarly trees.

Out of another I get a lovely view of the bay and a little private wharf belonging to the estate. There is a beautiful shaded lane that runs down there from the house. I always fancy I see people walking in these numerous paths and arbors, but John has cautioned me not to give way to fancy in the least. He says that with my imaginative power and habit of story-making, a nervous weakness like mine is sure to lead to all manner of excited fancies, and that I ought to use my will and good sense to check the tendency. So I try.

I think sometimes that if I were only well enough to write a little it would relieve the press of ideas and rest me.

But I find I get pretty tired when I try.

Despair is stopping to desire

It is so discouraging not to have any advice and companionship about my work. When I get really well, John says we will ask Cousin Henry and Julia down for a long visit; but he says he would as soon put fireworks in my pillow-case as to let me have those stimulating people about now.

I wish I could get well faster.

But I must not think about that. This paper looks to me as if it *knew* what a vicious influence it had!

There is a recurrent spot where the pattern lolls like a broken neck and two bulbous eyes stare at you upside down.

I get positively angry with the impertinence of it and the everlastingness. Up and down and sideways they crawl, and those absurd, unblinking eyes are everywhere. There is one place where two breadths didn't match, and the eyes go all up and down the line, one a little higher than the other.

I never saw so much expression in an inanimate thing before, and we all know how much expression they have! I used to lie awake as a child and get more entertainment and terror out of blank walls and plain furniture than most children could find in a toy-store.

I remember what a kindly wink the knobs of our big, old bureau used to have, and there was one chair that always seemed like a strong friend.

I used to feel that if any of the other things looked too fierce I could always hop into that chair and be safe.

The furniture in this room is no worse than inharmonious, however, for we had to bring it all from downstairs. I suppose when this was used as a playroom they had to take the nursery things out, and no wonder! I never saw such ravages as the children have made here.

The wallpaper, as I said before, is torn off in spots, and it sticketh closer than a brother—they must have had perseverance as well as hatred.

Then the floor is scratched and gouged and splintered, the plaster itself is dug out here and there, and this great heavy bed, which is all we found in the room, looks as if it had been through the wars.

But I don't mind it a bit—only the paper.

There comes John's sister. Such a dear girl as she is, and so careful of me! I must not let her find me writing.

She is a perfect and enthusiastic housekeeper, and hopes for no better profession. I verily believe she thinks it is the writing which made me sick!

But I can write when she is out, and see her a long way off from these windows.

There is one that commands the road, a lovely shaded winding road, and one that just looks off over the country. A lovely country, too, full of great elms and velvet meadows.

This wallpaper has a kind of sub-pattern in a different shade, a particularly irritating one, for you can only see it in certain lights, and not clearly then.

But in the places where it isn't faded and where the sun is just so—I can see a strange, provoking, formless sort of figure, that seems to skulk about behind that silly and conspicuous front design.

There's sister on the stairs!

Well, the Fourth of July is over! The people are all gone and I am tired out. John thought it might do me good to see a little company, so we just had mother and Nellie and the children down for a week.

Of course I didn't do a thing. Jennie sees to everything now.

But it tired me all the same.

John says if I don't pick up faster he shall send me to Weir Mitchell° in the fall.

But I don't want to go there at all. I had a friend who was in his hands once, and she says he is just like John and my brother, only more so!

Besides, it is such an undertaking to go so far.

I don't feel as if it was worthwhile to turn my hand over for anything, and I'm getting dreadfully fretful and querulous.

I cry at nothing, and cry most of the time.

Of course I don't when John is here, or anybody else, but when I am alone.

And I am alone a good deal just now. John is kept in town very often by serious cases, and Jennie is good and lets me alone when I want her to.

So I walk a little in the garden or down that lovely lane, sit on the porch under the roses, and lie down up here a good deal.

I'm getting really fond of the room in spite of the wallpaper. Perhaps *because* of the wallpaper.

It dwells in my mind so!

I lie here on this great immovable bed—it is nailed down, I believe—and follow that pattern about by the hour. It is as good as gymnastics, I assure you. I start, we'll say, at the bottom, down in the corner over there where it has not been touched, and I determine for the thousandth time that I *will* follow that pointless pattern to some sort of a conclusion.

I know a little of the principle of design, and I know this thing was not arranged on any laws of radiation, or alternation, or repetition, or symmetry, or anything else that I ever heard of.

It is repeated, of course, by the breadths, but not otherwise.

Weir Mitchell: Dr. S. Weir Mitchell (1829–1914) was an American neurologist and author who advocated "rest cures" for nervous illnesses.

Looked at in one way each breadth stands alone, the bloated curves and flourishes—a kind of "debased Romanesque" with *delirium tremens*—go waddling up and down in isolated columns of fatuity.

But, on the other hand, they connect diagonally, and the sprawling outlines run off in great slanting waves of optic horror, like a lot of wallowing sea-weeds in full chase.

The whole thing goes horizontally, too, at least it seems so, and I exhaust myself in trying to distinguish the order of its going in that direction.

They have used a horizontal breadth for a frieze, and that adds wonderfully to the confusion.

There is one end of the room where it is almost intact, and there, when the crosslights fade and the low sun shines directly upon it, I can almost fancy radiation after all,—the interminable grotesques seem to form around a common centre and rush off in headlong plunges of equal distraction.

It makes me tired to follow it. I will take a nap I guess.

I don't know why I should write this.

I don't want to.

I don't feel able.

And I know John would think it absurd. But I *must* say what I feel and think in some way—it is such a relief!

But the effort is getting to be greater than the relief.

Half the time now I am awfully lazy, and lie down ever so much.

John says I mustn't lose my strength, and has me take cod liver oil and lots of tonics and things, to say nothing of ale and wine and rare meat.

Dear John! He loves me very dearly, and hates to have me sick. I tried to have a real earnest reasonable talk with him the other day, and tell him how I wish he would let me go and make a visit to Cousin Henry and Julia.

But he said I wasn't able to go, nor able to stand it after I got there; and I did not make out a very good case for myself, for I was crying before I had finished.

It is getting to be a great effort for me to think straight. Just this nervous weakness I suppose.

And dear John gathered me up in his arms, and just carried me upstairs and laid me on the bed, and sat by me and read to me till it tired my head.

He said I was his darling and his comfort and all he had, and that I must take care of myself for his sake, and keep well.

He says no one but myself can help me out of it, that I must use my will and self-control and not let any silly fancies run away with me.

There's one comfort, the baby is well and happy, and does not have to occupy this nursery with the horrid wallpaper.

If we had not used it, that blessed child would have! What a fortunate escape! Why, I wouldn't have a child of mine, an impressionable little thing, live in such a room for worlds.

I never thought of it before, but it is lucky that John kept me here after all, I can stand it so much easier than a baby, you see.

Of course I never mention it to them any more—I am too wise, but I keep watch of it all the same.

There are things in the wallpaper that nobody knows but me, or ever will.

Behind that outside pattern the dim shapes get clearer every day.

It is always the same shape, only very numerous.

And it is like a woman stooping down and creeping about behind that pattern. I don't like it a bit. I wonder—I begin to think—I wish John would take me away from here!

It is so hard to talk with John about my case, because he is so wise, and because he loves me so.

But I tried it last night.

It was moonlight. The moon shines in all around just as the sun does.

I hate to see it sometimes, it creeps so slowly, and always comes in by one window or another.

John was asleep and I hated to waken him, so I kept still and watched the moonlight on that undulating wallpaper till I felt creepy.

The faint figure behind seemed to shake the pattern, just as if she wanted to get out.

I got up softly and went to feel and see if the paper *did* move, and when I came back John was awake.

"What is it, little girl?" he said. "Don't go walking about like that—you'll get cold."

I thought it was a good time to talk, so I told him that I really was not gaining here, and that I wished he would take me away.

"Why, darling!" said he, "our lease will be up in three weeks, and I can't see how to leave before.

"The repairs are not done at home, and I cannot possibly leave town just now. Of course if you were in any danger, I could and would, but you really are better, dear, whether you can see it or not. I am a doctor, dear, and I know. You are gaining flesh and color, your appetite is better, I feel really much easier about you."

"I don't weigh a bit more," said I, "nor as much; and my appetite may be better in the evening when you are here but it is worse in the morning when you are away!"

"Bless her little heart!" said he with a big hug, "she shall be as sick as she pleases! But now let's improve the shining hours by going to sleep, and talk about it in the morning!"

"And you won't go away?" I asked gloomily.

"Why, how can I, dear? It is only three weeks more and then we will take a nice little trip of a few days while Jennie is getting the house ready. Really dear you are better!"

"Better in body perhaps—" I began, and stopped short, for he sat up straight and looked at me with such a stern, reproachful look that I could not say another word.

"My darling," said he, "I beg you, for my sake and for our child's sake, as well as for your own, that you will never for one instant let that idea enter your mind! There is nothing so dangerous, so fascinating, to a temperament like yours. It is a false and foolish fancy. Can you trust me as a physician when I tell you so?"

So of course I said no more on that score, and we went to sleep before long. He thought I was asleep first, but I wasn't, and lay there for hours trying to decide whether that front pattern and the back pattern really did move together or separately.

On a pattern like this, by daylight, there is a lack of sequence, a defiance of law, that is a constant irritant to a normal mind.

The color is hideous enough, and unreliable enough, and infuriating enough, but the pattern is torturing.

You think you have mastered it, but just as you get well underway in following, it turns a back-somersault and there you are. It slaps you in the face, knocks you down, and tramples upon you. It is like a bad dream.

The outside pattern is a florid arabesque, reminding one of a fungus. If you can imagine a toadstool in joints, an interminable string of toadstools, budding and sprouting in endless convolutions—why, that is something like it.

That is, sometimes!

There is one marked peculiarity about this paper, a thing nobody seems to notice but myself, and that is that it changes as the light changes.

When the sun shoots in through the east window—I always watch for that first long, straight ray—it changes so quickly that I never can quite believe it.

That is why I watch it always.

By moonlight—the moon shines in all night when there is a moon—I wouldn't know it was the same paper.

At night in any kind of light, in twilight, candlelight, lamplight, and worst of all by moonlight, it becomes bars! The outside pattern I mean, and the woman behind it is as plain as can be.

I didn't realize for a long time what the thing was that showed behind, that dim sub-pattern, but now I am quite sure it is a woman.

By daylight she is subdued, quiet. I fancy it is the pattern that keeps her so still. It is so puzzling. It keeps me quiet by the hour.

I lie down ever so much now. John says it is good for me, and to sleep all I can.

Indeed he started the habit by making me lie down for an hour after each meal.

It is a very bad habit I am convinced, for you see I don't sleep.

And that cultivates deceit, for I don't tell them I'm awake—O, no!

The fact is I am getting a little afraid of John.

He seems very queer sometimes, and even Jennie has an inexplicable look.

It strikes me occasionally, just as a scientific hypothesis,—that perhaps it is the paper!

I have watched John when he did not know I was looking, and come into the room suddenly on the most innocent excuses, and I've caught him several times *looking at the paper!* And Jennie too. I caught Jennie with her hand on it once.

She didn't know I was in the room, and when I asked her in a quiet, a very quiet voice, with the most restrained manner possible, what she was doing with the paper—she turned around as if she had been caught stealing, and looked quite angry—asked me why I should frighten her so!

Then she said that the paper stained everything it touched, that she had found yellow smooches on all my clothes and John's, and she wished we would be more careful!

Did not that sound innocent? But I know she was studying that pattern, and I am determined that nobody shall find it out but myself!

Life is very much more exciting now than it used to be. You see I have something more to expect, to look forward to, to watch. I really do eat better, and am more quiet than I was.

John is so pleased to see me improve! He laughed a little the other day, and said I seemed to be flourishing in spite of my wallpaper.

I turned it off with a laugh. I had no intention of telling him it was *because* of the wallpaper—he would make fun of me. He might even want to take me away.

I don't want to leave now until I have found it out. There is a week more, and I think that will be enough.

I'm feeling ever so much better! I don't sleep much at night, for it is so interesting to watch developments; but I sleep a good deal in the daytime.

In the daytime it is tiresome and perplexing.

There are always new shoots on the fungus, and new shades of yellow all over it. I cannot keep count of them, though I have tried conscientiously.

It is the strangest yellow, that wallpaper! It makes me think of all the yellow things I ever saw—not beautiful ones like buttercups, but old foul, bad yellow things.

But there is something else about that paper—the smell! I noticed it the moment we came into the room, but with so much air and sun it was not bad. Now we have had a week of fog and rain, and whether the windows are open or not, the smell is here.

It creeps all over the house.

I find it hovering in the dining-room, skulking in the parlor, hiding in the hall, lying in wait for me on the stairs.

It gets into my hair.

Even when I go to ride, if I turn my head suddenly and surprise it—there is that smell!

Such a peculiar odor, too! I have spent hours in trying to analyze it, to find what it smelled like.

It is not bad—at first, and very gentle, but quite the subtlest, most enduring odor I ever met.

In this damp weather it is awful, I wake up in the night and find it hanging over me.

It used to disturb me at first. I thought seriously of burning the house—to reach the smell.

But now I am used to it. The only thing I can think of that it is like is the *color* of the paper! A yellow smell.

There is a very funny mark on this wall, low down, near the mopboard. A streak that runs round the room. It goes behind every piece of furniture, except the bed, a long, straight, even *smooch*, as if it had been rubbed over and over.

I wonder how it was done and who did it, and what they did it for. Round and round and round—round and round and round—it makes me dizzy!

I really have discovered something at last.

Through watching so much at night, when it changes so, I have finally found out.

The front pattern *does* move—and no wonder! The woman behind shakes it!

Sometimes I think there are a great many women behind, and sometimes only one, and she crawls around fast, and her crawling shakes it all over.

Then in the very bright spots she keeps still, and in the very shady spots she just takes hold of the bars and shakes them hard.

And she is all the time trying to climb through. But nobody could climb through that pattern—it strangles so; I think that is why it has so many heads.

They get through, and then the pattern strangles them off and turns them upside down, and makes their eyes white!

If those heads were covered or taken off it would not be half so bad.

I think that woman gets out in the daytime!

And I'll tell you why—privately—I've seen her!

I can see her out of every one of my windows!

It is the same woman, I know, for she is always creeping, and most women do not creep by daylight.

I see her in that long shaded lane, creeping up and down. I see her in those dark grape arbors, creeping all around the garden.

I see her on that long road under the trees, creeping along, and when a carriage comes she hides under the blackberry vines.

I don't blame her a bit. It must be very humiliating to be caught creeping by daylight!

I always lock the door when I creep by daylight. I can't do it at night, for I know John would suspect something at once.

And John is so queer now, that I don't want to irritate him. I wish he would take another room! Besides, I don't want anybody to get that woman out at night but myself.

I often wonder if I could see her out of all the windows at once.

But, turn as fast as I can, I can only see out of one at one time.

And though I always see her, she *may* be able to creep faster than I can turn!

I have watched her sometimes away off in the open country, creeping as fast as a cloud shadow in a high wind.

If only that top pattern could be gotten off from the under one! I mean to try it, little by little.

I have found out another funny thing, but I shan't tell it this time! It does not do to trust people too much.

There are only two more days to get this paper off, and I believe John is beginning to notice. I don't like the look in his eyes.

And I heard him ask Jennie a lot of professional questions, about me. She had a very good report to give.

She said I slept a good deal in the daytime.

John knows I don't sleep very well at night, for all I'm so quiet!

He asked me all sorts of questions too, and pretended to be very loving and kind.

As if I couldn't see through him!

Still, I don't wonder he acts so, sleeping under this paper for three months.

It only interests me, but I feel sure John and Jennie are secretly affected by it.

Hurrah! This is the last day, but it is enough. John to stay in town over night, and won't be out until this evening.

Jennie wanted to sleep with me—the sly thing! But I told her I should undoubtedly rest better for a night all alone.

That was clever, for really I wasn't alone a bit! As soon as it was moonlight and that poor thing began to crawl and shake the pattern, I got up and ran to help her.

I pulled and she shook, I shook and she pulled, and before morning we had peeled off yards of that paper.

A strip about as high as my head and half around the room.

And then when the sun came and that awful pattern began to laugh at me, I declared I would finish it to-day!

We go away to-morrow, and they are moving all my furniture down again to leave things as they were before.

Jennie looked at the wall in amazement, but I told her merrily that I did it out of pure spite at the vicious thing.

She laughed and said she wouldn't mind doing it herself, but I must not get tired.

How she betrayed herself that time!

But I am here, and no person touches this paper but me,—not *alive!*

She tried to get me out of the room—it was too patent! But I said it was so quiet and empty and clean now that I believed I would lie down again and sleep all I could, and not to wake me even for dinner—I would call when I woke.

So now she is gone, and the servants are gone, and the things are gone, and there is nothing left but that great bedstead nailed down, with the canvas mattress we found on it.

We shall sleep downstairs to-night, and take the boat home to-morrow.

I quite enjoy the room, now it is bare again.

How those children did tear about here!

This bedstead is fairly gnawed!

But I must get to work.

I have locked the door and thrown the key down into the front path.

I don't want to go out, and I don't want to have anybody come in, till John comes.

I want to astonish him.

I've got a rope up here that even Jennie did not find. If that woman does get out, and tries to get away, I can tie her!

But I forgot I could not reach far without anything to stand on!

This bed will *not* move!

I tried to lift and push it until I was lame, and then I got so angry I bit off a little piece at one corner—but it hurt my teeth.

Then I peeled off all the paper I could reach standing on the floor. It sticks horribly and the pattern just enjoys it! All those strangled heads and bulbous eyes and waddling fungus growths just shriek with derision!

I am getting angry enough to do something desperate. To jump out of the window would be admirable exercise, but the bars are too strong even to try.

Besides I wouldn't do it. Of course not. I know well enough that a step like that is improper and might be misconstrued.

I don't like to *look* out of the windows even—there are so many of those creeping women, and they creep so fast.

I wonder if they all come out of that wallpaper as I did?

But I am securely fastened now by my well-hidden rope—you don't get *me* out in the road there!

I suppose I shall have to get back behind the pattern when it comes night, and that is hard!

It is so pleasant to be out in this great room and creep around as I please!

I don't want to go outside. I won't, even if Jennie asks me to.

For outside you have to creep on the ground, and everything is green instead of yellow.

But here I can creep smoothly on the floor, and my shoulder just fits in that long smooch around the wall, so I cannot lose my way.

Why, there's John at the door!

It is no use, young man, you can't open it!

How he does call and pound!

Now he's crying for an axe.

It would be a shame to break down that beautiful door!

"John dear!" said I in the gentlest voice, "the key is down by the front steps, under a plantain leaf!"

That silenced him for a few moments.

Then he said—very quietly indeed, "Open the door, my darling!"

"I can't," said I. "The key is down by the front door under a plantain leaf!"

And then I said it again, several times, very gently and slowly, and said it so often that he had to go and see, and he got it of course, and came in. He stopped short by the door.

"What is the matter?" he cried. "For God's sake, what are you doing!"

I kept on creeping just the same, but I looked at him over my shoulder.

"I've got out at last," said I, "in spite of you and Jane. And I've pulled off most of the paper, so you can't put me back!"

Now why should that man have fainted? But he did, and right across my path by the wall, so that I had to creep over him every time!

[1892]

JAMES JOYCE   [1882–1941]

Araby

North Richmond Street, being blind, was a quiet street except at the hour when the Christian Brothers' School set the boys free. An uninhabited house of two storeys stood at the blind end, detached from its neighbours in a square ground. The other houses of the street, conscious of decent lives within them, gazed at one another with brown imperturbable faces.

The former tenant of our house, a priest, had died in the back drawing-room. Air, musty from having been long enclosed, hung in all the rooms, and the waste room behind the kitchen was littered with old useless papers. Among these I found a few paper-covered books, the pages of which were curled and damp: *The Abbot*, by Walter Scott, *The Devout Communicant*, and *The Memoirs of Vidocq*. I liked the last best because its leaves were yellow. The wild garden behind the house contained a central apple-tree and a few straggling bushes under one of which I found the late tenant's rusty bicycle-pump. He had been a very charitable priest; in his will he had left all his money to institutions and the furniture of his house to his sister.

When the short days of winter came dusk fell before we had well eaten our dinners. When we met in the street the houses had grown sombre. The space of sky above us was the colour of ever-changing violet and towards it the lamps of the street lifted their feeble lanterns. The cold air stung us and we played till our bodies glowed. Our shouts echoed in the silent street. The career of our play brought us through the dark muddy lanes behind the houses where we ran the gauntlet of the rough tribes from the cottages, to the back doors of the dark dripping gardens where odours arose from the ashpits, to the dark odorous stables where a coachman smoothed and combed the horse or shook music from the buckled harness. When we returned to the street light from the kitchen windows had filled the areas. If my uncle was seen turning the corner we hid in the shadow until we had seen him safely housed. Or if Mangan's sister came out on the doorstep to call her brother in to his tea we watched her from our shadow peer up and down the street. We waited to see whether she would remain or go in and, if she remained, we left our shadow and walked up to Mangan's steps resignedly. She was waiting for us, her figure defined by the light from the half-opened door. Her brother always teased her before he obeyed and I stood by the railings looking at her. Her dress swung as she moved her body and the soft rope of her hair tossed from side to side.

Every morning I lay on the floor in the front parlour watching her door. The blind was pulled down to within an inch of the sash so that I could not be seen. When she came out on the doorstep my heart leaped. I ran to the hall, seized my books, and followed her. I kept her brown figure always in my eye and, when we came near the point at which our ways diverged, I quickened my pace and passed her. This happened morning after morning. I had never spoken to her, except for a few casual words, and yet her name was like a summons to all my foolish blood.

Her image accompanied me even in places the most hostile to romance. On Saturday evenings when my aunt went marketing I had to go to carry some of the parcels. We walked through the flaring streets, jostled by drunken men and bargaining women, amid the curses of labourers, the shrill litanies of shop-boys who stood on guard by the barrel of pigs' cheeks, the nasal chanting of street-singers, who sang a *come-all-you* about O'Donovan Rossa,° or a ballad about the troubles in our native land. These noises converged in a single sensation of life for me: I imagined that I bore my chalice safely through a throng of foes. Her name sprang to my lips at moments in strange prayers and praises which I myself did not understand. My eyes were often full of tears (I could not tell why) and at times a flood from my heart seemed to pour itself out into my bosom. I thought little of the future. I did not know whether I would ever speak to her or not or, if I spoke to her, how I could tell her of my confused adoration. But my body was like a harp and her words and gestures were like fingers running upon the wires.

One evening I went into the back drawing-room in which the priest had died. It was a dark rainy evening and there was no sound in the

O'Donovan Rossa: Jeremiah O'Donovan (1831–1915) was nicknamed "Dynamite Rossa" for his militant pursuit of Irish independence.

house. Through one of the broken panes I heard the rain impinge upon the earth, the fine incessant needles of water playing in the sodden beds. Some distant lamp or lighted window gleamed below me. I was thankful that I could see so little. All my senses seemed to desire to veil themselves and, feeling that I was about to slip from them, I pressed the palms of my hands together until they trembled, murmuring: *"O love! O love!"* many times.

At last she spoke to me. When she addressed the first words to me I was so confused that I did not know what to answer. She asked me was I going to *Araby*. I forgot whether I answered yes or no. It would be a splendid bazaar, she said she would love to go.

"And why can't you?" I asked.

While she spoke she turned a silver bracelet round and round her wrist. She could not go, she said, because there would be a retreat that week in her convent. Her brother and two other boys were fighting for their caps and I was alone at the railings. She held one of the spikes, bowing her head towards me. The light from the lamp opposite our door caught the white curve of her neck, lit up her hair that rested there and, falling, lit up the hand upon the railing. It fell over one side of her dress and caught the white border of a petticoat, just visible as she stood at ease.

"It's well for you," she said.

"If I go," I said, "I will bring you something."

What innumerable follies laid waste my waking and sleeping thoughts after that evening! I wished to annihilate the tedious intervening days. I chafed against the work of school. At night in my bedroom and by day in the classroom her image came between me and the page I strove to read. The syllables of the word *Araby* were called to me through the silence in which my soul luxuriated and cast an Eastern enchantment over me. I asked for leave to go to the bazaar on Saturday night. My aunt was surprised and hoped it was not some Freemason affair. I answered few questions in class. I watched my master's face pass from amiability to sternness; he hoped I was not beginning to idle. I could not call my wandering thoughts together. I had hardly any patience with the serious work of life which, now that it stood between me and my desire, seemed to me child's play, ugly monotonous child's play.

On Saturday morning I reminded my uncle that I wished to go to the bazaar in the evening. He was fussing at the hallstand, looking for the hat-brush, and answered me curtly:

"Yes, boy, I know."

As he was in the hall I could not go into the front parlour and lie at the window. I left the house in bad humour and walked slowly towards the school. The air was pitilessly raw and already my heart misgave me.

When I came home to dinner my uncle had not yet been home. Still it was early. I sat staring at the clock for some time and, when its ticking began to irritate me, I left the room. I mounted the staircase and gained the upper part of the house. The high cold empty gloomy rooms liberated me and I went from room to room singing. From the front window I saw my companions playing below in the street. Their cries reached me weakened and indistinct and, leaning my forehead against the cool glass, I looked over at the dark house where she lived. I may have stood there for an hour, seeing nothing but the brown-clad figure cast by my imagination, touched discreetly by the lamplight at the curved neck, at the hand upon the railings and at the border below the dress.

When I came downstairs again I found Mrs. Mercer sitting at the fire. She was an old garrulous woman, a pawnbroker's widow, who collected used stamps for some pious purpose. I had to endure the gossip of the tea-table. The meal was prolonged beyond an hour and still my uncle did not come. Mrs. Mercer stood up to go: she was sorry she couldn't wait any longer, but it was after eight o'clock and she did not like to be out late, as the night air was bad for her. When she had gone I began to walk up and down the room, clenching my fists. My aunt said:

"I'm afraid you may put off your bazaar for this night of Our Lord."

At nine o'clock I heard my uncle's latchkey in the halldoor. I heard him talking to himself and heard the hallstand rocking when it had received the weight of his overcoat. I could interpret these signs. When he was midway through his dinner I asked him to give me the money to go to the bazaar. He had forgotten.

"The people are in bed and after their first sleep now," he said.

I did not smile. My aunt said to him energetically:

"Can't you give him the money and let him go? You've kept him late enough as it is."

My uncle said he was very sorry he had forgotten. He said he believed in the old saying: "All work and no play makes Jack a dull boy." He asked me where I was going and, when I had told him a second time he asked me did I know *The Arab's Farewell to his Steed*. When I left the kitchen he was about to recite the opening lines of the piece to my aunt.

I held a florin° tightly in my hand as I strode down Buckingham Street towards the station. The sight of the streets thronged with buyers and glaring with gas recalled to me the purpose of my journey. I took my seat in a third-class carriage of a deserted train. After an intolerable delay the train moved out of the station slowly. It crept onward among ruinous houses and over the twinkling river. At Westland Row Station a crowd of people pressed to the carriage doors; but the porters moved them back, saying that it was a special train for the bazaar. I remained alone in the bare carriage. In a few minutes the train drew up beside an improvised wooden platform. I passed out on to the road and saw by the lighted dial

Florin: A silver coin worth two shillings.

of a clock that it was ten minutes to ten. In front of me was a large build-ing which displayed the magical name.

I could not find any sixpenny entrance and, fearing that the bazaar would be closed, I passed in quickly through a turnstile, handing a shilling to a weary-looking man. I found myself in a big hall girdled at half its height by a gallery. Nearly all the stalls were closed and the greater part of the hall was in darkness. I recognised a silence like that which pervades a church after a service. I walked into the centre of the bazaar timidly. A few people were gathered about the stalls which were still open. Before a curtain, over which the words *Café Chantant* were written in coloured lamps, two men were counting money on a salver. I listened to the fall of the coins.

Remembering with difficulty why I had come I went over to one of the stalls and examined porcelain vases and flowered tea-sets. At the door of the stall a young lady was talking and laughing with two young gentle-men. I remarked their English accents and listened vaguely to their con-versation.

"O, I never said such a thing!"

"O, but you did!"

"O, but I didn't!"

"Didn't she say that?"

"Yes. I heard her."

"O, there's a . . . fib!"

Observing me the young lady came over and asked me did I wish to buy anything. The tone of her voice was not encouraging; she seemed to have spoken to me out of a sense of duty. I looked humbly at the great jars that stood like eastern guards at either side of the dark entrance to the stall and murmured:

"No, thank you."

The young lady changed the position of one of the vases and went back to the two young men. They began to talk of the same subject. Once or twice the young lady glanced at me over her shoulder.

I lingered before her stall, though I knew my stay was useless, to make my interest in her wares seem the more real. Then I turned away slowly and walked down the middle of the bazaar. I allowed the two pennies to fall against the sixpence in my pocket. I heard a voice call from one end of the gallery that the light was out. The upper part of the hall was now completely dark.

Gazing up into the darkness I saw myself as a creature driven and derided by vanity; and my eyes burned with anguish and anger.

[1914]

FRANZ KAFKA [1883–1924]

The Metamorphosis

TRANSLATED BY WILLA AND EDWIN MUIR, 1948

I

As Gregor Samsa awoke one morning from uneasy dreams he found himself transformed in his bed into a gigantic insect. He was lying on his hard, as it were armor-plated, back and when he lifted his head a little he could see his dome-like brown belly divided into stiff arched segments on top of which the bed quilt could hardly keep in position and was about to slide off completely. His numerous legs, which were pitifully thin compared to the rest of his bulk, waved helplessly before his eyes.

What has happened to me? he thought. It was no dream. His room, a regular human bedroom, only rather too small, lay quiet between the four familiar walls. Above the table on which a collection of cloth samples was unpacked and spread out — Samsa was a commercial traveler — hung the picture which he had recently cut out of an illustrated magazine and put into a pretty gilt frame. It showed a lady, with a fur cap on and a fur stole, sitting upright and holding out to the spectator a huge fur muff into which the whole of her forearm had vanished!

Gregor's eyes turned next to the window, and the overcast sky — one could hear rain drops beating on the window gutter — made him quite melancholy. What about sleeping a little longer and forgetting all this nonsense, he thought, but it could not be done, for he was accustomed to sleep on his right side and in his present condition he could not turn himself over. However violently he forced himself towards his right side he always rolled on to his back again. He tried it at least a hundred times, shutting his eyes to keep from seeing his struggling legs, and only desisted when he began to feel in his side a faint dull ache he had never experienced before.

Oh God, he thought, what an exhausting job I've picked on! Traveling about day in, day out. It's much more irritating work than doing the actual business in the office, and on top of that there's the trouble of constant traveling, of worrying about train connections, the bed and irregular meals, casual acquaintances that are always new and never become

101

intimate friends. The devil take it all! He felt a slight itching up on his belly; slowly pushed himself on his back nearer to the top of the bed so that he could lift his head more easily; identified the itching place which was surrounded by many small white spots the nature of which he could not understand and made to touch it with a leg, but drew the leg back immediately, for the contact made a cold shiver run through him.

He slid down again into his former position. This getting up early, he thought, makes one quite stupid. A man needs his sleep. Other commercials live like harem women. For instance, when I come back to the hotel of a morning to write up the orders I've got, these others are only sitting down to breakfast. Let me just try that with my chief; I'd be sacked on the spot. Anyhow, that might be quite a good thing for me, who can tell? If I didn't have to hold my hand because of my parents I'd have given notice long ago, I'd have gone to the chief and told him exactly what I think of him. That would knock him endways from his desk! It's a queer way of doing, too, this sitting on high at a desk and talking down to employees, especially when they have to come quite near because the chief is hard of hearing. Well, there's still hope; once I've saved enough money to pay back my parents' debts to him—that should take another five or six years—I'll do it without fail. I'll cut myself completely loose then. For the moment, though, I'd better get up, since my train goes at five.

He looked at the alarm clock ticking on the chest. Heavenly Father! he thought. It was half-past six o'clock and the hands were quietly moving on, it was even past the half-hour, it was getting on toward a quarter to seven. Had the alarm clock not gone off? From the bed one could see that it had been properly set for four o'clock; of course it must have gone off. Yes, but was it possible to sleep quietly through that ear-splitting noise? Well, he had not slept quietly, yet apparently all the more soundly for that. But what was he to do now? The next train went at seven o'clock; to catch that he would need to hurry like mad and his samples weren't even packed up, and he himself wasn't feeling particularly fresh and active. And even if he did catch the train he wouldn't avoid a row with the chief, since the firm's porter would have been waiting for the five o'clock train and would have long since reported his failure to turn up. The porter was a creature of the chief's, spineless and stupid. Well, supposing he were to say he was sick? But that would be most unpleasant and would look suspicious, since during his five years' employment he had not been ill once. The chief himself would be sure to come with the sick-insurance doctor, would reproach his parents with their son's laziness and would cut all excuses short by referring to the insurance doctor, who of course regarded all mankind as perfectly healthy malingerers. And would he be so far wrong on this occasion? Gregor really felt quite well, apart from a drowsiness that was utterly superfluous after such a long sleep, and he was even unusually hungry.

As all this was running through his mind at top speed without his being able to decide to leave his bed—the alarm clock had just struck a quarter to seven—there came a cautious tap at the door behind the head of his bed. "Gregor," said a voice—it was his mother's—"it's a quarter to seven. Hadn't you a train to catch?" That gentle voice! Gregor had a shock as he heard his own voice answering hers, unmistakably his own voice, it was true, but with a persistent horrible twittering squeak behind it like an undertone, that left the words in their clear shape only for the first moment and then rose up reverberating round them to destroy their sense, so that one could not be sure one had heard them rightly. Gregor wanted to answer at length and explain everything, but in the circumstances he confined himself to saying: "Yes, yes, thank you, Mother, I'm getting up now." The wooden door between them must have kept the change in his voice from being noticeable outside, for his mother contented herself with this statement and shuffled away. Yet this brief exchange of words had made the other members of the family aware that Gregor was still in the house, as they had not expected, and at one of the side doors his father was already knocking, gently, yet with his fist. "Gregor, Gregor," he called, "what's the matter with you?" And after a little while he called again in a deeper voice: "Gregor! Gregor!" At the other side door his sister was saying in a low, plaintive tone: "Gregor? Aren't you well? Are you needing anything?" He answered them both at once: "I'm just ready," and did his best to make his voice sound as normal as possible by enunciating the words very clearly and leaving long pauses between them. So his father went back to his breakfast, but his sister whispered: "Gregor, open the door, do." However, he was not thinking of opening the door, and felt thankful for the prudent habit he had acquired in traveling of locking all doors during the night, even at home.

His immediate intention was to get up quietly without being disturbed, to put on his clothes and above all eat his breakfast, and only then to consider what else was to be done, since in bed, he was well aware, his meditations would come to no sensible conclusion. He remembered that often enough in bed he had felt small aches and pains, probably caused by awkward postures, which had proved purely imaginary once he got up, and he looked forward eagerly to seeing this morning's delusions gradually fall away. That the change in his voice was nothing but the precursor of a severe chill, a standing ailment of commercial travelers, he had not the least possible doubt.

To get rid of the quilt was quite easy; he had only to inflate himself a little and it fell off by itself. But the next move was difficult, especially because he was so uncommonly broad. He would have needed arms and hands to hoist himself up; instead he had only the numerous little legs which never stopped waving in all directions and which he could not control in the least. When he tried to bend one of them it was the first to stretch itself straight; and did he succeed at last in making it do what he wanted, all the other legs meanwhile waved the more wildly in a high degree of unpleasant agitation. "But what's the use of lying idle in bed," said Gregor to himself.

He thought that he might get out of bed with the lower part of his body first, but this lower part, which he had not yet seen and of which he could form no clear conception, proved too difficult to move; it shifted so slowly; and when finally, almost wild with annoyance, he gathered his forces together and thrust out recklessly, he had miscalculated the direction and bumped heavily against the lower end of the bed, and the stinging pain he felt informed him that precisely this lower part of his body was at the moment probably the most sensitive.

So he tried to get the top part of himself out first, and cautiously moved his head towards the edge of the bed. That proved easy enough, and despite its breadth and mass the bulk of his body at last slowly followed the movement of his head. Still, when he finally got his head free over the edge of the bed he felt too scared to go on advancing, for after all if he let himself fall in this way it would take a miracle to keep his head from being injured. And at all costs he must not lose consciousness now, precisely now; he would rather stay in bed.

But when after a repetition of the same efforts he lay in his former position again, sighing, and watched his little legs struggling against each other more wildly than ever, if that were possible, and saw no way of bringing any order into this arbitrary confusion, he told himself again that it was impossible to stay in bed and that the most sensible course was to risk everything for the smallest hope of getting away from it. At the same time he did not forget meanwhile to remind himself that cool reflection, the coolest possible, was much better than desperate resolves. In such moments he focused his eyes as sharply as possible on the window, but, unfortunately, the prospect of the morning fog, which muffled even the other side of the narrow street, brought him little encouragement and comfort. "Seven o'clock already," he said to himself when the alarm clock chimed again, "seven o'clock already and still such a thick fog." And for a little while he lay quiet, breathing lightly, as if perhaps expecting such complete repose to restore all things to their real and normal condition.

But then he said to himself: "Before it strikes a quarter past seven I must be quite out of this bed, without fail. Anyhow, by that time some-one will have come from the office to ask for me, since it opens before seven." And he set himself to rocking his whole body at once in a regular rhythm, with the idea of swinging it out of the bed. If he tipped himself out in that way he could keep his head from injury by lifting it at an acute angle when he fell. His back seemed to be hard and was not likely to suffer from a fall on the carpet. His biggest worry was the loud crash he would not be able to help making, which would probably cause anxiety, if not terror, behind all the doors. Still, he must take the risk.

When he was already half out of the bed—the new method was more a game than an effort, for he needed only to hitch himself across by rocking to and fro—it struck him how simple it would be if he could get help. Two strong people—he thought of his father and the servant girl— would be amply sufficient; they would only have to thrust their arms under his convex back, lever him out of the bed, bend down with their burden and then be patient enough to let him turn himself right over on to the floor, where it was to be hoped his legs would then find their proper function. Well, ignoring the fact that the doors were all locked, ought he really to call for help? In spite of his misery he could not suppress a smile at the very idea of it.

He had got so far that he could barely keep his equilibrium when he rocked himself strongly, and he would have to nerve himself very soon for the final decision since in five minutes' time it would be a quarter past seven—when the front doorbell rang. "That's someone from the office," he said to himself, and grew almost rigid, while his little legs only jigged about all the faster. For a moment everything stayed quiet. "They're not going to open the door," said Gregor to himself, catching at some kind of irrational hope. But then of course the servant girl went as usual to the door with her heavy tread and opened it. Gregor needed only to hear the first good morning of the visitor to know immediately who it was—the chief clerk himself. What a fate, to be condemned to work for a firm where the smallest omission at once gave rise to the gravest suspicion! Were all employees in a body nothing but scoundrels, was there not among them one single loyal devoted man who, had he wasted only an hour or so of the firm's time in a morning, was so tormented by conscience as to be driven out of his mind and actually incapable of leaving his bed? Wouldn't it really have been sufficient to send an apprentice to inquire—if any inquiry were necessary at all—did the chief clerk himself have to come and thus indicate to the entire family, an innocent family, that this suspicious circumstance could be investigated by no one less versed in affairs than himself? And more through the agitation caused by these reflections than through any act of will Gregor swung himself out of bed with all his strength. There was a loud thump, but it was not really a crash. His fall was broken to some extent by the carpet, his back, too, was less stiff than he thought, and so there was merely a dull thud, not so very startling. Only he had not lifted his head carefully enough and had hit it; he turned it and rubbed it on the carpet in pain and irritation.

"That was something falling down in there," said the chief clerk in the next room to the left. Gregor tried to suppose to himself that something like what had happened to him today might some day happen to the chief clerk; one really could not deny that it was possible. But as if in brusque reply to this supposition the chief clerk took a couple of firm steps in the next-door room and his patent leather boots creaked. From the right-hand room his sister was whispering to inform him of the situation: "Gregor, the chief clerk's here." "I know," muttered Gregor to himself; but he didn't dare to make his voice loud enough for his sister to hear it.

"Gregor," said his father now from the left-hand room, "the chief clerk has come and wants to know why you didn't catch the early train. We don't know what to say to him. Besides, he wants to talk to you in person. So open the door, please. He will be good enough to excuse the untidiness of your room." "Good morning, Mr. Samsa," the chief clerk was calling amiably meanwhile. "He's not well," said his mother to the visitor, while his father was still speaking through the door, "he's not well, sir, believe me. What else would make him miss a train! The boy thinks about nothing but his work. It makes me almost cross the way he never goes out in the evenings; he's been here the last eight days and has stayed at home every single evening. He just sits there quietly at the table reading a newspaper or looking through railway timetables. The only amusement he gets is doing fretwork. For instance, he spent two or three evenings cutting out a little picture frame; you would be surprised to see how pretty it is; it's hanging in his room; you'll see it in a minute when Gregor opens the door. I must say I'm glad you've come, sir; we should never have got him to unlock the door by ourselves; he's so obstinate; and I'm sure he's unwell, though he wouldn't have it to be so this morning." "I'm just coming," said Gregor slowly and carefully, not moving an inch for fear of losing one word of the conversation. "I can't think of any other explanation, madam," said the chief clerk, "I hope it's nothing serious. Although on the other hand I must say that we men of business—fortunately or unfortunately—very often simply have to ignore any slight indisposition, since business must be attended to." "Well, can the chief clerk come in now?" asked Gregor's father impatiently, again knocking on the door. "No," said Gregor. In the left-hand room a painful silence followed this refusal, in the right-hand room his sister began to sob.

Why didn't his sister join the others? She was probably newly out of bed and hadn't even begun to put on her clothes yet. Well, why was she crying? Because he wouldn't get up and let the chief clerk in, because he was in danger of losing his job, and because the chief would begin dunning his parents again for the old debts? Surely these were things one didn't need to worry about for the present. Gregor was still at home and not in the least thinking of deserting the family. At the moment, true, he was lying on the carpet and no one who knew the condition he was in could seriously expect him to admit the chief clerk. But for such a small discourtesy, which could plausibly be explained away somehow later on, Gregor could hardly be dismissed on the spot. And it seemed to Gregor that it would be much more sensible to leave him in peace for the present than to trouble him with tears and entreaties. Still, of course, their uncertainty bewildered them all and excused their behavior.

"Mr. Samsa," the chief clerk called now in a louder voice, "what's the matter with you? Here you are, barricading yourself in your room, giving only 'yes' and 'no' for answers, causing your parents a lot of unnecessary trouble and neglecting—I mention this only in passing—neglecting your business duties in an incredible fashion. I am speaking here in the name of your parents and of your chief, and I beg you quite seriously to give me an immediate and precise explanation. You amaze me, you amaze me. I thought you were a quiet, dependable person, and now all at once you seem bent on making a disgraceful exhibition of yourself. The chief did hint to me early this morning a possible explanation for your disappearance—with reference to the cash payments that were entrusted to you recently—but I almost pledged my solemn word of honor that this could not be so. But now that I see how incredibly obstinate you are, I no longer have the slightest desire to take your part at all. And your position in the firm is not so unassailable. I came with the intention of telling you all this in private, but since you are wasting my time so needlessly I don't see why your parents shouldn't hear it too. For some time past your work has been most unsatisfactory; this is not the season of the year for a business boom, of course, we admit that, but a season of the year for doing no business at all, that does not exist, Mr. Samsa, must not exist."

"But, sir," cried Gregor, beside himself and in his agitation forgetting everything else, "I'm just going to open the door this very minute. A slight illness, an attack of giddiness, has kept me from getting up. I'm still lying in bed. But I feel all right again. I'm getting out of bed now. Just give me a moment or two longer! I'm not quite so well as I thought. But I'm all right, really. How a thing like that can suddenly strike one down! Only last night I was quite well, my parents can tell you, or rather I did have a slight presentiment. I must have showed some sign of it. Why didn't I report it at the office! But one always thinks that an indisposition can be got over without staying in the house. Oh sir, do spare my parents! All that you're reproaching me with now has no foundation;

no one has ever said a word to me about it. Perhaps you haven't looked at the last orders I sent in. Anyhow, I can still catch the eight o'clock train, I'm much the better for my few hours' rest. Don't let me detain you here, sir; I'll be attending to business very soon, and do be good enough to tell the chief so and to make my excuses to him!"

And while all this was tumbling out pell-mell and Gregor hardly knew what he was saying, he had reached the chest quite easily, perhaps because of the practice he had had in bed, and was now trying to lever himself upright by means of it. He meant actually to open the door, actually to show himself and speak to the chief clerk; he was eager to find out what the others, after all their insistence, would say at the sight of him. If they were horrified then the responsibility was no longer his and he could stay quiet. But if they took it calmly, then he had no reason either to be upset, and could really get to the station for the eight o'clock train if he hurried. At first he slipped down a few times from the polished surface of the chest, but at length with a last heave he stood upright; he paid no more attention to the pains in the lower part of his body, however they smarted. Then he let himself fall against the back of a near-by chair, and clung with his little legs to the edges of it. That brought him into control of himself again and he stopped speaking, for now he could listen to what the chief clerk was saying.

"Did you understand a word of it?" the chief clerk was asking; "surely he can't be trying to make fools of us?" "Oh dear," cried his mother, in tears, "perhaps he's terribly ill and we're tormenting him. Grete! Grete!" she called out then. "Yes, Mother?" called his sister from the other side. They were calling to each other across Gregor's room. "You must go this minute for the doctor. Gregor is ill. Go for the doctor, quick. Did you hear how he was speaking?" "That was no human voice," said the chief clerk in a voice noticeably low beside the shrillness of the mother's. "Anna! Anna!" his father was calling through the hall to the kitchen, clapping his hands, "get a locksmith at once!" And the two girls were already running through the hall with a swish of skirts—how could his sister have got dressed so quickly?—and were tearing the front door open. There was no sound of its closing again; they had evidently left it open, as one does in houses where some great misfortune has happened.

But Gregor was now much calmer. The words he uttered were no longer understandable, apparently, although they seemed clear enough to him, even clearer than before, perhaps because his ear had grown accustomed to the sound of them. Yet at any rate people now believed that something was wrong with him, and were ready to help him. The positive certainty with which these first measures had been taken comforted him. He felt himself drawn once more into the human circle and hoped for great and remarkable results from both the doctor and the locksmith, without really distinguishing precisely between them. To make his voice as clear as possible for the decisive conversation that was now imminent he coughed a little, as quietly as he could, of course, since this noise too might not sound like a human cough for all he was able to judge. In the next room meanwhile there was complete silence. Perhaps his parents were sitting at the table with the chief clerk, whispering, perhaps they were all leaning against the door and listening.

Slowly Gregor pushed the chair towards the door, then let go of it, caught hold of the door for support—the soles at the end of his little legs were somewhat sticky—and rested against it for a moment after his efforts. Then he set himself to turning the key in the lock with his mouth. It seemed, unhappily, that he hadn't really any teeth—what could he grip the key with?—but on the other hand his jaws were certainly very strong; with their help he did manage to set the key in motion, heedless of the fact that he was undoubtedly damaging them somewhere, since a brown fluid issued from his mouth, flowed over the key and dripped on the floor. "Just listen to that," said the chief clerk next door; "he's turning the key." That was a great encouragement to Gregor; but they should all have shouted encouragement to him, his father and mother too: "Go on, Gregor," they should have called out, "keep going, hold on to that key!" And in the belief that they were all following his efforts intently, he clenched his jaws recklessly on the key with all the force at his command. As the turning of the key progressed he circled round the lock, holding on now only with his mouth, pushing on the key, as required, or pulling it down again with all the weight of his body. The louder click of the finally yielding lock literally quickened Gregor. With a deep breath of relief he said to himself: "So I didn't need the locksmith," and laid his head on the handle to open the door wide.

Since he had to pull the door towards him, he was still invisible when it was really wide open. He had to edge himself slowly round the near half of the double door, and to do it very carefully if he was not to fall plump upon his back just on the threshold. He was still carrying out this difficult manoeuvre, with no time to observe anything else, when he heard the chief clerk utter a loud "Oh!"—it sounded like a gust of wind—and now he could see the man, standing as he was nearest to the door, clapping one hand before his open mouth and slowly backing away as if driven by some invisible steady pressure. His mother—in spite of the chief clerk's being there her hair was still undone and sticking up in all directions—first clasped her hands and looked at his father, then took two steps towards Gregor and fell on the floor among her outspread skirts, her face hidden on her breast. His father knotted his fist with a fierce expression on his face as if he meant to knock Gregor back into his room, then looked uncertainly round the living room, covered his eyes with his hands and wept till his great chest heaved.

Gregor did not go now into the living room, but leaned against the inside of the firmly shut wing of the door, so that only half his body was visible and his head above it bending sideways to look at the others. The light had meanwhile strengthened; on the other side of the street one could see clearly a section of the endlessly long, dark gray building opposite—it was a hospital—abruptly punctuated by its row of regular windows; the rain was still falling, but only in large singly discernible and literally singly splashing drops. The breakfast dishes were set out on the table lavishly, for breakfast was the most important meal of the day to Gregor's father, who lingered it out for hours over various newspapers. Right opposite Gregor on the wall hung a photograph of himself on military service, as a lieutenant, hand on sword, a carefree smile on his face, inviting one to respect his uniform and military bearing. The door leading to the hall was open, and one could see that the front door stood open too, showing the landing beyond and the beginning of the stairs going down.

"Well," said Gregor, knowing perfectly that he was the only one who had retained any composure, "I'll put my clothes on at once, pack up my samples and start off. Will you only let me go? You see, sir, I'm not obstinate, and I'm willing to work; traveling is a hard life, but I couldn't live without it. Where are you going, sir? To the office? Yes? Will you give a true account of all this? One can be temporarily incapacitated, but that's just the moment for remembering former services and bearing in mind that later on, when the incapacity has been got over, one will certainly work with all the more industry and concentration. I'm loyally bound to serve the chief, you know that very well. Besides, I have to provide for my parents and my sister. I'm in great difficulties, but I'll get out of them again. Don't make things any worse for me than they are. Stand up for me in the firm. Travelers are not popular there, I know. People think they earn sacks of money and just have a good time. A prejudice there's no particular reason for revising. But you, sir, have a more comprehensive view of affairs than the rest of the staff, yes, let me tell you in confidence, a more comprehensive view than the chief himself, who, being the owner, lets his judgment easily be swayed against one of his employees. And you know very well that the traveler, who is never seen in the office almost the whole year round, can so easily fall a victim to gossip and ill luck and unfounded complaints, which he mostly knows nothing about, except when he comes back exhausted from his rounds, and only then suffers in person from their evil consequences, which he can no longer trace back to the original causes. Sir, sir, don't go away without a word to me to show that you think me in the right at least to some extent!"

But at Gregor's very first words the chief clerk had already backed away and only stared at him with parted lips over one twitching shoulder. And while Gregor was speaking he did not stand still one moment but stole away towards the door, without taking his eyes off Gregor, yet only an inch at a time, as if obeying some secret injunction to leave the room. He was already at the hall, and the suddenness with which he took his last step out of the living room would have made one believe he had burned the sole of his foot. Once in the hall he stretched his right arm before him towards the staircase, as if some supernatural power were waiting there to deliver him.

Gregor perceived that the chief clerk must on no account be allowed to go away in this frame of mind if his position in the firm were not to be endangered to the utmost. His parents did not understand this so well; they had convinced themselves in the course of years that Gregor was settled for life in this firm, and besides they were so occupied with their immediate troubles that all foresight had forsaken them. Yet Gregor had this foresight. The chief clerk must be detained, soothed, persuaded and finally won over; the whole future of Gregor and his family depended on it! If only his sister had been there! She was intelligent; she had begun to cry while Gregor was still lying quietly on his back. And no doubt the chief clerk, so partial to ladies, would have been guided by her; she would have shut the door of the flat and in the hall talked him out of his horror. But she was not there, and Gregor would have to handle the situation himself. And without remembering that he was still unaware what powers of movement he possessed, without even remembering that his words in all possibility, indeed in all likelihood, would again be unintelligible, he let go the wing of the door, pushed himself through the opening, started to walk towards the chief clerk, who was already ridiculously clinging with both hands to the railing on the landing; but immediately, as he was feeling for a support, he fell down with a little cry upon all his numerous legs. Hardly was he down when he experienced for the first time this morning a sense of physical comfort; his legs had firm ground under them; they were completely obedient, as he noted with joy; they even strove to carry him forward in whatever direction he chose; and he was inclined to believe that a final relief from all his sufferings was at hand. But in the same moment as he found himself on the floor, rocking with suppressed eagerness to move, not far from his mother, indeed just in front of her, she, who had seemed so completely crushed, sprang all at once to her feet, her arms and fingers outspread, cried: "Help, for God's sake, help!" bent her head down as if to see Gregor better, yet on the contrary kept backing senselessly away; had quite forgotten that the laden table stood behind her; sat upon it hastily, as if in absence of mind, when she bumped into it; and seemed altogether unaware that the big coffee pot beside her was upset and pouring coffee in a flood over the carpet.

"Mother, Mother," said Gregor in a low voice, and looked up at her. The chief clerk, for the moment, had quite slipped from his mind; instead, he could not resist snapping his jaws together at the sight of the streaming coffee. That made his mother scream again, she fled from the table and fell into the arms of his father, who hastened to catch her. But Gregor had now no time to spare for his parents; the chief clerk was already on the stairs; with his chin on the banisters he was taking one last backward look. Gregor made a spring, to be as sure as possible of overtaking him; the chief clerk must have divined his intention, for he leaped down several steps and vanished; he was still yelling "Ugh!" and it echoed through the whole staircase.

Unfortunately, the flight of the chief clerk seemed completely to upset Gregor's father, who had remained relatively calm until now, for instead of running after the man himself, or at least not hindering Gregor in his pursuit, he seized in his right hand the walking stick which the chief clerk had left behind on a chair, together with a hat and greatcoat, snatched in his left hand a large newspaper from the table and began stamping his feet and flourishing the stick and the newspaper to drive Gregor back into his room. No entreaty of Gregor's availed, indeed no entreaty was even understood, however humbly he bent his head his father only stamped on the floor the more loudly. Behind his father his mother had torn open a window, despite the cold weather, and was leaning far out of it with her face in her hands. A strong draught set in from the street to the staircase, the window curtains blew in, the newspapers on the table fluttered, stray pages whisked over the floor. Pitilessly Gregor's father drove him back, hissing and crying "Shoo!" like a savage. But Gregor was quite unpracticed in walking backwards, it really was a slow business. If he only had a chance to turn round he could get back to his room at once, but he was afraid of exasperating his father by the slowness of such a rotation and at any moment the stick in his father's hand might hit him a fatal blow on the back or on the head. In the end, however, nothing else was left for him to do since to his horror he observed that in moving backwards he could not even control the direction he took; and so, keeping an anxious eye on his father all the time over his shoulder, he began to turn round as quickly as he could, which was in reality very slowly. Perhaps his father noted his good intentions, for he did not interfere except every now and then to help him in the manoeuvre from a distance with the point of the stick. If only he would have stopped making that unbearable hissing noise! It made Gregor quite lose his head. He had turned almost completely round when the hissing noise so distracted him that he even turned a little the wrong way again.

But when at last his head was fortunately right in front of the doorway, it appeared that his body was too broad simply to get through the opening. His father, of course, in his present mood was far from thinking of such a thing as opening the other half of the door, to let Gregor have enough space. He had merely the fixed idea of driving Gregor back into his room as quickly as possible. He would never have suffered Gregor to make the circumstantial preparations for standing up on end and perhaps slipping his way through the door. Maybe he was now making more noise than ever to urge Gregor forward, as if no obstacle impeded him; to Gregor, anyhow, the noise in his rear sounded no longer like the voice of one single father; this was really no joke, and Gregor thrust himself—come what might—into the doorway. One side of his body rose up, he was tilted at an angle in the doorway, his flank was quite bruised, horrid blotches stained the white door, soon he was stuck fast and, left to himself, could not have moved at all, his legs on one side fluttered trembling to the air, those on the other were crushed painfully to the floor—when from behind his father gave him a strong push which was literally a deliverance and he flew far into the room, bleeding freely. The door was slammed behind him with the stick, and then at last there was silence.

II

Not until it was twilight did Gregor awake out of a deep sleep, more like a swoon than a sleep. He would certainly have waked up of his own accord not much later, for he felt himself sufficiently rested and well-slept, but it seemed to him as if a fleeting step and a cautious shutting of the door leading into the hall had aroused him. The electric lights in the street cast a pale sheen here and there on the ceiling and the upper surfaces of the furniture, but down below, where he lay, it was dark. Slowly, awkwardly trying out his feelers, which he now first learned to appreciate, he pushed his way to the door to see what had been happening there. His left side felt like one single long, unpleasant tense scar, and he had actually to limp on his two rows of legs. One little leg, moreover, had been severely damaged in the course of that morning's events—it was almost a miracle that only one had been damaged—and trailed uselessly behind him.

He had reached the door before he discovered what had really drawn him to it: the smell of food. For there stood a basin filled with fresh milk in which floated little sops of white bread. He could almost have laughed with joy, since he was now still hungrier than in the morning, and he dipped his head almost over the eyes straight into the milk. But soon in disappointment he withdrew it again; not only did he find it difficult to feed because of his tender left side—and he could only feed with the palpitating collaboration of his whole body—he did not like the milk either, although milk had been his favorite drink and that was certainly why his sister had set it there for him, indeed it was almost with repulsion that he turned away from the basin and crawled back to the middle of the room.

He could see through the crack of the door that the gas was turned on in the living room, but while usually at this time his father made a habit of reading the afternoon newspaper in a loud voice to his mother and occasionally to his sister as well, not a sound was now to be heard. Well, perhaps his father had recently given up this habit of reading aloud, which his sister had mentioned so often in conversation and in her letters. But there was the same silence all around, although the flat was certainly not empty of occupants. "What a quiet life our family has been leading," said Gregor to himself, and as he sat there motionless staring into the darkness he felt great pride in the fact that he had been able to provide such a life for his parents and sister in such a fine flat. But what if all the quiet, the comfort, the contentment were now to end in horror? To keep himself from being lost in such thoughts Gregor took refuge in movement and crawled up and down the room.

Once during the long evening one of the side doors was opened a little and quickly shut again, later the other side door too; someone had apparently wanted to come in and then thought better of it. Gregor now stationed himself immediately before the living room door, determined to persuade any hesitating visitor to come in or at least to discover who it might be; but the door was not opened again and he waited in vain. In the early morning, when the doors were locked, they had all wanted to come in, now that he had opened one door and the other had apparently been opened during the day, no one came in and even the keys were on the other side of the doors.

It was late at night before the gas went out in the living room, and Gregor could easily tell that his parents and his sister had all stayed awake until then, for he could clearly hear the three of them stealing away on tiptoe. No one was likely to visit him, not until the morning, that was certain; so he had plenty of time to meditate at his leisure on how he was to arrange his life afresh. But the lofty, empty room in which he had to lie flat on the floor filled him with an apprehension he could not account for, since it had been his very own room for the past five years—and with a half-unconscious action, not without a slight feeling of shame, he scuttled under the sofa, where he felt comfortable at once, although his back was a little cramped and he could not lift his head up, and his only regret was that his body was too broad to get the whole of it under the sofa.

He stayed there all night, spending the time partly in a light slumber, from which his hunger kept waking him up with a start, and partly in worrying and sketching vague hopes, which all led to the same conclusion, that he must lie low for the present and, by exercising patience, and the utmost consideration, help the family to bear the inconvenience he was bound to cause them in his present condition.

Very early in the morning, it was still almost night, Gregor had the chance to test the strength of his new resolutions, for his sister, nearly fully dressed, opened the door from the hall and peered in. She did not see him at once, yet when she caught sight of him under the sofa—well, he had to be somewhere, he couldn't have flown away, could he?—she was so startled that without being able to help it she slammed the door shut again. But as if regretting her behavior she opened the door again immediately and came in on tiptoe, as if she were visiting an invalid or even a stranger. Gregor had pushed his head forward to the very edge of the sofa and watched her. Would she notice that he had left the milk standing, and not for lack of hunger, and would she bring in some other kind of food more to his taste? If she did not do it of her own accord, he would rather starve than draw her attention to the fact, although he felt a wild impulse to dart out from under the sofa, throw himself at her feet and beg her for something to eat. But his sister at once noticed, with surprise, that the basin was still full, except for a little milk that had been spilt all around it, she lifted it immediately, not with her bare hands, true, but with a cloth and carried it away. Gregor was wildly curious to know what she would bring instead, and made various speculations about it. Yet what she actually did next, in the goodness of her heart, he could never have guessed at. To find out what he liked she brought him a whole selection of food, all set out on an old newspaper. There were old, half-decayed vegetables, bones from last night's supper covered with a white sauce that had thickened; some raisins and almonds; a piece of cheese that Gregor would have called uneatable two days ago; a dry roll of bread, a buttered roll, and a roll both buttered and salted. Besides all that, she set down again the same basin, into which she had poured some water, and which was apparently to be reserved for his exclusive use. And with fine tact, knowing that Gregor would not eat in her presence, she withdrew quickly and even turned the key, to let him understand that he could take his ease as much as he liked. Gregor's legs all whizzed towards the food. His wounds must have healed completely, moreover, for he felt no disability, which amazed him and made him reflect how more than a month ago he had cut one finger a little with a knife and had still suffered pain from the wound only the day before yesterday. Am I less sensitive now? he thought, and sucked greedily at the cheese, which above all the other edibles attracted him at once and strongly. One after another and with tears of satisfaction in his eyes he quickly devoured the cheese, the vegetables and the sauce; the fresh food, on the other hand, had no charms for him, he could not even stand the smell of it and actually dragged away to some little distance the things he could eat. He had long finished his meal and was only lying lazily on the same spot when his sister turned the key slowly as a sign for him to retreat. That roused him at once, although he was nearly asleep, and he hurried under the sofa again. But it took considerable self-control for him to stay under the sofa, even for the short time his sister was in the room, since the large meal had swollen his body somewhat and he was so cramped he could hardly breathe. Slight attacks of breathlessness afflicted him and his eyes were starting a little out of his head as he watched his unsuspecting sister sweeping together with a broom not only the remains of what he had eaten but even the things he had not touched, as if these were now of no use to anyone, and hastily shoveling it all into a bucket, which she covered with a wooden lid and carried away. Hardly had she turned her back when Gregor came from under the sofa and stretched and puffed himself out.

In this manner Gregor was fed, once in the early morning while his parents and the servant girl were still asleep, and a second time after they had all had their midday dinner, for then his parents took a short nap and the servant girl could be sent out on some errand or other by his sister. Not that they would have wanted him to starve, of course, but perhaps they could not have borne to know more about his feeding than from hearsay, perhaps too his sister wanted to spare them such little anxieties wherever possible, since they had quite enough to bear as it was.

Under what pretext the doctor and the locksmith had been got rid of on that first morning Gregor could not discover, for since what he had said was not understood by the others it never struck any of them, not even his sister, that he could understand what they said, and so whenever his sister came into his room he had to content himself with hearing her utter only a sigh now and then and an occasional appeal to the saints. Later on, when she had got a little used to the situation—of course she could never get completely used to it—she sometimes threw out a remark which was kindly meant or could be so interpreted. "Well, he liked his dinner today," she would say when Gregor had made a good clearance of his food; and when he had not eaten, which gradually happened more and more often, she would say almost sadly: "Everything's been left standing again."

But although Gregor could get no news directly, he overheard a lot from the neighboring rooms, and as soon as voices were audible, he would run to the door of the room concerned and press his whole body against it. In the first few days especially there was no conversation that did not refer to him somehow, even if only indirectly. For two whole days there were family consultations at every mealtime about what should be done; but also between meals the same subject was discussed, for there were always at least two members of the family at home, since no one wanted to be alone in the flat and to leave it quite empty was unthinkable. And on the very first of these days the household cook—it was not quite clear what and how much she knew of the situation—went down on her knees to his mother and begged leave to go, and when she departed, a quarter of an hour later, gave thanks for her dismissal with tears in her eyes as if for the greatest benefit that could have been conferred on her, and without any prompting swore a solemn oath that she would never say a single word to anyone about what had happened.

Now Gregor's sister had to cook too, helping her mother; true, the cooking did not amount to much, for they ate scarcely anything. Gregor was always hearing one of the family vainly urging another to eat and getting no answer but: "Thanks, I've had all I want," or something similar. Perhaps they drank nothing either. Time and again his sister kept asking his father if he wouldn't like some beer and offered kindly to go and fetch it herself, and when he made no answer suggested that she could ask the concierge to fetch it, so that he need feel no sense of obligation, but then a round "No" came from his father and no more was said about it.

In the course of that very first day Gregor's father explained the family's financial position and prospects to both his mother and his sister. Now and then he rose from the table to get some voucher or memorandum out of the small safe he had rescued from the collapse of his business five years earlier. One could hear him opening the complicated lock and rustling papers out and shutting it again. This statement made by his father was the first cheerful information Gregor had heard since his imprisonment. He had been of the opinion that nothing at all was left over from his father's business, at least his father had never said anything to the contrary, and of course he had not asked him directly. At the time Gregor's sole desire was to do his utmost to help the family to forget as soon as possible the catastrophe which had overwhelmed the business and thrown them all into a state of complete despair. And so he had set to work with unusual ardor and almost overnight had become a commercial traveler instead of a little clerk, with of course much greater chances of earning money, and his success was immediately translated into good round coin which he could lay on the table for his amazed and happy family. These had been fine times, and they had never recurred, at least not with the same sense of glory, although later on Gregor had earned so much money that he was able to meet the expenses of the whole household and did so. They had simply got used to it, both the family and Gregor; the money was gratefully accepted and gladly given, but there was no special uprush of warm feeling. With his sister alone had he remained intimate, and it was a secret plan of his that she, who loved music, unlike himself, and could play movingly on the violin, should be sent next year to study at the Conservatorium, despite the great expense that would entail, which must be made up in some other way. During his brief visits home the Conservatorium was often mentioned in the talks he had with his sister, but always merely as a beautiful dream which could never come true, and his parents discouraged even these innocent references to it; yet Gregor had made up his mind firmly about it and meant to announce the fact with due solemnity on Christmas Day.

Such were the thoughts, completely futile in his present condition, that went through his head as he stood clinging upright to the door and listening. Sometimes out of sheer weariness he had to give up listening and let his head fall negligently against the door, but he always had to pull himself together again at once, for even the slight sound his head made was audible next door and brought all conversation to a stop. "What can he be doing now?" his father would say after a while, obviously turning towards the door, and only then would the interrupted conversation gradually be set going again.

Gregor was now informed as amply as he could wish—for his father tended to repeat himself in his explanations, partly because it was a long time since he had handled such matters and partly because his mother could not always grasp things at once—that a certain amount of investments, a very small amount it was true, had survived the wreck of their fortunes and had even increased a little because the dividends had not been touched meanwhile. And besides that, the money Gregor brought home every month—he had kept only a few dollars for himself—had never been quite used up and now amounted to a small capital sum. Behind the door Gregor nodded his head eagerly, rejoiced at this evidence of unexpected thrift and foresight. True, he could really have paid off some more of his father's debts to the chief with his extra money, and so brought much nearer the day on which he could quit his job, but doubtless it was better the way his father had arranged it.

Yet this capital was by no means sufficient to let the family live on the interest of it; for one year, perhaps, or at the most two, they could live on the principal, that was all. It was simply a sum that ought not to be touched and should be kept for a rainy day; money for living expenses would have to be earned. Now his father was still hale enough but an old man, and he had done no work for the past five years and could not be expected to do much; during these five years, the first years of leisure in his laborious though unsuccessful life, he had grown rather fat and become sluggish. And Gregor's old mother, how was she to earn a living with her asthma, which troubled her even when she walked through the flat and kept her lying on a sofa every other day panting for breath beside an open window? And was his sister to earn her bread, she who was still a child of seventeen and whose life hitherto had been so pleasant, consisting as it did in dressing herself nicely, sleeping long, helping in the housekeeping, going out to a few modest entertainments and above all playing the violin? At first whenever the need for earning money was mentioned Gregor let go his hold on the door and threw himself down on the cool leather sofa beside it, he felt so hot with shame and grief.

Often he just lay there the long nights through without sleeping at all, scrabbling for hours on the leather. Or he nerved himself to the great effort of pushing an armchair to the window, then crawled up over the window sill and, braced against the chair, leaned against the windowpanes, obviously in some recollection of the sense of freedom that looking out of a window always used to give him. For in reality day by day things that were even a little way off were growing dimmer to his sight; the hospital across the street, which he used to execrate for being all too often before his eyes, was now quite beyond his range of vision, and if he had not known that he lived in Charlotte Street, a quiet street but still a city street, he might have believed that his window gave on a desert waste where gray sky and gray land blended indistinguishably into each other. His quick-witted sister only needed to observe twice that the armchair stood by the window; after that whenever she had tidied the room she always pushed the chair back to the same place at the window and even left the inner casements open.

If he could have spoken to her and thanked her for all she had to do for him, he could have borne her ministrations better; as it was, they oppressed him. She certainly tried to make as light as possible of whatever was disagreeable in her task, and as time went on she succeeded, of course, more and more, but time brought more enlightenment to Gregor too. The very way she came in distressed him. Hardly was she in the room when she rushed to the window, without even taking time to shut the door, careful as she was usually to shield the sight of Gregor's room from the others, and as if she were almost suffocating tore the casements open with hasty fingers, standing then in the open draught for a while even in the bitterest cold and drawing deep breaths. This noisy scurry of hers upset Gregor twice a day; he would crouch trembling under the sofa all the time, knowing quite well that she would certainly have spared him such a disturbance had she found it at all possible to stay in his presence without opening a window.

On one occasion, about a month after Gregor's metamorphosis, when there was surely no reason for her to be still startled at his appearance, she came a little earlier than usual and found him gazing out of the window, quite motionless, and thus well placed to look like a bogey. Gregor would not have been surprised had she not come in at all, for she could not immediately open the window while he was there, but not only did she retreat, she jumped back as if in alarm and banged the door shut; a stranger might well have thought that he had been lying in wait for her there meaning to bite her. Of course he hid himself under the sofa at once, but he had to wait until midday before she came again, and she seemed more ill at ease than usual. This made him realize how repulsive the sight of him still was to her, and that it was bound to go on being repulsive, and what an effort it must cost her not to run away even from the sight of the small portion of his body that stuck out from under the sofa. In order to spare her that, therefore, one day he carried a sheet on his back to the sofa—it cost him four hours' labor—and arranged it there in such a way as to hide him completely, so that even if she were to bend down she could not see him. Had she considered the sheet unnecessary, she would certainly have stripped it off the sofa again, for it was clear enough that this curtaining and confining of himself was not likely to conduce Gregor's comfort, but she left it where it was, and Gregor even fancied that he caught a thankful glance from her eye when he lifted the sheet carefully a very little with his head to see how she was taking the new arrangement.

For the first fortnight his parents could not bring themselves to the point of entering his room, and he often heard them expressing their appreciation of his sister's activities, whereas formerly they had frequently scolded her for being as they thought a somewhat useless daughter. But now, both of them often waited outside the door, his father and his mother, while his sister tidied his room, and as soon as she came out she had to tell them exactly how things were in the room, what Gregor had eaten, how he had conducted himself this time and whether there was not perhaps some slight improvement in his condition. His mother, moreover, began relatively soon to want to visit him, but his father and sister dissuaded her at first with arguments which Gregor listened to very attentively and altogether approved. Later, however, she had to be held back by main force, and when she cried out: "Do let me in to Gregor, he is my unfortunate son! Can't you understand that I must go to him?" Gregor thought that it might be well to have her come in, not every day, of course, but perhaps once a week; she understood things, after all, much better than his sister, who was only a child despite the efforts she was making and had perhaps taken on so difficult a task merely out of childish thoughtlessness.

Gregor's desire to see his mother was soon fulfilled. During the day-time he did not want to show himself at the window, out of considera-tion for his parents, but he could not crawl very far around the few square yards of floor space he had, nor could he bear lying quietly at rest all during the night, while he was fast losing any interest he had ever taken in food, so that for mere recreation he had formed the habit of crawling crisscross over the walls and ceiling. He especially enjoyed hanging suspended from the ceiling; it was much better than lying on the floor; one could breathe more freely; one's body swung and rocked lightly; and in the almost blissful absorption induced by this suspension it could happen to his own surprise that he let go and fell plump on the floor. Yet he now had his body much better under control than formerly, and even such a big fall did him no harm. His sister at once remarked the new distraction Gregor had found for himself—he left traces behind him of the sticky stuff on his soles wherever he crawled—and she got the idea in her head of giving him as wide a field as possible to crawl in and of removing the pieces of furniture that hindered him, above all the chest of drawers and the writing desk. But that was more than she could manage all by herself; she did not dare ask her father to help her; and as for the servant girl, a young creature of sixteen who had had the courage to stay on after the cook's departure, she could not be asked to help, for she had begged as an especial favor that she might keep the kitchen door locked and open it only on a definite summons; so there was nothing left but to apply to her mother at an hour when her father was out. And the old lady did come, with exclamations of joyful eagerness, which, how-ever, died away at the door of Gregor's room. Gregor's sister, of course, went in first, to see that everything was in order before letting his mother enter. In great haste Gregor pulled the sheet lower and rucked it more in folds so that it really looked as if it had been thrown accidentally over the sofa. And this time he did not peer out from under it; he renounced the pleasure of seeing his mother on this occasion and was only glad that she had come at all. "Come in, he's out of sight," said his sister, obviously leading her mother in by the hand. Gregor could now hear the two women struggling to shift the heavy old chest from its place, and his sis-ter claiming the greater part of the labor for herself, without listening to the admonitions of her mother who feared she might overstrain herself. It took a long time. After at least a quarter of an hour's tugging his mother objected that the chest had better be left where it was, for in the first place it was too heavy and could never be got out before his father came home, and standing in the middle of the room like that it would only hamper Gregor's movements, while in the second place it was not at all certain that removing the furniture would be doing a service to Gre-gor. She was inclined to think to the contrary; the sight of the naked walls made her own heart heavy, and why shouldn't Gregor have the same feeling, considering that he had been used to his furniture for so long and might feel forlorn without it. "And doesn't it look," she concluded in a low voice — in fact she had been almost whispering all the time as if to avoid letting Gregor, whose exact whereabouts she did not know, hear even the tones of her voice, for she was convinced that he could not understand her words — "doesn't it look as if we were showing him, by taking away his furniture, that we have given up hope of his ever getting better and are just leaving him coldly to himself? I think it would be best to keep his room exactly as it has always been, so that when he comes back to us he will find everything unchanged and be able all the more easily to forget what has happened in between."

On hearing these words from his mother Gregor realized that the lack of all direct human speech for the past two months together with the monotony of family life must have confused his mind, otherwise he could not account for the fact that he had quite earnestly looked forward to having his room emptied of furnishing. Did he really want his warm room, so comfortably fitted with old family furniture, to be turned into a naked den in which he would certainly be able to crawl unhampered in all directions but at the price of shedding simultaneously all recollection of his human background? He had indeed been so near the brink of forgetfulness that only the voice of his mother, which he had not heard for so long, had drawn him back from it. Nothing should be taken out of his room; everything must stay as it was; he could not dispense with the good influence of the furniture on his state of mind; and even if the furniture did hamper him in his senseless crawling round and round, that was no drawback but a great advantage.

Unfortunately his sister was of the contrary opinion; she had grown accustomed, and not without reason, to consider herself an expert in Gregor's affairs as against her parents, and so her mother's advice was now enough to make her determined on the removal not only of the chest and the writing desk, which had been her first intention, but of all the furniture except the indispensable sofa. This determination was not, of course, merely the outcome of childish recalcitrance and of the self-confidence she had recently developed so unexpectedly and at such cost; she had in fact perceived that Gregor needed a lot of space to crawl about in, while on the other hand he never used the furniture at all, so far as could be seen. Another factor might have been also the enthusiastic temperament of an adolescent girl, which seeks to indulge itself on every opportunity and which now tempted Grete to exaggerate the horror of her brother's circumstances in order that she might do all the more for him. In a room where Gregor lorded it all alone over empty walls no one save herself was likely ever to set foot.

And so she was not to be moved from her resolve by her mother who seemed moreover to be ill at ease in Gregor's room and therefore unsure of herself, was soon reduced to silence and helped her daughter as best she could to push the chest outside. Now, Gregor could do without the chest, if need be, but the writing desk he must retain. As soon as the two women had got the chest out of his room, groaning as they pushed it, Gregor stuck his head out from under the sofa to see how he might intervene as kindly and cautiously as possible. But as bad luck would have it, his mother was the first to return, leaving Grete clasping the chest in the room next door where she was trying to shift it all by herself, without of course moving it from the spot. His mother however was not accustomed to the sight of him, it might sicken her and so in alarm Gregor backed quickly to the other end of the sofa, yet could not prevent the sheet from swaying a little in front. That was enough to put her on the alert. She paused, stood still for a moment and then went back to Grete.

Although Gregor kept reassuring himself that nothing out of the way was happening, but only a few bits of furniture were being changed round, he soon had to admit that all this trotting to and fro of the two women, their little ejaculations and the scraping of furniture along the floor affected him like a vast disturbance coming from all sides at once, and however much he tucked in his head and legs and cowered to the very floor he was bound to confess that he would not be able to stand it for long. They were clearing his room out; taking away everything he loved; the chest in which he kept his fret saw and other tools was already dragged off; they were now loosening the writing desk which had almost sunk into the floor, the desk at which he had done all his homework when he was at the commercial academy, at the grammar school before that, and, yes, even at the primary school—he had no more time to waste in weighing the good intentions of the two women, whose existence he had by now almost forgotten, for they were so exhausted that they were laboring in silence and nothing could be heard but the heavy scuffling of their feet.

And so he rushed out—the women were just leaning against the writing desk in the next room to give themselves a breather—and four times changed his direction, since he really did not know what to rescue first, then on the wall opposite, which was already otherwise cleared, he was struck by the picture of the lady muffled in so much fur and quickly crawled up to it and pressed himself to the glass, which was a good surface to hold on to and comforted his hot belly. This picture at least, which was entirely hidden beneath him, was going to be removed by nobody. He turned his head towards the door of the living room so as to observe the women when they came back.

They had not allowed themselves much of a rest and were already coming; Grete had twined her arm round her mother and was almost supporting her. "Well, what shall we take now?" said Grete, looking round. Her eyes met Gregor's from the wall. She kept her composure, presumably because of her mother, bent her head down to her mother, to keep her from looking up, and said, although in a fluttering, unpremeditated voice: "Come, hadn't we better go back to the living room for a moment?" Her intentions were clear enough to Gregor, she wanted to bestow her mother in safety and then chase him down from the wall. Well, just let her try it! He clung to his picture and would not give it up. He would rather fly in Grete's face.

But Grete's words had succeeded in disquieting her mother, who took a step to one side, caught sight of the huge brown mass on the flowered wallpaper, and before she was really conscious that what she saw was Gregor screamed in a loud, hoarse voice: "Oh God, oh God!" fell with outspread arms over the sofa as if giving up and did not move. "Gregor!" cried his sister, shaking her fist and glaring at him. This was the first time she had directly addressed him since his metamorphosis. She ran into the next room for some aromatic essence with which to rouse her mother from her fainting fit. Gregor wanted to help too—there was still time to rescue the picture—but he was stuck fast to the glass and had to tear himself loose; he then ran after his sister into the next room as if he could advise her, as he used to do; but then had to stand helplessly behind her; she meanwhile searched among various small bottles and when she turned round started in alarm at the sight of him; one bottle fell on the floor and broke; a splinter of glass cut Gregor's face and some kind of corrosive medicine splashed him; without pausing a moment longer Grete gathered up all the bottles she could carry and ran to her mother with them; she banged the door shut with her foot. Gregor was now cut off from his mother, who was perhaps nearly dying because of him; he dared not open the door for fear of frightening away his sister, who had to stay with her mother; there was nothing he could do but wait; and harassed by self-reproach and worry he began now to crawl to and fro, over everything, walls, furniture and ceiling, and finally in his despair, when the whole room seemed to be reeling round him, fell down on to the middle of the big table.

A little while elapsed, Gregor was still lying there feebly and all around was quiet, perhaps that was a good omen. Then the doorbell rang. The servant girl was of course locked in her kitchen, and Grete would have to open the door. It was his father. "What's been happening?" were his first words; Grete's face must have told him everything. Grete answered in a muffled voice, apparently hiding her head on his breast: "Mother has been fainting, but she's better now. Gregor's broken loose."

"Just what I expected," said his father, "just what I've been telling you, but you women would never listen." It was clear to Gregor that his father had taken the worst interpretation of Grete's all too brief statement and was assuming that Gregor had been guilty of some violent act. Therefore Gregor must now try to propitiate his father, since he had neither time nor means for an explanation. And so he fled to the door of his own room and crouched against it, to let his father see as soon as he came in from the hall that his son had the good intention of getting back into his room immediately and that it was not necessary to drive him there, but that if only the door were opened he would disappear at once.

Yet his father was not in the mood to perceive such fine distinctions. "Ah!" he cried as soon as he appeared, in a tone which sounded at once angry and exultant. Gregor drew his head back from the door and lifted it to look at his father. Truly, this was not the father he had imagined to himself; admittedly he had been too absorbed of late in his new recreation of crawling over the ceiling to take the same interest as before in what was happening elsewhere in the flat, and he ought really to be prepared for some changes. And yet, and yet, could that be his father? The man who used to lie wearily sunk in bed whenever Gregor set out on a business journey; who welcomed him back of an evening lying in a long chair in a dressing gown; who could not really rise to his feet but only lifted his arms in greeting, and on the rare occasions when he did go out with his family, on one or two Sundays a year and on high holidays, walked between Gregor and his mother, who were slow walkers anyhow, even more slowly than they did, muffled in his old greatcoat, shuffling laboriously forward with the help of his crook-handled stick which he set down most cautiously at every step and, whenever he wanted to say anything, nearly always came to a full stop and gathered his escort around him? Now he was standing there in fine shape; dressed in a smart blue uniform with gold buttons, such as bank messengers wear; his strong double chin bulged over the stiff high collar of his jacket; from under his bushy eyebrows his black eyes darted fresh and penetrating glances; his onetime tangled white hair had been combed flat on either side of a shining and carefully exact parting. He pitched his cap, which bore a gold monogram, probably the badge of some bank, in a wide sweep across the whole room on to a sofa and with the tail-ends of his jacket thrown back, his hands in his trouser pockets, advanced with a grim visage towards Gregor. Likely enough he did not himself know what he meant to do; at any rate he lifted his feet uncommonly high, and Gregor was dumbfounded at the enormous size of his shoe soles. But Gregor could not risk standing up to him, aware as he had been from the very first day of his new life that his father believed only the severest measures suitable for dealing with him. And so he ran before his father, stopping when he stopped and scuttling forward again when his father made any kind of move. In this way they circled the room several times without anything decisive happening; indeed the whole operation did not even look like a pursuit because it was carried out so slowly. And so Gregor did not leave the floor, for he feared that his father might take as a piece of peculiar wickedness any excursion of his over the walls or the ceiling. All the same, he could not stay this course much longer, for while his father took one step he had to carry out a whole series of movements. He was already beginning to feel breathless, just as in his former life his lungs had not been very dependable. As he was staggering along, trying to concentrate his energy on running, hardly keeping his eyes open; in his dazed state never even thinking of any other escape than simply going forward; and having almost forgotten that the walls were free to him, which in this room were well provided with finely carved pieces of furniture full of knobs and crevices—suddenly something lightly flung landed close behind him and rolled before him. It was an apple; a second apple followed immediately; Gregor came to a stop in alarm; there was no point in running on, for his father was determined to bombard him. He had filled his pockets with fruit from the dish on the sideboard and was now shying apple after apple, without taking particularly good aim for the moment. The small red apples rolled about the floor as if magnetized and cannoned into each other. An apple thrown without much force grazed Gregor's back and glanced off harmlessly. But another following immediately landed right on his back and sank in; Gregor wanted to drag himself forward, as if this startling, incredible pain could be left behind him: but he felt as if nailed to the spot and flattened himself out in a complete derangement of all his senses. With his last conscious look he saw the door of his room being torn open and his mother rushing out ahead of his screaming sister, in her underbodice, for her daughter had loosened her clothing to let her breathe more freely and recover from her swoon, he saw his mother rushing towards his father, leaving one after another behind her on the floor her loosened petticoats, stumbling over her petticoats straight to his father and embracing him, in complete union with him—but here Gregor's sight began to fail—with her hands clasped round his father's neck as she begged for her son's life.

III

The serious injury done to Gregor, which disabled him for more than a month—the apple went on sticking in his body as a visible reminder, since no one ventured to remove it—seemed to have made even his father recollect that Gregor was a member of the family, despite his present unfortunate and repulsive shape, and ought not to be treated as an enemy, that, on the contrary, family duty required the suppression of disgust and the exercise of patience, nothing but patience.

And although his injury had impaired, probably forever, his power of movement, and for the time being it took him long, long minutes to creep across his room like an old invalid—there was no question now of crawling up the wall—yet in his own opinion he was sufficiently compensated for this worsening of his condition by the fact that towards evening the living-room door, which he used to watch intently for an hour or two beforehand, was always thrown open, so that lying in the darkness of his room, invisible to the family, he could see them all at the lamp-lit table and listen to their talk, by general consent as it were, very different from his earlier eavesdropping.

True, their intercourse lacked the lively character of former times, which he had always called to mind with a certain wistfulness in the small hotel bedrooms where he had been wont to throw himself down, tired out, on damp bedding. They were now mostly very silent. Soon after supper his father would fall asleep in his armchair; his mother and sister would admonish each other to be silent; his mother, bending low over the lamp, stitched at fine sewing for an underwear firm; his sister, who had taken a job as a salesgirl, was learning shorthand and French in the evenings on the chance of bettering herself. Sometimes his father woke up, and as if quite unaware that he had been sleeping said to his mother: "What a lot of sewing you're doing today!" and at once fell asleep again, while the two women exchanged a tired smile.

With a kind of mulishness his father persisted in keeping his uniform on even in the house; his dressing gown hung uselessly on its peg and he slept fully dressed where he sat, as if he were ready for service at any moment and even here only at the beck and call of his superior. As a result, his uniform, which was not brand-new to start with, began to look dirty, despite all the loving care of the mother and sister to keep it clean, and Gregor often spent whole evenings gazing at the many greasy spots on the garment, gleaming with gold buttons always in a high state of polish, in which the old man sat sleeping in extreme discomfort and yet quite peacefully.

As soon as the clock struck ten his mother tried to rouse his father with gentle words and to persuade him after that to get into bed, for sitting there he could not have a proper sleep and that was what he needed most, since he had to go to duty at six. But with the mulishness that had obsessed him since he became a bank messenger he always insisted on staying longer at the table, although he regularly fell asleep again and in the end only with the greatest trouble could be got out of his armchair and into his bed. However insistently Gregor's mother and sister kept urging him with gentle reminders, he would go on slowly shaking his head for a quarter of an hour, keeping his eyes shut, and refuse to get to his feet. The mother plucked at his sleeve, whispering endearments in his ear, the sister left her lessons to come to her mother's help, but Gregor's father was not to be caught. He would only sink down deeper in his chair. Not until the two women hoisted him up by the armpits did he open his eyes and look at them both, one after the other, usually with the remark: "This is a life. This is the peace and quiet of my old age." And leaning on the two of them he would heave himself up, with difficulty, as if he were a great burden to himself, suffer them to lead him as far as the door and then wave them off and go on alone, while the mother abandoned her needlework and the sister her pen in order to run after him and help him farther.

Who could find time, in this overworked and tired-out family, to bother about Gregor more than was absolutely needful? The household was reduced more and more; the servant girl was turned off; a gigantic bony charwoman with white hair flying round her head came in morning and evening to do the rough work; everything else was done by Gregor's mother, as well as great piles of sewing. Even various family ornaments, which his mother and sister used to wear with pride at parties and celebrations, had to be sold, as Gregor discovered of an evening from hearing them all discuss the prices obtained. But what they lamented most was the fact that they could not leave the flat which was much too big for their present circumstances, because they could not think of any way to shift Gregor. Yet Gregor saw well enough that consideration for him was not the main difficulty preventing the removal, for they could have easily shifted him in some suitable box with a few air holes in it; what really kept them from moving into another flat was rather their own complete hopelessness and the belief that they had been singled out for a misfortune such as had never happened to any of their relations or acquaintances. They fulfilled to the uttermost all that the world demands of poor people, the father fetched breakfast for the small clerks in the bank, the mother devoted her energy to making underwear for strangers, the sister trotted to and fro behind the counter at the behest of customers, but more than this they had not the strength to do. And the wound in Gregor's back began to nag at him afresh when his mother and sister, after getting his father into bed, came back again, left their work lying, drew close to each other and sat cheek by cheek; when his mother, pointing towards his room, said: "Shut that door now, Grete," and he was left again in darkness, while next door the women mingled their tears or perhaps sat dry-eyed staring at the table.

Gregor hardly slept at all by night or by day. He was often haunted by the idea that next time the door opened he would take the family's affairs in hand again just as he used to do; once more, after this long interval, there appeared in his thoughts the figures of the chief and the chief clerk, the commercial travelers and the apprentices, the porter who was so dull-witted, two or three friends in other firms, a chambermaid in one of the rural hotels, a sweet and fleeting memory, a cashier in a milliner's shop, whom he had wooed earnestly but too slowly—they all appeared, together with strangers or people he had quite forgotten, but instead of helping him and his family they were one and all unapproachable and he was glad when they vanished. At other times he would not be in the mood to bother about his family, he was only filled with rage at the way they were neglecting him, and although he had no clear idea of what he might care to eat he would make plans for getting into the larder to take the food that was after all his due, even if he were not hungry. His sister no longer took thought to bring him what might especially please him, but in the morning and at noon before she went to business hurriedly pushed into his room with her foot any food that was available, and in the evening cleared it out again with one sweep of the broom, heedless of whether it had been merely tasted, or—as most frequently happened—left untouched. The cleaning of his room, which she now did always in the evenings, could not have been more hastily done. Streaks of dirt stretched along the walls, here and there lay balls of dust and filth. At first Gregor used to station himself in some particularly filthy corner when his sister arrived, in order to reproach her with it, so to speak. But he could have sat there for weeks without getting her to make any improvements; she could see the dirt as well as he did, but she had simply made up her mind to leave it alone. And yet, with a touchiness that was new to her, which seemed anyhow to have infected the whole family, she jealously guarded her claim to be the sole caretaker of Gregor's room. His mother once subjected his room to a thorough cleaning, which was achieved only by means of several buckets of water—all this dampness of course upset Gregor too and he lay widespread, sulky and motionless on the sofa—but she was well punished for it. Hardly had his sister noticed the changed aspect of his room than she rushed in high dudgeon into the living room and, despite the imploringly raised hands of her mother, burst into a storm of weeping, while her parents—her father had of course been startled out of his chair—looked on at first in helpless amazement; then they too began to go into action; the father reproached the mother on his right for not having left the cleaning of Gregor's room to his sister; shrieked at the sister on his left that never again was she to be allowed to clean Gregor's room; while the mother tried to pull the father into his bedroom, since he was beyond himself with agitation; the sister, shaken with sobs, then beat upon the table with her small fists; and Gregor hissed loudly with rage because not one of them thought of shutting the door to spare him such a spectacle and so much noise.

Still, even if the sister, exhausted by her daily work, had grown tired of looking after Gregor as she did formerly, there was no need for his mother's intervention or for Gregor's being neglected at all. The char-woman was there. This old widow, whose strong bony frame had en-abled her to survive the worst a long life could offer, by no means recoiled from Gregor. Without being in the least curious she had once by chance opened the door of his room and at the sight of Gregor, who, taken by surprise, began to rush to and fro although no one was chas-ing him, merely stood there with her arms folded. From that time she never failed to open his door a little for a moment, morning and eve-ning, to have a look at him. At first she even used to call him to her, with words which apparently she took to be friendly, such as: "Come along, then, you old dung beetle!" or "Look at the old dung beetle, then!" To such allocutions Gregor made no answer, but stayed motion-less where he was, as if the door had never been opened. Instead of being allowed to disturb him so senselessly whenever the whim took her, she should rather have been ordered to clean out his room daily, that charwoman! Once, early in the morning—heavy rain was lashing on the windowpanes, perhaps a sign that spring was on the way—Gre-gor was so exasperated when she began addressing him again that he ran at her, as if to attack her, although slowly and feebly enough. But the charwoman instead of showing fright merely lifted high a chair that happened to be beside the door, and as she stood there with her mouth wide open it was clear that she meant to shut it only when she brought the chair down on Gregor's back. "So you're not coming any nearer?" she asked, as Gregor turned away again, and quietly put the chair back into the corner.

Gregor was now eating hardly anything. Only when he happened to pass the food laid out for him did he take a bit of something in his mouth as a pastime, kept it there for an hour at a time and usually spat it out again. At first he thought it was chagrin over the state of his room that prevented him from eating, yet he soon got used to the various changes in his room. It had become a habit in the family to push into his room things there was no room for elsewhere, and there were plenty of these now, since one of the rooms had been let to three lodgers. These serious gentlemen—all three of them with full beards, as Gregor once observed through a crack in the door—had a passion for order, not only in their own room but, since they were now members of the household, in all its arrangements, especially in the kitchen. Superfluous, not to say dirty, objects they could not bear. Besides, they had brought with them most of the furnishings they needed. For this reason many things could be dispensed with that it was no use trying to sell but that should not be thrown away either. All of them found their way into Gregor's room. The ash can likewise and the kitchen garbage can. Anything that was not needed for the moment was simply flung into Gregor's room by the charwoman, who did everything in a hurry; fortunately Gregor usually saw only the object, whatever it was, and the hand that held it. Perhaps she intended to take the things away again as time and opportunity offered, or to collect them until she could throw them all out in a heap, but in fact they just lay wherever she happened to throw them, except when Gregor pushed his way through the junk heap and shifted it somewhat, at first out of necessity, because he had not room enough to crawl, but later with increasing enjoyment, although after such excursions, being sad and weary to death, he would lie motionless for hours. And since the lodgers often ate their supper at home in the common living room, the living room door stayed shut many an evening, yet Gregor reconciled himself quite easily to the shutting of the door, for often enough on evenings when it was opened he had disregarded it entirely and lain in the darkest corner of his room, quite unnoticed by the family. But on one occasion the charwoman left the door open a little and it stayed ajar even when the lodgers came in for supper and the lamp was lit. They set themselves at the top end of the table where formerly Gregor and his father and mother had eaten their meals, unfolded their napkins and took knife and fork in hand. At once his mother appeared in the other doorway with a dish of meat and close behind her his sister with a dish of potatoes piled high. The food steamed with a thick vapor. The lodgers bent over the food set before them as if to scrutinize it before eating, in fact the man in the middle, who seemed to pass for an authority with the other two, cut a piece of meat as it lay on the dish, obviously to discover if it were tender or should be sent back to the kitchen. He showed satisfaction, and Gregor's mother and sister, who had been watching anxiously, breathed freely and began to smile.

The family itself took its meals in the kitchen. Nonetheless, Gregor's father came into the living room before going in to the kitchen and with one prolonged bow, cap in hand, made a round of the table. The lodgers all stood up and murmured something in their beards. When they were alone again they ate their food in almost complete silence. It seemed remarkable to Gregor that among the various noises coming from the table he could always distinguish the sound of their masticating teeth, as if this were a sign to Gregor that one needed teeth in order to eat, and that with toothless jaws even of the finest make one could do nothing. "I'm hungry enough," said Gregor sadly to himself, "but not for that kind of food. How these lodgers are stuffing themselves, and here am I dying of starvation!"

On that very evening—during the whole of his time there Gregor could not remember ever having heard the violin—the sound of violin-playing came from the kitchen. The lodgers had already finished their supper, the one in the middle had brought out a newspaper and given the other two a page apiece, and now they were leaning back at ease reading and smoking. When the violin began to play they pricked up their ears, got to their feet, and went on tiptoe to the hall door where they stood huddled together. Their movements must have been heard in the kitchen, for Gregor's father called out: "Is the violin-playing disturbing you, gentlemen? It can be stopped at once." "On the contrary," said the middle lodger, "could not Fräulein Samsa come and play in this room, beside us, where it is much more convenient and comfortable?" "Oh certainly," cried Gregor's father, as if he were the violin-player. The lodgers came back into the living room and waited. Presently Gregor's father arrived with the music stand, his mother carrying the music and his sister with the violin. His sister quietly made everything ready to start playing; his parents, who had never let rooms before and so had an exaggerated idea of the courtesy due to lodgers, did not venture to sit down on their own chairs; his father leaned against the door, the right hand thrust between two buttons of his livery coat, which was formally buttoned up; but his mother was offered a chair by one of the lodgers and, since she left the chair just where he had happened to put it, sat down in a corner to one side.

Gregor's sister began to play; the father and mother, from either side, intently watched the movements of her hands. Gregor, attracted by the playing, ventured to move forward a little until his head was actually inside the living room. He felt hardly any surprise at his growing lack of consideration for the others; there had been a time when he prided himself on being considerate. And yet just on this occasion he had more reason than ever to hide himself, since owing to the amount of dust which lay thick in his room and rose into the air at the slightest movement, he too was covered with dust; fluff and hair and remnants of food trailed with him, caught on his back and along his sides; his indifference to everything was much too great for him to turn on his back and scrape himself clean on the carpet, as once he had done several times a day. And in spite of his condition, no shame deterred him from advancing a little over the spotless floor of the living room.

To be sure, no one was aware of him. The family was entirely absorbed in the violin-playing; the lodgers, however, who first of all had stationed themselves, hands in pockets, much too close behind the music stand so that they could all have read the music, which must have bothered his sister, had soon retreated to the window, half-whispering with downbent heads, and stayed there while his father turned an anxious eye on them. Indeed, they were making it more than obvious that they had been disappointed in their expectation of hearing good or enjoyable violin-playing, that they had had more than enough of the performance and only out of courtesy suffered a continued disturbance of their peace. From the way they all kept blowing the smoke of their cigars high in the air through nose and mouth one could divine their irritation. And yet Gregor's sister was playing so beautifully. Her face leaned sideways, intently and sadly her eyes followed the notes of music. Gregor crawled a little farther forward and lowered his head to the ground so that it might be possible for his eyes to meet hers. Was he an animal, that music had such an effect upon him? He felt as if the way were opening before him to the unknown nourishment he craved. He was determined to push forward till he reached his sister, to pull at her skirt and so let her know that she was to come into his room with her violin, for no one here appreciated her playing as he would appreciate it. He would never let her out of his room, at least, not so long as he lived; his frightful appearance would become, for the first time, useful to him; he would watch all the doors of his room at once and spit at intruders; but his sister should need no constraint, she should stay with him of her own free will; she should sit beside him on the sofa, bend down her ear to him and hear him confide that he had had the firm intention of sending her to the Conservatorium, and that, but for his mishap, last Christmas—surely Christmas was long past?—he would have announced it to everybody without allowing a single objection. After this confession his sister would be so touched that she would burst into tears, and Gregor would then raise himself to her shoulder and kiss her on the neck, which, now that she went to business, she kept free of any ribbon or collar.

"Mr. Samsa!" cried the middle lodger, to Gregor's father, and pointed, without wasting any more words, at Gregor, now working himself slowly forwards. The violin fell silent, the middle lodger first smiled to his friends with a shake of the head and then looked at Gregor again. Instead of driving Gregor out, his father seemed to think it more needful to begin by soothing down the lodgers, although they were not at all agitated and apparently found Gregor more entertaining than the violin-playing. He hurried toward them and, spreading out his arms, tried to urge them back into their own room and at the same time to block their view of Gregor. They now began to be really a little angry, one could not tell whether because of the old man's behavior or because it had just dawned on them that all unwittingly they had such a neighbor as Gregor next door. They demanded explanations of his father, they waved their arms like him, tugged uneasily at their beards, and only with reluctance backed towards their room. Meanwhile Gregor's sister, who stood there as if lost when her playing was so abruptly broken off, came to life again, pulled herself together all at once after standing for a while holding violin and bow in nervelessly hanging hands and staring at her music, pushed her violin into the lap of her mother, who was still sitting in her chair fighting asthmatically for breath, and ran into the lodgers' room to which they were now being shepherded by her father rather more quickly than before. One could see the pillows and blankets on the beds flying under her accustomed fingers and being laid in order. Before the lodgers had actually reached their room she had finished making the beds and slipped out.

The old man seemed once more to be so possessed by his mulish self-assertiveness that he was forgetting all the respect he should show to his lodgers. He kept driving them on and driving them on until in the very door of the bedroom the middle lodger stamped his foot loudly on the floor and so brought him to a halt. "I beg to announce," said the lodger, lifting one hand and looking also at Gregor's mother and sister, "that because of the disgusting conditions prevailing in this household and family"—here he spat on the floor with emphatic brevity—"I give you notice on the spot. Naturally I won't pay you a penny for the days I have lived here, on the contrary I shall consider bringing an action for damages against you, based on claims—believe me—that will be easily susceptible of proof." He ceased and stared straight in front of him, as if he expected something. In fact his two friends at once rushed into the breach with these words: "And we too give notice on the spot." On that he seized the door-handle and shut the door with a slam.

Gregor's father, groping with his hands, staggered forward and fell into his chair; it looked as if he were stretching himself there for his ordinary evening nap, but the marked jerkings of his head, which was as if uncontrollable, showed that he was far from asleep. Gregor had simply stayed quietly all the time on the spot where the lodgers had espied him. Disappointment at the failure of his plan, perhaps also the weakness arising from extreme hunger, made it impossible for him to move. He feared, with a fair degree of certainty, that at any moment the general tension would discharge itself in a combined attack upon him, and he lay waiting. He did not react even to the noise made by the violin as it fell off his mother's lap from under her trembling fingers and gave out a resonant note.

"My dear parents," said his sister, slapping her hand on the table by way of introduction, "things can't go on like this. Perhaps you don't realize that, but I do. I won't utter my brother's name in the presence of this creature, and so all I say is: we must try to get rid of it. We've tried to look after it and to put up with it as far as is humanly possible, and I don't think anyone could reproach us in the slightest."

"She is more than right," said Gregor's father to himself. His mother, who was still choking for lack of breath, began to cough hollowly into her hand with a wild look in her eyes.

His sister rushed over to her and held her forehead. His father's thoughts seemed to have lost their vagueness at Grete's words, he sat more upright, fingering his service cap that lay among the plates still lying on the table from the lodgers' supper, and from time to time looked at the still form of Gregor.

"We must try to get rid of it," his sister now said explicitly to her father, since her mother was coughing too much to hear a word, "it will be the death of both of you, I can see that coming. When one has to work as hard as we do, all of us, one can't stand this continual torment at home on top of it. At least I can't stand it any longer." And she burst into such a passion of sobbing that her tears dropped on her mother's face, where she wiped them off mechanically.

"My dear," said the old man sympathetically, and with evident understanding, "but what can we do?"

Gregor's sister merely shrugged her shoulders to indicate the feeling of helplessness that had now overmastered her during her weeping fit, in contrast to her former confidence.

"If he could understand us," said her father, half questioningly; Grete, still sobbing, vehemently waved a hand to show how unthinkable that was.

"If he could understand us," repeated the old man, shutting his eyes to consider his daughter's conviction that understanding was impossible, "then perhaps we might come to some agreement with him. But as it is—"

"He must go," cried Gregor's sister. "That's the only solution, Father. You must just try to get rid of the idea that this is Gregor. The fact that we've believed it for so long is the root of all our trouble. But how can it be Gregor? If this were Gregor, he would have realized long ago that human beings can't live with such a creature, and he'd have gone away on his own accord. Then we wouldn't have any brother, but we'd be able to go on living and keep his memory in honor. As it is, this creature persecutes us, drives away our lodgers, obviously wants the whole apartment to himself and would have us all sleep in the gutter. Just look, Father," she shrieked all at once, "he's at it again!" And in an access of panic that was quite incomprehensible to Gregor she even quitted her mother, literally thrusting the chair from her as if she would rather sacrifice her mother than stay so near to Gregor, and rushed behind her father, who also rose up, being simply upset by her agitation, and half-spread his arms out as if to protect her.

Yet Gregor had not the slightest intention of frightening anyone, far less his sister. He had only begun to turn round in order to crawl back to his room, but it was certainly a startling operation to watch, since because of his disabled condition he could not execute the difficult turning movements except by lifting his head and then bracing it against the floor over and over again. He paused and looked round. His good intentions seemed to have been recognized; the alarm had only been momentary. Now they were all watching him in melancholy silence. His mother lay in her chair, her legs stiffly outstretched and pressed together, her eyes almost closing for sheer weariness; his father and his sister were sitting beside each other, his sister's arm around the old man's neck.

Perhaps I can go on turning round now, thought Gregor, and began his labors again. He could not stop himself from panting with the effort, and had to pause now and then to take breath. Nor did anyone harass him, he was left entirely to himself. When he had completed the turn-round he began at once to crawl straight back. He was amazed at the distance separating him from his room and could not understand how in his weak state he had managed to accomplish the same journey so recently, almost without remarking it. Intent on crawling as fast as possible, he barely noticed that not a single word, not an ejaculation from his family, interfered with his progress. Only when he was already in the doorway did he turn his head round, not completely, for his neck muscles were getting stiff, but enough to see that nothing had changed behind him except that his sister had risen to her feet. His last glance fell on his mother, who was not quite overcome by sleep.

Hardly was he well inside his room when the door was hastily pushed shut, bolted, and locked. The sudden noise in his rear startled him so much that his little legs gave beneath him. It was his sister who had shown such haste. She had been standing ready waiting and had made a light spring forward, Gregor had not even heard her coming, and she cried "At last!" to her parents as she turned the key in the lock.

"And what now?" said Gregor to himself, looking round in the darkness. Soon he made the discovery that he was now unable to stir a limb. This did not surprise him, rather it seemed unnatural that he should ever actually have been able to move on these feeble little legs. Otherwise he felt relatively comfortable. True, his whole body was aching, but it seemed that the pain was gradually growing less and would finally pass away. The rotting apple in his back and the inflamed area around it, all covered with soft dust, already hardly troubled him. He thought of his family with tenderness and love. The decision that he must disappear was one that he held to even more strongly than his sister, if that were possible. In this state of vacant and peaceful meditation he remained until the tower clock struck three in the morning. The first broadening of light in the world outside the window entered his consciousness once more. Then his head sank to the floor of its own accord and from his nostrils came the last faint flicker of his breath.

When the charwoman arrived early in the morning—what between her strength and her impatience she slammed all the doors so loudly, never mind how often she had been begged not to do so, that no one in the whole apartment could enjoy any quiet sleep after her arrival — she noticed nothing unusual as she took her customary peep into Gregor's room. She thought he was lying motionless on purpose, pretending to be in the sulks; she credited him with every kind of intelligence. Since she happened to have the long-handled broom in her hand she tried to tickle him up with it from the doorway. When that too produced no reaction she felt provoked and poked at him a little harder, and only when she had pushed him along the floor without meeting any resistance was her attention aroused. It did not take her long to establish the truth of the matter, and her eyes widened, she let out a whistle, yet did not waste much time over it but tore open the door of the Samsas' bedroom and yelled into the darkness at the top of her voice: "Just look at this, it's dead; it's lying here dead and done for!"

Mr. and Mrs. Samsa started up in their double bed and before they realized the nature of the charwoman's announcement had some difficulty in overcoming the shock of it. But then they got out of bed quickly, one on either side, Mr. Samsa throwing a blanket over his shoulders, Mrs. Samsa in nothing but her nightgown; in this array they entered Gregor's room. Meanwhile the door of the living room opened, too, where Grete had been sleeping since the advent of the lodgers; she was completely dressed as if she had not been to bed, which seemed to be confirmed also by the paleness of her face. "Dead?" said Mrs. Samsa, looking questioningly at the charwoman, although she could have investigated for herself, and the fact was obvious enough without investigation. "I should say so," said the charwoman, proving her words by pushing Gregor's corpse a long way to one side with her broomstick. Mrs. Samsa made a movement as if to stop her, but checked it. "Well," said Mr. Samsa, "now thanks be to God." He crossed himself, and the three women followed his example. Grete, whose eyes never left the corpse, said: "Just see how thin he was. It's such a long time since he's eaten anything. The food came out again just as it went in." Indeed, Gregor's body was completely flat and dry, as could only now be seen when it was no longer supported by the legs and nothing prevented one from looking closely at it.

"Come in beside us, Grete, for a little while," said Mrs. Samsa with a tremulous smile, and Grete, not without looking back at the corpse, followed her parents into their bedroom. The charwoman shut the door and opened the window wide. Although it was so early in the morning a certain softness was perceptible in the fresh air. After all, it was already the end of March.

The three lodgers emerged from their room and were surprised to see no breakfast; they had been forgotten. "Where's our breakfast?" said the middle lodger peevishly to the charwoman. But she put her finger to her lips and hastily, without a word, indicated by gestures that they should go into Gregor's room. They did so and stood, their hands in the pockets of their somewhat shabby coats, around Gregor's corpse in the room where it was now fully light.

At that the door of the Samsas' bedroom opened and Mr. Samsa appeared in his uniform, his wife on one arm, his daughter on the other. They all looked a little as if they had been crying; from time to time Grete hid her face on her father's arm.

"Leave my house at once!" said Mr. Samsa, and pointed to the door without disengaging himself from the women. "What do you mean by that?" said the middle lodger, taken somewhat aback, with a feeble smile. The two others put their hands behind them and kept rubbing them together, as if in gleeful expectation of a fine set-to in which they were bound to come off the winners. "I mean just what I say," answered Mr. Samsa, and advanced in a straight line with his two companions towards the lodger. He stood his ground at first quietly, looking at the floor as if his thoughts were taking a new pattern in his head. "Then let us go, by all means," he said, and looked up at Mr. Samsa as if in a sudden access of humility he were expecting some renewed sanction for this decision. Mr. Samsa merely nodded briefly once or twice with meaning eyes. Upon that the lodger really did go with long strides into the hall, his two friends had been listening and had quite stopped rubbing their hands for some moments and now went scuttling after him as if afraid that Mr. Samsa might get into the hall before them and cut them off from their leader. In the hall they all three took their hats from the rack, their sticks from the umbrella stand, bowed in silence and quitted the apartment. With a suspiciousness which proved quite unfounded Mr. Samsa and the two women followed them out to the landing; leaning over the banister they watched the three figures slowly but surely going down the long stairs, vanishing from sight at a certain turn of the staircase on every floor and coming into view again after a moment or so; the more they dwindled, the more the Samsa family's interest in them dwindled, and when a butcher's boy met them and passed them on the stairs coming up proudly with a tray on his head, Mr. Samsa and the two women soon left the landing and as if a burden had been lifted from them went back into their apartment.

They decided to spend this day in resting and going for a stroll; they had not only deserved such a respite from work but absolutely needed it. And so they sat down at the table and wrote three notes of excuse, Mr. Samsa to his board of management, Mrs. Samsa to her employer and Grete to the head of her firm. While they were writing, the charwoman came in to say that she was going now, since her morning's work was finished. At first they only nodded without looking up, but as she kept hovering there they eyed her irritably. "Well?" said Mr. Samsa. The charwoman stood grinning in the doorway as if she had good news to impart to the family but meant not to say a word unless properly questioned. The small ostrich feather standing upright on her hat, which had annoyed Mr. Samsa ever since she was engaged, was waving gaily in all directions. "Well, what is it then?" asked Mrs. Samsa, who obtained more respect from the charwoman than the others. "Oh," said the charwoman, giggling so amiably that she could not at once continue, "just this, you don't need to bother about how to get rid of the thing next door. It's been seen to already." Mrs. Samsa and Grete bent over their letters again, as if preoccupied; Mr. Samsa, who perceived that she was eager to begin describing it all in detail, stopped her with a decisive hand. But since she was not allowed to tell her story, she remembered the great hurry she was in, being obviously deeply huffed: "Bye, everybody," she said, whirling off violently, and departed with a frightful slamming of doors.

"She'll be given notice tonight," said Mr. Samsa, but neither from his wife nor his daughter did he get any answer, for the charwoman seemed to have shattered again the composure they had barely achieved. They rose, went to the window and stayed there, clasping each other tight. Mr. Samsa turned in his chair to look at them and quietly observed them for a little. Then he called out: "Come along, now, do. Let bygones be bygones. And you might have some consideration for me." The two of them complied at once, hastened to him, caressed him and quickly finished their letters.

Then they all three left the apartment together, which was more than they had done for months, and went by tram into the open country outside the town. The tram, in which they were the only passengers, was filled with warm sunshine. Leaning comfortably back in their seats they canvassed their prospects for the future, and it appeared on closer inspection that these were not at all bad, for the jobs they had got, which so far they had never really discussed with each other, were all three admirable and likely to lead to better things later on. The greatest immediate improvement in their condition would of course arise from moving to another house; they wanted to take a smaller and cheaper but also better situated and more easily run apartment than the one they had, which Gregor had selected. While they were thus conversing, it struck both Mr. and Mrs. Samsa, almost at the same moment, as they became aware of their daughter's increasing vivacity, that in spite of all the sorrow of recent times, which had made her cheeks pale, she had bloomed into a pretty girl with a good figure. They grew quieter and half unconsciously exchanged glances of complete agreement, having come to the conclusion that it would soon be time to find a good husband for her. And it was like a confirmation of their new dreams and excellent intentions that at the end of their journey their daughter sprang to her feet first and stretched her young body.

[1915]

D. H. LAWRENCE   [1885–1930]

The Rocking-Horse Winner

There was a woman who was beautiful, who started with all the advantages, yet she had no luck. She married for love, and the love turned to dust. She had bonny children, yet she felt they had been thrust upon her, and she could not love them. They looked at her coldly, as if they were finding fault with her. And hurriedly she felt she must cover up some fault in herself. Yet what it was that she must cover up she never knew. Nevertheless, when her children were present, she always felt the center of her heart go hard. This troubled her, and in her manner she was all the more gentle and anxious for her children, as if she loved them very much. Only she herself knew that at the center of her heart was a hard little place that could not feel love, no, not for anybody. Everybody else said of her: "She is such a good mother. She adores her children." Only she herself, and her children themselves, knew it was not so. They read it in each other's eyes.

There were a boy and two little girls. They lived in a pleasant house, with a garden, and they had discreet servants, and felt themselves superior to anyone in the neighborhood.

Although they lived in style, they felt always an anxiety in the house. There was never enough money. The mother had a small income, and the father had a small income, but not nearly enough for the social position which they had to keep up. The father went into town to some office. But though he had good prospects, these prospects never materialized. There was always the grinding sense of the shortage of money, though the style was always kept up.

At last the mother said: "I will see if *I* can't make something." But she did not know where to begin. She racked her brains, and tried this thing and the other, but could not find anything successful. The failure made deep lines come into her face. Her children were growing up, they would have to go to school. There must be more money, there must be more money. The father, who was always very handsome and expensive in his tastes, seemed as if he never *would* be able to do anything worth doing. And the mother, who had a great belief in herself, did not succeed any better, and her tastes were just as expensive.

And so the house came to be haunted by the unspoken phrase: *There must be more money! There must be more money!* The children could hear it all the time though nobody said it aloud. They heard it at Christmas, when the expensive and splendid toys filled the nursery. Behind the shining modern rocking horse, behind the smart doll's house, a voice would start whispering: "There *must* be more money! There *must* be more money!" And the children would stop playing, to listen for a moment. They would look into each other's eyes, to see if they had all heard. And each one saw in the eyes of the other two that they too had heard. "There *must* be more money! There *must* be more money!"

It came whispering from the springs of the still-swaying rocking horse, and even the horse, bending his wooden, champing head, heard it. The big doll, sitting so pink and smirking in her new pram, could hear it quite plainly, and seemed to be smirking all the more self-consciously because of it. The foolish puppy, too, that took the place of the teddy bear, he was looking so extraordinarily foolish for no other reason but that he heard the secret whisper all over the house: "There *must* be more money!"

Yet nobody ever said it aloud. The whisper was everywhere, and therefore no one spoke it. Just as no one ever says: "We are breathing!" in spite of the fact that breath is coming and going all the time.

"Mother," said the boy Paul one day, "why don't we keep a car of our own? Why do we always use Uncle's, or else a taxi?"

"Because we're the poor members of the family," said the mother.

"But why *are* we, Mother?"

"Well—I suppose," she said slowly and bitterly, "it's because your father has no luck."

The boy was silent for some time.

"Is luck money, Mother?" he asked rather timidly.

"No, Paul. Not quite. It's what causes you to have money."

"Oh!" said Paul vaguely. "I thought when Uncle Oscar said *filthy lucker*, it meant money."

"*Filthy lucre* does mean money," said the mother. "But it's lucre, not luck."

"Oh!" said the boy. "Then what *is* luck, Mother?"

"It's what causes you to have money. If you're lucky you have money. That's why it's better to be born lucky than rich. If you're rich, you may lose your money. But if you're lucky, you will always get more money."

"Oh! Will you? And is Father not lucky?"

"Very unlucky, I should say," she said bitterly.

The boy watched her with unsure eyes.

"Why?" he asked.

"I don't know. Nobody ever knows why one person is lucky and another unlucky."

"Don't they? Nobody at all? Does *nobody* know?"

"Perhaps God. But He never tells."

"He ought to, then. And aren't you lucky either, Mother?"

"I can't be, if I married an unlucky husband."

"But by yourself, aren't you?"

"I used to think I was, before I married. Now I think I am very unlucky indeed."

"Why?"

"Well—never mind! Perhaps I'm not really," she said.

The child looked at her, to see if she meant it. But he saw, by the lines of her mouth, that she was only trying to hide something from him.

"Well, anyhow," he said stoutly, "I'm a lucky person."

"Why?" said his mother, with a sudden laugh.

He stared at her. He didn't even know why he had said it.

"God told me," he asserted, brazening it out.

"I hope He did, dear!" she said, again with a laugh, but rather bitter.

"He did, Mother!"

"Excellent!" said the mother.

The boy saw she did not believe him; or, rather, that she paid no attention to his assertion. This angered him somewhat, and made him want to compel her attention.

He went off by himself, vaguely, in a childish way, seeking for the clue to "luck." Absorbed, taking no heed of other people, he went about with a sort of stealth, seeking inwardly for luck. He wanted luck, he wanted it, he wanted it. When the two girls were playing dolls in the nursery, he would sit on his big rocking horse, charging madly into space, with a frenzy that made the little girls peer at him uneasily. Wildly the horse careered, the waving dark hair of the boy tossed, his eyes had a strange glare in them. The little girls dared not speak to him.

When he had ridden to the end of his mad little journey, he climbed down and stood in front of his rocking horse, staring fixedly into its lowered face. Its red mouth was slightly open, its big eye was wide and glassy-bright.

Now! he could silently command the snorting steed. Now, take me to where there is luck! Now take me!

And he would slash the horse on the neck with the little whip he had asked Uncle Oscar for. He *knew* the horse could take him to where there was luck, if only he forced it. So he would mount again, and start on his furious ride, hoping at last to get there. He knew he could get there.

"You'll break your horse, Paul!" said the nurse.

"He's always riding like that! I wish he'd leave off!" said his elder sister Joan.

But he only glared down on them in silence. Nurse gave him up. She could make nothing of him. Anyhow he was growing beyond her.

One day his mother and his uncle Oscar came in when he was on one of his furious rides. He did not speak to them.

"Hallo, you young jockey! Riding a winner?" said his uncle.

"Aren't you growing too big for a rocking horse? You're not a very little boy any longer, you know," said his mother.

But Paul only gave a blue glare from his big, rather close-set eyes. He would speak to nobody when he was in full tilt. His mother watched him with an anxious expression on her face.

At last he suddenly stopped forcing his horse into the mechanical gallop, and slid down.

"Well, I got there!" he announced fiercely, his blue eyes still flaring, and his sturdy long legs straddling apart.

"Where did you get to?" asked his mother.

"Where I wanted to go," he flared back at her.

"That's right, son!" said Uncle Oscar. "Don't you stop till you get there. What's the horse's name?"

"He doesn't have a name," said the boy.

"Gets on without all right?" asked the uncle.

"Well, he has different names. He was called Sansovino last week."

"Sansovino, eh? Won the Ascot. How did you know his name?"

"He always talks about horse races with Bassett," said Joan.

The uncle was delighted to find that his small nephew was posted with all the racing news. Bassett, the young gardener, who had been wounded in the left foot in the war and had got his present job through Oscar Cresswell, whose batman he had been, was a perfect blade of the "turf." He lived in the racing events, and the small boy lived with him.

Oscar Cresswell got it all from Bassett.

"Master Paul comes and asks me, so I can't do more than tell him, sir," said Bassett, his face terribly serious, as if he were speaking of religious matters.

"And does he ever put anything on a horse he fancies?"

"Well—I don't want to give him away—he's a young sport, a fine sport, sir. Would you mind asking him himself? He sort of takes a pleasure in it, and perhaps he'd feel I was giving him away, sir, if you don't mind."

Bassett was serious as a church.

The uncle went back to his nephew and took him off for a ride in the car.

"Say, Paul, old man, do you ever put anything on a horse?" the uncle asked.

The boy watched the handsome man closely.

"Why, do you think I oughtn't to?" he parried.

"Not a bit of it! I thought perhaps you might give me a tip for the Lincoln."

The car sped on into the country, going down to Uncle Oscar's place in Hampshire.

"Honor bright?" said the nephew.

"Honor bright, son!" said the uncle.

"Well, then, Daffodil."

"Daffodil! I doubt it, sonny. What about Mirza?"

"I only know the winner," said the boy. "That's Daffodil."

"Daffodil, eh?"

There was a pause. Daffodil was an obscure horse comparatively.

"Uncle!"

"Yes, son?"

"You won't let it go any further, will you? I promised Bassett."

"Bassett be damned, old man! What's he got to do with it?"

"We're partners. We've been partners from the first. Uncle, he lent me my first five shillings, which I lost. I promised him, honor bright, it was only between me and him; only you gave me that ten-shilling note I started winning with, so I thought you were lucky. You won't let it go any further, will you?"

The boy gazed at his uncle from those big, hot, blue eyes, set rather close together. The uncle stirred and laughed uneasily.

"Right you are, son! I'll keep your tip private. Daffodil, eh? How much are you putting on him?"

"All except twenty pounds," said the boy. "I keep that in reserve."

The uncle thought it a good joke.

"You keep twenty pounds in reserve, do you, you young romancer? What are you betting, then?"

"I'm betting three hundred," said the boy gravely. "But it's between you and me, Uncle Oscar! Honor bright?"

The uncle burst into a roar of laughter.

"It's between you and me all right, you young Nat Gould,"° he said, laughing. "But where's your three hundred?"

Nat Gould: Nathaniel Gould (1857–1919), British novelist and sports columnist who wrote novels about horse racing.

"Bassett keeps it for me. We're partners."

"You are, are you! And what is Bassett putting on Daffodil?"

"He won't go quite as high as I do, I expect. Perhaps he'll go a hundred and fifty."

"What, pennies?" laughed the uncle.

"Pounds," said the child, with a surprised look at his uncle. "Bassett keeps a bigger reserve than I do."

Between wonder and amusement Uncle Oscar was silent. He pursued the matter no further, but he determined to take his nephew with him to the Lincoln races.

"Now, son," he said, "I'm putting twenty on Mirza, and I'll put five for you on any horse you fancy. What's your pick?"

"Daffodil, Uncle."

"No, not the fiver on Daffodil!"

"I should if it was my own fiver," said the child.

"Good! Good! Right you are! A fiver for me and a fiver for you on Daffodil."

The child had never been to a race meeting before, and his eyes were blue fire. He pursed his mouth tight, and watched. A Frenchman just in front had put his money on Lancelot. Wild with excitement, he flailed his arms up and down, yelling *Lancelot! Lancelot!* in his French accent.

Daffodil came in first, Lancelot second, Mirza third. The child, flushed and with eyes blazing, was curiously serene. His uncle brought him four five-pound notes, four to one.

"What am I to do with these?" he cried, waving them before the boy's eyes.

"I suppose we'll talk to Bassett," said the boy. "I expect I have fifteen hundred now; and twenty in reserve; and this twenty."

His uncle studied him for some moments.

"Look here, son!" he said. "You're not serious about Bassett and that fifteen hundred, are you?"

"Yes, I am. But it's between you and me, Uncle. Honor bright!"

"Honor bright all right, son! But I must talk to Bassett."

"If you'd like to be a partner, Uncle, with Bassett and me, we could all be partners. Only, you'd have to promise, honor bright, Uncle, not to let it go beyond us three. Bassett and I are lucky, and you must be lucky, because it was your ten shillings I started winning with. . . ."

Uncle Oscar took both Bassett and Paul into Richmond Park for an afternoon, and there they talked.

"It's like this, you see, sir," Bassett said. "Master Paul would get me talking about racing events, spinning yarns, you know, sir. And he was always keen on knowing if I'd made or if I'd lost. It's about a year since, now, that I put five shillings on Blush of Dawn for him—and we lost.

Then the luck turned, with that ten shillings he had from you, that we put on Singhalese. And since then, it's been pretty steady, all things considering. What do you say, Master Paul?"

"We're all right when we're sure," said Paul. "It's when we're not quite sure that we go down."

"Oh, but we're careful then," said Bassett.

"But when are you *sure*?" Uncle Oscar smiled.

"It's Master Paul, sir," said Bassett, in a secret, religious voice. "It's as if he had it from heaven. Like Daffodil, now, for the Lincoln. That was as sure as eggs."

"Did you put anything on Daffodil?" asked Oscar Cresswell.

"Yes, sir. I made my bit."

"And my nephew?"

Bassett was obstinately silent, looking at Paul.

"I made twelve hundred, didn't I, Bassett? I told Uncle I was putting three hundred on Daffodil."

"That's right," said Bassett, nodding.

"But where's the money?" asked the uncle.

"I keep it safe locked up, sir. Master Paul he can have it any minute he likes to ask for it."

"What, fifteen hundred pounds?"

"And twenty! And *forty*, that is, with the twenty he made on the course."

"It's amazing!" said the uncle.

"If Master Paul offers you to be partners, sir, I would, if I were you; if you'll excuse me," said Bassett.

Oscar Cresswell thought about it.

"I'll see the money," he said.

They drove home again, and sure enough, Bassett came round to the garden house with fifteen hundred pounds in notes. The twenty pounds reserve was left with Joe Glee, in the Turf Commission deposit.

"You see, it's all right, Uncle, when I'm *sure*! Then we go strong, for all we're worth. Don't we, Bassett?"

"We do that, Master Paul."

"And when are you sure?" said the uncle, laughing.

"Oh, well, sometimes I'm *absolutely* sure, like about Daffodil," said the boy; "and sometimes I have an idea; and sometimes I haven't even an idea, have I, Bassett? Then we're careful, because we mostly go down."

"You do, do you! And when you're sure, like about Daffodil, what makes you sure, sonny?"

"Oh, well, I don't know," said the boy uneasily. "I'm sure, you know, Uncle; that's all."

"It's as if he had it from heaven, sir," Bassett reiterated.

"I should say so!" said the uncle.

But he became a partner. And when the Leger was coming on, Paul was "sure" about Lively Spark, which was a quite inconsiderable horse. The boy insisted on putting a thousand on the horse, Bassett went for five hundred, and Oscar Cresswell two hundred. Lively Spark came in first, and the betting had been ten to one against him. Paul had made ten thousand.

"You see," he said, "I was absolutely sure of him."

Even Oscar Cresswell had cleared two thousand.

"Look here, son," he said, "this sort of thing makes me nervous."

"It needn't, Uncle! Perhaps I shan't be sure again for a long time."

"But what are you going to do with your money?" asked the uncle.

"Of course," said the boy. "I started it for Mother. She said she had no luck, because Father is unlucky, so I thought if *I* was lucky, it might stop whispering."

"What might stop whispering?"

"Our house. I *hate* our house for whispering."

"What does it whisper?"

"Why—why"—the boy fidgeted—"why, I don't know. But it's always short of money, you know, Uncle."

"I know it, son, I know it."

"You know people send Mother writs, don't you, Uncle?"

"I'm afraid I do," said the uncle.

"And then the house whispers, like people laughing at you behind your back. It's awful, that is! I thought if I was lucky. . . ."

"You might stop it," added the uncle.

The boy watched him with big blue eyes, that had an uncanny cold fire in them, and he said never a word.

"Well, then!" said the uncle. "What are we doing?"

"I shouldn't like Mother to know I was lucky," said the boy.

"Why not, son?"

"She'd stop me."

"I don't think she would."

"Oh!"—and the boy writhed in an odd way—"I *don't* want her to know, Uncle."

"All right, son! We'll manage it without her knowing."

They managed it very easily. Paul, at the other's suggestion, handed over five thousand pounds to his uncle, who deposited it with the family lawyer, who was then to inform Paul's mother that a relative had put five thousand pounds into his hands, which sum was to be paid out a thousand pounds at a time, on the mother's birthday, for the next five years.

"So she'll have a birthday present of a thousand pounds for five successive years," said Uncle Oscar. "I hope it won't make it all the harder for her later."

Paul's mother had her birthday in November. The house had been "whispering" worse than ever lately, and, even in spite of his luck, Paul could not bear up against it. He was very anxious to see the effect of the birthday letter, telling his mother about the thousand pounds.

When there were no visitors, Paul now took his meals with his parents, as he was beyond the nursery control. His mother went into town nearly every day. She had discovered that she had an odd knack of sketching furs and dress materials, so she worked secretly in the studio of a friend who was the chief artist for the leading drapers. She drew the figures of ladies in furs and ladies in silk and sequins for the newspaper advertisements. This young woman artist earned several thousand pounds a year, but Paul's mother only made several hundreds, and she was again dissatisfied. She so wanted to be first in something, and she did not succeed, even in making sketches for drapery advertisements.

She was down to breakfast on the morning of her birthday. Paul watched her face as she read her letters. He knew the lawyer's letter. As his mother read it, her face hardened and became more expressionless. Then a cold, determined look came on her mouth. She hid the letter under the pile of others, and said not a word about it.

"Didn't you have anything nice in the post for your birthday, Mother?" said Paul.

"Quite moderately nice," she said, her voice cold and absent.

She went away to town without saying more.

But in the afternoon Uncle Oscar appeared. He said Paul's mother had had a long interview with the lawyer, asking if the whole five thousand could not be advanced at once, as she was in debt.

"What do you think, Uncle?" said the boy.

"I leave it to you, son."

"Oh, let her have it, then! We can get some more with the other," said the boy.

"A bird in the hand is worth two in the bush, laddie!" said Uncle Oscar.

"But I'm sure to *know* for the Grand National; or the Lincolnshire; or else the Derby. I'm sure to know for *one* of them," said Paul.

So Uncle Oscar signed the agreement, and Paul's mother touched the whole five thousand. Then something very curious happened. The voices in the house suddenly went mad, like a chorus of frogs on a spring evening. There were certain new furnishings, and Paul had a tutor. He was *really* going to Eton, his father's school, in the following autumn. There were flowers in the winter, and a blossoming of the luxury Paul's mother had been used to. And yet the voices in the house, behind the sprays of mimosa and almond blossom, and from under the piles of iridescent cushions, simply trilled and screamed in a sort of ecstasy: "There *must* be more money! Oh-h-h; there *must* be more money. Oh, now, now-w! Now-w-w—there *must* be more money!—more than ever! More than ever!"

It frightened Paul terribly. He studied away at his Latin and Greek. But his intense hours were spent with Bassett. The Grand National had gone by; he had not "known," and had lost a hundred pounds. Summer was at hand. He was in agony for the Lincoln. But even for the Lincoln he didn't "know," and he lost fifty pounds. He became wild-eyed and strange, as if something were going to explode in him.

"Let it alone, son! Don't you bother about it!" urged Uncle Oscar. But it was as if the boy couldn't really hear what his uncle was saying.

"I've got to know for the Derby! I've got to know for the Derby!" the child reiterated, his big blue eyes blazing with a sort of madness.

His mother noticed how overwrought he was.

"You'd better go to the seaside. Wouldn't you like to go now to the seaside, instead of waiting? I think you'd better," she said, looking down at him anxiously, her heart curiously heavy because of him.

But the child lifted his uncanny blue eyes. "I couldn't possibly go before the Derby, Mother!" he said. "I couldn't possibly!"

"Why not?" she said, her voice becoming heavy when she was opposed. "Why not? You can still go from the seaside to see the Derby with your uncle Oscar, if that's what you wish. No need for you to wait here. Besides, I think you care too much about these races. It's a bad sign. My family has been a gambling family, and you won't know till you grow up how much damage it has done. But it has done damage. I shall have to send Bassett away, and ask Uncle Oscar not to talk racing to you, unless you promise to be reasonable about it; go away to the seaside and forget it. You're all nerves!"

"I'll do what you like, Mother, so long as you don't send me away till after the Derby," the boy said.

"Send you away from where? Just from this house?"

"Yes," he said, gazing at her.

"Why, you curious child, what makes you care about this house so much, suddenly? I never knew you loved it."

He gazed at her without speaking. He had a secret within a secret, something he had not divulged, even to Bassett or to his uncle Oscar.

But his mother, after standing undecided and a little bit sullen for some moments, said:

"Very well, then! Don't go to the seaside till after the Derby, if you don't wish it. But promise me you won't let your nerves go to pieces. Promise you won't think so much about horse racing and *events*, as you call them!"

"Oh, no," said the boy casually. "I won't think much about them, Mother. You needn't worry. I wouldn't worry, Mother, if I were you."

"If you were me and I were you," said his mother, "I wonder what we *should* do!"

"But you know you needn't worry, Mother, don't you?" the boy repeated.

"I should be awfully glad to know it," she said wearily.

"Oh, well you *can*, you know. I mean, you *ought* to know you needn't worry," he insisted.

"Ought I? Then I'll see about it," she said.

Paul's secret of secrets was his wooden horse, that which had no name. Since he was emancipated from a nurse and a nursery governess, he had had his rocking horse removed to his own bedroom at the top of the house.

"Surely, you're too big for a rocking horse!" his mother had remonstrated.

"Well, you see, Mother, till I can have a *real* horse, I like to have *some* sort of animal about," had been his quaint answer.

"Do you feel he keeps you company?" She laughed.

"Oh, yes! He's very good, he always keeps me company, when I'm there," said Paul.

So the horse, rather shabby, stood in an arrested prance in the boy's bedroom.

The Derby was drawing near, and the boy grew more and more tense. He hardly heard what was spoken to him, he was very frail, and his eyes were really uncanny. His mother had sudden strange seizures of uneasiness about him. Sometimes, for half an hour, she would feel a sudden anxiety about him that was almost anguish. She wanted to rush to him at once, and know he was safe.

Two nights before the Derby, she was at a big party in town, when one of her rushes of anxiety about her boy, her firstborn, gripped her heart till she could hardly speak. She fought with the feeling, might and main, for she believed in common sense. But it was too strong. She had to leave the dance and go downstairs to telephone to the country. The children's nursery governess was terribly surprised and startled at being rung up in the night.

"Are the children all right, Miss Wilmot?"

"Oh, yes, they are quite all right."

"Master Paul? Is he all right?"

"He went to bed as right as a trivet. Shall I run up and look at him?"

"No," said Paul's mother reluctantly. "No! Don't trouble. It's all right. Don't sit up. We shall be home fairly soon." She did not want her son's privacy intruded upon.

"Very good," said the governess.

It was about one o'clock when Paul's mother and father drove up to their house. All was still. Paul's mother went to her room and slipped off her white fur cloak. She had told her maid not to wait up for her. She heard her husband downstairs, mixing a whisky and soda.

And then, because of the strange anxiety at her heart, she stole upstairs to her son's room. Noiselessly she went along the upper corridor. Was there a faint noise? What was it?

She stood, with arrested muscles, outside his door, listening. There was a strange, heavy, and yet not loud noise. Her heart stood still. It was a soundless noise, yet rushing and powerful. Something huge, in violent, hushed motion. What was it? What in God's name was it? She ought to know. She felt that she knew the noise. She knew what it was.

Yet she could not place it. She couldn't say what it was. And on and on it went, like a madness.

Softly, frozen with anxiety and fear, she turned the door handle.

The room was dark. Yet in the space near the window, she heard and saw something plunging to and fro. She gazed in fear and amazement.

Then suddenly she switched on the light, and saw her son, in his green pajamas, madly surging on the rocking horse. The blaze of light suddenly lit him up, as he urged the wooden horse, and lit her up, as she stood, blonde, in her dress of pale green and crystal, in the doorway.

"Paul!" she cried. "Whatever are you doing?"

"It's Malabar!" he screamed, in a powerful, strange voice. "It's Malabar!"

His eyes blazed at her for one strange and senseless second, as he ceased urging his wooden horse. Then he fell with a crash to the ground, and she, all her tormented motherhood flooding upon her, rushed to gather him up.

But he was unconscious, and unconscious he remained, with some brain fever. He talked and tossed, and his mother sat stonily by his side.

"Malabar! It's Malabar! Bassett, Bassett, I *know*! It's Malabar!"

So the child cried, trying to get up and urge the rocking horse that gave him his inspiration.

"What does he mean by Malabar?" asked the heart-frozen mother.

"I don't know," said the father stonily.

"What does he mean by Malabar?" she asked her brother Oscar.

"It's one of the horses running for the Derby," was the answer.

And, in spite of himself, Oscar Cresswell spoke to Bassett, and himself put a thousand on Malabar: at fourteen to one.

The third day of the illness was critical: they were waiting for a change. The boy, with his rather long, curly hair, was tossing ceaselessly on the pillow. He never slept nor regained consciousness, and his eyes were like blue stones. His mother sat, feeling her heart had gone, turned actually into a stone.

In the evening, Oscar Cresswell did not come, but Bassett sent a message, saying could he come up for one moment, just one moment? Paul's mother was very angry at the intrusion, but on second thought she agreed. The boy was the same. Perhaps Bassett might bring him to consciousness.

The gardener, a shortish fellow with a little brown mustache, and sharp little brown eyes, tiptoed into the room, touched his imaginary cap to Paul's mother, and stole to the bedside, staring with glittering, smallish eyes at the tossing, dying child.

"Master Paul!" he whispered. "Master Paul! Malabar came in first all right, a clean win. I did as you told me. You've made over seventy thousand pounds, you have; you've got over eighty thousand. Malabar came in all right, Master Paul."

"Malabar! Malabar! Did I say Malabar, Mother? Did I say Malabar? Do you think I'm lucky, Mother? I knew Malabar, didn't I? Over eighty thousand pounds! I call that lucky, don't you, Mother? Over eighty thousand pounds! I knew, didn't I know I knew? Malabar came in all right. If I ride my horse till I'm sure, then I tell you, Bassett, you can go as high as you like. Did you go for all you were worth, Bassett?"

"I went a thousand on it, Master Paul."

"I never told you, Mother, that if I can ride my horse, and *get there*, then I'm absolutely sure—oh, absolutely! Mother, did I ever tell you? I *am* lucky!"

"No, you never did," said the mother.

But the boy died in the night.

And even as he lay dead, his mother heard her brother's voice saying to her: "My God, Hester, you're eighty-odd thousand to the good, and a poor devil of a son to the bad. But, poor devil, poor devil, he's best gone out of a life where he rides his rocking horse to find a winner."

[1926]

KATHERINE ANNE PORTER [1890–1980]

The Jilting of
Granny Weatherall

She flicked her wrist neatly out of Doctor Harry's pudgy careful fingers
and pulled the sheet up to her chin. The brat ought to be in knee
breeches. Doctoring around the country with spectacles on his nose!
"Get along now, take your schoolbooks and go. There's nothing wrong
with me."

Doctor Harry spread a warm paw like a cushion on her forehead
where the forked green vein danced and made her eyelids twitch. "Now,
now, be a good girl, and we'll have you up in no time."

"That's no way to speak to a woman nearly eighty years old just
because she's down. I'd have you respect your elders, young man."

"Well, Missy, excuse me." Doctor Harry patted her cheek. "But I've got
to warn you, haven't I? You're a marvel, but you must be careful or
you're going to be good and sorry."

"Don't tell me what I'm going to be. I'm on my feet now, morally
speaking. It's Cornelia. I had to go to bed to get rid of her."

Her bones felt loose, and floated around in her skin, and Doctor Harry
floated like a balloon around the foot of the bed. He floated and pulled
down his waistcoat and swung his glasses on a cord. "Well, stay where
you are, it certainly can't hurt you."

"Get along and doctor your sick," said Granny Weatherall. "Leave a
well woman alone. I'll call for you when I want you. . . . Where were you
forty years ago when I pulled through milk-leg and double pneumonia?
You weren't even born. Don't let Cornelia lead you on," she shouted,
because Doctor Harry appeared to float up to the ceiling and out. "I pay
my own bills, and I don't throw my money away on nonsense!"

She meant to wave good-by, but it was too much trouble. Her eyes
closed of themselves, it was like a dark curtain drawn around the bed.
The pillow rose and floated under her, pleasant as a hammock in a light
wind. She listened to the leaves rustling outside the window. No, somebody was swishing newspapers: no, Cornelia and Doctor Harry were
whispering together. She leaped broad awake, thinking they whispered
in her ear.

"She was never like this, *never* like this!" "Well, what can we expect?" "Yes, eighty years old. . . ."

Well, and what if she was? She still had ears. It was like Cornelia to whisper around doors. She always kept things secret in such a public way. She was always being tactful and kind. Cornelia was dutiful; that was the trouble with her. Dutiful and good: "So good and dutiful," said Granny, "that I'd like to spank her." She saw herself spanking Cornelia and making a fine job of it.

"What'd you say, Mother?"

Granny felt her face tying up in hard knots.

"Can't a body think, I'd like to know?"

"I thought you might want something."

"I do. I want a lot of things. First off, go away and don't whisper."

She lay and drowsed, hoping in her sleep that the children would keep out and let her rest a minute. It had been a long day. Not that she was tired. It was always pleasant to snatch a minute now and then. There was always so much to be done, let me see: tomorrow.

Tomorrow was far away and there was nothing to trouble about. Things were finished somehow when the time came; thank God there was always a little margin over for peace: then a person could spread out the plan of life and tuck in the edges orderly. It was good to have everything clean and folded away, with the hair brushes and tonic bottles sitting straight on the white embroidered linen: the day started without fuss and the pantry shelves laid out with rows of jelly glasses and brown jugs and white stone-china jars with blue whirligigs and words painted on them: coffee, tea, sugar, ginger, cinnamon, allspice: and the bronze clock with the lion on top nicely dusted off. The dust that lion could collect in twenty-four hours! The box in the attic with all those letters tied up, well, she'd have to go through that tomorrow. All those letters— George's letters and John's letters and her letters to them both—lying around for the children to find afterwards made her uneasy. Yes, that would be tomorrow's business. No use to let them know how silly she had been once.

While she was rummaging around she found death in her mind and it felt clammy and unfamiliar. She had spent so much time preparing for death there was no need for bringing it up again. Let it take care of itself now. When she was sixty she had felt very old, finished, and went around making farewell trips to see her children and grandchildren, with a secret in her mind: This is the very last of your mother, children! Then she made her will and came down with a long fever. That was all just a notion like a lot of other things, but it was lucky too, for she had once for all got over the idea of dying for a long time. Now she couldn't be worried. She hoped she had better sense now. Her father had lived to be one hundred and two years old and had drunk a noggin of strong hot toddy on his last birthday. He told the reporters it was his daily habit, and he owed his long life to that. He had made quite a scandal and was very pleased about it. She believed she'd just plague Cornelia a little.

"Cornelia! Cornelia!" No footsteps, but a sudden hand on her cheek. "Bless you, where have you been?"

"Here, Mother."

"Well, Cornelia, I want a noggin of hot toddy."

"Are you cold, darling?"

"I'm chilly, Cornelia. Lying in bed stops the circulation. I must have told you that a thousand times."

Well, she could just hear Cornelia telling her husband that Mother was getting a little childish and they'd have to humor her. The thing that most annoyed her was that Cornelia thought she was deaf, dumb, and blind. Little hasty glances and tiny gestures tossed around her and over her head saying, "Don't cross her, let her have her way, she's eighty years old," and she sitting there as if she lived in a thin glass cage. Sometimes Granny almost made up her mind to pack up and move back to her own house where nobody could remind her every minute that she was old. Wait, wait, Cornelia, till your own children whisper behind your back!

In her day she had kept a better house and had got more work done. She wasn't too old yet for Lydia to be driving eighty miles for advice when one of the children jumped the track, and Jimmy still dropped in and talked things over: "Now, Mammy, you've a good business head, I want to know what you think of this? . . ." Old. Cornelia couldn't change the furniture around without asking. Little things, little things! They had been so sweet when they were little. Granny wished the old days were back again with the children young and everything to be done over. It had been a hard puff, but not too much for her. When she thought of all the food she had cooked, and all the clothes she had cut and sewed, and all the gardens she had made—well, the children showed it. There they were, made out of her, and they couldn't get away from that. Sometimes she wanted to see John again and point to them and say, Well, I didn't do so badly, did I? But that would have to wait. That was for tomorrow. She used to think of him as a man, but now all the children were older than their father, and he would be a child beside her if she saw him now. It seemed strange and there was something wrong in the idea. Why, he couldn't possibly recognize her. She had fenced in a hundred acres once, digging the post holes herself and clamping the wires with just a negro boy to help. That changed a woman. John would be looking for a young woman with the peaked Spanish comb in her hair and the painted fan. Digging post holes changed a woman. Riding country roads in the winter when women had their babies was another thing: sitting up nights with sick horses and sick negroes and sick children and hardly ever losing one. John, I hardly ever lost one of them! John would see that in a minute, that would be something he could understand, she wouldn't have to explain anything!

It made her feel like rolling up her sleeves and putting the whole place to rights again. No matter if Cornelia was determined to be everywhere at once, there were a great many things left undone on this place. She would start tomorrow and do them. It was good to be strong enough for everything, even if all you made melted and changed and slipped under your hands, so that by the time you finished you almost forgot what you were working for. What was it I set out to do? she asked herself intently, but she could not remember. A fog rose over the valley, she saw it marching across the creek swallowing the trees and moving up the hill like an army of ghosts. Soon it would be at the near edge of the orchard, and then it was time to go in and light the lamps. Come in, children, don't stay out in the night air.

Lighting the lamps had been beautiful. The children huddled up to her and breathed like little calves waiting at the bars in the twilight. Their eyes followed the match and watched the flame rise and settle in a blue curve, then they moved away from her. The lamp was lit, they didn't have to be scared and hang on to mother any more. Never, never, never more. God, for all my life I thank Thee. Without Thee, my God, I could never have done it. Hail, Mary, full of grace.

I want you to pick all the fruit this year and see that nothing is wasted. There's always someone who can use it. Don't let good things rot for want of using. You waste life when you waste good food. Don't let things get lost. It's bitter to lose things. Now, don't let me get to thinking, not when I am tired and taking a little nap before supper. . . .

The pillow rose about her shoulders and pressed against her heart and the memory was being squeezed out of it: oh, push down the pillow, somebody: it would smother her if she tried to hold it. Such a fresh breeze blowing and such a green day with no threats in it. But he had not come, just the same. What does a woman do when she has put on the white veil and set out the white cake for a man and he doesn't come? She tried to remember. No, I swear he never harmed me but in that. He never harmed me but in that . . . and what if he did? There was the day, the day, but a whirl of dark smoke rose and covered it, crept up and over into the bright field where everything was planted so carefully in orderly rows. That was hell, she knew hell when she saw it. For sixty years she had prayed against remembering him and against losing her soul in the deep pit of hell, and now the two things were mingled in one and the thought of him was a smoky cloud from hell that moved and crept in her head when she had just got rid of Doctor Harry and was trying to rest a minute. Wounded vanity, Ellen, said a sharp voice in the top of her mind. Don't let your wounded vanity get the upper hand of you. Plenty of girls get jilted. You were jilted, weren't you? Then stand up to it. Her eyelids wavered and let in streamers of blue-gray light like tissue paper over her eyes. She must get up and pull the shades down or she'd never sleep. She was in bed again and the shades were not down. How could that happen? Better turn over, hide from the light, sleeping in the light gave you nightmares. "Mother, how do you feel now?" and a stinging wetness on her forehead. But I don't like having my face washed in cold water!

Hapsy? George? Lydia? Jimmy? No, Cornelia, and her features were swollen and full of little puddles. "They're coming, darling, they'll all be here soon." Go wash your face, child, you look funny.

Instead of obeying, Cornelia knelt down and put her head on the pillow. She seemed to be talking but there was no sound. "Well, are you tongue-tied? Whose birthday is it? Are you going to give a party?"

Cornelia's mouth moved urgently in strange shapes. "Don't do that, you bother me, daughter."

"Oh, no, Mother. Oh, no. . . ."

Nonsense. It was strange about children. They disputed your every word. "No what, Cornelia?"

"Here's Doctor Harry."

"I won't see that boy again. He just left five minutes ago."

"That was this morning, Mother. It's night now. Here's the nurse!"

"This is Doctor Harry, Mrs. Weatherall. I never saw you look so young and happy!"

"Ah, I'll never be young again—but I'd be happy if they'd let me lie in peace and get rested."

She thought she spoke up loudly, but no one answered. A warm weight on her forehead, a warm bracelet on her wrist, and a breeze went on whispering, trying to tell her something. A shuffle of leaves in the everlasting hand of God, He blew on them and they danced and rattled. "Mother, don't mind, we're going to give you a little hypodermic." "Look here, daughter, how do ants get in this bed? I saw sugar ants yesterday." Did you send for Hapsy too?

It was Hapsy she really wanted. She had to go a long way back through a great many rooms to find Hapsy standing with a baby on her arm. She seemed to herself to be Hapsy also, and the baby on Hapsy's arm was Hapsy and himself and herself, all at once, and there was no surprise in the meeting. Then Hapsy melted from within and turned flimsy as gray gauze and the baby was a gauzy shadow, and Hapsy came up close and said, "I thought you'd never come," and looked at her very searchingly and said, "You haven't changed a bit!" They leaned forward to kiss, when Cornelia began whispering from a long way off, "Oh, is there anything you want to tell me? Is there anything I can do for you?"

Yes, she had changed her mind after sixty years and she would like to see George. I want you to find George. Find him and be sure to tell him I forgot him. I want him to know I had my husband just the same and my children and my house like any other woman. A good house too and a good husband that I loved and fine children out of him. Better than I hoped for even. Tell him I was given back everything he took away and more. Oh, no, oh, God, no, there was something else besides the house and the man and the children. Oh, surely they were not all? What was it? Something not given back. . . . Her breath crowded down under her ribs and grew into a monstrous frightening shape with cutting edges; it bored up into her head, and the agony was unbelievable: Yes, John, get the Doctor now, no more talk, my time has come.

When this one was born it should be the last. The last. It should have been born first, for it was the one she had truly wanted. Everything came in good time. Nothing left out, left over. She was strong, in three days she would be as well as ever. Better. A woman needed milk in her to have her full health.

"Mother, do you hear me?"

"I've been telling you—"

"Mother, Father Connolly's here."

"I went to Holy Communion only last week. Tell him I'm not so sinful as all that."

"Father just wants to speak to you."

He could speak as much as he pleased. It was like him to drop in and inquire about her soul as if it were a teething baby, and then stay on for a cup of tea and a round of cards and gossip. He always had a funny story of some sort, usually about an Irishman who made his little mistakes and confessed them, and the point lay in some absurd thing he would blurt out in the confessional showing his struggles between native piety and original sin. Granny felt easy about her soul. Cornelia, where are your manners? Give Father Connolly a chair. She had her secret comfortable understanding with a few favorite saints who cleared a straight road to God for her. All as surely signed and sealed as the papers for the new Forty Acres. Forever . . . heirs and assigns forever. Since the day the wedding cake was not cut, but thrown out and wasted. The whole bottom dropped out of the world, and there she was blind and sweating with nothing under her feet and the walls falling away. His hand had caught her under the breast, she had not fallen, there was the freshly polished floor with the green rug on it, just as before. He had cursed like a sailor's parrot and said, "I'll kill him for you." Don't lay a hand on him, for my sake leave something to God. "Now, Ellen, you must believe what I tell you. . . ."

So there was nothing, nothing to worry about any more, except some-times in the night one of the children screamed in a nightmare, and they both hustled out shaking and hunting for the matches and calling, "There, wait a minute, here we are!" John, get the doctor now, Hapsy's time has come. But there was Hapsy standing by the bed in a white cap. "Cornelia, tell Hapsy to take off her cap. I can't see her plain."

Her eyes opened very wide and the room stood out like a picture she had seen somewhere. Dark colors with the shadows rising towards the ceiling in long angles. The tall black dresser gleamed with nothing on it but John's picture, enlarged from a little one, with John's eyes very black when they should have been blue. You never saw him, so how do you know how he looked? But the man insisted the copy was perfect, it was very rich and handsome. For a picture, yes, but it's not my husband. The table by the bed had a linen cover and a candle and a crucifix. The light was blue from Cornelia's silk lampshades. No sort of light at all, just frip-pery. You had to live forty years with kerosene lamps to appreciate hon-est electricity. She felt very strong and she saw Doctor Harry with a rosy nimbus around him.

"You look like a saint, Doctor Harry, and I vow that's as near as you'll ever come to it."

"She's saying something."

"I heard you, Cornelia. What's all this carrying-on?"

"Father Connolly's saying—"

Cornelia's voice staggered and bumped like a cart in a bad road. It rounded corners and turned back again and arrived nowhere. Granny stepped up in the cart very lightly and reached for the reins, but a man sat beside her and she knew him by his hands, driving the cart. She did not look in his face, for she knew without seeing, but looked instead down the road where the trees leaned over and bowed to each other and a thousand birds were singing a Mass. She felt like singing too, but she put her hand in the bosom of her dress and pulled out a rosary, and Father Connolly murmured Latin in a very solemn voice and tickled her feet. My God, will you stop that nonsense? I'm a married woman. What if he did run away and leave me to face the priest by myself? I found another a whole world better. I wouldn't have exchanged my husband for anybody except St. Michael himself, and you may tell him that for me with a thank you in the bargain.

Light flashed on her closed eyelids, and a deep roaring shook her. Cor-nelia, is that lightning? I hear thunder. There's going to be a storm. Close all the windows. Call the children in. . . . "Mother, here we are, all of us." "Is that you, Hapsy?" "Oh, no, I'm Lydia. We drove as fast as we could." Their faces drifted above her, drifted away. The rosary fell out of her hands and Lydia put it back. Jimmy tried to help, their hands fumbled together, and Granny closed two fingers around Jimmy's thumb. Beads wouldn't do, it must be something alive. She was so amazed her thoughts ran round and round. So, my dear Lord, this is my death and I wasn't even thinking about it. My children have come to see me die. But I can't, it's not time. Oh, I always hated surprises. I wanted to give Cornelia the amethyst set—Cornelia, you're to have the amethyst set, but Hapsy's to wear it when she wants, and, Doctor Harry, do shut up. Nobody sent for you. Oh, my dear Lord, do wait a minute. I meant to do something about the Forty Acres, Jimmy doesn't need it and Lydia will later on, with that worthless husband of hers. I meant to finish the altar cloth and send six bottles of wine to Sister Borgia for her dyspepsia. I want to send six bottles of wine to Sister Borgia, Father Connolly, now don't let me forget.

Cornelia's voice made short turns and tilted over and crashed. "Oh, Mother, oh, Mother, oh, Mother. . . ."

"I'm not going, Cornelia. I'm taken by surprise. I can't go."

You'll see Hapsy again. What about her? "I thought you'd never come." Granny made a long journey outward, looking for Hapsy. What if I don't find her? What then? Her heart sank down and down, there was no bottom to death, she couldn't come to the end of it. The blue light from Cornelia's lampshade drew into a tiny point in the center of her brain, it flickered and winked like an eye, quietly it fluttered and dwindled. Granny lay curled down within herself, amazed and watchful, staring at the point of light that was herself; her body was now only a deeper mass of shadow in an endless darkness and this darkness would curl around the light and swallow it up. God, give a sign!

For the second time there was no sign. Again no bridegroom and the priest in the house. She could not remember any other sorrow because this grief wiped them all away. Oh, no, there's nothing more cruel than this—I'll never forgive it. She stretched herself with a deep breath and blew out the light.

[1930]

WILLIAM FAULKNER [1897–1962]

Barn Burning

The store in which the Justice of the Peace's court was sitting smelled of cheese. The boy, crouched on his nail keg at the back of the crowded room, knew he smelled cheese, and more: from where he sat he could see the ranked shelves close-packed with the solid, squat, dynamic shapes of tin cans whose labels his stomach read, not from the lettering which meant nothing to his mind but from the scarlet devils and the silver curve of fish—this, the cheese which he knew he smelled and the hermetic meat which his intestines believed he smelled coming in intermittent gusts momentary and brief between the other constant one, the smell and sense just a little of fear because mostly of despair and grief, the old fierce pull of blood. He could not see the table where the Justice sat and before which his father and his father's enemy (*our enemy* he thought in that despair; *ourn! mine and hisn both! He's my father!*) stood, but he could hear them, the two of them that is, because his father had said no word yet:

"But what proof have you, Mr. Harris?"

"I told you. The hog got into my corn. I caught it up and sent it back to him. He had no fence that would hold it. I told him so, warned him. The next time I put the hog in my pen. When he came to get it I gave him enough wire to patch up his pen. The next time I put the hog up and kept it. I rode down to his house and saw the wire I gave him still rolled on to the spool in his yard. I told him he could have the hog when he paid me a dollar pound fee. That evening a nigger came with the dollar and got the hog. He was a strange nigger. He said, 'He say to tell you wood and hay kin burn.' I said, 'What?' 'That whut he say to tell you,' the nigger said. 'Wood and hay kin burn.' That night my barn burned. I got the stock out but I lost the barn."

"Where is the nigger? Have you got him?"

"He was a strange nigger, I tell you. I don't know what became of him."

"But that's not proof. Don't you see that's not proof?"

"Get that boy up here. He knows." For a moment the boy thought too that the man meant his older brother until Harris said, "Not him. The little one. The boy," and, crouching, small for his age, small and wiry

161

like his father, in patched and faded jeans even too small for him, with straight, uncombed, brown hair and eyes gray and wild as storm scud, he saw the men between himself and the table part and become a lane of grim faces, at the end of which he saw the Justice, a shabby, collarless, graying man in spectacles, beckoning him. He felt no floor under his bare feet; he seemed to walk beneath the palpable weight of the grim turning faces. His father, stiff in his black Sunday coat donned not for the trial but for the moving, did not even look at him. *He aims for me to lie,* he thought, again with that frantic grief and despair. *And I will have to do hit.*

"What's your name, boy?" the Justice said.

"Colonel Sartoris Snopes," the boy whispered.

"Hey?" the Justice said. "Talk louder. Colonel Sartoris? I reckon anybody named for Colonel Sartoris in this country can't help but tell the truth, can they?" The boy said nothing. *Enemy! Enemy!* he thought; for a moment he could not even see, could not see that the Justice's face was kindly nor discern that his voice was troubled when he spoke to the man named Harris: "Do you want me to question this boy?" But he could hear, and during those subsequent long seconds while there was absolutely no sound in the crowded little room save that of quiet and intent breathing it was as if he had swung outward at the end of a grape vine, over a ravine, and at the top of the swing had been caught in a prolonged instant of mesmerized gravity, weightless in time.

"No!" Harris said violently, explosively. "Damnation! Send him out of here!" Now time, the fluid world, rushed beneath him again, the voices coming to him again through the smell of cheese and sealed meat, the fear and despair and the old grief of blood:

"This case is closed. I can't find against you, Snopes, but I can give you advice. Leave this country and don't come back to it."

His father spoke for the first time, his voice cold and harsh, level, without emphasis: "I aim to. I don't figure to stay in a country among people who . . ." he said something unprintable and vile, addressed to no one.

"That'll do," the Justice said. "Take your wagon and get out of this country before dark. Case dismissed."

His father turned, and he followed the stiff black coat, the wiry figure walking a little stiffly from where a Confederate provost's man's musket ball had taken him in the heel on a stolen horse thirty years ago, followed the two backs now, since his older brother had appeared from somewhere in the crowd, no taller than the father but thicker, chewing tobacco steadily, between the two lines of grim-faced men and out of the store and across the worn gallery and down the sagging steps and among the dogs and half-grown boys in the mild May dust, where as he passed a voice hissed:

"Barn burner!"

Again he could not see, whirling; there was a face in a red haze, moon-like, bigger than the full moon, the owner of it half again his size, he leaping in the red haze toward the face, feeling no blow, feeling no shock when his head struck the earth, scrabbling up and leaping again, feeling no blow this time either and tasting no blood, scrabbling up to see the other boy in full flight and himself already leaping into pursuit as his father's hand jerked him back, the harsh, cold voice speaking above him: "Go get in the wagon."

It stood in a grove of locusts and mulberries across the road. His two hulking sisters in their Sunday dresses and his mother and her sister in calico and sunbonnets were already in it, sitting on or among the sorry residue of the dozen and more movings which even the boy could remember—the battered stove, the broken beds and chairs, the clock inlaid with mother-of-pearl, which would not run, stopped at some four-teen minutes past two o'clock of a dead and forgotten day and time, which had been his mother's dowry. She was crying, though when she saw him she drew her sleeve across her face and began to descend from the wagon. "Get back," the father said.

"He's hurt. I got to get some water and wash his . . ."

"Get back in the wagon," his father said. He got in too, over the tail-gate. His father mounted to the seat where the older brother already sat and struck the gaunt mules two savage blows with the peeled willow, but without heat. It was not even sadistic; it was exactly that same quality which in later years would cause his descendants to over-run the engine before putting a motor car in motion, striking and reining back in the same movement. The wagon went on, the store with its quiet crowd of grimly watching men dropped behind; a curve in the road hid it. *Forever* he thought. *Maybe he's done satisfied now, now that he has . . .* stopping himself, not to say it aloud even to himself. His mother's hand touched his shoulder.

"Does hit hurt?" she said.

"Naw," he said. "Hit don't hurt. Lemme be."

"Can't you wipe some of the blood off before hit dries?"

"I'll wash to-night," he said. "Lemme be, I tell you."

The wagon went on. He did not know where they were going. None of them ever did or ever asked, because it was always somewhere, always a house of sorts waiting for them a day or two days or even three days away. Likely his father had already arranged to make a crop on another farm before he . . . Again he had to stop himself. He (the father) always did. There was something about his wolflike independence and even courage when the advantage was at least neutral which impressed strangers, as if they got from his latent ravening ferocity not so much a sense of dependability as a feeling that his ferocious conviction in the rightness of his own actions would be of advantage to all whose interest lay with his.

That night they camped, in a grove of oaks and beeches where a spring ran. The nights were still cool and they had a fire against it, of a rail lifted from a nearby fence and cut into lengths—a small fire, neat, niggard almost, a shrewd fire; such fires were his father's habit and custom always, even in freezing weather. Older, the boy might have remarked this and wondered why not a big one; why should not a man who had not only seen the waste and extravagance of war, but who had in his blood an inherent voracious prodigality with material not his own, have burned everything in sight? Then he might have gone a step farther and thought that that was the reason: that niggard blaze was the living fruit of nights passed during those four years in the woods hiding from all men, blue or gray, with his strings of horses (captured horses, he called them). And older still, he might have divined the true reason: that the element of fire spoke to some deep mainspring of his father's being, as the element of steel or of powder spoke to other men, as the one weapon for the preservation of integrity, else breath were not worth the breathing, and hence to be regarded with respect and used with discretion.

But he did not think this now and he had seen those same niggard blazes all his life. He merely ate his supper beside it and was already half asleep over his iron plate when his father called him, and once more he followed the stiff back, the stiff and ruthless limp, up the slope and on to the starlit road where, turning, he could see his father against the stars but without face or depth—a shape black, flat, and bloodless as though cut from tin in the iron folds of the frockcoat which had not been made for him, the voice harsh like tin and without heat like tin:

"You were fixing to tell them. You would have told him."

He didn't answer. His father struck him with the flat of his hand on the side of the head, hard but without heat, exactly as he had struck the two mules at the store, exactly as he would strike either of them with any stick in order to kill a horse fly, his voice still without heat or anger. "You're getting to be a man. You got to learn. You got to learn to stick to your own blood or you ain't going to have any blood to stick to you. Do you think either of them, any man there this morning, would? Don't you know all they wanted was a chance to get at me because they knew I had them beat? Eh?" Later, twenty years later, he was to tell himself, "If I had said they wanted only truth, justice, he would have hit me again." But now he said nothing. He was not crying. He just stood there. "Answer me," his father said.

"Yes," he whispered. His father turned.

"Get on to bed. We'll be there tomorrow."

Tomorrow they were there. In the early afternoon the wagon stopped before a paintless two-room house identical almost with the dozen others it had stopped before even in the boy's ten years, and again, as on the other dozen occasions, his mother and aunt got down and began to unload the wagon, although his two sisters and his father and brother had not moved.

"Likely hit ain't fitten for hawgs," one of the sisters said.

"Nevertheless, fit it will and you'll hog it and like it," his father said. "Get out of them chairs and help your Ma unload."

The two sisters got down, big, bovine, in a flutter of cheap ribbons; one of them drew from the jumbled wagon bed a battered lantern, the other a worn broom. His father handed the reins to the older son and began to climb stiffly over the wheel. "When they get unloaded, take the team to the barn and feed them." Then he said, and at first the boy thought he was still speaking to his brother: "Come with me."

"Me?" he said.

"Yes," his father said. "You."

"Abner," his mother said. His father paused and looked back—the harsh level stare beneath the shaggy, graying, irascible brows.

"I reckon I'll have a word with the man that aims to begin tomorrow owning me body and soul for the next eight months."

They went back up the road. A week ago—or before last night, that is—he would have asked where they were going, but not now. His father had struck him before last night but never before had he paused afterward to explain why; it was as if the blow and the following calm, outrageous voice still rang, repercussed, divulging nothing to him save the terrible handicap of being young, the light weight of his few years, just heavy enough to prevent his soaring free of the world as it seemed to be ordered but not heavy enough to keep him footed solid in it, to resist it and try to change the course of events.

Presently he could see the grove of oaks and cedars and the other flowering trees and shrubs where the house would be, though not the house yet. They walked beside a fence massed with honeysuckle and Cherokee roses and came to a gate swinging open between two brick pillars, and now, beyond a sweep of drive, he saw the house for the first time and at that instant he forgot his father and the terror and despair both, and even when he remembered his father again (who had not stopped) the terror and despair did not return. Because, for all the twelve movings, they had sojourned until now in a poor country, a land of small farms and fields and houses, and he had never seen a house like this before. *Hit's big as a courthouse* he thought quietly, with a surge of peace and joy whose reason he could not have thought into words, being too young for that: *They are safe from him. People whose lives are a part of this peace and dignity are beyond his touch, he no more to them than a buzzing wasp: capable of stinging for a little moment but that's all; the spell of this peace and dignity rendering even the barns and stable and cribs which belong to it impervious to the puny flames he might contrive* . . . this, the peace and joy, ebbing for an instant as he looked again at the stiff black back, the stiff and implacable limp of the figure which was not dwarfed by the house, for the reason that it had never looked big anywhere and which now, against the serene columned backdrop, had more than ever that impervious quality of something cut ruthlessly from tin, depthless, as though, sidewise to the sun, it would cast no shadow. Watching him, the boy remarked the absolutely undeviating course which his father held and saw the stiff foot come squarely down in a pile of fresh droppings where a horse had stood in the drive and which his father could have avoided by a simple change of stride. But it ebbed only for a moment, though he could not have thought this into words either, walking on in the spell of the house, which he could even want but without envy, without sorrow, certainly never with that ravening and jealous rage which unknown to him walked in the ironlike black coat before him: *Maybe he will feel it too. Maybe it will even change him now from what maybe he couldn't help but be.*

They crossed the portico. Now he could hear his father's stiff foot as it came down on the boards with clocklike finality, a sound out of all proportion to the displacement of the body it bore and which was not dwarfed either by the white door before it, as though it had attained to a sort of vicious and ravening minimum not to be dwarfed by anything — the flat, wide, black hat, the formal coat of broadcloth which had once been black but which had now that friction-glazed greenish cast of the bodies of old house flies, the lifted sleeve which was too large, the lifted hand like a curled claw. The door opened so promptly that the boy knew the Negro must have been watching them all the time, an old man with neat grizzled hair, in a linen jacket, who stood barring the door with his body, saying, "Wipe yo foots, white man, fo you come in here. Major ain't home nohow."

"Get out of my way, nigger," his father said, without heat too, flinging the door back and the Negro also and entering, his hat still on his head. And now the boy saw the prints of the stiff foot on the doorjamb and saw them appear on the pale rug behind the machinelike deliberation of the foot which seemed to bear (or transmit) twice the weight which the body compassed. The Negro was shouting "Miss Lula! Miss Lula!" somewhere behind them, then the boy, deluged as though by a warm wave by a suave turn of the carpeted stair and a pendant glitter of chandeliers and a mute gleam of gold frames, heard the swift feet and saw her too, a lady—perhaps he had never seen her like before either—in a gray, smooth gown with lace at the throat and an apron tied at the waist and the sleeves turned back, wiping cake or biscuit dough from her hands with a towel as she came up the hall, looking not at his father at all but at the tracks on the blond rug with an expression of incredulous amazement.

"I tried," the Negro cried. "I tole him to . . ."

"Will you please go away?" she said in a shaking voice. "Major de Spain is not at home. Will you please go away?"

His father had not spoken again. He did not speak again. He did not even look at her. He just stood stiff in the center of the rug, in his hat, the shaggy iron-gray brows twitching slightly above the pebble-colored eyes as he appeared to examine the house with brief deliberation. Then with the same deliberation he turned; the boy watched him pivot on the good leg and saw the stiff foot drag round the arc of the turning, leaving a final long and fading smear. His father never looked at it, he never once looked down at the rug. The Negro held the door. It closed behind them, upon the hysteric and indistinguishable woman-wail. His father stopped at the top of the steps and scraped his boot clean on the edge of it. At the gate he stopped again. He stood for a moment, planted stiffly on the stiff foot, looking back at the house. "Pretty and white, ain't it?" he said. "That's sweat. Nigger sweat. Maybe it ain't white enough yet to suit him. Maybe he wants to mix some white sweat with it."

Two hours later the boy was chopping wood behind the house within which his mother and aunt and the two sisters (the mother and aunt, not the two girls, he knew that; even at this distance and muffled by walls the flat loud voices of the two girls emanated an incorrigible idle inertia) were setting up the stove to prepare a meal; when he heard the hooves and saw the linen-clad man on a fine sorrel mare, whom he recognized even before he saw the rolled rug in front of the Negro youth following on a fat bay carriage horse—a suffused, angry face vanishing, still at full gallop, beyond the corner of the house where his father and brother were sitting in the two tilted chairs; and a moment later, almost before he could have put the axe down, he heard the hooves again and watched the sorrel mare go back out of the yard, already galloping again. Then his father began to shout one of the sisters' names, who presently emerged backward from the kitchen door dragging the rolled rug along the ground by one end while the other sister walked behind it.

"If you ain't going to tote, go on and set up the wash pot," the first said.

"You, Sarty!" the second shouted. "Set up the wash pot!" His father appeared at the door, framed against that shabbiness, as he had been against that other bland perfection, impervious to either, the mother's anxious face at his shoulder.

"Go on," the father said. "Pick it up." The two sisters stopped, broad, lethargic; stooping, they presented an incredible expanse of pale cloth and a flutter of tawdry ribbons.

"If I thought enough of a rug to have to git hit all the way from France I wouldn't keep hit where folks coming in would have to tromp on hit," the first said. They raised the rug.

"Abner," the mother said. "Let me do it."

"You go back and git dinner," his father said. "I'll tend to this."

From the woodpile through the rest of the afternoon the boy watched them, the rug spread flat in the dust beside the bubbling wash pot, the two sisters stooping over it with that profound and lethargic reluctance, while the father stood over them in turn, implacable and grim, driving them though never raising his voice again. He could smell the harsh homemade lye they were using; he saw his mother come to the door once and look toward them with an expression not anxious now but very like despair; he saw his father turn, and he fell to with the axe and saw from the corner of his eye his father raise from the ground a flattish fragment of field stone and examine it and return to the pot, and this time his mother actually spoke: "Abner. Abner. Please don't. Please, Abner."

Then he was done too. It was dusk; the whippoorwills had already begun. He could smell coffee from the room where they would presently eat the cold food remaining from the midafternoon meal, though when he entered the house he realized they were having coffee again probably because there was a fire on the hearth, before which the rug now lay spread over the backs of the two chairs. The tracks of his father's foot were gone. Where they had been were now long, water-cloudy scoriations resembling the sporadic course of a lilliputian mowing machine.

It still hung there while they ate the cold food and then went to bed, scattered without order or claim up and down the two rooms, his mother in one bed, where his father would later lie, the older brother in the other, himself, the aunt, and the two sisters on pallets on the floor. But his father was not in bed yet. The last thing the boy remembered was the depthless, harsh silhouette of the hat and coat bending over the rug and it seemed to him that he had not even closed his eyes when the silhouette was standing over him, the fire almost dead behind it, the stiff foot prodding him awake. "Catch up the mule," his father said.

When he returned with the mule his father was standing in the black door, the rolled rug over his shoulder. "Ain't you going to ride?" he said.

"No. Give me your foot."

He bent his knee into his father's hand, the wiry, surprising power flowed smoothly, rising, he rising with it, on to the mule's bare back (they had owned a saddle once; the boy could remember it though not when or where) and with the same effortlessness his father swung the rug up in front of him. Now in the starlight they retraced the afternoon's path, up the dusty road rife with honeysuckle, through the gate and up the black tunnel of the drive to the lightless house, where he sat on the mule and felt the rough warp of the rug drag across his thighs and vanish.

"Don't you want me to help?" he whispered. His father did not answer and now he heard again that stiff foot striking the hollow portico with that wooden and clocklike deliberation, that outrageous overstatement of the weight it carried. The rug, hunched, not flung (the boy could tell that even in the darkness) from his father's shoulder struck the angle of wall and floor with a sound unbelievably loud, thunderous, then the foot again, unhurried and enormous; a light came on in the house and the boy sat, tense, breathing steadily and quietly and just a little fast, though the foot itself did not increase its beat at all, descending the steps now; now the boy could see him.

"Don't you want to ride now?" he whispered. "We kin both ride now," the light within the house altering now, flaring up and sinking. *He's coming down the stairs now,* he thought. He had already ridden the mule up beside the horse block; presently his father was up behind him and he doubled the reins over and slashed the mule across the neck, but before the animal could begin to trot the hard, thin arm came around him, the hard, knotted hand jerking the mule back to a walk.

In the first red rays of the sun they were in the lot, putting plow gear on the mules. This time the sorrel mare was in the lot before he heard it at all, the rider collarless and even bareheaded, trembling, speaking in a shaking voice as the woman in the house had done, his father merely looking up once before stooping again to the hame he was buckling, so that the man on the mare spoke to his stooping back:

"You must realize you have ruined that rug. Wasn't there anybody here, any of your women . . ." he ceased, shaking, the boy watching him, the older brother leaning now in the stable door, chewing, blinking slowly and steadily at nothing apparently. "It cost a hundred dollars. But you never had a hundred dollars. You never will. So I'm going to charge you twenty bushels of corn against your crop. I'll add it in your contract and when you come to the commissary you can sign it. That won't keep Mrs. de Spain quiet but maybe it will teach you to wipe your feet before you enter her house again."

Then he was gone. The boy looked at his father, who still had not spoken or even looked up again, who was now adjusting the logger-head in the hame.

"Pap," he said. His father looked at him—the inscrutable face, the shaggy brows beneath which the gray eyes glinted coldly. Suddenly the boy went toward him, fast, stopping as suddenly. "You done the best you could!" he cried. "If he wanted hit done different why didn't he wait and tell you how? He won't git no twenty bushels! He won't git none! We'll gether hit and hide hit! I kin watch . . ."

"Did you put the cutter back in that straight stock like I told you?"

"No, sir," he said.

"Then go do it."

That was Wednesday. During the rest of that week he worked steadily, at what was within his scope and some which was beyond it, with an industry that did not need to be driven nor even commanded twice; he had this from his mother, with the difference that some at least of what he did he liked to do, such as splitting wood with the half-size axe which his mother and aunt had earned, or saved money somehow, to present him with at Christmas. In company with the two older women (and on one afternoon, even one of the sisters), he built pens for the shoat and the cow which were part of his father's contract with the landlord, and one afternoon, his father being absent, gone somewhere on one of the mules, he went to the field.

They were running a middle buster now, his brother holding the plow straight while he handled the reins, and walking beside the straining mule, the rich black soil shearing cool and damp against his bare ankles, he thought *Maybe this is the end of it. Maybe even that twenty bushels that seems hard to have to pay for just a rug will be a cheap price for him to stop forever and always from being what he used to be;* thinking, dreaming now, so that his brother had to speak sharply to him to mind the mule: *Maybe he even won't collect the twenty bushels. Maybe it will all add up and balance and vanish—corn, rug, fire; the terror and grief; the being pulled two ways like between two teams of horses—gone, done with for ever and ever.*

Then it was Saturday; he looked up from beneath the mule he was harnessing and saw his father in the black coat and hat. "Not that," his father said. "The wagon gear." And then, two hours later, sitting in the wagon bed behind his father and brother on the seat, the wagon accomplished a final curve, and he saw the weathered paintless store with its tattered tobacco- and patent-medicine posters and the tethered wagons and saddle animals below the gallery. He mounted the gnawed steps behind his father and brother, and there again was the lane of quiet, watching faces for the three of them to walk through. He saw the man in spectacles sitting at the plank table and he did not need to be told this was a Justice of the Peace; he sent one glare of fierce, exultant, partisan defiance at the man in collar and cravat now, whom he had seen but twice before in his life, and that on a galloping horse, who now wore on his face an expression not of rage but of amazed unbelief which the boy could not have known was at the incredible circumstance of being sued by one of his own tenants, and came and stood against his father and cried at the Justice: "He ain't done it! He aint' burnt . . ."

"Go back to the wagon," his father said.

"Burnt?" the Justice said. "Do I understand this rug was burned too?"

"Does anybody here claim it was?" his father said. "Go back to the wagon." But he did not, he merely retreated to the rear of the room, crowded as that other had been, but not to sit down this time, instead, to stand pressing among the motionless bodies, listening to the voices:

"And you claim twenty bushels of corn is too high for the damage you did to the rug?"

"He brought the rug to me and said he wanted the tracks washed out of it. I washed the tracks out and took the rug back to him."

"But you didn't carry the rug back to him in the same condition it was in before you made the tracks on it."

His father did not answer, and now for perhaps half a minute there was no sound at all save that of breathing, the faint, steady suspiration of complete and intent listening.

"You decline to answer that, Mr. Snopes?" Again his father did not answer. "I'm going to find against you, Mr. Snopes. I'm going to find that you were responsible for the injury to Major de Spain's rug and hold you liable for it. But twenty bushels of corn seems a little high for a man in your circumstances to have to pay. Major de Spain claims it cost a hundred dollars. October corn will be worth about fifty cents. I figure that if Major de Spain can stand a ninety-five dollar loss on something he paid cash for, you can stand a five-dollar loss you haven't earned yet. I hold you in damages to Major de Spain to the amount of ten bushels of corn over and above your contract with him, to be paid to him out of your crop at gathering time. Court adjourned."

It had taken no time hardly, the morning was but half begun. He thought they would return home and perhaps back to the field, since they were late, far behind all other farmers. But instead his father passed on behind the wagon, merely indicating with his hand for the older brother to follow with it, and crossed the road toward the blacksmith shop opposite, pressing on after his father, overtaking him, speaking, whispering up at the harsh, calm face beneath the weathered hat: "He won't git no ten bushels neither. He won't git one. We'll . . ." until his father glanced for an instant down at him, the face absolutely calm, the grizzled eyebrows tangled above the cold eyes, the voice almost pleasant, almost gentle:

"You think so? Well, we'll wait till October anyway."

The matter of the wagon—the setting of a spoke or two and the tightening of the tires—did not take long either, the business of the tires accomplished by driving the wagon into the spring branch behind the shop and letting it stand there, the mules nuzzling into the water from time to time, and the boy on the seat with the idle reins, looking up the slope and through the sooty tunnel of the shed where the slow hammer rang and where his father sat on an upended cypress bolt, easily, either talking or listening, still sitting there when the boy brought the dripping wagon up out of the branch and halted it before the door.

"Take them on to the shade and hitch," his father said. He did so and returned. His father and the smith and a third man squatting on his heels inside the door were talking, about crops and animals; the boy, squatting too in the ammoniac dust and hoof-parings and scales of rust, heard his father tell a long and unhurried story out of the time before the birth of the older brother even when he had been a professional horse-trader. And then his father came up beside him where he stood before a tattered last year's circus poster on the other side of the store, gazing rapt and quiet at the scarlet horses, the incredible poisings and convolutions of tulle and tights and the painted leers of comedians, and said, "It's time to eat."

But not at home. Squatting beside his brother against the front wall, he watched his father emerge from the store and produce from a paper sack a segment of cheese and divide it carefully and deliberately into three with his pocket knife and produce crackers from the same sack. They all three squatted on the gallery and ate, slowly, without talking; then in the store again, they drank from a tin dipper tepid water smelling of the cedar bucket and of living beech trees. And still they did not go home. It was a horse lot this time, a tall rail fence upon and along which men stood and sat and out of which one by one horses were led, to be walked and trotted and then cantered back and forth along the road while the slow swapping and buying went on and the sun began to slant westward, they—the three of them—watching and listening, the older brother with his muddy eyes and his steady, inevitable tobacco, the father commenting now and then on certain of the animals, to no one in particular.

It was after sundown when they reached home. They ate supper by lamplight, then, sitting on the doorstep, the boy watched the night fully accomplish, listening to the whippoorwills and the frogs, when he heard his mother's voice: "Abner! No! No! Oh, God. Oh, God. Abner!" and he rose, whirled, and saw the altered light through the door where a candle stub now burned in a bottle neck on the table and his father, still in the hat and coat, at once formal and burlesque as though dressed carefully for some shabby and ceremonial violence, emptying the reservoir of the lamp back into the five-gallon kerosene can from which it had been filled, while the mother tugged at his arm until he shifted the lamp to the other hand and flung her back, not savagely or viciously, just hard, into the wall, her hands flung out against the wall for balance, her mouth open and in her face the same quality of hopeless despair as had been in her voice. Then his father saw him standing in the door.

"Go to the barn and get that can of oil we were oiling the wagon with," he said. The boy did not move. Then he could speak.

"What . . ." he cried. "What are you . . ."

"Go get that oil," his father said. "Go."

Then he was moving, running, outside the house, toward the stable: this the old habit, the old blood which he had not been permitted to choose for himself, which had been bequeathed him willy nilly and which had run for so long (and who knew where, battening on what of outrage and savagery and lust) before it came to him. *I could keep on,* he thought. *I could run on and on and never look back, never need to see his face again. Only I can't. I can't,* the rusted can in his hand now, the liquid sploshing in it as he ran back to the house and into it, into the sound of his mother's weeping in the next room, and handed the can to his father.

"Ain't you going to even send a nigger?" he cried. "At least you sent a nigger before!"

This time his father didn't strike him. The hand came even faster than the blow had, the same hand which had set the can on the table with almost excruciating care flashing from the can toward him too quick for him to follow it, gripping him by the back of his shirt and on to tiptoe before he had seen it quit the can, the face stooping at him in breathless and frozen ferocity, the cold, dead voice speaking over him to the older brother who leaned against the table, chewing with that steady, curious, sidewise motion of cows:

"Empty the can into the big one and go on. I'll catch up with you."

"Better tie him up to the bedpost," the brother said.

"Do like I told you," the father said. Then the boy was moving, his bunched shirt and the hard, bony hand between his shoulder-blades, his toes just touching the floor, across the room and into the other one, past the sisters sitting with spread heavy thighs in the two chairs over the cold hearth, and to where his mother and aunt sat side by side on the bed, the aunt's arms about his mother's shoulders.

"Hold him," the father said. The aunt made a startled movement. "Not you," the father said. "Lennie. Take hold of him. I want to see you do it." His mother took him by the wrist. "You'll hold him better than that. If he gets loose don't you know what he is going to do? He will go up yonder." He jerked his head toward the road. "Maybe I'd better tie him."

"I'll hold him," his mother whispered.

"See you do then." Then his father was gone, the stiff foot heavy and measured upon the boards, ceasing at last.

Then he began to struggle. His mother caught him in both arms, he jerking and wrenching at them. He would be stronger in the end, he knew that. But he had no time to wait for it. "Lemme go!" he cried. "I don't want to have to hit you!"

"Let him go!" the aunt said. "If he don't go, before God, I am going up there myself!"

"Don't you see I can't?" his mother cried. "Sarty! Sarty! No! No! Help me, Lizzie!"

Then he was free. His aunt grasped at him but it was too late. He whirled, running, his mother stumbled forward on to her knees behind him, crying to the nearer sister. "Catch him, Net! Catch him!" But that was too late too, the sister (the sisters were twins, born at the same time, yet either of them now gave the impression of being, encompassing as much living meat and volume and weight as any other two of the family) not yet having begun to rise from the chair, her head, face, alone merely turned, presenting to him in the flying instant an astonishing expanse of young female features untroubled by any surprise even, wearing only an expression of bovine interest. Then he was out of the room, out of the house, in the mild dust of the starlit road and the heavy rifeness of honeysuckle, the pale ribbon unspooling with terrific slowness under his running feet, reaching the gate at last and turning in, running, his heart and lungs drumming, on up the drive toward the lighted house, the lighted door. He did not knock, he burst in, sobbing for breath, incapable for the moment of speech; he saw the astonished face of the Negro in the linen jacket without knowing when the Negro had appeared.

"De Spain!" he cried, panted. "Where's . . ." then he saw the white man too emerging from a white door down the hall. "Barn!" he cried. "Barn!"

"What?" the white man said. "Barn?"

"Yes!" the boy cried. "Barn!"

"Catch him!" the white man shouted.

But it was too late this time too. The Negro grasped his shirt, but the entire sleeve, rotten with washing, carried away, and he was out that door too and in the drive again, and had actually never ceased to run even while he was screaming into the white man's face.

Behind him the white man was shouting, "My horse! Fetch my horse!" and he thought for an instant of cutting across the park and climbing the fence into the road, but he did not know the park nor how high the vine-massed fence might be and he dared not risk it. So he ran on down the drive, blood and breath roaring; presently he was in the road again though he could not see it. He could not hear either: the galloping mare was almost upon him before he heard her, and even then he held his course, as if the very urgency of his wild grief and need must in a moment more find him wings, waiting until the ultimate instant to hurl himself aside and into the weed-choked roadside ditch as the horse thundered past and on, for an instant in furious silhouette against the stars, the tranquil early summer night sky which, even before the shape of the horse and rider vanished, strained abruptly and violently upward: a long, swirling roar incredible and soundless, blotting the stars, and he springing up and into the road again, running again, knowing it was too late yet still running even after he heard the shot and, an instant later, two shots, pausing now without knowing he had ceased to run, crying "Pap! Pap!," running again before he knew he had begun to run, stumbling, tripping over something and scrabbling up again without ceasing to run, looking backward over his shoulder at the glare as he got up, running on among the invisible trees, panting, sobbing, "Father! Father!"

At midnight he was sitting on the crest of a hill. He did not know it was midnight and he did not know how far he had come. But there was no glare behind him now and he sat now, his back toward what he had called home for four days anyhow, his face toward the dark woods which he would enter when breath was strong again, small, shaking steadily in the chill darkness, hugging himself into the remainder of his thin, rotten shirt, the grief and despair now no longer terror and fear but just grief and despair. *Father. My father,* he thought. "He was brave!" he cried suddenly, aloud but not loud, no more than a whisper: "He was! He was in the war! He was in Colonel Sartoris' cav'ry!" not knowing that his father had gone to that war a private in the fine old European sense, wearing no uniform, admitting the authority of and giving fidelity to no man or army or flag, going to war as Malbrouck° himself did: for booty—it meant nothing and less than nothing to him if it were enemy booty or his own.

The slow constellations wheeled on. It would be dawn and then sunup after a while and he would be hungry. But that would be tomorrow and now he was only cold, and walking would cure that. His breathing was easier now and he decided to get up and go on, and then he found that he had been asleep because he knew it was almost dawn, the night almost over. He could tell that from the whippoorwills. They were everywhere now among the dark trees below him, constant and inflectioned and ceaseless, so that, as the instant for giving over to the day birds drew nearer and nearer, there was no interval at all between them. He got up. He was a little stiff, but walking would cure that too as it would the cold, and soon there would be the sun. He went on down the hill, toward the dark woods within which the liquid silver voices of the birds called unceasing—the rapid and urgent beating of the urgent and quiring heart of the late spring night. He did not look back.

[1939]

Malbrouck: John Churchill (1650–1722), duke of Marlborough.

ERNEST HEMINGWAY [1899–1961]

A Clean, Well-Lighted Place

It was late and everyone had left the café except an old man who sat in the shadow the leaves of the tree made against the electric light. In the day time the street was dusty, but at night the dew settled the dust and the old man liked to sit late because he was deaf and now at night it was quiet and he felt the difference. The two waiters inside the café knew that the old man was a little drunk, and while he was a good client they knew that if he became too drunk he would leave without paying, so they kept watch on him.

"Last week he tried to commit suicide," one waiter said.

"Why?"

"He was in despair."

"What about?"

"Nothing."

"How do you know it was nothing?"

"He has plenty of money."

They sat together at a table that was close against the wall near the door of the café and looked at the terrace where the tables were all empty except where the old man sat in the shadow of the leaves of the tree that moved slightly in the wind. A girl and a soldier went by in the street. The street light shone on the brass number on his collar. The girl wore no head covering and hurried beside him.

"The guard will pick him up," one waiter said.

"What does it matter if he gets what he's after?"

"He had better get off the street now. The guard will get him. They went by five minutes ago."

The old man sitting in the shadow rapped on his saucer with his glass. The younger waiter went over to him.

"What do you want?"

The old man looked at him. "Another brandy," he said.

"You'll be drunk," the waiter said. The old man looked at him. The waiter went away.

"He'll stay all night," he said to his colleague. "I'm sleepy now. I never get into bed before three o'clock. He should have killed himself last week."

The waiter took the brandy bottle and another saucer from the

176

counter inside the café and marched out to the old man's table. He put down the saucer and poured the glass full of brandy.

"You should have killed yourself last week," he said to the deaf man. The old man motioned with his finger. "A little more," he said. The waiter poured on into the glass so that the brandy slopped over and ran down the stem into the top saucer of the pile. "Thank you," the old man said. The waiter took the bottle back inside the café. He sat down at the table with his colleague again.

"He's drunk now," he said.

"He's drunk every night."

"What did he want to kill himself for?"

"How should I know."

"How did he do it?"

"He hung himself with a rope."

"Who cut him down?"

"His niece."

"Why did they do it?"

"Fear for his soul."

"How much money has he got?"

"He's got plenty."

"He must be eighty years old."

"Anyway I should say he was eighty."

"I wish he would go home. I never get to bed before three o'clock. What kind of hour is that to go to bed?"

"He stays up because he likes it."

"He's lonely. I'm not lonely. I have a wife waiting in bed for me."

"He had a wife once too."

"A wife would be no good to him now."

"You can't tell. He might be better with a wife."

"His niece looks after him. You said she cut him down."

"I know."

"I wouldn't want to be that old. An old man is a nasty thing."

"Not always. This old man is clean. He drinks without spilling. Even now, drunk. Look at him."

"I don't want to look at him. I wish he would go home. He has no regard for those who must work."

The old man looked from his glass across the square, then over at the waiters.

"Another brandy," he said, pointing to his glass. The waiter who was in a hurry came over.

"Finished," he said, speaking with that omission of syntax stupid people employ when talking to drunken people or foreigners. "No more tonight. Close now."

"Another," said the old man.

"No. Finished." The waiter wiped the edge of the table with a towel and shook his head.

The old man stood up, slowly counted the saucers, took a leather coin purse from his pocket and paid for the drinks, leaving half a peseta tip.

The waiter watched him go down the street, a very old man walking unsteadily but with dignity.

"Why didn't you let him stay and drink?" the unhurried waiter asked. They were putting up the shutters. "It is not half-past two."

"I want to go home to bed."

"What is an hour?"

"More to me than to him."

"An hour is the same."

"You talk like an old man yourself. He can buy a bottle and drink at home."

"It's not the same."

"No, it is not," agreed the waiter with a wife. He did not wish to be unjust. He was only in a hurry.

"And you? You have no fear of going home before your usual hour?"

"Are you trying to insult me?"

"No, hombre, only to make a joke."

"No," the waiter who was in a hurry said, rising from pulling down the metal shutters. "I have confidence. I am all confidence."

"You have youth, confidence, and a job," the older waiter said. "You have everything."

"And what do you lack?"

"Everything but work."

"You have everything I have."

"No. I have never had confidence and I am not young."

"Come on. Stop talking nonsense and lock up."

"I am of those who like to stay late at the café," the older waiter said. "With all those who do not want to go to bed. With all those who need a light for the night."

"I want to go home and into bed."

"We are of two different kinds," the older waiter said. He was now dressed to go home. "It is not only a question of youth and confidence although those things are very beautiful. Each night I am reluctant to close up because there may be some one who needs the café."

"Hombre, there are bodegas open all night long."

"You do not understand. This is a clean and pleasant café. It is well lighted. The light is very good and also, now, there are shadows of the leaves."

"Good night," said the younger waiter.

"Good night," the other said. Turning off the electric light he continued the conversation with himself. It is the light of course but it is necessary that the place be clean and pleasant. You do not want music. Certainly you do not want music. Nor can you stand before a bar with dignity although that is all that is provided for these hours. What did he fear? It was not fear or dread. It was a nothing that he knew too well. It was all a nothing and a man was nothing too. It was only that and light was all it needed and a certain cleanness and order. Some lived in it and never felt it but he knew it was nada y pues nada y pues nada. Our nada who art in nada, nada be thy name thy kingdom nada thy will be nada in nada as it is in nada. Give us this nada our daily nada and nada us our nada as we nada our nadas and nada us not into nada but deliver us from nada; pues nada. Hail nothing full of nothing, nothing is with thee. He smiled and stood before a bar with a shining steam pressure coffee machine.

"What's yours?" asked the barman.

"Nada."

"Otro loco mas," said the barman and turned away.

"A little cup," said the waiter.

The barman poured it for him.

"The light is very bright and pleasant but the bar is unpolished," the waiter said.

The barman looked at him but did not answer. It was too late at night for conversation.

"You want another copita?" the barman asked.

"No, thank you," said the waiter and went out. He disliked bars and bodegas. A clean, well-lighted café was a very different thing. Now, without thinking further, he would go home to his room. He would lie in the bed and finally, with daylight, he would go to sleep. After all, he said to himself, it is probably only insomnia. Many must have it.

[1933]

JOHN STEINBECK [1902–1968]

The Chrysanthemums

The high grey-flannel fog of winter closed off the Salinas Valley from the sky and from all the rest of the world. On every side it sat like a lid on the mountains and made of the great valley a closed pot. On the broad, level land floor the gang plows bit deep and left the black earth shining like metal where the shares had cut. On the foothill ranches across the Salinas River, the yellow stubble fields seemed to be bathed in pale cold sunshine, but there was no sunshine in the valley now in December. The thick willow scrub along the river flamed with sharp and positive yellow leaves.

It was a time of quiet and of waiting. The air was cold and tender. A light wind blew up from the southwest so that the farmers were mildly hopeful of a good rain before long; but fog and rain do not go together.

Across the river, on Henry Allen's foothill ranch there was little work to be done, for the hay was cut and stored and the orchards were plowed up to receive the rain deeply when it should come. The cattle on the higher slopes were becoming shaggy and rough-coated.

Elisa Allen, working in her flower garden, looked down across the yard and saw Henry, her husband, talking to two men in business suits. The three of them stood by the tractor shed, each man with one foot on the side of the little Fordson. They smoked cigarettes and studied the machine as they talked.

Elisa watched them for a moment and then went back to her work. She was thirty-five. Her face was lean and strong and her eyes were as clear as water. Her figure looked blocked and heavy in her gardening costume, a man's black hat pulled low down over her eyes, clod-hopper shoes, a figured print dress almost completely covered by a big corduroy apron with four big pockets to hold the snips, the trowel and scratcher, the seeds, and the knife she worked with. She wore heavy leather gloves to protect her hands while she worked.

She was cutting down the old year's chrysanthemum stalks with a pair of short and powerful scissors. She looked down toward the men by the tractor shed now and then. Her face was eager and mature and handsome; even her work with the scissors was overeager, overpowerful. The chrysanthemum stems seemed too small and easy for her energy.

180

She brushed a cloud of hair out of her eyes with the back of her glove, and left a smudge of earth on her cheek in doing it. Behind her stood the neat white farm house with red geraniums close-banked around it as high as the windows. It was a hard-swept looking little house with hard-polished windows, and a clean mud-mat on the front steps.

Elisa cast another glance toward the tractor shed. The strangers were getting into their Ford coupe. She took off a glove and put her strong fingers down into the forest of new green chrysanthemum sprouts that were growing around the old roots. She spread the leaves and looked down among the close-growing stems. No aphids were there, no sow-bugs or snails or cutworms. Her terrier fingers destroyed such pests before they could get started.

Elisa started at the sound of her husband's voice. He had come near quietly, and he leaned over the wire fence that protected her flower garden from cattle and dogs and chickens.

"At it again," he said. "You've got a strong new crop coming."

Elisa straightened her back and pulled on the gardening glove again. "Yes. They'll be strong this coming year." In her tone and on her face there was a little smugness.

"You've got a gift with things," Henry observed. "Some of those yellow chrysanthemums you had this year were ten inches across. I wish you'd work out in the orchard and raise some apples that big."

Her eyes sharpened. "Maybe I could do it, too. I've a gift with things, all right. My mother had it. She could stick anything in the ground and make it grow. She said it was having planters' hands that knew how to do it."

"Well, it sure works with flowers," he said.

"Henry, who were those men you were talking to?"

"Why, sure, that's what I came to tell you. They were from the Western Meat Company. I sold thirty head of three-year-old steers. Got nearly my own price, too."

"Good," she said. "Good for you."

"And I thought," he continued, "I thought how it's Saturday afternoon, and we might go into Salinas for dinner at a restaurant, and then to a picture show—to celebrate, you see."

"Good," she repeated. "Oh, yes. That will be good."

Henry put on his joking tone. "There's fights tonight. How'd you like to go to the fights?"

"Oh, no," she said breathlessly. "No, I wouldn't like fights."

"Just fooling, Elisa. We'll go to a movie. Let's see. It's two now. I'm going to take Scotty and bring down those steers from the hill. It'll take us maybe two hours. We'll go in town about five and have dinner at the Cominos Hotel. Like that?"

"Of course I'll like it. It's good to eat away from home."

"All right, then. I'll go get up a couple of horses."

She said, "I'll have plenty of time to transplant some of these sets, I guess."

She heard her husband calling Scotty down by the barn. And a little later she saw the two men ride up the pale yellow hillside in search of the steers.

There was a little square sandy bed kept for rooting the chrysanthemums. With her trowel she turned the soil over and over, and smoothed it and patted it firm. Then she dug ten parallel trenches to receive the sets. Back at the chrysanthemum bed she pulled out the little crisp shoots, trimmed off the leaves at each one with her scissors, and laid it on a small orderly pile.

A squeak of wheels and plod of hoofs came from the road. Elisa looked up. The country road ran along the dense bank of willows and cottonwoods that bordered the river, and up this road came a curious vehicle, curiously drawn. It was an old spring-wagon, with a round canvas top on it like the corner of a prairie schooner. It was drawn by an old bay horse and a little grey-and-white burro. A big stubble-bearded man sat between the cover flaps and drove the crawling team. Underneath the wagon, between the hind wheels, a lean and rangy mongrel dog walked sedately. Words were painted on the canvas, in clumsy, crooked letters. "Pots, pans, knives, sisors, lawn mores, Fixed." Two rows of articles, and the triumphantly definitive "Fixed" below. The black paint had run down in little sharp points beneath each letter.

Elisa, squatting on the ground, watched to see the crazy, loose-jointed wagon pass by. But it didn't pass. It turned into the farm road in front of her house, crooked old wheels skirling and squeaking. The rangy dog darted from between the wheels and ran ahead. Instantly the two ranch shepherds flew out at him. Then all three stopped, and with stiff and quivering tails, with taut straight legs, with ambassadorial dignity, they slowly circled, sniffing daintily. The caravan pulled up to Elisa's wire fence and stopped. Now the newcomer dog, feeling outnumbered, lowered his tail and retired under the wagon with raised hackles and bared teeth.

The man on the seat called out, "That's a bad dog in a fight when he gets started."

Elisa laughed. "I see he is. How soon does he generally get started?"

The man caught up her laughter and echoed it heartily. "Sometimes not for weeks and weeks," he said. He climbed stiffly down, over the wheel. The horse and the donkey dropped like unwatered flowers.

Elisa saw that he was a very big man. Although his hair and beard were greying, he did not look old. His worn black suit was wrinkled and spotted with grease. The laughter had disappeared from his face and eyes the moment his laughing voice ceased. His eyes were dark, and they were full of the brooding that gets in the eyes of teamsters and of sailors. The calloused hands he rested on the wire fence were cracked, and every crack was a black line. He took off his battered hat.

"I'm off my general road, ma'am," he said. "Does this dirt road cut over across the river to the Los Angeles highway?"

Elisa stood up and shoved the thick scissors in her apron pocket. "Well, yes, it does, but it winds around and then fords the river. I don't think your team could pull through the sand."

He replied with some asperity, "It might surprise you what them beasts can pull through."

"When they get started?" she asked.

He smiled for a second. "Yes. When they get started."

"Well," said Elisa, "I think you'll save time if you go back to the Salinas road and pick up the highway there."

He drew a big finger down the chicken wire and made it sing. "I ain't in any hurry, ma'am. I go from Seattle to San Diego and back every year. Takes all my time. About six months each way. I aim to follow nice weather."

Elisa took off her gloves and stuffed them in the apron pocket with the scissors. She touched the under edge of her man's hat, searching for fugitive hairs. "That sounds like a nice kind of a way to live," she said.

He leaned confidentially over the fence. "Maybe you noticed the writing on my wagon. I mend pots and sharpen knives and scissors. You got any of them things to do?"

"Oh, no," she said, quickly. "Nothing like that." Her eyes hardened with resistance.

"Scissors is the worst thing," he explained. "Most people just ruin scissors trying to sharpen 'em, but I know how. I got a special tool. It's a little bobbit kind of thing, and patented. But it sure does the trick."

"No. My scissors are all sharp."

"All right, then. Take a pot," he continued earnestly, "a bent pot, or a pot with a hole. I can make it like new so you don't have to buy no new ones. That's a savings for you."

"No," she said shortly. "I tell you I have nothing like that for you to do."

His face fell to an exaggerated sadness. His voice took on a whining undertone. "I ain't had a thing to do today. Maybe I won't have no supper tonight. You see I'm off my regular road. I know folks on the highway clear from Seattle to San Diego. They save their things for me to sharpen up because they know I do it so good and save them money."

"I'm sorry," Elisa said irritably. "I haven't anything for you to do."

His eyes left her face and fell to searching the ground. They roamed about until they came to the chrysanthemum bed where she had been working. "What's them plants, ma'am?"

The irritation and resistance melted from Elisa's face. "Oh, those are chrysanthemums, giant whites and yellows. I raise them every year, bigger than anybody around here."

"Kind of a long-stemmed flower? Looks like a quick puff of colored smoke?" he asked.

"That's it. What a nice way to describe them."

"They smell kind of nasty till you get used to them," he said.

"It's a good bitter smell," she retorted, "not nasty at all."

He changed his tone quickly, "I like the smell myself."

"I had ten-inch-blooms this year," she said.

The man leaned farther over the fence. "Look, I know a lady down the road a piece, has got the nicest garden you ever seen. Got nearly every kind of flower but no chrysanthemums. Last time I was mending a copper-bottom washtub for her (that's a hard job but I do it good), she said to me, 'If you ever run acrost some nice chrysanthemums I wish you'd try to get me a few seeds.' That's what she told me."

Elisa's eyes grew alert and eager. "She couldn't have known much about chrysanthemums. You *can* raise them from seed, but it's much easier to root the little sprouts you see there."

"Oh," he said. "I s'pose I can't take none to her, then."

"Why yes you can," Elisa cried. "I can put some in damp sand, and you can carry them right along with you. They'll take root in the pot if you keep them damp. And then she can transplant them."

"She'd sure like to have some, ma'am. You say they're nice ones?"

"Beautiful," she said. "Oh, beautiful." Her eyes shone. She tore off the battered hat and shook out her dark pretty hair. "I'll put them in a flower pot, and you can take them right with you. Come into the yard."

While the man came through the picket gate Elisa ran excitedly along the geranium-bordered path to the back of the house. And she returned carrying a big red flower pot. The gloves were forgotten now. She kneeled on the ground by the starting bed and dug up the sandy soil with her fingers and scooped it into the bright new flower pot. Then she picked up the little pile of shoots she had prepared. With her strong fingers she pressed them into the sand and tamped around them with her knuckles. The man stood over her. "I'll tell you what to do," she said. "You remember so you can tell the lady."

"Yes, I'll try to remember."

"Well, look. These will take root in about a month. Then she must set them out, about a foot apart in good rich earth like this, see?" She lifted a handful of dark soil for him to look at. "They'll grow fast and tall. Now remember this: In July tell her to cut them down, about eight inches from the ground."

"Before they bloom?" he asked.

"Yes, before they bloom." Her face was tight with eagerness. "They'll grow right up again. About the last of September the buds will start."

She stopped and seemed perplexed. "It's the budding that takes the most care," she said hesitantly. "I don't know how to tell you." She looked deep into his eyes, searchingly. Her mouth opened a little, and she seemed to be listening. "I'll try to tell you," she said. "Did you ever hear of planting hands?"

"Can't say I have, ma'am."

"Well, I can only tell you what it feels like. It's when you're picking off the buds you don't want. Everything goes right down into your finger-tips. You watch your fingers work. They do it themselves. You can feel how it is. They pick and pick the buds. They never make a mistake. They're with the plant. Do you see? Your fingers and the plant. You can feel that, right up your arm. They know. They never make a mistake. You can feel it. When you're like that you can't do anything wrong. Do you see that? Can you understand that?"

She was kneeling on the ground looking up at him. Her breast swelled passionately.

The man's eyes narrowed. He looked away self-consciously. "Maybe I know," he said. "Sometimes in the night in the wagon there—"

Elisa's voice grew husky. She broke in on him, "I've never lived as you do, but I know what you mean. When the night is dark—why, the stars are sharp-pointed, and there's quiet. Why, you rise up and up! Every pointed star gets driven into your body. It's like that. Hot and sharp and—lovely."

Kneeling there, her hand went out toward his legs in the greasy black trousers. Her hesitant fingers almost touched the cloth. Then her hand dropped to the ground. She crouched low like a fawning dog.

He said, "It's nice, just like you say. Only when you don't have no dinner, it ain't."

She stood up then, very straight, and her face was ashamed. She held the flower pot out to him and placed it gently in his arms. "Here. Put it in your wagon, on the seat, where you can watch it. Maybe I can find something for you to do."

At the back of the house she dug in the can pile and found two old and battered aluminum saucepans. She carried them back and gave them to him. "Here, maybe you can fix these."

His manner changed. He became professional. "Good as new I can fix them." At the back of his wagon he set a little anvil, and out of an oily tool box dug a small machine hammer. Elisa came through the gate to watch him while he pounded out the dents in the kettles. His mouth grew sure and knowing. At a difficult part of the work he sucked his underlip.

"You sleep right in the wagon?" Elisa asked.

"Right in the wagon, ma'am. Rain or shine I'm dry as a cow in there."

"It must be nice," she said. "It must be very nice. I wish women could do such things."

"It ain't the right kind of a life for a woman."

Her upper lip raised a little, showing her teeth. "How do you know? How can you tell?" she said.

"I don't know, ma'am," he protested. "Of course I don't know. Now here's your kettles, done. You don't have to buy no new ones."

"How much?"

"Oh, fifty cents'll do. I keep my prices down and my work good. That's why I have all them satisfied customers up and down the highway."

Elisa brought him a fifty-cent piece from the house and dropped it in his hand. "You might be surprised to have a rival some time. I can sharpen scissors, too. And I can beat the dents out of little pots. I could show you what a woman might do."

He put his hammer back in the oily box and shoved the little anvil out of sight. "It would be a lonely life for a woman, ma'am, and a scarey life, too, with animals creeping under the wagon all night." He climbed over the singletree, steadying himself with a hand on the burro's white rump. He settled himself in the seat, picked up the lines. "Thank you kindly, ma'am," he said. "I'll do like you told me; I'll go back and catch the Salinas road."

"Mind," she called, "if you're long in getting there, keep the sand damp."

"Sand, ma'am? . . . Sand? Oh, sure. You mean around the chrysanthemums. Sure I will." He clucked his tongue. The beasts leaned luxuriously into their collars. The mongrel dog took his place between the back wheels. The wagon turned and crawled out the entrance road and back the way it had come, along the river.

Elisa stood in front of her wire fence watching the slow progress of the caravan. Her shoulders were straight, her head thrown back, her eyes half-closed, so that the scene came vaguely into them. Her lips moved silently, forming the words "Good-bye—good-bye." Then she whispered, "That's a bright direction. There's a glowing there." The sound of her whisper startled her. She shook herself free and looked about to see whether anyone had been listening. Only the dogs had heard. They lifted their heads toward her from their sleeping in the dust, and then stretched out their chins and settled asleep again. Elisa turned and ran hurriedly into the house.

In the kitchen she reached behind the stove and felt the water tank. It was full of hot water from the noonday cooking. In the bathroom she tore off her soiled clothes and flung them into the corner. And then she scrubbed herself with a little block of pumice, legs and thighs, loins and chest and arms, until her skin was scratched and red. When she had dried herself she stood in front of a mirror in her bedroom and looked at her body. She tightened her stomach and threw out her chest. She turned and looked over her shoulder at her back.

After a while she began to dress, slowly. She put on her newest under-clothing and her nicest stockings and the dress which was the symbol of her prettiness. She worked carefully on her hair, penciled her eyebrows and rouged her lips.

Before she was finished she heard the little thunder of hoofs and the shouts of Henry and his helper as they drove the red steers into the cor-ral. She heard the gate bang shut and set herself for Henry's arrival.

His step sounded on the porch. He entered the house calling, "Elisa, where are you?"

"In my room, dressing. I'm not ready. There's hot water for your bath. Hurry up. It's getting late."

When she heard him splashing in the tub, Elisa laid his dark suit on the bed, and shirt and socks and tie beside it. She stood his polished shoes on the floor beside the bed. Then she went to the porch and sat primly and stiffly down. She looked toward the river road where the willow-line was still yellow with frosted leaves so that under the high grey fog they seemed a thin band of sunshine. This was the only color in the grey afternoon. She sat unmoving for a long time. Her eyes blinked rarely.

Henry came banging out of the door, shoving his tie inside his vest as he came. Elisa stiffened and her face grew tight. Henry stopped short and looked at her. "Why — why, Elisa. You look so nice!"

"Nice? You think I look nice? What do you mean by 'nice'?"

Henry blundered on. "I don't know. I mean you look different, strong and happy."

"I am strong? Yes, strong. What do you mean 'strong'?"

He looked bewildered. "You're playing some kind of a game," he said helplessly. "It's a kind of a play. You look strong enough to break a calf over your knee, happy enough to eat it like a watermelon."

For a second she lost her rigidity. "Henry! Don't talk like that. You didn't know what you said." She grew complete again. "I'm strong," she boasted, "I never knew before how strong."

Henry looked down toward the tractor shed, and when he brought his eyes back to her, they were his own again. "I'll get out the car. You can put on your coat while I'm starting."

Elisa went into the house. She heard him drive to the gate and idle down his motor, and then she took a long time to put on her hat. She pulled it here and pressed it there. When Henry turned the motor off she slipped into her coat and went out.

The little roadster bounced along on the dirt road by the river, raising the birds and driving the rabbits into the brush. Two cranes flapped heavily over the willow-line and dropped into the river-bed.

Far ahead on the road Elisa saw a dark speck. She knew.

She tried not to look as they passed it, but her eyes would not obey. She whispered to herself sadly, "He might have thrown them off the road. That wouldn't have been much trouble, not very much. But he kept the pot," she explained. "He had to keep the pot. That's why he couldn't get them off the road."

The roadster turned a bend and she saw the caravan ahead. She swung full around toward her husband so she could not see the little covered wagon and the mismatched team as the car passed them.

In a moment it was over. The thing was done. She did not look back.

She said loudly, to be heard above the motor. "It will be good, tonight, a good dinner."

"Now you're changed again," Henry complained. He took one hand from the wheel and patted her knee. "I ought to take you in to dinner oftener. It would be good for both of us. We get so heavy out on the ranch."

"Henry," she asked, "could we have wine at dinner?"

"Sure we could. Say! That will be fine."

She was silent for a while; then she said, "Henry, at those prize fights, do the men hurt each other very much?"

"Sometimes a little, not often. Why?"

"Well, I've read how they break noses, and blood runs down their chests. I've read how the fighting gloves get heavy and soggy with blood."

He looked around at her. "What's the matter, Elisa? I didn't know you read things like that." He brought the car to a stop, then turned to the right over the Salinas River bridge.

"Do any women ever go to the fights?" she asked.

"Oh, sure, some. What's the matter Elisa? Do you want to go? I don't think you'd like it, but I'll take you if you really want to go."

She relaxed limply in the seat. "Oh, no. No. I don't want to go. I'm sure I don't." Her face was turned away from him. "It will be enough if we can have wine. It will be plenty." She turned up her coat collar so he could not see that she was crying weakly—like an old woman.

[1938]

EUDORA WELTY [1909–2001]

A Worn Path

It was December—a bright frozen day in the early morning. Far out in the country there was an old Negro woman with her head tied in a red rag, coming along a path through the pinewoods. Her name was Phoenix Jackson. She was very old and small and she walked slowly in the dark pine shadows, moving a little from side to side in her steps, with the balanced heaviness and lightness of a pendulum in a grandfather clock. She carried a thin, small cane made from an umbrella, and with this she kept tapping the frozen earth in front of her. This made a grave and persistent noise in the still air, that seemed meditative like the chirping of a solitary little bird.

She wore a dark striped dress reaching down to her shoe tops, and an equally long apron of bleached sugar sacks, with a full pocket: all neat and tidy, but every time she took a step she might have fallen over her shoelaces, which dragged from her unlaced shoes. She looked straight ahead. Her eyes were blue with age. Her skin had a pattern all its own of numberless branching wrinkles and as though a whole little tree stood in the middle of her forehead, but a golden color ran underneath, and the two knobs of her cheeks were illumined by a yellow burning under the dark. Under the red rag her hair came down on her neck in the frailest of ringlets, still black, and with an odor like copper.

Now and then there was a quivering in the thicket. Old Phoenix said, "Out of my way, all you foxes, owls, beetles, jack rabbits, coons and wild animals! . . . Keep out from under these feet, little bobwhites. . . . Keep the big wild hogs out of my path. Don't let none of those come running my direction. I got a long way." Under her small black-freckled hand her cane, limber as a buggy whip, would switch at the brush as if to rouse up any hiding things.

On she went. The woods were deep and still. The sun made the pine needles almost too bright to look at, up where the wind rocked. The cones dropped as light as feathers. Down in the hollow was the mourning dove—it was not too late for him.

The path ran up a hill. "Seem like there is chains about my feet, time I get this far," she said, in the voice of argument old people keep to use with themselves. "Something always take a hold of me on this hill—pleads I should stay."

After she got to the top she turned and gave a full, severe look behind her where she had come. "Up through pines," she said at length. "Now down through oaks."

Her eyes opened their widest, and she started down gently. But before she got to the bottom of the hill a bush caught her dress.

Her fingers were busy and intent, but her skirts were full and long, so that before she could pull them free in one place they were caught in another. It was not possible to allow the dress to tear. "I in the thorny bush," she said. "Thorns, you doing your appointed work. Never want to let folks pass, no sir. Old eyes thought you was a pretty little *green* bush."

Finally, trembling all over, she stood free, and after a moment dared to stoop for her cane.

"Sun so high!" she cried, leaning back and looking, while the thick tears went over her eyes. "The time getting all gone here."

At the foot of this hill was a place where a log was laid across the creek.

"Now comes the trial," said Phoenix.

Putting her right foot out, she mounted the log and shut her eyes. Lifting her skirt, leveling her cane fiercely before her, like a festival figure in some parade, she began to march across. Then she opened her eyes and she was safe on the other side.

"I wasn't as old as I thought," she said.

But she sat down to rest. She spread her skirts on the bank around her and folded her hands over her knees. Up above her was a tree in a pearly cloud of mistletoe. She did not dare to close her eyes, and when a little boy brought her a plate with a slice of marble-cake on it she spoke to him. "That would be acceptable," she said. But when she went to take it there was just her own hand in the air.

So she left that tree, and had to go through a barbed-wire fence. There she had to creep and crawl, spreading her knees and stretching her fingers like a baby trying to climb the steps. But she talked loudly to herself: she could not let her dress be torn now, so late in the day, and she could not pay for having her arm or her leg sawed off if she got caught fast where she was.

At last she was safe through the fence and risen up out in the clearing. Big dead trees, like black men with one arm, were standing in the purple stalks of the withered cotton field. There sat a buzzard.

"Who you watching?"

In the furrow she made her way along.

"Glad this not the season for bulls," she said, looking sideways, "and the good Lord made his snakes to curl up and sleep in the winter. A pleasure I don't see no two-headed snake coming around that tree, where it come once. It took a while to get by him, back in the summer."

She passed through the old cotton and went into a field of dead corn. It whispered and shook and was taller than her head. "Through the maze now," she said, for there was no path.

Then there was something tall, black, and skinny there, moving before her.

At first she took it for a man. It could have been a man dancing in the field. But she stood still and listened, and it did not make a sound. It was as silent as a ghost.

"Ghost," she said sharply, "who be you the ghost of? For I have heard of nary death close by."

But there was no answer — only the ragged dancing in the wind.

She shut her eyes, reached out her hand, and touched a sleeve. She found a coat and inside that an emptiness, cold as ice.

"You scarecrow," she said. Her face lighted. "I ought to be shut up for good," she said with laughter. "My senses is gone. I too old. I the oldest people I ever know. Dance, old scarecrow," she said, "while I dancing with you."

She kicked her foot over the furrow, and with mouth drawn down, shook her head once or twice in a little strutting way. Some husks blew down and whirled in streamers about her skirts.

Then she went on, parting her way from side to side with the cane, through the whispering field. At last she came to the end, to a wagon track where the silver grass blew between the red ruts. The quail were walking around like pullets, seeming all dainty and unseen.

"Walk pretty," she said. "This the easy place. This the easy going."

She followed the track, swaying through the quiet bare fields, through the little strings of trees silver in their dead leaves, past cabins silver from weather, with the doors and windows boarded shut, all like old women under a spell sitting there. "I walking in their sleep," she said, nodding her head vigorously.

In a ravine she went where a spring was silently flowing through a hollow log. Old Phoenix bent and drank. "Sweet-gum makes the water sweet," she said, and drank more. "Nobody know who made this well, for it was here when I was born."

The track crossed a swampy part where the moss hung as white as lace from every limb. "Sleep on, alligators, and blow your bubbles." Then the track went into the road.

Deep, deep the road went down between the high green-colored banks. Overhead the live-oaks met, and it was as dark as a cave.

A black dog with a lolling tongue came up out of the weeds by the ditch. She was meditating, and not ready, and when he came at her she only hit him a little with her cane. Over she went in the ditch, like a little puff of milkweed.

Down there, her senses drifted away. A dream visited her, and she reached her hand up, but nothing reached down and gave her a pull. So she lay there and presently went to talking. "Old woman," she said to herself, "that black dog come up out of the weeds to stall you off, and now there he sitting on his fine tail, smiling at you."

A white man finally came along and found her—a hunter, a young man, with his dog on a chain.

"Well, Granny!" he laughed. "What are you doing there?"

"Lying on my back like a June-bug waiting to be turned over, mister," she said, reaching up her hand.

He lifted her up, gave her a swing in the air, and set her down. "Anything broken, Granny?"

"No sir, them old dead weeds is springy enough," said Phoenix, when she had got her breath. "I thank you for your trouble."

"Where do you live, Granny?" he asked, while the two dogs were growling at each other.

"Away back yonder, sir, behind the ridge. You can't even see it from here."

"On your way home?"

"No sir, I going to town."

"Why, that's too far! That's as far as I walk when I come out myself, and I get something for my trouble." He patted the stuffed bag he carried, and there hung down a little closed claw. It was one of the bob-whites, with its beak hooked bitterly to show it was dead. "Now you go on home, Granny!"

"I bound to go to town, mister," said Phoenix. "The time come around."

He gave another laugh, filling the whole landscape. "I know you old colored people! Wouldn't miss going to town to see Santa Claus!"

But something held old Phoenix very still. The deep lines in her face went into a fierce and different radiation. Without warning, she had seen with her own eyes a flashing nickel fall out of the man's pocket onto the ground.

"How old are you, Granny?" he was saying.

"There is no telling, mister," she said, "no telling."

Then she gave a little cry and clapped her hands and said, "Git on away from here, dog! Look! Look at that dog!" She laughed as if in admiration. "He ain't scared of nobody. He a big black dog." She whispered, "Sic him!"

"Watch me get rid of that cur," said the man. "Sic him, Pete! Sic him!"

Phoenix heard the dogs fighting, and heard the man running and throwing sticks. She even heard a gunshot. But she was slowly bending forward by that time, further and further forward, the lid stretched down over her eyes, as if she were doing this in her sleep. Her chin was lowered almost to her knees. The yellow palm of her hand came out from the fold of her apron. Her fingers slid down and along the ground under the piece of money with the grace and care they would have in lifting an egg from under a setting hen. Then she slowly straightened up, she stood erect, and the nickel was in her apron pocket. A bird flew by. Her lips moved. "God watching me the whole time. I come to stealing."

The man came back, and his own dog panted about them. "Well, I scared him off that time," he said, and then he laughed and lifted his gun and pointed it at Phoenix.

She stood straight and faced him.

"Doesn't the gun scare you?" he said, still pointing it.

"No, sir, I seen plenty go off closer by, in my day, and for less than what I done," she said, holding utterly still.

He smiled, and shouldered the gun. "Well, Granny," he said, "you must be a hundred years old, and scared of nothing. I'd give you a dime if I had any money with me. But you take my advice and stay home, and nothing will happen to you."

"I bound to go on my way, mister," said Phoenix. She inclined her head in the red rag. Then they went in different directions, but she could hear the gun shooting again and again over the hill.

She walked on. The shadows hung from the oak trees to the road like curtains. Then she smelled wood-smoke, and smelled the river, and she saw a steeple and the cabins on their steep steps. Dozens of little black children whirled around her. There ahead was Natchez shining. Bells were ringing. She walked on.

In the paved city it was Christmas time. There were red and green electric lights strung and crisscrossed everywhere, and all turned on in the daytime. Old Phoenix would have been lost if she had not distrusted her eyesight and depended on her feet to know where to take her.

She paused quietly on the sidewalk where people were passing by. A lady came along in the crowd, carrying an armful of red-, green-, and silver-wrapped presents; she gave off perfume like the red roses in hot summer, and Phoenix stopped her.

"Please, missy, will you lace up my shoe?" She held up her foot.

"What do you want, Grandma?"

"See my shoe," said Phoenix. "Do all right for out in the country, but wouldn't look right to go in a big building."

"Stand still then, Grandma," said the lady. She put her packages down on the sidewalk beside her and laced and tied both shoes tightly.

"Can't lace 'em with a cane," said Phoenix. "Thank you, missy. I doesn't mind asking a nice lady to tie up my shoe, when I gets out on the street."

Moving slowly and from side to side, she went into the big building, and into a tower of steps, where she walked up and around and around until her feet knew to stop.

She entered a door, and there she saw nailed up on the wall the document that had been stamped with the gold seal and framed in the gold frame, which matched the dream that was hung up in her head.

"Here I be," she said. There was a fixed and ceremonial stiffness over her body.

"A charity case, I suppose," said an attendant who sat at the desk before her.

But Phoenix only looked above her head. There was sweat on her face, the wrinkles in her skin shone like a bright net.

"Speak up, Grandma," the woman said. "What's your name? We must have your history, you know. Have you been here before? What seems to be the trouble with you?"

Old Phoenix only gave a twitch to her face as if a fly were bothering her.

"Are you deaf?" cried the attendant.

But then the nurse came in.

"Oh, that's just old Aunt Phoenix," she said. "She doesn't come for herself—she has a little grandson. She makes these trips just as regular as clockwork. She lives away back off the Old Natchez Trace." She bent down. "Well, Aunt Phoenix, why don't you just take a seat? We won't keep you standing after your long trip." She pointed.

The old woman sat down, bolt upright in the chair.

"Now, how is the boy?" asked the nurse.

Old Phoenix did not speak.

"I said, how is the boy?"

But Phoenix only waited and stared straight ahead, her face very solemn and withdrawn into rigidity.

"Is his throat any better?" asked the nurse. "Aunt Phoenix, don't you hear me? Is your grandson's throat any better since the last time you came for the medicine?"

With her hands on her knees, the old woman waited, silent, erect and motionless, just as if she were in armor.

"You mustn't take up our time this way, Aunt Phoenix," the nurse said. "Tell us quickly about your grandson, and get it over. He isn't dead, is he?"

At last there came a flicker and then a flame of comprehension across her face, and she spoke.

"My grandson. It was my memory had left me. There I sat and forgot why I made my long trip."

"Forgot?" The nurse frowned. "After you came so far?"

Then Phoenix was like an old woman begging a dignified forgiveness for waking up frightened in the night. "I never did go to school, I was too old at the Surrender," she said in a soft voice. "I'm an old woman without an education. It was my memory fail me. My little grandson, he is just the same, and I forgot it in the coming."

"Throat never heals, does it?" said the nurse, speaking in a loud, sure voice to old Phoenix. By now she had a card with something written on it, a little list. "Yes. Swallowed lye. When was it?—January—two, three years ago—"

Phoenix spoke unasked now. "No, missy, he not dead, he just the same. Every little while his throat began to close up again, and he not able to swallow. He not get his breath. He not able to help himself. So the time come around, and I go on another trip for the soothing medicine."

"All right. The doctor said as long as you came to get it, you could have it," said the nurse. "But it's an obstinate case."

"My little grandson, he sit up there in the house all wrapped up, waiting by himself," Phoenix went on. "We is the only two left in the world. He suffer and it don't seem to put him back at all. He got a sweet look. He going to last. He wear a little patch quilt and peep out holding his mouth open like a little bird. I remembers so plain now. I not going to forget him again, no, the whole enduring time. I could tell him from all the others in creation."

"All right." The nurse was trying to hush her now. She brought her a bottle of medicine. "Charity," she said, making a check mark in a book.

Old Phoenix held the bottle close to her eyes, and then carefully put it into her pocket.

"I thank you," she said.

"It's Christmas time, Grandma," said the attendant. "Could I give you a few pennies out of my purse?"

"Five pennies is a nickel," said Phoenix stiffly.

"Here's a nickel," said the attendant.

Phoenix rose carefully and held out her hand. She received the nickel and then fished the other nickel out of her pocket and laid it beside the new one. She stared at her palm closely, with her head on one side.

Then she gave a tap with her cane on the floor.

"This is what come to me to do," she said. "I going to the store and buy my child a little windmill they sells, made out of paper. He going to find it hard to believe there such a thing in the world. I'll march myself back where he waiting, holding it straight up in this hand."

She lifted her free hand, gave a little nod, turned around, and walked out of the doctor's office. Then her slow step began on the stairs, going down.

[1941]

Battle Royal

It goes a long way back, some twenty years. All my life I had been looking for something, and everywhere I turned someone tried to tell me
what it was. I accepted their answers too, though they were often in contradiction and even self-contradictory. I was naïve. I was looking for
myself and asking everyone except myself questions which I, and only I,
could answer. It took me a long time and much painful boomeranging of
my expectations to achieve a realization everyone else appears to have
been born with: That I am nobody but myself. But first I had to discover
that I am an invisible man!

And yet I am no freak of nature, nor of history. I was in the cards,
other things having been equal (or unequal) eighty-five years ago. I am
not ashamed of my grandparents for having been slaves. I am only
ashamed of myself for having at one time been ashamed. About eighty-
five years ago they were told that they were free, united with others of
our country in everything pertaining to the common good, and, in everything social, separate like the fingers of the hand. And they believed it.
They exulted in it. They stayed in their place, worked hard, and brought
up my father to do the same. But my grandfather is the one. He was an
odd old guy, my grandfather, and I am told I take after him. It was he
who caused the trouble. On his deathbed he called my father to him and
said, "Son, after I'm gone I want you to keep up the good fight. I never
told you, but our life is a war and I have been a traitor all my born days,
a spy in the enemy's country ever since I give up my gun back in the
Reconstruction. Live with your head in the lion's mouth. I want you to
overcome 'em with yeses, undermine 'em with grins, agree 'em to death
and destruction, let 'em swoller you till they vomit or bust wide open."
They thought the old man had gone out of his mind. He had been the
meekest of men. The younger children were rushed from the room, the
shades drawn, and the flame of the lamp turned so low that it sputtered
on the wick like the old man's breathing. "Learn it to the younguns," he
whispered fiercely; then he died.

But my folks were more alarmed over his last words than over his
dying. It was as though he had not died at all, his words caused so much
anxiety. I was warned emphatically to forget what he had said and,

indeed, this is the first time it has been mentioned outside the family circle. It had a tremendous effect upon me, however. I could never be sure of what he meant. Grandfather had been a quiet old man who never made any trouble, yet on his deathbed he had called himself a traitor and a spy, and he had spoken of his meekness as a dangerous activity. It became a constant puzzle which lay unanswered in the back of my mind. And whenever things went well for me I remembered my grandfather and felt guilty and uncomfortable. It was as though I was carrying out his advice in spite of myself. And to make it worse, everyone loved me for it. I was praised by the most lily-white men of the town. I was considered an example of desirable conduct—just as my grandfather had been. And what puzzled me was that the old man had defined it as *treachery*. When I was praised for my conduct I felt a guilt that in some way I was doing something that was really against the wishes of the white folks, that if they had understood they would have desired me to act just the opposite, that I should have been sulky and mean, and that that really would have been what they wanted, even though they were fooled and thought they wanted me to act as I did. It made me afraid that some day they would look upon me as a traitor and I would be lost. Still I was more afraid to act any other way because they didn't like that at all. The old man's words were like a curse. On my graduation day I delivered an oration in which I showed that humility was the secret, indeed, the very essence of progress. (Not that I believed this—how could I, remembering my grandfather?—I only believed that it worked.) It was a great success. Everyone praised me and I was invited to give the speech at a gathering of the town's leading white citizens. It was a triumph for our whole community.

It was in the main ballroom of the leading hotel. When I got there I discovered that it was on the occasion of a smoker, and I was told that since I was to be there anyway I might as well take part in the battle royal to be fought by some of my schoolmates as part of the entertainment. The battle royal came first.

All of the town's big shots were there in their tuxedoes, wolfing down the buffet foods, drinking beer and whiskey and smoking black cigars. It was a large room with a high ceiling. Chairs were arranged in neat rows around three sides of a portable boxing ring. The fourth side was clear, revealing a gleaming space of polished floor. I had some misgivings over the battle royal, by the way. Not from a distaste for fighting, but because I didn't care too much for the other fellows who were to take part. They were tough guys who seemed to have no grandfather's curse worrying their minds. No one could mistake their toughness. And besides, I suspected that fighting a battle royal might detract from the dignity of my speech. In those pre-invisible days I visualized myself as a potential

Booker T. Washington. But the other fellows didn't care too much for me either, and there were nine of them. I felt superior to them in my way, and I didn't like the manner in which we were all crowded together into the servants' elevator. Nor did they like my being there. In fact, as the warmly lighted floors flashed past the elevator we had words over the fact that I, by taking part in the fight, had knocked one of their friends out of a night's work.

We were led out of the elevator through a rococo hall into an ante-room and told to get into our fighting togs. Each of us was issued a pair of boxing gloves and ushered out into the big mirrored hall, which we entered looking cautiously about us and whispering, lest we might accidentally be heard above the noise of the room. It was foggy with cigar smoke. And already the whiskey was taking effect. I was shocked to see some of the most important men of the town quite tipsy. They were all there — bankers, lawyers, judges, doctors, fire chiefs, teachers, merchants. Even one of the more fashionable pastors. Something we could not see was going on up front. A clarinet was vibrating sensuously and the men were standing up and moving eagerly forward. We were a small tight group, clustered together, our bare upper bodies touching and shining with anticipatory sweat; while up front the big shots were becoming increasingly excited over something we still could not see. Suddenly I heard the school superintendent, who had told me to come, yell, "Bring up the shines, gentlemen! Bring up the little shines!"

We were rushed up to the front of the ballroom, where it smelled even more strongly of tobacco and whiskey. Then we were pushed into place. I almost wet my pants. A sea of faces, some hostile, some amused, ringed around us, and in the center, facing us, stood a magnificent blonde — stark naked. There was dead silence. I felt a blast of cold air chill me. I tried to back away, but they were behind me and around me. Some of the boys stood with lowered heads, trembling. I felt a wave of irrational guilt and fear. My teeth chattered, my skin turned to goose flesh, my knees knocked. Yet I was strongly attracted and looked in spite of myself. Had the price of looking been blindness, I would have looked. The hair was yellow like that of a circus kewpie doll, the face heavily powdered and rouged, as though to form an abstract mask, the eyes hollow and smeared a cool blue, the color of a baboon's butt. I felt a desire to spit upon her as my eyes brushed slowly over her body. Her breasts were firm and round as the domes of East Indian temples, and I stood so close as to see the fine skin texture and beads of pearly perspiration glistening like dew around the pink and erected buds of her nipples. I wanted at one and the same time to run from the room, to sink through the floor, or go to her and cover her from my eyes and the eyes of the others with my body; to feel the soft thighs, to caress her and destroy her, to love her and murder her, to hide from her, and yet to stroke where below the small American flag tattooed upon her belly her thighs formed a capital V. I had a notion that of all in the room she saw only me with her impersonal eyes.

And then she began to dance, a slow sensuous movement; the smoke of a hundred cigars clinging to her like the thinnest of veils. She seemed like a fair bird-girl girdled in veils calling to me from the angry surface of some gray and threatening sea. I was transported. Then I became aware of the clarinet playing and the big shots yelling at us. Some threatened us if we looked and others if we did not. On my right I saw one boy faint. And now a man grabbed a silver pitcher from a table and stepped close as he dashed ice water upon him and stood him up and forced two of us to support him as his head hung and moans issued from his thick bluish lips. Another boy began to plead to go home. He was the largest of the group, wearing dark red fighting trunks much too small to conceal the erection which projected from him as though in answer to the insinuating low-registered moaning of the clarinet. He tried to hide himself with his boxing gloves.

And all the while the blonde continued dancing, smiling faintly at the big shots who watched her with fascination, and faintly smiling at our fear. I noticed a certain merchant who followed her hungrily, his lips loose and drooling. He was a large man who wore diamond studs in a shirtfront which swelled with the ample paunch underneath, and each time the blonde swayed her undulating hips he ran his hand through the thin hair of his bald head and, with his arms upheld, his posture clumsy like that of an intoxicated panda, wound his belly in a slow and obscene grind. This creature was completely hypnotized. The music had quickened. As the dancer flung herself about with a detached expression on her face, the men began reaching out to touch her. I could see their beefy fingers sink into her soft flesh. Some of the others tried to stop them and she began to move around the floor in graceful circles, as they gave chase, slipping and sliding over the polished floor. It was mad. Chairs went crashing, drinks were spilt, as they ran laughing and howling after her. They caught her just as she reached a door, raised her from the floor, and tossed her as college boys are tossed at a hazing, and above her red fixed-smiling lips I saw the terror and disgust in her eyes, almost like my own terror and that which I saw in some of the other boys. As I watched, they tossed her twice and her soft breasts seemed to flatten against the air and her legs flung wildly as she spun. Some of the more sober ones helped her to escape. And I started off the floor, heading for the anteroom with the rest of the boys.

Some were still crying and in hysteria. But as we tried to leave we were stopped and ordered to get into the ring. There was nothing to do but what we were told. All ten of us climbed under the ropes and allowed ourselves to be blindfolded with broad bands of white cloth. One of the men seemed to feel a bit sympathetic and tried to cheer us up as we stood with our backs against the ropes. Some of us tried to grin. "See that boy over there?" one of the men said. "I want you to run across at the bell and give it to him right in the belly. If you don't get him, I'm going to get you. I don't like his looks." Each of us was told the same. The blindfolds were put on. Yet even then I had been going over my speech. In my mind each word was as bright as flame. I felt the cloth pressed into place, and frowned so that it would be loosened when I relaxed.

But now I felt a sudden fit of blind terror. I was unused to darkness. It was as though I had suddenly found myself in a dark room filled with poisonous cottonmouths. I could hear the bleary voices yelling insistently for the battle royal to begin.

"Get going in there!"

"Let me at that big nigger!"

I strained to pick up the school superintendent's voice, as though to squeeze some security out of that slightly more familiar sound.

"Let me at those black sonsabitches!" someone yelled.

"No, Jackson, no!" another voice yelled. "Here, somebody, help me hold Jack."

"I want to get at that ginger-colored nigger. Tear him limb from limb," the first voice yelled.

I stood against the ropes trembling. For in those days I was what they called ginger-colored, and he sounded as though he might crunch me between his teeth like a crisp ginger cookie.

Quite a struggle was going on. Chairs were being kicked about and I could hear voices grunting as with a terrific effort. I wanted to see, to see more desperately than ever before. But the blindfold was as tight as a thick skin-puckering scab and when I raised my gloved hands to push the layers of white aside a voice yelled, "Oh, no you don't, black bastard! Leave that alone!"

"Ring the bell before Jackson kills him a coon!" someone boomed in the sudden silence. And I heard the bell clang and the sound of the feet scuffling forward.

A glove smacked against my head. I pivoted, striking out stiffly as someone went past, and felt the jar ripple along the length of my arm to my shoulder. Then it seemed as though all nine of the boys had turned upon me at once. Blows pounded me from all sides while I struck out as best I could. So many blows landed upon me that I wondered if I were not the only blindfolded fighter in the ring, or if the man called Jackson hadn't succeeded in getting me after all.

Blindfolded, I could no longer control my motions. I had no dignity. I stumbled about like a baby or a drunken man. The smoke had become thicker and with each new blow it seemed to sear and further restrict my lungs. My saliva became like hot bitter glue. A glove connected with my head, filling my mouth with warm blood. It was everywhere. I could not tell if the moisture I felt upon my body was sweat or blood. A blow landed hard against the nape of my neck. I felt myself going over, my head hitting the floor. Streaks of blue light filled the black world behind the blindfold. I lay prone, pretending that I was knocked out, but felt myself seized by hands and yanked to my feet. "Get going, black boy! Mix it up!" My arms were like lead, my head smarting from blows. I managed to feel my way to the ropes and held on, trying to catch my breath. A glove landed in my mid-section and I went over again, feeling as though the smoke had become a knife jabbed into my guts. Pushed this way and that by the legs milling around me, I finally pulled erect and discovered that I could see the black, sweat-washed forms weaving in the smoky-blue atmosphere like drunken dancers weaving to the rapid drum-like thuds of blows.

Everyone fought hysterically. It was complete anarchy. Everybody fought everybody else. No group fought together for long. Two, three, four, fought one, then turned to fight each other, were themselves attacked. Blows landed below the belt and in the kidney, with the gloves open as well as closed, and with my eye partly opened now there was not so much terror. I moved carefully, avoiding blows, although not too many to attract attention, fighting from group to group. The boys groped about like blind, cautious crabs crouching to protect their mid-sections, their heads pulled in short against their shoulders, their arms stretched nervously before them, with their fists testing the smoke-filled air like the knobbed feelers of hypersensitive snails. In one corner I glimpsed a boy violently punching the air and heard him scream in pain as he smashed his hand against a ring post. For a second I saw him bent over holding his hand, then going down as a blow caught his unprotected head. I played one group against the other, slipping in and throwing a punch then stepping out of range while pushing the others into the melee to take the blows blindly aimed at me. The smoke was agonizing and there were no rounds, no bells at three minute intervals to relieve our exhaustion. The room spun round me, a swirl of lights, smoke, sweating bodies surrounded by tense white faces. I bled from both nose and mouth, the blood spattering upon my chest.

The men kept yelling, "Slug him, black boy! Knock his guts out!"

"Uppercut him! Kill him! Kill that big boy!"

Taking a fake fall, I saw a boy going down heavily beside me as though we were felled by a single blow, saw a sneaker-clad foot shoot into his groin as the two who had knocked him down stumbled upon him. I rolled out of range, feeling a twinge of nausea.

The harder we fought the more threatening the men became. And yet, I had begun to worry about my speech again. How would it go? Would they recognize my ability? What would they give me?

I was fighting automatically and suddenly I noticed that one after another of the boys was leaving the ring. I was surprised, filled with panic, as though I had been left alone with an unknown danger. Then I understood. The boys had arranged it among themselves. It was the custom for the two men left in the ring to slug it out for the winner's prize. I discovered this too late. When the bell sounded two men in tuxedoes leaped into the ring and removed the blindfold. I found myself facing Tatlock, the biggest of the gang. I felt sick at my stomach. Hardly had the bell stopped ringing in my ears than it clanged again and I saw him moving swiftly toward me. Thinking of nothing else to do I hit him smash on the nose. He kept coming, bringing the rank sharp violence of stale sweat. His face was a black blank of a face, only his eyes alive—with hate of me and aglow with a feverish terror from what had happened to us all. I became anxious. I wanted to deliver my speech and he came at me as though he meant to beat it out of me. I smashed him again and again, taking his blows as they came. Then on a sudden impulse I struck him lightly and as we clinched, I whispered, "Fake like I knocked you out, you can have the prize."

"I'll break your behind," he whispered hoarsely.

"For *them*?"

"For *me*, sonofabitch!"

They were yelling for us to break it up and Tatlock spun me half around with a blow, and as a joggled camera sweeps in a reeling scene, I saw the howling red faces crouching tense beneath the cloud of blue-gray smoke. For a moment the world wavered, unraveled, flowed, then my head cleared and Tatlock bounced before me. That fluttering shadow before my eyes was his jabbing left hand. Then falling forward, my head against his damp shoulder, I whispered,

"I'll make it five dollars more."

"Go to hell!"

But his muscles relaxed a trifle beneath my pressure and I breathed, "Seven!"

"Give it to your ma," he said, ripping me beneath the heart.

And while I still held him I butted him and moved away. I felt myself bombarded with punches. I fought back with hopeless desperation. I wanted to deliver my speech more than anything else in the world, because I felt that only these men could judge truly my ability, and now this stupid clown was ruining my chances. I began fighting carefully now, moving in to punch him and out again with my greater speed. A lucky blow to his chin and I had him going too—until I heard a loud voice yell, "I got my money on the big boy."

Hearing this, I almost dropped my guard. I was confused: Should I try to win against the voice out there? Would not this go against my speech, and was not this a moment for humility, for nonresistance? A blow to my head as I danced about sent my right eye popping like a jack-in-the-box and settled my dilemma. The room went red as I fell. It was a dream fall, my body languid and fastidious as to where to land, until the floor became impatient and smashed up to meet me. A moment later I came to. An hypnotic voice said FIVE emphatically. And I lay there, hazily watching a dark red spot of my own blood shaping itself into a butterfly, glistening and soaking into the soiled gray world of the canvas.

When the voice drawled TEN I was lifted up and dragged to a chair. I sat dazed. My eye pained and swelled with each throb of my pounding heart and I wondered if now I would be allowed to speak. I was wringing wet, my mouth still bleeding. We were grouped along the wall now. The other boys ignored me as they congratulated Tatlock and speculated as to how much they would be paid. One boy whimpered over his smashed hand. Looking up front, I saw attendants in white jackets rolling the portable ring away and placing a small square rug in the vacant space surrounded by chairs. Perhaps, I thought, I will stand on the rug to deliver my speech.

Then the M.C. called to us, "Come on up here boys and get your money."

We ran forward to where the men laughed and talked in their chairs, waiting. Everyone seemed friendly now.

"There it is on the rug," the man said. I saw the rug covered with coins of all dimensions and a few crumpled bills. But what excited me, scattered here and there, were the gold pieces.

"Boys, it's all yours," the man said. "You get all you grab."

"That's right, Sambo," a blond man said, winking at me confidentially.

I trembled with excitement, forgetting my pain. I would get the gold and the bills, I thought. I would use both hands. I would throw my body against the boys nearest me to block them from the gold.

"Get down around the rug now," the man commanded, "and don't anyone touch it until I give the signal."

"This ought to be good," I heard.

As told, we got around the square rug on our knees. Slowly the man raised his freckled hand as we followed it upward with our eyes.

I heard, "These niggers look like they're about to pray!"

Then, "Ready," the man said. "Go!"

I lunged for a yellow coin lying on the blue design of the carpet, touching it and sending a surprised shriek to join those rising around me. I tried frantically to remove my hand but could not let go. A hot, violent force tore through my body, shaking me like a wet rat. The rug was electrified. The hair bristled up on my head as I shook myself free. My muscles jumped, my nerves jangled, writhed. But I saw that this was not stopping the other boys. Laughing in fear and embarrassment, some were holding back and scooping up the coins knocked off by the painful contortions of the others. The men roared above us as we struggled.

"Pick it up, goddamnit, pick it up!" someone called like a bass-voiced parrot. "Go on, get it!"

I crawled rapidly around the floor, picking up the coins, trying to avoid the coppers and to get greenbacks and the gold. Ignoring the shock by laughing, as I brushed the coins off quickly, I discovered that I could contain the electricity—a contradiction, but it works. Then the men began to push us onto the rug. Laughing embarrassedly, we struggled out of their hands and kept after the coins. We were all wet and slippery and hard to hold. Suddenly I saw a boy lifted into the air, glistening with sweat like a circus seal, and dropped, his wet back landing flush upon the charged rug, heard him yell and saw him literally dance upon his back, his elbows beating a frenzied tatoo upon the floor, his muscles twitching like the flesh of a horse stung by many flies. When he finally rolled off, his face was gray and no one stopped him when he ran from the floor amid booming laughter.

"Get the money," the M.C. called. "That's good hard American cash!"

And we snatched and grabbed, snatched and grabbed. I was careful not to come too close to the rug now, and when I felt the hot whiskey breath descend upon me like a cloud of foul air I reached out and grabbed the leg of a chair. It was occupied and I held on desperately.

"Leggo, nigger! Leggo!"

The huge face wavered down to mine as he tried to push me free. But my body was slippery and he was too drunk. It was Mr. Colcord, who owned a chain of movie houses and "entertainment palaces." Each time he grabbed me I slipped out of his hands. It became a real struggle. I feared the rug more than I did the drunk, so I held on, surprising myself for a moment by trying to topple *him* upon the rug. It was such an enormous idea that I found myself actually carrying it out. I tried not to be obvious, yet when I grabbed his leg, trying to tumble him out of the chair, he raised up roaring with laughter, and, looking at me with soberness dead in the eye, kicked me viciously in the chest. The chair leg flew out of my hand. I felt myself going and rolled. It was as though I had rolled through a bed of hot coals. It seemed a whole century would pass before I would roll free, a century in which I was seared through the deepest levels of my body to the fearful breath within me and the breath seared and heated to the point of explosion. It'll all be over in a flash, I thought as I rolled clear. It'll all be over in a flash.

But not yet, the men on the other side were waiting, red faces swollen as though from apoplexy as they bent forward in their chairs. Seeing their fingers coming toward me I rolled away as a fumbled football rolls off the receiver's fingertips, back into the coals. That time I luckily sent the rug sliding out of place and heard the coins ringing against the floor and the boys scuffling to pick them up and the M.C. calling, "All right, boys, that's all. Go get dressed and get your money."

I was limp as a dish rag. My back felt as though it had been beaten with wires.

When we had dressed the M.C. came in and gave us each five dollars, except Tatlock, who got ten for being last in the ring. Then he told us to leave. I was not to get a chance to deliver my speech, I thought. I was going out into the dim alley in despair when I was stopped and told to go back. I returned to the ballroom, where the men were pushing back their chairs and gathering in groups to talk.

The M.C. knocked on a table for quiet. "Gentlemen," he said, "we almost forgot an important part of the program. A most serious part, gentlemen. This boy was brought here to deliver a speech which he made at his graduation yesterday. . . ."

"Bravo!"

"I'm told that he is the smartest boy we've got out there in Greenwood. I'm told that he knows more big words than a pocket-sized dictionary."

Much applause and laughter.

"So now, gentlemen, I want you to give him your attention."

There was still laughter as I faced them, my mouth dry, my eye throbbing. I began slowly, but evidently my throat was tense, because they began shouting, "Louder! Louder!"

"We of the younger generation extol the wisdom of that great leader and educator," I shouted, "who first spoke these flaming words of wisdom: 'A ship lost at sea for many days suddenly sighted a friendly vessel. From the mast of the unfortunate vessel was seen a signal: "Water, water; we die of thirst!" The answer from the friendly vessel came back: "Cast down your bucket where you are." The captain of the distressed vessel, at last heeding the injunction, cast down his bucket, and it came up full of fresh sparkling water from the mouth of the Amazon River.' And like him I say, and in his words, 'To those of my race who depend upon bettering their condition in a foreign land, or who underestimate the importance of cultivating friendly relations with the Southern white man, who is his next-door neighbor, I would say: "Cast down your bucket where you are"—cast it down in making friends in every manly way of the people of all races by whom we are surrounded. . . .'"

I spoke automatically and with such fervor that I did not realize that the men were still talking and laughing until my dry mouth, filling up with blood from the cut, almost strangled me. I coughed, wanting to stop and go to one of the tall brass, sand-filled spittoons to relieve myself, but a few of the men, especially the superintendent, were listening and I was afraid. So I gulped it down, blood, saliva, and all, and continued. (What powers of endurance I had during those days! What enthusiasm! What a belief in the rightness of things!) I spoke even louder in spite of the pain. But still they talked and still they laughed, as though deaf with cotton in dirty ears. So I spoke with greater emotional emphasis. I closed my ears and swallowed blood until I was nauseated. The speech seemed a hundred times as long as before, but I could not leave out a single word. All had to be said, each memorized nuance considered, rendered. Nor was that all. Whenever I uttered a word of three or more syllables a group of voices would yell for me to repeat it. I used the phrase "social responsibility" and they yelled:

"What's the word you say, boy?"

"Social responsibility," I said.

"What?"

"Social . . ."

"Louder."

". . . responsibility."

"More!"

"Respon—"

"Repeat!"

"—sibility."

The room filled with the uproar of laughter until, no doubt, distracted by having to gulp down my blood, I made a mistake and yelled a phrase I had often seen denounced in newspaper editorials, heard debated in private.

"Social . . ."

"What?" they yelled.

". . . equality—"

The laughter hung smokelike in the sudden stillness. I opened my eyes, puzzled. Sounds of displeasure filled the room. The M.C. rushed forward. They shouted hostile phrases at me. But I did not understand.

A small dry mustached man in the front row blared out, "Say that slowly, son!"

"What sir?"

"What you just said!"

"Social responsibility, sir," I said.

"You weren't being smart, were you, boy?" he said, not unkindly.

"No, sir!"

"You sure that about 'equality' was a mistake?"

"Oh, yes, sir," I said. "I was swallowing blood."

"Well, you had better speak more slowly so we can understand. We mean to do right by you, but you've got to know your place at all times. All right, now, go on with your speech."

I was afraid. I wanted to leave but I wanted also to speak and I was afraid they'd snatch me down.

"Thank you, sir," I said, beginning where I had left off, and having them ignore me as before.

Yet when I finished there was a thunderous applause. I was surprised to see the superintendent come forth with a package wrapped in white tissue paper, and, gesturing for quiet, address the men.

"Gentlemen, you see that I did not overpraise this boy. He makes a good speech and some day he'll lead his people in the proper paths. And I don't have to tell you that that is important in these days and times. This is a good, smart boy, and so to encourage him in the right direction, in the name of the Board of Education I wish to present him a prize in the form of this . . ."

He paused, removing the tissue paper and revealing a gleaming calf-skin brief case.

". . . in the form of this first-class article from Shad Whitmore's shop."

"Boy," he said, addressing me, "take this prize and keep it well. Consider it a badge of office. Prize it. Keep developing as you are and some day it will be filled with important papers that will help shape the destiny of your people."

I was so moved that I could hardly express my thanks. A rope of bloody saliva forming a shape like an undiscovered continent drooled upon the leather and I wiped it quickly away. I felt an importance that I had never dreamed.

"Open it and see what's inside," I was told.

My fingers a-tremble, I complied, smelling the fresh leather and finding an official-looking document inside. It was a scholarship to the state college for Negroes. My eyes filled with tears and I ran awkwardly off the floor.

I was overjoyed; I did not even mind when I discovered that the gold pieces I had scrambled for were brass pocket tokens advertising a certain make of automobile.

When I reached home everyone was excited. Next day the neighbors came to congratulate me. I even felt safe from grandfather, whose deathbed curse usually spoiled my triumphs. I stood beneath his photograph with my brief case in hand and smiled triumphantly into his stolid black peasant's face. It was a face that fascinated me. The eyes seemed to follow everywhere I went.

That night I dreamed I was at a circus with him and that he refused to laugh at the clowns no matter what they did. Then later he told me to open my brief case and read what was inside and I did, finding an official envelope stamped with the state seal; and inside the envelope I found another and another, endlessly, and I thought I would fall of weariness. "Them's years," he said. "Now open that one." And I did and in it I found an engraved document containing a short message in letters of gold. "Read it," my grandfather said. "Out loud."

"To Whom It May Concern," I intoned. "Keep This Nigger-Boy Running."

I awoke with the old man's laughter ringing in my ears.

(It was a dream I was to remember and dream again for many years after. But at the time I had no insight into its meaning. First I had to attend college.)

[1952]

SHIRLEY JACKSON   [1919–1965]

The Lottery

The morning of June 27th was clear and sunny, with the fresh warmth of a full-summer day; the flowers were blossoming profusely and the grass was richly green. The people of the village began to gather in the square, between the post office and the bank, around ten o'clock; in some towns there were so many people that the lottery took two days and had to be started on June 26th, but in this village, where there were only about three hundred people, the whole lottery took less than two hours, so it could begin at ten o'clock in the morning and still be through in time to allow the villagers to get home for noon dinner.

The children assembled first, of course. School was recently over for the summer, and the feeling of liberty sat uneasily on most of them; they tended to gather together quietly for a while before they broke into boisterous play, and their talk was still of the classroom and teacher, of books and reprimands. Bobby Martin had already stuffed his pockets full of stones, and the other boys soon followed his example, selecting the smoothest and roundest stones; Bobby and Harry Jones and Dickie Delacroix—the villagers pronounced this name "Dellacroy"—eventually made a great pile of stones in one corner of the square and guarded it against the raids of the other boys. The girls stood aside, talking among themselves, looking over their shoulders at the boys, and the very small children rolled in the dust or clung to the hands of their older brothers or sisters.

Soon the men began to gather, surveying their own children, speaking of planting and rain, tractors and taxes. They stood together, away from the pile of stones in the corner, and their jokes were quiet and they smiled rather than laughed. The women, wearing faded house dresses and sweaters, came shortly after their menfolk. They greeted one another and exchanged bits of gossip as they went to join their husbands. Soon the women, standing by their husbands, began to call to their children, and the children came reluctantly, having to be called four or five times. Bobby Martin ducked under his mother's grasping hand and ran, laughing, back to the pile of stones. His father spoke up sharply, and Bobby came quickly and took his place between his father and his oldest brother.

The lottery was conducted—as were the square dances, the teen-age club, the Halloween program—by Mr. Summers, who had time and energy to devote to civic activities. He was a round-faced, jovial man and he ran the coal business, and people were sorry for him, because he had no children and his wife was a scold. When he arrived in the square, carrying the black wooden box, there was a murmur of conversation among the villagers, and he waved and called, "Little late today, folks." The postmaster, Mr. Graves, followed him, carrying a three-legged stool, and the stool was put in the center of the square and Mr. Summers set the black box down on it. The villagers kept their distance, leaving a space between themselves and the stool, and when Mr. Summers said, "Some of you fellows want to give me a hand?" there was a hesitation before two men, Mr. Martin and his oldest son, Baxter, came forward to hold the box steady on the stool while Mr. Summers stirred up the papers inside it.

The original paraphernalia for the lottery had been lost long ago, and the black box now resting on the stool had been put into use even before Old Man Warner, the oldest man in town, was born. Mr. Summers spoke frequently to the villagers about making a new box, but no one liked to upset even as much tradition as was represented by the black box. There was a story that the present box had been made with some pieces of the box that had preceded it, the one that had been constructed when the first people settled down to make a village here. Every year, after the lottery, Mr. Summers began talking again about a new box, but every year the subject was allowed to fade off without anything's being done. The black box grew shabbier each year; by now it was no longer completely black but splintered badly along one side to show the original wood color, and in some places faded or stained.

Mr. Martin and his oldest son, Baxter, held the black box securely on the stool until Mr. Summers had stirred the papers thoroughly with his hand. Because so much of the ritual had been forgotten or discarded, Mr. Summers had been successful in having slips of paper substituted for the chips of wood that had been used for generations. Chips of wood, Mr. Summers had argued, had been all very well when the village was tiny, but now that the population was more than three hundred and likely to keep on growing, it was necessary to use something that would fit more easily into the black box. The night before the lottery, Mr. Summers and Mr. Graves made up the slips of paper and put them in the box, and it was then taken to the safe of Mr. Summers's coal company and locked up until Mr. Summers was ready to take it to the square next morning. The rest of the year, the box was put away, sometimes one place, sometimes another; it had spent one year in Mr. Graves's barn and another year underfoot in the post office, and sometimes it was set on a shelf in the Martin grocery and left there.

There was a great deal of fussing to be done before Mr. Summers declared the lottery open. There were the lists to make up—of heads of families, heads of households in each family, members of each household in each family. There was the proper swearing-in of Mr. Summers by the postmaster, as the official of the lottery; at one time, some people remembered, there had been a recital of some sort, performed by the official of the lottery, a perfunctory, tuneless chant that had been rattled off duly each year; some people believed that the official of the lottery used to stand just so when he said or sang it, others believed that he was supposed to walk among the people, but years and years ago this part of the ritual had been allowed to lapse. There had been, also, a ritual salute, which the official of the lottery had had to use in addressing each person who came up to draw from the box, but this also had changed with time, until now it was felt necessary only for the official to speak to each person approaching. Mr. Summers was very good at all this; in his clean white shirt and blue jeans, with one hand resting carelessly on the black box, he seemed very proper and important as he talked interminably to Mr. Graves and the Martins.

Just as Mr. Summers finally left off talking and turned to the assembled villagers, Mrs. Hutchinson came hurriedly along the path to the square, her sweater thrown over her shoulders, and slid into place in the back of the crowd. "Clean forgot what day it was," she said to Mrs. Delacroix, who stood next to her, and they both laughed softly. "Thought my old man was out back stacking wood," Mrs. Hutchinson went on, "and then I looked out the window and the kids was gone, and then I remembered it was the twenty-seventh and came a-running." She dried her hands on her apron, and Mrs. Delacroix said, "You're in time, though. They're still talking away up there."

Mrs. Hutchinson craned her neck to see through the crowd and found her husband and children standing near the front. She tapped Mrs. Delacroix on the arm as a farewell and began to make her way through the crowd. The people separated good-humoredly to let her through; two or three people said, in voices just loud enough to be heard across the crowd, "Here comes your Missus, Hutchinson," and "Bill, she made it after all." Mrs. Hutchinson reached her husband, and Mr. Summers, who had been waiting, said cheerfully, "Thought we were going to have to get on without you, Tessie." Mrs. Hutchinson said, grinning, "Wouldn't have me leave m'dishes in the sink, now, would you, Joe?" and soft laughter ran through the crowd as the people stirred back into position after Mrs. Hutchinson's arrival.

"Well, now," Mr. Summers said soberly, "guess we better get started, get this over with, so's we can go back to work. Anybody ain't here?"

"Dunbar," several people said. "Dunbar, Dunbar."

Mr. Summers consulted his list. "Clyde Dunbar," he said. "That's right. He's broke his leg, hasn't he? Who's drawing for him?"

"Me, I guess," a woman said, and Mr. Summers turned to look at her. "Wife draws for her husband," Mr. Summers said. "Don't you have a grown boy to do it for you, Janey?" Although Mr. Summers and everyone else in the village knew the answer perfectly well, it was the business of the official of the lottery to ask such questions formally. Mr. Summers waited with an expression of polite interest while Mrs. Dunbar answered.

"Horace's not but sixteen yet," Mrs. Dunbar said regretfully. "Guess I gotta fill in for the old man this year."

"Right," Mr. Summers said. He made a note on the list he was holding. Then he asked, "Watson boy drawing this year?"

A tall boy in the crowd raised his hand. "Here," he said. "I'm drawing for m'mother and me." He blinked his eyes nervously and ducked his head as several voices in the crowd said things like "Good fellow, Jack," and "Glad to see your mother's got a man to do it."

"Well," Mr. Summers said, "guess that's everyone. Old Man Warner make it?"

"Here," a voice said, and Mr. Summers nodded.

A sudden hush fell on the crowd as Mr. Summers cleared his throat and looked at the list. "All ready?" he called. "Now, I'll read the names—

heads of families first—and the men come up and take a paper out of the box. Keep the paper folded in your hand without looking at it until everyone has had a turn. Everything clear?"

The people had done it so many times that they only half listened to the directions; most of them were quiet, wetting their lips, not looking around. Then Mr. Summers raised one hand high and said, "Adams." A man disengaged himself from the crowd and came forward. "Hi, Steve," Mr. Summers said, and Mr. Adams said, "Hi, Joe." They grinned at one another humorlessly and nervously. Then Mr. Adams reached into the black box and took out a folded paper. He held it firmly by one corner as he turned and went hastily back to his place in the crowd, where he stood a little apart from his family, not looking down at his hand.

"Allen," Mr. Summers said, "Anderson. . . . Bentham."

"Seems like there's no time at all between lotteries any more," Mrs. Delacroix said to Mrs. Graves in the back row. "Seems like we got through with the last one only last week."

"Time sure goes fast," Mrs. Graves said.

"Clark. . . . Delacroix."

"There goes my old man," Mrs. Delacroix said. She held her breath while her husband went forward.

"Dunbar," Mr. Summers said, and Mrs. Dunbar went steadily to the box while one of the women said, "Go on, Janey," and another said, "There she goes."

"We're next," Mrs. Graves said. She watched while Mr. Graves came around from the side of the box, greeted Mr. Summers gravely, and selected a slip of paper from the box. By now, all through the crowd there were men holding the small folded papers in their large hands, turning them over and over nervously. Mrs. Dunbar and her two sons stood together, Mrs. Dunbar holding the slip of paper.

"Harburt. . . . Hutchinson."

"Get up there, Bill," Mrs. Hutchinson said, and the people near her laughed.

"Jones."

"They do say," Mr. Adams said to Old Man Warner, who stood next to him, "that over in the north village they're talking of giving up the lottery."

Old Man Warner snorted. "Pack of crazy fools," he said. "Listening to the young folks, nothing's good enough for *them*. Next thing you know, they'll be wanting to go back to living in caves, nobody work any more, live *that* way for a while. Used to be a saying about 'Lottery in June, corn be heavy soon.' First thing you know, we'd all be eating stewed chickweed and acorns. There's *always* been a lottery," he added petulantly. "Bad enough to see young Joe Summers up there joking with everybody."

"Some places have already quit lotteries," Mrs. Adams said.

"Nothing but trouble in *that*," Old Man Warner said stoutly. "Pack of young fools."

"Martin." And Bobby Martin watched his father go forward. "Overdyke. . . . Percy."

"I wish they'd hurry," Mrs. Dunbar said to her older son. "I wish they'd hurry."

"They're almost through," her son said.

"You get ready to run tell Dad," Mrs. Dunbar said.

Mr. Summers called his own name and then stepped forward precisely and selected a slip from the box. Then he called, "Warner."

"Seventy-seventh year I been in the lottery," Old Man Warner said as he went through the crowd. "Seventy-seventh time."

"Watson." The tall boy came awkwardly through the crowd. Someone said, "Don't be nervous, Jack," and Mr. Summers said, "Take your time, son."

"Zanini."

After that, there was a long pause, a breathless pause, until Mr. Summers, holding his slip of paper in the air, said, "All right, fellows." For a minute, no one moved, and then all the slips of paper were opened. Suddenly, all the women began to speak at once, saying, "Who is it?" "Who's got it?" "Is it the Dunbars?" "Is it the Watsons?" Then the voices began to say, "It's Hutchinson. It's Bill," "Bill Hutchinson's got it."

"Go tell your father," Mrs. Dunbar said to her older son.

People began to look around to see the Hutchinsons. Bill Hutchinson was standing quiet, staring down at the paper in his hand. Suddenly, Tessie Hutchinson shouted to Mr. Summers, "You didn't give him time enough to take any paper he wanted. I saw you. It wasn't fair!"

"Be a good sport, Tessie," Mrs. Delacroix called, and Mrs. Graves said, "All of us took the same chance."

"Shut up, Tessie," Bill Hutchinson said.

"Well, everyone," Mr. Summers said, "that was done pretty fast, and now we've got to be hurrying a little more to get done in time." He consulted his next list. "Bill," he said, "you draw for the Hutchinson family. You got any other households in the Hutchinsons?"

"There's Don and Eva," Mrs. Hutchinson yelled. "Make *them* take their chance!"

"Daughters drew with their husbands' families, Tessie," Mr. Summers said gently. "You know that as well as anyone else."

"It wasn't *fair*," Tessie said.

"I guess not, Joe," Bill Hutchinson said regretfully. "My daughter draws with her husband's family, that's only fair. And I've got no other family except the kids."

"Then, as far as drawing for families is concerned, it's you," Mr. Summers said in explanation, "and as far as drawing for households is concerned, that's you, too. Right?"

"Right," Bill Hutchinson said.

"How many kids, Bill?" Mr. Summers asked formally.

"Three," Bill Hutchinson said. "There's Bill, Jr., and Nancy, and little Dave. And Tessie and me."

"All right, then," Mr. Summers said. "Harry, you got their tickets back?"

Mr. Graves nodded and held up the slips of paper. "Put them in the box, then," Mr. Summers directed. "Take Bill's and put it in."

"I think we ought to start over," Mrs. Hutchinson said, as quietly as she could. "I tell you it wasn't *fair*. You didn't give him time enough to choose. *Every*body saw that."

Mr. Graves had selected the five slips and put them in the box, and he dropped all the papers but those onto the ground, where the breeze caught them and lifted them off.

"Listen, everybody," Mrs. Hutchinson was saying to the people around her.

"Ready, Bill?" Mr. Summers asked, and Bill Hutchinson, with one quick glance around at his wife and children, nodded.

"Remember," Mr. Summers said, "take the slips and keep them folded until each person has taken one. Harry, you help little Dave." Mr. Graves took the hand of the little boy, who came willingly with him up to the box. "Take a paper out of the box, Davy," Mr. Summers said. Davy put his hand into the box and laughed. "Take just *one* paper," Mr. Summers said. "Harry, you hold it for him." Mr. Graves took the child's hand and removed the folded paper from the tight fist and held it while little Dave stood next to him and looked up at him wonderingly.

"Nancy next," Mr. Summers said. Nancy was twelve, and her school friends breathed heavily as she went forward, switching her skirt, and took a slip daintily from the box. "Bill, Jr.," Mr. Summers said, and Billy, his face red and his feet overlarge, nearly knocked the box over as he got a paper out. "Tessie," Mr. Summers said. She hesitated for a minute, looking around defiantly, and then set her lips and went up to the box. She snatched a paper out and held it behind her.

"Bill," Mr. Summers said, and Bill Hutchinson reached into the box and felt around, bringing his hand out at last with the slip of paper in it.

The crowd was quiet. A girl whispered, "I hope it's not Nancy," and the sound of the whisper reached the edges of the crowd.

"It's not the way it used to be," Old Man Warner said clearly. "People ain't the way they used to be."

"All right," Mr. Summers said. "Open the papers. Harry, you open little Dave's."

Mr. Graves opened the slip of paper and there was a general sigh through the crowd as he held it up and everyone could see that it was blank. Nancy and Bill, Jr., opened theirs at the same time, and both beamed and laughed, turning around to the crowd and holding their slips of paper above their heads.

"Tessie," Mr. Summers said. There was a pause, and then Mr. Summers looked at Bill Hutchinson, and Bill unfolded his paper and showed it. It was blank.

"It's Tessie," Mr. Summers said, and his voice was hushed. "Show us her paper, Bill."

Bill Hutchinson went over to his wife and forced the slip of paper out of her hand. It had a black spot on it, the black spot Mr. Summers had made the night before with the heavy pencil in the coal-company office. Bill Hutchinson held it up and there was a stir in the crowd.

"All right, folks," Mr. Summers said. "Let's finish quickly."

Although the villagers had forgotten the ritual and lost the original black box, they still remembered to use stones. The pile of stones the boys had made earlier was ready; there were stones on the ground with the blowing scraps of paper that had come out of the box. Mrs. Delacroix selected a stone so large she had to pick it up with both hands and turned to Mrs. Dunbar. "Come on," she said. "Hurry up."

Mrs. Dunbar had small stones in both hands, and she said, gasping for breath, "I can't run at all. You'll have to go ahead and I'll catch up with you."

The children had stones already, and someone gave little Davy Hutchinson a few pebbles.

Tessie Hutchinson was in the center of a cleared space by now, and she held her hands out desperately as the villagers moved in on her. "It isn't fair," she said. A stone hit her on the side of the head.

Old Man Warner was saying, "Come on, come on, everyone." Steve Adams was in the front of the crowd of villagers, with Mrs. Graves beside him.

"It isn't fair, it isn't right," Mrs. Hutchinson screamed and then they were upon her.

[1948]

A Conversation
with My Father

My father is eighty-six years old and in bed. His heart, that bloody
motor, is equally old and will not do certain jobs any more. It still floods
his head with brainy light. But it won't let his legs carry the weight of his
body around the house. Despite my metaphors, this muscle failure is
not due to his old heart, he says, but to a potassium shortage. Sitting on
one pillow, leaning on three, he offers last-minute advice and makes a
request.

"I would like you to write a simple story just once more," he says, "the
kind de Maupassant wrote, or Chekhov, the kind you used to write. Just
recognizable people and then write down what happened to them next."

I say, "Yes, why not? That's possible." I want to please him, though I
don't remember writing that way. I *would* like to try to tell such a story, if
he means the kind that begins: "There was a woman . . ." followed by
plot, the absolute line between two points which I've always despised.
Not for literary reasons, but because it takes all hope away. Everyone,
real or invented, deserves the open destiny of life.

Finally I thought of a story that had been happening for a couple of
years right across the street. I wrote it down, then read it aloud. "Pa," I
said, "how about this? Do you mean something like this?"

> Once in my time there was a woman and she had a son. They lived
> nicely, in a small apartment in Manhattan. This boy at about fifteen
> became a junkie, which is not unusual in our neighborhood. In order to
> maintain her close friendship with him, she became a junkie too. She
> said it was part of the youth culture, with which she felt very much at
> home. After a while, for a number of reasons, the boy gave it all up and
> left the city and his mother in disgust. Hopeless and alone, she grieved.
> We all visit her.

"O.K., Pa, that's it," I said, "an unadorned and miserable tale."

"But that's not what I mean," my father said. "You misunderstood me
on purpose. You know there's a lot more to it. You know that. You left

216

everything out. Turgenev wouldn't do that. Chekhov wouldn't do that. There are in fact Russian writers you never heard of, you don't have an inkling of, as good as anyone, who can write a plain ordinary story, who would not leave out what you have left out. I object not to facts but to people sitting in trees talking senselessly, voices from who knows where. . . ."

"Forget that one, Pa, what have I left out now? In this one?"

"Her looks, for instance."

"Oh. Quite handsome, I think. Yes."

"Her hair?"

"Dark, with heavy braids, as though she were a girl or a foreigner."

"What were her parents like, her stock? That she became such a person. It's interesting, you know."

"From out of town. Professional people. The first to be divorced in their county. How's that? Enough?" I asked.

"With you, it's all a joke," he said. "What about the boy's father? Why didn't you mention him? Who was he? Or was the boy born out of wedlock?"

"Yes," I said. "He was born out of wedlock."

"For Godsakes, doesn't anyone in your stories get married? Doesn't anyone have the time to run down to City Hall before they jump into bed?"

"No," I said. "In real life, yes. But in my stories, no."

"Why do you answer me like that?"

"Oh, Pa, this is a simple story about a smart woman who came to N.Y.C. full of interest love trust excitement very up to date, and about her son, what a hard time she had in this world. Married or not, it's of small consequence."

"It is of great consequence," he said.

"O.K.," I said.

"O.K. O.K. yourself," he said, "but listen. I believe you that she's good-looking, but I don't think she was so smart."

"That's true," I said. "Actually that's the trouble with stories. People start out fantastic. You think they're extraordinary, but it turns out as the work goes along, they're just average with a good education. Sometimes the other way around, the person's a kind of dumb innocent, but he outwits you and you can't even think of an ending good enough."

"What do you do then?" he asked. He had been a doctor for a couple of decades and then an artist for a couple of decades and he's still interested in details, craft, technique.

"Well, you just have to let the story lie around till some agreement can be reached between you and the stubborn hero."

"Aren't you talking silly now?" he asked. "Start again," he said. "It so happens I'm not going out this evening. Tell the story again. See what you can do this time."

"O.K.," I said. "But it's not a five-minute job." Second attempt:

Once, across the street from us, there was a fine handsome woman, our neighbor. She had a son whom she loved because she'd known him since birth (in helpless chubby infancy, and in the wrestling, hugging ages, seven to ten, as well as earlier and later). This boy, when he fell into the fist of adolescence, became a junkie. He was not a hopeless one. He was in fact hopeful, an ideologue and successful converter. With his busy brilliance, he wrote persuasive articles for his high-school newspaper. Seeking a wider audience, using important connections, he drummed into Lower Manhattan newsstand distribution a periodical called *Oh! Golden Horse!*

In order to keep him from feeling guilty (because guilt is the stony heart of nine tenths of all clinically diagnosed cancers in America today, she said), and because she had always believed in giving bad habits room at home where one could keep an eye on them, she too became a junkie. Her kitchen was famous for a while—a center for intellectual addicts who knew what they were doing. A few felt artistic like Coleridge° and others were scientific and revolutionary like Leary.° Although she was often high herself, certain good mothering reflexes remained, and she saw to it that there was lots of orange juice around and honey and milk and vitamin pills. However, she never cooked anything but chili, and that no more than once a week. She explained, when we talked to her, seriously, with neighborly concern, that it was her part in the youth culture and she would rather be with the young, it was an honor, than with her own generation.

One week, while nodding through an Antonioni film, this boy was severely jabbed by the elbow of a stern and proselytizing girl, sitting beside him. She offered immediate apricots and nuts for his sugar level, spoke to him sharply, and took him home.

She had heard of him and his work and she herself published, edited, and wrote a competitive journal called *Man Does Live by Bread Alone*. In the organic heat of her continuous presence he could not help but become interested once more in his muscles, his arteries, and nerve connections. In fact he began to love them, treasure them, praise them with funny little songs in *Man Does Live*. . . .

Coleridge: Samuel Taylor Coleridge (1772–1834), English Romantic poet, was an opium addict.
Leary: Timothy Leary (1920–1996), professor of psychology and early advocate of the use of LSD.

the fingers of my flesh transcend
my transcendental soul
the tightness in my shoulders end
my teeth have made me whole

To the mouth of his head (that glory of will and determination) he brought hard apples, nuts, wheat germ, and soybean oil. He said to his old friends, From now on, I guess I'll keep my wits about me. I'm going on the natch. He said he was about to begin a spiritual deep-breathing journey. How about you too, Mom? he asked kindly.

His conversion was so radiant, splendid, that neighborhood kids his age began to say that he had never been a real addict at all, only a journalist along for the smell of the story. The mother tried several times to give up what had become without her son and his friends a lonely habit. This effort only brought it to supportable levels. The boy and his girl took their electronic mimeograph and moved to the bushy edge of another borough. They were very strict. They said they would not see her again until she had been off drugs for sixty days.

At home alone in the evening, weeping, the mother read and reread the seven issues of *Oh! Golden Horse!* They seemed to her as truthful as ever. We often crossed the street to visit and console. But if we mentioned any of our children who were at college or in the hospital or dropouts at home, she would cry out, My baby! My baby! and burst into terrible, face-scarring, time-consuming tears. The End.

First my father was silent, then he said, "Number One: You have a nice sense of humor. Number Two: I see you can't tell a plain story. So don't waste time." Then he said sadly, "Number Three: I suppose that means she was alone, she was left like that, his mother. Alone. Probably sick?"

I said, "Yes."

"Poor woman. Poor girl, to be born in a time of fools, to live among fools. The end. The end. You were right to put that down. The end."

I didn't want to argue, but I had to say, "Well, it is not necessarily the end, Pa."

"Yes," he said, "what a tragedy. The end of a person."

"No, Pa," I begged him. "It doesn't have to be. She's only about forty. She could be a hundred different things in this world as time goes on. A teacher or a social worker. An ex-junkie! Sometimes it's better than having a master's in education."

"Jokes," he said. "As a writer that's your main trouble. You don't want to recognize it. Tragedy! Plain tragedy! Historical tragedy! No hope. The end."

"Oh, Pa," I said. "She could change."

"In your own life, too, you have to look it in the face." He took a couple of nitroglycerin. "Turn to five," he said, pointing to the dial on the oxygen tank. He inserted the tubes into his nostrils and breathed deep. He closed his eyes and said, "No."

I had promised the family to always let him have the last word when arguing, but in this case I had a different responsibility. That woman lives across the street. She's my knowledge and my invention. I'm sorry for her. I'm not going to leave her there in that house crying. (Actually neither would Life, which unlike me has no pity.)

Therefore: She did change. Of course her son never came home again. But right now, she's the receptionist in a storefront community clinic in the East Village. Most of the customers are young people, some old friends. The head doctor has said to her, "If we only had three people in this clinic with your experiences. . . ."

"The doctor said that?" My father took the oxygen tubes out of his nostrils and said, "Jokes. Jokes again."

"No, Pa, it could really happen that way, it's a funny world nowadays."

"No," he said. "Truth first. She will slide back. A person must have character. She does not."

"No, Pa," I said. "That's it. She's got a job. Forget it. She's in that storefront working."

"How long will it be?" he asked. "Tragedy! You too. When will you look it in the face?"

[1974]

JAMES BALDWIN   [1924–1987]

Sonny's Blues

I read about it in the paper, in the subway, on my way to work. I read it, and I couldn't believe it, and I read it again. Then perhaps I just stared at it, at the newsprint spelling out his name, spelling out the story. I stared at it in the swinging lights of the subway car, and in the faces and bodies of the people, and in my own face, trapped in the darkness which roared outside.

It was not to be believed and I kept telling myself that, as I walked from the subway station to the high school. And at the same time I couldn't doubt it. I was scared, scared for Sonny. He became real to me again. A great block of ice got settled in my belly and kept melting there slowly all day long, while I taught my classes algebra. It was a special kind of ice. It kept melting, sending trickles of ice water all up and down my veins, but it never got less. Sometimes it hardened and seemed to expand until I felt my guts were going to come spilling out or that I was going to choke or scream. This would always be at a moment when I was remembering some specific thing Sonny had once said or done.

When he was about as old as the boys in my classes his face had been bright and open, there was a lot of copper in it; and he'd had wonderfully direct brown eyes, and great gentleness and privacy. I wondered what he looked like now. He had been picked up, the evening before, in a raid on an apartment downtown, for peddling and using heroin.

I couldn't believe it: but what I mean by that is that I couldn't find any room for it anywhere inside me. I had kept it outside me for a long time. I hadn't wanted to know. I had had suspicions, but I didn't name them, I kept putting them away. I told myself that Sonny was wild, but he wasn't crazy. And he'd always been a good boy, he hadn't ever turned hard or evil or disrespectful, the way kids can, so quick, so quick, especially in Harlem. I didn't want to believe that I'd ever see my brother going down, coming to nothing, all that light in his face gone out, in the condition I'd already seen so many others. Yet it had happened and here I was, talking about algebra to a lot of boys who might, every one of them for all I knew, be popping off needles every time they went to the head. Maybe it did more for them than algebra could.

I was sure that the first time Sonny had ever had horse, he couldn't have been much older than these boys were now. These boys, now, were living as we'd been living then, they were growing up with a rush and their heads bumped abruptly against the low ceiling of their actual possibilities. They were filled with rage. All they really knew were two darknesses, the darkness of their lives, which was now closing in on them, and the darkness of the movies, which had blinded them to that other darkness, and in which they now, vindictively, dreamed, at once more together than they were at any other time, and more alone.

When the last bell rang, the last class ended, I let out my breath. It seemed I'd been holding it for all that time. My clothes were wet—I may have looked as though I'd been sitting in a steam bath, all dressed up, all afternoon. I sat alone in the classroom a long time. I listened to the boys outside, downstairs, shouting and cursing and laughing. Their laughter struck me for perhaps the first time. It was not the joyous laughter which—God knows why—one associates with children. It was mocking and insular, its intent to denigrate. It was disenchanted, and in this, also, lay the authority of their curses. Perhaps I was listening to them because I was thinking about my brother and in them I heard my brother. And myself.

One boy was whistling a tune, at once very complicated and very simple, it seemed to be pouring out of him as though he were a bird, and it sounded very cool and moving through all that harsh, bright air, only just holding its own through all those other sounds.

I stood up and walked over to the window and looked down into the courtyard. It was the beginning of the spring and the sap was rising in the boys. A teacher passed through them every now and again, quickly, as though he or she couldn't wait to get out of that courtyard, to get those boys out of their sight and off their minds. I started collecting my stuff. I thought I'd better get home and talk to Isabel.

The courtyard was almost deserted by the time I got downstairs. I saw this boy standing in the shadow of a doorway, looking just like Sonny. I almost called his name. Then I saw that it wasn't Sonny, but somebody we used to know, a boy from around our block. He'd been Sonny's friend. He'd never been mine, having been too young for me, and, anyway, I'd never liked him. And now, even though he was a grown-up man, he still hung around that block, still spent hours on the street corners, was always high and raggy. I used to run into him from time to time and he'd often work around to asking me for a quarter or fifty cents. He always had some real good excuse, too, and I always gave it to him, I don't know why.

But now, abruptly, I hated him. I couldn't stand the way he looked at me, partly like a dog, partly like a cunning child. I wanted to ask him what the hell he was doing in the school courtyard.

He sort of shuffled over to me, and he said, "I see you got the papers. So you already know about it."

"You mean about Sonny? Yes, I already know about it. How come they didn't get you?"

He grinned. It made him repulsive and it also brought to mind what he'd looked like as a kid. "I wasn't there. I stay away from them people."

"Good for you." I offered him a cigarette and I watched him through the smoke. "You come all the way down here just to tell me about Sonny?"

"That's right." He was sort of shaking his head and his eyes looked strange, as though they were about to cross. The bright sun deadened his damp dark brown skin and it made his eyes look yellow and showed up the dirt in his kinked hair. He smelled funky. I moved a little away from him and I said, "Well, thanks. But I already know about it and I got to get home."

"I'll walk you a little ways," he said. We started walking. There were a couple of kids still loitering in the courtyard and one of them said good-night to me and looked strangely at the boy beside me.

"What're you going to do?" he asked me. "I mean, about Sonny?"

"Look. I haven't seen Sonny for over a year. I'm not sure I'm going to do anything. Anyway, what the hell *can* I do?"

"That's right," he said quickly, "ain't nothing you can do. Can't much help old Sonny no more, I guess."

It was what I was thinking and so it seemed to me he had no right to say it.

"I'm surprised at Sonny, though," he went on—he had a funny way of talking, he looked straight ahead as though he were talking to himself—"I thought Sonny was a smart boy, I thought he was too smart to get hung."

"I guess he thought so too," I said sharply, "and that's how he got hung. And how about you? You're pretty goddamn smart, I bet."

Then he looked directly at me, just for a minute. "I ain't smart," he said. "If I was smart, I'd have reached for a pistol a long time ago."

"Look. Don't tell *me* your sad story, if it was up to me, I'd give you one." Then I felt guilty—guilty, probably, for never having supposed that the poor bastard *had* a story of his own, much less a sad one, and I asked, quickly, "What's going to happen to him now?"

He didn't answer this. He was off by himself some place. "Funny thing," he said, and from his tone we might have been discussing the quickest way to get to Brooklyn, "when I saw the papers this morning, the first thing I asked myself was if I had anything to do with it. I felt sort of responsible."

I began to listen more carefully. The subway station was on the corner, just before us, and I stopped. He stopped, too. We were in front of a bar and he ducked slightly, peering in, but whoever he was looking for didn't seem to be there. The juke box was blasting away with something black and bouncy and I half watched the barmaid as she danced her way from the juke box to her place behind the bar. And I watched her face as she laughingly responded to something someone said to her, still keeping time to the music. When she smiled one saw the little girl, one sensed the doomed, still-struggling woman beneath the battered face of the semi-whore.

"I never *give* Sonny nothing," the boy said finally, "but a long time ago I come to school high and Sonny asked me how it felt." He paused, I couldn't bear to watch him, I watched the barmaid, and I listened to the music which seemed to be causing the pavement to shake. "I told him it felt great." The music stopped, the barmaid paused and watched the juke box until the music began again. "It did."

All this was carrying me some place I didn't want to go. I certainly didn't want to know how it felt. It filled everything, the people, the houses, the music, the dark, quicksilver barmaid, with menace; and this menace was their reality.

"What's going to happen to him now?" I asked again.

"They'll send him away some place and they'll try to cure him." He shook his head. "Maybe he'll even think he's kicked the habit. Then they'll let him loose"—he gestured, throwing his cigarette into the gutter. "That's all."

"What do you mean, that's all?"

But I knew what he meant.

"I *mean*, that's *all*." He turned his head and looked at me, pulling down the corners of his mouth. "Don't you know what I mean?" he asked, softly.

"How the hell *would* I know what you mean?" I almost whispered it, I don't know why.

"That's right," he said to the air, "how would *he* know what I mean?" He turned toward me again, patient and calm, and yet I somehow felt him shaking, shaking as though he were going to fall apart. I felt that ice in my guts again, the dread I'd felt all afternoon; and again I watched the barmaid, moving about the bar, washing glasses, and singing. "Listen. They'll let him out and then it'll just start all over again. That's what I mean."

"You mean—they'll let him out. And then he'll just start working his way back in again. You mean he'll never kick the habit. Is that what you mean?"

"That's right," he said, cheerfully. "*You* see what I mean."

"Tell me," I said at last, "why does he want to die? He must want to die, he's killing himself, why does he want to die?"

He looked at me in surprise. He licked his lips. "He don't want to die. He wants to live. Don't nobody want to die, ever."

Then I wanted to ask him—too many things. He could not have answered, or if he had, I could not have borne the answers. I started walking. "Well, I guess it's none of my business."

"It's going to be rough on old Sonny," he said. We reached the subway station. "This is your station?" he asked. I nodded. I took one step down. "Damn!" he said, suddenly. I looked up at him. He grinned again. "Damn it if I didn't leave all my money home. You ain't got a dollar on you, have you? Just for a couple of days, is all."

All at once something inside gave and threatened to come pouring out of me. I didn't hate him any more. I felt that in another moment I'd start crying like a child.

"Sure," I said. "Don't sweat." I looked in my wallet and didn't have a dollar, I only had a five. "Here," I said. "That hold you?"

He didn't look at it—he didn't want to look at it. A terrible closed look came over his face, as though he were keeping the number on the bill a secret from him and me. "Thanks," he said, and now he was dying to see me go. "Don't worry about Sonny. Maybe I'll write him or something."

"Sure," I said. "You do that. So long."

"Be seeing you," he said. I went on down the steps.

And I didn't write Sonny or send him anything for a long time. When I finally did, it was just after my little girl died, he wrote me back a letter which made me feel like a bastard.

Here's what he said:

Dear brother,

You don't know how much I needed to hear from you. I wanted to write you many a time but I dug how much I must have hurt you and so I didn't write. But now I feel like a man who's been trying to climb up out of some deep, real deep and funky hole and just saw the sun up there, outside. I got to get outside.

I can't tell you much about how I got here. I mean I don't know how to tell you. I guess I was afraid of something or I was trying to escape from something and you know I have never been very strong in the head (smile). I'm glad Mama and Daddy are dead and can't see what's happened to their son and I swear if I'd known what I was doing I would never have hurt you so, you and a lot of other fine people who were nice to me and who believed in me.

I don't want you to think it had anything to do with me being a musician. It's more than that. Or maybe less than that. I can't get anything straight in my head down here and I try not to think about what's going to happen to me when I get outside again. Sometime I think I'm going to flip and *never* get outside and sometime I think I'll come straight back. I tell you one thing, though, I'd rather blow my brains out than go through this again. But that's what they all say, so they tell me. If I tell you when I'm coming to New York and if you could meet me, I sure would appreciate it. Give my love to Isabel and the kids and I was sure sorry to hear about little Gracie. I wish I could be like Mama and say the Lord's will be done, but I don't know it seems to me that trouble is the one thing that never does get stopped and I don't know what good it does to blame it on the Lord. But maybe it does some good if you believe it.

Your brother,
Sonny

Then I kept in constant touch with him and I sent him whatever I could and I went to meet him when he came back to New York. When I saw him many things I thought I had forgotten came flooding back to me. This was because I had begun, finally, to wonder about Sonny, about the life that Sonny lived inside. This life, whatever it was, had made him older and thinner and it had deepened the distant stillness in which he had always moved. He looked very unlike my baby brother. Yet, when he smiled, when we shook hands, the baby brother I'd never known looked out from the depths of his private life, like an animal waiting to be coaxed into the light.

"How you been keeping?" he asked me.

"All right. And you?"

"Just fine." He was smiling all over his face. "It's good to see you again."

"It's good to see you."

The seven years' difference in our ages lay between us like a chasm: I wondered if these years would ever operate between us as a bridge. I was remembering, and it made it hard to catch my breath, that I had been there when he was born; and I had heard the first words he had ever spoken. When he started to walk, he walked from our mother straight to me. I caught him just before he fell when he took the first steps he ever took in this world.

"How's Isabel?"

"Just fine. She's dying to see you."

"And the boys?"

"They're fine, too. They're anxious to see their uncle."

"Oh, come on. You know they don't remember me."

"Are you kidding? Of course they remember you."

He grinned again. We got into a taxi. We had a lot to say to each other, far too much to know how to begin.

As the taxi began to move, I asked, "You still want to go to India?"

He laughed. "You still remember that. Hell, no. This place is Indian enough for me."

"It used to belong to them," I said.

And he laughed again. "They damn sure knew what they were doing when they got rid of it."

Years ago, when he was around fourteen, he'd been all hipped on the idea of going to India. He read books about people sitting on rocks, naked, in all kinds of weather, but mostly bad, naturally, and walking barefoot through hot coals and arriving at wisdom. I used to say that it sounded to me as though they were getting away from wisdom as fast as they could. I think he sort of looked down on me for that.

"Do you mind," he asked, "if we have the driver drive alongside the park? On the west side—I haven't seen the city in so long."

"Of course not," I said. I was afraid that I might sound as though I were humoring him, but I hoped he wouldn't take it that way.

So we drove along, between the green of the park and the stony, lifeless elegance of hotels and apartment buildings, toward the vivid, killing streets of our childhood. These streets hadn't changed, though housing projects jutted up out of them now like rocks in the middle of a boiling sea. Most of the houses in which we had grown up had vanished, as had the stores from which we had stolen, the basements in which we had first tried sex, the rooftops from which we had hurled tin cans and bricks. But houses exactly like the houses of our past yet dominated the landscape, boys exactly like the boys we once had been found themselves smothering in these houses, came down into the streets for light and air and found themselves encircled by disaster. Some escaped the trap, most didn't. Those who got out always left something of themselves behind, as some animals amputate a leg and leave it in the trap. It might be said, perhaps, that I had escaped, after all, I was a school teacher; or that Sonny had, he hadn't lived in Harlem for years. Yet, as the cab moved uptown through streets which seemed, with a rush, to darken with dark people, and as I covertly studied Sonny's face, it came to me that what we both were seeking through our separate cab windows was that part of ourselves which had been left behind. It's always at the hour of trouble and confrontation that the missing member aches.

We hit 110th Street and started rolling up Lenox Avenue. And I'd known this avenue all my life, but it seemed to me again, as it had seemed on the day I'd first heard about Sonny's trouble, filled with a hidden menace which was its very breath of life.

"We almost there," said Sonny.

"Almost." We were both too nervous to say anything more.

We live in a housing project. It hasn't been up long. A few days after it was up it seemed uninhabitably new, now, of course, it's already run-down. It looks like a parody of the good, clean, faceless life—God knows the people who live in it do their best to make it a parody. The beat-looking grass lying around isn't enough to make their lives green, the hedges will never hold out the streets, and they know it. The big windows fool no one, they aren't big enough to make space out of no space. They don't bother with the windows, they watch the TV screen instead. The playground is most popular with the children who don't play at jacks, or skip rope, or roller skate, or swing, and they can be found in it after dark. We moved in partly because it's not too far from where I teach, and partly for the kids; but it's really just like the houses in which Sonny and I grew up. The same things happen, they'll have the same things to remember. The moment Sonny and I started into the house I had the feeling that I was simply bringing him back into the danger he had almost died trying to escape.

Sonny has never been talkative. So I don't know why I was sure he'd be dying to talk to me when supper was over the first night. Everything went fine, the oldest boy remembered him, and the youngest boy liked him, and Sonny had remembered to bring something for each of them;

and Isabel, who is really much nicer than I am, more open and giving, had gone to a lot of trouble about dinner and was genuinely glad to see him. And she's always been able to tease Sonny in a way that I haven't. It was nice to see her face so vivid again and to hear her laugh and watch her make Sonny laugh. She wasn't, or, anyway, she didn't seem to be, at all uneasy or embarrassed. She chatted as though there were no subject which had to be avoided and she got Sonny past his first, faint stiffness. And thank God she was there, for I was filled with that icy dread again. Everything I did seemed awkward to me, and everything I said sounded freighted with hidden meaning. I was trying to remember everything I'd heard about dope addiction and I couldn't help watching Sonny for signs. I wasn't doing it out of malice. I was trying to find out something about my brother. I was dying to hear him tell me he was safe.

"Safe!" my father grunted, whenever Mama suggested trying to move to a neighborhood which might be safer for children. "Safe, hell! Ain't no place safe for kids, nor nobody."

He always went on like this, but he wasn't, ever, really as bad as he sounded, not even on weekends, when he got drunk. As a matter of fact, he was always on the lookout for "something a little better," but he died before he found it. He died suddenly, during a drunken weekend in the middle of the war, when Sonny was fifteen. He and Sonny hadn't ever got on too well. And this was partly because Sonny was the apple of his father's eye. It was because he loved Sonny so much and was frightened for him, that he was always fighting with him. It doesn't do any good to fight with Sonny. Sonny just moves back, inside himself, where he can't be reached. But the principal reason that they never hit it off is that they were so much alike. Daddy was big and rough and loud-talking, just the opposite of Sonny, but they both had—that same privacy.

Mama tried to tell me something about this, just after Daddy died. I was home on leave from the army.

This was the last time I ever saw my mother alive. Just the same, this picture gets all mixed up in my mind with pictures I had of her when she was younger. The way I always see her is the way she used to be on a Sunday afternoon, say, when the old folks were talking after the big Sunday dinner. I always see her wearing pale blue. She'd be sitting on the sofa. And my father would be sitting in the easy chair, not far from her. And the living room would be full of church folks and relatives. There they sit, in chairs all around the living room, and the night is creeping up outside, but nobody knows it yet. You can see the darkness growing against the windowpanes and you hear the street noises every now and again, or maybe the jangling beat of a tambourine from one of the churches close by, but it's real quiet in the room. For a moment nobody's talking, but every face looks darkening, like the sky outside. And my mother rocks a little from the waist, and my father's eyes are closed. Everyone is looking at something a child can't see. For a minute they've forgotten the children. Maybe a kid is lying on the rug, half asleep. Maybe somebody's got a kid in his lap and is absent-mindedly stroking the kid's head. Maybe there's a kid, quiet and big-eyed, curled up in a big chair in the corner. The silence, the darkness coming, and the darkness in the faces frightens the child obscurely. He hopes that the hand which strokes his forehead will never stop—will never die. He hopes that there will never come a time when the old folks won't be sitting around the living room, talking about where they've come from, and what they've seen, and what's happened to them and their kinfolk.

But something deep and watchful in the child knows that this is bound to end, is already ending. In a moment someone will get up and turn on the light. Then the old folks will remember the children and they won't talk any more that day. And when light fills the room, the child is filled with darkness. He knows that every time this happens he's moved just a little closer to that darkness outside. The darkness outside is what the old folks have been talking about. It's what they've come from. It's what they endure. The child knows that they won't talk any more because if he knows too much about what's happened to *them*, he'll know too much too soon, about what's going to happen to *him*.

The last time I talked to my mother, I remember I was restless. I wanted to get out and see Isabel. We weren't married then and we had a lot to straighten out between us.

There Mama sat, in black, by the window. She was humming an old church song, *Lord, you brought me from a long ways off.* Sonny was out somewhere. Mama kept watching the streets.

"I don't know," she said, "if I'll ever see you again, after you go off from here. But I hope you'll remember the things I tried to teach you."

"Don't talk like that," I said, and smiled. "You'll be here a long time yet."

She smiled, too, but she said nothing. She was quiet for a long time. And I said, "Mama, don't you worry about nothing. I'll be writing all the time, and you be getting the checks. . . ."

"I want to talk to you about your brother," she said, suddenly. "If anything happens to me he ain't going to have nobody to look out for him."

"Mama," I said, "ain't nothing going to happen to you *or* Sonny. Sonny's all right. He's a good boy and he's got good sense."

"It ain't a question of his being a good boy," Mama said, "nor of his having good sense. It ain't only the bad ones, nor yet the dumb ones that gets sucked under." She stopped, looking at me. "Your Daddy once had a brother," she said, and she smiled in a way that made me feel she was in pain. "You didn't never know that, did you?"

"No," I said, "I never knew that," and I watched her face.

"Oh, yes," she said, "your Daddy had a brother." She looked out of the window again. "I know you never saw your Daddy cry. But *I* did—many a time, through all these years."

I asked her, "What happened to his brother? How come nobody's ever talked about him?"

This was the first time I ever saw my mother look old.

"His brother got killed," she said, "when he was just a little younger than you are now. I knew him. He was a fine boy. He was maybe a little full of the devil, but he didn't mean nobody no harm."

Then she stopped and the room was silent, exactly as it had sometimes been on those Sunday afternoons. Mama kept looking out into the streets.

"He used to have a job in the mill," she said, "and, like all young folks, he just liked to perform on Saturday nights. Saturday nights, him and your father would drift around to different places, go to dances and things like that, or just sit around with people they knew, and your father's brother would sing, he had a fine voice, and play along with himself on his guitar. Well, this particular Saturday night, him and your father was coming home from some place, and they were both a little drunk and there was a moon that night, it was bright like day. Your father's brother was feeling kind of good, and he was whistling to himself, and he had his guitar slung over his shoulder. They was coming down a hill and beneath them was a road that turned off from the highway. Well, your father's brother, being always kind of frisky, decided to run down this hill, and he did, with that guitar banging and clanging behind him, and he ran across the road, and he was making water behind a tree. And your father was sort of amused at him and he was still coming down the hill, kind of slow. Then he heard a car motor and that same minute his brother stepped from behind the tree, into the road, in the moonlight. And he started to cross the road. And your father started to run down the hill, he says he don't know why. This car was full of white men. They was all drunk, and when they seen your father's brother they let out a great whoop and holler and they aimed the car straight at him. They was having fun, they just wanted to scare him, the way they do sometimes, you know. But they was drunk. And I guess the boy, being drunk, too, and scared, kind of lost his head. By the time he jumped it was too late. Your father says he heard his brother scream when the car rolled over him, and he heard the wood of that guitar when it give, and he heard them strings go flying, and he heard them white men shouting, and the car kept on a-going and it ain't stopped till this day. And, time your father got down the hill, his brother weren't nothing but blood and pulp."

Tears were gleaming on my mother's face. There wasn't anything I could say.

"He never mentioned it," she said, "because I never let him mention it before you children. Your Daddy was like a crazy man that night and for many a night thereafter. He says he never in his life seen anything as dark as that road after the lights of that car had gone away. Weren't nothing, weren't nobody on that road, just your Daddy and his brother and that busted guitar. Oh, yes. Your Daddy never did really get right again. Till the day he died he weren't sure but that every white man he saw was the man that killed his brother."

She stopped and took out her handkerchief and dried her eyes and looked at me.

"I ain't telling you all this," she said, "to make you scared or bitter or to make you hate nobody. I'm telling you this because you got a brother. And the world ain't changed."

I guess I didn't want to believe this. I guess she saw this in my face. She turned away from me, toward the window again, searching those streets.

"But I praise my Redeemer," she said at last, "that He called your Daddy home before me. I ain't saying it to throw no flowers at myself, but, I declare, it keeps me from feeling too cast down to know I helped your father get safely through this world. Your father always acted like he was the roughest, strongest man on earth. And everybody took him to be like that. But if he hadn't had *me* there—to see his tears!"

She was crying again. Still, I couldn't move. I said, "Lord, Lord, Mama, I didn't know it was like that."

"Oh, honey," she said, "there's a lot that you don't know. But you are going to find it out." She stood up from the window and came over to me. "You got to hold on to your brother," she said, "and don't let him fall, no matter what it looks like is happening to him and no matter how evil you gets with him. You going to be evil with him many a time. But don't you forget what I told you, you hear?"

"I won't forget," I said. "Don't you worry, I won't forget. I won't let nothing happen to Sonny."

My mother smiled as though she were amused at something she saw in my face. Then, "You may not be able to stop nothing from happening. But you got to let him know you's *there.*"

Two days later I was married, and then I was gone. And I had a lot of things on my mind and I pretty well forgot my promise to Mama until I got shipped home on a special furlough for her funeral.

And, after the funeral, with just Sonny and me alone in the empty kitchen, I tried to find out something about him.

"What do you want to do?" I asked him.

"I'm going to be a musician," he said.

For he had graduated, in the time I had been away, from dancing to the juke box to finding out who was playing what, and what they were doing with it, and he had bought himself a set of drums.

"You mean, you want to be a drummer?" I somehow had the feeling that being a drummer might be all right for other people but not for my brother Sonny.

"I don't think," he said, looking at me very gravely, "that I'll ever be a good drummer. But I think I can play a piano."

I frowned. I'd never played the role of the older brother quite so seriously before, had scarcely ever, in fact, *asked* Sonny a damn thing. I sensed myself in the presence of something I didn't really know how to handle, didn't understand. So I made my frown a little deeper as I asked: "What kind of musician do you want to be?"

He grinned. "How many kinds do you think there are?"

"Be *serious*," I said.

He laughed, throwing his head back, and then looked at me. "I *am* serious."

"Well, then, for Christ's sake, stop kidding around and answer a serious question. I mean, do you want to be a concert pianist, you want to play classical music and all that, or—or what?" Long before I finished he was laughing again. "For Christ's *sake*, Sonny!"

He sobered, but with difficulty. "I'm sorry. But you sound so—*scared!*" and he was off again.

"Well, you may think it's funny now, baby, but it's not going to be so funny when you have to make your living at it, let me tell you *that*." I was furious because I knew he was laughing at me and I didn't know why.

"No," he said, very sober now, and afraid, perhaps, that he'd hurt me, "I don't want to be a classical pianist. That isn't what interests me. I mean"—he paused, looking hard at me, as though his eyes would help me to understand, and then gestured helplessly, as though perhaps his hand would help—"I mean, I'll have a lot of studying to do, and I'll have to study *everything*, but, I mean, I want to play *with*—jazz musicians." He stopped. "I want to play jazz," he said.

Well, the word had never before sounded as heavy, as real, as it sounded that afternoon in Sonny's mouth. I just looked at him and I was probably frowning a real frown by this time. I simply couldn't see why on earth he'd want to spend his time hanging around night-clubs, clowning around on bandstands, while people pushed each other around a dance floor. It seemed—beneath him, somehow. I had never thought about it before, had never been forced to, but I suppose I had always put jazz musicians in a class with what Daddy called "good-time people."

"Are you *serious*?"

"Hell, *yes*, I'm serious."

He looked more helpless than ever, and annoyed, and deeply hurt.

I suggested, helpfully: "You mean—like Louis Armstrong?"

His face closed as though I'd struck him. "No. I'm not talking about none of that old-time, down home crap."

"Well, look, Sonny, I'm sorry, don't get mad. I just don't altogether get it, that's all. Name somebody—you know, a jazz musician you admire."

"Bird."

"Who?"

"Bird! Charlie Parker! Don't they teach you nothing in the goddamn army?"

I lit a cigarette. I was surprised and then a little amused to discover that I was trembling. "I've been out of touch," I said. "You'll have to be patient with me. Now. Who's this Parker character?"

"He's just one of the greatest jazz musicians alive," said Sonny, sullenly, his hands in his pockets, his back to me. "Maybe *the* greatest," he added, bitterly, "that's probably why *you* never heard of him."

"All right," I said, "I'm ignorant. I'm sorry. I'll go out and buy all the cat's records right away, all right?"

"It don't," said Sonny, with dignity, "make any difference to me. I don't care what you listen to. Don't do me no favors."

I was beginning to realize that I'd never seen him so upset before. With another part of my mind I was thinking that this would probably turn out to be one of those things kids go through and that I shouldn't make it seem important by pushing it too hard. Still, I didn't think it would do any harm to ask: "Doesn't all this take a lot of time? Can you make a living at it?"

He turned back to me and half leaned, half sat, on the kitchen table. "Everything takes time," he said, "and—well, yes, sure, I can make a living at it. But what I don't seem to be able to make you understand is that it's the only thing I want to do."

"Well, Sonny," I said, gently, "you know people can't always do exactly what they *want* to do—"

"*No*, I don't know that," said Sonny, surprising me. "I think people *ought* to do what they want to do, what else are they alive for?"

"You getting to be a big boy," I said desperately, "it's time you started thinking about your future."

"I'm thinking about my future," said Sonny, grimly. "I think about it all the time."

I gave up. I decided, if he didn't change his mind, that we could always talk about it later. "In the meantime," I said, "you got to finish school." We had already decided that he'd have to move in with Isabel and her folks. I knew this wasn't the ideal arrangement because Isabel's folks are inclined to be dicty and they hadn't especially wanted Isabel to marry me. But I didn't know what else to do. "And we have to get you fixed up at Isabel's."

There was a long silence. He moved from the kitchen table to the window. "That's a terrible idea. You know it yourself."

"Do you have a *better* idea?"

He just walked up and down the kitchen for a minute. He was as tall as I was. He had started to shave. I suddenly had the feeling that I didn't know him at all.

He stopped at the kitchen table and picked up my cigarettes. Looking at me with a kind of mocking, amused defiance, he put one between his lips. "You mind?"

"You smoking already?"

He lit the cigarette and nodded, watching me through the smoke. "I just wanted to see if I'd have the courage to smoke in front of you." He grinned and blew a great cloud of smoke to the ceiling. "It was easy." He looked at my face. "Come on, now. I bet you was smoking at my age, tell the truth."

I didn't say anything but the truth was on my face, and he laughed. But now there was something very strained in his laugh. "Sure. And I bet that ain't all you was doing."

He was frightening me a little. "Cut the crap," I said. "We already decided that you was going to go and live at Isabel's. Now what's got into you all of a sudden?"

"*You* decided it," he pointed out. "*I* didn't decide nothing." He stopped in front of me, leaning against the stove, arms loosely folded. "Look, brother. I don't want to stay in Harlem no more, I really don't." He was very earnest. He looked at me, then over toward the kitchen window. There was something in his eyes I'd never seen before, some thoughtfulness, some worry all his own. He rubbed the muscle of one arm. "It's time I was getting out of here."

"Where do you want to *go*, Sonny?"

"I want to join the army. Or the navy, I don't care. If I say I'm old enough, they'll believe me."

Then I got mad. It was because I was so scared. "You must be crazy. You goddamn fool, what the hell do you want to go and join the *army* for?"

"I just told you. To get out of Harlem."

"Sonny, you haven't even finished *school*. And if you really want to be a musician, how do you expect to study if you're in the *army*?"

He looked at me, trapped, and in anguish. "There's ways. I might be able to work out some kind of deal. Anyway, I'll have the G.I. Bill when I come out."

"*If* you come out." We stared at each other. "Sonny, please. Be reasonable. I know the setup is far from perfect. But we got to do the best we can."

"I ain't learning nothing in school," he said. "Even when I go." He turned away from me and opened the window and threw his cigarette out into the narrow alley. I watched his back. "At least, I ain't learning nothing you'd want me to learn." He slammed the window so hard I thought the glass would fly out, and turned back to me. "And I'm sick of the stink of these garbage cans!"

"Sonny," I said, "I know how you feel. But if you don't finish school now, you're going to be sorry later that you didn't." I grabbed him by the shoulders. "And you only got another year. It ain't so bad. And I'll come back and I swear I'll help you do *whatever* you want to do. Just try to put up with it till I come back. Will you please do that? For me?"

He didn't answer and he wouldn't look at me.

"Sonny. You hear me?"

He pulled away. "I hear you. But you never hear anything *I* say."

I didn't know what to say to that. He looked out of the window and then back at me. "OK," he said, and sighed. "I'll try."

Then I said, trying to cheer him up a little, "They got a piano at Isabel's. You can practice on it."

And as a matter of fact, it did cheer him up for a minute. "That's right," he said to himself. "I forgot that." His face relaxed a little. But the worry, the thoughtfulness, played on it still, the way shadows play on a face which is staring into the fire.

But I thought I'd never hear the end of that piano. At first, Isabel would write me, saying how nice it was that Sonny was so serious about his music and how, as soon as he came in from school, or wherever he had been when he was supposed to be at school, he went straight to that piano and stayed there until suppertime. And, after supper, he went back to that piano and stayed there until everybody went to bed. He was at the piano all day Saturday and all day Sunday. Then he bought a record player and started playing records. He'd play one record over and over again, all day long sometimes, and he'd improvise along with it on the piano. Or he'd play one section of the record, one chord, one change, one progression, then he'd do it on the piano. Then back to the record. Then back to the piano.

Well, I really don't know how they stood it. Isabel finally confessed that it wasn't like living with a person at all, it was like living with sound. And the sound didn't make any sense to her, didn't make any sense to any of them—naturally. They began, in a way, to be afflicted by this presence that was living in their home. It was as though Sonny were some sort of god, or monster. He moved in an atmosphere which wasn't like theirs at all. They fed him and he ate, he washed himself, he walked in and out of their door; he certainly wasn't nasty or unpleasant or rude, Sonny isn't any of those things; but it was as though he were all wrapped up in some cloud, some fire, some vision all his own; and there wasn't any way to reach him.

At the same time, he wasn't really a man yet, he was still a child, and they had to watch out for him in all kinds of ways. They certainly couldn't throw him out. Neither did they dare to make a great scene about that piano because even they dimly sensed, as I sensed, from so many thousands of miles away, that Sonny was at that piano playing for his life.

But he hadn't been going to school. One day a letter came from the school board and Isabel's mother got it—there had, apparently, been other letters but Sonny had torn them up. This day, when Sonny came in, Isabel's mother showed him the letter and asked where he'd been spending his time. And she finally got it out of him that he'd been down in Greenwich Village, with musicians and other characters, in a white girl's apartment. And this scared her and she started to scream at him and what came up, once she began—though she denies it to this day— was what sacrifices they were making to give Sonny a decent home and how little he appreciated it.

Sonny didn't play the piano that day. By evening, Isabel's mother had calmed down but then there was the old man to deal with, and Isabel herself. Isabel says she did her best to be calm but she broke down and started crying. She says she just watched Sonny's face. She could tell, by watching him, what was happening with him. And what was happening was that they penetrated his cloud, they had reached him. Even if their fingers had been a thousand times more gentle than human fingers ever are, he could hardly help feeling that they had stripped him naked and were spitting on that nakedness. For he also had to see that his presence, that music, which was life or death to him, had been torture for them and that they had endured it, not at all for his sake, but only for mine. And Sonny couldn't take that. He can take it a little better today than he could then but he's still not very good at it and, frankly, I don't know any-body who is.

The silence of the next few days must have been louder than the sound of all the music ever played since time began. One morning, before she went to work, Isabel was in his room for something and she suddenly realized that all of his records were gone. And she knew for certain that he was gone. And he was. He went as far as the navy would carry him. He finally sent me a postcard from some place in Greece and that was the first I knew that Sonny was still alive. I didn't see him any more until we were both back in New York and the war had long been over.

He was a man by then, of course, but I wasn't willing to see it. He came by the house from time to time, but we fought almost every time we met. I didn't like the way he carried himself, loose and dreamlike all the time, and I didn't like his friends, and his music seemed to be merely an excuse for the life he led. It sounded just that weird and dis-ordered.

Then we had a fight, a pretty awful fight, and I didn't see him for months. By and by I looked him up, where he was living, in a furnished room in the Village, and I tried to make it up. But there were lots of people in the room and Sonny just lay on his bed, and he wouldn't come downstairs with me, and he treated these other people as though they were his family and I weren't. So I got mad and then he got mad, and then I told him that he might just as well be dead as live the way he was living. Then he stood up and he told me not to worry about him any more in life, that he *was* dead as far as I was concerned. Then he pushed me to the door and the other people looked on as though nothing were happening, and he slammed the door behind me. I stood in the hallway, staring at the door. I heard somebody laugh in the room and then the tears came to my eyes. I started down the steps, whistling to keep from crying, I kept whistling to myself, *You going to need me, baby, one of these cold, rainy days.*

I read about Sonny's trouble in the spring. Little Grace died in the fall. She was a beautiful little girl. But she only lived a little over two years. She died of polio and she suffered. She had a slight fever for a couple of days, but it didn't seem like anything and we just kept her in bed. And we would certainly have called the doctor, but the fever dropped, she seemed to be all right. So we thought it had just been a cold. Then, one day, she was up, playing, Isabel was in the kitchen fixing lunch for the two boys when they'd come in from school, and she heard Grace fall down in the living room. When you have a lot of children you don't always start running when one of them falls, unless they start screaming or something. And, this time, Grace was quiet. Yet, Isabel says that when she heard that *thump* and then that silence, something happened in her to make her afraid. And she ran to the living room and there was little Grace on the floor, all twisted up, and the reason she hadn't screamed was that she couldn't get her breath. And when she did scream, it was the worst sound, Isabel says, that she'd ever heard in all her life, and she still hears it sometimes in her dreams. Isabel will sometimes wake me up with a low, moaning, strangled sound and I have to be quick to awaken her and hold her to me and where Isabel is weeping against me seems a mortal wound.

I think I may have written Sonny the very day that little Grace was buried. I was sitting in the living room in the dark, by myself, and I suddenly thought of Sonny. My trouble made his real.

One Saturday afternoon, when Sonny had been living with us, or, anyway, been in our house, for nearly two weeks, I found myself wandering aimlessly about the living room, drinking from a can of beer, and trying to work up the courage to search Sonny's room. He was out, he was usually out whenever I was home, and Isabel had taken the children to see their grandparents. Suddenly I was standing still in front of the living room window, watching Seventh Avenue. The idea of searching Sonny's room made me still. I scarcely dared to admit to myself what I'd be searching for. I didn't know what I'd do if I found it. Or if I didn't.

On the sidewalk across from me, near the entrance to a barbecue joint, some people were holding an old-fashioned revival meeting. The barbecue cook, wearing a dirty white apron, his conked hair reddish and metallic in the pale sun, and a cigarette between his lips, stood in the doorway, watching them. Kids and older people paused in their errands and stood there, along with some older men and a couple of very tough-looking women who watched everything that happened on the avenue, as though they owned it, or were maybe owned by it. Well, they were watching this, too. The revival was being carried on by three sisters in black, and a brother. All they had were their voices and their Bibles and a tambourine. The brother was testifying and while he testified two of the sisters stood together, seeming to say, amen, and the third sister walked around with the tambourine outstretched and a couple of people dropped coins into it. Then the brother's testimony ended and the sister who had been taking up the collection dumped the coins into her palm and transferred them to the pocket of her long black robe. Then she raised both hands, striking the tambourine against the air, and then against one hand, and she started to sing. And the two other sisters and the brother joined in.

It was strange, suddenly, to watch, though I had been seeing these street meetings all my life. So, of course, had everybody else down there. Yet, they paused and watched and listened and I stood still at the window. *"Tis the old ship of Zion,"* they sang, and the sister with the tambourine kept a steady, jangling beat, *"it has rescued many a thousand!"* Not a soul under the sound of their voices was hearing this song for the first time, not one of them had been rescued. Nor had they seen much in the way of rescue work being done around them. Neither did they especially believe in the holiness of the three sisters and the brother, they knew too much about them, knew where they lived, and how. The woman with the tambourine, whose voice dominated the air, whose face was bright with joy, was divided by very little from the woman who stood watching her, a cigarette between her heavy, chapped lips, her hair a cuckoo's nest, her face scarred and swollen from many beatings, and her black eyes glittering like coal. Perhaps they both knew this, which was why, when, as rarely, they addressed each other, they addressed each other as Sister. As the singing filled the air the watching, listening faces underwent a change, the eyes focusing on something within; the music seemed to soothe a poison out of them; and time seemed, nearly, to fall away from the sullen, belligerent, battered faces, as though they were fleeing back to their first condition, while dreaming of their last. The barbecue cook half shook his head and smiled, and dropped his cigarette and disappeared into his joint. A man fumbled in his pockets for change and stood holding it in his hand impatiently, as though he had just remembered a pressing appointment further up the avenue. He looked furious. Then I saw Sonny, standing on the edge of the crowd. He was carrying a wide, flat notebook with a green cover, and it made him look, from where I was standing, almost like a schoolboy. The coppery sun brought out the copper in his skin, he was very faintly smiling, standing very still. Then the singing stopped, the tambourine turned into a collection plate again. The furious man dropped in his coins and vanished, so did a couple of the women, and Sonny dropped some change in the plate, looking directly at the woman with a little smile. He started across the avenue, toward the house. He has a slow, loping walk, something like the way Harlem hipsters walk, only he's imposed on this his own half-beat. I had never really noticed it before.

I stayed at the window, both relieved and apprehensive. As Sonny disappeared from my sight, they began singing again. And they were still singing when his key turned in the lock.

"Hey," he said.

"Hey, yourself. You want some beer?"

"No. Well, maybe." But he came up to the window and stood beside me, looking out. "What a warm voice," he said.

They were singing *If I could only hear my mother pray again!*

"Yes," I said, "and she can sure beat that tambourine."

"But what a terrible song," he said, and laughed. He dropped his notebook on the sofa and disappeared into the kitchen. "Where's Isabel and the kids?"

"I think they went to see their grandparents. You hungry?"

"No." He came back into the living room with his can of beer. "You want to come some place with me tonight?"

I sensed, I don't know how, that I couldn't possibly say no. "Sure. Where?"

He sat down on the sofa and picked up his notebook and started leafing through it. "I'm going to sit in with some fellows in a joint in the Village."

"You mean, you're going to play, tonight?"

"That's right." He took a swallow of his beer and moved back to the window. He gave me a sidelong look. "If you can stand it."

"I'll try," I said.

He smiled to himself and we both watched as the meeting across the way broke up. The three sisters and the brother, heads bowed, were singing *God be with you till we meet again*. The faces around them were very quiet. Then the song ended. The small crowd dispersed. We watched the three women and the lone man walk slowly up the avenue.

"When she was singing before," said Sonny, abruptly, "her voice reminded me for a minute of what heroin feels like sometimes—when it's in your veins. It makes you feel sort of warm and cool at the same time. And distant. And—and sure." He sipped his beer, very deliberately not looking at me. I watched his face. "It makes you feel—in control. Sometimes you've got to have that feeling."

"Do you?" I sat down slowly in the easy chair.

"Sometimes." He went to the sofa and picked up his notebook again. "Some people do."

"In order," I asked, "to play?" And my voice was very ugly, full of contempt and anger.

"Well"—he looked at me with great, troubled eyes, as though, in fact, he hoped his eyes would tell me things he could never otherwise say— "they *think* so. And *if* they think so—!"

"And what do *you* think?" I asked.

He sat on the sofa and put his can of beer on the floor. "I don't know," he said, and I couldn't be sure if he were answering my question or pursuing his thoughts. His face didn't tell me. "It's not so much to *play*. It's to *stand* it, to be able to make it at all. On any level." He frowned and smiled: "In order to keep from shaking to pieces."

"But these friends of yours," I said, "they seem to shake themselves to pieces pretty goddamn fast."

"Maybe." He played with the notebook. And something told me that I should curb my tongue, that Sonny was doing his best to talk, that I should listen. "But of course you only know the ones that've gone to pieces. Some don't—or at least they haven't *yet* and that's just about all *any* of us can say." He paused. "And then there are some who just live, really, in hell, and they know it and they see what's happening and they go right on. I don't know." He sighed, dropped the notebook, folded his arms. "Some guys, you can tell from the way they play, they on something *all* the time. And you can see that, well, it makes something real for them. But of course," he picked up his beer from the floor and sipped it and put the can down again, "they *want* to, too, you've got to see that. Even some of them that say they don't—*some*, not all."

"And what about you?" I asked—I couldn't help it. "What about you? Do *you* want to?"

He stood up and walked to the window and remained silent for a long time. Then he sighed. "Me," he said. Then: "While I was downstairs before, on my way here, listening to that woman sing, it struck me all of a sudden how much suffering she must have had to go through—to sing like that. It's *repulsive* to think you have to suffer that much."

I said: "But there's no way not to suffer—is there, Sonny?"

"I believe not," he said and smiled, "but that's never stopped anyone from trying." He looked at me. "Has it?" I realized, with this mocking look, that there stood between us, forever, beyond the power of time or forgiveness, the fact that I had held silence—so long!—when he had needed human speech to help him. He turned back to the window. "No, there's no way not to suffer. But you try all kinds of ways to keep from drowning in it, to keep on top of it, and to make it seem—well, like *you*. Like you did something, all right, and now you're suffering for it. You know?" I said nothing. "Well you know," he said, impatiently, "why *do* people suffer? Maybe it's better to do something to give it a reason, *any* reason."

"But we just agreed," I said, "that there's no way not to suffer. Isn't it better, then, just to—take it?"

"But nobody just takes it," Sonny cried, "that's what I'm telling you! *Everybody* tries not to. You're just hung up on the *way* some people try—it's not *your* way!"

The hair on my face began to itch, my face felt wet. "That's not true," I said, "that's not true. I don't give a damn what other people do, I don't even care how they suffer. I just care how *you* suffer." And he looked at me. "Please believe me," I said, "I don't want to see you—die—trying not to suffer."

"I won't," he said, flatly, "die trying not to suffer. At least, not any faster than anybody else."

"But there's no need," I said, trying to laugh, "is there? in killing yourself."

I wanted to say more, but I couldn't. I wanted to talk about will power and how life could be—well, beautiful. I wanted to say that it was all within; but was it? or, rather, wasn't that exactly the trouble? And I wanted to promise that I would never fail him again. But it would all have sounded—empty words and lies.

So I made the promise to myself and prayed that I would keep it.

"It's terrible sometimes, inside," he said, "that's what's the trouble. You walk these streets, black and funky and cold, and there's not really a

living ass to talk to, and there's nothing shaking, and there's no way of
getting it out—that storm inside. You can't talk it and you can't make
love with it, and when you finally try to get with it and play it, you realize
nobody's listening. So *you've* got to listen. You got to find a way to listen."

And then he walked away from the window and sat on the sofa again,
as though all the wind had suddenly been knocked out of him. "Sometimes you'll do *anything* to play, even cut your mother's throat." He
laughed and looked at me. "Or your brother's." Then he sobered. "Or
your own." Then: "Don't worry. I'm all right now and I think I'll *be* all
right. But I can't forget—where I've been. I don't mean just the physical
place I've been, I mean where I've *been*. And *what* I've been."

"What have you been, Sonny?" I asked.

He smiled—but sat sideways on the sofa, his elbow resting on the
back, his fingers playing with his mouth and chin, not looking at me.
"I've been something I didn't recognize, didn't know I could be. Didn't
know anybody could be." He stopped, looking inward, looking helplessly
young, looking old. "I'm not talking about it now because I feel *guilty* or
anything like that—maybe it would be better if I did, I don't know. Anyway, I can't really talk about it. Not to you, not to anybody," and now he
turned and faced me. "Sometimes, you know, and it was actually when I
was most *out* of the world, I felt that I was in it, that I was *with* it, really,
and I could play or I didn't really have to *play*, it just came out of me, it
was there. And I don't know how I played, thinking about it now, but I
know I did awful things, those times, sometimes, to people. Or it wasn't
that I *did* anything to them—it was that they weren't real." He picked up
the beer can; it was empty; he rolled it between his palms: "And other
times—well, I needed a fix, I needed to find a place to lean, I needed to
clear a space to *listen*—and I couldn't find it, and I—went crazy, I did
terrible things to *me*, I was terrible *for* me." He began pressing the beer
can between his hands, I watched the metal begin to give. It glittered, as
he played with it, like a knife, and I was afraid he would cut himself, but
I said nothing. "Oh well. I can never tell you. I was all by myself at the
bottom of something, stinking and sweating and crying and shaking,
and I smelled it, you know? *my* stink, and I thought I'd die if I couldn't
get away from it and yet, all the same, I knew that everything I was doing
was just locking me in with it. And I didn't know," he paused, still flatten-
ing the beer can, "I didn't know, I still *don't* know, something kept telling
me that maybe it was good to smell your own stink, but I didn't think
that *that* was what I'd been trying to do—and—who can stand it?" and
he abruptly dropped the ruined beer can, looking at me with a small, still
smile, and then rose, walking to the window as though it were the lode-
stone rock. I watched his face, he watched the avenue. "I couldn't tell
you when Mama died—but the reason I wanted to leave Harlem so bad

was to get away from drugs. And then, when I ran away, that's what I was running from—really. When I came back, nothing had changed, *I* hadn't changed, I was just—older." And he stopped, drumming with his fingers on the windowpane. The sun had vanished, soon darkness would fall. I watched his face. "It can come again," he said, almost as though speaking to himself. Then he turned to me. "It can come again," he repeated. "I just want you to know that."

"All right," I said, at last. "So it can come again. All right."

He smiled, but the smile was sorrowful. "I had to try to tell you," he said.

"Yes," I said. "I understand that."

"You're my brother," he said, looking straight at me, and not smiling at all.

"Yes," I repeated, "yes. I understand that."

He turned back to the window, looking out. "All that hatred down there," he said, "all that hatred and misery and love. It's a wonder it doesn't blow the avenue apart."

We went to the only nightclub on a short, dark street, downtown. We squeezed through the narrow, chattering, jam-packed bar to the entrance of the big room, where the bandstand was. And we stood there for a moment, for the lights were very dim in this room and we couldn't see. Then, "Hello, boy," said a voice and an enormous black man, much older than Sonny or myself, erupted out of all that atmospheric lighting and put an arm around Sonny's shoulder. "I been sitting right here," he said, "waiting for you."

He had a big voice, too, and heads in the darkness turned toward us.

Sonny grinned and pulled a little away, and said, "Creole, this is my brother. I told you about him."

Creole shook my hand. "I'm glad to meet you, son," he said, and it was clear that he was glad to meet me *there*, for Sonny's sake. And he smiled, "You got a real musician in *your* family," and he took his arm from Sonny's shoulder and slapped him, lightly, affectionately, with the back of his hand.

"Well. Now I've heard it all," said a voice behind us. This was another musician, and a friend of Sonny's, a coal-black, cheerful-looking man, built close to the ground. He immediately began confiding to me, at the top of his lungs, the most terrible things about Sonny, his teeth gleaming like a lighthouse and his laugh coming up out of him like the beginning of an earthquake. And it turned out that everyone at the bar knew Sonny, or almost everyone; some were musicians, working there, or nearby, or not working, some were simply hangers-on, and some were there to hear Sonny play. I was introduced to all of them and they were all very polite to me. Yet, it was clear that, for them, I was only Sonny's brother. Here, I was in Sonny's world. Or, rather: his kingdom. Here, it was not even a question that his veins bore royal blood.

They were going to play soon and Creole installed me, by myself, at a table in a dark corner. Then I watched them, Creole, and the little black man, and Sonny, and the others, while they horsed around, standing just below the bandstand. The light from the bandstand spilled just a little short of them and, watching them laughing and gesturing and moving about, I had the feeling that they, nevertheless, were being most careful not to step into that circle of light too suddenly: that if they moved into the light too suddenly, without thinking, they would perish in flame. Then, while I watched, one of them, the small, black man, moved into the light and crossed the bandstand and started fooling around with his drums. Then—being funny and being, also, extremely ceremonious— Creole took Sonny by the arm and led him to the piano. A woman's voice called Sonny's name and a few hands started clapping. And Sonny, also being funny and being ceremonious, and so touched, I think, that he could have cried, but neither hiding it nor showing it, riding it like a man, grinned, and put both hands to his heart and bowed from the waist.

Creole then went to the bass fiddle and a lean, very bright-skinned brown man jumped up on the bandstand and picked up his horn. So there they were, and the atmosphere on the bandstand and in the room began to change and tighten. Someone stepped up to the microphone and announced them. Then there were all kinds of murmurs. Some people at the bar shushed others. The waitress ran around, frantically getting in the last orders, guys and chicks got closer to each other, and the lights on the bandstand, on the quartet, turned to a kind of indigo. Then they all looked different there. Creole looked about him for the last time, as though he were making certain that all his chickens were in the coop, and then he—jumped and struck the fiddle. And there they were.

All I know about music is that not many people ever really hear it. And even then, on the rare occasions when something opens within, and the music enters, what we mainly hear, or hear corroborated, are personal, private, vanishing evocations. But the man who creates the music is hearing something else, is dealing with the roar rising from the void and imposing order on it as it hits the air. What is evoked in him, then, is of another order, more terrible because it has no words, and triumphant, too, for that same reason. And his triumph, when he triumphs, is ours. I just watched Sonny's face. His face was troubled, he was working hard, but he wasn't with it. And I had the feeling that, in a way, everyone on the bandstand was waiting for him, both waiting for him and pushing him along. But as I began to watch Creole, I realized that it was Creole who held them all back. He had them on a short rein. Up there, keeping the beat with his whole body, wailing on the fiddle, with his eyes half closed, he was listening to everything, but he was listening to Sonny. He was having a dialogue with Sonny. He wanted Sonny to leave the shoreline and strike out for the deep water. He was Sonny's witness that deep water and drowning were not the same thing—he had been there, and he knew. And he wanted Sonny to know. He was waiting for Sonny to do the things on the keys which would let Creole know that Sonny was in the water.

And, while Creole listened, Sonny moved, deep within, exactly like someone in torment. I had never before thought of how awful the relationship must be between the musician and his instrument. He has to fill it, this instrument, with the breath of life, his own. He has to make it do what he wants it to do. And a piano is just a piano. It's made out of so much wood and wires and little hammers and big ones, and ivory. While there's only so much you can do with it, the only way to find this out is to try; to try and make it do everything.

And Sonny hadn't been near a piano for over a year. And he wasn't on much better terms with his life, not the life that stretched before him now. He and the piano stammered, started one way, got scared, stopped; started another way, panicked, marked time, started again; then seemed to have found a direction, panicked again, got stuck. And the face I saw on Sonny I'd never seen before. Everything had been burned out of it, and, at the same time, things usually hidden were being burned in, by the fire and fury of the battle which was occurring in him up there.

Yet, watching Creole's face as they neared the end of the first set, I had the feeling that something had happened, something I hadn't heard. Then they finished, there was scattered applause, and then, without an instant's warning, Creole started into something else, it was almost sardonic, it was *Am I Blue*. And, as though he commanded, Sonny began to play. Something began to happen. And Creole let out the reins. The dry, low, black man said something awful on the drums, Creole answered, and the drums talked back. Then the horn insisted, sweet and high, slightly detached perhaps, and Creole listened, commenting now and then, dry, and driving, beautiful and calm and old. Then they all came together again, and Sonny was part of the family again. I could tell this from his face. He seemed to have found, right there beneath his fingers, a damn brand-new piano. It seemed that he couldn't get over it. Then, for awhile, just being happy with Sonny, they seemed to be agreeing with him that brand-new pianos certainly were a gas.

Then Creole stepped forward to remind them that what they were playing was the blues. He hit something in all of them, he hit something

in me, myself, and the music tightened and deepened, apprehension
began to beat the air. Creole began to tell us what the blues were all
about. They were not about anything very new. He and his boys up there
were keeping it new, at the risk of ruin, destruction, madness, and death,
in order to find new ways to make us listen. For, while the tale of how we
suffer, and how we are delighted, and how we may triumph is never new,
it always must be heard. There isn't any other tale to tell, it's the only
light we've got in all this darkness.

And this tale, according to that face, that body, those strong hands on
those strings, has another aspect in every country, and a new depth in
every generation. Listen, Creole seemed to be saying, listen. Now these
are Sonny's blues. He made the little black man on the drums know it,
and the bright, brown man on the horn. Creole wasn't trying any longer
to get Sonny in the water. He was wishing him Godspeed. Then he
stepped back, very slowly, filling the air with the immense suggestion
that Sonny speak for himself.

Then they all gathered around Sonny and Sonny played. Every now
and again one of them seemed to say, amen. Sonny's fingers filled the air
with life, his life. But that life contained so many others. And Sonny
went all the way back, he really began with the spare, flat statement of
the opening phrase of the song. Then he began to make it his. It was very
beautiful because it wasn't hurried and it was no longer a lament. I
seemed to hear with what burning he had made it his, with what burning we had yet to make it ours, how we could cease lamenting. Freedom
lurked around us and I understood, at last, that he could help us to be
free if we would listen, that he would never be free until we did. Yet,
there was no battle in his face now. I heard what he had gone through,
and would continue to go through until he came to rest in earth. He had
made it his: that long line, of which we knew only Mama and Daddy. And
he was giving it back, as everything must be given back, so that, passing
through death, it can live forever. I saw my mother's face again, and felt,
for the first time, how the stones of the road she had walked on must
have bruised her feet. I saw the moonlit road where my father's brother
died. And it brought something else back to me, and carried me past it. I
saw my little girl again and felt Isabel's tears again, and I felt my own
tears begin to rise. And I was yet aware that this was only a moment,
that the world waited outside, as hungry as a tiger, and that trouble
stretched above us, longer than the sky.

Then it was over. Creole and Sonny let out their breath, both soaking
wet, and grinning. There was a lot of applause and some of it was real. In
the dark, the girl came by and I asked her to take drinks to the bandstand. There was a long pause, while they talked up there in the indigo
light and after awhile I saw the girl put a Scotch and milk on top of the

piano for Sonny. He didn't seem to notice it, but just before they started playing again, he sipped from it and looked toward me, and nodded. Then he put it back on top of the piano. For me, then, as they began to play again, it glowed and shook above my brother's head like the very cup of trembling.

[1957]

FLANNERY O'CONNOR   [1925–1964]

A Good Man Is Hard to Find

The dragon is by the side of the road, watching those who pass. Beware lest he devour you. We go to the Father of Souls, but it is necessary to pass by the dragon. —ST. CYRIL OF JERUSALEM

The grandmother didn't want to go to Florida. She wanted to visit some of her connections in east Tennessee and she was seizing at every chance to change Bailey's mind. Bailey was the son she lived with, her only boy. He was sitting on the edge of his chair at the table, bent over the orange sports section of the *Journal.* "Now look here, Bailey," she said, "see here, read this," and she stood with one hand on her thin hip and the other rattling the newspaper at his bald head. "Here this fellow that calls himself The Misfit is aloose from the Federal Pen and headed toward Florida and you read here what it says he did to these people. Just you read it. I wouldn't take my children in any direction with a criminal like that aloose in it. I couldn't answer to my conscience if I did."

Bailey didn't look up from his reading so she wheeled around then and faced the children's mother, a young woman in slacks, whose face was as broad and innocent as a cabbage and was tied around with a green head-kerchief that had two points on the top like rabbit's ears. She was sitting on the sofa, feeding the baby his apricots out of a jar. "The children have been to Florida before," the old lady said. "You all ought to take them somewhere else for a change so they would see different parts of the world and be broad. They never have been to east Tennessee."

The children's mother didn't seem to hear her but the eight-year-old boy, John Wesley, a stocky child with glasses, said, "If you don't want to go to Florida, why dontcha stay at home?" He and the little girl, June Star, were reading the funny papers on the floor.

"She wouldn't stay at home to be queen for a day," June Star said without raising her yellow head.

"Yes and what would you do if this fellow, The Misfit, caught you?" the grandmother asked.

"I'd smack his face," John Wesley said.

"She wouldn't stay at home for a million bucks," June Star said. "Afraid she'd miss something. She has to go everywhere we go."

"All right, Miss," the grandmother said. "Just remember that the next time you want me to curl your hair."

June Star said her hair was naturally curly.

The next morning the grandmother was the first one in the car, ready to go. She had her big black valise that looked like the head of a hippopotamus in one corner, and underneath it she was hiding a basket with Pitty Sing, the cat, in it. She didn't intend for the cat to be left alone in the house for three days because he would miss her too much and she was afraid he might brush against one of the gas burners and accidentally asphyxiate himself. Her son, Bailey, didn't like to arrive at a motel with a cat.

She sat in the middle of the back seat with John Wesley and June Star on either side of her. Bailey and the children's mother and the baby sat in front and they left Atlanta at eight forty-five with the mileage on the car at 55890. The grandmother wrote this down because she thought it would be interesting to say how many miles they had been when they got back. It took them twenty minutes to reach the outskirts of the city.

The old lady settled herself comfortably, removing her white cotton gloves and putting them up with her purse on the shelf in front of the back window. The children's mother still had on slacks and still had her head tied up in a green kerchief, but the grandmother had on a navy blue straw sailor hat with a bunch of white violets on the brim and a navy blue dress with a small white dot in the print. Her collars and cuffs were white organdy trimmed with lace and at her neckline she had pinned a purple spray of cloth violets containing a sachet. In case of an accident, anyone seeing her dead on the highway would know at once that she was a lady.

She said she thought it was going to be a good day for driving, neither too hot nor too cold, and she cautioned Bailey that the speed limit was fifty-five miles an hour and that the patrolmen hid themselves behind billboards and small clumps of trees and sped out after you before you had a chance to slow down. She pointed out interesting details of the scenery: Stone Mountain; the blue granite that in some places came up to both sides of the highway; the brilliant red clay banks slightly streaked with purple; and the various crops that made rows of green lace-work on the ground. The trees were full of silver-white sunlight and the meanest of them sparkled. The children were reading comic magazines and their mother had gone back to sleep.

"Let's go through Georgia fast so we won't have to look at it much," John Wesley said.

"If I were a little boy," said the grandmother, "I wouldn't talk about my native state that way. Tennessee has the mountains and Georgia has the hills."

"Tennessee is just a hillbilly dumping ground," John Wesley said, "and Georgia is a lousy state too."

"You said it," June Star said.

"In my time," said the grandmother, folding her thin veined fingers, "children were more respectful of their native states and their parents and everything else. People did right then. Oh look at the cute little pickaninny!" she said and pointed to a Negro child standing in the door of a shack. "Wouldn't that make a picture, now?" she asked and they all turned and looked at the little Negro out of the back window. He waved.

"He didn't have any britches on," June Star said.

"He probably didn't have any," the grandmother explained. "Little niggers in the country don't have things like we do. If I could paint, I'd paint that picture," she said.

The children exchanged comic books.

The grandmother offered to hold the baby and the children's mother passed him over the front seat to her. She set him on her knee and bounced him and told him about the things they were passing. She rolled her eyes and screwed up her mouth and stuck her leathery thin face into his smooth bland one. Occasionally he gave her a faraway smile. They passed a large cotton field with five or six graves fenced in the middle of it, like a small island. "Look at the graveyard!" the grandmother said, pointing it out. "That was the old family burying ground. That belonged to the plantation."

"Where's the plantation?" John Wesley asked.

"Gone with the Wind," said the grandmother. "Ha. Ha."

When the children finished all the comic books they had brought, they opened the lunch and ate it. The grandmother ate a peanut butter sandwich and an olive and would not let the children throw the box and the paper napkins out the window. When there was nothing else to do they played a game by choosing a cloud and making the other two guess what shape it suggested. John Wesley took one the shape of a cow and June Star guessed a cow and John Wesley said, no, an automobile, and June

Star said he didn't play fair, and they began to slap each other over the grandmother.

The grandmother said she would tell them a story if they would keep quiet. When she told a story, she rolled her eyes and waved her head and was very dramatic. She said once when she was a maiden lady she had been courted by a Mr. Edgar Atkins Teagarden from Jasper, Georgia. She said he was a very good-looking man and a gentleman and that he brought her a watermelon every Saturday afternoon with his initials cut in it, E. A. T. Well, one Saturday, she said, Mr. Teagarden brought the watermelon and there was nobody at home and he left it on the front porch and returned in his buggy to Jasper, but she never got the watermelon, she said, because a nigger boy ate it when he saw the initials, E. A. T.! This story tickled John Wesley's funny bone and he giggled and giggled but June Star didn't think it was any good. She said she wouldn't marry a man that just brought her a watermelon on Saturday. The grandmother said she would have done well to marry Mr. Teagarden because he was a gentleman and had bought Coca-Cola stock when it first came out and that he had died only a few years ago, a very wealthy man.

They stopped at The Tower for barbecued sandwiches. The Tower was a part stucco and part wood filling station and dance hall set in a clearing outside of Timothy. A fat man named Red Sammy Butts ran it and there were signs stuck here and there on the building and for miles up and down the highway saying, TRY RED SAMMY'S FAMOUS BARBE-CUE. NONE LIKE FAMOUS RED SAMMY'S! RED SAM! THE FAT BOY WITH THE HAPPY LAUGH. A VETERAN! RED SAMMY'S YOUR MAN!

Red Sammy was lying on the bare ground outside The Tower with his head under a truck while a gray monkey about a foot high, chained to a small chinaberry tree, chattered nearby. The monkey sprang back into the tree and got on the highest limb as soon as he saw the children jump out of the car and run toward him.

Inside, The Tower was a long dark room with a counter at one end and tables at the other and dancing space in the middle. They all sat down at a board table next to the nickelodeon and Red Sam's wife, a tall burnt-brown woman with hair and eyes lighter than her skin, came and took their order. The children's mother put a dime in the machine and played "The Tennessee Waltz," and the grandmother said that tune always made her want to dance. She asked Bailey if he would like to dance but he only glared at her. He didn't have a naturally sunny disposition like she did and trips made him nervous. The grandmother's brown eyes were very bright. She swayed her head from side to side and pretended she was dancing in her chair. June Star said play something she could tap to so the children's mother put in another dime and played a fast number and June Star stepped out onto the dance floor and did her tap routine.

"Ain't she cute?" Red Sam's wife said, leaning over the counter. "Would you like to come be my little girl?"

"No I certainly wouldn't," June Star said. "I wouldn't live in a broken-down place like this for a million bucks!" and she ran back to the table.

"Ain't she cute?" the woman repeated, stretching her mouth politely.

"Aren't you ashamed?" hissed the grandmother.

Red Sam came in and told his wife to quit lounging on the counter and hurry up with these people's order. His khaki trousers reached just to his hip bones and his stomach hung over them like a sack of meal swaying under his shirt. He came over and sat down at a table nearby and let out a combination sigh and yodel. "You can't win," he said. "You can't win," and he wiped his sweating red face off with a gray handkerchief. "These days you don't know who to trust," he said. "Ain't that the truth?"

"People are certainly not nice like they used to be," said the grandmother.

"Two fellers come in here last week," Red Sammy said, "driving a Chrysler. It was a old beat-up car but it was a good one and these boys looked all right to me. Said they worked at the mill and you know I let them fellers charge the gas they bought? Now why did I do that?"

"Because you're a good man!" the grandmother said at once.

"Yes'm, I suppose so," Red Sam said as if he were struck with this answer.

His wife brought the orders, carrying the five plates all at once without a tray, two in each hand and one balanced on her arm. "It isn't a soul in this green world of God's that you can trust," she said. "And I don't count nobody out of that, not nobody," she repeated, looking at Red Sammy.

"Did you read about that criminal, The Misfit, that's escaped?" asked the grandmother.

"I wouldn't be a bit surprised if he didn't attack this place right here," said the woman. "If he hears about it being here, I wouldn't be none surprised to see him. If he hears it's two cent in the cash register, I wouldn't be a tall surprised if he . . ."

"That'll do," Red Sam said. "Go bring these people their Co'-Colas," and the woman went off to get the rest of the order.

"A good man is hard to find," Red Sammy said. "Everything is getting terrible. I remember the day you could go off and leave your screen door unlatched. Not no more."

He and the grandmother discussed better times. The old lady said that in her opinion Europe was entirely to blame for the way things were now. She said the way Europe acted you would think we were made of

money and Red Sam said it was no use talking about it, she was exactly
right. The children ran outside into the white sunlight and looked at
the monkey in the lacy chinaberry tree. He was busy catching fleas on
himself and biting each one carefully between his teeth as if it were a
delicacy.

They drove off again into the hot afternoon. The grandmother took
cat naps and woke up every few minutes with her own snoring. Outside
of Toombsboro she woke up and recalled an old plantation that she had
visited in this neighborhood once when she was a young lady. She said
the house had six white columns across the front and that there was an
avenue of oaks leading up to it and two little wooden trellis arbors on
either side in front where you sat down with your suitor after a stroll in
the garden. She recalled exactly which road to turn off to get to it. She
knew that Bailey would not be willing to lose any time looking at an old
house, but the more she talked about it, the more she wanted to see it
once again and find out if the little twin arbors were still standing.
"There was a secret panel in this house," she said craftily, not telling the
truth but wishing that she were, "and the story went that all the family
silver was hidden in it when Sherman came through but it was never
found . . ."

"Hey!" John Wesley said. "Let's go see it! We'll find it! We'll poke all the
woodwork and find it! Who lives there? Where do you turn off at? Hey
Pop, can't we turn off there?"

"We never have seen a house with a secret panel!" June Star shrieked.
"Let's go to the house with the secret panel! Hey Pop, can't we go see the
house with the secret panel!"

"It's not far from here, I know," the grandmother said. "It wouldn't
take over twenty minutes."

Bailey was looking straight ahead. His jaw was as rigid as a horse-
shoe. "No," he said.

The children began to yell and scream that they wanted to see the
house with the secret panel. John Wesley kicked the back of the front
seat and June Star hung over her mother's shoulder and whined desperately into her ear that they never had any fun even on their vacation, that
they could never do what THEY wanted to do. The baby began to scream
and John Wesley kicked the back of the seat so hard that his father could
feel the blows in his kidney.

"All right!" he shouted and drew the car to a stop at the side of the
road. "Will you all shut up? Will you all just shut up for one second? If
you don't shut up, we won't go anywhere."

"It would be very educational for them," the grandmother murmured.

"All right," Bailey said, "but get this: this is the only time we're going
to stop for anything like this. This is the one and only time."

"The dirt road that you have to turn down is about a mile back," the grandmother directed. "I marked it when we passed."

"A dirt road," Bailey groaned.

After they had turned around and were headed toward the dirt road, the grandmother recalled other points about the house, the beautiful glass over the front doorway and the candle-lamp in the hall. John Wesley said that the secret panel was probably in the fireplace.

"You can't go inside this house," Bailey said. "You don't know who lives there."

"While you all talk to the people in front, I'll run around behind and get in a window," John Wesley suggested.

"We'll all stay in the car," his mother said.

They turned onto the dirt road and the car raced roughly along in a swirl of pink dust. The grandmother recalled the times when there were no paved roads and thirty miles was a day's journey. The dirt road was hilly and there were sudden washes in it and sharp curves on dangerous embankments. All at once they would be on a hill, looking down over the blue tops of trees for miles around, then the next minute, they would be in a red depression with the dust-coated trees looking down on them.

"This place had better turn up in a minute," Bailey said, "or I'm going to turn around."

The road looked as if no one had traveled on it in months.

"It's not much farther," the grandmother said and just as she said it, a horrible thought came to her. The thought was so embarrassing that she turned red in the face and her eyes dilated and her feet jumped up, upsetting her valise in the corner. The instant the valise moved, the newspaper top she had over the basket under it rose with a snarl and Pitty Sing, the cat, sprang onto Bailey's shoulder.

The children were thrown to the floor and their mother, clutching the baby, was thrown out the door onto the ground; the old lady was thrown into the front seat. The car turned over once and landed right-side-up in a gulch off the side of the road. Bailey remained in the driver's seat with the cat—gray-striped with a broad white face and an orange nose—clinging to his neck like a caterpillar.

As soon as the children saw they could move their arms and legs, they scrambled out of the car, shouting, "We've had an ACCIDENT!" The grandmother was curled up under the dashboard, hoping she was injured so that Bailey's wrath would not come down on her all at once. The horrible thought she had had before the accident was that the house she had remembered so vividly was not in Georgia but in Tennessee.

Bailey removed the cat from his neck with both hands and flung it out the window against the side of a pine tree. Then he got out of the car and started looking for the children's mother. She was sitting against the side of the red gutted ditch, holding the screaming baby, but she only had a cut down her face and a broken shoulder. "We've had an ACCIDENT!" the children screamed in a frenzy of delight.

"But nobody's killed," June Star said with disappointment as the grandmother limped out of the car, her hat still pinned to her head but the broken front brim standing up at a jaunty angle and the violet spray hanging off the side. They all sat down in the ditch, except the children, to recover from the shock. They were all shaking.

"Maybe a car will come along," said the children's mother hoarsely.

"I believe I have injured an organ," said the grandmother, pressing her side, but no one answered her. Bailey's teeth were clattering. He had on a yellow sport shirt with bright blue parrots designed in it and his face was as yellow as the shirt. The grandmother decided that she would not mention that the house was in Tennessee.

The road was about ten feet above and they could only see the tops of the trees on the other side of it. Behind the ditch they were sitting in there were more woods, tall and dark and deep. In a few minutes they saw a car some distance away on top of a hill, coming slowly as if the occupants were watching them. The grandmother stood up and waved both arms dramatically to attract their attention. The car continued to come on slowly, disappeared around a bend and appeared again, moving even slower, on top of the hill they had gone over. It was a big black battered hearse-like automobile. There were three men in it.

It came to a stop just over them and for some minutes, the driver looked down with a steady expressionless gaze to where they were sitting, and didn't speak. Then he turned his head and muttered something to the other two and they got out. One was a fat boy in black trousers and a red sweat shirt with a silver stallion embossed on the front of it. He moved around on the right side of them and stood staring, his mouth partly open in a kind of loose grin. The other had on khaki pants and a blue striped coat and a gray hat pulled very low, hiding most of his face. He came around slowly on the left side. Neither spoke.

The driver got out of the car and stood by the side of it, looking down at them. He was an older man than the other two. His hair was just beginning to gray and he wore silver-rimmed spectacles that gave him a scholarly look. He had a long creased face and didn't have on any shirt or undershirt. He had on blue jeans that were too tight for him and was holding a black hat and a gun. The two boys also had guns.

"We've had an ACCIDENT!" the children screamed.

The grandmother had the peculiar feeling that the bespectacled man was someone she knew. His face was as familiar to her as if she had known him all her life but she could not recall who he was. He moved away from the car and began to come down the embankment, placing his feet carefully so that he wouldn't slip. He had on tan and white shoes and no socks, and his ankles were red and thin. "Good afternoon," he said. "I see you all had you a little spill."

"We turned over twice!" said the grandmother.

"Oncet," he corrected. "We seen it happen. Try their car and see will it run, Hiram," he said quietly to the boy with the gray hat.

"What you got that gun for?" John Wesley asked. "Whatcha gonna do with that gun?"

"Lady," the man said to the children's mother, "would you mind calling them children to sit down by you? Children make me nervous. I want all you all to sit down right together there where you're at."

"What are you telling US what to do for?" June Star asked.

Behind them the line of woods gaped like a dark open mouth. "Come here," said the mother.

"Look here now," Bailey began suddenly, "we're in a predicament! We're in . . ."

The grandmother shrieked. She scrambled to her feet and stood staring. "You're The Misfit!" she said. "I recognized you at once!"

"Yes'm," the man said, smiling slightly as if he were pleased in spite of himself to be known, "but it would have been better for all of you, lady, if you hadn't of reckernized me."

Bailey turned his head sharply and said something to his mother that shocked even the children. The old lady began to cry and The Misfit reddened.

"Lady," he said, "don't you get upset. Sometimes a man says things he don't mean. I don't reckon he meant to talk to you thataway."

"You wouldn't shoot a lady, would you?" the grandmother said and removed a clean handkerchief from her cuff and began to slap at her eyes with it.

The Misfit pointed the toe of his shoe into the ground and made a little hole and then covered it up again. "I would hate to have to," he said.

"Listen," the grandmother almost screamed, "I know you're a good man. You don't look a bit like you have common blood. I know you must come from nice people!"

"Yes mam," he said, "finest people in the world." When he smiled he showed a row of strong white teeth. "God never made a finer woman than my mother and my daddy's heart was pure gold," he said. The boy with the red sweat shirt had come around behind them and was standing with his gun at his hip. The Misfit squatted down on the ground. "Watch them children, Bobby Lee," he said. "You know they make me nervous." He looked at the six of them huddled together in front of him and he seemed to be embarrassed as if he couldn't think of anything to say. "Ain't a cloud in the sky," he remarked, looking up at it. "Don't see no sun but don't see no cloud neither."

"Yes, it's a beautiful day," said the grandmother. "Listen," she said, "you shouldn't call yourself The Misfit because I know you're a good man at heart. I can just look at you and tell."

"Hush!" Bailey yelled. "Hush! Everybody shut up and let me handle this!" He was squatting in the position of a runner about to sprint forward but he didn't move.

"I pre-chate that, lady," The Misfit said and drew a little circle in the ground with the butt of his gun.

"It'll take a half a hour to fix this here car," Hiram called, looking over the raised hood of it.

"Well, first you and Bobby Lee get him and that little boy to step over yonder with you," The Misfit said, pointing to Bailey and John Wesley. "The boys want to ast you something," he said to Bailey. "Would you mind stepping back in them woods there with them?"

"Listen," Bailey began, "we're in a terrible predicament! Nobody realizes what this is," and his voice cracked. His eyes were as blue and intense as the parrots in his shirt and he remained perfectly still.

The grandmother reached up to adjust her hat brim as if she were going to the woods with him but it came off in her hand. She stood staring at it and after a second she let it fall on the ground. Hiram pulled Bailey up by the arm as if he were assisting an old man. John Wesley caught hold of his father's hand and Bobby Lee followed. They went off toward the woods and just as they reached the dark edge, Bailey turned and supporting himself against a gray naked pine trunk, he shouted, "I'll be back in a minute, Mamma, wait on me!"

"Come back this instant!" his mother shrilled but they all disappeared into the woods.

"Bailey Boy!" the grandmother called in a tragic voice but she found she was looking at The Misfit squatting on the ground in front of her. "I just know you're a good man," she said desperately. "You're not a bit common!"

"Nome, I ain't a good man," The Misfit said after a second as if he had considered her statement carefully, "but I ain't the worst in the world neither. My daddy said I was a different breed of dog from my brothers and sisters. 'You know,' Daddy said, 'it's some that can live their whole life out without asking about it and it's others has to know why it is, and this boy is one of the latters. He's going to be into everything!'" He put on his black hat and looked up suddenly and then away deep into the woods as if he were embarrassed again. "I'm sorry I don't have on a shirt before you ladies," he said, hunching his shoulders slightly. "We buried our clothes that we had on when we escaped and we're just making do until we can get better. We borrowed these from some folks we met," he explained.

"That's perfectly all right," the grandmother said. "Maybe Bailey has an extra shirt in his suitcase."

"I'll look and see terrectly," The Misfit said.

"Where are they taking him?" the children's mother screamed.

"Daddy was a card himself," The Misfit said. "You couldn't put anything over on him. He never got in trouble with the Authorities though. Just had the knack of handling them."

"You could be honest too if you'd only try," said the grandmother. "Think how wonderful it would be to settle down and live a comfortable life and not have to think about somebody chasing you all the time."

The Misfit kept scratching in the ground with the butt of his gun as if he were thinking about it. "Yes'm, somebody is always after you," he murmured.

The grandmother noticed how thin his shoulder blades were just behind his hat because she was standing up looking down at him. "Do you ever pray?" she asked.

He shook his head. All she saw was the black hat wiggle between his shoulder blades. "Nome," he said.

There was a pistol shot from the woods, followed closely by another. Then silence. The old lady's head jerked around. She could hear the wind move through the tree tops like a long satisfied insuck of breath. "Bailey Boy!" she called.

"I was a gospel singer for a while," The Misfit said. "I been most everything. Been in the arm service, both land and sea, at home and abroad, been twict married, been an undertaker, been with the railroads, plowed Mother Earth, been in a tornado, seen a man burnt alive oncet," and he looked up at the children's mother and the little girl who were sitting close together, their faces white and their eyes glassy; "I even seen a woman flogged," he said.

"Pray, pray," the grandmother began, "pray, pray . . ."

"I never was a bad boy that I remember of," The Misfit said in an almost dreamy voice, "but somewheres along the line I done something wrong and got sent to the penitentiary. I was buried alive," and he looked up and held her attention to him by a steady stare.

"That's when you should have started to pray," she said. "What did you do to get sent to the penitentiary, that first time?"

"Turn to the right, it was a wall," The Misfit said, looking up again at the cloudless sky. "Turn to the left, it was a wall. Look up it was a ceiling, look down it was a floor. I forgot what I done, lady. I set there and set there, trying to remember what it was I done and I ain't recalled it to this day. Oncet in a while, I would think it was coming to me, but it never come."

"Maybe they put you in by mistake," the old lady said vaguely.

"Nome," he said. "It wasn't no mistake. They had the papers on me."

"You must have stolen something," she said.

The Misfit sneered slightly. "Nobody had nothing I wanted," he said. "It was a head-doctor at the penitentiary said what I had done was kill my daddy but I known that for a lie. My daddy died in nineteen ought nineteen of the epidemic flu and I never had a thing to do with it. He was buried in the Mount Hopewell Baptist churchyard and you can go there and see for yourself."

"If you would pray," the old lady said, "Jesus would help you."

"That's right," The Misfit said.

"Well then, why don't you pray?" she asked trembling with delight suddenly.

"I don't want no hep," he said. "I'm doing all right by myself."

Bobby Lee and Hiram came ambling back from the woods. Bobby Lee was dragging a yellow shirt with bright blue parrots in it.

"Thow me that shirt, Bobby Lee," The Misfit said. The shirt came flying at him and landed on his shoulder and he put it on. The grandmother couldn't name what the shirt reminded her of. "No, lady," The Misfit said while he was buttoning it up, "I found out the crime don't matter. You can do one thing or you can do another, kill a man or take a tire off his car, because sooner or later you're going to forget what it was you done and just be punished for it."

The children's mother had begun to make heaving noises as if she couldn't get her breath. "Lady," he asked, "would you and that little girl like to step off yonder with Bobby Lee and Hiram and join your husband?"

"Yes, thank you," the mother said faintly. Her left arm dangled helplessly and she was holding the baby, who had gone to sleep, in the other. "Hep that lady up, Hiram," The Misfit said as she struggled to climb out of the ditch, "and Bobby Lee, you hold onto that little girl's hand."

"I don't want to hold hands with him," June Star said. "He reminds me of a pig."

The fat boy blushed and laughed and caught her by the arm and pulled her off into the woods after Hiram and her mother.

Alone with The Misfit, the grandmother found that she had lost her voice. There was not a cloud in the sky nor any sun. There was nothing around her but woods. She wanted to tell him that he must pray. She opened and closed her mouth several times before anything came out. Finally she found herself saying, "Jesus. Jesus," meaning, Jesus will help you, but the way she was saying it, it sounded as if she might be cursing.

"Yes'm," The Misfit said as if he agreed. "Jesus thown everything off balance. It was the same case with Him as with me except He hadn't committed any crime and they could prove I had committed one because they had the papers on me. Of course," he said, "they never shown me my papers. That's why I sign myself now. I said long ago, you get you a signature and sign everything you do and keep a copy of it. Then you'll know what you done and you can hold up the crime to the punishment and see do they match and in the end you'll have something to prove you ain't been treated right. I call myself The Misfit," he said, "because I can't make what all I done wrong fit what all I gone through in punishment."

There was a piercing scream from the woods, followed closely by a pistol report. "Does it seem right to you, lady, that one is punished a heap and another ain't punished at all?"

"Jesus!" the old lady cried. "You've got good blood! I know you wouldn't shoot a lady! I know you come from nice people! Pray! Jesus, you ought not to shoot a lady. I'll give you all the money I've got!"

"Lady," The Misfit said, looking beyond her far into the woods, "there never was a body that give the undertaker a tip."

There were two more pistol reports and the grandmother raised her head like a parched old turkey hen crying for water and called, "Bailey Boy, Bailey Boy!" as if her heart would break.

"Jesus was the only One that ever raised the dead," The Misfit continued, "and He shouldn't have done it. He thown everything off balance. If He did what He said, then it's nothing for you to do but thow away everything and follow Him, and if He didn't, then it's nothing for you to do but enjoy the few minutes you got left the best you can—by killing somebody or burning down his house or doing some other meanness to him. No pleasure but meanness," he said and his voice had become almost a snarl.

"Maybe He didn't raise the dead," the old lady mumbled, not knowing what she was saying and feeling so dizzy that she sank down in the ditch with her legs twisted under her.

"I wasn't there so I can't say He didn't," The Misfit said. "I wisht I had of been there," he said, hitting the ground with his fist. "It ain't right I wasn't there because if I had of been there I would of known. Listen lady," he said in a high voice, "if I had of been there I would of known and I wouldn't be like I am now." His voice seemed about to crack and the grandmother's head cleared for an instant. She saw the man's face twisted close to her own as if he were going to cry and she murmured, "Why you're one of my babies. You're one of my own children!" She reached out and touched him on the shoulder. The Misfit sprang back as if a snake had bitten him and shot her three times through the chest. Then he put his gun down on the ground and took off his glasses and began to clean them.

Hiram and Bobby Lee returned from the woods and stood over the ditch, looking down at the grandmother who half sat and half lay in a puddle of blood with her legs crossed under her like a child's and her face smiling up at the cloudless sky.

Without his glasses, The Misfit's eyes were red-rimmed and pale and defenseless-looking. "Take her off and thow her where you thown the others," he said, picking up the cat that was rubbing itself against his leg.

"She was a talker, wasn't she?" Bobby Lee said, sliding down the ditch with a yodel.

"She would of been a good woman," The Misfit said, "if it had been somebody there to shoot her every minute of her life."

"Some fun!" Bobby Lee said.

"Shut up, Bobby Lee," The Misfit said. "It's no real pleasure in life."

[1955]

GABRIEL GARCÍA MÁRQUEZ [b. 1928]

A Very Old Man
with Enormous Wings

TRANSLATED BY GREGORY RABASSA, 1971

On the third day of rain they had killed so many crabs inside the house that Pelayo had to cross his drenched courtyard and throw them into the sea, because the newborn child had a temperature all night and they thought it was due to the stench. The world had been sad since Tuesday. Sea and sky were a single ash-gray thing and the sands of the beach, which on March nights glimmered like powdered light, had become a stew of mud and rotten shellfish. The light was so weak at noon that when Pelayo was coming back to the house after throwing away the crabs, it was hard for him to see what it was that was moving and groaning in the rear of the courtyard. He had to go very close to see that it was an old man, a very old man, lying face down in the mud, who, in spite of his tremendous efforts, couldn't get up, impeded by his enormous wings.

Frightened by that nightmare, Pelayo ran to get Elisenda, his wife, who was putting compresses on the sick child, and he took her to the rear of the courtyard. They both looked at the fallen body with mute stupor. He was dressed like a ragpicker. There were only a few faded hairs left on his bald skull and very few teeth in his mouth, and his pitiful condition of a drenched great-grandfather had taken away any sense of grandeur he might have had. His huge buzzard wings, dirty and half-plucked, were forever entangled in the mud. They looked at him so long and so closely that Pelayo and Elisenda very soon overcame their surprise and in the end found him familiar. Then they dared speak to him, and he answered in an incomprehensible dialect with a strong sailor's voice. That was how they skipped over the inconvenience of the wings and quite intelligently concluded that he was a lonely castaway from some foreign ship wrecked by the storm. And yet, they called in a neighbor woman who knew everything about life and death to see him, and all she needed was one look to show them their mistake.

"He's an angel," she told them. "He must have been coming for the child, but the poor fellow is so old that the rain knocked him down."

On the following day everyone knew that a flesh-and-blood angel was held captive in Pelayo's house. Against the judgment of the wise neighbor woman, for whom angels in those times were the fugitive survivors of a celestial conspiracy, they did not have the heart to club him to death. Pelayo watched over him all afternoon from the kitchen, armed with his bailiff's club, and before going to bed he dragged him out of the mud and locked him up with the hens in the wire chicken coop. In the middle of the night, when the rain stopped, Pelayo and Elisenda were still killing crabs. A short time afterward the child woke up without a fever and with a desire to eat. Then they felt magnanimous and decided to put the angel on a raft with fresh water and provisions for three days and leave him to his fate on the high seas. But when they went out into the courtyard with the first light of dawn, they found the whole neighborhood in front of the chicken coop having fun with the angel, without the slightest reverence, tossing him things to eat through the openings in the wire as if he weren't a supernatural creature but a circus animal.

Father Gonzaga arrived before seven o'clock, alarmed at the strange news. By that time onlookers less frivolous than those at dawn had already arrived and they were making all kinds of conjectures concerning the captive's future. The simplest among them thought that he should be named mayor of the world. Others of sterner mind felt that he should be promoted to the rank of five-star general in order to win all wars. Some visionaries hoped that he could be put to stud in order to implant on earth a race of winged wise men who could take charge of the universe. But Father Gonzaga, before becoming a priest, had been a robust woodcutter. Standing by the wire, he reviewed his catechism in an instant and asked them to open the door so that he could take a close look at that pitiful man who looked more like a huge decrepit hen among the fascinated chickens. He was lying in a corner drying his open wings in the sunlight among the fruit peels and breakfast leftovers that the early risers had thrown him. Alien to the impertinences of the world, he only lifted his antiquarian eyes and murmured something in his dialect when Father Gonzaga went into the chicken coop and said good morning to him in Latin. The parish priest had his first suspicion of an impostor when he saw that he did not understand the language of God or know how to greet His ministers. Then he noticed that seen close up he was much too human: he had an unbearable smell of the outdoors, the back side of his wings was strewn with parasites and his main feathers had been mistreated by terrestrial winds, and nothing about him measured up to the proud dignity of angels. Then he came out of the chicken coop and in a brief sermon warned the curious against the risks of being ingenuous. He reminded them that the devil had the bad habit of making use of carnival tricks in order to confuse the unwary. He argued that if wings were not the essential element in determining the difference between a hawk and an airplane, they were even less so in the recognition of angels. Nevertheless, he promised to write a letter to his bishop so that the latter would write to his primate so that the latter would write to the Supreme Pontiff in order to get the final verdict from the highest courts.

His prudence fell on sterile hearts. The news of the captive angel spread with such rapidity that after a few hours the courtyard had the bustle of a marketplace and they had to call in troops with fixed bayonets to disperse the mob that was about to knock the house down. Elisenda, her spine all twisted from sweeping up so much marketplace trash, then got the idea of fencing in the yard and charging five cents admission to see the angel.

The curious came from far away. A traveling carnival arrived with a flying acrobat who buzzed over the crowd several times, but no one paid any attention to him because his wings were not those of an angel but, rather, those of a sidereal° bat. The most unfortunate invalids on earth came in search of health: a poor woman who since childhood had been counting her heartbeats and had run out of numbers; a Portuguese man who couldn't sleep because the noise of the stars disturbed him; a sleepwalker who got up at night to undo the things he had done while awake; and many others with less serious ailments. In the midst of that shipwreck disorder that made the earth tremble, Pelayo and Elisenda were happy with fatigue, for in less than a week they had crammed their

Sidereal: Coming from the stars.

rooms with money and the line of pilgrims waiting their turn to enter still reached beyond the horizon.

The angel was the only one who took no part in his own act. He spent his time trying to get comfortable in his borrowed nest, befuddled by the hellish heat of the oil lamps and sacramental candles that had been placed along the wire. At first they tried to make him eat some moth-balls, which, according to the wisdom of the wise neighbor woman, were the food prescribed for angels. But he turned them down, just as he turned down the papal lunches that the penitents brought him, and they never found out whether it was because he was an angel or because he was an old man that in the end he ate nothing but eggplant mush. His only supernatural virtue seemed to be patience. Especially during the first days, when the hens pecked at him, searching for the stellar para-sites that proliferated in his wings, and the cripples pulled out feathers to touch their defective parts with, and even the most merciful threw stones at him, trying to get him to rise so they could see him standing. The only time they succeeded in arousing him was when they burned his side with an iron for branding steers, for he had been motionless for so many hours that they thought he was dead. He awoke with a start, rant-ing in his hermetic language and with tears in his eyes, and he flapped his wings a couple of times, which brought on a whirlwind of chicken dung and lunar dust and a gale of panic that did not seem to be of this world. Although many thought that his reaction had been one not of rage but of pain, from then on they were careful not to annoy him, because the majority understood that his passivity was not that of a hero taking his ease but that of a cataclysm in repose.

Father Gonzaga held back the crowd's frivolity with formulas of maid-servant inspiration while awaiting the arrival of a final judgment on the nature of the captive. But the mail from Rome showed no sense of urgency. They spent their time finding out if the prisoner had a navel, if his dialect had any connection with Aramaic, how many times he could fit on the head of a pin, or whether he wasn't just a Norwegian with wings. Those meager letters might have come and gone until the end of time if a providential event had not put an end to the priest's tribulations.

It so happened that during those days, among so many other carnival attractions, there arrived in town the traveling show of the woman who had been changed into a spider for having disobeyed her parents. The admission to see her was not only less than the admission to see the angel, but people were permitted to ask her all manner of questions about her absurd state and to examine her up and down so that no one would ever doubt the truth of her horror. She was a frightful tarantula the size of a ram and with the head of a sad maiden. What was most heart-rending, however, was not her outlandish shape but the sincere affliction with which she recounted the details of her misfortune. While still practically a child she had sneaked out of her parents' house to go to a dance, and while she was coming back through the woods after having danced all night without permission, a fearful thunderclap rent the sky in two and through the crack came the lightning bolt of brimstone that changed her into a spider. Her only nourishment came from the meatballs that charitable souls chose to toss into her mouth. A spectacle like that, full of so much human truth and with such a fearful lesson, was bound to defeat without even trying that of a haughty angel who scarcely deigned to look at mortals. Besides, the few miracles attributed to the angel showed a certain mental disorder, like the blind man who didn't recover his sight but grew three new teeth, or the paralytic who didn't get to walk but almost won the lottery, and the leper whose sores sprouted sunflowers. Those consolation miracles, which were more like mocking fun, had already ruined the angel's reputation when the woman who had been changed into a spider finally crushed him completely. That was how Father Gonzaga was cured forever of his insomnia and Pelayo's courtyard went back to being as empty as during the time it had rained for three days and crabs walked through the bedrooms.

The owners of the house had no reason to lament. With the money they saved they built a two-story mansion with balconies and gardens and high netting so that crabs wouldn't get in during the winter, and with iron bars on the windows so that angels wouldn't get in. Pelayo also set up a rabbit warren close to town and gave up his job as bailiff for good, and Elisenda bought some satin pumps with high heels and many dresses of iridescent silk, the kind worn on Sunday by the most desirable women in those times. The chicken coop was the only thing that didn't receive any attention. If they washed it down with creolin and burned tears of myrrh inside it every so often, it was not in homage to the angel but to drive away the dungheap stench that still hung everywhere like a ghost and was turning the new house into an old one. At first, when the child learned to walk, they were careful that he not get too close to the chicken coop. But then they began to lose their fears and got used to the smell, and before the child got his second teeth he'd gone inside the chicken coop to play, where the wires were falling apart. The angel was no less standoffish with him than with other mortals, but he tolerated the most ingenious infamies with the patience of a dog who had no illusions. They both came down with chicken pox at the same time. The doctor who took care of the child couldn't resist the temptation to listen to the angel's heart, and he found so much whistling in the heart and so many sounds in his kidneys that it seemed impossible for him to be alive. What surprised him most, however, was the logic of his wings. They seemed so natural on that completely human organism that he couldn't understand why other men didn't have them too.

When the child began school it had been some time since the sun and rain had caused the collapse of the chicken coop. The angel went dragging himself about here and there like a stray dying man. They would drive him out of the bedroom with a broom and a moment later find him in the kitchen. He seemed to be in so many places at the same time that they grew to think that he'd been duplicated, that he was reproducing himself all through the house, and the exasperated and unhinged Elisenda shouted that it was awful living in that hell full of angels. He could scarcely eat and his antiquarian eyes had also become so foggy that he went about bumping into posts. All he had left were the bare cannulae° of his last feathers. Pelayo threw a blanket over him and extended him the charity of letting him sleep in the shed, and only then did they notice that he had a temperature at night, and was delirious with the tongue twisters of an old Norwegian. That was one of the few times they became alarmed, for they thought he was going to die and not even the wise neighbor woman had been able to tell them what to do with dead angels.

And yet he not only survived his worst winter, but seemed improved with the first sunny days. He remained motionless for several days in the farthest corner of the courtyard, where no one would see him, and at the beginning of December some large, stiff feathers began to grow on his wings, the feathers of a scarecrow, which looked more like another misfortune of decrepitude. But he must have known the reason for those changes, for he was quite careful that no one should notice them, that no one should hear the sea chanteys that he sometimes sang under the stars. One morning Elisenda was cutting some bunches of onions for lunch when a wind that seemed to come from the high seas blew into the kitchen. Then she went to the window and caught the angel in his first attempts at flight. They were so clumsy that his fingernails opened a furrow in the vegetable patch and he was on the point of knocking the shed down with the ungainly flapping that slipped on the light and couldn't get a grip on the air. But he did manage to gain altitude. Elisenda let out a sigh of relief, for herself and for him, when she saw him pass over the last houses, holding himself up in some way with the risky flapping of a senile vulture. She kept watching him even when she was through cutting the onions and she kept on watching until it was no longer possible for her to see him, because then he was no longer an annoyance in her life but an imaginary dot on the horizon of the sea.

[1955]

Cannulae: The tubular pieces by which feathers are attached to a body.

CHINUA ACHEBE [b. 1930]

Civil Peace

Jonathan Iwegbu counted himself extraordinarily lucky. "Happy survival!" meant so much more to him than just a current fashion of greeting old friends in the first hazy days of peace. It went deep to his heart. He had come out of the war with five inestimable blessings—his head, his wife Maria's head, and the heads of three out of their four children. As a bonus he also had his old bicycle—a miracle too but naturally not to be compared to the safety of five human heads.

The bicycle had a little history of its own. One day at the height of the war it was commandeered "for urgent military action." Hard as its loss would have been to him he would still have let it go without a thought had he not had some doubts about the genuineness of the officer. It wasn't his disreputable rags, nor the toes peeping out of one blue and one brown canvas shoes, nor yet the two stars of his rank done obviously in a hurry in biro, that troubled Jonathan; many good and heroic soldiers looked the same or worse. It was rather a certain lack of grip and firmness in his manner. So Jonathan, suspecting he might be amenable to influence, rummaged in his raffia bag and produced the two pounds with which he had been going to buy firewood which his wife, Maria, retailed to camp officials for extra stock-fish and corn meal, and got his bicycle back. That night he buried it in the little clearing in the bush where the dead of the camp, including his own youngest son, were buried. When he dug it up again a year later after the surrender all it needed was a little palm-oil greasing. "Nothing puzzles God," he said in wonder.

He put it to immediate use as a taxi and accumulated a small pile of Biafran money ferrying camp officials and their families across the four-mile stretch to the nearest tarred road. His standard charge per trip was six pounds and those who had the money were only glad to be rid of some of it in this way. At the end of a fortnight he had made a small fortune of one hundred and fifteen pounds.

Then he made the journey to Enugu and found another miracle waiting for him. It was unbelievable. He rubbed his eyes and looked again and it was still standing there before him. But, needless to say, even that monumental blessing must be accounted also totally inferior to the five

266

heads in the family. This newest miracle was his little house in Ogui Overside. Indeed nothing puzzles God! Only two houses away a huge concrete edifice some wealthy contractor had put up just before the war was a mountain of rubble. And here was Jonathan's little zinc house of no regrets built with mud blocks quite intact! Of course the doors and windows were missing and five sheets off the roof. But what was that? And anyhow he had returned to Enugu early enough to pick up bits of old zinc and wood and soggy sheets of cardboard lying around the neighbourhood before thousands more came out of their forest holes looking for the same things. He got a destitute carpenter with one old hammer, a blunt plane, and a few bent and rusty nails in his tool bag to turn this assortment of wood, paper, and metal into door and window shutters for five Nigerian shillings or fifty Biafran pounds. He paid the pounds, and moved in with his overjoyed family carrying five heads on their shoulders.

His children picked mangoes near the military cemetery and sold them to soldiers' wives for a few pennies — real pennies this time — and his wife started making breakfast akara balls for neighbours in a hurry to start life again. With his family earnings he took his bicycle to the villages around and bought fresh palm-wine which he mixed generously in his rooms with the water which had recently started running again in the public tap down the road, and opened up a bar for soldiers and other lucky people with good money.

At first he went daily, then every other day, and finally once a week, to the offices of the Coal Corporation where he used to be a miner, to find out what was what. The only thing he did find out in the end was that that little house of his was even a greater blessing than he had thought. Some of his fellow ex-miners who had nowhere to return at the end of the day's waiting just slept outside the doors of the offices and cooked what meal they could scrounge together in Bournvita tins. As the weeks lengthened and still nobody could say what was what Jonathan discontinued his weekly visits altogether and faced his palm-wine bar.

But nothing puzzles God. Came the day of the windfall when after five days of endless scuffles in queues and counter-queues in the sun outside the Treasury he had twenty pounds counted into his palms as ex-gratia award for the rebel money he had turned in. It was like Christmas for him and for many others like him when the payments began. They called it (since few could manage its proper official name) *egg-rasher.*

As soon as the pound notes were placed in his palm Jonathan simply closed it tight over them and buried fist and money inside his trouser pocket. He had to be extra careful because he had seen a man a couple of days earlier collapse into near-madness in an instant before that oceanic crowd because no sooner had he got his twenty pounds than some heartless ruffian picked it off him. Though it was not right that a man in such an extremity of agony should be blamed yet many in the queues that day were able to remark quietly on the victim's carelessness, especially after he pulled out the innards of his pocket and revealed a hole in it big enough to pass a thief's head. But of course he had insisted that the money had been in the other pocket, pulling it out too to show its comparative wholeness. So one had to be careful.

Jonathan soon transferred the money to his left hand and pocket so as to leave his right free for shaking hands should the need arise, though by fixing his gaze at such an elevation as to miss all approaching human faces he made sure that the need did not arise, until he got home.

He was normally a heavy sleeper but that night he heard all the neighbourhood noises die down one after another. Even the night watchman who knocked the hour on some metal somewhere in the distance had fallen silent after knocking one o'clock. That must have been the last thought in Jonathan's mind before he was finally carried away himself. He couldn't have been gone for long, though, when he was violently awakened again.

"Who is knocking?" whispered his wife lying beside him on the floor.

"I don't know," he whispered back breathlessly.

The second time the knocking came it was so loud and imperious that the rickety old door could have fallen down.

"Who is knocking?" he asked then, his voice parched and trembling.

"Na tief-man and him people," came the cool reply. "Make you hopen de door." This was followed by the heaviest knocking of all.

Maria was the first to raise the alarm, then he followed and all their children.

"Police-o! Thieves-o! Neighbours-o! Police-o! We are lost! We are dead! Neighbours, are you asleep? Wake up! Police-o!"

This went on for a long time and then stopped suddenly. Perhaps they had scared the thief away. There was total silence. But only for a short while.

"You done finish?" asked the voice outside. "Make we help you small. Oya, everybody!"

"Police-o! Tief-man-o! Neighbours-o! we done loss-o! Police-o! . . ."

There were at least five other voices besides the leader's.

Jonathan and his family were now completely paralysed by terror. Maria and the children sobbed inaudibly like lost souls. Jonathan groaned continuously.

The silence that followed the thieves' alarm vibrated horribly. Jonathan all but begged their leader to speak again and be done with it.

"My frien," said he at long last, "we don try our best for call dem but I tink say dem all done sleep-o . . . So wetin we go do now? Sometaim you wan call soja? Or you wan make we call dem for you? Soja better pass police. No be so?"

"Na so!" replied his men. Jonathan thought he heard even more voices now than before and groaned heavily. His legs were sagging under him and his throat felt like sandpaper.

"My frien, why you no de talk again. I de ask you say you wan make we call soja?"

"No."

"Awrighto. Now make we talk business. We no be bad tief. We no like for make trouble. Trouble done finish. War done finish and all the katakata wey de for inside. No Civil War again. This time na Civil Peace. No be so?"

"Na so!" answered the horrible chorus.

"What do you want from me? I am a poor man. Everything I had went with this war. Why do you come to me? You know people who have money. We . . ."

"Awright! We know say you no get plenty money. But we sef no get even anini. So derefore make you open dis window and give us one hundred pound and we go commot. Orderwise we de come for inside now to show you guitar-boy like dis . . ."

A volley of automatic fire rang through the sky. Maria and the children began to weep aloud again.

"Ah, missisi de cry again. No need for dat. We done talk say we na good tief. We just take our small money and go nwayorly. No molest. Abi we de molest?"

"At all!" sang the chorus.

"My friends," began Jonathan hoarsely. "I hear what you say and I thank you. If I had one hundred pounds . . ."

"Lookia my frien, no be play we come play for your house. If we make mistake and step for inside you no go like am-o. So derefore . . ."

"To God who made me; if you come inside and find one hundred pounds, take it and shoot me and shoot my wife and children. I swear to God. The only money I have in this life is this twenty pounds *egg-rasher* they gave me today . . ."

"OK. Time de go. Make you open dis window and bring the twenty pound. We go manage am like dat."

There were now loud murmurs of dissent among the chorus: "Na lie de man de lie; e get plenty money . . . Make we go inside and search properly well . . . Wetin be twenty pound? . ."

"Shurrup!" rang the leader's voice like a lone shot in the sky and silenced the murmuring at once. "Are you dere? Bring the money quick!"

"I am coming," said Jonathan fumbling in the darkness with the key of the small wooden box he kept by his side on the mat.

*   *   *

At the first sign of light as neighbours and others assembled to commiserate with him he was already strapping his five-gallon demijohn to his bicycle carrier and his wife, sweating in the open fire, was turning over akara balls in a wide clay bowl of boiling oil. In the corner his eldest son was rinsing out dregs of yesterday's palm-wine from old beer bottles.

"I count it as nothing," he told his sympathizers, his eyes on the rope he was tying. "What is *egg-rasher*? Did I depend on it last week? Or is it greater than other things that went with the war? I say, let *egg-rasher* perish in the flames! Let it go where everything else has gone. Nothing puzzles God."

[1971]

JOHN UPDIKE   [b. 1932]

A & P

In walks these three girls in nothing but bathing suits. I'm in the third checkout slot, with my back to the door, so I don't see them until they're over by the bread. The one that caught my eye first was the one in the plaid green two-piece. She was a chunky kid, with a good tan and a sweet broad soft-looking can with those two crescents of white just under it, where the sun never seems to hit, at the top of the backs of her legs. I stood there with my hand on a box of HiHo crackers trying to remember if I rang it up or not. I ring it up again and the customer starts giving me hell. She's one of these cash-register-watchers, a witch about fifty with rouge on her cheekbones and no eyebrows, and I know it made her day to trip me up. She'd been watching cash registers for fifty years and probably never seen a mistake before.

By the time I got her feathers smoothed and her goodies into a bag — she gives me a little snort in passing, if she'd been born at the right time they would have burned her over in Salem — by the time I get her on her way the girls had circled around the bread and were coming back, without a pushcart, back my way along the counters, in the aisle between the checkouts and the Special bins. They didn't even have shoes on. There was this chunky one, with the two-piece—it was bright green and the seams on the bra were still sharp and her belly was still pretty pale so I guessed she just got it (the suit)—there was this one, with one of those chubby berry-faces, the lips all bunched together under her nose, this one, and a tall one, with black hair that hadn't quite frizzed right, and one of these sunburns right across under the eyes, and a chin that was too long—you know, the kind of girl other girls think is very "striking" and "attractive" but never quite makes it, as they very well know, which is why they like her so much—and then the third one, that wasn't quite so tall. She was the queen. She kind of led them, the other two peeking around and making their shoulders round. She didn't look around, not this queen, she just walked straight on slowly, on these long white prima-donna legs. She came down a little hard on her heels, as if she didn't walk in her bare feet that much, putting down her heels and then letting the weight move along to her toes as if she was testing the floor with every step, putting a little deliberate extra action into it. You never know for sure how girls' minds work (do you really think it's a mind in there or just a little buzz like a bee in a glass jar?) but you got the idea she had talked the other two into coming in here with her, and now she was showing them how to do it, walk slow and hold yourself straight.

She had on a kind of dirty-pink—beige maybe, I don't know—bathing suit with a little nubble all over it, and what got me, the straps were down. They were off her shoulders looped loose around the cool tops of her arms, and I guess as a result the suit had slipped a little on her, so all around the top of the cloth there was this shining rim. If it hadn't been there you wouldn't have known there could have been anything whiter than those shoulders. With the straps pushed off, there was nothing between the top of the suit and the top of her head except just *her*, this clean bare plane of the top of her chest down from the shoulder bones like a dented sheet of metal tilted in the light. I mean, it was more than pretty.

She had sort of oaky hair that the sun and salt had bleached, done up in a bun that was unravelling, and a kind of prim face. Walking into the A & P with your straps down, I suppose it's the only kind of face you *can* have. She held her head so high her neck, coming up out of those white shoulders, looked kind of stretched, but I didn't mind. The longer her neck was, the more of her there was.

She must have felt in the corner of her eye me and over my shoulder Stokesie in the second slot watching, but she didn't tip. Not this queen. She kept her eyes moving across the racks, and stopped, and turned so slow it made my stomach rub the inside of my apron, and buzzed to the other two, who kind of huddled against her for relief, and then they all three of them went up the cat-and-dog-food-breakfast-cereal-macaroni-rice-raisins-seasonings-spreads-spaghetti-soft-drinks-crackers-and-cookies aisle. From the third slot I look straight up this aisle to the meat counter, and I watched them all the way. The fat one with the tan sort of fumbled with the cookies, but on second thought she put the package back. The sheep pushing their carts down the aisle—the girls were walking against the usual traffic (not that we have one-way signs or anything)—were pretty hilarious. You could see them, when Queenie's white shoulders dawned on them, kind of jerk, or hop, or hiccup, but their eyes snapped back to their own baskets and on they pushed. I bet you could set off dynamite in an A & P and the people would by and large keep reaching and checking oatmeal off their lists and muttering "Let me see, there was a third thing, began with A, asparagus, no, ah, yes, applesauce!" or whatever it is they do mutter. But there was no doubt, this jiggled them. A few houseslaves in pin curlers even looked around after pushing their carts past to make sure what they had seen was correct.

You know, it's one thing to have a girl in a bathing suit down on the beach, where what with the glare nobody can look at each other much anyway, and another thing in the cool of the A & P, under the fluorescent lights, against all those stacked packages, with her feet paddling along naked over our checkerboard green-and-cream rubber-tile floor.

"Oh Daddy," Stokesie said beside me. "I feel so faint."

"Darling," I said. "Hold me tight." Stokesie's married, with two babies chalked up on his fuselage already, but as far as I can tell that's the only difference. He's twenty-two, and I was nineteen this April.

"Is it done?" he asks, the responsible married man finding his voice. I forgot to say he thinks he's going to be manager some sunny day, maybe in 1990 when it's called the Great Alexandrov and Petrooshki Tea Company or something.

What he meant was, our town is five miles from a beach, with a big summer colony out on the Point, but we're right in the middle of town, and the women generally put on a shirt or shorts or something before they get out of the car into the street. And anyway these are usually women with six children and varicose veins mapping their legs and nobody, including them, could care less. As I say, we're right in the middle of town, and if you stand at our front doors you can see two banks and the Congregational church and the newspaper store and three real-estate offices and about twenty-seven old freeloaders tearing up Central Street because the sewer broke again. It's not as if we're on the Cape; we're north of Boston and there's people in this town haven't seen the ocean for twenty years.

The girls had reached the meat counter and were asking McMahon something. He pointed, they pointed, and they shuffled out of sight behind a pyramid of Diet Delight peaches. All that was left for us to see was old McMahon patting his mouth and looking after them sizing up their joints. Poor kids, I began to feel sorry for them, they couldn't help it.

Now here comes the sad part of the story, at least my family says it's sad, but I don't think it's so sad myself. The store's pretty empty, it being Thursday afternoon, so there was nothing much to do except lean on the register and wait for the girls to show up again. The whole store was like a pinball machine and I didn't know which tunnel they'd come out of. After a while they come around out of the far aisle, around the light bulbs, records at discount of the Caribbean Six or Tony Martin Sings or some such gunk you wonder they waste the wax on, sixpacks of candy bars, and plastic toys done up in cellophane that fall apart when a kid looks at them anyway. Around they come, Queenie still leading the way, and holding a little gray jar in her hand. Slots Three through Seven are unmanned and I could see her wondering between Stokes and me, but Stokesie with his usual luck draws an old party in baggy gray pants who stumbles up with four giant cans of pineapple juice (what do these bums *do* with all that pineapple juice? I've often asked myself) so the girls come to me. Queenie puts down the jar and I take it into my fingers icy cold. Kingfish Fancy Herring Snacks in Pure Sour Cream: 49¢. Now her hands are empty, not a ring or a bracelet, bare as God made them, and I wonder where the money's coming from. Still with that prim look she lifts a folded dollar bill out of the hollow at the center of her nubbled pink top. The jar went heavy in my hand. Really, I thought that was so cute.

Then everybody's luck begins to run out. Lengel comes in from haggling with a truck full of cabbages on the lot and is about to scuttle into that door marked MANAGER behind which he hides all day when the girls touch his eye. Lengel's pretty dreary, teaches Sunday school and the rest, but he doesn't miss that much. He comes over and says, "Girls, this isn't the beach."

Queenie blushes, though maybe it's just a brush of sunburn I was noticing for the first time, now that she was so close. "My mother asked me to pick up a jar of herring snacks." Her voice kind of startled me, the way voices do when you see the people first, coming out so flat and dumb yet kind of tony, too, the way it ticked over "pick up" and "snacks." All of a sudden I slid right down her voice into her living room. Her father and the other men were standing around in ice-cream coats and bow ties and the women were in sandals picking up herring snacks on toothpicks off a big glass plate and they were all holding drinks the color of water with olives and sprigs of mint in them. When my parents have somebody over they get lemonade and if it's a real racy affair Schlitz in tall glasses with "They'll Do It Every Time" cartoons stencilled on.

"That's all right," Lengel said. "But this isn't the beach." His repeating this struck me as funny, as if it had just occurred to him, and he had been thinking all these years the A & P was a great big sand dune and he was the head lifeguard. He didn't like my smiling—as I say he doesn't miss much—but he concentrates on giving the girls that sad Sunday-school–superintendent stare.

Queenie's blush is no sunburn now, and the plump one in plaid, that I liked better from the back—a really sweet can—pipes up, "We weren't doing any shopping. We just came in for the one thing."

"That makes no difference," Lengel tells her, and I could see from the way his eyes went that he hadn't noticed she was wearing a two-piece before. "We want you decently dressed when you come in here."

"We *are* decent," Queenie says suddenly, her lower lip pushing, getting sore now that she remembers her place, a place from which the crowd that runs the A & P must look pretty crummy. Fancy Herring Snacks flashed in her very blue eyes.

"Girls, I don't want to argue with you. After this come in here with your shoulders covered. It's our policy." He turns his back. That's policy for you. Policy is what the kingpins want. What the others want is juvenile delinquency.

All this while, the customers had been showing up with their carts but, you know, sheep, seeing a scene, they had all bunched up on Stokesie, who shook open a paper bag as gently as peeling a peach, not wanting to miss a word. I could feel in the silence everybody getting nervous, most of all Lengel, who asks me, "Sammy, have you rung up their purchase?"

I thought and said "No" but it wasn't about that I was thinking. I go through the punches, 4, 9, GROC, TOT—it's more complicated than you think, and after you do it often enough, it begins to make a little song, that you hear words to, in my case "Hello *(bing)* there, you *(gung)* hap-py pee-pul *(splat)!*"—the *splat* being the drawer flying out. I uncrease the bill, tenderly as you may imagine, it just having come from between the two smoothest scoops of vanilla I had ever known were there, and pass a half and a penny into her narrow pink palm, and nestle the herrings in a bag and twist its neck and hand it over, all the time thinking.

The girls, and who'd blame them, are in a hurry to get out, so I say "I quit" to Lengel enough for them to hear, hoping they'll stop and watch me, their unsuspected hero. They keep right on going, into the electric eye; the door flies open and they flicker across the lot to their car, Queenie and Plaid and Big Tall Goony-Goony (not that as raw material she was so bad), leaving me with Lengel and a kink in his eyebrow.

"Did you say something, Sammy?"

"I said I quit."

"I thought you did."

"You didn't have to embarrass them."

"It was they who were embarrassing us."

I started to say something that came out "Fiddle-de-doo." It's a saying of my grandmother's, and I know she would have been pleased.

"I don't think you know what you're saying," Lengel said.

"I know you don't," I said. "But I do." I pull the bow at the back of my apron and start shrugging it off my shoulders. A couple customers that had been heading for my slot begin to knock against each other, like scared pigs in a chute.

Lengel sighs and begins to look very patient and old and gray. He's been a friend of my parents for years. "Sammy, you don't want to do this to your Mom and Dad," he tells me. It's true, I don't. But it seems to me that once you begin a gesture it's fatal not to go through with it. I fold the apron, "Sammy" stitched in red on the pocket, and put it on the counter, and drop the bow tie on top of it. The bow tie is theirs, if you've ever wondered. "You'll feel this for the rest of your life," Lengel says, and I know that's true, too, but remembering how he made that pretty girl blush makes me so scrunchy inside I punch the No Sale tab and the machine whirs "pee-pul" and the drawer splats out. One advantage to this scene taking place in summer, I can follow this up with a clean exit, there's no fumbling around getting your coat and galoshes, I just saunter into the electric eye in my white shirt that my mother ironed the night before, and the door heaves itself open, and outside the sunshine is skating around on the asphalt.

I look around for my girls, but they're gone, of course. There wasn't anybody but some young married screaming with her children about some candy they didn't get by the door of a powder-blue Falcon station wagon. Looking back in the big windows, over the bags of peat moss and aluminum lawn furniture stacked on the pavement, I could see Lengel in my place in the slot, checking the sheep through. His face was dark gray and his back stiff, as if he'd just had an injection of iron, and my stomach kind of fell as I felt how hard the world was going to be to me hereafter.

[1961]

JOYCE CAROL OATES [b. 1938]

Where Are You Going, Where Have You Been?

For Bob Dylan

Her name was Connie. She was fifteen and she had a quick nervous giggling habit of craning her neck to glance into mirrors, or checking other people's faces to make sure her own was all right. Her mother, who noticed everything and knew everything and who hadn't much reason any longer to look at her own face, always scolded Connie about it. "Stop gawking at yourself, who are you? You think you're so pretty?" she would say. Connie would raise her eyebrows at these familiar complaints and look right through her mother, into a shadowy vision of herself as she was right at that moment: she knew she was pretty and that was everything. Her mother had been pretty once too, if you could believe those old snapshots in the album, but now her looks were gone and that was why she was always after Connie.

"Why don't you keep your room clean like your sister? How've you got your hair fixed—what the hell stinks? Hair spray? You don't see your sister using that junk."

Her sister June was twenty-four and still lived at home. She was a secretary in the high school Connie attended, and if that wasn't bad enough—with her in the same building—she was so plain and chunky and steady that Connie had to hear her praised all the time by her mother and her mother's sisters. June did this, June did that, she saved money and helped clean the house and cooked and Connie couldn't do a thing, her mind was all filled with trashy daydreams. Their father was away at work most of the time and when he came home he wanted supper and he read the newspaper at supper and after supper he went to bed. He didn't bother talking much to them, but around his bent head Connie's mother kept picking at her until Connie wished her mother was dead and she herself was dead and it was all over. "She makes me want to throw up sometimes," she complained to her friends. She had a high, breathless, amused voice which made everything she said a little forced, whether it was sincere or not.

276

There was one good thing: June went places with girl friends of hers, girls who were just as plain and steady as she, and so when Connie wanted to do that her mother had no objections. The father of Connie's best girl friend drove the girls the three miles to town and left them off at a shopping plaza, so that they could walk through the stores or go to a movie, and when he came to pick them up again at eleven he never bothered to ask what they had done.

They must have been familiar sights, walking around that shopping plaza in their shorts and flat ballerina slippers that always scuffed the sidewalk, with charm bracelets jingling on their thin wrists; they would lean together to whisper and laugh secretly if someone passed by who amused or interested them. Connie had long dark blond hair that drew anyone's eye to it, and she wore part of it pulled up on her head and puffed out and the rest of it she let fall down her back. She wore a pullover jersey blouse that looked one way when she was at home and another way when she was away from home. Everything about her had two sides to it, one for home and one for anywhere that was not home: her walk that could be childlike and bobbing, or languid enough to make anyone think she was hearing music in her head, her mouth which was pale and smirking most of the time, but bright and pink on these evenings out, her laugh which was cynical and drawling at home—"Ha, ha, very funny"—but high-pitched and nervous anywhere else, like the jingling of the charms on her bracelet.

Sometimes they did go shopping or to a movie, but sometimes they went across the highway, ducking fast across the busy road, to a drive-in restaurant where older kids hung out. The restaurant was shaped like a big bottle, though squatter than a real bottle, and on its cap was a revolving figure of a grinning boy who held a hamburger aloft. One night in midsummer they ran across, breathless with daring, and right away someone leaned out a car window and invited them over, but it was just a boy from high school they didn't like. It made them feel good to be able to ignore him. They went up through the maze of parked and cruising cars to the bright-lit, fly-infested restaurant, their faces pleased and expectant as if they were entering a sacred building that loomed out of the night to give them what haven and what blessing they yearned for. They sat at the counter and crossed their legs at the ankles, their thin shoulders rigid with excitement and listened to the music that made everything so good: the music was always in the background like music at a church service, it was something to depend upon.

A boy named Eddie came in to talk with them. He sat backwards on his stool, turning himself jerkily around in semi-circles and then stopping and turning again, and after a while he asked Connie if she would like something to eat. She said she did and so she tapped her friend's arm on her way out—her friend pulled her face up into a brave droll look—and Connie said she would meet her at eleven, across the way. "I just hate to leave her like that," Connie said earnestly, but the boy said that she wouldn't be alone for long. So they went out to his car and on the way Connie couldn't help but let her eyes wander over the windshields and faces all around her, her face gleaming with the joy that had nothing to do with Eddie or even this place; it might have been the music. She drew her shoulders up and sucked in her breath with the pure pleasure of being alive, and just at that moment she happened to glance at a face just a few feet from hers. It was a boy with shaggy black hair, in a convertible jalopy painted gold. He stared at her and then his lips widened into a grin. Connie slit her eyes at him and turned away, but she couldn't help glancing back and there he was still watching her. He wagged a finger and laughed and said, "Gonna get you, baby," and Connie turned away again without Eddie noticing anything.

She spent three hours with him, at the restaurant where they ate hamburgers and drank Cokes in wax cups that were always sweating, and then down an alley a mile or so away, and when he left her off at five to eleven only the movie house was still open at the plaza. Her girl friend was there, talking with a boy. When Connie came up the two girls smiled at each other and Connie said, "How was the movie?" and the girl said, "*You* should know." They rode off with the girl's father, sleepy and pleased, and Connie couldn't help but look at the darkened shopping plaza with its big empty parking lot and its signs that were faded and ghostly now, and over at the drive-in restaurant where cars were still circling tirelessly. She couldn't hear the music at this distance.

Next morning June asked her how the movie was and Connie said, "So-so."

She and that girl and occasionally another girl went out several times a week that way, and the rest of the time Connie spent around the house—it was summer vacation—getting in her mother's way and thinking, dreaming, about the boys she met. But all the boys fell back and dissolved into a single face that was not even a face, but an idea, a feeling, mixed up with the urgent insistent pounding of the music and the humid night air of July. Connie's mother kept dragging her back to the daylight by finding things for her to do or saying suddenly, "What's this about the Pettinger girl?"

And Connie would say nervously, "Oh, her. That dope." She always drew thick clear lines between herself and such girls, and her mother was simple and kindly enough to believe her. Her mother was so simple, Connie thought, that it was maybe cruel to fool her so much. Her mother went scuffling around the house in old bedroom slippers and complained over the telephone to one sister about the other, then the other called up and the two of them complained about the third one. If

June's name was mentioned her mother's tone was approving, and if Connie's name was mentioned it was disapproving. This did not really mean she disliked Connie and actually Connie thought that her mother preferred her to June because she was prettier, but the two of them kept up a pretense of exasperation, a sense that they were tugging and struggling over something of little value to either of them. Sometimes, over coffee, they were almost friends, but something would come up—some vexation that was like a fly buzzing suddenly around their heads—and their faces went hard with contempt.

One Sunday Connie got up at eleven—none of them bothered with church—and washed her hair so that it could dry all day long, in the sun. Her parents and sister were going to a barbecue at an aunt's house and Connie said no, she wasn't interested, rolling her eyes, to let mother know just what she thought of it. "Stay home alone then," her mother said sharply. Connie sat out back in a lawn chair and watched them drive away, her father quiet and bald, hunched around so that he could back the car out, her mother with a look that was still angry and not at all softened through the windshield, and in the back seat poor old June all dressed up as if she didn't know what a barbecue was, with all the running yelling kids and the flies. Connie sat with her eyes closed in the sun, dreaming and dazed with the warmth about her as if this were a kind of love, the caresses of love, and her mind slipped over onto thoughts of the boy she had been with the night before and how nice he had been, how sweet it always was, not the way someone like June would suppose but sweet, gentle, the way it was in movies and promised in songs; and when she opened her eyes she hardly knew where she was, the back yard ran off into weeds and a fenceline of trees and behind it the sky was perfectly blue and still. The asbestos "ranch house" that was now three years old startled her—it looked small. She shook her head as if to get awake.

It was too hot. She went inside the house and turned on the radio to drown out the quiet. She sat on the edge of her bed, barefoot, and listened for an hour and a half to a program called XYZ Sunday Jamboree, record after record of hard, fast, shrieking songs she sang along with, interspersed by exclamations from "Bobby King": "An' look here you girls at Napoleon's—Son and Charley want you to pay real close attention to this song coming up!"

And Connie paid close attention herself, bathed in a glow of slow-pulsed joy that seemed to rise mysteriously out of the music itself and lay languidly about the airless little room, breathed in and breathed out with each gentle rise and fall of her chest.

After a while she heard a car coming up the drive. She sat up at once, startled, because it couldn't be her father so soon. The gravel kept crunching all the way in from the road—the driveway was long—and

Connie ran to the window. It was a car she didn't know. It was an open jalopy, painted a bright gold that caught the sun opaquely. Her heart began to pound and her fingers snatched at her hair, checking it, and she whispered "Christ. Christ," wondering how bad she looked. The car came to a stop at the side door and the horn sounded four short taps as if this were a signal Connie knew.

She went into the kitchen and approached the door slowly, then hung out the screen door, her bare toes curling down off the step. There were two boys in the car and now she recognized the driver: he had shaggy, shabby black hair that looked crazy as a wig and he was grinning at her.

"I ain't late, am I?" he said.

"Who the hell do you think you are?" Connie said.

"Toldja I'd be out, didn't I?"

"I don't even know who you are."

She spoke sullenly, careful to show no interest or pleasure, and he spoke in a fast bright monotone. Connie looked past him to the other boy, taking her time. He had fair brown hair, with a lock that fell onto his forehead. His sideburns gave him a fierce, embarrassed look, but so far he hadn't even bothered to glance at her. Both boys wore sunglasses. The driver's glasses were metallic and mirrored everything in miniature.

"You wanta come for a ride?" he said.

Connie smirked and let her hair fall loose over one shoulder.

"Don'tcha like my car? New paint job," he said. "Hey."

"What?"

"You're cute."

She pretended to fidget, chasing flies away from the door.

"Don'tcha believe me, or what?" he said.

"Look, I don't even know who you are," Connie said in disgust.

"Hey, Ellie's got a radio, see. Mine's broke down." He lifted his friend's arm and showed her the little transistor the boy was holding, and now Connie began to hear the music. It was the same program that was playing inside the house.

"Bobby King?" she said.

"I listen to him all the time. I think he's great."

"He's kind of great," Connie said reluctantly.

"Listen, that guy's *great*. He knows where the action is."

Connie blushed a little, because the glasses made it impossible for her to see just what this boy was looking at. She couldn't decide if she liked him or if he was just a jerk, and so she dawdled in the doorway and wouldn't come down or go back inside. She said, "What's all that stuff painted on your car?"

"Can'tcha read it?" He opened the door very carefully, as if he was afraid it might fall off. He slid out just as carefully, planting his feet firmly on the ground, the tiny metallic world in his glasses slowing down like gelatine hardening and in the midst of it Connie's bright green blouse. "This here is my name, to begin with," he said. ARNOLD FRIEND was written in tar-like black letters on the side, with a drawing of a round grinning face that reminded Connie of a pumpkin, except it wore sunglasses. "I wanta introduce myself, I'm Arnold Friend and that's my real name and I'm gonna be your friend, honey, and inside the car's Ellie Oscar, he's kinda shy." Ellie brought his transistor up to his shoulder and balanced it there. "Now these numbers are a secret code, honey," Arnold Friend explained. He read off the numbers 33, 19, 17 and raised his eyebrows at her to see what she thought of that, but she didn't think much of it. The left rear fender had been smashed and around it was written, on the gleaming gold background: DONE BY CRAZY WOMAN DRIVER. Connie had to laugh at that. Arnold Friend was pleased at her laughter and looked up at her. "Around the other side's a lot more—you wanta come and see them?"

"No."

"Why not?"

"Why should I?"

"Don'tcha wanta see what's on the car? Don'tcha wanta go for a ride?"

"I don't know."

"Why not?"

"I got things to do."

"Like what?"

"Things."

He laughed as if she had said something funny. He slapped his thighs. He was standing in a strange way, leaning back against the car as if he were balancing himself. He wasn't tall, only an inch or so taller than she would be if she came down to him. Connie liked the way he was dressed, which was the way all of them dressed: tight faded jeans stuffed into black, scuffed boots, a belt that pulled his waist in and showed how lean he was, and a white pull-over shirt that was a little soiled and showed the hard small muscles of his arms and shoulders. He looked as if he probably did hard work, lifting and carrying things. Even his neck looked muscular. And his face was a familiar face, somehow: the jaw and chin and cheeks slightly darkened, because he hadn't shaved for a day or two, and the nose long and hawk-like, sniffing as if she were a treat he was going to gobble up and it was all a joke.

"Connie, you ain't telling the truth. This is your day set aside for a ride with me and you know it," he said, still laughing. The way he straightened and recovered from his fit of laughing showed that it had been all fake.

"How do you know what my name is?" she said suspiciously.

"It's Connie."

"Maybe and maybe not."

"I know my Connie," he said, wagging his finger. Now she remembered him even better, back at the restaurant, and her cheeks warmed at the thought of how she sucked in her breath just at the moment she passed him—how she must have looked to him. And he had remembered her. "Ellie and I come out here especially for you," he said. "Ellie can sit in back. How about it?"

"Where?"

"Where what?"

"Where're we going?"

He looked at her. He took off the sunglasses and she saw how pale the skin around his eyes was, like holes that were not in shadow but instead in light. His eyes were like chips of broken glass that catch the light in an amiable way. He smiled. It was as if the idea of going for a ride somewhere, to some place, was a new idea to him.

"Just for a ride, Connie sweetheart."

"I never said my name was Connie," she said.

"But I know what it is. I know your name and all about you, lots of things," Arnold Friend said. He had not moved yet but stood still leaning back against the side of his jalopy. "I took a special interest in you, such a pretty girl, and found out all about you like I know your parents and sister are gone somewheres and I know where and how long they're going to be gone, and I know who you were with last night, and your best friend's name is Betty. Right?"

He spoke in a simple lilting voice, exactly as if he were reciting the words to a song. His smile assured her that everything was fine. In the car Ellie turned up the volume on his radio and did not bother to look around at them.

"Ellie can sit in the back seat," Arnold Friend said. He indicated his friend with a casual jerk of his chin, as if Ellie did not count and she could not bother with him.

"How'd you find out all that stuff?" Connie said.

"Listen: Betty Schultz and Tony Fitch and Jimmy Pettinger and Nancy Pettinger," he said, in a chant. "Raymond Stanley and Bob Hutter—"

"Do you know all those kids?"

"I know everybody."

"Look, you're kidding. You're not from around here."

"Sure."

"But—how come we never saw you before?"

"Sure you saw me before," he said. He looked down at his boots, as if he were a little offended. "You just don't remember."

"I guess I'd remember you," Connie said.

"Yeah?" He looked up at this, beaming. He was pleased. He began to mark time with the music from Ellie's radio, tapping his fists lightly together. Connie looked away from his smile to the car, which was painted so bright it almost hurt her eyes to look at it. She looked at that name, ARNOLD FRIEND. And up at the front fender was an expression that was familiar—MAN THE FLYING SAUCERS. It was an expression kids had used the year before, but didn't use this year. She looked at it for a while as if the words meant something to her that she did not yet know.

"What're you thinking about? Huh?" Arnold Friend demanded. "Not worried about your hair blowing around in the car, are you?"

"No."

"Think I maybe can't drive good?"

"How do I know?"

"You're a hard girl to handle. How come?" he said. "Don't you know I'm your friend? Didn't you see me put my sign in the air when you walked by?"

"What sign?"

"My sign." And he drew an X in the air, leaning out toward her. They were maybe ten feet apart. After his hand fell back to his side the X was still in the air, almost visible. Connie let the screen door close and stood perfectly still inside it, listening to the music from her radio and the boy's blend together. She stared at Arnold Friend. He stood there so stiffly relaxed, pretending to be relaxed, with one hand idly on the door handle as if he were keeping himself up that way and had no intention of ever moving again. She recognized most things about him, the tight jeans that showed his thighs and buttocks and the greasy leather boots and the tight shirt, and even that slippery friendly smile of his, that sleepy dreamy smile that all the boys used to get across ideas they didn't want to put into words. She recognized all this and also the singsong way he talked, slightly mocking, kidding, but serious and a little melancholy, and she recognized the way he tapped one fist against the other in homage to the perpetual music behind him. But all these things did not come together.

She said suddenly, "Hey, how old are you?"

His smile faded. She could see then that he wasn't a kid, he was much older—thirty, maybe more. At this knowledge her heart began to pound faster.

"That's a crazy thing to ask. Can'tcha see I'm your own age?"

"Like hell you are."

"Or maybe a coupla years older, I'm eighteen."

"Eighteen?" she said doubtfully.

He grinned to reassure her and lines appeared at the corners of his mouth. His teeth were big and white. He grinned so broadly his eyes became slits and she saw how thick the lashes were, thick and black as if painted with a black tar-like material. Then he seemed to become embarrassed, abruptly, and looked over his shoulder at Ellie. *"Him,* he's crazy," he said. "Ain't he a riot, he's a nut, a real character." Ellie was still listening to the music. His sunglasses told nothing about what he was thinking. He wore a bright orange shirt unbuttoned halfway to show his chest, which was a pale, bluish chest and not muscular like Arnold Friend's. His shirt collar was turned up all around and the very tips of the collar pointed out past his chin as if they were protecting him. He was pressing the transistor radio up against his ear and sat there in a kind of daze, right in the sun.

"He's kinda strange," Connie said.

"Hey, she says you're kinda strange! Kinda strange!" Arnold Friend cried. He pounded on the car to get Ellie's attention. Ellie turned for the first time and Connie saw with shock that he wasn't a kid either—he had a fair, hairless face, cheeks reddened slightly as if the veins grew too close to the surface of his skin, the face of a forty-year-old baby. Connie felt a wave of dizziness rise in her at this sight and she stared at him as if waiting for something to change the shock of the moment, make it all right again. Ellie's lips kept shaping words, mumbling along with the words blasting his ear.

"Maybe you two better go away," Connie said faintly.

"What? How come?" Arnold Friend cried. "We come out here to take you for a ride. It's Sunday." He had the voice of the man on the radio now. It was the same voice, Connie thought. "Don'tcha know it's Sunday all day and honey, no matter who you were with last night today you're with Arnold Friend and don't you forget it!—Maybe you better step out here," he said, and this last was in a different voice. It was a little flatter, as if the heat was finally getting to him.

"No. I got things to do."

"Hey."

"You two better leave."

"We ain't leaving until you come with us."

"Like hell I am—"

"Connie, don't fool around with me. I mean—I mean, don't fool *around,*" he said, shaking his head. He laughed incredulously. He placed his sunglasses on top of his head, carefully, as if he were indeed wearing a wig, and brought the stems down behind his ears. Connie stared at him, another wave of dizziness and fear rising in her so that for a moment he wasn't even in focus but was just a blur, standing there against his gold car, and she had the idea that he had driven up the driveway all right but had come from nowhere before that and belonged nowhere and that everything about him and even the music that was so familiar to her was only half real.

"If my father comes and sees you—"

"He ain't coming. He's at a barbecue."

"How do you know that?"

"Aunt Tillie's. Right now they're—uh—they're drinking. Sitting around," he said vaguely, squinting as if he were staring all the way to town and over to Aunt Tillie's back yard. Then the vision seemed to clear and he nodded energetically. "Yeah. Sitting around. There's your sister in a blue dress, huh? And high heels, the poor sad bitch—nothing like you, sweetheart! And your mother's helping some fat woman with the corn, they're cleaning the corn—husking the corn—"

"What fat woman?" Connie cried.

"How do I know what fat woman. I don't know every goddamn fat woman in the world!" Arnold Friend laughed.

"Oh, that's Mrs. Hornby.... Who invited her?" Connie said. She felt a little light-headed. Her breath was coming quickly.

"She's too fat. I don't like them fat. I like them the way you are, honey," he said, smiling sleepily at her. They stared at each other for a while, through the screen door. He said softly, "Now what you're going to do is this: you're going to come out that door. You're going to sit up front with me and Ellie's going to sit in the back, the hell with Ellie, right? This isn't Ellie's date. You're my date. I'm your lover, honey."

"What? You're crazy—"

"Yes, I'm your lover. You don't know what that is but you will," he said. "I know that too. I know all about you. But look: it's real nice and you couldn't ask for nobody better than me, or more polite. I always keep my word. I'll tell you how it is, I'm always nice at first, the first time. I'll hold you so tight you won't think you have to try to get away or pretend anything because you'll know you can't. And I'll come inside you where it's all secret and you'll give in to me and you'll love me—"

"Shut up! You're crazy!" Connie said. She backed away from the door. She put her hands against her ears as if she'd heard something terrible, something not meant for her. "People don't talk like that, you're crazy," she muttered. Her heart was almost too big now for her chest and its pumping made sweat break out all over her. She looked out to see Arnold Friend pause and then take a step toward the porch lurching. He almost fell. But, like a clever drunken man, he managed to catch his balance. He wobbled in his high boots and grabbed hold of one of the porch posts.

"Honey?" he said. "You still listening?"

"Get the hell out of here!"

"Be nice, honey. Listen."

"I'm going to call the police—"

He wobbled again and out of the side of his mouth came a fast spat curse, an aside not meant for her to hear. But even this "Christ!" sounded forced. Then he began to smile again. She watched this smile come, awkward as if he were smiling from inside a mask. His whole face was a mask, she thought wildly, tanned down onto his throat but then running out as if he had plastered make-up on his face but had forgotten about his throat.

"Honey—? Listen, here's how it is. I always tell the truth and I promise you this: I ain't coming in that house after you."

"You better not! I'm going to call the police if you—if you don't—"

"Honey," he said, talking right through her voice, "honey, I'm not coming in there but you are coming out here. You know why?"

She was panting. The kitchen looked like a place she had never seen before, some room she had run inside but which wasn't good enough, wasn't going to help her. The kitchen window had never had a curtain, after three years, and there were dishes in the sink for her to do—probably—and if you ran your hand across the table you'd probably feel something sticky there.

"You listening, honey? Hey?"

"—going to call the police—"

"Soon as you touch the phone I don't need to keep my promise and can come inside. You won't want that."

She rushed forward and tried to lock the door. Her fingers were shaking. "But why lock it," Arnold Friend said gently, talking right into her face. "It's just a screen door. It's just nothing." One of his boots was at a strange angle, as if his foot wasn't in it. It pointed out to the left, bent at the ankle. "I mean, anybody can break through a screen door and glass and wood and iron or anything else if he needs to, anybody at all and specially Arnold Friend. If the place got lit up with a fire, honey, you'd come runnin' out into my arms, right into my arms an' safe at home—like you knew I was your lover and'd stopped fooling around, I don't mind a nice shy girl but I don't like no fooling around." Part of those words were spoken with a slight rhythmic lilt, and Connie somehow recognized them—the echo of a song from last year, about a girl rushing into her boy friend's arms and coming home again—

Connie stood barefoot on the linoleum floor, staring at him. "What do you want?" she whispered.

"I want you," he said.

"What?"

"Seen you that night and thought, that's the one, yes sir. I never needed to look any more."

"But my father's coming back. He's coming to get me. I had to wash my hair first—" She spoke in a dry, rapid voice, hardly raising it for him to hear.

"No, your daddy is not coming and yes, you had to wash your hair and you washed it for me. It's nice and shining and all for me. I thank you, sweetheart," he said, with a mock bow, but again he almost lost his balance. He had to bend and adjust his boots. Evidently his feet did not go all the way down; the boots must have been stuffed with something so that he would seem taller. Connie stared out at him and behind him at Ellie in the car, who seemed to be looking off toward Connie's right, into nothing. Then Ellie said, pulling the words out of the air one after another as if he were just discovering them, "You want me to pull out the phone?"

"Shut your mouth and keep it shut," Arnold Friend said, his face red from bending over or maybe from embarrassment because Connie had seen his boots. "This ain't none of your business."

"What—what are you doing? What do you want?" Connie said. "If I call the police they'll get you, they'll arrest you—"

"Promise was not to come in unless you touch that phone, and I'll keep that promise," he said. He resumed his erect position and tried to force his shoulders back. He sounded like a hero in a movie, declaring something important. He spoke too loudly and it was as if he were speaking to someone behind Connie. "I ain't made plans for coming in that house where I don't belong but just for you to come out to me, the way you should. Don't you know who I am?"

"You're crazy," she whispered. She backed away from the door but did not want to go into another part of the house, as if this would give him permission to come through the door. "What do you . . . You're crazy, you. . . ."

"Huh? What're you saying, honey?"

Her eyes darted everywhere in the kitchen. She could not remember what it was, this room.

"This is how it is, honey: you come out and we'll drive away, have a nice ride. But if you don't come out we're gonna wait till your people come home and then they're all going to get it."

"You want that telephone pulled out?" Ellie said. He held the radio away from his ear and grimaced, as if without the radio the air was too much for him.

"I toldja shut up, Ellie," Arnold Friend said, "you're deaf, get a hearing aid, right? Fix yourself up. This little girl's no trouble and's gonna be nice to me, so Ellie keep to yourself, this ain't your date—right? Don't hem in on me, don't hog, don't crush, don't bird dog, don't trail me," he said in a rapid, meaningless voice, as if he were running through all the expressions he'd learned but was no longer sure which one of them was in style, then rushing on to new ones, making them up with his eyes closed. "Don't crawl under my fence, don't squeeze in my chipmunk hole, don't sniff my glue, suck my popsicle, keep your own greasy fingers on yourself!" He shaded his eyes and peered in at Connie, who was backed against the kitchen table. "Don't mind him, honey, he's just a creep. He's a dope. Right? I'm the boy for you and like I said, you come out here nice like a lady and give me your hand, and nobody else gets hurt, I mean, your nice old bald-headed daddy and your mummy and your sister in her high heels. Because listen: why bring them in this?"

"Leave me alone," Connie whispered.

"Hey, you know that old woman down the road, the one with the chickens and stuff—you know her?"

"She's dead!"

"Dead? What? You know her?" Arnold Friend said.

"She's dead—"

"Don't you like her?"

"She's dead—she's—she isn't here any more—"

"But don't you like her, I mean, you got something against her? Some grudge or something?" Then his voice dipped as if he were conscious of rudeness. He touched the sunglasses on top of his head as if to make sure they were still there. "Now you be a good girl."

"What are you going to do?"

"Just two things, or maybe three," Arnold Friend said. "But I promise it won't last long and you'll like me that way you get to like people you're close to. You will. It's all over for you here, so come on out. You don't want your people in any trouble, do you?"

She turned and bumped against a chair or something, hurting her leg, but she ran into the back room and picked up the telephone. Something roared in her ear, a tiny roaring, and she was so sick with fear that she could do nothing but listen to it—the telephone was clammy and very heavy and her fingers groped down to the dial but were too weak to touch it. She began to scream into the phone, into the roaring. She cried out, she cried for her mother, she felt her breath start jerking back and forth in her lungs as if it were something Arnold Friend was stabbing her with again and again with no tenderness. A noisy sorrowful wailing rose all about her and she was locked inside it the way she was locked inside this house.

After a while she could hear again. She was sitting on the floor, with her wet back against the wall.

Arnold Friend was saying from the door, "That's a good girl. Put the phone back."

She kicked the phone away from her.

"No, honey. Pick it up. Put it back right."

She picked it up and put it back. The dial tone stopped.

"That's a good girl. Now you come outside."

She was hollow with what had been fear but what was now just an emptiness. All that screaming had blasted it out of her. She sat, one leg cramped under her, and deep inside her brain was something like a pinpoint of light that kept going and would not let her relax. She thought,

I'm not going to see my mother again. She thought, I'm not going to sleep in my bed again. Her bright green blouse was all wet.

Arnold Friend said, in a gentle-loud voice that was like a stage voice, "The place where you came from ain't there any more, and where you had in mind to go is cancelled out. This place you are now—inside your daddy's house—is nothing but a cardboard box I can knock down any time. You know that and always did know it. You hear me?"

She thought, I have got to think. I have got to know what to do.

"We'll go out to a nice field, out in the country here where it smells so nice and it's sunny," Arnold Friend said. "I'll have my arms tight around you so you won't need to try to get away and I'll show you what love is like, what it does. The hell with this house! It looks solid all right," he said. He ran a fingernail down the screen and the noise did not make Connie shiver, as it would have the day before. "Now put your hand on your heart, honey. Feel that? That feels solid too but we know better. Be nice to me, be sweet like you can because what else is there for a girl like you but to be sweet and pretty and give in?—and get away before her people get back?"

She felt her pounding heart. Her hand seemed to enclose it. She thought for the first time in her life that it was nothing that was hers, that belonged to her, but just a pounding, living thing inside this body that wasn't really hers either.

"You don't want them to get hurt," Arnold Friend went on. "Now get up, honey. Get up all by yourself."

She stood.

"Now turn this way. That's right. Come over to me—Ellie, put that away, didn't I tell you? You dope. You miserable creepy dope," Arnold Friend said. His words were not angry but only part of an incantation. The incantation was kindly. "Now come out through the kitchen to me honey and let's see a smile, try it, you're a brave sweet little girl and now they're eating corn and hotdogs cooked to bursting over an outdoor fire, and they don't know one thing about you and never did and honey you're better than them because not a one of them would have done this for you."

Connie felt the linoleum under her feet; it was cool. She brushed her hair back out of her eyes. Arnold Friend let go of the post tentatively and opened his arms for her, his elbows pointing in toward each other and his wrists limp, to show that this was an embarrassed embrace and a little mocking, he didn't want to make her self-conscious.

She put out her hand against the screen. She watched herself push the door slowly open as if she were back safe somewhere in the other doorway, watching this body and this head of long hair moving out into the sunlight where Arnold Friend waited.

"My sweet little blue-eyed girl," he said in a half-sung sigh that had nothing to do with her brown eyes but was taken up just the same by the vast sunlit reaches of the land behind him and on all sides of him—so much land that Connie had never seen before and did not recognize except to know that she was going to it.

[1966]

RAYMOND CARVER   [1938–1988]

What We Talk About When We Talk About Love

My friend Mel McGinnis was talking. Mel McGinnis is a cardiologist, and sometimes that gives him the right.

The four of us were sitting around his kitchen table drinking gin. Sunlight filled the kitchen from the big window behind the sink. There were Mel and me and his second wife, Teresa—Terri, we called her—and my wife, Laura. We lived in Albuquerque then. But we were all from somewhere else.

There was an ice bucket on the table. The gin and the tonic water kept going around, and we somehow got on the subject of love. Mel thought real love was nothing less than spiritual love. He said he'd spent five years in a seminary before quitting to go to medical school. He said he still looked back on those years in the seminary as the most important years in his life.

Terri said the man she lived with before she lived with Mel loved her so much he tried to kill her. Then Terri said, "He beat me up one night. He dragged me around the living room by my ankles. He kept saying, 'I love you, I love you, you bitch.' He went on dragging me around the living room. My head kept knocking on things." Terri looked around the table. "What do you do with love like that?"

She was a bone-thin woman with a pretty face, dark eyes, and brown hair that hung down her back. She liked necklaces made of turquoise, and long pendant earrings.

"My God, don't be silly. That's not love, and you know it," Mel said. "I don't know what you'd call it, but I sure know you wouldn't call it love."

"Say what you want to, but I know it was," Terri said. "It may sound crazy to you, but it's true just the same. People are different, Mel. Sure, sometimes he may have acted crazy. Okay. But he loved me. In his own way maybe, but he loved me. There was love there, Mel. Don't say there wasn't."

Mel let out his breath. He held his glass and turned to Laura and me. "The man threatened to kill me," Mel said. He finished his drink and reached for the gin bottle. "Terri's a romantic. Terri's of the kick-me-so-I'll-know-you-love-me school. Terri, hon, don't look that way." Mel reached across the table and touched Terri's cheek with his fingers. He grinned at her.

"Now he wants to make up," Terri said.

"Make up what?" Mel said. "What is there to make up? I know what I know. That's all."

"How'd we get started on this subject, anyway?" Terri said. She raised her glass and drank from it. "Mel always has love on his mind," she said. "Don't you, honey?" She smiled, and I thought that was the last of it.

"I just wouldn't call Ed's behavior love. That's all I'm saying, honey," Mel said. "What about you guys?" Mel said to Laura and me. "Does that sound like love to you?"

"I'm the wrong person to ask," I said. "I didn't even know the man. I've only heard his name mentioned in passing. I wouldn't know. You'd have to know the particulars. But I think what you're saying is that love is an absolute."

Mel said, "The kind of love I'm talking about is. The kind of love I'm talking about, you don't try to kill people."

Laura said, "I don't know anything about Ed, or anything about the situation. But who can judge anyone else's situation?"

I touched the back of Laura's hand. She gave me a quick smile. I picked up Laura's hand. It was warm, the nails polished, perfectly manicured. I encircled the broad wrist with my fingers, and I held her.

"When I left, he drank rat poison," Terri said. She clasped her arms with her hands. "They took him to the hospital in Sante Fe. That's where we lived then, about ten miles out. They saved his life. But his gums went crazy from it. I mean they pulled away from his teeth. After that, his teeth stood out like fangs. My God," Terri said. She waited a minute, then let go of her arms and picked up her glass.

"What people won't do!" Laura said.

"He's out of the action now," Mel said. "He's dead."

Mel handed me the saucer of limes. I took a section, squeezed it over my drink, and stirred the ice cubes with my finger.

"It gets worse," Terri said. "He shot himself in the mouth. But he bungled that too. Poor Ed," she said. Terri shook her head.

"Poor Ed nothing," Mel said. "He was dangerous."

Mel was forty-five years old. He was tall and rangy with curly soft hair. His face and arms were brown from the tennis he played. When he was sober, his gestures, all his movements, were precise, very careful.

"He did love me though, Mel. Grant me that," Terri said. "That's all I'm asking. He didn't love me the way you love me. I'm not saying that. But he loved me. You can grant me that, can't you?"

"What do you mean, he bungled it?" I said.

Laura leaned forward with her glass. She put her elbows on the table and held her glass in both hands. She glanced from Mel to Terri and waited with a look of bewilderment on her open face, as if amazed that such things happened to people you were friendly with.

"How'd he bungle it when he killed himself?" I said.

"I'll tell you what happened," Mel said. "He took this twenty-two pistol he'd bought to threaten Terri and me with. Oh, I'm serious, the man was always threatening. You should have seen the way we lived in those days. Like fugitives. I even bought a gun myself. Can you believe it? A guy like me? But I did. I bought one for self-defense and carried it in the glove compartment. Sometimes I'd have to leave the apartment in the middle of the night. To go to the hospital, you know? Terri and I weren't married then, and my first wife had the house and kids, the dog, everything, and Terri and I were living in this apartment here. Sometimes, as I say, I'd get a call in the middle of the night and have to go in to the hospital at two or three in the morning. It'd be dark out there in the parking lot, and I'd break into a sweat before I could even get to my car. I never knew if he was going to come up out of the shrubbery or from behind a car and start shooting. I mean, the man was crazy. He was capable of wiring a bomb, anything. He used to call my service at all hours and say he needed to talk to the doctor, and when I'd return the call, he'd say, 'Son of a bitch, your days are numbered.' Little things like that. It was scary, I'm telling you."

"I still feel sorry for him," Terri said.

"It sounds like a nightmare," Laura said. "But what exactly happened after he shot himself?"

Laura is a legal secretary. We'd met in a professional capacity. Before we knew it, it was a courtship. She's thirty-five, three years younger than I am. In addition to being in love, we like each other and enjoy one another's company. She's easy to be with.

"What happened?" Laura said.

Mel said, "He shot himself in the mouth in his room. Someone heard the shot and told the manager. They came in with a passkey, saw what had happened, and called an ambulance. I happened to be there when they brought him in, alive but past recall. The man lived for three days. His head swelled up to twice the size of a normal head. I'd never seen anything like it, and I hope I never do again. Terri wanted to go in and sit with him when she found out about it. We had a fight over it. I didn't think she should see him like that. I didn't think she should see him, and I still don't."

"Who won the fight?" Laura said.

"I was in the room with him when he died," Terri said. "He never came up out of it. But I sat with him. He didn't have anyone else."

"He was dangerous," Mel said. "If you call that love, you can have it."

"It was love," Terri said. "Sure, it's abnormal in most people's eyes. But he was willing to die for it. He did die for it."

"I sure as hell wouldn't call it love," Mel said. "I mean, no one knows what he did it for. I've seen a lot of suicides, and I couldn't say anyone ever knew what they did it for."

Mel put his hands behind his neck and tilted his chair back. "I'm not interested in that kind of love," he said. "If that's love, you can have it."

Terri said, "We were afraid. Mel even made a will out and wrote to his brother in California who used to be a Green Beret. Mel told him who to look for if something happened to him."

Terri drank from her glass. She said, "But Mel's right—we lived like fugitives. We were afraid. Mel was, weren't you, honey? I even called the police at one point, but they were no help. They said they couldn't do anything until Ed actually did something. Isn't that a laugh?" Terri said.

She poured the last of the gin into her glass and waggled the bottle. Mel got up from the table and went to the cupboard. He took down another bottle.

"Well, Nick and I know what love is," Laura said. "For us, I mean," Laura said. She bumped my knee with her knee. "You're supposed to say something now," Laura said, and turned her smile on me.

For an answer, I took Laura's hand and raised it to my lips. I made a big production out of kissing her hand. Everyone was amused.

"We're lucky," I said.

"You guys," Terri said. "Stop that now. You're making me sick. You're still on the honeymoon, for God's sake. You're still gaga, for crying out loud. Just wait. How long have you been together now? How long has it been? A year? Longer than a year?"

"Going on a year and a half," Laura said, flushed and smiling.

"Oh, now," Terri said. "Wait awhile."

She held her drink and gazed at Laura.

"I'm only kidding," Terri said.

Mel opened the gin and went around the table with the bottle.

"Here, you guys," he said. "Let's have a toast. I want to propose a toast. A toast to love. To true love," Mel said.

We touched glasses.

"To love," we said.

Outside in the backyard, one of the dogs began to bark. The leaves of the aspen that leaned past the window ticked against the glass. The afternoon sun was like a presence in this room, the spacious light of ease and generosity. We could have been anywhere, somewhere enchanted. We raised our glasses again and grinned at each other like children who had agreed on something forbidden.

"I'll tell you what real love is," Mel said. "I mean, I'll give you a good example. And then you can draw your own conclusions." He poured more gin into his glass. He added an ice cube and a sliver of lime. We waited and sipped our drinks. Laura and I touched knees again. I put a hand on her warm thigh and left it there.

"What do any of us really know about love?" Mel said. "It seems to me we're just beginners at love. We say we love each other and we do, I don't doubt it. I love Terri and Terri loves me, and you guys love each other too. You know the kind of love I'm talking about now. Physical love, that impulse that drives you to someone special, as well as love of the other person's being, his or her essence, as it were. Carnal love and, well, call it sentimental love, the day-to-day caring about the other person. But sometimes I have a hard time accounting for the fact that I must have loved my first wife too. But I did, I know I did. So I suppose I am like Terri in that regard. Terri and Ed." He thought about it and then he went on. "There was a time when I thought I loved my first wife more than life itself. But now I hate her guts. I do. How do you explain that? What happened to that love? What happened to it, is what I'd like to know. I wish someone could tell me. Then there's Ed. Okay, we're back to Ed. He loves Terri so much he tries to kill her and he winds up killing himself." Mel stopped talking and swallowed from his glass. "You guys have been together eighteen months and you love each other. It shows all over you. You glow with it. But you both loved other people before you met each other. You've both been married before, just like us. And you probably loved other people before that too, even. Terri and I have been together five years, been married for four. And the terrible thing, the terrible thing is, but the good thing too, the saving grace, you might say, is that if something happened to one of us—excuse me for saying this—but if something happened to one of us tomorrow I think the other one, the other person, would grieve for a while, you know, but then the surviving party would go out and love again, have someone else soon enough. All this, all of this love we're talking about, it would just be a memory. Maybe not even a memory. Am I wrong? Am I way off base? Because I want you to set me straight if you think I'm wrong. I want to know. I mean, I don't know anything, and I'm the first one to admit it."

"Mel, for God's sake," Terri said. She reached out and took hold of his wrist. "Are you getting drunk? Honey? Are you drunk?"

"Honey, I'm just talking," Mel said. "All right? I don't have to be drunk to say what I think. I mean, we're all just talking, right?" Mel said. He fixed his eyes on her.

"Sweetie, I'm not criticizing," Terri said.

She picked up her glass.

"I'm not on call today," Mel said. "Let me remind you of that. I am not on call," he said.

"Mel, we love you," Laura said.

Mel looked at Laura. He looked at her as if he could not place her, as if she was not the woman she was.

"Love you too, Laura," Mel said. "And you, Nick, love you too. You know something?" Mel said. "You guys are our pals," Mel said.

He picked up his glass.

Mel said, "I was going to tell you about something. I mean, I was going to prove a point. You see, this happened a few months ago, but it's still going on right now, and it ought to make us feel ashamed when we talk like we know what we're talking about when we talk about love."

"Come on now," Terri said. "Don't talk like you're drunk if you're not drunk."

"Just shut up for once in your life," Mel said very quietly. "Will you do me a favor and do that for a minute? So as I was saying, there's this old couple who had this car wreck out on the interstate. A kid hit them and they were all torn to shit and nobody was giving them much chance to pull through."

Terri looked at us and then back at Mel. She seemed anxious, or maybe that's too strong a word.

Mel was handing the bottle around the table.

"I was on call that night," Mel said. "It was May or maybe it was June. Terri and I had just sat down to dinner when the hospital called. There'd been this thing out on the interstate. Drunk kid, teenager, plowed his dad's pickup into this camper with this old couple in it. They were up in their mid-seventies, that couple. The kid — eighteen, nineteen, something — he was DOA. Taken the steering wheel through his sternum. The old couple, they were alive, you understand. I mean, just barely. But they had everything. Multiple fractures, internal injuries, hemorrhaging, contusions, lacerations, the works, and they each of them had themselves concussions. They were in a bad way, believe me. And, of course, their age was two strikes against them. I'd say she was worse off than he was. Ruptured spleen along with everything else. Both kneecaps broken. But they'd been wearing their seatbelts and, God knows, that's what saved them for the time being."

"Folks, this is an advertisement for the National Safety Council," Terri said. "This is your spokesman, Dr. Melvin R. McGinnis, talking." Terri laughed. "Mel," she said, "sometimes you're just too much. But I love you, hon," she said.

"Honey, I love you," Mel said.

He leaned across the table. Terri met him halfway. They kissed.

"Terri's right," Mel said as he settled himself again. "Get those seatbelts on. But seriously, they were in some shape, those oldsters. By the time I got down there, the kid was dead, as I said. He was off in a corner, laid out on a gurney. I took one look at the old couple and told the ER nurse to get me a neurologist and an orthopedic man and a couple of surgeons down there right away."

He drank from his glass. "I'll try to keep this short," he said. "So we took the two of them up to the OR and worked like fuck on them most of the night. They had these incredible reserves, those two. You see that once in a while. So we did everything that could be done, and toward morning we're giving them a fifty-fifty chance, maybe less than that for her. So here they are, still alive the next morning. So, okay, we move them into the ICU, which is where they both kept plugging away at it for two weeks, hitting it better and better on all the scopes. So we transfer them out to their own room."

Mel stopped talking. "Here," he said, "let's drink this cheapo gin the hell up. Then we're going to dinner, right? Terri and I know a new place. That's where we'll go, to this new place we know about. But we're not going until we finish up this cut-rate, lousy gin."

Terri said, "We haven't actually eaten there yet. But it looks good. From the outside, you know."

"I like food," Mel said. "If I had it to do all over again, I'd be a chef, you know? Right, Terri?" Mel said.

He laughed. He fingered the ice in his glass.

"Terri knows," he said. "Terri can tell you. But let me say this. If I could come back again in a different life, a different time and all, you know what? I'd like to come back as a knight. You were pretty safe wearing all that armor. It was all right being a knight until gunpowder and muskets and pistols came along."

"Mel would like to ride a horse and carry a lance," Terri said.

"Carry a woman's scarf with you everywhere," Laura said.

"Or just a woman," Mel said.

"Shame on you," Laura said.

Terri said, "Suppose you came back as a serf. The serfs didn't have it so good in those days," Terri said.

"The serfs never had it good," Mel said. "But I guess even the knights were vessels to someone. Isn't that the way it worked? But then everyone is always a vessel to someone. Isn't that right? Terri? But what I liked about knights, besides their ladies, was that they had that suit of armor, you know, and they couldn't get hurt very easy. No cars in those days, you know? No drunk teenagers to tear into your ass."

"Vassals," Terri said.

"What?" Mel said.

"Vassals," Terri said. "They were called vassals, not vessels."

"Vassals, vessels," Mel said, "what the fuck's the difference? You knew what I meant anyway. All right," Mel said. "So I'm not educated. I learned my stuff. I'm a heart surgeon, sure, but I'm just a mechanic. I go in and I fuck around and I fix things. Shit," Mel said.

"Modesty doesn't become you," Terri said.

"He's just a humble sawbones," I said. "But sometimes they suffocated in all that armor, Mel. They'd even have heart attacks if it got too hot and they were too tired and worn out. I read somewhere that they'd fall off their horses and not be able to get up because they were too tired to stand with all that armor on them. They got trampled by their own horses sometimes."

"That's terrible," Mel said. "That's a terrible thing, Nicky. I guess they'd just lay there and wait until somebody came along and made a shish kebab out of them."

"Some other vessel," Terri said.

"That's right," Mel said. "Some vassal would come along and spear the bastard in the name of love. Or whatever the fuck it was they fought over in those days."

"Same things we fight over these days," Terri said.

Laura said, "Nothing's changed."

The color was still high in Laura's cheeks. Her eyes were bright. She brought her glass to her lips.

Mel poured himself another drink. He looked at the label closely as if studying a long row of numbers. Then he slowly put the bottle down on the table and slowly reached for the tonic water.

"What about the old couple?" Laura said. "You didn't finish that story you started."

Laura was having a hard time lighting her cigarette. Her matches kept going out.

The sunshine inside the room was different now, changing, getting thinner. But the leaves outside the window were still shimmering, and I stared at the pattern they made on the panes and on the Formica counter. They weren't the same patterns, of course.

"What about the old couple?" I said.

"Older but wiser," Terri said.

Mel stared at her.

Terri said, "Go on with your story, hon. I was only kidding. Then what happened?"

"Terri, sometimes," Mel said.

"Please, Mel," Terri said. "Don't always be so serious, sweetie. Can't you take a joke?"

"Where's the joke?" Mel said.

He held his glass and gazed steadily at his wife.

"What happened?" Laura said.

Mel fastened his eyes on Laura. He said, "Laura, if I didn't have Terri and if I didn't love her so much, and if Nick wasn't my best friend, I'd fall in love with you, I'd carry you off, honey," he said.

"Tell your story," Terri said. "Then we'll go to that new place, okay?"

"Okay," Mel said. "Where was I?" he said. He stared at the table and then he began again.

"I dropped in to see each of them every day, sometimes twice a day if I was up doing other calls anyway. Casts and bandages, head to foot, the both of them. You know, you've seen it in the movies. That's just the way they looked, just like in the movies. Little eye-holes and nose-holes and mouth-holes. And she had to have her legs slung up on top of it. Well, the husband was very depressed for the longest while. Even after he found out that his wife was going to pull through, he was still very depressed. Not about the accident, though. I mean, the accident was one thing, but it wasn't everything. I'd get up to his mouth-hole, you know, and he'd say no, it wasn't the accident exactly but it was because he couldn't see her through his eye-holes. He said that was what was making him feel so bad. Can you imagine? I'm telling you, the man's heart was breaking because he couldn't turn his goddamn head and *see* his goddamn wife."

Mel looked around the table and shook his head at what he was going to say.

"I mean, it was killing the old fart just because he couldn't *look* at the fucking woman."

We all looked at Mel.

"Do you see what I'm saying?" he said.

* * *

Maybe we were a little drunk by then. I know it was hard keeping things in focus. The light was draining out of the room, going back through the window where it had come from. Yet nobody made a move to get up from the table to turn on the overhead light.

"Listen," Mel said. "Let's finish this fucking gin. There's about enough left here for one shooter all around. Then let's go eat. Let's go to the new place."

"He's depressed," Terri said. "Mel, why don't you take a pill?"

Mel shook his head. "I've taken everything there is."

"We all need a pill now and then," I said.

"Some people are born needing them," Terri said.

She was using her finger to rub at something on the table. Then she stopped rubbing.

"I think I want to call my kids," Mel said. "Is that all right with everybody? I'll call my kids," he said.

Terri said, "What if Marjorie answers the phone? You guys, you've heard us on the subject of Marjorie? Honey, you know you don't want to talk to Marjorie. It'll make you feel even worse."

"I don't want to talk to Marjorie," Mel said. "But I want to talk to my kids."

"There isn't a day goes by that Mel doesn't say he wishes she'd get married again. Or else die," Terri said. "For one thing," Terri said, "she's bankrupting us. Mel says it's just to spite him that she won't get married again. She has a boyfriend who lives with her and the kids, so Mel is supporting the boyfriend too."

"She's allergic to bees," Mel said. "If I'm not praying she'll get married again, I'm praying she'll get herself stung to death by a swarm of fucking bees."

"Shame on you," Laura said.

"Bzzzzzzz," Mel said, turning his fingers into bees and buzzing them at Terri's throat. Then he let his hands drop all the way to his sides.

"She's vicious," Mel said. "Sometimes I think I'll go up there dressed like a beekeeper. You know, that hat that's like a helmet with the plate that comes down over your face, the big gloves, and the padded coat? I'll knock on the door and let loose a hive of bees in the house. But first I'd make sure the kids were out, of course."

He crossed one leg over the other. It seemed to take him a lot of time to do it. Then he put both feet on the floor and leaned forward, elbows on the table, his chin cupped in his hands.

"Maybe I won't call the kids, after all. Maybe it isn't such a hot idea. Maybe we'll just go eat. How does that sound?"

"Sounds fine to me," I said. "Eat or not eat. Or keep drinking. I could head right on out into the sunset."

"What does that mean, honey?" Laura said.

"It just means what I said," I said. "It means I could just keep going. That's all it means."

"I could eat something myself," Laura said. "I don't think I've ever been so hungry in my life. Is there something to nibble on?"

"I'll put out some cheese and crackers," Terri said.

But Terri just sat there. She did not get up to get anything.

Mel turned his glass over. He spilled it out on the table.

"Gin's gone," Mel said.

Terri said, "Now what?"

I could hear my heart beating. I could hear everyone's heart. I could hear the human noise we sat there making, not one of us moving, not even when the room went dark.

[1981]

MARGARET ATWOOD [b. 1939]

Happy Endings

John and Mary meet.
   What happens next?
   If you want a happy ending, try A.

A

John and Mary fall in love and get married. They both have worthwhile and remunerative jobs which they find stimulating and challenging. They buy a charming house. Real estate values go up. Eventually, when they can afford live-in help, they have two children, to whom they are devoted. The children turn out well. John and Mary have a stimulating and challenging sex life and worthwhile friends. They go on fun vacations together. They retire. They both have hobbies which they find stimulating and challenging. Eventually they die. This is the end of the story.

B

Mary falls in love with John but John doesn't fall in love with Mary. He merely uses her body for selfish pleasure and ego gratification of a tepid kind. He comes to her apartment twice a week and she cooks him dinner, you'll notice that he doesn't even consider her worth the price of a dinner out, and after he's eaten the dinner he fucks her and after that he falls asleep, while she does the dishes so he won't think she's untidy, having all those dirty dishes lying around, and puts on fresh lipstick so she'll look good when he wakes up, but when he wakes up he doesn't even notice, he puts on his socks and his shorts and his pants and his shirt and his tie and his shoes, the reverse order from the one in which he took them off. He doesn't take off Mary's clothes, she takes them off herself, she acts as if she's dying for it every time, not because she likes sex exactly, she doesn't, but she wants John to think she does because if they do it often enough surely he'll get used to her, he'll come to depend on her and they will get married, but John goes out the door with hardly so much as a good-night and three days later he turns up at six o'clock and they do the whole thing over again.

Mary gets run-down. Crying is bad for your face, everyone knows that and so does Mary but she can't stop. People at work notice. Her friends tell her John is a rat, a pig, a dog, he isn't good enough for her, but she can't believe it. Inside John, she thinks, is another John, who is much nicer. This other John will emerge like a butterfly from a cocoon, a Jack from a box, a pit from a prune, if the first John is only squeezed enough.

One evening John complains about the food. He has never complained about the food before. Mary is hurt.

Her friends tell her they've seen him in a restaurant with another woman, whose name is Madge. It's not even Madge that finally gets to Mary: it's the restaurant. John has never taken Mary to a restaurant. Mary collects all the sleeping pills and aspirins she can find, and takes them and a half a bottle of sherry. You can see what kind of a woman she is by the fact that it's not even whiskey. She leaves a note for John. She hopes he'll discover her and get her to the hospital in time and repent and then they can get married, but this fails to happen and she dies.

John marries Madge and everything continues as in A.

C

John, who is an older man, falls in love with Mary, and Mary, who is only twenty-two, feels sorry for him because he's worried about his hair falling out. She sleeps with him even though she's not in love with him. She met him at work. She's in love with someone called James, who is twenty-two also and not yet ready to settle down.

John on the contrary settled down long ago: this is what is bothering him. John has a steady, respectable job and is getting ahead in his field, but Mary isn't impressed by him, she's impressed by James, who has a motorcycle and a fabulous record collection. But James is often away on his motorcycle, being free. Freedom isn't the same for girls, so in the meantime Mary spends Thursday evenings with John. Thursdays are the only days John can get away.

John is married to a woman called Madge and they have two children, a charming house which they bought just before the real estate values went up, and hobbies which they find stimulating and challenging, when they have the time. John tells Mary how important she is to him, but of course he can't leave his wife because a commitment is a commitment. He goes on about this more than is necessary and Mary finds it boring, but older men can keep it up longer so on the whole she has a fairly good time.

One day James breezes in on his motorcycle with some top-grade California hybrid and James and Mary get higher than you'd believe possible and they climb into bed. Everything becomes very underwater, but along comes John, who has a key to Mary's apartment. He finds them stoned and entwined. He's hardly in any position to be jealous, considering Madge, but nevertheless he's overcome with despair. Finally he's middle-aged, in two years he'll be bald as an egg and he can't stand it. He purchases a handgun, saying he needs it for target practice—this is the thin part of the plot, but it can be dealt with later—and shoots the two of them and himself.

Madge, after a suitable period of mourning, marries an understanding man called Fred and everything continues as in A, but under different names.

D

Fred and Madge have no problems. They get along exceptionally well and are good at working out any little difficulties that may arise. But their charming house is by the seashore and one day a giant tidal wave approaches. Real estate values go down. The rest of the story is about what caused the tidal wave and how they escape from it. They do, though thousands drown, but Fred and Madge are virtuous and lucky. Finally on high ground they clasp each other, wet and dripping and grateful, and continue as in A.

E

Yes, but Fred has a bad heart. The rest of the story is about how kind and understanding they both are until Fred dies. Then Madge devotes herself to charity work until the end of A. If you like, it can be "Madge," "cancer," "guilty and confused," and "bird watching."

F

If you think this is all too bourgeois, make John a revolutionary and Mary a counterespionage agent and see how far that gets you. Remember, this is Canada. You'll still end up with A, though in between you may get a lustful brawling saga of passionate involvement, a chronicle of our times, sort of.

You'll have to face it, the endings are the same however you slice it. Don't be deluded by any other endings, they're all fake, either deliberately fake, with malicious intent to deceive, or just motivated by excessive optimism if not by downright sentimentality.

The only authentic ending is the one provided here:

John and Mary die. John and Mary die. John and Mary die.

So much for endings. Beginnings are always more fun. True connoisseurs, however, are known to favor the stretch in between, since it's the hardest to do anything with.

That's about all that can be said for plots, which anyway are just one thing after another, a what and a what and a what.

Now try How and Why.

[1983]

TONI CADE BAMBARA [1939–1995]

The Lesson

Back in the days when everyone was old and stupid or young and foolish and me and Sugar were the only ones just right, this lady moved on our block with nappy hair and proper speech and no makeup. And quite naturally we laughed at her, laughed the way we did at the junk man who went about his business like he was some big-time president and his sorry-ass horse his secretary. And we kinda hated her too, hated the way we did the winos who cluttered up our parks and pissed on our handball walls and stank up our hallways and stairs so you couldn't halfway play hide-and-seek without a goddamn gas mask. Miss Moore was her name. The only woman on the block with no first name. And she was black as hell, cept for her feet, which were fish-white and spooky. And she was always planning these boring-ass things for us to do, us being my cousin, mostly, who lived on the block cause we all moved North the same time and to the same apartment then spread out gradual to breathe. And our parents would yank our heads into some kinda shape and crisp up our clothes so we'd be presentable for travel with Miss Moore, who always looked like she was going to church, though she never did. Which is just one of the things the grownups talked about when they talked behind her back like a dog. But when she came calling with some sachet she'd sewed up or some gingerbread she'd made or some book, why then they'd all be too embarrassed to turn her down and we'd get handed over all spruced up. She'd been to college and said it was only right that she should take responsibility for the young ones' education, and she not even related by marriage or blood. So they'd go for it. Specially Aunt Gretchen. She was the main gofer in the family. You got some ole dumb shit foolishness you want somebody to go for, you send for Aunt Gretchen. She been screwed into the go-along for so long, it's a blood-deep natural thing with her. Which is how she got saddled with me and Sugar and Junior in the first place while our mothers were in a la-de-da apartment up the block having a good ole time.

So this one day, Miss Moore rounds us all up at the mailbox and it's puredee hot and she's knockin herself out about arithmetic. And school suppose to let up in summer I heard, but she don't never let up. And the starch in my pinafore scratching the shit outta me and I'm really hating this nappy-head bitch and her goddamn college degree. I'd much rather go to the pool or to the show where it's cool. So me and Sugar leaning on the mailbox being surly, which is a Miss Moore word. And Flyboy checking out what everybody brought for lunch. And Fat Butt already wasting his peanut-butter-and-jelly sandwich like the pig he is. And Junebug punchin on Q.T.'s arm for potato chips. And Rosie Giraffe shifting from one hip to the other waiting for somebody to step on her foot or ask her if she from Georgia so she can kick ass, preferably Mercedes'. And Miss Moore asking us do we know what money is, like we a bunch of retards. I mean real money, she say, like it's only poker chips or monopoly papers we lay on the grocer. So right away I'm tired of this and say so. And would much rather snatch Sugar and go to the Sunset and terrorize the West Indian kids and take their hair ribbons and their money too. And Miss Moore files that remark away for next week's lesson on brotherhood, I can tell. And finally I say we oughta get to the subway cause it's cooler and besides we might meet some cute boys. Sugar done swiped her mama's lipstick, so we ready.

So we heading down the street and she's boring us silly about what things cost and what our parents make and how much goes for rent and how money ain't divided up right in this country. And then she gets to the part about we all poor and live in the slums, which I don't feature. And I'm ready to speak on that, but she steps out in the street and hails two cabs just like that. Then she hustles half the crew in with her and hands me a five-dollar bill and tells me to calculate 10 percent tip for the driver. And we're off. Me and Sugar and Junebug and Flyboy hangin out the window and hollering to everybody, putting lipstick on each other cause Flyboy a faggot anyway, and making farts with our sweaty armpits. But I'm mostly trying to figure how to spend this money. But they all fascinated with the meter ticking and Junebug starts laying bets as to how much it'll read when Flyboy can't hold his breath no more. Then Sugar lays bets as to how much it'll be when we get there. So I'm stuck. Don't nobody want to go for my plan, which is to jump out at the next light and run off to the first bar-b-que we can find. Then the driver tells us to get the hell out cause we there already. And the meter reads eighty-five cents. And I'm stalling to figure out the tip and Sugar say give him a dime. And I decide he don't need it bad as I do, so later for him. But then he tries to take off with Junebug foot still in the door so we talk about his mama something ferocious. Then we check out that we on Fifth Avenue and everybody dressed up in stockings. One lady in a fur coat, hot as it is. White folks crazy.

"This is the place," Miss Moore say, presenting it to us in the voice she uses at the museum. "Let's look in the windows before we go in."

"Can we steal?" Sugar asks very serious like she's getting the ground rules squared away before she plays. "I beg your pardon," say Miss Moore, and we fall out. So she leads us around the windows of the toy store and me and Sugar screamin, "This is mine, that's mine, I gotta have that, that was made for me, I was born for that," till Big Butt drowns us out.

"Hey, I'm going to buy that there."

"That there? You don't even know what it is, stupid."

"I do so," he say punchin on Rosie Giraffe. "It's a microscope."

"Whatcha gonna do with a microscope, fool?"

"Look at things."

"Like what, Ronald?" ask Miss Moore. And Big Butt ain't got the first notion. So here go Miss Moore gabbing about the thousands of bacteria in a drop of water and the somethinorother in a speck of blood and the million and one living things in the air around us is invisible to the naked eye. And what she say that for? Junebug go to town on that "naked" and we rolling. Then Miss Moore ask what it cost. So we all jam into the window smudgin it up and the price tag say $300. So then she ask how long'd take for Big Butt and Junebug to save up their allowances. "Too long," I say. "Yeh," adds Sugar, "outgrown it by that time." And Miss Moore say no, you never outgrow learning instruments. "Why, even medical students and interns and," blah, blah, blah. And we ready to choke Big Butt for bringing it up in the first damn place.

"This here costs four hundred eighty dollars," say Rosie Giraffe. So we pile up all over her to see what she pointin out. My eyes tell me it's a chunk of glass cracked with something heavy, and different-color inks dripped into the splits, then the whole thing put into a oven or something. But for $480 it don't make sense.

"That's a paperweight made of semi-precious stones fused together under tremendous pressure," she explains slowly, with her hands doing the mining and all the factory work.

"So what's a paperweight?" ask Rosie Giraffe.

"To weigh paper with, dumbbell," say Flyboy, the wise man from the East.

"Not exactly," say Miss Moore, which is what she say when you warm or way off too. "It's to weigh paper down so it won't scatter and make your desk untidy." So right away me and Sugar curtsy to each other and then to Mercedes who is more the tidy type.

"We don't keep paper on top of the desk in my class," say Junebug, figuring Miss Moore crazy or lyin one.

"At home, then," she say. "Don't you have a calendar and a pencil case and a blotter and a letter-opener on your desk at home where you do your homework?" And she know damn well what our homes look like cause she nosys around in them every chance she gets.

"I don't even have a desk," say Junebug. "Do we?"

"No. And I don't get no homework neither," say Big Butt.

"And I don't even have a home," say Flyboy like he do at school to keep the white folks off his back and sorry for him. Send this poor kid to camp posters, is his specialty.

"I do," says Mercedes. "I have a box of stationery on my desk and a picture of my cat. My godmother bought the stationery and the desk. There's a big rose on each sheet and the envelopes smell like roses."

"Who wants to know about your smelly-ass stationery," say Rosie Giraffe fore I can get my two cents in.

"It's important to have a work area all your own so that . . ."

"Will you look at this sailboat, please," say Flyboy, cutting her off and pointin to the thing like it was his. So once again we tumble all over each other to gaze at this magnificent thing in the toy store which is just big enough to maybe sail two kittens across the pond if you strap them to the posts tight. We all start reciting the price tag like we in assembly. "Handcrafted sailboat of fiberglass at one thousand one hundred ninety-five dollars."

"Unbelievable," I hear myself say and am really stunned. I read it again for myself just in case the group recitation put me in a trance. Same thing. For some reason this pisses me off. We look at Miss Moore and she lookin at us, waiting for I dunno what.

"Who'd pay all that when you can buy a sailboat set for a quarter at Pop's, a tube of glue for a dime, and a ball of string for eight cents? It must have a motor and a whole lot else besides," I say. "My sailboat cost me about fifty cents."

"But will it take water?" say Mercedes with her smart ass.

"Took mine to Alley Pond Park once," say Flyboy. "String broke. Lost it. Pity."

"Sailed mine in Central Park and it keeled over and sank. Had to ask my father for another dollar."

"And you got the strap," laugh Big Butt. "The jerk didn't even have a string on it. My old man wailed on his behind."

Little Q.T. was staring hard at the sailboat and you could see he wanted it bad. But he too little and somebody'd just take it from him. So what the hell. "This boat for kids, Miss Moore?"

"Parents silly to buy something like that just to get all broke up," say Rosie Giraffe.

"That much money it should last forever," I figure.

"My father'd buy it for me if I wanted it."

"Your father, my ass," say Rosie Giraffe getting a chance to finally push Mercedes.

"Must be rich people shop here," say Q.T.

"You are a very bright boy," say Flyboy. "What was your first clue?" And he rap him on the head with the back of his knuckles, since Q.T. the only one he could get away with. Though Q.T. liable to come up behind you years later and get his licks in when you half expect it.

"What I want to know is," I says to Miss Moore though I never talk to her, I wouldn't give the bitch that satisfaction, "is how much a real boat costs? I figure a thousand'd get you a yacht any day."

"Why don't you check that out," she says, "and report back to the group?" Which really pains my ass. If you gonna mess up a perfectly good swim day least you could do is have some answers. "Let's go in," she say like she got something up her sleeve. Only she don't lead the way. So me and Sugar turn the corner to where the entrance is, but when we get there I kinda hang back. Not that I'm scared, what's there to be afraid of, just a toy store. But I feel funny, shame. But what I got to be shamed about? Got as much right to go in as anybody. But somehow I can't seem to get hold of the door, so I step away from Sugar to lead. But she hangs back too. And I look at her and she looks at me and this is ridiculous. I mean, damn, I have never been shy about doing nothing or going nowhere. But then Mercedes steps up and then Rosie Giraffe and Big Butt crowd in behind and shove, and next thing we all stuffed into the doorway with only Mercedes squeezing past us, smoothing out her jumper and walking right down the aisle. Then the rest of us tumble in like a glued-together jigsaw done all wrong. And people lookin at us. And it's like the time me and Sugar crashed into the Catholic church on a dare. But once we got in there and everything so hushed and holy and the candles and the bowin and the handkerchiefs on all the drooping heads, I just couldn't go through with the plan. Which was for me to run up to the altar and do a tap dance while Sugar played the nose flute and messed around in the holy water. And Sugar kept given me the elbow. Then later teased me so bad I tied her up in the shower and turned it on and locked her in. And she'd be there till this day if Aunt Gretchen hadn't finally figured I was lying about the boarder takin a shower.

Same thing in the store. We all walkin on tiptoe and hardly touchin the games and puzzles and things. And I watched Miss Moore who is steady watchin us like she waitin for a sign. Like Mama Drewery watches the sky and sniffs the air and takes note of just how much slant is in the bird formation. Then me and Sugar bump smack into each other, so busy gazing at the toys, 'specially the sailboat. But we don't laugh and go into our fat-lady bump-stomach routine. We just stare at that price tag. Then Sugar run a finger over the whole boat. And I'm jealous and want to hit her. Maybe not her, but I sure want to punch somebody in the mouth.

"Watcha bring us here for, Miss Moore?"

"You sound angry, Sylvia. Are you mad about something?" Givin me one of them grins like she tellin a grown-up joke that never turns out to be funny. And she's lookin very closely at me like maybe she plannin to do my portrait from memory. I'm mad, but I won't give her that satisfaction. So I slouch around the store being very bored and say, "Let's go."

Me and Sugar at the back of the train watchin the tracks whizzin by large then small then getting gobbled up in the dark. I'm thinkin about this tricky toy I saw in the store. A clown that somersaults on a bar then does chin-ups just cause you yank lightly at his leg. Cost $35. I could see me askin my mother for a $35 birthday clown. "You wanna who that costs what?" she'd say, cocking her head to the side to get a better view of the hole in my head. Thirty-five dollars could buy new bunk beds for Junior and Gretchen's boy. Thirty-five dollars and the whole household could go visit Grand-daddy Nelson in the country. Thirty-five dollars would pay for the rent and the piano bill too. Who are these people that spend that much for performing clowns and $1000 for toy sailboats? What kinda work they do and how they live and how come we ain't in on it? Where we are is who we are, Miss Moore always pointin out. But it don't necessarily have to be that way, she always adds then waits for somebody to say that poor people have to wake up and demand their share of the pie and don't none of us know what kind of pie she talking about in the first damn place. But she ain't so smart cause I still got her four dollars from the taxi and she sure ain't gettin it. Messin up my day with this shit. Sugar nudges me in my pocket and winks.

Miss Moore lines us up in front of the mailbox where we started from, seem like years ago, and I got a headache for thinkin so hard. And we lean all over each other so we can hold up under the draggy-ass lecture she always finishes us off with at the end before we thank her for borin us to tears. But she just looks at us like she readin tea leaves. Finally she say, "Well, what did you think of F.A.O. Schwarz?"

Rosie Giraffe mumbles, "White folks crazy."

"I'd like to go there again when I get my birthday money," says Mercedes, and we shove her out the pack so she has to lean on the mailbox by herself.

"I'd like a shower. Tiring day," say Flyboy.

Then Sugar surprises me by sayin, "You know, Miss Moore, I don't think all of us here put together eat in a year what that sailboat costs." And Miss Moore lights up like somebody goosed her. "And?" she say, urging Sugar on. Only I'm standin on her foot so she don't continue.

"Imagine for a minute what kind of society it is in which some people can spend on a toy what it would cost to feed a family of six or seven. What do you think?"

"I think," say Sugar pushing me off her feet like she never done before, cause I whip her ass in a minute, "that this is not much of a democracy if you ask me. Equal chance to pursue happiness means an equal crack at the dough, don't it?" Miss Moore is besides herself and I am disgusted with Sugar's treachery. So I stand on her foot one more time to see if she'll shove me. She shuts up, and Miss Moore looks at me, sorrowfully I'm thinkin. And somethin weird is goin on, I can feel it in my chest.

"Anybody else learn anything today?" lookin dead at me. I walk away and Sugar has to run to catch up and don't even seem to notice when I shrug her arm off my shoulder.

"Well, we got four dollars anyway," she says.

"Uh, hunh."

"We could go to Hascombs and get half a chocolate layer and then go to the Sunset and still have plenty money for potato chips and ice cream sodas."

"Uh, hunh."

"Race you to Hascombs," she say.

We start down the block and she gets ahead which is O.K. by me cause I'm going to the West End and then over to the Drive to think this day through. She can run if she want to and even run faster. But ain't nobody gonna beat me at nuthin.

[1972]

BHARATI MUKHERJEE   [b. 1940]

The Management of Grief

A woman I don't know is boiling tea the Indian way in my kitchen. There are a lot of women I don't know in my kitchen, whispering and moving tactfully. They open doors, rummage through the pantry, and try not to ask me where things are kept. They remind me of when my sons were small, on Mother's Day or when Vikram and I were tired, and they would make big, sloppy omelets. I would lie in bed pretending I didn't hear them.

Dr. Sharma, the treasurer of the Indo-Canada Society, pulls me into the hallway. He wants to know if I am worried about money. His wife, who has just come up from the basement with a tray of empty cups and glasses, scolds him. "Don't bother Mrs. Bhave with mundane details." She looks so monstrously pregnant her baby must be days overdue. I tell her she shouldn't be carrying heavy things. "Shaila," she says, smiling, "this is the fifth." Then she grabs a teenager by his shirttails. He slips his Walkman off his head. He has to be one of her four children; they have the same domed and dented foreheads. "What's the official word now?" she demands. The boy slips the headphones back on. "They're acting evasive, Ma. They're saying it could be an accident or a terrorist bomb."

All morning, the boys have been muttering, Sikh bomb, Sikh bomb. The men, not using the word, bow their heads in agreement. Mrs. Sharma touches her forehead at such a word. At least they've stopped talking about space debris and Russian lasers.

Two radios are going in the dining room. They are tuned to different stations. Someone must have brought the radios down from my boys' bedrooms. I haven't gone into their rooms since Kusum came running across the front lawn in her bathrobe. She looked so funny, I was laughing when I opened the door.

The big TV in the den is being whizzed through American networks and cable channels.

"Damn!" some man swears bitterly. "How can these preachers carry on like nothing's happened?" I want to tell him we're not that important. You look at the audience, and at the preacher in his blue robe with his beautiful white hair, the potted palm trees under a blue sky, and you know they care about nothing.

The phone rings and rings. Dr. Sharma's taken charge. "We're with her," he keeps saying. "Yes, yes, the doctor has given calming pills. Yes, yes, pills are having necessary effect." I wonder if pills alone explain this calm. Not peace, just a deadening quiet. I was always controlled, but never repressed. Sound can reach me, but my body is tensed, ready to scream. I hear their voices all around me. I hear my boys and Vikram cry, "Mommy, Shaila!" and their screams insulate me, like headphones.

The woman boiling water tells her story again and again. "I got the news first. My cousin called from Halifax before six A.M., can you imagine? He'd gotten up for prayers and his son was studying for medical exams and heard on a rock channel that something had happened to a plane. They said first it had disappeared from the radar, like a giant eraser just reached out. His father called me, so I said to him, what do you mean, 'something bad'? You mean a hijacking? And he said, *Behn,* there is no confirmation of anything yet, but check with your neighbors because a lot of them must be on that plane. So I called poor Kusum straight-away. I knew Kusum's husband and daughter were booked to go yesterday."

Kusum lives across the street from me. She and Satish had moved in less than a month ago. They said they needed a bigger place. All these people, the Sharmas and friends from the Indo-Canada Society, had been there for the housewarming. Satish and Kusum made tandoori on their big gas grill and even the white neighbors piled their plates high with that luridly red, charred, juicy chicken. Their younger daughter had danced, and even our boys had broken away from the Stanley Cup telecast to put in a reluctant appearance. Everyone took pictures for their albums and for the community newspapers—another of our families had made it big in Toronto—and now I wonder how many of those happy faces are gone. "Why does God give us so much if all along He intends to take it away?" Kusum asks me.

I nod. We sit on carpeted stairs, holding hands like children. "I never once told him that I loved him," I say. I was too much the well-brought-up woman. I was so well brought up I never felt comfortable calling my husband by his first name.

"It's all right," Kusum says. "He knew. My husband knew. They felt it. Modern young girls have to say it because what they feel is fake."

Kusum's daughter Pam runs in with an overnight case. Pam's in her McDonald's uniform. "Mummy! You have to get dressed!" Panic makes her cranky. "A reporter's on his way here."

"Why?"

"You want to talk to him in your bathrobe?" She starts to brush her mother's long hair. She's the daughter who's always in trouble. She dates Canadian boys and hangs out in the mall, shopping for tight sweaters. The younger one, the goody-goody one according to Pam, the one with a voice so sweet that when she sang *bhajans* for Ethiopian relief even a frugal man like my husband wrote out a hundred-dollar check, *she* was on that plane. *She* was going to spend July and August with grandparents because Pam wouldn't go. Pam said she'd rather waitress at McDonald's. "If it's a choice between Bombay and Wonderland, I'm picking Wonderland," she'd said.

"Leave me alone," Kusum yells. "You know what I want to do? If I didn't have to look after you now, I'd hang myself."

Pam's young face goes blotchy with pain. "Thanks," she says, "don't let me stop you."

"Hush," pregnant Mrs. Sharma scolds Pam. "Leave your mother alone. Mr. Sharma will tackle the reporters and fill out the forms. He'll say what has to be said."

Pam stands her ground. "You think I don't know what Mummy's thinking? *Why her?* That's what. That's sick! Mummy wishes my little sister were alive and I were dead."

Kusum's hand in mine is trembly hot. We continue to sit on the stairs.

She calls before she arrives, wondering if there's anything I need. Her name is Judith Templeton and she's an appointee of the provincial government. "Multiculturalism?" I ask, and she says "partially," but that her mandate is bigger. "I've been told you knew many of the people on the flight," she says. "Perhaps if you'd agree to help us reach the others . . . ?"

She gives me time at least to put on tea water and pick up the mess in the front room. I have a few *samosas* from Kusum's housewarming that I could fry up, but then I think, why prolong this visit?

Judith Templeton is much younger than she sounded. She wears a blue suit with a white blouse and a polka-dot tie. Her blond hair is cut short, her only jewelry is pearl-drop earrings. Her briefcase is new and expensive looking, a gleaming cordovan leather. She sits with it across her lap. When she looks out the front windows onto the street, her contact lenses seem to float in front of her light blue eyes.

"What sort of help do you want from me?" I ask. She has refused the tea, out of politeness, but I insist, along with some slightly stale biscuits.

"I have no experience," she admits. "That is, I have an M.S.W. and I've worked in liaison with accident victims, but I mean I have no experience with a tragedy of this scale—"

"Who could?" I ask.

"—and with the complications of culture, language, and customs. Someone mentioned that Mrs. Bhave is a pillar—because you've taken it more calmly."

At this, perhaps I frown, for she reaches forward, almost to take my hand. "I hope you understand my meaning, Mrs. Bhave. There are hundreds of people in Metro directly affected, like you, and some of them speak no English. There are some widows who've never handled money or gone on a bus, and there are old parents who still haven't eaten or gone outside their bedrooms. Some houses and apartments have been looted. Some wives are still hysterical. Some husbands are in shock and profound depression. We want to help, but our hands are tied in so many ways. We have to distribute money to some people, and there are legal documents—these things can be done. We have interpreters, but we don't always have the human touch, or maybe the right human touch. We don't want to make mistakes, Mrs. Bhave, and that's why we'd like to ask you to help us."

"More mistakes, you mean," I say.

"Police matters are not in my hands," she answers.

"Nothing I can do will make any difference," I say. "We must all grieve in our own way."

"But you are coping very well. All the people said, Mrs. Bhave is the strongest person of all. Perhaps if the others could see you, talk with you, it would help them."

"By the standards of the people you call hysterical, I am behaving very oddly and very badly, Miss Templeton." I want to say to her, *I wish I could scream, starve, walk into Lake Ontario, jump from a bridge.* "They would not see me as a model. I do not see myself as a model."

I am a freak. No one who has ever known me would think of me reacting this way. This terrible calm will not go away.

She asks me if she may call again, after I get back from a long trip that we all must make. "Of course," I say. "Feel free to call, anytime."

Four days later, I find Kusum squatting on a rock overlooking a bay in Ireland. It isn't a big rock, but it juts sharply out over water. This is as close as we'll ever get to them. June breezes balloon out her sari and unpin her knee-length hair. She has the bewildered look of a sea creature whom the tides have stranded.

It's been one hundred hours since Kusum came stumbling and screaming across my lawn. Waiting around the hospital, we've heard many stories. The police, the diplomats, they tell us things thinking that we're strong, that knowledge is helpful to the grieving, and maybe it is. Some, I know, prefer ignorance, or their own versions. The plane broke into two, they say. Unconsciousness was instantaneous. No one suffered. My boys must have just finished their breakfasts. They loved eating on planes, they loved the smallness of plates, knives, and forks. Last year they saved the airline salt and pepper shakers. Half an hour more and they would have made it to Heathrow.

Kusum says that we can't escape our fate. She says that all those people—our husbands, my boys, her girl with the nightingale voice, all those Hindus, Christians, Sikhs, Muslims, Parsis, and atheists on that plane—were fated to die together off this beautiful bay. She learned this from a swami in Toronto.

I have my Valium.

Six of us "relatives"—two widows and four widowers—choose to spend the day today by the waters instead of sitting in a hospital room and scanning photographs of the dead. That's what they call us now: relatives. I've looked through twenty-seven photos in two days. They're very kind to us, the Irish are very understanding. Sometimes understanding means freeing a tourist bus for this trip to the bay, so we can pretend to spy our loved ones through the glassiness of waves or in sun-speckled cloud shapes.

I could die here, too, and be content.

"What is that, out there?" She's standing and flapping her hands, and for a moment I see a head shape bobbing in the waves. She's standing in the water, I, on the boulder. The tide is low, and a round, black, head-sized rock has just risen from the waves. She returns, her sari end dripping and ruined and her face is a twisted remnant of hope, the way mine was a hundred hours ago, still laughing but inwardly knowing that nothing but the ultimate tragedy could bring two women together at six o'clock on a Sunday morning. I watch her face sag into blankness.

"That water felt warm, Shaila," she says at length.

"You can't," I say. "We have to wait for our turn to come."

I haven't eaten in four days, haven't brushed my teeth.

"I know," she says. "I tell myself I have no right to grieve. They are in a better place than we are. My swami says I should be thrilled for them. My swami says depression is a sign of our selfishness."

Maybe I'm selfish. Selfishly I break away from Kusum and run, sandals slapping against stones, to the water's edge. What if my boys aren't lying pinned under the debris? What if they aren't stuck a mile below that innocent blue chop? What if, given the strong currents. . . .

Now I've ruined my sari, one of my best. Kusum has joined me, knee-deep in water that feels to me like a swimming pool. I could settle in the water, and my husband would take my hand and the boys would slap water in my face just to see me scream.

"Do you remember what good swimmers my boys were, Kusum?"

"I saw the medals," she says.

One of the widowers, Dr. Ranganathan from Montreal, walks out to us, carrying his shoes in one hand. He's an electrical engineer. Someone at the hotel mentioned his work is famous around the world, something about the place where physics and electricity come together. He has lost a huge family, something indescribable. "With some good luck," Dr. Ranganathan suggests to me, "a good swimmer could make it safely to some island. It is quite possible that there may be many, many microscopic islets scattered around."

"You're not just saying that?" I tell Dr. Ranganathan about Vinod, my elder son. Last year he took diving as well.

"It's a parent's duty to hope," he says. "It is foolish to rule out possibilities that have not been tested. I myself have not surrendered hope."

Kusum is sobbing once again. "Dear lady," he says, laying his free hand on her arm, and she calms down.

"Vinod is how old?" he asks me. He's very careful, as we all are. *Is*, not was.

"Fourteen. Yesterday he was fourteen. His father and uncle were going to take him down to the Taj and give him a big birthday party. I couldn't go with them because I couldn't get two weeks off from my stupid job in June." I process bills for a travel agent. June is a big travel month.

Dr. Ranganathan whips the pockets of his suit jacket inside out. Squashed roses, in darkening shades of pink, float on the water. He tore the roses off creepers in somebody's garden. He didn't ask anyone if he could pluck the roses, but now there's been an article about it in the local papers. When you see an Indian person, it says, please give him or her flowers.

"A strong youth of fourteen," he says, "can very likely pull to safety a younger one."

My sons, though four years apart, were very close. Vinod wouldn't let Mithun drown. *Electrical engineering*, I think, foolishly perhaps: this man knows important secrets of the universe, things closed to me. Relief spins me lightheaded. No wonder my boys' photographs haven't turned up in the gallery of photos of the recovered dead. "Such pretty roses," I say.

"My wife loved pink roses. Every Friday I had to bring a bunch home. I used to say, Why? After twenty-odd years of marriage you're still needing proof positive of my love?" He has identified his wife and three of his children. Then others from Montreal, the lucky ones, intact families with no survivors. He chuckles as he wades back to shore. Then he swings around to ask me a question. "Mrs. Bhave, you are wanting to throw in some roses for your loved ones? I have two big ones left."

But I have other things to float: Vinod's pocket calculator; a half-painted model B-52 for my Mithun. They'd want them on their island. And for my husband? For him I let fall into the calm, glassy waters a poem I wrote in the hospital yesterday. Finally he'll know my feelings for him.

"Don't tumble, the rocks are slippery," Dr. Ranganathan cautions. He holds out a hand for me to grab.

Then it's time to get back on the bus, time to rush back to our waiting posts on hospital benches.

Kusum is one of the lucky ones. The lucky ones flew here, identified in multiplicate their loved ones, then will fly to India with the bodies for proper ceremonies. Satish is one of the few males who surfaced. The photos of faces we saw on the walls in an office at Heathrow and here in the hospital are mostly of women. Women have more body fat, a nun said to me matter-of-factly. They float better.

Today I was stopped by a young sailor on the street. He had loaded bodies, he'd gone into the water when— he checks my face for signs of strength—when the sharks were first spotted. I don't blush, and he breaks down. "It's all right," I say. "Thank you." I heard about the sharks from Dr. Ranganathan. In his orderly mind, science brings understanding, it holds no terror. It is the shark's duty. For every deer there is a hunter, for every fish a fisherman.

The Irish are not shy; they rush to me and give me hugs and some are crying. I cannot imagine reactions like that on the streets of Toronto. Just strangers, and I am touched. Some carry flowers with them and give them to any Indian they see.

After lunch, a policeman I have gotten to know quite well catches hold of me. He says he thinks he has a match for Vinod. I explain what a good swimmer Vinod is.

"You want me with you when you look at photos?" Dr. Ranganathan walks ahead of me into the picture gallery. In these matters, he is a scientist, and I am grateful. It is a new perspective. "They have performed miracles," he says. "We are indebted to them."

The first day or two the policemen showed us relatives only one picture at a time; now they're in a hurry, they're eager to lay out the possibles, and even the probables.

The face on the photo is of a boy much like Vinod; the same intelligent eyes, the same thick brows dipping into a V. But this boy's features, even his cheeks, are puffier, wider, mushier.

"No." My gaze is pulled by other pictures. There are five other boys who look like Vinod.

The nun assigned to console me rubs the first picture with a fingertip. "When they've been in the water for a while, love, they look a little heavier." The bones under the skin are broken, they said on the first day — try to adjust your memories. It's important.

"It's not him. I'm his mother. I'd know."

"I know this one!" Dr. Ranganathan cries out, and suddenly from the back of the gallery. "And this one!" I think he senses that I don't want to find my boys. "They are the Kutty brothers. They were also from Montreal." I don't mean to be crying. On the contrary, I am ecstatic. My suitcase in the hotel is packed heavy with dry clothes for my boys.

The policeman starts to cry. "I am so sorry, I am so sorry, ma'am. I really thought we had a match."

With the nun ahead of us and the policeman behind, we, the unlucky ones without our children's bodies, file out of the makeshift gallery.

From Ireland most of us go on to India. Kusum and I take the same direct flight to Bombay, so I can help her clear customs quickly. But we have to argue with a man in uniform. He has large boils on his face. The boils swell and glow with sweat as we argue with him. He wants Kusum to wait in line and he refuses to take authority because his boss is on a tea break. But Kusum won't let her coffins out of sight, and I shan't desert her though I know that my parents, elderly and diabetic, must be waiting in a stuffy car in a scorching lot.

"You bastard!" I scream at the man with the popping boils. Other passengers press closer. "You think we're smuggling contraband in those coffins!"

Once upon a time we were well-brought-up women; we were dutiful wives who kept our heads veiled, our voices shy and sweet.

In India, I become, once again, an only child of rich, ailing parents. Old friends of the family come to pay their respects. Some are Sikh, and inwardly, involuntarily, I cringe. My parents are progressive people; they do not blame communities for a few individuals.

In Canada it is a different story now.

"Stay longer," my mother pleads. "Canada is a cold place. Why would you want to be all by yourself?" I stay.

Three months pass. Then another.

"Vikram wouldn't have wanted you to give up things!" they protest. They call my husband by the name he was born with. In Toronto he'd changed to Vik so the men he worked with at his office would find his name as easy as Rod or Chris. "You know, the dead aren't cut off from us!"

My grandmother, the spoiled daughter of a rich zamindar,° shaved her head with rusty razor blades when she was widowed at sixteen. My grandfather died of childhood diabetes when he was nineteen, and she saw herself as the harbinger of bad luck. My mother grew up without parents, raised indifferently by an uncle, while her true mother slept in a hut behind the main estate house and took her food with the servants. She grew up a rationalist. My parents abhor mindless mortification.

The zamindar's daughter kept stubborn faith in Vedic rituals; my parents rebelled. I am trapped between two modes of knowledge. At thirty-six, I am too old to start over and too young to give up. Like my husband's spirit, I flutter between worlds.

Courting aphasia, we travel. We travel with our phalanx of servants and poor relatives. To hill stations and to beach resorts. We play contract bridge in dusty gymkhana clubs. We ride stubby ponies up crumbly mountain trails. At tea dances, we let ourselves be twirled twice round the ballroom. We hit the holy spots we hadn't made time for before. In Varanasi, Kalighat, Rishikesh, Hardwar, astrologers and palmists seek me out and for a fee offer me cosmic consolations.

Zamindar: Feudal landlord.

Already the widowers among us are being shown new bride candidates. They cannot resist the call of custom, the authority of their parents and older brothers. They must marry; it is the duty of a man to look after a wife. The new wives will be young widows with children, destitute but of good family. They will make loving wives, but the men will shun them. I've had calls from the men over crackling Indian telephone lines. "Save me," they say, these substantial, educated, successful men of forty. "My parents are arranging a marriage for me." In a month they will have buried one family and returned to Canada with a new bride and partial family.

I am comparatively lucky. No one here thinks of arranging a husband for an unlucky widow.

Then, on the third day of the sixth month into this odyssey, in an abandoned temple in a tiny Himalayan village, as I make my offering of flowers and sweetmeats to the god of a tribe of animists, my husband descends to me. He is squatting next to a scrawny sadhu° in moth-eaten robes. Vikram wears the vanilla suit he wore the last time I hugged him. The sadhu tosses petals on a butter-fed flame, reciting Sanskrit mantras, and sweeps his face of flies. My husband takes my hands in his.

You're beautiful, he starts. Then, *What are you doing here?*

Shall I stay? I ask. He only smiles, but already the image is fading. *You must finish alone what we started together.* No seaweed wreathes his mouth. He speaks too fast, just as he used to when we were an envied family in our pink split-level. He is gone.

In the windowless altar room, smoky with joss sticks and clarified butter lamps, a sweaty hand gropes for my blouse. I do not shriek. The sadhu arranges his robe. The lamps hiss and sputter out.

When we come out of the temple, my mother says, "Did you feel something weird in there?"

My mother has no patience with ghosts, prophetic dreams, holy men, and cults.

"No," I lie. "Nothing."

But she knows that she's lost me. She knows that in days I shall be leaving.

Kusum's put up her house for sale. She wants to live in an ashram in Hardwar. Moving to Hardwar was her swami's idea. Her swami runs two ashrams, the one in Hardwar and another here in Toronto.

"Don't run away," I tell her.

"I'm not running away," she says. "I'm pursuing inner peace. You think you or that Ranganathan fellow are better off?"

Sadhu: Holy man.

Pam's left for California. She wants to do some modeling, she says. She says when she comes into her share of the insurance money she'll open a yoga-cum-aerobics studio in Hollywood. She sends me postcards so naughty I daren't leave them on the coffee table. Her mother has withdrawn from her and the world.

The rest of us don't lose touch, that's the point. Talk is all we have, says Dr. Ranganathan, who has also resisted his relatives and returned to Montreal and to his job, alone. He says, Whom better to talk with than other relatives? We've been melted down and recast as a new tribe.

He calls me twice a week from Montreal. Every Wednesday night and every Saturday afternoon. He is changing jobs, going to Ottawa. But Ottawa is over a hundred miles away, and he is forced to drive two hundred and twenty miles a day from his home in Montreal. He can't bring himself to sell his house. The house is a temple, he says; the king-sized bed in the master bedroom is a shrine. He sleeps on a folding cot. A devotee.

There are still some hysterical relatives. Judith Templeton's list of those needing help and those who've "accepted" is in nearly perfect balance. Acceptance means you speak of your family in the past tense and you make active plans for moving ahead with your life. There are courses at Seneca and Ryerson we could be taking. Her gleaming leather briefcase is full of college catalogues and lists of cultural societies that need our help. She has done impressive work, I tell her.

"In the textbooks on grief management," she replies—I am her confidante, I realize, one of the few whose grief has not sprung bizarre obsessions—"there are stages to pass through: rejection, depression, acceptance, reconstruction." She has compiled a chart and finds that six months after the tragedy, none of us still rejects reality, but only a handful are reconstructing. "Depressed acceptance" is the plateau we've reached. Remarriage is a major step in reconstruction (though she's a little surprised, even shocked, over *how* quickly some of the men have taken on new families). Selling one's house and changing jobs and cities is healthy.

How to tell Judith Templeton that my family surrounds me, and that like creatures in epics, they've changed shapes? She sees me as calm and accepting but worries that I have no job, no career. My closest friends are worse off than I. I cannot tell her my days, even my nights, are thrilling.

She asks me to help with families she can't reach at all. An elderly couple in Agincourt whose sons were killed just weeks after they had brought their parents over from a village in Punjab. From their names, I know they are Sikh. Judith Templeton and a translator have visited them twice with offers of money for airfare to Ireland, with bank forms, power-of-attorney forms, but they have refused to sign, or to leave their tiny apartment. Their sons' money is frozen in the bank. Their sons' investment apartments have been trashed by tenants, the furnishings sold off. The parents fear that anything they sign or any money they receive will end the company's or the country's obligations to them. They fear they are selling their sons for two airline tickets to a place they've never seen.

The high-rise apartment is a tower of Indians and West Indians, with a sprinkling of Orientals. The nearest bus-stop kiosk is lined with women in saris. Boys practice cricket in the parking lot. Inside the building, even I wince a bit from the ferocity of onion fumes, the distinctive and immediate Indianness of frying ghee, but Judith Templeton maintains a steady flow of information. These poor old people are in imminent danger of losing their place and all their services.

I say to her, "They are Sikh. They will not open up to a Hindu woman." And what I want to add is, as much as I try not to, I stiffen now at the sight of beards and turbans. I remember a time when we all trusted each other in this new country, it was only the new country we worried about.

The two rooms are dark and stuffy. The lights are off, and an oil lamp sputters on the coffee table. The bent old lady has let us in, and her husband is wrapping a white turban over his oiled, hip-length hair. She immediately goes to the kitchen, and I hear the most familiar sound of an Indian home, tap water hitting and filling a teapot.

They have not paid their utility bills, out of fear and inability to write a check. The telephone is gone, electricity and gas and water are soon to follow. They have told Judith their sons will provide. They are good boys, and they have always earned and looked after their parents.

We converse a bit in Hindi. They do not ask about the crash and I wonder if I should bring it up. If they think I am here merely as a translator, then they may feel insulted. There are thousands of Punjabi speakers, Sikhs, in Toronto to do a better job. And so I say to the old lady, "I too have lost my sons, and my husband, in the crash."

Her eyes immediately fill with tears. The man mutters a few words which sound like a blessing. "God provides and God takes away," he says.

I want to say, But only men destroy and give back nothing. "My boys and my husband are not coming back," I say. "We have to understand that."

Now the old woman responds. "But who is to say? Man alone does not decide these things." To this her husband adds his agreement.

Judith asks about the bank papers, the release forms. With a stroke of the pen, they will have a provincial trustee to pay their bills, invest their money, send them a monthly pension.

"Do you know this woman?" I ask them.

The man raises his hand from the table, turns it over, and seems to regard each finger separately before he answers. "This young lady is always coming here, we make tea for her, and she leaves papers for us to sign." His eyes scan a pile of papers in the corner of the room. "Soon we will be out of tea, then will she go away?"

The old lady adds, "I have asked my neighbors and no one else gets *angrezi*° visitors. What have we done?"

"It's her job," I try to explain. "The government is worried. Soon you will have no place to stay, no lights, no gas, no water."

"Government will get its money. Tell her not to worry, we are honorable people."

I try to explain the government wishes to give money, not take. He raises his hand. "Let them take," he says. "We are accustomed to that. That is no problem."

"We are strong people," says the wife. "Tell her that."

"Who needs all this machinery?" demands the husband. "It is unhealthy, the bright lights, the cold air on a hot day, the cold food, the four gas rings. God will provide, not government."

"When our boys return," the mother says.

Her husband sucks his teeth. "Enough talk," he says.

Judith breaks in. "Have you convinced them?" The snaps on her cordovan briefcase go off like firecrackers in that quiet apartment. She lays the sheaf of legal papers on the coffee table. "If they can't write their names, an X will do—I've told them that."

Now the old lady has shuffled to the kitchen and soon emerges with a pot of tea and two cups. "I think my bladder will go first on a job like this," Judith says to me, smiling. "If only there was some way of reaching them. Please thank her for the tea. Tell her she's very kind."

I nod in Judith's direction and tell them in Hindi, "She thanks you for the tea. She thinks you are being very hospitable but she doesn't have the slightest idea what it means."

I want to say, Humor her. I want to say, My boys and my husband are with me too, more than ever. I look in the old man's eyes and I can read his stubborn, peasant's message: *I have protected this woman as best I can. She is the only person I have left. Give to me or take from me what you will, but I will not sign for it. I will not pretend that I accept.*

In the car, Judith says, "You see what I'm up against? I'm sure they're lovely people, but their stubbornness and ignorance are driving me crazy. They think signing a paper is signing their sons' death warrants, don't they?"

Angrezi: English or Anglo.

I am looking out the window. I want to say, *In our culture, it is a parent's duty to hope.*

"Now Shaila, this next woman is a real mess. She cries day and night, and she refuses all medical help. We may have to—"

"Let me out at the subway," I say.

"I beg your pardon?" I can feel those blue eyes staring at me.

It would not be like her to disobey. She merely disapproves, and slows at a corner to let me out. Her voice is plaintive. "Is there anything I said? Anything I did?"

I could answer her suddenly in a dozen ways, but I choose not to. "Shaila? Let's talk about it," I hear, then slam the door.

A wife and mother begins her life in a new country, and that life is cut short. Yet her husband tells her: Complete what we have started. We, who stayed out of politics and came half way around the world to avoid religious and political feuding, have been the first in the New World to die from it. I no longer know what we started, nor how to complete it. I write letters to the editors of local papers and to members of Parliament. Now at least they admit it was a bomb. One MP answers back, with sympathy, but with a challenge. You want to make a difference? Work on a campaign. Work on mine. Politicize the Indian voter.

My husband's old lawyer helps me set up a trust. Vikram was a saver and a careful investor. He had saved the boys' boarding school and college fees. I sell the pink house at four times what we paid for it and take a small apartment downtown. I am looking for a charity to support.

We are deep in the Toronto winter, gray skies, icy pavements. I stay indoors, watching television. I have tried to assess my situation, how best to live my life, to complete what we began so many years ago. Kusum has written me from Hardwar that her life is now serene. She has seen Satish and has heard her daughter sing again. Kusum was on a pilgrimage, passing through a village, when she heard a young girl's voice, singing one of her daughter's favorite *bhajans*. She followed the music through the squalor of a Himalayan village, to a hut where a young girl, an exact replica of her daughter, was fanning coals under the kitchen fire. When she appeared, the girl cried out, "Ma!" and ran away. What did I think of that?

I think I can only envy her.

Pam didn't make it to California, but writes me from Vancouver. She works in a department store, giving makeup hints to Indian and Oriental girls. Dr. Ranganathan has given up his commute, given up his house and job, and accepted an academic position in Texas, where no one knows his story and he has vowed not to tell it. He calls me now once a week.

I wait, I listen and I pray, but Vikram has not returned to me. The voices and the shapes and the nights filled with visions ended abruptly several weeks ago.

I take it as a sign.

One rare, beautiful, sunny day last week, returning from a small errand on Yonge Street, I was walking through the park from the subway to my apartment. I live equidistant from the Ontario Houses of Parliament and the University of Toronto. The day was not cold, but something in the bare trees caught my attention. I looked up from the gravel, into the branches and the clear blue sky beyond. I thought I heard the rustling of larger forms, and I waited a moment for voices. Nothing.

"What?" I asked.

Then as I stood in the path looking north to Queen's Park and west to the university, I heard the voices of my family one last time. *Your time has come*, they said. *Go, be brave.*

I do not know where this voyage I have begun will end. I do not know which direction I will take. I dropped the package on a park bench and started walking.

[1988]

ALICE WALKER [b. 1944]

Everyday Use

For Your Grandmama

I will wait for her in the yard that Maggie and I made so clean and wavy yesterday afternoon. A yard like this is more comfortable than most people know. It is not just a yard. It is like an extended living room. When the hard clay is swept clean as a floor and the fine sand around the edges lined with tiny, irregular grooves, anyone can come and sit and look up into the elm tree and wait for the breezes that never come inside the house.

Maggie will be nervous until after her sister goes: she will stand hope-lessly in corners, homely and ashamed of the burn scars down her arms and legs, eying her sister with a mixture of envy and awe. She thinks her sister has held life always in the palm of one hand, that "no" is a word the world never learned to say to her.

You've no doubt seen those TV shows where the child who has "made it" is confronted, as a surprise, by her own mother and father, tottering in weakly from backstage. (A pleasant surprise, of course: What would they do if parent and child came on the show only to curse out and insult each other?) On TV mother and child embrace and smile into each other's faces. Sometimes the mother and father weep, the child wraps them in her arms and leans across the table to tell how she would not have made it without their help. I have seen these programs.

Sometimes I dream a dream in which Dee and I are suddenly brought together on a TV program of this sort. Out of a dark and soft-seated lim-ousine I am ushered into a bright room filled with many people. There I meet a smiling, gray, sporty man like Johnny Carson who shakes my hand and tells me what a fine girl I have. Then we are on the stage and Dee is embracing me with tears in her eyes. She pins on my dress a large orchid, even though she has told me once that she thinks orchids are tacky flowers.

In real life I am a large, big-boned woman with rough, man-working hands. In the winter I wear flannel nightgowns to bed and overalls dur-ing the day. I can kill and clean a hog as mercilessly as a man. My fat keeps me hot in zero weather. I can work outside all day, breaking ice to get water for washing; I can eat pork liver cooked over the open fire min-utes after it comes steaming from the hog. One winter I knocked a bull calf straight in the brain between the eyes with a sledge hammer and had the meat hung up to chill before nightfall. But of course all this does not show on television. I am the way my daughter would want me to be: a hundred pounds lighter, my skin like an uncooked barley pancake. My hair glistens in the hot bright lights. Johnny Carson has much to do to keep up with my quick and witty tongue.

But that is a mistake. I know even before I wake up. Who ever knew a Johnson with a quick tongue? Who can even imagine me looking a strange white man in the eye? It seems to me I have talked to them always with one foot raised in flight, with my head turned in whichever way is farthest from them. Dee, though. She would always look anyone in the eye. Hesitation was no part of her nature.

"How do I look, Mama?" Maggie says, showing just enough of her thin body enveloped in pink skirt and red blouse for me to know she's there, almost hidden by the door.

"Come out into the yard," I say.

Have you ever seen a lame animal, perhaps a dog run over by some careless person rich enough to own a car, sidle up to someone who is ignorant enough to be kind to him? That is the way my Maggie walks. She has been like this, chin on chest, eyes on ground, feet in shuffle, ever since the fire that burned the other house to the ground.

Dee is lighter than Maggie, with nicer hair and a fuller figure. She's a woman now, though sometimes I forget. How long ago was it that the other house burned? Ten, twelve years? Sometimes I can still hear the flames and feel Maggie's arms sticking to me, her hair smoking and her dress falling off her in little black papery flakes. Her eyes seemed stretched open, blazed open by the flames reflected in them. And Dee. I see her standing off under the sweet gum tree she used to dig gum out of; a look of concentration on her face as she watched the last dingy gray board of the house fall in toward the red-hot brick chimney. Why don't you do a dance around the ashes? I'd want to ask her. She had hated the house that much.

I used to think she hated Maggie, too. But that was before we raised the money, the church and me, to send her to Augusta to school. She used to read to us without pity; forcing words, lies, other folks' habits, whole lives upon us two, sitting trapped and ignorant underneath her voice. She washed us in a river of make-believe, burned us with a lot of knowledge we didn't necessarily need to know. Pressed us to her with the serious way she read, to shove us away at just the moment, like dimwits, we seemed about to understand.

Dee wanted nice things. A yellow organdy dress to wear to her graduation from high school; black pumps to match a green suit she'd made from an old suit somebody gave me. She was determined to stare down any disaster in her efforts. Her eyelids would not flicker for minutes at a time. Often I fought off the temptation to shake her. At sixteen she had a style of her own: and knew what style was.

I never had an education myself. After second grade the school was closed down. Don't ask me why: in 1927 colored asked fewer questions than they do now. Sometimes Maggie reads to me. She stumbles along good-naturedly but can't see well. She knows she is not bright. Like good looks and money, quickness passed her by. She will marry John Thomas (who has mossy teeth in an earnest face) and then I'll be free to sit here and I guess just sing church songs to myself. Although I never was a good singer. Never could carry a tune. I was always better at a man's job. I used to love to milk till I was hooked in the side in '49. Cows are soothing and slow and don't bother you, unless you try to milk them the wrong way.

I have deliberately turned my back on the house. It is three rooms, just like the one that burned, except the roof is tin; they don't make shingle roofs any more. There are no real windows, just some holes cut in the sides, like the portholes in a ship, but not round and not square, with rawhide holding the shutters up on the outside. This house is in a pasture, too, like the other one. No doubt when Dee sees it she will want to tear it down. She wrote me once that no matter where we "choose" to live, she will manage to come see us. But she will never bring her friends. Maggie and I thought about this and Maggie asked me, "Mama, when did Dee ever *have* any friends?"

She had a few. Furtive boys in pink shirts hanging about on washday after school. Nervous girls who never laughed. Impressed with her they worshipped the well-turned phrase, the cute shape, the scalding humor that erupted like bubbles in lye. She read to them.

When she was courting Jimmy T she didn't have much time to pay to us, but turned all her faultfinding power on him. He *flew* to marry a cheap city girl from a family of ignorant flashy people. She hardly had time to recompose herself.

When she comes I will meet—but there they are!

Maggie attempts to make a dash for the house, in her shuffling way, but I stay her with my hand. "Come back here," I say. And she stops and tries to dig a well in the sand with her toe.

It is hard to see them clearly through the strong sun. But even the first glimpse of leg out of the car tells me it is Dee. Her feet were always neat-looking, as if God himself had shaped them with a certain style. From the other side of the car comes a short, stocky man. Hair is all over his head a foot long and hanging from his chin like a kinky mule tail. I hear Maggie suck in her breath. "Uhnnnh," is what it sounds like. Like when you see the wriggling end of a snake just in front of your foot on the road. "Uhnnnh."

Dee next. A dress down to the ground, in this hot weather. A dress so loud it hurts my eyes. There are yellows and oranges enough to throw back the light of the sun. I feel my whole face warming from the heat waves it throws out. Earrings gold, too, and hanging down to her shoulders. Bracelets dangling and making noises when she moves her arm up to shake the folds of the dress out of her armpits. The dress is loose and flows, and as she walks closer, I like it. I hear Maggie go "Uhnnnh" again. It is her sister's hair. It stands straight up like the wool on a sheep. It is black as night and around the edges are two long pigtails that rope about like small lizards disappearing behind her ears.

"Wa-su-zo-Tean-o!" she says, coming on in that gliding way the dress makes her move. The short stocky fellow with the hair to his navel is all grinning and he follows up with "Asalamalakim, my mother and sister!" He moves to hug Maggie but she falls back, right up against the back of my chair. I feel her trembling there and when I look up I see the perspiration falling off her chin.

"Don't get up," says Dee. Since I am stout it takes something of a push. You can see me trying to move a second or two before I make it. She turns, showing white heels through her sandals, and goes back to the car. Out she peeks next with a Polaroid. She stoops down quickly and lines up picture after picture of me sitting there in front of the house with Maggie cowering behind me. She never takes a shot without making sure the house is included. When a cow comes nibbling around the edge of the yard she snaps it and me and Maggie *and* the house. Then she puts the Polaroid in the back seat of the car, and comes up and kisses me on the forehead.

Meanwhile Asalamalakim is going through motions with Maggie's hand. Maggie's hand is as limp as a fish, and probably as cold, despite the sweat, and she keeps trying to pull it back. It looks like Asalamalakim wants to shake hands but wants to do it fancy. Or maybe he don't know how people shake hands. Anyhow, he soon gives up on Maggie.

"Well," I say. "Dee."

"No, Mama," she says. "Not 'Dee,' Wangero Leewanika Kemanjo!"

"What happened to 'Dee'?" I wanted to know.

"She's dead," Wangero said. "I couldn't bear it any longer, being named after the people who oppress me."

"You know as well as me you was named after your aunt Dicie," I said. Dicie is my sister. She named Dee. We called her "Big Dee" after Dee was born.

"But who was *she* named after?" asked Wangero.

"I guess after Grandma Dee," I said.

"And who was she named after?" asked Wangero.

"Her mother," I said, and saw Wangero was getting tired. "That's about as far back as I can trace it," I said. Though, in fact, I probably could have carried it back beyond the Civil War through the branches.

"Well," said Asalamalakim, "there you are."

"Uhnnnh," I heard Maggie say.

"There I was not," I said, "before 'Dicie' cropped up in our family, so why should I try to trace it that far back?"

He just stood there grinning, looking down on me like somebody inspecting a Model A car. Every once in a while he and Wangero sent eye signals over my head.

"How do you pronounce this name?" I asked.

"You don't have to call me by it if you don't want to," said Wangero.

"Why shouldn't I?" I asked. "If that's what you want us to call you, we'll call you."

"I know it might sound awkward at first," said Wangero.

"I'll get used to it," I said. "Ream it out again."

Well, soon we got the name out of the way. Asalamalakim had a name twice as long and three times as hard. After I tripped over it two or three times he told me to just call him Hakim-a-barber. I wanted to ask him was he a barber, but I didn't really think he was, so I didn't ask.

"You must belong to those beef-cattle peoples down the road," I said. They said "Asalamalakim" when they met you, too, but they didn't shake hands. Always too busy: feeding the cattle, fixing the fences, putting up salt-lick shelters, throwing down hay. When the white folks poisoned some of the herd the men stayed up all night with rifles in their hands. I walked a mile and a half just to see the sight.

Hakim-a-barber said, "I accept some of their doctrines, but farming and raising cattle is not my style." (They didn't tell me, and I didn't ask, whether Wangero (Dee) had really gone and married him.)

We sat down to eat and right away he said he didn't eat collards and pork was unclean. Wangero, though, went on through the chitlins and corn bread, the greens and everything else. She talked a blue streak over the sweet potatoes. Everything delighted her. Even the fact that we still used the benches her daddy made for the table when we couldn't afford to buy chairs.

"Oh, Mama!" she cried. Then turned to Hakim-a-barber. "I never knew how lovely these benches are. You can feel the rump prints," she said, running her hands underneath her and long the bench. Then she gave a sigh and her hand closed over Grandma Dee's butter dish. "That's it!" she said. "I knew there was something I wanted to ask you if I could have." She jumped up from the table and went over in the corner where the churn stood, the milk in it clabber by now. She looked at the churn and looked at it.

"This churn top is what I need," she said. "Didn't Uncle Buddy whittle it out of a tree you all used to have?"

"Yes," I said.

"Uh huh," she said happily. "And I want the dasher, too."

"Uncle Buddy whittle that, too?" asked the barber.

Dee (Wangero) looked up at me.

"Aunt Dee's first husband whittled the dash," said Maggie so low you almost couldn't hear her. "His name was Henry, but they called him Stash."

"Maggie's brain is like an elephant's," Wangero said, laughing. "I can use the churn top as a centerpiece for the alcove table," she said, sliding a plate over the churn, "and I'll think of something artistic to do with the dasher."

When she finished wrapping the dasher the handle stuck out. I took it for a moment in my hands. You didn't even have to look close to see where hands pushing the dasher up and down to make butter had left a kind of sink in the wood. In fact, there were a lot of small sinks; you could see where thumbs and fingers had sunk into the wood. It was beautiful light yellow wood, from a tree that grew in the yard where Big Dee and Stash had lived.

After dinner Dee (Wangero) went to the trunk at the foot of my bed and started rifling through it. Maggie hung back in the kitchen over the dishpan. Out came Wangero with two quilts. They had been pieced by Grandma Dee and then Big Dee and me had hung them on the quilt frames on the front porch and quilted them. One was in the Lone Star pattern. The other was Walk Around the Mountain. In both of them were scraps of dresses Grandma Dee had worn fifty and more years ago. Bits and pieces of Grandpa Jarrell's Paisley shirts. And one teeny faded blue piece, about the size of a penny matchbox, that was from Great Grandpa Ezra's uniform that he wore in the Civil War.

"Mama," Wangero said sweet as a bird. "Can I have these old quilts?"

I heard something fall in the kitchen, and a minute later the kitchen door slammed.

"Why don't you take one or two of the others?" I asked. "These old things was just done by me and Big Dee from some tops your grandma pieced before she died."

"No," said Wangero. "I don't want those. They are stitched around the borders by machine."

"That'll make them last better," I said.

"That's not the point," said Wangero. "These are all pieces of dresses Grandma used to wear. She did all this stitching by hand. Imagine!" She held the quilts securely in her arms, stroking them.

"Some of the pieces, like those lavender ones, come from old clothes her mother handed down to her," I said, moving up to touch the quilts. Dee (Wangero) moved back just enough so that I couldn't reach the quilts. They already belonged to her.

"Imagine!" she breathed again, clutching them closely to her bosom.

"The truth is," I said, "I promised to give them quilts to Maggie, for when she marries John Thomas."

She gasped like a bee had stung her.

"Maggie can't appreciate these quilts!" she said. "She'd probably be backward enough to put them to everyday use."

"I reckon she would," I said. "God knows I been saving 'em for long enough with nobody using 'em. I hope she will!" I didn't want to bring up how I had offered Dee (Wangero) a quilt when she went away to college. Then she had told me they were old-fashioned, out of style.

"But they're *priceless*!" she was saying now, furiously; for she has a temper. "Maggie would put them on the bed and in five years they'd be in rags. Less than that!"

"She can always make some more," I said. "Maggie knows how to quilt."

Dee (Wangero) looked at me with hatred. "You just will not understand. The point is these quilts, *these* quilts!"

"Well," I said, stumped. "What would *you* do with them?"

"Hang them," she said. As if that was the only thing you *could* do with quilts.

Maggie by now was standing in the door. I could almost hear the sound her feet made as they scraped over each other.

"She can have them, Mama," she said, like somebody used to never winning anything, or having anything reserved for her. "I can 'member Grandma Dee without the quilts."

I looked at her hard. She had filled her bottom lip with checkerberry snuff and it gave her face a kind of dopey, hangdog look. It was Grandma Dee and Big Dee who taught her how to quilt herself. She stood there with her scarred hands hidden in the folds of her skirt. She looked at her sister with something like fear but she wasn't mad at her. This was Maggie's portion. This was the way she knew God to work.

When I looked at her like that something hit me in the top of my head and ran down to the soles of my feet. Just like when I'm in church and the spirit of God touches me and I get happy and shout. I did something I never had done before: hugged Maggie to me, then dragged her on into the room, snatched the quilts out of Miss Wangero's hands and dumped them into Maggie's lap. Maggie just sat there on my bed with her mouth open.

"Take one or two of the others," I said to Dee.

But she turned without a word and went out to Hakim-a-barber.

"You just don't understand," she said, as Maggie and I came out to the car.

"What don't I understand?" I wanted to know.

"Your heritage," she said. And then she turned to Maggie, kissed her, and said, "You ought to try to make something of yourself, too, Maggie. It's really a new day for us. But from the way you and Mama still live you'd never know it."

She put on some sunglasses that hid everything above the tip of her nose and her chin.

Maggie smiled; maybe at the sunglasses. But a real smile, not scared. After we watched the car dust settle I asked Maggie to bring me a dip of snuff. And then the two of us sat there just enjoying, until it was time to go in the house and go to bed.

[1973]

TIM O'BRIEN [b. 1946]

The Things They Carried

First Lieutenant Jimmy Cross carried letters from a girl named Martha, a junior at Mount Sebastian College in New Jersey. They were not love letters, but Lieutenant Cross was hoping, so he kept them folded in plastic at the bottom of his rucksack. In the late afternoon, after a day's march, he would dig his foxhole, wash his hands under a canteen, unwrap the letters, hold them with the tips of his fingers, and spend the last hour of light pretending. He would imagine romantic camping trips into the White Mountains in New Hampshire. He would sometimes taste the envelope flaps, knowing her tongue had been there. More than anything, he wanted Martha to love him as he loved her, but the letters were mostly chatty, elusive on the matter of love. She was a virgin, he was almost sure. She was an English major at Mount Sebastian, and she wrote beautifully about her professors and roommates and midterm exams, about her respect for Chaucer and her great affection for Virginia Woolf. She often quoted lines of poetry; she never mentioned the war, except to say, Jimmy, take care of yourself. The letters weighed ten ounces. They were signed "Love, Martha," but Lieutenant Cross understood that "Love" was only a way of signing and did not mean what he sometimes pretended it meant. At dusk, he would carefully return the letters to his rucksack. Slowly, a bit distracted, he would get up and move among his men, checking the perimeter, then at full dark he would return to his hole and watch the night and wonder if Martha was a virgin.

The things they carried were largely determined by necessity. Among the necessities or near necessities were P-38 can openers, pocket knives, heat tabs, wrist watches, dog tags, mosquito repellant, chewing gum, candy, cigarettes, salt tablets, packets of Kool-Aid, lighters, matches, sewing kits, Military Payment Certificates, C rations, and two or three canteens of water. Together, these items weighed between fifteen and twenty pounds, depending upon a man's habits or rate of metabolism. Henry Dobbins, who was a big man, carried extra rations; he was especially fond of canned peaches in heavy syrup over pound cake. Dave Jensen, who practiced field hygiene, carried a toothbrush, dental floss, and several hotel-size bars of soap he'd stolen on R&R in Sydney, Australia. Ted Lavender, who was scared, carried tranquilizers until he was shot in the head outside the village of Than Khe in mid-April. By necessity, and because it was SOP,° they all carried steel helmets that weighed five pounds including the liner and camouflage cover. They carried the standard fatigue jackets and trousers. Very few carried underwear. On their feet they carried jungle boots—2.1 pounds—and Dave Jensen carried three pairs of socks and a can of Dr. Scholl's foot powder as a precaution against trench foot. Until he was shot, Ted Lavender carried six or seven ounces of premium dope, which for him was a necessity. Mitchell Sanders, the RTO,° carried condoms. Norman Bowker carried a diary. Rat Kiley carried comic books. Kiowa, a devout Baptist, carried an illustrated New Testament that had been presented to him by his father, who taught Sunday school in Oklahoma City, Oklahoma. As a hedge against bad times, however, Kiowa also carried his grandmother's distrust of the white man, his grandfather's old hunting hatchet. Necessity dictated. Because the land was mined and booby-trapped, it was SOP for each man to carry a steel-centered, nylon-covered flak jacket, which weighed 6.7 pounds, but which on hot days seemed much heavier. Because you could die so quickly, each man carried at least one large compress bandage, usually in the helmet band for easy access. Because the nights were cold, and because the monsoons were wet, each carried a green plastic poncho that could be used as a raincoat or ground sheet or makeshift tent. With its quilted liner, the poncho weighed almost two pounds, but it was worth every ounce. In April, for instance, when Ted Lavender was shot, they used his poncho to wrap him up, then to carry him across the paddy, then to lift him into the chopper that took him away.

They were called legs or grunts.

To carry something was to "hump" it, as when Lieutenant Jimmy Cross humped his love for Martha up the hills and through the swamps. In its intransitive form, "to hump" meant "to walk," or "to march," but it implied burdens far beyond the intransitive.

Almost everyone humped photographs. In his wallet, Lieutenant Cross carried two photographs of Martha. The first was a Kodachrome snapshot signed "Love," though he knew better. She stood against a brick wall. Her eyes were gray and neutral, her lips slightly open as she stared straight-on at the camera. At night, sometimes, Lieutenant Cross wondered who had taken the picture, because he knew she had boyfriends, because he loved her so much, and because he could see the shadow of the picture taker spreading out against the brick wall. The

SOP: Standard operating procedure.
RTO: Radiotelephone operator.

second photograph had been clipped from the 1968 Mount Sebastian yearbook. It was an action shot—women's volleyball—and Martha was bent horizontal to the floor, reaching, the palms of her hands in sharp focus, the tongue taut, the expression frank and competitive. There was no visible sweat. She wore white gym shorts. Her legs, he thought, were almost certainly the legs of a virgin, dry and without hair, the left knee cocked and carrying her entire weight, which was just over one hundred pounds. Lieutenant Cross remembered touching that left knee. A dark theater, he remembered, and the movie was *Bonnie and Clyde,* and Martha wore a tweed skirt, and during the final scene, when he touched her knee, she turned and looked at him in a sad, sober way that made him pull his hand back, but he would always remember the feel of the tweed skirt and the knee beneath it and the sound of the gunfire that killed Bonnie and Clyde, how embarrassing it was, how slow and oppressive. He remembered kissing her good night at the dorm door. Right then, he thought, he should've done something brave. He should've carried her up the stairs to her room and tied her to the bed and touched that left knee all night long. He should've risked it. Whenever he looked at the photographs, he thought of new things he should've done.

What they carried was partly a function of rank, partly of field specialty.

As a first lieutenant and platoon leader, Jimmy Cross carried a compass, maps, code books, binoculars, and a .45-caliber pistol that weighed 2.9 pounds fully loaded. He carried a strobe light and the responsibility for the lives of his men.

As an RTO, Mitchell Sanders carried the PRC-25 radio, a killer, twenty-six pounds with its battery.

As a medic, Rat Kiley carried a canvas satchel filled with morphine and plasma and malaria tablets and surgical tape and comic books and all the things a medic must carry, including M&M's for especially bad wounds, for a total weight of nearly twenty pounds.

As a big man, therefore a machine gunner, Henry Dobbins carried the M-60, which weighed twenty-three pounds unloaded, but which was almost always loaded. In addition, Dobbins carried between ten and fifteen pounds of ammunition draped in belts across his chest and shoulders.

As PFCs or Spec 4s, most of them were common grunts and carried the standard M-16 gas-operated assault rifle. The weapon weighed 7.5 pounds unloaded, 8.2 pounds with its full twenty-round magazine. Depending on numerous factors, such as topography and psychology, the riflemen carried anywhere from twelve to twenty magazines, usually in cloth bandoliers, adding on another 8.4 pounds at minimum, fourteen pounds at maximum. When it was available, they also carried M-16 maintenance gear—rods and steel brushes and swabs and tubes of LSA oil—all of which weighed about a pound. Among the grunts, some carried the M-79 grenade launcher, 5.9 pounds unloaded, a reasonably light weapon except for the ammunition, which was heavy. A single round weighed ten ounces. The typical load was twenty-five rounds. But Ted Lavender, who was scared, carried thirty-four rounds when he was shot and killed outside Than Khe, and he went down under an exceptional burden, more than twenty pounds of ammunition, plus the flak jacket and helmet and rations and water and toilet paper and tranquilizers and all the rest, plus the unweighed fear. He was dead weight. There was no twitching or flopping. Kiowa, who saw it happen, said it was like watching a rock fall, or a big sandbag or something—just boom, then down—not like the movies where the dead guy rolls around and does fancy spins and goes ass over teakettle—not like that, Kiowa said, the poor bastard just flat-fuck fell. Boom. Down. Nothing else. It was a bright morning in mid-April. Lieutenant Cross felt the pain. He blamed himself. They stripped off Lavender's canteens and ammo, all the heavy things, and Rat Kiley said the obvious, the guy's dead, and Mitchell Sanders used his radio to report one U.S. KIA° and to request a chopper. Then they wrapped Lavender in his poncho. They carried him out to a dry paddy, established security, and sat smoking the dead man's dope until the chopper came. Lieutenant Cross kept to himself. He pictured Martha's smooth young face, thinking he loved her more than anything, more than his men, and now Ted Lavender was dead because he loved her so much and could not stop thinking about her. When the dust-off arrived, they carried Lavender aboard. Afterward they burned Than Khe. They marched until dusk, then dug their holes, and that night Kiowa kept explaining how you had to be there, how fast it was, how the poor guy just dropped like so much concrete. Boom-down, he said. Like cement.

In addition to the three standard weapons—the M-60, M-16, and M-79—they carried whatever presented itself, or whatever seemed appropriate as a means of killing or staying alive. They carried catch-as-catch-can. At various times, in various situations, they carried M-14s and CAR-15s and Swedish Ks and grease guns and captured AK-47s and Chi-Coms and RPGs and Simonov carbines and black-market Uzis and .38-caliber Smith & Wesson handguns and 66 mm LAWs and shotguns and silencers and blackjacks and bayonets and C-4 plastic explosives. Lee Strunk carried a slingshot; a weapon of last resort, he called it. Mitchell Sanders carried brass knuckles. Kiowa carried his grandfather's feathered hatchet. Every third or fourth man carried a Claymore antipersonnel mine—3.5 pounds with its firing device. They all carried

KIA: Killed in action.

fragmentation grenades—fourteen ounces each. They all carried at least one M-18 colored smoke grenade—twenty-four ounces. Some carried CS or tear-gas grenades. Some carried white-phosphorus grenades. They carried all they could bear, and then some, including a silent awe for the terrible power of the things they carried.

In the first week of April, before Lavender died, Lieutenant Jimmy Cross received a good-luck charm from Martha. It was a simple pebble, an ounce at most. Smooth to the touch, it was a milky-white color with flecks of orange and violet, oval-shaped, like a miniature egg. In the accompanying letter, Martha wrote that she had found the pebble on the Jersey shoreline, precisely where the land touched water at high tide, where things came together but also separated. It was this separate-but-together quality, she wrote, that had inspired her to pick up the pebble and to carry it in her breast pocket for several days, where it seemed weightless, and then to send it through the mail, by air, as a token of her truest feelings for him. Lieutenant Cross found this romantic. But he wondered what her truest feelings were, exactly, and what she meant by separate-but-together. He wondered how the tides and waves had come into play on that afternoon along the Jersey shoreline when Martha saw the pebble and bent down to rescue it from geology. He imagined bare feet. Martha was a poet, with the poet's sensibilities, and her feet would be brown and bare, the toenails unpainted, the eyes chilly and somber like the ocean in March, and though it was painful, he wondered who had been with her that afternoon. He imagined a pair of shadows moving along the strip of sand where things came together but also separated. It was phantom jealousy, he knew, but he couldn't help himself. He loved her so much. On the march, through the hot days of early April, he carried the pebble in his mouth, turning it with his tongue, tasting sea salts and moisture. His mind wandered. He had difficulty keeping his attention on the war. On occasion he would yell at his men to spread out the column, to keep their eyes open, but then he would slip away into daydreams, just pretending, walking barefoot along the Jersey shore, with Martha, carrying nothing. He would feel himself rising. Sun and waves and gentle winds, all love and lightness.

What they carried varied by mission.

When a mission took them to the mountains, they carried mosquito netting, machetes, canvas tarps, and extra bug juice.

If a mission seemed especially hazardous, or if it involved a place they knew to be bad, they carried everything they could. In certain heavily mined AOs,° where the land was dense with Toe Poppers and Bouncing

AOs: Areas of operations.

Betties, they took turns humping a twenty-eight-pound mine detector. With its headphones and big sensing plate, the equipment was a stress on the lower back and shoulders, awkward to handle, often useless because of the shrapnel in the earth, but they carried it anyway, partly for safety, partly for the illusion of safety.

On ambush, or other night missions, they carried peculiar little odds and ends. Kiowa always took along his New Testament and a pair of moccasins for silence. Dave Jensen carried night-sight vitamins high in carotin. Lee Strunk carried his slingshot; ammo, he claimed, would never be a problem. Rat Kiley carried brandy and M&M's. Until he was shot, Ted Lavender carried the starlight scope, which weighed 6.3 pounds with its aluminum carrying case. Henry Dobbins carried his girlfriend's pantyhose wrapped around his neck as a comforter. They all carried ghosts. When dark came, they would move out single file across the meadows and paddies to their ambush coordinates, where they would quietly set up the Claymores and lie down and spend the night waiting.

Other missions were more complicated and required special equipment. In mid-April, it was their mission to search out and destroy the elaborate tunnel complexes in the Than Khe area south of Chu Lai. To blow the tunnels, they carried one-pound blocks of pentrite high explosives, four blocks to a man, sixty-eight pounds in all. They carried wiring, detonators, and battery-powered clackers. Dave Jensen carried earplugs. Most often, before blowing the tunnels, they were ordered by higher command to search them, which was considered bad news, but by and large they just shrugged and carried out orders. Because he was a big man, Henry Dobbins was excused from tunnel duty. The others would draw numbers. Before Lavender died there were seventeen men in the platoon, and whoever drew the number seventeen would strip off his gear and crawl in head first with a flashlight and Lieutenant Cross's .45-caliber pistol. The rest of them would fan out as security. They would sit down or kneel, not facing the hole, listening to the ground beneath them, imagining cobwebs and ghosts, whatever was down there—the tunnel walls squeezing in—how the flashlight seemed impossibly heavy in the hand and how it was tunnel vision in the very strictest sense, compression in all ways, even time, and how you had to wiggle in—ass and elbows—a swallowed-up feeling—and how you found yourself worrying about odd things—will your flashlight go dead? Do rats carry rabies? If you screamed, how far would the sound carry? Would your buddies hear it? Would they have the courage to drag you out? In some respects, though not many, the waiting was worse than the tunnel itself. Imagination was a killer.

On April 16, when Lee Strunk drew the number seventeen, he laughed and muttered something and went down quickly. The morning was hot and very still. Not good, Kiowa said. He looked at the tunnel opening, then out across a dry paddy toward the village of Than Khe. Nothing moved. No clouds or birds or people. As they waited, the men smoked and drank Kool-Aid, not talking much, feeling sympathy for Lee Strunk but also feeling the luck of the draw. You win some, you lose some, said Mitchell Sanders, and sometimes you settle for a rain check. It was a tired line and no one laughed.

Henry Dobbins ate a tropical chocolate bar. Ted Lavender popped a tranquilizer and went off to pee.

After five minutes, Lieutenant Jimmy Cross moved to the tunnel, leaned down, and examined the darkness. Trouble, he thought—a cave-in maybe. And then suddenly, without willing it, he was thinking about Martha. The stresses and fractures, the quick collapse, the two of them buried alive under all that weight. Dense, crushing love. Kneeling, watching the hole, he tried to concentrate on Lee Strunk and the war, all the dangers, but his love was too much for him, he felt paralyzed, he wanted to sleep inside her lungs and breathe her blood and be smothered. He wanted her to be a virgin and not a virgin, all at once. He wanted to know her. Intimate secrets—why poetry? Why so sad? Why the grayness in her eyes? Why so alone? Not lonely, just alone—riding her bike across campus or sitting off by herself in the cafeteria. Even dancing, she danced alone—and it was the aloneness that filled him with love. He remembered telling her that one evening. How she nodded and looked away. And how, later, when he kissed her, she received the kiss without returning it, her eyes wide open, not afraid, not a virgin's eyes, just flat and uninvolved.

Lieutenant Cross gazed at the tunnel. But he was not there. He was buried with Martha under the white sand at the Jersey shore. They were pressed together, and the pebble in his mouth was her tongue. He was smiling. Vaguely, he was aware of how quiet the day was, the sullen paddies, yet he could not bring himself to worry about matters of security. He was beyond that. He was just a kid at war, in love. He was twenty-two years old. He couldn't help it.

A few moments later Lee Strunk crawled out of the tunnel. He came up grinning, filthy but alive. Lieutenant Cross nodded and closed his eyes while the others clapped Strunk on the back and made jokes about rising from the dead.

Worms, Rat Kiley said. Right out of the grave. Fuckin' zombie.

The men laughed. They all felt great relief.

Spook City, said Mitchell Sanders.

Lee Strunk made a funny ghost sound, a kind of moaning, yet very happy, and right then, when Strunk made that high happy moaning sound, when he went *Ahhooooo*, right then Ted Lavender was shot in the

head on his way back from peeing. He lay with his mouth open. The
teeth were broken. There was a swollen black bruise under his left eye.
The cheekbone was gone. Oh shit, Rat Kiley said, the guy's dead. The
guy's dead, he kept saying, which seemed profound—the guy's dead. I
mean really.

The things they carried were determined to some extent by superstition. Lieutenant Cross carried his good-luck pebble. Dave Jensen carried
a rabbit's foot. Norman Bowker, otherwise a very gentle person, carried a
thumb that had been presented to him as a gift by Mitchell Sanders. The
thumb was dark brown, rubbery to the touch, and weighed four ounces
at most. It had been cut from a VC corpse, a boy of fifteen or sixteen.
They'd found him at the bottom of an irrigation ditch, badly burned,
flies in his mouth and eyes. The boy wore black shorts and sandals. At
the time of his death he had been carrying a pouch of rice, a rifle, and
three magazines of ammunition.

You want my opinion, Mitchell Sanders said, there's a definite moral
here.

He put his hand on the dead boy's wrist. He was quiet for a time, as if
counting a pulse, then he patted the stomach, almost affectionately, and
used Kiowa's hunting hatchet to remove the thumb.

Henry Dobbins asked what the moral was.

Moral?

You know. *Moral.*

Sanders wrapped the thumb in toilet paper and handed it across to
Norman Bowker. There was no blood. Smiling, he kicked the boy's head,
watched the flies scatter, and said, It's like with that old TV show—
Paladin. Have gun, will travel.

Henry Dobbins thought about it.

Yeah, well, he finally said. I don't see no moral.

There it *is*, man.

Fuck off.

They carried USO stationery and pencils and pens. They carried
Sterno, safety pins, trip flares, signal flares, spools of wire, razor blades,
chewing tobacco, liberated joss sticks and statuettes of the smiling
Buddha, candles, grease pencils, *The Stars and Stripes*, fingernail clip-
pers, Psy Ops° leaflets, bush hats, bolos, and much more. Twice a week,
when the resupply choppers came in, they carried hot chow in green
Mermite cans and large canvas bags filled with iced beer and soda pop.
They carried plastic water containers, each with a two-gallon capacity.

Psy Ops: Psychological operations.

Mitchell Sanders carried a set of starched tiger fatigues for special occasions. Henry Dobbins carried Black Flag insecticide. Dave Jensen carried empty sandbags that could be filled at night for added protection. Lee Strunk carried tanning lotion. Some things they carried in common. Taking turns, they carried the big PRC-77 scrambler radio, which weighed thirty pounds with its battery. They shared the weight of memory. They took up what others could no longer bear. Often, they carried each other, the wounded or weak. They carried infections. They carried chess sets, basketballs, Vietnamese-English dictionaries, insignia of rank, Bronze Stars and Purple Hearts, plastic cards imprinted with the Code of Conduct. They carried diseases, among them malaria and dysentery. They carried lice and ringworm and leeches and paddy algae and various rots and molds. They carried the land itself—Vietnam, the place, the soil—a powdery orange-red dust that covered their boots and fatigues and faces. They carried the sky. The whole atmosphere, they carried it, the humidity, the monsoons, the stink of fungus and decay, all of it, they carried gravity. They moved like mules. By daylight they took sniper fire, at night they were mortared, but it was not battle, it was just the endless march, village to village, without purpose, nothing won or lost. They marched for the sake of the march. They plodded along slowly, dumbly, leaning forward against the heat, unthinking, all blood and bone, simple grunts, soldiering with their legs, toiling up the hills and down into the paddies and across the rivers and up again and down, just humping, one step and then the next and then another, but no volition, no will, because it was automatic, it was anatomy, and the war was entirely a matter of posture and carriage, the hump was everything, a kind of inertia, a kind of emptiness, a dullness of desire and intellect and conscience and hope and human sensibility. Their principles were in their feet. Their calculations were biological. They had no sense of strategy or mission. They searched the villages without knowing what to look for, not caring, kicking over jars of rice, frisking children and old men, blowing tunnels, sometimes setting fires and sometimes not, then forming up and moving on to the next village, then other villages, where it would always be the same. They carried their own lives. The pressures were enormous. In the heat of early afternoon, they would remove their helmets and flak jackets, walking bare, which was dangerous but which helped ease the strain. They would often discard things along the route of march. Purely for comfort, they would throw away rations, blow their Claymores and grenades, no matter, because by nightfall the resupply choppers would arrive with more of the same, then a day or two later still more, fresh watermelons and crates of ammunition and sunglasses and woolen sweaters—the resources were stunning—sparklers for the Fourth of July, colored eggs for Easter. It was the great American war chest—the fruits of science, the smokestacks, the canneries, the arsenals at Hartford, the Minnesota forests, the machine shops, the vast fields of corn and wheat—they carried like freight trains; they carried it on their backs and shoulders—and for all the ambiguities of Vietnam, all the mysteries and unknowns, there was at least the single abiding certainty that they would never be at a loss for things to carry.

After the chopper took Lavender away, Lieutenant Jimmy Cross led his men into the village of Than Khe. They burned everything. They shot chickens and dogs, they trashed the village well, they called in artillery and watched the wreckage, then they marched for several hours through the hot afternoon, and then at dusk, while Kiowa explained how Lavender died, Lieutenant Cross found himself trembling.

He tried not to cry. With his entrenching tool, which weighed five pounds, he began digging a hole in the earth.

He felt shame. He hated himself. He had loved Martha more than his men, and as a consequence Lavender was now dead, and this was something he would have to carry like a stone in his stomach for the rest of the war.

All he could do was dig. He used his entrenching tool like an ax, slashing, feeling both love and hate, and then later, when it was full dark, he sat at the bottom of his foxhole and wept. It went on for a long while. In part, he was grieving for Ted Lavender, but mostly it was for Martha, and for himself, because she belonged to another world, which was not quite real, and because she was a junior at Mount Sebastian College in New Jersey, a poet and a virgin and uninvolved, and because he realized she did not love him and never would.

Like cement, Kiowa whispered in the dark. I swear to God—boom-down. Not a word.

I've heard this, said Norman Bowker.

A pisser, you know? Still zipping himself up. Zapped while zipping.

All right, fine. That's enough.

Yeah, but you had to see it, the guy just—

I *heard*, man. Cement. So why not shut the fuck *up?*

Kiowa shook his head sadly and glanced over at the hole where Lieutenant Jimmy Cross sat watching the night. The air was thick and wet. A warm, dense fog had settled over the paddies and there was the stillness that precedes rain.

After a time Kiowa sighed.

One thing for sure, he said. The Lieutenant's in some deep hurt. I mean that crying jag—the way he was carrying on—it wasn't fake or anything, it was real heavy-duty hurt. The man cares.

Sure, Norman Bowker said.

Say what you want, the man does care.

We all got problems.

Not Lavender.

No, I guess not, Bowker said. Do me a favor, though.

Shut up?

That's a smart Indian. Shut up.

Shrugging, Kiowa pulled off his boots. He wanted to say more, just to lighten up his sleep, but instead he opened his New Testament and arranged it beneath his head as a pillow. The fog made things seem hollow and unattached. He tried not to think about Ted Lavender, but then he was thinking how fast it was, no drama, down and dead, and how it was hard to feel anything except surprise. It seemed un-Christian. He wished he could find some great sadness, or even anger, but the emotion wasn't there and he couldn't make it happen. Mostly he felt pleased to be alive. He liked the smell of the New Testament under his cheek, the leather and ink and paper and glue, whatever the chemicals were. He liked hearing the sounds of night. Even his fatigue, it felt fine, the stiff muscles and the prickly awareness of his own body, a floating feeling. He enjoyed not being dead. Lying there, Kiowa admired Lieutenant Jimmy Cross's capacity for grief. He wanted to share the man's pain, he wanted to care as Jimmy Cross cared. And yet when he closed his eyes, all he could think was Boom-down, and all he could feel was the pleasure of having his boots off and the fog curling in around him and the damp soil and the Bible smells and the plush comfort of night.

After a moment Norman Bowker sat up in the dark.

What the hell, he said. You want to talk, *talk*. Tell it to me.

Forget it.

No, man, go on. One thing I hate, it's a silent Indian.

For the most part they carried themselves with poise, a kind of dignity. Now and then, however, there were times of panic, when they squealed or wanted to squeal but couldn't, when they twitched and made moaning sounds and covered their heads and said Dear Jesus and flopped around on the earth and fired their weapons blindly and cringed and sobbed and begged for the noise to stop and went wild and made stupid promises to themselves and to God and to their mothers and fathers, hoping not to die. In different ways, it happened to all of them. Afterward, when the firing ended, they would blink and peek up. They would touch their bodies, feeling shame, then quickly hiding it. They would force themselves to stand. As if in slow motion, frame by frame, the world would take on the old logic—absolute silence, then the wind, then sunlight, then voices. It was the burden of being alive. Awkwardly, the men would reassemble themselves, first in private, then in groups, becoming soldiers again. They would repair the leaks in their eyes. They would check for casualties, call in dust-offs, light cigarettes, try to smile, clear their throats and spit and begin cleaning their weapons. After a time someone would shake his head and say, No lie, I almost shit my pants, and someone else would laugh, which meant it was bad, yes, but the guy had obviously not shit his pants, it wasn't that bad, and in any case nobody would ever do such a thing and then go ahead and talk about it. They would squint into the dense, oppressive sunlight. For a few moments, perhaps, they would fall silent, lighting a joint and tracking its passage from man to man, inhaling, holding in the humiliation. Scary stuff, one of them might say. But then someone else would grin or flick his eyebrows and say, Roger-dodger, almost cut me a new asshole, *almost.*

There were numerous such poses. Some carried themselves with a sort of wistful resignation, others with pride or stiff soldierly discipline or good humor or macho zeal. They were afraid of dying but they were even more afraid to show it.

They found jokes to tell.

They used a hard vocabulary to contain the terrible softness. *Greased,* they'd say. *Offed, lit up, zapped while zipping.* It wasn't cruelty, just stage presence. They were actors and the war came at them in 3-D. When someone died, it wasn't quite dying, because in a curious way it seemed scripted, and because they had their lines mostly memorized, irony mixed with tragedy, and because they called it by other names, as if to encyst and destroy the reality of death itself. They kicked corpses. They cut off thumbs. They talked grunt lingo. They told stories about Ted Lavender's supply of tranquilizers, how the poor guy didn't feel a thing, how incredibly tranquil he was.

There's a moral here, said Mitchell Sanders.

They were waiting for Lavender's chopper, smoking the dead man's dope.

The moral's pretty obvious, Sanders said, and winked. Stay away from drugs. No joke, they'll ruin your day every time.

Cute, said Henry Dobbins.

Mind-blower, get it? Talk about wiggy—nothing left, just blood and brains.

They made themselves laugh.

There it is, they'd say, over and over, as if the repetition itself were an act of poise, a balance between crazy and almost crazy, knowing without going. There it is, which meant be cool, let it ride, because oh yeah, man, you can't change what can't be changed, there it is, there it absolutely and positively and fucking well *is.*

They were tough.

They carried all the emotional baggage of men who might die. Grief, terror, love, longing—these were intangibles, but the intangibles had their own mass and specific gravity, they had tangible weight. They carried shameful memories. They carried the common secret of cowardice barely restrained, the instinct to run or freeze or hide, and in many respects this was the heaviest burden of all, for it could never be put down, it required perfect balance and perfect posture. They carried their reputations. They carried the soldier's greatest fear, which was the fear of blushing. Men killed, and died, because they were embarrassed not to. It was what had brought them to the war in the first place, nothing positive, no dreams of glory or honor, just to avoid the blush of dishonor. They died so as not to die of embarrassment. They crawled into tunnels and walked point and advanced under fire. Each morning, despite the unknowns, they made their legs move. They endured. They kept humping. They did not submit to the obvious alternative, which was simply to close the eyes and fall. So easy, really. Go limp and tumble to the ground and let the muscles unwind and not speak and not budge until your buddies picked you up and lifted you into the chopper that would roar and dip its nose and carry you off to the world. A mere matter of falling, yet no one ever fell. It was not courage, exactly; the object was not valor. Rather, they were too frightened to be cowards.

By and large they carried these things inside, maintaining the masks of composure. They sneered at sick call. They spoke bitterly about guys who had found release by shooting off their own toes or fingers. Pussies, they'd say. Candyasses. It was fierce, mocking talk, with only a trace of envy or awe, but even so, the image played itself out behind their eyes.

They imagined the muzzle against flesh. They imagined the quick, sweet pain, then the evacuation to Japan, then a hospital with warm beds and cute geisha nurses.

They dreamed of freedom birds.

At night, on guard, staring into the dark, they were carried away by jumbo jets. They felt the rush of takeoff. *Gone!* they yelled. And then velocity, wings and engines, a smiling stewardess—but it was more than a plane, it was a real bird, a big sleek silver bird with feathers and talons and high screeching. They were flying. The weights fell off, there was nothing to bear. They laughed and held on tight, feeling the cold slap of wind and altitude, soaring, thinking *It's over, I'm gone!*—they were naked, they were light and free—it was all lightness, bright and fast and buoyant, light as light, a helium buzz in the brain, a giddy bubbling in the lungs as they were taken up over the clouds and the war, beyond duty, beyond gravity and mortification and global entanglements—*Sin loi!°* they yelled, *I'm sorry, motherfuckers, but I'm out of it, I'm goofed, I'm*

Sin loi!: "Sorry about that!"

on a space cruise, I'm gone!—and it was a restful, disencumbered sensation, just riding the light waves, sailing that big silver freedom bird over the mountains and oceans, over America, over the farms and great sleeping cities and cemeteries and highways and the golden arches of McDonald's. It was flight, a kind of fleeing, a kind of falling, falling higher and higher, spinning off the edge of the earth and beyond the sun and through the vast, silent vacuum where there were no burdens and where everything weighed exactly nothing. *Gone!* they screamed, *I'm sorry but I'm gone!* And so at night, not quite dreaming, they gave themselves over to lightness, they were carried, they were purely borne.

On the morning after Ted Lavender died, First Lieutenant Jimmy Cross crouched at the bottom of his foxhole and burned Martha's letters. Then he burned the two photographs. There was a steady rain falling, which made it difficult, but he used heat tabs and Sterno to build a small fire, screening it with his body, holding the photographs over the tight blue flame with the tips of his fingers.

He realized it was only a gesture. Stupid, he thought. Sentimental, too, but mostly just stupid.

Lavender was dead. You couldn't burn the blame.

Besides, the letters were in his head. And even now, without photographs, Lieutenant Cross could see Martha playing volleyball in her white gym shorts and yellow T-shirt. He could see her moving in the rain.

When the fire died out, Lieutenant Cross pulled his poncho over his shoulders and ate breakfast from a can.

There was no great mystery, he decided.

In those burned letters Martha had never mentioned the war, except to say, Jimmy, take care of yourself. She wasn't involved. She signed the letters "Love," but it wasn't love, and all the fine lines and technicalities did not matter.

The morning came up wet and blurry. Everything seemed part of everything else, the fog and Martha and the deepening rain.

It was a war, after all.

Half smiling, Lieutenant Jimmy Cross took out his maps. He shook his head hard, as if to clear it, then bent forward and began planning the day's march. In ten minutes, or maybe twenty, he would rouse the men and they would pack up and head west, where the maps showed the country to be green and inviting. They would do what they had always done. The rain might add some weight, but otherwise it would be one more day layered upon all the other days.

He was realistic about it. There was that new hardness in his stomach.

No more fantasies, he told himself.

Henceforth, when he thought about Martha, it would be only to think that she belonged elsewhere. He would shut down the daydreams. This was not Mount Sebastian, it was another world, where there were no pretty poems or midterm exams, a place where men died because of carelessness and gross stupidity. Kiowa was right. Boom-down, and you were dead, never partly dead.

Briefly, in the rain, Lieutenant Cross saw Martha's gray eyes gazing back at him.

He understood.

It was very sad, he thought. The things men carried inside. The things men did or felt they had to do.

He almost nodded at her, but didn't.

Instead he went back to his maps. He was now determined to perform his duties firmly and without negligence. It wouldn't help Lavender, he knew that, but from this point on he would comport himself as a soldier. He would dispose of his good-luck pebble. Swallow it, maybe, or use Lee Strunk's slingshot, or just drop it along the trail. On the march he would impose strict field discipline. He would be careful to send out flank security, to prevent straggling or bunching up, to keep his troops moving at the proper pace and at the proper interval. He would insist on clean weapons. He would confiscate the remainder of Lavender's dope. Later in the day, perhaps, he would call the men together and speak to them plainly. He would accept the blame for what had happened to Ted Lavender. He would be a man about it. He would look them in the eyes, keeping his chin level, and he would issue the new SOPs in a calm, impersonal tone of voice, an officer's voice, leaving no room for argument or discussion. Commencing immediately, he'd tell them, they would no longer abandon equipment along the route of march. They would police up their acts. They would get their shit together, and keep it together, and maintain it neatly and in good working order.

He would not tolerate laxity. He would show strength, distancing himself.

Among the men there would be grumbling, of course, and maybe worse, because their days would seem longer and their loads heavier, but Lieutenant Cross reminded himself that his obligation was not to be loved but to lead. He would dispense with love; it was not now a factor. And if anyone quarreled or complained, he would simply tighten his lips and arrange his shoulders in the correct command posture. He might give a curt little nod. Or he might not. He might just shrug and say Carry on, then they would saddle up and form into a column and move out toward the villages of Than Khe.

[1986]

Girl

Wash the white clothes on Monday and put them on the stone heap; wash the color clothes on Tuesday and put them on the clothesline to dry; don't walk barehead in the hot sun; cook pumpkin fritters in very hot sweet oil; soak your little cloths right after you take them off; when buying cotton to make yourself a nice blouse, be sure that it doesn't have gum on it, because that way it won't hold up well after a wash; soak salt fish overnight before you cook it; is it true that you sing benna° in Sunday school?; always eat your food in such a way that it won't turn someone else's stomach; on Sundays try to walk like a lady and not like the slut you are so bent on becoming; don't sing benna in Sunday school; you mustn't speak to wharf-rat boys, not even to give directions; don't eat fruits on the street—flies will follow you; *but I don't sing benna on Sundays at all and never in Sunday school;* this is how to sew on a button; this is how to make a button-hole for the button you have just sewed on; this is how to hem a dress when you see the hem coming down and so to prevent yourself from looking like the slut I know you are so bent on becoming; this is how you iron your father's khaki shirt so that it doesn't have a crease; this is how you iron your father's khaki pants so that they don't have a crease; this is how you grow okra—far from the house, because okra tree harbors red ants; when you are growing dasheen, make sure it gets plenty of water or else it makes your throat itch when you are eating it; this is how you sweep a corner; this is how you sweep a whole house; this is how you sweep a yard; this is how you smile to someone you don't like too much; this is how you smile to someone you don't like at all; this is how you smile to someone you like completely; this is how you set a table for tea; this is how you set a table for dinner; this is how you set a table for dinner with an important guest; this is how you set a table for lunch; this is how you set a table for breakfast; this is how to behave in the presence of men who don't know you very well, and this way they won't recognize immediately the slut I have warned you against becoming; be sure to wash every day, even if it is

Benna: Calypso music.

347

with your own spit; don't squat down to play marbles—you are not a
boy, you know; don't pick people's flowers—you might catch something;
don't throw stones at blackbirds, because it might not be a blackbird at
all; this is how to make a bread pudding; this is how to make doukona;[2]
this is how to make pepper pot; this is how to make a good medicine for
a cold; this is how to make a good medicine to throw away a child before
it even becomes a child; this is how to catch a fish; this is how to throw
back a fish you don't like, and that way something bad won't fall on you;
this is how to bully a man; this is how a man bullies you; this is how to
love a man, and if this doesn't work there are other ways, and if they
don't work don't feel too bad about giving up; this is how to spit up in the
air if you feel like it, and this is how to move quick so that it doesn't fall
on you; this is how to make ends meet; always squeeze bread to make
sure it's fresh; *but what if the baker won't let me feel the bread?;* you mean
to say that after all you are really going to be the kind of woman who the
baker won't let near the bread?

[1978]

Doukona: A spicy plantain pudding.

AMY TAN [b. 1952]

Two Kinds

My mother believed you could be anything you wanted to be in America.
You could open a restaurant. You could work for the government and get
good retirement. You could buy a house with almost no money down. You
could become rich. You could become instantly famous.

"Of course you can be prodigy, too," my mother told me when I was
nine. "You can be best anything. What does Auntie Lindo know? Her
daughter, she is only best tricky."

America was where all my mother's hopes lay. She had come here in
1949 after losing everything in China: her mother and father, her family
home, her first husband, and two daughters, twin baby girls. But she

never looked back with regret. There were so many ways for things to get better.

We didn't immediately pick the right kind of prodigy. At first my mother thought I could be a Chinese Shirley Temple. We'd watch Shirley's old movies on TV as though they were training films. My mother would poke my arm and say, *"Ni kan"*—You watch. And I would see Shirley tapping her feet, or singing a sailor song, or pursing her lips into a very round O while saying, "Oh my goodness."

"Ni kan," said my mother as Shirley's eyes flooded with tears. "You already know how. Don't need talent for crying!"

Soon after my mother got this idea about Shirley Temple, she took me to a beauty training school in the Mission district and put me in the hands of a student who could barely hold the scissors without shaking. Instead of getting big fat curls, I emerged with an uneven mass of crinkly black fuzz. My mother dragged me off to the bathroom and tried to wet down my hair.

"You look like Negro Chinese," she lamented, as if I had done this on purpose.

The instructor of the beauty training school had to lop off these soggy clumps to make my hair even again. "Peter Pan is very popular these days," the instructor assured my mother. I now had hair the length of a boy's, with straight-across bangs that hung at a slant two inches above my eyebrows. I liked the haircut and it made me actually look forward to my future fame.

In fact, in the beginning, I was just as excited as my mother, maybe even more so. I pictured this prodigy part of me as many different images, trying each one on for size. I was a dainty ballerina girl standing by the curtains, waiting to hear the right music that would send me floating on my tiptoes. I was like the Christ child lifted out of the straw manger, crying with holy indignity. I was Cinderella stepping from her pumpkin carriage with sparkly cartoon music filling the air.

In all of my imaginings, I was filled with a sense that I would soon become *perfect*. My mother and father would adore me. I would be beyond reproach. I would never feel the need to sulk for anything.

But sometimes the prodigy in me became impatient. "If you don't hurry up and get me out of here, I'm disappearing for good," it warned. "And then you'll always be nothing."

Every night after dinner, my mother and I would sit at the Formica kitchen table. She would present new tests, taking her examples from stories of amazing children she had read in *Ripley's Believe It or Not,* or *Good Housekeeping, Reader's Digest,* and a dozen other magazines she kept in a pile in our bathroom. My mother got these magazines from people whose houses she cleaned. And since she cleaned many houses each week, we had a great assortment. She would look through them all, searching for stories about remarkable children.

The first night she brought out a story about a three-year-old boy who knew the capitals of all the states and even most of the European countries. A teacher was quoted as saying the little boy could also pronounce the names of the foreign cities correctly.

"What's the capital of Finland?" my mother asked me, looking at the magazine story.

All I knew was the capital of California, because Sacramento was the name of the street we lived on in Chinatown. "Nairobi!" I guessed, saying the most foreign word I could think of. She checked to see if that was possibly one way to pronounce "Helsinki" before showing me the answer.

The tests got harder—multiplying numbers in my head, finding the queen of hearts in a deck of cards, trying to stand on my head without using my hands, predicting the daily temperatures in Los Angeles, New York, and London.

One night I had to look at a page from the Bible for three minutes and then report everything I could remember. "Now Jehoshaphat had riches and honor in abundance and . . . that's all I remember, Ma," I said.

And after seeing my mother's disappointed face once again, something inside of me began to die. I hated the tests, the raised hopes and failed expectations. Before going to bed that night, I looked in the mirror above the bathroom sink and when I saw only my face staring back— and that it would always be this ordinary face—I began to cry. Such a sad, ugly girl! I made high-pitched noises like a crazed animal, trying to scratch out the face in the mirror.

And then I saw what seemed to be the prodigy side of me—because I had never seen that face before. I looked at my reflection, blinking so I could see more clearly. The girl staring back at me was angry, powerful. This girl and I were the same. I had new thoughts, willful thoughts, or rather thoughts filled with lots of won'ts. I won't let her change me, I promised myself. I won't be what I'm not.

So now on nights when my mother presented her tests, I performed listlessly, my head propped on one arm. I pretended to be bored. And I was. I got so bored I started counting the bellows of the foghorns out on the bay while my mother drilled me in other areas. The sound was comforting and reminded me of the cow jumping over the moon. And the next day, I played a game with myself, seeing if my mother would give up on me before eight bellows. After a while I usually counted only one, maybe two bellows at most. At last she was beginning to give up hope.

* * *

Two or three months had gone by without any mention of my being a prodigy again. And then one day my mother was watching *The Ed Sullivan Show* on TV. The TV was old and the sound kept shorting out. Every time my mother got halfway up from the sofa to adjust the set, the sound would go back on and Ed would be talking. As soon as she sat down, Ed would go silent again. She got up, the TV broke into loud piano music. She sat down. Silence. Up and down, back and forth, quiet and loud. It was like a stiff embraceless dance between her and the TV set. Finally she stood by the set with her hand on the sound dial.

She seemed entranced by the music, a little frenzied piano piece with this mesmerizing quality, sort of quick passages and then teasing lilting ones before it returned to the quick playful parts.

"*Ni kan,*" my mother said, calling me over with hurried hand gestures. "Look here."

I could see why my mother was fascinated by the music. It was being pounded out by a little Chinese girl, about nine years old, with a Peter Pan haircut. The girl had the sauciness of a Shirley Temple. She was proudly modest like a proper Chinese child. And she also did this fancy sweep of a curtsy, so that the fluffy skirt of her white dress cascaded slowly to the floor like the petals of a large carnation.

In spite of these warning signs, I wasn't worried. Our family had no piano and we couldn't afford to buy one, let alone reams of sheet music and piano lessons. So I could be generous in my comments when my mother bad-mouthed the little girl on TV.

"Play note right, but doesn't sound good! No singing sound," complained my mother.

"What are you picking on her for?" I said carelessly. "She's pretty good. Maybe she's not the best, but she's trying hard." I knew almost immediately I would be sorry I said that.

"Just like you," she said. "Not the best. Because you not trying." She gave a little huff as she let go of the sound dial and sat down on the sofa.

The little Chinese girl sat down also to play an encore of "Anitra's Dance" by Grieg. I remember the song, because later on I had to learn how to play it.

Three days after watching *The Ed Sullivan Show,* my mother told me what my schedule would be for piano lessons and piano practice. She had talked to Mr. Chong, who lived on the first floor of our apartment building. Mr. Chong was a retired piano teacher and my mother had traded housecleaning services for weekly lessons and a piano for me to practice on every day, two hours a day, from four until six.

When my mother told me this, I felt as though I had been sent to hell. I whined and then kicked my foot a little when I couldn't stand it anymore.

"Why don't you like me the way I am? I'm *not* a genius! I can't play the piano. And even if I could, I wouldn't go on TV if you paid me a million dollars!" I cried.

My mother slapped me. "Who ask you be genius?" she shouted. "Only ask you be your best. For you sake. You think I want you be genius? Hnnh! What for! Who ask you!"

"So ungrateful," I heard her mutter in Chinese. "If she had as much talent as she has temper, she would be famous now."

Mr. Chong, whom I secretly nicknamed Old Chong, was very strange, always tapping his fingers to the silent music of an invisible orchestra. He looked ancient in my eyes. He had lost most of the hair on top of his head and he wore thick glasses and had eyes that always looked tired and sleepy. But he must have been younger than I thought, since he lived with his mother and was not yet married.

I met Old Lady Chong once and that was enough. She had this peculiar smell like a baby that had done something in its pants. And her fingers felt like a dead person's, like an old peach I once found in the back of the refrigerator; the skin just slid off the meat when I picked it up.

I soon found out why Old Chong had retired from teaching piano. He was deaf. "Like Beethoven!" he shouted to me. "We're both listening only in our head!" And he would start to conduct his frantic silent sonatas.

Our lessons went like this. He would open the book and point to different things, explaining their purpose: "Key! Treble! Bass! No sharps or flats! So this is C major! Listen now and play after me!"

And then he would play the C scale a few times, a simple chord, and then, as if inspired by an old, unreachable itch, he gradually added more notes and running trills and a pounding bass until the music was really something quite grand.

I would play after him, the simple scale, the simple chord, and then I just played some nonsense that sounded like a cat running up and down on top of garbage cans. Old Chong smiled and applauded and then said, "Very good! But now you must learn to keep time!"

So that's how I discovered that Old Chong's eyes were too slow to keep up with the wrong notes I was playing. He went through the motions in half-time. To help me keep rhythm, he stood behind me, pushing down on my right shoulder for every beat. He balanced pennies on top of my wrists so I would keep them still as I slowly played scales and arpeggios. He had me curve my hand around an apple and keep that shape when playing chords. He marched stiffly to show me how to make each finger dance up and down, staccato like an obedient little soldier.

He taught me all these things, and that was how I also learned I could be lazy and get away with mistakes, lots of mistakes. If I hit the wrong notes because I hadn't practiced enough, I never corrected myself. I just kept playing in rhythm. And Old Chong kept conducting his own private reverie.

So maybe I never really gave myself a fair chance. I did pick up the basics pretty quickly, and I might have become a good pianist at that young age. But I was so determined not to try, not to be anybody different that I learned to play only the most ear-splitting preludes, the most discordant hymns.

Over the next year, I practiced like this, dutifully in my own way. And then one day I heard my mother and her friend Lindo Jong both talking in a loud bragging tone of voice so others could hear. It was after church, and I was leaning against the brick wall wearing a dress with stiff white petticoats. Auntie Lindo's daughter, Waverly, who was about my age, was standing farther down the wall about five feet away. We had grown up together and shared all the closeness of two sisters squabbling over crayons and dolls. In other words, for the most part, we hated each other. I thought she was snotty. Waverly Jong had gained a certain amount of fame as "Chinatown's Littlest Chinese Chess Champion."

"She bring home too many trophy," lamented Auntie Lindo that Sunday. "All day she play chess. All day I have no time do nothing but dust off her winnings." She threw a scolding look at Waverly, who pretended not to see her.

"You lucky you don't have this problem," said Auntie Lindo with a sigh to my mother.

And my mother squared her shoulders and bragged: "Our problem worser than yours. If we ask Jing-mei wash dish, she hear nothing but music. It's like you can't stop this natural talent."

And right then, I was determined to put a stop to her foolish pride.

A few weeks later, Old Chong and my mother conspired to have me play in a talent show which would be held in the church hall. By then, my parents had saved up enough to buy me a secondhand piano, a black Wurlitzer spinet with a scarred bench. It was the showpiece of our living room.

For the talent show, I was to play a piece called "Pleading Child" from Schumann's *Scenes from Childhood*. It was a simple, moody piece that sounded more difficult than it was. I was supposed to memorize the whole thing, playing the repeat parts twice to make the piece sound longer. But I dawdled over it, playing a few bars and then cheating, looking up to see what notes followed. I never really listened to what I was playing. I daydreamed about being somewhere else, about being someone else.

The part I liked to practice best was the fancy curtsy: right foot out, touch the rose on the carpet with a pointed foot, sweep to the side, left leg bends, look up and smile.

My parents invited all the couples from the Joy Luck Club to witness my debut. Auntie Lindo and Uncle Tin were there. Waverly and her two older brothers had also come. The first two rows were filled with children both younger and older than I was. The littlest ones got to go first. They recited simple nursery rhymes, squawked out tunes on miniature violins, twirled Hula Hoops, pranced in pink ballet tutus, and when they bowed or curtsied, the audience would sigh in unison, "Awww," and then clap enthusiastically.

When my turn came, I was very confident. I remember my childish excitement. It was as if I knew, without a doubt, that the prodigy side of me really did exist. I had no fear whatsoever, no nervousness. I remember thinking to myself, This is it! This is it! I looked out over the audience, at my mother's blank face, my father's yawn, Auntie Lindo's stiff-lipped smile, Waverly's sulky expression. I had on a white dress layered with sheets of lace, and a pink bow in my Peter Pan haircut. As I sat down I envisioned people jumping to their feet and Ed Sullivan rushing up to introduce me to everyone on TV.

And I started to play. It was so beautiful. I was so caught up in how lovely I looked that at first I didn't worry how I would sound. So it was a surprise to me when I hit the first wrong note and I realized something didn't sound quite right. And then I hit another and another followed that. A chill started at the top of my head and began to trickle down. Yet I couldn't stop playing, as though my hands were bewitched. I kept thinking my fingers would adjust themselves back, like a train switching to the right track. I played this strange jumble through two repeats, the sour notes staying with me all the way to the end.

When I stood up, I discovered my legs were shaking. Maybe I had just been nervous and the audience, like Old Chong, had seen me go through the right motions and had not heard anything wrong at all. I swept my right foot out, went down on my knee, looked up and smiled. The room was quiet, except for Old Chong, who was beaming and shouting, "Bravo! Bravo! Well done!" But then I saw my mother's face, her stricken face. The audience clapped weakly, and as I walked back to my chair, with my whole face quivering as I tried not to cry, I heard a little boy whisper loudly to his mother, "That was awful," and the mother whispered back, "Well, she certainly tried."

And now I realized how many people were in the audience, the whole world it seemed. I was aware of eyes burning into my back. I felt the shame of my mother and father as they sat stiffly throughout the rest of the show.

We could have escaped during intermission. Pride and some strange sense of honor must have anchored my parents to their chairs. And so we watched it all: the eighteen-year-old boy with a fake mustache who did a magic show and juggled flaming hoops while riding a unicycle. The breasted girl with white makeup who sang from *Madama Butterfly* and got honorable mention. And the eleven-year-old boy who won first prize playing a tricky violin song that sounded like a busy bee.

After the show, the Hsus, the Jongs, and the St. Clairs from the Joy Luck Club came up to my mother and father.

"Lots of talented kids," Auntie Lindo said vaguely, smiling broadly.

"That was somethin' else," said my father, and I wondered if he was referring to me in a humorous way, or whether he even remembered what I had done.

Waverly looked at me and shrugged her shoulders. "You aren't a genius like me," she said matter-of-factly. And if I hadn't felt so bad, I would have pulled her braids and punched her stomach.

But my mother's expression was what devastated me: a quiet, blank look that said she had lost everything. I felt the same way, and it seemed as if everybody were now coming up, like gawkers at the scene of an accident, to see what parts were actually missing. When we got on the bus to go home, my father was humming the busy-bee tune and my mother was silent. I kept thinking she wanted to wait until we got home before shouting at me. But when my father unlocked the door to our apartment, my mother walked in and then went to the back, into the bedroom. No accusations. No blame. And in a way, I felt disappointed. I had been waiting for her to start shouting, so I could shout back and cry and blame her for all my misery.

I assumed my talent-show fiasco meant I never had to play the piano again. But two days later, after school, my mother came out of the kitchen and saw me watching TV.

"Four clock," she reminded me as if it were any other day. I was stunned, as though she were asking me to go through the talent-show torture again. I wedged myself more tightly in front of the TV.

"Turn off TV," she called from the kitchen five minutes later.

I didn't budge. And then I decided. I didn't have to do what my mother said anymore. I wasn't her slave. This wasn't China. I had listened to her before and look what happened. She was the stupid one.

She came out from the kitchen and stood in the arched entryway of the living room. "Four clock," she said once again, louder.

"I'm not going to play anymore," I said nonchalantly. "Why should I? I'm not a genius."

She walked over and stood in front of the TV. I saw her chest was heaving up and down in an angry way.

"No!" I said, and I now felt stronger, as if my true self had finally emerged. So this was what had been inside me all along.

"No! I won't!" I screamed.

She yanked me by the arm, pulled me off the floor, snapped off the TV. She was frighteningly strong, half pulling, half carrying me toward the piano as I kicked the throw rugs under my feet. She lifted me up and onto the hard bench. I was sobbing by now, looking at her bitterly. Her chest was heaving even more and her mouth was open, smiling crazily as if she were pleased I was crying.

"You want me to be someone that I'm not!" I sobbed. "I'll never be the kind of daughter you want me to be!"

"Only two kinds of daughters," she shouted in Chinese. "Those who are obedient and those who follow their own mind! Only one kind of daughter can live in this house. Obedient daughter!"

"Then I wish I wasn't your daughter. I wish you weren't my mother," I shouted. As I said these things I got scared. I felt like worms and toads and slimy things were crawling out of my chest, but it also felt good, as if this awful side of me had surfaced, at last.

"Too late change this," said my mother shrilly.

And I could sense her anger rising to its breaking point. I wanted to see it spill over. And that's when I remembered the babies she had lost in China, the ones we never talked about. "Then I wish I'd never been born!" I shouted. "I wish I were dead! Like them."

It was as if I had said the magic words, Alakazam! — and her face went blank, her mouth closed, her arms went slack, and she backed out of the room, stunned, as if she were blowing away like a small brown leaf, thin, brittle, lifeless.

It was not the only disappointment my mother felt in me. In the years that followed, I failed her so many times, each time asserting my own will, my right to fall short of expectations. I didn't get straight As. I didn't become class president. I didn't get into Stanford. I dropped out of college.

For unlike my mother, I did not believe I could be anything I wanted to be. I could only be me.

And for all those years, we never talked about the disaster at the recital or my terrible accusations afterward at the piano bench. All that remained unchecked, like a betrayal that was now unspeakable. So I never found a way to ask her why she had hoped for something so large that failure was inevitable.

And even worse, I never asked her what frightened me the most: Why had she given up hope?

For after our struggle at the piano, she never mentioned my playing again. The lessons stopped, the lid to the piano was closed, shutting out the dust, my misery, and her dreams.

So she surprised me. A few years ago, she offered to give me the piano, for my thirtieth birthday. I had not played in all those years. I saw the offer as a sign of forgiveness, a tremendous burden removed.

"Are you sure?" I asked shyly. "I mean, won't you and Dad miss it?"

"No, this your piano," she said firmly. "Always your piano. You only one can play."

"Well, I probably can't play anymore," I said. "It's been years."

"You pick up fast," said my mother, as if she knew this was certain. "You have natural talent. You could been genius if you want to."

"No I couldn't."

"You just not trying," said my mother. And she was neither angry nor sad. She said it as if to announce a fact that could never be disproved. "Take it," she said.

But I didn't at first. It was enough that she had offered it to me. And after that, every time I saw it in my parents' living room, standing in front of the bay windows, it made me feel proud, as if it were a shiny trophy I had won back.

Last week I sent a tuner over to my parents' apartment and had the piano reconditioned, for purely sentimental reasons. My mother had died a few months before and I had been getting things in order for my father, a little bit at a time. I put the jewelry in special silk pouches. The sweaters she had knitted in yellow, pink, bright orange—all the colors I hated—I put those in moth-proof boxes. I found some old Chinese silk dresses, the kind with little slits up the sides. I rubbed the old silk against my skin, then wrapped them in tissue and decided to take them home with me.

After I had the piano tuned, I opened the lid and touched the keys. It sounded even richer than I remembered. Really, it was a very good piano. Inside the bench were the same exercise notes with handwritten scales, the same secondhand music books with their covers held together with yellow tape.

I opened up the Schumann book to the dark little piece I had played at the recital. It was on the left-hand side of the page, "Pleading Child." It looked more difficult than I remembered. I played a few bars, surprised at how easily the notes came back to me.

And for the first time, or so it seemed, I noticed the piece on the right-hand side. It was called "Perfectly Contented." I tried to play this one as well. It had a lighter melody but the same flowing rhythm and turned out to be quite easy. "Pleading Child" was shorter but slower; "Perfectly Contented" was longer but faster. And after I played them both a few times, I realized they were two halves of the same song.

[1989]

SANDRA CISNEROS [b. 1954]

The House on Mango Street

We didn't always live on Mango Street. Before that we lived on Loomis on the third floor, and before that we lived on Keeler. Before Keeler it was Paulina, and before that I can't remember. But what I remember most is moving a lot. Each time it seemed there'd be one more of us. By the time we got to Mango Street we were six — Mama, Papa, Carlos, Kiki, my sister Nenny, and me.

The house on Mango Street is ours, and we don't have to pay rent to anybody, or share the yard with the people downstairs, or be careful not to make too much noise, and there isn't a landlord banging on the ceiling with a broom. But even so, it's not the house we'd thought we'd get.

We had to leave the flat on Loomis quick. The water pipes broke and the landlord wouldn't fix them because the house was too old. We had to leave fast. We were using the washroom next door and carrying water over in empty milk gallons. That's why Mama and Papa looked for a house, and that's why we moved into the house on Mango Street, far away, on the other side of town.

They always told us that one day we would move into a house, a real house that would be ours for always so we wouldn't have to move each year. And our house would have running water and pipes that worked. And inside it would have real stairs, not hallway stairs, but stairs inside like the houses on T.V. And we'd have a basement and at least three washrooms so when we took a bath we wouldn't have to tell everybody. Our house would be white with trees around it, a great big yard and grass growing without a fence. This was the house Papa talked about when he held a lottery ticket and this was the house Mama dreamed up in the stories she told us before we went to bed.

But the house on Mango Street is not the way they told it at all. It's small and red with tight steps in front and windows so small you'd think they were holding their breath. Bricks are crumbling in places, and the front door is so swollen you have to push hard to get in. There is no front yard, only four little elms the city planted by the curb. Out back is a small garage for the car we don't own yet and a small yard that looks smaller between the two buildings on either side. There are stairs in our house, but they're ordinary hallway stairs, and the house has only one washroom. Everybody has to share a bedroom—Mama and Papa, Carlos and Kiki, me and Nenny.

Once when we were living on Loomis, a nun from my school passed by and saw me playing out front. The laundromat downstairs had been boarded up because it had been robbed two days before and the owner had painted on the wood YES WE'RE OPEN so as not to lose business.

Where do you live? she asked.

There, I said pointing up to the third floor.

You live *there?*

There. I had to look to where she pointed—the third floor, the paint peeling, wooden bars Papa had nailed on the windows so we wouldn't fall out. You live *there?* The way she said it made me feel like nothing. *There.* I lived *there.* I nodded.

I knew then I had to have a house. A real house. One I could point to. But this isn't it. The house on Mango Street isn't it. For the time being, Mama says. Temporary, says Papa. But I know how those things go.

[1983]

LOUISE ERDRICH [b. 1954]

The Red Convertible

Lyman Lamartine

I was the first one to drive a convertible on my reservation. And of course it was red, a red Olds. I owned that car along with my brother Henry Junior. We owned it together until his boots filled with water on a windy night and he bought out my share. Now Henry owns the whole car, and his younger brother Lyman (that's myself), Lyman walks everywhere he goes.

How did I earn enough money to buy my share in the first place? My own talent was I could always make money. I had a touch for it, unusual in a Chippewa. From the first I was different that way, and everyone recognized it. I was the only kid they let in the American Legion Hall to shine shoes, for example, and one Christmas I sold spiritual bouquets for the mission door to door. The nuns let me keep a percentage. Once I started, it seemed the more money I made the easier the money came. Everyone encouraged it. When I was fifteen I got a job washing dishes at the Joliet Café, and that was where my first big break happened.

It wasn't long before I was promoted to busing tables, and then the short-order cook quit and I was hired to take her place. No sooner than you know it I was managing the Joliet. The rest is history. I went on managing. I soon became part owner, and of course there was no stopping me then. It wasn't long before the whole thing was mine.

After I'd owned the Joliet for one year, it blew over in the worst tornado ever seen around here. The whole operation was smashed to bits. A total loss. The fryalator was up in a tree, the grill torn in half like it was paper. I was only sixteen. I had it all in my mother's name, and I lost it quick, but before I lost it I had every one of my relatives, and their relatives, to dinner, and I also bought that red Olds I mentioned, along with Henry.

The first time we saw it! I'll tell you when we first saw it. We had gotten a ride up to Winnipeg, and both of us had money. Don't ask me why, because we never mentioned a car or anything, we just had all our money. Mine was cash, a big bankroll from the Joliet's insurance. Henry had two checks—a week's extra pay for being laid off, and his regular check from the Jewel Bearing Plant.

We were walking down Portage anyway, seeing the sights, when we saw it. There it was, parked, large as life. Really as *if* it was alive. I thought of the word *repose*, because the car wasn't simply stopped, parked, or whatever. That car reposed, calm and gleaming, a FOR SALE sign in its left front window. Then, before we had thought it over at all, the car belonged to us and our pockets were empty. We had just enough money for gas back home.

We went places in that car, me and Henry. We took off driving all one whole summer. We started off toward the Little Knife River and Mandaree in Fort Berthold and then we found ourselves down in Wakpala somehow, and then suddenly we were over in Montana on the Rocky Boy, and yet the summer was not even half over. Some people hang on to details when they travel, but we didn't let them bother us and just lived our everyday lives here to there.

I do remember this one place with willows. I remember I laid under those trees and it was comfortable. So comfortable. The branches bent down all around me like a tent or a stable. And quiet, it was quiet, even though there was a powwow close enough so I could see it going on. The air was not too still, not too windy either. When the dust rises up and hangs in the air around the dancers like that, I feel good. Henry was asleep with his arms thrown wide. Later on, he woke up and we started driving again. We were somewhere in Montana, or maybe on the Blood Reserve—it could have been anywhere. Anyway it was where we met the girl.

All her hair was in buns around her ears, that's the first thing I noticed about her. She was posed alongside the road with her arm out, so we stopped. That girl was short, so short her lumber shirt looked comical on her, like a nightgown. She had jeans on and fancy moccasins and she carried a little suitcase.

"Hop on in," says Henry. So she climbs in between us.

"We'll take you home," I says. "Where do you live?"

"Chicken," she says.

"Where the hell's that?" I ask her.

"Alaska."

"Okay," says Henry, and we drive.

We got up there and never wanted to leave. The sun doesn't truly set there in summer, and the night is more a soft dusk. You might doze off, sometimes, but before you know it you're up again, like an animal in nature. You never feel like you have to sleep hard or put away the world. And things would grow up there. One day just dirt or moss, the next day flowers and long grass. The girl's name was Susy. Her family really took to us. They fed us and put us up. We had our own tent to live in by their house, and the kids would be in and out of there all day and night. They couldn't get over me and Henry being brothers, we looked so different. We told them we knew we had the same mother, anyway.

One night Susy came in to visit us. We sat around in the tent talking of this and that. The season was changing. It was getting darker by that time, and the cold was even getting just a little mean. I told her it was time for us to go. She stood up on a chair.

"You never seen my hair," Susy said.

That was true. She was standing on a chair, but still, when she unclipped her buns the hair reached all the way to the ground. Our eyes opened. You couldn't tell how much hair she had when it was rolled up so neatly. Then my brother Henry did something funny. He went up to the chair and said, "Jump on my shoulders." So she did that, and her hair reached down past his waist, and he started twirling, this way and that, so her hair was flung out from side to side.

"I always wondered what it was like to have long pretty hair," Henry says. Well we laughed. It was a funny sight, the way he did it. The next morning we got up and took leave of those people.

*   *   *

On to greener pastures, as they say. It was down through Spokane and across Idaho then Montana and very soon we were racing the weather right along under the Canadian border through Columbus, Des Lacs, and then we were in Bottineau County and soon home. We'd made most of the trip, that summer, without putting up the car hood at all. We got home just in time, it turned out, for the army to remember Henry had signed up to join it.

I don't wonder that the army was so glad to get my brother that they turned him into a Marine. He was built like a brick outhouse anyway. We liked to tease him that they really wanted him for his Indian nose. He had a nose big and sharp as a hatchet, like the nose on Red Tomahawk, the Indian who killed Sitting Bull, whose profile is on signs all along the North Dakota highways. Henry went off to training camp, came home once during Christmas, then the next thing you know we got an overseas letter from him. It was 1970, and he said he was stationed up in the northern hill country. Whereabouts I did not know. He wasn't such a hot letter writer, and only got off two before the enemy caught him. I could never keep it straight, which direction those good Vietnam soldiers were from.

I wrote him back several times, even though I didn't know if those letters would get through. I kept him informed all about the car. Most of the time I had it up on blocks in the yard or half taken apart, because that long trip did a hard job on it under the hood.

I always had good luck with numbers, and never worried about the draft myself. I never even had to think about what my number was. But Henry was never lucky in the same way as me. It was at least three years before Henry came home. By then I guess the whole war was solved in the government's mind, but for him it would keep on going. In those years I'd put his car into almost perfect shape. I always thought of it as his car while he was gone, even though when he left he said, "Now it's yours," and threw me his key.

"Thanks for the extra key," I'd said. "I'll put it up in your drawer just in case I need it." He laughed.

When he came home, though, Henry was very different, and I'll say this: the change was no good. You could hardly expect him to change for the better, I know. But he was quiet, so quiet, and never comfortable sitting still anywhere but always up and moving around. I thought back to times we'd sat still for whole afternoons, never moving a muscle, just shifting our weight along the ground, talking to whoever sat with us, watching things. He'd always had a joke, then, too, and now you couldn't get him to laugh, or when he did it was more the sound of a man choking, a sound that stopped up the throats of other people around him.

They got to leaving him alone most of the time, and I didn't blame them. It was a fact: Henry was jumpy and mean.

I'd bought a color TV set for my mom and the rest of us while Henry was away. Money still came very easy. I was sorry I'd ever bought it though, because of Henry. I was also sorry I'd bought color, because with black-and-white the pictures seem older and farther away. But what are you going to do? He sat in front of it, watching it, and that was the only time he was completely still. But it was the kind of stillness that you see in a rabbit when it freezes and before it will bolt. He was not easy. He sat in his chair gripping the armrests with all his might, as if the chair itself was moving at a high speed and if he let go at all he would rocket forward and maybe crash right through the set.

Once I was in the room watching TV with Henry and I heard his teeth click at something. I looked over, and he'd bitten through his lip. Blood was going down his chin. I tell you right then I wanted to smash that tube to pieces. I went over to it but Henry must have known what I was up to. He rushed from his chair and shoved me out of the way, against the wall. I told myself he didn't know what he was doing.

My mom came in, turned the set off real quiet, and told us she had made something for supper. So we went and sat down. There was still blood going down Henry's chin, but he didn't notice it and no one said anything, even though every time he took a bit of his bread his blood fell onto it until he was eating his own blood mixed in with the food.

While Henry was not around we talked about what was going to happen to him. There were no Indian doctors on the reservation, and my mom was afraid of trusting the old man, Moses Pillager, because he courted her long ago and was jealous of her husbands. He might take revenge through her son. We were afraid that if we brought Henry to a regular hospital they would keep him.

"They don't fix them in those places," Mom said; "they just give them drugs."

"We wouldn't get him there in the first place," I agreed, "so let's just forget about it."

Then I thought about the car.

Henry had not even looked at the car since he'd gotten home, though like I said, it was in tip-top condition and ready to drive. I thought the car might bring the old Henry back somehow. So I bided my time and waited for my chance to interest him in the vehicle.

One night Henry was off somewhere. I took myself a hammer. I went out to that car and I did a number on its underside. Whacked it up. Bent the tail pipe double. Ripped the muffler loose. By the time I was done with the car it looked worse than any typical Indian car that has been driven all its life on reservation roads, which they always say are like government promises—full of holes. It just about hurt me, I'll tell you that! I threw dirt in the carburetor and I ripped all the electric tape off the seats. I made it look just as beat up as I could. Then I sat back and waited for Henry to find it.

Still, it took him over a month. That was all right, because it was just getting warm enough, not melting, but warm enough to work outside.

"Lyman," he says, walking in one day, "that red car looks like shit."

"Well it's old," I says. "You got to expect that."

"No way!" says Henry. "That car's a classic! But you went and ran the piss right out of it, Lyman, and you know it don't deserve that. I kept that car in A-one shape. You don't remember. You're too young. But when I left, that car was running like a watch. Now I don't even know if I can get it to start again, let alone get it anywhere near its old condition."

"Well you try," I said, like I was getting mad, "but I say it's a piece of junk."

Then I walked out before he could realize I knew he'd strung together more than six words at once.

After that I thought he'd freeze himself to death working on that car. He was out there all day, and at night he rigged up a little lamp, ran a cord out the window, and had himself some light to see by while he worked. He was better than he had been before, but that's still not saying much. It was easier for him to do the things rest of us did. He ate more slowly and didn't jump up and down during the meal to get this or that or look out the window. I put my hand in the back of the TV set, I admit, and fiddled around with it good, so that it was almost impossible now to get a clear picture. He didn't look at it very often anyway. He was always out with that car or going off to get parts for it. By the time it was really melting outside, he had it fixed.

I had been feeling down in the dumps about Henry around this time. We had always been together before. Henry and Lyman. But he was such a loner now that I didn't know how to take it. So I jumped at the chance one day when Henry seemed friendly. It's not that he smiled or anything. He just said, "Let's take that old shitbox for a spin." Just the way he said it made me think he could be coming around.

We went out to the car. It was spring. The sun was shining very bright. My only sister, Bonita, who was just eleven years old, came out and made us stand together for a picture. Henry leaned his elbow on the red car's windshield, and he took his other arm and put it over my shoulder, very carefully, as though it was heavy for him to lift and he didn't want to bring the weight down all at once.

"Smile," Bonita said, and he did.

* * *

That picture, I never look at it anymore. A few months ago, I don't know why, I got his picture out and tacked it on the wall. I felt good about Henry at the time, close to him. I felt good having his picture on the wall, until one night when I was looking at television. I was a little drunk and stoned. I looked up at the wall and Henry was staring at me. I don't know what it was, but his smile had changed, or maybe it was gone. All I know is I couldn't stay in the same room with that picture. I was shaking. I got up, closed the door, and went into the kitchen. A little later my friend Ray came over and we both went back into that room. We put the picture in a brown bag, folded the bag over and over tightly, then put it way back in a closet.

I still see that picture now, as if it tugs at me, whenever I pass that closet door. The picture is very clear in my mind. It was so sunny that day Henry had to squint against the glare. Or maybe the camera Bonita held flashed like a mirror, blinding him, before she snapped the picture. My face is right out in the sun, big and round. But he might have drawn back, because the shadows on his face are deep as holes. There are two shadows curved like little hooks around the ends of his smile, as if to frame it and try to keep it there—that one, first smile that looked like it might have hurt his face. He has his field jacket on and the worn-in clothes he'd come back in and kept wearing ever since. After Bonita took the picture, she went into the house and we got into the car. There was a full cooler in the trunk. We started off, east, toward Pembina and the Red River because Henry said he wanted to see the high water.

The trip over there was beautiful. When everything starts changing, drying up, clearing off, you feel like your whole life is starting. Henry felt it, too. The top was down and the car hummed like a top. He'd really put it back in shape, even the tape on the seats was very carefully put down and glued back in layers. It's not that he smiled again or even joked, but his face looked to me as if it was clear, more peaceful. It looked as though he wasn't thinking of anything in particular except the bare fields and windbreaks and houses we were passing.

The river was high and full of winter trash when we got there. The sun was still out, but it was colder by the river. There were still little clumps of dirty snow here and there on the banks. The water hadn't gone over the banks yet, but it would, you could tell. It was just at its limit, hard swollen glossy like an old gray scar. We made ourselves a fire, and we sat down and watched the current go. As I watched it I felt something squeezing inside me and tightening and trying to let go all at the same time. I knew I was not just feeling it myself; I knew I was feeling what Henry was going through at that moment. Except that I couldn't stand it, the closing and opening. I jumped to my feet. I took Henry by the shoulders and I started shaking him. "Wake up," I says, "wake up, wake up, wake up!" I didn't know what had come over me. I sat down beside him again.

His face was totally white and hard. Then it broke, like stones break all of a sudden when water boils up inside them.

"I know it," he says. "I know it. I can't help it. It's no use."

We start talking. He said he knew what I'd done with the car. It was obvious it had been whacked out of shape and not just neglected. He said he wanted to give the car to me for good now, it was no use. He said he'd fixed it just to give it back and I should take it.

"No way," I says, "I don't want it."

"That's okay," he says, "you take it."

"I don't want it, though," I says back to him, and then to emphasize, just to emphasize, you understand, I touch his shoulder. He slaps my hand off.

"Take that car," he says.

"No," I say. "Make me," I say, and then he grabs my jacket and rips the arm loose. That jacket is a class act, suede with tags and zippers. I push Henry backwards, off the log. He jumps up and bowls me over. We go down in a clinch and come up swinging hard, for all we're worth, with our fists. He socks my jaw so hard I feel like it swings loose. Then I'm at his rib cage and land a good one under his chin so his head snaps back. He's dazzled. He looks at me and I look at him and then his eyes are full of tears and blood and at first I think he's crying. But no, he's laughing. "Ha! Ha!" he says. "Ha! Ha! Take good care of it."

"Okay," I says, "okay, no problem. Ha! Ha!"

I can't help it, and I start laughing, too. My face feels fat and strange, and after a while I get a beer from the cooler in the trunk, and when I hand it to Henry he takes his shirt and wipes my germs off. "Hoof-and-mouth disease," he says. For some reason this cracks me up, and so we're really laughing for a while, and then we drink all the rest of the beers one by one and throw them in the river and see how far, how fast, the current takes them before they fill up and sink.

"You want to go on back?" I ask after a while. "Maybe we could snag a couple nice Kashpaw girls."

He says nothing. But I can tell his mood is turning again.

"They're all crazy, the girls up here, every damn one of them."

"You're crazy too," I say, to jolly him up. "Crazy Lamartine boys!"

He looks as though he will take this wrong at first. His face twists, then clears, and he jumps up on his feet. "That's right!" he says. "Crazier 'n hell. Crazy Indians!"

I think it's the old Henry again. He throws off his jacket and starts swinging his legs out from the knees like a fancy dancer. He's down doing something between a grass dance and a bunny hop, no kind of dance I ever saw before, but neither has anyone else on all this green growing earth. He's wild. He wants to pitch whoopee! He's up and at me and all over. All this time I'm laughing so hard, so hard my belly is getting tied up in a knot.

"Got to cool me off!" he shouts all of a sudden. Then he runs over to the river and jumps in.

There's boards and other things in the current. It's so high. No sound comes from the river after the splash he makes, so I run right over. I look around. It's getting dark. I see he's halfway across the water already, and I know he didn't swim there but the current took him. It's far. I hear his voice, though, very clearly across it.

"My boots are filling," he says.

He says this in a normal voice, like he just noticed and he doesn't know what to think of it. Then he's gone. A branch comes by. Another branch. And I go in.

By the time I get out of the river, off the snag I pulled myself onto, the sun is down. I walk back to the car, turn on the high beams, and drive it up the bank. I put it in first gear and then I take my foot off the clutch. I get out, close the door, and watch it plow softly into the water. The headlights reach in as they go down, searching, still lighted even after the water swirls over the back end. I wait. The wires short out. It is all finally dark. And then there is only the water, the sound of it going and running and going and running and running.

[1984]

PART TWO

250 Poems

ANONYMOUS

Sir Patrick Spens

The king sits in Dumferling town,
   Drinking the blude-reid° wine; *blood-red*
"O whar will I get guid sailor,
   To sail this ship of mine?"

Up and spak an eldern° knicht,° *elderly/knight*   5
   Sat at the king's richt° knee: *right*
"Sir Patrick Spens is the best sailor
   That sails upon the sea."

The king has written a braid° letter *broad (clear)*
   And signed it wi' his hand, 10
And sent it to Sir Patrick Spens,
   Was walking on the sand.

The first line that Sir Patrick read,
   A loud lauch° lauched he; *laugh*
The next line that Sir Patrick read, 15
   The tear blinded his ee.° *eye*

"O wha° is this has done this deed, *who*
   This ill deed done to me,
To send me out this time o' the year,
   To sail upon the sea? 20

"Mak haste, mak haste, my mirry men all,
   Our guid ship sails the morn."
"O say na° sae,° my master dear, *not/so*
   For I fear a deadly storm.

"Late, late yestre'en I saw the new moon 25
   Wi' the auld moon in hir arm,
And I fear, I fear, my dear master,
   That we will come to harm."

O our Scots nobles were richt laith° *loath*
   To weet° their cork-heeled shoon,° *wet/shoes* 30

But lang or° a' the play were played   *before*
  Their hats they swam aboon.°   *above*

O lang, lang may their ladies sit,
  Wi' their fans into their hand,
Or ere they see Sir Patrick Spens   35
  Come sailing to the land.

O lang, lang may the ladies stand
  Wi' their gold kems° in their hair,   *combs*
Waiting for their ain° dear lords,   *own*
· For they'll see them na mair.°   *more* 40

Half o'er, half o'er to Aberdour
  It's fifty fadom° deep,   *fathoms*
And there lies guid Sir Patrick Spens
  Wi' the Scots lords at his feet.

[1765]

ANONYMOUS

Lord Randal

1

"O where ha' you been, Lord Randal, my son?
And where ha' you been, my handsome young man?"
"I ha' been at the greenwood; mother, mak my bed soon,
For I'm wearied wi' huntin', and fain wad° lie down."   *gladly would*

2

"And wha° met ye there, Lord Randal, my son?   *who* 5
And wha met you there, my handsome young man?"
"O I met wi' my true-love; mother, mak my bed soon,
For I'm wearied wi' huntin', and fain wad lie down."

3

"And what did she give you, Lord Randal, my son?
And what did she give you, my handsome young man?"   10
"Eels fried in a pan; mother, mak my bed soon,
For I'm wearied wi' huntin', and fain wad lie down."

4

"And wha gat your leavin's, Lord Randal, my son?
And wha gat your leavin's, my handsome young man?"
"My hawks and my hounds; mother, mak my bed soon,   15
For I'm wearied wi' huntin', and fain wad lie down."

5

"And what becam of them, Lord Randal, my son?
And what becam of them, my handsome young man?"
"They stretched their legs out and died; mother, mak my bed soon,
For I'm wearied wi' huntin', and fain wad lie down."   20

6

"O I fear you are poisoned, Lord Randal, my son!
I fear you are poisoned, my handsome young man!"
"O yes, I am poisoned; mother, mak my bed soon,
For I'm sick at the heart, and I fain wad lie down."

7

"What d' ye leave to your mother, Lord Randal, my son?   25
What d' ye leave to your mother, my handsome young man?"
"Four and twenty milk kye;° mother, mak my bed soon,   *cows*
For I'm sick at the heart, and I fain wad lie down."

8

"What d' ye leave to your sister, Lord Randal, my son?
What d' ye leave to your sister, my handsome young man?"   30
"My gold and my silver; mother, mak my bed soon,
For I'm sick at the heart, and I fain wad lie down."

9

"What d' ye leave to your brother, Lord Randal, my son?
What d' ye leave to your brother, my handsome young man?"
"My houses and my lands; mother, mak my bed soon,   35
For I'm sick at the heart, and I fain wad lie down."

10

"What d' ye leave to your true-love, Lord Randal, my son?
What d' ye leave to your true-love, my handsome young man?"
"I leave her hell and fire; mother, mak my bed soon,
For I'm sick at the heart, and I fain wad lie down."   40

[1803]

SIR THOMAS WYATT   [1503–1542]

They flee from me

They flee from me, that sometime did me seek,
With naked foot stalking in my chamber.
I have seen them, gentle, tame, and meek,
That now are wild, and do not remember
That sometime they put themselves in danger   5
To take bread at my hand; and now they range,
Busily seeking with a continual change.

Thankèd be fortune it hath been otherwise,
Twenty times better; but once in special,
In thin array, after a pleasant guise,°   *manner of dress* 10
When her loose gown from her shoulders did fall,
And she me caught in her arms long and small,°   *slender*
Therewithall sweetly did me kiss
And softly said, "Dear heart,° how like you this?"

It was no dream, I lay broad waking.   15
But all is turned, thorough° my gentleness,   *through*
Into a strange fashion of forsaking;
And I have leave to go, of° her goodness,   *out of (motivated by)*
And she also to use newfangleness.
But since that I so kindly° am served,   20
I fain would know what she hath deserved.

[from an undated manuscript]

14. **Dear heart** (pun): Heart, and hart (deer).
20. **kindly** (pun): Graciously (ironic), and "in kind"; i.e., in a way typical of female nature.

QUEEN ELIZABETH I   [1533–1603]

When I was fair and young

When I was fair and young, and favor graced me,
Of many was I sought, their mistress for to be;
But I did scorn them all, and answered them therefore,
    "Go, go, go seek some otherwhere,
        Importune me no more!"   5

How many weeping eyes I made to pine with woe,
How many sighing hearts, I have no skill to show;
Yet I the prouder grew, and answered them therefore,
    "Go, go, go seek some otherwhere,
        Importune me no more!"   10

Then spake fair Venus' son,° that proud victorious boy,   *Cupid*
And said: "Fine dame, since that you be so coy,
I will so pluck your plumes that you shall say no more,
    'Go, go, go seek some otherwhere,
        Importune me no more!'"   15

When he had spake these words, such change grew in my breast
That neither night nor day since that, I could take any rest.
Then lo! I did repent that I had said before,
    "Go, go, go seek some otherwhere,
        Importune me no more!"   20

                        [*c. 1580s*]

EDMUND SPENSER   [1552–1599]

One day I wrote her name
upon the strand

One day I wrote her name upon the strand,
But came the waves and washèd it away:
Again I wrote it with a second hand,
But came the tide, and made my pains his prey.

"Vain man," said she, "that dost in vain assay,   5
A mortal thing so to immortalize,
For I myself shall like to this decay,
And eek° my name be wipèd out likewise."   *also*
"Not so," quod° I, "let baser things devise,   *quoth (said)*
To die in dust, but you shall live by fame: 10
My verse your virtues rare shall eternize,
And in the heavens write your glorious name.
Where whenas death shall all the world subdue,
Our love shall live, and later life renew."

[1595]

SIR PHILIP SIDNEY   [1554–1586]

Loving in truth, and fain in verse my love to show

Loving in truth, and fain° in verse my love to show,   *glad*
That the dear she might take some pleasure of my pain,
Pleasure might cause her read, reading might make her know,
Knowledge might pity win, and pity grace obtain,
    I sought fit words to paint the blackest face of woe: 5
Studying inventions fine, her wits to entertain,
Oft turning others' leaves, to see if thence would flow
Some fresh and fruitful showers upon my sunburned brain.
    But words came halting forth, wanting° Invention's stay;°
Invention, Nature's child, fled step-dame Study's blows,   10
And others' feet still seemed but strangers in my way.
Thus great with child to speak, and helpless in my throes,
    Biting my truant pen, beating myself for spite,
    "Fool," said my Muse to me, "look in thy heart and write."

[1582]

9. **wanting:** Lacking; **stay:** Support.

MARY (SIDNEY) HERBERT, COUNTESS OF PEMBROKE [1561–1621]

Psalm 100 *Jubilate Deo*

O all you lands, the treasures of your joy
  In merry shout upon the Lord bestow:
Your service cheerfully on him employ,
  With triumph song into his presence go.
Know first that he is God; and after know   5
  This God did us, not we ourselves create:
We are his flock, for us his feedings grow:
  We are his folk, and he upholds our state.
With thankfulness O enter then his gate:
  Make through each porch of his your praises ring,   10
All good, all grace, of his high name relate,
  He of all grace and goodness is the spring.
Time in no terms his mercy comprehends,
From age to age his truth itself extends.

[*c. 1595;* 1823]

MICHAEL DRAYTON [1563–1631]

Since there's no help, come let us kiss and part

Since there's no help, come let us kiss and part;
Nay, I have done, you get no more of me,
And I am glad, yea glad with all my heart
That thus so cleanly I myself can free;
Shake hands forever, cancel all our vows,   5
And when we meet at any time again,
Be it not seen in either of our brows
That we one jot of former love retain.
Now at the last gasp of love's latest breath,
When, his pulse failing, passion speechless lies,   10
When faith is kneeling by his bed of death,

And innocence is closing up his eyes,
  Now if thou wouldst, when all have given him over,
  From death to life thou mightst him yet recover.

[1619]

CHRISTOPHER MARLOWE   [1564–1593]

The Passionate Shepherd to His Love

Come live with me and be my love,
And we will all the pleasures prove
That valleys, groves, hills, and fields,
Woods, or steepy mountain yields.

And we will sit upon the rocks,   5
Seeing the shepherds feed their flocks,
By shallow rivers, to whose falls
Melodious birds sing madrigals.

And I will make thee beds of roses
And a thousand fragrant posies,   10
A cap of flowers, and a kirtle
Embroidered all with leaves of myrtle.

A gown made of the finest wool
Which from our pretty lambs we pull,
Fair lined slippers for the cold,   15
With buckles of the purest gold.

A belt of straw and ivy buds,
With coral clasps and amber studs,
And if these pleasures may thee move,
Come live with me, and be my love.   20

The shepherd swains shall dance and sing
For thy delight each May morning.
If these delights thy mind may move,
Then live with me and be my love.

[1599]

WILLIAM SHAKESPEARE   [1564–1616]

Sonnet 18

Shall I compare thee to a summer's day?
Thou art more lovely and more temperate:
Rough winds do shake the darling buds of May,
And summer's lease° hath all too short a date;°   *allotted time/duration*
Sometimes too hot the eye of heaven shines,   5
And often is his gold complexion dimmed;
And every fair° from fair° sometimes declines,   *beautiful thing/beauty*
By chance or nature's changing course untrimmed;°   *stripped of its beauty*
But thy eternal summer shall not fade,
Nor lose possession of that fair thou ow'st;°   *beauty you own*   10
Nor shall death brag thou wand'rest in his shade,
When in eternal lines° to time thou grow'st:°
   So long as men can breathe, or eyes can see,
   So long lives this,° and this gives life to thee.   *this sonnet*

[1609]

12. **lines:** (Of poetry); **grow'st:** You are grafted to time.

WILLIAM SHAKESPEARE   [1564–1616]

Sonnet 73

That time of year thou mayst in me behold
When yellow leaves, or none, or few, do hang
Upon those boughs which shake against the cold,
Bare ruined choirs,° where late° the sweet birds sang.   *choirstalls/lately*
In me thou seest the twilight of such day   5
As after sunset fadeth in the west,
Which by and by black night doth take away,
Death's second self, that seals up all in rest.
In me thou seest the glowing of such fire
That on the ashes of his youth doth lie,   10
As the deathbed whereon it must expire,
Consumed with that which it was nourished by.

This thou perceiv'st, which makes thy love more strong,
To love that well which thou must leave ere long.

[1609]

WILLIAM SHAKESPEARE   [1564–1616]

Sonnet 116

Let me not to the marriage of true minds
Admit impediments. Love is not love
Which alters when it alteration finds,
Or bends with the remover to remove.
O, no, it is an ever-fixèd mark   5
That looks on tempests and is never shaken;
It is the star to every wandering bark,°   *ship*
Whose worth's unknown, although his height be taken.°   *is measured*
Love's not time's fool, though rosy lips and cheeks
Within his bending sickle's compass come;   10
Love alters not with his brief hours and weeks,
But bears it out even to the edge of doom.°   *Judgment Day*
    If this be error and upon me proved,
    I never writ, nor no man ever loved.

[1609]

WILLIAM SHAKESPEARE   [1564–1616]

Sonnet 130

My mistress' eyes are nothing like the sun;
Coral is far more red than her lips' red;
If snow be white, why then her breasts are dun;°   *dull grayish brown*
If hairs be wires, black wires grow on her head.
I have seen roses damasked,° red and white,   *variegated* 5
But no such roses see I in her cheeks;

And in some perfumes is there more delight
Than in the breath that from my mistress reeks.
I love to hear her speak, yet well I know
That music hath a far more pleasing sound.   10
I grant I never saw a goddess go;°   *walk*
My mistress, when she walks, treads on the ground.
   And yet, by heaven, I think my love as rare
   As any she° belied° with false compare.   *woman/misrepresented*

[1609]

THOMAS CAMPION [1567–1620]

When thou must home

When thou must home to shades of underground,
And there arrived, a new admirèd guest,
The beauteous spirits do engirt° thee round,   *encircle*
White Iope, blithe Helen,° and the rest,
To hear the stories of thy finished love   5
From that smooth tongue whose music hell can move,

Then wilt thou speak of banqueting delights,
Of masques and revels which sweet youth did make,
Of tourneys and great challenges of knights,
And all these triumphs for thy beauty's sake;   10
When thou hast told these honors done to thee,
Then tell, Oh tell, how thou didst murther° me.   *murder*

[1601]

4. **Iope, Helen:** In Greek mythology, Iope, or Cassiopeia, was known for her beauty and vanity; Helen was known for loveliness, liveliness, and inconstancy.

JOHN DONNE [1572–1631]

A Valediction:
Forbidding Mourning

As virtuous men pass mildly away,
   And whisper to their souls to go,
Whilst some of their sad friends do say
   The breath goes now, and some say, No;

So let us melt, and make no noise,   5
   No tear-floods, nor sigh-tempests move;
'Twere profanation of our joys
   To tell the laity our love.

Moving of th' earth brings harms and fears,
   Men reckon what it did and meant;   10
But trepidation of the spheres,
   Though greater far, is innocent.°

Dull sublunary° lovers' love   *under the moon; hence, inconstant*
   (Whose soul is sense) cannot admit
Absence, because it doth remove   15
   Those things which elemented° it.   *composed*

But we, by a love so much refined
   That our selves know not what it is,
Inter-assurèd of the mind,
   Care less, eyes, lips, and hands to miss.   20

Our two souls therefore, which are one,
   Though I must go, endure not yet
A breach, but an expansion,
   Like gold to airy thinness beat.

If they be two, they are two so   25
   As stiff twin compasses° are two;   *drawing compasses*
Thy soul, the fixed foot, makes no show
   To move, but doth, if th' other do.

9–12. **Moving . . . innocent:** Earthquakes cause damage and were taken as portending further changes or dangers. Trepidation (an oscillating motion of the eighth or ninth sphere, in the Ptolemaic cosmological system) is greater than an earthquake, but not harmful or ominous.

And though it in the center sit,
   Yet when the other far doth roam,   30
It leans and hearkens after it,
   And grows erect, as that comes home.

Such wilt thou be to me, who must,
   Like th' other foot, obliquely run;
Thy firmness makes my circle just,   35
   And makes me end where I begun.

                             [1633]

JOHN DONNE   [1572–1631]

The Flea

Mark but this flea, and mark in this,
How little that which thou deny'st me is;
Me it sucked first, and now sucks thee,
And in this flea, our two bloods mingled be;°
Confess it, this cannot be said°   *called*   5
A sin, or shame, or loss of maidenhead,°   *virginity*
   Yet this enjoys before it woo,
   And pampered swells with one blood made of two,
   And this, alas, is more than we would do.

Oh stay,° three lives in one flea spare,   10
Where we almost, nay more than married are.
This flea is you and I, and this
Our marriage bed, and marriage temple is;
Though parents grudge, and you, we are met,
And cloistered in these living walls of jet.   15
   Though use° make you apt to kill me,   *habit*
   Let not to this, self murder added be,
   And sacrilege, three sins in killing three.°

4. our two bloods mingled be: Renaissance medical theory held that blood was mingled during sexual intercourse, the "little" act the lady is denying the speaker (l. 2); such mingling leads to conception and pregnancy (l. 8).
10. stay: Stop; refrain from killing the flea. "Die" and "kill" were Renaissance slang terms for orgasm (the sexual act, with its loss of blood, was believed to reduce the length of a man's life).
18. three sins: Murder, suicide, and sacrilege (destroying a "marriage temple").

Cruel and sudden, hast thou since
Purpled thy nail, in blood of innocence?   20
In what could this flea guilty be,
Except in that drop which it sucked from thee?
Yet thou triumph'st, and say'st that thou
Find'st not thyself, nor me the weaker now;
   'Tis true, then learn how false, fears be;   25
   Just so much honour, when thou yield'st to me,
   Will waste, as this flea's death took life from thee.

[1633]

JOHN DONNE   [1572–1631]

Batter my heart, three-personed God

Batter my heart, three-personed God, for you
As yet but knock, breathe, shine, and seek to mend;
That I may rise and stand, o'erthrow me, and bend
Your force to break, blow, burn, and make me new.
I, like an usurped town, to another due,   5
Labor to admit you, but oh, to no end;
Reason, your viceroy in me, me should defend,
But is captived, and proves weak or untrue.
Yet dearly I love you, and would be lovèd fain,
But am betrothed unto your enemy;   10
Divorce me, untie or break that knot again,
Take me to you, imprison me, for I,
Except you enthrall me, never shall be free,
Nor ever chaste, except you ravish me.

[1633]

BEN JONSON   [1572–1637]

On My First Son

Farewell, thou child of my right hand,° and joy;
My sin was too much hope of thee, loved boy:
Seven years thou'wert lent to me, and I thee pay,
Exacted by thy fate, on the just day.
O could I lose all father now! for why   5
Will man lament the state he should envy,
To have so soon 'scaped world's and flesh's rage,
And, if no other misery, yet age?
Rest in soft peace, and asked, say, "Here doth lie
Ben Jonson his best piece of poetry."   10
For whose sake henceforth all his° vows be such   *(the father's)*
As what he loves may never like° too much.

[1616]

1. child . . . hand: A literal translation of the Hebrew name "Benjamin." The boy, named for his father, was born in 1596 and died on his birthday ("the just day") in 1603.
12. like: Archaic meaning "please."

LADY MARY WROTH   [c. 1587–c. 1651]

Am I thus conquered?

Am I thus conquered? Have I lost the powers
   That° to withstand, which joys° to ruin me?   *(love)/delights*
   Must I be still while it my strength devours,
   And captive leads me prisoner, bound, unfree?
Love first shall leave men's fant'sies to them free,   5
   Desire shall quench love's flames, spring hate sweet showers,
   Love shall loose all his darts, have sight, and see
   His shame, and wishings hinder happy hours.
Why should we not love's purblind° charms resist?   *completely blind*
   Must we be servile, doing what he list?°   *pleases* 10
   No, seek some host to harbor thee: I fly

Thy babish° tricks, and freedom do profess. *childish*
 But O my hurt makes my lost heart confess
 I love, and must: So farewell liberty.

[1621]

ROBERT HERRICK [1591–1674]

To the Virgins, to Make Much of Time

Gather ye rosebuds while ye may,
 Old time is still a-flying;
And this same flower that smiles today
 Tomorrow will be dying.

The glorious lamp of heaven, the sun,   5
 The higher he's a-getting,
The sooner will his race be run,
 And nearer he's to setting.

That age is best which is the first,
 When youth and blood are warmer;   10
But being spent, the worse, and worst
 Times still succeed the former.

Then be not coy, but use your time,
 And while ye may, go marry;
For having lost but once your prime,   15
 You may forever tarry.

[1648]

GEORGE HERBERT   [1593–1633]

Easter-wings°

Lord, who createdst man in wealth and store,°
Though foolishly he lost the same,°
Decaying more and more
Till   he   became
Most   poor:
    With   thee
    O   let   me   rise
    As   larks,   harmoniously,
    And sing this day thy victories:
Then shall the fall further the flight in me.   10

My tender age in sorrow did begin:
And still with sicknesses and shame
Thou didst so punish sin,
That   I   became
Most   thin.
    With   thee
    Let   me   combine,
    And   feel   thy   victory;
For, if I imp° my wing on thine,
Affliction shall advance the flight in me.   20

[1633]

Easter-wings: Originally the stanzas were printed on facing pages, lines 1–10 on the left page, to be read first, then lines 11–20 on the right page. **1. Store:** Abundance. **2. "lost the same":** Through the Fall in the Garden of Eden. Early editions include the words "this day" in line 18 (perhaps repeated by mistake from line 9); they do not appear in the only surviving manuscript and are not required for the meter. **19. imp:** A term from falconry—to graft additional feathers onto the wings of a hawk to improve its flight.

GEORGE HERBERT   [1593–1633]

The Pulley

When God at first made man,
Having a glass of blessings standing by,
"Let us," said he, "pour on him all we can.

Let the world's riches, which dispersèd lie,
   Contract into a span."   5

So strength first made a way;
Then beauty flowed, then wisdom, honor, pleasure.
When almost all was out, God made a stay,
Perceiving that, alone of all his treasure,
   Rest in the bottom lay.   10

"For if I should," said he,
"Bestow this jewel also on my creature,
He would adore my gifts instead of me,
And rest in Nature, not the God of Nature;
   So both should losers be.   15

"Yet let him keep the rest,
But keep them with repining restlessness.
Let him be rich and weary, that at least,
If goodness lead him not, yet weariness
   May toss him to my breast."   20

[1633]

EDMUND WALLER   [1606–1687]

Song

Go, lovely rose!
Tell her that wastes her time and me
   That now she knows,
When I resemble her to thee,
How sweet and fair she seems to be.   5

Tell her that's young,
And shuns to have her graces spied,
   That hadst thou sprung
In deserts, where no men abide,
Thou must have uncommended died.   10

Small is the worth
Of beauty from the light retired;
   Bid her come forth,

Suffer herself to be desired,
And not blush so to be admired.   15

   Then die! that she
The common fate of all things rare
   May read in thee;
How small a part of time they share
That are so wondrous sweet and fair!   20

[1645]

JOHN MILTON   [1608–1674]

Lycidas

In this monody° the author bewails a learned friend, unfortunately drowned in his passage from Chester on the Irish Seas, 1637. And by occasion foretells the ruin of our corrupted clergy, then in their height.

Yet once more, O ye laurels,° and once more,
Ye myrtles brown,° with ivy never sere,   *dark*
I come to pluck your berries harsh and crude,°   *unripe*
And with forced fingers rude
Shatter your leaves before the mellowing year.   5
Bitter constraint, and sad occasion dear,
Compels me to disturb your season due:
For Lycidas is dead, dead ere his prime,
Young Lycidas, and hath not left his peer.
Who would not sing for Lycidas? He knew   10
Himself to sing, and build the lofty rhyme.
He must not float upon his watery bier
Unwept, and welter° to the parching wind,   *roll about*
Without the meed° of some melodious tear.   *reward*

monody: A monody is an elegy or dirge sung by a single voice. The poem draws on the traditions of the pastoral elegy. It appeared in a collection of poems published as a tribute to Edward King, Milton's "learned friend" and fellow student at Cambridge.
1. ye laurels: Laurel, sacred to Apollo, was the emblem of poetic achievement. Myrtle is the crown of Venus and ivy of Bacchus. All three are evergreen, thus "never sere" (dry, withered).

Begin then, sisters of the sacred well°   15
That from beneath the seat of Jove doth spring,
Begin, and somewhat loudly sweep the string.
Hence with denial vain, and coy° excuse,   *reticent*
So may some gentle Muse
With lucky words favor my destined urn,   20
And as he passes turn,
And bid fair peace be to my sable° shroud.   *black*
For we were nursed upon the self-same hill,
Fed the same flock, by fountain, shade, and rill.
    Together both, ere the high lawns° appeared   *pastures*   25
Under the opening eyelids of the morn,
We drove afield, and both together heard
What time the grey-fly winds° her sultry horn,   *blows*
Battening° our flocks with the fresh dews of night,   *fattening*
Oft till the star that rose, at evening, bright   30
Toward heaven's descent had sloped his westering wheel.
Meanwhile the rural ditties were not mute,
Tempered to the oaten flute;°
Rough satyrs danced, and fauns with cloven heel
From the glad sound would not be absent long,   35
And old Damaetas° loved to hear our song.
    But O the heavy change, now thou art gone,
Now thou art gone, and never must return!
Thee, shepherd, thee the woods and desert caves,
With wild thyme and the gadding° vine o'ergrown,   *wandering*   40
And all their echoes mourn.
The willows and the hazel copses° green   *thickets*
Shall now no more be seen
Fanning their joyous leaves to thy soft lays.
As killing as the canker° to the rose,   *cankerworm*   45
Or taint-worm to the weanling herds that graze,
Or frost to flowers, that their gay wardrobe wear,
When first the white-thorn blows;°   *hawthorn blossoms*
Such, Lycidas, thy loss to shepherd's ear.
    Where were ye, nymphs, when the remorseless deep   50
Closed o'er the head of your loved Lycidas?
For neither were ye playing on the steep

---

15. sisters . . . well: The muses; the well sacred to them was Aganippe near
Mount Helicon.
33. oaten flute: Instrument symbolic of pastoral poetry.
36. Damaetas: A pastoral name, referring probably to a Cambridge tutor.

Where your old bards, the famous Druids, lie,
Nor on the shaggy top of Mona high,
Nor yet where Deva spreads her wizard stream.°   55
Ay me, I fondly° dream,   *foolishly*
Had ye been there!—for what could that have done?
What could the Muse herself that Orpheus bore,
The Muse herself,° for her enchanting son
Whom universal nature did lament,   60
When by the rout that made the hideous roar
His gory visage down the stream was sent,
Down the swift Hebrus to the Lesbian shore?
    Alas! what boots° it with uncessant care   *profits*
To tend the homely slighted shepherd's trade,   65
And strictly meditate the thankless Muse?
Were it not better done as others use,
To sport with Amaryllis in the shade,
Or with the tangles of Neaera's hair?°
Fame is the spur that the clear spirit doth raise   70
(That last infirmity of noble mind)
To scorn delights, and live laborious days;
But the fair guerdon° when we hope to find,   *reward*
And think to burst out into sudden blaze,
Comes the blind Fury with the abhorrèd shears,°   75
And slits the thin-spun life. "But not the praise,"
Phoebus replied, and touched my trembling ears:
"Fame is no plant that grows on mortal soil,
Nor in the glistering foil°
Set off to the world, nor in broad rumor lies,   80
But lives and spreads aloft by those pure eyes
And perfect witness of all-judging Jove;
As he pronounces lastly on each deed,

55. Deva . . . stream: The River Dee in Cheshire, "wizard" because it was said to
be able to change the size and position of its channel. "Mona" is the island of
Anglesey, in northwest Wales. Both are in the west country near where King died.
59. The Muse herself: Calliope. Her son Orpheus was torn apart by a mob
("rout") of screaming Thracian women (Bacchantes). His bloody head floated
down the river Hebrus, across the Aegean to the island of Lesbos.
68–69. Amaryllis, Neaera: Conventional names for shepherdesses.
75. Fury: Atropos, one of the three Fates in Greek mythology, used her scissors to
cut the thread of human life, after it had been spun and measured by her sisters.
For the Greeks and Romans the Furies had a different role, but even in classical
literature "Fury" and "Fate" were often used interchangeably.
79. glistering foil: Gold or silver leaf set under jewels to increase their brilliance.

Of so much fame in heaven expect thy meed.'
　O fountain Arethuse,° and thou honored flood,   85
Smooth-sliding Mincius,° crowned with vocal reeds,
That strain I heard was of a higher mood.
But now my oat proceeds,
And listens to the herald of the sea°
That came in Neptune's plea.   90
He asked the waves, and asked the felon winds,
What hard mishap hath doomed this gentle swain?
And questioned every gust of rugged wings
That blows from off each beakèd promontory—
They knew not of his story,   95
And sage Hippotades° their answer brings,
That not a blast was from his dungeon strayed;
The air was calm, and on the level brine
Sleek Panope° with her all sisters played.
It was that fatal and perfidious bark,   100
Built in the eclipse, and rigged with curses dark,
That sunk so low that sacred head of thine.
　Next Camus,° reverend sire, went footing slow,
His mantle hairy, and his bonnet sedge,°   *plants growing near water*
Inwrought with figures dim, and on the edge   105
Like to that sanguine flower° inscribed with woe.
"Ah, who hath reft," quoth he, "my dearest pledge?"°   *child (hopefulness)*
Last came, and last did go,
The Pilot° of the Galilean lake;
Two massy keys he bore of metals twain   110
(The golden opes, the iron shuts amain).°   *with force*
He shook his mitred locks, and stern bespake:
"How well could I have spared for thee, young swain,

85. **Arethuse:** A fountain in Sicily associated with the pastoral poetry of Theocritus.
86. **Mincius:** A river in Lombardy associated with the *Eclogues* of Virgil.
89. **herald of the sea:** The merman Triton, who pleads Neptune's innocence in Lycidas's death.
96. **Hippotades:** Aeolus, the wind god, son of Hippotas.
99. **Panope:** The greatest of the Nereids (sea nymphs).
103. **Camus:** God of the river Cam, representing the ancient University of Cambridge.
106. **sanguine flower:** The blood-colored hyacinth; marks on its leaves supposedly are the Greek letters AIAI, expressing woe.
109. **The Pilot:** Saint Peter, Galilean fisherman, first bishop of the church (thus his "mitred" locks—entitled to wear a bishop's mitre); to him Christ promised "the keys of the kingdom" (Matthew 16:19) to open and close the gates of heaven.

Enow° of such as for their bellies' sake   *enough*
Creep and intrude and climb into the fold!°   115
Of other care they little reckoning make
Than how to scramble at the shearers' feast,
And shove away the worthy bidden guest.
Blind mouths!° that scarce themselves know how to hold
A sheep-hook, or have learned aught else the least   120
That to the faithful herdman's art belongs!
What recks° it them? What need they? They are sped;°
And when they list,° their lean and flashy songs   *want*
Grate on their scrannel° pipes of wretched straw   *thin, feeble*
The hungry sheep look up, and are not fed,   125
But swoln with wind, and the rank mist they draw,
Rot inwardly, and foul contagion spread,
Besides what the grim wolf° with privy paw
Daily devours apace, and nothing said;
But that two-handed engine° at the door   130
Stands ready to smite once, and smite no more,"
    Return, Alpheus,° the dread voice is past
That shrunk thy streams; return, Sicilian Muse,
And call the vales, and bid them hither cast
Their bells and flowerets of a thousand hues.   135
Ye valleys low where the mild whispers use°   *frequent (verb)*
Of shades and wanton winds and gushing brooks,
On whose fresh lap the swart star° sparely looks,   *Sirius*
Throw hither all your quaint enamelled eyes,
That on the green turf suck the honied showers,   140
And purple all the ground with vernal flowers.
Bring the rathe° primrose that forsaken dies,   *early*
The tufted crowtoe, and pale jessamine,
The white pink, and the pansy freaked° with jet,   *flecked*
The glowing violet,   145

115. **Creep . . . fold:** Alluding to John 10:1 — "Anyone who does not enter the sheepfold by the gate but climbs in by another way is a thief and a bandit."
119. **Blind mouths!:** A reference to the greed of the bishops: a bishop *(episcopus)* is one who oversees, and a pastor is one who feeds his flock.
122. **recks:** Matters to them; **are sped:** Have more than enough.
128. **grim wolf:** The Roman Catholic Church, secretly ("privy") opposing Protestantism.
130. **two-handed engine:** An apocalyptic instrument of revenge against clergy who neglect their responsibilities.
132. **Alpheus:** The reference to this river god who fell in love with the nymph Arethusa brings the poem back to the pastoral mode.

The musk-rose, and the well-attired woodbine,
With cowslips wan that hang the pensive head,
And every flower that sad embroidery wears.
Bid amaranthus all his beauty shed,
And daffadillies fill their cups with tears,   150
To strew the laureate hearse where Lycid lies.
For so to interpose a little ease,
Let our frail thoughts dally with false surmise;
Ay me! whilst thee the shores and sounding seas
Wash far away, where'er thy bones are hurled,   155
Whether beyond the stormy Hebrides,
Where thou perhaps under the whelming° tide   *engulfing*
Visit'st the bottom of the monstrous world;
Or whether thou, to our moist vows° denied,   *tearful prayers*
Sleep'st by the fable of Bellerus° old,   160
Where the great vision of the guarded mount°
Looks toward Namancos and Bayona's hold:°
Look homeward, Angel,° now, and melt with ruth;°
And, O ye dolphins,° waft the hapless youth.
    Weep no more, woeful shepherds, weep no more,   165
For Lycidas your sorrow is not dead,
Sunk though he be beneath the watery floor;
So sinks the day-star° in the ocean bed,   *the sun*
And yet anon repairs° his drooping head,   *returns (raises)*
And tricks° his beams, and with new-spangled ore   *plays tricks with* 170
Flames in the forehead of the morning sky:
So Lycidas sunk low, but mounted high,
Through the dear might of him that walked the waves,°   *(Christ)*
Where, other groves and other streams along,
With nectar pure his oozy locks he laves,°   *bathes* 175
And hears the unexpressive° nuptial song   *inexpressible*
In the blest kingdoms meek of joy and love.
There entertain him all the saints above,
In solemn troops and sweet societies

---

160. **Bellerus:** A fabulous giant for whom Land's End (the southwestern tip of Cornwall) was called Bellerium in Roman times.
161. **the guarded mount:** Saint Michael's Mount, in Cornwall.
162. **Namancos and Bayona:** A mountain range and a fortress on the coast of northern Spain.
163. **Angel:** The archangel Michael, patron of mariners, imagined as standing on Saint Michael's Mount, looking southward; **ruth:** Pity.
164. **ye dolphins:** Dolphins brought the Greek poet Arion safely to shore and carried Melicertes to land, where he was transformed to a sea god, Palaemon.

That sing, and singing in their glory move,   180
And wipe the tears for ever from his eyes.
Now, Lycidas, the shepherds weep no more;
Henceforth thou art the Genius of the Shore,
In thy large recompense, and shalt be good
To all that wander in that perilous flood.   185
    Thus sang the uncouth° swain to the oaks and rills,   *uneducated*
While the still morn went out with sandals grey;
He touched the tender stops of various quills,
With eager thought warbling his Doric lay.°   *pastoral song*
And now the sun had stretched out all the hills,   190
And now was dropped into the western bay;
At last he rose, and twitched his mantle blue:
Tomorrow to fresh woods, and pastures new.

                                                                        [1638]

JOHN MILTON   [1608–1674]

When I consider
how my light is spent

When I consider how my light is spent°
  Ere half my days, in this dark world and wide,
  And that one talent which is death to hide
  Lodged with me useless, though my soul more bent
To serve therewith my Maker, and present   5
  My true account, lest he returning chide.
  "Doth God exact day-labor, light denied?"
  I fondly ask; but patience to prevent
That murmur, soon replies, "God doth not need
  Either man's work or his own gifts; who best   10
  Bear his mild yoke, they serve him best. His state
Is kingly. Thousands at his bidding speed
  And post o'er land and ocean without rest:
  They also serve who only stand and wait."

                                                               [*c. 1652;* 1673]

1. when . . . spent: Milton went blind in 1652. Lines 1–2 allude to Matthew
25:1–13; line 3, to Matthew 25:14–30; and line 11, to Matthew 11:30.

ANNE BRADSTREET [c. 1612–1672]

To My Dear and Loving Husband

If ever two were one, then surely we.
If ever man were loved by wife, then thee;
If ever wife was happy in a man,
Compare with me ye women if you can.
I prize thy love more than whole mines of gold,   5
Or all the riches that the East doth hold.
My love is such that rivers cannot quench,
Nor ought but love from thee give recompense.
Thy love is such I can no way repay;
The heavens reward thee manifold, I pray.   10
Then while we live, in love let's so persever,
That when we live no more we may live ever.

[1678]

RICHARD LOVELACE [1618–1657]

To Lucasta, Going to the Wars

Tell me not, Sweet, I am unkind,
   That from the nunnery
Of thy chaste breast and quiet mind
   To war and arms I fly.

True, a new mistress now I chase,   5
   The first foe in the field;
And with a stronger faith embrace
   A sword, a horse, a shield.

Yet this inconstancy is such
   As you too shall adore;   10

I could not love thee, dear, so much,
  Loved I not honor more.

[1649]

ANDREW MARVELL [1621–1678]

To His Coy Mistress°

   Had we but world enough, and time,
This coyness, lady, were no crime.
We would sit down, and think which way
To walk, and pass our long love's day.
Thou by the Indian Ganges' side   5
Shouldst rubies find; I by the tide
Of Humber would complain.° I would
Love you ten years before the Flood,
And you should, if you please, refuse
Till the conversion of the Jews.°   10
My vegetable° love should grow   *living and growing*
Vaster than empires, and more slow;
An hundred years should go to praise
Thine eyes, and on thy forehead gaze;
Two hundred to adore each breast,   15
But thirty thousand to the rest;
An age at least to every part,
And the last age should show your heart.
For, lady, you deserve this state,°   *dignity*
Nor would I love at lower rate.   20
   But at my back I always hear
Time's wingèd chariot hurrying near;
And yonder all before us lie

Coy: In the seventeenth century, "coy" could carry its older meaning, "shy," or the modern sense of "coquettish."
5–7. Indian Ganges', Humber: The Ganges River in India, with its distant, romantic associations, contrasts with the Humber River, running through Hull in northeast England, Marvell's home town.
10. conversion . . . Jews: An occurrence foretold, in some traditions, as one of the concluding events of human history.

Deserts of vast eternity.
Thy beauty shall no more be found,   25
Nor, in thy marble vault, shall sound
My echoing song; then worms shall try
That long-preserved virginity,
And your quaint honor turn to dust,
And into ashes all my lust: 30
The grave's a fine and private place,
But none, I think, do there embrace.
    Now therefore, while the youthful hue
Sits on thy skin like morning dew,
And while thy willing soul transpires°   *breathes forth* 35
At every pore with instant fires,°   *urgent passion*
Now let us sport us while we may,
And now, like amorous birds of prey,
Rather at once our time devour
Than languish in his slow-chapped° power.   40
Let us roll all our strength and all
Our sweetness up into one ball,
And tear our pleasures with rough strife
Thorough° the iron gates of life;   *through*
Thus, though we cannot make our sun   45
Stand still,° yet we will make him run.

                                             [*c. 1650;* 1681]

40. slow-chapped: Slow-jawed, devouring slowly.
45–46. make our sun stand still: An allusion to Joshua 10:12. In answer to
Joshua's prayer, God made the sun stand still, to prolong the day and give the
Israelites more time to defeat the Amorites.

APHRA BEHN   [1640–1689]

On Her Loving Two Equally

I

How strong does my passion flow,
Divided equally twixt two?
Damon had ne'er subdued my heart
Had not Alexis° took his part;

3–4. Damon, Alexis: Traditional names in poetry.

Nor could Alexis powerful prove,   5
Without my Damon's aid, to gain my love.

II

When my Alexis present is,
Then I for Damon sigh and mourn;
But when Alexis I do miss,
Damon gains nothing but my scorn.   10
But if it chance they both are by,
For both alike I languish, sigh, and die.

III

Cure then, thou mighty wingèd god,
This restless fever in my blood;
One golden-pointed dart take back: 15
But which, O Cupid, wilt thou take?
If Damon's, all my hopes are crossed;
Or that of my Alexis, I am lost.

                                                          [1684]

EDWARD TAYLOR   [c. 1642–1729]

Housewifery

Make me, O Lord, thy spinning wheel complete.°
   Thy holy word my distaff make for me.
Make mine affections thy swift flyers neat,
   And make my soul thy holy spool to be.
   My conversation make to be thy reel,   5
   And reel the yarn thereon spun on thy wheel.

Make me thy loom then, knit therein this twine;
   And make thy holy spirit, Lord, wind quills.°
Then weave the web thyself. The yarn is fine.
   Thine ordinances make my fulling mills.   10

---

1. **spinning wheel complete:** In a spinning wheel, the distaff holds the raw wool
or flax to be spun; the flyers twist and guide the thread; the thread is wound onto
the spool as it is spun; and the reel receives the finished thread.
8. **quills:** The spools of a loom.

Then dye the same in heavenly colors choice,
All pinked° with varnished° flowers of paradise.   *ornamented/lustrous*

Then clothe therewith mine understanding, will,
  Affections, judgment, conscience, memory,
My words, and actions, that their shine may fill   15
  My ways with glory and thee glorify.
  Then mine apparel shall display before ye
  That I am clothed in holy robes for glory.

                                        [*1682–1683;* 1939]

ANNE FINCH, COUNTESS OF WINCHILSEA [1661–1720]

From The Introduction

Did I my lines intend for public view,
How many censures° would their faults pursue,   *criticisms*
Some would, because such words they do affect,
Cry they're insipid, empty, uncorrect.
And many have attained, dull and untaught,   5
The name of wit,° only by finding fault.   *perceptive person*
True judges might condemn their want° of wit,°   *lack/cleverness*
And all might say, they're by a woman writ.
Alas! a woman that attempts the pen,
Such an intruder on the rights of men,   10
Such a presumptuous creature, is esteemed,
The° fault can by no virtue be redeemed.   *That the*
They tell us we mistake our sex and way;
Good breeding, fashion, dancing, dressing, play
Are the accomplishments we should desire;   15
To write, or read, or think, or to inquire
Would cloud our beauty, and exhaust our time,
And interrupt the conquests° of our prime;°   *(amorous)/best years*
Whilst the dull manage of a servile house°   *household with servants*
Is held by some our utmost art, and use.   20
    Sure 'twas not ever thus, nor are we told
Fables° of women that excelled of old;   *stories conveying lessons*
To whom, by the diffusive° hand of Heaven   *scattering*
Some share of wit and poetry was given.

• • •

How are we fallen, fallen by mistaken rules?
And education's, more than nature's, fools,
Debarred from all improvements of the mind,
And to be dull, expected and designed;°   *shaped, formed*
And if someone would soar above the rest,   55
With warmer fancy° and ambition pressed,   *inventiveness*
So strong th' opposing faction still appears,
The hopes to thrive can ne'er outweigh the fears.
Be cautioned then my Muse, and still retired;
Nor be despised, aiming to be admired;   60
Conscious of wants, still with contracted wing,
To some few friends and to thy sorrows sing;
For groves of laurel° thou wert never meant;
Be dark enough thy shades, and be thou
    there content.

[1689]

63. **groves of laurel:** Leaves worn as a mark of distinction.

JONATHAN SWIFT [1667-1745]

A Description
of the Morning

Now hardly here and there a hackney-coach
Appearing, showed the ruddy morn's approach.
Now Betty from her master's bed had flown,
And softly stole to discompose her own;
The slip-shod 'prentice from his master's door   5
Had pared the dirt and sprinkled round the floor.
Now Moll had whirled her mop with dext'rous airs,
Prepared to scrub the entry and the stairs.
The youth with broomy stumps° began to trace   *worn broom*
The kennel-edge,° where wheels had worn the place.   *gutter* 10
The small-coal man° was heard with cadence deep,   *coal vendor*
Till drowned in shriller notes of chimney-sweep:
Duns° at his lordship's gate began to meet;   *debt collectors*

And brickdust Moll° had screamed through half the street
The turnkey now his flock returning sees,   15
Duly let out a-nights to steal for fees:
The watchful bailiffs take their silent stands,
And schoolboys lag with satchels in their hands.

[1709]

14. **brickdust Moll:** Woman selling powdered brick.

ALEXANDER POPE   [1688–1744]

The Rape of the Lock°

CANTO I

What dire offence from amorous causes springs,
What mighty quarrels rise from trivial things,
I sing—This verse to Caryll, Muse, is due:
This, even Belinda may vouchsafe to view:
Slight is the subject, but not so the praise,   5
If she inspire, and he approve my lays.
     Say what strange motive, Goddess, could compel
A well-bred lord to assault a gentle belle?
Oh, say what stranger cause, yet unexplored,
Could make a gentle belle reject a lord?   10
And dwells such rage in softest bosoms then?
And lodge such daring souls in little men?
     Sol° through white curtains did his beams display,   *the sun*
And oped those eyes which brighter shine than they.
Shock° just had given himself the rowzing shake,   15

The Rape of the Lock: The poem is based on an actual incident: Lord Petre had cut a lock of hair from the head of Arabella Fermor, which led to an estrangement between the two prominent families. Pope's friend John Caryll, to whom the poem is addressed (I.3), suggested that Pope write a humorous poem about the incident that might lead to a reconciliation. The poem printed here is the original version in two cantos, which Pope said was written in less than two weeks. It was widely admired and praised when it appeared in 1712. Two years later Pope published an expanded version in five cantos.
I.15. Shock: The conventional name for a lapdog with very long hair.

And nymphs° prepared their chocolate to take.   *beautiful young women*
Thrice the wrought slipper knocked against the ground,°
And striking watches the tenth hour resound.
Belinda rose, and 'midst attending dames,
Launched on the bosom of the silver Thames.   20
A train of well-dressed youths around her shone,
And every eye was fixed on her alone;
On her white breast a sparkling cross she wore,
Which Jews might kiss, and infidels adore.
Her lively looks a sprightly mind disclose,   25
Quick as her eyes, and as unfixed as those:
Favors to none, to all she smiles extends;
Oft she rejects, but never once offends.
Bright as the sun, her eyes the gazers strike,
And, like the sun, they shine on all alike.   30
Yet graceful ease, and sweetness void of pride,
Might hide her faults, if belles had faults to hide:
If to her share some female errors fall,
Look on her face, and you'll forgive 'em all.
   This nymph, to the destruction of mankind,   35
Nourished two locks which graceful hung behind
In equal curls, and well conspired to deck
With shining ringlets her smooth ivory neck.
Love in these labyrinths his slaves detains,
And mighty hearts are held in slender chains.   40
With hairy springes° we the birds betray,   *snares*
Slight lines of hair surprize the finny prey,°   *fish*
Fair tresses man's imperial race ensnare,
And beauty draws us with a single hair.
   The adventrous baron the bright locks admired,   45
He saw, he wished, and to the prize aspired.
Resolved to win, he meditates the way,
By force to ravish, or by fraud betray;
For when success a lover's toil attends,
Few ask if fraud or force attained his ends.   50
   For this, ere Phoebus° rose, he had implored   *the sun*
Propitious heaven, and every power adored,
But chiefly love—to love an altar built,
Of twelve vast French romances, neatly gilt.

I.17. slipper . . . ground: To summon a servant; bells were not introduced until
the late 1700s.

There lay the sword-knot° Sylvia's hands had sewn,   55
With Flavia's busk° that oft had wrapped his own:
A fan, a garter, half a pair of gloves,
And all the trophies of his former loves.
With tender billet-doux° he lights the pyre,   *love letters*
And breaths three amorous sighs to raise the fire.   60
Then prostrate falls, and begs with ardent eyes
Soon to obtain, and long possess the prize:
The powers gave ear, and granted half his prayer,
The rest, the winds dispersed in empty air.
    Close by those meads° forever crowned with flowers,   *meadows* 65
Where Thames with pride surveys his rising towers,
There stands a structure of majestic frame,
Which from the neighboring Hampton° takes its name.
Here Britain's statesmen oft the fall foredoom
Of foreign tyrants, and of nymphs at home;   70
Here thou, great Anna,° whom three realms obey,
Dost sometimes counsel take—and sometimes tea.°
    Hither our nymphs and heroes did resort,
To taste awhile the pleasures of a court;
In various talk the cheerful hours they passed,   75
Of, who was bit,° or who capotted last:°
This speaks the glory of the British Queen,
And that describes a charming Indian screen;
A third interprets motions, looks, and eyes;
At every word a reputation dies.   80
Snuff, or the fan, supply each pause of chat,
With singing, laughing, ogling, and all that.

I.55. sword-knot: A ribbon or tassel tied to the hilt of a sword, sometimes the work of the sword owner's lady.

I.56. busk: Usually a strip of wood, whalebone, steel, or other rigid material used to stiffen the front of a corset. It probably refers here to the whole corset, which the baron often has wrapped around his hand (or waist).

I.68. Hampton: Hampton Court Palace, about fifteen miles up the Thames from central London.

I.71. Anna: Queen Anne (1665–1714) was ruler of Great Britain and Ireland (1702–1714), and the English Crown continued its old claim to rule France as well.

I.72. tea: In seventeenth-century pronunciation, "tea" and "obey" were perfect rhymes, as were "found" and "wound" (II. 102–03) and "hair" and "sphere" (II. 183–84).

I.76. was bit: Taken in, made the butt of a joke, or cheated in a card game; **capotted:** Lost all the tricks in the card game Piquet.

Now, when declining from the noon of day,
The sun obliquely shoots his burning ray;
When hungry judges soon the sentence sign,   85
And wretches hang that jurymen may dine;
When merchants from the Exchange return in peace,
And the long labors of the toilet° cease—   *dressing-table*
The board's with cups and spoons, alternate, crowned;
The berries crackle, and the mill turns round;°   90
On shining altars of Japan° they raise
The silver lamp, and fiery spirits blaze:
From silver spouts the grateful liquors glide,
And China's earth receives the smoking tide.
At once they gratify their smell and taste,   95
While frequent cups prolong the rich repast.
Coffee (which makes the politician wise,
And see through all things with his half-shut eyes)
Sent up in vapors to the Baron's brain
New stratagems, the radiant lock to gain.   100
Ah, cease, rash youth! desist ere 'tis too late,
Fear the just Gods, and think of Scylla's fate!°
Changed to a bird, and sent to flit in air,
She dearly pays for Nisus' injured hair!
But when to mischief mortals bend their mind,   105
How soon fit instruments of ill they find.
Just then, Clarissa drew with tempting grace
A two-edged weapon° from her shining case: *scissors*
So ladies in romance assist their knight,
Present the spear, and arm him for the fight.   110
He takes the gift with reverence, and extends
The little engine on his fingers' ends;
This just behind Belinda's neck he spread,
As o'er the fragrant steams she bends her head.
He first expands the glittering forfex° wide   115

I.90. berries . . . round: Denotes the roasting and grinding of coffee beans.
I.91. altars of Japan: A table work decorated and finished in the Japanese style, with a varnish of exceptional hardness.
I.102. Scylla's fate!: This Scylla, daughter of Ninus, cut from his head a lock of hair that protected him to give it to her lover, Minos of Crete, who was laying siege to her father's city of Megara. Minos was shocked and refused to accept it, and Scylla was turned into a seabird (Ovid, *Metamorphoses*, VIII).
I.115. forfex: Latin for scissors.

To enclose the lock; then joins it, to divide;
One fatal stroke the sacred hair does sever
From the fair head, forever and forever!
   The living fires come flashing from her eyes,
And screams of horror rend the affrighted skies.   120
Not louder shrieks by dames to heaven are cast,
When husbands die, or lapdogs breathe their last,
Or when rich china vessels fallen from high,
In glittering dust and painted fragments lie.
   "Let wreaths of triumph now my temples twine,"   125
The victor cried, "The glorious prize is mine!
While fish in streams, or birds delight in air,
Or in a coach and six the British fair,
As long as *Atalantis*° shall be read,
Or the small pillow grace a lady's bed,   130
While visits shall be paid on solemn days,
When numerous wax-lights in bright order blaze,
While nymphs take treats, or assignations give,
So long my honor, name, and praise shall live!
   "What time would spare, from steel receives its date,   135
And monuments, like men, submit to fate!
Steel did the labor of the Gods destroy,
And strike to dust the aspiring towers of Troy;
Steel could the works of mortal pride confound,
And hew triumphal arches to the ground.   140
What wonders then, fair nymph, thy hairs should feel
The conquering force of unresisted steel?"

CANTO II

But anxious cares the pensive nymph oppressed,
And secret passions labored in her breast.
Not youthful kings in battle seized alive,
Not scornful virgins who their charms survive,
Not ardent lover robbed of all his bliss,   5
Not ancient lady when refused a kiss,
Not tyrants fierce that unrepenting die,
Not Cynthia° when her manteau's pinned awry,   *conventional name*
E'er felt such rage, resentment, and despair,
As thou, sad virgin, for thy ravished hair.   10

I.129. *Atalantis*: *New Atlantis* (1709) by Delarivière Manley was popular at the time because of its accounts of court scandal.

While her racked soul repose and peace requires,
The fierce Thalestris° fans the rising fires.
"O wretched maid!" she spreads her hands, and cried,
And Hampton's echoes, "Wretched maid!" replied,
"Was it for this you took such constant care,   15
Combs, bodkins, leads, pomatums to prepare?°
For this your locks in paper durance bound,
For this with torturing irons wreathed around?
Oh, had the youth but been content to seize
Hairs less in sight—or any hairs but these!   20
Gods! shall the ravisher display this hair,
While the fops envy, and the ladies stare?
Honor forbid! at whose unrivaled shrine
Ease, pleasure, virtue, all, our sex resign.
Methinks already I your tears survey,   25
Already hear the horrid things they say,
Already see you a degraded toast,°
And all your honor in a whisper lost!
How shall I, then, your helpless fame defend?
'Twill then be infamy to seem your friend!   30
And shall this prize, the inestimable prize,
Exposed through crystal to the gazing eyes,
And heightened by the diamond's circling rays,
On that rapacious hand forever blaze?°
Sooner shall grass in Hyde Park Circus° grow,   35
And wits take lodgings in the sound of Bow;°
Sooner let earth, air, sea, to chaos fall,
Men, monkeys, lapdogs, parrots, perish all!"
    She said; then raging to Sir Plume repairs,
And bids her beau demand the precious hairs   40

II.12. Thalestris: A character named for a queen of the Amazons, thus a fierce and militant warrior.
II.16. bodkin: A long pin or pin-shaped ornament used by women to fasten up their hair; leads: Black lead combs were used to darken hair.
II.27. toast: "A celebrated woman whose health is often drunk" (from Samuel Johnson's *Dictionary of the English Language* [1755]).
II.33–34. diamond's . . . blaze: The baron intends to encase the lock in crystal and mount it on a ring.
II.35. Hyde Park Circus: A circular drive in Hyde Park, a popular gathering place for the upper classes.
II.36. Bow: Lodgings within hearing distance of the bells of Saint Mary-le-Bow Church would be in an unfashionable part of London.

(Sir Plume, of amber snuffbox justly vain,
And the nice conduct of a clouded cane).°
With earnest eyes, and round unthinking face,
He first the snuffbox opened, then the case,
And thus broke out—"My Lord, why, what the devil?   45
Zounds!° damn the lock! 'fore Gad, you must be civil!
Plague on 't! 'tis past a jest—nay prithee, pox!
Give her the hair"—he spoke, and rapped his box.
    "It grieves me much," replied the Peer again,
"Who speaks so well should ever speak in vain.   50
But by this lock, this sacred lock, I swear
(Which never more shall join its parted hair,
Which never more its honors shall renew,
Clipped from the lovely head where once it grew),
That while my nostrils draw the vital air,   55
This hand, which won it, shall forever wear."
He spoke, and speaking, in proud triumph spread
The long-contended honors of her head.
    But see! the nymph in sorrow's pomp appears,
Her eyes half languishing, half drowned in tears;   60
Now livid pale her cheeks, now glowing red;⎫
On her heaved bosom hung her drooping head, ⎬
Which, with a sigh, she raised; and thus she said:⎭
    "Forever cursed be this detested day,
Which snatched my best, my favorite curl away!   65
Happy! ah, ten times happy had I been,
If Hampton Court these eyes had never seen!
Yet am not I the first mistaken maid,
By love of courts to numerous ills betrayed.
Oh, had I rather unadmired remained   70
In some lone isle, or distant northern land;
Where the gilt chariot never marked the way,
Where none learn ombre, none e'er taste bohea!°
There kept my charms concealed from mortal eye,
Like roses that in deserts bloom and die.   75
What moved my mind with youthful lords to roam?

II.42. clouded cane: Canes with heads of mottled or veined stones were considered stylish.
II.46. Zounds!: A euphemistic abbreviation of "by God's wounds" used in oaths
and asseverations.
II.73. ombre: A popular card game played by three persons; bohea: In the early
1700s, referred to the finest kinds of black tea.

Oh, had I stayed, and said my prayers at home!
'Twas this the morning omens did foretell;
Thrice from my trembling hand the patch box° fell;
The tottering china shook without a wind,   80
Nay, Poll sat mute, and shock was most unkind.
See the poor remnants of this slighted hair:
My hands shall rend what ev'n thy own did spare.
This, in two sable ringlets taught to break,
Once gave new beauties to the snowy neck.   85
The sister lock now sits uncouth, alone,
And in its fellow's fate foresees its own;
Uncurled it hangs! the fatal shears demands,
And tempts once more thy sacrilegious hands."
    She said: the pitying audience melt in tears,   90
But fate and Jove had stopped the baron's ears.
In vain Thalestris with reproach assails,
For who can move when fair Belinda fails?
Not half so fixed the Trojan° could remain,
While Anna begged and Dido raged in vain.   95
"To arms, to arms!" the bold Thalestris cries,
And swift as lightning to the combat flies.
All side in parties, and begin the attack;
Fans clap, silks rustle, and tough whalebones crack;
Heroes' and heroines' shouts confusedly rise,   100
And bass and treble voices strike the skies.
No common weapons in their hands are found,
Like Gods they fight, nor dread a mortal wound.
    So when bold Homer makes the Gods engage,
And heavenly breasts with human passions rage;   105
'Gainst Pallas, Mars; Latona, Hermes arms;°
And all Olympus rings with loud alarms.
Jove's thunder roars, heaven trembles all around;

II.79. patch box: A box for holding patches, the small pieces of black silk or
court-plaster worn on the face by men and especially women of fashion in the
1600s and 1700s, either to hide a blemish or to show off the complexion by contrast.
II.94–95. the Trojan: Aeneas, who abandoned Dido at the bidding of the gods,
despite Dido's reproaches (*Aeneid* 4.305–92) and the pleadings of her sister Anna
that he stay (4.416–49).
II.106. Pallas . . . Hermes: In the *Iliad* 20.91ff, Pallas (Athena) and Hermes sided
with the Greeks, Mars and Latona (Leto, mother of Apollo and Diana), with the
Trojans.

Blue Neptune storms, the bellowing deeps resound;
Earth shakes her nodding towers, the ground gives way,   110
And the pale ghosts start at the flash of day.
　　While through the press enraged Thalestris flies,
And scatters deaths around from both her eyes,°
A beau and witling perished in the throng,
One died in metaphor, and one in song.   115
"O cruel nymph! a living death I bear,"
Cried Dapperwit, and sunk beside his chair.
A mournful glance Sir Fopling° upwards cast,
"Those eyes are made so killing"—was his last.
Thus on Meander's flowery margin lies   120
The expiring swan, and as he sings he dies.°
　　As bold Sir Plume had drawn Clarissa down,
Chloe stepped in, and killed him with a frown;
She smiled to see the doughty hero slain,
But at her smile, the beau revived again.   125
　　Now Jove suspends his golden scales in air,°
Weighs the men's wits against the lady's hair;
The doubtful beam long nods from side to side;
At length the wits mount up, the hairs subside.
　　See, fierce Belinda on the baron flies,   130
With more than usual lightning in her eyes;
Nor feared the chief the unequal fight to try,
Who sought no more than on his foe to die.
But this bold lord, with manly strength indued,
She with one finger and a thumb subdued: 135
Just where the breath of life his nostrils drew,
A charge of snuff the wily virgin threw;
Sudden, with starting tears each eye o'erflows,
And the high dome re-echoes to his nose.

II.113. Lines 113–47 include sexual innuendos, particularly the double entendre
in which "die" or "kill" can mean orgasm as well as physical death.
II.117–18. **Dapperwit, Fopling:** Names of characters borrowed from recent
satiric comedies.
II.120–21. **Meander's flowery margin:** "Thus, at the summons of fate, casting
himself down amid the watery grasses by the shallows of Meander, sings the
white swan" (Ovid, *Heroides* 7:1–2). **expiring swan:** Legends hold that the mute
swan, a royal bird in England since 1462, uses its voice only as it dies.
II.126. **Jove . . . air:** In the *Iliad* (16.783ff, 22.271ff), the *Aeneid* (12.725ff), and
Paradise Lost (4.996ff), scales are used by the gods to determine the course of
future events.

"Now meet thy fate," the incensed Virago° cried,   *female warrior*   140
And drew a deadly bodkin° from her side.
"Boast not my fall," he said, "insulting foe!
Thou by some other shalt be laid as low.
Nor think, to die dejects my lofty mind;
All that I dread, is leaving you behind!   145
Rather than so, ah, let me still survive,
And still burn on, in Cupid's flames, alive."
    "Restore the lock!" she cries; and all around
"Restore the lock!" the vaulted roofs rebound.
Not fierce Othello in so loud a strain   150
Roared for the handkerchief that caused his pain.°
But see how oft ambitious aims are crossed,
And chiefs contend till all the prize is lost.
The lock, obtained with guilt, and kept with pain,
In every place is sought, but sought in vain: 155
With such a prize no mortal must be blessed,
So heaven decrees! with heaven who can contest?
    Some thought it mounted to the lunar sphere,
Since all that man e'er lost is treasured there.
There heroes' wits are kept in ponderous vases,   160
And beaux' in snuffboxes and tweezer cases.
There broken vows and deathbed alms are found,
And lovers' hearts with ends of riband bound;
The courtiers' promises, and sick man's prayers,
The smiles of harlots, and the tears of heirs;   165
Cages for gnats, and chains to yoke a flea,
Dried butterflies, and tomes of casuistry.
    But trust the Muse—she saw it upward rise,
Though marked by none but quick, poetic eyes
(Thus Rome's great founder to the heavens withdrew,   170
To Proculus alone confessed in view).°
A sudden star, it shot through liquid air,
And drew behind a radiant trail of hair.
Not Berenice's locks first rose so bright,°

II.141. **bodkin:** A short pointed weapon, or dagger, or (as in II.16 above) a long pin or pin-shaped ornament used to fasten up the hair.
II.150–51. **Othello . . . pain:** *Othello* 3.4.55–98.
II.170–71. **(Thus . . . view):** Romulus' removal to heaven in a storm cloud was observed only by the senator Proculus.
II.174. **Berenice:** Wife of Ptolemy III who offered a lock of her hair to Aphrodite to ensure her husband's safe return from war; the hair disappeared from Aphrodite's temple and was turned into a constellation.

The skies bespangling with disheveled light.   175
This, the beau monde shall from the Mall survey,
As through the moonlight shade they nightly stray,   ⎫
And hail with music its propitious ray.   ⎬
This Partridge soon shall view in cloudless skies,   ⎭
When next he looks through Galileo's eyes;°   *telescope* 180
And hence the egregious wizard shall foredoom
The fate of Louis,° and the fall of Rome.
    Then cease, bright nymph, to mourn the ravished hair,
Which adds new glory to the shining sphere.
Not all the tresses that fair head can boast   185
Shall draw such envy as the lock you lost.
For, after all the murders of your eye,
When, after millions slain, yourself shall die;
When those fair suns shall set, as set they must,
And all those tresses shall be laid in dust;   190
This lock the Muse shall consecrate to fame,
And 'midst the stars inscribe Belinda's name.

                                                          [1712]

II.179–82. "John Partridge was a ridiculous Star-gazer, who in his Almanacks
every year, never fail'd to predict the downfall of the Pope, and the King of
France, then at war with the English" [Pope's note].

THOMAS GRAY   [1716–1771]

Elegy Written in a Country Churchyard

The curfew° tolls the knell of parting day,   *evening bell*
    The lowing herd wind slowly o'er the lea,
The plowman homeward plods his weary way,
    And leaves the world to darkness and to me.

Now fades the glimmering landscape on the sight,   5
    And all the air a solemn stillness holds,
Save where the beetle wheels his droning flight,
    And drowsy tinklings lull the distant folds;

Save that from yonder ivy-mantled tower
    The moping owl does to the moon complain   10
Of such, as wandering near her secret bower,
    Molest her ancient solitary reign.

Beneath those rugged elms, that yew tree's shade,
    Where heaves the turf in many a moldering heap,
Each in his narrow cell forever laid,   15
    The rude forefathers° of the hamlet sleep.   *humble ancestors*

The breezy call of incense-breathing morn,
    The swallow twittering from the straw-built shed,
The cock's shrill clarion, or the echoing horn,°   *(of a hunter)*
    No more shall rouse them from their lowly bed.   20

For them no more the blazing hearth shall burn,
    Or busy housewife ply her evening care;
No children run to lisp their sire's return,
    Or climb his knees the envied kiss to share.

Oft did the harvest to their sickle yield,   25
    Their furrow oft the stubborn glebe° has broke;   *soil*
How jocund did they drive their team afield!
    How bowed the woods beneath their sturdy stroke!

Let not Ambition mock their useful toil,
    Their homely joys, and destiny obscure;   30
Nor Grandeur hear with a disdainful smile
    The short and simple annals of the poor.

The boast of heraldry,° the pomp of power,   *noble ancestry*
    And all that beauty, all that wealth e'er gave,
Awaits alike the inevitable hour.   35
    The paths of glory lead but to the grave.

Nor you, ye proud, impute to these the fault,
    If memory o'er their tomb no trophies° raise,   *memorials*
Where through the long-drawn aisle and fretted° vault   *ornamented*
    The pealing anthem swells the note of praise.   40

Can storied° urn or animated° bust   *decorated/lifelike*
    Back to its mansion call the fleeting breath?
Can Honor's voice provoke° the silent dust,   *call forth*
    Or Flattery soothe the dull cold ear of Death?

Perhaps in this neglected spot is laid   45
    Some heart once pregnant with celestial fire;

Hands that the rod of empire might have swayed,
   Or waked to ecstasy the living lyre.

But Knowledge to their eyes her ample page
   Rich with the spoils of time did ne'er unroll;   50
Chill Penury repressed their noble rage,
   And froze the genial current of the soul.

Full many a gem of purest ray serene,
   The dark unfathomed caves of ocean bear:
Full many a flower is born to blush unseen,   55
   And waste its sweetness on the desert air.

Some village Hampden,° that with dauntless breast
   The little tyrant of his fields withstood;
Some mute inglorious Milton here may rest,
   Some Cromwell guiltless of his country's blood.   60

The applause of listening senates to command,
   The threats of pain and ruin to despise,
To scatter plenty o'er a smiling land,
   And read their history in a nation's eyes,

Their lot forbade: nor° circumscribed alone   *not* 65
   Their growing virtues, but their crimes confined;
Forbade to wade through slaughter to a throne,
   And shut the gates of mercy on mankind,

The struggling pangs of conscious truth to hide,
   To quench the blushes of ingenuous shame,   70
Or heap the shrine of Luxury and Pride
   With incense kindled at the Muse's flame.

Far from the madding crowd's ignoble strife,
   Their sober wishes never learned to stray;
Along the cool sequestered vale of life   75
   They kept the noiseless tenor of their way.

Yet even these bones from insult to protect
   Some frail memorial° still erected nigh,   *(simple tombstone)*
With uncouth rhymes and shapeless sculpture decked,
   Implores the passing tribute of a sigh.   80

Their name, their years, spelt by the unlettered Muse,
   The place of fame and elegy supply:

57–60. Hampden, Cromwell: John Hampden (1594–1643) refused to pay a special tax imposed in 1636 and led a defense of the people's rights in Parliament.
Oliver Cromwell (1599–1658) was a rebel leader in the English Civil War.

And many a holy text around she strews,
That teach the rustic moralist to die.

For who to dumb Forgetfulness a prey,   85
This pleasing anxious being e'er resigned,
Left the warm precincts of the cheerful day,
Nor cast one longing lingering look behind?

On some fond breast the parting soul relies,
Some pious drops° the closing eye requires;   *tears*   90
Even from the tomb the voice of Nature cries,
Even in our ashes live their wonted fires.

For thee,° who mindful of the unhonored dead   *(the poet himself)*
Dost in these lines their artless tale relate;
If chance, by lonely contemplation led,   95
Some kindred spirit shall inquire thy fate,

Haply° some hoary-headed swain° may say,   *perhaps, elderly shepherd*
"Oft have we seen him° at the peep of dawn   *the poet*
Brushing with hasty steps the dews away
To meet the sun upon the upland lawn.   100

"There at the foot of yonder nodding beech
That wreathes its old fantastic roots so high,
His listless length at noontide would he stretch,
And pore upon the brook that babbles by.

"Hard by yon wood, now smiling as in scorn,   105
Muttering his wayward fancies he would rove,
Now drooping, woeful wan, like one forlorn,
Or crazed with care, or crossed in hopeless love.

"One morn I missed him on the customed hill,
Along the heath and near his favorite tree;   110
Another° came; nor yet beside the rill,   *(another day)*
Nor up the lawn, nor at the wood was he;

"The next with dirges due in sad array
Slow through the churchway path we saw him borne.
Approach and read (for thou canst read) the lay,   115
Graved on the stone beneath yon aged thorn."

THE EPITAPH

Here rests his head upon the lap of Earth
A youth to fortune and to Fame unknown.
Fair Science° frowned not on his humble birth,   *learning*
And Melancholy marked him for her own.   120

Large was his bounty, and his soul sincere,
    Heaven did a recompense as largely send:
He gave to Misery all he had, a tear,
    He gained from Heaven ('twas all he wished) a friend.

No farther seek his merits to disclose,   125
    Or draw his frailties from their dread abode
(There they alike in trembling hope repose),
    The bosom of his Father and his God.

[1751]

CHRISTOPHER SMART   [1722–1771]

From Jubilate Agno°

For I will consider my Cat Jeoffry.
For he is the servant of the Living God, duly and daily serving him.
For at the first glance of the glory of God in the East he worships
    in his way.
For is this done by wreathing his body seven times round with elegant
    quickness.
For then he leaps up to catch the musk, which is the blessing of God
    upon his prayer.   5
For he rolls upon prank° to work it in.   *prankishly*
For having done duty and received blessing he begins to consider
    himself.
For this he performs in ten degrees.
For first he looks upon his forepaws to see if they are clean.
For secondly he kicks up behind to clear away there.   10
For thirdly he works it upon stretch with the forepaws extended.
For fourthly he sharpens his paws by wood.
For fifthly he washes himself.
For sixthly he rolls upon wash.

Jubilate Agno: "Rejoice in the Lamb" (Latin); i.e., in Jesus, the Lamb of God. The
poem was written while Smart was confined for madness from 1759 to 1763. It is
influenced by the form of Hebrew poetry, particularly the biblical psalms. The
best-known section is that concerning his cat Jeoffry, his companion during his
confinement.

For seventhly he fleas himself, that he may not be interrupted
    upon the beat.°   15
For eighthly he rubs himself against a post.
For ninthly he looks up for his instructions.
For tenthly he goes in quest of food.
For having considered God and himself he will consider his neighbor.
For if he meets another cat he will kiss her in kindness.   20
For when he takes his prey he plays with it to give it a chance.
For one mouse in seven escapes by his dallying.
For when his day's work is done his business more properly begins.
For he keeps the Lord's watch in the night against the adversary.
For he counteracts the powers of darkness by his electrical skin and
    glaring eyes.   25
For he counteracts the Devil, who is death, by brisking about the life.
For in his morning orisons he loves the sun and the sun loves him.
For he is of the tribe of Tiger.
For the Cherub Cat is a term of the Angel Tiger.°
For he has the subtlety and hissing of a serpent, which in goodness
    he suppresses.   30
For he will not do destruction if he is well-fed, neither will he spit
    without provocation.
For he purrs in thankfulness when God tells him he's a good Cat.
For he is an instrument for the children to learn benevolence upon.
For every house is incomplete without him, and a blessing is lacking
    in the spirit.
For the Lord commanded Moses concerning the cats at the departure
    of the Children of Israel from Egypt.   35
For every family had one cat at least in the bag.°
For the English Cats are the best in Europe.
For he is the cleanest in the use of his forepaws of any quadruped.
For the dexterity of his defense is an instance of the love of God to him
    exceedingly.
For he is the quickest to his mark of any creature.   40
For he is tenacious of his point.
For he is a mixture of gravity and waggery.
For he knows that God is his Savior.

15. that . . . beat: Not need to stop to scratch while on his daily rounds of hunting.
29. Cherub . . . Tiger: As a cherub is a small angel, so a cat is like a small tiger.
36. cat . . . bag: No cats are mentioned in the biblical account of the Exodus, but
Smart may have been aware that images of cats were among the Egyptian gods
and may be speculating that cats were among the jewelry of silver and gold the
Egyptians gave the Israelites as they left (Exodus 12:35–36).

For there is nothing sweeter than his peace when at rest.
For there is nothing brisker than his life when in motion.   45
For he is of the Lord's poor, and so indeed is he called by benevolence
    perpetually—Poor Jeoffry! poor Jeoffry! the rat has bit thy throat.
For I bless the name of the Lord Jesus that Jeoffry is better.
For the divine spirit comes about his body to sustain it in complete cat.
For his tongue is exceeding pure so that it has in purity what
    it wants° in music.   *lacks*
For he is docile and can learn certain things.   50
For he can sit up with gravity, which is patience upon approbation.
For he can fetch and carry, which is patience in employment.
For he can jump over a stick, which is patience upon proof positive.
For he can spraggle upon waggle° at the word of command.
For he can jump from an eminence into his master's bosom.   55
For he can catch the cork and toss it again.
For he is hated by the hypocrite and miser.
For the former is afraid of detection.
For the latter refuses the charge.
For he camels his back to bear the first notion of business.   60
For he is good to think on, if a man would express himself neatly.
For he made a great figure in Egypt for his signal services.
For he killed the Ichneumon rat, very pernicious by land.°
For his ears are so acute that they sting again.
For from this proceeds the passing quickness of his attention.   65
For by stroking of him I have found out electricity.
For I perceived God's light about him both wax and fire.
For the electrical fire is the spiritual substance which God sends from
    heaven to sustain the bodies both of man and beast.
For God has blessed him in the variety of his movements.
For, though he cannot fly, he is an excellent clamberer.   70
For his motions upon the face of the earth are more than any other
    quadruped.
For he can tread to all the measures upon the music.
For he can swim for life.
For he can creep.

                    [*c. 1760;* 1939]

---

54. **spraggle upon waggle:** Sprawl when his master waggles a finger.
63. **Ichneumon:** Egyptian species of mongoose that somewhat resembles a large
rat. It is, however, regarded as beneficial and was domesticated by the ancient
Egyptians.

PHILIP FRENEAU   [1752–1832]

The Indian Burying Ground

In spite of all the learned have said,
　I still my opinion keep;
The posture, that we give the dead,
　Points out the soul's eternal sleep.

Not so the ancients of these lands°—   5
　The Indian, when from life released,
Again is seated with his friends,°
　And shares again the joyous feast.

His imaged birds, and painted bowl,
　And venison, for a journey dressed,°   10
Bespeak the nature of the soul,
　Activity, that knows no rest.

His bow, for action ready bent,
　And arrows, with a head of stone,
Can only mean that life is spent,   15
　And not the old ideas gone.

Thou, stranger, that shalt come this way,
　No fraud upon the dead commit—
Observe the swelling turf, and say
　They do not lie, but here they sit.   20

Here still a lofty rock remains,
　On which the curious eye may trace
(Now wasted, half, by wearing rains)
　The fancies of a ruder° race.   *more primitive*

Here still an aged elm aspires,   25
　Beneath whose far-projecting shade
(And which the shepherd still admires)
　The children of the forest played!

5. these lands: America or the Americas.
7. seated . . . friends: Refers to the Native American custom of burying the dead
in a sitting position.
10. for a journey dressed (pun): To prepare for cooking as well as to clothe.

There oft a restless Indian queen
  (Pale Shebah,° with her braided hair)   30
And many a barbarous form is seen
  To chide the man that lingers there.

By midnight moons, o'er moistening dews;
  In habit for the chase arrayed,
The hunter still the deer pursues,   35
  The hunter and the deer, a shade!

And long shall timorous fancy see
  The painted chief, and pointed spear,
And Reason's self shall bow the knee
  To shadows and delusions here.   40

[1788]

30. **Pale Shebah:** The Queen of Sheba (here thought of as in Africa) visited
Solomon (1 Kings 10:1–13). The queen of line 29 is pale by contrast with her
African counterpart.

WILLIAM BLAKE   [1757–1827]

The Lamb

  Little Lamb, who made thee?
  Dost thou know who made thee?
Gave thee life & bid thee feed,
By the stream & o'er the mead;
Gave thee clothing of delight,   5
Softest clothing wooly bright;
Gave thee such a tender voice,
Making all the vales rejoice!
  Little Lamb who made thee?
  Dost thou know who made thee?   10

  Little Lamb I'll tell thee,
  Little Lamb I'll tell thee!
He is callèd by thy name,
For he calls himself a Lamb:
He is meek & he is mild,   15

He became a little child:
I a child & thou a lamb,
We are callèd by his name.
  Little Lamb God bless thee.
  Little Lamb God bless thee.   20

[1789]

WILLIAM BLAKE   [1757–1827]

The Tyger

Tyger, Tyger, burning bright
In the forests of the night,
What immortal hand or eye
Could frame thy fearful symmetry?

In what distant deeps or skies   5
Burnt the fire of thine eyes?
On what wings dare he aspire?
What the hand, dare seize the fire?

And what shoulder, & what art,
Could twist the sinews of thy heart?   10
And when thy heart began to beat,
What dread hand? & what dread feet?

What the hammer? what the chain?
In what furnace was thy brain?
What the anvil? what dread grasp   15
Dare its deadly terrors clasp?

When the stars threw down their spears
And water'd heaven with their tears,
Did he smile his work to see?
Did he who made the Lamb make thee?   20

Tyger, Tyger, burning bright
In the forests of the night,
What immortal hand or eye
Dare frame thy fearful symmetry?

[1794]

WILLIAM BLAKE   [1757–1827]

London

I wander through each chartered street,
Near where the chartered Thames does flow,
And mark in every face I meet
Marks of weakness, marks of woe.

In every cry of every man,   5
In every infant's cry of fear,
In every voice, in every ban,
The mind-forged manacles I hear.

How the chimney-sweeper's cry
Every black'ning church appalls;   10
And the hapless soldier's sigh
Runs in blood down palace walls.

But most through midnight streets I hear
How the youthful harlot's curse
Blasts the new-born infant's tear,   15
And blights with plagues the marriage hearse.

[1794]

ROBERT BURNS   [1759–1796]

A Red, Red Rose

O my luve's like a red, red rose,
   That's newly sprung in June;
O my luve's like the melodie
   That's sweetly played in tune.

As fair art thou, my bonnie lass,   5
   So deep in luve am I;
And I will luve thee still, my dear,
   Till a' the seas gang dry.

Till a' the seas gang dry, my dear,
   And the rocks melt wi' the sun: 10
O I will love thee still, my dear,
   While the sands o' life shall run.

And fare thee weel, my only luve,
   And fare thee weel awhile!
And I will come again, my luve,   15
   Though it were ten thousand mile.

[1796]

WILLIAM WORDSWORTH [1770–1850]

Lines

*Composed a Few Miles above Tintern Abbey°
on Revisiting the Banks of the Wye
During a Tour. July 13, 1798*

Five years have passed; five summers, with the length
Of five long winters! and again I hear
These waters, rolling from their mountain-springs
With a soft inland murmur. Once again
Do I behold these steep and lofty cliffs,   5
That on a wild secluded scene impress
Thoughts of more deep seclusion; and connect
The landscape with the quiet of the sky.
The day is come when I again repose
Here, under this dark sycamore, and view   10
These plots of cottage ground, these orchard tufts,
Which at this season, with their unripe fruits,
Are clad in one green hue, and lose themselves
'Mid groves and copses. Once again I see
These hedgerows, hardly hedgerows, little lines   15

Tintern Abbey: The ruins of a medieval abbey that Wordsworth had visited in August 1793. Wordsworth says that he composed the poem in his head in four or five hours as he walked from Tintern to Bristol in 1798, and then wrote it down without revisions.

Of sportive wood run wild; these pastoral farms,
Green to the very door; and wreaths of smoke
Sent up, in silence, from among the trees!
With some uncertain notice, as might seem
Of vagrant dwellers in the houseless woods,   20
Or of some Hermit's cave, where by his fire
The Hermit sits alone.

          These beauteous forms,
Through a long absence, have not been to me
As is a landscape to a blind man's eye;
But oft, in lonely rooms, and 'mid the din   25
Of towns and cities, I have owed to them,
In hours of weariness, sensations sweet,
Felt in the blood, and felt along the heart;
And passing even into my purer mind,
With tranquil restoration—feelings too   30
Of unremembered pleasure; such, perhaps,
As have no slight or trivial influence
On that best portion of a good man's life,
His little, nameless, unremembered, acts
Of kindness and of love. Nor less, I trust,   35
To them I may have owed another gift,
Of aspect more sublime; that blessed mood,
In which the burthen of the mystery,
In which the heavy and the weary weight
Of all this unintelligible world,   40
Is lightened—that serene and blessed mood,
In which the affections gently lead us on—
Until, the breath of this corporeal frame
And even the motion of our human blood
Almost suspended, we are laid asleep   45
In body, and become a living soul;
While with an eye made quiet by the power
Of harmony, and the deep power of joy,
We see into the life of things.

          If this
Be but a vain belief, yet, oh! how oft—   50
In darkness and amid the many shapes
Of joyless daylight; when the fretful stir
Unprofitable, and the fever of the world,
Have hung upon the beatings of my heart—
How oft, in spirit, have I turned to thee,   55

O sylvan° Wye! thou wanderer through the woods,   *wooded*
How often has my spirit turned to thee!

   An now, with gleams of half-extinguished thought,
With many recognitions dim and faint,
And somewhat of a sad perplexity,   60
The picture of the mind revives again;
While here I stand, not only with the sense
Of present pleasure, but with pleasing thoughts
That in this moment there is life and food
For future years. And so I dare to hope,   65
Though changed, no doubt, from what I was when first
I came among these hills; when like a roe
I bounded o'er the mountains, by the sides
Of the deep rivers, and the lonely streams,
Wherever nature led—more like a man   70
Flying from something that he dreads than one
Who sought the thing he loved. For nature then
(The coarser pleasures of my boyish days,
And their glad animal movements all gone by)
To me was all in all.—I cannot paint   75
What then I was. The sounding cataract
Haunted me like a passion; the tall rock,
The mountain, and the deep and gloomy wood,
Their colors and their forms, were then to me
An appetite; a feeling and a love,   80
That had no need of a remoter charm,
By thought supplied, nor any interest
Unborrowed from the eye.—That time is past,
And all its aching joys are now no more,
And all its dizzy raptures. Not for this   85
Faint° I, nor mourn nor murmur; other gifts   *become discouraged*
Have followed; for such loss, I would believe,
Abundant recompense. For I have learned
To look on nature, not as in the hour
Of thoughtless youth; but hearing oftentimes   90
The still, sad music of humanity,
Nor harsh nor grating, though of ample power
To chasten and subdue. And I have felt
A presence that disturbs me with the joy
Of elevated thoughts; a sense sublime   95
Of something far more deeply interfused,
Whose dwelling is the light of setting suns,
And the round ocean and the living air,

And the blue sky, and in the mind of man:
A motion and a spirit, that impels   100
All thinking things, all objects of all thought,
And rolls through all things. Therefore am I still
A lover of the meadows and the woods,
And mountains; and of all that we behold
From this green earth; of all the mighty world   105
Of eye, and ear—both what they half create,
And what perceive; well pleased to recognize
In nature and the language of the sense
The anchor of my purest thoughts, the nurse,
The guide, the guardian of my heart, and soul   110
Of all my moral being.

             Nor perchance,
If I were not thus taught, should I the more
Suffer my genial spirits° to decay: *creative powers*
For thou art with me here upon the banks
Of this fair river; thou my dearest Friend,°   115
My dear, dear Friend; and in thy voice I catch
The language of my former heart, and read
My former pleasures in the shooting lights
Of thy wild eyes. Oh! yet a little while
May I behold in thee what I was once,   120
My dear, dear Sister! and this prayer I make,
Knowing that Nature never did betray
The heart that loved her; 'tis her privilege,
Through all the years of this our life, to lead
From joy to joy: for she can so inform   125
The mind that is within us, so impress
With quietness and beauty, and so feed
With lofty thoughts, that neither evil tongues,
Rash judgments, nor the sneers of selfish men,
Nor greetings where no kindness is, nor all   130
The dreary intercourse of daily life,
Shall e'er prevail against us, or disturb
Our cheerful faith, that all which we behold
Is full of blessings. Therefore let the moon
Shine on thee in thy solitary walk;   135
And let the misty mountain winds be free

---

115. Friend: Wordsworth's sister Dorothy, who is made to sound younger by
more than the year and a half that separated them.

To blow against thee: and, in after years,
When these wild ecstasies shall be matured
Into a sober pleasure; when thy mind
Shall be a mansion for all lovely forms,   140
Thy memory be as a dwelling place
For all sweet sounds and harmonies; oh! then,
If solitude, or fear, or pain, or grief
Should be thy portion, with what healing thoughts
Of tender joy wilt thou remember me,   145
And these my exhortations! Nor, perchance—
If I should be where I no more can hear
Thy voice, nor catch from thy wild eyes these gleams
Of past existence—wilt thou then forget
That on the banks of this delightful stream   150
We stood together; and that I, so long
A worshiper of Nature, hither came
Unwearied in that service; rather say
With warmer love—oh! with far deeper zeal
Of holier love. Nor wilt thou then forget,   155
That after many wanderings, many years
Of absence, these steep woods and lofty cliffs,
And this green pastoral landscape, were to me
More dear, both for themselves and for thy sake!

                                                          [1798]

WILLIAM WORDSWORTH   [1770–1850]

I wandered lonely as a cloud

I wandered lonely as a cloud
That floats on high o'er vales and hills,
When all at once I saw a crowd,
A host, of golden daffodils;
Beside the lake, beneath the trees,   5
Fluttering and dancing in the breeze.

Continuous as the stars that shine
And twinkle on the milky way,
They stretched in never-ending line

Along the margin of a bay: 10
Ten thousand saw I at a glance,
Tossing their heads in sprightly dance.

The waves beside them danced; but they
Outdid the sparkling waves in glee:
A poet could not but be gay,   15
In such a jocund company:
I gazed—and gazed—but little thought
What wealth the show to me had brought:

For oft, when on my couch I lie
In vacant or in pensive mood,   20
They flash upon that inward eye
Which is the bliss of solitude;
And then my heart with pleasure fills,
And dances with the daffodils.

                                                      [1807]

WILLIAM WORDSWORTH   [1770–1850]

Ode

Intimations of Immortality from Recollections
of Early Childhood

The Child is father of the Man;
And I could wish my days to be
Bound each to each by natural piety.°

1

There was a time when meadow, grove, and stream,
The earth, and every common sight,
            To me did seem
            Appareled in celestial light,
The glory and the freshness of a dream.   5
It is not now as it hath been of yore—

Epigraph: The final lines of Wordsworth's "My Heart Leaps Up."

Turn whereso'er I may,
      By night or day,
The things which I have seen I now can see no more.

2

The Rainbow comes and goes,   10
And lovely is the Rose,
The Moon doth with delight
Look round her when the heavens are bare,
      Waters on a starry night
      Are beautiful and fair;   15
   The sunshine is a glorious birth;
   But yet I know, where'er I go,
That there hath passed away a glory from the earth.

3

Now, while the birds thus sing a joyous song,
   And while the young lambs bound   20
      As to the tabor's° sound,
To me alone there came a thought of grief:
A timely utterance gave that thought relief,
      And I again am strong:
The cataracts blow their trumpets from the steep;   25
No more shall grief of mine the season wrong;
I hear the Echoes through the mountains throng,
The Winds come to me from the fields of sleep,
      And all the earth is gay;
         Land and sea   30
      Give themselves up to jollity,
         And with the heart of May
      Doth every Beast keep holiday—
         Thou Child of Joy,
Shout round me, let me hear thy shouts, thou happy Shepherd-boy! 35

4

Ye blessèd Creatures, I have heard the call
   Ye to each other make; I see
The heavens laugh with you in your jubilee;
      My heart is at your festival,
         My head hath its coronal,°   40

---

21. **tabor:** A small drum, used chiefly as an accompaniment to the pipe or trumpet.
40. **coronal:** A wreath of flowers or leaves for the head; a garland.

The fullness of your bliss, I feel—I feel it all.
    Oh, evil day! if I were sullen
    While Earth herself is adorning,
      This sweet May morning,
    And the Children are culling   45
      On every side,
    In a thousand valleys far and wide,
    Fresh flowers; while the sun shines warm,
And the Babe leaps up on his Mother's arm—
    I hear, I hear, with joy I hear!   50
    —But there's a Tree, of many, one,
A single Field which I have looked upon,
Both of them speak of something that is gone:
      The Pansy at my feet
      Doth the same tale repeat: 55
Whither is fled the visionary gleam?
Where is it now, the glory and the dream?

5

Our birth is but a sleep and a forgetting:
The Soul that rises with us, our life's Star,
    Hath had elsewhere its setting,   60
      And cometh from afar:
    Not in entire forgetfulness,
    And not in utter nakedness,
But trailing clouds of glory do we come
      From God, who is our home: 65
Heaven lies about us in our infancy!
Shades of the prison-house begin to close
      Upon the growing Boy
      But he
Beholds the light, and whence it flows,   70
    He sees it in his joy;
The Youth, who daily farther from the east
      Must travel, still is Nature's Priest,
      And by the vision splendid
      Is on his way attended;   75
At length the Man perceives it die away,
And fade into the light of common day.°

---

77. Lines 58–77 reflect Plato's belief that human souls inhabit "a pre-existent state" (in Wordsworth's terms) before being born into this world. Though imprisoned in a physical body and the material world, the soul of the infant has recollections of

6

Earth fills her lap with pleasures of her own;
Yearnings she hath in her own natural kind,
And, even with something of a Mother's mind,   80
          And no unworthy aim,
     The homely° Nurse doth all she can   *simple, kindly*
To make her foster child, her Inmate Man,
          Forget the glories he hath known,
And that imperial palace whence he came.   85

7

Behold the Child among his newborn blisses,
A six-years' Darling of a pygmy size!
See, where 'mid work of his own hand he lies,
Fretted° by sallies of his mother's kisses,   *annoyed*
With light upon him from his father's eyes!   90
See, at his feet, some little plan or chart,
Some fragrant from his dream of human life,
Shaped by himself with newly-learnèd art;
          A wedding or a festival,
          A mourning or a funeral;   95
               And this hath now his heart,
          And unto this he frames his song;
               Then will he fit his tongue
To dialogues of business, love, or strife;
          But it will not be long   100
          Ere this be thrown aside,
          And with new joy and pride
The little Actor cons° another part;   *learns*
Filling from time to time his "humorous stage"°
With all the Persons,° down to palsied Age,   *dramatis personae* 105
That Life brings with her in her equipage;°

---

and longs to return to the perfect world of ideas. As the child grows older, those memories begin to fade, though reminders of that primal glory recur (usually from experiences with things in nature). By adulthood, such glimpses become rare and the adult becomes reconciled to the material world and its values.

104. "humorous stage": Quoted from a sonnet by the Elizabethan poet Samuel Daniel: the varied temperaments (humors) of characters represented on the stage. Lines 103–05 echo Jaques's "All the world's a stage" speech in Shakespeare's *As You Like It* (2.7.138–65), with its description of the "seven ages" in the life of a person.

105–06. all . . . equipage: All that is needed for a military operation, a journey, or a domestic establishment.

As if his whole vocation
Were endless imitation.

8

Thou, whose exterior semblance doth belie
  Thy Soul's immensity;   110
Thou best Philosopher, who yet dost keep
Thy heritage, thou Eye among the blind,
That, deaf and silent, read'st the eternal deep,
Haunted forever by the eternal mind—
  Mighty Prophet! Seer blest!   115
  On whom those truths do rest,
Which we are toiling all our lives to find,
In darkness lost, the darkness of the grave;
Thou, over whom thy Immortality
Broods like the Day, a Master o'er a Slave,   120
A Presence which is not to be put by;
Thou little Child, yet glorious in the might
Of heaven-born freedom on thy being's height,
Why with such earnest pains dost thou provoke
The years to bring the inevitable yoke,   125
Thus blindly with thy blessedness at strife?
Full soon thy Soul shall have her earthly freight,
And custom lie upon thee with a weight,
Heavy as frost, and deep almost as life!

9

  O joy! that in our embers   130
  Is something that doth live,
  That nature yet remembers
  What was so fugitive!
The thought of our past years in me doth breed
Perpetual benediction: not indeed   135
For that which is most worthy to be blest;
Delight and liberty, the simple creed
Of Childhood, whether busy or at rest,
With new-fledged hope still fluttering in his breast—
  Not for these I raise   140
  The song of thanks and praise;
  But for those obstinate questionings
  Of sense and outward things,
  Fallings from us, vanishings;

Blank misgivings of a Creature   145
Moving about in worlds not realized,°   *not seeming real*
High instincts before which our mortal Nature
Did tremble like a guilty Thing surprised;
    But for those first affections,
    Those shadowy recollections,   150
    Which, be they what they may,
Are yet the fountain light of all our day,
Are yet a master light of all our seeing;
    Uphold us, cherish, and have power to make
Our noisy years seem moments in the being   155
Of the eternal Silence: truths that wake,
      To perish never;
Which neither listlessness, nor mad endeavor,
      Nor Man nor Boy,
Nor all that is at enmity with joy,   160
Can utterly abolish or destroy!
    Hence in a season of calm weather
    Though inland far we be,
Our Souls have sight of that immortal sea
    Which brought us hither,   165
    Can in a moment travel thither,
And see the Children sport upon the shore,
And hear the mighty waters rolling evermore.

10

Then sing, ye Birds, sing, sing a joyous song!
    And let the young Lambs bound   170
    As to the tabor's sound!
We in thought will join your throng,
    Ye that pipe and ye that play,
    Ye that through your hearts today
    Feel the gladness of the May!   175
What though the radiance which was once so bright
Be now forever taken from my sight,
    Though nothing can bring back the hour
Of splendor in the grass, of glory in the flower;
    We will grieve not, rather find   180
    Strength in what remains behind;
    In the primal sympathy
    Which having been must ever be;
    In the soothing thoughts that spring

     Out of human suffering;   185
       In the faith that looks through death,
In years that bring the philosophic mind.

11

And O, ye Fountains, Meadows, Hills, and Groves,
Forebode not any severing of our loves!
Yet in my heart of hearts I feel your might;   190
I only have relinquished one delight
To live beneath your more habitual sway.
I love the Brooks which down their channels fret,°   *move in agitated waves*
Even more than when I tripped lightly as they;
The innocent brightness of a newborn Day   195
      Is lovely yet;
The clouds that gather round the setting sun
Do take a sober coloring from an eye
That hath kept watch o'er man's mortality;
Another race hath been, and other palms° are won.   *symbols of victory* 200
Thanks to the human heart by which we live,
Thanks to its tenderness, its joys, and fears,
To me the meanest° flower that blows° can give   *most ordinary/blooms*
Thoughts that do often lie too deep for tears.

[1807]

WILLIAM WORDSWORTH [1770–1850]

The world is too much with us

The world is too much with us; late and soon,
Getting and spending, we lay waste our powers;
Little we see in Nature that is ours;
We have given our hearts away, a sordid boon!°   *gift*
This Sea that bares her bosom to the moon,   5
The winds that will be howling at all hours,
And are up-gathered now like sleeping flowers,
For this, for everything, we are out of tune;
It moves us not.—Great God! I'd rather be
A Pagan suckled in a creed outworn;   10
So might I, standing on this pleasant lea,°   *open meadow*

Have glimpses that would make me less forlorn;
Have sight of Proteus° rising from the sea;
Or hear old Triton° blow his wreathèd° horn.

[1807]

13. **Proteus:** In Greek mythology, a sea god who could change his own form or appearance at will.
14. **Triton:** A Greek sea god with the head and upper body of a man and the tail of a fish, usually pictured as playing on a conch-shell trumpet; **wreathèd:** Curved.

SAMUEL TAYLOR COLERIDGE [1772–1834]

Kubla Khan

Or, a Vision in a Dream. A Fragment°

In Xanadu did Kubla Khan
A stately pleasure dome decree:°
Where Alph,° the sacred river, ran
Through caverns measureless to man
 Down to a sunless sea.   5
So twice five miles of fertile ground
With walls and towers were girdled round:
And there were gardens bright with sinuous rills,
Where blossomed many an incense-bearing tree;
And here were forests ancient as the hills,   10
Enfolding sunny spots of greenery.

Or, a Vision . . . A Fragment: Coleridge stated in a preface that this poem composed itself in his mind during "a profound sleep" (actually an opium-induced reverie); that he began writing it down immediately upon waking but was interrupted by a caller; and that when he returned to his room an hour later he could not complete it.
1–2. In . . . decree: "In Xamdu did Cublai Can build a stately Palace, encompassing sixteene miles of plaine ground with a wall" (Samuel Purchas, *Purchas his Pilgrimage* [1613]). The historical Kublai Khan (1215–1294) was the founder of the Yüan dynasty of China and overlord of the Mongol Empire.
3. Alph: Probably derived from the name of the River Alpheus in southern Greece, which according to mythology ran under the sea and emerged at Syracuse (Italy) in the fountain of Arethusa.

But oh! that deep romantic chasm which slanted
Down the green hill athwart a cedarn cover!
A savage place! as holy and enchanted
As e'er beneath a waning moon was haunted   15
By woman wailing for her demon lover!
And from this chasm, with ceaseless turmoil seething,
As if this earth in fast thick pants were breathing,
A mighty fountain momently was forced:
Amid whose swift half-intermitted burst   20
Huge fragments vaulted like rebounding hail,
Or chaffy grain beneath the thresher's flail:
And 'mid these dancing rocks at once and ever
It flung up momently the sacred river.
Five miles meandering with a mazy motion   25
Through wood and dale the sacred river ran,
Then reached the caverns measureless to man,
And sank in tumult to a lifeless ocean:
And 'mid this tumult Kubla heard from far
Ancestral voices prophesying war!   30
    The shadow of the dome of pleasure
    Floated midway on the waves;
    Where was heard the mingled measure
    From the fountain and the caves.
It was a miracle of rare device,   35
A sunny pleasure dome with caves of ice!

    A damsel with a dulcimer
    In a vision once I saw:
    It was an Abyssinian maid,
    And on her dulcimer she played,   40
    Singing of Mount Abora.°
    Could I revive within me
    Her symphony and song,
    To such a deep delight 'twould win me,
That with music loud and long,   45
I would build that dome in air,
That sunny dome! those caves of ice!
And all who heard should see them there,

39–41. **Abyssinian . . . Abora:** See *Paradise Lost* 4.280–82: "where Abassin Kings
their issue Guard, / Mount Amara, though this by some supposed / True Paradise
under the Ethiop Line."

And all should cry, Beware! Beware!
His flashing eyes, his floating hair!   50
Weave a circle round him thrice,
And close your eyes with holy dread,
For he on honey-dew hath fed,
And drunk the milk of Paradise.

[*c. 1797–1798;* 1813]

GEORGE GORDON, LORD BYRON

[1788–1824]

She walks in beauty

1

She walks in beauty, like the night
  Of cloudless climes and starry skies;
And all that's best of dark and bright
  Meet in her aspect and her eyes:
Thus mellowed to that tender light   5
  Which heaven to gaudy day denies.

2

One shade the more, one ray the less,
  Had half impaired the nameless grace
Which waves in every raven tress,
  Or softly lightens o'er her face;   10
Where thoughts serenely sweet express
  How pure, how dear their dwelling place.

3

And on that cheek, and o'er that brow,
  So soft, so calm, yet eloquent,
The smiles that win, the tints that glow,   15
  But tell of days in goodness spent,
A mind at peace with all below,
  A heart whose love is innocent!

[1815]

PERCY BYSSHE SHELLEY [1792–1822]

Ozymandias°

I met a traveler from an antique land
Who said: Two vast and trunkless legs of stone
Stand in the desert. Near them, on the sand,
Half sunk, a shattered visage lies, whose frown,
And wrinkled lip, and sneer of cold command,   5
Tell that its sculptor well those passions read
Which yet survive, stamped on these lifeless things,
The hand that mocked them, and the heart that fed:
And on the pedestal these words appear:
"My name is Ozymandias, king of kings: 10
Look on my works, ye Mighty, and despair!"
Nothing beside remains. Round the decay
Of that colossal wreck, boundless and bare
The lone and level sands stretch far away.

[1818]

Ozymandias: The Greek name for Ramses II of Egypt (thirteenth century B.C.E.), who erected the largest statue in Egypt as a memorial to himself.

PERCY BYSSHE SHELLEY [1792–1822]

Ode to the West Wind

1

O wild West Wind, thou breath° of Autumn's being,
Thou, from whose unseen presence the leaves dead
Are driven, like ghosts from an enchanter fleeing,

1. breath: In many ancient languages, the words for *breath, wind, soul,* and *inspiration* are the same or closely related: in Latin, *spiritus.* Shelley uses this to interconnect nature and artistic inspiration (poetry) in his poem.

Yellow, and black, and pale, and hectic red,
Pestilence-stricken multitudes: O thou,   5
Who chariotest to their dark wintry bed

The wingèd seeds, where they lie cold and low,
Each like a corpse within its grave, until
Thine azure sister of the Spring shall blow

Her clarion o'er the dreaming earth, and fill   10
(Driving sweet buds like flocks to feed in air)
With living hues and odors plain and hill:

Wild Spirit, which art moving everywhere;
Destroyer and preserver; hear, oh, hear!

2

Thou on whose stream, mid the steep sky's commotion,   15
Loose clouds like earth's decaying leaves are shed,
Shook from the tangled boughs of Heaven and Ocean,

Angels of rain and lightning: there are spread
On the blue surface of thine airy surge,
Like the bright hair uplifted from the head   20

Of some fierce Maenad,° even from the dim verge
Of the horizon to the zenith's height,
The locks of the approaching storm. Thou dirge

Of the dying year, to which this closing night
Will be the dome of a vast sepulcher,   25
Vaulted with all thy congregated might

Of vapors, from whose solid atmosphere
Black rain, and fire, and hail will burst: oh, hear!

3

Thou who didst waken from his summer dreams
The blue Mediterranean, where he lay,   30
Lulled by the coil of his crystàlline streams,

Beside a pumice isle in Baiae's bay,°
And saw in sleep old palaces° and towers
Quivering within the wave's intenser day,

21. **Maenad:** A female votary of Dionysus, Greek god of wine and vegetation, who took part in the wild, orgiastic rites that characterize his worship.
32. **pumice:** Porous volcanic stone; **Baiae's bay:** West of Naples, Italy.
33. **old palaces:** Villas built by the Roman emperors.

All overgrown with azure moss and flowers   35
So sweet, the sense faints picturing them! Thou
For whose path the Atlantic's level powers

Cleave themselves into chasms, while far below
The sea-blooms and the oozy woods which wear
The sapless foliage of the ocean, know   40

Thy voice, and suddenly grow gray with fear,
And tremble and despoil themselves: oh, hear!

4

If I were a dead leaf thou mightest bear;
If I were a swift cloud to fly with thee;
A wave to pant beneath thy power, and share   45

The impulse of thy strength, only less free
Than thou, O uncontrollable! If even
I were as in my boyhood, and could be

The comrade of thy wanderings over Heaven,
As then, when to outstrip thy skyey speed   50
Scarce seemed a vision; I would ne'er have striven

As thus with thee in prayer in my sore need.
Oh, lift me as a wave, a leaf, a cloud!
I fall upon the thorns of life! I bleed!

A heavy weight of hours has chained and bowed   55
One too like thee: tameless, and swift, and proud.

5

Make me thy lyre,° even as the forest is:
What if my leaves are falling like its own!
The tumult of thy mighty harmonies

Will take from both a deep, autumnal tone,   60
Sweet though in sadness. Be thou, Spirit fierce,
My spirit! Be thou me, impetuous one!

Drive my dead thoughts over the universe
Like withered leaves to quicken a new birth!
And, by the incantation of this verse,   65

---

57. lyre: An Aeolian harp, whose strings produce a sequence of rising and falling harmonies as air blows over them.

Scatter, as from an unextinguished hearth
Ashes and sparks, my words among mankind!
Be through my lips to unawakened earth

The trumpet of a prophecy! O Wind,
If Winter comes, can Spring be far behind?   70

[1820]

JOHN KEATS [1795–1821]

When I have fears
that I may cease to be

When I have fears that I may cease to be
    Before my pen has gleaned my teeming brain,
Before high piled books, in charactry,°   *writing*
    Hold like rich garners the full ripened grain;
When I behold, upon the night's starred face,   5
    Huge cloudy symbols of a high romance,
And think that I may never live to trace
    Their shadows, with the magic hand of chance;
And when I feel, fair creature of an hour,
    That I shall never look upon thee more,   10
Never have relish in the fairy power
    Of unreflecting love;—then on the shore
Of the wide world I stand alone, and think
Till love and fame to nothingness do sink.

[*1818;* 1848]

JOHN KEATS   [1795–1821]

The Eve of St. Agnes°

1

St. Agnes' Eve—Ah, bitter chill it was!
The owl, for all his feathers, was a-cold;
The hare limped trembling through the frozen grass,
And silent was the flock in woolly fold:
Numb were the Beadsman's° fingers, while he told   5
His rosary, and while his frosted breath,
Like pious incense from a censer old,
Seemed taking flight for heaven, without a death,
Past the sweet Virgin's picture, while his prayer he saith.

2

His prayer he saith, this patient, holy man;   10
Then takes his lamp, and riseth from his knees,
And back returneth, meagre, barefoot, wan,
Along the chapel aisle by slow degrees:
The sculptured dead, on each side, seem to freeze,
Emprisoned in black, purgatorial rails: 15
Knights, ladies, praying in dumb orat'ries,°   *silent chapels*
He passeth by; and his weak spirit fails
To think how they may ache in icy hoods and mails.

3

Northward he turneth through a little door,
And scarce three steps, ere Music's golden tongue   20
Flattered° to tears this aged man and poor;   *beguiled*
But no—already had his deathbell rung;
The joys of all his life were said and sung:
His was harsh penance on St. Agnes' Eve:

St. Agnes: According to legend, a young woman who performs the proper ritual will dream of her future husband on Saint Agnes's Eve (January 20). Keats unites this legend with the Romeo and Juliet theme of young love hindered by feuding families. (Saint Agnes, martyred c. 303 at the age of thirteen, is the patron saint of virgins.)
5. Beadsman: Someone paid to pray for a benefactor, counting ("telling") the beads of the rosary.

Another way he went, and soon among   25
Rough ashes sat he for his soul's reprieve,
And all night kept awake, for sinners' sake to grieve.

4

That ancient Beadsman heard the prelude soft;
And so it chanced, for many a door was wide,
From hurry to and fro. Soon, up aloft,   30
The silver, snarling trumpets 'gan to chide:
The level chambers, ready with their pride,
Were glowing to receive a thousand guests:
The carved angels, ever eager-eyed,
Star'd, where upon their heads the cornice rests,   35
With hair blown back, and wings put cross-wise on their breasts.

5

At length burst in the argent revelry,°   *revelers adorned with silver*
With plume, tiara, and all rich array,
Numerous as shadows haunting fairily°   *in a fairy-like manner*
The brain, new stuffed, in youth, with triumphs gay   40
Of old romance. These let us wish away,
And turn, sole-thoughted, to one Lady there,
Whose heart had brooded, all that wintry day,
On love, and winged St. Agnes' saintly care,
As she had heard old dames full many times declare.   45

6

They told her how, upon St. Agnes' Eve,
Young virgins might have visions of delight,
And soft adorings from their loves receive
Upon the honeyed middle of the night,
If ceremonies due they did aright;   50
As, supperless to bed they must retire,
And couch supine their beauties,° lily white;
Nor look behind, nor sideways, but require
Of heaven with upward eyes for all that they desire.

7

Full of this whim was thoughtful Madeline: 55
The music, yearning like a god in pain,
She scarcely heard: her maiden eyes divine,

52. couch supine their beauties: To lay themselves (their beauties) face-up.

Fix'd on the floor, saw many a sweeping train
Pass by—she heeded not at all: in vain
Came many a tiptoe,° amorous cavalier,   *ambitious (straining upwards)* 60
And back retired, not cooled by high disdain;
But she saw not: her heart was otherwhere:
She sighed for Agnes' dreams, the sweetest of the year.

8

She danced along with vague, regardless eyes,
Anxious her lips, her breathing quick and short: 65
The hallowed hour was near at hand: she sighs
Amid the timbrels,° and the thronged resort
Of whisperers in anger, or in sport;
'Mid looks of love, defiance, hate, and scorn,
Hoodwinked with faery° fancy; all amort,°   *visionary, unreal/as if dead* 70
Save to St. Agnes and her lambs unshorn,°
And all the bliss to be before to-morrow morn.

9

So, purposing each moment to retire,
She lingered still. Meantime, across the moors,
Had come young Porphyro, with heart on fire   75
For Madeline. Beside the portal doors,
Buttressed° from moonlight, stands he, and implores
All saints to give him sight of Madeline,
But for one moment in the tedious hours,
That he might gaze and worship all unseen;   80
Perchance speak, kneel, touch, kiss—in sooth such things have been.

10

He ventures in: let no buzzed whisper tell:
All eyes be muffled, or a hundred swords
Will storm his heart, Love's feverous citadel:
For him, those chambers held barbarian hordes,   85
Hyena foemen, and hot-blooded lords,
Whose very dogs would execrations howl
Against his lineage: not one breast affords
Him any mercy, in that mansion foul,
Save one old beldame,° weak in body and in soul.   *old woman, hag* 90

---

67. timbrels: Hand-held percussion instruments, similar to a tambourine.
71. Save . . . unshorn: On Saint Agnes's Day, the wool of two lambs was offered
at the altar during Mass and later spun and woven into cloth by nuns.
77. Buttressed: Sheltered by buttresses.

11

Ah, happy chance! the aged creature came,
Shuffling along with ivory-headed wand,°   *staff*
To where he stood, hid from the torch's flame,
Behind a broad hall-pillar, far beyond
The sound of merriment and chorus bland:°   *soft*   95
He startled her; but soon she knew his face,
And grasped his fingers in her palsied hand,
Saying, "Mercy, Porphyro! hie thee from this place;
They are all here to-night, the whole blood-thirsty race!

12

"Get hence! get hence! there's dwarfish Hildebrand;   100
He had a fever late, and in the fit
He cursed thee and thine, both house and land:
Then there's that old Lord Maurice, not a whit
More tame for his gray hairs—Alas me! flit!
Flit like a ghost away."—"Ah, Gossip° dear,   *friend*   105
We're safe enough; here in this arm-chair sit,
And tell me how"—"Good Saints! not here, not here;
Follow me, child, or else these stones will be thy bier."

13

He followed through a lowly arched way,
Brushing the cobwebs with his lofty plume,   110
And as she muttered "Well-a—well-a-day!"
He found him in a little moonlight room,
Pale, latticed, chill, and silent as a tomb.
"Now tell me where is Madeline," said he,
"O tell me, Angela, by the holy loom   115
Which none but secret sisterhood may see,
When they St. Agnes' wool are weaving piously."

14

"St. Agnes! Ah! it is St. Agnes' Eve—
Yet men will murder upon holy days:
Thou must hold water in a witch's sieve,°   120
And be liege-lord of all the Elves and Fays,
To venture so: it fills me with amaze
To see thee, Porphyro!—St. Agnes' Eve!
God's help! my lady fair the conjuror plays

120. witch's sieve: A sieve bewitched so that it can hold water.

This very night: good angels her deceive!   125
But let me laugh awhile, I've mickle° time to grieve."   *much*

15

Feebly she laugheth in the languid moon,
While Porphyro upon her face doth look,
Like puzzled urchin on an aged crone
Who keepeth closed a wonderous riddle-book,   130
As spectacled she sits in chimney nook.
But soon his eyes grew brilliant, when she told
His lady's purpose; and he scarce could brook°
Tears, at the thought of those enchantments cold,
And Madeline asleep in lap of legends old.   135

16

Sudden a thought came like a full-blown rose,
Flushing his brow, and in his pained heart
Made purple riot: then doth he propose
A stratagem, that makes the beldame start:
"A cruel man and impious thou art: 140
Sweet lady, let her pray, and sleep, and dream
Alone with her good angels, far apart
From wicked men like thee. Go, go! — I deem
Thou canst not surely be the same that thou didst seem."

17

"I will not harm her, by all saints I swear,"   145
Quoth Porphyro: "O may I ne'er find grace
When my weak voice shall whisper its last prayer,
If one of her soft ringlets I displace,
Or look with ruffian passion in her face:
Good Angela, believe me by these tears;   150
Or I will, even in a moment's space,
Awake, with horrid shout, my foemen's ears,
And beard them, though they be more fanged than wolves and bears."

18

"Ah! why wilt thou affright a feeble soul?
A poor, weak, palsy-stricken, churchyard thing,   155
Whose passing-bell may ere the midnight toll;
Whose prayers for thee, each morn and evening,

---

133. brook: Usually "endure," but here "hold back."

Were never miss'd."—Thus plaining, doth she bring
A gentler speech from burning Porphyro;
So woeful, and of such deep sorrowing,   160
That Angela gives promise she will do
Whatever he shall wish, betide her weal or woe.

19

Which was, to lead him, in close secrecy,
Even to Madeline's chamber, and there hide
Him in a closet, of such privacy   165
That he might see her beauty unespied,
And win perhaps that night a peerless bride,
While legioned fairies paced the coverlet,
And pale enchantment held her sleepy-eyed.
Never on such a night have lovers met,   170
Since Merlin paid his Demon° all the monstrous debt.

20

"It shall be as thou wishest," said the Dame:
"All cates° and dainties shall be stored there   *delicacies*
Quickly on this feast-night: by the tambour frame°
Her own lute thou wilt see: no time to spare,   175
For I am slow and feeble, and scarce dare
On such a catering trust my dizzy head.
Wait here, my child, with patience; kneel in prayer
The while: Ah! thou must needs the lady wed,
Or may I never leave my grave among the dead."   180

21

So saying, she hobbled off with busy fear.
The lover's endless minutes slowly passed;
The dame returned, and whispered in his ear
To follow her; with aged eyes aghast
From fright of dim espial. Safe at last,   185
Through many a dusky gallery, they gain
The maiden's chamber, silken, hushed, and chaste;
Where Porphyro took covert,° pleased amain.°   *a hiding place/greatly*
His poor guide hurried back with agues° in her brain. *feverish disturbance*

---

171. his Demon: Presumably the temptress Vivian, in the Arthurian legends, who
turned one of Merlin's own spells against him.
174. tambour frame: A drum-shaped embroidery frame.

22

Her faltering hand upon the balustrade,   190
Old Angela was feeling for the stair,
When Madeline, St. Agnes' charmed maid,
Rose, like a missioned spirit,° unaware:
With silver taper's light, and pious care,
She turned, and down the aged gossip led   195
To a safe level matting. Now prepare,
Young Porphyro, for gazing on that bed;
She comes, she comes again, like ring-dove frayed° and fled.   *frightened*

23

Out went the taper as she hurried in;
Its little smoke, in pallid moonshine, died: 200
She closed the door, she panted, all akin
To spirits of the air, and visions wide:
No uttered syllable, or, woe betide!
But to her heart, her heart was voluble,
Paining with eloquence her balmy side;   205
As though a tongueless nightingale should swell
Her throat in vain, and die, heart-stifled, in her dell.

24

A casement° high and triple-arched there was,   *a type of window*
All garlanded with carven imag'ries
Of fruits, and flowers, and bunches of knot-grass,   210
And diamonded with panes of quaint device,
Innumerable of stains and splendid dyes,
As are the tiger-moth's deep-damasked° wings;   *variegated*
And in the midst, 'mong thousand heraldries,
And twilight saints, and dim emblazonings,   215
A shielded scutcheon blushed with blood of queens and kings.°

25

Full on this casement shone the wintry moon,
And threw warm gules° on Madeline's fair breast,
As down she knelt for heaven's grace and boon;°   *gift, blessing*

193. **missioned spirit:** An angel on a mission.
216. **scutcheon:** The escutcheon (shield emblazoned with a coat of arms) reveals the royal lineage of the family. **Blushed:** Points to "gules" (red) in line 218 as the moon reflecting off the shield reddening her breast.
218. **gules:** The heraldic name for red.

Rose-bloom fell on her hands, together prest,   220
And on her silver cross soft amethyst,
And on her hair a glory, like a saint:
She seemed a splendid angel, newly drest,
Save wings, for heaven: — Porphyro grew faint:
She knelt, so pure a thing, so free from mortal taint.   225

26

Anon his heart revives: her vespers° done,   *evening prayers*
Of all its wreathed pearls her hair she frees;
Unclasps her warmed jewels one by one;
Loosens her fragrant bodice; by degrees
Her rich attire creeps rustling to her knees: 230
Half-hidden, like a mermaid in sea-weed,
Pensive awhile she dreams awake, and sees,
In fancy, fair St. Agnes in her bed,
But dares not look behind, or all the charm is fled.

27

Soon, trembling in her soft and chilly nest,   235
In sort of wakeful swoon, perplexed she lay,
Until the poppied warmth of sleep oppressed
Her soothed limbs, and soul fatigued away;
Flown, like a thought, until the morrow-day;
Blissfully havened both from joy and pain;   240
Clasped like a missal where swart Paynims pray;°
Blinded alike from sunshine and from rain,
As though a rose should shut, and be a bud again.

28

Stol'n to this paradise, and so entranced,
Porphyro gazed upon her empty dress,   245
And listened to her breathing, if it chanced
To wake into a slumberous tenderness;
Which when he heard, that minute did he bless,
And breathed himself: then from the closet crept,
Noiseless as fear° in a wide wilderness,   *a fearful person* 250
And over the hushed carpet, silent, stepped,
And 'tween the curtains peeped, where, lo! — how fast she slept.

---

241. Clasped . . . pray: Kept shut as a Christian prayer book would be where
dark-skinned pagans (presumably Muslims) pray.

29

Then by the bed-side, where the faded moon
Made a dim, silver twilight, soft he set
A table, and, half anguished, threw thereon   255
A cloth of woven crimson, gold, and jet:—
O for some drowsy Morphean amulet!°   *sleep-inducing charm*
The boisterous, midnight, festive clarion,°   *a shrill-sounding trumpet*
The kettle-drum, and far-heard clarionet,°   *clarinet*
Affray° his ears, though but in dying tone:—   *assault*   260
The hall door shuts again, and all the noise is gone.

30

And still she slept an azure-lidded sleep,
In blanchèd linen, smooth, and lavendered,
While he from forth the closet brought a heap
Of candied apple, quince, and plum, and gourd;   265
With jellies soother° than the creamy curd,   *smoother*
And lucent syrups, tinct° with cinnamon;   *tinctured*
Manna and dates, in argosy transferred
From Fez,° and spiced dainties, every one,
From silken Samarcand° to cedared Lebanon.   270

31

These delicates he heaped with glowing hand
On golden dishes and in baskets bright
Of wreathed silver: sumptuous they stand
In the retired quiet of the night,
Filling the chilly room with perfume light.—   275
"And now, my love, my seraph fair, awake!
Thou art my heaven, and I thine eremite:°   *hermit*
Open thine eyes, for meek St. Agnes' sake,
Or I shall drowse beside thee, so my soul doth ache."

32

Thus whispering, his warm, unnervèd arm   280
Sank in her pillow. Shaded was her dream
By the dusk curtains:—'twas a midnight charm
Impossible to melt as iced stream:

---

269. Fez: A commercial city in northern Morocco.
270. Samarcand: A city now in southern Russia, still noted for its silks.

The lustrous salvers in the moonlight gleam;
Broad golden fringe upon the carpet lies: 285
It seemed he never, never could redeem
From such a stedfast spell his lady's eyes;
So mused awhile, entoiled in woofèd° phantasies.   *woven*

33

Awakening up, he took her hollow lute,—
Tumultuous,—and, in chords that tenderest be,   290
He played an ancient ditty, long since mute,
In Provence called, "La belle dame sans mercy":°
Close to her ear touching the melody;—
Wherewith disturbed, she uttered a soft moan:
He ceased—she panted quick—and suddenly   295
Her blue affrayed eyes wide open shone:
Upon his knees he sank, pale as smooth-sculptured stone.

34

Her eyes were open, but she still beheld,
Now wide awake, the vision of her sleep:
There was a painful change, that nigh expelled   300
The blisses of her dream so pure and deep:
At which fair Madeline began to weep,
And moan forth witless words with many a sigh;
While still her gaze on Porphyro would keep;
Who knelt, with joinèd hands and piteous eye,   305
Fearing to move or speak, she look'd so dreamingly.

35

"Ah, Porphyro!" said she, "but even now
Thy voice was at sweet tremble in mine ear,
Made tuneable with every sweetest vow;
And those sad eyes were spiritual and clear: 310
How changed thou art! how pallid, chill, and drear!
Give me that voice again, my Porphyro,
Those looks immortal, those complainings dear!
Oh leave me not in this eternal woe,
For if thou diest, my love, I know not where to go."   315

---

292. "La . . . mercy": "The Beautiful Lady without Pity": title of a poem by the
medieval French poet Alain Chartier and later of a poem by Keats.

36

Beyond a mortal man impassioned far
At these voluptuous accents, he arose,
Ethereal, flushed, and like a throbbing star
Seen mid the sapphire heaven's deep repose;
Into her dream he melted, as the rose   320
Blendeth its odor with the violet, —
Solution sweet: meantime the frost-wind blows
Like Love's alarum pattering the sharp sleet
Against the window-panes; St. Agnes' moon hath set.

37

'Tis dark: quick pattereth the flaw-blown° sleet: *gust-blown* 325
"This is no dream, my bride, my Madeline!"
'Tis dark: the icèd gusts still rave and beat:
"No dream, alas! alas! and woe is mine!
Porphyro will leave me here to fade and pine. —
Cruel! what traitor could thee hither bring?   330
I curse not, for my heart is lost in thine,
Though thou forsakest a deceived thing; —
A dove forlorn and lost with sick unprunèd wing."

38

"My Madeline! sweet dreamer! lovely bride!
Say, may I be for aye thy vassal blest?   335
Thy beauty's shield, heart-shaped and vermeil° dyed?   *vermilion*
Ah, silver shrine, here will I take my rest
After so many hours of toil and quest,
A famished pilgrim, — saved by miracle.
Though I have found, I will not rob thy nest   340
Saving of thy sweet self; if thou thinkest well
To trust, fair Madeline, to no rude infidel.

39

"Hark! 'tis an elfin-storm from faery land,
Of haggard° seeming, but a boon indeed: *wild*
Arise — arise! the morning is at hand; —   345
The bloated wassaillers° will never heed: —   *drunken revelers*
Let us away, my love, with happy speed;
There are no ears to hear, or eyes to see, —
Drowned all in Rhenish° and the sleepy mead:°

349. Rhenish: Rhine wine; mead: A heavy fermented liquor made of malt and
honey.

Awake! arise! my love, and fearless be,   350
For o'er the southern moors I have a home for thee."

40

She hurried at his words, beset with fears,
For there were sleeping dragons° all around,
At glaring watch, perhaps, with ready spears—
Down the wide stairs a darkling way they found.—   355
In all the house was heard no human sound.
A chain-drooped lamp was flickering by each door;
The arras,° rich with horseman, hawk, and hound,   *tapestry*
Fluttered in the besieging wind's uproar;
And the long carpets rose along the gusty floor.   360

41

They glide, like phantoms, into the wide hall;
Like phantoms, to the iron porch, they glide;
Where lay the Porter, in uneasy sprawl,
With a huge empty flaggon by his side:
The wakeful bloodhound rose, and shook his hide,   365
But his sagacious eye an inmate owns:°
By one, and one, the bolts full easy slide:—
The chains lie silent on the footworn stones;—
The key turns, and the door upon its hinges groans.

42

And they are gone: aye, ages long ago   370
These lovers fled away into the storm.
That night the Baron dreamt of many a woe,
And all his warrior-guests, with shade and form
Of witch, and demon, and large coffin-worm,
Were long be-nightmared. Angela the old   375
Died palsy-twitched, with meagre face deform;
The Beadsman, after thousand aves° told,
For aye unsought for slept among his ashes cold.

[1820]

353. **sleeping dragons:** Sentries; i.e., commissioned to watch like dragons over a treasure.
366. **sagacious . . . owns:** Recognizes a member of his household.
377. **aves:** Prayers beginning *Ave Maria* ("Hail Mary").

JOHN KEATS   [1795–1821]

Ode on a Grecian Urn

1

Thou still unravished bride of quietness,
    Thou foster child of silence and slow time,
Sylvan historian, who canst thus express
    A flowery tale more sweetly than our rhyme:
What leaf-fringed legend haunts about thy shape   5
    Of deities or mortals, or of both,
        In Tempe or the dales of Arcady?°
    What men or gods are these? What maidens loath?
What mad pursuit? What struggle to escape?
        What pipes and timbrels? What wild ecstasy?   10

2

Heard melodies are sweet, but those unheard
    Are sweeter; therefore, ye soft pipes, play on;
Not to the sensual ear,° but, more endeared,
    Pipe to the spirit ditties of no tone:
Fair youth, beneath the trees, thou canst not leave   15
    Thy song, nor ever can those trees be bare;
        Bold lover, never, never canst thou kiss,
Though winning near the goal—yet, do not grieve;
    She cannot fade, though thou hast not thy bliss,
    Forever wilt thou love, and she be fair!   20

3

Ah, happy, happy boughs! that cannot shed
    Your leaves, nor ever bid the spring adieu;
And, happy melodist, unwearièd,
    Forever piping songs forever new;
More happy love! more happy, happy love!   25
    Forever warm and still to be enjoyed,
        Forever panting, and forever young;

---

7. **Tempe, Arcady:** Tempe, a valley in Greece, and Arcadia ("Arcady"), a region of
ancient Greece, represent ideal pastoral landscapes.
13. **not . . . ear:** Not to the ear of the senses, but to the imagination.

All breathing human passion far above,
　That leaves a heart high-sorrowful and cloyed,
　　A burning forehead, and a parching tongue.　　　　30

4

Who are these coming to the sacrifice?
　To what green altar, O mysterious priest,
Lead'st thou that heifer lowing at the skies,
　And all her silken flanks with garlands dressed?
What little town by river or sea shore,　　　　35
　Or mountain-built with peaceful citadel,
　　Is emptied of this folk, this pious morn?
And, little town, thy streets forevermore
　Will silent be; and not a soul to tell
　　Why thou art desolate, can e'er return.　　　　40

5

O Attic° shape! Fair attitude! with brede°
Of marble men and maidens overwrought,
With forest branches and the trodden weed;
　Thou, silent form, dost tease us out of thought
As doth eternity: Cold Pastoral!　　　　45
　When old age shall this generation waste,
　　Thou shalt remain, in midst of other woe
Than ours, a friend to man, to whom thou say'st,
"Beauty is truth, truth beauty,"°— that is all
　Ye know on earth, and all ye need to know.　　　　50

[1820]

41. Attic: Greek, specifically Athenian; brede: Interwoven pattern.
49. Beauty . . . beauty: The quotation marks around this phrase were found in its earliest printing, in an 1820 volume of poetry by Keats, but not in a printing later that year or in written transcripts. This discrepancy has led to considerable critical controversy concerning the last two lines. Critics disagree whether "Beauty is truth, truth beauty" is spoken by the urn (and thus perhaps expressing a limited perspective not to be taken at face value) or by the speaker in the poem, or whether the last two lines in their entirety are said by the urn (some recent editors enclose both lines in parentheses to make this explicit) or by the speaker.

JOHN KEATS   [1795–1821]

To Autumn

I

Season of mists and mellow fruitfulness,
   Close bosom-friend of the maturing sun;
Conspiring with him how to load and bless
   With fruit the vines that round the thatch-eves run;
To bend with apples the mossed cottage-trees,   5
   And fill all fruit with ripeness to the core;
     To swell the gourd, and plump the hazel shells
With a sweet kernel; to set budding more,
   And still more, later flowers for the bees,
   Until they think warm days will never cease,   10
     For Summer has o'er-brimmed their clammy cells.

II

Who hath not seen thee oft amid thy store?
   Sometimes whoever seeks abroad may find
Thee sitting careless on a granary floor,
   Thy hair soft-lifted by the winnowing wind;   15
Or on a half-reaped furrow sound asleep,
   Drowsed with the fume of poppies, while thy hook°   *scythe*
     Spares the next swath and all its twinèd flowers:
And sometimes like a gleaner thou dost keep
   Steady thy laden head across a brook;   20
   Or by a cider-press, with patient look,
     Thou watchest the last oozings hours by hours.

III

Where are the songs of Spring? Aye, where are they?
   Think not of them, thou hast thy music too,—
While barrèd clouds bloom the soft-dying day,   25
   And touch the stubble-plains with rosy hue;
Then in a wailful choir the small gnats mourn
   Among the river sallows,° borne aloft   *willows*
     Or sinking as the light wind lives or dies;
And full-grown lambs loud bleat from hilly bourn;°   *region* 30
   Hedge-crickets sing; and now with treble soft

The red-breast whistles from a garden-croft;
And gathering swallows twitter in the skies.

[1820]

ELIZABETH   BARRETT   BROWNING
[1806–1861]

How do I love thee?
Let me count the ways

How do I love thee? Let me count the ways.
I love thee to the depth and breadth and height
My soul can reach, when feeling out of sight
For the ends of Being and ideal Grace.
I love thee to the level of everyday's   5
Most quiet need, by sun and candlelight.
I love thee freely, as men strive for Right;
I love thee purely, as they turn from Praise.
I love thee with the passion put to use
In my old griefs, and with my childhood's faith.   10
I love thee with a love I seemed to lose
With my lost saints—I love thee with the breath,
Smiles, tears, of all my life!—and, if God choose,
I shall but love thee better after death.

[1850]

EDGAR ALLAN POE [1809–1849]

To Helen

Helen,° thy beauty is to me
  Like those Nicéan barks° of yore,
That gently, o'er a perfumed sea,
  The weary, way-worn wanderer bore
  To his own native shore.   5

On desperate seas long wont to roam,
  Thy hyacinth hair,° thy classic face,
Thy Naiad° airs have brought me home
  To the glory that was Greece
And the grandeur that was Rome.   10

Lo! in yon brilliant window-niche
  How statue-like I see thee stand,
  The agate lamp within thy hand!
Ah! Psyche, from the regions which
  Are Holy Land!   15

[*1823;* 1831]

1. **Helen:** Daughter of Leda and Zeus, the most beautiful woman in the world; her abduction by Paris gave rise to the Trojan War.
2. **barks:** Small sailing boats; Poe probably invented "Nicéan" for its sound and suggestiveness.
7. **hyacinth:** "Raven-black" and "naturally curling" (from Poe's story "Ligeia").
8. **Naiads:** Fresh-water nymphs in classical myths.

EDGAR ALLAN POE [1809–1849]

Annabel Lee

It was many and many a year ago,
  In a kingdom by the sea,
That a maiden there lived whom you may know
  By the name of Annabel Lee;

And this maiden she lived with no other thought   5
　　Than to love and be loved by me.

She was a child and *I* was a child,
　　In this kingdom by the sea,
But we loved with a love that was more than love—
　　I and my Annabel Lee—   10
With a love that the wingèd seraphs° of Heaven   *angels of the highest order*
　　Coveted her and me.

And this was the reason that, long ago,
　　In this kingdom by the sea,
A wind blew out of a cloud by night   15
　　Chilling my Annabel Lee;
So that her highborn kinsmen came
　　And bore her away from me,
To shut her up in a sepulchre
　　In this kingdom by the sea.   20

The angels, not half so happy in Heaven,
　　Went envying her and me:
Yes! that was the reason (as all men know,
　　In this kingdom by the sea)
That the wind came out of the cloud, chilling   25
　　And killing my Annabel Lee.

But our love it was stronger by far than the love
　　Of those who were older than we—
　　Of many far wiser than we—
And neither the angels in Heaven above   30
　　Nor the demons down under the sea,
Can ever dissever my soul from the soul
　　Of the beautiful Annabel Lee:

For the moon never beams without bringing me dreams
　　Of the beautiful Annabel Lee;   35
And the stars never rise but I see the bright eyes
　　Of the beautiful Annabel Lee;
And so, all the night-tide, I lie down by the side
Of my darling, my darling, my life and my bride,
　　In her sepulchre there by the sea—   40
　　In her tomb by the side of the sea.

[1849]

ALFRED, LORD TENNYSON   [1809–1892]

Ulysses°

It little profits that an idle king,
By this still hearth, among these barren crags,
Matched with an agèd wife, I mete and dole
Unequal laws unto a savage race,°
That hoard, and sleep, and feed, and know not me.   5

I cannot rest from travel; I will drink
Life to the lees. All times I have enjoyed
Greatly, have suffered greatly, both with those
That loved me, and alone; on shore, and when
Through scudding drifts° the rainy Hyades°   10
Vexed the dim sea. I am become a name;
For always roaming with a hungry heart
Much have I seen and known — cities of men
And manners, climates, councils, governments,
Myself not least, but honored of them all —   15
And drunk delight of battle with my peers,
Far on the ringing plains of windy Troy.
I am a part of all that I have met;
Yet all experience is an arch wherethrough
Gleams that untraveled world whose margin fades   20
Forever and forever when I move.

Ulysses (the Roman form of Odysseus): The hero of Homer's epic *The Odyssey*, which tells the story of Odysseus's adventures on his voyage back to his home, the little island of Ithaca, after he and the other Greek heroes defeated Troy. It took Odysseus ten years to reach Ithaca, the small, rocky island of which he was king, where his wife (Penelope) and son (Telemachus) were waiting for him. Upon his return he defeated the suitors who had been trying to marry the faithful Penelope, and he resumed the kingship and his old ways of life. Here Homer's story ends, but in Canto 26 of the *Inferno*, Dante extended the story: Odysseus eventually became restless and dissatisfied with his settled life and decided to return to the sea and sail west, into the unknown sea, and seek whatever adventures he might find there. Tennyson's poem amplifies the speech delivered in Dante's poem as Ulysses challenges his men to accompany him on this new voyage.
3–4. mete . . . race: Administer inadequate (unequal to what is needed) laws to a still somewhat lawless race.
10. scudding drifts: Wind-driven spray; **Hyades:** Five stars in the constellation Taurus whose rising was assumed would be followed by rain.

How dull it is to pause, to make an end,
To rust unburnished, not to shine in use!
As though to breathe were life! Life piled on life
Were all too little, and of one to me   25
Little remains; but every hour is saved
From that eternal silence, something more,
A bringer of new things; and vile it were
For some three suns° to store and hoard myself,   *years*
And this gray spirit yearning in desire   30
To follow knowledge like a sinking star,
Beyond the utmost bound of human thought.

     This is my son, mine own Telemachus,
To whom I leave the scepter and the isle—
Well-loved of me, discerning to fulfill   35
This labor, by slow prudence to make mild
A rugged people, and through soft degrees
Subdue them to the useful and the good.
Most blameless is he, centered in the sphere
Of common duties, decent not to fail   40
In offices of tenderness, and pay
Meet adoration to my household gods,
When I am gone. He works his work, I mine.

     There lies the port; the vessel puffs her sail;
There gloom the dark, broad seas. My mariners,   45
Souls that have toiled, and wrought, and thought with me—
That ever with a frolic welcome took
The thunder and the sunshine, and opposed
Free hearts, free foreheads—you and I are old;
Old age hath yet his honor and his toil.   50
Death closes all; but something ere the end,
Some work of noble note, may yet be done,
Not unbecoming men that strove with Gods.
The lights begin to twinkle from the rocks;
The long day wanes; the slow moon climbs; the deep   55
Moans round with many voices. Come, my friends,
'Tis not too late to seek a newer world.
Push off, and sitting well in order smite
The sounding furrows; for my purpose holds
To sail beyond the sunset, and the baths°   60

60. **baths:** The outer river or ocean surrounding the flat earth, in Greek cosmology, into which the stars descended upon setting.

Of all the western stars, until I die.
It may be that the gulfs will wash us down;
It may be we shall touch the Happy Isles,°
And see the great Achilles,° whom we knew.
Though much is taken, much abides; and though   65
We are not now that strength which in old days
Moved earth and heaven, that which we are, we are—
One equal temper of heroic hearts,
Made weak by time and fate, but strong in will
To strive, to seek, to find, and not to yield.   70

[1833]

63. **Happy Isles:** The Islands of the Blessed, or Elysian Fields, in Greek myth, which lay in the western seas beyond the Strait of Gibraltar and were the abode of heroes after death.
64. **Achilles:** The hero of the Greeks, and Odysseus's comrade, in Homer's *Iliad*.

ALFRED, LORD TENNYSON   [1809–1892]

Tears, idle tears

Tears, idle tears, I know not what they mean,
Tears from the depth of some divine despair
Rise in the heart, and gather to the eyes,
In looking on the happy Autumn-fields,
And thinking of the days that are no more.   5

Fresh as the first beam glittering on a sail,
That brings our friends up from the underworld,
Sad as the last which reddens over one
That sinks with all we love below the verge;
So sad, so fresh, the days that are no more.   10

Ah, sad and strange as in dark summer dawns
The earliest pipe of half-awakened birds
To dying ears, when unto dying eyes
The casement slowly grows a glimmering square;
So sad, so strange, the days that are no more.   15

Dear as remembered kisses after death,
And sweet as those by hopeless fancy feigned
On lips that are for others; deep as love,
Deep as first love, and wild with all regret;
O Death in Life, the days that are no more!   20

[1847]

ALFRED, LORD TENNYSON   [1809–1892]

Crossing the Bar

Sunset and evening star,
    And one clear call for me!
And may there be no moaning of the bar,
    When I put out to sea,

But such a tide as moving seems asleep,   5
    Too full for sound and foam,
When that which drew from out the boundless deep
    Turns again home.

Twilight and evening bell,
    And after that the dark!   10
And may there be no sadness of farewell,
    When I embark;

For though from out our bourne of Time and Place
    The flood may bear me far,
I hope to see my Pilot face to face   15
    When I have crossed the bar.

[1889]

ROBERT BROWNING [1812–1889]

My Last Duchess

Ferrara°

That's my last Duchess° painted on the wall,
Looking as if she were alive. I call
That piece a wonder, now: Frà Pandolf's° hands
Worked busily a day, and there she stands.
Will't please you sit and look at her? I said   5
"Frà Pandolf" by design, for never read
Strangers like you that pictured countenance,
The depth and passion of its earnest glance,
But to myself they turned (since none puts by
The curtain I have drawn for you, but I)   10
And seemed as they would ask me, if they durst,
How such a glance came there; so, not the first
Are you to turn and ask thus. Sir, 'twas not
Her husband's presence only, called that spot
Of joy into the Duchess' cheek: perhaps   15
Frà Pandolf chanced to say "Her mantle laps
Over my lady's wrist too much," or "Paint
Must never hope to reproduce the faint
Half-flush that dies along her throat:" such stuff
Was courtesy, she thought, and cause enough   20
For calling up that spot of joy. She had
A heart—how shall I say?—too soon made glad,
Too easily impressed; she liked whate'er
She looked on, and her looks went everywhere.
Sir, 'twas all one! My favor at her breast,   25
The dropping of the daylight in the West,
The bough of cherries some officious fool
Broke in the orchard for her, the white mule
She rode with round the terrace—all and each
Would draw from her alike the approving speech,   30
Or blush, at least. She thanked men,—good! but thanked

Ferrara: The poem is based on events that occurred in the life of Alfonso II, duke
of Ferrara in Italy, in the sixteenth century.
1. last Duchess: Ferrara's first wife, Lucrezia, died in 1561 at age seventeen after
three years of marriage.
3. Frà Pandolf: Brother Pandolf, a fictional painter.

Somehow—I know not how—as if she ranked
My gift of a nine-hundred-years-old name
With anybody's gift. Who'd stoop to blame
This sort of trifling? Even had you skill   35
In speech—(which I have not)—to make your will
Quite clear to such an one, and say, "Just this
Or that in you disgusts me; here you miss,
Or there exceed the mark"—and if she let
Herself be lessoned so, nor plainly set   40
Her wits to yours, forsooth, and made excuse,
—E'en then would be some stooping; and I choose
Never to stoop. Oh sir, she smiled, no doubt,
Whene'er I passed her; but who passed without
Much the same smile? This grew; I gave commands;   45
Then all smiles stopped together. There she stands
As if alive. Will't please you rise? We'll meet
The company below, then. I repeat,
The Count your master's known munificence
Is ample warrant that no just pretence   50
Of mine for dowry will be disallowed;
Though his fair daughter's self, as I avowed
At starting, is my object. Nay, we'll go
Together down, sir. Notice Neptune, though,
Taming a sea-horse, thought a rarity,   55
Which Claus of Innsbruck° cast in bronze for me!

[1842]

56. Claus of Innsbruck: A fictional sculptor.

ROBERT BROWNING [1812–1889]

Home-Thoughts, from Abroad

1

Oh, to be in England
Now that April's there,
And whoever wakes in England
Sees, some morning, unaware,

That the lowest boughs and the brushwood sheaf   5
Round the elm-tree bole are in tiny leaf,
While the chaffinch sings on the orchard bough
In England—now!

2

And after April, when May follows,
And the whitethroat builds, and all the swallows!   10
Hark, where my blossomed pear-tree in the hedge
Leans to the field and scatters on the clover
Blossoms and dewdrops—at the bent spray's edge—
That's the wise thrush; he sings each song twice over,
Lest you should think he never could recapture   15
The first fine careless rapture!
And though the fields look rough with hoary dew
All will be gay when noontide wakes anew
The buttercups, the little children's dower
—Far brighter than this gaudy melon-flower!   20

[1845]

EMILY BRONTË [1818–1848]

Riches I hold in light esteem

Riches I hold in light esteem
And Love I laugh to scorn
And lust of Fame was but a dream
That vanished with the morn—

And if I pray, the only prayer   5
That moves my lips for me
Is—"Leave the heart that now I bear
And give me liberty."

Yes, as my swift days near their goal
'Tis all that I implore—   10
Through life and death, a chainless soul
With courage to endure!

[1846]

WALT WHITMAN   [1819–1892]

From Song of Myself

1

I celebrate myself, and sing myself,
And what I assume you shall assume,
For every atom belonging to me as good belongs to you.

I loafe and invite my soul,
I lean and loafe at my ease observing a spear of summer grass.   5

My tongue, every atom of my blood, form'd from this soil, this air,
Born here of parents born here from parents the same, and their
    parents the same,
I, now thirty-seven years old in perfect health begin,
Hoping to cease not till death.

Creeds and schools in abeyance,   10
Retiring back a while sufficed at what they are, but never forgotten,
I harbor for good or bad, I permit to speak at every hazard,
Nature without check with original energy.

2

Houses and rooms are full of perfumes, the shelves are crowded with
    perfumes,
I breathe the fragrance myself and know it and like it,   15
The distillation would intoxicate me also, but I shall not let it.

The atmosphere is not a perfume, it has no taste of the distillation, it is
    odorless,
It is for my mouth forever, I am in love with it,
I will go to the bank by the wood and become undisguised and naked,
I am mad for it to be in contact with me.   20

The smoke of my own breath,
Echoes, ripples, buzz'd whispers, love-root, silk-thread, crotch and vine,
My respiration and inspiration, the beating of my heart, the passing of
    blood and air through my lungs,
The sniff of green leaves and dry leaves, and of the shore and dark-
    color'd sea-rocks, and of hay in the barn,
The sound of the belch'd words of my voice loos'd to the eddies of the
    wind,   25

A few light kisses, a few embraces, a reaching around of arms,
The play of shine and shade on the trees as the supple boughs wag,
The delight alone or in the rush of the streets, or along the fields and
    hill-sides,
The feeling of health, the full-noon trill, the song of me rising from bed
    and meeting the sun.

Have you reckon'd a thousand acres much? have you reckon'd the earth
    much?   30
Have you practis'd so long to learn to read?
Have you felt so proud to get at the meaning of poems?

Stop this day and night with me and you shall possess the origin of all
    poems,
You shall possess the good of the earth and sun, (there are millions of
    suns left,)
You shall no longer take things at second or third hand, nor look
    through the eyes of the dead, nor feed on the spectres in books,   35
You shall not look through my eyes either, nor take things from me,
You shall listen to all sides and filter them from your self.

3

I have heard what the talkers were talking, the talk of the beginning and
    the end,
But I do not talk of the beginning or the end.

There was never any more inception than there is now,   40
Nor any more youth or age than there is now,
And will never be any more perfection than there is now,
Nor any more heaven or hell than there is now.
Urge and urge and urge,
Always the procreant urge of the world.   45

Out of the dimness opposite equals advance, always substance and
    increase, always sex,
Always a knit of identity, always distinction, always a breed of life.

To elaborate is no avail, learn'd and unlearn'd feel that it is so.

Sure as the most certain sure, plumb in the uprights, well entretied,°
    braced in the beams,
Stout as a horse, affectionate, haughty, electrical,   50
I and this mystery here we stand.

Clear and sweet is my soul, and clear and sweet is all that is not my soul.

49. entretied: Cross-braced, as between two joists in carpentry.

Lack one lacks both, and the unseen is proved by the seen,
Till that becomes unseen and receives proof in its turn.

Showing the best and dividing it from the worst age vexes age,   55
Knowing the perfect fitness and equanimity of things, while they
    discuss I am silent, and go bathe and admire myself.

Welcome is every organ and attribute of me, and of any man hearty and
    clean,
Not an inch nor a particle of an inch is vile, and none shall be less
    familiar than the rest.

I am satisfied—I see, dance, laugh, sing;
As the hugging and loving bed-fellow sleeps at my side through the
    night, and withdraws at the peep of the day with stealthy tread,   60
Leaving me baskets cover'd with white towels swelling the house with
    their plenty,
Shall I postpone my acceptation and realization and scream at my eyes,
That they turn from gazing after and down the road,
And forthwith cipher and show me to a cent,
Exactly the value of one and exactly the value of two, and which is ahead?   65

• • •

6

A child said *What is the grass?* fetching it to me with full hands;
How could I answer the child? I do not know what it is any more
    than he.   100

I guess it must be the flag of my disposition, out of hopeful green stuff
    woven.

Or I guess it is the handkerchief of the Lord,
A scented gift and remembrancer designedly dropt,
Bearing the owner's name someway in the corners, that we may see and
    remark, and say *Whose?*

Or I guess the grass is itself a child, the produced babe of the vegetation.   105

Or I guess it is a uniform hieroglyphic,
And it means, Sprouting alike in broad zones and narrow zones,
Growing among black folks as among white,
Kanuck, Tuckahoe, Congressman, Cuff,° I give them the same, I receive
    them the same.

And now it seems to me the beautiful uncut hair of graves.   110

---

109. Kanuck: A French Canadian; **Tuckahoe:** A Virginian living in the tidewater
region and eating tuckahoe, a fungus; **Cuff:** A black person.

Tenderly will I use you curling grass,
It may be you transpire from the breasts of young men,
It may be if I had known them I would have loved them,
It may be you are from old people, or from offspring taken soon out of
    their mothers' laps,
And here you are the mothers' laps.   115

This grass is very dark to be from the white heads of old mothers,
Darker than the colorless beards of old men,
Dark to come from under the faint red roofs of mouths.

O I perceive after all so many uttering tongues,
And I perceive they do not come from the roofs of mouths for nothing.   120

I wish I could translate the hints about the dead young men and
    women,
And the hints about old men and mothers, and the offspring taken soon
    out of their laps.
What do you think has become of the young and old men?
And what do you think has become of the women and children?

They are alive and well somewhere,   125
The smallest sprout shows there is really no death,
And if ever there was it led forward life, and does not wait at the end to
    arrest it,
And ceas'd the moment life appear'd.

All goes onward and outward, nothing collapses,
And to die is different from what any one supposed, and luckier.   130

7

Has any one supposed it lucky to be born?
I hasten to inform him or her it is just as lucky to die, and I know it.

I pass death with the dying and birth with the new-wash'd babe, and am
    not contain'd between my hat and boots,
And peruse manifold objects, no two alike and every one good,
The earth good and the stars good, and their adjuncts all good.   135

I am not an earth nor an adjunct of an earth,
I am the mate and companion of people, all just as immortal and
    fathomless as myself,
(They do not know how immortal, but I know.)

Every kind for itself and its own, for me mine male and female,
For me those that have been boys and that love women,   140
For me the man that is proud and feels how it stings to be slighted,

For me the sweet-heart and the old maid, for me mothers and the
    mothers of mothers,
For me lips that have smiled, eyes that have shed tears,
For me children and the begetters of children.

Undrape! you are not guilty to me, nor stale nor discarded,   145
I see through the broadcloth and gingham whether or no,
And am around, tenacious, acquisitive, tireless, and cannot be shaken
    away.

                                    8

The little one sleeps in its cradle,
I lift the gauze and look a long time, and silently brush away flies with
    my hand.

The youngster and the red-faced girl turn aside up the bushy hill,   150
I peeringly view them from the top.

The suicide sprawls on the bloody floor of the bedroom,
I witness the corpse with its dabbled hair, I note where the pistol has
    fallen.

The blab of the pave, tires of carts, sluff of boot-soles, talk of the
    promenaders,
The heavy omnibus, the driver with his interrogating thumb, the clank
    of the shod horses on the granite floor,   155
The snow-sleighs, clinking, shouted jokes, pelts of snow-balls,
The hurrahs for popular favorites, the fury of rous'd mobs,
The flap of the curtain'd litter, a sick man inside borne to the hospital,
The meeting of enemies, the sudden oath, the blows and fall,
The excited crowd, the policeman with his star quickly working his
    passage to the centre of the crowd,   160
The impassive stones that receive and return so many echoes,
What groans of over-fed or half-starv'd who fall sunstruck or in fits,
What exclamations of women taken suddenly who hurry home and give
    birth to babes,
What living and buried speech is always vibrating here, what howls
    restrain'd by decorum,
Arrests of criminals, slights, adulterous offers made, acceptances,
    rejections with convex lips,   165
I mind them or the show or resonance of them—I come and I depart.

                                    9

The big doors of the country barn stand open and ready,
The dried grass of the harvest-time loads the slow-drawn wagon,

The clear light plays on the brown gray and green intertinged,
The armfuls are pack'd to the sagging mow.   170

I am there, I help, I came stretch'd atop of the load,
I felt its soft jolts, one leg reclined on the other,
I jump from the cross-beams and seize the clover and timothy,
And roll head over heels and tangle my hair full of wisps.

10

Alone far in the wilds and mountains I hunt,   175
Wandering amazed at my own lightness and glee,
In the late afternoon choosing a safe spot to pass the night,
Kindling a fire and broiling the fresh-kill'd game,
Falling asleep on the gather'd leaves with my dog and gun by my side.

The Yankee clipper is under her sky-sails, she cuts the sparkle and scud,   180
My eyes settle the land, I bend at her prow or shout joyously from the
    deck.

The boatmen and clam-diggers arose early and stopt for me,
I tuck'd my trowser-ends in my boots and went and had a good time;
You should have been with us that day round the chowder-kettle.

I saw the marriage of the trapper in the open air in the far west, the
    bride was a red girl,   185
Her father and his friends sat near cross-legged and dumbly smoking,
    they had moccasins to their feet and large thick blankets hanging
    from their shoulders,
On a bank lounged the trapper, he was drest mostly in skins, his
    luxuriant beard and curls protected his neck, he held his bride by the
    hand,
She had long eyelashes, her head was bare, her coarse straight locks
    descended upon her voluptuous limbs and reach'd to her feet.

The runaway slave came to my house and stopt outside,
I heard his motions crackling the twigs of the woodpile,   190
Through the swung half-door of the kitchen I saw him limpsy and weak,
And went where he sat on a log and led him in and assured him,
And brought water and fill'd a tub for his sweated body and bruis'd feet,
And gave him a room that enter'd from my own, and gave him some
    coarse clean clothes,
And remember perfectly well his revolving eyes and his awkwardness, 195
And remember putting plasters on the galls of his neck and ankles;
He staid with me a week before he was recuperated and pass'd north,
I had him sit next me at table, my fire-lock lean'd in the corner.

14

The wild gander leads his flock through the cool night,   245
Ya-honk he says, and sounds it down to me like an invitation,
The pert may suppose it meaningless, but I listening close,
Find its purpose and place up there toward the wintry sky.

The sharp-hoof'd moose of the north, the cat on the house-sill, the
    chickadee, the prairie-dog,
The litter of the grunting sow as they tug at her teats,   250
The brood of the turkey-hen and she with her half-spread wings,
I see in them and myself the same old law.

The press of my foot to the earth springs a hundred affections,
They scorn the best I can do to relate them.

I am enamour'd of growing out-doors,   255
Of men that live among cattle or taste of the ocean or woods,
Of the builders and steerers of ships and the wielders of axes and mauls,
    and the drivers of horses,
I can eat and sleep with them week in and week out.

What is commonest, cheapest, nearest, easiest, is Me,
Me going in for my chances, spending for vast returns,   260
Adorning myself to bestow myself on the first that will take me,
Not asking the sky to come down to my good will,
Scattering it freely forever.

21

I am the poet of the Body and I am the poet of the Soul,
The pleasures of heaven are with me and the pains of hell are with me,
The first I graft and increase upon myself, the latter I translate into a
    new tongue.

I am the poet of the woman the same as the man,   425
And I say it is as great to be a woman as to be a man,
And I say there is nothing greater than the mother of men.

I chant the chant of dilation or pride,
We have had ducking and deprecating about enough,
I show that size is only development.   430

Have you outstript the rest? are you the President?
It is a trifle, they will more than arrive there every one, and still pass on.

I am he that walks with the tender and growing night,
I call to the earth and sea half-held by the night.

Press close bare-bosom'd night—press close magnetic nourishing night!   435
Night of south winds—night of the large few stars!
Still nodding night—mad naked summer night.

Smile O voluptuous cool-breath'd earth!
Earth of the slumbering and liquid trees!
Earth of departed sunset—earth of the mountains misty-topt!   440
Earth of the vitreous pour of the full moon just tinged with blue!
Earth of shine and dark mottling the tide of the river!
Earth of the limpid gray of clouds brighter and clearer for my sake!
Far-swooping elbow'd earth—rich apple-blossom'd earth!
Smile, for your lover comes.   445

Prodigal, you have given me love—therefore I to you give love!
O unspeakable passionate love.

24

Walt Whitman, a kosmos, of Manhattan the son,
Turbulent, fleshy, sensual, eating, drinking and breeding,
No sentimentalist, no stander above men and women or apart from
   them,
No more modest than immodest.   500

Unscrew the locks from the doors!
Unscrew the doors themselves from their jambs!

Whoever degrades another degrades me,
And whatever is done or said returns at last to me.

Through me the afflatus° surging and surging, through me the current
   and index.   505

I speak the pass-word primeval, I give the sign of democracy,
By God! I will accept nothing which all cannot have their counterpart of
   on the same terms.

Through me many long dumb voices,
Voices of the interminable generations of prisoners and slaves,
Voices of the diseas'd and despairing and of thieves and dwarfs,   510
Voices of cycles of preparation and accretion,
And of the threads that connect the stars, and of wombs and of the
   father-stuff,
And of the rights of them the others are down upon,
Of the deform'd, trivial, flat, foolish, despised,
Fog in the air, beetles rolling balls of dung.   515

505. afflatus: Inspiration (from the Latin for "to blow on").

Through me forbidden voices,
Voices of sexes and lusts, voices veil'd and I remove the veil,
Voices indecent by me clarified and transfigur'd.

I do not press my fingers across my mouth,
I keep as delicate around the bowels as around the head and heart,   520
Copulation is no more rank to me than death is.

I believe in the flesh and the appetites,
Seeing, hearing, feeling, are miracles, and each part and tag of me is a
    miracle.

Divine am I inside and out, and I make holy whatever I touch or am
    touch'd from,
The scent of these arm-pits aroma finer than prayer,   525
This head more than churches, bibles, and all the creeds.

If I worship one thing more than another it shall be the spread of my
    own body, or any part of it,
Translucent mould of me it shall be you!
Shaded ledges and rests it shall be you!
Firm masculine colter° it shall be you!   530
Whatever goes to the tilth° of me it shall be you!
You my rich blood! your milky stream pale strippings of my life!
Breast that presses against other breasts it shall be you!
My brain it shall be your occult convolutions!
Root of wash'd sweet-flag! timorous pond-snipe! nest of guarded
    duplicate eggs! it shall be you!   535
Mix'd tussled hay of head, beard, brawn, it shall be you!
Trickling sap of maple, fibre of manly wheat, it shall be you!
Sun so generous it shall be you!
Vapors lighting and shading my face it shall be you!
You sweaty brooks and dews it shall be you!   540
Winds whose soft-tickling genitals rub against me it shall be you!
Broad muscular fields, branches of live oak, loving lounger in my
    winding paths, it shall be you!
Hands I have taken, face I have kiss'd, mortal I have ever touch'd, it
    shall be you.

46

I know I have the best of time and space, and was never measured and
    never will be measured.

530. colter: Blade or disk on a plow for cutting the earth.
531. tilth: Cultivation of land.

I tramp a perpetual journey, (come listen all!)
My signs are a rain-proof coat, good shoes, and a staff cut from the woods,
No friend of mine takes his ease in my chair,
I have no chair, no church, no philosophy,   1205
I lead no man to a dinner-table, library, exchange,
But each man and each woman of you I lead upon a knoll,
My left hand hooking you round the waist,
My right hand pointing to landscapes of continents and the public road.

Not I, not any one else can travel that road for you,   1210
You must travel it for yourself.

It is not far, it is within reach,
Perhaps you have been on it since you were born and did not know,
Perhaps it is everywhere on water and on land.

Shoulder your duds dear son, and I will mine, and let us hasten forth,   1215
Wonderful cities and free nations we shall fetch as we go.

If you tire, give me both burdens, and rest the chuff° of your hand on
    my hip,
And in due time you shall repay the same service to me,
For after we start we never lie by again.

This day before dawn I ascended a hill and look'd at the crowded heaven,   1220
And I said to my spirit *When we become the enfolders of those orbs, and
    the pleasure and knowledge of every thing in them, shall we be fill'd and
    satisfied then?*
And my spirit said *No, we but level that lift to pass and continue beyond.*

You are also asking me questions and I hear you,
I answer that I cannot answer, you must find out for yourself.

Sit a while dear son,   1225
Here are biscuits to eat and here is milk to drink,
But as soon as you sleep and renew yourself in sweet clothes, I kiss you
    with a good-by kiss and open the gate for your egress hence.

Long enough have you dream'd contemptible dreams,
Now I wash the gum from your eyes,
You must habit yourself to the dazzle of the light and of every moment
    of your life.   1230

Long have you timidly waded holding a plank by the shore,
Now I will you to be a bold swimmer,
To jump off in the midst of the sea, rise again, nod to me, shout, and
    laughingly dash with your hair.

1217. chuff: Weight.

48

I have said that the soul is not more than the body,
And I have said that the body is not more than the soul,   1270
And nothing, not God, is greater to one than one's self is,
And whoever walks a furlong without sympathy walks to his own
    funeral drest in his shroud,
And I or you pocketless of a dime may purchase the pick of the earth,
And to glance with an eye or show a bean in its pod confounds the
    learning of all times,
And there is no trade or employment but the young man following it
    may become a hero,   1275
And there is no object so soft but it makes a hub for the wheel'd universe,
And I say to any man or woman, Let your soul stand cool and composed
    before a million universes.

And I say to mankind, Be not curious about God,
For I who am curious about each am not curious about God,
(No array of terms can say how much I am at peace about God and
    about death.)   1280

I hear and behold God in every object, yet understand God not in the
    least,
Nor do I understand who there can be more wonderful than myself.

Why should I wish to see God better than this day?
I see something of God each hour of the twenty-four, and each moment
    then,
In the faces of men and women I see God, and in my own face in the glass, 1285
I find letters from God dropt in the street, and every one is sign'd by
    God's name,
And I leave them where they are, for I know that wheresoe'er I go,
Others will punctually come for ever and ever.

51

The past and present wilt—I have fill'd them, emptied them,
And proceed to fill my next fold of the future.   1320

Listener up there! what have you to confide to me?
Look in my face while I snuff° the sidle° of evening,
(Talk honestly, no one else hears you, and I stay only a minute longer.)

Do I contradict myself?
Very well then I contradict myself,
(I am large, I contain multitudes.)   1325

1322: snuff: Snuff out; **sidle:** Sidewise or stealthy movement.

I concentrate toward them that are nigh, I wait on the door-slab.

Who has done his day's work? who will soonest be through with his
    supper?
Who wishes to walk with me?

Will you speak before I am gone? will you prove already too late?

52

The spotted hawk swoops by and accuses me, he complains of my gab
    and my loitering.   1330

I too am not a bit tamed, I too am untranslatable,
I sound my barbaric yawp over the roofs of the world.

The last scud of day holds back for me,
It flings my likeness after the rest and true as any on the shadow'd wilds,
It coaxes me to the vapor and the dusk.   1335

I depart as air, I shake my white locks at the runaway sun,
I effuse my flesh in eddies, and drift it in lacy jags.

I bequeath myself to the dirt to grow from the grass I love,
If you want me again look for me under your boot-soles.

You will hardly know who I am or what I mean,   1340
But I shall be good health to you nevertheless,
And filter and fibre your blood.

Failing to fetch me at first keep encouraged,
Missing me one place search another,
I stop somewhere waiting for you.   1345

[*1855*/1891–1892]°

Date: The poem was first published in 1855 as an untitled section of *Leaves
of Grass*. It was a rough, rude, and vigorous example of antebellum American
cultural politics and free verse experimentation. The version used here, from the
sixth edition (1891–1892), is much longer, more carefully crafted, and more con-
ventionally punctuated. Sections 1–3 introduce the persona and the scope and
method of the poem; section 6 explains grass as a symbol; sections 7–10, examples
of Whitman's dynamic panoramic miniatures, are also of historical significance
regarding Native and African Americans; section 14 extends the outward sweep of
7–10; section 21 develops Whitman's theme of sex and nature; section 24 extends
the handling of the poem's persona; sections 46 and 48 offer a recapitulation of
the major themes of the poem; sections 51 and 52 deal with the absorption of the
poet's persona into the converted reader.

WALT WHITMAN [1819–1892]

When Lilacs Last in the Dooryard Bloom'd

1

When lilacs last in the dooryard bloom'd,
And the great star early droop'd in the western sky in the night,
I mourn'd, and yet shall mourn with ever-returning spring.

Ever-returning spring, trinity sure to me you bring,
Lilac blooming perennial and drooping star in the west,   5
And thought of him I love.

2

O powerful western fallen star!
O shades of night—O moody, tearful night!
O great star disappear'd—O the black murk that hides the star!
O cruel hands that hold me powerless—O helpless soul of me!   10
O harsh surrounding cloud that will not free my soul.

3

In the dooryard fronting an old farm-house near the white-wash'd
    palings,
Stands the lilac-bush tall-growing with heart-shaped leaves of rich green,
With many a pointed blossom rising delicate, with the perfume strong
    I love,
With every leaf a miracle—and from this bush in the dooryard, 15
With delicate-color'd blossoms and heart-shaped leaves of rich green,
A sprig with its flower I break.

4

In the swamp in secluded recesses,
A shy and hidden bird is warbling a song.

Solitary the thrush,   20
The hermit withdrawn to himself, avoiding the settlements,
Sings by himself a song.

Song of the bleeding throat,
Death's outlet song of life, (for well dear brother I know,
If thou wast not granted to sing thou would'st surely die.)   25

5

Over the breast of the spring, the land, amid cities,
Amid lanes and through old woods, where lately the violets peep'd from
  the ground, spotting the gray debris,
Amid the grass in the fields each side of the lanes, passing the endless
  grass,
Passing the yellow-spear'd wheat, every grain from its shroud in the
  dark-brown fields uprisen,
Passing the apple-tree blows of white and pink in the orchards,   30
Carrying a corpse to where it shall rest in the grave,
Night and day journeys a coffin.

6

Coffin that passes through lanes and streets,°
Through day and night with the great cloud darkening the land,
With the pomp of the inloop'd flags with the cities draped in black,   35
With the show of the States themselves as of crape-veil'd women
  standing,
With processions long and winding and the flambeaus° of the night,
With the countless torches lit, with the silent sea of faces and the
  unbared heads,
With the waiting depot, the arriving coffin, and the sombre faces,
With dirges through the night, with the thousand voices rising strong
  and solemn,   40
With all the mournful voices of the dirges pour'd around the coffin,
The dim-lit churches and the shuddering organs—where amid these
  you journey,
With the tolling tolling bells' perpetual clang,
Here, coffin that slowly passes,
I give you my sprig of lilac.   45

7

(Nor for you, for one alone,
Blossoms and branches green to coffins all I bring,
For fresh as the morning, thus would I chant a song for you O sane and
  sacred death.

---

33. lanes and streets: President Lincoln's funeral procession traveled from Washington to Springfield, Illinois, with stops at cities and towns to enable people to honor their assassinated president.
37. flambeaus: Flaming torches.

All over bouquets of roses,
O death, I cover you over with roses and early lilies,   50
But mostly and now the lilac that blooms the first,
Copious I break, I break the sprigs from the bushes,
With loaded arms I come, pouring for you,
For you and the coffins all of you O death.)

8

O western orb sailing the heaven,   55
Now I know what you must have meant as a month since I walk'd,
As I walk'd in silence the transparent shadowy night,
As I saw you had something to tell as you bent to me night after
    night,
As you droop'd from the sky low down as if to my side, (while the other
    stars all look'd on,)
As we wander'd together the solemn night, (for something I know not
    what kept me from sleep,)   60
As the night advanced, and I saw on the rim of the west how full you
    were of woe,
As I stood on the rising ground in the breeze in the cool transparent
    night,
As I watch'd where you pass'd and was lost in the netherward black of
    the night,
As my soul in its trouble dissatisfied sank, as where you sad orb,
Concluded, dropt in the night, and was gone.   65

9

Sing on there in the swamp,
O singer bashful and tender, I hear your notes, I hear your call,
I hear, I come presently, I understand you,
But a moment I linger, for the lustrous star has detain'd me,
The star my departing comrade holds and detains me.   70

10

O how shall I warble myself for the dead one there I loved?
And how shall I deck my song for the large sweet soul that has gone?
And what shall my perfume be for the grave of him I love?

Sea-winds blown from east and west,
Blown from the Eastern sea and blown from the Western sea, till there
    on the prairies meeting,   75
These and with these and the breath of my chant,
I'll perfume the grave of him I love.

11

O what shall I hang on the chamber walls?
And what shall the pictures be that I hang on the walls,
To adorn the burial-house of him I love?   80

Pictures of growing spring and farms and homes,
With the Fourth-month eve at sundown, and the gray smoke lucid and
      bright,
With floods of the yellow gold of the gorgeous, indolent, sinking sun,
      burning, expanding the air,
With the fresh sweet herbage under foot, and the pale green leaves of
      the trees prolific,
In the distance the flowing glaze, the breast of the river, with a wind-
      dapple here and there,   85
With ranging hills on the banks, with many a line against the sky, and
      shadows,
And the city at hand with dwellings so dense, and stacks of chimneys,
And all the scenes of life and the workshops, and the workmen
      homeward returning.

12

Lo, body and soul—this land,
My own Manhattan with spires, and the sparkling and hurrying tides,
      and the ships,   90
The varied and ample land, the South and the North in the light, Ohio's
      shores and flashing Missouri,
And ever the far-spreading prairies cover'd with grass and corn.

Lo, the most excellent sun so calm and haughty,
The violet and purple morn with just-felt breezes,
The gentle soft-born measureless light,   95
The miracle spreading, bathing all, the fulfill'd noon,
The coming eve delicious, the welcome night and the stars,
Over my cities shining all, enveloping man and land.

13

Sing on, sing on you gray-brown bird,
Sing from the swamps, the recesses, pour your chant from the bushes,   100
Limitless out of the dusk, out of the cedars and pines.

Sing on dearest brother, warble your reedy song,
Loud human song, with voice of uttermost woe.

O liquid and free and tender!
O wild and loose to my soul—O wondrous singer!   105

You only I hear—yet the star holds me, (but will soon depart,)
Yet the lilac with mastering odor holds me.

14

Now while I sat in the day and look'd forth,
In the close of the day with its light and the fields of spring, and the
     farmers preparing their crops,
In the large unconscious scenery of my land with its lakes and forests,   110
In the heavenly aerial beauty, (after the perturb'd winds and the
     storms,)
Under the arching heavens of the afternoon swift passing, and the
     voices of children and women,
The many-moving sea-tides, and I saw the ships how they sail'd,
And the summer approaching with richness, and the fields all busy with
     labor,
And the infinite separate houses, how they all went on, each with its
     meals and minutia of daily usages,   115
And the streets how their throbbings throbb'd, and the cities pent—lo,
     then and there.
Falling upon them all and among them all, enveloping me with the rest,
Appear'd the cloud, appear'd the long black trail,
And I knew death, its thought, and the sacred knowledge of death.

Then with the knowledge of death as walking one side of me,   120
And the thought of death close-walking the other side of me,
And I in the middle as with companions, and as holding the hands of
     companions,
I fled forth to the hiding receiving night that talks not,
Down to the shores of the water, the path by the swamp in the dimness,
To the solemn shadowy cedars and ghostly pines so still.   125

And the singer so shy to the rest receiv'd me,
The gray-brown bird I know receiv'd us comrades three,
And he sang the carol of death, and a verse for him I love.

From deep secluded recesses,
From the fragrant cedars and the ghostly pines so still,   130
Came the carol of the bird.

And the charm of the carol rapt me,
As I held as if by their hands my comrades in the night,
And the voice of my spirit tallied the song of the bird.

Come lovely and soothing death,   135
Undulate round the world, serenely arriving, arriving,

In the day, in the night, to all, to each,
Sooner or later delicate death.

Prais'd be the fathomless universe,
For life and joy, and for objects and knowledge curious,   140
And for love, sweet love—but praise! praise! praise!
For the sure-enwinding arms of cool-enfolding death.

Dark mother always gliding near with soft feet,
Have none chanted for thee a chant of fullest welcome?
Then I chant it for thee, I glorify thee above all,   145
I bring thee a song that when thou must indeed come, come
    unfalteringly.

Approach strong deliveress,
When it is so, when thou hast taken them I joyously sing the dead,
Lost in the loving floating ocean of thee,
Laved in the flood of thy bliss O death.   150

From me to thee glad serenades,
Dances for thee I propose saluting thee, adornments and feastings for thee,
And the sights of the open landscape and the high-spread sky are fitting,
And life and the fields, and the huge and thoughtful night.

The night in silence under many a star,   155
The ocean shore and the husky whispering wave whose voice I know,
And the soul turning to thee O vast and well-veil'd death,
And the body gratefully nestling close to thee.

Over the tree-tops I float thee a song,
Over the rising and sinking waves, over the myriad fields and the prairies
    wide,   160
Over the dense-pack'd cities all and the teeming wharves and ways,
I float this carol with joy, with joy to thee O death.

15

To the tally of my soul,
Loud and strong kept up the gray-brown bird,
With pure deliberate notes spreading filling the night.   165

Loud in the pines and cedars dim,
Clear in the freshness moist and the swamp-perfume,
And I with my comrades there in the night.

While my sight that was bound in my eyes unclosed,
As to long panoramas of visions.   170

And I saw askant the armies,
I saw as in noiseless dreams hundreds of battle-flags,
Borne through the smoke of the battles and pierc'd with missiles I saw
  them,
And carried hither and yon through the smoke, and torn and bloody,
And at last but a few shreds left on the staffs, (and all in silence,)   175
And the staffs all splinter'd and broken.

I saw battle-corpses, myriads of them,
And the white skeletons of young men, I saw them,
I saw the debris and debris of all the slain soldiers of the war,
But I saw they were not as was thought,   180
They themselves were fully at rest, they suffer'd not,
The living remain'd and suffer'd, the mother suffer'd,
And the wife and the child and the musing comrade suffer'd,
And the armies that remain'd suffer'd.

16

Passing the visions, passing the night,   185
Passing, unloosing the hold of my comrades' hands,
Passing the song of the hermit bird and the tallying song of my soul,
Victorious song, death's outlet song, yet varying ever-altering song,
As low and wailing, yet clear the notes, rising and falling, flooding the
  night,
Sadly sinking and fainting, as warning and warning, and yet again
  bursting with joy,   190
Covering the earth and filling the spread of the heaven,
As that powerful psalm in the night I heard from recesses,
Passing, I leave thee lilac with heart-shaped leaves,
I leave thee there in the door-yard, blooming, returning with spring.

I cease from my song for thee,   195
From my gaze on thee in the west, fronting the west, communing with
  thee,
O comrade lustrous with silver face in the night.

Yet each to keep and all, retrievements out of the night,
The song, the wondrous chant of the gray-brown bird,
And the tallying chant, the echo arous'd in my soul,   200
With the lustrous and drooping star with the countenance full of woe,
With the holders holding my hand nearing the call of the bird,
Comrades mine and I in the midst, and their memory ever to keep, for
  the dead I loved so well,
For the sweetest, wisest soul of all my days and lands — and this for his
  dear sake,

Lilac and star and bird twined with the chant of my soul,   205
There in the fragrant pines and the cedars dusk and dim.

[*1865;* 1891–1892]°

Date: This is one of four elegies written by Whitman on the death of President
Abraham Lincoln, 14 April 1865, and first published as an addendum to *Drum-
Taps* called "Sequel to *Drum-Taps.*" Whitman later added the *Drum-Taps* volume
to *Leaves of Grass.* The version used here is from the sixth edition of *Leaves of
Grass* (1891–1892).

WALT WHITMAN [1819–1892]

A Noiseless Patient Spider

A noiseless patient spider,
I mark'd where on a little promontory it stood isolated,
Mark'd how to explore the vacant vast surrounding,
It launch'd forth filament, filament, filament, out of itself,
Ever unreeling them, ever tirelessly speeding them.   5

And you O my soul where you stand,
Surrounded, detached, in measureless oceans of space,
Ceaselessly musing, venturing, throwing, seeking the spheres to connect
    them,
Till the bridge you will need be form'd, till the ductile anchor hold,
Till the gossamer thread you fling catch somewhere, O my soul.   10

[1868–1881]

MATTHEW ARNOLD [1822–1888]

Dover Beach

The sea is calm tonight.
The tide is full, the moon lies fair
Upon the straits; on the French coast the light

Gleams and is gone; the cliffs of England stand,
Glimmering and vast, out in the tranquil bay.   5
Come to the window, sweet is the night-air!
Only, from the long line of spray
Where the sea meets the moon-blanched land,
Listen! you hear the grating roar
Of pebbles which the waves draw back, and fling,   10
At their return, up the high strand,
Begin, and cease, and then again begin,
With tremulous cadence slow, and bring
The eternal note of sadness in.

Sophocles long ago   15
Heard it on the Aegean, and it brought
Into his mind the turbid ebb and flow
Of human misery; we
Find also in the sound a thought,
Hearing it by this distant northern sea.   20

The Sea of Faith
Was once, too, at the full, and round earth's shore
Lay like the folds of a bright girdle furled.
But now I only hear
Its melancholy, long, withdrawing roar,   25
Retreating, to the breath
Of the night-wind, down the vast edges drear
And naked shingles° of the world.   *pebble-covered beaches*

Ah, love, let us be true
To one another! for the world, which seems   30
To lie before us like a land of dreams,
So various, so beautiful, so new,
Hath really neither joy, nor love, nor light,
Nor certitude, nor peace, nor help for pain;
And we are here as on a darkling plain   35
Swept with confused alarms of struggle and flight,
Where ignorant armies clash by night.

[*c. 1851;* 1867]

EMILY DICKINSON   [1830–1886]

I felt a Funeral, in my Brain

I felt a Funeral, in my Brain,
And Mourners to and fro
Kept treading—treading—till it seemed
That Sense was breaking through—

And when they all were seated,   5
A Service, like a Drum—
Kept beating—beating—till I thought
My Mind was going numb—

And then I heard them lift a Box
And creak across my Soul   10
With those same Boots of Lead, again,
Then Space—began to toll,

As all the Heavens were a Bell,
And Being, but an Ear,
And I, and Silence, some strange Race   15
Wrecked, solitary, here—

And then a Plank in Reason, broke,
And I dropped down, and down—
And hit a World, at every plunge,
And Finished knowing—then—   20

[c. 1861; 1896]

EMILY DICKINSON   [1830–1886]

Much Madness is divinest Sense

Much Madness is divinest Sense—
To a discerning Eye—
Much Sense—the starkest Madness—
'Tis the Majority

In this, as All, prevail—   5
Assent—and you are sane—
Demur—you're straightway dangerous—
And handled with a Chain—

[*c. 1862;* 1890]

EMILY DICKINSON   [1830–1886]

I heard a Fly buzz—
when I died

I heard a Fly buzz—when I died—
The Stillness in the Room
Was like the Stillness in the Air—
Between the Heaves of Storm—

The Eyes around—had wrung them dry—   5
And Breaths were gathering firm
For that last Onset—when the King
Be witnessed—in the Room—

I willed my Keepsakes—Signed away
What portion of me be   10
Assignable—and then it was
There interposed a Fly—

With Blue—uncertain stumbling Buzz—
Between the light—and me—
And then the Windows failed—and then   15
I could not see to see—

[*c. 1862;* 1890]

EMILY DICKINSON   [1830–1886]

Because I could not stop for Death

Because I could not stop for Death—
He kindly stopped for me—
The Carriage held but just Ourselves—
And Immortality.

We slowly drove—He knew no haste   5
And I had put away
My labor and my leisure too,
For His Civility—

We passed the School, where Children strove
At Recess—in the Ring—   10
We passed the Fields of Gazing Grain—
We passed the Setting Sun—

Or rather—He passed Us—
The Dews drew quivering and chill—
For only Gossamer, my Gown—   15
My Tippet°—only Tulle°—   *scarf/silk net*

We paused before a House that seemed
A Swelling of the Ground—
The Roof was scarcely visible—
The Cornice—in the Ground—   20

Since then—'tis Centuries—and yet
Feels shorter than the Day
I first surmised the Horses' Heads
Were toward Eternity—

                                                        [*c. 1863;* 1890]

CHRISTINA ROSSETTI [1830–1894]

Song

When I am dead, my dearest,
  Sing no sad songs for me;
Plant thou no roses at my head,
  Nor shady cypress tree:
Be the green grass above me   5
  With showers and dewdrops wet;
And if thou wilt, remember,
  And if thou wilt, forget.

I shall not see the shadows,
  I shall not feel the rain;   10
I shall not hear the nightingale
  Sing on, as if in pain:
And dreaming through the twilight
  That doth not rise nor set,
Haply I may remember,   15
  And haply may forget.

[1862]

THOMAS HARDY [1840–1928]

The Convergence of the Twain

Lines on the Loss of the Titanic°

1

In a solitude of the sea
Deep from human vanity,
And the Pride of Life that planned her, stilly couches she.

Titanic: A famous luxury ocean liner, largest of its time and considered unsink-
able. It collided with an iceberg on its maiden voyage, 15 April 1912, and sank. Of
some 2,200 people aboard, more than 1,500 were lost.

2

Steel chambers, late the pyres
Of her salamandrine° fires,   5
Cold currents thrid,° and turn to rhythmic tidal lyres.   *thread*

3

Over the mirrors meant
To glass the opulent
The sea-worm crawls—grotesque, slimed, dumb, indifferent.

4

Jewels in joy designed   10
To ravish the sensuous mind
Lie lightless, all their sparkles bleared and black and blind.

5

Dim moon-eyed fishes near
Gaze at the gilded gear
And query: "What does this vaingloriousness down here?"   15

6

Well: while was fashioning
This creature of cleaving wing,
The Immanent Will that stirs and urges everything

7

Prepared a sinister mate
For her—so gaily great—   20
A Shape of Ice, for the time far and dissociate.

8

And as the smart ship grew
In stature, grace, and hue,
In shadowy silent distance grew the Iceberg too.

9

Alien they seemed to be: 25
No mortal eye could see
The intimate welding of their later history,

5. salamandrine: Fierce, inextinguishable (the lizardlike salamander supposedly
is able to resist or live in fire).

10

Or sign that they were bent
    By paths coincident
On being anon twin halves of one august event,   30

11

Till the Spinner of the Years
    Said "Now!" And each one hears,
And consummation comes, and jars two hemispheres.

[1912]

GERARD MANLEY HOPKINS   [1844–1889]

The Windhover°

To Christ Our Lord

I caught this morning morning's minion,° king-   *darling, favorite*
    dom of daylight's dauphin,° dapple-dáwn-drawn Falcon,
        in his riding
Of the rólling level úndernéath him steady air, and stríding
Hígh there, how he rung upon the rein of a wimpling° wing   *rippling*
In his ecstasy! then off, off forth on swing,   5
    As a skate's heel sweeps smooth on a bow-bend: the hurl and gliding
    Rebuffed the big wind. My heart in hiding
Stírred for a bird,—the achieve of, the mastery of the thing!

Brute beauty and valour and act, oh, air, pride, plume, here
    Buckle! AND the fire that breaks from thee then, a billion   10
Times told lovelier, more dangerous, O my chevalier!°   *knight, nobleman*
    Nó wonder of it: shéer plód makes plóugh down síllion°   *furrow*
Shíne, and blue-bleak embers, ah my dear,
    Fall, gáll themselves, and gásh gold-vermilion.

[*1877;* 1918]

Windhover: A kestrel (a species of small hawk), which seems to hover in the wind.
2. dauphin: Heir (eldest son of the king of France).

GERARD MANLEY HOPKINS   [1844–1889]

God's Grandeur

The world is charged with the grándeur of God.
  It will flame out, like shining from shook foil;°   *shaken gold foil*
  It gathers to a greatness, like the ooze of oil°   *(from olives)*
Crushed. Why do men then now not reck° his rod°?   *recognize/discipline*
Génerátions have trod, have trod, have trod;   5
  And all is seared with trade; bleared, smeared, with toil;
  And wears man's smudge and shares man's smell: the soil
Is bare now, nor can foot feel, being shod.

Ánd, for° all this, náture is never spent;   *despite*
  There lives the dearest freshness deep down things;   10
And though the last lights off the black West went
  Oh, morning, at the brown brink eastward, springs—
Because the Holy Ghost óver the bent
  World broods with warm breast and with ah! bright wings.

[*1877*; 1918]

GERARD MANLEY HOPKINS   [1844–1889]

Pied° Beauty   *multicolored, variegated*

Glóry be to God for dappled things—
  For skies of couple-colour as a brinded° cow;   *streaked*
    For rose-moles all in stipple upon trout that swim;
Fresh-firecoal chestnut-fálls; fínches' wings;
  Lándscape plotted and pieced—fold, fallow, and plough;   5
    And áll trádes, their gear and tackle and trim.

All things counter, original, spáre, stránge;
  Whatever is fickle, freckled (who knows how?)
    With swift, slow; sweet, sour; adazzle, dim;
He fathers-forth whose beauty is pást chánge: 10
          Práise hím.

[*1877*; 1918]

GERARD MANLEY HOPKINS   [1844–1889]

Spring and Fall

to a young child

Márgarét, áre you gríeving
Over Goldengrove unleaving?
Leáves, líke the things of mán, you
With your fresh thoughts care for, can you?
Áh! ás the héart grows ólder   5
It will come to such sights colder
By and by, nor spare a sigh
Though worlds of wanwood leafmeal° lie;
And yet you *will* weep and know why.
Now no matter, child, the name: 10
Sórrow's spríngs áre the sáme.
Nor mouth had, no nor mind, expressed
What héart héard of, ghóst° guéssed: *spirit*
It ís the blíght man was bórn for,
It is Margaret you mourn for.   15

[*1880;* 1918]

8. **wanwood leafmeal:** Colorless forest with scattered leaves.

A. E. HOUSMAN   [1859–1936]

Loveliest of trees,
the cherry now

Loveliest of trees, the cherry now
Is hung with bloom along the bough,
And stands about the woodland ride
Wearing white for Eastertide.

Now, of my threescore years and ten,   5
Twenty will not come again,

And take from seventy springs a score,
It only leaves me fifty more.

And since to look at things in bloom
Fifty springs are little room,   10
About the woodlands I will go
To see the cherry hung with snow.

[1896]

A. E. HOUSMAN   [1859–1936]

To an Athlete Dying Young

The time you won your town the race
We chaired you through the market-place;
Man and boy stood cheering by,
And home we brought you shoulder-high.

To-day, the road all runners come,   5
Shoulder-high we bring you home,
And set you at your threshold down,
Townsman of a stiller town.

Smart lad, to slip betimes away
From fields where glory does not stay   10
And early though the laurel grows
It withers quicker than the rose.

Eyes the shady night has shut
Cannot see the record cut,°   *broken*
And silence sounds no worse than cheers   15
After earth has stopped the ears:

Now you will not swell the rout
Of lads that wore their honours out,
Runners whom renown outran
And the name died before the man.   20

So set, before its echoes fade,
The fleet foot on the sill of shade,
And hold to the low lintel up
The still-defended challenge-cup.

And round that early-laurelled head   25
Will flock to gaze the strengthless dead,
And find unwithered on its curls
The garland briefer than a girl's.

[1896]

A. E. HOUSMAN   [1859–1936]

"Terence, this is stupid stuff"

"Terence,° this is stupid stuff:
You eat your victuals fast enough;
There can't be much amiss, 'tis clear,
To see the rate you drink your beer.
But oh, good Lord, the verse you make,   5
It gives a chap the belly-ache.
The cow, the old cow, she is dead;
It sleeps well, the horned head:
We poor lads, 'tis our turn now
To hear such tunes as killed the cow.   10
Pretty friendship 'tis to rhyme
Your friends to death before their time
Moping melancholy mad:
Come, pipe a tune to dance to, lad."

Why, if 'tis dancing you would be,   15
There's brisker pipes than poetry.
Say, for what were hop-yards meant,
Or why was Burton° built on Trent?°   *famous brewing town/river in England*
Oh many a peer of England brews
Livelier liquor than the Muse,   20
And malt does more than Milton can
To justify God's ways to man.°
Ale, man, ale's the stuff to drink
For fellows whom it hurts to think:

1. **Terence:** *The Poems of Terence Hearsay* was the title Housman originally intended for the volume in which this poem was published. Later he changed it to *The Shropshire Lad.*
22. **justify . . . man:** See *Paradise Lost* 1.26.

Look into the pewter pot   25
To see the world as the world's not.
And faith, 'tis pleasant till 'tis past:
The mischief is that 'twill not last.
Oh I have been to Ludlow° fair   *market town in Shropshire*
And left my necktie God knows where,   30
And carried half-way home, or near,
Pints and quarts of Ludlow beer:
Then the world seemed none so bad,
And I myself a sterling lad;
And down in lovely muck I've lain,   35
Happy till I woke again.
Then I saw the morning sky:
Heigho, the tale was all a lie;
The world, it was the old world yet,
I was I, my things were wet,   40
And nothing now remained to do
But begin the game anew.

    Therefore, since the world has still
Much good, but much less good than ill,
And while the sun and moon endure   45
Luck's a chance, but trouble's sure,
I'd face it as a wise man would,
And train for ill and not for good.
'Tis true, the stuff I bring for sale
Is not so brisk a brew as ale: 50
Out of a stem that scored° the hand   *cut*
I wrung it in a weary land.
But take it: if the smack is sour,
The better for the embittered hour;
It should do good to heart and head   55
When your soul is in my soul's stead;
And I will friend you, if I may,
In the dark and cloudy day.

    There was a king reigned in the East:
There, when kings will sit to feast,   60
They get their fill before they think
With poisoned meat and poisoned drink.
He gathered all that springs to birth
From the many-venomed earth;
First a little, thence to more,   65
He sampled all her killing store;

And easy, smiling, seasoned sound,
Sate the king when healths went round.
They put arsenic in his meat
And stared aghast to watch him eat;   70
They poured strychnine in his cup
And shook to see him drink it up:
They shook, they stared as white's their shirt:
Them it was their poison hurt.
—I tell the tale that I heard told.   75
Mithridates,° he died old.

[1896]

76. **Mithridates:** King of Pontus, first century B.C.E., who according to Pliny's
Natural History made himself immune to poison by taking small doses daily.

WILLIAM BUTLER YEATS [1865–1939]

The Second Coming°

Turning and turning in the widening gyre
The falcon cannot hear the falconer;
Things fall apart; the centre cannot hold;
Mere anarchy is loosed upon the world,
The blood-dimmed tide is loosed, and everywhere   5
The ceremony of innocence is drowned;
The best lack all conviction, while the worst
Are full of passionate intensity.

Surely some revelation is at hand;
Surely the Second Coming is at hand.   10

The Second Coming: Alludes to Matthew 24:3–44, on the return of Christ at the
end of the present age. Yeats viewed history as a series of 2,000-year cycles
(imaged as gyres, cone-shaped motions). The birth of Christ in Bethlehem
brought to an end the cycle that ran from the Babylonians through the Greeks
and Romans. The approach of the year 2000, then, anticipated for Yeats the end
of another era (the Christian age). Yeats wrote this poem shortly after the Russian
Revolution of 1917 (lines 4–8), which may have confirmed his sense of imminent
change and of a new beginning of an unpredictable nature (Yeats expected the
new era to be violent and despotic).

The Second Coming! Hardly are those words out
When a vast image out of *Spiritus Mundi*°
Troubles my sight: somewhere in sands of the desert
A shape with lion body and the head of a man,
A gaze blank and pitiless as the sun,   15
Is moving its slow thighs, while all about it
Reel shadows of the indignant desert birds.
The darkness drops again; but now I know
That twenty centuries of stony sleep
Were vexed to nightmare by a rocking cradle,   20
And what rough beast, its hour come round at last,
Slouches towards Bethlehem to be born?

[1921]

12. *Spiritus Mundi*: Latin, "the spirit of the universe." Yeats believed in a Great Memory, a universal storehouse of symbolic images from the past. Individuals, drawing on it for images, are put in touch with the soul of the universe.

WILLIAM BUTLER YEATS   [1865–1939]

Leda and the Swan°

A sudden blow: the great wings beating still
Above the staggering girl, her thighs caressed
By the dark webs, her nape caught in his bill,
He holds her helpless breast upon his breast.

How can those terrified vague fingers push   5
The feathered glory from her loosening thighs?
And how can body, laid in that white rush,
But feel the strange heart beating where it lies?

Leda and the Swan: In Greek mythology, Leda was seduced (or raped) by Zeus, who approached her in the form of a swan. She gave birth to Helen, whose abduction by Paris gave rise to the Trojan War (referred to in line 10). The Greek forces were headed by Agamemnon, who was killed (line 11) upon his return to Greece by his wife, Clytemnestra, daughter of Leda by her husband, Tyndareus. Yeats regarded Zeus's visit as a "violent annunciation" of the founding of Greek civilization, with parallels to the annunciation to Mary (Luke 1:26–38), 2,000 years later, of the coming of the Christian age. See the note to "The Second Coming" for Yeats's view of historical eras (p. 499).

A shudder in the loins engenders there
The broken wall, the burning roof and tower   10
And Agamemnon dead.
                          Being so caught up,
So mastered by the brute blood of the air,
Did she put on his knowledge with his power
Before the indifferent beak could let her drop?   15

                                                              [1928]

WILLIAM BUTLER YEATS [1865–1939]

Among School Children°

1

I walk through the long schoolroom questioning;
A kind old nun in a white hood replies;
The children learn to cipher° and to sing,   *do arithmetic*
To study reading-books and history,
To cut and sew, be neat in everything   5
In the best modern way — the children's eyes
In momentary wonder stare upon
A sixty-year-old smiling public man.

2

I dream of a Ledaean° body, bent
Above a sinking fire, a tale that she   10
Told of a harsh reproof, or trivial event
That changed some childish day to tragedy —
Told, and it seemed that our two natures blent
Into a sphere from youthful sympathy,

Among School Children: In February 1926, Yeats visited a Montessori school as
part of his duties as a senator. In March he wrote in his diary the following topic
for a poem: "School children and the thought that life will waste them, perhaps
that no possible life can fulfill their own dreams or even their teacher's hope.
Bring in the old thought that life prepares for what never happens."
9. Ledaean: Helen-like (referring to Helen, daughter of Leda — see the note to
"Leda and the Swan" on p. 500). Here and in lines 19–28 Yeats was thinking of
Maud Gonne, a beautiful actress and Irish nationalist whom he loved desperately
for many years but who refused to marry him.

Or else, to alter Plato's parable,   15
Into the yolk and white of the one shell.°

3

And thinking of that fit of grief or rage
I look upon one child or t'other there
And wonder if she stood so at that age—
For even daughters of the swan can share   20
Something of every paddler's heritage—
And had that colour upon cheek or hair,
And thereupon my heart is driven wild:
She stands before me as a living child.

4

Her present image floats into the mind—   25
Did Quattrocento° finger fashion it
Hollow of cheek as though it drank the wind
And took a mess of shadows for its meat?
And I though never of Ledaean kind
Had pretty plumage once—enough of that,   30
Better to smile on all that smile, and show
There is a comfortable kind of old scarecrow.

5

What youthful mother, a shape upon her lap
Honey of generation had betrayed,°
And that must sleep, shriek, struggle to escape   35
As recollection or the drug decide,

16. Into . . . shell: To explain love, in Plato's *Symposium*, Aristophanes describes
primeval humans as round with "four hands and four feet, back and sides forming a circle, one head with two faces." Fearful of their power, Zeus cut them in
two, as one would divide an egg. After separation, each half desired to be reunited
with its opposite: "Each of us is . . . but the half of a human being, . . . forever
seeking his missing half."
26. Quattrocento: The fifteenth century, as a period in Italian art and literature.
34. Honey . . . betrayed: Yeats wrote in a note, "I have taken the 'honey of generation' from Porphyry's essay on 'The Cave of the Nymphs' but find no warrant in
Porphyry for considering it the 'drug' that destroys the 'recollection' of pre-natal
freedom." Porphyry (a third-century Neoplatonic philosopher) described the
sweetness of honey as allegorically representing "the pleasure arising from copulation." For Yeats, however, the honey of generation seems to blot out the memory
of prenatal happiness, thus "betraying" an infant into consenting to be born into
this world.

Would think her son, did she but see that shape
With sixty or more winters on its head,
A compensation for the pang of his birth,
Or the uncertainty of his setting forth?   40

6

Plato thought nature but a spume that plays
Upon a ghostly paradigm of things;°
Solider Aristotle played the taws
Upon the bottom of a king of kings;°
World-famous golden-thighed Pythagoras°   45
Fingered upon a fiddle-stick or strings
What a star sang and careless Muses heard:
Old clothes upon old sticks to scare a bird.°

7

Both nuns and mothers worship images,°
But those the candles light are not as those   50
That animate a mother's reveries,
But keep a marble or a bronze repose.
And yet they too break hearts—O Presences
That passion, piety or affection knows,
And that all heavenly glory symbolize—   55
O self-born mockers of man's enterprise;

8

Labour is blossoming or dancing where
The body is not bruised to pleasure soul,
Nor beauty born out of its own despair,
Nor blear-eyed wisdom out of midnight oil.   60

41–42. but . . . things: Plato thought that the world of nature is merely an appearance ("spume") that covers the world of ideal, spiritual, and mathematical realities ("ghostly paradigm").

43–44. Solider . . . kings: Aristotle, who was tutor to Alexander the Great and presumably disciplined him by whippings ("played the taws"), was "solider" than Plato in that he believed that nature itself had reality.

45. Pythagoras: Greek philosopher (6th century B.C.E.) whose study of mathematics and music supposedly led to his discovery of the music of the spheres, the harmonies that hold the universe in order.

48. Old . . . bird: Yeats's dismissal of the three philosophers just named.

49. nuns . . . images: Nuns worship religious images; mothers worship mental images of their own children.

O chestnut-tree, great-rooted blossomer,
Are you the leaf, the blossom or the bole?°   *trunk*
O body swayed to music, O brightening glance,
How can we know the dancer from the dance?

[1928]

WILLIAM BUTLER YEATS   [1865–1939]

Sailing to Byzantium°

1

That is no country for old men. The young
In one another's arms, birds in the trees
— Those dying generations — at their song,
The salmon-falls, the mackerel-crowded seas,
Fish, flesh, or fowl, commend all summer long   5
Whatever is begotten, born, and dies.
Caught in that sensual music all neglect
Monuments of unaging intellect.

2

An aged man is but a paltry thing,
A tattered coat upon a stick, unless   10
Soul clap its hands and sing, and louder sing
For every tatter in its mortal dress,
Nor is there singing school but studying

Sailing to Byzantium: Yeats wrote in *A Vision* (1925): "I think if I could be given
a month of Antiquity and leave to spend it where I chose, I would spend it in
Byzantium [modern Istanbul] a little before Justinian [ruled 527 to 565] opened
St. Sophia and closed the Academy of Plato. . . . I think that in early Byzantium,
and maybe never before or since in recorded history, religious, aesthetic and practical life were one, and that architect and artificers . . . spoke to the multitude
and the few alike. The painter and the mosaic worker, the worker in gold and
silver, the illuminator of Sacred Books were almost impersonal, almost perhaps
without the consciousness of individual design, absorbed in their subject matter
and that the vision of a whole people" (3.3). Byzantium becomes for Yeats a symbol of eternity, a place of perfection where the growth and change that characterize nature and physical life do not occur.

Monuments of its own magnificence;
And therefore I have sailed the seas and come   15
To the holy city of Byzantium.

3

O sages standing in God's holy fire
As in the gold mosaic of a wall,
Come from the holy fire, perne in a gyre,°
And be the singing-masters of my soul.   20
Consume my heart away; sick with desire
And fastened to a dying animal
It knows not what it is; and gather me
Into the artifice of eternity.

4

Once out of nature I shall never take   25
My bodily form from any natural thing,
But such a form as Grecian goldsmiths make
Of hammered gold and gold enamelling
To keep a drowsy Emperor awake;°
Or set upon a golden bough to sing   30
To lords and ladies of Byzantium
Of what is past, or passing, or to come.

                                                          [1928]

19. perne . . . gyre: Whirl in a spiral motion (a *perne* is a spool or bobbin on
which something is wound; a *gyre* is a spiral).
25–29. Yeats wrote in a note, "I have read somewhere that in the Emperor's
palace at Byzantium was a tree made of gold and silver, and artificial birds that
sang." He may have been thinking of Hans Christian Andersen's *The Emperor's
Nightingale*.

EDWIN ARLINGTON ROBINSON   [1869–1935]

Richard Cory

Whenever Richard Cory went down town,
We people on the pavement looked at him:
He was a gentleman from sole to crown,
Clean favored, and imperially slim.

And he was always quietly arrayed,   5
And he was always human when he talked;
But still he fluttered pulses when he said,
"Good-morning," and he glittered when he walked.

And he was rich—yes, richer than a king—
And admirably schooled in every grace: 10
In fine, we thought that he was everything
To make us wish that we were in his place.

So on we worked, and waited for the light,
And went without the meat, and cursed the bread;
And Richard Cory, one calm summer night,   15
Went home and put a bullet through his head.

[1897]

STEPHEN CRANE   [1871–1900]

Do not weep, maiden,
for war is kind

Do not weep, maiden, for war is kind.
Because your lover threw wild hands toward the sky
And the affrighted steed ran on alone,
Do not weep.
War is kind.   5

    Hoarse, booming drums of the regiment,
    Little souls who thirst for fight,
    These men were born to drill and die.
    The unexplained glory flies above them,
    Great is the Battle-God, great, and his Kingdom—   10
    A field where a thousand corpses lie.

Do not weep, babe, for war is kind.
Because your father tumbled in the yellow trenches,
Raged at his breast, gulped and died,
Do not weep.   15
War is kind.

Swift blazing flag of the regiment,
Eagle with crest of red and gold,
These men were born to drill and die.
Point for them the virtue of slaughter,   20
Make plain to them the excellence of killing
And a field where a thousand corpses lie.

Mother whose heart hung humble as a button
On the bright splendid shroud of your son,
Do not weep.   25
War is kind.

[1899]

PAUL LAURENCE DUNBAR   [1872–1906]

We Wear the Mask

We wear the mask that grins and lies,
It hides our cheeks and shades our eyes,—
This debt we pay to human guile;
With torn and bleeding hearts we smile,
And mouth with myriad subtleties.   5

Why should the world be over-wise,
In counting all our tears and sighs?
Nay, let them only see us, while
    We wear the mask.

We smile, but, O great Christ, our cries   10
To thee from tortured souls arise.
We sing, but oh the clay is vile
Beneath our feet, and long the mile;
But let the world dream otherwise,
    We wear the mask!   15

[1896]

ROBERT FROST [1874–1963]

After Apple-Picking

My long two-pointed ladder's sticking through a tree
Toward heaven still,
And there's a barrel that I didn't fill
Beside it, and there may be two or three
Apples I didn't pick upon some bough.   5
But I am done with apple-picking now.
Essence of winter sleep is on the night,
The scent of apples: I am drowsing off.
I cannot rub the strangeness from my sight
I got from looking through a pane of glass   10
I skimmed this morning from the drinking trough
And held against the world of hoary grass.
It melted, and I let it fall and break.
But I was well
Upon my way to sleep before it fell,   15
And I could tell
What form my dreaming was about to take.
Magnified apples appear and disappear,
Stem end and blossom end,
And every fleck of russet showing clear.   20
My instep arch not only keeps the ache,
It keeps the pressure of a ladder-round.
I feel the ladder sway as the boughs bend.
And I keep hearing from the cellar bin
The rumbling sound   25
Of load on load of apples coming in.
For I have had too much
Of apple-picking: I am overtired
Of the great harvest I myself desired.
There were ten thousand thousand fruit to touch,   30
Cherish in hand, lift down, and not let fall.
For all
That struck the earth,
No matter if not bruised or spiked with stubble,
Went surely to the cider-apple heap   35
As of no worth.
One can see what will trouble

This sleep of mine, whatever sleep it is.
Were he not gone,
The woodchuck could say whether it's like his   40
Long sleep, as I describe its coming on,
Or just some human sleep.

[1914]

ROBERT FROST   [1874–1963]

The Road Not Taken

Two roads diverged in a yellow wood,
And sorry I could not travel both
And be one traveler, long I stood
And looked down one as far as I could
To where it bent in the undergrowth;   5

Then took the other, as just as fair,
And having perhaps the better claim,
Because it was grassy and wanted wear;
Though as for that, the passing there
Had worn them really about the same,   10

And both that morning equally lay
In leaves no step had trodden black.
Oh, I kept the first for another day!
Yet knowing how way leads on to way,
I doubted if I should ever come back.   15

I shall be telling this with a sigh
Somewhere ages and ages hence:
Two roads diverged in a wood, and I—
I took the one less traveled by,
And that has made all the difference.   20

[1916]

ROBERT FROST   [1874–1963]

Birches

When I see birches bend to left and right
Across the lines of straighter darker trees,
I like to think some boy's been swinging them.
But swinging doesn't bend them down to stay
As ice storms do. Often you must have seen them   5
Loaded with ice a sunny winter morning
After a rain. They click upon themselves
As the breeze rises, and turn many-colored
As the stir cracks and crazes their enamel.
Soon the sun's warmth makes them shed crystal shells   10
Shattering and avalanching on the snow crust—
Such heaps of broken glass to sweep away
You'd think the inner dome of heaven had fallen.
They are dragged to the withered bracken by the load,
And they seem not to break; though once they are bowed   15
So low for long, they never right themselves:
You may see their trunks arching in the woods
Years afterwards, trailing their leaves on the ground
Like girls on hands and knees that throw their hair
Before them over their heads to dry in the sun.   20
But I was going to say when Truth broke in
With all her matter of fact about the ice storm,
I should prefer to have some boy bend them
As he went out and in to fetch the cows—
Some boy too far from town to learn baseball,   25
Whose only play was what he found himself,
Summer or winter, and could play alone.
One by one he subdued his father's trees
By riding them down over and over again
Until he took the stiffness out of them,   30
And not one but hung limp, not one was left
For him to conquer. He learned all there was
To learn about not launching out too soon
And so not carrying the tree away
Clear to the ground. He always kept his poise   35
To the top branches, climbing carefully
With the same pains you use to fill a cup

Up to the brim, and even above the brim.
Then he flung outward, feet first, with a swish,
Kicking his way down through the air to the ground.   40
So was I once myself a swinger of birches.
And so I dream of going back to be.
It's when I'm weary of considerations,
And life is too much like a pathless wood
Where your face burns and tickles with the cobwebs   45
Broken across it, and one eye is weeping
From a twig's having lashed across it open.
I'd like to get away from earth awhile
And then come back to it and begin over.
May no fate willfully misunderstand me   50
And half grant what I wish and snatch me away
Not to return. Earth's the right place for love:
I don't know where it's likely to go better.
I'd like to go by climbing a birch tree,
And climb black branches up a snow-white trunk   55
Toward heaven, till the tree could bear no more,
But dipped its top and set me down again.
That would be good both going and coming back.
One could do worse than be a swinger of birches.

[1916]

ROBERT FROST   [1874–1963]

Stopping by Woods on a Snowy Evening

Whose woods these are I think I know.
His house is in the village, though;
He will not see me stopping here
To watch his woods fill up with snow.

My little horse must think it queer   5
To stop without a farmhouse near
Between the woods and frozen lake
The darkest evening of the year.

He gives his harness bells a shake
To ask if there is some mistake.   10
The only other sound's the sweep
Of easy wind and downy flake.

The woods are lovely, dark, and deep,
But I have promises to keep,
And miles to go before I sleep,   15
And miles to go before I sleep.

[1923]

GERTRUDE STEIN   [1874–1946]

Susie Asado

Sweet sweet sweet sweet sweet tea.
    Susie Asado.
Sweet sweet sweet sweet sweet tea.
    Susie Asado.
Susie Asado which is a told tray sure.   5
A lean on the shoe this means slips slips hers.
When the ancient light grey is clean it is yellow, it is a silver seller.
This is a please this is a please there are the saids to jelly. These are
the wets these say the sets to leave a crown to Incy.
Incy is short for incubus.   10
A pot. A pot is a beginning of a rare bit of trees. Trees tremble, the
old vats are in bobbles, bobbles which shade and shove and render
clean, render clean must.
    Drink pups.
Drink pups drink pups lease a sash hold, see it shine and a bobolink 15
has pins. It shows a nail.
What is a nail. A nail is unison.
Sweet sweet sweet sweet sweet tea.

[1913]

WALLACE STEVENS   [1879–1955]

The Emperor of Ice-Cream

Call the roller of big cigars,
The muscular one, and bid him whip
In kitchen cups concupiscent curds.
Let the wenches dawdle in such dress
As they are used to wear, and let the boys   5
Bring flowers in last month's newspapers.
Let be be finale of seem.
The only emperor is the emperor of ice-cream.

Take from the dresser of deal.
Lacking the three glass knobs, that sheet   10
On which she embroidered fantails once
And spread it so as to cover her face.
If her horny feet protrude, they come
To show how cold she is, and dumb.
Let the lamp affix its beam.   15
The only emperor is the emperor of ice-cream.

[1923]

WALLACE STEVENS   [1879–1955]

Disillusionment of Ten O'Clock

The houses are haunted
By white night-gowns.
None are green,
Or purple with green rings,
Or green with yellow rings,   5
Or yellow with blue rings.
None of them are strange,
With socks of lace
And beaded ceintures.°   *girdles*

People are not going   10
To dream of baboons and periwinkles.
Only, here and there, an old sailor,
Drunk and asleep in his boots,
Catches tigers
In red weather.   15

[1923]

WALLACE STEVENS [1879–1955]

Sunday Morning

I

Complacencies of the peignoir,° and late   *negligee*
Coffee and oranges in a sunny chair,
And the green freedom of a cockatoo
Upon a rug mingle to dissipate
The holy hush of ancient sacrifice.   5
She dreams a little, and she feels the dark
Encroachment of that old catastrophe,
As a calm darkens among water-lights.
The pungent oranges and bright, green wings
Seem things in some procession of the dead,   10
Winding across wide water, without sound.
The day is like wide water, without sound,
Stilled for the passing of her dreaming feet
Over the seas, to silent Palestine,
Dominion of the blood and sepulchre.   15

II

Why should she give her bounty to the dead?
What is divinity if it can come
Only in silent shadows and in dreams?
Shall she not find in comforts of the sun,
In pungent fruit and bright, green wings, or else   20
In any balm or beauty of the earth,
Things to be cherished like the thought of heaven?

Divinity must live within herself:
Passions of rain, or moods in falling snow;
Grievings in loneliness, or unsubdued   25
Elations when the forest blooms; gusty
Emotions on wet roads on autumn nights;
All pleasures and all pains, remembering
The bough of summer and the winter branch.
These are the measures destined for her soul.   30

III

Jove in the clouds had his inhuman birth.
No mother suckled him, no sweet land gave
Large-mannered motions to his mythy mind
He moved among us, as a muttering king,
Magnificent, would move among his hinds,   35
Until our blood, commingling, virginal,
With heaven, brought such requital to desire
The very hinds discerned it, in a star.
Shall our blood fail? Or shall it come to be
The blood of paradise? And shall the earth   40
Seem all of paradise that we shall know?
The sky will be much friendlier then than now,
A part of labor and a part of pain,
And next in glory to enduring love,
Not this dividing and indifferent blue.   45

IV

She says, "I am content when wakened birds,
Before they fly, test the reality
Of misty fields, by their sweet questionings;
But when the birds are gone, and their warm fields
Return no more, where, then, is paradise?"   50
There is not any haunt of prophecy,
Nor any old chimera of the grave,
Neither the golden underground, nor isle
Melodious, where spirits gat° them home,   *got*
Nor visionary south, nor cloudy palm   55
Remote on heaven's hill, that has endured
As April's green endures; or will endure
Like her remembrance of awakened birds,
Or her desire for June and evening, tipped
By the consummation of the swallow's wings.   60

V

She says, "But in contentment I still feel
The need of some imperishable bliss."
Death is the mother of beauty; hence from her,
Alone, shall come fulfilment to our dreams
And our desires. Although she strews the leaves   65
Of sure obliteration on our paths,
The path sick sorrow took, the many paths
Where triumph rang its brassy phrase, or love
Whispered a little out of tenderness,
She makes the willow shiver in the sun   70
For maidens who were wont to sit and gaze
Upon the grass, relinquished to their feet.
She causes boys to pile new plums and pears
On disregarded plate. The maidens taste
And stray impassioned in the littering leaves.   75

VI

Is there no change of death in paradise?
Does ripe fruit never fall? Or do the boughs
Hang always heavy in that perfect sky,
Unchanging, yet so like our perishing earth,
With rivers like our own that seek for seas   80
They never find, the same receding shores
That never touch with inarticulate pang?
Why set the pear upon those river-banks
Or spice the shores with odors of the plum?
Alas, that they should wear our colors there,   85
The silken weavings of our afternoons,
And pick the strings of our insipid lutes!
Death is the mother of beauty, mystical,
Within whose burning bosom we devise
Our earthly mothers waiting, sleeplessly.   90

VII

Supple and turbulent, a ring of men
Shall chant in orgy on a summer morn
Their boisterous devotion to the sun,
Not as a god, but as a god might be,
Naked among them, like a savage source.   95
Their chant shall be a chant of paradise,
Out of their blood, returning to the sky;
And in their chant shall enter, voice by voice,
The windy lake wherein their lord delights,

The trees, like serafin,° and echoing hills,   *seraphim* 100
That choir among themselves long afterward.
They shall know well the heavenly fellowship
Of men that perish and of summer morn.
And whence they came and whither they shall go
The dew upon their feet shall manifest.   105

VIII

She hears, upon that water without sound,
A voice that cries, "The tomb in Palestine
Is not the porch of spirits lingering.
It is the grave of Jesus, where he lay."
We live in an old chaos of the sun,   110
Or old dependency of day and night,
Or island solitude, unsponsored, free,
Of that wide water, inescapable.
Deer walk upon our mountains, and the quail
Whistle about us their spontaneous cries;   115
Sweet berries ripen in the wilderness;
And, in the isolation of the sky,
At evening, casual flocks of pigeons make
Ambiguous undulations as they sink,
Downward to darkness, on extended wings.   120

[1923]

WILLIAM CARLOS WILLIAMS [1883–1963]

The Red Wheelbarrow

so much depends
upon

a red wheel
barrow

glazed with rain   5
water

beside the white
chickens.

[1923]

WILLIAM CARLOS WILLIAMS [1883–1963]

Spring and All

By the road to the contagious hospital
under the surge of the blue
mottled clouds driven from the
northeast—a cold wind. Beyond, the
waste of broad, muddy fields   5
brown with dried weeds, standing and fallen

patches of standing water
the scattering of tall trees

All along the road the reddish
purplish, forked, upstanding, twiggy   10
stuff of bushes and small trees
with dead, brown leaves under them
leafless vines—

Lifeless in appearance, sluggish
dazed spring approaches—   15

They enter the new world naked,
cold, uncertain of all
save that they enter. All about them
the cold, familiar wind—

Now the grass, tomorrow   20
the stiff curl of wildcarrot leaf

One by one objects are defined—
It quickens: clarity, outline of leaf

But now the stark dignity of
entrance—Still, the profound change   25
has come upon them: rooted, they
grip down and begin to awaken

[1923]

WILLIAM CARLOS WILLIAMS   [1883–1963]

This Is Just to Say

I have eaten
the plums
that were in
the icebox

and which   5
you were probably
saving
for breakfast

Forgive me
they were delicious   10
so sweet
and so cold

[1934]

EZRA POUND   [1885–1972]

The River-Merchant's Wife:
A Letter

While my hair was still cut straight across my forehead
I played about the front gate, pulling flowers.
You came by on bamboo stilts, playing horse,
You walked about my seat, playing with blue plums.
And we went on living in the village of Chokan: 5
Two small people, without dislike or suspicion.

At fourteen I married My Lord you.
I never laughed, being bashful.
Lowering my head, I looked at the wall.
Called to, a thousand times, I never looked back.   10

At fifteen I stopped scowling,
I desired my dust to be mingled with yours

Forever and forever and forever.
Why should I climb the look out?

At sixteen you departed,   15
You went into far Ku-to-yen, by the river of swirling eddies,
And you have been gone five months.
The monkeys make sorrowful noise overhead.

You dragged your feet when you went out.
By the gate now, the moss is grown, the different mosses,   20
Too deep to clear them away!
The leaves fall early this autumn, in wind.
The paired butterflies are already yellow with August
Over the grass in the West garden;
They hurt me. I grow older.   25
If you are coming down through the narrows of the river Kiang,
Please let me know beforehand,
And I will come out to meet you
            As far as Cho-fu-Sa.

                                                                    By Rihaku°

                                                                    [1915]

By Rihaku: An adaptation of a Chinese poem by the famous poet Li Po (701–762
C.E.), whose Japanese name is Rihaku.

H. D. [HILDA DOOLITTLE]   [1886–1961]

Garden

I
You are clear
O rose, cut in rock,
hard as the descent of hail.

I could scrape the colour
from the petals   5
like spilt dye from a rock.

If I could break you
I could break a tree.

If I could stir
I could break a tree—   10
I could break you.

II

O wind, rend open the heat,
cut apart the heat,
rend it to tatters.

Fruit cannot drop   15
through this thick air—
fruit cannot fall into heat
that presses up and blunts
the points of pears
and rounds the grapes.   20

Cut the heat—
plough through it,
turning it on either side
of your path.

                                                              [1916]

MARIANNE MOORE   [1887–1972]

Poetry

I, too, dislike it: there are things that are important beyond all this fiddle.
   Reading it, however, with a perfect contempt for it, one discovers in
      it after all, a place for the genuine.
         Hands that can grasp, eyes
            that can dilate, hair that can rise   5
               if it must, these things are important not because a

high-sounding interpretation can be put upon them but because they are
   useful. When they become so derivative as to become unintelligible,
      the same thing may be said for all of us, that we
         do not admire what   10
            we cannot understand: the bat
               holding on upside down or in quest of something to

eat, elephants pushing, a wild horse taking a roll, a tireless wolf under
    a tree, the immovable critic twitching his skin like a horse that feels a
               flea, the base-
  ball fan, the statistician— 15
    nor is it valid
      to discriminate against "business documents and

school-books"; all these phenomena are important. One must make a
               distinction
  however: when dragged into prominence by half poets, the result is
               not poetry,
  nor till the poets among us can be 20
    "literalists of
    the imagination"—above
      insolence and triviality and can present

for inspection, "imaginary gardens with real toads in them," shall we
               have
  it. In the meantime, if you demand on the one hand, 25
  the raw material of poetry in
    all its rawness and
    that which is on the other hand
      genuine, you are interested in poetry.

                                         [1921]

EDITH SITWELL [1887–1964]

Lullaby

Though the world has slipped and gone,
Sounds my loud discordant cry
Like the steel birds' song on high:
"Still one thing is left—the Bone!"
Then out danced the Babioun.°   *baboon* 5

She sat in the hollow of the sea—
A socket whence the eye's put out—
She sang to the child a lullaby
(The steel birds' nest was thereabout).

"Do, do, do, do—   10
Thy mother's hied to the vaster race:
The Pterodactyl made its nest
And laid a steel egg in her breast—
Under the Judas-colored sun.
She'll work no more, nor dance, nor moan,   15
And I am come to take her place
Do, do.

There's nothing left but earth's low bed—
(The Pterodactyl fouls its nest):
But steel wings fan thee to thy rest,   20
And wingless truth and larvae lie
And eyeless hope and handless fear—
All these for thee as toys are spread,
Do—do—

Red is the bed of Poland, Spain,   25
And thy mother's breast, who has grown wise
In that fouled nest. If she could rise.
Give birth again,
In wolfish pelt she'd hide thy bones
To shield thee from the world's long cold,   30
And down on all fours shouldst thou crawl
For thus from no height canst thou fall—
Do, do.

She'd give no hands: there's nought to hold
And nought to make: there's dust to sift,   35
But no food for the hands to lift.
Do, do.

Heed my ragged lullaby,
Fear not living, fear not chance;
All is equal—blindness, sight,   40
There is no depth, there is no height:
Do, do.

The Judas-colored sun is gone,
And with the Ape thou art alone—
Do,   45
    Do."

[1942]

ROBINSON JEFFERS   [1887–1962]

Hurt Hawks

I

The broken pillar of the wing jags from the clotted shoulder,
The wing trails like a banner in defeat,
No more to use the sky forever but live with famine
And pain a few days: cat nor coyote
Will shorten the week of waiting for death, there is game without talons.   5
He stands under the oak-bush and waits
The lame feet of salvation; at night he remembers freedom
And flies in a dream, the dawns ruin it.
He is strong and pain is worse to the strong, incapacity is worse.
The curs of the day come and torment him   10
At distance, no one but death the redeemer will humble that head,
The intrepid readiness, the terrible eyes.
The wild God of the world is sometimes merciful to those
That ask mercy, not often to the arrogant.
You do not know him, you communal people, or you have forgotten
    him;   15
Intemperate and savage, the hawk remembers him;
Beautiful and wild, the hawks, and men that are dying, remember him.

II

I'd sooner, except the penalties, kill a man than a hawk; but the great
    redtail
Had nothing left but unable misery
From the bone too shattered for mending, the wing that trailed under
    his talons when he moved.   20
We had fed him six weeks, I gave him freedom,
He wandered over the foreland hill and returned in the evening, asking
    for death,
Not like a beggar, still eyed with the old
Implacable arrogance. I gave him the lead gift in the twilight. What fell
    was relaxed,
Owl-downy, soft feminine feathers; but what   25
Soared: the fierce rush: the night-herons by the flooded river cried fear
    at its rising
Before it was quite unsheathed from reality.

[1928]

T. S. ELIOT [1888–1965]

The Love Song of
J. Alfred Prufrock

S'io credesse che mia risposta fosse
A persona che mai tornasse al mondo,
Questa fiamma staria senza piu scosse.
Ma perciocche giammai di questo fondo
Non torno vivo alcun, s'i'odo il vero,
Senza tema d'infamia ti rispondo.°

Let us go then, you and I,
When the evening is spread out against the sky
Like a patient etherised upon a table;
Let us go, through certain half-deserted streets,
The muttering retreats   5
Of restless nights in one-night cheap hotels
And sawdust restaurants with oyster-shells:
Streets that follow like a tedious argument
Of insidious intent
To lead you to an overwhelming question . . .   10
Oh, do not ask, "What is it?"
Let us go and make our visit.

In the room the women come and go
Talking of Michelangelo.

The yellow fog that rubs its back upon the window-panes,   15
The yellow smoke that rubs its muzzle on the window-panes
Licked its tongue into the corners of the evening,

Epigraph: "If I thought that my answer were being made to someone who would
ever return to earth, this flame would remain without further movement; but
since no one has ever returned alive from this depth, if what I hear is true, I
answer you without fear of infamy" (Dante, *Inferno* 27.61–66). Dante encounters
Guido de Montefeltro in the eighth circle of hell, where souls are trapped within
flames (tongues of fire) as punishment for giving evil counsel. Guido tells Dante
details about his evil life only because he assumes that Dante is on his way to an
even deeper circle in hell and will never return to earth and be able to repeat what
he has heard.

Lingered upon the pools that stand in drains,
Let fall upon its back the soot that falls from chimneys,
Slipped by the terrace, made a sudden leap,   20
And seeing that it was a soft October night,
Curled once about the house, and fell asleep.

　　And indeed there will be time
For the yellow smoke that slides along the street,
Rubbing its back upon the window-panes;   25
There will be time, there will be time
To prepare a face to meet the faces that you meet;
There will be time to murder and create,
And time for all the works and days° of hands
That lift and drop a question on your plate;   30
Time for you and time for me,
And time yet for a hundred indecisions,
And for a hundred visions and revisions,
Before the taking of a toast and tea.

　　In the room the women come and go   35
Talking of Michelangelo.

　　And indeed there will be time
To wonder, "Do I dare?" and, "Do I dare?"
Time to turn back and descend the stair,
With a bald spot in the middle of my hair—   40
[They will say: "How his hair is growing thin!"]
My morning coat, my collar mounting firmly to the chin,
My necktie rich and modest, but asserted by a simple pin—
[They will say: "But how his arms and legs are thin!"]
Do I dare   45
Disturb the universe?
In a minute there is time
For decisions and revisions which a minute will reverse.

　　For I have known them all already, known them all:—
Have known the evenings, mornings, afternoons,   50
I have measured out my life with coffee spoons;
I know the voices dying with a dying fall°

---

29. works and days: *Works and Days* is the title of a didactic poem about farming by the Greek poet Hesiod (eighth century B.C.E.) that includes instruction about doing each task at the proper time.
52. a dying fall: An allusion to Shakespeare's *Twelfth Night* (1.1.4): "That strain [of music] again! It had a dying fall" (a cadence that falls away).

Beneath the music from a farther room.
    So how should I presume?

And I have known the eyes already, known them all—   55
The eyes that fix you in a formulated phrase,
And when I am formulated, sprawling on a pin,
When I am pinned and wriggling on the wall,
Then how should I begin
To spit out all the butt-ends of my days and ways?   60
    And how should I presume?

And I have known the arms already, known them all—
Arms that are braceleted and white and bare
[But in the lamplight, downed with light brown hair!]
Is it perfume from a dress   65
That makes me so digress?
Arms that lie along a table, or wrap about a shawl.
    And should I then presume?
    And how should I begin?

                    .   .   .

Shall I say, I have gone at dusk through narrow streets   70
And watched the smoke that rises from the pipes
Of lonely men in shirt-sleeves, leaning out of windows? . . .

    I should have been a pair of ragged claws
Scuttling across the floors of silent seas.

                    .   .   .

And the afternoon, the evening, sleeps so peacefully!   75
Smoothed by long fingers,
Asleep . . . tired . . . or it malingers,
Stretched on the floor, here beside you and me.
Should I, after tea and cakes and ices,
Have the strength to force the moment to its crisis?   80
But though I have wept and fasted, wept and prayed,
Though I have seen my head [grown slightly bald] brought in upon a
            platter,°
I am no prophet—and here's no great matter;
I have seen the moment of my greatness flicker,

---

82. head . . . platter: As a reward for dancing before King Herod, Salome, his
stepdaughter, asked for the head of John the Baptist to be presented to her on a
platter (Matthew 14:1–12; Mark 6:17–28).

And I have seen the eternal Footman hold my coat, and snicker,   85
And in short, I was afraid.

   And would it have been worth it, after all,
After the cups, the marmalade, the tea,
Among the porcelain, among some talk of you and me,
Would it have been worth while,   90
To have bitten off the matter with a smile,
To have squeezed the universe into a ball
To roll it toward some overwhelming question,
To say: "I am Lazarus,° come from the dead,
Come back to tell you all, I shall tell you all"—   95
If one, settling a pillow by her head,
   Should say: "That is not what I meant at all.
   That is not it, at all."

   And would it have been worth it, after all,
Would it have been worth while,   100
After the sunsets and the dooryards and the sprinkled streets,
After the novels, after the teacups, after the skirts that trail along the
      floor—
And this, and so much more?—
It is impossible to say just what I mean!
But as if a magic lantern threw the nerves in patterns on a screen: 105
Would it have been worth while
If one, settling a pillow or throwing off a shawl,
And turning toward the window, should say:
   "That is not it at all,
   That is not what I meant, at all."   110

       •   •   •

No! I am not Prince Hamlet, nor was meant to be;
Am an attendant lord, one that will do
To swell a progress,° start a scene or two,
Advise the prince; no doubt, an easy tool,
Deferential, glad to be of use,   115
Politic, cautious, and meticulous;
Full of high sentence,° but a bit obtuse;   *sententiousness*
At times, indeed, almost ridiculous—
Almost, at times, the Fool.

94. Lazarus: Either the beggar Lazarus, who in Luke 16:19–31 did not return
from the dead, or Jesus' friend Lazarus, who did (John 11:1–44).
113. progress: Ceremonial journey made by a royal court.

I grow old . . . I grow old . . .   120
I shall wear the bottoms of my trousers rolled.°   *turned up, with cuffs*

 Shall I part my hair behind? Do I dare to eat a peach?
I shall wear white flannel trousers, and walk upon the beach.
I have heard the mermaids singing, each to each.

 I do not think that they will sing to me.   125

 I have seen them riding seaward on the waves
Combing the white hair of the waves blown back
When the wind blows the water white and black.

 We have lingered in the chambers of the sea
By sea-girls wreathed with seaweed red and brown   130
Till human voices wake us, and we drown.

[1917]

T. S. ELIOT   [1888–1965]

Preludes

I

The winter evening settles down
With smell of steaks in passageways.
Six o'clock.
The burnt-out ends of smoky days.
And now a gusty shower wraps   5
The grimy scraps
Of withered leaves about your feet
And newspapers from vacant lots;
The showers beat
On broken blinds and chimney-pots,   10
And at the corner of the street
A lonely cab-horse steams and stamps.
And then the lighting of the lamps.

II

The morning comes to consciousness
Of faint stale smells of beer   15
From the sawdust-trampled street
With all its muddy feet that press

To early coffee-stands.
With the other masquerades
That time resumes,   20
One thinks of all the hands
That are raising dingy shades
In a thousand furnished rooms.

III

You tossed a blanket from the bed,
You lay upon your back, and waited;   25
You dozed, and watched the night revealing
The thousand sordid images
Of which your soul was constituted;
They flickered against the ceiling.
And when all the world came back   30
And the light crept up between the shutters
And you heard the sparrows in the gutters,
You had such a vision of the street
As the street hardly understands;
Sitting along the bed's edge, where   35
You curled the papers from your hair,
Or clasped the yellow soles of feet
In the palms of both soiled hands.

IV

His soul stretched tight across the skies
That fade behind a city block,   40
Or trampled by insistent feet
At four and five and six o'clock;
And short square fingers stuffing pipes,
And evening newspapers, and eyes
Assured of certain certainties,   45
The conscience of a blackened street
Impatient to assume the world.

    I am moved by fancies that are curled
Around these images, and cling:
The notion of some infinitely gentle   50
Infinitely suffering thing.

    Wipe your hand across your mouth, and laugh;
The worlds revolve like ancient women
Gathering fuel in vacant lots.

                                                              [1917]

JOHN CROWE RANSOM [1888–1974]

Bells for John Whiteside's Daughter

There was such speed in her little body,
And such lightness in her footfall,
It is no wonder her brown study°
Astonishes us all.

Her wars were bruited in our high window.   5
We looked among orchard trees and beyond
Where she took arms against her shadow,
Or harried unto the pond

The lazy geese, like a snow cloud
Dripping their snow on the green grass,   10
Tricking and stopping, sleepy and proud,
Who cried in goose, Alas,

For the tireless heart within the little
Lady with rod that made them rise
From their noon apple-dreams and scuttle   15
Goose-fashion under the skies!

But now go the bells, and we are ready,
In one house we are sternly stopped
To say we are vexed at her brown study,
Lying so primly propped.   20

[1924]

3. **brown study:** Being deeply absorbed in one's thoughts; reverie.

CLAUDE McKAY [1890–1948]

America

Although she feeds me bread of bitterness,
And sinks into my throat her tiger's tooth,
Stealing my breath of life, I will confess

I love this cultured hell that tests my youth!
Her vigor flows like tides into my blood,   5
Giving me strength erect against her hate.
Her bigness sweeps my being like a flood.
Yet as a rebel fronts a king in state,
I stand within her walls with not a shred
Of terror, malice, not a word of jeer.   10
Darkly I gaze into the days ahead,
And see her might and granite wonders there,
Beneath the touch of Time's unerring hand,
Like priceless treasures sinking in the sand.

[1922]

EDNA ST. VINCENT MILLAY   [1892–1950]

Wild Swans

I looked in my heart while the wild swans went over.
And what did I see I had not seen before?
Only a question less or a question more;
Nothing to match the flight of wild birds flying.
Tiresome heart, forever living and dying,   5
House without air, I leave you and lock your door.
Wild swans, come over the town, come over
The town again, trailing your legs and crying!

[1921]

WILFRED OWEN   [1893–1918]

Dulce et Decorum Est

Bent double, like old beggars under sacks,
Knock-kneed, coughing like hags, we cursed through sludge,
Till on the haunting flares we turned our backs
And towards our distant rest began to trudge.

Men marched asleep. Many had lost their boots   5
But limped on, blood-shod. All went lame; all blind;
Drunk with fatigue; deaf even to the hoots
Of tired, outstripped Five-Nines° that dropped behind.

Gas! GAS! Quick, boys!—An ecstasy of fumbling,
Fitting the clumsy helmets just in time;   10
But someone still was yelling out and stumbling
And flound'ring like a man in fire or lime . . .
Dim, through the misty panes° and thick green light,   *of a gas mask*
As under a green sea, I saw him drowning.

In all my dreams, before my helpless sight,   15
He plunges at me, guttering, choking, drowning.

If in some smothering dreams you too could pace
Behind the wagon that we flung him in,
And watch the white eyes writhing in his face,
His hanging face, like a devil's sick of sin;   20
If you could hear, at every jolt, the blood
Come gargling from the froth-corrupted lungs,
Obscene as cancer, bitter as the cud
Of vile, incurable sores on innocent tongues,—
My friend, you would not tell with such high zest   25
To children ardent for some desperate glory,
The old Lie: Dulce et decorum est
Pro patria mori.°

                                                                    [1920]

8. **Five-Nines:** 5.9-inch caliber shells.
27–28. **Dulce . . . mori:** It is sweet and fitting / to die for one's country (Horace, *Odes* 3.12.13).

E. E. CUMMINGS [1894–1962]

in Just-

in Just-
spring   when the world is mud-
luscious the little
lame balloonman

whistles   far   and wee

and eddieandbill come
running from marbles and
piracies and it's
spring

when the world is puddle-wonderful   10

the queer
old balloonman whistles
far   and   wee
and bettyandisbel come dancing

from hop-scotch and jump-rope and   15

it's
spring
and
   the

      goat-footed   20

balloonMan   whistles
far
and
wee

[1923]

E. E. CUMMINGS [1894–1962]

pity this busy monster,manunkind

pity this busy monster,manunkind,

not. Progress is a comfortable disease:
your victim(death and life safely beyond)

plays with the bigness of his littleness
—electrons deify one razorblade
into a mountainrange;lenses extend   5

unwish through curving wherewhen till unwish
returns on its unself.

                    A world of made
is not a world of born—pity poor flesh   10

and trees,poor stars and stones,but never this
fine specimen of hypermagical

ultraomnipotence. We doctors know

a hopeless case if—listen:there's a hell
of a good universe next door;let's go   15

                                                        [1944]

JEAN TOOMER   [1894–1967]

Reapers

Black reapers with the sound of steel on stones
Are sharpening scythes. I see them place the hones
In their hip-pockets as a thing that's done.
And start their silent swinging, one by one.
Black horses drive a mower through the weeds.   5
And there, a field rat, startled, squealing bleeds.
His belly close to ground. I see the blade,
Blood-stained, continue cutting weeds and shade.

                                                        [1923]

LOUISE BOGAN   [1897–1970]

Women

Women have no wilderness in them,
They are provident instead,
Content in the tight hot cell of their hearts
To eat dusty bread.

They do not see cattle cropping red winter grass,   5
They do not hear
Snow water going down under culverts
Shallow and clear.

They wait, when they should turn to journeys,
They stiffen, when they should bend.   10
They use against themselves that benevolence
To which no man is friend.

They cannot think of so many crops to a field
Or of clean wood cleft by an axe.
Their love is an eager meaninglessness   15
Too tense, or too lax.

They hear in every whisper that speaks to them
A shout and a cry.
As like as not, when they take life over their door-sills
They should let it go by.   20

[1923]

HART CRANE   [1899–1932]

My Grandmother's Love Letters

There are no stars tonight
But those of memory.
Yet how much room for memory there is
In the loose girdle of soft rain.

There is even room enough   5
For the letters of my mother's mother,
Elizabeth,
That have been pressed so long
Into a corner of the roof
That they are brown and soft,   10
And liable to melt as snow.

Over the greatness of such space
Steps must be gentle.

It is all hung by an invisible white hair.
It trembles as birch limbs webbing the air.   15

And I ask myself:

"Are your fingers long enough to play
Old keys that are but echoes:
Is the silence strong enough
To carry back the music to its source   20
And back to you again
As though to her?"

Yet I would lead my grandmother by the hand
Through much of what she would not understand;
And so I stumble. And the rain continues on the roof   25
With such a sound of gently pitying laughter.

[1926]

STERLING A. BROWN   [1901–1989]

Riverbank Blues

A man git his feet set in a sticky mudbank,
A man git dis yellow water in his blood,
No need for hopin', no need for doin',
Muddy streams keep him fixed for good.

Little Muddy, Big Muddy, Moreau and Osage,   5
Little Mary's, Big Mary's, Cedar Creek,
Flood deir muddy water roundabout a man's roots,
Keep him soaked and stranded and git him weak.

Lazy sun shinin' on a little cabin,
Lazy moon glistenin' over river trees;   10
Ole river whisperin', lappin' 'gainst de long roots:
"Plenty of rest and peace in these. . . ."

Big mules, black loam, apple and peach trees,
But seems lak de river washes us down
Past de rich farms, away from de fat lands,   15
Dumps us in some ornery riverbank town.

Went down to the river, sot me down an' listened,
Heard de water talkin' quiet, quiet lak an' slow:
"Ain' no need fo' hurry, take yo' time, take yo' time. . . ."
Heard it sayin'—*"Baby, hyeahs de way life go. . . ."*   20

Dat is what it tole me as I watched it slowly rollin',
But somp'n way inside me rared up an' say,
"Better be movin'. . . better be travelin'. . .
Riverbank'll git you ef you stay. . . ."

Towns are sinkin' deeper, deeper in de riverbank,   25
Takin' on de ways of deir sulky Ole Man—
Takin' on his creepy ways, takin' on his evil ways,
"Bes' git way, a long way . . . whiles you can.

"Man got his sea too lak de Mississippi
Ain't got so long for a whole lot longer way,   30
Man better move some, better not git rooted
Muddy water fool you, ef you stay. . . ."

[1932]

LANGSTON HUGHES   [1902–1967]

The Negro Speaks of Rivers

I've known rivers:
I've known rivers ancient as the world and older than the flow of human
    blood in human veins.

My soul has grown deep like the rivers.

I bathed in the Euphrates when dawns were young.
I built my hut near the Congo and it lulled me to sleep.   5
I looked upon the Nile and raised the pyramids above it.
I heard the singing of the Mississippi when Abe Lincoln went down to
    New Orleans, and I've seen its muddy bosom turn all golden in the
    sunset.

I've known rivers:
Ancient, dusky rivers.

My soul has grown deep like the rivers.   10

[1926]

LANGSTON HUGHES [1902–1967]

Harlem

What happens to a dream deferred?

   Does it dry up
   like a raisin in the sun?
   Or fester like a sore—
   And then run?   5
   Does it stink like rotten meat?
   Or crust and sugar over—
   like a syrupy sweet?

   Maybe it just sags
   like a heavy load.   10

   Or does it explode?

[1951]

COUNTEE CULLEN [1903–1946]

Incident

for Eric Walrond

Once riding in old Baltimore,
   Heart-filled, head-filled with glee,
I saw a Baltimorean
   Keep looking straight at me.

Now I was eight and very small,   5
   And he was no whit bigger,
And so I smiled, but he poked out
   His tongue, and called me, "Nigger."

I saw the whole of Baltimore
   From May until December;   10
Of all the things that happened there
   That's all that I remember.

[1925]

LOUIS ZUKOFSKY [1904–1978]

From "A" 15

An
   hinny
by
   stallion
out of   5
   she-ass

He neigh ha lie low h'who y'he gall mood
So roar cruel hire
Lo to achieve an eye leer rot off
Mass th'lo low o loam echo   10
How deal me many coeval yammer
Naked on face of white rock — sea.
Then I said: Liveforever my nest
Is arable hymn
Shore she root to water   15
Dew anew to branch.

Wind: Yahweh° at Iyyob°   *Israel's deity/Job*
Mien His roar "Why yammer
Measly make short hates oh
By milling bleat doubt?   20
Eye sore gnaw key heaver haul its core
Weigh as I lug where hide any?
If you — had you towed beside the roots?
How goad Him — you'd do it by now —
My sum My made day a key to daw?   25
O Me not there allheal — a cave.

All mouth deny hot bough?
O Me you're raw — Heaven pinned Dawn stars
Brine I heard choir and weigh by care —
Why your ear would call by now Elohim:°   *Hebrew for God* 30
Where was soak — bid lot tie in hum —
How would you have known to hum
How would you all oats rose snow lay
Assáy how'd a rock light rollick ore
Had the rush in you curb, ah bay,   35
Bay the shophar yammer *heigh horse*"

Wind: Yahweh at Iyyob "Why yammer,"
Wind: Iyyob at Yahweh, "Why yammer
How cold the mouth achieved echo."
Wind: Yahweh at Iyyob "Why yammer   40
Ha neigh now behēmoth° and share I see see your make   *beast*
Giddy pair—stones—whose rages go
Weigh raw all gay where how spill lay who"
Wind: Iyyob
"Rain without sun hated? *hurt no one*   45
In two we shadow, how hide any."

The traffic below,
sound of it a wind
eleven stories
below: *The Parkway*   50
no parking there ever:
the deaths as
after it might be said
"ordered," the one
the two old   55
songsters would not
live to see—
the death of
the young man,
who had possibly   60
alleviated
the death of
the oldest
vagrantly back he
might have thought   65
from vying culturally
with the Russian
Puritan Bear—
to vagary of
Bear hug and King   70
Charles° losing his head—   *Charles I of England*
and the other
a decade younger
never international
emissary   75
at least not
for his President,
aged in a suburb
dying maundering

the language —   80
American — impatient now
sometimes extreme clarity —
to hurrȳ
his compost
to the hill
his grave —   85
(distance
   a gastank)

he would
miss   90
living thru the
assassination

[1978]

STANLEY KUNITZ [b. 1905]

Father and Son

Now in the suburbs and the falling light
I followed him, and now down sandy road
Whiter than bone-dust, through the sweet
Curdle of fields, where the plums
Dropped with their load of ripeness, one by one.   5
Mile after mile I followed, with skimming feet,
After the secret master of my blood,
Him, steeped in the odor of ponds, whose indomitable love
Kept me in chains. Strode years; stretched into bird;
Raced through the sleeping country where I was young,   10
The silence unrolling before me as I came,
The night nailed like an orange to my brow.

How should I tell him my fable and the fears,
How bridge the chasm in a casual tone,
Saying, "The house, the stucco one you built,   15
We lost. Sister married and went from home,
And nothing comes back, it's strange, from where she goes.
I lived on a hill that had too many rooms:
Light we could make, but not enough of warmth,

And when the light failed, I climbed under the hill.   20
The papers are delivered every day;
I am alone and never shed a tear."

At the water's edge, where the smothering ferns lifted
Their arms, "Father!" I cried, "Return! You know
The way. I'll wipe the mudstains from your clothes;   25
No trace, I promise, will remain. Instruct
Your son, whirling between two wars,
In the Gemara° of your gentleness,
For I would be a child to those who mourn
And brother to the foundlings of the field   30
And friend of innocence and all bright eyes.
O teach me how to work and keep me kind."

Among the turtles and the lilies he turned to me
The white ignorant hollow of his face.

[1944]

28. **Gemara:** The second division of the Talmud; it is a commentary on Jewish
civil and religious laws.

W. H. AUDEN   [1907–1973]

As I Walked Out One Evening

As I walked out one evening,
   Walking down Bristol Street,
The crowds upon the pavement
   Were fields of harvest wheat.

And down by the brimming river   5
   I heard a lover sing
Under an arch of the railway:
   "Love has no ending.

"I'll love you, dear, I'll love you
   Till China and Africa meet,   10
And the river jumps over the mountain
   And the salmon sing in the street,

"I'll love you till the ocean
   Is folded and hung up to dry
And the seven stars° go squawking   15
   Like geese about the sky.

The years shall run like rabbits,
   For in my arms I hold
The Flower of the Ages,
   And the first love of the world."   20

But all the clocks in the city
   Began to whirr and chime:
"O let not Time deceive you,
   You cannot conquer Time.

"In the burrows of the Nightmare   25
   Where Justice naked is,
Time watches from the shadow
   And coughs when you would kiss.

"In headaches and in worry
   Vaguely life leaks away,   30
And Time will have his fancy
   To-morrow or to-day.

"Into many a green valley
   Drifts the appalling snow;
Time breaks the threaded dances   35
   And the diver's brilliant bow.

"O plunge your hands in water,
   Plunge them in up to the wrist;
Stare, stare in the basin
   And wonder what you've missed.   40

"The glacier knocks in the cupboard,
   The desert sighs in the bed,
And the crack in the tea-cup opens
   A lane to the land of the dead.

"Where the beggars raffle the banknotes°   45
   And the Giant° is enchanting to Jack,

---

15. the seven stars: An echo of the traditional counting song "Green Grow the Rushes, O": "What are your seven, O? / Seven for the seven stars in the sky."
45–48. "Where the beggars . . .": This stanza alludes to and—through social satire and sexual innuendo—inverts the milieu of nursery rhymes and a counting song.
46. Giant: From the fairy tale "Jack the Giant-Killer."

And the Lily-white Boy° is a Roarer,°
   And Jill° goes down on her back.

"O look, look in the mirror,
   O look in your distress;   50
Life remains a blessing
   Although you cannot bless.

"O stand, stand at the window
   As the tears scald and start;
You shall love your crooked neighbour   55
   With your crooked heart."°

It was late, late in the evening,
   The lovers they were gone;
The clocks had ceased their chiming,
   And the deep river ran on.   60

[1937]

47. Lily-white Boy: Echoing "Green Grow the Rushes, O": "What are your two,
O? / Two, two the lily-white boys / Clothed all in green, O"; **Roarer:** Hell-raiser.
48. Jill: From the nursery rhyme "Jack and Jill."
55–56. "You . . . heart.": Perhaps a distorted conflation of Matthew 22:37 and
22:39: "Thou shalt love the Lord thy God with all thy heart . . . [and] thy neighbor
as thyself."

W. H. AUDEN   [1907–1973]

Musée des Beaux Arts°

About suffering they were never wrong,
The Old Masters: how well they understood
Its human position; how it takes place
While someone else is eating or opening a window or just walking dully
   along;
How, when the aged are reverently, passionately waiting   5
For the miraculous birth, there always must be
Children who did not specially want it to happen, skating

Musée des Beaux Arts: The painting *Landscape with the Fall of Icarus* by Pieter
Brueghel the Elder, on which the poem is based, is in the Musées Royaux des
Beaux-Arts in Brussels.

Brueghel, *Landscape with the Fall of Icarus*

On a pond at the edge of the wood:
They never forgot
That even the dreadful martyrdom must run its course   10
Anyhow in a corner, some untidy spot
Where the dogs go on with their doggy life and the torturer's horse
Scratches its innocent behind on a tree.

In Breughel's *Icarus*, for instance: how everything turns away
Quite leisurely from the disaster; the ploughman may   15
Have heard the splash, the forsaken cry,
But for him it was not an important failure; the sun shone
As it had to on the white legs disappearing into the green
Water; and the expensive delicate ship that must have seen
Something amazing, a boy falling out of the sky,   20
Had somewhere to get to and sailed calmly on.

[1940]

THEODORE ROETHKE   [1908–1963]

My Papa's Waltz

The whiskey on your breath
Could make a small boy dizzy;
But I hung on like death:
Such waltzing was not easy.

We romped until the pans   5
Slid from the kitchen shelf;
My mother's countenance
Could not unfrown itself.

The hand that held my wrist
Was battered on one knuckle;   10
At every step you missed
My right ear scraped a buckle.

You beat time on my head
With a palm caked hard by dirt,
Then waltzed me off to bed   15
Still clinging to your shirt.

                                    [1948]

GEORGE OPPEN   [1908–1984]

The Forms of Love

Parked in the fields
All night
So many years ago,
We saw
A lake beside us   5
When the moon rose.
I remember

Leaving that ancient car
Together. I remember
Standing in the white grass   10

Beside it. We groped
Our way together
Downhill in the bright
Incredible light

Beginning to wonder   15
Whether it could be lake
Or fog
We saw, our heads
Ringing under the stars. We walked
To where it would have wet our feet   20
Had it been water

[1965]

ELIZABETH BISHOP [1911–1979]

The Fish

I caught a tremendous fish
and held him beside the boat
half out of water, with my hook
fast in a corner of his mouth.
He didn't fight.   5
He hadn't fought at all.
He hung a grunting weight,
battered and venerable
and homely. Here and there
his brown skin hung in strips   10
like ancient wallpaper,
and its pattern of darker brown
was like wallpaper:
shapes like full-blown roses
stained and lost through age.   15
He was speckled with barnacles,
fine rosettes of lime,
and infested
with tiny white sea-lice,
and underneath two or three   20
rags of green weed hung down.
While his gills were breathing in

the terrible oxygen
—the frightening gills,
fresh and crisp with blood,   25
that can cut so badly—
I thought of the coarse white flesh
packed in like feathers,
the big bones and the little bones,
the dramatic reds and blacks   30
of his shiny entrails,
and the pink swim-bladder
like a big peony.
I looked into his eyes
which were far larger than mine   35
but shallower, and yellowed,
the irises backed and packed
with tarnished tinfoil
seen through the lenses
of old scratched isinglass.°   *transparent sheet of mica* 40
They shifted a little, but not
to return my stare.
—It was more like the tipping
of an object toward the light.
I admired his sullen face,   45
the mechanism of his jaw,
and then I saw
that from his lower lip
—if you could call it a lip—
grim, wet, and weaponlike,   50
hung five old pieces of fish-line,
or four and a wire leader
with the swivel still attached,
with all their five big hooks
grown firmly in his mouth.   55
A green line, frayed at the end
where he broke it, two heavier lines,
and a fine black thread
still crimped from the strain and snap
when it broke and he got away.   60
Like medals with their ribbons
frayed and wavering,
a five-haired beard of wisdom
trailing from his aching jaw.
I stared and stared   65

and victory filled up
the little rented boat,
from the pool of bilge
where oil had spread a rainbow
around the rusted engine   70
to the bailer rusted orange,
the sun-cracked thwarts,
the oarlocks on their strings,
the gunnels—until everything
was rainbow, rainbow, rainbow!   75
And I let the fish go.

[1946]

ELIZABETH BISHOP   [1911–1979]

One Art

The art of losing isn't hard to master;
so many things seem filled with the intent
to be lost that their loss is no disaster.

Lose something every day. Accept the fluster
of lost door keys, the hour badly spent.   5
The art of losing isn't hard to master.

Then practice losing farther, losing faster:
places, and names, and where it was you meant
to travel. None of these will bring disaster.

I lost my mother's watch. And look! my last, or   10
next-to-last, of three loved houses went.
The art of losing isn't hard to master.

I lost two cities, lovely ones. And, vaster,
some realms I owned, two rivers, a continent.
I miss them, but it wasn't a disaster.   15

—Even losing you (the joking voice, a gesture
I love) I shan't have lied. It's evident
the art of losing's not too hard to master
though it may look like (*Write* it!) like disaster.

[1976]

JOHN FREDERICK NIMS   [1913–1999]

Love Poem

My clumsiest dear, whose hands shipwreck vases,
At whose quick touch all glasses chip and ring,
Whose palms are bulls in china, burs in linen,
And have no cunning with any soft thing

Except all ill-at-ease fidgeting people: 5
The refugee uncertain at the door
You make at home; deftly you steady
The drunk clambering on his undulant floor.

Unpredictable dear, the taxi drivers' terror,
Shrinking from far headlights pale as a dime   10
Yet leaping before red apoplectic streetcars —
Misfit in any space. And never on time.

A wrench in clocks and the solar system, Only
With words and people and love you move at ease;
In traffic of wit expertly maneuver   15
And keep us, all devotion, at your knees.

Forgetting your coffee spreading on our flannel,
Your lipstick grinning on our coat,
So gaily in love's unbreakable heaven
Our souls on glory of spilt bourbon float.   20

Be with me, darling, early and late. Smash glasses —
I will study wry music for your sake.
For should your hands drop white and empty
All the toys of the world would break.

[1947]

ROBERT HAYDEN   [1913–1980]

Those Winter Sundays

Sundays too my father got up early
and put his clothes on in the blueblack cold,
then with cracked hands that ached
from labor in the weekday weather made
banked fires blaze. No one ever thanked him.   5

I'd wake and hear the cold splintering, breaking.
When the rooms were warm, he'd call,
and slowly I would rise and dress,
fearing the chronic angers of that house,

Speaking indifferently to him,   10
who had driven out the cold
and polished my good shoes as well.
What did I know, what did I know
of love's austere and lonely offices?

[1962]

DUDLEY RANDALL   [1914–2000]

Ballad of Birmingham

On the bombing of a church in Birmingham, Alabama, 1963

"Mother dear, may I go downtown
Instead of out to play,
And march the streets of Birmingham
In a Freedom March today?"

"No, baby, no, you may not go,   5
For the dogs are fierce and wild,
And clubs and hoses, guns and jails
Aren't good for a little child."

"But, mother, I won't be alone.
Other children will go with me,   10

And march the streets of Birmingham
To make our country free."

"No, baby, no, you may not go,   10
For I fear those guns will fire.
But you may go to church instead   15
And sing in the children's choir."

She has combed and brushed her night-dark hair,
And bathed rose petal sweet,
And drawn white gloves on her small brown hands,
And white shoes on her feet.   20

The mother smiled to know her child
Was in the sacred place,
But that smile was the last smile
To come upon her face.

For when she heard the explosion,   25
Her eyes grew wet and wild.
She raced through the streets of Birmingham
Calling for her child.

She clawed through bits of glass and brick,
Then lifted out a shoe.   30
"Oh, here's the shoe my baby wore,
But, baby, where are you?"

                                                       [1969]

JOHN BERRYMAN   [1914–1972]

Henry's Confession

from *The Dream Songs* 76

Nothin very bad happen to me lately.
How you explain that?—I explain that, Mr Bones,°   *minstrel figure*
terms o' your bafflin odd sobriety.
Sober as man can get, no girls, no telephones,
what could happen bad to Mr Bones?   5
—*If* life is a handkerchief sandwich,

in a modesty of death I join my father
who dared so long agone leave me.
A bullet on a concrete stoop
close by a smothering southern sea   10
spreadeagled on an island, by my knee.
—You is from hunger, Mr Bones,

I offers you this handkerchief, now set
your left foot by my right foot,
shoulder to shoulder, all that jazz,   15
arm in arm, by the beautiful sea,
hum a little, Mr Bones.
—I saw nobody coming, so I went instead.

[1964]

WILLIAM STAFFORD [1914–1995]

Traveling through the Dark

Traveling through the dark I found a deer
dead on the edge of the Wilson River road.
It is usually best to roll them into the canyon:
that road is narrow; to swerve might make more dead.

By glow of the tail-light I stumbled back of the car   5
and stood by the heap, a doe, a recent killing;
she had stiffened already, almost cold.
I dragged her off; she was large in the belly.

My fingers touching her side brought me the reason—
her side was warm; her fawn lay there waiting,   10
alive, still, never to be born.
Beside that mountain road I hesitated.

The car aimed ahead its lowered parking lights;
under the hood purred the steady engine.
I stood in the glare of the warm exhaust turning red;   15
around our group I could hear the wilderness listen.

I thought hard for us all—my only swerving—,
then pushed her over the edge into the river.

[1962]

DYLAN THOMAS   [1914–1953]

Fern Hill

Now as I was young and easy under the apple boughs
About the lilting house and happy as the grass was green,
   The night above the dingle° starry,   *small wooded valley*
      Time let me hail and climb
     Golden in the heydays of his eyes,   5
And honoured among wagons I was prince of the apple towns
And once below a time I lordly had the trees and leaves
     Trail with daisies and barley
    Down the rivers of the windfall light.

And as I was green and carefree, famous among the barns   10
About the happy yard and singing as the farm was home,
    In the sun that is young once only,
      Time let me play and be
    Golden in the mercy of his means,
And green and golden I was huntsman and herdsman, the calves   15
Sang to my horn, the foxes on the hills barked clear and cold,
     And the sabbath rang slowly
    In the pebbles of the holy streams.

All the sun long it was running, it was lovely, the hay
Fields high as the house, the tunes from the chimneys, it was air   20
    And playing, lovely and watery
      And fire green as grass.
    And nightly under the simple stars
As I rode to sleep the owls were bearing the farm away,
All the moon long I heard, blessed among stables, the nightjars   25
    Flying with the ricks, and the horses
      Flashing into the dark.

And then to awake, and the farm, like a wanderer white
With the dew, come back, the cock on his shoulder: it was all
    Shining, it was Adam and maiden,   30
      The sky gathered again
    And the sun grew round that very day.
So it must have been after the birth of the simple light
In the first, spinning place, the spellbound horses walking warm
    Out of the whinnying green stable   35
      On to the fields of praise.

And honoured among foxes and pheasants by the gay house
Under the new made clouds and happy as the heart was long,
   In the sun born over and over,
     I ran my heedless ways,   40
   My wishes raced through the house high hay
And nothing I cared, at my sky blue trades, that time allows
In all his tuneful turning so few and such morning songs
   Before the children green and golden
     Follow him out of grace,   45

Nothing I cared, in the lamb white days, that time would take me
Up to the swallow thronged loft by the shadow of my hand,
   In the moon that is always rising,
     Nor that riding to sleep
I should hear him fly with the high fields   50
And wake to the farm forever fled from the childless land.
Oh as I was young and easy in the mercy of his means,
   Time held me green and dying
   Though I sang in my chains like the sea.

[1946]

DYLAN THOMAS   [1914–1953]

Do not go gentle into that good night

Do not go gentle into that good night,
Old age should burn and rave at close of day;
Rage, rage against the dying of the light.

Though wise men at their end know dark is right,
Because their words had forked no lightning they   5
Do not go gentle into that good night.

Good men, the last wave by, crying how bright
Their frail deeds might have danced in a green bay,
Rage, rage against the dying of the light.

Wild men who caught and sang the sun in flight,   10
And learn, too late, they grieved it on its way,
Do not go gentle into that good night.

Grave men, near death, who see with blinding sight
Blind eyes could blaze like meteors and be gay,
Rage, rage against the dying of the light. 15

And you, my father, there on the sad height,
Curse, bless, me now with your fierce tears, I pray.
Do not go gentle into that good night.
Rage, rage against the dying of the light.

[1952]

HENRY REED [1914–1986]

Naming of Parts

Today we have naming of parts. Yesterday,
We had daily cleaning. And tomorrow morning,
We shall have what to do after firing. But today,
Today we have naming of parts. Japonica
Glistens like coral in all of the neighbouring gardens, 5
    And today we have naming of parts.

This is the lower sling swivel. And this
Is the upper sling swivel, whose use you will see,
When you are given your slings. And this is the piling swivel,
Which in your case you have not got. The branches 10
Hold in the gardens their silent, eloquent gestures,
    Which in our case we have not got.

This is the safety-catch, which is always released
With an easy flick of the thumb. And please do not let me
See anyone using his finger. You can do it quite easy 15
If you have any strength in your thumb. The blossoms
Are fragile and motionless, never letting anyone see
    Any of them using their finger.

And this you can see is the bolt. The purpose of this
Is to open the breech, as you see. We can slide it 20
Rapidly backwards and forwards: we call this
Easing the spring. And rapidly backwards and forwards
The early bees are assaulting and fumbling the flowers:
    They call it easing the Spring.

They call it easing the Spring: it is perfectly easy   25
If you have any strength in your thumb: like the bolt,
And the breech, and the cocking-piece, and the point of balance,
Which in our case we have not got; and the almond-blossom
Silent in all of the gardens and the bees going backwards and forwards,
    For today we have naming of parts.   30

[1946]

RANDALL JARRELL   [1914–1965]

The Woman at the Washington Zoo

The saris go by me from the embassies.

Cloth from the moon. Cloth from another planet.
They look back at the leopard like the leopard.

And I. . . .
            this print of mine, that has kept its color   5
Alive through so many cleanings; this dull null
Navy I wear to work, and wear from work, and so
To my bed, so to my grave, with no
Complaints, no comment: neither from my chief,
The Deputy Chief Assistant, nor his chief—   10
Only I complain. . . . this serviceable
Body that no sunlight dyes, no hand suffuses
But, dome-shadowed, withering among columns,
Wavy beneath fountains—small, far-off, shining
In the eyes of animals, these beings trapped   15
As I am trapped but not, themselves, the trap,
Aging, but without knowledge of their age,
Kept safe here, knowing not of death, for death—
Oh, bars of my own body, open, open!

The world goes by my cage and never sees me.   20
And there come not to me, as come to these,
The wild beasts, sparrows pecking the llamas' grain,
Pigeons settling on the bears' bread, buzzards
Tearing the meat the flies have clouded. . . .

Vulture,   25
When you come for the white rat that the foxes left,
Take off the red helmet of your head, the black
Wings that have shadowed me, and step to me as man:
The wild brother at whose feet the white wolves fawn,
To whose hand of power the great lioness   30
Stalks, purring. . . .
                    You know what I was,
You see what I am: change me, change me!

[1960]

GWENDOLYN BROOKS [1917–2000]

We Real Cool

The Pool Players.
Seven at the Golden Shovel.

We real cool. We
Left school. We

Lurk late. We
Strike straight. We

Sing sin. We   5
Thin gin. We

Jazz June.° We   *sexual intercourse*
Die soon.

[1960]

GWENDOLYN BROOKS [1917–2000]

The Bean Eaters

They eat beans mostly, this old yellow pair.
Dinner is a casual affair.
Plain chipware on a plain and creaking wood,
Tin flatware.

Two who are Mostly Good.   5
Two who have lived their day,
But keep on putting on their clothes
and putting things away.

And remembering . . .
Remembering, with twinklings and twinges,   10
As they lean over the beans in their rented back room that
   is full of beads and receipts and dolls and cloths,
     tobacco crumbs, vases and fringes.

                                   [1960]

ROBERT LOWELL [1917–1978]

Skunk Hour

for Elizabeth Bishop

Nautilus Island's hermit
heiress still lives through winter in her Spartan cottage;
her sheep still graze above the sea.
Her son's a bishop. Her farmer
is first selectman in our village;   5
she's in her dotage.

Thirsting for
the hierarchic privacy
of Queen Victoria's century,
she buys up all   10
the eyesores facing her shore,
and lets them fall.

The season's ill—
we've lost our summer millionaire,
who seemed to leap from an L. L. Bean   15
catalogue. His nine-knot yawl
was auctioned off to lobstermen.
A red fox stain covers Blue Hill.

And now our fairy
decorator brightens his shop for fall;   20
his fishnet's filled with orange cork,

orange, his cobbler's bench and awl;
there is no money in his work,
he'd rather marry.

One dark night,   25
my Tudor Ford climbed the hill's skull;
I watched for love-cars. Lights turned down,
they lay together, hull to hull,
where the graveyard shelves on the town. . . .
My mind's not right.   30

A car radio bleats,
"Love, O careless Love. . . ." I hear
my ill-spirit sob in each blood cell,
as if my hand were at its throat. . . .
I myself am hell;   35
nobody's here—

only skunks, that search
in the moonlight for a bite to eat.
They march on their soles up Main Street:
white stripes, moonstruck eyes' red fire   40
under the chalk-dry and spar spire
of the Trinitarian Church.

I stand on top
of our back steps and breathe the rich air—
a mother skunk with her column of kittens swills the garbage pail. 45
She jabs her wedge-head in a cup
of sour cream, drops her ostrich tail,
and will not scare.

[1963]

ROBERT DUNCAN [1919–1988]

The Torso

Passages 18

Most beautiful!   the red-flowering eucalyptus,
        the madrone, the yew
    Is he . . .

    So thou wouldst smile, and take me in thine arms
    The sight of London to my exiled eyes   5
    Is as Elysium° to a new-come soul   *paradise*

       If he be Truth
       I would dwell in the illusion of him

His hands unlocking from chambers of my male body

          such an idea in man's image   10

    rising tides that sweep me towards him

         . . . *homosexual?*

            and at the treasure of his mouth

       pour forth my soul

             his soul   commingling   15

    I thought a Being more than vast, His body leading
       into Paradise,   his eyes
           quickening a fire in me,   a trembling

    hieroglyph:°   At the root of the neck

the clavicle, for the neck is the stem of the great artery   20
    upward into his head that is beautiful

          At the rise of the pectoral muscle,

the nipples, for the breasts are like sleeping fountains
    of feeling in man, waiting above the beat of his heart,
    shielding the rise and fall of his breath, to be   25
    awakend

         At the axis of his mid hriff

the navel, for in the pit of his stomach the chord from
    which first he was fed has its temple

         At the root of the groin   30

the pubic hair, for the torso is the stem in which the man
    flowers forth and leads to the stamen of flesh in which
    his seed rises

a wave of need and desire over   taking me

---

19. **hieroglyph:** A picture or symbol representing a word or sound.

cried out my name   35

(This was long ago.   It was another life)

and said,

What do you want of me?

I do not know, I said.   I have fallen in love.   He
has brought me into heights and depths my heart   40
would fear   without him.   His look

pierces my side   •   fire eyes   •

I have been waiting for you, he said:
I know what you desire

you do not yet know   but through me   •   45

And I am with you everywhere.   In your falling

I have fallen from a high place.   I have raised myself

from darkness in your   rising

wherever you are

my hand in your hand   seeking   the locks, the keys   50

I am there.   Gathering me, you gather

your Self   •

For my Other is not a woman but a man

the King upon whose bosom let me lie.

[1968]

CHARLES BUKOWSKI   [1920–1994]

my old man

16 years old
during the depression
I'd come home drunk
and all my clothing—
shorts, shirts, stockings—   5

suitcase, and pages of
short stories
would be thrown out on the
front lawn and about the
street.   10

my mother would be
waiting behind a tree:
"Henry, Henry, don't
go in . . . he'll
kill you, he's read   15
your stories . . ."

"I can whip his
ass . . ."

"Henry, please take
this . . . and   20
find yourself a room."

but it worried him
that I might not
finish high school
so I'd be back   25
again.

one evening he walked in
with the pages of
one of my short stories
(which I had never submitted   30
to him)
and he said, "this is
a great short story."
I said, "o.k.,"
and he handed it to me   35
and I read it.
it was a story about
a rich man
who had a fight with
his wife and had   40
gone out into the night
for a cup of coffee
and had observed
the waitress and the spoons
and forks and the   45

salt and pepper shakers
and the neon sign
in the window
and then had gone back
to his stable   50
to see and touch his
favorite horse
who then
kicked him in the head
and killed him.   55

somehow
the story held
meaning for him
though
when I had written it   60
I had no idea
of what I was
writing about.

so I told him,
"o.k., old man, you can   65
have it."
and he took it
and walked out
and closed the door.
I guess that's   70
as close
as we ever got.

[1977]

RICHARD WILBUR   [b. 1921]

Love Calls Us to the Things
of This World

The eyes open to a cry of pulleys,
And spirited from sleep, the astounded soul
Hangs for a moment bodiless and simple

As false dawn.
                    Outside the open window
The morning air is all awash with angels.   5

    Some are in bed-sheets, some are in blouses,
Some are in smocks: but truly there they are.
Now they are rising together in calm swells
Of halcyon feeling, filling whatever they wear
With the deep joy of their impersonal breathing;   10

    Now they are flying in place, conveying
The terrible speed of their omnipresence, moving
And staying like white water; and now of a sudden
They swoon down into so rapt a quiet
That nobody seems to be there.   The soul shrinks   15

    From all that it is about to remember,
From the punctual rape of every blessèd day,
And cries,
              "Oh, let there be nothing on earth but laundry,
Nothing but rosy hands in the rising steam
And clear dances done in the sight of heaven."   20

    Yet, as the sun acknowledges
With a warm look the world's hunks and colors,
The soul descends once more in bitter love
To accept the waking body, saying now
In a changed voice as the man yawns and rises,   25

    "Bring them down from their ruddy gallows;
Let there be clean linen for the backs of thieves;
Let lovers go fresh and sweet to be undone,
And the heaviest nuns walk in a pure floating
Of dark habits,
              keeping their difficult balance."   30

                                [1956]

HAYDEN CARRUTH   [b. 1921]

Regarding Chainsaws

The first chainsaw I owned was years ago,
an old yellow McCulloch that wouldn't start.
Bo Bremmer give it to me that was my friend,
though I've had enemies couldn't of done
no worse. I took it to Ward's over to Morrisville,   5
and no doubt they tinkered it as best they could,
but it still wouldn't start. One time later
I took it down to the last bolt and gasket
and put it together again, hoping somehow
I'd do something accidental-like that would   10
make it go, and then I yanked on it
450 times, as I figured afterwards,
and give myself a bursitis in the elbow
that went five years even after
Doc Arrowsmith shot it full of cortisone   15
and near killed me when he hit a nerve
dead on. Old Stan wanted that saw, wanted it bad.
Figured I was a greenhorn that didn't know
nothing and he could fix it. Well, I was,
you could say, being only forty at the time,   20
but a fair hand at tinkering. "Stan," I said,
"you're a neighbor. I like you. I wouldn't
sell that thing to nobody, except maybe
Vice-President Nixon." But Stan persisted.
He always did. One time we was loafing and   25
gabbing in his front dooryard, and he spied
that saw in the back of my pickup. He run
quick inside, then come out and stuck a double
sawbuck° in my shirt pocket, and he grabbed   *twenty dollar bill*
that saw and lugged it off. Next day, when I   30
drove past, I seen he had it snugged down tight
with a tow-chain on the bed of his old Dodge
Powerwagon, and he was yanking on it
with both hands. Two or three days after,
I asked him, "How you getting along with that   35
McCulloch, Stan?" "Well," he says, "I tooken
it down to scrap, and I buried it in three

separate places yonder on the upper side
of the potato piece. You can't be too careful,"
he says, "when you're disposing of a hex."   40
The next saw I had was a godawful ancient
Homelite that I give Dry Dryden thirty bucks for,
temperamental as a ram too, but I liked it.
It used to remind me of Dry and how he'd
clap that saw a couple times with the flat   45
of his double-blade axe to make it go
and how he honed the chain with a worn-down
file stuck in an old baseball. I worked
that saw for years. I put up forty-five
run them days each summer and fall to keep   50
my stoves het through the winter. I couldn't now.
It'd kill me. Of course they got these here
modern Swedish saws now that can take
all the worry out of it. What's the good
of that? Takes all the fun out too, don't it?   55
Why, I reckon. I mind when Gilles Boivin snagged
an old sap spout buried in a chunk of maple
and it tore up his mouth so bad he couldn't play
"Tea for Two" on his cornet in the town band
no more, and then when Toby Fox was holding   60
a beech limb that Rob Bowen was bucking up
and the saw skidded crossways and nipped off
one of Toby's fingers. Ain't that more like it?
Makes you know you're living. But mostly they wan't
dangerous, and the only thing they broke was your   65
back. Old Stan, he was a buller and a jammer
in his time, no two ways about that, but he
never sawed himself. Stan had the sugar
all his life, and he wan't always too careful
about his diet and the injections. He lost   70
all the feeling in his legs from the knees down.
One time he started up his Powerwagon
out in the barn, and his foot slipped off the clutch,
and she jumped forwards right through the wall
and into the manure pit. He just set there,   75
swearing like you could of heard it in St.
Johnsbury, till his wife come out and said,
"Stan, what's got into you?" "Missus," he says,
"ain't nothing got into me. Can't you see?
It's me that's got into this here pile of shit."   80

Not much later they took away one of his
legs, and six months after that they took
the other and left him sitting in his old chair
with a tank of oxygen to sip at whenever
he felt himself sinking. I remember that chair.   85
Stan reupholstered it with an old bearskin
that must of come down from his great-great-
grandfather and had grit in it left over
from the Civil War and a bullet-hole as big
as a yawning cat. Stan latched the pieces together   90
with rawhide, cross fashion, but the stitches was
always breaking and coming undone. About then
I quit stopping by to see old Stan, and I
don't feel so good about that neither. But my mother
was having her strokes then. I figured   95
one person coming apart was as much
as a man can stand. Then Stan was taken away
to the nursing home, and then he died. I always
remember how he planted them pieces of spooked
McCulloch up above the potatoes. One time   100
I went up and dug, and I took the old
sprocket, all pitted and et away, and set it
on the windowsill right there next to the
butter mold. But I'm damned if I know why.

[1983]

PHILIP LARKIN   [1922–1985]

High Windows

When I see a couple of kids
And guess he's fucking her and she's
Taking pills or wearing a diaphragm,
I know this is paradise

Everyone old has dreamed of all their lives —   5
Bonds and gestures pushed to one side
Like an outdated combine harvester,
And everyone young going down the long slide

To happiness, endlessly. I wonder if
Anyone looked at me, forty years back,   10
And thought, *That'll be the life;*
No God any more, or sweating in the dark

About hell and that, or having to hide
What you think of the priest. He
And his lot will all go down the long slide   15
Like free bloody birds. And immediately

Rather than words comes the thought of high windows:
The sun-comprehending glass,
And beyond it, the deep blue air, that shows
Nothing, and is nowhere, and is endless.   20

[1974]

DENISE LEVERTOV   [1923–1997]

February Evening in New York

As the stores close, a winter light
    opens air to iris blue,
    glint of frost through the smoke
    grains of mica, salt of the sidewalk.
As the buildings close, released autonomous   5
    feet pattern the streets
    in hurry and stroll; balloon heads
    drift and dive above them; the bodies
    aren't really there.
As the lights brighten, as the sky darkens,   10
    a woman with crooked heels says to another woman
    while they step along at a fair pace,
    "You know, I'm telling you, what I love best
    is life. I love life! Even if I ever get
    to be old and wheezy—or limp! You know?   15
    Limping along?—I'd still . . ." Out of hearing.
To the multiple disordered tones
    of gears changing, a dance

to the compass points, out, four-way river.
Prospect of sky   20
wedged into avenues, left at the ends of streets,
west sky, east sky: more life tonight! A range
of open time at winter's outskirts.

[1959]

MAXINE KUMIN [b. 1925]

The Excrement Poem

It is done by us all, as God disposes, from
the least cast of worm to what must have been
in the case of the brontosaur, say, spoor
of considerable heft, something awesome.

We eat, we evacuate, survivors that we are.   5
I think these things each morning with shovel
and rake, drawing the risen brown buns
toward me, fresh from the horse oven, as it were,

or culling the alfalfa-green ones, expelled
in a state of ooze, through the sawdust bed   10
to take a serviceable form, as putty does,
so as to lift out entire from the stall.

And wheeling to it, storming up the slope,
I think of the angle of repose the manure
pile assumes, how sparrows come to pick   15
the redelivered grain, how inky-cap

coprinus mushrooms spring up in a downpour.
I think of what drops from us and must then
be moved to make way for the next and next.
However much we stain the world, spatter   20

it with our leavings, make stenches, defile
the great formal oceans with what leaks down,
trundling off today's last barrowful,
I honor shit for saying: We go on.

[1978]

KENNETH KOCH   [1925–2002]

The History of Jazz

1

The leaves of blue came drifting down.
In the corner Madeleine Reierbacher was reading *Lorna Doone.*°
The bay's water helped to implement the structuring of the garden hose.
The envelope fell. Was it pink or was it red? Consult *Lorna Doone.*
There, voyager, you will find your answer. The savant grapeade stands   5
Remember Madeleine Reierbacher. Madeleine Reierbacher says,
"If you are happy, there is no one to keep you from being happy;
Don't let them!" Madeleine Reierbacher went into the racing car.
The racing car was orange and red. Madeleine Reierbacher drove to
    Beale Street.
There Maddy doffed her garments to get into some more comfortable
    clothes.   10
Jazz was already playing in Beale Street when Madeleine Reierbacher
    arrived there.
Madeleine Reierbacher picked up the yellow horn and began to play.
No one had ever heard anything comparable to the playing of
    Madeleine Reierbacher.
What a jazz musician! The pianist missed his beats because he was so
    excited.
The drummer stared out the window in ecstasy at the yellow wooden
    trees.   15
The orchestra played "September in the Rain," "Mugging," and "I'm Full
    of Love."
Madeleine Reierbacher rolled up her sleeves; she picked up her horn;
    she played "Blues in the Rain."
It was the best jazz anyone had ever heard. It was mentioned in the
    newspapers. St. Louis!
Madeleine Reierbacher became a celebrity. She played with Pesky
    Summerton and Muggsy Pierce.
Madeleine cut numerous disks. Her best waxings are "Alpha Beta and
    Gamma"   20
And "Wing Song." One day Madeleine was riding on a donkey
When she came to a yellow light; the yellow light did not change.

2. *Lorna Doone*:   Romance novel (1869) by Richard Doddridge Blackmore.

Madeleine kept hoping it would change to green or red. She said, "As
    long as you have confidence,
You need be afraid of nothing." Madeleine saw the red smokestacks, she
    looked at the thin trees,
And she regarded the railroad tracks. The yellow light was unchanging.
    Madeleine's donkey dropped dead   25
From his mortal load. Madeleine Reierbacher, when she fell to earth,
Picked up a blade of grass and began to play. "The Blues!" cried the
    workmen of the vicinity.
And they ran and came in great numbers to where Madeleine
    Reierbacher was.
They saw her standing in that simple field beside the railroad track
Playing, and they saw that light changing to green and red, and they
    saw that donkey stand up   30
And rise into the sky; and Madeleine Reierbacher was like a clot of blue
In the midst of the blue of all that sky, and the young farmers screamed
In excitement, and the workmen dropped their heavy boards and stones
    in their excitement,
And they cried, "O Madeleine Reierbacher, play us the 'Lead Flint Blues'
    once again!"

O railroad stations, pennants, evenings, and lumberyards!   35
When will you ever bring us such a beautiful soloist again?
An argent strain shows on the reddish face of the sun.
Madeleine Reierbacher stands up and screams, "I am getting wet! You
    are all egotists!"
Her brain floats up into the lyric atmosphere of the sky.
We must figure out a way to keep our best musicians with us.   40
The finest we have always melt into the light blue sky!
In the middle of a concert, sometimes, they disappear, like anvils.
(The music comes down to us with sweet white hands on our
    shoulders.)
We stare up in surprise; and we hear Madeleine's best-known tune once
    again,
"If you ain't afraid of life, life can't be afraid for you."   45
Madeleine! Come back and sing to us!

2

Dick looked up from his blackboard.
Had he really written a history of the jazz age?
He stared at his television set; the technicolor jazz program was
    coming on.

The program that day was devoted to pictures of Madeleine Reierbacher   50
Playing her saxophone in the golden age of jazz.
Dick looked at his blackboard. It was a mass of green and orange lines.
Here and there a red chalk line interlaced with the others.
He stared attentively at the program.

It was a clear and blue white day. Amos said, "The calibration is
    finished. Now there need be no more jazz."   55

In his mountain home old Lucas Dog laughed when he heard what
    Amos had said.
He smilingly picked up his yellow horn to play, but all that came out of
    it was steam.

                                                              [1961]

GERALD STERN   [b. 1925]

Cow Worship

I love the cows best when they are a few feet away
from my dining-room window and my pine floor,
when they reach in to kiss me with their wet
mouths and their white noses.
I love them when they walk over the garbage cans   5
and across the cellar doors,
over the sidewalk and through the metal chairs
and the birdseed.
—Let me reach out through the thin curtains
and feel the warm air of May.   10
It is the temperature of the whole galaxy,
all the bright clouds and clusters,
beasts and heroes,
glittering singers and isolated thinkers
at pasture.   15

                                                              [1981]

JACK GILBERT [b. 1925]

Michiko Dead

He manages like somebody carrying a box
that is too heavy, first with his arms
underneath. When their strength gives out,
he moves the hands forward, hooking them
on the corners, pulling the weight against   5
his chest. He moves his thumbs slightly
when the fingers begin to tire, and it makes
different muscles take over. Afterward,
he carries it on his shoulder, until the blood
drains out of the arm that is stretched up   10
to steady the box and the arm goes numb. But now
the man can hold underneath again, so that
he can go on without ever putting the box down.

[1994]

FRANK O'HARA [1926–1966]

The Day Lady° Died   *jazz singer*
                                        Billie Holliday

It is 12:20 in New York a Friday
three days after Bastille day,° yes   *(July 14)*
it is 1959 and I go get a shoeshine
because I will get off the 4:19 in Easthampton
at 7:15 and then go straight to dinner   5
and I don't know the people who will feed me

I walk up the muggy street beginning to sun
and have a hamburger and a malted and buy
an ugly NEW WORLD WRITING to see what the poets
in Ghana are doing these days   10
                    I go on to the bank
and Miss Stillwagon (first name Linda I once heard)
doesn't even look up my balance for once in her life
and in the GOLDEN GRIFFIN I get a little Verlaine°   *French poet*

for Patsy with drawings by Bonnard° although I do   15
think of Hesiod,° trans. Richmond Lattimore or   *Greek poet*
Brendan Behan's° new play or *Le Balcon* or *Les Nègres*   *Irish playwright*
of Genet,° but I don't, I stick with Verlaine   *French playwright and novelist*
after practically going to sleep with quandariness

and for Mike I just stroll into the PARK LANE   20
Liquor Store and ask for a bottle of Strega and
then I go back where I came from to 6th Avenue
and the tobacconist in the Ziegfeld Theatre and
casually ask for a carton of Gauloises° and a carton   *French cigarettes*
of Picayunes,° and a NEW YORK POST with her face on it   *Southern cigarettes*   25

and I am sweating a lot by now and thinking of
leaning on the john door in the 5 SPOT
while she whispered a song along the keyboard
to Mal Waldron and everyone and I stopped breathing

                                                                          [1964]

15. Bonnard: French modernist painter.

ALLEN GINSBERG   [1926–1997]

A Supermarket in California

What thoughts I have of you tonight, Walt Whitman, for I walked down
the sidestreets under the trees with a headache self-conscious looking at
the full moon.

In my hungry fatigue, and shopping for images, I went into the neon
fruit supermarket, dreaming of your enumerations!

What peaches and what penumbras! Whole families shopping at night!
Aisles full of husbands! Wives in the avocados, babies in the tomatoes!—
and you, García Lorca,° what were you doing down by the watermelons?

I saw you, Walt Whitman, childless, lonely old grubber, poking among
the meats in the refrigerator and eyeing the grocery boys.

3. García Lorca: (1899–1936), Spanish surrealist poet and playwright.

I heard you asking questions of each: Who killed the pork chops? What price bananas? Are you my Angel?   5

I wandered in and out of the brilliant stacks of cans following you, and followed in my imagination by the store detective.

We strode down the open corridors together in our solitary fancy tasting artichokes, possessing every frozen delicacy, and never passing the cashier.

Where are we going, Walt Whitman? The doors close in an hour. Which way does your beard point tonight?

(I touch your book and dream of our odyssey in the supermarket and feel absurd.)

Will we walk all night through solitary streets? The trees add shade to shade, lights out in the houses, we'll both be lonely.   10

Will we stroll dreaming of the lost America of love past blue automobiles in driveways, home to our silent cottage?

Ah, dear father, graybeard, lonely old courage-teacher, what America did you have when Charon° quit poling his ferry and you got out on a smoking bank and stood watching the boat disappear on the black waters of Lethe?°

Berkeley, 1955

[1956]

12. **Charon:** The boatman in Greek mythology who carried the dead across the river Styx to Hades. **Lethe:** River of Forgetfulness in Hades.

ROBERT CREELEY [b. 1926]

Time

Moment to
moment the
body seems

to me to
be there: a   5
catch of

air, pattern
of space— Let's
walk today

all the way   10
to the beach,
let's think

of where we'll be
in two years'
time, of where   15

we *were*. Let
the days go.
Each moment is

of such paradoxical
definition—a   20
waterfall that would

flow backward
if it could. It
can? My time,

one thinks,   25
is drawing to
some close. This

feeling comes
and goes. No
measure ever serves   30

enough, enough—
so "finish it"
gets done, alone.

[1972]

JAMES MERRILL   [1926–1995]

The Pier: Under Pisces

The shallows, brighter,
Wetter than water,
Tepidly glitter with the fingerprint-
Obliterating feel of kerosene.

Each piling like a totem   5
Rises from rock bottom
Straight through the ceiling
Aswirl with suns, clear ones or pale bluegreen,

And beyond! where bubbles burst,
Sphere of their worst dreams,   10
If dream is what they do,
These floozy fish—

Ceramic-lipped in filmy
Peekaboo blouses,
Fluorescent body   15
Stockings, hot stripes,

Swayed by the hypnotic ebb and flow
Of supermarket Muzak,
Bolero° beat the undertow's   *a Spanish dance*
Pebble-filled gourds repeat;   20

Jailbait consumers of subliminal
Hints dropped from on high
In gobbets° none   *fragments, bits*
Eschews as minced kin;

Who, hooked themselves—bamboo diviner   25
Bent their way
Vigorously nodding
Encouragement—

Are one by one hauled kisswise, oh
Into some blinding hell   30
Policed by leathery ex-
Justices each

Minding his catch, if catch is what he can,
If mind is what one means—
The torn mouth   35
Stifled by newsprint, working still. If . . . if . . .

The little scales
Grow stiff. Dusk plugs her dryer in,
Buffs her nails, riffles through magazines,
While far and wide and deep   40

Rover the great sharkskin-suited criminals
And safe in this lit shrine

A boy sits. He'll be eight.
We've drunk our milk, we've eaten our stringbeans,

But left untasted on the plate   45
The fish. An eye, a broiled pearl, meeting mine,
I lift his fork . . .
The bite. The tug of fate.

[1985]

ROBERT BLY   [b. 1926]

Driving to Town Late
to Mail a Letter

It is a cold and snowy night. The main street is deserted.
The only things moving are swirls of snow.
As I lift the mailbox door, I feel its cold iron.
There is a privacy I love in this snowy night.
Driving around, I will waste more time.   5

[1962]

W. S. MERWIN   [b. 1927]

Yesterday

My friend says I was not a good son
you understand
I say yes I understand

he says I did not go
to see my parents very often you know
and I say yes I know

even when I was living in the same city he says
maybe I would go there once   5

a month or maybe even less
I say oh yes   10

he says the last time I went to see my father
I say the last time I saw my father

he says the last time I saw my father
he was asking me about my life
how I was making out and he   15
went into the next room
to get something to give me

oh I say
feeling again the cold
of my father's hand the last time   20

he says and my father turned
in the doorway and saw me
look at my wristwatch and he
said you know I would like you to stay
and talk with me   25

oh yes I say

but if you are busy he said
I don't want you to feel that you
have to
just because I'm here   30

I say nothing

he says my father
said maybe
you have important work you are doing
or maybe you should be seeing   35
somebody I don't want to keep you

I look out the window
my friend is older than I am
he says and I told my father it was so
and I got up and left him then   40
you know

though there was nowhere I had to go
and nothing I had to do

[1983]

JOHN ASHBERY   [b. 1927]

One Coat of Paint

We will all have to just hang on for a while,
It seems, now. This could mean "early retirement"
For some, if only for an afternoon of pottering around
Buying shoelaces and the like. Or it could mean a spell
In some enchanter's cave, after several centuries of which   5
You wake up curiously refreshed, eager to get back
To the crossword puzzle, only no one knows your name
Or who you are, really, or cares much either. To seduce
A fact into becoming an object, a pleasing one, with some
Kind of esthetic quality, which would also add to the store   10
Of knowledge and even extend through several strata
Of history, like a pin through a cracked wrist bone,
Connecting these in such a dynamic way that one would be forced
To acknowledge a new kind of superiority without which the world
Could no longer conduct its business, even simple stuff like bringing   15
Water home from wells, coals to hearths, would of course be
An optimal form of it but in any case the thing's got to
Come into being, something has to happen, or all
We'll have left is disagreements, *désagréments,*° to name a few.
O don't you see how necessary it is to be around,   20
To be ferried from here to that near, smiling shore
And back again into the arms of those that love us,
Not many, but of such infinite, superior sweetness
That their lie is for us and it becomes stained, encrusted,
Finally gilded in some exasperating way that turns it   25
To a truth plus something, delicate and dismal as a star,
Cautious as a drop of milk, so that they let us
Get away with it, some do at any rate?

[1987]

19. *désagréments:* Unpleasantness, difficulties.

GALWAY KINNELL   [b. 1927]

The Bear

1

In late winter
I sometimes glimpse bits of steam
coming up from
some fault in the old snow
and bend close and see it is lung-colored   5
and put down my nose
and know
the chilly, enduring odor of bear.

2

I take a wolf's rib and whittle
it sharp at both ends   10
and coil it up
and freeze it in blubber and place it out
on the fairway of the bears.

And when it has vanished
I move out on the bear tracks,   15
roaming in circles
until I come to the first, tentative, dark
splash on the earth.

And I set out
running, following the splashes   20
of blood wandering over the world.
At the cut, gashed resting places
I stop and rest,
at the crawl-marks
where he lay out on his belly   25
to overpass some stretch of bauchy ice
I lie out
dragging myself forward with bear-knives in my fists.

3

On the third day I begin to starve,
at nightfall I bend down as I knew I would   30
at a turd sopped in blood,

and hesitate, and pick it up,
and thrust it in my mouth, and gnash it down,
and rise
and go on running.   35

4

On the seventh day,
living by now on bear blood alone,
I can see his upturned carcass far out ahead, a scraggled,
steamy hulk,
the heavy fur riffling in the wind.   40

I come up to him
and stare at the narrow-spaced, petty eyes,
the dismayed
face laid back on the shoulder, the nostrils
flared, catching   45
perhaps the first taint of me as he
died.

I hack
a ravine in his thigh, and eat and drink,
and tear him down his whole length   50
and open him and climb in
and close him up after me, against the wind,
and sleep.

5

And dream
of lumbering flatfooted   55
over the tundra,
stabbed twice from within,
splattering a trail behind me,
splattering it out no matter which way I lurch,
no matter which parabola of bear-transcendence,   60
which dance of solitude I attempt,
which gravity-clutched leap,
which trudge, which groan.

6

Until one day I totter and fall—
fall on this   65
stomach that has tried so hard to keep up,
to digest the blood as it leaked in,

to break up
and digest the bone itself: and now the breeze
blows over me, blows off   70
the hideous belches of ill-digested bear blood
and rotted stomach
and the ordinary, wretched odor of bear,

blows across
my sore, lolled tongue a song   75
or screech, until I think I must rise up
and dance. And I lie still.

7

I awaken I think. Marshlights
reappear, geese
come trailing again up the flyway.   80
In her ravine under old snow the dam-bear
lies, licking
lumps of smeared fur
and drizzly eyes into shapes
with her tongue. And one   85
hairy-soled trudge stuck out before me,
the next groaned out,
the next,
the next,
the rest of my days I spend   90
wandering: wondering
what, anyway,
was that sticky infusion, that rank flavor of blood, that poetry, by which
    I lived?

[1967]

JAMES WRIGHT   [1927–1980]

A Blessing

Just off the highway to Rochester, Minnesota,
Twilight bounds softly forth on the grass.
And the eyes of those two Indian ponies
Darken with kindness.

They have come gladly out of the willows   5
To welcome my friend and me.
We step over the barbed wire into the pasture
Where they have been grazing all day, alone.

They ripple tensely, they can hardly contain their happiness
That we have come.   10
They bow shyly as wet swans. They love each other.
There is no loneliness like theirs.
At home once more,
They begin munching the young tufts of spring in the darkness.
I would like to hold the slenderer one in my arms,   15
For she has walked over to me
And nuzzled my left hand.
She is black and white,
Her mane falls wild on her forehead,
And the light breeze moves me to caress her long ear   20
That is delicate as the skin over a girl's wrist.
Suddenly I realize
That if I stepped out of my body I would break
Into blossom.

[1963]

PHILIP LEVINE   [b. 1928]

What Work Is

We stand in the rain in a long line
waiting at Ford Highland Park. For work.
You know what work is—if you're
old enough to read this you know what
work is, although you may not do it.   5
Forget you. This is about waiting,
shifting from one foot to another.
Feeling the light rain falling like mist
into your hair, blurring your vision
until you think you see your own brother   10
ahead of you, maybe ten places.
You rub your glasses with your fingers,
and of course it's someone else's brother,

narrower across the shoulders than
yours but with the same sad slouch, the grin   15
that does not hide the stubbornness,
the sad refusal to give in to
rain, to the hours wasted waiting,
to the knowledge that somewhere ahead
a man is waiting who will say, "No,   20
we're not hiring today," for any
reason he wants. You love your brother,
now suddenly you can hardly stand
the love flooding you for your brother,
who's not beside you or behind or   25
ahead because he's home trying to
sleep off a miserable night shift
at Cadillac so he can get up
before noon to study his German.
Works eight hours a night so he can sing   30
Wagner, the opera you hate most,
the worst music ever invented.
How long has it been since you told him
you loved him, held his wide shoulders,
opened your eyes wide and said those words,   35
and maybe kissed his cheek? You've never
done something so simple, so obvious,
not because you're too young or too dumb,
not because you're jealous or even mean
or incapable of crying in   40
the presence of another man, no,
just because you don't know what work is.

[1991]

CONRAD HILBERRY [b. 1928]

Player Piano

She was right: basement was the place for it.
Who wants a Pianola in the dining room?
It's not an instrument, not a household
object even, more a curiosity.

So with a rented dolly and four big friends   5
from work, he eased it down the cellar stairs,
across the concrete to its place against
the wall. Now he leans back on the bench

and pumps the Basement Rag. His youngest daughter
sits beside him on the bench within   10
the light of the gooseneck lamp, the dog curls
on the rug, and always the ghostly fingers move,

the left hand striding and the right hand climbing
down out of the high notes. Four of them,
father, daughter, dog, and piano player,   15
all in a circle of light, the roll unwinding

its dots and dashes, music clattering out,
and no one saying anything. "Hey,
Cosby's on,"° his wife calls down the stairs.
"Why not come on up?" And so they sit   20

in the kitchen, laughing at Rudy and the Cos.
Afterwards, homework and bed—and he drifts
back to the basement, back to the wooden music.
Gradually, his wife becomes sarcastic,

as if he were counterfeiting bills down there,   25
or dissecting cats. His daughter says she isn't
coming down. But he believes the piano
brings him closer to them all. It's something

he can count on, almost like a law
of nature, not needing praise or inspiration,   30
sticking to its version of the story.
The roll scrolling in front of him is

Morse code talking to people in other basements
or in huts or lean-to's—Sarasota, Caracas,
up-country Liberia. The key taps out   35
news of high winds, the river rising, families

sheltered in the local school, news
of people he's never met, clicking in a voice
without inflection, neither speech
nor silence. The longs and shorts, the steady   40

19. Cosby's on: *The Cosby Show* was a popular television situation comedy (1984–1992) starring Bill Cosby and Phylicia Rashad.

white keys and the black must carry
through the studs of the house, he thinks,
easing the children into sleep.
He hears a pipe muttering

and knows his wife is drawing water for   45
a bath. It stops. She must be in the tub.
He taps a message on the pipe, binary,
the way nerves talk, signaling across

the gaps, need and love condensed to dots
and dashes. She must hear it as she steams   50
and lathers in the bath, metallic music
played by no one's fingers on the pipes.

[1999]

SAMUEL HAZO [b. 1928]

For Fawzi in Jerusalem

Leaving a world too old to name
and too undying to forsake,
I flew the cold, expensive sea
toward Columbus' mistake
where life could never be the same   5

for me. In Jerash° on the sand
I saw the colonnades of Rome
bleach in the sun like skeletons.
Behind a convalescent home,
armed soldiers guarded no man's land   10

between Jordanians and Jews.
Opposing sentries frowned and spat.
Fawzi, you mocked in Arabic
this justice from Jehoshophat°
before you shined my Pittsburgh shoes   15

6. **Jerash:** The ancient city of Gerasa, twenty-two miles north of Amman in present-day Jordan. Called Jerash by the Romans who rebuilt it in 65 C.E., it is the best-preserved Palestinian city of Roman times.
14. **Jehoshophat:** Hebrew king of Judah (c. 873–849 B.C.E.), the first to make a treaty with the neighboring kingdom of Israel.

for nothing. Why you never kept
the coins I offered you is still
your secret and your victory.
Saying you saw marauders kill
your father while Beershebans° wept   20

for mercy in their holy war,
you told me how you stole to stay
alive. You must have thought I thought
your history would make me pay
a couple of piastres more   25

than any shine was worth—and I
was ready to—when you said, "No,
I never take. I never want
America to think I throw
myself on you. I never lie."   30

I watched your young but old man's stare
demand the sword to flash again
in blood and flame from Jericho°
and leave the bones of these new men
of Judah bleaching in the air   35

like Roman stones upon the plain
of Jerash. Then you faced away.
Jerusalem, Jerusalem,
I asked myself if I could pray
for peace and not recall the pain   40

you spoke. But what could praying do?
Today I live your loss in no
man's land but mine, and every time
I talk of fates not just but so,
Fawzi, my friend, I think of you.   45

[1968]

20. **Beershebans:** Inhabitants of Beersheba, a city in southern Israel. Given to
the Arabs in the partition of Palestine (1948), it was retaken by Israel in the Arab-
Israeli war of 1948.
33. **Jericho:** Ancient city in biblical Palestine, in the Jordan valley north of the
Dead Sea, captured from the Canaanites by Joshua and destroyed (Joshua 6:1–21).

ANNE SEXTON [1928–1974]

Cinderella

You always read about it:
the plumber with twelve children
who wins the Irish Sweepstakes.
From toilets to riches.
That story.   5

Or the nursemaid,
some luscious sweet from Denmark
who captures the oldest son's heart.
From diapers to Dior.°
That story.   10

Or a milkman who serves the wealthy,
eggs, cream, butter, yogurt, milk,
the white truck like an ambulance
who goes into real estate
and makes a pile.   15
From homogenized to martinis at lunch.

Or the charwoman
who is on the bus when it cracks up
and collects enough from the insurance.
    From mops to Bonwit Teller.°   20
    That story.

Once
the wife of a rich man was on her deathbed
and she said to her daughter Cinderella:
Be devout. Be good. Then I will smile   25
down from heaven in the seam of a cloud.
The man took another wife who had
two daughters, pretty enough
but with hearts like blackjacks.
Cinderella was their maid.   30
She slept on the sooty hearth each night

9. Dior: Fashions designed by the French house of Dior, established by Christian
Dior (1905–1957).
20. Bonwit Teller: A fashionable and expensive department store.

and walked around looking like Al Jolson.°
Her father brought presents home from town,
jewels and gowns for the other women
but the twig of a tree for Cinderella.   35
She planted that twig on her mother's grave
and it grew to a tree where a white dove sat.
Whenever she wished for anything the dove
would drop it like an egg upon the ground.
The bird is important, my dears, so heed him.   40

Next came the ball, as you all know.
It was a marriage market.
The prince was looking for a wife.
All but Cinderella were preparing
and gussying up for the big event.   45
Cinderella begged to go too.
Her stepmother threw a dish of lentils
into the cinders and said: Pick them
up in an hour and you shall go.
The white dove brought all his friends;   50
all the warm wings of the fatherland came,
and picked up the lentils in a jiffy.
No, Cinderella, said the stepmother,
you have no clothes and cannot dance.
That's the way with stepmothers.   55

Cinderella went to the tree at the grave
and cried forth like a gospel singer:
Mama! Mama! My turtledove,
send me to the prince's ball!
The bird dropped down a golden dress   60
and delicate little gold slippers.
Rather a large package for a simple bird.
So she went. Which is no surprise.
Her stepmother and sisters didn't
recognize her without her cinder face   65
and the prince took her hand on the spot
and danced with no other the whole day.

As nightfall came she thought she'd better
get home. The prince walked her home

32. Al Jolson: American entertainer (1888–1950), known particularly for singing
in blackface.

and she disappeared into the pigeon house   70
and although the prince took an axe and broke
it open she was gone. Back to her cinders.
These events repeated themselves for three days.
However on the third day the prince
covered the palace steps with cobbler's wax   75
and Cinderella's gold shoe stuck upon it.

Now he would find whom the shoe fit
and find his strange dancing girl for keeps.
He went to their house and the two sisters
were delighted because they had lovely feet.   80
The eldest went into a room to try the slipper on
but her big toe got in the way so she simply
sliced it off and put on the slipper.
The prince rode away with her until the white dove
told him to look at the blood pouring forth.   85
That is the way with amputations.
They don't just heal up like a wish.
The other sister cut off her heel
but the blood told as blood will.
The prince was getting tired.   90
He began to feel like a shoe salesman.
But he gave it one last try.
This time Cinderella fit into the shoe
like a love letter into its envelope.

At the wedding ceremony   95
the two sisters came to curry favor
and the white dove pecked their eyes out.
Two hollow spots were left
like soup spoons.

Cinderella and the prince   100
lived, they say, happily ever after,
like two dolls in a museum case
never bothered by diapers or dust,
never arguing over the timing of an egg,
never telling the same story twice,   105
never getting a middle-aged spread,
their darling smiles pasted on for eternity.
Regular Bobbsey Twins.
That story.

[1971]

ADRIENNE RICH   [b. 1929]

Diving into the Wreck

First having read the book of myths,
and loaded the camera,
and checked the edge of the knife-blade,
I put on
the body-armor of black rubber   5
the absurd flippers
the grave and awkward mask.
I am having to do this
not like Cousteau° with his
assiduous team   10
aboard the sun-flooded schooner
but here alone.

There is a ladder.
The ladder is always there
hanging innocently   15
close to the side of the schooner.
We know what it is for,
we who have used it.
Otherwise
it's a piece of maritime floss   20
some sundry equipment.

I go down.
Rung after rung and still
the oxygen immerses me
the blue light   25
the clear atoms
of our human air.
I go down.
My flippers cripple me,
I crawl like an insect down the ladder   30
and there is no one
to tell me when the ocean
will begin.

---

9. **Cousteau:** Jacques-Yves Cousteau (1910–1997), French underwater explorer,
photographer, and author.

First the air is blue and then
it is bluer and then green and then   35
black I am blacking out and yet
my mask is powerful
it pumps my blood with power
the sea is another story
the sea is not a question of power   40
I have to learn alone
to turn my body without force
in the deep element.

And now: it is easy to forget
what I came for   45
among so many who have always
lived here
swaying their crenellated° fans
between the reefs
and besides   50
you breathe differently down here.

I came to explore the wreck.
The words are purposes.
The words are maps.
I came to see the damage that was done   55
and the treasures that prevail.
I stroke the beam of my lamp
slowly along the flank
of something more permanent
than fish or weed   60

the thing I came for:
the wreck and not the story of the wreck
the thing itself and not the myth
the drowned face° always staring
toward the sun   65
the evidence of damage
worn by salt and sway into this threadbare beauty
the ribs of the disaster
curving their assertion
among the tentative haunters.   70

48. crenellated: Notched; *crenels* are the open spaces between the solid portions
of a battlement.
64. drowned face: The ornamental female figurehead on the prow of an old sailing ship.

This is the place.
And I am here, the mermaid whose dark hair
streams black, the merman in his armored body
We circle silently
about the wreck   75
we dive into the hold.
I am she: I am he

whose drowned face sleeps with open eyes
whose breasts still bear the stress
whose silver, copper, vermeil° cargo lies   80
obscurely inside barrels
half-wedged and left to rot
we are the half-destroyed instruments
that once held to a course
the water-eaten log   85
the fouled compass

We are, I am, you are
by cowardice or courage
the one who find our way
back to this scene   90
carrying a knife, a camera
a book of myths
in which
our names do not appear.

                                                        [1973]

80. vermeil: Gilded silver, bronze, or copper.

GARY SNYDER   [b. 1930]

Hitch Haiku

They didn't hire him
          so he ate his lunch alone:
the noon whistle
                  • • •

Cats shut down
               deer thread through   5
men all eating lunch
        • • •

Frying hotcakes in a dripping shelter
            Fu Manchu°
Queets Indian Reservation in the rain
        • • •

A truck went by   10
              three hours ago:
Smoke Creek desert
        • • •

Jackrabbit eyes all night
  breakfast in Elko.
        • • •

Old kanji hid by dirt   15
on skidroad Jap town walls
          down the hill
to the Wobbly hall

Seattle
        • • •

Spray drips from the cargo-booms
a fresh-chipped winch   20
          spotted with red lead
young fir—
        soaking in summer rain
             • • •

Over the Mindanao Deep

Scrap bass
          dumpt off the fantail   25
falling six miles
        • • •

[*The following two were written on classical
themes while traveling through Sappho, Washington.
The first is by Thomas L. Hoodlatch.*]

Moonlight on the burned-out temple—
        wooden horse shit.

8. Fu Manchu: Master criminal in a series of "Yellow Peril Thrillers" by Sax
Rohmer (pen name of Arthur Henry Sarsfield Ward, 1883–1959) that were immensely popular in the first half of the twentieth century.

Sunday dinner in Ithaca—
       the twang of a bowstring   30
             • • •

After weeks of watching the roof leak
       I fixed it tonight
by moving a single board
             • • •

A freezing morning in October in the high
Sierra crossing Five Lakes Basin to the
Kaweahs with Bob Greensfelder and Claude Dalenburg

Stray white mare
           neck rope dangling   35
forty miles from farms.
             • • •

Back from the Kaweahs

Sundown, Timber Gap
        —sat down—
             dark firs.
  dirty;   cold;   40
too tired to talk
             • • •

Cherry blossoms at Hood river
          rusty sand near Tucson
mudflats of Willapa Bay
             • • •

Pronghorn country

Steering into the sun   45
          glittering jewel-road
shattered obsidian
             • • •

The mountain walks over the water!
Rain down from the mountain!
          high bleat of a   50
cow elk
        over blackberries
             • • •

A great freight truck
        lit like a town
through the dark stony desert   55
             • • •

Drinking hot saké
          toasting fish on coals
  the motorcycle
out   parked in the rain.
                • • •

Switchback

turn, turn,
and again,   hard-
scrabble
steep travel a-
head.

                           60

                          [1968]

DEREK WALCOTT   [b. 1930]

Sea Grapes

That sail which leans on light,
tired of islands,
a schooner beating up the Caribbean

for home, could be Odysseus,°
home-bound on the Aegean;
that father and husband's   5

longing, under gnarled sour grapes, is
like the adulterer hearing Nausicaa's name
in every gull's outcry.

This brings nobody peace. The ancient war   10
between obsession and responsibility
will never finish and has been the same

4. Odysseus: For background, see page 460. Princess Nausicaa (line 8) fell in love with Odysseus when he was carried by a storm to Phaiacia; he could have married her and stayed there, but he chose to go home (responsibility) rather than to enjoy an indulgent life with her (obsession). Odysseus blinded Polyphemus (line 16), a giant one-eyed Cyclops, who held him prisoner; as Odysseus escaped, Polyphemus threw great rocks in front of his boat to wash it back to shore. The *Odyssey* was written in hexameter verse (line 17).

for the sea-wanderer or the one on shore
now wriggling on his sandals to walk home,
since Troy sighed its last flame,   15

and the blind giant's boulder heaved the trough
from whose groundswell the great hexameters come
to the conclusions of exhausted surf.

The classics can console. But not enough.

[1976]

GEOFFREY HILL [b. 1932]

In Memory of Jane Fraser

When snow like sheep lay in the fold
And winds went begging at each door,
And the far hills were blue with cold,
And a cold shroud lay on the moor,

She kept the siege. And every day   5
We watched her brooding over death
Like a strong bird above its prey.
The room filled with the kettle's breath.

Damp curtains glued against the pane
Sealed time away. Her body froze   10
As if to freeze us all, and chain
Creation to a stunned repose.

She died before the world could stir.
In March the ice unloosed the brook
And water ruffled the sun's hair.   15
Dead cones upon the alder shook.

[1959]

LINDA PASTAN   [b. 1932]

An Early Afterlife

. . . a wise man in time of peace, shall
make the necessary preparations for war.
— HORACE

Why don't we say goodbye right now
in the fallacy of perfect health
before whatever is going to happen
happens. We could perfect our parting,   5
like those characters in *On the Beach*
who said farewell in the shadow
of the bomb as we sat watching,
young and holding hands at the movies.
We could use the loving words   10
we otherwise might not have time to say.
We could hold each other for hours
in a quintessential dress rehearsal.

Then we would just continue
for however many years were left.   15
The ragged things that are coming next—
arteries closing like rivers silting over,
or rampant cells stampeding us to the exit—
would be like postscripts to our lives
and wouldn't matter. And we would bask   20
in an early afterlife of ordinary days,
impervious to the inclement weather
already in our long-range forecast.
Nothing could touch us. We'd never
have to say goodbye again.

[1995]

SYLVIA PLATH [1932–1963]

Metaphors

I'm a riddle in nine syllables,
An elephant, a ponderous house,
A melon strolling on two tendrils.
O red fruit, ivory, fine timbers!
This loaf's big with its yeasty rising.   5
Money's new-minted in this fat purse.
I'm a means, a stage, a cow in calf.
I've eaten a bag of green apples,
Boarded the train there's no getting off.

[1960]

SYLVIA PLATH [1932–1963]

Daddy

You do not do, you do not do
Any more, black shoe
In which I have lived like a foot
For thirty years, poor and white,
Barely daring to breathe or Achoo.   5

Daddy, I have had to kill you.
You died before I had time—
Marble-heavy, a bag full of God,
Ghastly statue with one grey toe
Big as a Frisco seal   10

And a head in the freakish Atlantic
Where it pours bean green over blue
In the waters off beautiful Nauset.
I used to pray to recover you.
Ach, du.°   *Oh, you (German)*   15

In the German tongue, in the Polish town
Scraped flat by the roller

Of wars, wars, wars.
But the name of the town is common.
My Polack friend   20

Says there are a dozen or two.
So I never could tell where you
Put your foot, your root,
I never could talk to you.
The tongue stuck in my jaw.   25

It stuck in a barb wire snare.
Ich, ich, ich, ich,°   *I (German)*
I could hardly speak.
I thought every German was you.
And the language obscene   30

An engine, an engine
Chuffing me off like a Jew.
A Jew to Dachau, Auschwitz, Belsen.°
I began to talk like a Jew.
I think I may well be a Jew.   35

The snows of the Tyrol,° the clear beer of Vienna
Are not very pure or true.
With my gypsy ancestress and my weird luck
And my Taroc pack and my Taroc pack
I may be a bit of a Jew.   40

I have always been scared of *you,*
With your Luftwaffe,° your gobbledygoo.
And your neat moustache
And your Aryan eye, bright blue.
Panzer°-man, panzer-man, O You—   45

Not God but a swastika
So black no sky could squeak through.
Every woman adores a Fascist,
The boot in the face, the brute
Brute heart of a brute like you.   50

You stand at the blackboard, daddy,
In the picture I have of you,

33. **Dachau, Auschwitz, Belsen:** Nazi concentration camps.
36. **the Tyrol:** An alpine region in western Austria and northern Italy.
42. **Luftwaffe:** The Nazi air force in World War II.
45. **Panzer:** An armored unit in the German army in World War II.

A cleft in your chin instead of your foot
But no less a devil for that, no not
Any less the black man who   55

Bit my pretty red heart in two.
I was ten when they buried you.
At twenty I tried to die
And get back, back, back to you.
I thought even the bones would do.   60

But they pulled me out of the sack,
And they stuck me together with glue.
And then I knew what to do.
I made a model of you,
A man in black with a Meinkampf° look   65

And a love of the rack and the screw.
And I said I do, I do.
So daddy, I'm finally through.
The black telephone's off at the root,
The voices just can't worm through.   70

If I've killed one man, I've killed two—
The vampire who said he was you
And drank my blood for a year,
Seven years, if you want to know.
Daddy, you can lie back now.   75

There's a stake in your fat black heart
And the villagers never liked you.
They are dancing and stamping on you.
They always *knew* it was you.
Daddy, daddy, you bastard, I'm through.   80

                                                        [1962]

65. *Mein Kampf*: *My Struggle,* the title of Adolf Hitler's autobiography.

ETHERIDGE KNIGHT [1933–1991]

Hard Rock Returns to Prison from the Hospital for the Criminal Insane

Hard Rock / was / "known not to take no shit
From nobody," and he had the scars to prove it:
Split purple lips, lumbed ears, welts above
His yellow eyes, and one long scar that cut
Across his temple and plowed through a thick   5
Canopy of kinky hair.

The WORD / was / that Hard Rock wasn't a mean nigger
Anymore, that the doctors had bored a hole in his head,
Cut out part of his brain, and shot electricity
Through the rest. When they brought Hard Rock back,   10
Handcuffed and chained, he was turned loose,
Like a freshly gelded stallion, to try his new status.
And we all waited and watched, like a herd of sheep,
To see if the WORD was true.

As we waited we wrapped ourselves in the cloak   15
Of his exploits: "Man, the last time, it took eight
Screws° to put him in the Hole."° "Yeah, remember when he
Smacked the captain with his dinner tray?" "He set
The record for time in the Hole—67 straight days!"
"Ol Hard Rock! man, that's one crazy nigger."   20
And then the jewel of a myth that Hard Rock had once bit
A screw on the thumb and poisoned him with syphilitic spit.

The testing came, to see if Hard Rock was really tame.
A hillbilly called him a black son of a bitch
And didn't lose his teeth, a screw who knew Hard Rock   25
From before shook him down and barked in his face.
And Hard Rock did *nothing*. Just grinned and looked silly,
His eyes empty like knot holes in a fence.

And even after we discovered that it took Hard Rock
Exactly 3 minutes to tell you his first name,   30

17. **Screws:** Guards; **Hole:** Solitary confinement.

We told ourselves that he had just wised up,
Was being cool; but we could not fool ourselves for long,
And we turned away, our eyes on the ground. Crushed.
He had been our Destroyer, the doer of things
We dreamed of doing but could not bring ourselves to do,   35
The fears of years, like a biting whip,
Had cut deep bloody grooves
Across our backs.

[1968]

JIM BARNES   [b. 1933]

Return to La Plata, Missouri

The warping bandstand reminds you of the hard rage
you felt in the heart of the town the day you said goodbye
to the park, silver jet, and cicadas dead in the sage.

The town is basic red, although it browns. A cry
of murder, rape, or wrong will always bend the night   5
hard into the broken grass. You listen close for sighs

of lovers on the ground. The darkness gathers light
and throws it down: something glows that you cannot name,
something fierce, abstract, given time and space you might

on a journey leave behind, a stone to carve your fame   10
on, or a simple word like *love*. The sun is down
or always going down in La Plata, the same

sun. Same too the child's cry that turns the mother's frown
brittle as chalk or the town's face against the moon.
Same too the moan of dog and diesel circling the town   15

in an air so heavy with cloud that there is little room
for breath or moon. Strange: in a town so country, so
foreign, you never hear a song nor see a loom

pattern dark threads into a history you would know
and would not know. You think you see one silver star.   20
But the town offers only itself, and you must go.

[1982]

JEAN VALENTINE   [b. 1934]

December 21st

How will I think of you
"God-with-us"
a name: a word

and trees paths stars this earth
how will I think of them   5

and the dead I love   and all absent friends
here-with-me

and table: hand: white coffee mug:
a northern still life:

and you   10
without a body

quietness

and the infant's red-brown mouth   a star
at the star of a girl's nipple . . .

[1979]

SONIA SANCHEZ   [b. 1934]

An Anthem

for the anc and brandywine peace community

Our vision is our voice
we cut through the country
where madmen goosestep in tune to Guernica.°

3. **Guernica:** A town in northern Spain that was destroyed in 1937 by insurgents
in the Spanish civil war, aided by German planes; the indiscriminate killing of
women and children aroused world opinion, and the bombing of Guernica made
it a symbol of fascist brutality.

we are people made of fire
we walk with ceremonial breaths   5
we have condemned talking mouths.

we run without legs
we see without eyes
loud laughter breaks over our heads.

give me courage so I can spread   10
it over my face and mouth.

we are secret rivers
with shaking hips and crests
come awake in our thunder
so that our eyes can see behind trees.   15

for the world is split wide open
and you hide your hands behind your backs
for the world is broken into little pieces
and you beg with tin cups for life.

are we not more than hunger and music?   20
are we not more than harlequins and horns?
are we not more than color and drums?
are we not more than anger and dance?
give me courage so I can spread it
over my face and mouth.   25

we are the shakers
walking from top to bottom in a day
we are like Shango°
involving ourselves in acts
that bring life to the middle   30
of our stomachs

we are coming towards you madmen
shredding your death talk
standing in front with mornings around our waist
we have inherited our prayers from   35
the rain
our eyes from the children of Soweto.°

28. Shango: One of the orishas, or gods, of the Yoruba tribe of western Nigeria.
The legendary fourth king of the ancient kingdom of Oyo, he is lord of lightning,
thunder, rain, and testicular fertility.
37. Soweto: A group of segregated townships inhabited by blacks near Johannes-
burg, South Africa. It was the scene of a massive uprising in 1976 against the poli-
cies of apartheid.

red rain pours over the land
and our fire mixes with the water.

give me courage so I can spread   40
it over my face and mouth.

[1987]

PAUL ZIMMER   [b. 1934]

Zimmer Imagines Heaven

for Merrill Leffler

I sit with Joseph Conrad in Monet's garden.
We are listening to Yeats chant his poems,
A breeze stirs through Thomas Hardy's moustache,
John Skelton has gone to the house for beer,
Wanda Landowska lightly fingers a harpsichord,   5
Along the spruce tree walk Roberto Clemente and
Thurman Munson whistle a baseball back and forth.
Mozart chats with Ellington in the roses.

Monet smokes and dabs his canvas in the sun,
Brueghel and Turner set easels behind the wisteria.   10
The band is warming up in the Big Studio:
Bean, Brute, Bird, and Serge on saxes,
Kai, Bill Harris, Lawrence Brown trombones,
Little Jazz, Clifford, Fats, Diz on trumpets,
Klook plays drums, Mingus bass, Bud the piano.   15
Later Madam Schuman-Heink will sing Schubert,
The monks of Benedictine Abbey will chant.
There will be more poems from Emily Dickinson,
James Wright, John Clare, Walt Whitman.
Shakespeare rehearses players for *King Lear*.   20

At dusk Alice Toklas brings out platters
Of sweetbreads, Salad Livonière,
And a tureen of Gazpacho of Málaga.
After the meal Brahms passes fine cigars.
God comes then, radiant with a bottle of cognac,   25
She pours generously into the snifters,

I tell Her I have begun to learn what
Heaven is about. She wants to hear.
It is, I say, being thankful for eternity.
Her smile is the best part of the day.   30

[1996]

AUDRE LORDE [1934–1992]

Coal

I   is the total black
being spoken
from the earth's inside.

There are many kinds of open
how a diamond comes   5
into a knot of flame
how sound comes into a word
colored
by who pays what for speaking.

Some words are open   10
diamonds on a glass window
singing out within the crash
of passing sun
other words are stapled wagers
in a perforated book   15
buy and sign and tear apart
and come whatever wills all chances
the stub remains
an ill-pulled tooth
with a ragged edge.   20

Some words live in my throat
breeding like adders
others
know sun
seeking like gypsies   25
over my tongue

to explode through my lips
like young sparrows
bursting from shell.

Some words   30
bedevil me.

Love is a word, another kind of open.
As the diamond comes
into a knot of flame
I am Black   35
because I come from the earth's inside
take my word for jewel
in the open light.

[1962; rev. 1992]

CHARLES WRIGHT [b. 1935]

March Journal

—After the Rapture comes, and everyone goes away
Quicker than cream in a cat's mouth,
                              all of them gone
In an endless slipknot down the sky
                              and its pink tongue   5
Into the black hole of Somewhere Else,

What will we do, left with the empty spaces of our lives
Intact,
        the radio frequencies still unchanged,
The same houses up for sale,   10
Same books unread,
                all comfort gone and its comforting . . .

For us, the earth is a turbulent rest,
                                    a different bed
Altogether, and kinder than that—   15
After the first death is the second,
A little fire in the afterglow,
                        somewhere to warm your hands.

—The clean, clear line, incised, unbleeding,
Sharp and declarative as a cut   20
                    the instant before the blood wells out . . .

—*March Blues*
·The insides were blue, the color of Power Putty,
When Luke dissected the dogfish,
                              a plastic blue   25
In the whey
          sharkskin infenestrated:
Its severed tailfin bobbed like a wing nut in another pan
As he explained the dye job
                    and what connected with what,   30
Its pursed lips skewed and pointed straight-lined at the ceiling,
The insides so blue, so blue . . .

March gets its second wind,
                    starlings high shine in the trees
As dread puts its left foot down and then the other.   35
Buds hold their breaths and sit tight.
The weeping cherries
          lower their languorous necks and nibble the grass
Sprout ends that jump headfirst from the ground,
Magnolia drums blue weight   40
                    next door when the sun is right.

—Rhythm comes from the roots of the world,
                              rehearsed and expandable.

—After the ice storm a shower of crystal down from the trees
Shattering over the ground   45
                    like cut glass twirling its rainbows,
Sunlight in flushed layers under the clouds,
Twirling and disappearing into the clenched March grass.

—Structure is binary, intent on a resolution,
Its parts tight but the whole loose   50
                    and endlessly repetitious.

—And here we stand, caught
In the crucifixal noon
                    with its bled, attendant bells,
And nothing to answer back with.   55
Forsythia purrs in its burning shell,
Jonquils, like Dante's angels, appear from their blue shoots.

How can we think to know of another's desire for darkness,
That low coo like a dove's
                              insistent outside the heart's window?   60
How can we think to think this?
How can we sit here, crossing out line after line,
Such five-finger exercises
                              up and down, learning our scales,

And say that all quartets are eschatological°   *pertaining to the end times*   65
Heuristically
                  when the willows swim like medusas through the trees,
Their skins beginning to blister into a thousand green welts?
How can we think to know these things,
Clouds like full suds in the sky   70
                              keeping away, keeping away?

— Form is finite, an undestroyable hush over all things.

                                                                    [1988]

MARY OLIVER   [b. 1935]

August

When the blackberries hang
swollen in the woods, in the brambles
nobody owns, I spend

all day among the high
branches, reaching   5
my ripped arms, thinking

of nothing, cramming
the black honey of summer
into my mouth; all day my body

accepts what it is. In the dark   10
creeks that run by there is
this thick paw of my life darting among

the black bells, the leaves; there is
this happy tongue.

                                                                    [1983]

JAYNE CORTEZ   [b. 1936]

Into This Time

for Charles Mingus°

Into this time
of steel feathers blowing from hearts
into this turquoise flame time in the mouth
into this sonic boom time in the conch
into this musty stone-fly time sinking into   5
the melancholy buttocks of dawn
sinking into lacerated whelps
into gun holsters
into breast bones
into a manganese field of uranium nozzles   10
into a nuclear tube full of drunk rodents
into the massive vein of one interval
into one moment's hair plucked down into
the timeless droning fixed into
long pauses   15
fixed into a lash of ninety-eight minutes screeching into
the internal heat of an ice ball melting time into
a configuration of commas on strike
into a work force armed with a calendar of green wings
into a collection of nerves   20
into magnetic mucus
into tongueless shrines
into water pus of a silver volcano
into the black granite face of Morelos°
into the pigeon toed dance of Mingus   25
into a refuge of air bubbles
into a cylinder of snake whistles
into clusters of slow spiders
into spade fish skulls
into rosin coated shadows of women wrapped in live iguanas   30
into coins into crosses into St. Martin De Porres°

Charles Mingus: An innovative American jazz bassist (1929–1979).
24. Morelos: José Maria Morelos (1765–1815), a Mexican revolutionary leader.
31. Martin De Porres: A seventeenth-century Peruvian saint.

into the pain of this place changing pitches beneath
fingers swelling into
night shouts
into day trembles   35
into month of precious bloods flowing into
this fiesta of sadness year
into this city of eternal spring
into this solo
on the road of young bulls   40
on the street of lost children
on the avenue of dead warriors
on the frisky horse tail fuzz zooming
into ears of every madman
stomping into every new composition   45
everyday of the blues
penetrating into this time

This time of loose strings in low tones
pulling boulders of Olmec heads into the sun
into tight wires uncoiling from body of a strip teaser on the table   50
into half-tones wailing between snap and click
of two castanets smoking into
scales jumping from tips of sacrificial flints
into frogs yodeling across grieving cults
yodeling up into word stuffed smell of flamingo stew   55
into wind packed fuel of howling dog throats slit into
this January flare of aluminum dust falling into
laminated stomach of a bass violin rubbed into red ashes
rubbed into the time sequence of
this time of salmonella leaking from eyeballs of a pope   60
into this lavender vomit time in the chest into
this time plumage of dried bats in the brain into
this wallowing time weed of invisible wakes on cassettes into
this off-beat time syncopation in a leopard skin suit
into this radiated protrusion of time in the desert into   65
this frozen cheek time of dead infants in the cellar
into this time flying with the rotten bottoms of used tuxedos
into this purple   brown   grey   gold minus zero time trilling into
a lime stone crusted Yucatan belching
into fifty six medallions shaking   70
into armadillo drums thumping
into tambourines of fetishes rattling
into an oil slick of poverty symbols flapping

into flat-footed shuffle of two birds advancing
into back spine of luminous impulses tumbling   75
into metronomes of colossal lips ticking
into a double zigzag of callouses splitting
into foam of electric snow flashing into this time
of steel feathers blowing from hearts
into this turquoise flame time in the mouth into   80
this sonic boom time in the conch
into this musty stone fly time sinking into
the melancholy buttocks of dawn

                                                        [1991]

LUCILLE CLIFTON [b. 1936]

at the cemetery,
walnut grove plantation,
south carolina, 1989

among the rocks
at walnut grove
your silence drumming
in my bones,
tell me your names.   5

nobody mentioned slaves
and yet the curious tools
shine with your fingerprints.
nobody mentioned slaves
but somebody did this work   10
who had no guide, no stone,
who moulders under rock.

tell me your names,
tell me your bashful names
and i will testify.   15

the inventory lists ten slaves
but only men were recognized.

among the rocks
at walnut grove
some of these honored dead   20
were dark
some of these dark
were slaves
some of these slaves
were women   25
some of them did this
honored work.
tell me your names
foremothers, brothers,
tell me your dishonored names.   30
here lies
here lies
here lies
here lies
hear   35

[1991]

NANCY WILLARD   [b. 1936]

Questions My Son Asked Me, Answers I Never Gave Him

1. Do gorillas have birthdays?
    Yes. Like the rainbow, they happen.
    Like the air, they are not observed.

2. Do butterflies make a noise?
    The wire in the butterfly's tongue
    hums gold. Some men hear butterflies
    even in winter.

3. Are they part of our family?
    They forgot us, who forgot how to fly.

4. Who tied my navel? Did God tie it?
    God made the thread: O man, live forever!
    Man made the knot: enough is enough.

5. If I drop my tooth in the telephone
    will it go through the wires and bite someone's ear?
    I have seen earlobes pierced by a tooth of steel.
    It loves what lasts.
    It does not love flesh.
    It leaves a ring of gold in the wound.

6. If I stand on my head
    will the sleep in my eye roll up into my head?
    Does the dream know its own father?
    Can bread go back to the field of its birth?

7. Can I eat a star?
    Yes, with the mouth of time
    that enjoys everything.

8. Could we Xerox the moon?
    This is the first commandment:
    I am the moon, thy moon.
    Thou shalt have no other moons before thee.

9. Who invented water?
    The hands of the air, that wanted to wash each other.

10. What happens at the end of numbers?
    I see three men running toward a field.
    At the edge of the tall grass, they turn into light.

11. Do the years ever run out?
    God said, I will break time's heart.
    Time ran down like an old phonograph.
    It lay flat as a carpet.
    At rest on its threads, I am learning to fly.

[1982]

DAVID YOUNG [b. 1936]

The Portable Earth-Lamp

The planet on the desk, illuminated globe
we ordered for Bo's birthday,
sits in its Lucite crescent, a medicine ball

of Rand McNally plastic. A brown cord
runs from the South Pole toward a socket.   5

It's mostly a night-light for the boys
and it blanches their dreaming faces
a blue sphere patched with continents
mottled by deeps and patterned currents,
its capital cities bright white dots.   10

Our models: they're touching and absurd,
magical for both their truth and falsehood.

I like its shine at night. Moth-light.
I sleepwalk toward it, musing.
This globe's a bible, a bubble of myth-   15
light, a blue eye, a double
bowl: empty of all but its bulb and clever skin,
full of whatever we choose to lodge there.

I haven't been able to shake off all my grief,
my globe's cold poles and arid wastes,   20
the weight of death, disease and history.
But see how the oceans heave and shine,
see how the clouds and mountains glisten!

We float through space. Days pass.
Sometimes we know we are part of a crystal   25
where light is sorted and stored,
sharing an iridescence
cobbled and million-featured.

Oh, tiny beacon in the hurting dark.
Oh, soft blue glow.   30

[1988]

MARGE PIERCY   [b. 1936]

Barbie Doll

This girlchild was born as usual
and presented dolls that did pee-pee
and miniature GE stoves and irons

and wee lipsticks the color of cherry candy.
Then in the magic of puberty, a classmate said: 5
You have a great big nose and fat legs.

She was healthy, tested intelligent,
possessed strong arms and back,
abundant sexual drive and manual dexterity.
She went to and fro apologizing.   10
Everyone saw a fat nose on thick legs.

She was advised to play coy,
exhorted to come on hearty,
exercise, diet, smile and wheedle.
Her good nature wore out   15
like a fan belt.
So she cut off her nose and her legs
and offered them up.

In the casket displayed on satin she lay
with the undertaker's cosmetics painted on,   20
a turned-up putty nose,
dressed in a pink and white nightie.
Doesn't she look pretty? everyone said.
Consummation at last.
To every woman a happy ending.   25

[1973]

SUSAN HOWE   [b. 1937]

From Speeches at
the Barriers

2.

Right or ruth
rent

to the winds shall be thrown

words being wind or web

What (pine-cone wheat-ear   35
sea-shell) what

volume of secrets to teach
Socrates

Banks of wild bees in story
sing in no wood so on   40

cornstalk and cornsheaf

prodigal benevolence
wealth washed up by the sea

What I find
signal seen by my eye   45

This winter falls froward
forever

sound and suggestion speared
open

Free will in blind duel   50

sees in secret houses in sand

each day's last purpose
each day's firm progress

schoolgirls sleeping
schoolboys sleeping and stemmed   55

I will dream you
Draw you

dawn and horses of the sun
dawn galloped in greek before flame

fugitive dialogue of masterwork   60

[1983]

CHARLES SIMIC [b. 1938]

Begotten of the Spleen°

The Virgin Mother° walked barefoot
Among the land mines.
She carried an old man in her arms
Like a howling babe.

The earth was an old people's home.   5
Judas was the night nurse,
Emptying bedpans into the river Jordan,
Tying people on a dog chain.

The old man had two stumps for legs.
St. Peter came pushing a cart   10
Loaded with flying carpets.
They were not flying carpets.

They were piles of bloody diapers.
The Magi° stood around
Cleaning their nails with bayonets.   15
The old man gave little Mary Magdalene°

A broke piece of a mirror.
She hid in the church outhouse.
When she got thirsty she licked
the steam off the glass.   20

That leaves Joseph.° Poor Joseph,
Standing naked in the snow.
He only had a rat
To load his suitcases on.

The rat wouldn't run into its hole.   25
Even when the lights came on—
And the lights came on:
The floodlights in the guard towers.

[1980; 1999]

Spleen: The seat or source in a person either of high spirit, courage, and resolute
mind or of ill-nature, ill-humor, and irritable or peevish temper.
1. The Virgin Mother: Mary, the mother of Jesus.
14. Magi: The wise men from the East who visited the baby Jesus.
16. Mary Magdalene: A follower of Jesus who was present at his crucifixion and
burial and who went to the tomb on Easter Sunday to anoint his body.
21. Joseph: The husband of Mary, the mother of Jesus.

MICHAEL S. HARPER [b. 1938]

Nightmare Begins Responsibility

I place these numbed wrists to the pane
watching white uniforms whisk over
him in the tube-kept
prison
fear what they will do in experiment   5
watch my gloved stickshifting gasolined hands
breathe *boxcar-information-please* infirmary tubes
distrusting white-pink mending paperthin
silkened end hairs, distrusting tubes
shrunk in his *trunk-skincapped*   10
shaven head, in thighs
distrusting-white-hands-picking-baboon-light
on this son who will not make his second night
of this wardstrewn intensive airpocket
where his father's asthmatic   15
hymns of *night-train,* train done gone
his mother can only know that he has flown
up into essential calm unseen corridor
going boxscarred home, *mamaborn, sweetsonchild*
gonedowntown into *researchtestingwarehousebatteryacid* 20
mama-son-done-gone/me telling her 'nother
train tonight, no music, no breathstroked
heartbeat in my infinite distrust of them:

and of my distrusting self
white-doctor-who-breathed-for-him-all-night   25
say it for two sons gone,
say nightmare, say it loud
panebreaking heartmadness:
nightmare begins responsibility.

[1975]

SEAMUS HEANEY   [b. 1939]

Digging

Between my finger and my thumb
The squat pen rests; snug as a gun.

Under my window, a clean rasping sound
When the spade sinks into gravelly ground:
My father, digging. I look down   5

Till his straining rump among the flowerbeds
Bends low, comes up twenty years away
Stooping in rhythm through potato drills
Where he was digging.

The coarse boot nestled on the lug, the shaft   10
Against the inside knee was levered firmly.
He rooted out tall tops, buried the bright edge deep
To scatter new potatoes that we picked
Loving their cool hardness in our hands.

By God, the old man could handle a spade.   15
Just like his old man.

My grandfather cut more turf in a day
Than any other man on Toner's bog.
Once I carried him milk in a bottle
Corked sloppily with paper. He straightened up   20
To drink it, then fell to right away
Nicking and slicing neatly, heaving sods
Over his shoulder, going down and down
For the good turf. Digging.

The cold smell of potato mould, the squelch and slap   25
Of soggy peat, the curt cuts of an edge
Through living roots awaken in my head.
But I've no spade to follow men like them.

Between my finger and my thumb
The squat pen rests.   30
I'll dig with it.

[1966]

MARGARET ATWOOD [b. 1939]

The Woman Who Could Not Live with Her Faulty Heart

I do not mean the symbol
of love, a candy shape
to decorate cakes with,
the heart that is supposed
to belong or break;   5

I mean this lump of muscle
that contracts like a flayed biceps,
purple-blue, with its skin of suet,
its skin of gristle, this isolate,
this caved hermit, unshelled   10
turtle, this one lungful of blood,
no happy plateful.

All hearts float in their own
deep oceans of no light,
wetblack and glimmering,   15
their four mouths gulping like fish.
Hearts are said to pound:
this is to be expected, the heart's
regular struggle against being drowned.

But most hearts say, I want, I want,   20
I want, I want. My heart
is more duplicitous,
though no twin as I once thought.
It says, I want, I don't want, I
want, and then a pause.   25
It forces me to listen,

and at night it is the infra-red
third eye that remains open
while the other two are sleeping
but refuses to say what it has seen.   30

It is a constant pestering
in my ears, a caught moth, limping drum,
a child's first beating

itself against the bedsprings:
I want, I don't want.   35
How can one live with such a heart?

Long ago I gave up singing
to it, it will never be satisfied or lulled.
One night I will say to it:
Heart, be still,   40
and it will.

[1978]

AL YOUNG   [b. 1939]

A Dance for Ma Rainey°

I'm going to be just like you, Ma
Rainey this monday morning
clouds puffing up out of my head
like those balloons
that float above the faces of white people   5
in the funnypapers

I'm going to hover in the corners
of the world, Ma
& sing from the bottom of hell
up to the tops of high heaven   10
& send out scratchless waves of yellow
& brown & that basic black honey
misery

I'm going to cry so sweet
& so low   15
& so dangerous,
Ma,
that the message is going to reach you
back in 1922
where you shimmer   20

Ma Rainey: Gertrude Pridgett (1886–1939), known after her marriage as Ma
Rainey, was a noted vaudeville entertainer and blues singer, credited as being the
"Mother of the Blues."

snaggle-toothed
perfumed &
powdered
in your bauble beads

hair pressed & tied back   25
throbbing with that sick pain
I know
& hide so well
that pain that blues
jives the world with   30
aching to be heard
that downness
that bottomlessness
first felt by some stolen delta nigger
swamped under with redblooded american agony;   35
reduced to the sheer shit
of existence
that bred
& battered us all,
Ma,   40
the beautiful people
our beautiful brave black people
who no longer need to jazz
or sing to themselves in murderous vibrations
or play the veins of their strong tender arms   45
with needles
to prove we're still here

[1969]

JAMES WELCH   [b. 1940]

Christmas Comes to
Moccasin Flat

Christmas comes like this: Wise men
unhurried, candles bought on credit (poor price
for calves), warriors face down in wine sleep.
Winds cheat to pull heat from smoke.

Friends sit in chinked cabins, stare out   5
plastic windows and wait for commodities.
Charlie Blackbird, twenty miles from church
and bar, stabs his fire with flint.

When drunks drain radiators for love
or need, chiefs eat snow and talk of change,   10
an urge to laugh pounding their ribs.
Elk play games in high country.

Medicine Woman, clay pipe and twist tobacco,
calls each blizzard by name and predicts
five o'clock by spitting at her television.   15
Children lean into her breath to beg a story:

Something about honor and passion,
warriors back with meat and song,
a peculiar evening star, quick vision of birth.
Blackbird feeds his fire. Outside, a quick 30 below.   20

[1976]

NELLIE   WONG   [b. 1940]

Grandmother's Song

Grandmothers sing their song
Blinded by the suns' rays
Grandchildren for whom they long
For pomelo°-golden days   *grapefruit*

Blinded by the sun's rays   5
Gold bracelets, opal rings
For pomelo-golden days
Tiny fingers, ancient things

Gold bracelets, opal rings
Sprinkled with Peking dust   10
Tiny fingers, ancient things
So young they'll never rust

Sprinkled with Peking dust
To dance in fields of mud

So young they'll never rust   15
Proud as if of royal blood

To dance in fields of mud
Or peel shrimp for pennies a day
Proud as if of royal blood
Coins and jade to put away   20

Or peel shrimp for pennies a day
Seaweed washes up the shore
Coins and jade to put away
A camphor chest is home no more

Seaweed washes up the shore   25
Bound feet struggle to loosen free
A camphor chest is home no more
A foreign tongue is learned at three

Bound feet struggle to loosen free
Grandchildren for whom they long   30
A foreign tongue is learned at three
Grandmothers sing their song

[1977]

ROBERT PINSKY   [b. 1940]

Shirt

The back, the yoke, the yardage. Lapped seams,
The nearly invisible stitches along the collar
Turned in a sweatshop by Koreans or Malaysians

Gossiping over tea and noodles on their break
Or talking money or politics while one fitted   5
This armpiece with its overseam to the band

Of cuff I button at my wrist. The presser, the cutter,
The wringer, the mangle. The needle, the union,
The treadle, the bobbin. The code. The infamous blaze

At the Triangle Factory° in nineteen-eleven.   *(in New York City)* 10
One hundred and forty-six died in the flames
On the ninth floor, no hydrants, no fire escapes —

The witness in a building across the street
Who watched how a young man helped a girl to step
Up to the windowsill, then held her out   15

Away from the masonry wall and let her drop.
And then another. As if he were helping them up
To enter a streetcar, and not eternity.

A third before he dropped her put her arms
Around his neck and kissed him. Then he held   20
Her into space, and dropped her. Almost at once

He stepped to the sill himself, his jacket flared
And fluttered up from his shirt as he came down,
Air filling up the legs of his gray trousers—

Like Hart Crane's Bedlamite, "shrill shirt ballooning."   25
Wonderful how the pattern matches perfectly
Across the placket and over the twin bar-tacked

Corners of both pockets, like a strict rhyme
Or a major chord. Prints, plaids, checks,
Houndstooth, Tattersall, Madras. The clan tartans   30

Invented by mill-owners inspired by the hoax of Ossian,°
To control their savage Scottish workers, tamed
By a fabricated heraldry: MacGregor,

Bailey, MacMartin. The kilt, devised for workers
To wear among the dusty clattering looms.   35
Weavers, carders, spinners. The loader,

The docker, the navvy. The planter, the picker, the sorter
Sweating at her machine in a litter of cotton
As slaves in calico headrags sweated in fields:

George Herbert,° your descendant is a Black   40
Lady in South Carolina, her name is Irma
And she inspected my shirt. Its color and fit

---

31. Ossian: Legendary Gaelic poet, hero of a cycle of traditional tales and poems that place him in the third century C.E. The hoax involved Scottish author James Macpherson (1736–1796), who published two epic poems that he said were translations of works written by Ossian but were in fact mostly composed by Macpherson himself.
40. George Herbert: (1593–1633), English metaphysical poet. See Biographical Notes (p. 1394).

And feel and its clean smell have satisfied
Both her and me. We have culled its cost and quality
Down to the buttons of simulated bone,   45

The buttonholes, the sizing, the facing, the characters
Printed in black on neckband and tail. The shape,
The label, the labor, the color, the shade. The shirt.

[1990]

ROBERT HASS   [b. 1941]

Late Spring

And then in mid-May the first morning of steady heat,

the morning, Leif says, when you wake up, put on shorts, and that's it for
the day,

when you pour coffee and walk outside, blinking in the sun.

Strawberries have appeared in the markets, and peaches will soon;

squid is so cheap in the fishstores you begin to consult Japanese and
Italian cookbooks for the various and ingenious ways of preparing *ika*
and *calamari*;°   5

and because the light will enlarge your days, your dreams at night will
be as strange as the jars of octopus you saw once in a fisherman's boat
under the summer moon;

and after swimming, white wine; and the sharing of stories before dinner is prolonged because the relations of the children in the neighborhood have acquired village intensity and the stories take longer telling;

and there are the nights when the fog rolls in that nobody likes—hey,
fog, the Miwok° sang, who lived here first, you better go home, pelican is
beating your wife—

and after dark in the first cool hour, your children sleep so heavily in
their beds exhausted from play, it is a pleasure to watch them,

5. *ika* and *calamari*: Squid, in Japanese and Italian.
8. the Miwok: Native American people formerly living in California.

Leif does not move a muscle as he lies there; no, wait; it is Luke who lies
there in his eight-year-old body,   10

Leif is taller than you are and he isn't home; when he is, his feet will
extend past the end of the mattress, and Kristin is at the corner in the
dark, talking to neighborhood boys;

things change; there is no need for this dream-compelled narration; the
rhythm will keep me awake, changing.

[1989]

BILLY COLLINS   [b. 1941]

Aristotle

This is the beginning.
Almost anything can happen.
This is where you find
the creation of light, a fish wriggling onto land,
the first word of *Paradise Lost* on an empty page.   5
Think of an egg, the letter *A*,
a woman ironing on a bare stage
as the heavy curtain rises.
This is the very beginning.
The first-person narrator introduces himself,   10
tells us about his lineage.
The mezzo-soprano stands in the wings.
Here the climbers are studying a map
or pulling on their long woolen socks.
This is early on, years before the Ark, dawn.   15
The profile of an animal is being smeared
on the wall of a cave,
and you have not yet learned to crawl.
This is the opening, the gambit,
a pawn moving forward an inch.   20
This is your first night with her,
your first night without her.
This is the first part
where the wheels begin to turn,

where the elevator begins its ascent,   25
before the doors lurch apart.

This is the middle.
Things have had time to get complicated,
messy, really. Nothing is simple anymore.
Cities have sprouted up along the rivers   30
teeming with people at cross-purposes—
a million schemes, a million wild looks.
Disappointment unshoulders his knapsack
here and pitches his ragged tent.
This is the sticky part where the plot congeals,   35
where the action suddenly reverses
or swerves off in an outrageous direction.
Here the narrator devotes a long paragraph
to why Miriam does not want Edward's child.
Someone hides a letter under a pillow.   40
Here the aria rises to a pitch,
a song of betrayal, salted with revenge.
And the climbing party is stuck on a ledge
halfway up the mountain.
This is the bridge, the painful modulation.   45
This is the thick of things.
So much is crowded into the middle—
the guitars of Spain, piles of ripe avocados,
Russian uniforms, noisy parties,
lakeside kisses, arguments heard through a wall—   50
too much to name, too much to think about.

And this is the end,
the car running out of road,
the river losing its name in an ocean,
the long nose of the photographed horse   55
touching the white electronic line.
This is the colophon, the last elephant in the parade,
the empty wheelchair,
and pigeons floating down in the evening.
Here the stage is littered with bodies,   60
the narrator leads the characters to their cells,
and the climbers are in their graves.
It is me hitting the period
and you closing the book.
It is Sylvia Plath in the kitchen   65

and St. Clement with an anchor around his neck.
This is the final bit
thinning away to nothing.
This is the end, according to Aristotle,
that we have all been waiting for,   70
what everything comes down to,
the destination we cannot help imagining,
a streak of light in the sky,
a hat on a peg, and outside the cabin, falling leaves.

[1998]

RICHARD GARCIA   [b. 1941]

Why I Left the Church

Maybe it was
because the only time
I hit a baseball
it smashed the neon cross
on the church across   5
the street. Even
twenty-five years later
when I saw Father Harris
I would wonder
if he knew it was me.   10
Maybe it was the demon-stoked
rotisseries of purgatory
where we would roast
hundreds of years
for the smallest of sins.   15
Or was it the day
I wore my space helmet
to catechism? Clear plastic
with a red-and-white
inflatable rim.   20
Sister Mary Bernadette
pointed toward the door
and said, "Out! Come back
when you're ready."
I rose from my chair   25

and kept rising
toward the ceiling
while the children
screamed and Sister
kept crossing herself.   30
The last she saw of me
was my shoes disappearing
through cracked plaster.
I rose into the sky and beyond.
It is a good thing   35
I am wearing my helmet,
I thought as I floated
and turned in the blackness
and brightness of outer space,
my body cold on one side and hot   40
on the other. It would
have been very quiet
if my blood had not been
rumbling in my ears so loud.
I remember thinking,   45
Maybe I will come back
when I'm ready.
But I won't tell
the other children
what it was like.   50
I'll have to make something up.

[1993]

SIMON J. ORTIZ   [b. 1941]

Speaking

I take him outside
under the trees,
have him stand on the ground.
We listen to the crickets,
cicadas, million years old sound.   5
Ants come by us.
I tell them,
"This is he, my son.

This boy is looking at you.
I am speaking for him."   10

The crickets, cicadas,
the ants, the millions of years
are watching us,
hearing us.
My son murmurs infant words,   15
speaking, small laughter
bubbles from him.
Tree leaves tremble.
They listen to this boy
speaking for me.   20

[1977]

TOI DERRICOTTE   [b. 1941]

A Note on My Son's Face

I

Tonight, I look, thunderstruck
at the gold head of my grandchild.
Almost asleep, he buries his feet
between my thighs;
his little straw eyes   5
close in the near dark.
I smell the warmth of his raw
slightly foul breath, the new death
waiting to rot inside him.
Our breaths equalize our heartbeats;   10
every muscle of the chest uncoils,
the arm bones loosen in the nest
of nerves. I think of the peace
of walking through the house,
pointing to the name of this, the name of that,   15
an educator of a new man.

Mother. Grandmother. Wise
Snake-woman who will show the way;
Spider-woman whose black tentacles

hold him precious. Or will tear off his head,   20
her teeth over the little husband,
the small fist clotted in trust at her breast.

This morning, looking at the face of his father,
I remembered how, an infant, his face was too dark,
nose too broad, mouth too wide.   25
I did not look in that mirror
and see the face that could save me
from my own darkness.
Did he, looking in my eye, see
what I turned from: 30
my own dark grandmother
bending over gladioli in the field,
her shaking black hand defenseless
at the shining cock of flower?

I wanted that face to die,   35
to be reborn in the face of a white child.

I wanted the soul to stay the same,
for I loved to death,
to damnation and God-death,
the soul that broke out of me.   40
I crowed: My Son! My Beautiful!
But when I peeked in the basket,
I saw the face of a black man.

Did I bend over his nose
and straighten it with my fingers   45
like a vine growing the wrong way?
Did he feel my hand in malice?

Generations we prayed and fucked
for this light child,
the shining god of the second coming;   50
we bow down in shame
and carry the children of the past
in our wallets, begging forgiveness.

II

A picture in a book,
a lynching.   55
The bland faces of men who watch
a Christ go up in flames, smiling,

as if he were a hooked
fish, a felled antelope, some
wild thing tied to boards and burned.   60
His charring body
gives off light—a halo
burns out of him.
His face scorched featureless;
the hair matted to the scalp   65
like feathers.
One man stands with his hand on his hip,
another with his arm
slung over the shoulder of a friend,
as if this moment were large enough   70
to hold affection.

III

How can we wake
from a dream
we are born into,
that shines around us,   75
the terrible bright air?

Having awakened,
having seen our own bloody hands,
how can we ask forgiveness,
bring before our children the real   80
monster of their nightmares?

The worst is true.
Everything you did not want to know.

                                                  [1989]

LYN HEJINIAN   [b. 1941]

A Mask of Anger

he said I should try something harder
a mask of rage

says of snakes
says of broken glass

says of aged foundations   5
unconsolable wildness,
an imagination uncomforted,
says without comfort

where are the gods who support the event

crashed into the circle   10

took the blue out of the sky

walled the warbler; turned the walker

wrong and wrong

there's no song but what's said
felt it   15
and no thought but what's bitten

[1977]

SHARON OLDS   [b. 1942]

I Go Back to May 1937

I see them standing at the formal gates of their colleges,
I see my father strolling out
under the ochre sandstone arch, the
red tiles glinting like bent
plates of blood behind his head, I   5
see my mother with a few light books at her hip
standing at the pillar made of tiny bricks with the
wrought-iron gate still open behind her, its
sword-tips black in the May air,
they are about to graduate, they are about to get married,   10
they are kids, they are dumb, all they know is they are
innocent, they would never hurt anybody.
I want to go up to them and say Stop,
don't do it—she's the wrong woman,
he's the wrong man, you are going to do things   15
you cannot imagine you would ever do,
you are going to do bad things to children,
you are going to suffer in ways you never heard of,
you are going to want to die. I want to go

up to them there in the late May sunlight and say it,   20
her hungry pretty blank face turning to me,
her pitiful beautiful untouched body,
his arrogant handsome blind face turning to me,
his pitiful beautiful untouched body,
but I don't do it. I want to live. I   25
take them up like the male and female
paper dolls and bang them together
at the hips like chips of flint as if to
strike sparks from them, I say
Do what you are going to do, and I will tell about it.   30

[1987]

MARILYN HACKER   [b. 1942]

Villanelle

Every day our bodies separate,
explode torn and dazed.
Not understanding what we celebrate

we grope through languages and hesitate
and touch each other, speechless and amazed;   5
and every day our bodies separate

us further from our planned, deliberate
ironic lives. I am afraid, disphased,
not understanding what we celebrate

when our fused limbs and lips communicate   10
the unlettered power we have raised.
Every day our bodies' separate

routines are harder to perpetuate.
In wordless darkness we learn wordless praise,
not understanding what we celebrate;   15

wake to ourselves, exhausted, in the late
morning as the wind tears off the haze,
not understanding how we celebrate
our bodies. Every day we separate.

[1974]

ELLEN BRYANT VOIGT   [b. 1943]

Woman Who Weeps

Up from the valley, ten children working the fields
and three in the ground, plus four who'd slipped like fish
from a faulty seine, she wept to the priest:
    Father, I saw the Virgin on a hill,
    she was a lion, lying on her side,   5
    grooming her blond shoulders with her tongue.

Six months weeping as she hulled the corn,
gathered late fruit and milked the goats,
planted grain and watched the hillside blossom,
before she went to the Bishop, kissed his ring.   10
    Father, I saw Our Lady in a tree,
    swaddled in black, she was a raven,
    on one leg, on one bent claw
    she hunched in the tree but she was the tree,
    charred trunk in a thicket of green.   15

After seven years of weeping,
not as other stunned old women weep,
she baked flat bread, washed the cooking stones,
cut a staff from a sapling by the road.
The Holy Father sat in a gilded chair: 20
    Father, I saw Christ's Mother in a stream,
    she was a rock, the water
    parted on either side of her,
    from one stream she made two—
    two tresses loosened across her collarbone—   25
    until the pouring water met at her breast
    and made a single stream again—

Then from the marketplace, from the busiest stall
she stole five ripened figs
and carried her weeping back to the countryside,   30
with a cloth sack, with a beggar's cup,
village to village and into the smoky huts,
her soul a well, an eye, an open door.

[1992]

LOUISE GLÜCK [b. 1943]

Parable of Flight

A flock of birds leaving the side of the mountain.
Black against the spring evening, bronze in early summer,
rising over blank lake water.

Why is the young man disturbed suddenly,
his attention slipping from his companion?   5
His heart is no longer wholly divided; he's trying to think
how to say this compassionately.

Now we hear the voices of the others, moving through the library
toward the veranda, the summer porch; we see them
taking their usual places on the various hammocks and chairs,   10
the white wood chairs of the old house, rearranging
the striped cushions.

Does it matter where the birds go? Does it even matter
what species they are?
They leave here, that's the point,   15
first their bodies, then their sad cries.
And from that moment, cease to exist for us.

You must learn to think of our passion that way.
Each kiss was real, then
each kiss left the face of the earth.   20

[1996]

JAMES TATE [b. 1943]

The Wheelchair Butterfly

O sleepy city of reeling wheelchairs
where a mouse can commit suicide if he can

concentrate long enough
on the history book of rodents
in this underground town   5

of electrical wheelchairs!
The girl who is always pregnant and bruised
like a pear

rides her many-stickered bicycle
backward up the staircase   10
of the abandoned trolleybarn.

Yesterday was warm. Today a butterfly froze
in midair; and was plucked like a grape
by a child who swore he could take care

of it. O confident city where   15
the seeds of poppies pass for carfare,

where the ordinary hornets in a human's heart
may slumber and snore, where bifocals bulge

in an orange garage of daydreams,
we wait in our loose attics for a new season   20

as if for an ice-cream truck.
An Indian pony crosses the plains

whispering Sanskrit prayers to a crater of fleas.
Honeysuckle says: I thought I could swim.

The Mayor is urinating on the wrong side   25
of the street! A dandelion sends off sparks:
beware your hair is locked!

Beware the trumpet wants a glass of water!
Beware a velvet tabernacle!

Beware the Warden of Light has married   30
an old piece of string!

[1969]

QUINCY TROUPE   [b. 1943]

Snake-Back Solo 2

for Louis Armstrong, Steve Cannon, Miles Davis,
& Eugene Redmond

with the music up high, boogalooin
bass down way way low
up & under, eye come slidin on in, mojoin
on in, spacin on in on a riff full of rain
riffin on in full of rain & pain   5
spacin on in on a sound
like coltrane°

& my metaphor is a blues
hot pain dealin blues, is a blues
axin guitar voices, whiskey broken, niggah   10
deep in the heart, is a blues in a glass filled with rain
is a blues in the dark
slurred voices of straight bourbon
is a blues, dagger stuck off in the heart
of night, moanin like bessie smith°   15
is a blues filling up, glooming under
the wings of darkness, is a blues
is a blues, a blues

& looking through the heart
a dream can become a raindrop window to see through   20
can become a window, to see through this moment
to see yourself hanging around the dark
to see through this moment
& see yourself as a river catching rain there
feeding time there with your movement   25
to wash time clean as a window
to see through to the other side
while outside windows, flames trigger
the deep explosion, time steals rivers that move on
& stay where they are, inside yourself, moving   30

7. **coltrane:** John Coltrane (1926–1967), a well-known jazz saxophonist.
15. **bessie smith:** Bessie Smith (1894–1937), an influential classic blues singer of
the 1920s.

soon there will be daylight
breaking the darkness
to point the way home, soon there will be
voices breaking music, to come on home by
down & up river, breaking the darkness   35
to come on home by, stroking with the music
swimming up river
the sound of louie armstrong
swinging up river, carrying river boats
upstream, on the back of his honky-tonk jazz rhythms   40
licks of vibratos climbing up from new orleans, close heat & rain
swimming up river, up the river of mud & rain
satchmo° breaking the darkness, his cornet speaking
flames bouncing off the river's back
at sunset, snake river's back, big muddy, mississippi   45
up from naw leans, to east st. louis, illinois
cross river from st. louis
to come on home by, up river now
the music swims, breaking silence to land
in miles dewey davis's° horn, then leap off again   50
& fly up in space to create
new music in time with place
to create new music in time with this place
to pass it on, pass it on
pass it on, into space   55

where eye catch it now, inside myself
inside this poem eye am (w)riting here
where eye am soloing, now
soloing of rivers catching rains & dreams & sunsets
solo of trane tracks screaming through the night, stark   60
a dagger in the heart
solo of bird° spreading wings for the wind
to lift up by, solo of miles, pied piper, prince of darkness
river rain voice now, eye solo at the root of the flower
leaning against promises of shadows   65
solo of bones leering beneath the river's snake-back
solo of trees cut down by double-bladed axes
river rain voice now eye solo
of the human condition, solo of the matrix

43. satchmo: Louis "Satchmo" Armstrong (1901–1971), American jazz trumpeter.
50. miles dewey davis: Miles Davis (1926–1991), jazz trumpet player, composer,
and bandleader.
62. bird: Charlie Parker (1920–1955), jazz saxophonist and composer.

mojoin new blues, river rain voice   70
now, eye solo   solo
solo now to become the wings & eyes of an owl
to see through this darkness, eye solo now
to become a simple skybreak shattering darkness
to become lightning's jagged-sword-like thunder   75
eye solo now to become, to become
eye solo now to become

with the music up high
up way, way high, boogalooin bass down
way, way low   80
up & under, eye come slidin on in, mojoin on in
spacin on in on a poetic riff full of rain
river riff full of rain & trains & dreams
lookin through ajax° clean windows
eye come slidin on through   85
these blues metaphors
riffin on in through rain & pain
ridin on a tongue of poetic flame
leanin & glidin, eye solo   solo
loopin & flyin eye solo now   solo   90

[1979]

84. ajax: A brand name for household cleaning products.

EAVAN BOLAND [b. 1944]

The Pomegranate

The only legend I have ever loved is
The story of a daughter lost in hell.
And found and rescued there.
Love and blackmail are the gist of it.
Ceres° and Persephone the names.   5

5. Ceres: Roman name of Demeter, the goddess of crops and harvest. Her daughter Persephone was kidnapped by Pluto (or Hades) and taken to the underworld. Demeter, grieving and angry, refused to let seeds germinate or crops grow. To save the human race from extinction, Zeus finally ordered Pluto to release Persephone.

And the best thing about the legend is
I can enter it anywhere. And have.
As a child in exile in
A city of fogs and strange consonants,
I read it first and at first I was   10
An exiled child in the crackling dusk of
The underworld, the stars blighted. Later
I walked out in a summer twilight
Searching for my daughter at bedtime.
When she came running I was ready   15
To make any bargain to keep her.
I carried her back past whitebeams.
And wasps and honey-scented buddleias.
But I was Ceres then and I knew
Winter was in store for every leaf   20
On every tree on that road.
Was inescapable for each one we passed.
And for me.
It is winter
And the stars are hidden.   25
I climb the stairs and stand where I can see
My child asleep beside her teen magazines,
Her can of Coke, her plate of uncut fruit.
The pomegranate! How did I forget it?
She could have come home and been safe   30
And ended the story and all
Our heartbroken searching but she reached
Out a hand and plucked a pomegranate.
She put out her hand and pulled down
The French sound for apple° and   *pomme*   35
The noise of stone° and the proof   *granite*
That even in the place of death,
At the heart of legend, in the midst
Of rocks full of unshed tears
Ready to be diamonds by the time   40
The story was told, a child can be
Hungry. I could warn her. There is still a chance.

Pluto told her she was free to leave but tricked her by offering a pomegranate
seed; anyone who eats food in the underworld must return there. Zeus therefore
arranged a compromise: Persephone would spend a third of each year in the land
of the dead with Pluto (winter, when Demeter went into mourning); but she would
be with her mother for the other two-thirds of each year (spring and summer).

The rain is cold. The road is flint-coloured.
The suburb has cars and cable television.
The veiled stars are above ground.   45
It is another world. But what else
Can a mother give her daughter but such
Beautiful rifts in time?
If I defer the grief I will diminish the gift.
The legend must be hers as well as mine.   50
She will enter it. As I have.
She will wake up. She will hold
The papery, flushed skin in her hand.
And to her lips. I will say nothing.

[1994]

ROBERT MORGAN   [b. 1944]

Mountain Bride

They say Revis found a flatrock
on the ridge just
perfect for a natural hearth,
and built his cabin with a stick

and clay chimney right over it.   5
On their wedding night he lit
the fireplace to dry away the mountain
chill of late spring, and flung on

applewood to dye
the room with molten color while   10
he and Martha that was a Parrish
warmed the sheets between the tick

stuffed with leaves and its feather
cover. Under that wide hearth
a nest of rattlers,   15
they'll knot a hundred together,

had wintered and were coming awake.
The warming rock
flushed them out early.
It was she   20

who wakened to their singing near
the embers and roused him to go look.
Before he reached the fire
more than a dozen struck

and he died yelling her to stay   25
on the big four-poster.
Her uncle coming up the hollow
with a gift bearham two days later

found her shivering there
marooned above a pool   30
of hungry snakes,
and the body beginning to swell.

[1979]

ANNE WALDMAN [b. 1945]

Makeup on Empty Space

I am putting makeup on empty space
all patinas convening on empty space
rouge blushing on empty space
I am putting makeup on empty space
pasting eyelashes on empty space   5
painting the eyebrows of empty space
piling creams on empty space
painting the phenomenal world
I am hanging ornaments on empty space
gold clips, lacquer combs, plastic hairpins on empty space   10
I am sticking wire pins into empty space
I pour words over empty space, enthrall the empty space
packing, stuffing jamming empty space
spinning necklaces around empty space
Fancy this, imagine this: painting the phenomenal world   15
bangles on wrists
pendants hung on empty space
I am putting my memory into empty space
undressing you
hanging the wrinkled clothes on a nail   20
hanging the green coat on a nail

dancing in the evening it ended with dancing in the evening
I am still thinking about putting makeup on empty space
I want to scare you: the hanging night, the drifting night,
the moaning night, daughter of troubled sleep I want to scare you   25
you
I bind as far as cold day goes
I bind the power of 20 husky men
I bind the seductive colorful women, all of them
I bind the massive rock   30
I bind the hanging night, the drifting night, the
moaning night, daughter of troubled sleep
I am binding my debts, I magnetize the phone bill
bind the root of my pointed tongue
I cup my hands in water, splash water on empty space   35
water drunk by empty space
Look what thoughts will do   Look what words will do
from nothing to the face
from nothing to the root of the tongue
from nothing to speaking of empty space   40
I bind the ash tree
I bind the yew
I bind the willow
I bind uranium
I bind the uneconomical unrenewable energy of uranium   45
dash uranium to empty space
I bind the color red I seduce the color red to empty space
I put the sunset in empty space
I take the blue of his eyes and make an offering to empty space
renewable blue   50
I take the green of everything coming to life, it grows &
climbs into empty space
I put the white of the snow at the foot of empty space
I clasp the yellow of the cat's eyes sitting in the
black space I clasp them to my heart, empty space   55
I want the brown of this floor to rise up into empty space
Take the floor apart to find the brown,
bind it up again under spell of empty space
I want to take this old wall apart I am rich in my mind thinking
of this, I am thinking of putting makeup on empty space   60
Everything crumbles around empty space
the thin dry weed crumbles, the milkweed is blown into empty space
I bind the stars reflected in your eye
from nothing to these typing fingers

from nothing to the legs of the elk   65
from nothing to the neck of the deer
from nothing to porcelain teeth
from nothing to the fine stand of pine in the forest
I kept it going when I put the water on
when I let the water run   70
sweeping together in empty space
There is a better way to say empty space
Turn yourself inside out and you might disappear
you have a new definition in empty space
What I like about impermanence is the clash   75
of my big body with empty space
I am putting the floor back together again
I am rebuilding the wall
I am slapping mortar on bricks
I am fastening the machine together with delicate wire   80
There is no eternal thread, maybe there is thread of pure gold
I am starting to sing inside about the empty space
there is some new detail every time
I am taping the picture I love so well on the wall:
moonless black night beyond country-plaid curtains   85
everything illuminated out of empty space
I hang the black linen dress on my body
the hanging night, the drifting night, the moaning night
daughter of troubled sleep
This occurs to me   90
I hang up a mirror to catch stars, everything occurs to me out in the
night in my skull of empty space
I go outside in starry ice
I build up the house again in memory of empty space
This occurs to me about empty space   95
that it is nevered to be mentioned again
Fancy this
imagine this
painting the phenomenal world
there's talk of dressing the body with strange adornments   100
to remind you of a vow to empty space
there's talk of the discourse in your mind like a silkworm
I wish to venture into a not-chiseled place
I pour sand on the ground
Objects and vehicles emerge from the fog   105
the canyon is dangerous tonight
suddenly there are warning lights

The patrol is helpful in the manner of guiding
there is talk of slowing down
there is talk of a feminine deity   110
I bind her with a briar
I bind with the tooth of a tiger
I bind with my quartz crystal
I magnetize the worlds
I cover myself with jewels   115
I drink amrita
there is some new detail
there is a spangle on her shoe
there is a stud on her boot
the tires are studded for the difficult climb   120
I put my hands to my face
I am putting makeup on empty space
I wanted to scare you with the night that scared me
the drifting night, the moaning night
Someone was always intruding to make you forget empty space   125
you put it all on
you paint your nails
you put on scarves
all the time adorning empty space
Whatever-your-name-is I tell you "empty space"   130
with your fictions with dancing come around to it
with your funny way of singing come around to it
with your smiling come to it
with your enormous retinue & accumulation come around to it
with your extras come round to it   135
with your good fortune, with your lazy fortune come round to it
when you look most like a bird, that is the time to come around to it
when you are cheating, come to it
when you are in your anguished head
when you are not sensible   140
when you are insisting on the
praise from many tongues
It begins with the root of the tongue
it begins with the root of the heart
there is a spinal cord of wind   145
singing & moaning in empty space

[1984]

LARRY LEVIS   [1946–1996]

The Poem You Asked For

My poem would eat nothing.
I tried giving it water
but it said no,

worrying me.
Day after day,   5
I held it up to the light,

turning it over,
but it only pressed its lips
more tightly together.

It grew sullen, like a toad   10
through with being teased.
I offered it all my money,

my clothes, my car with a full tank.
But the poem stared at the floor.
Finally I cupped it in   15

my hands, and carried it gently
out into the soft air, into the
evening traffic, wondering how

to end things between us.
For now it had begun breathing,   20
putting on more and

more hard rings of flesh.
And the poem demanded the food,
it drank up all the water,

beat me and took my money,   25
tore the faded clothes
off my back,

said Shit,
and walked slowly away,
slicking its hair down.   30

Said it was going
over to your place.

[1972]

LINDA HOGAN   [b. 1947]

The History of Red

First
there was some other order of things
never spoken
but in dreams of darkest creation.

Then there was black earth,   5
lake, the face of light on water.
Then the thick forest all around
that light,
and then the human clay
whose blood we still carry   10
rose up in us
who remember caves with red bison
painted in their own blood,
after their kind.

A wildness   15
swam inside our mothers,
desire through closed eyes,
a new child
wearing the red, wet mask of birth,
delivered into this land   20
already wounded,
stolen and burned
beyond reckoning.

Red is this yielding land
turned inside out   25
by a country of hunters
with iron, flint and fire.
Red is the fear
that turns a knife back
against men, holds it at their throats,   30
and they cannot see the claw on the handle,
the animal hand
that haunts them
from some place inside their blood.

So that is hunting, birth,   35
and one kind of death.

Then there was medicine, the healing of wounds.
Red was the infinite fruit
of stolen bodies.
The doctors wanted to know   40
what invented disease
how wounds healed
from inside themselves
how life stands up in skin,
if not by magic.   45

They divined the red shadows of leeches
that swam in white bowls of water;
they believed stars
in the cup of sky,
They cut the wall of skin   50
to let
what was bad escape
but they were reading the story of fire
gone out
and that was science.   55

As for the animal hand on death's knife,
knives have as many sides
as the red father of war
who signs his name
in the blood of other men.   60

And red was the soldier
who crawled
through a ditch
of human blood in order to live.
It was the canal of his deliverance.   65
It is his son who lives near me.
Red is the thunder in our ears
when we meet.
Love, like creation,
is some other order of things.   70

Red is the share of fire
I have stolen
from root, hoof, fallen fruit.
And this was hunger.

Red is the human house   75
I come back to at night
swimming inside the cave of skin

that remembers bison.
In that round nation
of blood
we are all burning,   80
red, inseparable fires
the living have crawled
and climbed through
in order to live   85
so nothing will be left
for death at the end.

This life in the fire, I love it,
I want it,
this life.   90

[1993]

AI [b. 1947]

Why Can't I Leave You?

You stand behind the old black mare,
dressed as always in that red shirt,
stained from sweat, the crying of the armpits,
that will not stop for anything,
stroking her rump, while the barley goes unplanted.   5
I pick up my suitcase and set it down,
as I try to leave you again.
I smooth the hair back from your forehead.
I think with your laziness and the drought too,
you'll be needing my help more than ever.   10
You take my hands, I nod
and go to the house to unpack,
having found another reason to stay.

I undress, then put on my white lace slip
for you to take off, because you like that   15
and when you come in, you pull down the straps
and I unbutton your shirt.
I know we can't give each other any more
or any less than what we have.

There is safety in that, so much   20
that I can never get past the packing,
the begging you to please, if I can't make you happy,
come close between my thighs
and let me laugh for you from my second mouth.

[1972]

YUSEF KOMUNYAKAA   [b. 1947]

Facing It

My black face fades,
hiding inside the black granite.
I said I wouldn't,
dammit: No tears.
I'm stone. I'm flesh.   5
My clouded reflection eyes me
like a bird of prey, the profile of night
slanted against morning. I turn
this way—the stone lets me go.
I turn that way—I'm inside   10
the Vietnam Veterans Memorial
again, depending on the light
to make a difference.
I go down the 58,022 names,
half-expecting to find   15
my own in letters like smoke.
I touch the name Andrew Johnson;
I see the booby trap's white flash.
Names shimmer on a woman's blouse
but when she walks away   20
the names stay on the wall.
Brushstrokes flash, a red bird's
wings cutting across my stare.
The sky. A plane in the sky.
A white vet's image floats   25
closer to me, then his pale eyes
look through mine. I'm a window.
He's lost his right arm

inside the stone. In the black mirror
a woman's trying to erase names: 30
No, she's brushing a boy's hair.

                                              [1988]

JANE KENYON   [1947–1995]

From Room to Room

Here in this house, among photographs
of your ancestors, their hymnbooks and old
shoes . . .

           I move from room to room,
a little dazed, like the fly. I watch it   5
bump against each window.

I am clumsy here, thrusting
slabs of maple into the stove.
Out of my body for a while,
weightless in space. . . .   10

                Sometimes
the wind against the clapboard
sounds like a car driving up to the house.

My people are not here, my mother
and father, my brother. I talk   15
to the cats about weather.

"Blessed be the tie that binds . . ."
we sing in the church down the road.
And how does it go from there? The tie . . .

the tether, the hose carrying   20
oxygen to the astronaut,
turning, turning outside the hatch,
taking a look around.

                                              [1978]

HEATHER McHUGH   [b. 1948]

What He Thought

for Fabbio Doplicher

We were supposed to do a job in Italy
and, full of our feeling for
ourselves (our sense of being
Poets from America) we went
from Rome to Fano, met   5
the mayor, mulled
a couple matters over (what's
cheap date, they asked us; what's
flat drink). Among Italian literati

we could recognize our counterparts: 10
the academic, the apologist,
the arrogant, the amorous,
the brazen and the glib—and there was one

administrator (the conservative), in suit
of regulation gray, who like a good tour guide   15
with measured pace and uninflected tone narrated
sights and histories the hired van hauled us past.
Of all, he was most politic and least poetic,
so it seemed. Our last few days in Rome
(when all but three of the New World Bards had flown)   20
I found a book of poems this
unprepossessing one had written: it was there
in the *pensione* room (a room he'd recommended)
where it must have been abandoned by
the German visitor (was there a bus of *them*?)   25
to whom he had inscribed and dated it a month before.
I couldn't read Italian, either, so I put the book
back into the wardrobe's dark. We last Americans

were due to leave tomorrow. For our parting evening then
our host chose something in a family restaurant, and there   30
we sat and chatted, sat and chewed,
till, sensible it was our last
big chance to be poetic, make

our mark, one of us asked
          "What's poetry?   35
Is it the fruits and vegetables and
marketplace of Campo dei Fiori, or
the statue there?" Because I was

the glib one, I identified the answer
instantly, I didn't have to think—"The truth   40
is both, it's both," I blurted out. But that
was easy. That was easiest to say. What followed
taught me something about difficulty,
for our underestimated host spoke out,
all of a sudden, with a rising passion, and he said: 45

The statue represents Giordano Bruno,
brought to be burned in the public square
because of his offense against
authority, which is to say
the Church. His crime was his belief   50
the universe does not revolve around
the human being: God is no
fixed point or central government, but rather is
poured in waves through all things. All things
move. "If God is not the soul itself, He is   55
the soul of the soul of the world." Such was
his heresy. The day they brought him
forth to die, they feared he might
incite the crowd (the man was famous
for his eloquence). And so his captors   60
placed upon his face
an iron mask, in which

he could not speak. That's
how they burned him. That is how
he died: without a word, in front   65
of everyone.
           And poetry—
               (we'd all
put down our forks by now, to listen to
the man in gray; he went on   70
softly)—
          poetry is what

he thought, but did not say.

                           [1994]

LESLIE MARMON SILKO   [b. 1948]

Prayer to the Pacific

I traveled to the ocean
      distant
            from my southwest land of sandrock
            to the moving blue water
         Big as the myth of origin.   5

Pale
pale water in the yellow-white light of
            sun   floating west
                to China
            where ocean herself was born.   10
Clouds that blow across the sand are wet.

Squat in the wet sand and speak to the Ocean:
        I return to you   turquoise   the red coral you sent us,
             sister spirit of Earth.
Four round stones in my pocket   I carry back the ocean   15
            to suck and to taste.

Thirty thousand years ago
           Indians came riding across the ocean
           carried by giant sea turtles.

Waves were high that day   20
        great sea turtles waded   slowly out
            from the gray sundown sea.

Grandfather Turtle rolled in the sand   four times
        and disappeared
           swimming into the sun.   25

And so   from that time
        immemorial,
           as the old people say,
rain clouds drift from the west
          gift from the ocean.   30

Green leaves in the wind
Wet earth on my feet
      swallowing raindrops
         clear from China.

                    [1981]

SEKOU SUNDIATA   [b. 1948]

Blink Your Eyes

Remembering Sterling A. Brown

I was on my way to see my woman
but the Law said I was on my way
thru a red light red light red light
and if you saw my woman
you could understand,   5
I was just being a man
It wasn't about no light
it was about my ride
and if you saw my ride
you could dig that too, you dig?   10
Sunroof stereo radio black leather
bucket seats sit low you know,
the body's cool, but the tires are worn.
Ride when the hard time come, ride
when they're gone, in other words   15
the light was green.

I could wake up in the morning
without a warning
and my world could change:
blink your eyes.   20
All depends, all depends on the skin,
all depends on the skin you're living in.

Up to the window comes the Law
with his hand on his gun
what's up? what's happening?   25
I said I guess
that's when I really broke the law.
He said *a routine, step out the car*
a routine, assume the position.
Put your hands up in the air   30
you know the routine, like you just don't care.
License and registration.
Deep was the night and the light
from the North Star on the car door, deja vu
we've been through this before,   35

why did you stop me?
Somebody had to stop you.
I watch the news, you always lose.
You're unreliable, that's undeniable.
This is serious, you could be dangerous.   40

I could wake up in the morning
without a warning
and my world could change:
blink your eyes.
All depends, all depends on the skin,   45
all depends on the skin you're living in.

New York City, they got laws
can't no bruthas drive outdoors,
in certain neighborhoods, on particular streets
near and around certain types of people.   50
They got laws.
All depends, all depends on the skin,
all depends on the skin you're living in.

[1995]

AGHA SHAHID ALI   [1949–2001]

I Dream It Is Afternoon
When I Return to Delhi

At Purana Qila I am alone, waiting
for the bus to Daryaganj. I see it coming,
but my hands are empty.
"Jump on, jump on," someone shouts,
"I've saved this change for you   5
for years. Look!"
A hand opens, full of silver rupees.
"Jump on, jump on." The voice doesn't stop.
There's no one I know. A policeman,
handcuffs silver in his hands,   10
asks for my ticket.

I jump off the running bus,
sweat pouring from my hair.
I run past the Doll Museum, past
headlines on the Times of India   15
building, PRISONERS BLINDED IN A BIHAR
JAIL, HARIJAN VILLAGES BURNED BY LANDLORDS.
Panting, I stop in Daryaganj,
outside Golcha Cinema.

Sunil is there, lighting   20
a cigarette, smiling. I say,
"It must be ten years, you haven't changed,
it was your voice on the bus!"
He says, "The film is about to begin,
I've bought an extra ticket for you,"   25
and we rush inside:

Anarkali is being led away,
her earrings lying on the marble floor.
Any moment she'll be buried alive.
"But this is the end," I turn   30
toward Sunil. He is nowhere.
The usher taps my shoulder, says
my ticket is ten years old.

Once again my hands are empty.
I am waiting, alone, at Purana Qila.   35
Bus after empty bus is not stopping.
Suddenly, beggar women with children
are everywhere, offering
me money, weeping for me.

[1987]

VICTOR HERNÁNDEZ CRUZ [b. 1949]

Problems with Hurricanes

A campesino looked at the air
And told me:
With hurricanes it's not the wind

or the noise or the water.
I'll tell you he said: 5
it's the mangoes, avocados
Green plantains and bananas
flying into town like projectiles.

How would your family
feel if they had to tell   10
The generations that you
got killed by a flying
Banana.

Death by drowning has honor
If the wind picked you up   15
and slammed you
Against a mountain boulder
This would not carry shame
But
to suffer a mango smashing   20
Your skull
or a plantain hitting your
Temple at 70 miles per hour
is the ultimate disgrace.

The campesino takes off his hat—   25
As a sign of respect
towards the fury of the wind
And says:
Don't worry about the noise
Don't worry about the water   30
Don't worry about the wind—
If you are going out
beware of mangoes
And all such beautiful
sweet things.   35

[1991]

MARK HALLIDAY   [b. 1949]

Functional Poem

Is there any reason why a poem shouldn't
at least occasionally
come through for us in a concrete way and
get something done?

Because I need to get something across   5
to a particular individual
with whom I have no normal contact,
I mean I never see this guy, and yet
I've got something to say to him—
and me being a poet I naturally   10
have to use
the means at my disposal.

The individual to whom I refer
is a young man with blond hair,
I admit from a certain point of view   15
many people would consider him handsome although
he's what I call rather heavy-set i.e.
chubby. Well-dressed, the guy has money, I'm sure
he wears those yellow-white cotton pants
made for people like golfers and princes   20
who can take everything slow and cool—
not that he does. Because

the one time I saw this guy
on a hot inter-suburban street some years ago
he was driving his white Camaro   25
with his radio on terrifically loud with
some old Beach Boys song which I normally like
but it seemed a sacrilege for this rich guy to have
that old gentle lighthearted music in his Camaro—
the song was a hit when this character was about   30
five years old, for god's sake!—
but anyway he cuts right in front of me,
I'm driving my father's old VW,
he almost clips my fender, gives me this look,
like "You're over the hill, man, get off the road"—   35
I'm under 35 and this guy is telling me

I'm over the hill! So naturally
I give him a blast on the horn.
So then the bastard slows way way down.
So I pass him, except all of a sudden   40
he speeds up to keep even with me,
I'm stuck out in the left lane
and here comes a frigging truck or something!
So I hit the brakes and duck in behind him
in his beautiful creamy white Camaro   45
with the Beach Boys and a little cooler of
Miller High Life in the back seat, I'm sure.
Almost immediately he does the slow-down thing again—

and this time he lets me pass him.
But then about thirty seconds later   50
vrrrrooooooommm!—he's passing me
but there's traffic coming toward us,
God, my heart seized up like a broken clutch—
but
he made it, the bastard,   55
I admit he had great acceleration,
and nerve, too, the guy had nerve—
he pulled away into the distance,
going even faster to show me that
the near-miss never scared him for a second.   60

Okay. Now, I've thought it over,
and I realize that what's wrong with this individual
is not that he's rich, or that he's young,
or that he's a little on the heavy side.
That stuff is his business, and the same goes   65
for the loud radio as far as I'm concerned and
the fast driving too, even, in most situations.
But what's wrong with the guy is
that he made me run the risk of
severe damage to life and limb or   70
possibly a fatality, i.e. I could have been killed.
And that is just not acceptable.
I'm saying, this person cannot be permitted
to do such a thing.

Now, I know all your theories, by the way,   75
about "Poetry makes nothing happen"
and art is not a tool or weapon et cetera.

But on the other hand it *is* a way of giving messages,
and if I'm being a little more honest about this
than most poets, then so be it;   80
and I'm just giving that blond individual
this message:

Don't go around interfering with somebody else's
right to live, you stupid jerk.
Why don't you consider some other life-style   85
less dangerous to others and yourself as well?
Why don't you read some poetry once in a while?
If this poem can do a job on you,
maybe others can, too. Why don't you
take some of your gas money and   90
subscribe to a few poetry magazines?
Think about it.

Readers, if you see the above individual,
or somebody like him, could you
please just pass along this message.   95

[1987]

RAY A. YOUNG BEAR   [b. 1950]

From the Spotted Night

In the blizzard
while chopping wood
the mystical whistler
beckons my attention.
Once there were longhouses   5
here. A village.
In the abrupt spring floods
swimmers retrieved our belief.
So their spirit remains.
From the spotted night   10
distant jets transform
into fireflies who float
towards me like incandescent
snowflakes.

The leather shirt   15
which is suspended
on a wire hanger
above the bed's headboard
is humanless; yet when one
stands outside the house,   20
the strenuous sounds
of dressers and boxes
being moved can be heard.
We believe someone wears
the shirt and rearranges   25
the heavy furniture,
although nothing
is actually changed.
Unlike the Plains Indian shirts
which repelled lead bullets,   30
ricocheting from them
in fiery sparks,
this shirt is the means;
this shirt *is* the bullet.

[1990]

CAROLYN FORCHÉ [b. 1950]

The Colonel

What you have heard is true. I was in his house. His wife carried a tray
of coffee and sugar. His daughter filed her nails, his son went out for the
night. There were daily papers, pet dogs, a pistol on the cushion beside
him. The moon swung bare on its black cord over the house. On the television was a cop show. It was in English. Broken bottles were embedded
in the walls around the house to scoop the kneecaps from a man's legs or
cut his hands to lace. On the windows there were gratings like those in
liquor stores. We had dinner, rack of lamb, good wine, a gold bell was on
the table for calling the maid. The maid brought green mangoes, salt, a
type of bread. I was asked how I enjoyed the country. There was a brief
commercial in Spanish. His wife took everything away. There was some
talk then of how difficult it had become to govern. The parrot said hello
on the terrace. The colonel told it to shut up, and pushed himself from

the table. My friend said to me with his eyes: say nothing. The colonel
returned with a sack used to bring groceries home. He spilled many
human ears on the table. They were like dried peach halves. There is no
other way to say this. He took one of them in his hands, shook it in our
faces, dropped it into a water glass. It came alive there. I am tired of fooling around he said. As for the rights of anyone, tell your people they can
go fuck themselves. He swept the ears to the floor with his arm and held
the last of his wine in the air. Something for your poetry, no? he said.
Some of the ears on the floor caught this scrap of his voice. Some of the
ears on the floor were pressed to the ground.

[1978]

ANNE CARSON   [b. 1950]

Sumptuous Destitution

"Sumptuous destitution"
*Your opinion gives me a serious feeling: I would like to be what you deem
me.*
              (Emily Dickinson letter 319 to Thomas Higginson)

is a phrase
You see my position is benighted.   5
              (Emily Dickinson letter 268 to Thomas Higginson)

scholars use
*She was much too enigmatical a being for me to solve in an hour's inter-
view.*   (Thomas Higginson letter 342a to Emily Dickinson)

of female   10
God made me [Sir] Master—I didn't be—myself.
              (Emily Dickinson letter 233 to Thomas Higginson)

silence.
Rushing among my small heart—and pushing aside the blood—
              (Emily Dickinson letter 248 to Thomas Higginson)   15

Save what you can, Emily.
*And when I try to organize—my little Force explodes—and leaves me bare
and charred.*   (Emily Dickinson letter 271 to Thomas Higginson)

Save every bit of thread.
Have you a little chest to put the Alive in?   20
            (Emily Dickinson letter 233 to Thomas Higginson)

One of them may be
By Cock, said Ophelia.
            (Emily Dickinson letter 268 to Thomas Higginson)

the way out of here.

                                                              [2000]

JOHN YAU   [b. 1950]

Chinese Villanelle

I have been with you, and I have thought of you
Once the air was dry and drenched with light
I was like a lute filling the room with description

We watched glum clouds reject their shape
We dawdled near a fountain, and listened   5
I have been with you, and I have thought of you

Like a river worthy of its gown
And like a mountain worthy of its insolence . . .
Why am I like a lute left with only description

How does one cut an axe handle with an axe   10
What shall I do to tell you all my thoughts
When I have been with you, and thought of you

A pelican sits on a dam, while a duck
Folds its wings again; the song does not melt
I remember you looking at me without description   15

Perhaps a king's business is never finished,
Though "perhaps" implies a different beginning
I have been with you, and I have thought of you
Now I am a lute filled with this wandering description

                                                              [1979]

JORIE GRAHAM   [b. 1950]

Reading Plato

This is the story
   of a beautiful
lie, what slips
   through my fingers,
your fingers. It's winter,   5
   it's far

in the lifespan
   of man.
Bareheaded, in a soiled
   shirt,   10
speechless, my friend
   is making

lures, his hobby. Flies
   so small
he works with tweezers and   15
   a magnifying glass.
They must be
   so believable

they're true—feelers,
   antennae,   20
quick and frantic
   as something
drowning. His heart
   beats wildly
in his hands. It is   25
   blinding
and who will forgive him
   in his tiny
garden? He makes them
   out of hair,   30

deer hair, because it's hollow
   and floats.
Past death, past sight,
   this is
his good idea, what drives   35
   the silly days

together. Better than memory. Better
    than love.
Then they are done, a hook
    under each pair   40
of wings, and it's Spring,
    and the men

wade out into the riverbed
    at dawn. Above,
the stars still connect-up   45
    their hungry animals.
Soon they'll be satisfied
    and go. Meanwhile

upriver, downriver, imagine, quick
    in the air,   50
in flesh, in a blue
    swarm of
flies, our knowledge of
    the graceful

deer skips easily across   55
    the surface.
Dismembered, remembered,
    it's finally
alive. Imagine
    the body   60

they were all once
    a part of,
these men along the lush
    green banks
trying to slip in   65
    and pass

for the natural world.

                                                                   [1983]

JOY HARJO   [b. 1951]

She Had Some Horses

She had some horses.

She had horses who were bodies of sand.
She had horses who were maps drawn of blood.
She had horses who were skins of ocean water.
She had horses who were the blue air of sky.   5
She had horses who were fur and teeth.
She had horses who were clay and would break.
She had horses who were splintered red cliff.

She had some horses.

She had horses with long, pointed breasts.   10
She had horses with full, brown thighs.
She had horses who laughed too much.
She had horses who threw rocks at glass houses.
She had horses who licked razor blades.

She had some horses.   15

She had horses who danced in their mothers' arms.
She had horses who thought they were the sun and their
bodies shone and burned like stars.
She had horses who waltzed nightly on the moon.
She had horses who were much too shy, and kept quiet   20
in stalls of their own making.

She had some horses.

She had horses who liked Creek Stomp Dance songs.
She had horses who cried in their beer.
She had horses who spit at male queens who made   25
them afraid of themselves.
She had horses who said they weren't afraid.
She had horses who lied.
She had horses who told the truth, who were stripped
bare of their tongues.   30

She had some horses.

She had horses who called themselves, "horse."
She had horses who called themselves, "spirit," and kept

their voices secret and to themselves.
She had horses who had no names.   35
She had horses who had books of names.

She had some horses.

She had horses who whispered in the dark, who were afraid to speak.
She had horses who screamed out of fear of the silence, who
carried knives to protect themselves from ghosts.   40
She had horses who waited for destruction.
She had horses who waited for resurrection.

She had some horses.

She had horses who got down on their knees for any saviour.
She had horses who thought their high price had saved them.   45
She had horses who tried to save her, who climbed in her
bed at night and prayed as they raped her.

She had some horses.

She had some horses she loved.
She had some horses she hated.   50

These were the same horses.

                                                           [1983]

GARRETT KAORU HONGO [b. 1951]

Yellow Light

One arm hooked around the frayed strap
of a tar-black, patent-leather purse,
the other cradling something for dinner:
fresh bunches of spinach from a J-Town *yaoya*,°   *vegetable stand or seller*
sides of split Spanish mackerel from Alviso's,   5
maybe a loaf of Langendorf;° she steps
off the hissing bus at Olympic and Fig,
begins the three-block climb up the hill,
passing gangs of schoolboys playing war,

6. **Langendorf:** A well-known bakery in California.

Japs against Japs, Chicanas chalking sidewalks   10
with the holy double-yoked crosses of hopscotch,
and the Korean grocer's wife out for a stroll
around this neighborhood of Hawaiian apartments
just starting to steam with cooking
and the anger of young couples coming home   15
from work, yelling at kids, flicking on
TV sets for the Wednesday Night Fights.

If it were May, hydrangeas and jacaranda
flowers in the streetside trees would be
blooming through the smog of late spring.   20
Wisteria in Masuda's front yard would be
shaking out the long tresses of its purple hair.
Maybe mosquitoes, moths, a few orange butterflies
settling on the lattice of monkey flowers
tangled in chain-link fences by the trash.   25

But this is October, and Los Angeles
seethes like a billboard under twilight.
From used-car lots and the movie houses uptown,
long silver sticks of light probe the sky.
From the Miracle Mile, whole freeways away,   30
a brilliant fluorescence breaks out
and makes war with the dim squares
of yellow kitchen light winking on
in all the side streets of the Barrio.

She climbs up the two flights of flagstone   35
stairs to 201-B, the spikes of her high heels
clicking like kitchen knives on a cutting board,
props the groceries against the door,
fishes through memo pads, a compact,
empty packs of chewing gum, and finds her keys.   40

The moon then, cruising from behind
a screen of eucalyptus across the street,
covers everything, everything in sight,
in a heavy light like yellow onions.

[1982]

DAVID MURA   [b. 1952]

Grandfather-in-Law

It's nothing really, and really, it could have been worse, and of course,
    he's now several years dead,
and his widow, well, if oftentimes she's somewhat distracted, overly
    cautious when we visit—
after all, Boston isn't New York—she seems, for some reason, enormously
    proud that there's now a writer in the family,
and periodically, sends me clippings about the poet laureate, Thoreau,
    Anne Sexton's daughter, Lowell, New England literary lore—
in which I fit, if I fit at all, simply because I write in English—as if color
    of skin didn't matter anymore.   5
Still, years ago, during my first visit to Boston, when we were all asleep,
he, who used to require that my wife memorize lines of Longfellow or
    Poe and recite them on the phone,
so that, every time he called, she ran outdoors and had to be coaxed
    back, sometimes with threats, to talk to Pops
(though she remembers too his sly imitations of Lincoln, ice cream at
    Brighams, burgers and fries, all the usual grandfatherly treats),
he, who for some reason was prejudiced against Albanians—where on
    earth did he find them I wondered—   10
who, in the thirties, would vanish to New York, catch a show, buy a suit,
    while up north,
the gas and water bills pounded the front door (his spendthrift ways
    startled me with my grandfather's resemblance),
who for over forty years came down each morning, "How's the old goat?"
    with a tie only his wife could knot circling his neck,
he slipped into my wife's room—we were unmarried at the time—and
    whispered so softly she thought
he almost believed she was really asleep, and was saying this like a wish
    or spell, some bohunk miscalculated Boston sense of duty: 15
"Don't make a mistake with your life, Susie. Don't make a mistake . . ."
Well. The thing that gets me now, despite the dangling rantings I've let
    go, is that, at least at that time,
he was right: There was, inside me, some pressing, raw unpeeled
    persistence, some libidinous desire for dominance
that, in the scribbled first drafts of my life, seemed to mark me as wastrel
    and rageful, bound to be unfaithful,
to destroy, in some powerful, nuclear need, fissioned both by childhood
    and racism, whatever came near—   20

And I can't help but feel, forgiving him now, that if she had listened, if
    she had been awake,
if this flourishing solace, this muscled-for-happiness, shared by us now,
    had never awakened,
he would have become for me a symbol of my rage and self-destruction,
    another raw, never healing wound,
and not this silenced grandfatherly presence, a crank and scoundrel, red-
    necked Yankee who created the delicate seed of my wife, my child.

[1989]

RITA DOVE [b. 1952]

The Satisfaction Coal Company

1

What to do with a day.
Leaf through *Jet*. Watch T.V.
Freezing on the porch
but he goes anyhow, snow too high
for a walk, the ice treacherous.   5
Inside, the gas heater takes care of itself;
he doesn't even notice being warm.

Everyone says he looks great.
Across the street a drunk stands smiling
at something carved in a tree.   10
The new neighbor with the floating hips
scoots out to get the mail
and waves once, brightly,
storm door clipping her heel on the way in.

2

Twice a week he had taken the bus down Glendale hill   15
to the corner of Market. Slipped through
the alley by the canal and let himself in.
Started to sweep
with terrible care, like a woman

brushing shine into her hair,   20
same motion, same lullaby.
No curtains—the cop on the beat
stopped outside once in the hour
to swing his billy club and glare.

It was better on Saturdays   25
when the children came along:
he mopped while they emptied
ashtrays, clang of glass on metal
then a dry scutter. Next they counted
nailheads studding the leather cushions.   30
Thirty-four! they shouted,
that was the year and
they found it mighty amusing.

But during the week he noticed more—
lights when they gushed or dimmed   35
at the Portage Hotel, the 10:32
picking up speed past the B & O switchyard,
floorboards trembling and the explosive
kachook kachook kachook kachook
and the oiled rails ticking underneath.   40

3

They were poor then but everyone had been poor.
He hadn't minded the sweeping,
just the thought of it—like now
when people ask him what he's thinking
and he says *I'm listening.*   45

Those nights walking home alone,
the bucket of coal scraps banging his knee,
he'd hear a roaring furnace
with its dry, familiar heat. Now the nights
take care of themselves—as for the days,   50
there is the canary's sweet curdled song,
the wino smiling through his dribble.
Past the hill, past the gorge
choked with wild sumac in summer,
the corner has been upgraded.   55
Still, he'd like to go down there someday
to stand for a while, and get warm.

[1986]

NAOMI SHIHAB NYE   [b. 1952]

The Small Vases from Hebron°

Tip their mouths open to the sky.
Turquoise, amber,
the deep green with fluted handle,
pitcher the size of two thumbs,
tiny lip and graceful waist.   5

Here we place the smallest flower
which could have lived invisibly
in loose soil beside the road,
sprig of succulent rosemary,
bowing mint.   10

They grow deeper in the center of the table.

Here we entrust the small life,
thread, fragment, breath.
And it bends. It waits all day.
As the bread cools and the children   15
open their gray copybooks
to shape the letter that looks like
a chimney rising out of a house.

And what do the headlines say?

Nothing of the smaller petal   20
perfectly arranged inside the larger petal
or the way tinted glass filters light.
Men and boys, praying when they died,
fall out of their skins.
The whole alphabet of living,   25
heads and tails of words,
sentences, the way they said,
"Ya'Allah!" when astonished,
or "ya'ani" for "I mean"—

Hebron: An ancient city in the West Bank area of Israel, a sacred place for both
Muslims and Jews. It has been a focus of tension between Israelis and Palestin-
ians since the 1967 Arab-Israeli war.

a crushed glass under the feet   30
still shines.
But the child of Hebron sleeps
with the thud of her brothers falling
and the long sorrow of the color red.

[1998]

ALICE FULTON [b. 1952]

You Can't Rhumboogie in a Ball and Chain

for Janis Joplin°

You called the blues' loose black belly lover
and in Port Arthur they called you pig-face.
The way you chugged booze straight, without a glass,
your brass-assed language, slingbacks with jeweled heel,
proclaimed you no kin to their muzzled blood.   5
No Chiclet-toothed Baptist boyfriend for you.

Strung-out, street hustling showed men wouldn't buy you.
Once you clung to the legs of a lover,
let him drag you till your knees turned to blood,
mouth hardened to a thin scar on your face,   10
cracked under songs, screams, never left to heal.
Little Girl Blue, soul pressed against the glass.

That voice rasping like you'd guzzled fiberglass,
stronger than the four armed men behind you.
But a pale horse lured you, docile, to heel: 15
warm snow flanks pillowed you like a lover.
Men feared the black holes in your body and face,
knew what they put in would return as blood.

Janis Joplin: (1943–1970), Blues singer in the 1960s and 1970s. Born and raised in Port Arthur, Texas, her life was blessed by an innate musical talent and cursed by alcohol and drugs. She died of an overdose at age twenty-seven.

Craving fast food, cars, garish as fresh blood,
diners with flies and doughnuts under glass,   20
Formica bars and a surfer's gold face,
in nameless motels, after sign-off, you
let TV's blank bright stare play lover,
lay still, convinced its cobalt rays could heal.

Your songs that sound ground under some stud's heel,   25
swallowed and coughed up in a voice like blood:
translation unavailable, lover!
No prince could shoe you in unyielding glass,
stories of exploding pumpkins bored you
who flaunted tattooed breast and hungry face.   30

That night needing a sweet-legged sugar's face,
a hot, sky-eyed Southern comfort to heal
the hurt of senior proms for all but you,
plain Janis Lyn, self-hatred laced your blood.
You knew they worshiped drained works, emptied glass,   35
legend's last gangbang the wildest lover.

Like clerks we face your image in the glass,
suggest lovers, as accessories, heels.
"It's your shade, this blood dress," we say. "It's you."

[1983]

ALBERTO RÍOS   [b. 1952]

Nani°   *diminutive for "grandmother"*

Sitting at her table, she serves
the sopa de arroz to me
instinctively, and I watch her,
the absolute *mamá*, and eat words
I might have had to say more   5
out of embarrassment. To speak,
now-foreign words I used to speak,
too, dribble down her mouth as she serves
me albondigas. No more
than a third are easy to me.   10

By the stove she does something with words
and looks at me only with her
back. I am full. I tell her
I taste the mint, and watch her speak
smiles at the stove. All my words   15
make her smile. Nani never serves
herself, she only watches me
with her skin, her hair. I ask for more.

I watch the *mamá* warming more
tortillas for me. I watch her   20
fingers in the flame for me.
Near her mouth, I see a wrinkle speak
of a man whose body serves
the ants like she serves me, then more words
from more wrinkles about children, words   25
about this and that, flowing more
easily from these other mouths. Each serves
as a tremendous string around her,
holding her together. They speak
nani was this and that to me   30
and I wonder just how much of me
will die with her, what were the words
I could have been, was. Her insides speak
through a hundred wrinkles, now, more
than she can bear, steel around her,   35
shouting, then, What is this thing she serves?

She asks me if I want more.
I own no words to stop her.
Even before I speak, she serves.

[1982]

GARY SOTO [b. 1952]

The Elements of San Joaquin

for César Chávez°

FIELD

The wind sprays pale dirt into my mouth
The small, almost invisible scars
On my hands.

The pores in my throat and elbows
Have taken in a seed of dirt of their own.   5

After a day in the grape fields near Rolinda
A fine silt, washed by sweat,
Has settled into the lines
On my wrists and palms.

Already I am becoming the valley,   10
A soil that sprouts nothing.
For any of us.

WIND

A dry wind over the valley
Peeled mountains, grain by grain,
To small slopes, loose dirt   15
Where red ants tunnel.
The wind strokes
The skulls and spines of cattle
To white dust, to nothing,

Covers the spiked tracks of beetles,   20
Of tumbleweed, of sparrows
That pecked the ground for insects.

César Chávez: (1927–1993), Hispanic-American labor leader and activist known
for creating the United Farm Workers and for leading a nationwide boycott of
California table grapes in 1968 as part of an effort to achieve labor contracts for
field workers.

Evenings, when I am in the yard weeding,
The wind picks up the breath of my armpits
Like dust, swirls it   25
Miles away

And drops it
On the ear of a rabid dog,
And I take on another life.

WIND

When you got up this morning the sun   30
Blazed an hour in the sky,

A lizard hid
Under the curled leaves of manzanita°
And winked its dark lids.

Later, the sky grayed,   35
And the cold wind you breathed
Was moving under your skin and already far
From the small hives of your lungs.

STARS

At dusk the first stars appear.
Not one eager finger points toward them.   40
A little later the stars spread with the night
And an orange moon rises
To lead them, like a shepherd, toward dawn.

SUN

In June the sun is a bonnet of light
Coming up,   45
Little by little,
From behind a skyline of pine.

The pastures sway with fiddle-neck,
Tassels of foxtail.

At Piedra   50
A couple fish on the river's edge,
Their shadows deep against the water.
Above, in the stubbled slopes,

---

33. manzanita: An evergreen shrub or small tree found in arid regions of the
western United States.

Cows climb down
As the heat rises   55
In a mist of blond locusts,
Returning to the valley.

RAIN

When autumn rains flatten sycamore leaves,
The tiny volcanos of dirt
Ants raised around their holes,   60
I should be out of work.

My silverware and stack of plates will go unused
Like the old, my two good slacks
Will smother under a growth of lint
And smell of the old dust   65
That rises
When the closet door opens or closes.

The skin of my belly will tighten like a belt
And there will be no reason for pockets.

HARVEST

East of the sun's slant, in the vineyard that never failed, 70
A wind crossed my face, moving the dust
And a portion of my voice a step closer to a new year.

The sky went black in the ninth hour of rolling trays,
And in the distance ropes of rain dropped to pull me
From the thick harvest that was not mine.   75

FOG

If you go to your window
You will notice a fog drifting in.

The sun is no stronger than a flashlight.
Not all the sweaters
Hung in closets all summer   80

Could soak up this mist. The fog:
A mouth nibbling everything to its origin,
Pomegranate trees, stolen bicycles,

The string of lights at a used-car lot,
A Pontiac with scorched valves.   85

In Fresno the fog is passing
The young thief prying a window screen,
Graying my hair that falls

And goes unfound, my fingerprints
Slowly growing a fur of dust—
One hundred years from now
There should be no reason to believe
I lived.   90

DAYBREAK

In this moment when the light starts up
In the east and rubs   95
The horizon until it catches fire,

We enter the fields to hoe,
Row after row, among the small flags of onion,
Waving off the dragonflies
That ladder the air.   100

And tears the onions raise
Do not begin in your eyes but in ours,
In the salt blown
From one blister into another;

They begin in knowing   105
You will never waken to bear
The hour timed to a heart beat,
The wind pressing us closer to the ground.

When the season ends,
And the onions are unplugged from their sleep,   110
We won't forget what you failed to see,
And nothing will heal
Under the rain's broken fingers.

[1977; rev. 1995]

JIMMY SANTIAGO BACA   [b. 1952]

Family Ties

Mountain barbecue.
They arrive, young cousins singly,
older aunts and uncles in twos and threes,
like trees. I play with a new generation
of children, my hands in streambed silt   5

of their lives, a scuba diver's hands, dusting
surface sand for buried treasure.
Freshly shaved and powdered faces
of uncles and aunts surround taco
and tamale tables. Mounted elk head on wall,   10
brass rearing horse cowboy clock
on fireplace mantle. Sons and daughters
converse round beer and whiskey table.
Tempers ignite on land grant issues.
Children scurry round my legs.   15
Old bow-legged men toss horseshoes on lawn,
other farmhands from Mexico sit on a bench,
broken lives repaired for this occasion.
I feel no love or family tie here. I rise
to go hiking, to find abandoned rock cabins   20
in the mountains. We come to a grass clearing,
my wife rolls her jeans up past ankles,
wades ice cold stream, and I barefooted,
carry a son in each arm and follow.
We cannot afford a place like this.   25
At the party again, I eat bean and chile
burrito, and after my third glass of rum,
we climb in the car and my wife drives
us home. My sons sleep in the back,
dream of the open clearing,   30
they are chasing each other with cattails
in the sunlit pasture, giggling,
as I stare out the window
at no trespassing signs white flashing past.

                                                    [1989]

JUDITH ORTIZ COFER [b. 1952]

Cold as Heaven

Before there is a breeze again
before the cooling days of Lent, she may be gone.
My grandmother asks me to tell her
again about the snow.

We sit on her white bed   5
in this white room, while outside
the Caribbean sun winds up the world
like an old alarm clock. I tell her
about the enveloping blizzard I lived through
that made everything and everyone the same;   10
how we lost ourselves in drifts so tall
we fell through our own footprints;
how wrapped like mummies in layers of wool
that almost immobilized us, we could only
take hesitant steps like toddlers   15
toward food, warmth, shelter.
I talk winter real for her,
as she would once conjure for me to dream
at sweltering siesta time,
cool stone castles in lands far north.   20
Her eyes wander to the window,
to the teeming scene of children
pouring out of a yellow bus, then to the bottle
dripping minutes through a tube
into her veins. When her eyes return to me,   25
I can see she's waiting to hear more
about the purifying nature of ice,
how snow makes way for a body,
how you can make yourself an angel
by just lying down and waving your arms   30
as you do when you say
good-bye.

                                                                    [1995]

ANITA ENDREZZE [b. 1952]

The Girl Who Loved the Sky

Outside the second grade room,
the jacaranda tree blossomed
into purple lanterns, the papery petals
drifted, darkening the windows.
Inside, the room smelled like glue.   5

The desks were made of yellowed wood,
the tops littered with eraser rubbings,
rulers, and big fat pencils.
Colored chalk meant special days.
The walls were covered with precise   10
bright tulips and charts with shiny stars
by certain names. There, I learned
how to make butter by shaking a jar
until the pale cream clotted
into one sweet mass. There, I learned   15
that numbers were fractious beasts
with dens like dim zeros. And there,
I met a blind girl who thought the sky
tasted like cold metal when it rained
and whose eyes were always covered   20
with the bruised petals of her lids.

She loved the formless sky, defined
only by sounds, or the cool umbrellas
of clouds. On hot, still days
we listened to the sky falling   25
like chalk dust. We heard the noon
whistle of the pig-mash factory,
smelled the sourness of home-bound men.
I had no father; she had no eyes;
we were best friends. The other girls   30
drew shaky hop-scotch squares
on the dusty asphalt, talked about
pajama parties, weekend cook-outs,
and parents who bought sleek-finned cars.
Alone, we sat in the canvas swings,   35
our shoes digging into the sand, then pushing,
until we flew high over their heads,
our hands streaked with red rust
from the chains that kept us safe.

I was born blind, she said, an act of nature.   40
Sure, I thought, like birds born
without wings, trees without roots.
I didn't understand. The day she moved
I saw the world clearly; the sky
backed away from me like a departing father.   45
I sat under the jacaranda, catching

the petals in my palm, enclosing them
until my fist was another lantern
hiding a small and bitter flame.

[1988]

RAY GONZÁLEZ   [b. 1952]

Praise the Tortilla, Praise the Menudo, Praise the Chorizo

I praise the tortilla in honor of El Panzón,
who hit me in school every day and made me see
how the bruises on my arms looked like
the brown clouds on my mother's tortillas.
I praise the tortilla because I know   5
they can fly into our hands like
eager flesh of the one we love,
those soft yearnings we delight in biting
as we tear the tortilla and wipe the plate clean.

I praise the menudo as visionary food that it is,   10
the tripas y posole tight flashes of color
we see as the red caldo smears across our notebooks
like a vision we have not had in years,
our lives going down like the empty bowl
of menudo exploding in our stomachs   15
with the chili piquin of our poetic dreams.

I praise the chorizo and smear it
across my face and hands,
the dayglow brown of it painting me
with the desire to find out   20
what happened to la familia,
why the chorizo sizzled in the pan
and covered the house with a smell
of childhood we will never have again,

the chorizo burrito hot in our hands,   25
as we ran out to play and show the vatos
it's time to cut the chorizo,
tell it like it is before la manteca runs down
our chins and drips away.

[1992]

MARK DOTY   [b. 1953]

Tiara

Peter died in a paper tiara
cut from a book of princess paper dolls;
he loved royalty, sashes

and jewels. I don't know,
he said, when he woke in the hospice,   5
I was watching the Bette Davis film festival

on Channel 57 and then —
At the wake, the tension broke
when someone guessed

the casket closed because   10
he was *in there in a big wig*
and heels, and someone said,

You know he's always late,
he probably isn't here yet —
he's still fixing his makeup.   15

And someone said he asked for it.
Asked for it —
when all he did was go down

into the salt tide
of wanting as much as he wanted,   20
giving himself over so drunk

or stoned it almost didn't matter who,
though they were beautiful,
stampeding into him in the simple,

ravishing music of their hurry.   25
I think heaven is perfect stasis
poised over the realms of desire,

where dreaming and waking men lie
on the grass while wet horses
roam among them, huge fragments   30

of the music we die into
in the body's paradise.
Sometimes we wake not knowing

how we came to lie here,
or who has crowned us with these temporary,   35
precious stones. And given

the world's perfectly turned shoulders,
the deep hollows blued by longing,
given the irreplaceable silk

of horses rippling in orchards,   40
fruit thundering and chiming down,
given the ordinary marvels of form

and gravity, what could he do,
what could any of us ever do
but ask for it?   45

[1991]

RICHARD JONES   [b. 1953]

Cathedral

Songbirds live
in the old cathedral,
caged birds bought at the street market
and freed as a kind of offering.
Now doves and finches and parakeets   5
nest in the crooks of the nave's highest arches,
roosting on the impossibly high
sills of stained glass windows,

looking down into the valley of the altar
as if from cliffs.   10

Twice a day, you'll hear them singing:
at dawn
when the blue light
of angels' wings
and the yellow light of halos   15
flood into their nests to wake them;
and during mass
when the organ fills
the valley below with thunder.
These birds love thunder,   20
never having seen a drop of rain.
They love it when the people below stand up
and sing. They fly
in mad little loops
from window to window,   25
from the tops of arches
down toward the candles and tombs,
making the sign of the cross.

If you look up during mass
to the world's light falling   30
through the arms of saints,
you can see birds flying
through blue columns of incense
as if it were simple wood smoke
rising from a cabin's chimney   35
in a remote and hushed forest.

[1994]

JANE HIRSHFIELD   [b. 1953]

The Stone of Heaven

Here, where the rivers dredge up
the very stone of Heaven, we name its colors—
muttonfat jade, kingfisher jade, jade of appleskin green.

And here, in the glittering
hues of the Flemish Masters, we sample their wine;   5
rest in their windows' sun-warmth,
cross with pleasure their scrubbed tile floors.
Everywhere the details leap like fish — bright shards
of water out of water, facet-cut, swift-moving
on the myriad bones.   10

Any woodthrush shows it — he sings,
not to fill the world, but because he is filled.

But the world does not fill with us,
it spills and spills, whirs with owl-wings,
rises, sets, stuns us with planet-rings, stars.   15
A carnival tent, a fluttering of banners.

O baker of yeast-scented loaves,
sword dancer,
seamstress, weaver of shattering glass,
O whirler of winds, boat-swallower,   20
germinant seed,
O seasons that sing in our ears in the shape of O —
we name your colors muttonfat, kingfisher, jade,
we name your colors anthracite, orca, growth-tip of pine,
we name them arpeggio, pond,   25
we name them flickering helix within the cell, burning coal tunnel,
    blossom of salt,
we name them roof flashing copper, frost-scent at morning, smoke-
    singe of pearl,
from black-flowering to light-flowering we name them,
from barest conception, the almost not thought of, to heaviest matter,
    we name them,
from glacier-lit blue to the gold of iguana we name them,   30
and naming, begin to see,
and seeing, begin to assemble the plain stones of earth.

                                                        [1994]

LORNA DEE CERVANTES   [b. 1954]

Freeway 280

Las casitas° near the gray cannery,   *little houses*
nestled amid wild abrazos° of climbing roses   *bear hugs*
and man-high red geraniums
are gone now. The freeway conceals it
all beneath a raised scar.   5

But under the fake windsounds of the open lanes,
in the abandoned lots below, new grasses sprout,
wild mustard remembers, old gardens
come back stronger than they were,
trees have been left standing in their yards.   10
Albaricoqueros, cerezos, nogales° . . .   *apple, cherry, walnut trees*
Viejitas° come here with paper bags to gather greens.   *old women*
Espinaca, verdolagas, yerbabuena° . . .   *spinach, purslane, mint*

I scramble over the wire fence
that would have kept me out.   15
Once, I wanted out, wanted the rigid lanes
to take me to a place without sun,
without the smell of tomatoes burning
on swing shift in the greasy summer air.

Maybe it's here   20
en los campos extraños de esta ciudad°
where I'll find it, that part of me
mown under
like a corpse
or a loose seed.   25

[1981]

21. en . . . ciudad: In the strange fields of this city.

THYLIAS MOSS [b. 1954]

Tornados

Truth is, I envy them
not because they dance; I out jitterbug them
as I'm shuttled through and through legs
strong as looms, weaving time. They
do black more justice than I, frenzy   5
of conductor of philharmonic and electricity, hair
on end, result of the charge when horns and strings release
the pent up Beethoven and Mozart. Ions played

instead of notes. The movement
is not wrath, not hormone swarm because   10
I saw my first forming above the church a surrogate
steeple. The morning of my first baptism and
salvation already tangible, funnel for the spirit
coming into me without losing a drop, my black
guardian angel come to rescue me before all the words   15

get out, *I looked over Jordan and what did I see coming for
to carry me home. Regardez,*° it all comes back, even the first   *look*
grade French, when the tornado stirs up the past, bewitched spoon
lost in its own spin, like a roulette wheel that won't
be steered, like the world. They drove me underground,   20
tornado watches and warnings, atomic bomb drills. Adult
storms so I had to leave the room. Truth is

the tornado is a perfect nappy curl, tightly wound,
spinning wildly when I try to tamper with its nature, shunning
the hot comb and pressing oil even though if absolutely straight   25
I'd have the longest hair in the world. Bouffant tornadic
crown taking the royal path on a trip to town, stroll down
Tornado Alley where it intersects Memory Lane. Smoky spirit-
clouds, shadows searching for what cast them.

[1991]

LOUISE ERDRICH   [b. 1954]

A Love Medicine

Still it is raining lightly
in Wahpeton. The pickup trucks
sizzle beneath the blue neon
bug traps of the dairy bar.

Theresa goes out in green halter and chains   5
that glitter at her throat.
This dragonfly, my sister,
she belongs more than I
to this night of rising water.

The Red River swells to take the bridge.   10
She laughs and leaves her man in his Dodge.
He shoves off to search her out.
He wears a long rut in the fog.

And later, at the crest of the flood,
when the pilings are jarred from their sockets   15
and pitch into the current,
she steps against the fistwork of a man.
She goes down in wet grass
and his boot plants its grin
among the arches of her face.   20

Now she feels her way home in the dark.
The white-violet bulbs of the streetlamps
are seething with insects,
and the trees lean down aching and empty.
The river slaps at the dike works, insistent.   25

I find her curled up in the roots of a cottonwood.
I find her stretched out in the park, where all night
the animals are turning in their cages.
I find her in a burnt-over ditch, in a field
that is gagging on rain,   30
sheets of rain sweep up down
to the river held tight against the bridge.

We see that now the moon is leavened and the water,
as deep as it will go,

stops rising. Where we wait for the night to take us   35
the rain ceases. *Sister, there is nothing*
I would not do.

[1984]

CORNELIUS EADY   [b. 1954]

My Mother, If She Had Won Free Dance Lessons

Would she have been a person
With a completely different outlook on life?
There are times when I visit
And find her settled on a chair
In our dilapidated house,   5
The neighborhood crazy lady
Doing what the neighborhood crazy lady is supposed to do,
Which is absolutely nothing

And I wonder as we talk our sympathetic talk,
Abandoned in easy dialogue,   10
I, the son of the crazy lady,
Who crosses easily into her point of view
As if yawning
Or taking off an overcoat.
Each time I visit   15
I walk back into our lives

And I wonder, like any child who wakes up one day to find themself
Abandoned in a world larger than their
    Bad dreams,
I wonder as I see my mother sitting there,   20
Landed to the right-hand window in the living room,
Pausing from time to time in the endless loop of our dialogue
To peek for rascals through the
Venetian blinds,

I wonder a small thought.   25
I walk back into our lives.

Given the opportunity,
How would she have danced?
Would it have been as easily

As we talk to each other now,   30
The crazy lady
And the crazy lady's son,
As if we were old friends from opposite coasts
Picking up the thread of a long conversation,

Or two ballroom dancers   35
Who only know
One step?

What would have changed
If the phone had rung like a suitor,
If the invitation had arrived in the mail   40
Like Jesus, extending a hand?

[1986]

MARILYN CHIN   [b. 1955]

Turtle Soup

for Ben Huang

You go home one evening tired from work,
and your mother boils you turtle soup.
Twelve hours hunched over the hearth
(who knows what else is in that cauldron).

You say, "Ma, you've poached the symbol of long life;   5
that turtle lived four thousand years, swam
the Wei, up the Yellow, over the Yangtze.
Witnessed the Bronze Age, the High Tang,
grazed on splendid sericulture."
(So, she boils the life out of him.)   10

"All our ancestors have been fools.
Remember Uncle Wu who rode ten thousand miles

to kill a famous Manchu and ended up
with his head on a pole? Eat, child,
its liver will make you strong." 15

"Sometimes you're the life, sometimes the sacrifice."
Her sobbing is inconsolable.
So, you spread that gentle napkin
over your lap in decorous Pasadena.

Baby, some high priestess has got it wrong. 20
The golden decal on the green underbelly
says "Made in Hong Kong."

Is there nothing left but the shell
and humanity's strange inscriptions,
the songs, the rites, the oracles? 25

[1987]

CATHY SONG   [b. 1955]

Girl Powdering Her Neck

From a Ukiyo-e Print by Utamaro

The light is the inside
sheen of an oyster shell,
sponged with talc and vapor,
moisture from a bath.

A pair of slippers 5
are placed outside
the rice-paper doors.
She kneels at a low table
in the room,
her legs folded beneath her 10
as she sits on a buckwheat pillow.

Her hair is black
with hints of red,
the color of seaweed
spread over rocks. 15

Kitagawa Utamaro (1753–1806), *Girl Powdering Her Neck*
(Musée Guimet, Paris).

Morning begins the ritual
wheel of the body,
the application of translucent skins.
She practices pleasure:
the pressure of three fingertips   20
applying powder.
Fingerprints of pollen
some other hand will trace.

The peach-dyed kimono
patterned with maple leaves   25
drifting across the silk,
falls from right to left
in a diagonal, revealing
the nape of her neck
and the curve of a shoulder   30
like the slope of a hill
set deep in snow in a country
of huge white solemn birds.
Her face appears in the mirror,
a reflection in a winter pond,   35
rising to meet itself.

She dips a corner of her sleeve
like a brush into water
to wipe the mirror;
she is about to paint herself.   40
The eyes narrow
in a moment of self-scrutiny.
The mouth parts
as if desiring to disturb
the placid plum face;   45
break the symmetry of silence.
But the berry-stained lips,
stenciled into the mask of beauty,
do not speak.

Two chrysanthemums   50
touch in the middle of the lake
and drift apart.

                                                        [1983]

KIMIKO HAHN   [b. 1955]

When You Leave

This sadness could only be a color
if we call it *momoiro*, Japanese

for *peach-color*, as in the first story
Mother told us: It is the color of the hero's skin

when the barren woman discovered him   5
inside a peach floating down the river.

And of the banner and gloves she sewed
when he left her to battle the horsemen, then found himself

torn, like fruit off a tree. Even when he met a monkey
dog and bird he could not release   10

the color he saw when he closed his eyes.
   In his boat
the lap of the waves against the hold

was too intimate as he leaned back to sleep.
   He wanted   15
to leave all thoughts of peach behind him—

the fruit that brought him to her
and she, the one who opened the color forever.

[1989]

JIM DANIELS   [b. 1956]

Short-order Cook

An average joe comes in
and orders thirty cheeseburgers and thirty fries.

I wait for him to pay before I start cooking.
He pays.
He ain't no average joe.   5

The grill is just big enough for ten rows of three.
I slap the burgers down
throw two buckets of fries in the deep frier
and they pop pop spit spit . . .
psss . . .   10
The counter girls laugh.
I concentrate.
It is the crucial point—
they are ready for the cheese:
my fingers shake as I tear off slices   15
toss them on the burgers/fries done/dump/
refill buckets/burgers ready/flip into buns/
beat that melting cheese/wrap burgers in plastic/
into paper bags/fries done/fill thirty bags/
bring them to the counter/wipe sweat on sleeve   20
and smile at the counter girls.
I puff my chest out and bellow:
"Thirty cheeseburgers, thirty fries!"
They look at me funny.
I grab a handful of ice, toss it in my mouth   25
do a little dance and walk back to the grill.
Pressure, responsibility, success,
thirty cheeseburgers, thirty fries.

[1985]

LI-YOUNG LEE [b. 1957]

Eating Alone

I've pulled the last of the year's young onions.
The garden is bare now. The ground is cold,
brown and old. What is left of the day flames
in the maples at the corner of my
eye. I turn, a cardinal vanishes.   5
By the cellar door, I wash the onions,
then drink from the icy metal spigot.

Once, years back, I walked beside my father
among the windfall pears. I can't recall

our words. We may have strolled in silence. But   10
I still see him bend that way—left hand braced
on knee, creaky—to lift and hold to my
eye a rotten pear. In it, a hornet
spun crazily, glazed in slow, glistening juice.

It was my father I saw this morning   15
waving to me from the trees. I almost
called to him, until I came close enough
to see the shovel, leaning where I had
left it, in the flickering, deep green shade.

White rice steaming, almost done. Sweet green peas   20
fried in onions. Shrimp braised in sesame
oil and garlic. And my own loneliness.
What more could I, a young man, want.

[1986]

MARTÍN ESPADA   [b. 1957]

The Saint Vincent de Paul
Food Pantry Stomp

Madison, Wisconsin, 1980

Waiting for the carton of food
given with Christian suspicion
even to agency-certified charity cases
like me,
thin and brittle   5
as uncooked linguini,
anticipating the factory-damaged cans
of tomato soup, beets, three-bean salad
in a welfare cornucopia,
I spotted a squashed dollar bill   10
on the floor, and with
a Saint Vincent de Paul food pantry stomp
pinned it under my sneaker,
tied my laces meticulously,
and stuffed the bill in my sock   15

like a smuggler of diamonds,
all beneath the plaster statue wingspan
of Saint Vinnie,
who was unaware
of the dance   20
named in his honor
by a maraca shaker
in the salsa band
of the unemployed.

[1990]

WANG PING   [b. 1957]

Syntax

She walks to a table
She walk to table

She is walking to a table
She walk to table now

What difference does it make   5
What difference it make

In Nature, no completeness
No sentence really complete thought

Language, like woman,
Look best when free, undressed.   10

[1999]

TOM ANDREWS [1961–2001]

The Hemophiliac's Motorcycle

For the sin against the holy ghost is ingratitude.
—CHRISTOPHER SMART, *JUBILATE AGNO*°

May the Lord Jesus Christ bless the hemophiliac's motorcycle, the smell
    of knobby tires,
Bel-Ray oil mixed with gasoline, new brake and clutch cables and
    handlebar grips,
the whole bike smothered in WD40 (to prevent rust, and to make the
    bike shine),
may He divine that the complex smell that simplified my life was
    performing the work of the spirit,
a window into the net of gems, linkages below and behind the given
    material world,   5
my little corner of the world's danger and sweet risk, a hemophiliac
    dicing on motocross tracks
in Pennsylvania and Ohio and West Virginia each Sunday from April
    through November,
the raceway names to my mind then a perfect sensual music, Hidden
    Hills, Rocky Fork, Mt. Morris, Salt Creek,
and the tracks themselves part of that music, the double jumps and off-
    camber turns, whoop-de-doos and fifth-gear downhills,
and me with my jersey proclaiming my awkward faith—"Powered By
    Christ," it said above a silk-screened picture of a rider in a radical
    cross-up,   10
the bike flying sideways off a jump like a ramp, the rider leaning his
    whole body into a left-hand corner—
may He find His name glorified in such places and smells,

Epigraph: In 1756 Christopher Smart (1722–1771) was seized by an urge to pray
publicly, sometimes forcing passersby to kneel with him. He was placed in an institution, where he began pouring out innovative poetry, including *Jubilate Agno
(Rejoice in the Lamb)*. It is, in part, a liturgy of worship, joining the material and
spiritual universe in prayers of praise and thanksgiving. The most famous section
is on his cat Jeoffry (see p. 416).

and in the people, Mike Bias, Charles Godby, Tracy Woods, David and
Tommy Hill, Bill Schultz° —
their names and faces snowing down to me now as I look upward to the
past —
friends who taught me to look at the world luminously in front of my eyes,   15
to find for myself the right rhythm of wildness and precision, when to
hold back and when to let go,
each of them with a style, a thumbprint, a way of tilting the bike this
way or that out of a berm shot, or braking heavily into a corner,
may He hear a listening to the sure song of His will in those years,
for they flooded me with gratitude that His informing breath was
breathed into me,
gratitude that His silence was the silence of all things, His presence
palpable everywhere in His absence,   20
gratitude that the sun flashed on the Kanawha River, making it
shimmer and wink,
gratitude that the river twisted like a wrist in its socket of bottomland,
its water part of our speech
as my brother and I drifted in inner tubes fishing the Great White Carp,
gratitude that plump squirrels tight-walked telephone lines and trellises
of honeysuckle vines
and swallows dove and banked through the limbs of sycamore trees,
word-perfect and sun-stunned   25
in the middle of the afternoon, my infusion of factor VIII° sucked in and
my brother's dialysis sucked in and out —
both of us bewildered by the body's deep swells and currents and eerie
backwaters,
our eyes widening at the white bursts on the mountain ash, at
earthworms inching into oil-rainbowed roads —
gratitude that the oak tops on the high hills beyond the lawns fingered
the denim sky
as cicadas drilled a shrill voice into the roadside sumac and
peppergrass,   30
gratitude that after a rain catbirds crowded the damp air, bees spiraling
from one exploding blossom to another,
gratitude that at night the star clusters were like nun buoys moored to
a second sky, where God made room for us all,
may He adore each moment alive in the whirring world,
as now sitting up in this hospital bed brings a bright gladness for the
human body, membrane of web and dew

13. **Mike Bias . . . Bill Schultz:** Motocross racers.
26. **factor VIII:** An enzyme essential to blood clotting.

I want to hymn and abide by, splendor of tissue, splendor of cartilage
    and bone,   35
splendor of the taillike spine's desire to stretch as it fills with blood
after a mundane backward plunge on an iced sidewalk in Ann Arbor,
splendor of fibrinogen and cryoprecipitate, loosening the blood pooled
    in the stiffened joints
so I can sit up oh sit up in radiance, like speech after eight weeks of
    silence,
and listen for Him in the blood-rush and clairvoyance of the healing
    body,   40
in the sweet impersonal luck that keeps me now
from bleeding into the kidney or liver, or further into the spine,
listen for Him in the sound of my wife and my father weeping and
    rejoicing,
listen as my mother kneels down on the tiled floor like Christopher
    Smart
praying with strangers on a cobbled London street, kneels here in broad
    daylight   45
singing a "glorious hosanna from the den"
as nurses and orderlies and patients rolling their IV stands behind them
    like luggage
stall and stare into the room and smile finally and shuffle off, having
    heard God's great goodness lifted up
on my mother's tongue, each face transformed for a moment by
    ridicule
or sympathy before disappearing into the shunt-light of the hallway,   50
listen for Him in the snap and jerk of my roommate's curtain as he
    draws it open
to look and look at my singing mother and her silent choir
and to wink at me with an understanding that passeth peace, this kind,
    skeletal man
suffering from end-stage heart disease who loves science fiction and
    okra,
who on my first night here read aloud his grandson's bar mitzvah
    speech to me,   55
". . . In my haftorah portion, the Lord takes Ezekiel to a valley full of
    bones,
the Lord commands him to prophesy over the bones so they will
    become people. . . ,"
and solemnly recited the entire text of the candlelighting ceremony,
"I would like to light the first candle in memory of Grandma Ruth, for
    whom I was named,
I would like Grandma Dot and Grandpa Dan to come up and light the
    second candle,   60

I would like Aunt Mary Ann and my Albuquerque cousins Alanna and
    Susanna to come up and light the third candle. . . ,"
his voice rising steadily through the vinegary smell and brutal hush in
    the room,
may the Lord hear our listening, His word like matchlight cupped to a
    cigarette
the instant before the intake of breath, like the smoke clouds pooled in
    the lit tobacco
before flooding the lungs and bloodstream, filtering into pith and
    marrow,   65
may He see Himself again in the hemophiliac's motorcycle
on a certain Sunday in 1975 — Hidden Hills Raceway, Gallipolis, Ohio,
a first moto holeshot and wire-to-wire win, a miraculously benign
    sideswipe early on in the second moto
bending the handlebars and front brake lever before the possessed
    rocketing up through the pack
to finish third after passing Brian Kloser on his tricked-out Suzuki RM125   70
midair over the grandstand double jump —
may His absence arrive like that again here in this hygienic room,
not with the rush of a peaked power band and big air over the jumps
but with the strange intuitive calm of that race, a stillness somehow
    poised
in the body even as it pounded and blasted and held its line across the
    washboard track,   75
may His silence plague us like that again,
may He bless our listening and our homely tongues.

                                                                    [1994]

VIRGIL SUÁREZ [b. 1962]

The Ways of Guilt

Guilt is magical.
— FROM "ADULTERY," A POEM BY JAMES DICKEY

My father calls a day
too late, merely to remind
me that once again
I've forgotten my mother's

birthday, never mind his,   5
which is a month earlier,
and which I have also
forgotten. He lowers

his voice so that he can
tell me that he will call   10
my mother and tell her
that I have just called

to wish her a happy
birthday—never mind
that I'm a day too late.   15
My mother, after he puts

her on, manages to say
that it's all right, all right
for a son to forget a parent's
birthday, but a mother   20

or father (I'm a father
of two)—and she stops
at "father" to suck
in her breath—should never

forget a son or daughter's   25
birthday, that would certainly
be unpardonable, like a tiger
eating her cubs. After we

hang up, I think of all those
moments, painfully awkward   30
and embarrassing when my
parents, left without any other

alternative, reverted to what always
works: guilt. As I hang up
my three-year-old daughter   35
Alexandria walks into the kitchen

for a glass of cold water. She
looks up at me & must sense
something in the way I look
for she asks, "Daddy, are you   40

happy?" This is something
she's learned at school,

from hearing her teacher say
bad behavior doesn't make

her happy. This is also the   45
same child who's asked
in the past where laughter
goes. I look at her & smile

just to reassure her that yes,
I am happy, for the moment,   50
anyway. Perhaps happiest
to know that when the moment

comes in her own life, I too
will know what buttons to push.
What strings   55
to pull.

[1997]

TIMOTHY LIU   [b. 1965]

Thoreau

My father and I have no place to go.
His wife will not let us in the house—
afraid of catching AIDS. She thinks
sleeping with men is more than a sin,
my father says, as we sit on the curb   5
in front of someone else's house.
Sixty-four years have made my father
impotent. Silver roots, faded black
dye mottling his hair make him look
almost comical, as if his shame   10
belonged to me. Last night we read
Thoreau in a steak house down the road
and wept: *If a man does not keep pace*
with his companions, let him travel
to the music that he hears, however   15
measured or far away. The orchards
are gone, his village near Shanghai

bombed by the Japanese, the groves
I have known in Almaden—apricot,
walnut, peach and plum—hacked down.   20

                                                              [1995]

SHERMAN ALEXIE   [b. 1966]

Postcards to Columbus

Beginning at the front door of the White House, travel west
for 500 years, pass through small towns and house fires, ignore
hitchhikers and stranded motorists, until you find yourself
back at the beginning of this journey, this history and country

folded over itself like a Mobius strip. Christopher Columbus   5
where have you been? Lost between Laramie and San Francisco
or in the reservation HUD house, building a better mousetrap?
Seymour saw you shooting free throws behind the Tribal School

in a thunderstorm. Didn't you know lightning strikes the earth
800 times a second? But, Columbus, how could you ever imagine   10
how often our lives change? *Electricity is lightning pretending
to be permanent* and when the Indian child pushes the paper clip

into the electrical outlet, it's applied science, insane economics
of supply and demand, the completion of a 20th century circuit.
Christopher Columbus, you are the most successful real estate agent   15
who ever lived, sold acres and acres of myth, a house built on stilts

above the river salmon travel by genetic memory. Beneath the burden
of 15,000 years my tribe celebrated this country's 200th birthday
by refusing to speak English and we'll honor the 500th anniversary
of your invasion, Columbus, by driving blindfolded cross-country   20

naming the first tree we destroy *America*. We'll make the first guardrail
we crash through our national symbol. Our flag will be a white sheet
stained with blood and piss. Columbus, can you hear me over white noise
of your television set? Can you hear ghosts of drums approaching?

                                                              [1993]

ALLISON JOSEPH   [b. 1967]

On Being Told I Don't Speak
Like a Black Person

Emphasize the "h," you hignorant ass,
was what my mother was told
when colonial-minded teachers
slapped her open palm with a ruler
in that Jamaican schoolroom.   5
Trained in England, they tried
to force their pupils to speak
like Eliza Doolittle after
her transformation, fancying themselves
British as Henry Higgins,   10
despite dark, sun-ripened skin.
Mother never lost her accent,
though, the music of her voice
charming everyone, an infectious lilt
I can imitate, not duplicate.   15
No one in the States told her
to eliminate the accent,
my high school friends adoring
the way her voice would lift
when she called me to the phone,   20
A-ll-i-son, it's friend Cathy.
Why don't you sound like her?,
they'd ask. I didn't sound
like anyone or anything,
no grating New Yorker nasality,   25
no fastidious British mannerisms
like the ones my father affected
when he wanted to sell someone
something. And I didn't sound
like a Black American,   30
college acquaintances observed,
sure they knew what a black person
was supposed to sound like.
Was I supposed to sound lazy,
dropping syllables here, there,   35
not finishing words but

slurring the final letter so that
each sentence joined the next,
sliding past the listener?
Were certain words off limits,   40
too erudite, too scholarly
for someone with a natural tan?
I asked what they meant,
and they stuttered, blushed,
said you know, Black English,   45
applying what they'd learned
from that semester's text.
Does everyone in your family
speak alike?, I'd question,
and they'd say don't take this the   50
wrong way, nothing personal.

Now I realize there's nothing
more personal than speech,
that I don't have to defend
how I speak, how any person,   55
black, white, chooses to speak.
Let us speak. Let us talk
with the sounds of our mothers
and fathers still reverberating
in our minds, wherever our mothers   60
or fathers come from:
Arkansas, Belize, Alabama,
Brazil, Aruba, Arizona.
Let us simply speak
to one another,   65
listen and prize the inflections,
differences, never assuming
how any person will sound
until her mouth opens,
until his mouth opens,   70
greetings familiar
in any language.

[1999]

9 Plays

SOPHOCLES [c. 496–c. 406 B.C.E.]

Oedipus Rex

TRANSLATED BY DUDLEY FITTS AND ROBERT FITZGERALD

Characters

OEDIPUS, *King of Thebes, supposed son of Polybos and Merope, King and Queen of Corinth*
IOKASTE,° *wife of Oedipus and widow of the late King Laios*
KREON,° *brother of Iokaste, a prince of Thebes*
TEIRESIAS, *a blind seer who serves Apollo*
PRIEST
MESSENGER, *from Corinth*
SHEPHERD, *former servant of Laios*
SECOND MESSENGER, *from the palace*
CHORUS OF THEBAN ELDERS
CHORAGOS, *leader of the Chorus*
ANTIGONE and ISMENE, *young daughters of Oedipus and Iokaste. They appear in the Exodos but do not speak.*
SUPPLIANTS, GUARDS, SERVANTS

Scene: *Before the palace of Oedipus, King of Thebes. A central door and two lateral doors open onto a platform which runs the length of the facade. On the platform, right and left, are altars; and three steps lead down into the orchestra, or chorus-ground. At the beginning of the action these steps are crowded by suppliants who have brought branches and chaplets of olive leaves and who sit in various attitudes of despair. Oedipus enters.*

PROLOGUE°

OEDIPUS: My children, generations of the living
  In the line of Kadmos,° nursed at his ancient hearth:

Iokaste: Traditional Western spelling is *Jocasta*. **Kreon:** Traditional Western spelling is *Creon*. **Prologue:** First part of the play explaining the background and introducing the scene. **2. Kadmos:** Founder of Thebes.

Why have you strewn yourselves before these altars
In supplication, with your boughs and garlands?
The breath of incense rises from the city   5
With a sound of prayer and lamentation.
   Children,
I would not have you speak through messengers,
And therefore I have come myself to hear you—
I, Oedipus, who bear the famous name.
(*To a Priest.*) You, there, since you are eldest in the company,   10
Speak for them all, tell me what preys upon you,
Whether you come in dread, or crave some blessing:
Tell me, and never doubt that I will help you
In every way I can; I should be heartless
Were I not moved to find you suppliant here.   15
PRIEST: Great Oedipus, O powerful king of Thebes!
  You see how all the ages of our people
  Cling to your altar steps: here are boys
  Who can barely stand alone, and here are priests
  By weight of age, as I am a priest of God,   20
  And young men chosen from those yet unmarried;
  As for the others, all that multitude,
  They wait with olive chaplets in the squares,
  At the two shrines of Pallas,° and where Apollo°
  Speaks in the glowing embers.
                         Your own eyes   25
Must tell you: Thebes is tossed on a murdering sea
And can not lift her head from the death surge.
A rust consumes the buds and fruits of the earth;
The herds are sick; children die unborn,
And labor is vain. The god of plague and pyre   30
Raids like detestable lightning through the city,
And all the house of Kadmos is laid waste,
All emptied, and all darkened: Death alone
Battens upon the misery of Thebes.

You are not one of the immortal gods, we know;   35
Yet we have come to you to make our prayer
As to the man surest in mortal ways
And wisest in the ways of God. You saved us

---

24. Pallas: Daughter of Zeus, goddess of wisdom, and protectress of Athens.
Apollo: Son of Zeus and god of the sun, of light, and of healing.

From the Sphinx,° that flinty singer, and the tribute
We paid to her so long; yet you were never   40
Better informed than we, nor could we teach you:
A god's touch, it seems, enabled you to help us.

Therefore, O mighty power, we turn to you:
Find us our safety, find us a remedy,
Whether by counsel of the gods or of men.   45
A king of wisdom tested in the past
Can act in a time of troubles, and act well.
Noblest of men, restore
Life to your city! Think how all men call you
Liberator for your boldness long ago;   50
Ah, when your years of kingship are remembered,
Let them not say *We rose, but later fell* —
Keep the State from going down in the storm!
Once, years ago, with happy augury,
You brought us fortune; be the same again!   55
No man questions your power to rule the land:
But rule over men, not over a dead city!
Ships are only hulls, high walls are nothing,
When no life moves in the empty passageways.

OEDIPUS: Poor children! You may be sure I know   60
All that you longed for in your coming here.
I know that you are deathly sick; and yet,
Sick as you are, not one is as sick as I.
Each of you suffers in himself alone
His anguish, not another's; but my spirit   65
Groans for the city, for myself, for you.

I was not sleeping, you are not waking me.
No, I have been in tears for a long while
And in my restless thought walked many ways.
In all my search I found one remedy,   70
And I have adopted it: I have sent Kreon,
Son of Menoikeus, brother of the queen,

---

39. Sphinx: A winged monster with the body of a lion and the face of a woman.
The Sphinx tormented Thebes with a riddle — "What goes on four legs in the
morning, two at noon, and three in the evening?" — and killed those who could
not answer correctly. When Oedipus solved the riddle, the Sphinx killed herself.

To Delphi,° Apollo's place of revelation,
To learn there, if he can,
What act or pledge of mine may save the city.   75
I have counted the days, and now, this very day,
I am troubled, for he has overstayed his time.
What is he doing? He has been gone too long.
Yet whenever he comes back, I should do ill
Not to take any action the god orders.   80
PRIEST: It is a timely promise. At this instant
   They tell me Kreon is here.
OEDIPUS: O Lord Apollo!
   May his news be fair as his face is radiant!
PRIEST: Good news, I gather! he is crowned with bay,
   The chaplet is thick with berries.
OEDIPUS: We shall soon know;   85
   He is near enough to hear us now. (*Enter Kreon.*) O prince:
   Brother: son of Menoikeus:
   What answer do you bring us from the god?
KREON: A strong one. I can tell you, great afflictions
   Will turn out well, if they are taken well.   90
OEDIPUS: What was the oracle? These vague words
   Leave me still hanging between hope and fear.
KREON: Is it your pleasure to hear me with all these
   Gathered around us? I am prepared to speak,
   But should we not go in?
OEDIPUS: Speak to them all,   95
   It is for them I suffer, more than for myself.
KREON: Then I will tell you what I heard at Delphi.
   In plain words
   The god commands us to expel from the land of Thebes
   An old defilement we are sheltering.   100
   It is a deathly thing, beyond cure;
   We must not let it feed upon us longer.
OEDIPUS: What defilement? How shall we rid ourselves of it?
KREON: By exile or death, blood for blood. It was
   Murder that brought the plague-wind on the city.   105
OEDIPUS: Murder of whom? Surely the god has named him?
KREON: My Lord: Laios once ruled this land,
   Before you came to govern us.
OEDIPUS: I know;
   I learned of him from others; I never saw him.

73. **Delphi:** Site of the oracle, the preeminent shrine of Apollo.

KREON: He was murdered; and Apollo commands us now   110
  To take revenge upon whoever killed him.
OEDIPUS: Upon whom? Where are they? Where shall we find a clue
  To solve that crime, after so many years?
KREON: Here in this land, he said. Search reveals
  Things that escape an inattentive man.   115
OEDIPUS: Tell me: Was Laios murdered in his house,
  Or in the fields, or in some foreign country?
KREON: He said he planned to make a pilgrimage.
  He did not come home again.
OEDIPUS: And was there no one,
  No witness, no companion, to tell what happened?   120
KREON: They were all killed but one, and he got away
  So frightened that he could remember one thing only.
OEDIPUS: What was that one thing? One may be the key
  To everything, if we resolve to use it.
KREON: He said that a band of highwaymen attacked them,   125
  Outnumbered them, and overwhelmed the king.
OEDIPUS: Strange, that a highwayman should be so daring —
  Unless some faction here bribed him to do it.
KREON: We thought of that. But after Laios' death
  New troubles arose and we had no avenger.   130
OEDIPUS: What troubles could prevent your hunting down the killers?
KREON: The riddling Sphinx's song
  Made us deaf to all mysteries but her own.
OEDIPUS: Then once more I must bring what is dark to light.
  It is most fitting that Apollo shows,   135
  As you do, this compunction for the dead.
  You shall see how I stand by you, as I should,
  Avenging this country and the god as well,
  And not as though it were for some distant friend,
  But for my own sake, to be rid of evil.   140
  Whoever killed King Laios might — who knows? —
  Lay violent hands even on me — and soon.
  I act for the murdered king in my own interest.

  Come, then, my children: leave the altar steps,
  Lift up your olive boughs!
                         One of you go   145
  And summon the people of Kadmos to gather here.
  I will do all that I can; you may tell them that.   (*Exit a Page.*)
  So, with the help of God,
  We shall be saved — or else indeed we are lost.

PRIEST: Let us rise, children. It was for this we came,   150
    And now the king has promised it.
    Phoibos° has sent us an oracle; may he descend
    Himself to save us and drive out the plague.

(*Exeunt° Oedipus and Kreon into the palace by the central door. The Priest and the Suppliants disperse right and left. After a short pause the Chorus enters the orchestra.*)

PARODOS°   *Strophe° 1*

CHORUS: What is God singing in his profound
    Delphi of gold and shadow?
    What oracle for Thebes, the Sunwhipped city?
    Fear unjoints me, the roots of my heart tremble.
    Now I remember, O Healer, your power, and wonder: 5
    Will you send doom like a sudden cloud, or weave it
    Like nightfall of the past?
    Speak to me, tell me, O
    Child of golden Hope, immortal Voice.

Antistrophe° 1

Let me pray to Athene, the immortal daughter of Zeus,   10
And to Artemis° her sister
Who keeps her famous throne in the market ring,
And to Apollo, archer from distant heaven—
O gods, descend! Like three streams leap against
The fires of our grief, the fires of darkness;   15
Be swift to bring us rest!
As in the old time from the brilliant house
Of air you stepped to save us, come again!

Strophe 2

Now our afflictions have no end,
Now all our stricken host lies down   20

152. Phoibos: Apollo.   **[S.D.]** *Exeunt:* Latin for "they go out."   **Parodos:** The song chanted by the Chorus on their entry.   **Strophe:** Song sung by the Chorus as they danced from stage right to stage left.   **Antistrophe:** Song sung by the Chorus as they danced from stage left back to stage right.   **11. Artemis:** Daughter of Zeus, twin sister of Apollo, goddess of the hunt and female chastity.

And no man fights off death with his mind;
The noble plowland bears no grain,
And groaning mothers can not bear—
See, how our lives like birds take wing,
Like sparks that fly when a fire soars,   25
To the shore of the god of evening.

Antistrophe 2

The plague burns on, it is pitiless,
Though pallid children laden with death
Lie unwept in the stony ways,
And old gray women by every path   30
Flock to the strand about the altars
There to strike their breasts and cry
Worship of Phoibos in wailing prayers:
Be kind, God's golden child!

Strophe 3

There are no swords in this attack by fire,   35
No shields, but we are ringed with cries.
Send the besieger plunging from our homes
Into the vast sea-room of the Atlantic
Or into the waves that foam eastward of Thrace—
For the day ravages what the night spares—   40
Destroy our enemy, lord of the thunder!
Let him be riven by lightning from heaven!

Antistrophe 3

Phoibos Apollo, stretch the sun's bowstring,
That golden cord, until it sing for us,
Flashing arrows in heaven!
                              Artemis, Huntress,   45
Race with flaring lights upon our mountains!
O scarlet god,° O golden-banded brow,
O Theban Bacchos in a storm of Maenads,°

(*Enter Oedipus, center.*)

---

47. scarlet god: Bacchus, god of wine (also called Dionysus).   **48. Maenads:**
Bacchus's female devotees.

Whirl upon Death, that all the Undying hate!
Come with blinding torches, come in joy!   50

SCENE 1

OEDIPUS: Is this your prayer? It may be answered. Come,
Listen to me, act as the crisis demands,
And you shall have relief from all these evils.

Until now I was a stranger to this tale,
As I had been a stranger to the crime.   5
Could I track down the murderer without a clue?
But now, friends,
As one who became a citizen after the murder,
I make this proclamation to all Thebans:
If any man knows by whose hand Laios, son of Labdakos,   10
Met his death, I direct that man to tell me everything,
No matter what he fears for having so long withheld it.
Let it stand as promised that no further trouble
Will come to him, but he may leave the land in safety.
Moreover: If anyone knows the murderer to be foreign,   15
Let him not keep silent: he shall have his reward from me.
However, if he does conceal it; if any man
Fearing for his friend or for himself disobeys this edict,
Hear what I propose to do:

I solemnly forbid the people of this country,   20
Where power and throne are mine, ever to receive that man
Or speak to him, no matter who he is, or let him
Join in sacrifice, lustration, or in prayer.
I decree that he be driven from every house,
Being, as he is, corruption itself to us: the Delphic   25
Voice of Apollo has pronounced this revelation.
Thus I associate myself with the oracle
And take the side of the murdered king.

As for the criminal, I pray to God—
Whether it be a lurking thief, or one of a number—   30
I pray that that man's life be consumed in evil and wretchedness.
And as for me, this curse applies no less
If it should turn out that the culprit is my guest here,

Sharing my hearth.
                    You have heard the penalty.
I lay it on you now to attend to this   35
For my sake, for Apollo's, for the sick
Sterile city that heaven has abandoned.
Suppose the oracle had given you no command:
Should this defilement go uncleansed for ever?
You should have found the murderer: your king,   40
A noble king, had been destroyed!
                              Now I,
Having the power that he held before me,
Having his bed, begetting children there
Upon his wife, as he would have, had he lived—
Their son would have been my children's brother,   45
If Laios had had luck in fatherhood!
(And now his bad fortune has struck him down)—
I say I take the son's part, just as though
I were his son, to press the fight for him
And see it won! I'll find the hand that brought   50
Death to Labdakos' and Polydoros' child,
Heir of Kadmos' and Agenor's line.°
And as for those who fail me,
May the gods deny them the fruit of the earth,
Fruit of the womb, and may they rot utterly!   55
Let them be wretched as we are wretched, and worse!

For you, for loyal Thebans, and for all
Who find my actions right, I pray the favor
Of justice, and of all the immortal gods.
CHORAGOS:° Since I am under oath, my lord, I swear   60
I did not do the murder, I can not name
The murderer. Phoibos ordained the search;
Why did he not say who the culprit was?
OEDIPUS: An honest question. But no man in the world
Can make the gods do more than the gods will.   65
CHORAGOS: There is an alternative, I think—
OEDIPUS: Tell me.
Any or all, you must not fail to tell me.
CHORAGOS: A lord clairvoyant to the lord Apollo,

51–52. Labdakos, Polydoros, Kadmos, and Agenor: Father, grandfather, great-grandfather, and great-great-grandfather of Laios.   **60. Choragos:** Chorus leader.

As we all know, is the skilled Teiresias.
One might learn much about this from him, Oedipus.   70
OEDIPUS: I am not wasting time:
    Kreon spoke of this, and I have sent for him—
    Twice, in fact; it is strange that he is not here.
CHORAGOS: The other matter—that old report—seems useless.
OEDIPUS: What was that? I am interested in all reports.   75
CHORAGOS: The king was said to have been killed by highwaymen.
OEDIPUS: I know. But we have no witnesses to that.
CHORAGOS: If the killer can feel a particle of dread,
    Your curse will bring him out of hiding!
OEDIPUS: No.
    The man who dared that act will fear no curse.   80

(*Enter the blind seer Teiresias, led by a Page.*)

CHORAGOS: But there is one man who may detect the criminal.
    This is Teiresias, this is the holy prophet
    In whom, alone of all men, truth was born.
OEDIPUS: Teiresias: seer: student of mysteries,
    Of all that's taught and all that no man tells,   85
    Secrets of Heaven and secrets of the earth:
    Blind though you are, you know the city lies
    Sick with plague; and from this plague, my lord,
    We find that you alone can guard or save us.

    Possibly you did not hear the messengers?   90
    Apollo, when we sent to him,
    Sent us back word that this great pestilence
    Would lift, but only if we established clearly
    The identity of those who murdered Laios.
    They must be killed or exiled.
                                    Can you use   95
    Birdflight° or any art of divination
    To purify yourself, and Thebes, and me
    From this contagion? We are in your hands.
    There is no fairer duty
    Than that of helping others in distress.   100
TEIRESIAS: How dreadful knowledge of the truth can be
    When there's no help in truth! I knew this well,
    But did not act on it; else I should not have come.

96. **Birdflight:** Prophets believed they could predict the future based on the flight
of birds.

OEDIPUS: What is troubling you? Why are your eyes so cold?

TEIRESIAS: Let me go home. Bear your own fate, and I'll   105
   Bear mine. It is better so: trust what I say.

OEDIPUS: What you say is ungracious and unhelpful
   To your native country. Do not refuse to speak.

TEIRESIAS: When it comes to speech, your own is neither temperate
   Nor opportune. I wish to be more prudent.   110

OEDIPUS: In God's name, we all beg you—

TEIRESIAS: You are all ignorant.
   No; I will never tell you what I know.
   Now it is my misery; then, it would be yours.

OEDIPUS: What! You do know something, and will not tell us?
   You would betray us all and wreck the State?   115

TEIRESIAS: I do not intend to torture myself, or you.
   Why persist in asking? You will not persuade me.

OEDIPUS: What a wicked old man you are! You'd try a stone's
   Patience! Out with it! Have you no feeling at all?

TEIRESIAS: You call me unfeeling. If you could only see   120
   The nature of your own feelings . . .

OEDIPUS: Why,
   Who would not feel as I do? Who could endure
   Your arrogance toward the city?

TEIRESIAS: What does it matter?
   Whether I speak or not, it is bound to come.

OEDIPUS: Then, if "it" is bound to come, you are bound to tell me.   125

TEIRESIAS: No, I will not go on. Rage as you please.

OEDIPUS: Rage? Why not!
                 And I'll tell you what I think:
   You planned it, you had it done, you all but
   Killed him with your own hands: if you had eyes,
   I'd say the crime was yours, and yours alone.   130

TEIRESIAS: So? I charge you, then,
   Abide by the proclamation you have made:
   From this day forth
   Never speak again to these men or to me;
   You yourself are the pollution of this country.   135

OEDIPUS: You dare say that! Can you possibly think you have
   Some way of going free, after such insolence?

TEIRESIAS: I have gone free. It is the truth sustains me.

OEDIPUS: Who taught you shamelessness? It was not your craft.

TEIRESIAS: You did. You made me speak. I did not want to.   140

OEDIPUS: Speak what? Let me hear it again more clearly.

TEIRESIAS: Was it not clear before? Are you tempting me?

OEDIPUS: I did not understand it. Say it again.
TEIRESIAS: I say that you are the murderer whom you seek.
OEDIPUS: Now twice you have spat out infamy. You'll pay for it! 145
TEIRESIAS: Would you care for more? Do you wish to be really angry?
OEDIPUS: Say what you will. Whatever you say is worthless.
TEIRESIAS: I say you live in hideous shame with those
 Most dear to you. You can not see the evil.
OEDIPUS: Can you go on babbling like this for ever? 150
TEIRESIAS: I can, if there is power in truth.
OEDIPUS: There is:
 But not for you, not for you,
 You sightless, witless, senseless, mad old man!
TEIRESIAS: You are the madman. There is no one here
 Who will not curse you soon, as you curse me. 155
OEDIPUS: You child of total night! I would not touch you;
 Neither would any man who sees the sun.
TEIRESIAS: True: it is not from you my fate will come.
 That lies within Apollo's competence,
 As it is his concern.
OEDIPUS: Tell me, who made 160
 These fine discoveries? Kreon? or someone else?
TEIRESIAS: Kreon is no threat. You weave your own doom.
OEDIPUS: Wealth, power, craft of statemanship!
 Kingly position, everywhere admired!
 What savage envy is stored up against these, 165
 If Kreon, whom I trusted, Kreon my friend,
 For this great office which the city once
 Put in my hands unsought—if for this power
 Kreon desires in secret to destroy me!

 He has bought this decrepit fortune-teller, this 170
 Collector of dirty pennies, this prophet fraud—
 Why, he is no more clairvoyant than I am!
             Tell us:
 Has your mystic mummery ever approached the truth?
 When that hellcat the Sphinx was performing here,
 What help were you to these people? 175
 Her magic was not for the first man who came along:
 It demanded a real exorcist. Your birds—
 What good were they? or the gods, for the matter of that?
 But I came by,
 Oedipus, the simple man, who knows nothing— 180
 I thought it out for myself, no birds helped me!
 And this is the man you think you can destroy,

That you may be close to Kreon when he's king!
Well, you and your friend Kreon, it seems to me,
Will suffer most. If you were not an old man,   185
You would have paid already for your plot.
CHORAGOS: We can not see that his words or yours
    Have been spoken except in anger, Oedipus,
    And of anger we have no need. How to accomplish
    The god's will best: that is what most concerns us.   190
TEIRESIAS: You are a king. But where argument's concerned
    I am your man, as much a king as you.
    I am not your servant, but Apollo's.
    I have no need of Kreon or Kreon's name.

    Listen to me. You mock my blindness, do you?   195
    But I say that you, with both your eyes, are blind:
    You can not see the wretchedness of your life,
    Nor in whose house you live, no, nor with whom.
    Who are your father and mother? Can you tell me?
    You do not even know the blind wrongs   200
    That you have done them, on earth and in the world below.
    But the double lash of your parents' curse will whip you
    Out of this land some day, with only night
    Upon your precious eyes.
    Your cries then—where will they not be heard?   205
    What fastness of Kithairon° will not echo them?
    And that bridal-descant of yours—you'll know it then,
    The song they sang when you came here to Thebes
    And found your misguided berthing.
    All this, and more, that you can not guess at now,   210
    Will bring you to yourself among your children.

    Be angry, then. Curse Kreon. Curse my words.
    I tell you, no man that walks upon the earth
    Shall be rooted out more horribly than you.
OEDIPUS: Am I to bear this from him?—Damnation   215
    Take you! Out of this place! Out of my sight!
TEIRESIAS: I would not have come at all if you had not asked me.
OEDIPUS: Could I have told that you'd talk nonsense, that
    You'd come here to make a fool of yourself, and of me?
TEIRESIAS: A fool? Your parents thought me sane enough.   220

---

206. **Kithairon:** The mountain near Thebes where Oedipus was abandoned as an
infant.

OEDIPUS: My parents again!—Wait: who were my parents?
TEIRESIAS: This day will give you a father, and break your heart.
OEDIPUS: Your infantile riddles! Your damned abracadabra!
TEIRESIAS: You were a great man once at solving riddles.
OEDIPUS: Mock me with that if you like; you will find it true.   225
TEIRESIAS: It was true enough. It brought about your ruin.
OEDIPUS: But if it saved this town?
TEIRESIAS (*to the Page*):   Boy, give me your hand.
OEDIPUS: Yes, boy; lead him away.
                                   —While you are here
   We can do nothing. Go; leave us in peace.
TEIRESIAS: I will go when I have said what I have to say.   230
   How can you hurt me? And I tell you again:
   The man you have been looking for all this time,
   The damned man, the murderer of Laios,
   That man is in Thebes. To your mind he is foreign-born,
   But it will soon be shown that he is a Theban,   235
   A revelation that will fail to please.
                                   A blind man,
   Who has his eyes now; a penniless man, who is rich now;
   And he will go tapping the strange earth with his staff.
   To the children with whom he lives now he will be
   Brother and father—the very same; to her   240
   Who bore him, son and husband—the very same
   Who came to his father's bed, wet with his father's blood.
   Enough. Go think that over.
   If later you find error in what I have said,
   You may say that I have no skill in prophecy.   245

         (*Exit Teiresias, led by his Page. Oedipus goes into the palace.*)

ODE° 1   *Strophe 1*

CHORUS: The Delphic stone of prophecies
         Remembers ancient regicide
         And a still bloody hand.
         That killer's hour of flight has come.
         He must be stronger than riderless   5
         Coursers of untiring wind,
         For the son of Zeus° armed with his father's thunder

Ode: Song sung by the Chorus.   **7. son of Zeus:** Apollo.

Leaps in lightning after him;
And the Furies° hold his track, the sad Furies.

Antistrophe 1

Holy Parnassos'° peak of snow   10
Flashes and blinds that secret man,
That all shall hunt him down:
Though he may roam the forest shade
Like a bull gone wild from pasture
To rage through glooms of stone.   15
Doom comes down on him; flight will not avail him;
For the world's heart calls him desolate,
And the immortal voices follow, for ever follow.

Strophe 2

But now a wilder thing is heard
From the old man skilled at hearing Fate in the wing-beat of a bird.   20
Bewildered as a blown bird, my soul hovers and can not find
Foothold in this debate, or any reason or rest of mind.
But no man ever brought—none can bring
Proof of strife between Thebes' royal house,
Labdakos' line,° and the son of Polybos;°   25
And never until now has any man brought word
Of Laios' dark death staining Oedipus the King.

Antistrophe 2

Divine Zeus and Apollo hold
Perfect intelligence alone of all tales ever told;
And well though this diviner works, he works in his own night;   30
No man can judge that rough unknown or trust in second sight,
For wisdom changes hands among the wise.
Shall I believe my great lord criminal
At a raging word that a blind old man let fall?
I saw him, when the carrion woman° faced him of old,   35
Prove his heroic mind. These evil words are lies.

9. **Furies:** Powerful avenging divinities.   10. **Parnassos:** Mountain sacred to
Apollo.   25. **Labdakos' line:** Laios's family.   **Polybos:** King of Corinth who
adopted Oedipus.   35. **woman:** The Sphinx.

SCENE 2

KREON: Men of Thebes:
 I am told that heavy accusations
 Have been brought against me by King Oedipus.

 I am not the kind of man to bear this tamely.

 If in these present difficulties   5
 He holds me accountable for any harm to him
 Through anything I have said or done—why, then,
 I do not value life in this dishonor.
 It is not as though this rumor touched upon
 Some private indiscretion. The matter is grave.   10
 The fact is that I am being called disloyal
 To the State, to my fellow citizens, to my friends.
CHORAGOS: He may have spoken in anger, not from his mind.
KREON: But did you not hear him say I was the one
 Who seduced the old prophet into lying?   15
CHORAGOS: The thing was said; I do not know how seriously.
KREON: But you were watching him! Were his eyes steady?
 Did he look like a man in his right mind?
CHORAGOS: I do not know.
 I can not judge the behavior of great men.
 But here is the king himself.

(*Enter Oedipus.*)

OEDIPUS: So you dared come back.   20
 Why? How brazen of you to come to my house,
 You murderer!
              Do you think I do not know
 That you plotted to kill me, plotted to steal my throne?
 Tell me, in God's name: am I coward, a fool,
 That you should dream you could accomplish this?   25
 A fool who could not see your slippery game?
 A coward, not to fight back when I saw it?
 You are the fool, Kreon, are you not? hoping
 Without support or friends to get a throne?
 Thrones may be won or bought: you could do neither.   30
KREON: Now listen to me. You have talked; let me talk, too.
 You can not judge unless you know the facts.
OEDIPUS: You speak well: there is one fact; but I find it hard
 To learn from the deadliest enemy I have.

KREON: That above all I must dispute with you.   35
OEDIPUS: That above all I will not hear you deny.
KREON: If you think there is anything good in being stubborn
    Against all reason, then I say you are wrong.
OEDIPUS: If you think a man can sin against his own kind
    And not be punished for it, I say you are mad.   40
KREON: I agree. But tell me: what have I done to you?
OEDIPUS: You advised me to send for that wizard, did you not?
KREON: I did. I should do it again.
OEDIPUS: Very well. Now tell me:
    How long has it been since Laios—
KREON: What of Laios?
OEDIPUS: Since he vanished in that onset by the road?   45
KREON: It was long ago, a long time.
OEDIPUS: And this prophet,
    Was he practicing here then?
KREON: He was; and with honor, as now.
OEDIPUS: Did he speak of me at that time?
KREON: He never did,
    At least, not when I was present.
OEDIPUS: But . . . the enquiry?
    I suppose you held one?
KREON: We did, but we learned nothing.   50
OEDIPUS: Why did the prophet not speak against me then?
KREON: I do not know; and I am the kind of man
    Who holds his tongue when he has no facts to go on.
OEDIPUS: There's one fact that you know, and you could tell it.
KREON: What fact is that? If I know it, you shall have it.   55
OEDIPUS: If he were not involved with you, he could not say
    That it was I who murdered Laios.
KREON: If he says that, you are the one that knows it!—
    But now it is my turn to question you.
OEDIPUS: Put your questions. I am no murderer.   60
KREON: First, then: You married my sister?
OEDIPUS: I married your sister.
KREON: And you rule the kingdom equally with her?
OEDIPUS: Everything that she wants she has from me.
KREON: And I am the third, equal to both of you?
OEDIPUS: That is why I call you a bad friend.   65
KREON: No. Reason it out, as I have done.
    Think of this first: would any sane man prefer
    Power, with all a king's anxieties,
    To that same power and the grace of sleep?

Certainly not I.   70
I have never longed for the king's power—only his rights.
Would any wise man differ from me in this?
As matters stand, I have my way in everything
With your consent, and no responsibilities.
If I were king, I should be a slave to policy.   75
How could I desire a scepter more
Than what is now mine—untroubled influence?
No, I have not gone mad; I need no honors,
Except those with the perquisites I have now.
I am welcome everywhere; every man salutes me,   80
And those who want your favor seek my ear,
Since I know how to manage what they ask.
Should I exchange this ease for that anxiety?
Besides, no sober mind is treasonable.
I hate anarchy   85
And never would deal with any man who likes it.
Test what I have said. Go to the priestess
At Delphi, ask if I quoted her correctly.
And as for this other thing: if I am found
Guilty of treason with Teiresias,   90
Then sentence me to death. You have my word
It is a sentence I should cast my vote for—
But not without evidence!
                            You do wrong
When you take good men for bad, bad men for good.
A true friend thrown aside—why, life itself   95
Is not more precious!
                          In time you will know this well:
For time, and time alone, will show the just man,
Though scoundrels are discovered in a day.
CHORAGOS: This is well said, and a prudent man would ponder it.
    Judgments too quickly formed are dangerous.   100
OEDIPUS: But is he not quick in his duplicity?
    And shall I not be quick to parry him?
    Would you have me stand still, hold my peace, and let
    This man win everything, through my inaction?
KREON: And you want—what is it, then? To banish me?   105
OEDIPUS: No, not exile. It is your death I want,
    So that all the world may see what treason means.
KREON: You will persist, then? You will not believe me?
OEDIPUS: How can I believe you?
KREON: Then you are a fool.

OEDIPUS: To save myself?
KREON: In justice, think of me.   110
OEDIPUS: You are evil incarnate.
KREON: But suppose that you are wrong?
OEDIPUS: Still I must rule.
KREON: But not if you rule badly.
OEDIPUS: O city, city!
KREON: It is my city, too!
CHORAGOS: Now, my lords, be still. I see the queen,
   Iokaste, coming from her palace chambers;   115
   And it is time she came, for the sake of you both.
   This dreadful quarrel can be resolved through her.

(*Enter Iokaste.*)

IOKASTE: Poor foolish men, what wicked din is this?
   With Thebes sick to death, is it not shameful
   That you should take some private quarrel up?   120
   (*To Oedipus.*) Come into the house.
                              —And you, Kreon, go now:
   Let us have no more of this tumult over nothing.
KREON: Nothing? No, sister: what your husband plans for me
   Is one of two great evils: exile or death.
OEDIPUS: He is right.
                          Why, woman I have caught him squarely   125
   Plotting against my life.
KREON: No! Let me die
   Accurst if ever I have wished you harm!
IOKASTE: Ah, believe it, Oedipus!
   In the name of the gods, respect this oath of his
   For my sake, for the sake of these people here!   130

Strophe 1

CHORAGOS: Open your mind to her, my lord. Be ruled by her, I beg you!
OEDIPUS: What would you have me do?
CHORAGOS: Respect Kreon's word. He has never spoken like a fool,
   And now he has sworn an oath.
OEDIPUS: You know what you ask?
CHORAGOS: I do.
OEDIPUS: Speak on, then.
CHORAGOS: A friend so sworn should not be baited so,   135
   In blind malice, and without final proof.

OEDIPUS: You are aware, I hope, that what you say
  Means death for me, or exile at the least.

Strophe 2

CHORAGOS: No, I swear by Helios, first in heaven!
    May I die friendless and accurst,   140
  The worst of deaths, if ever I meant that!
  It is the withering fields
    That hurt my sick heart:
  Must we bear all these ills,
  And now your bad blood as well?   145
OEDIPUS: Then let him go. And let me die, if I must,
  Or be driven by him in shame from the land of Thebes.
  It is your unhappiness, and not his talk,
  That touches me.
              As for him—
  Wherever he goes, hatred will follow him.   150
KREON: Ugly in yielding, as you were ugly in rage!
  Natures like yours chiefly torment themselves.
OEDIPUS: Can you not go? Can you not leave me?
KREON: I can.
  You do not know me; but the city knows me,
  And in its eyes I am just, if not in yours.   (*Exit Kreon.*)   155

Antistrophe 1

CHORAGOS: Lady Iokaste, did you not ask the King to go to his
  chambers?
IOKASTE: First tell me what has happened.
CHORAGOS: There was suspicion without evidence; yet it rankled
  As even false charges will.
IOKASTE: On both sides?
CHORAGOS: On both.
IOKASTE: But what was said?   160
CHORAGOS: Oh let it rest, let it be done with!
  Have we not suffered enough?
OEDIPUS: You see to what your decency has brought you:
  You have made difficulties where my heart saw none.

Antistrophe 2

CHORAGOS: Oedipus, it is not once only I have told you—   165
      You must know I should count myself unwise
      To the point of madness, should I now forsake you—
            You, under whose hand,
                In the storm of another time,
                  Our dear land sailed out free.   170
                But now stand fast at the helm!
IOKASTE: In God's name, Oedipus, inform your wife as well:
      Why are you so set in this hard anger?
OEDIPUS: I will tell you, for none of these men deserves
      My confidence as you do. It is Kreon's work,   175
      His treachery, his plotting against me.
IOKASTE: Go on, if you can make this clear to me.
OEDIPUS: He charges me with the murder of Laios.
IOKASTE: Has he some knowledge? Or does he speak from
      hearsay?
OEDIPUS: He would not commit himself to such a charge,   180
      But he has brought in that damnable soothsayer
      To tell his story.
IOKASTE: Set your mind at rest.
      If it is a question of soothsayers, I tell you
      That you will find no man whose craft gives knowledge
      Of the unknowable.
                      Here is my proof: 185
      An oracle was reported to Laios once
      (I will not say from Phoibos himself, but from
      His appointed ministers, at any rate)
      That his doom would be death at the hands of his own son—
      His son, born of his flesh and of mine!   190

      Now, you remember the story: Laios was killed
      By marauding strangers where three highways meet;
      But his child had not been three days in this world
      Before the king had pierced the baby's ankles
      And left him to die on a lonely mountainside.   195

      Thus, Apollo never caused that child
      To kill his father, and it was not Laios' fate
      To die at the hands of his son, as he had feared.
      This is what prophets and prophecies are worth!

Have no dread of them.
                        It is God himself   200
Who can show us what he wills, in his own way.

OEDIPUS: How strange a shadowy memory crossed my mind,
Just now while you were speaking; it chilled my heart.

IOKASTE: What do you mean? What memory do you speak of?

OEDIPUS: If I understand you, Laios was killed   205
At a place where three roads meet.

IOKASTE: So it was said;
We have no later story.

OEDIPUS: Where did it happen?

IOKASTE: Phokis, it is called: at a place where the Theban Way
Divides into the roads toward Delphi and Daulia.

OEDIPUS: When?

IOKASTE: We had the news not long before you came   210
And proved the right to your succession here.

OEDIPUS: Ah, what net has God been weaving for me?

IOKASTE: Oedipus! Why does this trouble you?

OEDIPUS: Do not ask me yet.
First, tell me how Laios looked, and tell me
How old he was.

IOKASTE: He was tall, his hair just touched   215
With white; his form was not unlike your own.

OEDIPUS: I think that I myself may be accurst
By my own ignorant edict.

IOKASTE: You speak strangely.
It makes me tremble to look at you, my king.

OEDIPUS: I am not sure that the blind man can not see.   220
But I should know better if you were to tell me—

IOKASTE: Anything—though I dread to hear you ask it.

OEDIPUS: Was the king lightly escorted, or did he ride
With a large company, as a ruler should?

IOKASTE: There were five men with him in all: one was a herald; 225
And a single chariot, which he was driving.

OEDIPUS: Alas, that makes it plain enough!
                                    But who—
Who told you how it happened?

IOKASTE: A household servant,
The only one to escape.

OEDIPUS: And is he still
A servant of ours?

IOKASTE: No; for when he came back at last   230

And found you enthroned in the place of the dead king,
He came to me, touched my hand with his, and begged
That I would send him away to the frontier district
Where only the shepherds go —
As far away from the city as I could send him.   235
I granted his prayer; for although the man was a slave,
He had earned more than this favor at my hands.
OEDIPUS: Can he be called back quickly?
IOKASTE: Easily.
But why?
OEDIPUS: I have taken too much upon myself   240
Without enquiry; therefore I wish to consult him.
IOKASTE: Then he shall come.
                              But am I not one also
To whom you might confide these fears of yours?
OEDIPUS: That is your right; it will not be denied you,
Now least of all; for I have reached a pitch   245
Of wild foreboding. Is there anyone
To whom I should sooner speak?

Polybos of Corinth is my father.
My mother is a Dorian: Merope.
I grew up chief among the men of Corinth   250
Until a strange thing happened —
Not worth my passion, it may be, but strange.
At a feast, a drunken man maundering in his cups
Cries out that I am not my father's son!
I contained myself that night, though I felt anger   255
And a sinking heart. The next day I visited
My father and mother, and questioned them. They stormed,
Calling it all the slanderous rant of a fool;
And this relieved me. Yet the suspicion
Remained always aching in my mind;   260
I knew there was talk; I could not rest;
And finally, saying nothing to my parents,
I went to the shrine at Delphi.

The god dismissed my question without reply;
He spoke of other things.
                          Some were clear,   265
Full of wretchedness, dreadful, unbearable:
As, that I should lie with my own mother, breed

Children from whom all men would turn their eyes;
And that I should be my father's murderer.

I heard all this, and fled. And from that day   270
Corinth to me was only in the stars
Descending in that quarter of the sky,
As I wandered farther and farther on my way
To a land where I should never see the evil
Sung by the oracle. And I came to this country   275
Where, so you say, King Laios was killed.

I will tell you all that happened there, my lady.
There were three highways
Coming together at a place I passed;
And there a herald came towards me, and a chariot   280
Drawn by horses, with a man such as you describe
Seated in it. The groom leading the horses
Forced me off the road at his lord's command;
But as this charioteer lurched over towards me
I struck him in my rage. The old man saw me   285
And brought his double goad down upon my head
As I came abreast.
                            He was paid back, and more!
Swinging my club in this right hand I knocked him
Out of his car, and he rolled on the ground.
                                          I killed him.

I killed them all.   290
Now if that stranger and Laios were — kin,
Where is a man more miserable than I?
More hated by the gods? Citizen and alien alike
Must never shelter me or speak to me —
I must be shunned by all.
                            And I myself   295
Pronounced this malediction upon myself!

Think of it: I have touched you with these hands,
These hands that killed your husband. What defilement!

Am I all evil, then? It must be so,
Since I must flee from Thebes, yet never again   300
See my own countrymen, my own country,
For fear of joining my mother in marriage

And killing Polybos, my father.
                              Ah,
If I was created so, born to this fate,
Who could deny the savagery of God?   305

O holy majesty of heavenly powers!
May I never see that day! Never!
Rather let me vanish from the race of men
Than know the abomination destined me!
CHORAGOS: We too, my lord, have felt dismay at this.   310
   But there is hope: you have yet to hear the shepherd.
OEDIPUS: Indeed, I fear no other hope is left me.
IOKASTE: What do you hope from him when he comes?
OEDIPUS: This much:
   If his account of the murder tallies with yours,
   Then I am cleared.
IOKASTE: What was it that I said   315
   Of such importance?
OEDIPUS: Why, "marauders," you said,
   Killed the king, according to this man's story.
   If he maintains that still, if there were several,
   Clearly the guilt is not mine: I was alone.
   But if he says one man, singlehanded, did it,   320
   Then the evidence all points to me.
IOKASTE: You may be sure that he said there were several;
   And can he call back that story now? He can not.
   The whole city heard it as plainly as I.
   But suppose he alters some detail of it: 325
   He can not ever show that Laios' death
   Fulfilled the oracle: for Apollo said
   My child was doomed to kill him; and my child —
   Poor baby! — it was my child that died first.

   No. From now on, where oracles are concerned,   330
   I would not waste a second thought on any.
OEDIPUS: You may be right.
                         But come: let someone go
   For the shepherd at once. This matter must be settled.
IOKASTE: I will send for him.
   I would not wish to cross you in anything,   335
   And surely not in this. — Let us go in.

                                 (*Exeunt into the palace.*)

ODE 2   *Strophe 1*

CHORUS: Let me be reverent in the ways of right,
    Lowly the paths I journey on;
    Let all my words and actions keep
    The laws of the pure universe
    From highest Heaven handed down.   5
    For Heaven is their bright nurse,
    Those generations of the realms of light;
    Ah, never of mortal kind were they begot,
    Nor are they slaves of memory, lost in sleep:
    Their Father is greater than Time, and ages not.   10

Antistrophe 1

The tyrant is a child of Pride
Who drinks from his great sickening cup
Recklessness and vanity,
Until from his high crest headlong
He plummets to the dust of hope.   15
That strong man is not strong.
But let no fair ambition be denied;
May God protect the wrestler for the State
In government, in comely policy,
Who will fear God, and on his ordinance wait.   20

Strophe 2

Haughtiness and the high hand of disdain
Tempt and outrage God's holy law;
And any mortal who dares hold
No immortal Power in awe
Will be caught up in a net of pain: 25
The price for which his levity is sold.
Let each man take due earnings, then,
And keep his hands from holy things,
And from blasphemy stand apart—
Else the crackling blast of heaven   30
Blows on his head, and on his desperate heart.
Though fools will honor impious men,
In their cities no tragic poet sings.

Antistrophe 2

Shall we lose faith in Delphi's obscurities,
We who have heard the world's core   35
Discredited, and the sacred wood
Of Zeus at Elis praised no more?
The deeds and the strange prophecies
Must make a pattern yet to be understood.
Zeus, if indeed you are lord of all,   40
Throned in light over night and day,
Mirror this in your endless mind:
Our masters call the oracle
Words on the wind, and the Delphic vision blind!
Their hearts no longer know Apollo,   45
And reverence for the gods has died away.

SCENE 3

(*Enter Iokaste.*)

IOKASTE: Princes of Thebes, it has occurred to me
    To visit the altars of the gods, bearing
    These branches as a suppliant, and this incense.
    Our king is not himself: his noble soul
    Is overwrought with fantasies of dread,   5
    Else he would consider
    The new prophecies in the light of the old.
    He will listen to any voice that speaks disaster,
    And my advice goes for nothing. (*She approaches the*
      altar, right.)
                To you, then, Apollo,
    Lycean lord, since you are nearest, I turn in prayer   10
    Receive these offerings, and grant us deliverance
    From defilement. Our hearts are heavy with fear
    When we see our leader distracted, as helpless sailors
    Are terrified by the confusion of their helmsman.

(*Enter Messenger.*)

MESSENGER: Friends, no doubt you can direct me: 15
    Where shall I find the house of Oedipus,
    Or, better still, where is the king himself?

CHORAGOS: It is this very place, stranger; he is inside.
This is his wife and mother of his children.
MESSENGER: I wish her happiness in a happy house,   20
Blest in all the fulfillment of her marriage.
IOKASTE: I wish as much for you: your courtesy
Deserves a like good fortune. But now, tell me:
Why have you come? What have you to say to us?
MESSENGER: Good news, my lady, for your house and your husband.   25
IOKASTE: What news? Who sent you here?
MESSENGER: I am from Corinth.
The news I bring ought to mean joy for you,
Though it may be you will find some grief in it.
IOKASTE: What is it? How can it touch us in both ways?
MESSENGER: The word is that the people of the Isthmus   30
Intend to call Oedipus to be their king.
IOKASTE: But old King Polybos—is he not reigning still?
MESSENGER: No. Death holds him in his sepulchre.
IOKASTE: What are you saying? Polybos is dead?
MESSENGER: If I am not telling the truth, may I die myself.   35
IOKASTE (*to a Maidservant*): Go in, go quickly; tell this to your master.
O riddlers of God's will, where are you now!
This was the man whom Oedipus, long ago,
Feared so, fled so, in dread of destroying him—
But it was another fate by which he died.   40

(*Enter Oedipus, center.*)

OEDIPUS: Dearest Iokaste, why have you sent for me?
IOKASTE: Listen to what this man says, and then tell me
What has become of the solemn prophecies.
OEDIPUS: Who is this man? What is his news for me?
IOKASTE: He has come from Corinth to announce your father's death!   45
OEDIPUS: Is it true, stranger? Tell me in your own words.
MESSENGER: I can not say it more clearly: the king is dead.
OEDIPUS: Was it by treason? Or by an attack of illness?
MESSENGER: A little thing brings old men to their rest.
OEDIPUS: It was sickness, then?
MESSENGER: Yes, and his many years.   50
OEDIPUS: Ah!
Why should a man respect the Pythian hearth,° or
Give heed to the birds that jangle above his head?
They prophesied that I should kill Polybos,

52. **Pythian hearth:** A site in Delphi where ritualistic offerings were made.

Kill my own father; but he is dead and buried,   55
And I am here—I never touched him, never,
Unless he died of grief for my departure,
And thus, in a sense, through me. No. Polybos
Has packed the oracles off with him underground.
They are empty words.
IOKASTE: Had I not told you so?   60
OEDIPUS: You had; it was my faint heart that betrayed me.
IOKASTE: From now on never think of those things again.
OEDIPUS: And yet—must I not fear my mother's bed?
IOKASTE: Why should anyone in this world be afraid
   Since Fate rules us and nothing can be foreseen?   65
   A man should live only for the present day.

   Have no more fear of sleeping with your mother:
   How many men, in dreams, have lain with their mothers!
   No reasonable man is troubled by such things.
OEDIPUS: That is true, only—   70
   If only my mother were not still alive!
   But she is alive. I can not help my dread.
IOKASTE: Yet this news of your father's death is wonderful.
OEDIPUS: Wonderful. But I fear the living woman.
MESSENGER: Tell me, who is this woman that you fear?   75
OEDIPUS: It is Merope, man; the wife of King Polybos.
MESSENGER: Merope? Why should you be afraid of her?
OEDIPUS: An oracle of the gods, a dreadful saying.
MESSENGER: Can you tell me about it or are you sworn to silence?
OEDIPUS: I can tell you, and I will.   80
   Apollo said through his prophet that I was the man
   Who should marry his own mother, shed his father's blood
   With his own hands. And so, for all these years
   I have kept clear of Corinth, and no harm has come—
   Though it would have been sweet to see my parents again.   85
MESSENGER: And is this the fear that drove you out of Corinth?
OEDIPUS: Would you have me kill my father?
MESSENGER: As for that
   You must be reassured by the news I gave you.
OEDIPUS: If you could reassure me, I would reward you.
MESSENGER: I had that in mind, I will confess: I thought   90
   I could count on you when you returned to Corinth.
OEDIPUS: No: I will never go near my parents again.
MESSENGER: Ah, son, you still do not know what you are doing—
OEDIPUS: What do you mean? In the name of God tell me!

MESSENGER: — If these are your reasons for not going home.   95
OEDIPUS: I tell you, I fear the oracle may come true.
MESSENGER: And guilt may come upon you through your parents?
OEDIPUS: That is the dread that is always in my heart.
MESSENGER: Can you not see that all your fears are groundless?
OEDIPUS: Groundless? Am I not my parents' son?   100
MESSENGER: Polybos was not your father.
OEDIPUS: Not my father?
MESSENGER: No more your father than the man speaking to you.
OEDIPUS: But you are nothing to me!
MESSENGER: Neither was he.
OEDIPUS: Then why did he call me son?
MESSENGER: I will tell you:
   Long ago he had you from my hands, as a gift.   105
OEDIPUS: Then how could he love me so, if I was not his?
MESSENGER: He had no children, and his heart turned to you.
OEDIPUS: What of you? Did you buy me? Did you find me by chance?
MESSENGER: I came upon you in the woody vales of Kithairon.
OEDIPUS: And what were you doing there?
MESSENGER: Tending my flocks.   110
OEDIPUS: A wandering shepherd?
MESSENGER: But your savior, son, that day.
OEDIPUS: From what did you save me?
MESSENGER: Your ankles should tell you that.
OEDIPUS: Ah, stranger, why do you speak of that childhood pain?
MESSENGER: I pulled the skewer that pinned your feet together.
OEDIPUS: I have had the mark as long as I can remember.   115
MESSENGER: That was why you were given the name you bear.°
OEDIPUS: God! Was it my father or my mother who did it?
   Tell me!
MESSENGER: I do not know. The man who gave you to me
   Can tell you better than I.
OEDIPUS: It was not you that found me, but another?   120
MESSENGER: It was another shepherd gave you to me.
OEDIPUS: Who was he? Can you tell me who he was?
MESSENGER: I think he was said to be one of Laios' people.
OEDIPUS: You mean the Laios who was king here years ago?
MESSENGER: Yes; King Laios; and the man was one of his herdsmen.   125
OEDIPUS: Is he still alive? Can I see him?
MESSENGER: These men here
   Know best about such things.

---

116. name you bear: "Oedipus" literally means swollen foot.

OEDIPUS: Does anyone here
  Know this shepherd that he is talking about?
  Have you seen him in the fields, or in the town?
  If you have, tell me. It is time things were made plain.   130
CHORAGOS: I think the man he means is that same shepherd
  You have already asked to see. Iokaste perhaps
  Could tell you something.
OEDIPUS: Do you know anything
  About him, Lady? Is he the man we have summoned?
  Is that the man this shepherd means?
IOKASTE: Why think of him?   135
  Forget this herdsman. Forget it all.
  This talk is a waste of time.
OEDIPUS: How can you say that,
  When the clues to my true birth are in my hands?
IOKASTE: For God's love, let us have no more questioning!
  Is your life nothing to you?   140
  My own is pain enough for me to bear.
OEDIPUS: You need not worry. Suppose my mother a slave,
  And born of slaves: no baseness can touch you.
IOKASTE: Listen to me, I beg you: do not do this thing!
OEDIPUS: I will not listen; the truth must be made known.   145
IOKASTE: Everything that I say is for your own good!
OEDIPUS: My own good
  Snaps my patience, then; I want none of it.
IOKASTE: You are fatally wrong! May you never learn who you are!
OEDIPUS: Go, one of you, and bring the shepherd here.
  Let us leave this woman to brag of her royal name.   150
IOKASTE: Ah, miserable!
  That is the only word I have for you now.
  That is the only word I can ever have.   (*Exit into the palace.*)
CHORAGOS: Why has she left us, Oedipus? Why has she gone
  In such a passion of sorrow? I fear this silence: 155
  Something dreadful may come of it.
OEDIPUS: Let it come!
  However base my birth, I must know about it.
  The Queen, like a woman, is perhaps ashamed
  To think of my low origin. But I
  Am a child of Luck, I can not be dishonored.   160
  Luck is my mother; the passing months, my brothers,
  Have seen me rich and poor.
              If this is so,
  How could I wish that I were someone else?
  How could I not be glad to know my birth?

ODE 3   *Strophe*

CHORUS: If ever the coming time were known
   To my heart's pondering,
   Kithairon, now by Heaven I see the torches
   At the festival of the next full moon
   And see the dance, and hear the choir sing   5
   A grace to your gentle shade:
   Mountain where Oedipus was found,
   O mountain guard of a noble race!
   May the god° who heals us lend his aid,
   And let that glory come to pass   10
   For our king's cradling-ground.

Antistrophe

Of the nymphs that flower beyond the years,
   Who bore you, royal child,
   To Pan° of the hills or the timberline Apollo,
   Cold in delight where the upland clears,   15
   Or Hermes° for whom Kyllene's° heights are piled?
   Or flushed as evening cloud,
   Great Dionysos, roamer of mountains,
   He—was it he who found you there,
   And caught you up in his own proud   20
   Arms from the sweet god-ravisher
   Who laughed by the Muses'° fountains?

SCENE 4

OEDIPUS: Sirs: though I do not know the man,
   I think I see him coming, this shepherd we want:
   He is old, like our friend here, and the men
   Bringing him seem to be servants of my house.
   But you can tell, if you have ever seen him.   5

(*Enter Shepherd escorted by Servants.*)

---

9. god: Apollo.   **14. Pan:** God of nature and fertility, depicted as an ugly man
with the horns and legs of a goat. Pan was considered playful and amorous.
16. Hermes: Son of Zeus, messenger of the gods.   **Kyllene:** Hermes' birthplace.
22. Muses: Nine sister goddesses of poetry, music, art, and sciences.

CHORAGOS: I know him, he was Laios' man. You can trust him.
OEDIPUS: Tell me first, you from Corinth: is this the shepherd
   We were discussing?
MESSENGER: This is the very man.
OEDIPUS (*to Shepherd*): Come here. No, look at me. You must answer
   Everything I ask. — You belonged to Laios?   10
SHEPHERD: Yes: born his slave, brought up in his house.
OEDIPUS: Tell me: what kind of work did you do for him?
SHEPHERD: I was a shepherd of his, most of my life.
OEDIPUS: Where mainly did you go for pasturage?
SHEPHERD: Sometimes Kithairon, sometimes the hills near-by.   15
OEDIPUS: Do you remember ever seeing this man out there?
SHEPHERD: What would he be doing there? This man?
OEDIPUS: This man standing here. Have you ever seen him before?
SHEPHERD: No. At least, not to my recollection.
MESSENGER: And that is not strange, my lord. But I'll refresh   20
   His memory: he must remember when we two
   Spent three whole seasons together, March to September,
   On Kithairon or thereabouts. He had two flocks;
   I had one. Each autumn I'd drive mine home
   And he would go back with his to Laios' sheepfold. —   25
   Is this not true, just as I have described it?
SHEPHERD: True, yes; but it was all so long ago.
MESSENGER: Well, then: do you remember, back in those days,
   That you gave me a baby boy to bring up as my own?
SHEPHERD: What if I did? What are you trying to say?   30
MESSENGER: King Oedipus was once that little child.
SHEPHERD: Damn you, hold your tongue!
OEDIPUS: No more of that!
   It is your tongue needs watching, not this man's.
SHEPHERD: My king, my master, what is it I have done wrong?
OEDIPUS: You have not answered his question about the boy.   35
SHEPHERD: He does not know . . . He is only making trouble . . .
OEDIPUS: Come, speak plainly, or it will go hard with you.
SHEPHERD: In God's name, do not torture an old man!
OEDIPUS: Come here, one of you; bind his arms behind him.
SHEPHERD: Unhappy king! What more do you wish to learn?   40
OEDIPUS: Did you give this man the child he speaks of?
SHEPHERD: I did.
   And I would to God I had died that very day.
OEDIPUS: You will die now unless you speak the truth.
SHEPHERD: Yet if I speak the truth, I am worse than dead.
OEDIPUS (*to Attendant*): He intends to draw it out, apparently —   45
SHEPHERD: No! I have told you already that I gave him the boy.

OEDIPUS: Where did you get him? From your house? From somewhere else?

SHEPHERD: Not from mine, no. A man gave him to me.

OEDIPUS: Is that man here? Whose house did he belong to?

SHEPHERD: For God's love, my king, do not ask me any more!   50

OEDIPUS: You are a dead man if I have to ask you again.

SHEPHERD: Then . . . Then the child was from the palace of Laios.

OEDIPUS: A slave child? or a child of his own line?

SHEPHERD: Ah, I am on the brink of dreadful speech!

OEDIPUS: And I of dreadful hearing. Yet I must hear.   55

SHEPHERD: If you must be told, then . . .

                                    They said it was Laios' child;

But it is your wife who can tell you about that.

OEDIPUS: My wife—Did she give it to you?

SHEPHERD: My lord, she did.

OEDIPUS: Do you know why?

SHEPHERD: I was told to get rid of it.

OEDIPUS: Oh heartless mother!

SHEPHERD: But in dread of prophecies . . .   60

OEDIPUS: Tell me.

SHEPHERD: It was said that the boy would kill his own father.

OEDIPUS: Then why did you give him over to this old man?

SHEPHERD: I pitied the baby, my king,

And I thought that this man would take him far away

To his own country.

                   He saved him—but for what a fate!   65

For if you are what this man says you are,

No man living is more wretched than Oedipus.

OEDIPUS: Ah God!

It was true!

              All the prophecies!

                     —Now,

O Light, may I look on you for the last time!   70

I, Oedipus,

Oedipus, damned in his birth, in his marriage damned,

Damned in the blood he shed with his own hand!

(*He rushes into the palace.*)

ODE 4   *Strophe 1*

CHORUS: Alas for the seed of men.

What measure shall I give these generations

That breathe on the void and are void

And exist and do not exist?
Who bears more weight of joy   5
Than mass of sunlight shifting in images,
Or who shall make his thought stay on
That down time drifts away?
Your splendor is all fallen.
O naked brow of wrath and tears,   10
O change of Oedipus!
I who saw your days call no man blest—
Your great days like ghosts gone.

Antistrophe 1

That mind was a strong bow.
Deep, how deep you drew it then, hard archer,   15
At a dim fearful range,
And brought dear glory down!
You overcame the stranger°—
The virgin with her hooking lion claws—
And though death sang, stood like a tower   20
To make pale Thebes take heart.
Fortress against our sorrow!
True king, giver of laws,
Majestic Oedipus!
No prince in Thebes had ever such renown,   25
No prince won such grace of power.

Strophe 2

And now of all men ever known
Most pitiful is this man's story:
His fortunes are most changed; his state
Fallen to a low slave's   30
Ground under bitter fate.
O Oedipus, most royal one!
The great door° that expelled you to the light
Gave at night—ah, gave night to your glory:
As to the father, to the fathering son.   35
All understood too late.
How could that queen whom Laios won,
The garden that he harrowed at his height,
Be silent when that act was done?

18. stranger: The Sphinx.   33. door: Iokaste's womb.

Antistrophe 2

But all eyes fail before time's eye,   40
All actions come to justice there.
Though never willed, though far down the deep past,
Your bed, your dread sirings,
Are brought to book at last.
Child by Laios doomed to die,   45
Then doomed to lose that fortunate little death,
Would God you never took breath in this air
That with my wailing lips I take to cry:
For I weep the world's outcast.
I was blind, and now I can tell why: 50
Asleep, for you had given ease of breath
To Thebes, while the false years went by.

EXODOS°

(Enter, from the palace, Second Messenger.)

SECOND MESSENGER: Elders of Thebes, most honored in this land,
    What horrors are yours to see and hear, what weight
    Of sorrow to be endured, if, true to your birth,
    You venerate the line of Labdakos!
    I think neither Istros nor Phasis, those great rivers,   5
    Could purify this place of all the evil
    It shelters now, or soon must bring to light—
    Evil not done unconsciously, but willed.

    The greatest griefs are those we cause ourselves.
CHORAGOS: Surely, friend, we have grief enough already;   20
    What new sorrow do you mean?
SECOND MESSENGER: The queen is dead.
CHORAGOS: O miserable queen! But at whose hand?
SECOND MESSENGER: Her own.
    The full horror of what happened you can not know,
    For you did not see it; but I, who did, will tell you
    As clearly as I can how she met her death.   15

    When she had left us,
    In passionate silence, passing through the court,

Exodos: Final scene.

She ran to her apartment in the house,
Her hair clutched by the fingers of both hands.
She closed the doors behind her; then, by that bed   20
Where long ago the fatal son was conceived—
That son who should bring about his father's death—
We heard her call upon Laios, dead so many years,
And heard her wail for the double fruit of her marriage,
A husband by her husband, children by her child.   25

Exactly how she died I do not know:
For Oedipus burst in moaning and would not let us
Keep vigil to the end: it was by him
As he stormed about the room that our eyes were caught.
From one to another of us he went, begging a sword,   30
Hunting the wife who was not his wife, the mother
Whose womb had carried his own children and himself.
I do not know: it was none of us aided him,
But surely one of the gods was in control!
For with a dreadful cry   35
He hurled his weight, as though wrenched out of himself,
At the twin doors: the bolts gave, and he rushed in.
And there we saw her hanging, her body swaying
From the cruel cord she had noosed about her neck.
A great sob broke from him, heartbreaking to hear,   40
As he loosed the rope and lowered her to the ground.

I would blot out from my mind what happened next!
For the king ripped from her gown the golden brooches
That were her ornament, and raised them, and plunged them down
Straight into his own eyeballs, crying, "No more,   45
No more shall you look on the misery about me,
The horrors of my own doing! Too long you have known
The faces of those whom I should never have seen,
Too long been blind to those for whom I was searching!
From this hour, go in darkness!" And as he spoke,   50
He struck at his eyes—not once, but many times;
And the blood spattered his beard,
Bursting from his ruined sockets like red hail.

So from the unhappiness of two this evil has sprung,
A curse on the man and woman alike. The old   55
Happiness of the house of Labdakos
Was happiness enough: where is it today?
It is all wailing and ruin, disgrace, death—all

The misery of mankind that has a name—
And it is wholly and for ever theirs.   60
CHORAGOS: Is he in agony still? Is there no rest for him?
SECOND MESSENGER: He is calling for someone to open the
    doors wide
So that all the children of Kadmos may look upon
His father's murderer, his mother's—no,
I can not say it!
                              And then he will leave Thebes,   65
Self-exiled, in order that the curse
Which he himself pronounced may depart from the house.
He is weak, and there is none to lead him,
So terrible is his suffering.
                              But you will see:
Look, the doors are opening; in a moment   70
You will see a thing that would crush a heart of stone.

(*The central door is opened; Oedipus, blinded, is led in.*)

CHORAGOS: Dreadful indeed for men to see.
    Never have my own eyes
    Looked on a sight so full of fear.

    Oedipus!   75
    What madness came upon you, what demon
    Leaped on your life with heavier
    Punishment than a mortal man can bear?
    No: I can not even
    Look at you, poor ruined one.   80
    And I would speak, question, ponder,
    If I were able. No.
    You make me shudder.
OEDIPUS: God. God.
    Is there a sorrow greater?   85
    Where shall I find harbor in this world?
    My voice is hurled far on a dark wind.
    What has God done to me?
CHORAGOS: Too terrible to think of, or to see.

Strophe 1

OEDIPUS: O cloud of night,   90
    Never to be turned away: night coming on,

I can not tell how: night like a shroud!
My fair winds brought me here.
                              O God. Again
The pain of the spikes where I had sight,
The flooding pain   95
Of memory, never to be gouged out.
CHORAGOS: This is not strange.
    You suffer it all twice over, remorse in pain,
    Pain in remorse.

Antistrophe 1

OEDIPUS: Ah dear friend   100
    Are you faithful even yet, you alone?
    Are you still standing near me, will you stay here,
    Patient, to care for the blind?
                              The blind man!
    Yet even blind I know who it is attends me,
    By the voice's tone—   105
    Though my new darkness hide the comforter.
CHORAGOS: Oh fearful act!
    What god was it drove you to rake black
    Night across your eyes?

Strophe 2

OEDIPUS: Apollo. Apollo. Dear   110
    Children, the god was Apollo.
    He brought my sick, sick fate upon me.
    But the blinding hand was my own!
    How could I bear to see
    When all my sight was horror everywhere?   115
CHORAGOS: Everywhere; that is true.
OEDIPUS: And now what is left?
    Images? Love? A greeting even,
    Sweet to the senses? Is there anything?
    Ah, no, friends: lead me away.   120
    Lead me away from Thebes.
                              Lead the great wreck
    And hell of Oedipus, whom the gods hate.
CHORAGOS: Your misery, you are not blind to that.
    Would God you had never found it out!

Antistrophe 2

OEDIPUS: Death take the man who unbound   125
　　My feet on that hillside
　　And delivered me from death to life! What life?
　　If only I had died,
　　This weight of monstrous doom
　　Could not have dragged me and my darlings down.   130
CHORAGOS: I would have wished the same.
OEDIPUS: Oh never to have come here
　　With my father's blood upon me! Never
　　To have been the man they call his mother's husband!
　　Oh accurst! Oh child of evil,   135
　　To have entered that wretched bed—
　　　　　　　　　　　　　　　　the selfsame one!
　　More primal than sin itself, this fell to me.
CHORAGOS: I do not know what words to offer you.
　　You were better dead than alive and blind.
OEDIPUS: Do not counsel me any more. This punishment   140
　　That I have laid upon myself is just.
　　If I had eyes,
　　I do not know how I could bear the sight
　　Of my father, when I came to the house of Death,
　　Or my mother: for I have sinned against them both   145
　　So vilely that I could not make my peace
　　By strangling my own life.
　　　　　　　　　　　Or do you think my children,
　　Born as they were born, would be sweet to my eyes?
　　Ah never, never! Nor this town with its high walls,
　　Nor the holy images of the gods.
　　　　　　　　　　　For I,   150
　　Thrice miserable!—Oedipus, noblest of all the line
　　Of Kadmos, have condemned myself to enjoy
　　These things no more, by my own malediction
　　Expelling that man whom the gods declared
　　To be a defilement in the house of Laios.   155
　　After exposing the rankness of my own guilt,
　　How could I look men frankly in the eyes?
　　No, I swear it,
　　If I could have stifled my hearing at its source,
　　I would have done it and made all this body   160
　　A tight cell of misery, blank to light and sound:
　　So I should have been safe in my dark mind
　　Beyond external evil.

Ah Kithairon!
Why did you shelter me? When I was cast upon you,
Why did I not die? Then I should never   165
Have shown the world my execrable birth.

Ah Polybos! Corinth, city that I believed
The ancient seat of my ancestors: how fair
I seemed, your child! And all the while this evil
Was cancerous within me!
                              For I am sick   170
In my own being, sick in my origin.
O three roads, dark ravine, woodland and way
Where three roads met; you, drinking my father's blood,
My own blood, spilled by my own hand: can you remember
The unspeakable things I did there, and the things   175
I went on from there to do?
                          O marriage, marriage!
The act that engendered me, and again the act
Performed by the son in the same bed—
                              Ah, the net
Of incest, mingling fathers, brothers, sons,
With brides, wives, mothers: the last evil   180
That can be known by men: no tongue can say
How evil!
          No. For the love of God, conceal me
Somewhere far from Thebes; or kill me; or hurl me
Into the sea, away from men's eyes for ever.

Come, lead me. You need not fear to touch me.   185
Of all men, I alone can bear this guilt.

(*Enter Kreon.*)

CHORAGOS: Kreon is here now. As to what you ask,
    He may decide the course to take. He only
    Is left to protect the city in your place.
OEDIPUS: Alas, how can I speak to him? What right have I   190
    To beg his courtesy whom I have deeply wronged?
KREON: I have not come to mock you, Oedipus,
    Or to reproach you, either.
    (*To Attendants.*)   —You, standing there:
    If you have lost all respect for man's dignity,
    At least respect the flame of Lord Helios:°   195
    Do not allow this pollution to show itself

195. Lord Helios: The sun god.

Openly here, an affront to the earth
And Heaven's rain and the light of day. No, take him
Into the house as quickly as you can.
For it is proper   200
That only the close kindred see his grief.
OEDIPUS: I pray you in God's name, since your courtesy
Ignores my dark expectation, visiting
With mercy this man of all men most execrable:
Give me what I ask—for your good, not for mine.   205
KREON: And what is it that you turn to me begging for?
OEDIPUS: Drive me out of this country as quickly as may be
To a place where no human voice can ever greet me.
KREON: I should have done that before now—only,
God's will had not been wholly revealed to me.   210
OEDIPUS: But his command is plain: the parricide
Must be destroyed. I am that evil man.
KREON: That is the sense of it, yes; but as things are,
We had best discover clearly what is to be done.
OEDIPUS: You would learn more about a man like me?   215
KREON: You are ready now to listen to the god.
OEDIPUS: I will listen. But it is to you
That I must turn for help. I beg you, hear me.

The woman is there—
Give her whatever funeral you think proper: 220
She is your sister.
                    —But let me go, Kreon!
Let me purge my father's Thebes of the pollution
Of my living here, and go out to the wild hills,
To Kithairon, that has won such fame with me,
The tomb my mother and father appointed for me,   225
And let me die there, as they willed I should.
And yet I know
Death will not ever come to me through sickness
Or in any natural way: I have been preserved
For some unthinkable fate. But let that be.   230

As for my sons, you need not care for them.
They are men, they will find some way to live.
But my poor daughters, who have shared my table,
Who never before have been parted from their father—
Take care of them, Kreon; do this for me.   235

And will you let me touch them with my hands
A last time, and let us weep together?

Be kind, my lord,
Great prince, be kind!
                    Could I but touch them,
They would be mine again, as when I had my eyes.   240

(*Enter Antigone and Ismene, attended.*)

   Ah, God!
Is it my dearest children I hear weeping?
Has Kreon pitied me and sent my daughters?
KREON: Yes, Oedipus: I knew that they were dear to you
In the old days, and know you must love them still.   245
OEDIPUS: May God bless you for this—and be a friendlier
Guardian to you than he has been to me!

Children, where are you?
Come quickly to my hands: they are your brother's—
Hands that have brought your father's once clear eyes   250
To this way of seeing—
                        Ah dearest ones,
I had neither sight nor knowledge then, your father
By the woman who was the source of his own life!
And I weep for you—having no strength to see you—,
I weep for you when I think of the bitterness   255
That men will visit upon you all your lives.
What homes, what festivals can you attend
Without being forced to depart again in tears?
And when you come to marriageable age,
Where is the man, my daughters, who would dare   260
Risk the bane that lies on all my children?
Is there any evil wanting? Your father killed
His father; sowed the womb of her who bore him;
Engendered you at the fount of his own existence!
That is what they will say of you.

                              Then, whom   265
Can you ever marry? There are no bridegrooms for you,
And your lives must wither away in sterile dreaming.

O Kreon, son of Menoikeus!
You are the only father my daughters have,
Since we, their parents, are both of us gone for ever.   270
They are your own blood: you will not let them
Fall into beggary and loneliness;
You will keep them from the miseries that are mine!

Take pity on them; see, they are only children,
Friendless except for you. Promise me this,   275
Great prince, and give me your hand in token of it.

(*Kreon clasps his right hand.*)

Children:
I could say much, if you could understand me,
But as it is, I have only this prayer for you:
Live where you can, be as happy as you can—   280
Happier, please God, than God has made your father.
KREON: Enough. You have wept enough. Now go within.
OEDIPUS: I must, but it is hard.
KREON: Time eases all things.
OEDIPUS: You know my mind, then?
KREON: Say what you desire.
OEDIPUS: Send me from Thebes!
KREON: God grant that I may!   285
OEDIPUS: But since God hates me . . .
KREON: No, he will grant your wish.
OEDIPUS: You promise?
KREON: I can not speak beyond my knowledge.
OEDIPUS: Then lead me in.
KREON: Come now, and leave your children.   290
OEDIPUS: No! Do not take them from me!
KREON: Think no longer
That you are in command here, but rather think
How, when you were, you served your own destruction.

(*Exeunt into the house all but the Chorus; the Choragos chants directly to the
audience.*)

CHORAGOS: Men of Thebes: look upon Oedipus.

This is the king who solved the famous riddle   295
And towered up, most powerful of men.
No mortal eyes but looked on him with envy,
Yet in the end ruin swept over him.

Let every man in mankind's frailty
Consider his last day; and let none   300
Presume on his good fortune until he find
Life, at his death, a memory without pain.

[c. 430 B.C.E.]

WILLIAM SHAKESPEARE [1564–1616]

Hamlet, Prince of Denmark

[Dramatis Personae
CLAUDIUS, *King of Denmark*
HAMLET, *son to the late King Hamlet, and nephew to the present King*
POLONIUS, *Lord Chamberlain*
HORATIO, *friend to Hamlet*
LAERTES, *son to Polonius*
VOLTIMAND,
CORNELIUS,
ROSENCRANTZ,
GUILDENSTERN, } *courtiers*
OSRIC,
GENTLEMAN,
PRIEST, OR DOCTOR OF DIVINITY
MARCELLUS, } *officers*
BERNARDO,
FRANCISCO, *a solider*
REYNALDO, *servant to Polonius*
PLAYERS
TWO CLOWNS, *grave-diggers*
FORTINBRAS, *Prince of Norway*
CAPTAIN
ENGLISH AMBASSADORS

GERTRUDE, *Queen of Denmark, mother to Hamlet*
OPHELIA, *daughter to Polonius*

LORDS, LADIES, OFFICERS, SOLDIERS, SAILORS, MESSENGERS, AND OTHER
ATTENDANTS
GHOST *of Hamlet's father*

Scene: *Denmark.*]

Note: The text of *Hamlet* has come down to us in different versions—such as the first quarto, the second quarto, and the first Folio. The copy of the text used here is largely drawn from the second quarto. Passages enclosed in square brackets are taken from one of the other versions, in most cases the first Folio.

{ACT I   *Scene 1*}°

(*Enter Bernardo and Francisco, two sentinels, [meeting].*)

BERNARDO: Who's there?
FRANCISCO: Nay, answer me.° Stand and unfold yourself.
BERNARDO: Long live the King!
FRANCISCO: Bernardo?
BERNARDO: He.   5
FRANCISCO: You come most carefully upon your hour.
BERNARDO: 'Tis now struck twelve. Get thee to bed, Francisco.
FRANCISCO: For this relief much thanks. 'Tis bitter cold,
    And I am sick at heart.
BERNARDO: Have you had quiet guard?
FRANCISCO: Not a mouse stirring.   10
BERNARDO: Well, good night.
    If you do meet Horatio and Marcellus,
    The rivals° of my watch, bid them make haste.

(*Enter Horatio and Marcellus.*)

FRANCISCO: I think I hear them. Stand, ho! Who is there?
HORATIO: Friends to this ground.
MARCELLUS: And liegemen to the Dane.°   15
FRANCISCO: Give you° good night.
MARCELLUS: O, farewell, honest soldier.
    Who hath relieved you?
FRANCISCO: Bernardo hath my place.
    Give you good night.   (*Exit Francisco.*)
MARCELLUS: Holla, Bernardo!
BERNARDO: Say,
    What, is Horatio there?
HORATIO: A piece of him.
BERNARDO: Welcome, Horatio. Welcome, good Marcellus.   20
HORATIO: What, has this thing appear'd again tonight?
BERNARDO: I have seen nothing.
MARCELLUS: Horatio says 'tis but our fantasy,
    And will not let belief take hold of him
    Touching this dreaded sight, twice seen of us.   25
    Therefore I have entreated him along

I, I. **Location:** Elsinore castle. A guard platform.   **2. me:** Francisco emphasizes
that *he* is the sentry currently on watch.   **13. rivals:** Partners.   **15. liegemen to
the Dane:** Men sworn to serve the Danish king.   **16. Give you:** God give you.

With us to watch the minutes of this night,
That if again this apparition come
He may approve° our eyes and speak to it.
HORATIO: Tush, tush, 'twill not appear.
BERNARDO: Sit down awhile,   30
And let us once again assail your ears,
That are so fortified against our story,
What we have two nights seen.
HORATIO: Well, sit we down,
And let us hear Bernardo speak of this.
BERNARDO: Last night of all,   35
When yond same star that's westward from the pole°
Had made his° course t' illume that part of heaven
Where now it burns, Marcellus and myself,
The bell then beating one—

(*Enter Ghost.*)

MARCELLUS: Peace, break thee off! Look where it comes again!   40
BERNARDO: In the same figure, like the King that's dead.
MARCELLUS: Thou art a scholar.° Speak to it, Horatio.
BERNARDO: Looks 'a° not like the King? Mark it, Horatio.
HORATIO: Most like. It harrows me with fear and wonder.
BERNARDO: It would be spoke to.
MARCELLUS: Speak to it,° Horatio.   45
HORATIO: What art thou that usurp'st this time of night,
Together with that fair and warlike form
In which the majesty of buried Denmark°
Did sometimes° march? By heaven I charge thee speak!
MARCELLUS: It is offended.
BERNARDO: See, it stalks away.   50
HORATIO: Stay! Speak, speak. I charge thee, speak.

(*Exit Ghost.*)

MARCELLUS: 'Tis gone, and will not answer.
BERNARDO: How now, Horatio? You tremble and look pale.
Is not this something more than fantasy?
What think you on 't?   55

29. approve: Corroborate. 36. pole: Polestar. 37. his: Its. 42. scholar: One
learned in Latin and able to address spirits. 43. 'a: He. 45. It . . . it: A ghost
could not speak until spoken to. 48. buried Denmark: The buried king of
Denmark. 49. sometimes: Formerly.

HORATIO: Before my God, I might not this believe
  Without the sensible° and true avouch
  Of mine own eyes.
MARCELLUS: Is it not like the King?
HORATIO: As thou art to thyself.
  Such was the very armor he had on   60
  When he the ambitious Norway° combated.
  So frown'd he once when, in an angry parle,°
  He smote the sledded° Polacks° on the ice.
  'Tis strange.
MARCELLUS: Thus twice before, and jump° at this dead hour,   65
  With martial stalk hath he gone by our watch.
HORATIO: In what particular thought to work I know not,
  But, in the gross and scope° of mine opinion,
  This bodes some strange eruption to our state.
MARCELLUS: Good now,° sit down, and tell me, he that knows,   70
  Why this same strict and most observant watch
  So nightly toils° the subject° of the land,
  And why such daily cast° of brazen cannon,
  And foreign mart° for implements of war,
  Why such impress° of shipwrights, whose sore task   75
  Does not divide the Sunday from the week.
  What might be toward,° that this sweaty haste
  Doth make the night joint-laborer with the day?
  Who is 't that can inform me?
HORATIO: That can I,
  At least, the whisper goes so. Our last king,   80
  Whose image even but now appear'd to us,
  Was, as you know, by Fortinbras of Norway,
  Thereto prick'd on° by a most emulate° pride,
  Dar'd to the combat; in which our valiant Hamlet—
  For so this side of our known world esteem'd him—   85
  Did slay this Fortinbras; who, by a seal'd compact,
  Well ratified by law and heraldry,
  Did forfeit, with his life, all those his lands
  Which he stood seiz'd° of, to the conqueror;

---

57. sensible: Confirmed by the senses.   **61. Norway:** King of Norway.   **62. parle:**
Parley.   **63. sledded:** Traveling on sleds.   **Polacks:** Poles.   **65. jump:** Exactly.
68. gross and scope: General view.   **70. Good now:** An expression denoting
entreaty or expostulation.   **72. toils:** Causes to toil.   **subject:** Subjects.   **73. cast:**
Casting.   **74. mart:** Buying and selling.   **75. impress:** Impressment, conscrip-
tion.   **77. toward:** In preparation.   **83. prick'd on:** Incited.   **emulate:** Ambitious.
89. seiz'd: Possessed.

Against the° which a moi'ty competent°   90
Was gaged° by our king, which had return'd
To the inheritance of Fortinbras
Had he been vanquisher, as, by the same comart°
And carriage° of the article design'd,
His fell to Hamlet. Now, sir, young Fortinbras,   95
Of unimproved° mettle hot and full,
Hath in the skirts° of Norway here and there
Shark'd up° a list of lawless resolutes°
For food and diet° to some enterprise
That hath a stomach° in 't, which is no other—   100
As it doth well appear unto our state—
But to recover of us, by strong hand
And terms compulsatory, those foresaid lands
So by his father lost. And this, I take it,
Is the main motive of our preparations,   105
The source of this our watch, and the chief head°
Of this post-haste and romage° in the land.
BERNARDO: I think it be no other but e'en so.
Well may it sort° that this portentous figure
Comes armed through our watch so like the King   110
That was and is the question of these wars.
HORATIO: A mote° it is to trouble the mind's eye.
In the most high and palmy° state of Rome,
A little ere the mightiest Julius fell,
The graves stood tenantless and the sheeted° dead   115
Did squeak and gibber in the Roman streets;
As° stars with trains of fire and dews of blood,
Disasters° in the sun; and the moist star°
Upon whose influence Neptune's° empire stands°
Was sick almost to doomsday° with eclipse.   120

90. Against the: In return for. . . . **moi'ty competent:** Sufficient portion.
91. gaged: Engaged, pledged. **93. comart:** Joint bargain (?). **94. carriage:**
Import, bearing. **96. unimproved:** Not turned to account (?) or untested (?).
97. skirts: Outlying regions, outskirts. **98. Shark'd up:** Got together in haphaz-
ard fashion. **resolutes:** Desperadoes. **99. food and diet:** No pay but their
keep. **100. stomach:** Relish of danger. **106. head:** Source. **107. romage:**
Bustle, commotion. **109. sort:** Suit. **112. mote:** Speck of dust. **113. palmy:**
Flourishing. **115. sheeted:** Shrouded. **117. As:** This abrupt transition suggests that matter is possibly omitted between lines 116 and 117. **118. Disas-
ters:** Unfavorable signs of aspects. **moist star:** Moon, governing tides.
119. Neptune: God of the sea. **stands:** Depends. **120. sick . . . doomsday:**
See Matt. 24:29 and Rev. 6:12.

And even the like precurse° of fear'd events,
As harbingers° preceding still° the fates
And prologue to the omen° coming on,
Have heaven and earth together demonstrated
Unto our climatures° and countrymen.   125

(*Enter Ghost.*)

But soft, behold! Lo where it comes again!
I'll cross° it, though it blast me. Stay, illusion!
If thou hast any sound, or use of voice,
Speak to me!   (*It spreads his arms.*)
If there be any good thing to be done   130
That may to thee do ease and grace to me,
Speak to me!
If thou art privy to thy country's fate,
Which, happily,° foreknowing may avoid,
O, speak!   135
Or if thou hast uphoarded in thy life
Extorted treasure in the womb of earth,
For which, they say, you spirits oft walk in death,

(*The cock crows.*)

Speak of it. Stay, and speak! Stop it, Marcellus.
MARCELLUS: Shall I strike at it with my partisan?°   140
HORATIO: Do, if it will not stand.   [*They strike at it.*]
BERNARDO: 'Tis here!
HORATIO: 'Tis here!
MARCELLUS: 'Tis gone.   [*Exit Ghost.*]
We do it wrong, being so majestical,
To offer it the show of violence;
For it is, as the air, invulnerable,   145
And our vain blows malicious mockery.
BERNARDO: It was about to speak when the cock crew.
HORATIO: And then it started like a guilty thing
Upon a fearful summons. I have heard,
The cock, that is the trumpet to the morn,   150
Doth with his lofty and shrill-sounding throat
Awake the god of day, and, at his warning,
Whether in sea or fire, in earth or air,

---

121. precurse: Heralding, foreshadowing. 122. harbingers: Forerunners.
still: Continually. 123. omen: Calamitous event. 125. climatures: Regions.
127. cross: Meet, face directly. 134. happily: Haply, perchance. 140. partisan: Long-handled spear.

Th' extravagant and erring° spirit hies
To his confine; and of the truth herein   155
This present object made probation.°
MARCELLUS: It faded on the crowing of the cock.
Some say that ever 'gainst° that season comes
Wherein our Savior's birth is celebrated,
The bird of dawning singeth all night long,   160
And then, they say, no spirit dare stir abroad;
The nights are wholesome, then no planets strike,°
No fairy takes,° nor witch hath power to charm,
So hallowed and so gracious° is that time.
HORATIO: So have I heard and do in part believe it.   165
But, look, the morn, in russet mantle clad,
Walks o'er the dew of yon high eastward hill.
Break we our watch up, and by my advice
Let us impart what we have seen tonight
Unto young Hamlet; for, upon my life,   170
This spirit, dumb to us, will speak to him.
Do you consent we shall acquaint him with it,
As needful in our loves, fitting our duty?
MARCELLUS: Let's do 't, I pray, and I this morning know
Where we shall find him most conveniently.   175

(Exeunt.)°

[*Scene II*]°

(*Flourish. Enter Claudius, King of Denmark, Gertrude the Queen, Councilors, Polonius and his son Laertes, Hamlet, cum aliis*° [*including Voltimand and Cornelius*].)

KING: Though yet of Hamlet our dear brother's death
The memory be green, and that it us befitted
To bear our hearts in grief and our whole kingdom
To be contracted in one brow of woe,
Yet so far hath discretion fought with nature   5
That we with wisest sorrow think on him,
Together with remembrance of ourselves.

---

154. extravagant and erring: Wandering. (The words have similar meaning.)
156. probation: Proof. **158. 'gainst:** Just before. **162. strike:** Exert evil influence. **163. takes:** Bewitches. **164. gracious:** Full of goodness. [S.D.] *Exeunt:* Latin for "they go out." I, II. **Location:** The castle. [S.D.] *cum aliis:* With others.

Therefore our sometime sister, now our queen,
Th' imperial jointress° to this warlike state,
Have we, as 'twere with a defeated joy—   10
With an auspicious and a dropping eye,
With mirth in funeral and with dirge in marriage,
In equal scale weighing delight and dole—
Taken to wife. Nor have we herein barr'd
Your better wisdoms, which have freely gone   15
With this affair along. For all, our thanks.
Now follows that you know° young Fortinbras,
Holding a weak supposal° of our worth,
Or thinking by our late dear brother's death
Our state to be disjoint and out of frame,   20
Colleagued with° this dream of his advantage,°
He hath not fail'd to pester us with message
Importing° the surrender of those lands
Lost by his father, with all bands° of law,
To our most valiant brother. So much for him.   25
Now for ourself and for this time of meeting.
Thus much the business is: we have here writ
To Norway, uncle of young Fortinbras—
Who, impotent and bed-rid, scarcely hears
Of this his nephew's purpose—to suppress   30
His° further gait° herein, in that the levies,
The lists, and full proportions are all made
Out of his subject;° and we here dispatch
You, good Cornelius, and you, Voltimand,
For bearers of this greeting to old Norway,   35
Giving to you no further personal power
To business with the King, more than the scope
Of these delated° articles allow.   [Gives a paper.]
Farewell, and let your haste commend your duty.
CORNELIUS, VOLTIMAND: In that, and all things, will we show our duty.   40
KING: We doubt it nothing. Heartily farewell.

                        [Exit Voltimand and Cornelius.]

---

9. jointress: Woman possessed of a joint tenancy of an estate.   17. know: Be
informed (that).   18. weak supposal: Low estimate.   21. Colleagued with:
Joined to, allied with.   dream . . . advantage: Illusory hope of success.
23. Importing: Pertaining to.   24. bands: Contracts.   31. His: Fortinbras's.
gait: Proceeding.   31–33. in that . . . subject: Since the levying of troops and
supplies is drawn entirely from the King of Norway's own subjects.   38. delated:
Detailed. (Variant of dilated.)

And now, Laertes, what's the news with you?
You told us of some suit; what is 't, Laertes?
You cannot speak of reason to the Dane°
And lose your voice.° What wouldst thou beg, Laertes,   45
That shall not be my offer, not thy asking?
The head is not more native° to the heart,
The hand more instrumental° to the mouth,
Than is the throne of Denmark to thy father.
What wouldst thou have, Laertes?

LAERTES: My dread lord,   50
Your leave and favor to return to France,
From whence though willingly I came to Denmark
To show my duty in your coronation,
Yet now I must confess, that duty done,
My thoughts and wishes bend again toward France   55
And bow them to your gracious leave and pardon.°

KING: Have you your father's leave? What says Polonius?

POLONIUS: H'ath, my lord, wrung from me my slow leave
By laborsome petition, and at last
Upon his will I seal'd my hard° consent.   60
I do beseech you, give him leave to go.

KING: Take thy fair hour, Laertes. Time be thine,
And thy best graces spend it at thy will!
But now, my cousin° Hamlet, and my son—

HAMLET: A little more than kin, and less than kind.°   65

KING: How is it that the clouds still hang on you?

HAMLET: Not so, my lord. I am too much in the sun.°

QUEEN: Good Hamlet, cast thy nighted color off,
And let thine eye look like a friend on Denmark.
Do not forever with thy veiled° lids   70
Seek for thy noble father in the dust.
Thou know'st 'tis common,° all that lives must die,
Passing through nature to eternity.

---

44. the Dane: The Danish king.   45. lose your voice: Waste your speech.
47. native: Closely connected, related.   48. instrumental: Serviceable.   56. leave
and pardon: Permission to depart.   60. hard: Reluctant.   64. cousin: Any kin
not of the immediate family.   65. A little ... kind: Closer than an ordinary
nephew (since I am stepson), and yet more separated in natural feeling (with pun
on *kind*, meaning affectionate and natural, lawful). This line is often read as an
aside, but it need not be.   67. sun: The sunshine of the King's royal favor (with
pun on *son*).   70. veiled: Downcast.   72. common: Of universal occurrence.
(But Hamlet plays on the sense of *vulgar* in line 74.)

HAMLET: Ay, madam, it is common.
QUEEN: If it be,
    Why seems it so particular with thee?   75
HAMLET: Seems, madam! Nay, it is. I know not "seems."
    'Tis not alone my inky cloak, good mother,
    Nor customary suits of solemn black,
    Nor windy suspiration of forc'd breath,
    No, nor the fruitful° river in the eye,   80
    Nor the dejected havior of the visage,
    Together with all forms, moods, shapes of grief,
    That can denote me truly. These indeed seem,
    For they are actions that a man might play.
    But I have that within which passes show;   85
    These but the trappings and the suits of woe.
KING: 'Tis sweet and commendable in your nature, Hamlet,
    To give these mourning duties to your father.
    But you must know your father lost a father,
    That father lost, lost his, and the survivor bound   90
    In filial obligation for some term
    To do obsequious° sorrow. But to persever°
    In obstinate condolement° is a course
    Of impious stubbornness. 'Tis unmanly grief.
    It shows a will most incorrect to heaven,   95
    A heart unfortified, a mind impatient,
    An understanding simple and unschool'd.
    For what we know must be and is as common
    As any the most vulgar thing to sense,°
    Why should we in our peevish opposition   100
    Take it to heart? Fie, 'tis a fault to heaven,
    A fault against the dead, a fault to nature,
    To reason most absurd, whose common theme
    Is death of fathers, and who still hath cried,
    From the first corse° till he that died today,   105
    "This must be so." We pray you, throw to earth
    This unprevailing° woe, and think of us
    As of a father; for let the world take note,
    You are the most immediate° to our throne,
    And with no less nobility of love   110

80. fruitful: Abundant.   92. obsequious: Suited to obsequies or funerals.   persever: Persevere.   93. condolement: Sorrowing.   99. As . . . sense: As the most
ordinary experience.   105. corse: Corpse.   107. unprevailing: Unavailing.
109. most immediate: Next in succession.

Than that which dearest father bears his son
Do I impart toward you. For your intent
In going back to school in Wittenberg,°
It is most retrograde° to our desire,
And we beseech you, bend you° to remain   115
Here in the cheer and comfort of our eye,
Our chiefest courtier, cousin, and our son.
QUEEN: Let not thy mother lose her prayers, Hamlet.
  I pray thee stay with us, go not to Wittenberg.
HAMLET: I shall in all my best obey you, madam.   120
KING: Why, 'tis a loving and a fair reply.
  Be as ourself in Denmark. Madam, come.
  This gentle and unforc'd accord of Hamlet
  Sits smiling to my heart, in grace whereof
  No jocund° health that Denmark drinks today   125
  But the great cannon to the clouds shall tell,
  And the King's rouse° the heaven shall bruit again,°
  Respeaking earthly thunder.° Come away.

  (*Flourish. Exeunt all but Hamlet.*)

HAMLET: O, that this too too sullied° flesh would melt,
  Thaw, and resolve itself into a dew!   130
  Or that the Everlasting had not fix'd
  His canon° 'gainst self-slaughter! O God, God,
  How weary, stale, flat, and unprofitable
  Seem to me all the uses of this world!
  Fie on 't, ah, fie! 'Tis an unweeded garden   135
  That grows to seed. Things rank and gross in nature
  Possess it merely.° That it should come to this!
  But two months dead—nay, not so much, not two.
  So excellent a king, that was to° this
  Hyperion° to a satyr; so loving to my mother   140
  That he might not beteem° the winds of heaven
  Visit her face too roughly. Heaven and earth,
  Must I remember? Why, she would hang on him
  As if increase of appetite had grown

113. **Wittenberg:** Famous German university founded in 1502.   114. **retrograde:** Contrary.   115. **bend you:** Incline yourself.   125. **jocund:** Merry. 127. **rouse:** Draft of liquor.   **bruit again:** Loudly echo.   128. **thunder:** Of trumpet and kettledrum sounded when the King drinks, see I, IV, 8–12. 129. **sullied:** Defiled. (The early quartos read *sallied*, the Folio *solid*.) 132. **canon:** Law.   137. **merely:** Completely.   139. **to:** In comparison to. 140. **Hyperion:** Titan sun-god, father of Helios.   141. **beteem:** Allow.

By what it fed on, and yet, within a month—   145
Let me not think on 't. Frailty, thy name is woman!—
A little month, or ere those shoes were old
With which she followed my poor father's body,
Like Niobe,° all tears, why she, even she—
O God, a beast, that wants discourse of reason,°   150
Would have mourn'd longer—married with my uncle,
My father's brother, but no more like my father
Than I to Hercules. Within a month,
Ere yet the salt of most unrighteous tears
Had left the flushing in her galled° eyes,   155
She married. O, most wicked speed, to post
With such dexterity to incestuous° sheets!
It is not nor it cannot come to good.
But break, my heart, for I must hold my tongue.

(*Enter Horatio, Marcellus, and Bernardo.*)

HORATIO: Hail to your lordship!
HAMLET: I am glad to see you well.   160
    Horatio!—or I do forget myself.
HORATIO: The same, my lord, and your poor servant ever.
HAMLET: Sir, my good friend; I'll change° that name with you.
    And what make° you from Wittenberg, Horatio?
    Marcellus?   165
MARCELLUS: My good lord.
HAMLET: I am very glad to see you. [*To Bernardo.*] Good even, sir.—
    But what, in faith, make you from Wittenberg?
HORATIO: A truant disposition, good my lord.
HAMLET: I would not hear your enemy say so,   170
    Nor shall you do my ear that violence
    To make it truster of your own report
    Against yourself. I know you are no truant.
    But what is your affair in Elsinore?
    We'll teach you to drink deep ere you depart.   175
HORATIO: My lord, I came to see your father's funeral.

---

149. **Niobe:** Tantalus's daughter, Queen of Thebes, who boasted that she had
more sons and daughters than Leto; for this, Apollo and Artemis, children of
Leto, slew her fourteen children. She was turned by Zeus into a stone that continually dropped tears.   150. **wants . . . reason:** Lacks the faculty of reason.
155. **galled:** Irritated, inflamed.   157. **incestuous:** In Shakespeare's day, the marriage of a man like Claudius to his deceased brother's wife was considered incestuous.   163. **change:** Exchange (i.e., the name of friend).   164. **make:** Do.

HAMLET: I prithee do not mock me, fellow student;
   I think it was to see my mother's wedding.
HORATIO: Indeed, my lord, it followed hard° upon.
HAMLET: Thrift, thrift, Horatio! The funeral bak'd meats   180
   Did coldly furnish forth the marriage tables.
   Would I had met my dearest° foe in heaven
   Or° ever I had seen that day, Horatio!
   My father!—Methinks I see my father.
HORATIO: Where, my lord?
HAMLET: In my mind's eye, Horatio.   185
HORATIO: I saw him once. 'A° was a goodly king.
HAMLET: 'A was a man, take him for all in all,
   I shall not look upon his like again.
HORATIO: My lord, I think I saw him yesternight.
HAMLET: Saw? Who?   190
HORATIO: My lord, the King your father.
HAMLET: The King my father?
HORATIO: Season your admiration° for a while
   With an attent° ear, till I may deliver,
   Upon the witness of these gentlemen,
   This marvel to you.
HAMLET: For God's love, let me hear!   195
HORATIO: Two nights together had these gentlemen,
   Marcellus and Bernardo, on their watch,
   In the dead waste and middle of the night,
   Been thus encount'red. A figure like your father,
   Armed at point° exactly, cap-a-pe,°   200
   Appears before them, and with solemn march
   Goes slow and stately by them. Thrice he walk'd
   By their oppress'd and fear-surprised eyes
   Within his truncheon's° length, whilst they, distill'd
   Almost to jelly with the act° of fear,   205
   Stand dumb and speak not to him. This to me
   In dreadful secrecy impart they did,
   And I with them the third night kept the watch,
   Where, as they had delivered, both in time,
   Form of the thing, each word made true and good,   210
   The apparition comes. I knew your father;

---

179. **hard:** Close.   182. **dearest:** Direst.   183. **Or:** Ere, before.   186. **'A:** He.
192. **Season your admiration:** Restrain your astonishment.   193. **attent:** Attentive.   200. **at point:** Completely.   **cap-a-pe:** From head to foot.   204. **truncheon:** Officer's staff.   205. **act:** Action, operation.

These hands are not more like.
HAMLET: But where was this?
MARCELLUS: My lord, upon the platform where we watch.
HAMLET: Did you not speak to it?
HORATIO: My lord, I did,
   But answer made it none. Yet once methought   215
   It lifted up it° head and did address
   Itself to motion, like as it would speak;
   But even then the morning cock crew loud,
   And at the sound it shrunk in haste away,
   And vanish'd from our sight.
HAMLET: 'Tis very strange.   220
HORATIO: As I do live, my honor'd lord, 'tis true,
   And we did think it writ down in our duty
   To let you know of it.
HAMLET: Indeed, indeed, sirs. But this troubles me.
   Hold you the watch tonight?
ALL: We do, my lord.   225
HAMLET: Arm'd, say you?
ALL: Arm'd, my lord.
HAMLET: From top to toe?
ALL: My lord, from head to foot.
HAMLET: Then saw you not his face?
HORATIO: O, yes, my lord. He wore his beaver° up.   230
HAMLET: What, looked he frowningly?
HORATIO: A countenance more
   In sorrow than in anger.
HAMLET: Pale or red?
HORATIO: Nay, very pale.
HAMLET: And fix'd his eyes upon you?
HORATIO: Most constantly.
HAMLET: I would I had been there.
HORATIO: It would have much amaz'd you.   235
HAMLET: Very like, very like. Stay'd it long?
HORATIO: While one with moderate haste might tell° a hundred.
MARCELLUS, BERNARDO: Longer, longer.
HORATIO: Not when I saw 't.
HAMLET: His beard was grizzl'd,—no?
HORATIO: It was, as I have seen it in his life,   240
   A sable silver'd.°

216. it: Its.   **230. beaver:** Visor on the helmet.   **237. tell:** Count.   **241. sable
silver'd:** Black mixed with white.

HAMLET: I will watch tonight.
Perchance 'twill walk again.
HORATIO: I warr'nt it will.
HAMLET: If it assume my noble father's person,
I'll speak to it, though hell itself should gape
And bid me hold my peace. I pray you all,   245
If you have hitherto conceal'd this sight,
Let it be tenable° in your silence still,
And whatsomever else shall hap tonight,
Give it an understanding, but no tongue.
I will requite your loves. So, fare you well.   250
Upon the platform, 'twixt eleven and twelve,
I'll visit you.
ALL: Our duty to your honor.
HAMLET: Your loves, as mine to you. Farewell.

                                   (*Exeunt [all but Hamlet]*.)

My father's spirit in arms! All is not well.
I doubt° some foul play. Would the night were come!   255
Till then sit still, my soul. Foul deeds will rise,
Though all the earth o'erwhelm them, to men's eyes.

                                                    (*Exit.*)

                         [*Scene III*]°
(*Enter Laertes and Ophelia, his sister.*)

LAERTES: My necessaries are embark'd. Farewell.
And, sister, as the winds give benefit
And convoy is assistant,° do not sleep
But let me hear from you.
OPHELIA: Do you doubt that?
LAERTES: For Hamlet, and the trifling of his favor,   5
Hold it a fashion and a toy in blood,°
A violet in the youth of primy° nature,
Forward,° not permanent, sweet, not lasting,
The perfume and suppliance° of a minute—
No more.

---

247. **tenable:** Held tightly.   255. **doubt:** Suspect.   I, III. **Location:** Polonius's
chambers.   3. **convoy is assistant:** Means of conveyance are available.   6. **toy
in blood:** Passing amorous fancy.   7. **primy:** In its prime, springtime.
8. **Forward:** Precocious.   9. **suppliance:** Supply, filler.

OPHELIA: No more but so?
LAERTES: Think it no more.   10
  For nature crescent° does not grow alone
  In thews° and bulk, but, as this temple° waxes,
  The inward service of the mind and soul
  Grows wide withal.° Perhaps he loves you now,
  And now no soil° nor cautel° doth besmirch   15
  The virtue of his will;° but you must fear,
  His greatness weigh'd,° his will is not his own.
  [For he himself is subject to his birth.]
  He may not, as unvalued persons do,
  Carve° for himself; for on his choice depends   20
  The safety and health of this whole state,
  And therefore must his choice be circumscrib'd
  Unto the voice and yielding° of that body
  Whereof he is the head. Then if he says he loves you,
  It fits your wisdom so far to believe it   25
  As he in his particular act and place
  May give his saying deed,° which is no further
  Than the main voice of Denmark goes withal.
  Then weigh what loss your honor may sustain
  If with too credent° ear you list° his songs,   30
  Or lose your heart, or your chaste treasure open
  To his unmaster'd importunity.
  Fear it, Ophelia, fear it, my dear sister,
  And keep you in the rear of your affection,
  Out of the shot° and danger of desire.   35
  The chariest° maid is prodigal enough
  If she unmask her beauty to the moon.
  Virtue itself scapes not calumnious strokes.
  The canker galls° the infants of the spring
  Too oft before their buttons° be disclos'd,°   40
  And in the morn and liquid dew° of youth
  Contagious blastments° are most imminent.
  Be wary then; best safety lies in fear.

---

11. **crescent:** Growing, waxing.   12. **thews:** Bodily strength.   **temple:** Body.
14. **Grows wide withal:** Grows along with it.   15. **soil:** Blemish.   **cautel:**
Deceit.   16. **will:** Desire.   17. **greatness weigh'd:** High position considered.
20. **Carve:** Choose pleasure.   23. **voice and yielding:** Assent, approval.
27. **deed:** Effect.   30. **credent:** Credulous.   **list:** Listen to.   35. **shot:** Range.
36. **chariest:** Most scrupulously modest.   39. **canker galls:** Cankerworm destroys.   40. **buttons:** Buds.   **disclos'd:** Opened.   41. **liquid dew:** Time when
dew is fresh.   42. **blastments:** Blights.

Youth to itself rebels, though none else near.
OPHELIA: I shall the effect of this good lesson keep   45
As watchman to my heart. But, good my brother,
Do not, as some ungracious pastors do,
Show me the steep and thorny way to heaven,
Whiles, like a puff'd° and reckless libertine,
Himself the primrose path of dalliance treads,   50
And recks° not his own rede.°

(*Enter Polonius.*)

LAERTES: O, fear me not.
I stay too long. But here my father comes.
A double blessing is a double° grace;
Occasion° smiles upon a second leave.
POLONIUS: Yet here, Laertes? Aboard, aboard, for shame!   55
The wind sits in the shoulder of your sail,
And you are stay'd for. There—my blessing with thee!
And these few precepts in thy memory
Look thou character.° Give thy thoughts no tongue
Nor any unproportion'd thought his° act.   60
Be thou familiar,° but by no means vulgar.°
Those friends thou hast, and their adoption tried,°
Grapple them to thy soul with hoops of steel,
But do not dull thy palm with entertainment
Of each new-hatch'd, unfledg'd courage.° Beware   65
Of entrance to a quarrel, but, being in,
Bear't that° th' opposed may beware of thee.
Give every man thy ear, but few thy voice;
Take each man's censure,° but reserve thy judgment.
Costly thy habit as thy purse can buy,   70
But not express'd in fancy; rich, not gaudy,
For the apparel oft proclaims the man,
And they in France of the best rank and station
Are of a most select and generous chief° in that.
Neither a borrower nor a lender be,   75
For loan oft loses both itself and friend,
And borrowing dulleth edge of husbandry.°

49. puff'd: Bloated. **51. recks:** Heeds. **rede:** Counsel. **53. double:** I.e.,
Laertes has already bidden his father good-bye. **54. Occasion:** Opportu-
nity. **59. character:** Inscribe. **60. his:** Its. **61. familiar:** Sociable. **vulgar:**
Common. **62. tried:** Tested. **65. courage:** Young man of spirit. **67. Bear't
that:** Manage it so that. **69. censure:** Opinion, judgment. **74. generous chief:**
Noble eminence (?). **77. husbandry:** Thrift.

This above all: to thine own self be true,
And it must follow, as the night the day,
Thou canst not then be false to any man.   80
Farewell. My blessing season° this in thee!
LAERTES: Most humbly do I take my leave, my lord.
POLONIUS: The time invests° you. Go, your servants tend.°
LAERTES: Farewell, Ophelia, and remember well
What I have said to you.   85
OPHELIA: 'Tis in my memory lock'd,
And you yourself shall keep the key of it.
LAERTES: Farewell.   (*Exit Laertes.*)
POLONIUS: What is 't, Ophelia, he hath said to you?
OPHELIA: So please you, something touching the Lord Hamlet.   90
POLONIUS: Marry,° well bethought.
'Tis told me he hath very oft of late
Given private time to you, and you yourself
Have of your audience been most free and bounteous.
If it be so—as so 'tis put on° me,   95
And that in way of caution—I must tell you
You do not understand yourself so clearly
As it behooves my daughter and your honor.
What is between you? Give me up the truth.
OPHELIA: He hath, my lord, of late made many tenders°   100
Of his affection to me.
POLONIUS: Affection? Pooh! You speak like a green girl,
Unsifted° in such perilous circumstance.
Do you believe his tenders, as you call them?
OPHELIA: I do not know, my lord, what I should think.   105
POLONIUS: Marry, I will teach you. Think yourself a baby
That you have ta'en these tenders° for true pay,
Which are not sterling.° Tender° yourself more dearly,
Or—not to crack the wind° of the poor phrase,
Running it thus—you'll tender me a fool.°   110
OPHELIA: My lord, he hath importun'd me with love
In honorable fashion.
POLONIUS: Ay, fashion° you may call it. Go to, go to.

81. season: Mature.   83. invests: Besieges. . . .   tend: Attend, wait.   91. Marry:
By the Virgin Mary (a mild oath).   95. put on: Impressed on, told to.   100. tenders: Offers.   103. Unsifted: Untried.   107. tenders: With added meaning
here of *promises to pay*.   108. sterling: Legal currency.   Tender: Hold.
109. crack the wind: Run it until it is broken, winded.   110. tender me a fool:
(1) Show yourself to me as a fool, (2) show me up as a fool, (3) present me with a
grandchild (*fool* was a term of endearment for a child).   113. fashion: Mere
form, pretense.

OPHELIA: And hath given countenance° to his speech, my lord,
　　With almost all the holy vows of heaven.   115
POLONIUS: Ay, springes° to catch woodcocks.° I do know,
　　When the blood burns, how prodigal the soul
　　Lends the tongue vows. These blazes, daughter,
　　Giving more light than heat, extinct in both
　　Even in their promise, as it is a-making,   120
　　You must not take for fire. From this time
　　Be something scanter of your maiden presence.
　　Set your entreatments° at a higher rate
　　Than a command to parle.° For Lord Hamlet,
　　Believe so much in him° that he is young,   125
　　And with a larger tether may he walk
　　Than may be given you. In few,° Ophelia,
　　Do not believe his vows, for they are brokers,°
　　Not of that dye° which their investments° show,
　　But mere implorators° of unholy suits,   130
　　Breathing° like sanctified and pious bawds,
　　The better to beguile. This is for all:
　　I would not, in plain terms, from this time forth
　　Have you so slander° any moment leisure
　　As to give words or talk with the Lord Hamlet.   135
　　Look to 't, I charge you. Come your ways.
OPHELIA: I shall obey, my lord.   (*Exeunt.*)

{*Scene IV*}°

(*Enter Hamlet, Horatio, and Marcellus.*)

HAMLET: The air bites shrewdly; it is very cold.
HORATIO: It is a nipping and an eager air.
HAMLET: What hour now?
HORATIO: I think it lacks of twelve.
MARCELLUS: No, it is struck.

114. **countenance:** Credit, support.   116. **springes:** Snares.   **woodcocks:**
Birds easily caught; here used to connote gullibility.   123. **entreatments:**
Negotiations for surrender (a military term).   124. **parle:** Discuss terms with the
enemy. (Polonius urges his daughter, in the metaphor of military language, not to
meet with Hamlet and consider giving in to him merely because he requests an
interview.)   125. **so . . . him:** This much concerning him.   127. **In few:** Briefly.
128. **brokers:** Go-betweens, procurers.   129. **dye:** Color or sort.   **investments:**
Clothes (i.e., they are not what they seem).   130. **mere implorators:** Out-and-
out solicitors.   131. **Breathing:** Speaking.   134. **slander:** Bring disgrace or
reproach upon.   I, IV. **Location:** The guard platform.

HORATIO: Indeed? I heard it not.
It then draws near the season   5
Wherein the spirit held his wont to walk.

(*A flourish of trumpets, and two pieces*° *go off* [*within*].)

What does this mean, my lord?
HAMLET: The King doth wake° tonight and takes his rouse,°
Keeps wassail,° and the swagg'ring up-spring° reels;
And as he drains his draughts of Rhenish° down,   10
The kettle-drum and trumpet thus bray out
The triumph of his pledge.°
HORATIO: Is it a custom?
HAMLET: Ay, marry, is 't,
But to my mind, though I am native here
And to the manner° born, it is a custom   15
More honor'd in the breach than the observance.°
This heavy-headed revel east and west°
Makes us traduc'd and tax'd of° other nations.
They clepe° us drunkards, and with swinish phrase°
Soil our addition;° and indeed it takes   20
From our achievements, though perform'd at height,°
The pith and marrow of our attribute.
So, oft it chances in particular men,
That for some vicious mole of nature° in them,
As in their birth—wherein they are not guilty,   25
Since nature cannot choose his° origin—
By the o'ergrowth of some complexion,°
Oft breaking down the pales° and forts of reason,
Or by some habit that too much o'er-leavens°
The form of plausive° manners, that these men,   30
Carrying, I say, the stamp of one defect,

[S.D.] *pieces:* I.e., of ordnance, cannon.   8. **wake:** Stay awake and hold revel.
rouse: Carouse, drinking bout.   9. **wassail:** Carousal.   **up-spring:** Wild German dance.   10. **Rhenish:** Rhine wine.   12. **triumph . . . pledge:** His feat in
draining the wine in a single draft.   15. **manner:** Custom (of drinking).
16. **More . . . observance:** Better neglected than followed.   17. **east and west:**
I.e., everywhere.   18. **tax'd of:** Censured by.   19. **clepe:** Call.   **with swinish
phrase:** By calling us swine.   20. **addition:** Reputation.   21. **at height:**
Outstandingly.   24. **mole of nature:** Natural blemish in one's constitution.
26. **his:** Its.   27. **complexion:** Humor (i.e., one of the four humors or fluids
thought to determine temperament).   28. **pales:** Palings, fences (as of a fortifica-
tion).   29. **o'er-leavens:** Induces a change throughout (as yeast works in dough).
30. **plausive:** Pleasing.

Being nature's livery,° or fortune's star,°
Their virtues else, be they as pure as grace,
As infinite as man may undergo,
Shall in the general censure take corruption　　　　　　35
From that particular fault. The dram of eale°
Doth all the noble substance of a doubt°
To his own scandal.°

(*Enter Ghost.*)

HORATIO:　　　　　　Look, my lord, it comes!
HAMLET: Angels and ministers of grace defend us!
　Be thou a spirit of health° or goblin damn'd,　　　　40
　Bring with thee airs from heaven or blasts from hell,
　Be thy intents wicked or charitable,
　Thou com'st in such a questionable° shape
　That I will speak to thee. I'll call thee Hamlet,
　King, father, royal Dane. O, answer me!　　　　　　45
　Let me not burst in ignorance, but tell
　Why thy canoniz'd° bones, hearsed° in death,
　Have burst their cerements;° why the sepulcher
　Wherein we saw thee quietly interr'd
　Hath op'd his ponderous and marble jaws　　　　　　50
　To cast thee up again. What may this mean,
　That thou, dead corse, again in complete steel
　Revisits thus the glimpses of the moon,°
　Making night hideous, and we fools of nature°
　So horridly to shake our disposition　　　　　　　　55
　With thoughts beyond the reaches of our souls?
　Say, why is this? Wherefore? What should we do?

([*Ghost*] *beckons* [*Hamlet*].)

HORATIO: It beckons you to go away with it,
　As if it some impartment° did desire
　To you alone.

32. **nature's livery:** Endowment from nature. . . . **fortune's star:** Mark placed by fortune. 36. **dram of eale:** Small amount of evil (?). 37. **of a doubt:** A famous crux, sometimes emended to *oft about* or *often dout,* i.e., often erase or do out, or to *antidote,* counteract. 38. **To . . . scandal:** To the disgrace of the whole enterprise. 40. **of health:** Of spiritual good. 43. **questionable:** Inviting question or conversation. 47. **canoniz'd:** Buried according to the canons of the church. . . . **hearsed:** Coffined. 48. **cerements:** Grave-clothes. 53. **glimpses of the moon:** Earth by night. 54. **fools of nature:** Mere men, limited to natural knowledge. 59. **impartment:** Communication.

MARCELLUS: Look with what courteous action   60
  It waves you to a more removed ground.
  But do not go with it.
HORATIO: No, by no means.
HAMLET: It will not speak. Then I will follow it.
HORATIO: Do not, my lord.
HAMLET: Why, what should be the fear?
  I do not set my life at a pin's fee,°   65
  And for my soul, what can it do to that,
  Being a thing immortal as itself?
  It waves me forth again. I'll follow it.
HORATIO: What if it tempt you toward the flood, my lord
  Or to the dreadful summit of the cliff   70
  That beetles o'er° his° base into the sea,
  And there assume some other horrible form
  Which might deprive your sovereignty of reason,°
  And draw you into madness? Think of it.
  The very place puts toys of desperation,°   75
  Without more motive, into every brain
  That looks so many fathoms to the sea
  And hears it roar beneath.
HAMLET: It waves me still.
  Go on, I'll follow thee.
MARCELLUS: You shall not go, my lord.

                                      [*They try to stop him.*]

HAMLET: Hold off your hands!   80
HORATIO: Be rul'd, you shall not go.
HAMLET: My fate cries out,
  And makes each petty artery° in this body
  As hardy as the Nemean lion's° nerve.°
  Still am I call'd. Unhand me, gentlemen.
  By heaven, I'll make a ghost of him that lets° me!   85
  I say, away! Go on. I'll follow thee.

                                  (*Exeunt Ghost and Hamlet.*)

HORATIO: He waxes desperate with imagination.
MARCELLUS: Let's follow. 'Tis not fit thus to obey him.

---

65. fee: Value.   **71. beetles o'er:** Overhangs threateningly.   **his:** Its.   **73. deprive . . . reason:** Take away the rule of reason over your mind.   **75. toys of desperation:** Fancies of desperate acts, i.e., suicide.   **82. artery:** Sinew.   **83. Nemean
lion:** One of the monsters slain by Hercules in his twelve labors.   **nerve:** Sinew.
85. lets: Hinders.

HORATIO: Have after. To what issue° will this come?
MARCELLUS: Something is rotten in the state of Denmark.   90
HORATIO: Heaven will direct it.°
MARCELLUS: Nay, let's follow him.   (*Exeunt.*)

{*Scene v*}°

(*Enter Ghost and Hamlet.*)

HAMLET: Whither wilt thou lead me? Speak. I'll go no further.
GHOST: Mark me.
HAMLET: I will.
GHOST: My hour is almost come,
   When I to sulph'rous and tormenting flames
   Must render up myself.
HAMLET: Alas, poor ghost!
GHOST: Pity me not, but lend thy serious hearing   5
   To what I shall unfold.
HAMLET: Speak. I am bound to hear.
GHOST: So art thou to revenge, when thou shalt hear.
HAMLET: What?
GHOST: I am thy father's spirit,   10
   Doom'd for a certain term to walk the night,
   And for the day confin'd to fast° in fires,
   Till the foul crimes° done in my days of nature
   Are burnt and purg'd away. But that° I am forbid
   To tell the secrets of my prison-house,   15
   I could a tale unfold whose lightest word
   Would harrow up thy soul, freeze thy young blood,
   Make thy two eyes, like stars, start from their spheres,°
   Thy knotted and combined locks° to part,
   And each particular hair to stand an end,°   20
   Like quills upon the fearful porpentine.°
   But this eternal blazon° must not be
   To ears of flesh and blood. List, list, O, list!
   If thou didst ever thy dear father love—
HAMLET: O God!   25

---

89. issue: Outcome.   **91. it:** The outcome.   **I, v. Location:** The battlements of the castle.   **12. fast:** Do penance.   **13. crimes:** Sins.   **14. But that:** Were it not that.   **18. spheres:** Eye sockets, here compared to the orbits or transparent revolving spheres in which, according to Ptolemaic astronomy, the heavenly bodies were fixed.   **19. knotted . . . locks:** Hair neatly arranged and confined. **20. an end:** On end.   **21. fearful porpentine:** Frightened porcupine.   **22. eternal blazon:** Revelation of the secrets of eternity.

GHOST: Revenge his foul and most unnatural murder.

HAMLET: Murder?

GHOST: Murder most foul, as in the best it is,
But this most foul, strange, and unnatural.

HAMLET: Haste me to know 't, that I, with wings as swift   30
As meditation or the thoughts of love,
May sweep to my revenge.

GHOST: I find thee apt;
And duller shouldst thou be than the fat weed
That roots itself in ease on Lethe° wharf,°
Wouldst thou not stir in this. Now, Hamlet, hear.   35
'Tis given out that, sleeping in my orchard,
A serpent stung me. So the whole ear of Denmark
Is by a forged process° of my death
Rankly abus'd.° But know, thou noble youth,
The serpent that did sting thy father's life   40
Now wears his crown.

HAMLET: O my prophetic soul!
My uncle!

GHOST: Ay, that incestuous, that adulterate° beast,
With witchcraft of his wits, with traitorous gifts—
O wicked wit and gifts, that have the power   45
So to seduce!—won to his shameful lust
The will of my most seeming-virtuous queen.
O Hamlet, what a falling-off was there!
From me, whose love was of that dignity
That it went hand in hand even with the vow   50
I made to her in marriage, and to decline
Upon a wretch whose natural gifts were poor
To those of mine!
But virtue, as it never will be moved,
Though lewdness court it in a shape of heaven,°   55
So lust, though to a radiant angel link'd,
Will sate itself in a celestial bed,
And prey on garbage.
But, soft, methinks I scent the morning air.
Brief let me be. Sleeping within my orchard,   60
My custom always of the afternoon,
Upon my secure° hour thy uncle stole,

---

34. Lethe: The river of forgetfulness in Hades. **wharf:** Bank. **38. forged process:** Falsified account. **39. abus'd:** Deceived. **43. adulterate:** Adulterous. **55. shape of heaven:** Heavenly form. **62. secure:** Confident, unsuspicious.

With juice of cursed hebona° in a vial,
And in the porches of my ears did pour
The leprous° distillment, whose effect   65
Holds such an enmity with blood of man
That swift as quicksilver it courses through
The natural gates and alleys of the body,
And with a sudden vigor it doth posset°
And curd, like eager° droppings into milk,   70
The thin and wholesome blood. So did it mine,
And a most instant tetter° bark'd° about,
Most lazar-like,° with vile and loathsome crust,
All my smooth body.
Thus was I, sleeping, by a brother's hand   75
Of life, of crown, of queen, at once dispatch'd,°
Cut off even in the blossoms of my sin,
Unhous'led,° disappointed,° unanel'd,°
No reck'ning made, but sent to my account
With all my imperfections on my head.   80
O, horrible! O, horrible, most horrible!
If thou hast nature° in thee, bear it not.
Let not the royal bed of Denmark be
A couch for luxury° and damned incest.
But, howsomever thou pursues this act,   85
Taint not thy mind, nor let thy soul contrive
Against thy mother aught. Leave her to heaven
And to those thorns that in her bosom lodge,
To prick and sting her. Fare thee well at once.
The glow-worm shows the matin° to be near, 90
And 'gins to pale his uneffectual fire.°
Adieu, adieu, adieu! Remember me.   *[Exit.]*
HAMLET: O all you host of heaven! O earth! What else?
And shall I couple° hell? O fie! Hold, hold, my heart,
And you, my sinews, grow not instant old,   95

---

63. hebona: Poison. (The word seems to be a form of *ebony*, though it is thought perhaps to be related to *henbane*, a poison, or to *ebenus*, yew.) **65. leprous:** Causing leprosy-like disfigurement. **69. posset:** Coagulate, curdle. **70. eager:** Sour, acid. **72. tetter:** Eruption of scabs. **bark'd:** Covered with a rough covering, like bark on a tree. **73. lazar-like:** Leper-like. **76. dispatch'd:** Suddenly deprived. **78. Unhous'led:** Without having received the sacrament [of Holy Communion]. **disappointed:** Unready (spiritually) for the last journey. **unanel'd:** Without having received extreme unction. **82. nature:** The promptings of a son. **84. luxury:** Lechery. **90. matin:** Morning. **91. uneffectual fire:** Cold light. **94. couple:** Add.

But bear me stiffly up. Remember thee!
Ay, thou poor ghost, whiles memory holds a seat
In this distracted globe.° Remember thee!
Yea, from the table° of my memory
I'll wipe away all trivial fond° records,   100
All saws° of books, all forms,° all pressures° past
That youth and observation copied there,
And thy commandment all alone shall live
Within the book and volume of my brain,
Unmix'd with baser matter. Yes, by heaven!   105
O most pernicious woman!
O villain, villain, smiling, damned villain!
My tables—meet it is I set it down,
That one may smile, and smile, and be a villain.
At least I am sure it may be so in Denmark.   110

                                                          [*Writing.*]

So, uncle, there you are. Now to my word;
It is "Adieu, adieu! Remember me."
I have sworn 't.

(*Enter Horatio and Marcellus.*)

HORATIO: My lord, my lord!
MARCELLUS: Lord Hamlet!
HORATIO: Heavens secure him!
HAMLET: So be it!   115
MARCELLUS: Illo, ho, ho, my lord!
HAMLET: Hillo, ho, ho,° boy! Come, bird, come.
MARCELLUS: How is 't, my noble lord?
HORATIO: What news, my lord?
HAMLET: O, wonderful!
HORATIO: Good my lord, tell it.
HAMLET: No, you will reveal it.   120
HORATIO: Not I, my lord, by heaven.
MARCELLUS: Nor I, my lord.
HAMLET: How say you, then, would heart of man once think it?
   But you'll be secret?
HORATIO, MARCELLUS: Ay, by heaven, my lord.
HAMLET: There's never a villain dwelling in all Denmark
   But he's an arrant° knave.   125

98. globe: Head.   99. table: Writing tablet.   100. fond: Foolish.   101. saws:
Wise sayings.   forms: Images.   pressures: Impressions stamped.   117. Hillo,
ho, ho: A falconer's call to a hawk in air. Hamlet is playing upon Marcellus's *Illo*,
i.e., *halloo*.   125. arrant: Thoroughgoing.

HORATIO: There needs no ghost, my lord, come from the grave
 To tell us this.
HAMLET: Why, right, you are in the right.
  And so, without more circumstance° at all,
  I hold it fit that we shake hands and part,
  You, as your business and desire shall point you—   130
  For every man hath business and desire,
  Such as it is—and for my own poor part,
  Look you, I'll go pray.
HORATIO: These are but wild and whirling words, my lord.
HAMLET: I am sorry they offend you, heartily;   135
  Yes, faith, heartily.
HORATIO: There's no offense, my lord.
HAMLET: Yes, by Saint Patrick,° but there is, Horatio,
  And much offense too. Touching this vision here,
  It is an honest° ghost, that let me tell you.
  For your desire to know what is between us,   140
  O'ermaster 't as you may. And now, good friends
  As you are friends, scholars, and soldiers,
  Give me one poor request.
HORATIO: What is 't, my lord? We will.
HAMLET: Never make known what you have seen tonight.   145
HORATIO, MARCELLUS: My lord, we will not.
HAMLET: Nay, but swear 't.
HORATIO: In faith,
  My lord, not I.
MARCELLUS: Nor I, my lord, in faith.
HAMLET: Upon my sword.°   [*Holds out his sword.*]
MARCELLUS: We have sworn, my lord, already.
HAMLET: Indeed, upon my sword, indeed.

                          (*Ghost cries under the stage.*)

GHOST: Swear.   150
HAMLET: Ha, ha, boy, say'st thou so? Art thou there, truepenny?°
  Come on, you hear this fellow in the cellarage.
  Consent to swear.
HORATIO: Propose the oath, my lord.
HAMLET: Never to speak of this that you have seen,
  Swear by my sword.   155

---

128. **circumstance:** Ceremony. 137. **Saint Patrick:** The keeper of purgatory
and patron saint of all blunders and confusion. 139. **honest:** I.e., a real ghost
and not an evil spirit. 148. **sword:** The hilt in the form of a cross.
151. **truepenny:** Honest old fellow.

GHOST [*beneath*]: Swear.
HAMLET: Hic et ubique?° Then we'll shift our ground.

                             [*He moves to another spot.*]

   Come hither, gentlemen,
   And lay your hands again upon my sword.
   Swear by my sword   160
   Never to speak of this that you have heard.
GHOST [*beneath*]: Swear by his sword.
HAMLET: Well said, old mole! Canst work i' th' earth so fast?
   A worthy pioner!° Once more remove, good friends.

                                 [*Moves again.*]

HORATIO: O day and night, but this is wondrous strange!   165
HAMLET: And therefore as a stranger give it welcome.
   There are more things in heaven and earth, Horatio,
   Than are dreamt of in your philosophy.°
   But come;
   Here, as before, never, so help you mercy,   170
   How strange or odd soe'er I bear myself—
   As I perchance hereafter shall think meet
   To put an antic° disposition on—
   That you, at such times seeing me, never shall,
   With arms encumb'red° thus, or this headshake,   175
   Or by pronouncing of some doubtful phrase,
   As "Well, well, we know," or "We could, an if° we would,"
   Or "If we list° to speak," or "There be, an if they might,"
   Or such ambiguous giving out,° to note°
   That you know aught of me—this do swear,   180
   So grace and mercy at your most need help you.
GHOST [*beneath*]: Swear.   [*They swear.*]
HAMLET: Rest, rest, perturbed spirit! So, gentlemen,
   With all my love I do commend me to you;
   And what so poor a man as Hamlet is   185
   May do, t' express his love and friending to you,
   God willing, shall not lack. Let us go in together,
   And still° your fingers on your lips, I pray.

---

157. **Hic et ubique:** Here and everywhere (Latin).   164. **pioner:** Pioneer, digger, miner.   168. **your philosophy:** This subject called "natural philosophy" or "science" that people talk about.   173. **antic:** Fantastic.   175. **encumb'red:** Folded or entwined.   177. **an if:** If.   178. **list:** Were inclined.   179. **giving out:** Profession of knowledge.   **note:** Give a sign, indicate.   188. **still:** Always.

The time is out of joint. O cursed spite,
That ever I was born to set it right!   190

> [*They wait for him to leave first.*]

Nay, come, let's go together.   (*Exeunt.*)

{ACT II   *Scene I*}°

(*Enter old Polonius, with his man* [*Reynaldo*].)

POLONIUS: Give him this money and these notes, Reynaldo.
REYNALDO: I will, my lord.
POLONIUS: You shall do marvel's° wisely, good Reynaldo,
  Before you visit him, to make inquire
  Of his behavior.
REYNALDO: My lord, I did intend it.   5
POLONIUS: Marry, well said, very well said. Look you, sir,
  Inquire me first what Danskers° are in Paris,
  And how, and who, what means,° and where they keep,°
  What company, at what expense; and finding
  By this encompassment° and drift° of question   10
  That they do know my son, come you more nearer
  Than your particular demands will touch it.°
  Take° you, as 'twere, some distant knowledge of him,
  As thus, "I know his father and his friends,
  And in part him." Do you mark this, Reynaldo?   15
REYNALDO: Ay, very well, my lord.
POLONIUS: "And in part him, but," you may say, "not well.
  But, if 't be he I mean, he's very wild,
  Addicted so and so," and there put on° him
  What forgeries° you please—marry, none so rank   20
  As may dishonor him, take heed of that,
  But, sir, such wanton,° wild, and usual slips,
  As are companions noted and most known
  To youth and liberty.

II, I. Location: Polonius's chambers.   3. marvel's: Marvelous(ly).   7. Danskers:
Danes.   8. what means: What wealth (they have).   keep: Dwell.   10. en-
compassment: Roundabout talking.   drift: Gradual approach or course.
11–12. come . . . it: You will find out more this way than by asking pointed questions (particular demands).   13. Take: Assume, pretend.   19. put on: Impute
to.   20. forgeries: Invented tales.   22. wanton: Sportive, unrestrained.

REYNALDO:	As gaming, my lord.	
POLONIUS:	Ay, or drinking, fencing, swearing,	25

Quarreling, drabbing° — you may go so far.

REYNALDO: My lord, that would dishonor him.

POLONIUS: Faith, no, as you may season° it in the charge.
   You must not put another scandal on him
   That he is open to incontinency;°   30
   That's not my meaning. But breathe his faults so quaintly°
   That they may seem the taints of liberty,°
   The flash and outbreak of a fiery mind,
   A savageness in unreclaimed° blood,
   Of general assault.°

REYNALDO: But, my good lord —   35

POLONIUS: Wherefore should you do this?

REYNALDO: Ay, my lord,
   I would know that.

POLONIUS: Marry, sir, here's my drift,
   And, I believe, it is a fetch of wit.°
   You laying these slight sullies on my son,
   As 'twere a thing a little soil'd i' th' working,°   40
   Mark you,
   Your party in converse,° him you would sound,°
   Having ever° seen in the prenominate crimes°
   The youth you breathe° of guilty, be assur'd
   He closes with you in this consequence:°   45
   "Good sir," or so, or "friend," or "gentleman,"
   According to the phrase or the addition°
   Of man and country.

REYNALDO: Very good, my lord.

POLONIUS: And then, sir, does 'a this — 'a does — what was I about to
   say?
   By the mass, I was about to say something.   50
   Where did I leave?

REYNALDO: At "closes in the consequence."

---

26. drabbing: Whoring.   **28. season:** Temper, soften.   **30. incontinency:** Habitual loose behavior.   **31. quaintly:** Delicately, ingeniously.   **32. taints of liberty:** Faults resulting from freedom.   **34. unreclaimed:** Untamed.   **35. general assault:** Tendency that assails all unrestrained youth.   **38. fetch of wit:** Clever trick.   **40. soil'd i' th' working:** Shopworn.   **42. converse:** Conversation. **sound:** Sound out.   **43. Having ever:** If he has ever. **prenominate crimes:** Before-mentioned offenses.   **44. breathe:** Speak.   **45. closes . . . consequence:** Follows your lead in some fashion as follows.   **47. addition:** Title.

POLONIUS: At "closes in the consequence," ay, marry.
  He closes thus: "I know the gentleman;
  I saw him yesterday, or th' other day,
  Or then, or then, with such, or such, and, as you say,   55
  There was 'a gaming, there o'ertook in 's rouse,°
  There falling out° at tennis," or perchance,
  "I saw him enter such a house of sale,"
  Videlicet,° a brothel, or so forth. See you now,
  Your bait of falsehood takes this carp° of truth;   60
  And thus do we of wisdom and of reach,°
  With windlasses° and with assays of bias,°
  By indirections find directions° out.
  So by my former lecture and advice
  Shall you my son. You have me, have you not?   65
REYNALDO: My lord, I have.
POLONIUS: God buy ye; fare ye well.
REYNALDO: Good my lord.
POLONIUS: Observe his inclination in yourself.°
REYNALDO: I shall, my lord.
POLONIUS: And let him ply° his music.
REYNALDO: Well, my lord.   70
POLONIUS: Farewell.   (*Exit Reynaldo.*)

(*Enter Ophelia.*)

            How now, Ophelia, what's the matter?
OPHELIA: O, my lord, my lord, I have been so affrighted!
POLONIUS: With what, i' th' name of God?
OPHELIA: My lord, as I was sewing in my closet,°
  Lord Hamlet, with his doublet° all unbrac'd,°   75
  No hat upon his head, his stockings fouled,
  Ungart'red, and down-gyved to his ankle,°
  Pale as his shirt, his knees knocking each other,
  And with a look so piteous in purport

---

56. **o'ertook in 's rouse:** Overcome by drink.   57. **falling out:** Quarreling.
59. **Videlicet:** Namely.   60. **carp:** A fish.   61. **reach:** Capacity, ability.
62. **windlasses:** Circuitous paths (literally, circuits made to head off the game in
hunting).   **assays of bias:** Attempts through indirection (like the curving path of
the bowling ball, which is biased or weighted to one side).   63. **directions:** The
way things really are.   68. **in yourself:** In your own person (as well as by asking
questions).   70. **let him ply:** See that he continues to study.   74. **closet:** Private
chamber.   75. **doublet:** Close-fitting jacket.   **unbrac'd:** Unfastened.   77. **down-
gyved to his ankle:** Fallen to the ankles (like gyves or fetters).

As if he had been loosed out of hell   80
  To speak of horrors—he comes before me.
POLONIUS: Mad for thy love?
OPHELIA: My lord, I do not know,
  But truly I do fear it.
POLONIUS: What said he?
OPHELIA: He took me by the wrist and held me hard.
  Then goes he to the length of all his arm,   85
  And, with his other hand thus o'er his brow
  He falls to such perusal of my face
  As 'a would draw it. Long stay'd he so.
  At last, a little shaking of mine arm
  And thrice his head thus waving up and down,   90
  He rais'd a sigh so piteous and profound
  As it did seem to shatter all his bulk°
  And end his being. That done, he lets me go,
  And, with his head over his shoulder turn'd,
  He seem'd to find his way without his eyes,   95
  For out o' doors he went without their helps,
  And, to the last, bended their light on me.
POLONIUS: Come, go with me. I will go seek the King.
  This is the very ecstasy° of love
  Whose violent property° fordoes° itself   100
  And leads the will to desperate undertakings
  As oft as any passion under heaven
  That does afflict our natures. I am sorry.
  What, have you given him any hard words of late?
OPHELIA: No, my good lord, but, as you did command,   105
  I did repel his letters and denied
  His access to me.
POLONIUS: That hath made him mad.
  I am sorry that with better heed and judgment
  I had not quoted° him. I fear'd he did but trifle
  And meant to wrack thee; but, beshrew my jealousy!°   110
  By heaven, it is as proper to our age°
  To cast beyond° ourselves in our opinions
  As it is common for the younger sort
  To lack discretion. Come, go we to the King.

---

92. **bulk:** Body. 99. **ecstasy:** Madness. 100. **property:** Nature. **fordoes:**
Destroys. 109. **quoted:** Observed. 110. **beshrew my jealousy:** A plague upon
my suspicious nature. 111. **proper . . . age:** Characteristic of us (old) men.
112. **cast beyond:** Overshoot, miscalculate.

This must be known, which, being kept close,° might move   115
More grief to hide than hate to utter love.°
Come.   (*Exeunt.*)

[*Scene II*]°

(*Flourish. Enter King and Queen, Rosencrantz, and Guildenstern [with others].*)

KING: Welcome, dear Rosencrantz and Guildenstern.
   Moreover that° we much did long to see you,
   The need we have to use you did provoke
   Our hasty sending. Something have you heard
   Of Hamlet's transformation—so call it,   5
   Sith° nor th' exterior nor° the inward man
   Resembles that° it was. What it should be,
   More than his father's death, that thus hath put him
   So much from th' understanding of himself,
   I cannot dream of. I entreat you both   10
   That, being of so young days° brought up with him,
   And sith so neighbor'd to his youth and havior,
   That you vouchsafe your rest° here in our court
   Some little time, so by your companies
   To draw him on to pleasures, and to gather   15
   So much as from occasion you may glean,
   Whether aught to us unknown afflicts him thus,
   That, open'd,° lies within our remedy.
QUEEN: Good gentlemen, he hath much talk'd of you
   And sure I am two men there is not living   20
   To whom he more adheres. If it will please you
   To show us so much gentry° and good will
   As to expend your time with us awhile
   For the supply and profit° of our hope,
   Your visitation shall receive such thanks   25
   As fits a king's remembrance.
ROSENCRANTZ: Both your Majesties
   Might, by the sovereign power you have of us,

---

115. close: Secret. **115–16. might . . . love:** Might cause more grief (to others)
by hiding the knowledge of Hamlet's strange behavior to Ophelia than hatred by
telling it. **II, II. Location:** The castle. **2. Moreover that:** Besides the fact that.
6. Sith: Since. **nor . . . nor:** Neither . . . nor. **7. that:** What. **11. of . . . days:**
From such early youth. **13. vouchsafe your rest:** Please to stay. **18. open'd:**
Revealed. **22. gentry:** Courtesy. **24. supply and profit:** Aid and successful
outcome.

Put your dread pleasures more into command
Than to entreaty.
GUILDENSTERN: But we both obey,
And here give up ourselves in the full bent°   30
To lay our service freely at your feet,
To be commanded.
KING: Thanks, Rosencrantz and gentle Guildenstern.
QUEEN: Thanks, Guildenstern and gentle Rosencrantz.
And I beseech you instantly to visit   35
My too much changed son. Go, some of you,
And bring these gentlemen where Hamlet is.
GUILDENSTERN: Heavens make our presence and our practices
Pleasant and helpful to him!
QUEEN: Ay, amen!

(Exeunt Rosencrantz and Guildenstern [with some Attendants].)

(Enter Polonius.)

POLONIUS: Th' ambassadors from Norway, my good lord,   40
Are joyfully return'd.
KING: Thou still° hast been the father of good news.
POLONIUS: Have I, my lord? I assure my good liege
I hold my duty, as I hold my soul,
Both to my God and to my gracious king;   45
And I do think, or else this brain of mine
Hunts not the trail of policy so sure
As it hath us'd to do, that I have found
The very cause of Hamlet's lunacy.
KING: O, speak of that! That do I long to hear.   50
POLONIUS: Give first admittance to th' ambassadors.
My news shall be the fruit° to that great feast.
KING: Thyself do grace to them, and bring them in.

(Exit Polonius.)

He tells me, my dear Gertrude, he hath found
The head and source of all your son's distemper.   55
QUEEN: I doubt° it is no other but the main,°
His father's death, and our o'erhasty marriage.

(Enter Ambassadors [Voltimand and Cornelius, with Polonius].)

---

30. **in ... bent:** To the utmost degree of our capacity. **42. still:** Always.
52. **fruit:** Dessert. **56. doubt:** Fear, suspect. **main:** Chief point, principal
concern.

KING: Well, we shall sift him. — Welcome, my good friends!
    Say, Voltimand, what from our brother Norway?
VOLTIMAND: Most fair return of greetings and desires.   60
    Upon our first,° he sent out to suppress
    His nephew's levies, which to him appear'd
    To be a preparation 'gainst the Polack,
    But, better look'd into, he truly found
    It was against your Highness. Whereat griev'd   65
    That so his sickness, age, and impotence
    Was falsely borne in hand,° sends out arrests
    On Fortinbras, which he, in brief, obeys,
    Receives rebuke from Norway, and in fine°
    Makes vow before his uncle never more   70
    To give th' assay° of arms against your Majesty.
    Whereon old Norway, overcome with joy,
    Gives him three score thousand crowns in annual fee,
    And his commission to employ those soldiers,
    So levied as before, against the Polack,   75
    With an entreaty, herein further shown,

                                   [*Giving a paper.*]

    That it might please you to give quiet pass
    Through your dominions for this enterprise,
    On such regards of safety and allowance°
    As therein are set down.
KING: It likes° us well;   80
    And at our more consider'd'd° time we'll read,
    Answer, and think upon this business.
    Meantime we thank you for your well-took labor.
    Go to your rest; at night we'll feast together.
    Most welcome home!   (*Exeunt Ambassadors.*)
POLONIUS: This business is well ended.   85
    My liege, and madam, to expostulate°
    What majesty should be, what duty is,
    Why day is day, night night, and time is time,
    Were nothing but to waste night, day, and time.
    Therefore, since brevity is the soul of wit,°   90

---

61. **Upon our first:** At our first words on the business. 67. **borne in hand:**
Deluded, taken advantage of. 69. **in fine:** In the end. 71. **assay:** Trial.
79. **On . . . allowance:** With such pledges of safety and provisos. 80. **likes:**
Pleases. 81. **consider'd:** Suitable for deliberation. 86. **expostulate:** Expound.
90. **wit:** Sound sense or judgment.

And tediousness the limbs and outward flourishes,
I will be brief. Your noble son is mad.
Mad call I it, for, to define true madness,
What is 't but to be nothing else but mad?
But let that go.
QUEEN: More matter, with less art.   95
POLONIUS: Madam, I swear I use no art at all.
That he is mad, 'tis true; 'tis true 'tis pity,
And pity 'tis 'tis true—a foolish figure,°
But farewell it, for I will use no art.
Mad let us grant him, then, and now remains   100
That we find out the cause of this effect,
Or rather say, the cause of this defect,
For this effect defective comes by cause.°
Thus it remains, and the remainder thus.
Perpend.°   105
I have a daughter—have while she is mine—
Who, in her duty and obedience, mark,
Hath given me this. Now gather, and surmise.
[*Reads the letter.*] "To the celestial and my soul's idol,
the most beautified Ophelia"—   110
That's an ill phrase, a vile phrase; "beautified" is a vile
phrase. But you shall hear. Thus: [*Reads.*]
"In her excellent white bosom, these, etc."
QUEEN: Came this from Hamlet to her?
POLONIUS: Good madam, stay awhile; I will be faithful.   [*Reads.*] 115
"Doubt° thou the stars are fire,
   Doubt that the sun doth move,
Doubt truth to be a liar,
   But never doubt I love.
O dear Ophelia, I am ill at these numbers.° I have   120
not art to reckon° my groans. But that I love thee
best, O most best, believe it. Adieu.
            Thine evermore, most dear lady, whilst this
                   machine° is to him, Hamlet."
This in obedience hath my daughter shown me,   125
And, more above,° hath his solicitings,

---

98. figure: Figure of speech.   **103. For . . . cause:** I.e., for this defective behavior,
this madness has a cause.   **105. Perpend:** Consider.   **116. Doubt:** Suspect,
question.   **120. ill . . . numbers:** Unskilled at writing verses.   **121. reckon:**
(1) Count, (2) number metrically, scan.   **124. machine:** Body.   **126. more above:**
Moreover.

As they fell out° by time, by means, and place,
All given to mine ear.
KING: But how hath she
    Receiv'd his love?
POLONIUS: What do you think of me?
KING: As of a man faithful and honorable.   130
POLONIUS: I would fain prove so. But what might you think,
    When I had seen this hot love on the wing—
    As I perceiv'd it, I must tell you that,
    Before my daughter told me—what might you,
    Or my dear Majesty your Queen here, think,   135
    If I had play'd the desk or table-book,°
    Or given my heart a winking,° mute and dumb,
    Or look'd upon this love with idle sight?°
    What might you think? No, I went round° to work,
    And my young mistress thus I did bespeak:°   140
    "Lord Hamlet is a prince, out of thy star;°
    This must not be." And then I prescripts gave her,
    That she should lock herself from his resort,
    Admit no messengers, receive no tokens.
    Which done, she took the fruits of my advice;   145
    And he, repelled—a short tale to make—
    Fell into a sadness, then into a fast,
    Thence to a watch,° thence into a weakness,
    Thence to a lightness,° and, by this declension,°
    Into the madness wherein now he raves,   150
    And all we mourn for.
KING: Do you think this?
QUEEN: It may be, very like.
POLONIUS: Hath there been such a time—I would fain know that—
    That I have positively said "'Tis so,"
    When it prov'd otherwise?
KING: Not that I know.   155
POLONIUS [pointing to his head and shoulder]: Take this from this, if this
    be otherwise.
    If circumstances lead me, I will find

---

127. fell out: Occurred.   **136. play'd ... table-book:** Remained shut up, concealing the information.   **137. winking:** Closing of the eyes.   **138. with idle
sight:** Complacently or uncomprehendingly.   **139. round:** Roundly, plainly.
140. bespeak: Address.   **141. out of thy star:** Above your sphere, position.
148. watch: State of sleeplessness.   **149. lightness:** Light-headedness.   **declen-**
sion: Decline, deterioration.

Where truth is hid, though it were hid indeed
Within the center.°
KING: How may we try it further?
POLONIUS: You know, sometimes he walks four hours together   160
Here in the lobby.
QUEEN: So he does indeed.
POLONIUS: At such a time I'll loose my daughter to him.
Be you and I behind an arras° then.
Mark the encounter. If he love her not
And be not from his reason fall'n thereon,°   165
Let me be no assistant for a state,
But keep a farm and carters.
KING: We will try it.

(Enter Hamlet [reading on a book].)

QUEEN: But look where sadly the poor wretch comes reading.
POLONIUS: Away, I do beseech you both, away.
I'll board° him presently.

                    (Exeunt King and Queen [with Attendants].)

                            O, give me leave.   170
How does my good Lord Hamlet?
HAMLET: Well, God-a-mercy.°
POLONIUS: Do you know me, my lord?
HAMLET: Excellent well. You are a fishmonger.°
POLONIUS: Not I, my lord.   175
HAMLET: Then I would you were so honest a man.
POLONIUS: Honest, my lord?
HAMLET: Ay, sir. To be honest, as this world goes, is to be one man pick'd
out of ten thousand.
POLONIUS: That's very true, my lord.   180
HAMLET: For if the sun breed maggots in a dead dog, being a good kiss-
ing carrion° — Have you a daughter?
POLONIUS: I have, my lord.
HAMLET: Let her not walk i' th' sun.° Conception° is a blessing, but as
your daughter may conceive, friend, look to 't.   185

159. center: Middle point of the earth (which is also the center of the Ptolemaic
universe). 163. arras: Hanging, tapestry. 165. thereon: On that account.
170. board: Accost. 172. God-a-mercy: Thank you. 174. fishmonger: Fish
merchant (with connotation of *bawd, procurer*[?]). 181–82. good kissing carrion: A good piece of flesh for kissing, or for the sun to kiss. 184. i' th' sun:
With additional implication of the sunshine of princely favors. Conception:
(1) Understanding, (2) pregnancy.

POLONIUS [*aside*]: How say you by that? Still harping on my daughter. Yet he knew me not at first; 'a said I was a fishmonger. 'A is far gone. And truly in my youth I suff'red much extremity for love, very near this. I'll speak to him again. — What do you read, my lord?

HAMLET: Words, words, words.   190

POLONIUS: What is the matter,° my lord?

HAMLET: Between who?

POLONIUS: I mean, the matter that you read, my lord.

HAMLET: Slanders, sir, for the satirical rogue says here that old men have gray beards, that their faces are wrinkled, their eyes purging° thick   195 amber and plum-tree gum, and that they have a plentiful lack of wit, together with most weak hams. All which, sir, though I most power- fully and potently believe, yet I hold it not honesty° to have it thus set down, for you yourself, sir, shall grow old as I am, if like a crab you could go backward.   200

POLONIUS [*aside*]: Though this be madness, yet there is method in 't. — Will you walk out of the air, my lord?

HAMLET: Into my grave.

POLONIUS: Indeed, that's out of the air. [*Aside.*] How pregnant° some- times his replies are! A happiness° that often madness hits on, which   205 reason and sanity could not so prosperously° be deliver'd of. I will leave him, [and suddenly contrive the means of meeting between him] and my daughter. — My honorable lord, I will most humbly take my leave of you.

HAMLET: You cannot, sir, take from me any thing that I will more will-   210 ingly part withal — except my life, except my life, except my life.

(*Enter Guildenstern and Rosencrantz.*)

POLONIUS: Fare you well, my lord.

HAMLET: These tedious old fools!°

POLONIUS: You go to seek the Lord Hamlet; there he is.

ROSENCRANTZ [*to Polonius*]: God save you, sir!   215

[*Exit Polonius.*]

GUILDENSTERN: My honor'd lord!

ROSENCRANTZ: My most dear lord!

HAMLET: My excellent good friends! How dost thou, Guildenstern? Ah, Rosencrantz! Good lads, how do you both?

191. **matter:** Substance (but Hamlet plays on the sense of *basis for a dispute*). 195. **purging:** Discharging. 198. **honesty:** Decency. 204. **pregnant:** Full of meaning. 205. **happiness:** Felicity of expression. 206. **prosperously:** Suc- cessfully. 213. **old fools:** I.e., old men like Polonius.

ROSENCRANTZ: As the indifferent° children of the earth.   220
GUILDENSTERN: Happy in that we are not over-happy. On Fortune's cap
  we are not the very button.
HAMLET: Nor the soles of her shoe?
ROSENCRANTZ: Neither, my lord.
HAMLET: Then you live about her waist, or in the middle of her favors?   225
GUILDENSTERN: Faith, her privates° we.
HAMLET: In the secret parts of Fortune? O, most true; she is a strumpet.°
  What news?
ROSENCRANTZ: None, my lord, but the world's grown honest.
HAMLET: Then is doomsday near. But your news is not true. [Let me   230
  question more in particular. What have you, my good friends, deserv'd
  at the hands of Fortune that she sends you to prison hither?
GUILDENSTERN: Prison, my lord?
HAMLET: Denmark's a prison.
ROSENCRANTZ: Then is the world one.   235
HAMLET: A goodly one, in which there are many confines,° wards,° and
  dungeons, Denmark being one o' th' worst.
ROSENCRANTZ: We think not so, my lord.
HAMLET: Why then 'tis none to you, for there is nothing either good or
  bad but thinking makes it so. To me it is a prison.   240
ROSENCRANTZ: Why then, your ambition makes it one. 'Tis too narrow
  for your mind.
HAMLET: O God, I could be bounded in a nutshell and count myself a
  king of infinite space, were it not that I have bad dreams.
GUILDENSTERN: Which dreams indeed are ambition, for the very sub-   245
  stance of the ambitious° is merely the shadow of a dream.
HAMLET: A dream itself is but a shadow.
ROSENCRANTZ: Truly, and I hold ambition of so airy and light a quality
  that it is but a shadow's shadow.
HAMLET: Then are our beggars bodies,° and our monarchs and out-   250
  stretch'd° heroes the beggars' shadows. Shall we to th' court? For, by
  my fay,° I cannot reason.
ROSENCRANTZ, GUILDENSTERN: We'll wait upon° you.

220. indifferent: Ordinary.   **226. privates:** Close acquaintances (with sexual
pun on *private parts*).   **227. strumpet:** Prostitute (a common epithet for indiscriminate Fortune, see line 449 p. 809).   **236. confines:** Places of confinement.
wards: Cells.   **245–46. the very . . . ambitious:** That seemingly very substantial
thing which the ambitious pursue.   **250. bodies:** Solid substances rather than
shadows (since beggars are not ambitious).   **250–51. outstretch'd:** (1) Far-
reaching in their ambition, (2) elongated as shadows.   **252. fay:** Faith.
253. wait upon: Accompany, attend.

HAMLET: No such matter. I will not sort° you with the rest of my servants, for, to speak to you like an honest man, I am most dreadfully　255
attended.°] But, in the beaten way° of friendship, what make° you at
Elsinore?

ROSENCRANTZ: To visit you, my lord, no other occasion.

HAMLET: Beggar that I am, I am even poor in thanks; but I thank you,
and sure, dear friends, my thanks are too dear a halfpenny.° Were you　260
not sent for? Is it your own inclining? Is it a free visitation? Come,
come, deal justly with me. Come, come; nay, speak.

GUILDENSTERN: What should we say, my lord?

HAMLET: Why, anything, but to th' purpose. You were sent for; and there
is a kind of confession in your looks which your modesties have not　265
craft enough to color. I know the good King and Queen have sent
for you.

ROSENCRANTZ: To what end, my lord?

HAMLET: That you must teach me. But let me conjure° you, by the rights
of our fellowship, by the consonancy of our youth,° by the obligation　270
of our ever-preserv'd love, and by what more dear a better proposer°
could charge° you withal, be even° and direct with me, whether you
were sent for, or no?

ROSENCRANTZ [aside to Guildenstern]: What say you?

HAMLET [aside]: Nay then, I have an eye of° you.—If you love me, hold　275
not off.

GUILDENSTERN: My lord, we were sent for.

HAMLET: I will tell you why; so shall my anticipation prevent your discovery,° and your secrecy to the King and Queen molt no feather.° I
have of late—but wherefore I know not—lost all my mirth, forgone　280
all custom of exercises; and indeed it goes so heavily with my disposition that this goodly frame, the earth, seems to me a sterile promontory; this most excellent canopy, the air, look you, this brave°
o'erhanging firmament, this majestical roof fretted° with golden fire,
why, it appeareth nothing to me but a foul and pestilent congregation　285
of vapors. What a piece of work is a man! How noble in reason, how

254. **sort:** Class, associate.　255–56. **dreadfully attended:** Waited upon in
slovenly fashion.　256. **beaten way:** Familiar path.　**make:** Do.　260. **dear a
halfpenny:** Expensive at the price of a halfpenny, i.e., of little worth.　269. **conjure:** Adjure, entreat.　270. **consonancy of our youth:** The fact that we are of
the same age.　271. **better proposer:** More skillful propounder.　272. **charge:**
Urge. **even:** Straight, honest.　275. **of:** On.　278–79. **prevent your discovery:**
Forestall your disclosure.　279. **molt no feather:** Not diminish in the least.
283. **brave:** Splendid.　284. **fretted:** Adorned (with fret-work, as in a vaulted
ceiling).

infinite in faculties, in form and moving how express° and admirable,
in action how like an angel, in apprehension how like a god! The
beauty of the world, the paragon of animals! And yet, to me, what is
this quintessence° of dust? Man delights not me—no, nor woman nei-   290
ther, though by your smiling you seem to say so.

ROSENCRANTZ: My lord, there was no such stuff in my thoughts.

HAMLET: Why did you laugh then, when I said "man delights not me"?

ROSENCRANTZ: To think, my lord, if you delight not in man, what lenten
entertainment° the players shall receive from you. We coted° them on   295
the way, and hither are they coming, to offer you service.

HAMLET: He that plays the king shall be welcome; his Majesty shall have
tribute of me. The adventurous knight shall use his foil and target,°
the lover shall not sigh gratis, the humorous man° shall end his part in
peace, [the clown shall make those laugh whose lungs are tickle o' th'   300
sere°], and the lady shall say her mind freely, or the blank verse shall
halt° for 't. What players are they?

ROSENCRANTZ: Even those you were wont to take such delight in, the
tragedians of the city.

HAMLET: How chances it they travel? Their residence,° both in reputa-   305
tion and profit, was better both ways.

ROSENCRANTZ: I think their inhibition° comes by the means of the
innovation.°

HAMLET: Do they hold the same estimation they did when I was in the
city? Are they so follow'd?   310

ROSENCRANTZ: No, indeed, are they not.

[HAMLET: How comes it? Do they grow rusty?

ROSENCRANTZ: Nay, their endeavor keeps in the wonted° pace. But there
is, sir, an aery° of children, little eyases,° that cry out on the top of
question,° and are most tyrannically° clapp'd for 't. These are now the   315

---

287. express: Well-framed (?), exact (?).   **290. quintessence:** The fifth essence
of ancient philosophy, beyond earth, water, air, and fire, supposed to be the substance of the heavenly bodies and to be latent in all things.   **294–95. lenten
entertainment:** Meager reception (appropriate to Lent).   **295. coted:** Overtook
and passed beyond.   **298. foil and target:** Sword and shield.   **299. humorous
man:** Eccentric character, dominated by one trait or "humor."   **300–01. tickle o'
th' sere:** Easy on the trigger, ready to laugh easily. (*Sere* is part of a gunlock.)
302. halt: Limp.   **305. residence:** Remaining in one place, i.e., in the city.
307. inhibition: Formal prohibition (from acting plays in the city).   **308. innovation:** I.e., the new fashion in satirical plays performed by boy actors in the "private" theaters; or possibly a political uprising; or the strict limitations set on the
theater in London in 1600.   **313. wonted:** Usual.   **314. aery:** Nest.   **eyases:**
Young hawks.   **314–15. cry . . . question:** Speak shrilly, dominating the controversy (in decrying the public theaters).   **315. tyrannically:** Outrageous.

fashion, and so berattle° the common stages°—so they call them—
that many wearing rapiers° are afraid of goose-quills° and dare scarce
come thither.

HAMLET: What, are they children? Who maintains 'em? How are they
escoted?° Will they pursue the quality° no longer than they can sing?°   320
Will they not say afterwards, if they should grow themselves to
common° players—as it is most like, if their means are no better—
their writers do them wrong, to make them exclaim against their own
succession?°

ROSENCRANTZ: Faith, there has been much to do° on both sides, and the   325
nation holds it no sin to tarre° them to controversy. There was, for a
while, no money bid for argument° unless the poet and the player
went to cuffs in the question.°

HAMLET: Is 't possible?

GUILDENSTERN: O, there has been much throwing about of brains.   330

HAMLET: Do the boys carry it away?°

ROSENCRANTZ: Ay, that they do, my lord—Hercules and his load° too.°]

HAMLET: It is not very strange, for my uncle is King of Denmark, and
those that would make mouths° at him while my father liv'd, give
twenty, forty, fifty, a hundred ducats° apiece for his picture in little.°   335
'Sblood,° there is something in this more than natural, if philosophy
could find it out.

(A flourish [of trumpets within].)

GUILDENSTERN: There are the players.

HAMLET: Gentlemen, you are welcome to Elsinore. Your hands, come
then. Th' appurtenance of welcome is fashion and ceremony. Let me   340
comply° with you in this garb,° lest my extent° to the players, which, I

---

316. **berattle:** Berate. **common stages:** Public theaters. 317. **many wearing
rapiers:** Many men of fashion, who were afraid to patronize the common players
for fear of being satirized by the poets who wrote for the children. **goose-quills:**
Pens of satirists. 320. **escoted:** Maintained. **quality:** (Acting) profession.
no longer . . . sing: Only until their voices change. 322. **common:** Regular,
adult. 324. **succession:** Future careers. 325. **to do:** Ado. 326. **tarre:** Set on
(as dogs). 327. **argument:** Plot for a play. 328. **went . . . question:** Came to
blows in the play itself. 331. **carry it away:** Win the day. 332. **Hercules . . .
load:** Thought to be an allusion to the sign of the Globe Theatre, which was
Hercules bearing the world on his shoulder. 312–32. **How . . . load too:** The
passage, omitted from the early quartos, alludes to the so-called War of
the Theatres, 1599–1602, the rivalry between the children companies and the
adult actors. 334. **mouths:** Faces. 335. **ducats:** Gold coins. **in little:** In
miniature. 336. **'Sblood:** By His (God's, Christ's) blood. 341. **comply:** Observe the formalities of courtesy. **garb:** Manner. **my extent:** The extent of my
showing courtesy.

tell you, must show fairly outwards,° should more appear like enter-
tainment° than yours. You are welcome. But my uncle-father and
aunt-mother are deceiv'd.

GUILDENSTERN: In what, my dear lord?   345

HAMLET: I am but mad north-north-west.° When the wind is southerly I
know a hawk from a handsaw.°

(*Enter Polonius.*)

POLONIUS: Well be with you, gentlemen!

HAMLET: Hark you, Guildenstern, and you too; at each ear a hearer. That
great baby you see there is not yet out of his swaddling-clouts.°   350

ROSENCRANTZ: Happily° he is the second time come to them; for they say
an old man is twice a child.

HAMLET: I will prophesy he comes to tell me of the players; mark it.—
You say right, sir, o' Monday morning, 'twas then indeed.

POLONIUS: My lord, I have news to tell you.   355

HAMLET: My lord, I have news to tell you. When Roscius° was an actor in
Rome—

POLONIUS: The actors are come hither, my lord.

HAMLET: Buzz,° buzz!

POLONIUS: Upon my honor—   360

HAMLET: Then came each actor on his ass—

POLONIUS: The best actors in the world, either for tragedy, comedy,
history, pastoral, pastoral-comical, historical-pastoral, tragical-
historical, tragical-comical-historical-pastoral, scene individable,° or
poem unlimited.° Seneca° cannot be too heavy, nor Plautus° too light.   365
For the law of writ and the liberty,° these are the only men.

HAMLET: O Jephthah, judge of Israel,° what a treasure hadst thou!

POLONIUS: What a treasure had he, my lord?

---

342. **show fairly outwards:** Look cordial to outward appearances.   **342–43. entertainment:** A (warm) reception.   **346. north-north-west:** Only partly, at times.
347. hawk, handsaw: Mattock (or *hack*) and a carpenter's cutting tool respectively;
also birds, with a play on *hernshaw* or heron.   **350. swaddling-clouts:** Cloths in
which to wrap a newborn baby.   **351. Happily:** Haply, perhaps.   **356. Roscius:**
A famous Roman actor who died in 62 B.C.E.   **359. Buzz:** An interjection used to
denote stale news.   **364. scene individable:** A play observing the unity of place.
365. poem unlimited: A play disregarding the unities of time and place.
Seneca: Writer of Latin tragedies.   **Plautus:** Writer of Latin comedy.
366. law . . . liberty: Dramatic composition both according to rules and without
rules, i.e., "classical" and "romantic" dramas.   **367. Jephthah . . . Israel:**
Jephthah had to sacrifice his daughter; see Judges 11. Hamlet goes on to quote
from a ballad on the theme.

HAMLET: Why,
  "One fair daughter, and no more,   370
  The which he loved passing° well."
POLONIUS [*aside*]: Still on my daughter.
HAMLET: Am I not i' th' right, old Jephthah?
POLONIUS: If you call me Jephthah, my lord, I have a daughter that I love
  passing well.   375
HAMLET: Nay, that follows not.
POLONIUS: What follows, then, my lord?
HAMLET: Why,
  "As by lot, God wot,"°
  and then, you know,   380
  "It came to pass, as most like° it was."
  The first row° of the pious chanson° will show you more, for look
  where my abridgement° comes.

(*Enter the Players.*)

  You are welcome, masters; welcome, all. I am glad to see thee well.
  Welcome, good friends. O, old friend! Why, thy face is valanc'd° since I 385
  saw thee last. Com'st thou to beard° me in Denmark? What, my young
  lady° and mistress? By 'r lady, your ladyship is nearer to heaven than
  when I saw you last, by the altitude of a chopine.° Pray God your
  voice, like a piece of uncurrent° gold, be not crack'd within the ring.°
  Masters, you are all welcome. We'll e'en to 't like French falconers, fly 390
  at anything we see. We'll have a speech straight.° Come, give us a taste
  of your quality; come, a passionate speech.
FIRST PLAYER: What speech, my good lord?
HAMLET: I heard thee speak me a speech once, but it was never acted, or,
  if it was, not above once, for the play, I remember, pleas'd not the mil- 395
  lion; 'twas caviary to the general.° But it was—as I receiv'd it, and others, whose judgments in such matters cried in the top of° mine—an

---

371. passing: Surpassingly.   **379. wot:** Knows.   **381. like:** Likely, probable.
382. row: Stanza.   **chanson:** Ballad, song.   **383. my abridgement:** Something
that cuts short my conversation; also, a diversion.   **385. valanc'd:** Fringed (with a
beard).   **386. beard:** Confront (with obvious pun).   **386–87. young lady:** Boy
playing women's parts.   **388. chopine:** Thick-soled shoe of Italian fashion.
389. uncurrent: Not passable as lawful coinage.   **crack'd . . . ring:** Changed
from adolescent to male voice, no longer suitable for women's roles. (Coins fea-
tured rings enclosing the sovereign's head; if the coin was cracked within this ring,
it was unfit for currency.)   **391. straight:** At once.   **396. caviary to the general:**
Caviar to the multitude, i.e., a choice dish too elegant for coarse tastes.
397. cried in the top of: Spoke with greater authority than.

excellent play, well digested in the scenes, set down with as much
modesty as cunning.° I remember one said there were no sallets° in
the lines to make the matter savory, nor no matter in the phrase that   400
might indict° the author of affectation, but call'd it an honest method,
as wholesome as sweet, and by very much more handsome than fine.°
One speech in 't I chiefly lov'd: 'twas Aeneas' tale to Dido, and there-
about of it especially when he speaks of Priam's slaughter.° If it live in
your memory, begin at this line: let me see, let me see—   405
"The rugged Pyrrhus,° like th' Hyrcanian beast"°—
'Tis not so. It begins with Pyrrhus:
"The rugged Pyrrhus, he whose sable° arms,
Black as his purpose, did the night resemble
When he lay couched in the ominous horse,°   410
Hath now this dread and black complexion smear'd
With heraldry more dismal.° Head to foot
Now is he total gules,° horridly trick'd°
With blood of fathers, mothers, daughters, sons,
Bak'd and impasted° with the parching streets,°   415
That lend a tyrannous and a damned light
To their lord's° murder. Roasted in wrath and fire,
And thus o'er-sized° with coagulate gore,
With eyes like carbuncles, the hellish Pyrrhus
Old grandsire Priam seeks."   420
So proceed you.

POLONIUS: 'Fore God, my lord, well spoken, with good accent and good
discretion.

FIRST PLAYER: "Anon he finds him
Striking too short at Greeks. His antique sword,   425
Rebellious to his arm, lies where it falls,
Repugnant° to command. Unequal match'd,

---

399. cunning: Skill.   **sallets:** Salad, i.e., spicy improprieties.   **401. indict:**
Convict.   **402. fine:** Elaborately ornamented, showy.   **404. Priam's slaughter:**
The slaying of the ruler of Troy, when the Greeks finally took the city.
406. Pyrrhus: A Greek hero in the Trojan War, also known as Neoptolemus, son
of Achilles.   **Hyrcanian beast:** I.e., the tiger. (See Virgil, *Aeneid*, IV, 266; compare the whole speech with Marlowe's *Dido Queen of Carthage*, II, I, 214 ff.)
408. sable: Black (for reasons of camouflage during the episode of the Trojan
horse).   **410. ominous horse:** Trojan horse, by which the Greeks gained access
to Troy.   **412. dismal:** Ill-omened.   **413. gules:** Red (a heraldic term).   **trick'd:**
Adorned, decorated.   **415. impasted:** Crusted, like a thick paste.   **with . . .
streets:** By the parching heat of the streets (because of the fires everywhere).
417. their lord's: Priam's.   **418. o'er-sized:** Covered as with size or glue.
427. Repugnant: Disobedient, resistant.

Pyrrhus at Priam drives, in rage strikes wide,
But with the whiff and wind of his fell° sword
Th' unnerved father falls. [Then senseless Ilium,°]   430
Seeming to feel this blow, with flaming top
Stoops to his° base, and with a hideous crash
Takes prisoner Pyrrhus' ear. For, lo! His sword,
Which was declining on the milky head
Of reverend Priam, seem'd i' th' air to stick.   435
So as a painted° tyrant Pyrrhus stood,
And, like a neutral to his will and matter,°
Did nothing.
But, as we often see, against° some storm,
A silence in the heavens, the rack° stand still,   440
The bold winds speechless, and the orb below
As hush as death, anon the dreadful thunder
Doth rend the region,° so, after Pyrrhus' pause,
Aroused vengeance sets him new a-work,
And never did the Cyclops'° hammers fall   445
On Mars's armor forg'd for proof eterne°
With less remorse than Pyrrhus' bleeding sword
Now falls on Priam.
Out, out, thou strumpet Fortune! All you gods,
In general synod,° take away her power!   450
Break all the spokes and fellies° from her wheel,
And bowl the round nave° down the hill of heaven,
As low as to the fiends!"
POLONIUS: This is too long.
HAMLET: It shall to the barber's with your beard. — Prithee say on. He's   455
    for a jig° or a tale of bawdry, or he sleeps. Say on, come to Hecuba.°
FIRST PLAYER: "But who, ah woe! had seen the mobled° queen"—
HAMLET: "The mobled queen?"
POLONIUS: That's good. "Mobled queen" is good.
FIRST PLAYER: "Run barefoot up and down, threat'ning the flames   460
    With bisson rheum,° a clout° upon that head

429. fell: Cruel.   430. senseless Ilium: Insensate Troy.   432. his: Its.
436. painted: Painted in a picture.   437. like ... matter: As though poised inde-
cisively between his intention and its fulfillment.   439. against: Just before.
440. rack: Mass of clouds.   443. region: Sky.   445. Cyclops: Giant armor
makers in the smithy of Vulcan.   446. proof eterne: Eternal resistance to
assault.   450. synod: Assembly.   451. fellies: Pieces of wood forming the rim
of a wheel.   452. nave: Hub.   456. jig: Comic song and dance often given at
the end of a play.   Hecuba: Wife of Priam.   457. mobled: Muffled.   461. bis-
son rheum: Blinding tears.   clout: Cloth.

Where late the diadem stood, and for a robe,
About her lank and all o'er-teemed° loins,
A blanket, in the alarm of fear caught up—
Who this had seen, with tongue in venom steep'd,   465
'Gainst Fortune's state° would treason have pronounc'd.°
But if the gods themselves did see her then
When she saw Pyrrhus make malicious sport
In mincing with his sword her husband's limbs,
The instant burst of clamor that she made,   470
Unless things mortal move them not at all,
Would have made milch° the burning eyes of heaven,
And passion in the gods."

POLONIUS: Look whe'er° he has not turn'd his color and has tears in 's
  eyes. Prithee, no more.   475

HAMLET: 'Tis well; I'll have thee speak out the rest of this soon. Good my
  lord, will you see the players well bestow'd?° Do you hear, let them be
  well us'd, for they are the abstract° and brief chronicles of the time.
  After your death you were better have a bad epitaph than their ill
  report while you live.   480

POLONIUS: My lord, I will use them according to their desert.

HAMLET: God's bodkin,° man, much better! Use every man after his
  desert, and who shall scape whipping? Use them after your own honor
  and dignity. The less they deserve, the more merit is in your bounty.
  Take them in.   485

POLONIUS: Come, sirs.

HAMLET: Follow him, friends. We'll hear a play tomorrow. [*As they start to
  leave, Hamlet detains the First Player.*] Dost thou hear me, old friend? Can
  you play the Murder of Gonzago?

FIRST PLAYER: Ay, my lord.   490

HAMLET: We'll ha 't tomorrow night. You could, for need, study a speech
  of some dozen or sixteen lines, which I would set down and insert in 't,
  could you not?

FIRST PLAYER: Ay, my lord.

HAMLET: Very well. Follow that lord, and look you mock him not.—My   495
  good friends, I'll leave you till night. You are welcome to Elsinore.

                                            (*Exeunt Polonius and Players.*)

463. o'er-teemed: Worn out with bearing children.   466. state: Rule, managing.
pronounc'd: Proclaimed.   472. milch: Milky moist with tears.   474. whe'er:
Whether.   477.   bestow'd: Lodged.   478.   abstract: Summary   account.
482. God's bodkin: By God's (Christ's) little body, *bodykin* (not to be confused
with *bodkin*, dagger).

ROSENCRANTZ: Good my lord!

(*Exeunt [Rosencrantz and Guildenstern].*)

HAMLET: Ay, so, God buy you.—Now I am alone.
  O, what a rogue and peasant slave am I!
  Is it not monstrous that this player here,   500
  But in a fiction, in a dream of passion,
  Could force his soul so to his own conceit°
  That from her working all his visage wann'd,°
  Tears in his eyes, distraction in his aspect,
  A broken voice, and his whole function suiting   505
  With forms to his conceit?° And all for nothing!
  For Hecuba!
  What's Hecuba to him, or he to Hecuba,
  That he should weep for her? What would he do,
  Had he the motive and the cue for passion   510
  That I have? He would drown the stage with tears
  And cleave the general ear with horrid speech,
  Make mad the guilty and appall the free,°
  Confound the ignorant, and amaze indeed
  The very faculties of eyes and ears. Yet I,   515
  A dull and muddy-mettled° rascal, peak,°
  Like John-a-dreams,° unpregnant of° my cause,
  And can say nothing—no, not for a king
  Upon whose property° and most dear life
  A damn'd defeat was made. Am I a coward?   520
  Who calls me villain? Breaks my pate across?
  Plucks off my beard, and blows it in my face?
  Tweaks me by the nose? Gives me the lie° i' th' throat,
  As deep as to the lungs? Who does me this?
  Ha, 'swounds, I should take it; for it cannot be   525
  But I am pigeon-liver'd,° and lack gall
  To make oppression bitter, or ere this
  I should have fatted all the region kites°
  With this slave's offal. Bloody, bawdy villain!

502. **conceit:** Conception. 503. **wann'd:** Grew pale. 505–06. **his whole . . . conceit:** His whole being responded with actions to suit his thought. 513. **free:** Innocent. 516. **muddy-mettled:** Dull-spirited. **peak:** Mope, pine. 517. **John-a-dreams:** Sleepy dreaming idler. **unpregnant of:** Not quickened by. 519. **property:** The crown; perhaps also character, quality. 523. **Gives me the lie:** Calls me a liar. 526. **pigeon-liver'd:** The pigeon or dove was popularly supposed to be mild because it secreted no gall. 528. **region kites:** Kites (birds of prey) of the air, from the vicinity.

Remorseless, treacherous, lecherous, kindless° villain!   530
[O, vengeance!]
Why, what an ass am I! This is most brave,
That I, the son of a dear father murder'd,
Prompted to my revenge by heaven and hell,
Must, like a whore, unpack my heart with words,   535
And fall a-cursing, like a very drab,°
A stallion!° Fie upon 't, foh! About,° my brains!
Hum, I have heard
That guilty creatures sitting at a play
Have by the very cunning of the scene   540
Been struck so to the soul that presently°
They have proclaim'd their malefactions;
For murder, though it have no tongue, will speak
With most miraculous organ. I'll have these players
Play something like the murder of my father   545
Before mine uncle. I'll observe his looks;
I'll tent° him to the quick. If 'a do blench,°
I know my course. The spirit that I have seen
May be the devil, and the devil hath power
T' assume a pleasing shape; yea, and perhaps   550
Out of my weakness and my melancholy,
As he is very potent with such spirits,°
Abuses° me to damn me. I'll have grounds
More relative° than this. The play's the thing
Wherein I'll catch the conscience of the King.   555

                                                                    (*Exit.*)

[ACT III   *Scene I*]°

(*Enter King, Queen, Polonius, Ophelia, Rosencrantz, Guildenstern, Lords.*)

KING: And can you, by no drift of conference,°
    Get from him why he puts on this confusion,

---

530. kindless: Unnatural. **536. drab:** Prostitute. **537. stallion:** Prostitute
(male or female). (Many editors follow the Folio reading of *scullion*.) **About:**
About it, to work. **541. presently:** At once. **547. tent:** Probe. **blench:** Quail,
flinch. **552. spirits:** Humors (of melancholy). **553. Abuses:** Deludes.
554. relative: Closely related, pertinent. **III, I. Location:** The castle. **1. drift
of conference:** Direction of conversation.

Grating so harshly all his days of quiet
With turbulent and dangerous lunacy?
ROSENCRANTZ: He does confess he feels himself distracted,   5
But from what cause 'a will by no means speak.
GUILDENSTERN: Nor do we find him forward° to be sounded,°
But with a crafty madness keeps aloof
When we would bring him on to some confession
Of his true state.
QUEEN: Did he receive you well?   10
ROSENCRANTZ: Most like a gentleman.
GUILDENSTERN: But with much forcing of his disposition.°
ROSENCRANTZ: Niggard of question,° but of our demands
Most free in his reply.
QUEEN: Did you assay° him
To any pastime?   15
ROSENCRANTZ: Madam, it so fell out that certain players
We o'er-raught° on the way. Of these we told him,
And there did seem in him a kind of joy
To hear of it. They are here about the court,
And, as I think, they have already order   20
This night to play before him.
POLONIUS: 'Tis most true,
And he beseech'd me to entreat your Majesties
To hear and see the matter.
KING: With all my heart, and it doth much content me
To hear him so inclin'd.   25
Good gentlemen, give him a further edge,°
And drive his purpose into these delights.
ROSENCRANTZ: We shall, my lord.

(Exeunt Rosencrantz and Guildenstern.)

KING: Sweet Gertrude, leave us too,
For we have closely° sent for Hamlet hither,
That he, as 'twere by accident, may here   30
Affront° Ophelia.
Her father and myself, [lawful espials,°]
Will so bestow ourselves that seeing, unseen,
We may of their encounter frankly judge,

---

7. forward: Willing. **sounded:** Tested deeply. **12. disposition:** Inclination.
13. question: Conversation. **14. assay:** Try to win. **17. o'er-raught:** Overtook
and passed. **26. edge:** Incitement. **29. closely:** Privately. **31. Affront:** Confront, meet. **32. espials:** Spies.

And gather by him, as he is behav'd,   35
If 't be th' affliction of his love or no
That thus he suffers for.
QUEEN: I shall obey you.
And for your part, Ophelia, I do wish
That your good beauties be the happy cause
Of Hamlet's wildness. So shall I hope your virtues   40
Will bring him to his wonted way again,
To both your honors.
OPHELIA: Madam, I wish it may.

[*Exit Queen.*]

POLONIUS: Ophelia, walk you here.—Gracious,° so please you,
We will bestow ourselves. [*To Ophelia.*] Read on this book,

[*Gives her a book.*]

That show of such an exercise° may color°   45
Your loneliness. We are oft to blame in this—
'Tis too much prov'd°—that with devotion's visage
And pious action we do sugar o'er
The devil himself.
KING [*aside*]: O, 'tis too true!   50
How smart a lash that speech doth give my conscience!
The harlot's cheek, beautied with plast'ring art,
Is not more ugly to° the thing° that helps it
Than is my deed to my most painted word.
O heavy burden!   55
POLONIUS: I hear him coming. Let's withdraw, my lord.

[*King and Polonius withdraw.°*]

(*Enter Hamlet.* [*Ophelia pretends to read a book.*])

HAMLET: To be, or not to be, that is the question:
Whether 'tis nobler in the mind to suffer
The slings and arrows of outrageous fortune,
Or to take arms against a sea of troubles,   60
And by opposing end them. To die, to sleep—
No more—and by a sleep to say we end

43. Gracious: Your Grace (i.e., the King).   **45. exercise:** Act of devotion. (The book she reads is one of devotion.)   **color:** Give a plausible appearance to.   **47. too much prov'd:** Too often shown to be true, too often practiced.   **53. to:** Compared to.   **thing:** I.e., the cosmetic.   [S.D.] *withdraw:* The King and Polonius may retire behind an arras. The stage directions specify that they "enter" again near the end of the scene.

The heart-ache and the thousand natural shocks
That flesh is heir to. 'Tis a consummation
Devoutly to be wish'd. To die, to sleep;   65
To sleep, perchance to dream. Ay, there's the rub,°
For in that sleep of death what dreams may come
When we have shuffled° off this mortal coil,°
Must give us pause. There's the respect°
That makes calamity of so long life.°   70
For who would bear the whips and scorns of time,
Th' oppressor's wrong, the proud man's contumely,°
The pangs of despis'd° love, the law's delay,
The insolence of office,° and the spurns°
That patient merit of th' unworthy takes,   75
When he himself might his quietus° make
With a bare bodkin?° Who would fardels° bear,
To grunt and sweat under a weary life,
But that the dread of something after death,
The undiscover'd country from whose bourn°   80
No traveler returns, puzzles the will,
And makes us rather bear those ills we have
Than fly to others that we know not of?
Thus conscience does make cowards of us all
And thus the native hue° of resolution   85
Is sicklied o'er with the pale cast° of thought,
And enterprises of great pitch° and moment°
With this regard° their currents° turn awry,
And lose the name of action. — Soft you now,
The fair Ophelia. Nymph, in thy orisons°   90
Be all my sins remembr'red.
OPHELIA: Good my lord,
How does your honor for this many a day?
HAMLET: I humbly thank you; well, well, well.
OPHELIA: My lord, I have remembrances of yours,
That I have longed long to re-deliver.   95
I pray you, now receive them.   [Offers tokens.]

66. **rub:** Literally, an obstacle in the game of bowls. 68. **shuffled:** Sloughed,
cast. **coil:** Turmoil. 69. **respect:** Consideration. 70. **of . . . life:** So long-lived.
72. **contumely:** Insolent abuse. 73. **despis'd:** Rejected. 74. **office:** Officialdom.
spurns: Insults. 76. **quietus:** Acquittance; here, death. 77. **bodkin:** Dagger.
fardels: Burdens. 80. **bourn:** Boundary. 85. **native hue:** Natural color, complexion. 86. **cast:** Shade of color. 87. **pitch:** Height (as of a falcon's flight).
moment: Importance. 88. **regard:** Respect, consideration. **currents:** Courses.
90. **orisons:** Prayers.

HAMLET: No, not I, I never gave you aught.
OPHELIA: My honor'd lord, you know right well you did,
  And with them words of so sweet breath compos'd
  As made these things more rich. Their perfume lost,   100
  Take these again, for to the noble mind
  Rich gifts wax poor when givers prove unkind.
  There, my lord.   [*Gives tokens.*]
HAMLET: Ha, ha! Are you honest?°
OPHELIA: My lord?   105
HAMLET: Are you fair?°
OPHELIA: What means your lordship?
HAMLET: That if you be honest and fair, your honesty° should admit no
  discourse° to your beauty.
OPHELIA: Could beauty, my lord, have better commerce° than with   110
  honesty?
HAMLET: Ay, truly, for the power of beauty will sooner transform honesty
  from what it is to a bawd than the force of honesty can translate
  beauty into his likeness. This was sometime° a paradox,° but now the
  time° gives it proof. I did love you once.   115
OPHELIA: Indeed, my lord, you made me believe so.
HAMLET: You should not have believ'd me, for virtue cannot so inocu-
  late° our old stock but we shall relish of it.° I lov'd you not.
OPHELIA: I was the more deceiv'd.
HAMLET: Get thee to a nunn'ry.° Why wouldst thou be a breeder of sin-   120
  ners? I am myself indifferent honest;° but yet I could accuse me of
  such things that it were better my mother had not borne me: I am very
  proud, revengeful, ambitious, with more offenses at my beck° than I
  have thoughts to put them in, imagination to give them shape, or time
  to act them in. What should such fellows as I do crawling between   125
  earth and heaven? We are arrant knaves, all; believe none of us. Go thy
  ways to a nunn'ry. Where's your father?
OPHELIA: At home, my lord.
HAMLET: Let the doors be shut upon him, that he may play the fool
  nowhere but in 's own house.   130
  Farewell.

104. honest: (1) Truthful; (2) chaste.   106. fair: (1) Beautiful; (2) just, honorable.   108. your honesty: Your chastity.   109. discourse: Familiar dealings.
110. commerce: Dealings.   114. sometime: Formerly.   paradox: A view opposite to commonly held opinion.   114–15. the time: The present age.
117–18. inoculate: Graft, be engrafted to.   118. but . . . it: That we do not still
have about us a taste of the old stock; i.e., retain our sinfulness.   120. nunn'ry:
(1) Convent, (2) brothel.   121. indifferent honest: Reasonably virtuous.
123. beck: Command.

OPHELIA: O, help him, you sweet heavens!

HAMLET: If thou dost marry, I'll give thee this plague for thy dowry: be
thou as chaste as ice, as pure as snow, thou shalt not escape calumny.
Get thee to a nunn'ry, farewell. Or, if thou wilt needs marry, marry a   135
fool, for wise men know well enough what monsters° you° make of
them. To a nunn'ry, go, and quickly too. Farewell.

OPHELIA: Heavenly powers, restore him!

HAMLET: I have heard of your paintings too, well enough. God hath
given you one face, and you make yourselves another. You jig,° and   140
amble, and you lisp, you nickname God's creatures, and make your
wantonness your ignorance.° Go to, I'll no more on 't; it hath made me
mad. I say, we will have no moe marriage. Those that are married
already—all but one—shall live. The rest shall keep as they are. To a
nunn'ry, go.   (*Exit.*)   145

OPHELIA: O, what a noble mind is here o'erthrown!
The courtier's, soldier's, scholar's, eye, tongue, sword,
Th' expectancy and rose of the fair state,°
The glass of fashion and the mold of form,°
Th' observ'd of all observers,° quite, quite down!   150
And I, of ladies most deject and wretched,
That suck'd the honey of his music vows,
Now see that noble and most sovereign reason,
Like sweet bells jangled, out of time and harsh,
That unmatch'd form and feature of blown° youth   155
Blasted with ecstasy.° O, woe is me,
T' have seen what I have seen, see what I see!

(*Enter King and Polonius.*)

KING: Love? His affections do not that way tend;
Nor what he spake, though it lack'd form a little,
Was not like madness. There's something in his soul,   160
O'er which his melancholy sits on brood,
And I do doubt° the hatch and the disclose°
Will be some danger; which for to prevent,
I have in quick determination

---

136. monsters: An allusion to the horns of a cuckold. **you:** You women.
140. jig: Dance and sing affectedly and wantonly.   **141–42. make . . . ignorance:**
Excuse your affection on the grounds of your ignorance.   **148. Th' expectancy . . . state:** The hope and ornament of the kingdom made fair (by him).
149. The glass . . . form: The mirror of fashion and the pattern of courtly behavior.   **150. observ'd . . . observers:** The center of attention and honor in the
court.   **155. blown:** Blooming.   **156. ecstasy:** Madness.   **162. doubt:** Fear.
disclose: Disclosure.

Thus set it down: he shall with speed to England,   165
For the demand of° our neglected tribute.
Haply the seas and countries different
With variable° objects shall expel
This something-settled° matter in his heart,
Whereon his brains still beating puts him thus   170
From fashion of himself.° What think you on 't?
POLONIUS: It shall do well. But yet do I believe
The origin and commencement of his grief
Sprung from neglected love. — How now, Ophelia?
You need not tell us what Lord Hamlet said;   175
We heard it all. — My lord, do as you please,
But, if you hold it fit, after the play
Let his queen mother all alone entreat him
To show his grief. Let her be round° with him;
And I'll be plac'd, so please you, in the ear   180
Of all their conference. If she find him not,
To England send him, or confine him where
Your wisdom best shall think.
KING: It shall be so.
Madness in great ones must not unwatch'd go.

                                                        (*Exeunt.*)

                          [*Scene II*]°

(*Enter Hamlet and three of the Players.*)

HAMLET: Speak the speech, I pray you, as I pronounc'd it to you, trip-
    pingly on the tongue. But if you mouth it, as many of our players° do, I
    had as lief the town-crier spoke my lines. Nor do not saw the air too
    much with your hand, thus, but use all gently; for in the very torrent,
    tempest, and, as I may say, whirlwind of your passion, you must   5
    acquire and beget a temperance that may give it smoothness. O, it
    offends me to the soul to hear a robustious° periwig-pated° fellow tear
    a passion to tatters, to very rags, to split the ears of the groundlings,°
    who for the most part are capable of° nothing but inexplicable dumb-

---

166. For . . . of: To demand.   168. variable: Various.   169. something-settled:
Somewhat settled.   171. From . . . himself: Out of his natural manner.
179. round: Blunt.   III, II. Location: The castle.   2. our players: Indefinite
use; i.e., *players nowadays.*   7. robustious: Violent, boisterous.   periwig-pated:
Wearing a wig.   8. groundlings: Spectators who paid least and stood in the yard
of the theater.   9. capable of: Susceptible of being influenced by.

shows and noise. I would have such a fellow whipp'd for o'er-doing   10
Termagant.° It out-herods Herod.° Pray you, avoid it.

FIRST PLAYER: I warrant your honor.

HAMLET: Be not too tame neither, but let your own discretion be your
tutor. Suit the action to the word, the word to the action, with this special observance, that you o'erstep not the modesty of nature. For any-   15
thing so o'erdone is from° the purpose of playing, whose end, both at
the first and now, was and is, to hold, as 't were, the mirror up to
nature, to show virtue her feature, scorn her own image, and the very
age and body of the time his° form and pressure.° Now this overdone,
or come tardy off,° though it makes the unskillful laugh, cannot but   20
make the judicious grieve, the censure of which one° must in your
allowance o'erweigh a whole theater of others. O, there be players that
I have seen play, and heard others praise, and that highly, not to speak
it profanely, that, neither having th' accent of Christians nor the gait of
Christian, pagan, nor man, have so strutted and bellow'd that I have   25
thought some of nature's journeymen° had made men and not made
them well, they imitated humanity so abominably.

FIRST PLAYER: I hope we have reform'd that indifferently° with us, sir.

HAMLET: O, reform it altogether. And let those that play your clowns
speak no more than is set down for them; for there be of them° that   30
will themselves laugh, to set on some quantity of barren° spectators to
laugh too, though in the mean time some necessary question of the
play be then to be consider'd. That's villainous, and shows a most pitiful ambition in the fool that uses it. Go, make you ready.

[Exeunt Players.]

(*Enter Polonius, Guildenstern, and Rosencrantz.*)

How now, my lord? Will the King hear this piece of work?   35

POLONIUS: And the Queen too, and that presently.°

HAMLET: Bid the players make haste.

[Exit Polonius.]

Will you two help to hasten them?

11. Termagant: A god of the Saracens; a character in the St. Nicholas play, where
one of his worshipers, leaving him in charge of goods, returns to find them stolen;
whereupon he beats the god or idol, which howls vociferously.   **Herod:** Herod of
Jewry. (A character in *The Slaughter of the Innocents* and other cycle plays. The
part was played with great noise and fury.)   **16. from:** Contrary to.   **19. his:** Its.
pressure: Stamp, impressed character.   **20. come tardy off:** Inadequately done.
21. the censure . . . one: The judgment of even one of whom.   **26. journeymen:**
Laborers not yet masters in their trade.   **28. indifferently:** Tolerably.   **30. of
them:** Some among them.   **31. barren:** I.e., of wit.   **36. presently:** At once.

ROSENCRANTZ: Ay, my lord.   (*Exeunt they two.*)
HAMLET: What ho, Horatio!

(*Enter Horatio.*)

HORATIO: Here, sweet lord, at your service.   40
HAMLET: Horatio, thou art e'en as just a man
  As e'er my conversation cop'd withal.°
HORATIO: O, my dear lord —
HAMLET: Nay, do not think I flatter;
  For what advancement may I hope from thee
  That no revenue hast but thy good spirits,   45
  To feed and clothe thee? Why should the poor be flatter'd?
  No, let the candied° tongue lick absurd pomp,
  And crook the pregnant° hinges of the knee
  Where thrift° may follow fawning. Dost thou hear?
  Since my dear soul was mistress of her choice   50
  And could of men distinguish her election,
  Sh' hath seal'd thee for herself, for thou hast been
  As one, in suff'ring all, that suffers nothing,
  A man that Fortune's buffets and rewards
  Hast ta'en with equal thanks; and blest are those   55
  Whose blood° and judgment are so well commeddled°
  That they are not a pipe for Fortune's finger
  To sound what stop° she please. Give me that man
  That is not passion's slave, and I will wear him
  In my heart's core, ay, in my heart of heart,   60
  As I do thee. — Something too much of this. —
  There is a play tonight before the King.
  One scene of it comes near the circumstance
  Which I have told thee of my father's death.
  I prithee, when thou seest that act afoot,   65
  Even with the very comment of thy soul°
  Observe my uncle. If his occulted° guilt
  Do not itself unkennel in one speech,
  It is a damned° ghost that we have seen,
  And my imaginations are as foul   70
  As Vulcan's stithy.° Give him heedful note,

---

42. my . . . withal: My contact with people provided opportunity for encounter
with.   **47. candied:** Sugared, flattering.   **48. pregnant:** Compliant.   **49. thrift:**
Profit.   **56. blood:** Passion.   **commeddled:** Commingled.   **58. stop:** Hole in a
wind instrument for controlling the sound.   **66. very . . . soul:** Inward and sagacious criticism.   **67. occulted:** Hidden.   **69. damned:** In league with Satan.
71. stithy: Smithy, place of stiths (anvils).

For I mine eyes will rivet to his face,
And after we will both our judgments join
In censure of his seeming.°
HORATIO: Well, my lord.
If 'a steal aught the whilst this play is playing,   75
And scape detecting, I will pay the theft.

([*Flourish.*] *Enter trumpets and kettledrums, King, Queen, Polonius, Ophelia,*
[*Rosencrantz, Guildenstern, and other Lords, with Guards carrying torches*].)

HAMLET: They are coming to the play. I must be idle. Get you a place.

[*The King, Queen, and courtiers sit.*]

KING: How fares our cousin Hamlet?
HAMLET: Excellent, i' faith, of the chameleon's dish:° I eat the air, promise-
cramm'd. You cannot feed capons so.   80
KING: I have nothing with° this answer, Hamlet. These words are not
mine.°
HAMLET: No, nor mine now. [*To Polonius.*] My lord, you played once i' th'
university, you say?
POLONIUS: That did I, my lord; and was accounted a good actor.   85
HAMLET: What did you enact?
POLONIUS: I did enact Julius Caesar. I was killed i' th' Capitol; Brutus
kill'd me.
HAMLET: It was a brute part of him to kill so capital a calf there. Be the
players ready?   90
ROSENCRANTZ: Ay, my lord; they stay upon your patience.
QUEEN: Come hither, my dear Hamlet, sit by me.
HAMLET: No, good mother, here's metal more attractive.
POLONIUS [*to the King*]: O, ho, do you mark that?
HAMLET: Lady, shall I lie in your lap?   95

[*Lying down at Ophelia's feet.*]

OPHELIA: No, my lord.
[HAMLET: I mean, my head upon your lap?
OPHELIA: Ay, my lord.]
HAMLET: Do you think I meant country° matters?
OPHELIA: I think nothing, my lord.   100

---

74. censure of his seeming: Judgment of his appearance or behavior.
79. chameleon's dish: Chameleons were supposed to feed on air. Hamlet deliberately misinterprets the King's *fares* as *feeds*. By his phrase *eat the air* he also plays
on the idea of feeding himself with the promise of succession, of being the *heir*.
81. have . . . with: Make nothing of.   **81–82. are not mine:** Do not respond to
what I asked.   **99. country:** With a bawdy pun.

HAMLET: That's a fair thought to lie between maids' legs.
OPHELIA: What is, my lord?
HAMLET: Nothing.
OPHELIA: You are merry, my lord.
HAMLET: Who, I?   105
OPHELIA: Ay, my lord.
HAMLET: O God, your only jig-maker.° What should a man do but be
    merry? For look you how cheerfully my mother looks, and my father
    died within 's° two hours.
OPHELIA: Nay, 'tis twice two months, my lord.   110
HAMLET: So long? Nay then, let the devil wear black for I'll have a suit of
    sables.° O heavens! Die two months ago, and not forgotten yet? Then
    there's hope a great man's memory may outlive his life half a year. But,
    by 'r lady, 'a must build churches, then, or else shall 'a suffer not think-
    ing on,° with the hobby-horse, whose epitaph is "For, O, for, O, the   115
    hobby-horse is forgot."°

(*The trumpets sound. Dumb show follows.*)

(*Enter a King and a Queen [very lovingly]; the Queen embracing him, and he
her. [She kneels and makes show of protestation unto him.] He takes her up,
and declines his head upon her neck. He lies him down upon a bank of flowers.
She, seeing him asleep, leaves him. Anon comes in another man, takes off his
crown, kisses it, pours poison in the sleeper's ears, and leaves him. The Queen
returns; finds the King dead, makes passionate action. The Poisoner, with some
three or four, come in again, seem to condole with her. The dead body is carried
away. The Poisoner woos the Queen with gifts; she seems harsh awhile but in
the end accepts love.*)

                                                                    [*Exeunt.*]

OPHELIA: What means this, my lord?
HAMLET: Marry, this' miching mallecho;° it means mischief.
OPHELIA: Belike° this show imports the argument° of the play.

(*Enter Prologue.*)

---

107. only jig-maker: Very best composer of jigs (song and dance).   **109. within 's:**
Within this.   **111–12. suit of sables:** Garments trimmed with the fur of the sable
and hence suited for a wealthy person, not a mourner (with a pun on *sable* black).
114–15. suffer . . . on: Undergo oblivion.   **115–16. "For . . . forgot":** Verse of a
song occurring also in *Love's Labor's Lost*, III, I, 30. The hobby-horse was a character made up to resemble a horse, appearing in the Morris dance and such May-
game sports. This song laments the disappearance of such customs under
pressure from the Puritans.   **118. this' miching mallecho:** This is sneaking mischief.   **119. Belike:** Probably.   **argument:** Plot.

HAMLET: We shall know by this fellow. The players cannot keep counsel;°   120
   they'll tell all.
OPHELIA: Will 'a tell us what this show meant?
HAMLET: Ay, or any show that you will show him. Be not you° asham'd to
   show, he'll not shame to tell you what it means.
OPHELIA: You are naught, you are naught.° I'll mark the play.   125
PROLOGUE: For us, and for our tragedy,
   Here stooping° to your clemency,
   We beg your hearing patiently.   [*Exit.*]
HAMLET: Is this a prologue, or the posy of a ring?°
OPHELIA: 'Tis brief, my lord.   130
HAMLET: As woman's love.

(*Enter* [*two Players as*] *King and Queen.*)

PLAYER KING: Full thirty times hath Phoebus' cart° gone round
   Neptune's salt wash° and Tellus'° orbed ground,
   And thirty dozen moons with borrowed° sheen
   About the world have times twelve thirties been,   135
   Since love our hearts and Hymen° did our hands
   Unite commutual° in most sacred bands.
PLAYER QUEEN: So many journeys may the sun and moon
   Make us again count o'er ere love be done!
   But, woe is me, you are so sick of late,   140
   So far from cheer and from your former state,
   That I distrust you. Yet, though I distrust,°
   Discomfort you, my lord, it nothing° must.
   For women's fear and love hold quantity;°
   In neither aught, or in extremity.   145
   Now, what my love is, proof° hath made you know,
   And as my love is siz'd, my fear is so.
   Where love is great, the littlest doubts are fear;
   Where little fears grow great, great love grows there.
PLAYER KING: Faith, I must leave thee, love, and shortly too;   150
   My operant° powers their functions leave to do.°

---

120. **counsel:** Secret.   123. **Be not you:** If you are not.   125. **naught:** Indecent.
127. **stooping:** Bowing.   129. **posy . . . ring:** Brief motto in verse inscribed in a
ring.   132. **Phoebus' cart:** The sun god's chariot.   133. **salt wash:** The sea.
Tellus: Goddess of the earth, of the *orbed ground*.   134. **borrowed:** Reflected.
136. **Hymen:** God of matrimony.   137. **commutual:** Mutually.   142. **distrust:**
Am anxious about.   143. **nothing:** Not at all.   144. **hold quantity:** Keep proportion with one another.   146. **proof:** Experience.   151. **operant:** Active. **leave
to do:** Cease to perform.

And thou shalt live in this fair world behind,
Honor'd, belov'd; and haply one as kind
For husband shalt thou—

PLAYER QUEEN: O, confound the rest!
Such love must needs be treason in my breast.   155
In second husband let me be accurst!
None wed the second but who kill'd the first.

HAMLET: Wormwood, wormwood.

PLAYER QUEEN: The instances° that second marriage move°
Are base respects of thrift,° but none of love.   160
A second time I kill my husband dead,
When second husband kisses me in bed.

PLAYER KING: I do believe you think what now you speak,
But what we do determine oft we break.
Purpose is but the slave to memory,°   165
Of violent birth, but poor validity,°
Which now, like fruit unripe, sticks on the tree,
But fall unshaken when they mellow be.
Most necessary 'tis that we forget
To pay ourselves what to ourselves is debt.°   170
What to ourselves in passion we propose,
The passion ending, doth the purpose lose.
The violence of either grief or joy
Their own enactures° with themselves destroy.
Where joy most revels, grief doth most lament;   175
Grief joys, joy grieves, on slender accident.
This world is not for aye,° nor 'tis not strange
That even our loves should with our fortunes change;
For 'tis a question left us yet to prove,
Whether love lead fortune, or else fortune love.   180
The great man down, you mark his favorite flies;
The poor advanc'd makes friends of enemies.
And hitherto doth love on fortune tend;
For who not needs° shall never lack a friend,
And who in want° a hollow friend doth try,°   185

---

159. instances: Motives. **move:** Motivate. **160. base . . . thrift:** Ignoble considerations of material prosperity. **165. Purpose . . . memory:** Our good intentions are subject to forgetfulness. **166. validity:** Strength, durability. **169–70. Most . . . debt:** It's inevitable that in time we forget the obligations we have imposed on ourselves. **174. enactures:** Fulfillments. **177. aye:** Ever. **184. who not needs:** He who is not in need (of wealth). **185. who in want:** He who is in need. **try:** Test (his generosity).

Directly seasons him° his enemy.
But, orderly to end where I begun,
Our wills and fates do so contrary run
That our devices still° are overthrown;
Our thoughts are ours, their ends° none of our own.   190
So think thou wilt no second husband wed,
But die thy thoughts when thy first lord is dead.
PLAYER QUEEN: Nor earth to me give food, nor heaven light,
Sport and repose lock from me day and night,
To desperation turn my trust and hope,   195
An anchor's cheer° in prison be my scope!°
Each opposite° that blanks° the face of joy
Meet what I would have well and it destroy!
Both here and hence° pursue me lasting strife,
If, once a widow, ever I be wife!   200
HAMLET: If she should break it now!
PLAYER KING: 'Tis deeply sworn. Sweet, leave me here awhile;
My spirits grow dull, and fain I would beguile
The tedious day with sleep.   [*Sleeps.*]
PLAYER QUEEN: Sleep rock thy brain,
And never come mischance between us twain!   205

                                                    [*Exit.*]

HAMLET: Madam, how like you this play?
QUEEN: The lady doth protest too much, methinks.
HAMLET: O, but she'll keep her word.
KING: Have you heard the argument?° Is there no offense in 't?
HAMLET: No, no, they do but jest, poison in jest; no offense i' th' world.   210
KING: What do you call the play?
HAMLET: "The Mouse-trap." Marry, how? Tropically.° This play is the
   image of a murder done in Vienna. Gonzago is the Duke's name; his
   wife, Baptista. You shall see anon. 'Tis a knavish piece of work, but
   what of that? Your Majesty, and we that have free° souls, it touches us   215
   not. Let the gall'd jade° winch,° our withers° are unwrung.°

186. **seasons him:** Ripens him into.   189. **devices still:** Intentions continually.
190. **ends:** Results.   196. **anchor's cheer:** Anchorite's or hermit's fare.   **my
scope:** The extent of my happiness.   197. **opposite:** Adverse thing.   **blanks:**
Causes to blanch or grow pale.   199. **hence:** In the life hereafter.   209. **argument:**
Plot.   212. **Tropically:** Figuratively. (The first quarto reading, *tropically*, suggests a
pun on *trap* in *Mouse-trap*.)   215. **free:** Guiltless.   216. **gall'd jade:** Horse whose
hide is rubbed by saddle or harness.   **winch:** Wince.   **withers:** The part between
the horse's shoulder blades.   **unwrung:** Not rubbed sore.

(*Enter Lucianus.*)

    This is one Lucianus, nephew to the King.
OPHELIA: You are as good as a chorus,° my lord.
HAMLET: I could interpret between you and your love, if I could see the
    puppets dallying.°   220
OPHELIA: You are keen, my lord, you are keen.
HAMLET: It would cost you a groaning to take off mine edge.
OPHELIA: Still better, and worse.°
HAMLET: So° you mistake° your husbands. Begin, murderer, leave thy
    damnable faces, and begin. Come, the croaking raven doth bellow for 225
    revenge.
LUCIANUS: Thoughts black, hands apt, drugs fit, and time agreeing,
    Confederate season,° else no creature seeing,
    Thou mixture rank, of midnight weeds collected,
    With Hecate's ban° thrice blasted, thrice infected,   230
    Thy natural magic and dire property
    On wholesome life usurp immediately.

                 [*Pours the poison into the sleeper's ears.*]

HAMLET: 'A poisons him i' th' garden for his estate. His name's Gonzago.
    The story is extant, and written in very choice Italian. You shall see
    anon how the murderer gets the love of Gonzago's wife.   235

                       [*Claudius rises.*]

OPHELIA: The King rises.
[HAMLET: What, frighted with false fire?°]
QUEEN: How fares my lord?
POLONIUS: Give o'er the play.
KING: Give me some light. Away!   240
POLONIUS: Lights, lights, lights!

             (*Exeunt all but Hamlet and Horatio.*)

---

218. chorus: In many Elizabethan plays the forthcoming action was explained by
an actor known as the "chorus"; at a puppet show the actor who spoke the dialogue
was known as an "interpreter," as indicated by the lines following.   **220. dallying:**
With sexual suggestion, continued in *keen*, i.e., sexually aroused, *groaning*, i.e.,
moaning in pregnancy, and *edge*, i.e., sexual desire or impetuosity.   **223. Still . . .
worse:** More keen-witted and less decorous.   **224. So:** Even thus (in marriage).
mistake: Mistake, take erringly, falseheartedly.   **228. Confederate season:** The
time and occasion conspiring (to assist the murderer).   **230. Hecate's ban:** The
curse of Hecate, the goddess of witchcraft.   **237. false fire:** The blank discharge of
a gun loaded with powder but not shot.

HAMLET: "Why, let the strucken deer go weep,
   The hart ungalled° play.
For some must watch,° while some must sleep;
   Thus runs the world away."°   245
Would not this,° sir, and a forest of feathers°—if the rest of my for-
tunes turn Turk with° me—with two Provincial roses° on my raz'd°
shoes, get me a fellowship in a cry of players?°
HORATIO: Half a share.
HAMLET: A whole one, I.   250
   "For thou dost know, O Damon dear,
     This realm dismantled° was
   Of Jove himself, and now reigns here
     A very, very—pajock."°
HORATIO: You might have rhym'd.   255
HAMLET: O good Horatio, I'll take the ghost's word for a thousand
   pound. Didst perceive?
HORATIO: Very well, my lord.
HAMLET: Upon the talk of pois'ning?
HORATIO: I did very well note him.   260
HAMLET: Ah, ha! Come, some music! Come, the recorders!°
   "For if the King like not the comedy,
   Why then, belike, he likes it not, perdy"°
   Come, some music!

(*Enter Rosencrantz and Guildenstern.*)

GUILDENSTERN: Good my lord, vouchsafe me a word with you.   265
HAMLET: Sir, a whole history.
GUILDENSTERN: The King, sir—
HAMLET: Ay, sir, what of him?
GUILDENSTERN: Is in his retirement marvelous distemp'red.
HAMLET: With drink, sir?   270

---

243. ungalled: Unafflicted. **244. watch:** Remain awake. **242–45. Why . . .
away:** Probably from an old ballad, with allusion to the popular belief that a
wounded deer retires to weep and die; cf. *As You Like It*, II, i, 66. **246. this:** The
play. **feathers:** Allusion to the plumes that Elizabethan actors were fond of
wearing. **247. turn Turk with:** Turn renegade against, go back on. **Provincial
roses:** Rosettes of ribbon like the roses of a part of France. **raz'd:** With ornamental slashing. **248. fellowship . . . players:** Partnership in a theatrical company. **252. dismantled:** Stripped, divested. **254. pajock:** Peacock, a bird with
a bad reputation (here substituted for the obvious rhyme-word *ass*).
261. recorders: Wind instruments like the flute. **263. perdy:** A corruption of
the French *par dieu*, by God.

GUILDENSTERN: No, my lord, with choler.°

HAMLET: Your wisdom should show itself more richer to signify this to the doctor, for for me to put him to his purgation would perhaps plunge him into more choler.

GUILDENSTERN: Good my lord, put your discourse into some frame° and start not so wildly from my affair.   275

HAMLET: I am tame, sir. Pronounce.

GUILDENSTERN: The Queen, your mother, in most great affliction of spirit, hath sent me to you.

HAMLET: You are welcome.   280

GUILDENSTERN: Nay, good my lord, this courtesy is not of the right breed. If it shall please you to make me a wholesome answer, I will do your mother's commandment; if not, your pardon° and my return shall be the end of my business.

HAMLET: Sir, I cannot.   285

ROSENCRANTZ: What, my lord?

HAMLET: Make you a wholesome answer; my wit's diseas'd. But, sir, such answer as I can make, you shall command, or rather, as you say, my mother. Therefore no more, but to the matter. My mother, you say—

ROSENCRANTZ: Then thus she says: your behavior hath struck her into amazement and admiration.°   290

HAMLET: O wonderful son, that can so stonish a mother! But is there no sequel at the heels of this mother's admiration? Impart.

ROSENCRANTZ: She desires to speak with you in her closet,° ere you go to bed.   295

HAMLET: We shall obey, were she ten times our mother. Have you any further trade with us?

ROSENCRANTZ: My lord, you once did love me.

HAMLET: And do still, by these pickers and stealers.°

ROSENCRANTZ: Good my lord, what is your cause of distemper? You do   300
surely bar the door upon your own liberty, if you deny your griefs to your friend.

HAMLET: Sir, I lack advancement.

ROSENCRANTZ: How can that be, when you have the voice of the King himself for your succession in Denmark?   305

---

271. **choler:** Anger. (But Hamlet takes the word in its more basic humors sense of *bilious disorder.*)   275. **frame:** Order.   283. **pardon:** Permission to depart.
291. **admiration:** Wonder.   294. **closet:** Private chamber.   299. **pickers and stealers:** Hands (so called from the catechism, "to keep my hands from picking and stealing").

HAMLET: Ay, sir, but "While the grass grows"°—the proverb is something° musty.

(*Enter the Players with recorders.*)

O, the recorders! Let me see one. [*He takes a recorder.*] To withdraw° with you: why do you go about to recover the wind° of me, as if you would drive me into a toil?°   310

GUILDENSTERN: O, my lord, if my duty be too bold, my love is too unmannerly.°

HAMLET: I do not well understand that. Will you play upon this pipe?

GUILDENSTERN: My lord, I cannot.

HAMLET: I pray you.   315

GUILDENSTERN: Believe me, I cannot.

HAMLET: I do beseech you.

GUILDENSTERN: I know no touch of it, my lord.

HAMLET: It is as easy as lying. Govern these ventages° with your fingers and thumb, give it breath with your mouth, and it will discourse most   320 eloquent music. Look you, these are the stops.

GUILDENSTERN: But these cannot I command to any utt'rance of harmony; I have not the skill.

HAMLET: Why, look you now, how unworthy a thing you make of me! You would play upon me, you would seem to know my stops, you would   325 pluck out the heart of my mystery, you would sound me from my lowest note to the top of my compass,° and there is much music, excellent voice, in this little organ,° yet cannot you make it speak. 'Sblood, do you think I am easier to be play'd on than a pipe? Call me what instrument you will, though you can fret° me, you cannot play upon me.   330

(*Enter Polonius.*)

God bless you, sir!

POLONIUS: My lord, the Queen would speak with you, and presently.°

HAMLET: Do you see yonder cloud that's almost in shape of a camel?

POLONIUS: By th' mass, and 'tis like a camel, indeed.

HAMLET: Methinks it is like a weasel.   335

306. While . . . grows: The rest of the proverb is "the silly horse starves"; Hamlet may not live long enough to succeed to the kingdom.   306–07. something: Somewhat.   308. withdraw: Speak privately.   309. recover the wind: Get the windward side.   310. toil: Snare.   311–12. if . . . unmannerly: If I am using an unmannerly boldness, it is my love that occasions it.   319. ventages: Stops of the recorder.   327. compass: Range (of voice).   328. organ: Musical instrument.   330. fret: Irritate (with a quibble on *fret* meaning the piece of wood, gut, or metal that regulates the fingering on an instrument).   332. presently: At once.

POLONIUS: It is back'd like a weasel.
HAMLET: Or like a whale?
POLONIUS: Very like a whale.
HAMLET: Then I will come to my mother by and by.° [*Aside.*] They fool
   me° to the top of my bent.°—I will come by and by.   340
POLONIUS: I will say so.   [*Exit.*]
HAMLET: "By and by" is easily said. Leave me, friends.

                                  [*Exeunt all but Hamlet.*]

  'Tis now the very witching time° of night,
  When churchyards yawn and hell itself breathes out
  Contagion to this world. Now could I drink hot blood,   345
  And do such bitter business as the day
  Would quake to look on. Soft, now to my mother.
  O heart, lose not thy nature! Let not ever
  The soul of Nero° enter this firm bosom.
  Let me be cruel, not unnatural;   350
  I will speak daggers to her, but use none.
  My tongue and soul in this be hypocrites:
  How in my words somever° she be shent,°
  To give them seals° never, my soul, consent!

                                        (*Exit.*)

                          {*Scene III*}°
(*Enter King, Rosencrantz, and Guildenstern.*)

KING: I like him not, nor stands it safe with us
  To let his madness range. Therefore prepare you.
  I your commission will forthwith dispatch,°
  And he to England shall along with you.
  The terms° of our estate° may not endure   5
  Hazard so near 's as doth hourly grow
  Out of his brows.°

---

339. by and by: Immediately.   **339–40. fool me:** Make me play the fool.
340. top of my bent: Limit of my ability or endurance (literally, the extent to which
a bow may be bent).   **343. witching time:** Time when spells are cast and evil is
abroad.   **349. Nero:** Murderer of his mother, Agrippina.   **353. How . . . somever:**
However much by my words.   **shent:** Rebuked.   **354. give them seals:** Confirm
them with deeds.   **III, III. Location:** The castle.   **3. dispatch:** Prepare, cause to
be drawn up.   **5. terms:** Condition, circumstances.   **our estate:** My royal position.   **7. brows:** Effronteries, threatening frowns (?), brain (?).

GUILDENSTERN: We will ourselves provide.
  Most holy and religious fear it is
  To keep those many many bodies safe
  That live and feed upon your Majesty.   10
ROSENCRANTZ: The single and peculiar° life is bound
  With all the strength and armor of the mind
  To keep itself from noyance,° but much more
  That spirit upon whose weal depends and rests
  The lives of many. The cess° of majesty   15
  Dies not alone, but like a gulf° doth draw
  What's near it with it; or it is a messy wheel
  Fix'd on the summit of the highest mount,
  To whose huge spokes ten thousand lesser things
  Are mortis'd and adjoin'd, which, when it falls,   20
  Each small annexment, petty consequence,
  Attends° the boist'rous ruin. Never alone
  Did the King sigh, but with a general groan.
KING: Arm° you, I pray you, to this speedy voyage,
  For we will fetters put about this fear,   25
  Which now goes too free-footed.
ROSENCRANTZ: We will haste us.

                      (*Exeunt Gentlemen* [*Rosencrantz and Guildenstern*].)

(*Enter Polonius.*)

POLONIUS: My lord, he's going to his mother's closet.
  Behind the arras° I'll convey myself
  To hear the process.° I'll warrant she'll tax him home,°
  And, as you said, and wisely was it said,   30
  'Tis meet that some more audience than a mother,
  Since nature makes them partial, should o'erhear
  The speech, of vantage.° Fare you well, my liege.
  I'll call upon you ere you go to bed,
  And tell you what I know.
KING: Thanks, dear my lord.   35

                                        (*Exit* [*Polonius*].)

---

11. **single and peculiar:** Individual and private.   13. **noyance:** Harm.   15. **cess:**
Decease.   16. **gulf:** Whirlpool.   22. **Attends:** Participates in.   24. **Arm:** Prepare.
28. **arras:** Screen of tapestry placed around the walls of household apartments.
(On the Elizabethan stage, the arras was presumably over a door or discovery
space in the tiring-house façade.)   29. **process:** Proceedings.   **tax him home:**
Reprove him severely.   33. **of vantage:** From an advantageous place.

O, my offense is rank, it smells to heaven;
It hath the primal eldest curse° upon 't,
A brother's murder. Pray can I not,
Though inclination be as sharp as will.°
My stronger guilt defeats my strong intent,   40
And, like a man to double business bound,
I stand in pause where I shall first begin,
And both neglect. What if this cursed hand
Were thicker than itself with brother's blood,
Is there not rain enough in the sweet heavens   45
To wash it white as snow? Whereto serves mercy
But to confront the visage of offense?°
And what's in prayer but this twofold force,
To be forestalled° ere we come to fall,
Or pardon'd being down? Then I'll look up;   50
My fault is past. But, O, what form of prayer
Can serve my turn? "Forgive me my foul murder"?
That cannot be, since I am still possess'd
Of those effects for which I did the murder,
My crown, mine own ambition, and my queen.   55
May one be pardon'd and retain th' offense?
In the corrupted currents° of this world
Offense's gilded hand° may shove by justice,
And oft 'tis seen the wicked prize° itself
Buys out the law. But 'tis not so above.   60
There is no shuffling,° there the action lies°
In his° true nature, and we ourselves compell'd,
Even to the teeth and forehead° of our faults,
To give in evidence. What then? What rests?°
Try what repentance can. What can it not?   65
Yet what can it, when one cannot repent?
O wretched state! O bosom black as death!
O limed° soul, that, struggling to be free,

37. **primal eldest curse:** The curse of Cain, the first murderer; he killed his
brother Abel.   39. **Though . . . will:** Though my desire is as strong as my determination.   46–47. **Whereto . . . offense:** For what function does mercy serve
other than to undo the effects of sin?   49. **forestalled:** Prevented (from sinning).
57. **currents:** Courses.   58. **gilded hand:** Hand offering gold as a bribe.
59. **wicked prize:** Prize won by wickedness.   61. **shuffling:** Escape by trickery.
the action lies: The accusation is made manifest, comes up for consideration (a
legal metaphor).   62. **his:** Its.   63. **teeth and forehead:** Face to face, concealing nothing.   64. **rests:** Remains.   68. **limed:** Caught as with birdlime, a sticky
substance used to ensnare birds.

Art more engag'd!° Help, angels! Make assay.°
Bow, stubborn knees, and heart with strings of steel,   70
Be soft as sinews of the new-born babe!
All may be well.

> *[He kneels.]*

(Enter Hamlet [with sword drawn].)

HAMLET: Now might I do it pat,° now 'a is a-praying;
And now I'll do 't. And so 'a goes to heaven;
And so am I reveng'd. That would be scann'd:°   75
A villain kills my father, and for that,
I, his sole son, do this same villain send
To heaven.
Why, this is hire and salary, not revenge.
'A took my father grossly,° full of bread,°   80
With all his crimes broad blown,° as flush° as May;
And how his audit° stands who knows save heaven?
But in our circumstance and course° of thought,
'Tis heavy with him. And am I then reveng'd,
To take him in the purging of his soul,   85
When he is fit and season'd for his passage?
No!
Up, sword, and know thou a more horrid hent.°

> *[Puts up his sword.]*

When he is drunk asleep, or in his rage,
Or in th' incestuous pleasure of his bed,   90
At game a-swearing, or about some act
That has no relish of salvation in 't—
Then trip him, that his heels may kick at heaven,
And that his soul may be as damn'd and black
As hell, whereto it goes. My mother stays.   95
This physic° but prolongs thy sickly days.   *(Exit.)*
KING: My words fly up, my thoughts remain below.
Words without thoughts never to heaven go.

> *(Exit.)*

---

69. engag'd: Embedded. **assay:** Trial. **73. pat:** Opportunely. **75. would be scann'd:** Needs to be looked into. **80. grossly:** Not spiritually prepared. **full of bread:** Enjoying his worldly pleasures. (See Ezek. 16:49.) **81. crimes broad blown:** Sins in full bloom. **flush:** Lusty. **82. audit:** Account. **83. in . . . course:** As we see it in our mortal situation. **88. know . . . hent:** Await to be grasped by me on a more horrid occasion. **96. physic:** Purging (by prayer).

[*Scene IV*]°

(*Enter [Queen] Gertrude and Polonius.*)

POLONIUS: 'A will come straight. Look you lay° home to him.
  Tell him his pranks have been too broad° to bear with,
  And that your Grace hath screen'd and stood between
  Much heat° and him. I'll sconce° me even here.
  Pray you, be round° [with him.   5
HAMLET (*within*): Mother, mother, mother!]
QUEEN: I'll warrant you, fear me not.
  Withdraw, I hear him coming.

                                          [*Polonius hides behind the arras.*]

(*Enter Hamlet.*)

HAMLET: Now, mother, what's the matter?
QUEEN: Hamlet, thou hast thy father° much offended.   10
HAMLET: Mother, you have my father much offended.
QUEEN: Come, come, you answer with an idle° tongue.
HAMLET: Go, go, you question with a wicked tongue.
QUEEN: Why, how now, Hamlet?
HAMLET: What's the matter now?
QUEEN: Have you forgot me?
HAMLET: No, by the rood,° not so: 15
  You are the Queen, your husband's brother's wife
  And—would it were not so!—you are my mother.
QUEEN: Nay, then, I'll set those to you that can speak.
HAMLET: Come, come, and sit you down; you shall not budge.
  You go not till I set you up a glass   20
  Where you may see the inmost part of you.
QUEEN: What wilt thou do? Thou wilt not murder me?
  Help, ho!
POLONIUS [*behind*]: What, ho! Help!
HAMLET [*drawing*]: How now? A rat? Dead, for a ducat, dead!   25

                                          [*Makes a pass through the arras.*]

POLONIUS [*behind*]: O, I am slain! [*Falls and dies.*]
QUEEN: O me, what hast thou done?
HAMLET: Nay, I know not. Is it the King?

III, IV. **Location:** The queen's private chamber.   **1. lay:** Thrust (i.e., reprove him
soundly).   **2. broad:** Unrestrained.   **4. Much heat:** The king's anger.   **sconce:**
Ensconce, hide.   **5. round:** Blunt.   **10. thy father:** Your stepfather, Claudius.
12. idle: Foolish.   **15. rood:** Cross.

QUEEN: O, what a rash and bloody deed is this!
HAMLET: A bloody deed—almost as bad, good mother,
  As kill a king, and marry with his brother.   30
QUEEN: As kill a king!
HAMLET: Ay, lady, it was my word.

                    [*Parts the arras and discovers Polonius.*]

  Thou wretched, rash, intruding fool, farewell!
  I took thee for thy better. Take thy fortune.
  Thou find'st to be too busy is some danger.—
  Leave wringing of your hands. Peace, sit you down,   35
  And let me wring your heart, for so I shall,
  If it be made of penetrable stuff,
  If damned custom° have not braz'd° it so
  That it be proof° and bulwark against sense.°
QUEEN: What have I done, that thou dar'st wag thy tongue   40
  In noise so rude against me?
HAMLET: Such an art
  That blurs the grace and blush of modesty,
  Calls virtue hypocrite, takes off the rose
  From the fair forehead of an innocent love
  And sets a blister° there, makes marriage-vows   45
  As false as dicers' oaths. O, such a deed
  As from the body of contraction° plucks
  The very soul, and sweet religion° makes
  A rhapsody° of words. Heaven's face does glow
  O'er this solidity and compound mass   50
  With heated visage, as against the doom,
  Is thought-sick at the act.°
QUEEN: Ay me, what act,
  That roars so loud and thunders in the index?°
HAMLET: Look here, upon this picture, and on this,
  The counterfeit presentment° of two brothers.   55

                    [*Shows her two likenesses.*]

38. **damned custom:** Habitual wickedness. **braz'd:** Brazened, hardened. 39. **proof:** Armor. **sense:** Feeling. 45. **sets a blister:** Brands as a harlot. 47. **contraction:** The marriage contract. 48. **religion:** Religious vows. 49. **rhapsody:** Senseless string. **49–52. Heaven's . . . act:** Heaven's face flushes with anger to look down upon this solid world, this compound mass, with hot face as though the day of doom were near, and is thought-sick at the deed (i.e., Gertrude's marriage). 53. **index:** Table of contents, prelude, or preface. 55. **counterfeit presentment:** Portrayed representation.

See, what a grace was seated on this brow:
Hyperion's° curls, the front° of Jove himself,
An eye like Mars, to threaten and command,
A station° like the herald Mercury
New-lighted on a heaven-kissing hill—   60
A combination and a form indeed,
Where every god did seem to set his seal,
To give the world assurance of a man.
This was your husband. Look you now, what follows:
Here is your husband, like a mildew'd ear,°   65
Blasting his wholesome brother. Have you eyes?
Could you on this fair mountain leave to feed,
And batten° on this moor?° Ha, have you eyes?
You cannot call it love, for at your age
The heyday° in the blood is tame, it's humble,   70
And waits upon the judgment, and what judgment
Would step from this to this? Sense,° sure, you have,
Else could you not have motion, but sure that sense
Is apoplex'd,° for madness would not err,
Nor sense to ecstasy was ne'er so thrall'd   75
But it reserv'd some quantity of choice
To serve in such a difference. What devil was 't
That thus hath cozen'd° you at hoodman-blind?°
Eyes without feeling, feeling without sight,
Ears without hands or eyes, smelling sans° all,   80
Or but a sickly part of one true sense
Could not so mope.°
O shame, where is thy blush? Rebellious hell,
If thou canst mutine° in a matron's bones,
To flaming youth let virtue be as wax,   85
And melt in her own fire. Proclaim no shame
When the compulsive ardor gives the charge,
Since frost itself as actively doth burn,

57. Hyperion: The sun god. **front:** Brow. **59. station:** Manner of standing.
65. ear: I.e., of grain. **68. batten:** Gorge. **moor:** Barren upland. **70. hey-day:** State of excitement. **72. Sense:** Perception through the five senses (the functions of the middle or sensible soul). **74. apoplex'd:** Paralyzed. (Hamlet goes on to explain that without such a paralysis of will, mere madness would not so err, nor would the five senses so enthrall themselves to *ecstasy* or lunacy; even such deranged states of mind would be able to make the obvious choice between Hamlet Senior and Claudius.) **78. cozen'd:** Cheated. **hoodman-blind:** Blindman's bluff. **80. sans:** Without. **82. mope:** Be dazed, act aimlessly.
84. mutine: Mutiny.

And reason panders will.°
QUEEN: O Hamlet, speak no more!   90
Thou turn'st mine eyes into my very soul,
And there I see such black and grained° spots
As will not leave their tint.°
HAMLET: Nay, but to live
In the rank sweat of an enseamed° bed,
Stew'd in corruption, honeying and making love   95
Over the nasty sty—
QUEEN: O, speak to me no more.
These words, like daggers, enter in my ears.
No more, sweet Hamlet!
HAMLET: A murderer and a villain,
A slave that is not twentieth part the tithe°   100
Of your precedent° lord, a vice° of kings,
A cutpurse of the empire and the rule,
That from a shelf the precious diadem stole,
And put it in his pocket!
QUEEN: No more!   105

(*Enter Ghost* [*in his nightgown*].)

HAMLET: A king of shreds and patches°—
Save me, and hover o'er me with your wings,
You heavenly guards! What would your gracious figure?
QUEEN: Alas, he's mad!
HAMLET: Do you not come your tardy son to chide,   110
That, laps'd in time and passion,° lets go by
Th' important° acting of your dread command?
O, say!
GHOST: Do not forget. This visitation
Is but to whet thy almost blunted purpose.   115
But, look, amazement° on thy mother sits.
O, step between her and her fighting soul!

86–89. Proclaim . . . will: Call it no shameful business when the compelling
ardor of youth delivers the attack, i.e., commits lechery, since the frost of
advanced age burns with as active a fire of lust and reason perverts itself by
fomenting lust rather than restraining it.   92. grained: Dyed in grain, indelible.
93. tint: Color.   94. enseamed: Laden with grease.   100. tithe: Tenth part.
101. precedent: Former (i.e., the elder Hamlet).   vice: Buffoon (a reference to
the vice of the morality plays).   106. shreds and patches: Motley, the traditional
costume of the clown or fool.   111. laps'd . . . passion: Having allowed time to
lapse and passion to cool.   112. important: Importunate, urgent.   116. amazement: Distraction.

Conceit° in weakest bodies strongest works.
Speak to her, Hamlet.
HAMLET: How is it with you, lady?
QUEEN: Alas, how is 't with you,   120
    That you do bend your eye on vacancy,
    And with th' incorporal° air do hold discourse?
    Forth at your eyes your spirits wildly peep,
    And, as the sleeping soldiers in th' alarm,
    Your bedded° hair, like life in excrements,°   125
    Start up and stand an° end. O gentle son,
    Upon the heat and flame of thy distemper
    Sprinkle cool patience. Whereon do you look?
HAMLET: On him, on him! Look you how pale he glares!
    His form and cause conjoin'd,° preaching to stones,   130
    Would make them capable.° — Do not look upon me,
    Lest with this piteous action you convert
    My stern effects.° Then what I have to do
    Will want true color° — tears perchance for blood.
QUEEN: To whom do you speak this?   135
HAMLET: Do you see nothing there?
QUEEN: Nothing at all, yet all that is I see.
HAMLET: Nor did you nothing hear?
QUEEN: No, nothing but ourselves.
HAMLET: Why, look you there, look how it steals away!   140
    My father, in his habit° as he lived!
    Look, where he goes, even now, out at the portal!

                                            (*Exit Ghost.*)

QUEEN: This is the very coinage of your brain.
    This bodiless creation ecstasy°
    Is very cunning in.   145
HAMLET: Ecstasy?
    My pulse, as yours, doth temperately keep time,
    And makes as healthful music. It is not madness
    That I have utter'd. Bring me to the test,
    And I the matter will reword, which madness   150

118. **Conceit:** Imagination. 122. **incorporal:** Immaterial. 125. **bedded:** Laid
in smooth layers. **excrements:** Outgrowths. 126. **an:** On. 130. **His . . . con-
join'd:** His appearance joined to his cause for speaking. 131. **capable:**
Receptive. 132–33. **convert . . . effects:** Divert me from my stern duty.
134. **want true color:** Lack plausibility so that (with a play on the normal sense
of *color*) I shall shed tears instead of blood. 141. **habit:** Dress. 144. **ecstasy:**
Madness.

Would gambol° from. Mother, for love of grace,
Lay not that flattering unction° to your soul
That not your trespass but my madness speaks.
It will but skin and film the ulcerous place,
Whiles rank corruption, mining° all within,   155
Infects unseen. Confess yourself to heaven,
Repent what's past, avoid what is to come,
And do not spread the compost° on the weeds
To make them ranker. Forgive me this my virtue;°
For in the fatness° of these pursy° times   160
Virtue itself of vice must pardon beg,
Yea, curb° and woo for leave° to do him good.
QUEEN: O Hamlet, thou hast cleft my heart in twain.
HAMLET: O, throw away the worser part of it,
And live the purer with the other half.   165
Good night. But go not to my uncle's bed;
Assume a virtue, if you have it not.
That monster, custom, who all sense doth eat,°
Of habits devil,° is angel yet in this,
That to the use of actions fair and good   170
He likewise gives a frock or livery°
That aptly is put on. Refrain tonight,
And that shall lend a kind of easiness
To the next abstinence; the next more easy;
For use° almost can change the stamp of nature,   175
And either° . . . the devil, or throw him out
With wondrous potency. Once more, good night;
And when you are desirous to be bless'd,°
I'll blessing beg of you. For this same lord,

                                         [*Pointing to Polonius.*]

I do repent; but heaven hath pleas'd it so   180
To punish me with this, and this with me,

151. **gambol:** Skip away.   152. **unction:** Ointment.   155. **mining:** Working under the surface.   158. **compost:** Manure.   159. **this my virtue:** My virtuous talk in reproving you.   160. **fatness:** Grossness.   **pursy:** Short-winded, corpulent.   162. **curb:** Bow, bend the knee.   **leave:** Permission.   168. **who . . . eat:** Who consumes all proper or natural feeling.   169. **Of habits devil:** Devil-like in prompting evil habits.   171. **livery:** An outer appearance, a customary garb (and hence a predisposition easily assumed in time of stress).   175. **use:** Habit.   176. **And either:** A defective line usually emended by inserting the word *master* after *either,* following the fourth quarto and early editors.   178. **be bless'd:** Become blessed, i.e., repentant.

That I must be their scourge and minister.°
I will bestow° him, and will answer well
The death I gave him. So, again, good night.
I must be cruel only to be kind.   185
Thus bad begins and worse remains behind.°
One word more, good lady.
QUEEN: What shall I do?
HAMLET: Not this, by no means, that I bid you do:
    Let the bloat° king tempt you again to bed,
    Pinch wanton on your cheek, call you his mouse,   190
    And let him, for a pair of reechy° kisses,
    Or paddling in your neck with his damn'd fingers,
    Make you to ravel all this matter out,
    That I essentially am not in madness,
    But mad in craft. 'Twere good° you let him know,   195
    For who that's but a queen, fair, sober, wise,
    Would from a paddock,° from a bat, a gib,°
    Such dear concernings° hide? Who would do so?
    No, in despite of sense and secrecy,
    Unpeg the basket° on the house's top,   200
    Let the birds fly, and, like the famous ape,°
    To try conclusions,° in the basket creep
    And break your own neck down.
QUEEN: Be thou assur'd, if words be made of breath,
    And breath of life, I have no life to breathe   205
    What thou hast said to me.
HAMLET: I must to England; you know that?
QUEEN: Alack,
    I had forgot. 'Tis so concluded on.
HAMLET: There's letters seal'd, and my two school-fellows,
    Whom I will trust as I will adders fang'd,   210
    They bear the mandate; they must sweep my way,°
    And marshal me to knavery. Let it work.

182. their scourge and minister: Agent of heavenly retribution. (By *scourge*,
Hamlet also suggests that he himself will eventually suffer punishment in
the process of fulfilling heaven's will.) 183. bestow: Stow, dispose of.
186. behind: To come. 189. bloat: Bloated. 191. reechy: Dirty, filthy.
195. good: Said ironically; also the following eight lines. 197. paddock: Toad.
gib: Tomcat. 198. dear concernings: Important affairs. 200. Unpeg the basket: Open the cage, i.e., let out the secret. 201. famous ape: In a story now lost.
202. conclusions: Experiments (in which the ape apparently enters a cage from
which birds have been released and then tries to fly out of the cage as they have
done, falling to his death). 211. sweep my way: Go before me.

For 'tis the sport to have the enginer°
Hoist with° his own petar,° and 't shall go hard
But I will delve one yard below their mines,°   215
And blow them at the moon. O, 'tis most sweet,
When in one line two crafts° directly meet.
This man shall set me packing.°
I'll lug the guts into the neighbor room.
Mother, good night indeed. This counselor   220
Is now most still, most secret, and most grave,
Who was in life a foolish prating knave.
Come, sir, to draw toward an end° with you.
Good night, mother.

(Exeunt [severally, Hamlet dragging in Polonius].)

{ACT IV   Scene I}°

(Enter King and Queen, with Rosencrantz and Guildenstern.)

KING: There's matter in these sighs, these profound heaves
  You must translate; 'tis fit we understand them.
  Where is your son?
QUEEN: Bestow this place on us a little while.

[Exeunt Rosencrantz and Guildenstern.]

  Ah, mine own lord, what have I seen tonight!   5
KING: What, Gertrude? How does Hamlet?
QUEEN: Mad as the sea and wind when both contend
  Which is the mightier. In his lawless fit,
  Behind the arras hearing something stir,
  Whips out his rapier, cries, "A rat, a rat!"   10
  And, in this brainish apprehension,° kills
  The unseen good old man.

---

213. **enginer:** Constructor of military contrivances. 214. **Hoist with:** Blown up
by. **petar:** Petard, an explosive used to blow in a door or make a breach.
215. **mines:** Tunnels used in warfare to undermine the enemy's emplacements;
Hamlet will countermine by going under their mines. 217. **crafts:** Acts of guile,
plots. 218. **set me packing:** Set me to making schemes, and set me to lugging
(him) and, also, send me off in a hurry. 223. **draw . . . end:** Finish up (with a
pun on *draw*, pull). IV, I. **Location:** The castle. 11. **brainish apprehension:**
Headstrong conception.

KING: O heavy deed!
  It had been so with us, had we been there.
  His liberty is full of threats to all—
  To you yourself, to us, to everyone.   15
  Alas, how shall this bloody deed be answer'd?
  It will be laid to us, whose providence°
  Should have kept short,° restrain'd, and out of haunt°
  This mad young man. But so much was our love
  We would not understand what was most fit,   20
  But, like the owner of a foul disease,
  To keep it from divulging,° let it feed
  Even on the pith of life. Where is he gone?
QUEEN: To draw apart the body he hath kill'd,
  O'er whom his very madness, like some ore°   25
  Among a mineral° of metals base,
  Shows itself pure: 'a weeps for what is done.
KING: O Gertrude, come away!
  The sun no sooner shall the mountains touch
  But we will ship him hence, and this vile deed   30
  We must, with all our majesty and skill,
  Both countenance and excuse. Ho, Guildenstern!

(*Enter Rosencrantz and Guildenstern.*)

  Friends both, go join you with some further aid.
  Hamlet in madness hath Polonius slain,
  And from his mother's closet hath he dragg'd him.   35
  Go seek him out; speak fair, and bring the body
  Into the chapel. I pray you, haste in this.

                     [*Exeunt Rosencrantz and Guildenstern.*]

  Come, Gertrude, we'll call up our wisest friends
  And let them know both what we mean to do
  And what's untimely done°   40
  Whose whisper o'er the world's diameter,°
  As level° as the cannon to his blank,°
  Transports his pois'ned shot, may miss our name,

---

17. providence: Foresight.   18. short: On a short tether.   out of haunt:
Secluded.   22. divulging: Becoming evident.   25. ore: Vein of gold.   26. min-
eral: Mine.   40. And . . . done: A defective line; conjectures as to the missing
words include *so, haply, slander* (Capell and others); *for, haply, slander* (Theobald
and others).   41. diameter: Extent from side to side.   42. As level: With as
direct aim.   blank: White spot in the center of a target.

And hit the woundless° air. O, come away!
My soul is full of discord and dismay.   (*Exeunt.*) 45

{*Scene II*}°

(*Enter Hamlet.*)

HAMLET: Safely stow'd.
[ROSENCRANTZ, GUILDENSTERN (*within*): Hamlet! Lord Hamlet!]
HAMLET: But soft, what noise? Who calls on Hamlet? O, here they come.

(*Enter Rosencrantz and Guildenstern.*)

ROSENCRANTZ: What have you done, my lord, with the dead body?
HAMLET: Compounded it with dust, whereto 'tis kin.   5
ROSENCRANTZ: Tell us where 'tis, that we may take it thence
    And bear it to the chapel.
HAMLET: Do not believe it.
ROSENCRANTZ: Believe what?
HAMLET: That I can keep your counsel and not mine own. Besides, to be 10
    demanded of° a sponge, what replication° should be made by the son
    of a king?
ROSENCRANTZ: Take you me for a sponge, my lord?
HAMLET: Ay, sir, that soaks up the King's countenance,° his rewards, his
    authorities. But such officers do the King best service in the end. He 15
    keeps them, like an ape an apple, in the corner of his jaw, first
    mouth'd, to be last swallow'd. When he needs what you have glean'd, it
    is but squeezing you, and, sponge, you shall be dry again.
ROSENCRANTZ: I understand you not, my lord.
HAMLET: I am glad of it. A knavish speech sleeps in° a foolish ear.   20
ROSENCRANTZ: My lord, you must tell us where the body is, and go with
    us to the King.
HAMLET: The body is with the King, but the King is not with the body.°
    The King is a thing—
GUILDENSTERN: A thing, my lord?   25
HAMLET: Of nothing.° Bring me to him. [Hide fox, and all after.°]

                                                            (*Exeunt.*)

---

44. woundless: Invulnerable. **IV, II. Location:** The castle. **11. demanded of:**
Questioned by. **replication:** Reply. **14. countenance:** Favor. **20. sleeps in:**
Has no meaning to. **23. The . . . body:** Perhaps alludes to the legal commonplace of "the king's two bodies," which drew a distinction between the sacred
office of kingship and the particular mortal who possessed it at any given time.
26. Of nothing: Of no account. **Hide . . . after:** An old signal cry in the game of
hide-and-seek, suggesting that Hamlet now runs away from them.

[*Scene III*]°

(*Enter King, and two or three.*)

KING: I have sent to seek him, and to find the body.
How dangerous is it that this man goes loose!
Yet must not we put the strong law on him.
He's lov'd of the distracted° multitude,
Who like not in their judgment, but their eyes,   5
And where 'tis so, th' offender's scourge° is weigh'd,°
But never the offense. To bear° all smooth and even,
This sudden sending him away must seem
Deliberate pause.° Diseases desperate grown
By desperate appliance are reliev'd,   10
Or not at all.

(*Enter Rosencrantz, [Guildenstern,] and all the rest.*)

                    How now? What hath befall'n?
ROSENCRANTZ: Where the dead body is bestow'd, my lord,
We cannot get from him.
KING: But where is he?
ROSENCRANTZ: Without, my lord; guarded, to know your pleasure.
KING: Bring him before us.
ROSENCRANTZ: Ho! Bring in the lord.   15

(*They enter [with Hamlet].*)

KING: Now, Hamlet, where's Polonius?
HAMLET: At supper.
KING: At supper? Where?
HAMLET: Not where he eats, but where 'a is eaten. A certain convocation
of politic worms° are e'en at him. Your worm is your only emperor for   20
diet.° We fat all creatures else to fat us, and we fat ourselves for maggots. Your fat king and your lean beggar is but variable service,° two
dishes, but to one table—that's the end.
KING: Alas, alas!
HAMLET: A man may fish with the worm that hath eat° of a king, and eat   25
of the fish that hath fed of that worm.

IV, III. **Location:** The castle.   **4. distracted:** Fickle, unstable.   **6. scourge:**
Punishment.   **weigh'd:** Taken into consideration.   **7. bear:** Manage.   **9. Deliberate pause:** Carefully considered action.   **20. politic worms:** Crafty worms
(suited to a master spy like Polonius).   **21. diet:** Food, eating (with perhaps a
punning reference to the Diet of Worms, a famous convocation held in 1521).
22. variable service: Different courses of a single meal.   **25. eat:** Eaten (pronounced *et*).

KING: What dost thou mean by this?

HAMLET: Nothing but to show you how a king may go a progress°
through the guts of a beggar.

KING: Where is Polonius?   30

HAMLET: In heaven. Send thither to see. If your messenger find him not
there, seek him i' th' other place yourself. But if indeed you find him
not within this month, you shall nose him as you go up the stairs into
the lobby.

KING [to some Attendants]: Go seek him there.   35

HAMLET: 'A will stay till you come.

                            [Exit Attendants.]

KING: Hamlet, this deed, for thine especial safety.—
  Which we do tender,° as we dearly° grieve
  For that which thou hast done—must send thee hence
  [With fiery quickness.] Therefore prepare thyself.   40
  The bark° is ready, and the wind at help,
  Th' associates tend,° and everything is bent°
  For England.

HAMLET: For England!

KING: Ay, Hamlet.   45

HAMLET: Good.

KING: So is it, if thou knew'st our purposes.

HAMLET: I see a cherub° that sees them. But, come, for England! Farewell,
dear mother.

KING: Thy loving father, Hamlet.   50

HAMLET: My mother. Father and mother is man and wife, man and wife
is one flesh, and so, my mother. Come, for England!   *(Exit.)*

KING: Follow him at foot;° tempt him with speed aboard.
  Delay it not; I'll have him hence tonight.
  Away! For everything is seal'd and done   55
  That else leans on° th' affair. Pray you, make haste.

                     [Exeunt all but the King.]

  And, England,° if my love thou hold'st at aught—
  As my great power thereof may give thee sense,
  Since yet thy cicatrice° looks raw and red

---

28. progress: Royal journey of state.   **38. tender:** Regard, hold dear.   **dearly:**
Intensely.   **41. bark:** Sailing vessel.   **42. tend:** Wait.   **bent:** In readiness.
48. cherub: Cherubim are angels of knowledge.   **53. at foot:** Close behind, at
heel.   **56. leans on:** Bears upon, is related to.   **57. England:** King of England.
59. cicatrice: Scar.

After the Danish sword, and thy free awe°   60
Pays homage to us—thou mayst not coldly set°
Our sovereign process,° which imports at full,
By letters congruing° to that effect,
The present° death of Hamlet. Do it, England,
For like the hectic° in my blood he rages,   65
And thou must cure me. Till I know 'tis done,
Howe'er my haps,° my joys were ne'er begun.

                                                    (*Exit.*)

                            {*Scene IV*}°

(*Enter Fortinbras with his Army over the stage.*)

FORTINBRAS: Go, captain, from me greet the Danish king.
    Tell him that, by his license,° Fortinbras
    Craves the conveyance° of a promis'd march
    Over his kingdom. You know the rendezvous.
    If that his Majesty would aught with us,   5
    We shall express our duty in his eye;°
    And let him know so.
CAPTAIN: I will do 't, my lord.
FORTINBRAS: Go softly° on.   [*Exeunt all but the Captain.*]

(*Enter Hamlet, Rosencrantz, [Guildenstern,] etc.*)

HAMLET: Good sir, whose powers° are these?
CAPTAIN: They are of Norway, sir.   10
HAMLET: How purposed, sir, I pray you?
CAPTAIN: Against some part of Poland.
HAMLET: Who commands them, sir?
CAPTAIN: The nephew to old Norway, Fortinbras.
HAMLET: Goes it against the main° of Poland, sir,   15
    Or for some frontier?
CAPTAIN: Truly to speak, and with no addition,°
    We go to gain a little patch of ground
    That hath in it no profit but the name.

---

60. free awe: Voluntary show of respect. **61. set:** Esteem. **62. process:**
Command. **63. congruing:** Agreeing. **64. present:** Immediate. **65. hectic:**
Persistent fever. **67. haps:** Fortunes. **IV, IV. Location:** The coast of Denmark.
2. license: Permission. **3. conveyance:** Escort, convoy. **6. eye:** Presence.
8. softly: Slowly. **9. powers:** Forces. **15. main:** Main part. **17. addition:**
Exaggeration.

To pay° five ducats, five, I would not farm it;°   20
Nor will it yield to Norway or the Pole
A ranker° rate, should it be sold in fee.°
HAMLET: Why, then the Polack never will defend it.
CAPTAIN: Yes, it is already garrison'd.
HAMLET: Two thousand souls and twenty thousand ducats   25
Will not debate the question of this straw.°
This is th' imposthume° of much wealth and peace,
That inward breaks, and shows no cause without
Why the man dies. I humbly thank you, sir.
CAPTAIN: God buy you, sir.   [Exit.]
ROSENCRANTZ: Will 't please you go, my lord?   30
HAMLET: I'll be with you straight. Go a little before.

                                  [Exit all except Hamlet.]

How all occasions do inform against° me,
And spur my dull revenge! What is a man,
If his chief good and market of° his time
Be but to sleep and feed? A beast, no more.   35
Sure he that made us with such large discourse,°
Looking before and after, gave us not
That capability and god-like reason
To fust° in us unus'd. Now, whether it be
Bestial oblivion,° or some craven scruple   40
Of thinking too precisely on th' event° —
A thought which, quarter'd, hath but one part wisdom
And ever three parts coward—I do not know
Why yet I live to say "This thing's to do,"
Sith° I have cause and will and strength and means   45
To do 't. Examples gross° as earth exhort me:
Witness this army of such mass and charge°
Led by a delicate and tender prince,
Whose spirit, with divine ambition puff'd
Makes mouths° at the invisible event,   50
Exposing what is mortal and unsure
To all that fortune, death, and danger dare,

20. **To pay:** I.e., for a yearly rental of. **farm it:** Take a lease of it. **22. ranker:** Higher. **in fee:** Fee simple, outright. **26. debate . . . straw:** Settle this trifling matter. **27. imposthume:** Abscess. **32. inform against:** Denounce, betray; take shape against. **34. market of:** Profit of compensation for. **36. discourse:** Power of reasoning. **39. fust:** Grow moldy. **40. oblivion:** Forgetfulness. **41. event:** Outcome. **45. Sith:** Since. **46. gross:** Obvious. **47. charge:** Expense. **50. Makes mouths:** Makes scornful faces.

Even for an egg-shell. Rightly to be great
Is not to stir without great argument,
But greatly to find quarrel in a straw   55
When honor's at the stake. How stand I then,
That have a father kill'd, a mother stain'd,
Excitements of° my reason and my blood,
And let all sleep, while, to my shame, I see
The imminent death of twenty thousand men,   60
That, for a fantasy° and trick° of fame,
Go to their graves like beds, fight for a plot°
Whereon the numbers cannot try the cause,°
Which is not tomb enough and continent°
To hide the slain? O, from this time forth,   65
My thoughts be bloody, or be nothing worth!

                                                          (*Exit.*)

                              [*Scene v*]°

(*Enter Horatio, [Queen] Gertrude, and a Gentleman.*)

QUEEN: I will not speak with her.
GENTLEMAN: She is importunate, indeed distract.
    Her mood will needs be pitied.
QUEEN: What would she have?
GENTLEMAN: She speaks much of her father, says she hears
    There's tricks° i' th' world, and hems, and beats her heart,°   5
    Spurns enviously at straws,° speaks things in doubt°
    That carry but half sense. Her speech is nothing,
    Yet the unshaped use° of it doth move
    The hearers to collection;° they yawn° at it,
    And botch° the words up fit to their own thoughts,   10
    Which, as her winks and nods and gestures yield° them,
    Indeed would make one think there might be thought,°

---

58. **Excitements of:** Promptings by. 61. **fantasy:** Fanciful caprice. **trick:**
Trifle. 62. **plot:** I.e., of ground. 63. **Whereon . . . cause:** On which there is
insufficient room for the soldiers needed to engage in a military contest.
64. **continent:** Receptacle, container. **IV, v. Location:** The castle. 5. **tricks:**
Deceptions. **heart:** Breast. 6. **Spurns . . . straws:** Kicks spitefully, takes
offense at trifles. **in doubt:** Obscurely. 8. **unshaped use:** Distracted manner.
9. **collection:** Inference, a guess at some sort of meaning. **yawn:** Wonder,
grasp. 10. **botch:** Patch. 11. **yield:** Delivery, bring forth (her words).
12. **thought:** Conjectured.

Though nothing sure, yet much unhappily.
HORATIO: 'twere good she were spoken with, for she may strew
   Dangerous conjectures in ill-breeding° minds.   15
QUEEN: Let her come in.   [*Exit Gentlemen.*]
   [*Aside.*] To my sick soul, as sin's true nature is,
   Each toy° seems prologue to some great amiss.°
   So full of artless jealousy is guilt,
   It spills itself in fearing to be spilt.°   20

(*Enter Ophelia* [*distracted*].)

OPHELIA: Where is the beauteous majesty of Denmark?
QUEEN: How now, Ophelia?
OPHELIA (*she sings*): "How should I your true love know
    From another one?
  By his cockle hat° and staff,   25
    And his sandal shoon."°
QUEEN: Alas, sweet lady, what imports this song?
OPHELIA: Say you? Nay, pray you, mark.
  "He is dead and gone, lady,   (*Song.*)
    He is dead and gone;   30
  At his head a grass-green turf,
    At his heels a stone."
  O, ho!
QUEEN: Nay, but Ophelia—
OPHELIA: Pray you mark.   35
  [*Sings.*] "White his shroud as the mountain snow"—

(*Enter King.*)

QUEEN: Alas, look here, my lord.
OPHELIA: "Larded° all with flowers   (*Song.*)
  Which bewept to the ground did not go
    With true-love showers."   40
KING: How do you, pretty lady?
OPHELIA: Well, God 'ild° you! They say the owl° was a baker's daughter.
  Lord, we know what we are, but know not what we may be. God be at
  your table!

---

15. ill-breeding: Prone to suspect the worst.   **18. toy:** Trifle.   **amiss:** Calamity.
19–20. So . . . spilt: Guilt is so full of suspicion that it unskillfully betrays itself in
fearing betrayal.   **25. cockle hat:** Hat with cockleshell stuck in it as a sign that
the wearer had been a pilgrim to the shrine of St. James of Compostella in Spain.
26. shoon: Shoes.   **38. Larded:** Decorated.   **42. God 'ild:** God yield or reward.
owl: Refers to a legend about a baker's daughter who was turned into an owl for
refusing Jesus bread.

KING: Conceit° upon her father.   45
OPHELIA: Pray let's have no words of this; but when they ask you what it
    means, say you this:
    "Tomorrow is Saint Valentine's° day.   (*Song.*)
        All in the morning betime,
    And I a maid at your window,   50
        To be your Valentine.
    Then up he rose, and donn'd his clo'es,
        And dupp'd° the chamber-door,
    Let in the maid, that out a maid
        Never departed more."   55
KING: Pretty Ophelia!
OPHELIA: Indeed, la, without an oath, I'll make an end on 't:
    [*Sings.*] "By Gis° and by Saint Charity,
        Alack, and fie for shame!
    Young men will do 't, if they come to 't;   60
        By Cock,° they are to blame.
    Quoth she, 'Before you tumbled me,
        You promised me to wed.'"
He answers:
    "'So would I ha' done, by yonder sun,   65
        An thou hadst not come to my bed.'"
KING: How long hath she been thus?
OPHELIA: I hope all will be well. We must be patient, but I cannot choose
    but weep, to think they would lay him i' th' cold ground. My brother
    shall know of it; and so I thank you for your good counsel. Come, my   70
    coach! Good night, ladies; good night, sweet ladies; good night, good
    night.

                                                              [*Exit.*]

KING: Follow her close; give her good watch, I pray you.

                                                        [*Exit Horatio.*]

    O, this is the poison of deep grief; it springs
    All from her father's death—and now behold!   75
    O Gertrude, Gertrude,
    When sorrows come, they come not single spies,°
    But in battalions. First, her father slain;
    Next, your son gone, and he most violent author

---

45. Conceit: Brooding.   **48. Valentine's:** This song alludes to the belief that the
first girl seen by a man on the morning of this day was his valentine or true love.
53. dupp'd: Opened.   **58. Gis:** Jesus.   **61. Cock:** A perversion of *God* in oaths.
77. spies: Scouts sent in advance of the main force.

Of his own just remove; the people muddied,°   80
Thick and unwholesome in their thoughts and whispers,
For good Polonius' death; and we have done but greenly,°
In hugger-mugger° to inter him; poor Ophelia
Divided from herself and her fair judgment,
Without the which we are pictures, or mere beasts;   85
Last, and as much containing as all these,
Her brother is in secret come from France,
Feeds on his wonder, keeps himself in clouds,°
And wants° not buzzers° to infect his ear
With pestilent speeches of his father's death,   90
Wherein necessity, of matter beggar'd,°
Will nothing stick our person to arraign
In ear and ear.° O my dear Gertrude, this,
Like to a murd'ring-piece,° in many places
Gives me superfluous death.   (*A noise within.*)   95
[QUEEN: Alack, what noise is this?]
KING: Attend!
Where are my Switzers?° Let them guard the door.

(*Enter a Messenger.*)

What is the matter?
MESSENGER: Save yourself, my lord!
The ocean, overpeering of his list,°   100
Eats not the flats° with more impiteous° haste
Than young Laertes, in a riotous head,°
O'erbears your officers. The rabble call him lord,
And, as° the world were now but to begin,
Antiquity forgot, custom not known,   105
The ratifiers and props° of every word,°
They cry, "Choose we! Laertes shall be king!"
Caps, hands, and tongues applaud it to the clouds,
"Laertes shall be king, Laertes king!"

                                        (*A noise within.*)

---

80. **muddied:** Stirred up, confused. 82. **greenly:** Imprudently, foolishly.
83. **hugger-mugger:** Secret haste. 88. **in clouds:** I.e., of suspicion and rumor.
89. **wants:** Lacks. **buzzers:** Gossipers, informers. 91. **of matter beggar'd:**
Unprovided with facts. 92–93. **Will . . . and ear:** Will not hesitate to accuse my
(royal) person in everybody's ears. 94. **murd'ring-piece:** Cannon loaded so as to
scatter its shot. 98. **Switzers:** Swiss guards, mercenaries. 100. **overpeering of
his list:** Overflowing its shore. 101. **flats:** Flatlands near shore. **impiteous:**
Pitiless. 102. **head:** Armed force. 104. **as:** As if. 106. **ratifiers and props:**
Refer to *antiquity* and *custom*. **word:** Promise.

QUEEN: How cheerfully on the false trail they cry!   110
  O, this is counter,° you false Danish dogs!

(*Enter Laertes with others.*)

KING: The doors are broke.
LAERTES: Where is this King? Sirs, stand you all without.
ALL: No, let's come in.
LAERTES: I pray you, give me leave.
ALL: We will, we will.   115

> [*They retire without the door.*]

LAERTES: I thank you. Keep the door. O thou vile king,
  Give me my father!
QUEEN: Calmly, good Laertes.

> [*She tries to hold him back.*]

LAERTES: That drop of blood that's calm proclaims me bastard,
  Cries cuckold to my father, brands the harlot
  Even here, between the chaste unsmirched brow   120
  Of my true mother.
KING: What is the cause, Laertes,
  That thy rebellion looks so giant-like?
  Let him go, Gertrude. Do not fear our° person.
  There's such divinity doth hedge a king
  That treason can but peep to what it would,°   125
  Acts little of his will.° Tell me, Laertes,
  Why thou art thus incens'd. Let him go, Gertrude.
  Speak, man.
LAERTES: Where is my father?
KING: Dead.
QUEEN: But not by him.
KING: Let him demand his fill.
LAERTES: How came he dead? I'll not be juggled with.   130
  To hell, allegiance! Vows, to the blackest devil!
  Conscience and grace, to the profoundest pit!
  I dare damnation. To this point I stand,
  That both the worlds I give to negligence,°

---

111. counter: A hunting term meaning to follow the trail in a direction opposite to
that which the game has taken.   **123. fear our:** Fear for my.   **125. can . . . would:**
Can only glance; as from far off or through a barrier, at what it would intend.
126. Acts . . . will: (But) performs little of what it intends.   **134. both . . . negligence:** Both this world and the next are of no consequence to me.

Let come what comes, only I'll be reveng'd   135
Most throughly° for my father.
KING: Who shall stay you?
LAERTES: My will, not all the world's.°
And for my means, I'll husband them so well,
They shall go far with little.
KING: Good Laertes,
If you desire to know the certainty   140
Of your dear father, is 't writ in your revenge
That, swoopstake,° you will draw both friend and foe,
Winner and loser?
LAERTES: None but his enemies.
KING: Will you know them then?
LAERTES: To his good friends thus wide I'll ope my arms,   145
And, like the kind life-rend'ring pelican,°
Repast° them with my blood.
KING: Why, now you speak
Like a good child and a true gentleman.
That I am guiltless of your father's death,
And am most sensibly° in grief for it,   150
It shall as level° to your judgment 'pear
As day does to your eye.
                    (A noise within:) "Let her come in."
LAERTES: How now? What noise is that?

(Enter Ophelia.)

O heat, dry up my brains! Tears seven times salt
Burn out the sense and virtue° of mine eye!   155
By heaven, thy madness shall be paid with weight°
Till our scale turn the beam.° O rose of May!
Dear maid, kind sister, sweet Ophelia!
O heavens, is 't possible a young maid's wits
Should be as mortal as an old man's life?   160
[Nature is fine in° love, and where 'tis fine,
It sends some precious instance° of itself

136. **throughly:** Thoroughly.   137. **My will . . . world's:** I'll stop (*stay*) when my will is accomplished, not for anyone else's.   142. **swoopstake:** Literally, taking all stakes on the gambling table at once, i.e., indiscriminately; *draw* is also a gambling term.   146. **pelican:** Refers to the belief that the female pelican fed its young with its own blood.   147. **Repast:** Feed.   150. **sensibly:** Feelingly.   151. **level:** Plain.   155. **virtue:** Faculty, power.   156. **paid with weight:** Repaid, avenged equally or more.   157. **beam:** Crossbar of a balance.   161. **fine in:** Refined by.   162. **instance:** Token.

After the thing it loves.°]
OPHELIA: "They bore him barefac'd on the bier;

(*Song.*)

[Hey non nonny, nonny, hey nonny,]   165
And in his grave rain'd many a tear"—
Fare you well, my dove!
LAERTES: Hadst thou thy wits, and didst persuade° revenge,
It could not move thus.
OPHELIA: You must sing "A-down a-down,   170
And you call him a-down-a."
O, how the wheel° becomes it! It is the false steward° that stole his
master's daughter.
LAERTES: This nothing's more than matter.°
OPHELIA: There's rosemary,° that's for remembrance; pray you, love,   175
remember. And there is pansies,° that's for thoughts.
LAERTES: A document° in madness, thoughts and remembrance fitted.
OPHELIA: There's fennel° for you, and columbines.° There's rue° for you,
and here's some for me; we may call it herb of grace o' Sundays. You
may wear your rue with a difference.° There's a daisy.° I would give   180
you some violets,° but they wither'd all when my father died. They say
'a made a good end—
[*Sings.*] "For bonny sweet Robin is all my joy."
LAERTES: Thought° and affliction, passion, hell itself,
She turns to favor° and to prettiness.   185
OPHELIA: "And will 'a not come again? (*Song.*)
And will 'a not come again?
   No, no, he is dead,
   Go to thy death-bed,
He never will come again.   190

163. After . . . loves: Into the grave, along with Polonius.   168. persuade: Argue
cogently for.   172. wheel: Spinning wheel as accompaniment to the song, or
refrain.   false steward: The story is unknown.   174. This . . . matter: This
seeming nonsense is more meaningful than sane utterance.   175. rosemary:
Used as a symbol of remembrance both at weddings and at funerals.   176. pansies: Emblems of love and courtship; perhaps from French *pensées*, thoughts.
177. document: Instruction, lesson.   178. fennel: Emblem of flattery.
columbines: Emblems of unchastity (?) or ingratitude (?).   rue: Emblem of
repentance; when mingled with holy water, it was known as *herb of grace*.
180. with a difference: Suggests that Ophelia and the queen have different
causes of sorrow and repentance; perhaps with a play on *rue* in the sense of ruth,
pity.   daisy: Emblem of dissembling, faithlessness.   181. violets: Emblems of
faithfulness.   184. Thought: Melancholy.   185. favor: Grace.

"His beard was as white as snow,
All flaxen was his poll.°
  He is gone, he is gone,
  And we cast away moan.
God 'a' mercy on his soul!"   195
And of all Christians' souls, I pray God. God buy you.

                                             [*Exit.*]

LAERTES: Do you see this, O God?
KING: Laertes, I must commune with your grief,
  Or you deny me right. Go but apart,
  Make choice of whom your wisest friends you will,   200
  And they shall hear and judge 'twixt you and me.
  If by direct or by collateral° hand
  They find us touch'd,° we will our kingdom give,
  Our crown, our life, and all that we call ours,
  To you in satisfaction; but if not,   205
  Be you content to lend your patience to us,
  And we shall jointly labor with your soul
  To give it due content.
LAERTES: Let this be so.
  His means of death, his obscure funeral—
  No trophy,° sword, nor hatchment° o'er his bones,   210
  No noble rite nor formal ostentation°—
  Cry to be heard, as 'twere from heaven to earth,
  That I must call 't in question.
KING: So you shall;
  And where th' offense is, let the great ax fall.
  I pray you go with me.   (*Exeunt.*) 215

[*Scene VI*]°

(*Enter Horatio and others.*)

HORATIO: What are they that would speak with me?
GENTLEMAN: Seafaring men, sir. They say they have letters for you.
HORATIO: Let them come in.   [*Exit Gentleman.*]
  I do not know from what part of the world
  I should be greeted, if not from lord Hamlet.   5

---

192. poll: Head.   **202. collateral:** Indirect.   **203. us touch'd:** Me implicated.
210. trophy: Memorial.   **hatchment:** Tablet displaying the armorial bearings of
a deceased person.   **211. ostentation:** Ceremony.   **IV, VI. Location:** The castle.

(*Enter Sailors.*)

FIRST SAILOR: God bless you sir.
HORATIO: Let him bless thee too.
FIRST SAILOR: 'A shall, sir, an 't please him. There's a letter for you, sir—
   it came from th' ambassador that was bound for England—if your
   name be Horatio, as I am let to know it is.   [*Gives letter.*]   10
HORATIO [*reads*]: "Horatio, when thou shalt have over-look'd this, give
   these fellows some means° to the King; they have letters for him. Ere
   we were two days old at sea, a pirate of very warlike appointment°
   gave us chase. Finding ourselves too slow of sail, we put on a compell'd valor, and in the grapple I boarded them. On the instant they got   15
   clear of our ship, so I alone became their prisoner. They have dealt
   with me like thieves of mercy,° but they knew what they did: I am to do
   a good turn for them. Let the King have the letters I have sent, and
   repair thou to me with as much speed as thou wouldest fly death. I
   have words to speak in thine ear will make thee dumb; yet are they   20
   much too light for the bore° of the matter. These good fellows will
   bring thee where I am. Rosencrantz and Guildenstern hold their
   course for England. Of them I have much to tell thee. Farewell.

                      He that thou knowest thine, Hamlet."
Come, I will give you way for these your letters,   25
And do 't the speedier that you may direct me
To him from whom you brought them.   (*Exeunt.*)

                    [*Scene VII*]°

(*Enter King and Laertes.*)

KING: Now must your conscience my acquittance seal,°
   And you must put me in your heart for friend,
   Sith you have heard, and with a knowing ear,
   That he which hath your noble father slain
   Pursued my life.
LAERTES: It well appears. But tell me   5
   Why you proceeded not against these feats°
   So criminal and so capital° in nature,
   As by your safety, greatness, wisdom, all things else,
   You mainly° were stirr'd up.

---

12. means: Means of access.   **13. appointment:** Equipage.   **17. thieves of
mercy:** Merciful thieves.   **21. bore:** Caliber, i.e., importance.   **IV, VII. Location:**
The castle.   **1. my acquittance seal:** Confirm or acknowledge my innocence.
6. feats: Acts.   **7. capital:** Punishable by death.   **9. mainly:** Greatly.

KING:　　　　　　　　　　　　　O, for two special reasons,
　Which may to you, perhaps, seem much unsinew'd,°　　　　　　10
　But yet to me th' are strong. The Queen his mother
　Lives almost by his looks, and for myself—
　My virtue or my plague, be it either which—
　She's so conjunctive° to my life and soul
　That, as the star moves not but in his sphere,°　　　　　　　15
　I could not but by her. The other motive,
　Why to a public count° I might not go,
　Is the great love the general gender° bear him,
　Who, dipping all his faults in their affection,
　Would, like the spring° that turneth wood to stone,　　　　　20
　Convert his gyves° to graces, so that my arrows,
　Too slightly timber'd° for so loud° a wind,
　Would have reverted to my bow again
　And not where I had aim'd them.
LAERTES:　And so have I a noble father lost,　　　　　　　　25
　A sister driven into desp'rate terms,°
　Whose worth, if praises may go back° again,
　Stood challenger on mount° of all the age
　For her perfections. But my revenge will come.
KING:　Break not your sleeps for that. You must not think　30
　That we are made of stuff so flat and dull
　That we can let our beard be shook with danger
　And think it pastime. You shortly shall hear more.
　I lov'd your father, and we love ourself;
　And that, I hope, will teach you to imagine—　　　　　　　35

(*Enter a Messenger with letters.*)

　[How now? What news?]
MESSENGER:　　　　　　　　[Letters, my lord, from Hamlet:]
　These to your Majesty, this to the Queen.

　　　　　　　　　　　　　　　　　　　　　　[*Gives letters.*]

---

10. **unsinew'd:** Weak.　14. **conjunctive:** Closely united.　15. **sphere:** The hollow sphere in which, according to Ptolemaic astronomy, the planets moved. 17. **count:** Account, reckoning.　18. **general gender:** Common people. 20. **spring:** A spring with such a concentration of lime that it coats a piece of wood with limestone, in effect gilding it.　21. **gyves:** Fetters (which, gilded by the people's praise, would look like badges of honor).　22. **slightly timber'd:** Light. **loud:** Strong.　26. **terms:** State, condition.　27. **go back:** Recall Ophelia's former virtues.　28. **on mount:** On high.

KING: From Hamlet? Who brought them?
MESSENGER: Sailors, my lord, they say; I saw them not.
  They were given me by Claudio. He receiv'd them   40
  Of him that brought them.
KING: Laertes, you shall hear them.
  Leave us.   [*Exit Messenger.*]
  [*Reads.*] "High and mighty, you shall know I am set naked° on your
  kingdom. Tomorrow shall I beg leave to see your kingly eyes, when I
  shall, first asking your pardon° thereunto, recount the occasion of my   45
  sudden and more strange return.   Hamlet."
  What should this mean? Are all the rest come back?
  Or is it some abuse,° and no such thing?
LAERTES: Know you the hand?
KING: 'Tis Hamlet's character.° "Naked!"
  And in a postscript here, he says "alone."   50
  Can you devise° me?
LAERTES: I am lost in it, my lord. But let him come.
  It warms the very sickness in my heart
  That I shall live and tell him to his teeth,
  "Thus didst thou."
KING: If it be so, Laertes—   55
  As how should it be so? How otherwise?°—
  Will you be ruled by me?
LAERTES: Ay, my lord,
  So° you will not o'errule me to a peace.
KING: To thine own peace. If he be now returned,
  As checking at° his voyage, and that he means   60
  No more to undertake it, I will work him
  To an exploit, now ripe in my device,
  Under the which he shall not choose but fall;
  And for his death no wind of blame shall breathe,
  But even his mother shall uncharge the practice°   65
  And call it accident.
LAERTES: My lord, I will be rul'd,
  The rather if you could devise it so
  That I might be the organ.°

43. **naked:** Destitute, unarmed, without following. 45. **pardon:** Permission.
48. **abuse:** Deceit. 49. **character:** Handwriting. 51. **devise:** Explain to.
56. **As . . . otherwise:** How can this (Hamlet's return) be true? Yet how otherwise
than true (since we have the evidence of his letter). 58. **So:** Provided that.
60. **checking at:** Turning aside from (like a falcon leaving the quarry to fly at a
chance bird). 65. **uncharge the practice:** Acquit the stratagem of being a plot.
68. **organ:** Agent, instrument.

KING: It falls right.
  You have been talk'd of since your travel much,
  And that in Hamlet's hearing, for a quality   70
  Wherein, they say, you shine. Your sum of parts°
  Did not together pluck such envy from him
  As did that one, and that, in my regard,
  Of the unworthiest siege.°
LAERTES: What part is that, my lord?   75
KING: A very riband in the cap of youth,
  Yet needful too, for youth no less becomes
  The light and careless livery that it wears
  Than settled age his sables° and his weeds,°
  Importing health° and graveness. Two months since   80
  Here was a gentleman of Normandy.
  I have seen myself, and serv'd against, the French,
  And they can well° on horseback, but this gallant
  Had witchcraft in 't; he grew unto his seat,
  And to such wondrous doing brought his horse   85
  As had he been incorps'd and demi-natured°
  With the brave beast. So far he topp'd° my thought
  That I, in forgery° of shapes and tricks,
  Come short of what he did.
LAERTES: A Norman was 't?
KING: A Norman.   90
LAERTES: Upon my life, Lamord.
KING: The very same.
LAERTES: I know him well. He is the brooch° indeed
  And gem of all the nation.
KING: He made confession° of you,
  And gave you such a masterly report   95
  For art and exercise in your defense,
  And for your rapier most especial,
  That he cried out, 'twould be a sight indeed,
  If one could match you. The scrimers° of their nation,
  He swore, had neither motion, guard, nor eye,   100
  If you oppos'd them. Sir, this report of his

71. Your . . . parts: All your other virtues.   74. unworthiest siege: Least important rank.   79. sables: Rich robes furred with sable.   weeds: Garments.
80. Importing health: Indicating prosperity.   83. can well: Are skilled.
86. incorps'd and demi-natured: Of one body and nearly of one nature (like the
centaur).   87. topp'd: Surpassed.   88. forgery: Invention.   92. brooch: Ornament.   94. confession: Admission of superiority.   99. scrimers: Fencers.

Did Hamlet so envenom with his envy
That he could nothing do but wish and beg
Your sudden coming o'er to play° with you.
Now, out of this—
LAERTES: What out of this, my lord?   105
KING: Laertes, was your father dear to you?
   Or are you like the painting of a sorrow,
   A face without a heart?
LAERTES: Why ask you this?
KING: Not that I think you did not love your father,
   But that I know love is begun by time,°   110
   And that I see, in passages of proof,°
   Time qualifies° the spark and fire of it.
   There lives within the very flame of love
   A kind of wick or snuff° that will abate it,
   And nothing is at a like goodness still,°   115
   For goodness, growing to a plurisy,°
   Dies in his own too much.° That° we would do,
   We should do when we would; for this "would" changes
   And hath abatements° and delays as many
   As there are tongues, are hands, are accidents,°   120
   And then this "should" is like a spendthrift's sigh,°
   That hurts by easing.° But, to the quick o' th' ulcer;
   Hamlet comes back. What would you undertake
   To show yourself your father's son in deed
   More than in words?
LAERTES: To cut his throat i' th' church!   125
KING: No place, indeed, should murder sanctuarize;°
   Revenge should have no bounds. But, good Laertes,
   Will you do this,° keep close within your chamber.
   Hamlet return'd shall know you are come home.
   We'll put on those° shall praise your excellence   130

104. play: Fence.   110. begun by time: Subject to change.   111. passages of
proof: Actual instances.   112. qualifies: Weakens.   114. snuff: The charred
part of a candlewick.   115. nothing . . . still: Nothing remains at a constant
level of perfection.   116. plurisy: Excess, plethora.   117. in . . . much: Of its
own excess.   That: That which.   119. abatements: Diminutions.   120. accidents: Occurrences, incidents.   121. spendthrift's sigh: An allusion to the
belief that each sigh cost the heart a drop of blood.   122. hurts by easing: Costs
the heart blood even while it affords emotional relief.   126. sanctuarize: Protect
from punishment (alludes to the right of sanctuary with which certain religious
places were invested).   128. Will you do this: If you wish to do this.   130. put
on those: Instigate those who.

And set a double varnish on the fame
The Frenchman gave you, bring you in fine° together,
And wager on your heads. He, being remiss,°
Most generous,° and free from all contriving,
Will not peruse the foils, so that, with ease,   135
Or with a little shuffling, you may choose
A sword unbated,° and in a pass of practice°
Requite him for your father.
LAERTES: I will do 't.
And for that purpose I'll anoint my sword.
I bought an unction° of a mountebank°   140
So mortal that, but dip a knife in it,
Where it draws blood no cataplasm° so rare,
Collected from all simples° that have virtue
Under the moon, can save the thing from death
That is but scratch'd withal. I'll touch my point   145
With this contagion, that, if I gall° him slightly,
It may be death.
KING: Let's further think of this,
Weigh what convenience both of time and means
May fit us to our shape.° If this should fail,
And that our drift look through our bad performance,°   150
'Twere better not assay'd. Therefore this project
Should have a back or second, that might hold
If this did blast in proof.° Soft, let me see.
We'll make a solemn wager on your cunnings—
I ha 't!   155
When in your motion you are hot and dry—
As° make your bouts more violent to that end—
And that he calls for drink, I'll have prepar'd him
A chalice for the nonce,° whereon but sipping,
If he by chance escape your venom'd stuck,°   160
Our purpose may hold there. [*A cry within.*] But stay, what noise?

(*Enter Queen.*)

---

132. **in fine:** Finally.   133. **remiss:** Negligently unsuspicious.   134. **generous:**
Noble-minded.   137. **unbated:** Not blunted, having no button.   **pass of prac-
tice:** Treacherous thrust.   140. **unction:** Ointment.   **mountebank:** Quack doc-
tor.   142. **cataplasm:** Plaster or poultice.   143. **simples:** Herbs.   146. **gall:**
Graze, wound.   149. **shape:** Part that we propose to act.   150. **drift . . . per-
formance:** I.e., intention be disclosed by our bungling.   153. **blast in proof:**
Burst in the test (like a cannon).   157. **As:** And you should.   159. **nonce:**
Occasion.   160. **stuck:** Thrust (from *stoccado,* a fencing term).

QUEEN: One woe doth tread upon another's heel,
  So fast they follow. Your sister's drowned, Laertes.
LAERTES: Drown'd! O, where?
QUEEN: There is a willow grows askant° the brook   165
  That shows his hoar° leaves in the glassy stream;
  Therewith fantastic garlands did she make
  Of crow-flowers, nettles, daisies, and long purples°
  That liberal° shepherds give a grosser name,
  But our cold° maids do dead men's fingers call them.   170
  There on the pendent boughs her crownet° weeds
  Clamb'ring to hang, an envious sliver° broke,
  When down her weedy° trophies and herself
  Fell in the weeping brook. Her clothes spread wide,
  And mermaid-like awhile they bore her up,   175
  Which time she chanted snatches of old lauds,°
  As one incapable° of her own distress,
  Or like a creature native and indued°
  Unto that element. But long it could not be
  Till that her garments, heavy with their drink,   180
  Pull'd the poor wretch from her melodious lay
  To muddy death.
LAERTES: Alas, then she is drown'd?
QUEEN: Drown'd, drown'd.
LAERTES: Too much of water hast thou, poor Ophelia,
  And therefore I forbid my tears. But yet   185
  It is our trick;° nature her custom holds,
  Let shame say what it will. [*He weeps.*] When these are gone,
  The woman will be out.° Adieu, my lord.
  I have a speech of fire, that fain would blaze,
  But that this folly drowns it.   (*Exit.*)
KING: Let's follow, Gertrude.   190
  How much I had to do to calm his rage!
  Now fear I this will give it start again;
  Therefore let's follow.   (*Exeunt.*)

---

165. **askant:** Aslant.   166. **hoar:** White or gray.   168. **long purples:** Early purple orchids.   169. **liberal:** Free-spoken.   170. **cold:** Chaste.   171. **crownet:** Made into a chaplet or coronet.   172. **envious sliver:** Malicious branch. 173. **weedy:** I.e., of plants.   176. **lauds:** Hymns.   177. **incapable:** Lacking capacity to apprehend.   178. **indued:** Adapted by nature.   186. **It is our trick:** Weeping is our natural way (when sad).   187–88. **When . . . out:** When my tears are all shed, the woman in me will be expended, satisfied.

{ACT V   *Scene 1*}°

(*Enter two Clowns*° [*with spades, etc.*])

FIRST CLOWN: Is she to be buried in Christian burial when she willfully
seeks her own salvation?

SECOND CLOWN: I tell thee she is; therefore make her grave straight.° The
crowner° hath sat on her, and finds it Christian burial.

FIRST CLOWN: How can that be, unless she drown'd herself in her own   5
defense?

SECOND CLOWN: Why, 'tis found so.

FIRST CLOWN: It must be "se offendendo";° it cannot be else. For here lies
the point: if I drown myself wittingly, it argues an act, and an act hath
three branches—it is to act, to do, and to perform. Argal,° she   10
drown'd herself wittingly.

SECOND CLOWN: Nay, but hear you, goodman delver—

FIRST CLOWN: Give me leave. Here lies the water; good. Here stands the
man; good. If the man go to this water, and drown himself, it is, will
he,° nill he, he goes, mark you that. But if the water come to him and   15
drown him, he drowns not himself. Argal, he that is not guilty of his
own death shortens not his own life.

SECOND CLOWN: But is this law?

FIRST CLOWN: Ay, marry, is 't—crowner's quest° law.

SECOND CLOWN: Will you ha' the truth on 't? If this had not been a gentle- 20
woman, she should have been buried out o' Christian burial.

FIRST CLOWN: Why, there thou say'st.° And the more pity that great folk
should have count'nance° in this world to drown or hang themselves,
more than their even-Christen.° Come, my spade. There is no ancient
gentlemen but gard'ners, ditchers, and grave-makers. They hold up   25
Adam's profession.

SECOND CLOWN: Was he a gentleman?

FIRST CLOWN: 'A was the first that ever bore arms.

[SECOND CLOWN: Why, he had none.

FIRST CLOWN: What, art a heathen? How dost thou understand the   30
Scripture? The Scripture says "Adam digg'd." Could he dig without

---

V, I. Location: A churchyard. **[s.D.]** *Clowns:* Rustics. **3. straight:** Straightway,
immediately. **4. crowner:** Coroner. **8. se offendendo:** A comic mistake for *se
defendendo*, term used in verdicts of justifiable homicide. **10. Argal:** Corruption
of *ergo*, therefore. **14–15. will he:** Will he not. **19. quest:** Inquest. **22. there
thou say'st:** That's right. **23. count'nance:** Privilege. **24. even-Christen:** Fellow Christian.

arms?] I'll put another question to thee. If thou answerest me not to
the purpose, confess thyself° —

SECOND CLOWN: Go to.

FIRST CLOWN: What is he that builds stronger than either the mason, the   35
shipwright, or the carpenter?

SECOND CLOWN: The gallows-maker, for that frame outlives a thousand
tenants.

FIRST CLOWN: I like thy wit well, in good faith. The gallows does well, but
how does it well? It does well to those that do ill. Now thou dost ill to   40
say the gallows is built stronger than the church. Argal, the gallows
may do well to thee. To 't again, come.

SECOND CLOWN: "Who builds stronger than a mason, a shipwright, or a
carpenter?"

FIRST CLOWN: Ay, tell me that, and unyoke.°   45

SECOND CLOWN: Marry, now I can tell.

FIRST CLOWN: To 't.

SECOND CLOWN: Mass,° I cannot tell.

(*Enter Hamlet and Horatio [at a distance].*)

FIRST CLOWN: Cudgel thy brains no more about it, for your dull ass will
not mend his pace with beating; and, when you are ask'd this question   50
next, say "a grave-maker." The houses he makes lasts till doomsday.
Go, get thee in, and fetch me a stoup° of liquor.

                                             [*Exit Second Clown. First Clown digs.*]

                                                                        (*Song.*)

"In youth, when I did love, did love,°
    Methought it was very sweet,
To contract — O — the time for — a — my behove,°   55
    O, methought there — a — was nothing — a — meet."°

HAMLET: Has this fellow no feeling of his business, that 'a sings at grave-
making?

HORATIO: Custom hath made it in him a property of easiness.°

HAMLET: 'Tis e'en so. The hand of little employment hath the daintier   60
sense.°

33. confess thyself: The saying continues, "and be hanged."   45. unyoke: After
this great effort you may unharness the team of your wits.   48. Mass: By the
Mass.   52. stoup: Two-quart measure.   53. In . . . love: This and the two following stanzas, with nonsensical variations, are from a poem attributed to Lord
Vaux and printed in *Tottel's Miscellany* (1557). The *O* and *a* (for "ah") seemingly
are the grunts of the digger.   55. To contract . . . behove: To make a betrothal
agreement for my benefit (?).   56. meet: Suitable, i.e., more suitable.   59. property of easiness: Something he can do easily and without thinking.
60–61. daintier sense: More delicate sense of feeling.

(*Song.*)

FIRST CLOWN: "But age, with his stealing steps,
　　　Hath claw'd me in his clutch,
　　And hath shipped me into the land,°
　　　As if I had never been such."   65

[*Throws up a skull.*]

HAMLET: That skull had a tongue in it, and could sing once. How the
　　knave jowls° it to the ground, as if 'twere Cain's jaw-bone, that did the
　　first murder! This might be the pate of a politician,° which this ass
　　now o'erreaches,° one that would circumvent God, might it not?

HORATIO: It might, my lord.   70

HAMLET: Or of a courtier, which could say "Good morrow, sweet lord!
　　How dost thou, sweet lord?" This might be my Lord Such-a-one, that
　　prais'd my Lord Such-a-one's horse when 'a meant to beg it, might
　　it not?

HORATIO: Ay, my lord.   75

HAMLET: Why, e'en so, and now my Lady Worm's, chapless,° and knock'd
　　about the mazzard° with a sexton's spade. Here's fine revolution,° an°
　　we had the trick to see 't. Did these bones cost no more the breeding,°
　　but to play at loggats° with them? Mine ache to think on 't.

(*Song.*)

FIRST CLOWN: "A pick-axe, and a spade, a spade,   80
　　　For and° a shrouding sheet;
　　O, a pit of clay for to be made
　　　For such a guest is meet."

[*Throws up another skull.*]

HAMLET: There's another. Why may not that be the skull of a lawyer?
　　Where be his quiddities° now, his quillities,° his cases, his tenures,°   85
　　and his tricks? Why does he suffer this mad knave now to knock him
　　about the sconce° with a dirty shovel, and will not tell him of his

---

64. into the land: Toward my grave (?) (but note the lack of rhyme in *steps, land*). **67. jowls:** Dashes. **68. politician:** Schemer, plotter. **69. o'erreaches:** Circumvents, gets the better of (with a quibble on the literal sense). **76. chapless:** Having no lower jaw. **77. mazzard:** Head (literally, a drinking vessel). **revolution:** Change. **an:** If. **78. the breeding:** In the breeding, raising. **79. loggats:** A game in which pieces of hardwood are thrown to lie as near as possible to a stake. **81. For and:** And moreover. **85. quiddities:** Subtleties, quibbles (from Latin *quid*, a thing). **quillities:** Verbal niceties, subtle distinctions (variation of *quiddities*). **tenures:** The holding of a piece of property or office, or the conditions or period of such holding. **87. sconce:** Head.

action of battery? Hum! This fellow might be in 's time a great buyer
of land, with his statutes, his recognizances,° his fines, his double°
vouchers,° his recoveries.° [Is this the fine of his fines, and the recov-   90
ery of his recoveries,] to have his fine pate full of fine dirt?° Will his
vouchers vouch him no more of his purchases, and double [ones too],
than the length and breadth of a pair of indentures?° The very con-
veyances° of his lands will scarcely lie in this box,° and must th' inher-
itor° himself have no more, ha?   95
HORATIO: Not a jot more, my lord.
HAMLET: Is not parchment made of sheep-skins?
HORATIO: Ay, my lord, and of calf-skins too.
HAMLET: They are sheep and calves which seek out assurance in that.° I
will speak to this fellow. — Whose grave's this, sirrah?°   100
FIRST CLOWN: Mine, sir.
[*Sings.*] "O, a pit of clay for to be made
[For such a guest is meet]."
HAMLET: I think it be thine, indeed, for thou liest in 't.
FIRST CLOWN: You lie out on 't, sir, and therefore 'tis not yours. For my   105
part, I do not lie in 't, yet it is mine.
HAMLET: Thou dost lie in 't, to be in 't and say it is thine. 'Tis for the dead,
not for the quick;° therefore thou liest.
FIRST CLOWN: 'Tis a quick lie, sir; 'twill away again from me to you.
HAMLET: What man dost thou dig it for?   110
FIRST CLOWN: For no man, sir.
HAMLET: What woman, then?
FIRST CLOWN: For none, neither.
HAMLET: Who is to be buried in 't?
FIRST CLOWN: One that was a woman, sir, but, rest her soul, she's dead.   115
HAMLET: How absolute° the knave is! We must speak by the card,° or
equivocation° will undo us. By the Lord, Horatio, this three years I

---

89. statutes, recognizances: Legal documents guaranteeing a debt by attaching
land and property.   **89–90. fines, recoveries:** Ways of converting entailed estates
into "fee simple" or freehold.   **89. double:** Signed by two signatories.   **90. vouchers:** Guarantees of the legality of a title to real estate.   **90–91. fine of his fines . . .
fine pate . . . fine dirt:** End of his legal maneuvers . . . elegant head . . . minutely
sifted dirt.   **93. pair of indentures:** Legal document drawn up in duplicate on a
single sheet and then cut apart on a zigzag line so that each pair was uniquely
matched. (Hamlet may refer to two rows of teeth, or dentures.)   **93–94. con-
veyances:** Deeds.   **94. this box:** The skull.   **94–95. inheritor:** Possessor, owner.
99. assurance in that: Safety in legal parchments.   **100. sirrah:** Term of
address to inferiors.   **108. quick:** Living.   **116. absolute:** Positive, decided.
by the card: By the mariner's card on which the points of the compass were
marked, i.e., with precision.   **117. equivocation:** Ambiguity in the use of terms.

have taken note of it: the age is grown so pick'd° that the toe of the
peasant comes so near the heel of the courtier, he galls his kibe.° How
long hast thou been a grave-maker?   120

FIRST CLOWN: Of all the days i' th' year, I came to 't that day that our last
king Hamlet overcame Fortinbras.

HAMLET: How long is that since?

FIRST CLOWN: Cannot you tell that? Every fool can tell that. It was that
very day that young Hamlet was born—he that is mad, and sent into   125
England.

HAMLET: Ay, marry, why was he sent into England?

FIRST CLOWN: Why, because 'a was mad. 'A shall recover his wits there,
or, if 'a do not, 'tis no great matter there.

HAMLET: Why?   130

FIRST CLOWN: 'Twill not be seen in him there. There the men are as mad
as he.

HAMLET: How came he mad?

FIRST CLOWN: Very strangely, they say.

HAMLET: How strangely?   135

FIRST CLOWN: Faith, e'en with losing his wits.

HAMLET: Upon what ground?

FIRST CLOWN: Why, here in Denmark. I have been sexton here, man and
boy, thirty years.

HAMLET: How long will a man lie i' th' earth ere he rot?   140

FIRST CLOWN: Faith, if 'a be not rotten before 'a die—as we have many
pocky° corses [now-a-days], that will scarce hold the laying in—'a will
last you some eight year or nine year. A tanner will last you nine year.

HAMLET: Why he more than another?

FIRST CLOWN: Why, sir, his hide is so tann'd with his trade that 'a will 145
keep out water a great while, and your water is a sore decayer of your
whoreson dead body. [*Picks up a skull.*] Here's a skull now hath lain
you° i' th' earth three and twenty years.

HAMLET: Whose was it?

FIRST CLOWN: A whoreson mad fellow's it was. Whose do you think it   150
was?

HAMLET: Nay, I know not.

FIRST CLOWN: A pestilence on him for a mad rogue! 'A pour'd a flagon of
Rhenish° on my head once. This same skull, sir, was Yorick's skull, the
King's jester.   155

---

118. pick'd: Refined, fastidious.   **119. galls his kibe:** Chafes the courtier's
chilblain (a swelling or sore caused by cold).   **142. pocky:** Rotten, diseased (literally, with the pox, or syphilis).   **147–48. lain you:** Lain.   **154. Rhenish:**
Rhine wine.

HAMLET: This?
FIRST CLOWN: E'en that.
HAMLET: [Let me see.] [*Takes the skull.*] Alas, poor Yorick! I knew him,
  Horatio, a fellow of infinite jest, of most excellent fancy. He hath borne
  me on his back a thousand times; and now, how abhorr'd in my imagi-   160
  nation it is! My gorge rises at it. Here hung those lips that I have kiss'd
  I know not how oft. Where be your gibes now? Your gambols, your
  songs, your flashes of merriment that were wont to set the table on a
  roar? Not one now, to mock your own grinning? Quite chap-fall'n?°
  Now get you to my lady's chamber, and tell her, let her paint an inch   165
  thick, to this favor° she must come; make her laugh at that. Prithee,
  Horatio, tell me one thing.
HORATIO: What's that, my lord?
HAMLET: Dost thou think Alexander look'd o' this fashion i' th' earth?
HORATIO: E'en so.   170
HAMLET: And smelt so? Pah! [*Puts down the skull.*]
HORATIO: E'en so, my lord.
HAMLET: To what base uses we may return, Horatio! Why may not imag-
  ination trace the noble dust of Alexander, till 'a find it stopping a bung-
  hole?   175
HORATIO: 'twere to consider too curiously,° to consider so.
HAMLET: No, faith, not a jot, but to follow him thither with modesty°
  enough, and likelihood to lead it. [As thus]: Alexander died, Alexander
  was buried, Alexander returneth to dust; the dust is earth; of earth we
  make loam;° and why of that loam, whereto he was converted, might   180
  they not stop a beer-barrel?
  Imperious° Caesar, dead and turn'd to clay,
  Might stop a hole to keep the wind away.
  O, that that earth which kept the world in awe
  Should patch a wall t' expel the winter's flaw!°   185
  But soft, but soft awhile! Here comes the King.

(*Enter King, Queen, Laertes, and the Corse* [*of Ophelia, in procession, with
Priest, Lords etc.*].)

  The Queen, the courtiers. Who is this they follow?
  And with such maimed rites? This doth betoken
  The corse they follow did with desp'rate hand

---

164. chap-fall'n: (1) Lacking the lower jaw; (2) dejected.   166. favor: Aspect,
appearance.   176. curiously: Minutely.   177. modesty: Moderation.   180. loam:
Clay mixture for brickmaking or other clay use.   182. Imperious: Imperial.
185. flaw: Gust of wind.

Fordo it° own life. 'Twas of some estate.°   190
Couch° we awhile, and mark.

> [*He and Horatio conceal themselves.*
> *Ophelia's body is taken to the grave.*]

LAERTES: What ceremony else?
HAMLET [*to Horatio*]: That is Laertes, a very noble youth. Mark.
LAERTES: What ceremony else?
PRIEST: Her obsequies have been as far enlarg'd   195
  As we have warranty. Her death was doubtful,
  And, but that great command o'ersways the order,
  She should in ground unsanctified been lodg'd
  Till the last trumpet. For° charitable prayers,
  Shards,° flints, and pebbles should be thrown on her.   200
  Yet here she is allow'd her virgin crants,°
  Her maiden strewments,° and the bringing home
  Of bell and burial.°
LAERTES: Must there no more be done?
PRIEST: No more be done.
  We should profane the service of the dead   205
  To sing a requiem and such rest to her
  As to peace-parted souls.
LAERTES: Lay her i' th' earth,
  And from her fair and unpolluted flesh
  May violets° spring! I tell thee, churlish priest,
  A minist'ring angel shall my sister be   210
  When thou liest howling!
HAMLET [*to Horatio*]:   What, the fair Ophelia!
QUEEN [*scattering flowers*]: Sweets to the sweet! Farewell.
  I hoped thou shouldst have been my Hamlet's wife.
  I thought thy bride-bed to have deck'd, sweet maid,
  And not have strew'd thy grave.
LAERTES: O, treble woe   215
  Fall ten times treble on that cursed head
  Whose wicked deed thy most ingenious sense°
  Depriv'd thee of! Hold off the earth awhile,

190. Fordo it: Destroy its. **estate:** Rank. **191. Couch:** Hide, lurk. **199. For:** In place of. **200. Shards:** Broken bits of pottery. **201. crants:** Garland. **202. strewments:** Traditional strewing of flowers. **202–03. bringing . . . burial:** Laying to rest of the body in consecrated ground, to the sound of the bell. **209. violets:** See IV, v, 181 and note. **217. ingenious sense:** Mind endowed with finest qualities.

Till I have caught her once more in mine arms.

> *[Leaps into the grave and embraces Ophelia.]*

Now pile your dust upon the quick and dead,   220
Till of this flat a mountain you have made
T 'o'ertop old Pelion,° or the skyish head
Of blue Olympus.°
HAMLET [*coming forward*]: What is he whose grief
Bears such an emphasis, whose phrase of sorrow   225
Conjures the wand'ring stars,° and makes them stand
Like wonder-wounded hearers? This is I,
Hamlet the Dane.°
LAERTES: The devil take thy soul!

> *[Grappling with him.]*

HAMLET: Thou pray'st not well.
I prithee, take thy fingers from my throat;   230
For, though I am not splenitive° and rash,
Yet have I in me something dangerous,
Which let thy wisdom fear. Hold off thy hand.
KING: Pluck them asunder.
QUEEN: Hamlet, Hamlet!
ALL: Gentlemen!
HORATIO: Good my lord, be quiet.   235

> *[Hamlet and Laertes are parted.]*

HAMLET: Why, I will fight with him upon this theme
Until my eyelids will no longer wag.
QUEEN: O my son, what theme?
HAMLET: I lov'd Ophelia. Forty thousand brothers
Could not with all their quantity of love   240
Make up my sum. What wilt thou do for her?
KING: O, he is mad, Laertes.
QUEEN: For love of God, forbear him.
HAMLET: 'Swounds,° show me what thou' do.
Woo 't° weep? Woo 't fight? Woo 't fast? Woo 't tear thyself?   245
Woo 't drink up eisel?° Eat a crocodile?
I'll do 't. Dost thou come here to whine?

222, 223. Pelion, Olympus: Mountains in the north of Thessaly; see also *Ossa* at
line 253.   **226. wand'ring stars:** Planets.   **228. the Dane:** This title normally
signifies the king, see I, I, 15 and note.   **231. splenitive:** Quick-tempered.
244. 'Swounds: By His (Christ's) wounds.   **245. Woo 't:** Wilt thou.   **246. eisel:**
Vinegar.

To outface me with leaping in her grave?
Be buried quick° with her, and so will I.
And, if thou prate of mountains, let them throw   250
Millions of acres on us, till our ground,
Singeing his pate° against the burning zone,°
Make Ossa° like a wart! Nay, an thou 'lt mouth,°
I'll rant as well as thou.
QUEEN: This is mere° madness,
And thus a while the fit will work on him;   255
Anon, as patient as the female dove
When that her golden couplets° are disclos'd,°
His silence will sit drooping.
HAMLET: Hear you, sir.
What is the reason that you use me thus?
I lov'd you ever. But it is no matter.   260
Let Hercules himself do what he may,
The cat will mew, and dog will have his day.°
KING: I pray thee, good Horatio, wait upon him.

                                        (*Exit Hamlet and Horatio.*)

[*To Laertes.*] Strengthen your patience in° our last night's speech;
We'll put the matter to the present push.°—   265
Good Gertrude, set some watch over your son.—
This grave shall have a living° monument.
An hour of quiet shortly shall we see;
Till then, in patience our proceeding be.   (*Exeunt.*)

                        [*Scene II*]°

(*Enter Hamlet and Horatio.*)

HAMLET: So much for this, sir; now shall you see the other.°
    You do remember all the circumstance?
HORATIO: Remember it, my lord!
HAMLET: Sir, in my heart there was a kind of fighting

249. quick: Alive.   **252. his pate:** Its head, i.e., top.   **burning zone:** Sun's orbit.
253. Ossa: Another mountain in Thessaly. (In their war against the Olympian gods,
the giants attempted to heap Ossa, Pelion, and Olympus on one another to scale
heaven.)   **mouth:** Rant.   **254. mere:** Utter.   **257. golden couplets:** Two baby
pigeons, covered with yellow down.   **disclos'd:** Hatched.   **261–62. Let . . . day:**
Despite any blustering attempts at interference every person will sooner or later do
what he must do.   **264. in:** By recalling.   **265. present push:** Immediate test.
267. living: Lasting; also refers (for Laertes' benefit) to the plot against Hamlet.
V, II. Location: The castle.   **1. see the other:** Hear the other news.

That would not let me sleep. Methought I lay   5
Worse than the mutines° in the bilboes.° Rashly,°
And prais'd be rashness for it—let us know,°
Our indiscretion sometime serves us well
When our deep plots do pall,° and that should learn° us
There's a divinity that shapes our ends,   10
Rough-hew° them how we will—
HORATIO: That is most certain.
HAMLET: Up from my cabin,
My sea-gown scarf'd about me, in the dark
Grop'd I to find out them, had my desire,
Finger'd° their packet, and in fine° withdrew   15
To mine own room again, making so bold,
My fears forgetting manners, to unseal
Their grand commission; where I found, Horatio—
Ah, royal knavery!—an exact command,
Larded° with many several sorts of reasons   20
Importing° Denmark's health and England's too,
With, ho, such bugs° and goblins in my life,°
That, on the supervise,° no leisure bated,°
No, not to stay the grinding of the axe,
My head should be struck off.
HORATIO: Is 't possible?   25
HAMLET: Here's the commission; read it at more leisure.

                              [*Gives document.*]

But wilt thou hear now how I did proceed?
HORATIO: I beseech you.
HAMLET: Being thus benetted round with villainies,
Or I could make a prologue to my brains,   30
They had begun the play.° I sat me down,
Devis'd a new commission, wrote it fair.°
I once did hold it, as our statists° do,

6. **mutines:** Mutineers. **bilboes:** Shackles. **Rashly:** On impulse (this adverb goes with lines 12ff.). 7. **know:** Acknowledge. 9. **pall:** Fail. **learn:** Teach. 11. **Rough-hew:** Shape roughly. 15. **Finger'd:** Pilfered, pinched. **in fine:** Finally, in conclusion. 20. **Larded:** Enriched. 21. **Importing:** Relating to. 22. **bugs:** Bugbears, hobgoblins. **in my life:** To be feared if I were allowed to live. 23. **supervise:** Reading. **leisure bated:** Delay allowed. 30–31. **Or . . . play:** Before I could consciously turn my brain to the matter, it had started working on a plan. (*Or* means *ere.*) 32. **fair:** In a clear hand. 33. **statists:** Statesmen.

A baseness° to write fair, and labor'd much
How to forget that learning, but, sir, now   35
It did me yeoman's° service. Wilt thou know
Th' effect° of what I wrote?
HORATIO: Ay, good my lord.
HAMLET: An earnest conjuration from the King,
  As England was his faithful tributary,
  As love between them like the palm might flourish,   40
  As peace should still her wheaten garland° wear
  And stand a comma° 'tween their amities,
  And many such-like as's° of great charge,°
  That, on the view and knowing of these contents,
  Without debasement further, more or less,   45
  He should those bearers put to sudden death,
  Not shriving time° allow'd.
HORATIO: How was this seal'd?
HAMLET: Why, even in that was heaven ordinant.°
  I had my father's signet° in my purse,
  Which was the model of that Danish seal;   50
  Folded the writ up in the form of th' other,
  Subscrib'd° it, gave 't th' impression,° plac'd it safely,
  The changeling° never known. Now, the next day
  Was our sea-fight, and what to this was sequent
  Thou knowest already.   55
HORATIO: So Guildenstern and Rosencrantz go to 't.
HAMLET: [Why, man, they did make love to this employment.]
  They are not near my conscience. Their defeat
  Does by their own insinuation° grow.
  'Tis dangerous when the baser nature comes   60
  Between the pass° and fell° incensed points
  Of mighty opposites.
HORATIO: Why, what a king is this!
HAMLET: Does it not, think thee, stand° me now upon —
  He that hath killed my king and whor'd my mother,

34. **baseness:** Lower-class trait.   36. **yeoman's:** Substantial, workmanlike.
37. **effect:** Purport.   41. **wheaten garland:** Symbolic of fruitful agriculture, of
peace.   42. **comma:** Indicating continuity, link.   43. **as's:** (1) The "whereases"
of formal document, (2) asses.   **charge:** (1) Import, (2) burden.   47. **shriving
time:** Time for confession and absolution.   48. **ordinant:** Directing.
49. **signet:** Small seal.   52. **Subscrib'd:** Signed.   **impression:** With a wax seal.
53. **changeling:** The substituted letter (literally, a fairy child substituted for a
human one).   59. **insinuation:** Interference.   61. **pass:** Thrust.   **fell:** Fierce.
63. **stand:** Become incumbent.

Popp'd in between th' election° and my hopes,   65
Thrown out his angle° for my proper° life,
And with such coz'nage°—is 't not perfect conscience
[To quit° him with this arm? And is 't not to be damn'd
To let this canker° of our nature come
In further evil?   70
HORATIO: It must be shortly known to him from England
What is the issue of the business there.
HAMLET: It will be short. The interim is mine,
And a man's life 's no more than to say "One."°
But I am very sorry, good Horatio,   75
That to Laertes I forgot myself,
For by the image of my cause I see
The portraiture of his. I'll court his favors.
But, sure, the bravery° of his grief did put me
Into a tow'ring passion.
HORATIO: Peace, who comes here?]   80

(*Enter a Courtier [Osric].*)

OSRIC: Your lordship is right welcome back to Denmark.
HAMLET: I humbly thank you, sir. [*To Horatio.*] Dost know this water-fly?
HORATIO: No, my good lord.
HAMLET: Thy state is the more gracious, for 'tis a vice to know him. He
hath much land, and fertile. Let a beast be lord of beasts, and his crib   85
shall stand at the King's mess.° 'Tis a chough,° but, as I say, spacious in
the possession of dirt.
OSRIC: Sweet lord, if your lordship were at leisure, I should impart a
thing to you from his Majesty.
HAMLET: I will receive it, sir, with all diligence of spirit. Put your bonnet 90
to his right use; 'tis for the head.
OSRIC: I thank your lordship, it is very hot.
HAMLET: No, believe me, 'tis very cold; the wind is northerly.
OSRIC: It is indifferent° cold, my lord, indeed.
HAMLET: But yet methinks it is very sultry and hot for my complexion.°   95
OSRIC: Exceedingly, my lord; it is very sultry, as 'twere—I cannot tell
how. My lord, his Majesty bade me signify to you that 'a has laid a
great wager on your head. Sir, this is the matter—

---

65. **election:** The Danish monarch was "elected" by a small number of high-
ranking electors. 66. **angle:** Fishing line. **proper:** Very. 67. **coz'nage:**
Trickery. 68. **quit:** Repay. 69. **canker:** Ulcer. 74. **a man's . . . "One":** To take
a man's life requires no more than to count to one as one duels. 79. **bravery:**
Bravado. 85–86. **Let . . . mess:** If a man, no matter how beastlike, is as rich
in possessions as Osric, he may eat at the king's table. 86. **chough:** Chattering
jackdaw. 94. **indifferent:** Somewhat. 95. **complexion:** Temperament.

HAMLET: I beseech you, remember—

[*Hamlet moves him to put on his hat.*]

OSRIC: Nay, good my lord; for my ease,° in good faith. Sir, here is newly   100
come to court Laertes—believe me, an absolute gentleman, full of most
excellent differences,° of very soft society° and great showing.° Indeed,
to speak feelingly° of him, he is the card° or calendar° of gentry,° for you
shall find in him the continent of what part° a gentleman would see.

HAMLET: Sir, his definement° suffers no perdition° in you, though, I   105
know, to divide him inventorially° would dozy° th' arithmetic of memory, and yet but yaw° neither° in respect of° his quick sail. But, in the
verity of extolment,° I take him to be a soul of great article,° and his
infusion° of such dearth and rareness,° as, to make true diction° of
him, his semblable° is his mirror, and who else would trace° him, his   110
umbrage,° nothing more.

OSRIC: Your lordship speaks most infallibly of him.

HAMLET: The concernancy,° sir? Why do we wrap the gentleman in our
more rawer breath?°

OSRIC: Sir?   115

HORATIO: Is 't not possible to understand in another tongue?° You will do
't,° sir, really.

HAMLET: What imports the nomination° of this gentleman?

OSRIC: Of Laertes?

HORATIO [*to Hamlet*]: His purse is empty already; all 's golden words are   120
spent.

HAMLET: Of him, sir.

100. for my ease: A conventional reply declining the invitation to put his hat
back on.   **102. differences:** Special qualities.   **soft society:** Agreeable manners.
great showing: Distinguished appearance.   **103. feelingly:** With just perception.
card: Chart, map.   **calendar:** Guide.   **gentry:** Good breeding.   **104. the continent . . . part:** One who contains in him all the qualities (a *continent* is that
which contains).   **105. definement:** Definition. (Hamlet proceeds to mock Osric
by using his lofty diction back at him.)   **perdition:** Loss, diminution.
106. divide him inventorially: Enumerate his graces.   **dozy:** Dizzy.   **107. yaw:**
To move unsteadily (said of a ship).   **neither:** For all that.   **in respect of:** In
comparison with.   **107–08. in . . . extolment:** In true praise (of him).
108. article: Moment or importance.   **109. infusion:** Essence, character
imparted by nature.   **dearth and rareness:** Rarity.   **make true diction:** Speak
truly.   **110. semblable:** Only true likeness.   **who . . . trace:** Any other person
who would wish to follow.   **111. umbrage:** Shadow.   **113. concernancy:**
Import, relevance.   **114. breath:** Speech.   **116. to understand . . . tongue:** For
Osric to understand when someone else speaks in his manner. (Horatio twits
Osric for not being able to understand the kind of flowery speech he himself uses
when Hamlet speaks in such a vein.)   **116–17. You will do 't:** You can if you try.
118. nomination: Naming.

OSRIC: I know you are not ignorant—
HAMLET: I would you did, sir; yet, in faith, if you did, it would not much
approve° me. Well, sir?   125
OSRIC: You are not ignorant of what excellence Laertes is—
HAMLET: I dare not confess that, lest I should compare° with him in
excellence; but to know a man well were to know himself.°
OSRIC: I mean, sir, for his weapon; but in the imputation laid on him by
them,° in his meed° he's unfellow'd.°   130
HAMLET: What's his weapon?
OSRIC: Rapier and dagger.
HAMLET: That's two of his weapons—but well.
OSRIC: The King, sir, hath wager'd with him six Barbary horses, against
the which he has impawn'd,° as I take it, six French rapiers and   135
poniards, with their assigns,° as girdle, hangers,° and so. Three of the
carriages,° in faith, are very dear to fancy,° very responsive° to the
hilts, most delicate° carriages, and of very liberal conceit.°
HAMLET: What call you the carriages?
HORATIO [to Hamlet]: I knew you must be edified by the margent° ere you   140
had done.
OSRIC: The carriages, sir, are the hangers.
HAMLET: The phrase would be more germane to the matter if we could
carry a cannon by our sides; I would it might be hangers till then. But,
on: six Barb'ry horses against six French swords, their assigns, and   145
three liberal-conceited carriages; that's the French bet against the
Danish. Why is this impawn'd, as you call it?
OSRIC: The King, sir, hath laid,° sir, that in a dozen passes° between
yourself and him, he shall not exceed you three hits. He hath laid on
twelve for nine, and it would come to immediate trial, if your lordship   150
would vouchsafe the answer.
HAMLET: How if I answer no?

125. approve: Commend.   127. compare: Seem to compete.   128. but . . .
himself: For, to recognize excellence in another man, one must know
oneself.   129–30. imputation . . . them: Reputation given him by others.
130. meed: Merit.   unfellow'd: Unmatched.   135. impawn'd: Staked, wagered.
136. assigns: Appurtenances.   hangers: Straps on the sword belt (*girdle*) from
which the sword hung.   137. carriages: An affected way of saying *hangers;* literally, gun-carriages.   dear to fancy: Fancifully designed, tasteful.   responsive:
Corresponding closely, matching.   138. delicate: I.e., in workmanship.   liberal
conceit: Elaborate design.   140. margent: Margin of a book, place for explanatory notes.   148. laid: Wagered.   passes: Bouts. (The odds of the betting are
hard to explain. Possibly the king bets that Hamlet will win at least five out of
twelve, at which point Laertes raises the odds against himself by betting he will
win nine.)

OSRIC: I mean, my lord, the opposition of your person in trial.

HAMLET: Sir, I will walk here in the hall. If it please his Majesty, it is the breathing time° of day with me. Let the foils be brought, the gentle- 155 man willing, and the King hold his purpose, I will win for him an I can; if not, I will gain nothing but my shame and the odd hits.

OSRIC: Shall I deliver you so?

HAMLET: To this effect, sir—after what flourish your nature will.

OSRIC: I commend my duty to your lordship.   160

HAMLET: Yours, yours. [*Exit Osric.*] He does well to commend it himself; there are no tongues else for 's turn.

HORATIO: This lapwing° runs away with the shell on his head.

HAMLET: 'A did comply, sir, with his dug,° before 'a suck'd it. Thus has he—and many more of the same breed that I know the drossy° age 165 dotes on—only got the tune° of the time and, out of an habit of encounter,° a kind of yesty° collection,° which carries them through and through the most fann'd and winnow'd° opinions; and do but blow them to their trial, the bubbles are out.°

(*Enter a Lord.*)

LORD: My lord, his Majesty commended him to you by young Osric, who 170 brings back to him that you attend him in the hall. He sends to know if your pleasure hold to play with Laertes, or that you will take longer time.

HAMLET: I am constant to my purposes; they follow the King's pleasure. If his fitness speaks,° mine is ready; now or whensoever, provided I be 175 so able as now.

LORD: The King and Queen and all are coming down.

HAMLET: In happy time.°

LORD: The Queen desires you to use some gentle entertainment° to Laertes before you fall to play.   180

HAMLET: She well instructs me.   [*Exit Lord.*]

HORATIO: You will lose, my lord.

---

155. breathing time: Exercise period.   **163. lapwing:** A bird that draws intrud-ers away from its nest and was thought to run about when newly hatched with its head in the shell; a seeming reference to Osric's hat.   **164. comply . . . dug:** Observe ceremonious formality toward his mother's teat.   **165. drossy:** Frivolous.   **166. tune:** Temper, mood, manner of speech.   **166–67. habit of encounter:** Demeanor of social intercourse.   **167. yesty:** Yeasty, frothy.   **col-lection:** I.e., of current phrases.   **168. fann'd and winnow'd:** Select and refined.   **169. blow . . . out:** Put them to the test, and their ignorance is exposed.   **175. If . . . speaks:** If his readiness answers to the time.   **178. In happy time:** A phrase of courtesy indicating acceptance.   **179. entertainment:** Greeting.

HAMLET: I do not think so. Since he went into France, I have been in
   continual practice; I shall win at the odds. But thou wouldst not think
   how ill all's here about my heart; but it is no matter.   185
HORATIO: Nay, good my lord—
HAMLET: It is but foolery, but it is such a kind of gain-giving,° as would
   perhaps trouble a woman.
HORATIO: If your mind dislike anything, obey it. I will forestall their
   repair hither, and say you are not fit.   190
HAMLET: Not a whit, we defy augury. There is special providence in the
   fall of a sparrow. If it be now, 'tis not to come; if it be not to come, it
   will be now, if it be not now, yet it will come. The readiness is all. Since
   no man of aught he leaves knows what is 't to leave betimes,° let be.

(*A table prepar'd.* [*Enter*] *trumpets, drums, and Officers with cushions; King,
Queen,* [*Osric,*] *and all the State; foils, daggers,* [*and wine borne in;*] *and
Laertes.*)

KING: Come, Hamlet, come, and take this hand from me.   195

[*The King puts Laertes' hand into Hamlet's.*]

HAMLET: Give me your pardon, sir. I have done you wrong,
   But pardon 't, as you are a gentleman.
   This presence° knows,
   And you must needs have heard, how I am punish'd
   With a sore distraction. What I have done   200
   That might your nature, honor, and exception°
   Roughly awake, I here proclaim was madness.
   Was 't Hamlet wrong'd Laertes? Never Hamlet.
   If Hamlet from himself be ta'en away,
   And when he's not himself does wrong Laertes,   205
   Then Hamlet does it not, Hamlet denies it.
   Who does it, then? His madness. If 't be so,
   Hamlet is of the faction that is wrong'd;
   His madness is poor Hamlet's enemy.
   [Sir, in this audience,]   210
   Let my disclaiming from a purpos'd evil
   Free me so far in your most generous thoughts
   That I have shot my arrow o'er the house
   And hurt my brother.
LAERTES: I am satisfied in nature,°
   Whose motive in this case should stir me most   215

---

187. **gain-giving:** Misgiving.   194. **what . . . betimes:** What is the best time
to leave it.   198. **presence:** Royal assembly.   201. **exception:** Disapproval.
214. **in nature:** As to my personal feelings.

To my revenge. But in my terms of honor
I stand aloof, and will no reconcilement
Till by some elder masters of known honor
I have a voice° and precedent of peace
To keep my name ungor'd. But till that time,   220
I do receive your offer'd love like love,
And will not wrong it.
HAMLET: I embrace it freely,
And will this brothers' wager frankly play.
Give us the foils. Come on.
LAERTES: Come, one for me.
HAMLET: I'll be your foil,° Laertes. In mine ignorance   225
Your skill shall, like a star i' th' darkest night,
Stick fiery off° indeed.
LAERTES: You mock me, sir.
HAMLET: No, by this hand.
KING: Give them the foils, young Osric. Cousin Hamlet,
You know the wager?
HAMLET: Very well, my lord.   230
Your Grace has laid the odds o' th' weaker side.
KING: I do not fear it; I have seen you both.
But since he is better'd,° we have therefore odds.
LAERTES: This is too heavy, let me see another.

                              [*Exchanges his foil for another.*]

HAMLET: This likes me well. These foils have all a length?   235

                              [*They prepare to play.*]

OSRIC: Ay, my good lord.
KING: Set me the stoups of wine upon that table.
If Hamlet give the first or second hit,
Or quit° in answer of the third exchange,
Let all the battlements their ordnance fire.   240
The King shall drink to Hamlet's better breath,
And in the cup an union° shall he throw,
Richer than that which four successive kings
In Denmark's crown have worn. Give me the cups,
And let the kettle° to the trumpet speak,   245

219. voice: Authoritative pronouncement.   **225. foil:** Thin metal background
which sets a jewel off (with pun on the blunted rapier for fencing).   **227. Stick
fiery off:** Stand out brilliantly.   **233. is better'd:** Has improved; is the odds-on
favorite.   **239. quit:** Repay (with a hit).   **242. union:** Pearl (so called, according to Pliny's *Natural History*, IX, because pearls are *unique*, never identical).
245. kettle: Kettledrum.

The trumpet to the cannoneer without,
The cannons to the heavens, the heaven to earth,
"Now the King drinks to Hamlet." Come, begin.

(Trumpets the while.)

And you, the judges, bear a wary eye.
HAMLET: Come on sir.   250
LAERTES: Come, my lord.   [*They play. Hamlet scores a hit.*]
HAMLET: One.
LAERTES: No.
HAMLET: Judgment.
OSRIC: A hit, a very palpable hit.

(Drum, trumpets, and shot. Flourish.
A piece goes off.)

LAERTES: Well, again.   255
KING: Stay, give me drink. Hamlet, this pearl is thine.

[*He throws a pearl in Hamlet's cup and drinks.*]

Here's to thy health. Give him the cup.
HAMLET: I'll play this bout first, set it by awhile.
Come. [*They play.*] Another hit; what say you?
LAERTES: A touch, a touch. I do confess 't.   260
KING: Our son shall win.
QUEEN: He's fat,° and scant of breath.
Here, Hamlet, take my napkin,° rub thy brows.
The Queen carouses° to thy fortune, Hamlet.
HAMLET: Good madam!
KING: Gertrude, do not drink.   265
QUEEN: I will, my lord; I pray you pardon me.

[*Drinks.*]

KING [*aside*]: It is the pois'ned cup. It is too late.
HAMLET: I dare not drink yet, madam; by and by.
QUEEN: Come, let me wipe thy face.
LAERTES [*to King*]: My lord, I'll hit him now.
KING: I do not think 't.   270
LAERTES [*aside*]: And yet it is almost against my conscience.
HAMLET: Come, for the third Laertes. You do but dally.
I pray you, pass with your best violence;

---

261. fat: Not physically fit, out of training.   **262. napkin:** Handkerchief.
263. carouses: Drinks a toast.

I am afeard you make a wanton of me.°
LAERTES: Say you so? Come on.   [*They play.*] 275
OSRIC: Nothing, neither way.
LAERTES: Have at you now!

[*Laertes wounds Hamlet; then, in scuffling,*
they change rapiers,° and Hamlet wounds Laertes.]

KING: Part them! They are incens'd.
HAMLET: Nay, come, again.   [*The Queen falls.*]
OSRIC: Look to the Queen there, ho!
HORATIO: They bleed on both sides. How is it, my lord?
OSRIC: How is 't, Laertes?   280
LAERTES: Why, as a woodcock° to mine own springe,° Osric;
   I am justly kill'd with mine own treachery.
HAMLET: How does the Queen?
KING: She swoons to see them bleed.
QUEEN: No, no, the drink, the drink—O my dear Hamlet—
   The drink, the drink! I am pois'ned.   [*Dies.*] 285
HAMLET: O villainy! Ho, let the door be lock'd!
   Treachery! Seek it out.   [*Laertes falls.*]
LAERTES: It is here, Hamlet. Hamlet, thou art slain.
   No med'cine in the world can do thee good;
   In thee there is not half an hour's life.   290
   The treacherous instrument is in thy hand,
   Unbated° and envenom'd. The foul practice
   Hath turn'd itself on me. Lo, here I lie,
   Never to rise again. Thy mother's pois'ned.
   I can no more. The King, the King's to blame.   295
HAMLET: The point envenom'd too? Then, venom, to thy work.

[*Stabs the King.*]

ALL: Treason! Treason!
KING: O, yet defend me, friends; I am but hurt.
HAMLET: Here, thou incestuous, murd'rous, damned Dane,

[*He forces the King to drink the poisoned cup.*]

---

274. make . . . me: Treat me like a spoiled child, holding back to give me an advantage.   [S.D.] ***in scuffling, they change rapiers:*** This stage direction occurs in the Folio. According to a widespread stage tradition, Hamlet receives a scratch, realizes that Laertes' sword is unbated, and accordingly forces an exchange. **281. woodcock:** A bird, a type of stupidity or as a decoy.   **springe:** Trap, snare. **292. Unbated:** Not blunted with a button.

Drink off this potion. Is thy union° here?   300
Follow my mother.   [*King dies.*]
LAERTES: He is justly serv'd.
  It is a poison temper'd° by himself.
  Exchange forgiveness with me, noble Hamlet.
  Mine and my father's death come not upon thee,
  Nor thine on me!   [*Dies.*] 305
HAMLET: Heaven make thee free of it! I follow thee.
  I am dead, Horatio. Wretched Queen, adieu!
  You that look pale and tremble at this chance,
  That are but mutes° or audience to this act,
  Had I but time—as this fell° sergeant,° Death,   310
  Is strict in his arrest—O, I could tell you—
  But let it be. Horatio, I am dead;
  Thou livest. Report me and my cause aright
  To the unsatisfied.
HORATIO: Never believe it.
  I am more an antique Roman° than a Dane.   315
  Here's yet some liquor left.

> [*He attempts to drink from the poisoned cup.*
> *Hamlet prevents him.*]

HAMLET: As th' art a man,
  Give me the cup! Let go! By heaven, I'll ha 't.
  O God, Horatio, what a wounded name,
  Things standing thus unknown, shall I leave behind me!
  If thou didst ever hold me in thy heart,   320
  Absent thee from felicity awhile,
  And in this harsh world draw thy breath in pain
  To tell my story.

> (*A march afar off* [*and a volley within*].)

                What warlike noise is this?
OSRIC: Young Fortinbras, with conquest come from Poland,
  To the ambassadors of England gives   325
  This warlike volley.
HAMLET: O, I die, Horatio!
  The potent poison quite o'ercrows° my spirit.

---

300. union: Pearl (see line 242; with grim puns on the word's other
meanings: marriage, shared death[?]). **302. temper'd:** Mixed. **309. mutes:**
Silent observers. **310. fell:** Cruel. **sergeant:** Sheriff's officer. **315. Roman:**
It was the Roman custom to follow masters in death. **327. o'ercrows:** Triumphs
over.

I cannot live to hear the news from England,
But I do prophesy th' election lights
On Fortinbras. He has my dying voice.°   330
So tell him, with th' occurrents° more and less
Which have solicited°—the rest is silence.   [*Dies.*]
HORATIO: Now cracks a noble heart. Good night, sweet prince;
And flights of angels sing thee to thy rest!

[*March within.*]

Why does the drum come hither?   335

(*Enter Fortinbras, with the [English] Ambassadors [with drum, colors, and attendants].*)

FORTINBRAS: Where is this sight?
HORATIO: What is it you would see?
If aught of woe or wonder, cease your search.
FORTINBRAS: This quarry° cries on havoc.° O proud Death.
What feast is toward° in thine eternal cell,
That thou so many princes at a shot   340
So bloodily hast struck?
FIRST AMBASSADOR: The sight is dismal;
And our affairs from England come too late.
The ears are senseless that should give us hearing,
To tell him his commandment is fulfill'd,
That Rosencrantz and Guildenstern are dead.   345
Where should we have our thanks?
HORATIO: Not from his° mouth,
Had it th' ability of life to thank you.
He never gave commandment for their death.
But since, so jump° upon this bloody question,°
You from the Polack wars, and you from England,   350
Are here arriv'd, give order that these bodies
High on a stage° be placed to the view,
And let me speak to th' yet unknowing world
How these things came about. So shall you hear
Of carnal, bloody, and unnatural acts,   355
Of accidental judgments,° casual° slaughters,
Of deaths put on° by cunning and forc'd cause,

---

330. **voice:** Vote.   331. **occurrents:** Events, incidents.   332. **solicited:** Moved, urged.   338. **quarry:** Heap of dead.   **cries on havoc:** Proclaims a general slaughter.   339. **toward:** In preparation.   346. **his:** Claudius's.   349. **jump:** Precisely.   **question:** Dispute.   352. **stage:** Platform.   356. **judgments:** Retributions.   **casual:** Occurring by chance.   357. **put on:** Instigated.

And, in this upshot, purposes mistook
Fall'n on th' inventors' heads. All this can I
Truly deliver.
FORTINBRAS: Let us haste to hear it,   360
And call the noblest to the audience.
For me, with sorrow I embrace my fortune.
I have some rights of memory° in this kingdom,
Which now to claim my vantage° doth invite me.
HORATIO: Of that I shall have also cause to speak,   365
And from his mouth whose voice will draw on more.°
But let this same be presently° perform'd,
Even while men's minds are wild, lest more mischance
On° plots and errors happen.
FORTINBRAS: Let four captains
Bear Hamlet, like a soldier, to the stage,   370
For he was likely, had he been put on,°
To have prov'd most royal; and, for his passage,°
The soldiers' music and the rite of war
Speak loudly for him.
Take up the bodies. Such a sight as this   375
Becomes the field,° but here shows much amiss.
Go, bid the soldiers shoot.

                    (*Exeunt* [*marching, bearing off the dead bodies;*
                             a peal of ordnance is shot off].)

                                                            [c. 1600]

---

363. **of memory:** Traditional, remembered.   364. **vantage:** Presence at this
opportune moment.   366. **voice . . . more:** Vote will influence still others.
367. **presently:** Immediately.   369. **On:** On the basis of.   371. **put on:** Invested
in royal office and so put to the test.   372. **passage:** Death.   376. **field:** I.e., of
battle.

HENRIK IBSEN [1828–1906]

A Doll House

TRANSLATED BY ROLF FJELDE

The Characters

TORVALD HELMER, *a lawyer*
NORA, *his wife*
DR. RANK
MRS. LINDE
NILS KROGSTAD, *a bank clerk*
THE HELMERS' THREE SMALL CHILDREN
ANNE-MARIE, *their nurse*
HELENE, *a maid*
A DELIVERY BOY

The action takes place in Helmer's residence.

ACT I

(*A comfortable room, tastefully but not expensively furnished. A door to the right in the back wall leads to the entryway; another to the left leads to Helmer's study. Between these doors, a piano. Midway in the left-hand wall a door, and further back a window. Near the window a round table with an armchair and a small sofa. In the right-hand wall, toward the rear, a door, and nearer the foreground a porcelain stove with two armchairs and a rocking chair beside it. Between the stove and the side door, a small table. Engravings on the walls. An étagère° with china figures and other small art objects; a small bookcase with richly bound books; the floor carpeted; a fire burning in the stove. It is a winter day.*)

Note: As Fjelde explains in his foreword to the translation, he does not use the possessive "A Doll's House" because "the house is not Nora's, as the possessive implies." Fjelde believes that Ibsen includes Torvald with Nora in the original title, "for the two of them at the play's opening are still posing like the little marzipan bride and groom atop the wedding cake."
[S.D.] *étagère:* Cabinet with shelves.

(*A bell rings in the entryway; shortly after we hear the door being unlocked. Nora comes into the room, humming happily to herself; she is wearing street clothes and carries an armload of packages, which she puts down on the table to the right. She has left the hall door open, and through it a Delivery Boy is seen holding a Christmas tree and a basket, which he gives to the Maid who let them in.*)

NORA: Hide the tree well, Helene. The children mustn't get a glimpse of it till this evening, after it's trimmed. (*To the Delivery Boy, taking out her purse.*) How much?

DELIVERY BOY: Fifty, ma'am.

NORA: There's a crown. No, keep the change. (*The Boy thanks her and leaves. Nora shuts the door. She laughs softly to herself while taking off her street things. Drawing a bag of macaroons from her pocket, she eats a couple, then steals over and listens at her husband's study door.*) Yes, he's home. (*Hums again as she moves to the table right.*)

HELMER (*from the study*): Is that my little lark twittering out there?

NORA (*busy opening some packages*): Yes, it is.

HELMER: Is that my squirrel rummaging around?

NORA: Yes!

HELMER: When did my squirrel get in?

NORA: Just now. (*Putting the macaroon bag in her pocket and wiping her mouth.*) Do come in, Torvald, and see what I've bought.

HELMER: Can't be disturbed. (*After a moment he opens the door and peers in, pen in hand.*) Bought, you say? All that there? Has the little spend-thrift been out throwing money around again?

NORA: Oh, but Torvald, this year we really should let ourselves go a bit. It's the first Christmas we haven't had to economize.

HELMER: But you know we can't go squandering.

NORA: Oh yes, Torvald, we can squander a little now. Can't we? Just a tiny, wee bit. Now that you've got a big salary and are going to make piles and piles of money.

HELMER: Yes—starting New Year's. But then it's a full three months till the raise comes through.

NORA: Pooh! We can borrow that long.

HELMER: Nora! (*Goes over and playfully takes her by the ear.*) Are your scatterbrains off again? What if today I borrowed a thousand crowns, and you squandered them over Christmas week, and then on New Year's Eve a roof tile fell on my head, and I lay there—

NORA (*putting her hand on his mouth*): Oh! Don't say such things!

HELMER: Yes, but what if it happened—then what?

NORA: If anything so awful happened, then it just wouldn't matter if I had debts or not.

HELMER: Well, but the people I'd borrowed from?

NORA: Them? Who cares about them! They're strangers.

HELMER: Nora, Nora, how like a woman! No, but seriously, Nora, you know what I think about that. No debts! Never borrow! Something of freedom's lost—and something of beauty, too—from a home that's founded on borrowing and debt. We've made a brave stand up to now, the two of us; and we'll go right on like that the little while we have to.

NORA (*going toward the stove*): Yes, whatever you say, Torvald.

HELMER (*following her*): Now, now, the little lark's wings mustn't droop. Come on, don't be a sulky squirrel. (*Taking out his wallet.*) Nora, guess what I have here.

NORA (*turning quickly*): Money!

HELMER: There, see. (*Hands her some notes.*) Good grief, I know how costs go up in a house at Christmastime.

NORA: Ten—twenty—thirty—forty. Oh, thank you, Torvald; I can manage no end on this.

HELMER: You really will have to.

NORA: Oh yes, I promise I will! But come here so I can show you everything I bought. And so cheap! Look, new clothes for Ivar here—and a sword. Here a horse and a trumpet for Bob. And a doll and a doll's bed here for Emmy; they're nothing much, but she'll tear them to bits in no time anyway. And here I have dress material and handkerchiefs for the maids. Old Anne-Marie really deserves something more.

HELMER: And what's in that package there?

NORA (*with a cry*): Torvald, no! You can't see that till tonight!

HELMER: I see. But tell me now, you little prodigal, what have you thought of for yourself?

NORA: For myself? Oh, I don't want anything at all.

HELMER: Of course you do. Tell me just what—within reason—you'd most like to have.

NORA: I honestly don't know. Oh, listen, Torvald—

HELMER: Well?

NORA (*fumbling at his coat buttons, without looking at him*): If you want to give me something, then maybe you could—you could—

HELMER: Come on, out with it.

NORA (*hurriedly*): You could give me money, Torvald. No more than you think you can spare; then one of these days I'll buy something with it.

HELMER: But Nora—

NORA: Oh, please, Torvald darling, do that! I beg you, please. Then I could hang the bills in pretty gilt paper on the Christmas tree. Wouldn't that be fun?

HELMER: What are those little birds called that always fly through their fortunes?

NORA: Oh yes, spendthrifts; I know all that. But let's do as I say, Torvald; then I'll have time to decide what I really need most. That's very sensible, isn't it?

HELMER (*smiling*): Yes, very—that is, if you actually hung onto the money I give you, and you actually used it to buy yourself something. But it goes for the house and for all sorts of foolish things, and then I only have to lay out some more.

NORA: Oh, but Torvald—

HELMER: Don't deny it, my dear little Nora. (*Putting his arm around her waist.*) Spendthrifts are sweet, but they use up a frightful amount of money. It's incredible what it costs a man to feed such birds.

NORA: Oh, how can you say that! Really, I save everything I can.

HELMER (*laughing*): Yes, that's the truth. Everything you can. But that's nothing at all.

NORA (*humming, with a smile of quiet satisfaction*): Hm, if you only knew what expenses we larks and squirrels have, Torvald.

HELMER: You're an odd little one. Exactly the way your father was. You're never at a loss for scaring up money; but the moment you have it, it runs right out through your fingers; you never know what you've done with it. Well, one takes you as you are. It's deep in your blood. Yes, these things are hereditary, Nora.

NORA: Ah, I could wish I'd inherited many of Papa's qualities.

HELMER: And I couldn't wish you anything but just what you are, my sweet little lark. But wait; it seems to me you have a very—what should I call it?—a very suspicious look today—

NORA: I do?

HELMER: You certainly do. Look me straight in the eye.

NORA (*looking at him*): Well?

HELMER (*shaking an admonitory finger*): Surely my sweet tooth hasn't been running riot in town today, has she?

NORA: No. Why do you imagine that?

HELMER: My sweet tooth really didn't make a little detour through the confectioner's?

NORA: No, I assure you, Torvald—

HELMER: Hasn't nibbled some pastry?

NORA: No, not at all.

HELMER: Not even munched a macaroon or two?

NORA: No, Torvald, I assure you, really—

HELMER: There, there now. Of course I'm only joking.

NORA (*going to the table, right*): You know I could never think of going against you.

HELMER: No, I understand that; and you *have* given me your word. (*Going over to her.*) Well, you keep your little Christmas secrets to yourself, Nora darling. I expect they'll come to light this evening, when the tree is lit.

NORA: Did you remember to ask Dr. Rank?

HELMER: No. But there's no need for that, it's assumed he'll be dining with us. All the same, I'll ask him when he stops by here this morning.

I've ordered some fine wine. Nora, you can't imagine how I'm looking
forward to this evening.

NORA: So am I. And what fun for the children, Torvald!

HELMER: Ah, it's so gratifying to know that one's gotten a safe, secure
job, and with a comfortable salary. It's a great satisfaction, isn't it?

NORA: Oh, it's wonderful!

HELMER: Remember last Christmas? Three whole weeks before, you
shut yourself in every evening till long after midnight, making flowers
for the Christmas tree, and all the other decorations to surprise us.
Ugh, that was the dullest time I've ever lived through.

NORA: It wasn't at all dull for me.

HELMER (*smiling*): But the outcome *was* pretty sorry, Nora.

NORA: Oh, don't tease me with that again. How could I help it that the
cat came in and tore everything to shreds.

HELMER: No, poor thing, you certainly couldn't. You wanted so much to
please us all, and that's what counts. But it's just as well that the hard
times are past.

NORA: Yes, it's really wonderful.

HELMER: Now I don't have to sit here alone, boring myself, and you don't
have to tire your precious eyes and your fair little delicate hands

NORA (*clapping her hands*): No, is it really true, Torvald, I don't have to?
Oh, how wonderfully lovely to hear! (*Taking his arm.*) Now I'll tell you
just how I've thought we should plan things. Right after Christmas—
(*The doorbell rings.*) Oh, the bell. (*Straightening the room up a bit.*)
Somebody would have to come. What a bore!

HELMER: I'm not at home to visitors, don't forget.

MAID (*from the hall doorway*): Ma'am, a lady to see you—

NORA: All right, let her come in.

MAID (*to Helmer*): And the doctor's just come too.

HELMER: Did he go right to my study?

MAID: Yes, he did.

(*Helmer goes into his room. The Maid shows in Mrs. Linde, dressed in traveling
clothes, and shuts the door after her.*)

MRS. LINDE (*in a dispirited and somewhat hesitant voice*): Hello, Nora.

NORA (*uncertain*): Hello—

MRS. LINDE: You don't recognize me.

NORA: No, I don't know—but wait, I think—(*Exclaiming.*) What! Kristine!
Is it really you?

MRS. LINDE: Yes, it's me.

NORA: Kristine! To think I didn't recognize you. But then, how could I?
(*More quietly.*) How you've changed, Kristine!

MRS. LINDE: Yes, no doubt I have. In nine—ten long years.

NORA: Is it so long since we met! Yes, it's all of that. Oh, these last eight years have been a happy time, believe me. And so now you've come in to town, too. Made the long trip in the winter. That took courage.

MRS. LINDE: I just got here by ship this morning.

NORA: To enjoy yourself over Christmas, of course. Oh, how lovely! Yes, enjoy ourselves, we'll do that. But take your coat off. You're not still cold? (*Helping her.*) There now, let's get cozy here by the stove. No, the easy chair there! I'll take the rocker here. (*Seizing her hands.*) Yes, now you have your old look again; it was only in that first moment. You're a bit more pale, Kristine—and maybe a bit thinner.

MRS. LINDE: And much, much older, Nora.

NORA: Yes, perhaps a bit older; a tiny, tiny bit; not much at all. (*Stopping short; suddenly serious.*) Oh, but thoughtless me, to sit here, chattering away. Sweet, good Kristine, can you forgive me?

MRS. LINDE: What do you mean, Nora?

NORA (*softly*): Poor Kristine, you've become a widow.

MRS. LINDE: Yes, three years ago.

NORA: Oh, I knew it, of course; I read it in the papers. Oh, Kristine, you must believe me; I often thought of writing you then, but I kept postponing it, and something always interfered.

MRS. LINDE: Nora dear, I understand completely.

NORA: No, it was awful of me, Kristine. You poor thing, how much you must have gone through. And he left you nothing?

MRS. LINDE: No.

NORA: And no children?

MRS. LINDE: No.

NORA: Nothing at all, then?

MRS. LINDE: Not even a sense of loss to feed on.

NORA (*looking incredulously at her*): But Kristine, how could that be?

MRS. LINDE (*smiling wearily and smoothing her hair*): Oh, sometimes it happens, Nora.

NORA: So completely alone. How terribly hard that must be for you. I have three lovely children. You can't see them now; they're out with the maid. But now you must tell me everything—

MRS. LINDE: No, no, no, tell me about yourself.

NORA: No, you begin. Today I don't want to be selfish. I want to think only of you today. But there is something I must tell you. Did you hear of the wonderful luck we had recently?

MRS. LINDE: No, what's that?

NORA: My husband's been made manager in the bank, just think!

MRS. LINDE: Your husband? How marvelous!

NORA: Isn't it? Being a lawyer is such an uncertain living, you know, especially if one won't touch any cases that aren't clean and decent. And of course Torvald would never do that, and I'm with him com-

pletely there. Oh, we're simply delighted, believe me! He'll join the
bank right after New Year's and start getting a huge salary and lots of
commissions. From now on we can live quite differently—just as we
want. Oh, Kristine, I feel so light and happy! Won't it be lovely to have
stacks of money and not a care in the world?

MRS. LINDE: Well, anyway, it would be lovely to have enough for necessities.

NORA: No, not just for necessities, but stacks and stacks of money!

MRS. LINDE (*smiling*): Nora, Nora, aren't you sensible yet? Back in school
you were such a free spender.

NORA (*with a quiet laugh*): Yes, that's what Torvald still says. (*Shaking her
finger.*) But "Nora, Nora" isn't as silly as you all think. Really, we've
been in no position for me to go squandering. We've had to work, both
of us.

MRS. LINDE: You too?

NORA: Yes, at odd jobs—needlework, crocheting, embroidery, and
such—(*casually*) and other things too. You remember that Torvald left
the department when we were married? There was no chance of pro-
motion in his office, and of course he needed to earn more money. But
that first year he drove himself terribly. He took on all kinds of extra
work that kept him going morning and night. It wore him down, and
then he fell deathly ill. The doctors said it was essential for him to
travel south.

MRS. LINDE: Yes, didn't you spend a whole year in Italy?

NORA: That's right. It wasn't easy to get away, you know. Ivar had just
been born. But of course we had to go. Oh, that was a beautiful trip,
and it saved Torvald's life. But it cost a frightful sum, Kristine.

MRS. LINDE: I can well imagine.

NORA: Four thousand, eight hundred crowns it cost. That's really a lot of
money.

MRS. LINDE: But it's lucky you had it when you needed it.

NORA: Well, as it was, we got it from Papa.

MRS. LINDE: I see. It was just about the time your father died.

NORA: Yes, just about then. And, you know, I couldn't make that trip out
to nurse him. I had to stay here, expecting Ivar any moment, and with
my poor sick Torvald to care for. Dearest Papa, I never saw him again,
Kristine. Oh, that was the worst time I've known in all my marriage.

MRS. LINDE: I know how you loved him. And then you went off to Italy?

NORA: Yes. We had the means now, and the doctors urged us. So we left
a month after.

MRS. LINDE: And your husband came back completely cured?

NORA: Sound as a drum!

MRS. LINDE: But—the doctor?

NORA: Who?

MRS. LINDE: I thought the maid said he was a doctor, the man who came
in with me.

NORA: Yes, that was Dr. Rank—but he's not making a sick call. He's our
closest friend, and he stops by at least once a day. No, Torvald hasn't
had a sick moment since, and the children are fit and strong, and I am,
too. (*Jumping up and clapping her hands.*) Oh, dear God, Kristine, what a
lovely thing to live and be happy! But how disgusting of me—I'm talking of nothing but my own affairs. (*Sits on a stool close by Kristine, arms
resting across her knees.*) Oh, don't be angry with me! Tell me, is it really
true that you weren't in love with your husband? Why did you marry
him, then?

MRS. LINDE: My mother was still alive, but bedridden and helpless—and
I had my two younger brothers to look after. In all conscience, I didn't
think I could turn him down.

NORA: No, you were right there. But was he rich at the time?

MRS. LINDE: He was very well off, I'd say. But the business was shaky,
Nora. When he died, it all fell apart, and nothing was left.

NORA: And then—?

MRS. LINDE: Yes, so I had to scrape up a living with a little shop and a
little teaching and whatever else I could find. The last three years have
been like one endless workday without a rest for me. Now, it's over,
Nora. My poor mother doesn't need me, for she's passed on. Nor the
boys, either; they're working now and can take care of themselves.

NORA: How free you must feel—

MRS. LINDE: No—only unspeakably empty. Nothing to live for now.
(*Standing up anxiously.*) That's why I couldn't take it any longer out in
that desolate hole. Maybe here it'll be easier to find something to do
and keep my mind occupied. If I could only be lucky enough to get a
steady job, some office work—

NORA: Oh, but Kristine, that's so dreadfully tiring, and you already look
so tired. It would be much better for you if you could go off to a
bathing resort.

MRS. LINDE (*going toward the window*): I have no father to give me travel
money, Nora.

NORA (*rising*): Oh, don't be angry with me.

MRS. LINDE (*going to her*): Nora dear, don't you be angry with me. The
worst of my kind of situation is all the bitterness that's stored away. No
one to work for, and yet you're always having to snap up your opportunities. You have to live; and so you grow selfish. When you told me the
happy change in your lot, do you know I was delighted less for your
sakes than for mine?

NORA: How so? Oh, I see. You think maybe Torvald could do something for you.

MRS. LINDE: Yes, that's what I thought.

NORA: And he will, Kristine! Just leave it to me; I'll bring it up so delicately—find something attractive to humor him with. Oh, I'm so eager to help you.

MRS. LINDE: How very kind of you, Nora, to be so concerned over me—doubly kind, considering you really know so little of life's burdens yourself.

NORA: I—? I know so little—?

MRS. LINDE (smiling): Well, my heavens—a little needlework and such—Nora, you're just a child.

NORA (tossing her head and pacing the floor): You don't have to act so superior.

MRS. LINDE: Oh?

NORA: You're just like the others. You all think I'm incapable of anything serious—

MRS. LINDE: Come now—

NORA: That I've never had to face the raw world.

MRS. LINDE: Nora dear, you've just been telling me all your troubles.

NORA: Hm! Trivial! (Quietly.) I haven't told you the big thing.

MRS. LINDE: Big thing? What do you mean?

NORA: You look down on me so, Kristine, but you shouldn't. You're proud that you worked so long and hard for your mother.

MRS. LINDE: I don't look down on a soul. But it is true: I'm proud—and happy, too—to think it was given to me to make my mother's last days almost free of care.

NORA: And you're also proud thinking of what you've done for your brothers.

MRS. LINDE: I feel I've a right to be.

NORA: I agree. But listen to this, Kristine—I've also got something to be proud and happy for.

MRS. LINDE: I don't doubt it. But whatever do you mean?

NORA: Not so loud. What if Torvald heard! He mustn't, not for anything in the world. Nobody must know, Kristine. No one but you.

MRS. LINDE: But what is it, then?

NORA: Come here. (Drawing her down beside her on the sofa.) It's true—I've also got something to be proud and happy for. I'm the one who saved Torvald's life.

MRS. LINDE: Saved—? Saved how?

NORA: I told you about the trip to Italy. Torvald never would have lived if he hadn't gone south—

MRS. LINDE: Of course; your father gave you the means—

NORA (*smiling*): That's what Torvald and all the rest think, but—

MRS. LINDE: But—?

NORA: Papa didn't give us a pin. I was the one who raised the money.

MRS. LINDE: You? That whole amount?

NORA: Four thousand, eight hundred crowns. What do you say to that?

MRS. LINDE: But Nora, how was it possible? Did you win the lottery?

NORA (*disdainfully*): The lottery? Pooh! No art to that.

MRS. LINDE: But where did you get it from then?

NORA (*humming, with a mysterious smile*): Hmm, tra-la-la-la.

MRS. LINDE: Because you couldn't have borrowed it.

NORA: No? Why not?

MRS. LINDE: A wife can't borrow without her husband's consent.

NORA (*tossing her head*): Oh, but a wife with a little business sense, a wife who knows how to manage—

MRS. LINDE: Nora, I simply don't understand—

NORA: You don't have to. Whoever said I *borrowed* the money? I could have gotten it other ways. (*Throwing herself back on the sofa.*) I could have gotten it from some admirer or other. After all, a girl with my ravishing appeal—

MRS. LINDE: You lunatic.

NORA: I'll bet you're eaten up with curiosity, Kristine.

MRS. LINDE: Now listen here, Nora—you haven't done something indiscreet?

NORA (*sitting up again*): Is it indiscreet to save your husband's life?

MRS. LINDE: I think it's indiscreet that without his knowledge you—

NORA: But that's the point: He mustn't know! My Lord, can't you understand? He mustn't ever know the close call he had. It was to *me* the doctors came to say his life was in danger—that nothing could save him but a stay in the south. Didn't I try strategy then! I began talking about how lovely it would be for me to travel abroad like other young wives; I begged and I cried; I told him please to remember my condition, to be kind and indulge me; and then I dropped a hint that he could easily take out a loan. But at that, Kristine, he nearly exploded. He said I was frivolous, and it was his duty as man of the house not to indulge me in whims and fancies—as I think he called them. Aha, I thought, now you'll just have to be saved—and that's when I saw my chance.

MRS. LINDE: And your father never told Torvald the money wasn't from him?

NORA: No, never. Papa died right about then. I'd considered bringing him into my secret and begging him never to tell. But he was too sick at the time—and then, sadly, it didn't matter.

MRS. LINDE: And you've never confided in your husband since?

NORA: For heaven's sake, no! Are you serious? He's so strict on that subject. Besides—Torvald, with all his masculine pride—how painfully
humiliating for him if he ever found out he was in debt to me. That
would just ruin our relationship. Our beautiful, happy home would
never be the same.

MRS. LINDE: Won't you ever tell him?

NORA (*thoughtfully, half smiling*): Yes—maybe sometime years from now,
when I'm no longer so attractive. Don't laugh! I only mean when
Torvald loves me less than now, when he stops enjoying my dancing
and dressing up and reciting for him. Then it might be wise to have
something in reserve—(*Breaking off.*) How ridiculous! That'll never
happen—Well, Kristine, what do you think of my big secret? I'm
capable of something too, hm? You can imagine, of course, how this
thing hangs over me. It really hasn't been easy meeting the payments on
time. In the business world there's what they call quarterly interest and
what they call amortization, and these are always so terribly hard to
manage. I've had to skimp a little here and there, wherever I could, you
know. I could hardly spare anything from my house allowance, because
Torvald has to live well. I couldn't let the children go poorly dressed;
whatever I got for them, I felt I had to use up completely—the darlings!

MRS. LINDE: Poor Nora, so it had to come out of your own budget, then?

NORA: Yes, of course. But I was the one most responsible, too. Every
time Torvald gave me money for new clothes and such, I never used
more than half; always bought the simplest, cheapest outfits. It was a
godsend that everything looks so well on me that Torvald never
noticed. But it did weigh me down at times, Kristine. It *is* such a joy to
wear fine things. You understand.

MRS. LINDE: Oh, of course.

NORA: And then I found other ways of making money. Last winter I was
lucky enough to get a lot of copying to do. I locked myself in and sat
writing every evening till late in the night. Ah, I was tired so often,
dead tired. But still it was wonderful fun, sitting and working like that,
earning money. It was almost like being a man.

MRS. LINDE: But how much have you paid off this way so far?

NORA: That's hard to say, exactly. These accounts, you know, aren't easy
to figure. I only know that I've paid out all I could scrape together. Time
and again I haven't known where to turn. (*Smiling.*) Then I'd sit here
dreaming of a rich old gentleman who had fallen in love with me—

MRS. LINDE: What! Who is he?

NORA: Oh, really! And that he'd died, and when his will was opened,
there in big letters it said, "All my fortune shall be paid over in cash,
immediately, to that enchanting Mrs. Nora Helmer."

MRS. LINDE: But Nora dear—who *was* this gentleman?

NORA: Good grief, can't you understand? The old man never existed; that was only something I'd dream up time and again whenever I was at my wits' end for money. But it makes no difference now; the old fossil can go where he pleases for all I care; I don't need him or his will—because now I'm free. (*Jumping up.*) Oh, how lovely to think of that, Kristine! Carefree! To know you're carefree, utterly carefree; to be able to romp and play with the children, and to keep up a beautiful, charming home—everything just the way Torvald likes it! And think, spring is coming, with big blue skies. Maybe we can travel a little then. Maybe I'll see the ocean again. Oh yes, it *is* so marvelous to live and be happy!

(*The front doorbell rings.*)

MRS. LINDE (*rising*): There's the bell. It's probably best that I go.

NORA: No, stay. No one's expected. It must be for Torvald.

MAID (*from the hall doorway*): Excuse me, ma'am—there's a gentleman here to see Mr. Helmer, but I didn't know—since the doctor's with him—

NORA: Who is the gentleman?

KROGSTAD (*from the doorway*): It's me, Mrs. Helmer.

(*Mrs. Linde starts and turns away toward the window.*)

NORA (*stepping toward him, tense, her voice a whisper*): You? What is it? Why do you want to speak to my husband?

KROGSTAD: Bank business—after a fashion. I have a small job in the investment bank, and I hear now your husband is going to be our chief—

NORA: In other words, it's—

KROGSTAD: Just dry business, Mrs. Helmer. Nothing but that.

NORA: Yes, then please be good enough to step into the study. (*She nods indifferently as she sees him out by the hall door, then returns and begins stirring up the stove.*)

MRS. LINDE: Nora—who was that man?

NORA: That was a Mr. Krogstad—a lawyer.

MRS. LINDE: Then it really was him.

NORA: Do you know that person?

MRS. LINDE: I did once—many years ago. For a time he was a law clerk in our town.

NORA: Yes, he's been that.

MRS. LINDE: How he's changed.

NORA: I understand he had a very unhappy marriage.

MRS. LINDE: He's a widower now.

NORA: With a number of children. There now, it's burning. (*She closes the stove door and moves the rocker a bit to one side.*)

MRS. LINDE: They say he has a hand in all kinds of business.

NORA: Oh? That may be true; I wouldn't know. But let's not think about business. It's so dull.

(*Dr. Rank enters from Helmer's study.*)

RANK (*still in the doorway*): No, no, really—I don't want to intrude, I'd just as soon talk a little while with your wife. (*Shuts the door, then notices Mrs. Linde.*) Oh, beg pardon. I'm intruding here too.

NORA: No, not at all. (*Introducing him.*) Dr. Rank, Mrs. Linde.

RANK: Well now, that's a name much heard in this house. I believe I passed the lady on the stairs as I came.

MRS. LINDE: Yes, I take the stairs very slowly. They're rather hard on me.

RANK: Uh-hm, some touch of internal weakness?

MRS. LINDE: More overexertion, I'd say.

RANK: Nothing else? Then you're probably here in town to rest up in a round of parties?

MRS. LINDE: I'm here to look for work.

RANK: Is that the best cure for overexertion?

MRS. LINDE: One has to live, Doctor.

RANK: Yes, there's a common prejudice to that effect.

NORA: Oh, come on, Dr. Rank—you really do want to live yourself.

RANK: Yes, I really do. Wretched as I am, I'll gladly prolong my torment indefinitely. All my patients feel like that. And it's quite the same, too, with the morally sick. Right at this moment there's one of those moral invalids in there with Helmer—

MRS. LINDE (*softly*): Ah!

NORA: Who do you mean?

RANK: Oh, it's a lawyer, Krogstad, a type you wouldn't know. His character is rotten to the root—but even he began chattering all-importantly about how he had to *live*.

NORA: Oh? What did he want to talk to Torvald about?

RANK: I really don't know. I only heard something about the bank.

NORA: I didn't know that Krog—that this man Krogstad had anything to do with the bank.

RANK: Yes, he's gotten some kind of berth down there. (*To Mrs. Linde.*) I don't know if you also have, in your neck of the woods, a type of person who scuttles about breathlessly, sniffing out hints of moral corruption, and then maneuvers his victim into some sort of key position where he can keep an eye on him. It's the healthy these days that are out in the cold.

MRS. LINDE: All the same, it's the sick who most need to be taken in.

RANK (*with a shrug*): Yes, there we have it. That's the concept that's turning society into a sanatorium.

(*Nora, lost in her thoughts, breaks out into quiet laughter and claps her hands.*)

RANK: Why do you laugh at that? Do you have any real idea of what society is?

NORA: What do I care about dreary old society? I was laughing at something quite different—something terribly funny. Tell me, Doctor—is everyone who works in the bank dependent now on Torvald?

RANK: Is that what you find so terribly funny?

NORA (*smiling and humming*): Never mind, never mind! (*Pacing the floor.*) Yes, that's really immensely amusing: that we—that Torvald has so much power now over all those people. (*Taking the bag out of her pocket.*) Dr. Rank, a little macaroon on that?

RANK: See here, macaroons! I thought they were contraband here.

NORA: Yes, but these are some that Kristine gave me.

MRS. LINDE: What? I—?

NORA: Now, now, don't be afraid. You couldn't possibly know that Torvald had forbidden them. You see, he's worried they'll ruin my teeth. But hmp! Just this once! Isn't that so, Dr. Rank? Help yourself! (*Puts a macaroon in his mouth.*) And you too, Kristine. And I'll also have one, only a little one—or two, at the most. (*Walking about again.*) Now I'm really tremendously happy. Now's there's just one last thing in the world that I have an enormous desire to do.

RANK: Well! And what's that?

NORA: It's something I have such a consuming desire to say so Torvald could hear.

RANK: And why can't you say it?

NORA: I don't dare. It's quite shocking.

MRS. LINDE: Shocking?

RANK: Well, then it isn't advisable. But in front of us you certainly can. What do you have such a desire to say so Torvald could hear?

NORA: I have such a huge desire to say—to hell and be damned!

RANK: Are you crazy?

MRS. LINDE: My goodness, Nora!

RANK: Go on, say it. Here he is.

NORA (*hiding the macaroon bag*): Shh, shh, shh!

(*Helmer comes in from his study, hat in hand, overcoat over his arm.*)

NORA (*going toward him*): Well, Torvald dear, are you through with him?

HELMER: Yes, he just left.

NORA: Let me introduce you—this is Kristine, who's arrived here in town.

HELMER: Kristine—? I'm sorry, but I don't know—

NORA: Mrs. Linde, Torvald dear. Mrs. Kristine Linde.

HELMER: Of course. A childhood friend of my wife's, no doubt?

MRS. LINDE: Yes, we knew each other in those days.

NORA: And just think, she made the long trip down here in order to talk with you.

HELMER: What's this?

MRS. LINDE: Well, not exactly—

NORA: You see, Kristine is remarkably clever in office work, and so she's terribly eager to come under a capable man's supervision and add more to what she already knows—

HELMER: Very wise, Mrs. Linde.

NORA: And then when she heard that you'd become a bank manager— the story was wired out to the papers—then she came in as fast as she could and—Really, Torvald, for my sake you can do a little something for Kristine, can't you?

HELMER: Yes, it's not at all impossible. Mrs. Linde, I suppose you're a widow?

MRS. LINDE: Yes.

HELMER: Any experience in office work?

MRS. LINDE: Yes, a good deal.

HELMER: Well, it's quite likely that I can make an opening for you—

NORA (*clapping her hands*): You see, you see!

HELMER: You've come at a lucky moment, Mrs. Linde.

MRS. LINDE: Oh, how can I thank you?

HELMER: Not necessary. (*Putting his overcoat on.*) But today you'll have to excuse me—

RANK: Wait, I'll go with you. (*He fetches his coat from the hall and warms it at the stove.*)

NORA: Don't stay out long, dear.

HELMER: An hour; no more.

NORA: Are you going too, Kristine?

MRS. LINDE (*putting on her winter garments*): Yes, I have to see about a room now.

HELMER: Then perhaps we can all walk together.

NORA (*helping her*): What a shame we're so cramped here, but it's quite impossible for us to—

MRS. LINDE: Oh, don't even think of it! Good-bye, Nora dear, and thanks for everything.

NORA: Good-bye for now. Of course you'll be back this evening. And you too, Dr. Rank. What? If you're well enough? Oh, you've got to be! Wrap up tight now.

(*In a ripple of small talk the company moves out into the hall; children's voices are heard outside on the steps.*)

NORA: There they are! There they are! (*She runs to open the door. The children come in with their nurse, Anne-Marie.*) Come in, come in! (*Bends down and kisses them.*) Oh, you darlings—! Look at them, Kristine. Aren't they lovely!

RANK: No loitering in the draft here.

HELMER: Come, Mrs. Linde—this place is unbearable now for anyone but mothers.

(*Dr. Rank, Helmer, and Mrs. Linde go down the stairs. Anne-Marie goes into the living room with the children. Nora follows, after closing the hall door.*)

NORA: How fresh and strong you look. Oh, such red cheeks you have! Like apples and roses. (*The children interrupt her throughout the following.*) And it was so much fun? That's wonderful. Really? You pulled both Emmy and Bob on the sled? Imagine, all together! Yes, you're a clever boy, Ivar. Oh, let me hold her a bit, Anne-Marie. My sweet little doll baby! (*Takes the smallest from the nurse and dances with her.*) Yes, yes, Mama will dance with Bob as well. What? Did you throw snowballs? Oh, if I'd only been there! No, don't bother, Anne-Marie—I'll undress them myself. Oh yes, let me. It's such fun. Go in and rest; you look half frozen. There's hot coffee waiting for you on the stove. (*The nurse goes into the room to the left. Nora takes the children's winter things off, throwing them about, while the children talk to her all at once.*) Is that so? A big dog chased you? But it didn't bite? No, dogs never bite little, lovely doll babies. Don't peek in the packages, Ivar! What is it? Yes, wouldn't you like to know. No, no, it's an ugly something. Well? Shall we play? What shall we play? Hide-and-seek? Yes, let's play hide-and-seek. Bob must hide first. I must? Yes, let me hide first. (*Laughing and shouting, she and the children play in and out of the living room and the adjoining room to the right. At last Nora hides under the table. The children come storming in, search, but cannot find her, then hear her muffled laughter, dash over to the table, lift the cloth up and find her. Wild shouting. She creeps forward as if to scare them. More shouts. Meanwhile, a knock at the hall door; no one has noticed it. Now the door half opens, and Krogstad appears. He waits a moment; the game goes on.*)

KROGSTAD: Beg pardon, Mrs. Helmer—

NORA (*with a strangled cry, turning and scrambling to her knees*): Oh! What do you want?

KROGSTAD: Excuse me. The outer door was ajar; it must be someone forgot to shut it—

NORA (*rising*): My husband isn't home, Mr. Krogstad.

KROGSTAD: I know that.

NORA: Yes—then what do you want here?

KROGSTAD: A word with you.

NORA: With—? (*To the children, quietly.*) Go in to Anne-Marie. What? No, the strange man won't hurt Mama. When he's gone, we'll play some more. (*She leads the children into the room to the left and shuts the door after them. Then, tense and nervous:*) You want to speak to me?

KROGSTAD: Yes, I want to.

NORA: Today? But it's not yet the first of the month—

KROGSTAD: No, it's Christmas Eve. It's going to be up to you how merry a Christmas you have.

NORA: What is it you want? Today I absolutely can't—

KROGSTAD: We won't talk about that till later. This is something else. You do have a moment to spare, I suppose?

NORA: Oh yes, of course—I do, except—

KROGSTAD: Good. I was sitting over at Olsen's Restaurant when I saw your husband go down the street—

NORA: Yes?

KROGSTAD: With a lady.

NORA: Yes. So?

KROGSTAD: If you'll pardon my asking: Wasn't that lady a Mrs. Linde?

NORA: Yes.

KROGSTAD: Just now come into town?

NORA: Yes, today.

KROGSTAD: She's a good friend of yours?

NORA: Yes, she is. But I don't see—

KROGSTAD: I also knew her once.

NORA: I'm aware of that.

KROGSTAD: Oh? You know all about it. I thought so. Well, then let me ask you short and sweet: Is Mrs. Linde getting a job in the bank?

NORA: What makes you think you can cross-examine me, Mr. Krogstad— you, one of my husband's employees? But since you ask, you might as well know—yes, Mrs. Linde's going to be taken on at the bank. And I'm the one who spoke for her, Mr. Krogstad. Now you know.

KROGSTAD: So I guessed right.

NORA (*pacing up and down*): Oh, one does have a tiny bit of influence, I should hope. Just because I am a woman, don't think it means that— When one has a subordinate position, Mr. Krogstad, one really ought to be careful about pushing somebody who—hm—

KROGSTAD: Who has influence?

NORA: That's right.

KROGSTAD (*in a different tone*): Mrs. Helmer, would you be good enough to use your influence on my behalf?

NORA: What? What do you mean?

KROGSTAD: Would you please make sure that I keep my subordinate position in the bank?

NORA: What does that mean? Who's thinking of taking away your position?

KROGSTAD: Oh, don't play the innocent with me. I'm quite aware that your friend would hardly relish the chance of running into me again; and I'm also aware now whom I can thank for being turned out.

NORA: But I promise you—

KROGSTAD: Yes, yes, yes, to the point: There's still time, and I'm advising you to use your influence to prevent it.

NORA: But Mr. Krogstad, I have absolutely no influence.

KROGSTAD: You haven't? I thought you were just saying—

NORA: You shouldn't take me so literally. I! How can you believe that I have any such influence over my husband?

KROGSTAD: Oh, I've known your husband from our student days. I don't think the great bank manager's more steadfast than any other married man.

NORA: You speak insolently about my husband, and I'll show you the door.

KROGSTAD: The lady has spirit.

NORA: I'm not afraid of you any longer. After New Year's, I'll soon be done with the whole business.

KROGSTAD (*restraining himself*): Now listen to me, Mrs. Helmer. If necessary, I'll fight for my little job in the bank as if it were life itself.

NORA: Yes, so it seems.

KROGSTAD: It's not just a matter of income; that's the least of it. It's something else—All right, out with it! Look, this is the thing. You know, just like all the others, of course, that once, a good many years ago, I did something rather rash.

NORA: I've heard rumors to that effect.

KROGSTAD: The case never got into court; but all the same, every door was closed in my face from then on. So I took up those various activities you know about. I had to grab hold somewhere; and I dare say I haven't been among the worst. But now I want to drop all that. My boys are growing up. For their sakes, I'll have to win back as much respect as possible here in town. That job in the bank was like the first rung in my ladder. And now your husband wants to kick me right back down in the mud again.

NORA: But for heaven's sake, Mr. Krogstad, it's simply not in my power to help you.

KROGSTAD: That's because you haven't the will to—but I have the means to make you.

NORA: You certainly won't tell my husband that I owe you money?

KROGSTAD: Hm—what if I told him that?

NORA: That would be shameful of you. (*Nearly in tears.*) This secret—my joy and my pride—that he should learn it in such a crude and disgusting way—learn it from you. You'd expose me to the most horrible unpleasantness—

KROGSTAD: Only unpleasantness?

NORA (*vehemently*): But go on and try. It'll turn out the worse for you, because then my husband will really see what a crook you are, and then you'll never be able to hold your job.

KROGSTAD: I asked if it was just domestic unpleasantness you were afraid of?

NORA: If my husband finds out, then of course he'll pay what I owe at once, and then we'd be through with you for good.

KROGSTAD (*a step closer*): Listen, Mrs. Helmer—you've either got a very bad memory, or else no head at all for business. I'd better put you a little more in touch with the facts.

NORA: What do you mean?

KROGSTAD: When your husband was sick, you came to me for a loan of four thousand, eight hundred crowns.

NORA: Where else could I go?

KROGSTAD: I promised to get you that sum—

NORA: And you got it.

KROGSTAD: I promised to get you that sum, on certain conditions. You were so involved in your husband's illness, and so eager to finance your trip, that I guess you didn't think out all the details. It might just be a good idea to remind you. I promised you the money on the strength of a note I drew up.

NORA: Yes, and that I signed.

KROGSTAD: Right. But at the bottom I added some lines for your father to guarantee the loan. He was supposed to sign down there.

NORA: Supposed to? He did sign.

KROGSTAD: I left the date blank. In other words, your father would have dated his signature himself. Do you remember that?

NORA: Yes, I think—

KROGSTAD: Then I gave you the note for you to mail to your father. Isn't that so?

NORA: Yes.

KROGSTAD: And naturally you sent it at once—because only some five, six days later you brought me the note, properly signed. And with that, the money was yours.

NORA: Well, then; I've made my payments regularly, haven't I?

KROGSTAD: More or less. But—getting back to the point—those were hard times for you then, Mrs. Helmer.

NORA: Yes, they were.

KROGSTAD: Your father was very ill, I believe.

NORA: He was near the end.

KROGSTAD: He died soon after?

NORA: Yes.

KROGSTAD: Tell me, Mrs. Helmer, do you happen to recall the date of your father's death? The day of the month, I mean.

NORA: Papa died the twenty-ninth of September.

KROGSTAD: That's quite correct; I've already looked into that. And now we come to a curious thing—(*taking out a paper*) which I simply cannot comprehend.

NORA: Curious thing? I don't know—

KROGSTAD: This is the curious thing: that your father co-signed the note for your loan three days after his death.

NORA: How—? I don't understand.

KROGSTAD: Your father died the twenty-ninth of September. But look. Here your father dated his signature October second. Isn't that curious, Mrs. Helmer? (*Nora is silent.*) Can you explain it to me? (*Nora remains silent.*) It's also remarkable that the words "October second" and the year aren't written in your father's hand, but rather in one that I think I know. Well, it's easy to understand. Your father forgot perhaps to date his signature, and then someone or other added it, a bit sloppily, before anyone knew of his death. There's nothing wrong in that. It all comes down to the signature. And there's no question about *that*, Mrs. Helmer. It really *was* your father who signed his own name here, wasn't it?

NORA (*after a short silence, throwing her head back and looking squarely at him*): No, it wasn't. *I* signed Papa's name.

KROGSTAD: Wait, now—are you fully aware that this is a dangerous confession?

NORA: Why? You'll soon get your money.

KROGSTAD: Let me ask you a question—why didn't you send the paper to your father?

NORA: That was impossible. Papa was so sick. If I'd asked him for his signature, I also would have had to tell him what the money was for. But I couldn't tell him, sick as he was, that my husband's life was in danger. That was just impossible.

KROGSTAD: Then it would have been better if you'd given up the trip abroad.

NORA: I couldn't possibly. The trip was to save my husband's life. I couldn't give that up.

KROGSTAD: But didn't you ever consider that this was a fraud against me?

NORA: I couldn't let myself be bothered by that. You weren't any concern of mine. I couldn't stand you, with all those cold complications you made, even though you knew how badly off my husband was.

KROGSTAD: Mrs. Helmer, obviously you haven't the vaguest idea of what you've involved yourself in. But I can tell you this: It was nothing more and nothing worse that I once did—and it wrecked my whole reputation.

NORA: You? Do you expect me to believe that you ever acted bravely to save your wife's life?

KROGSTAD: Laws don't inquire into motives.

NORA: Then they must be very poor laws.

KROGSTAD: Poor or not—if I introduce this paper in court, you'll be judged according to law.

NORA: This I refuse to believe. A daughter hasn't a right to protect her dying father from anxiety and care? A wife hasn't a right to save her husband's life? I don't know much about laws, but I'm sure that some-where in the books these things are allowed. And you don't know any-thing about it—you who practice the law? You must be an awful lawyer, Mr. Krogstad.

KROGSTAD: Could be. But business—the kind of business we two are mixed up in—don't you think I know about that? All right. Do what you want now. But I'm telling you *this:* If I get shoved down a second time, you're going to keep me company. (*He bows and goes out through the hall.*)

NORA (*pensive for a moment, then tossing her head*): Oh, really! Trying to frighten me! I'm not so silly as all that. (*Begins gathering up the children's clothes, but soon stops.*) But—? No, but that's impossible! I did it out of love.

THE CHILDREN (*in the doorway, left*): Mama, that strange man's gone out the door.

NORA: Yes, yes, I know it. But don't tell anyone about the strange man. Do you hear? Not even Papa!

THE CHILDREN: No, Mama. But now will you play again?

NORA: No, not now.

THE CHILDREN: Oh, but Mama, you promised.

NORA: Yes, but I can't now. Go inside; I have too much to do. Go in, go in, my sweet darlings. (*She herds them gently back in the room and shuts the door after them. Settling on the sofa, she takes up a piece of embroidery and makes some stitches, but soon stops abruptly.*) No! (*Throws the work aside, rises, goes to the hall door and calls out.*) Helene! Let me have the tree in here. (*Goes to the table, left, opens the table drawer, and stops again.*) No, but that's utterly impossible!

MAID (*with the Christmas tree*): Where should I put it, ma'am?

NORA: There. The middle of the floor.

MAID: Should I bring anything else?

NORA: No, thanks. I have what I need.

(*The Maid, who has set the tree down, goes out.*)

NORA (*absorbed in trimming the tree*): Candles here—and flowers here. That terrible creature! Talk, talk, talk! There's nothing to it at all. The tree's going to be lovely. I'll do anything to please you Torvald. I'll sing for you, dance for you—

(*Helmer comes in from the hall, with a sheaf of papers under his arm.*)

NORA: Oh! You're back so soon?

HELMER: Yes. Has anyone been here?

NORA: Here? No.

HELMER: That's odd. I saw Krogstad leaving the front door.

NORA: So? Oh yes, that's true. Krogstad was here a moment.

HELMER: Nora, I can see by your face that he's been here, begging you to put in a good word for him.

NORA: Yes.

HELMER: And it was supposed to seem like your own idea? You were to hide it from me that he'd been here. He asked you that, too, didn't he?

NORA: Yes, Torvald, but—

HELMER: Nora, Nora, and you could fall for that? Talk with that sort of person and promise him anything? And then in the bargain, tell me an untruth.

NORA: An untruth—?

HELMER: Didn't you say that no one had been here? (*Wagging his finger.*) My little songbird must never do that again. A songbird needs a clean beak to warble with. No false notes. (*Putting his arm about her waist.*) That's the way it should be, isn't it? Yes, I'm sure of it. (*Releasing her.*) And so, enough of that. (*Sitting by the stove.*) Ah, how snug and cozy it is here. (*Leafing among his papers.*)

NORA (*busy with the tree, after a short pause*): Torvald!

HELMER: Yes.

NORA: I'm so much looking forward to the Stenborgs' costume party, day after tomorrow.

HELMER: And I can't wait to see what you'll surprise me with.

NORA: Oh, that stupid business!

HELMER: What?

NORA: I can't find anything that's right. Everything seems so ridiculous, so inane.

HELMER: So my little Nora's come to *that* recognition?

NORA (*going behind his chair, her arms resting on its back*): Are you very busy, Torvald?

HELMER: Oh—

NORA: What papers are those?

HELMER: Bank matters.

NORA: Already?

HELMER: I've gotten full authority from the retiring management to make all necessary changes in personnel and procedure. I'll need Christmas week for that. I want to have everything in order by New Year's.

NORA: So that was the reason this poor Krogstad—

HELMER: Hm.

NORA (*still leaning on the chair and slowly stroking the nape of his neck*): If you weren't so very busy, I would have asked you an enormous favor, Torvald.

HELMER: Let's hear. What is it?

NORA: You know, there isn't anyone who has your good taste—and I want so much to look well at the costume party. Torvald, couldn't you take over and decide what I should be and plan my costume?

HELMER: Ah, is my stubborn little creature calling for a lifeguard?

NORA: Yes, Torvald, I can't get anywhere without your help.

HELMER: All right—I'll think it over. We'll hit on something.

NORA: Oh, how sweet of you. (*Goes to the tree again. Pause.*) Aren't the red flowers pretty—? But tell me, was it really such a crime that this Krogstad committed?

HELMER: Forgery. Do you have any idea what that means?

NORA: Couldn't he have done it out of need?

HELMER: Yes, or thoughtlessness, like so many others. I'm not so heartless that I'd condemn a man categorically for just one mistake.

NORA: No, of course not, Torvald!

HELMER: Plenty of men have redeemed themselves by openly confessing their crimes and taking their punishment.

NORA: Punishment—?

HELMER: But now Krogstad didn't go that way. He got himself out by sharp practices, and that's the real cause of his moral breakdown.

NORA: Do you really think that would—?

HELMER: Just imagine how a man with that sort of guilt in him has to lie and cheat and deceive on all sides, has to wear a mask even with the nearest and dearest he has, even with his own wife and children. And with the children, Nora—that's where it's most horrible.

NORA: Why?

HELMER: Because that kind of atmosphere of lies infects the whole life of a home. Every breath the children take in is filled with the germs of something degenerate.

NORA (*coming closer behind him*): Are you sure of that?

HELMER: Oh, I've seen it often enough as a lawyer. Almost everyone who goes bad early in life has a mother who's a chronic liar.

NORA: Why just—the mother?

HELMER: It's usually the mother's influence that's dominant, but the father's works in the same way, of course. Every lawyer is quite familiar with it. And still this Krogstad's been going home year in, year out, poisoning his own children with lies and pretense; that's why I call him morally lost. (*Reaching his hands out toward her.*) So my sweet little Nora must promise me never to plead his cause. Your hand on it. Come, come, what's this? Give me your hand. There, now. All settled. I can tell you it'd be impossible for me to work alongside of him. I literally feel physically revolted when I'm anywhere near such a person.

NORA (*withdraws her hand and goes to the other side of the Christmas tree*): How hot it is here! And I've got so much to do.

HELMER (*getting up and gathering his papers*): Yes, and I have to think about getting some of these read through before dinner. I'll think about your costume, too. And something to hang on the tree in gilt paper, I may even see about that. (*Putting his hand on her head.*) Oh you, my darling little songbird. (*He goes into his study and closes the door after him.*)

NORA (*softly, after a silence*): Oh, really! It isn't so. It's impossible. It must be impossible.

ANNE-MARIE (*in the doorway left*): The children are begging so hard to come in to Mama.

NORA: No, no, no, don't let them in to me! You stay with them, Anne-Marie.

ANNE-MARIE: Of course, ma'am. (*Closes the door.*)

NORA (*pale with terror*): Hurt my children—! Poison my home? (*A moment's pause; then she tosses her head.*) That's not true. Never. Never in all the world.

ACT II

(*Same room. Beside the piano the Christmas tree now stands stripped of ornament, burned-down candle stubs on its ragged branches. Nora's street clothes lie on the sofa. Nora, alone in the room, moves restlessly about; at last she stops at the sofa and picks up her coat.*)

NORA (*dropping the coat again*): Someone's coming! (*Goes toward the door, listens.*) No—there's no one. Of course—nobody's coming today, Christmas Day—or tomorrow, either. But maybe—(*Opens the door and looks out.*) No, nothing in the mailbox. Quite empty. (*Coming forward.*) What nonsense! He won't do anything serious. Nothing terrible could happen. It's impossible. Why, I have three small children.

(*Anne-Marie, with a large carton, comes in from the room to the left.*)

ANNE-MARIE: Well, at last I found the box with the masquerade clothes.

NORA: Thanks. Put it on the table.

ANNE-MARIE (*does so*): But they're all pretty much of a mess.

NORA: Ahh! I'd love to rip them in a million pieces!

ANNE-MARIE: Oh, mercy, they can be fixed right up. Just a little patience.

NORA: Yes, I'll go get Mrs. Linde to help me.

ANNE-MARIE: Out again now? In this nasty weather? Miss Nora will catch cold—get sick.

NORA: Oh, worse things could happen—How are the children?

ANNE-MARIE: The poor mites are playing with their Christmas presents, but—

NORA: Do they ask for me much?

ANNE-MARIE: They're so used to having Mama around, you know.

NORA: Yes, but Anne-Marie, I *can't* be together with them as much as I was.

ANNE-MARIE: Well, small children get used to anything.

NORA: You think so? Do you think they'd forget their mother if she was gone for good?

ANNE-MARIE: Oh, mercy—gone for good!

NORA: Wait, tell me. Anne-Marie—I've wondered so often—how could you ever have the heart to give your child over to strangers?

ANNE-MARIE: But I had to, you know, to become little Nora's nurse.

NORA: Yes, but how could you *do* it?

ANNE-MARIE: When I could get such a good place? A girl who's poor and who's gotten in trouble is glad enough for that. Because that slippery fish, he didn't do a thing for me, you know.

NORA: But your daughter's surely forgotten you.

ANNE-MARIE: Oh, she certainly has not. She's written to me, both when she was confirmed and when she was married.

NORA (*clasping her about the neck*): You old Anne-Marie, you were a good mother for me when I was little.

ANNE-MARIE: Poor little Nora, with no other mother but me.

NORA: And if the babies didn't have one, then I know that you'd—What silly talk! (*Opening the carton.*) Go in to them. Now I'll have to—Tomorrow you can see how lovely I'll look.

ANNE-MARIE: Oh, there won't be anyone at the party as lovely as Miss Nora. (*She goes off into the room, left.*)

NORA (*begins unpacking the box, but soon throws it aside*): Oh, if I dared to go out. If only nobody would come. If only nothing would happen here while I'm out. What craziness—nobody's coming. Just don't think. This muff—needs a brushing. Beautiful gloves, beautiful gloves. Let it go. Let it go! One, two, three, four, five, six—(*With a cry.*) Oh, there they are! (*Poises to move toward the door, but remains irresolutely standing. Mrs. Linde enters from the hall, where she has removed her street clothes.*)

NORA: Oh, it's you, Kristine. There's no one else out there? How good that you've come.

MRS. LINDE: I hear you were up asking for me.

NORA: Yes, I just stopped by. There's something you really can help me with. Let's get settled on the sofa. Look, there's going to be a costume party tomorrow evening at the Stenborgs' right above us, and now Torvald wants me to go as a Neapolitan peasant girl and dance the tarantella that I learned in Capri.

MRS. LINDE: Really, are you giving a whole performance?

NORA: Torvald says yes, I should. See, here's the dress. Torvald had it made for me down there; but now it's all so tattered that I just don't know—

MRS. LINDE: Oh, we'll fix that up in no time. It's nothing more than the trimmings—they're a bit loose here and there. Needle and thread? Good, now we have what we need.

NORA: Oh, how sweet of you!

MRS. LINDE (*sewing*): So you'll be in disguise tomorrow, Nora. You know what? I'll stop by then for a moment and have a look at you all dressed up. But listen, I've absolutely forgotten to thank you for that pleasant evening yesterday.

NORA (*getting up and walking about*): I don't think it was as pleasant as usual yesterday. You should have come to town a bit sooner, Kristine— Yes, Torvald really knows how to give a home elegance and charm.

MRS. LINDE: And you do, too, if you ask me. You're not your father's daughter for nothing. But tell me, is Dr. Rank always so down in the mouth as yesterday?

NORA: No, that was quite an exception. But he goes around critically ill all the time—tuberculosis of the spine, poor man. You know, his father was a disgusting thing who kept mistresses and so on—and that's why the son's been sickly from birth.

MRS. LINDE (*lets her sewing fall to her lap*): But my dearest Nora, how do you know about such things?

NORA (*walking more jauntily*): Hmp! When you've had three children, then you've had a few visits from—from women who know something of medicine, and they tell you this and that.

MRS. LINDE (*resumes sewing; a short pause*): Does Dr. Rank come here every day?

NORA: Every blessed day. He's Torvald's best friend from childhood, and *my* good friend, too. Dr. Rank almost belongs to this house.

MRS. LINDE: But tell me—is he quite sincere? I mean, doesn't he rather enjoy flattering people?

NORA: Just the opposite. Why do you think that?

MRS. LINDE: When you introduced us yesterday, he was proclaiming that he'd often heard my name in this house; but later I noticed that your husband hadn't the slightest idea who I really was. So how could Dr. Rank—?

NORA: But it's all true, Kristine. You see, Torvald loves me beyond words, and, as he puts it, he'd like to keep me all to himself. For a long time he'd almost be jealous if I even mentioned any of my old friends back home. So of course I dropped that. But with Dr. Rank I talk a lot about such things because he likes hearing about them.

MRS. LINDE: Now listen, Nora; in many ways you're still like a child. I'm a good deal older than you, with a little more experience. I'll tell you something: You ought to put an end to all this with Dr. Rank.

NORA: What should I put an end to?

MRS. LINDE: Both parts of it, I think. Yesterday you said something about a rich admirer who'd provide you with money—

NORA: Yes, one who doesn't exist—worse luck. So?

MRS. LINDE: Is Dr. Rank well off?

NORA: Yes, he is.

MRS. LINDE: With no dependents?

NORA: No, no one. But—

MRS. LINDE: And he's over here every day?

NORA: Yes, I told you that.

MRS. LINDE: How can a man of such refinement be so grasping?

NORA: I don't follow you at all.

MRS. LINDE: Now don't try to hide it, Nora. You think I can't guess who loaned you the forty-eight hundred crowns?

NORA: Are you out of your mind? How could you think such a thing! A friend of ours, who comes here every single day. What an intolerable situation that would have been!

MRS. LINDE: Then it really wasn't him.

NORA: No, absolutely not. It never even crossed my mind for a moment—And he had nothing to lend in those days; his inheritance came later.

MRS. LINDE: Well, I think that was a stroke of luck for you, Nora dear.

NORA: No, it never would have occurred to me to ask Dr. Rank—Still, I'm quite sure that if I had asked him—

MRS. LINDE: Which you won't, of course.

NORA: No, of course not. I can't see that I'd ever need to. But I'm quite positive that if I talked to Dr. Rank—

MRS. LINDE: Behind your husband's back?

NORA: I've got to clear up this other thing; *that's* also behind his back. I've *got* to clear it all up.

MRS. LINDE: Yes, I was saying that yesterday, but—

NORA (*pacing up and down*): A man handles these problems so much better than a woman—

MRS. LINDE: One's husband does, yes.

NORA: Nonsense. (*Stopping.*) When you pay everything you owe, then you get your note back, right?

MRS. LINDE: Yes, naturally.

NORA: And can rip it into a million pieces and burn it up—that filthy scrap of paper!

MRS. LINDE (*looking hard at her, laying her sewing aside, and rising slowly*): Nora, you're hiding something from me.

NORA: You can see it in my face?

MRS. LINDE: Something's happened to you since yesterday morning. Nora, what is it?

NORA (*hurrying toward her*): Kristine! (*Listening.*) Shh! Torvald's home. Look, go in with the children a while. Torvald can't bear all this snipping and stitching. Let Anne-Marie help you.

MRS. LINDE (*gathering up some of the things*): All right, but I'm not leaving here until we've talked this out. (*She disappears into the room, left, as Torvald enters from the hall.*)

NORA: Oh, how I've been waiting for you, Torvald dear.

HELMER: Was that the dressmaker?

NORA: No, that was Kristine. She's helping me fix up my costume. You know, it's going to be quite attractive.

HELMER: Yes, wasn't that a bright idea I had?

NORA: Brilliant! But then wasn't I good as well to give in to you?

HELMER: Good—because you give in to your husband's judgment? All right, you little goose, I know you didn't mean it like that. But I won't disturb you. You'll want to have a fitting, I suppose.

NORA: And you'll be working?

HELMER: Yes. (*Indicating a bundle of papers.*) See. I've been down to the bank. (*Starts toward his study.*)

NORA: Torvald.

HELMER (*stops*): Yes.

NORA: If your little squirrel begged you, with all her heart and soul, for something—?

HELMER: What's that?

NORA: Then would you do it?

HELMER: First, naturally, I'd have to know what it was.

NORA: Your squirrel would scamper about and do tricks, if you'd only be sweet and give in.

HELMER: Out with it.

NORA: Your lark would be singing high and low in every room—

HELMER: Come on, she does that anyway.

NORA: I'd be a wood nymph and dance for you in the moonlight.

HELMER: Nora—don't tell me it's that same business from this morning?

NORA (*coming closer*): Yes, Torvald, I beg you, please!

HELMER: And you actually have the nerve to drag that up again?

NORA: Yes, yes, you've got to give in to me; you *have* to let Krogstad keep his job in the bank.

HELMER: My dear Nora, I've slated his job for Mrs. Linde.

NORA: That's awfully kind of you. But you could just fire another clerk instead of Krogstad.

HELMER: This is the most incredible stubbornness! Because you go and give an impulsive promise to speak up for him, I'm expected to—

NORA: That's not the reason, Torvald. It's for your own sake. That man does writing for the worst papers; you said it yourself. He could do you any amount of harm. I'm scared to death of him—

HELMER: Ah, I understand. It's the old memories haunting you.

NORA: What do you mean by that?

HELMER: Of course, you're thinking about your father.

NORA: Yes, all right. Just remember how those nasty gossips wrote in the papers about Papa and slandered him so cruelly. I think they'd have had him dismissed if the department hadn't sent you up to investigate, and if you hadn't been so kind and open-minded toward him.

HELMER: My dear Nora, there's a notable difference between your father and me. Your father's official career was hardly above reproach. But mine is; and I hope it'll stay that way as long as I hold my position.

NORA: Oh, who can ever tell what vicious minds can invent? We could be so snug and happy now in our quiet, carefree home—you and I and the children, Torvald! That's why I'm pleading with you so—

HELMER: And just by pleading for him you make it impossible for me to keep him on. It's already known at the bank that I'm firing Krogstad. What if it's rumored around now that the new bank manager was vetoed by his wife—

NORA: Yes, what then—?

HELMER: Oh yes—as long as our little bundle of stubbornness gets her way—! I should go and make myself ridiculous in front of the whole office—give people the idea I can be swayed by all kinds of outside pressure. Oh, you can bet I'd feel the effects of that soon enough! Besides—there's something that rules Krogstad right out at the bank as long as I'm the manager.

NORA: What's that?

HELMER: His moral failings I could maybe overlook if I had to—

NORA: Yes, Torvald, why not?

HELMER: And I hear he's quite efficient on the job. But he was a crony of mine back in my teens—one of those rash friendships that crop up again and again to embarrass you later in life. Well, I might as well say it straight out: We're on a first-name basis. And that tactless fool makes no effort at all to hide it in front of others. Quite the contrary— he thinks that entitles him to take a familiar air around me, and so every other second he comes booming out with his, "Yes, Torvald!" and "Sure thing, Torvald!" I tell you, it's been excruciating for me. He's out to make my place in the bank unbearable.

NORA: Torvald, you can't be serious about all this.

HELMER: Oh no? Why not?

NORA: Because these are such petty considerations.

HELMER: What are you saying? Petty? You think I'm petty!

NORA: No, just the opposite, Torvald dear. That's exactly why—

HELMER: Never mind. You call my motives petty; then I might as well be just that. Petty! All right! We'll put a stop to this for good. (*Goes to the hall door and calls.*) Helene!

NORA: What do you want?

HELMER (*searching among his papers*): A decision. (*The Maid comes in.*) Look here; take this letter; go out with it at once. Get hold of a messenger and have him deliver it. Quick now. It's already addressed. Wait, here's some money.

MAID: Yes, sir. (*She leaves with the letter.*)

HELMER (*straightening his papers*): There, now, little Miss Willful.

NORA (*breathlessly*): Torvald, what was that letter?

HELMER: Krogstad's notice.

NORA: Call it back, Torvald! There's still time. Oh, Torvald, call it back! Do it for my sake—for your sake, for the children's sake! Do you hear, Torvald; do it! You don't know how this can harm us.

HELMER: Too late.

NORA: Yes, too late.

HELMER: Nora, dear, I can forgive you this panic, even though basically you're insulting me. Yes, you are! Or isn't it an insult to think that *I* should be afraid of a courtroom hack's revenge? But I forgive you anyway, because this shows so beautifully how much you love me. (*Takes her in his arms.*) This is the way it should be, my darling Nora. Whatever comes, you'll see: When it really counts, I have strength and courage enough as a man to take on the whole weight myself.

NORA (*terrified*): What do you mean by that?

HELMER: The whole weight, I said.

NORA (*resolutely*): No, never in all the world.

HELMER: Good. So we'll share it, Nora, as man and wife. That's as it should be. (*Fondling her.*) Are you happy now? There, there, there—not these frightened dove's eyes. It's nothing at all but empty fantasies— Now you should run through your tarantella and practice your tambourine. I'll go to the inner office, and shut both doors, so I won't hear a thing; you can make all the noise you like. (*Turning in the doorway.*) And when Rank comes, just tell him where he can find me. (*He nods to her and goes with his papers into the study, closing the door.*)

NORA (*standing as though rooted, dazed with fright, in a whisper*): He really could do it. He will do it. He'll do it in spite of everything. No, not that, never, never! Anything but that! Escape! A way out—(*The doorbell rings.*) Dr. Rank! Anything but that! *Anything,* whatever it is! (*Her hands pass over her face, smoothing it; she pulls herself together, goes over and opens the hall door. Dr. Rank stands outside, hanging his fur coat up. During the following scene, it begins getting dark.*)

NORA: Hello, Dr. Rank. I recognized your ring. But you mustn't go in to Torvald yet; I believe he's working.

RANK: And you?

NORA: For you, I always have an hour to spare—you know that. (*He has entered, and she shuts the door after him.*)

RANK: Many thanks. I'll make use of these hours while I can.

NORA: What do you mean by that? While you can?

RANK: Does that disturb you?

NORA: Well, it's such an odd phrase. Is anything going to happen?

RANK: What's going to happen is what I've been expecting so long—but I honestly didn't think it would come so soon.

NORA (*gripping his arm*): What is it you've found out? Dr. Rank, you have to tell me!

RANK (*sitting by the stove*): It's all over with me. There's nothing to be done about it.

NORA (*breathing easier*): Is it you—then—?

RANK: Who else? There's no point in lying to one's self. I'm the most miserable of all my patients, Mrs. Helmer. These past few days I've been auditing my internal accounts. Bankrupt! Within a month I'll probably be laid out and rotting in the churchyard.

NORA: Oh, what a horrible thing to say.

RANK: The thing itself is horrible. But the worst of it is all the other horror before it's over. There's only one final examination left; when I'm finished with that, I'll know about when my disintegration will begin. There's something I want to say. Helmer with his sensitivity has such a sharp distaste for anything ugly. I don't want him near my sickroom.

NORA: Oh, but Dr. Rank—

RANK: I won't have him in there. Under no condition. I'll lock my door to him—As soon as I'm completely sure of the worst, I'll send you my calling card marked with a black cross, and you'll know then the wreck has started to come apart.

NORA: No, today you're completely unreasonable. And I wanted you so much to be in a really good humor.

RANK: With death up my sleeve? And then to suffer this way for somebody else's sins. Is there any justice in that? And in every single family, in some way or another, this inevitable retribution of nature goes on—

NORA (*her hands pressed over her ears*): Oh, stuff! Cheer up! Please— be gay!

RANK: Yes, I'd just as soon laugh at it all. My poor, innocent spine, serving time for my father's gay army days.

NORA (*by the table, left*): He was so infatuated with asparagus tips and pâté de foie gras, wasn't that it?

RANK: Yes—and with truffles.

NORA: Truffles, yes. And then with oysters, I suppose?

RANK: Yes, tons of oysters, naturally.

NORA: And then the port and champagne to go with it. It's so sad that all these delectable things have to strike at our bones.

RANK: Especially when they strike at the unhappy bones that never shared in the fun.

NORA: Ah, that's the saddest of all.

RANK (*looks searchingly at her*): Hm.

NORA (*after a moment*): Why did you smile?

RANK: No, it was you who laughed.

NORA: No, it was you who smiled, Dr. Rank!

RANK (*getting up*): You're even a bigger tease than I'd thought.

NORA: I'm full of wild ideas today.

RANK: That's obvious.

NORA (*putting both hands on his shoulders*): Dear, dear Dr. Rank, you'll never die for Torvald and me.

RANK: Oh, that loss you'll easily get over. Those who go away are soon forgotten.

NORA (*looks fearfully at him*): You believe that?

RANK: One makes new connections, and then—

NORA: Who makes new connections?

RANK: Both you and Torvald will when I'm gone. I'd say you're well under way already. What was that Mrs. Linde doing here last evening?

NORA: Oh, come—you can't be jealous of poor Kristine?

RANK: Oh yes, I am. She'll be my successor here in the house. When I'm down under, that woman will probably—

NORA: Shh! Not so loud. She's right in there.

RANK: Today as well. So you see.

NORA: Only to sew on my dress. Good gracious, how unreasonable you are. (*Sitting on the sofa.*) Be nice now, Dr. Rank. Tomorrow you'll see how beautifully I'll dance; and you can imagine then that I'm dancing only for you—yes, and of course for Torvald, too—that's understood. (*Takes various items out of the carton.*) Dr. Rank, sit over here and I'll show you something.

RANK (*sitting*): What's that?

NORA: Look here. Look.

RANK: Silk stockings.

NORA: Flesh-colored. Aren't they lovely? Now it's so dark here, but tomorrow—No, no, no, just look at the feet. Oh well, you might as well look at the rest.

RANK: Hm—

NORA: Why do you look so critical? Don't you believe they'll fit?

RANK: I've never had any chance to form an opinion on that.

NORA (*glancing at him a moment*): Shame on you. (*Hits him lightly on the ear with the stockings.*) That's for you. (*Puts them away again.*)

RANK: And what other splendors am I going to see now?

NORA: Not the least bit more, because you've been naughty. (*She hunts a little and rummages among her things.*)

RANK (*after a short silence*): When I sit here together with you like this, completely easy and open, then I don't know—I simply can't imagine— whatever would have become of me if I'd never come into this house.

NORA (*smiling*): Yes, I really think you feel completely at ease with us.

RANK (*more quietly, staring straight ahead*): And then to have to go away from it all—

NORA: Nonsense, you're not going away.

RANK (*his voice unchanged*):—and not even be able to leave some poor show of gratitude behind, scarcely a fleeting regret—no more than a vacant place that anyone can fill.

NORA: And if I asked you now for—No—

RANK: For what?

NORA: For a great proof of your friendship—

RANK: Yes, yes?

NORA: No, I mean—for an exceptionally big favor—

RANK: Would you really, for once, make me so happy?

NORA: Oh, you haven't the vaguest idea what it is.

RANK: All right, then tell me.

NORA: No, but I can't, Dr. Rank—it's all out of reason. It's advice and help, too—and a favor—

RANK: So much the better. I can't fathom what you're hinting at. Just speak out. Don't you trust me?

NORA: Of course. More than anyone else. You're my best and truest friend, I'm sure. That's why I want to talk to you. All right, then, Dr. Rank: There's something you can help me prevent. You know how deeply, how inexpressibly dearly Torvald loves me; he'd never hesitate a second to give up his life for me.

RANK (*leaning close to her*): Nora—do you think he's the only one—

NORA (*with a slight start*): Who—?

RANK: Who'd gladly give up his life for you.

NORA (*heavily*): I see.

RANK: I swore to myself you should know this before I'm gone. I'll never find a better chance. Yes, Nora, now you know. And also you know now that you can trust me beyond anyone else.

NORA (*rising, natural and calm*): Let me by.

RANK (*making room for her, but still sitting*): Nora—

NORA (*in the hall doorway*): Helene, bring the lamp in. (*Goes over to the stove.*) Ah, dear Dr. Rank, that was really mean of you.

RANK (*getting up*): That I've loved you just as deeply as somebody else? Was *that* mean?

NORA: No, but that you came out and told me. That was quite unnecessary—

RANK: What do you mean? Have you known—?

(*The Maid comes in with the lamp, sets it on the table, and goes out again.*)

RANK: Nora—Mrs. Helmer—I'm asking you: Have you known about it?

NORA: Oh, how can I tell what I know or don't know? Really, I don't know what to say—Why did you have to be so clumsy, Dr. Rank! Everything was so good.

RANK: Well, in any case, you now have the knowledge that my body and soul are at your command. So won't you speak out?

NORA (*looking at him*): After that?

RANK: Please, just let me know what it is.

NORA: You can't know anything now.

RANK: I have to. You mustn't punish me like this. Give me the chance to do whatever is humanly possible for you.

NORA: Now there's nothing you can do for me. Besides, actually, I don't need any help. You'll see—it's only my fantasies. That's what it is. Of course! (*Sits in the rocker, looks at him, and smiles.*) What a nice one you are, Dr. Rank. Aren't you a little bit ashamed, now that the lamp is here?

RANK: No, not exactly. But perhaps I'd better go—for good?

NORA: No, you certainly can't do that. You must come here just as you always have. You know Torvald can't do without you.

RANK: Yes, but *you*?

NORA: You know how much I enjoy it when you're here.

RANK: That's precisely what threw me off. You're a mystery to me. So many times I've felt you'd almost rather be with me than with Helmer.

NORA: Yes—you see, there are some people that one loves most and other people that one would almost prefer being with.

RANK: Yes, there's something to that.

NORA: When I was back home, of course I loved Papa most. But I always thought it was so much fun when I could sneak down to the maids' quarters, because they never tried to improve me, and it was always so amusing, the way they talked to each other.

RANK: Aha, so it's their place that I've filled.

NORA (*jumping up and going to him*): Oh, dear, sweet Dr. Rank, that's not what I meant at all. But you can understand that with Torvald it's just the same as with Papa—

(*The Maid enters from the hall.*)

MAID: Ma'am—please! (*She whispers to Nora and hands her a calling card.*)

NORA (*glancing at the card*): Ah! (*Slips it into her pocket.*)

RANK: Anything wrong?

NORA: No, no, not at all. It's only some—it's my new dress—

RANK: Really? But—there's your dress.

NORA: Oh, that. But this is another one—I ordered it—Torvald mustn't know—

RANK: Ah, now we have the big secret.

NORA: That's right. Just go in with him—he's back in the inner study. Keep him there as long as—

RANK: Don't worry. He won't get away. (*Goes into the study.*)

NORA (*to the Maid*): And he's standing waiting in the kitchen?

MAID: Yes, he came up by the back stairs.

NORA: But didn't you tell him somebody was here?

MAID: Yes, but that didn't do any good.

NORA: He won't leave?

MAID: No, he won't go till he's talked with you, ma'am.

NORA: Let him come in, then—but quietly. Helene, don't breathe a word about this. It's a surprise for my husband.

MAID: Yes, yes, I understand—(*Goes out.*)

NORA: This horror—it's going to happen. No, no, no, it can't happen, it mustn't. (*She goes and bolts Helmer's door. The Maid opens the hall door for Krogstad and shuts it behind him. He is dressed for travel in a fur coat, boots, and a fur cap.*)

NORA (*going toward him*): Talk softly. My husband's home.

KROGSTAD: Well, good for him.

NORA: What do you want?

KROGSTAD: Some information.

NORA: Hurry up, then. What is it?

KROGSTAD: You know, of course, that I got my notice.

NORA: I couldn't prevent it, Mr. Krogstad. I fought for you to the bitter end, but nothing worked.

KROGSTAD: Does your husband's love for you run so thin? He knows everything I can expose you to, and all the same he dares to—

NORA: How can you imagine he knows anything about this?

KROGSTAD: Ah, no—I can't imagine it either, now. It's not at all like my fine Torvald Helmer to have so much guts—

NORA: Mr. Krogstad, I demand respect for my husband!

KROGSTAD: Why, of course—all due respect. But since the lady's keeping it so carefully hidden, may I presume to ask if you're also a bit better informed than yesterday about what you've actually done?

NORA: More than you ever could teach me.

KROGSTAD: Yes, I *am* such an awful lawyer.

NORA: What is it you want from me?

KROGSTAD: Just a glimpse of how you are, Mrs. Helmer. I've been thinking about you all day long. A cashier, a night-court scribbler, a—well, a type like me also has a little of what they call a heart, you know.

NORA: Then show it. Think of my children.

KROGSTAD: Did you or your husband ever think of mine? But never mind. I simply wanted to tell you that you don't need to take this thing too seriously. For the present, I'm not proceeding with any action.

NORA: Oh no, really! Well—I knew that.

KROGSTAD: Everything can be settled in a friendly spirit. It doesn't have to get around town at all; it can stay just among us three.

NORA: My husband must never know anything of this.

KROGSTAD: How can you manage that? Perhaps you can pay me the balance?

NORA: No, not right now.

KROGSTAD: Or you know some way of raising the money in a day or two?

NORA: No way that I'm willing to use.

KROGSTAD: Well, it wouldn't have done you any good, anyway. If you stood in front of me with a fistful of bills, you still couldn't buy your signature back.

NORA: Then tell me what you're going to do with it.

KROGSTAD: I'll just hold onto it—keep it on file. There's no outsider who'll even get wind of it. So if you've been thinking of taking some desperate step—

NORA: I have.

KROGSTAD: Been thinking of running away from home—

NORA: I have!

KROGSTAD: Or even of something worse—

NORA: How could you guess that?

KROGSTAD: You can drop those thoughts.

NORA: How could you guess I was thinking of *that*?

KROGSTAD: Most of us think about *that* at first. I thought about it too, but I discovered I hadn't the courage—

NORA (*lifelessly*): I don't either.

KROGSTAD (*relieved*): That's true, you haven't the courage? You too?

NORA: I don't have it—I don't have it.

KROGSTAD: It would be terribly stupid, anyway. After that first storm at home blows out, why, then—I have here in my pocket a letter for your husband—

NORA: Telling everything?

KROGSTAD: As charitably as possible.

NORA (*quickly*): He mustn't ever get that letter. Tear it up. I'll find some way to get money.

KROGSTAD: Beg pardon, Mrs. Helmer, but I think I just told you—

NORA: Oh, I don't mean the money I owe you. Let me know how much you want from my husband, and I'll manage it.

KROGSTAD: I don't want any money from your husband.

NORA: What do you want, then?

KROGSTAD: I'll tell you what. I want to recoup, Mrs. Helmer; I want to get on in the world—and there's where your husband can help me. For a year and a half I've kept myself clean of anything disreputable—all that time struggling with the worst conditions; but I was satisfied, working my way up step by step. Now I've been written right off, and I'm just not in the mood to come crawling back. I tell you, I want to move on. I want to get back in the bank—in a better position. Your husband can set up a job for me—

NORA: He'll never do that!

KROGSTAD: He'll do it. I know him. He won't dare breathe a word of protest. And once I'm in there together with him, you just wait and see! Inside of a year, I'll be the manager's right-hand man. It'll be Nils Krogstad, not Torvald Helmer, who runs the bank.

NORA: You'll never see the day!

KROGSTAD: Maybe you think you can—

NORA: I have the courage now—for *that*.

KROGSTAD: Oh, you don't scare me. A smart, spoiled lady like you—

NORA: You'll see; you'll see!

KROGSTAD: Under the ice, maybe? Down in the freezing, coal-black water? There, till you float up in the spring, ugly unrecognizable, with your hair falling out—

NORA: You don't frighten me.

KROGSTAD: Nor do you frighten me. One doesn't do these things, Mrs. Helmer. Besides what good would it be? I'd still have him safe in my pocket.

NORA: Afterwards? When I'm no longer—?

KROGSTAD: Are you forgetting that *I'll* be in control then over your final reputation? (*Nora stands speechless, staring at him.*) Good; now I've warned you. Don't do anything stupid. When Helmer's read my letter, I'll be waiting for his reply. And bear in mind that it's your husband himself who's forced me back to my old ways. I'll never forgive him for that. Good-bye, Mrs. Helmer. (*He goes out through the hall.*)

NORA (*goes to the hall door, opens it a crack, and listens*): He's gone. Didn't leave the letter. Oh no, no, that's impossible too! (*Opening the door more and more.*) What's that? He's standing outside—not going downstairs. He's thinking it over? Maybe he'll—? (*A letter falls in the mailbox; then Krogstad's footsteps are heard, dying away down a flight of stairs. Nora gives a muffled cry and runs over toward the sofa table. A short pause.*) In the mailbox. (*Slips warily over to the hall door.*) It's lying there. Torvald, Torvald—now we're lost!

MRS. LINDE (*entering with the costume from the room, left*): There now, I can't see anything else to mend. Perhaps you'd like to try—

NORA (*in a hoarse whisper*): Kristine, come here.

MRS. LINDE (*tossing the dress on the sofa*): What's wrong? You look upset.

NORA: Come here. See that letter? There! Look—through the glass in the mailbox.

MRS. LINDE: Yes, yes, I see it.

NORA: That letter's from Krogstad—

MRS. LINDE: Nora—it's Krogstad who loaned you the money!

NORA: Yes, and now Torvald will find out everything.

MRS. LINDE: Believe me, Nora, it's best for both of you.

NORA: There's more you don't know. I forged a name.

MRS. LINDE: But for heaven's sake—?

NORA: I only want to tell you that, Kristine, so that you can be my witness.

MRS. LINDE: Witness? Why should I—?

NORA: If I should go out of my mind—it could easily happen—

MRS. LINDE: Nora!

NORA: Or anything else occurred—so I couldn't be present here—

MRS. LINDE: Nora, Nora, you aren't yourself at all!

NORA: And someone should try to take on the whole weight, all of the guilt, you follow me—

MRS. LINDE: Yes, of course, but why do you think—?

NORA: Then you're the witness that it isn't true, Kristine. I'm very much myself; my mind right now is perfectly clear; and I'm telling you:

Nobody else has known about this; I alone did everything. Remember that.

MRS. LINDE: I will. But I don't understand all this.

NORA: Oh, how could you ever understand it? It's the miracle now that's going to take place.

MRS. LINDE: The miracle?

NORA: Yes, the miracle. But it's so awful, Kristine. It mustn't take place, not for anything in the world.

MRS. LINDE: I'm going right over and talk with Krogstad.

NORA: Don't go near him; he'll do you some terrible harm!

MRS. LINDE: There was a time once when he'd gladly have done anything for me.

NORA: He?

MRS. LINDE: Where does he live?

NORA: Oh, how do I know? Yes. (*Searches in her pocket.*) Here's his card. But the letter, the letter—!

HELMER (*from the study, knocking on the door*): Nora!

NORA (*with a cry of fear*): Oh! What is it? What do you want?

HELMER: Now, now, don't be so frightened. We're not coming in. You locked the door—are you trying on the dress?

NORA: Yes, I'm trying it. I'll look just beautiful, Torvald.

MRS. LINDE (*who has read the card*): He's living right around the corner.

NORA: Yes, but what's the use? We're lost. The letter's in the box.

MRS. LINDE: And your husband has the key?

NORA: Yes, always.

MRS. LINDE: Krogstad can ask for his letter back unread; he can find some excuse—

NORA: But it's just this time that Torvald usually—

MRS. LINDE: Stall him. Keep him in there. I'll be back as quick as I can. (*She hurries out through the hall entrance.*)

NORA (*goes to Helmer's door, opens it, and peers in*): Torvald!

HELMER (*from the inner study*): Well—does one dare set foot in one's own living room at last? Come on, Rank, now we'll get a look—(*In the doorway.*) But what's this?

NORA: What, Torvald dear?

HELMER: Rank had me expecting some grand masquerade.

RANK (*in the doorway*): That was my impression, but I must have been wrong.

NORA: No one can admire me in my splendor—not till tomorrow.

HELMER: But Nora dear, you look so exhausted. Have you practiced too hard?

NORA: No, I haven't practiced at all yet.

HELMER: You know, it's necessary—

NORA: Oh, it's absolutely necessary, Torvald. But I can't get anywhere without your help. I've forgotten the whole thing completely.

HELMER: Ah, we'll soon take care of that.

NORA: Yes, take care of me, Torvald, please! Promise me that? Oh, I'm so nervous. That big party—You must give up everything this evening for me. No business—don't even touch your pen. Yes? Dear Torvald, promise?

HELMER: It's a promise. Tonight I'm totally at your service—you little helpless thing. Hm—but first there's one thing I want to—(*Goes toward the hall door.*)

NORA: What are you looking for?

HELMER: Just to see if there's any mail.

NORA: No, no, don't do that, Torvald!

HELMER: Now what?

NORA: Torvald, please. There isn't any.

HELMER: Let me look, though. (*Starts out. Nora, at the piano, strikes the first notes of the tarantella. Helmer, at the door, stops.*) Aha!

NORA: I can't dance tomorrow if I don't practice with you.

HELMER (*going over to her*): Nora dear, are you really so frightened?

NORA: Yes, so terribly frightened. Let me practice right now; there's still time before dinner. Oh, sit down and play for me, Torvald. Direct me. Teach me, the way you always have.

HELMER: Gladly, if it's what you want. (*Sits at the piano.*)

NORA (*snatches the tambourine up from the box, then a long, varicolored shawl, which she throws around herself, whereupon she springs forward and cries out*): Play for me now! Now I'll dance!

(*Helmer plays and Nora dances. Rank stands behind Helmer at the piano and looks on.*)

HELMER (*as he plays*): Slower. Slow down.

NORA: Can't change it.

HELMER: Not so violent, Nora!

NORA: Has to be just like this.

HELMER (*stopping*): No, no, that won't do at all.

NORA (*laughing and swinging her tambourine*): Isn't that what I told you?

RANK: Let me play for her.

HELMER (*getting up*): Yes, go on. I can teach her more easily then.

(*Rank sits at the piano and plays, Nora dances more and more wildly. Helmer has stationed himself by the stove and repeatedly gives her directions; she seems not to hear them; her hair loosens and falls over her shoulders; she does not notice, but goes on dancing. Mrs. Linde enters.*)

MRS. LINDE (*standing dumbfounded at the door*): Ah—!

NORA (*still dancing*): See what fun, Kristine!

HELMER: But Nora darling, you dance as if your life were at stake.

NORA: And it is.

HELMER: Rank, stop! This is pure madness. Stop it, I say!

(*Rank breaks off playing, and Nora halts abruptly.*)

HELMER (*going over to her*): I never would have believed it. You've forgotten everything I taught you.

NORA (*throwing away the tambourine*): You see for yourself.

HELMER: Well, there's certainly room for instruction here.

NORA: Yes, you see how important it is. You've got to teach me to the very last minute. Promise me that, Torvald?

HELMER: You can bet on it.

NORA: You mustn't, either today or tomorrow, think about anything else but me; you mustn't open any letters — or the mailbox —

HELMER: Ah, it's still the fear of that man —

NORA: Oh yes, yes, that too.

HELMER: Nora, it's written all over you — there's already a letter from him out there.

NORA: I don't know. I guess so. But you mustn't read such things now; there mustn't be anything ugly between us before it's all over.

RANK (*quietly to Helmer*): You shouldn't deny her.

HELMER (*putting his arm around her*): The child can have her way. But tomorrow night, after you've danced —

NORA: Then you'll be free.

MAID (*in the doorway, right*): Ma'am, dinner is served.

NORA: We'll be wanting champagne, Helene.

MAID: Very good, ma'am. (*Goes out.*)

HELMER: So — a regular banquet, hm?

NORA: Yes, a banquet — champagne till daybreak! (*Calling out.*) And some macaroons, Helene. Heaps of them — just this once.

HELMER (*taking her hands*): Now, now, now — no hysterics. Be my own little lark again.

NORA: Oh, I will soon enough. But go on in — and you, Dr. Rank. Kristine, help me put up my hair.

RANK (*whispering, as they go*): There's nothing wrong — really wrong, is there?

HELMER: Oh, of course not. It's nothing more than this childish anxiety I was telling you about. (*They go out, right.*)

NORA: Well?

MRS. LINDE: Left town.

NORA: I could see by your face.

MRS. LINDE: He'll be home tomorrow evening. I wrote him a note.

NORA: You shouldn't have. Don't try to stop anything now. After all, it's a wonderful joy, this waiting here for the miracle.

MRS. LINDE: What is it you're waiting for?

NORA: Oh, you can't understand that. Go in to them; I'll be along in a moment.

(*Mrs. Linde goes into the dining room. Nora stands a short while as if composing herself; then she looks at her watch.*)

NORA: Five. Seven hours to midnight. Twenty-four hours to the midnight after, and then the tarantella's done. Seven and twenty-four? Thirty-one hours to live.

HELMER (*in the doorway, right*): What's become of the little lark?

NORA (*going toward him with open arms*): Here's your lark!

ACT III

(*Same scene. The table, with chairs around it, has been moved to the center of the room. A lamp on the table is lit. The hall door stands open. Dance music drifts down from the floor above. Mrs. Linde sits at the table, absently paging through a book, trying to read, but apparently unable to focus her thoughts. Once or twice she pauses, tensely listening for a sound at the outer entrance.*)

MRS. LINDE (*glancing at her watch*): Not yet—and there's hardly any time left. If only he's not—(*Listening again.*) Ah, there it is. (*She goes out in the hall and cautiously opens the outer door. Quiet footsteps are heard on the stairs. She whispers.*) Come in. Nobody's here.

KROGSTAD (*in the doorway*): I found a note from you at home. What's back of all this?

MRS. LINDE: I just *had* to talk to you.

KROGSTAD: Oh? And it just *had* to be here in this house?

MRS. LINDE: At my place it was impossible; my room hasn't a private entrance. Come in, we're all alone. The maid's asleep, and the Helmers are at the dance upstairs.

KROGSTAD (*entering the room*): Well, well, the Helmers are dancing tonight? Really?

MRS. LINDE: Yes, why not?

KROGSTAD: How true—why not?

MRS. LINDE: All right, Krogstad, let's talk.

KROGSTAD: Do we two have anything more to talk about?

MRS. LINDE: We have a great deal to talk about.

KROGSTAD: I wouldn't have thought so.

MRS. LINDE: No, because you've never understood me, really.

KROGSTAD: Was there anything more to understand—except what's all too common in life? A calculating woman throws over a man the moment a better catch comes by.

MRS. LINDE: You think I'm so thoroughly calculating? You think I broke it off lightly?

KROGSTAD: Didn't you?

MRS. LINDE: Nils—is that what you really thought?

KROGSTAD: If you cared, then why did you write me the way you did?

MRS. LINDE: What else could I do? If I had to break off with you, then it was my job as well to root out everything you felt for me.

KROGSTAD (*wringing his hands*): So that was it. And this—all this, simply for money!

MRS. LINDE: Don't forget I had a helpless mother and two small brothers. We couldn't wait for you, Nils; you had such a long road ahead of you then.

KROGSTAD: That may be; but you still hadn't the right to abandon me for somebody else's sake.

MRS. LINDE: Yes—I don't know. So many, many times I've asked myself if I did have that right.

KROGSTAD (*more softly*): When I lost you, it was as if all the solid ground dissolved from under my feet. Look at me; I'm a half-drowned man now, hanging onto a wreck.

MRS. LINDE: Help may be near.

KROGSTAD: It was near—but then you came and blocked it off.

MRS. LINDE: Without my knowing it, Nils. Today for the first time I learned that it's you I'm replacing at the bank.

KROGSTAD: All right—I believe you. But now that you know, will you step aside?

MRS. LINDE: No, because that wouldn't benefit you in the slightest.

KROGSTAD: Not "benefit" me, hm! I'd step aside anyway.

MRS. LINDE: I've learned to be realistic. Life and hard, bitter necessity have taught me that.

KROGSTAD: And life's taught me never to trust fine phrases.

MRS. LINDE: Then life's taught you a very sound thing. But you do have to trust in actions, don't you?

KROGSTAD: What does that mean?

MRS. LINDE: You said you were hanging on like a half-drowned man to a wreck.

KROGSTAD: I've good reason to say that.

MRS. LINDE: I'm also like a half-drowned woman on a wreck. No one to suffer with; no one to care for.

KROGSTAD: You made your choice.

MRS. LINDE: There wasn't any choice then.

KROGSTAD: So—what of it?

MRS. LINDE: Nils, if only we two shipwrecked people could reach across to each other.

KROGSTAD: What are you saying?

MRS. LINDE: Two on one wreck are at least better off than each on his own.

KROGSTAD: Kristine!

MRS. LINDE: Why do you think I came into town?

KROGSTAD: Did you really have some thought of me?

MRS. LINDE: I have to work to go on living. All my born days, as long as I can remember, I've worked, and it's been my best and my only joy. But now I'm completely alone in the world; it frightens me to be so empty and lost. To work for yourself—there's no joy in that. Nils, give me something—someone to work for.

KROGSTAD: I don't believe all this. It's just some hysterical feminine urge to go out and make a noble sacrifice.

MRS. LINDE: Have you ever found me to be hysterical?

KROGSTAD: Can you honestly mean this? Tell me—do you know everything about my past?

MRS. LINDE: Yes.

KROGSTAD: And you know what they think I'm worth around here.

MRS. LINDE: From what you were saying before, it would seem that with me you could have been another person.

KROGSTAD: I'm positive of that.

MRS. LINDE: Couldn't it happen still?

KROGSTAD: Kristine—you're saying this in all seriousness? Yes, you are! I can see it in you. And do you really have the courage, then—?

MRS. LINDE: I need to have someone to care for, and your children need a mother. We both need each other. Nils, I have faith that you're good at heart—I'll risk everything together with you.

KROGSTAD (*gripping her hands*): Kristine, thank you, thank you—Now I know I can win back a place in their eyes. Yes—but I forgot—

MRS. LINDE (*listening*): Shh! The tarantella. Go now! Go on!

KROGSTAD: Why? What is it?

MRS. LINDE: Hear the dance up there? When that's over, they'll be coming down.

KROGSTAD: Oh, then I'll go. But—it's all pointless. Of course, you don't know the move I made against the Helmers.

MRS. LINDE: Yes, Nils, I know.

KROGSTAD: And all the same, you have the courage to—?

MRS. LINDE: I know how far despair can drive a man like you.

KROGSTAD: Oh, if I only could take it all back.

MRS. LINDE: You easily could—your letter's still lying in the mailbox.

KROGSTAD: Are you sure of that?

MRS. LINDE: Positive. But—

KROGSTAD (*looks at her searchingly*): Is that the meaning of it, then? You'll save your friend at any price. Tell me straight out. Is that it?

MRS. LINDE: Nils—anyone who's sold herself for somebody else once isn't going to do it again.

KROGSTAD: I'll demand my letter back.

MRS. LINDE: No, no.

KROGSTAD: Yes, of course. I'll stay here till Helmer comes down; I'll tell him to give me my letter again—that it only involves my dismissal— that he shouldn't read it—

MRS. LINDE: No, Nils, don't call the letter back.

KROGSTAD: But wasn't that exactly why you wrote me to come here?

MRS. LINDE: Yes, in that first panic. But it's been a whole day and night since then, and in that time I've seen such incredible things in this house. Helmer's got to learn everything; this dreadful secret has to be aired; those two have to come to a full understanding; all these lies and evasions can't go on.

KROGSTAD: Well, then, if you want to chance it. But at least there's one thing I can do, and do right away—

MRS. LINDE (*listening*): Go now, go, quick! The dance is over. We're not safe another second.

KROGSTAD: I'll wait for you downstairs.

MRS. LINDE: Yes, please do; take me home.

KROGSTAD: I can't believe it; I've never been so happy. (*He leaves by way of the outer door; the door between the room and the hall stays open.*)

MRS. LINDE (*straightening up a bit and getting together her street clothes*): How different now! How different! Someone to work for, to live for— a home to build. Well, it is worth the try! Oh, if they'd only come! (*Listening.*) Ah, there they are. Bundle up. (*She picks up her hat and coat. Nora's and Helmer's voices can be heard outside; a key turns in the lock, and Helmer brings Nora into the hall almost by force. She is wearing the Italian costume with a large black shawl about her; he has on evening dress, with a black domino open over it.*)

NORA (*struggling in the doorway*): No, no, no, not inside! I'm going up again. I don't want to leave so soon.

HELMER: But Nora dear—

NORA: Oh, I beg you, please, Torvald. From the bottom of my heart, *please*—only an hour more!

HELMER: Not a single minute, Nora darling. You know our agreement. Come on, in we go; you'll catch cold out here. (*In spite of her resistance, he gently draws her into the room.*)

MRS. LINDE: Good evening.

NORA: Kristine!
HELMER: Why, Mrs. Linde—are you here so late?
MRS. LINDE: Yes, I'm sorry, but I did want to see Nora in costume.
NORA: Have you been sitting here, waiting for me?
MRS. LINDE: Yes. I didn't come early enough; you were all upstairs; and then I thought I really couldn't leave without seeing you.
HELMER (*removing Nora's shawl*): Yes, take a good look. She's worth looking at, I can tell you that, Mrs. Linde. Isn't she lovely?
MRS. LINDE: Yes, I should say—
HELMER: A dream of loveliness, isn't she? That's what everyone thought at the party, too. But she's horribly stubborn—this sweet little thing. What's to be done with her? Can you imagine, I almost had to use force to pry her away.
NORA: Oh, Torvald, you're going to regret you didn't indulge me, even for just a half hour more.
HELMER: There, you see. She danced her tarantella and got a tumultuous hand—which was well earned, although the performance may have been a bit too naturalistic—I mean it rather overstepped the proprieties of art. But never mind—what's important is, she made a success, an overwhelming success. You think I could let her stay on after that and spoil the effect? Oh no; I took my lovely little Capri girl—my capricious little Capri girl, I should say—took her under my arm; one quick tour of the ballroom, a curtsy to every side, and then—as they say in novels—the beautiful vision disappeared. An exit should always be effective, Mrs. Linde, but that's what I can't get Nora to grasp. Phew, It's hot in here. (*Flings the domino on a chair and opens the door to his room.*) Why's it dark in here? Oh yes, of course. Excuse me. (*He goes in and lights a couple of candles.*)
NORA (*in a sharp, breathless whisper*): So?
MRS. LINDE (*quietly*): I talked with him.
NORA: And—?
MRS. LINDE: Nora—you must tell your husband everything.
NORA (*dully*): I knew it.
MRS. LINDE: You've got nothing to fear from Krogstad, but you have to speak out.
NORA: I won't tell.
MRS. LINDE: Then the letter will.
NORA: Thanks, Kristine. I know now what's to be done. Shh!
HELMER (*reentering*): Well, then, Mrs. Linde—have you admired her?
MRS. LINDE: Yes, and now I'll say good night.
HELMER: Oh, come, so soon? Is this yours, this knitting?
MRS. LINDE: Yes, thanks. I nearly forgot it.
HELMER: Do you knit, then?

MRS. LINDE: Oh yes.

HELMER: You know what? You should embroider instead.

MRS. LINDE: Really? Why?

HELMER: Yes, because it's a lot prettier. See here, one holds the embroidery so, in the left hand, and then one guides the needle with the right — so — in an easy, sweeping curve — right?

MRS. LINDE: Yes, I guess that's —

HELMER: But, on the other hand, knitting — it can never be anything but ugly. Look, see here, the arms tucked in, the knitting needles going up and down — there's something Chinese about it. Ah, that was really a glorious champagne they served.

MRS. LINDE: Yes, good night, Nora, and don't be stubborn anymore.

HELMER: Well put, Mrs. Linde!

MRS. LINDE: Good night, Mr. Helmer.

HELMER (*accompanying her to the door*): Good night, good night. I hope you get home all right. I'd be very happy to — but you don't have far to go. Good night, good night. (*She leaves. He shuts the door after her and returns.*) There, now, at last we got her out the door. She's a deadly bore, that creature.

NORA: Aren't you pretty tired, Torvald?

HELMER: No, not a bit.

NORA: You're not sleepy?

HELMER: Not at all. On the contrary, I'm feeling quite exhilarated. But you? Yes, you really look tired and sleepy.

NORA: Yes, I'm very tired. Soon now I'll sleep.

HELMER: See! You see! I was right all along that we shouldn't stay longer.

NORA: Whatever you do is always right.

HELMER (*kissing her brow*): Now my little lark talks sense. Say, did you notice what a time Rank was having tonight?

NORA: Oh, was he? I didn't get to speak with him.

HELMER: I scarcely did either, but it's a long time since I've seen him in such high spirits. (*Gazes at her a moment, then comes nearer her.*) Hm — it's marvelous, though, to be back home again — to be completely alone with you. Oh, you bewitchingly lovely young woman!

NORA: Torvald, don't look at me like that!

HELMER: Can't I look at my richest treasure? At all that beauty that's mine, mine alone — completely and utterly.

NORA (*moving around to the other side of the table*): You mustn't talk to me that way tonight.

HELMER (*following her*): The tarantella is still in your blood. I can see — and it makes you even more enticing. Listen. The guests are beginning to go. (*Dropping his voice.*) Nora — it'll soon be quiet through this whole house.

NORA: Yes, I hope so.

HELMER: You do, don't you, my love? Do you realize—when I'm out at a party like this with you—do you know why I talk to you so little, and keep such a distance away; just send you a stolen look now and then— you know why I do it? It's because I'm imagining then that you're my secret darling, my secret young bride-to-be, and that no one suspects there's anything between us.

NORA: Yes, yes; oh, yes, I know you're always thinking of me.

HELMER: And then when we leave and I place the shawl over those fine young rounded shoulders—over that wonderful curving neck—then I pretend that you're my young bride, that we're just coming from the wedding, that for the first time I'm bringing you into my house—that for the first time I'm alone with you—completely alone with you, your trembling young beauty! All this evening I've longed for nothing but you. When I saw you turn and sway in the tarantella—my blood was pounding till I couldn't stand it—that's why I brought you down here so early—

NORA: Go away, Torvald! Leave me alone. I don't want all this.

HELMER: What do you mean? Nora, you're teasing me. You will, won't you? Aren't I your husband—?

(*A knock at the outside door.*)

NORA (*startled*): What's that?

HELMER (*going toward the hall*): Who is it?

RANK (*outside*): It's me. May I come in a moment?

HELMER (*with quiet irritation*): Oh, what does he want now? (*Aloud.*) Hold on. (*Goes and opens the door.*) Oh, how nice that you didn't just pass us by!

RANK: I thought I heard your voice, and then I wanted so badly to have a look in. (*Lightly glancing about.*) Ah, me, these old familiar haunts. You have it snug and cozy in here, you two.

HELMER: You seemed to be having it pretty cozy upstairs, too.

RANK: Absolutely. Why shouldn't I? Why not take in everything in life? As much as you can, anyway, and as long as you can. The wine was superb—

HELMER: The champagne especially.

RANK: You noticed that too? It's amazing how much I could guzzle down.

NORA: Torvald also drank a lot of champagne this evening.

RANK: Oh?

NORA: Yes, and that always makes him so entertaining.

RANK: Well, why shouldn't one have a pleasant evening after a well-spent day?

HELMER: Well spent? I'm afraid I can't claim that.

RANK (*slapping him on the back*): But I can, you see!

NORA: Dr. Rank, you must have done some scientific research today.

RANK: Quite so.

HELMER: Come now—little Nora talking about scientific research!

NORA: And can I congratulate you on the results?

RANK: Indeed you may.

NORA: Then they were good?

RANK: The best possible for both doctor and patient—certainty.

NORA (*quickly and searchingly*): Certainty?

RANK: Complete certainty. So don't I owe myself a gay evening afterwards?

NORA: Yes, you're right, Dr. Rank.

HELMER: I'm with you—just so long as you don't have to suffer for it in the morning.

RANK: Well, one never gets something for nothing in life.

NORA: Dr. Rank—are you very fond of masquerade parties?

RANK: Yes, if there's a good array of odd disguises—

NORA: Tell me, what should we two go as at the next masquerade?

HELMER: You little featherhead—already thinking of the next!

RANK: We two? I'll tell you what: You must go as Charmed Life—

HELMER: Yes, but find a costume for that!

RANK: Your wife can appear just as she looks every day.

HELMER: That was nicely put. But don't you know what you're going to be?

RANK: Yes, Helmer, I've made up my mind.

HELMER: Well?

RANK: At the next masquerade I'm going to be invisible.

HELMER: That's a funny idea.

RANK: They say there's a hat—black, huge—have you never heard of the hat that makes you invisible? You put it on, and then no one on earth can see you.

HELMER (*suppressing a smile*): Ah, of course.

RANK: But I'm quite forgetting what I came for. Helmer, give me a cigar, one of the dark Havanas.

HELMER: With the greatest pleasure. (*Holds out his case.*)

RANK: Thanks. (*Takes one and cuts off the tip.*)

NORA (*striking a match*): Let me give you a light.

RANK: Thank you. (*She holds the match for him; he lights the cigar.*) And now good-bye.

HELMER: Good-bye, good-bye, old friend.

NORA: Sleep well, Doctor.

RANK: Thanks for that wish.

NORA: Wish me the same.

RANK: You? All right, if you like—Sleep well. And thanks for the light. (*He nods to them both and leaves.*)

HELMER (*his voice subdued*): He's been drinking heavily.

NORA (*absently*): Could be. (*Helmer takes his keys from his pocket and goes out in the hall.*) Torvald—what are you after?

HELMER: Got to empty the mailbox; it's nearly full. There won't be room for the morning papers.

NORA: Are you working tonight?

HELMER: You know I'm not. Why—what's this? Someone's been at the lock.

NORA: At the lock—?

HELMER: Yes, I'm positive. What do you suppose—? I can't imagine one of the maids—? Here's a broken hairpin. Nora, it's yours—

NORA (*quickly*): Then it must be the children—

HELMER: You'd better break them of that. Hm, hm—well, opened it after all. (*Takes the contents out and calls into the kitchen.*) Helene! Helene, would you put out the lamp in the hall. (*He returns to the room, shutting the hall door, then displays the handful of mail.*) Look how it's piled up. (*Sorting through them.*) Now what's this?

NORA (*at the window*): The letter! Oh, Torvald, no!

HELMER: Two calling cards—from Rank.

NORA: From Dr. Rank?

HELMER (*examining them*): "Dr. Rank, Consulting Physician." They were on top. He must have dropped them in as he left.

NORA: Is there anything on them?

HELMER: There's a black cross over the name. See? That's a gruesome notion. He could almost be announcing his own death.

NORA: That's just what he's doing.

HELMER: What! You've heard something? Something he's told you?

NORA: Yes. That when those cards came, he'd be taking his leave of us. He'll shut himself in now and die.

HELMER: Ah, my poor friend! Of course I knew he wouldn't be here much longer. But so soon—And then to hide himself away like a wounded animal.

NORA: If it has to happen, then it's best it happens in silence—don't you think so, Torvald?

HELMER (*pacing up and down*): He's grown right into our lives. I simply can't imagine him gone. He with his suffering and loneliness—like a dark cloud setting off our sunlit happiness. Well, maybe it's best this way. For him, at least. (*Standing still.*) And maybe for us too, Nora. Now we're thrown back on each other, completely. (*Embracing her.*) Oh you, my darling wife, how can I hold you close enough? You know what, Nora—time and again I've wished you were in some terrible danger, just so I could stake my life and soul and everything, for your sake.

NORA (*tearing herself away, her voice firm and decisive*): Now you must read your mail, Torvald.

HELMER: No, no, not tonight. I want to stay with you, dearest.

NORA: With a dying friend on your mind?

HELMER: You're right. We've both had a shock. There's ugliness between us—these thoughts of death and corruption. We'll have to get free of them first. Until then—we'll stay apart.

NORA (*clinging about his neck*): Torvald—good night! Good night!

HELMER (*kissing her on the cheek*): Good night, little songbird. Sleep well, Nora. I'll be reading my mail now. (*He takes the letters into his room and shuts the door after him.*)

NORA (*with bewildered glances, groping about, seizing Helmer's domino, throwing it around her, and speaking in short, hoarse, broken whispers*): Never see him again. Never, never. (*Putting her shawl over her head.*) Never see the children either—them, too. Never, never. Oh, the freezing black water! The depths—down—Oh, I wish it were over—He has it now; he's reading it—now. Oh no, no, not yet. Torvald, goodbye, you and the children—(*She starts for the hall; as she does, Helmer throws open his door and stands with an open letter in his hand.*)

HELMER: Nora!

NORA (*screams*): Oh—!

HELMER: What is this? You know what's in this letter?

NORA: Yes, I know. Let me go! Let me out!

HELMER (*holding her back*): Where are you going?

NORA (*struggling to break loose*): You can't save me, Torvald!

HELMER (*slumping back*): True! Then it's true what he writes? How horrible! No, no, it's impossible—it can't be true.

NORA: It *is* true. I've loved you more than all this world.

HELMER: Ah, none of your slippery tricks.

NORA (*taking one step toward him*): Torvald—!

HELMER: What *is* this you've blundered into!

NORA: Just let me loose. You're not going to suffer for my sake. You're not going to take on my guilt.

HELMER: No more playacting. (*Locks the hall door.*) You stay right here and give me a reckoning. You understand what you've done? Answer! You understand?

NORA (*looking squarely at him, her face hardening*): Yes. I'm beginning to understand everything now.

HELMER (*striding about*): Oh, what an awful awakening! In all these eight years—she who was my pride and joy—a hypocrite, a liar—worse, worse—a criminal! How infinitely disgusting it all is! The shame!

(*Nora says nothing and goes on looking straight at him. He stops in front of her.*) I should have suspected something of the kind. I should have known. All your father's flimsy values—Be still! All your father's flimsy values have come out in you. No religion, no morals, no sense of duty—Oh, how I'm punished for letting him off! I did it for your sake, and you repay me like this.

NORA: Yes, like this.

HELMER: Now you've wrecked all my happiness—ruined my whole future. Oh, it's awful to think of. I'm in a cheap little grafter's hands; he can do anything he wants with me, ask for anything, play with me like a puppet—and I can't breathe a word. I'll be swept down miserably into the depths on account of a featherbrained woman.

NORA: When I'm gone from this world, you'll be free.

HELMER: Oh, quit posing. Your father had a mess of those speeches too. What good would that ever do me if you were gone from this world, as you say? Not the slightest. He can still make the whole thing known; and if he does, I could be falsely suspected as your accomplice. They might even think that I was behind it—that I put you up to it. And all that I can thank you for—you that I've coddled the whole of our marriage. Can you see now what you've done to me?

NORA (*icily calm*): Yes.

HELMER: It's so incredible, I just can't grasp it. But we'll have to patch up whatever we can. Take off the shawl. I said, take it off! I've got to appease him somehow or other. The thing has to be hushed up at any cost. And as for you and me, it's got to seem like everything between us is just as it was—to the outside world, that is. You'll go right on living in this house, of course. But you can't be allowed to bring up the children; I don't dare trust you with them—Oh, to have to say this to someone I've loved so much! Well, that's done with. From now on happiness doesn't matter; all that matters is saving the bits and pieces, the appearance—(*The doorbell rings. Helmer starts.*) What's that? And so late. Maybe the worst—? You think he'd—? Hide, Nora! Say you're sick. (*Nora remains standing motionless. Helmer goes and opens the door.*)

MAID (*half dressed, in the hall*): A letter for Mrs. Helmer.

HELMER: I'll take it. (*Snatches the letter and shuts the door.*) Yes, it's from him. You don't get it; I'm reading it myself.

NORA: Then read it.

HELMER (*by the lamp*): I hardly dare. We may be ruined, you and I. But—I've got to know. (*Rips open the letter, skims through a few lines, glances at an enclosure, then cries out joyfully.*) Nora! (*Nora looks inquiringly at him.*) Nora! Wait—better check it again—Yes, yes, it's true. I'm saved. Nora, I'm saved!

NORA: And I?

HELMER: You too, of course. We're both saved, both of us. Look. He's sent back your note. He says he's sorry and ashamed—that a happy development in his life—oh, who cares what he says! Nora, we're saved! No one can hurt you. Oh, Nora, Nora—but first, this ugliness all has to go. Let me see—(*Takes a look at the note.*) No, I don't want to see it; I want the whole thing to fade like a dream. (*Tears the note and both letters to pieces, throws them into the stove and watches them burn.*) There—now there's nothing left—He wrote that since Christmas Eve you—Oh, they must have been three terrible days for you, Nora.

NORA: I fought a hard fight.

HELMER: And suffered pain and saw no escape but—No, we're not going to dwell on anything unpleasant. We'll just be grateful and keep on repeating: It's over now, it's over! You hear me, Nora? You don't seem to realize—it's over. What's it mean—that frozen look? Oh, poor little Nora, I understand. You can't believe I've forgiven you. But I have, Nora; I swear I have. I know that what you did, you did out of love for me.

NORA: That's true.

HELMER: You loved me the way a wife ought to love her husband. It's simply the means that you couldn't judge. But you think I love you any the less for not knowing how to handle your affairs? No, no—just lean on me; I'll guide you and teach you. I wouldn't be a man if this feminine helplessness didn't make you twice as attractive to me. You mustn't mind those sharp words I said—that was all in the first confusion of thinking my world had collapsed. I've forgiven you, Nora; I swear I've forgiven you.

NORA: My thanks for your forgiveness. (*She goes out through the door, right.*)

HELMER: No, wait—(*Peers in.*) What are you doing in there?

NORA (*inside*): Getting out of my costume.

HELMER (*by the open door*): Yes, do that. Try to calm yourself and collect your thoughts again, my frightened little songbird. You can rest easy now; I've got wide wings to shelter you with. (*Walking about close by the door.*) How snug and nice our home is, Nora. You're safe here; I'll keep you like a hunted dove I've rescued out of a hawk's claws. I'll bring peace to your poor, shuddering heart. Gradually it'll happen, Nora; you'll see. Tomorrow all this will look different to you; then everything will be as it was. I won't have to go on repeating I forgive you; you'll feel it for yourself. How can you imagine I'd ever conceivably want to disown you—or even blame you in any way? Ah, you don't know a man's heart, Nora. For a man there's something indescribably sweet and satisfying in knowing he's forgiven his wife—and forgiven her out of a full and open heart. It's as if she belongs to him in two ways now: In a sense he's given her fresh into the world again, and she's become his wife and his child as well. From now on that's what you'll be to me—you little, bewildered, helpless thing. Don't be afraid of anything, Nora; just open your heart to me, and I'll be conscience and will to you both—(*Nora enters in her regular clothes.*) What's this? Not in bed? You've changed your dress?

NORA: Yes, Torvald, I've changed my dress.

HELMER: But why now, so late?

NORA: Tonight I'm not sleeping.

HELMER: But Nora dear—

NORA (*looking at her watch*): It's still not so very late. Sit down, Torvald; we have a lot to talk over. (*She sits at one side of the table.*)

HELMER: Nora—what is this? That hard expression—

NORA: Sit down. This'll take some time. I have a lot to say.

HELMER (*sitting at the table directly opposite her*): You worry me, Nora. And I don't understand you.

NORA: No, that's exactly it. You don't understand me. And I've never understood you either—until tonight. No, don't interrupt. You can just listen to what I say. We're closing out accounts, Torvald.

HELMER: How do you mean that?

NORA (*after a short pause*): Doesn't anything strike you about our sitting here like this?

HELMER: What's that?

NORA: We've been married now eight years. Doesn't it occur to you that this is the first time we two, you and I, man and wife, have ever talked seriously together?

HELMER: What do you mean—seriously?

NORA: In eight whole years—longer even—right from our first acquaintance, we've never exchanged a serious word on any serious thing.

HELMER: You mean I should constantly go and involve you in problems you couldn't possibly help me with?

NORA: I'm not talking of problems. I'm saying that we've never sat down seriously together and tried to get to the bottom of anything.

HELMER: But dearest, what good would that ever do you?

NORA: That's the point right there: You've never understood me. I've been wronged greatly, Torvald—first by Papa, and then by you.

HELMER: What! By us—the two people who've loved you more than anyone else?

NORA (*shaking her head*): You never loved me. You've thought it fun to be in love with me, that's all.

HELMER: Nora, what a thing to say!

NORA: Yes, it's true now, Torvald. When I lived at home with Papa, he told me all his opinions, so I had the same ones too; or if they were different I hid them, since he wouldn't have cared for that. He used to call me his doll-child, and he played with me the way I played with my dolls. Then I came into your house—

HELMER: How can you speak of our marriage like that?

NORA (*unperturbed*): I mean, then I went from Papa's hands into yours. You arranged everything to your own taste, and so I got the same taste as you—or I pretended to; I can't remember. I guess a little of both, first one, then the other. Now when I look back, it seems as if I'd lived here like a beggar—just from hand to mouth. I've lived by doing tricks for you, Torvald. But that's the way you wanted it. It's a great sin what you and Papa did to me. You're to blame that nothing's become of me.

HELMER: Nora, how unfair and ungrateful you are! Haven't you been happy here?

NORA: No, never. I thought so—but I never have.

HELMER: Not—not happy!

NORA: No, only lighthearted. And you've always been so kind to me. But our home's been nothing but a playpen. I've been your doll-wife here, just as at home I was Papa's doll-child. And in turn the children have been my dolls. I thought it was fun when you played with me, just as they thought it fun when I played with them. That's been our marriage, Torvald.

HELMER: There's some truth in what you're saying—under all the raving exaggeration. But it'll all be different after this. Playtime's over; now for the schooling.

NORA: Whose schooling—mine or the children's?

HELMER: Both yours and the children's, dearest.

NORA: Oh, Torvald, you're not the man to teach me to be a good wife to you.

HELMER: And you can say that?

NORA: And I—how am I equipped to bring up children?

HELMER: Nora!

NORA: Didn't you say a moment ago that that was no job to trust me with?

HELMER: In a flare of temper! Why fasten on that?

NORA: Yes, but you were so very right. I'm not up to the job. There's another job I have to do first. I have to try to educate myself. You can't help me with that. I've got to do it alone. And that's why I'm leaving you now.

HELMER (*jumping up*): What's that?

NORA: I have to stand completely alone, if I'm ever going to discover myself and the world out there. So I can't go on living with you.

HELMER: Nora, Nora!

NORA: I want to leave right away. Kristine should put me up for the night—

HELMER: You're insane! You've no right! I forbid you!

NORA: From here on, there's no use forbidding me anything. I'll take with me whatever is mine. I don't want a thing from you, either now or later.

HELMER: What kind of madness is this!

NORA: Tomorrow I'm going home—I mean, home where I came from. It'll be easier up there to find something to do.

HELMER: Oh, you blind, incompetent child!

NORA: I must learn to be competent, Torvald.

HELMER: Abandon your home, your husband, your children! And you're not even thinking what people will say.

NORA: I can't be concerned about that. I only know how essential this is.

HELMER: Oh, it's outrageous. So you'll run out like this on your most sacred vows.

NORA: What do you think are my most sacred vows?

HELMER: And I have to tell you that! Aren't they your duties to your husband and children?

NORA: I have other duties equally sacred.

HELMER: That isn't true. What duties are they?

NORA: Duties to myself.

HELMER: Before all else, you're a wife and a mother.

NORA: I don't believe in that anymore. I believe that before all else, I'm a human being, no less than you—or anyway, I ought to try to become one. I know the majority thinks you're right, Torvald, and plenty of books agree with you, too. But I can't go on believing what the majority says, or what's written in books. I have to think over these things myself and try to understand them.

HELMER: Why can't you understand your place in your own home? On a point like that, isn't there one everlasting guide you can turn to? Where's your religion?

NORA: Oh, Torvald, I'm really not sure what religion is.

HELMER: What—?

NORA: I only know what the minister said when I was confirmed. He told me religion was this thing and that. When I get clear and away by myself, I'll go into that problem too. I'll see if what the minister said was right, or, in any case, if it's right for me.

HELMER: A young woman your age shouldn't talk like that. If religion can't move you, I can try to rouse your conscience. You do have some moral feeling? Or, tell me—has that gone too?

NORA: It's not easy to answer that, Torvald. I simply don't know. I'm all confused about these things. I just know I see them so differently from you. I find out for one thing, that the law's not at all what I'd thought— but I can't get it through my head that the law is fair. A woman hasn't a right to protect her dying father or save her husband's life! I can't believe that.

HELMER: You talk like a child. You don't know anything of the world you live in.

NORA: No, I don't. But now I'll begin to learn for myself. I'll try to discover who's right, the world or I.

HELMER: Nora, you're sick; you've got a fever. I almost think you're out of your head.

NORA: I've never felt more clearheaded and sure in my life.

HELMER: And—clearheaded and sure—you're leaving your husband and children?

NORA: Yes.

HELMER: Then there's only one possible reason.

NORA: What?

HELMER: You no longer love me.

NORA: No. That's exactly it.

HELMER: Nora! You can't be serious!

NORA: Oh, this is so hard, Torvald—you've been so kind to me always. But I can't help it. I don't love you anymore.

HELMER (*struggling for composure*): Are you also clearheaded and sure about that?

NORA: Yes, completely. That's why I can't go on staying here.

HELMER: Can you tell me what I did to lose your love?

NORA: Yes, I can tell you. It was this evening when the miraculous thing didn't come—then I knew you weren't the man I'd imagined.

HELMER: Be more explicit; I don't follow you.

NORA: I've waited now so patiently eight long years—for, my Lord, I know miracles don't come every day. Then this crisis broke over me, and such a certainty filled me: *Now* the miraculous event would occur. While Krogstad's letter was lying out there, I never for an instant dreamed that you could give in to his terms. I was so utterly sure you'd say to him: Go on, tell your tale to the whole wide world. And when he'd done that—

HELMER: Yes, what then? When I'd delivered my own wife into shame and disgrace—!

NORA: When he'd done that, I was so utterly sure that you'd step forward, take the blame on yourself and say: I am the guilty one.

HELMER: Nora—!

NORA: You're thinking I'd never accept such a sacrifice from you? No, of course not. But what good would my protests be against you? That was the miracle I was waiting for, in terror and hope. And to stave that off, I would have taken my life.

HELMER: I'd gladly work for you day and night, Nora—and take on pain and deprivation. But there's no one who gives up honor for love.

NORA: Millions of women have done just that.

HELMER: Oh, you think and talk like a silly child.

NORA: Perhaps. But you neither think nor talk like the man I could join myself to. When your big fright was over—and it wasn't from any threat against me, only for what might damage you—when all the danger was past, for you it was just as if nothing had happened. I was exactly the same, your little lark, your doll, that you'd have to handle with double care now that I'd turned out so brittle and frail. (*Gets up.*) Torvald—in that instant it dawned on me that for eight years I've been living here with a stranger, and that I'd even conceived three children—oh, I can't stand the thought of it! I could tear myself to bits.

HELMER (*heavily*): I see. There's a gulf that's opened between us—that's clear. Oh, but Nora, can't we bridge it somehow?

NORA: The way I am now, I'm no wife for you.

HELMER: I have the strength to make myself over.

NORA: Maybe—if your doll gets taken away.

HELMER: But to part! To part from you! No, Nora, no—I can't imagine it.

NORA (*going out, right*): All the more reason why it has to be. (*She reenters with her coat and a small overnight bag, which she puts on a chair by the table.*)

HELMER: Nora, Nora, not now! Wait till tomorrow.

NORA: I can't spend the night in a strange man's room.

HELMER: But couldn't we live here like brother and sister—

NORA: You know very well how long that would last. (*Throws her shawl about her.*) Good-bye, Torvald. I won't look in on the children. I know they're in better hands than mine. The way I am now, I'm no use to them.

HELMER: But someday, Nora—someday—?

NORA: How can I tell? I haven't the least idea what'll become of me.

HELMER: But you're my wife, now and wherever you go.

NORA: Listen, Torvald—I've heard that when a wife deserts her husband's house just as I'm doing, then the law frees him from all responsibility. In any case, I'm freeing you from being responsible. Don't feel yourself bound, any more than I will. There has to be absolute freedom for us both. Here, take your ring back. Give me mine.

HELMER: That too?

NORA: That too.

HELMER: There it is.

NORA: Good. Well, now it's all over. I'm putting the keys here. The maids know all about keeping up the house—better than I do. Tomorrow, after I've left town, Kristine will stop by to pack up everything that's mine from home. I'd like those things shipped up to me.

HELMER: Over! All over! Nora, won't you ever think about me?

NORA: I'm sure I'll think of you often, and about the children and the house here.

HELMER: May I write you?

NORA: No—never. You're not to do that.

HELMER: Oh, but let me send you—

NORA: Nothing. Nothing.

HELMER: Or help you if you need it.

NORA: No. I accept nothing from strangers.

HELMER: Nora—can I never be more than a stranger to you?

NORA (*picking up the overnight bag*): Ah, Torvald—it would take the greatest miracle of all—

HELMER: Tell me the greatest miracle!

NORA: You and I both would have to transform ourselves to the point that—Oh, Torvald, I've stopped believing in miracles.

HELMER: But I'll believe. Tell me! Transform ourselves to the point that—?

NORA: That our living together could be a true marriage. (*She goes out down the hall.*)

HELMER (*sinks down on a chair by the door, face buried in his hands*): Nora! Nora! (*Looking about and rising.*) Empty. She's gone. (*A sudden hope leaps in him.*) The greatest miracle—?

(*From below, the sound of a door slamming shut.*)

[1879]

SUSAN GLASPELL [1882-1948]

Trifles

Characters

GEORGE HENDERSON, *county attorney*
HENRY PETERS, *sheriff*
LEWIS HALE, *a neighboring farmer*
MRS. PETERS
MRS. HALE

Scene: *The kitchen in the now abandoned farmhouse of John Wright, a gloomy kitchen, and left without having been put in order—the walls covered with a faded wall paper. Down right is a door leading to the parlor. On the right wall above this door is a built-in kitchen cupboard with shelves in the upper portion and drawers below. In the rear wall at right, up two steps is a door opening onto stairs leading to the second floor. In the rear wall at left is a door to the shed and from there to the outside. Between these two doors is an old-fashioned black iron stove. Running along the left wall from the shed door is an old iron sink and sink shelf, in which is set a hand pump. Downstage of the sink is an uncurtained window. Near the window is an old wooden rocker. Center stage is an unpainted wooden kitchen table with straight chairs on either side. There is a small chair down right. Unwashed pans under the sink, a loaf of bread outside the breadbox, a dish towel on the table— other signs of incompleted work. At the rear the shed door opens and the Sheriff comes in followed by the County Attorney and Hale. The Sheriff and Hale are men in middle life, the County Attorney is a young man; all are much bundled up and go at once to the stove. They are followed by the two women—the Sheriff's wife, Mrs. Peters, first: she is a slight wiry woman, a thin nervous face. Mrs. Hale is larger and would ordinarily be called more comfortable looking, but she is disturbed now and looks fearfully about as she enters. The women have come in slowly, and stand close together near the door.*

COUNTY ATTORNEY (*at stove rubbing his hands*): This feels good. Come up to the fire, ladies.
MRS. PETERS (*after taking a step forward*): I'm not—cold.
SHERIFF (*unbuttoning his overcoat and stepping away from the stove to right of table as if to mark the beginning of official business*): Now, Mr. Hale, before we move things about, you explain to Mr. Henderson just what you saw when you came here yesterday morning.
COUNTY ATTORNEY (*crossing down to left of the table*): By the way, has anything been moved? Are things just as you left them yesterday?

SHERIFF (*looking about*): It's just about the same. When it dropped below zero last night I thought I'd better send Frank out this morning to make a fire for us—(*sits right of center table*) no use getting pneumonia with a big case on, but I told him not to touch anything except the stove—and you know Frank.

COUNTY ATTORNEY: Somebody should have been left here yesterday.

SHERIFF: Oh—yesterday. When I had to send Frank to Morris Center for that man who went crazy—I want you to know I had my hands full yesterday. I knew you could get back from Omaha by today and as long as I went over everything here myself———

COUNTY ATTORNEY: Well, Mr. Hale, tell just what happened when you came here yesterday morning.

HALE (*crossing down to above table*): Harry and I had started to town with a load of potatoes. We came along the road from my place and as I got here I said, "I'm going to see if I can't get John Wright to go in with me on a party telephone." I spoke to Wright about it once before and he put me off, saying folks talked too much anyway, and all he asked was peace and quiet—I guess you know about how much he talked himself; but I thought maybe if I went to the house and talked about it before his wife, though I said to Harry that I didn't know as what his wife wanted made much difference to John———

COUNTY ATTORNEY: Let's talk about that later, Mr. Hale. I do want to talk about that, but tell now just what happened when you got to the house.

HALE: I didn't hear or see anything; I knocked at the door, and still it was all quiet inside. I knew they must be up, it was past eight o'clock. So I knocked again, and I thought I heard someone say, "Come in." I wasn't sure, I'm not sure yet, but I opened the door—this door (*indicating the door by which the two women are still standing*) and there in that rocker—(*pointing to it*) sat Mrs. Wright. (*They all look at the rocker down left.*)

COUNTY ATTORNEY: What—was she doing?

HALE: She was rockin' back and forth. She had her apron in her hand and was kind of—pleating it.

COUNTY ATTORNEY: And how did she—look?

HALE: Well, she looked queer.

COUNTY ATTORNEY: How do you mean—queer?

HALE: Well, as if she didn't know what she was going to do next. And kind of done up.

COUNTY ATTORNEY (*takes out notebook and pencil and sits left of center table*): How did she seem to feel about your coming?

HALE: Why, I don't think she minded—one way or other. She didn't pay much attention. I said, "How do, Mrs. Wright, it's cold, ain't it?" And she said, "Is it?"—and went on kind of pleating at her apron. Well, I was surprised: she didn't ask me to come up to the stove, or to set down, but just sat there, not even looking at me, so I said, "I want to see John." And then she—laughed. I guess you would call it a laugh. I thought of Harry and the team outside, so I said a little sharp: "Can't I see John?" "No," she says, kind o' dull like. "Ain't he home?" says I. "Yes," says she, "he's home." "Then why can't I see him?" I asked her, out of patience. "'Cause he's dead," says she. *"Dead?"* says I. She just nodded her head, not getting a bit excited, but rockin' back and forth. "Why—where is he?" says I, not knowing what to say. She just pointed upstairs—like that. (*Himself pointing to the room above.*) I started for the stairs, with the idea of going up there. I walked from there to here—then I says, "Why, what did he die of?" "He died of a rope round his neck," says she, and just went on pleatin' at her apron. Well, I went out and called Harry. I thought I might—need help. We went upstairs and there he was lyin'——

COUNTY ATTORNEY: I think I'd rather have you go into that upstairs, where you can point it all out. Just go on now with the rest of the story.

HALE: Well, my first thought was to get that rope off. It looked . . . (*stops: his face twitches*) . . . but Harry, he went up to him, and he said, "No, he's dead all right, and we'd better not touch anything." So we went right back downstairs. She was still sitting that same way. "Has anybody been notified?" I asked. "No," says she, unconcerned. "Who did this, Mrs. Wright?" said Harry. He said it businesslike—and she stopped pleatin' of her apron. "I don't know," she says. "You don't *know?*" says Harry. "No," says she. "Weren't you sleepin' in the bed with him?" says Harry. "Yes," says she, "but I was on the inside." "Somebody slipped a rope round his head and strangled him and you didn't wake up?" says Harry. "I didn't wake up," she said after him. We must 'a' looked as if we didn't see how that could be, for after a minute she said, "I sleep sound." Harry was going to ask her more questions but I said maybe we ought to let her tell her story first to the coroner, or the sheriff, so Harry went fast as he could to Rivers' place, where there's a telephone.

COUNTY ATTORNEY: And what did Mrs. Wright do when she knew that you had gone for the coroner?

HALE: She moved from the rocker to that chair over there (*pointing to a small chair in the down right corner*) and just sat there with her hands held together and looking down. I got a feeling that I ought to make some conversation, so I said I had come in to see if John wanted to put in a telephone, and at that she started to laugh, and then she stopped and looked at me—scared. (*The County Attorney, who has had his notebook out, makes a note.*) I dunno, maybe it wasn't scared. I wouldn't like to say it was. Soon Harry got back, and then Dr. Lloyd came and you, Mr. Peters, and so I guess that's all I know that you don't.

COUNTY ATTORNEY (*rising and looking around*): I guess we'll go upstairs first—and then out to the barn and around there. (*To the Sheriff.*) You're convinced that there was nothing important here—nothing that would point to any motive?

SHERIFF: Nothing here but kitchen things. (*The County Attorney, after again looking around the kitchen, opens the door of a cupboard closet in right wall. He brings a small chair from right—gets on it and looks on a shelf. Pulls his hand away, sticky.*)

COUNTY ATTORNEY: Here's a nice mess. (*The women draw nearer up to center.*)

MRS. PETERS (*to the other woman*): Oh, her fruit; it did freeze. (*To the Lawyer.*) She worried about that when it turned so cold. She said the fire'd go out and her jars would break.

SHERIFF (*rises*): Well, can you beat the woman! Held for murder and worryin' about her preserves.

COUNTY ATTORNEY (*getting down from chair*): I guess before we're through she may have something more serious than preserves to worry about. (*Crosses down right center.*)

HALE: Well, women are used to worrying over trifles. (*The two women move a little closer together.*)

COUNTY ATTORNEY (*with the gallantry of a young politician*): And yet, for all their worries, what would we do without the ladies? (*The women do not unbend. He goes below the center table to the sink, takes a dipperful of water from the pail, and pouring it into a basin, washes his hands. While he is doing this the Sheriff and Hale cross to cupboard, which they inspect. The County Attorney starts to wipe his hands on the roller towel, turns it for a cleaner place.*) Dirty towels! (*Kicks his foot against the pans under the sink.*) Not much of a housekeeper, would you say, ladies?

MRS. HALE (*stiffly*): There's a great deal of work to be done on a farm.

COUNTY ATTORNEY: To be sure. And yet (*with a little bow to her*) I know there are some Dickson County farmhouses which do not have such roller towels. (*He gives it a pull to expose its full-length again.*)

MRS. HALE: Those towels get dirty awful quick. Men's hands aren't always clean as they might be.

COUNTY ATTORNEY: Ah, loyal to your sex, I see. But you and Mrs. Wright were neighbors. I suppose you were friends, too.

MRS. HALE (*shaking her head*): I've not seen much of her of late years. I've not been in this house—it's more than a year.

COUNTY ATTORNEY (*crossing to women up center*): And why was that? You didn't like her?

MRS. HALE: I liked her all well enough. Farmer's wives have their hands full, Mr. Henderson. And then——

COUNTY ATTORNEY: Yes——?

MRS. HALE (*looking about*): It never seemed a very cheerful place.

COUNTY ATTORNEY: No—it's not cheerful. I shouldn't say she had the homemaking instinct.

MRS. HALE: Well, I don't know as Wright had, either.

COUNTY ATTORNEY: You mean that they didn't get on very well?

MRS. HALE: No, I don't mean anything. But I don't think a place'd be any cheerfuller for John Wright's being in it.

COUNTY ATTORNEY: I'd like to talk more of that a little later. I want to get the lay of things upstairs now. (*He goes past the women to up right where the steps lead to a stair door.*)

SHERIFF: I suppose anything Mrs. Peters does'll be all right. She was to take in some clothes for her, you know, and a few little things. We left in such a hurry yesterday.

COUNTY ATTORNEY: Yes, but I would like to see what you take, Mrs. Peters, and keep an eye out for anything that might be of use to us.

MRS. PETERS: Yes, Mr. Henderson. (*The men leave by up right door to stairs. The women listen to the men's steps on the stairs, then look about the kitchen.*)

MRS. HALE (*crossing left to sink*): I'd hate to have men coming into my kitchen, snooping around and criticizing. (*She arranges the pans under sink which the lawyer had shoved out of place.*)

MRS. PETERS: Of course it's no more than their duty. (*Crosses to cupboard up right.*)

MRS. HALE: Duty's all right, but I guess that deputy sheriff that came out to make the fire might have got a little of this on. (*Gives the roller towel a pull.*) Wish I'd thought of that sooner. Seems mean to talk about her for not having things slicked up when she had to come away in such a hurry. (*Crosses right to Mrs. Peters at cupboard.*)

MRS. PETERS (*who has been looking through cupboard, lifts one end of towel that covers a pan*): She had bread set. (*Stands still.*)

MRS. HALE (*eyes fixed on a loaf of bread beside the breadbox, which is on a low shelf of the cupboard*): She was going to put this in there. (*Picks up loaf, abruptly drops it. In a manner of returning to familiar things.*) It's a shame about her fruit. I wonder if it's all gone. (*Gets up on chair and looks.*) I think there's some here that's all right, Mrs. Peters. Yes— here; (*holding it toward the window*) this is cherries, too. (*Looking again.*) I declare I believe that's the only one. (*Gets down, jar in hand. Goes to the sink and wipes it off on the outside.*) She'll feel awful bad after all her hard work in the hot weather. I remember the after- noon I put up my cherries last summer. (*She puts the jar on the big kitchen table, center of the room. With a sigh, is about to sit down in the rocking chair. Before she is seated realizes what chair it is; with a slow look at it, steps back. The chair which she has touched rocks back and forth. Mrs. Peters moves to center table and they both watch the chair rock for a moment or two.*)

MRS. PETERS (*shaking off the mood which the empty rocking chair has evoked. Now in a businesslike manner she speaks*): Well I must get those things from the front room closet. (*She goes to the door at the right but, after looking into the other room, steps back.*) You coming with me, Mrs. Hale? You could help me carry them. (*They go in the other room; reappear, Mrs. Peters carrying a dress, petticoat, and skirt, Mrs. Hale following with a pair of shoes.*) My, it's cold in there. (*She puts the clothes on the big table and hurries to the stove.*)

MRS. HALE (*right of center table examining the skirt*): Wright was close. I think maybe that's why she kept so much to herself. She didn't even belong to the Ladies' Aid. I suppose she felt she couldn't do her part, and then you don't enjoy things when you feel shabby. I heard she used to wear pretty clothes and be lively, when she was Minnie Foster, one of the town girls singing in the choir. But that — oh, that was thirty years ago. This all you want to take in?

MRS. PETERS: She said she wanted an apron. Funny thing to want, for there isn't much to get you dirty in jail, goodness knows. But I suppose just to make her feel more natural. (*Crosses to cupboard.*) She said they was in the top drawer in this cupboard. Yes, here. And then her little shawl that always hung behind the door. (*Opens stair door and looks.*) Yes, here it is. (*Quickly shuts door leading upstairs.*)

MRS. HALE (*abruptly moving toward her*): Mrs. Peters?

MRS. PETERS: Yes, Mrs. Hale? (*At up right door.*)

MRS. HALE: Do you think she did it?

MRS. PETERS (*in a frightened voice*): Oh, I don't know.

MRS. HALE: Well, I don't think she did. Asking for an apron and her little shawl. Worrying about her fruit.

MRS. PETERS (*starts to speak, glances up, where footsteps are heard in the room above. In a low voice*): Mr. Peters says it looks bad for her. Mr. Henderson is awful sarcastic in a speech and he'll make fun of her sayin' she didn't wake up.

MRS. HALE: Well, I guess John Wright didn't wake when they was slipping that rope under his neck.

MRS. PETERS (*crossing slowly to table and placing shawl and apron on table with other clothing*): No, it's strange. It must have been done awful crafty and still. They say it was such a — funny way to kill a man, rigging it all up like that.

MRS. HALE (*crossing to left of Mrs. Peters at table*): That's just what Mr. Hale said. There was a gun in the house. He says that's what he can't understand.

MRS. PETERS: Mr. Henderson said coming out that what was needed for the case was a motive: something to show anger, or—sudden feeling.

MRS. HALE (*who is standing by the table*): Well, I don't see any signs of anger around here. (*She puts her hand on the dish towel, which lies on the table, stands looking down at table, one-half of which is clean, the other half messy.*) It's wiped to here. (*Makes a move as if to finish work, then turns and looks at loaf of bread outside the breadbox. Drops towel. In that voice of coming back to familiar things.*) Wonder how they are finding things upstairs. (*Crossing below table to down right.*) I hope she had it a little more red-up up there. You know, it seems kind of *sneaking*. Locking her up in town and then coming out here and trying to get her own house to turn against her!

MRS. PETERS: But, Mrs. Hale, the law is the law.

MRS. HALE: I s'pose 'tis. (*Unbuttoning her coat.*) Better loosen up your things, Mrs. Peters. You won't feel them when you go out. (*Mrs. Peters takes off her fur tippet, goes to hang it on chair back left of table, stands looking at the work basket on floor near down left window.*)

MRS. PETERS: She was piecing a quilt. (*She brings the large sewing basket to the center table and they look at the bright pieces, Mrs. Hale above the table and Mrs. Peters left of it.*)

MRS. HALE: It's a log cabin pattern. Pretty, isn't it? I wonder if she was goin' to quilt it or just knot it? (*Footsteps have been heard coming down the stairs. The Sheriff enters followed by Hale and the County Attorney.*)

SHERIFF: They wonder if she was going to quilt it or just knot it! (*The men laugh, the women look abashed.*)

COUNTY ATTORNEY (*rubbing his hands over the stove*): Frank's fire didn't do much up there, did it? Well, let's go out to the barn and get that cleared up. (*The men go outside by up left door.*)

MRS. HALE (*resentfully*): I don't know as there's anything so strange, our takin' up our time with little things while we're waiting for them to get the evidence. (*She sits in chair right of table smoothing out a block with decision.*) I don't see as it's anything to laugh about.

MRS. PETERS (*apologetically*): Of course they've got awful important things on their minds. (*Pulls up a chair and joins Mrs. Hale at the left of the table.*)

MRS. HALE (*examining another block*): Mrs. Peters, look at this one. Here, this is the one she was working on, and look at the sewing! All the rest of it has been so nice and even. And look at this! It's all over the place! Why, it looks as if she didn't know what she was about! (*After she has said this they look at each other, then start to glance back at the door. After an instant Mrs. Hale has pulled at a knot and ripped the sewing.*)

MRS. PETERS: Oh, what are you doing, Mrs. Hale?

MRS. HALE (*mildly*): Just pulling out a stitch or two that's not sewed very good. (*Threading a needle.*) Bad sewing always made me fidgety.

MRS. PETERS (*with a glance at the door, nervously*): I don't think we ought to touch things.

MRS. HALE: I'll just finish up this end. (*Suddenly stopping and leaning forward.*) Mrs. Peters?

MRS. PETERS: Yes, Mrs. Hale?

MRS. HALE: What do you suppose she was so nervous about?

MRS. PETERS: Oh—I don't know. I don't know as she was nervous. I sometimes sew awful queer when I'm just tired. (*Mrs. Hale starts to say something, looks at Mrs. Peters, then goes on sewing.*) Well, I must get these things wrapped up. They may be through sooner than we think. (*Putting apron and other things together.*) I wonder where I can find a piece of paper, and string. (*Rises.*)

MRS. HALE: In that cupboard, maybe.

MRS. PETERS (*crosses right looking in cupboard*): Why, here's a bird-cage. (*Holds it up.*) Did she have a bird, Mrs. Hale?

MRS. HALE: Why, I don't know whether she did or not—I've not been here for so long. There was a man around last year selling canaries cheap, but I don't know as she took one; maybe she did. She used to sing real pretty herself.

MRS. PETERS (*glancing around*): Seems funny to think of a bird here. But she must have had one, or why would she have a cage? I wonder what happened to it?

MRS. HALE: I s'pose maybe the cat got it.

MRS. PETERS: No, she didn't have a cat. She's got that feeling some people have about cats—being afraid of them. My cat got in her room and she was real upset and asked me to take it out.

MRS. HALE: My sister Bessie was like that. Queer, ain't it?

MRS. PETERS (*examining the cage*): Why, look at this door. It's broke. One hinge is pulled apart. (*Takes a step down to Mrs. Hale's right.*)

MRS. HALE (*looking too*): Looks as if someone must have been rough with it.

MRS. PETERS: Why, yes. (*She brings the cage forward and puts it on the table.*)

MRS. HALE (*glancing toward up left door*): I wish if they're going to find any evidence they'd be about it. I don't like this place.

MRS. PETERS: But I'm awful glad you came with me, Mrs. Hale. It would be lonesome for me sitting here alone.

MRS. HALE: It would, wouldn't it? (*Dropping her sewing.*) But I tell you what I do wish, Mrs. Peters. I wish I had come over sometimes when *she* was here. I—(*looking around the room*)—wish I had.

MRS. PETERS: But of course you were awful busy, Mrs. Hale—your house and your children.

MRS. HALE (*rises and crosses left*): I could've come. I stayed away because it weren't cheerful—and that's why I ought to have come. I—(*looking out left window*)—I've never liked this place. Maybe it's because it's down in a hollow and you don't see the road. I dunno what it is, but it's a lonesome place and always was. I wish I had come over to see Minnie Foster sometimes. I can see now—(*Shakes her head.*)

MRS. PETERS (*left of table and above it*): Well, you mustn't reproach yourself, Mrs. Hale. Somehow we just don't see how it is with other folks until—something turns up.

MRS. HALE: Not having children makes less work—but it makes a quiet house, and Wright out to work all day, and no company when he did come in. (*Turning from window.*) Did you know John Wright, Mrs. Peters?

MRS. PETERS: Not to know him; I've seen him in town. They say he was a good man.

MRS. HALE: Yes—good; he didn't drink, and kept his word as well as most, I guess, and paid his debts. But he was a hard man, Mrs. Peters. Just to pass the time of day with him—(*Shivers.*) Like a raw wind that gets to the bone. (*Pauses, her eye falling on the cage.*) I should think she would 'a' wanted a bird. But what do you suppose went with it?

MRS. PETERS: I don't know, unless it got sick and died. (*She reaches over and swings the broken door, swings it again, both women watch it.*)

MRS. HALE: You weren't raised round here, were you? (*Mrs. Peters shakes her head.*) You didn't know—her?

MRS. PETERS: Not till they brought her yesterday.

MRS. HALE: She—come to think of it, she was kind of like a bird herself—real sweet and pretty, but kind of timid and—fluttery. How—she—did—change. (*Silence: then as if struck by a happy thought and relieved to get back to everyday things. Crosses right above Mrs. Peters to cupboard, replaces small chair used to stand on to its original place down right.*) Tell you what, Mrs. Peters, why don't you take the quilt in with you? It might take up her mind.

MRS. PETERS: Why, I think that's a real nice idea, Mrs. Hale. There couldn't possibly be any objection to it could there? Now, just what would I take? I wonder if her patches are in here—and her things. (*They look in the sewing basket.*)

MRS. HALE (*crosses to right of table*): Here's some red. I expect this has got sewing things in it. (*Brings out a fancy box.*) What a pretty box. Looks like something somebody would give you. Maybe her scissors are in here. (*Opens box. Suddenly puts her hand to her nose.*) Why———(*Mrs. Peters bends nearer, then turns her face away.*) There's something wrapped up in this piece of silk.

MRS. PETERS: Why, this isn't her scissors.

MRS. HALE (*lifting the silk*): Oh, Mrs. Peters—it's———(*Mrs. Peters bends closer.*)

MRS. PETERS: It's the bird.

MRS. HALE: But, Mrs. Peters—look at it! Its neck! Look at its neck! It's all—other side *to*.

MRS. PETERS: Somebody—wrung—its—neck. (*Their eyes meet. A look of growing comprehension, of horror. Steps are heard outside. Mrs. Hale slips box under quilt pieces, and sinks into her chair. Enter Sheriff and County Attorney. Mrs. Peters steps down left and stands looking out of window.*)

COUNTY ATTORNEY (*as one turning from serious things to little pleasantries*): Well, ladies, have you decided whether she was going to quilt it or knot it? (*Crosses to center above table.*)

MRS. PETERS: We think she was going to—knot it. (*Sheriff crosses to right of stove, lifts stove lid, and glances at fire, then stands warming hands at stove.*)

COUNTY ATTORNEY: Well, that's interesting, I'm sure. (*Seeing the bird-cage.*) Has the bird flown?

MRS. HALE (*putting more quilt pieces over the box*): We think the—cat got it.

COUNTY ATTORNEY (*preoccupied*): Is there a cat? (*Mrs. Hale glances in a quick covert way at Mrs. Peters.*)

MRS. PETERS (*turning from window takes a step in*): Well, not *now*. They're superstitious, you know. They leave.

COUNTY ATTORNEY (*to Sheriff Peters, continuing an interrupted conversation*): No sign at all of anyone having come from the outside. Their own rope. Now let's go up again and go over it piece by piece. (*They start upstairs.*) It would have to have been someone who knew just the———(*Mrs. Peters sits down left of table. The two women sit there not looking at one another, but as if peering into something and at the same time holding back. When they talk now it is in the manner of feeling their way over strange ground, as if afraid of what they are saying, but as if they cannot help saying it.*)

MRS. HALE (*hesitatively and in hushed voice*): She liked the bird. She was going to bury it in that pretty box.

MRS. PETERS (*in a whisper*): When I was a girl—my kitten—there was a boy took a hatchet, and before my eyes—and before I could get there———(*Covers her face an instant.*) If they hadn't held me back I would have—(*catches herself, looks upstairs where steps are heard, falters weakly*)—hurt him.

MRS. HALE (*with a slow look around her*): I wonder how it would seem never to have had any children around. (*Pause.*) No, Wright wouldn't like the bird—a thing that sang. She used to sing. He killed that, too.

MRS. PETERS (*moving uneasily*): We don't know who killed the bird.

MRS. HALE: I knew John Wright.

MRS. PETERS: It was an awful thing was done in this house that night, Mrs. Hale. Killing a man while he slept, slipping a rope around his neck that choked the life out of him.

MRS. HALE: His neck. Choked the life out of him. (*Her hand goes out and rests on the bird-cage.*)

MRS. PETERS (*with rising voice*): We don't know who killed him. We don't *know.*

MRS. HALE (*her own feelings not interrupted*): If there'd been years and years of nothing, then a bird to sing to you, it would be awful—still, after the bird was still.

MRS. PETERS (*something within her speaking*): I know what stillness is. When we homesteaded in Dakota, and my first baby died—after he was two years old, and me with no other then———

MRS. HALE (*moving*): How soon do you suppose they'll be through looking for the evidence?

MRS. PETERS: I know what stillness is. (*Pulling herself back.*) The law has got to punish crimes, Mrs. Hale.

MRS. HALE (*not as if answering that*): I wish you'd seen Minnie Foster when she wore a white dress with blue ribbons and stood up there in the choir and sang. (*A look around the room.*) Oh, I *wish* I'd come over here once in a while! That was a crime! That was a crime! Who's going to punish that?

MRS. PETERS (*looking upstairs*): We mustn't—take on.

MRS. HALE: I might have known she needed help! I know how things can be—for women. I tell you, it's queer, Mrs. Peters. We live close together and we live far apart. We all go through the same things— it's all just a different kind of the same thing. (*Brushes her eyes, noticing the jar of fruit, reaches out for it.*) If I was you I wouldn't tell her her fruit was gone. Tell her it *ain't.* Tell her it's all right. Take this in to prove it to her. She—she may never know whether it was broke or not.

MRS. PETERS (*takes the jar, looks about for something to wrap it in; takes petticoat from the clothes brought from the other room, very nervously begins winding this around the jar. In a false voice*): My, it's a good thing the men couldn't hear us. Wouldn't they just laugh! Getting all stirred up over a little thing like a—dead canary. As if that could have anything to do with—with—wouldn't they *laugh!* (*The men are heard coming downstairs.*)

MRS. HALE (*under her breath*): Maybe they would—maybe they wouldn't.

COUNTY ATTORNEY: No, Peters, it's all perfectly clear except a reason for doing it. But you know juries when it comes to women. If there was some definite thing. (*Crosses slowly to above table. Sheriff crosses down right. Mrs. Hale and Mrs. Peters remain seated at either side of table.*) Something to show—something to make a story about—a thing that would connect up with this strange way of doing it——— (*The women's eyes meet for an instant. Enter Hale from outer door.*)

HALE (*remaining by door*):   Well, I've got the team around. Pretty cold out there.

COUNTY ATTORNEY: I'm going to stay awhile by myself. (*To the Sheriff.*) You can send Frank out for me, can't you? I want to go over everything. I'm not satisfied that we can't do better.

SHERIFF: Do you want to see what Mrs. Peters is going to take in? (*The Lawyer picks up the apron, laughs.*)

COUNTY ATTORNEY: Oh, I guess they're not very dangerous things the ladies have picked out. (*Moves a few things about, disturbing the quilt pieces which cover the box. Steps back.*) No, Mrs. Peters doesn't need supervising. For that matter a sheriff's wife is married to the law. Ever think of it that way, Mrs. Peters?

MRS. PETERS: Not—just that way.

SHERIFF (*chuckling*):   Married to the law. (*Moves to down right door to the other room.*) I just want you to come in here a minute, George. We ought to take a look at these windows.

COUNTY ATTORNEY (*scoffingly*):   Oh, windows!

SHERIFF: We'll be right out, Mr. Hale. (*Hale goes outside. The Sheriff follows the County Attorney into the room. Then Mrs. Hale rises, hands tight together, looking intensely at Mrs. Peters, whose eyes make a slow turn, finally meeting Mrs. Hale's. A moment Mrs. Hale holds her, then her own eyes point the way to where the box is concealed. Suddenly Mrs. Peters throws back quilt pieces and tries to put the box in the bag she is carrying. It is too big. She opens box, starts to take bird out, cannot touch it, goes to pieces, stands there helpless. Sound of a knob turning in the other room. Mrs. Hale snatches the box and puts it in the pocket of her big coat. Enter County Attorney and Sheriff, who remains down right.*)

COUNTY ATTORNEY (*crosses to up left door facetiously*):   Well, Henry, at least we found out that she was not going to quilt it. She was going to— what is it you call it, ladies?

MRS. HALE (*standing center below table facing front, her hand against her pocket*):   We call it—knot it, Mr. Henderson.

[1916]

TENNESSEE WILLIAMS [1911–1983]

The Glass Menagerie

nobody, not even the rain, has such small hands
— E. E. CUMMINGS

Production Notes by Tennessee Williams

Being a "memory play," *The Glass Menagerie* can be presented with unusual freedom of convention. Because of its considerably delicate or tenuous material, atmospheric touches and subtleties of direction play a particularly important part. Expressionism and all other unconventional techniques in drama have only one valid aim, and this is a closer approach to truth. When a play employs unconventional techniques, it is not, or certainly shouldn't be, trying to escape its responsibility of dealing with reality, or interpreting experience, but is actually or should be attempting to find a closer approach, or more penetrating and vivid expression of things as they are. The straight realistic play with its genuine frigidaire and authentic ice cubes, its characters that speak exactly as its audience speaks, corresponds to the academic landscape and has the same virtue of a photographic likeness. Everyone should know nowadays the unimportance of the photographic in art: that truth, life, or reality is an organic thing which the poetic imagination can represent or suggest, in essence, only through transformation, through changing into other forms than those which were merely present in appearance.

These remarks are not meant as a preface only to this particular play. They have to do with a conception of a new, plastic theatre which must take the place of the exhausted theatre of realistic conventions if the theatre is to resume vitality as a part of our culture.

The Screen Device: There is *only one important difference between the original and acting version of the play* and that is the *omission* in the latter of the device which I tentatively included in my *original* script. This device was the use of a screen on which were projected magic-lantern slides bearing images or titles. I do not regret the omission of this device from the present Broadway production. The extraordinary power of Miss Taylor's performance made it suitable to have the utmost simplicity in the physical production. But I think it may be interesting to some readers to see how this device was conceived. So I am putting it into the published manuscript. These

956

images and legends, projected from behind, were cast on a section of wall between the front-room and dining-room areas, which should be indistinguishable from the rest when not in use.

The purpose of this will probably be apparent. It is to give accent to certain values in each scene. Each scene contains a particular point (or several) which is structurally the most important. In an episodic play, such as this, the basic structure or narrative line may be obscured from the audience; the effect may seem fragmentary rather than architectural. This may not be the fault of the play so much as a lack of attention in the audience. The legend or image upon the screen will strengthen the effect of what is merely allusion in the writing and allow the primary point to be made more simply and lightly than if the entire responsibility were on the spoken lines. Aside from this structural value, I think the screen will have a definite emotional appeal, less definable but just as important. An imaginative producer or director may invent many other uses for this device than those indicated in the present script. In fact the possibilities of the device seem much larger to me than the instance of this play can possibly utilize.

The Music: Another extra-literary accent in this play is provided by the use of music. A single recurring tune, "The Glass Menagerie," is used to give emotional emphasis to suitable passages. This tune is like circus music, not when you are on the grounds or in the immediate vicinity of the parade, but when you are at some distance and very likely thinking of something else. It seems under those circumstances to continue almost interminably and it weaves in and out of your preoccupied consciousness; then it is the lightest, most delicate music in the world and perhaps the saddest. It expresses the surface vivacity of life with the underlying strain of immutable and inexpressible sorrow. When you look at a piece of delicately spun glass you think of two things: how beautiful it is and how easily it can be broken. Both of those ideas should be woven into the recurring tune, which dips in and out of the play as if it were carried on a wind that changes. It serves as a thread of connection and allusion between the narrator with his separate point in time and space and the subject of his story. Between each episode it returns as reference to the emotion, nostalgia, which is the first condition of the play. It is primarily Laura's music and therefore comes out most clearly when the play focuses upon her and the lovely fragility of glass which is her image.

The Lighting: The lighting in the play is not realistic. In keeping with the atmosphere of memory, the stage is dim. Shafts of light are focused on selected areas or actors, sometimes in contradistinction to what is the apparent center. For instance, in the quarrel scene between Tom and Amanda, in which Laura has no active part, the clearest pool of light is on her figure. This is also true of the supper scene, when her silent figure on the sofa should remain the visual center. The light upon Laura should be distinct from the others, having a peculiar pristine clarity such as light used in early religious portraits of female saints or madonnas. A certain correspondence to light in religious paintings, such as El Greco's, where the figures are radiant in atmosphere that is relatively dusky, could be effectively used throughout the play. (It will also permit a more effective use of the screen.) A free, imaginative use of light can be of enormous value in giving a mobile, plastic quality to plays of a more or less static nature.

Characters

AMANDA WINGFIELD, *the mother. A little woman of great but confused vitality clinging frantically to another time and place. Her characterization must be carefully created, not copied from type. She is not paranoiac, but her life is paranoia. There is much to admire in Amanda, and as much to love and pity as there is to laugh at. Certainly she has endurance and a kind of heroism, and though her foolishness makes her unwittingly cruel at times, there is tenderness in her slight person.*

LAURA WINGFIELD, *her daughter. Amanda, having failed to establish contact with reality, continues to live vitally in her illusions, but Laura's situation is even graver. A childhood illness has left her crippled, one leg slightly shorter than the other, and held in a brace. This defect need not be more than suggested on the stage. Stemming from this, Laura's separation increases till she is like a piece of her own glass collection, too exquisitely fragile to move from the shelf.*

TOM WINGFIELD, *her son. And the narrator of the play. A poet with a job in a warehouse. His nature is not remorseless, but to escape from a trap he has to act without pity.*

JIM O'CONNOR, *the gentleman caller. A nice, ordinary, young man.*

Scene: *An alley in St. Louis.*
Part I: *Preparation for a Gentleman Caller.*
Part II: *The Gentleman Calls.*
Time: *Now and the Past.*

SCENE 1

(*The Wingfield apartment is in the rear of the building, one of those vast hive-like conglomerations of cellular living-units that flower as warty growths in overcrowded urban centers of lower middle-class population and are symptomatic of the impulse of this largest and fundamentally enslaved section of American society to avoid fluidity and differentiation and to exist and function as one interfused mass of automatism.*)

(*The apartment faces an alley and is entered by a fire escape, a structure whose name is a touch of accidental poetic truth, for all of these huge buildings are always*

burning with the slow and implacable fires of human desperation. The fire escape is
included in the set—that is, the landing of it and steps descending from it.)

(The scene is memory and is therefore nonrealistic. Memory takes a lot of poetic
license. It omits some details; others are exaggerated, according to the emotional
value of the articles it touches, for memory is seated predominantly in the heart. The
interior is therefore rather dim and poetic.)

(At the rise of the curtain, the audience is faced with the dark, grim rear wall of the
Wingfield tenement. This building, which runs parallel to the footlights, is flanked on
both sides by dark, narrow alleys which run into murky canyons of tangled clothes-
lines, garbage cans, and the sinister latticework of neighboring fire escapes. It is up
and down these side alleys that exterior entrances and exits are made, during the
play. At the end of Tom's opening commentary, the dark tenement wall slowly reveals
[by means of a transparency] the interior of the ground floor Wingfield apartment.)

(Downstage is the living room, which also serves as a sleeping room for Laura, the
sofa unfolding to make her bed. Upstage, center, and divided by a wide arch or sec-
ond proscenium with transparent faded portieres [or second curtain], is the dining
room. In an old-fashioned what-not in the living room are seen scores of transparent
glass animals. A blown-up photograph of the father hangs on the wall of the living
room, facing the audience, to the left of the archway. It is the face of a very hand-
some young man in a doughboy's First World War cap. He is gallantly smiling,
ineluctably smiling, as if to say, "I will be smiling forever.")

(The audience hears and sees the opening scene in the dining room through both
the transparent fourth wall of the building and the transparent gauze portieres of the
dining-room arch. It is during this revealing scene that the fourth wall slowly
ascends, out of sight. This transparent exterior wall is not brought down again until
the very end of the play, during Tom's final speech.)

(The narrator is an undisguised convention of the play. He takes whatever license
with dramatic convention as is convenient to his purposes.)

(Tom enters dressed as a merchant sailor from alley, stage left, and strolls across
the front of the stage to the fire escape. There he stops and lights a cigarette. He
addresses the audience.)

TOM: Yes, I have tricks in my pocket, I have things up my sleeve. But I
am the opposite of a stage magician. He gives you illusion that has the
appearance of truth. I give you truth in the pleasant disguise of illusion. To begin with, I turn back time. I reverse it to that quaint period,
the thirties, when the huge middle class of America was matriculating
in a school for the blind. Their eyes had failed them, or they had failed
their eyes, and so they were having their fingers pressed forcibly down
on the fiery Braille alphabet of a dissolving economy. In Spain there
was revolution. Here there was only shouting and confusion. In Spain
there was Guernica. Here there were disturbances of labor, sometimes
pretty violent, in otherwise peaceful cities such as Chicago, Cleveland,
Saint Louis. . . . This is the social background of the play.

(Music.)

The play is memory. Being a memory play, it is dimly lighted, it is sentimental, it is not realistic. In memory everything seems to happen to music. That explains the fiddle in the wings. I am the narrator of the play, and also a character in it. The other characters are my mother, Amanda, my sister, Laura, and a gentleman caller who appears in the final scenes. He is the most realistic character in the play, being an emissary from a world of reality that we were somehow set apart from. But since I have a poet's weakness for symbols, I am using this character also as a symbol; he is the long delayed but always expected something that we live for. There is a fifth character in the play who doesn't appear except in this larger-than-life photograph over the mantel. This is our father who left us a long time ago. He was a telephone man who fell in love with long distances; he gave up his job with the telephone company and skipped the light fantastic out of town . . . The last we heard of him was a picture postcard from Mazatlan, on the Pacific coast of Mexico, containing a message of two words— "Hello—Good-bye!" and no address. I think the rest of the play will explain itself. . . .

(*Amanda's voice becomes audible through the portieres.*)
    (*Legend on Screen: "Où Sont les Neiges."*)°
    (*He divides the portieres and enters the upstage area.*)
    (*Amanda and Laura are seated at a drop-leaf table. Eating is indicated by gestures without food or utensils. Amanda faces the audience. Tom and Laura are seated in profile.*)
    (*The interior has lit up softly and through the scrim we see Amanda and Laura seated at the table in the upstage area.*)

AMANDA (*calling*): Tom?
TOM: Yes, Mother.
AMANDA: We can't say grace until you come to the table!
TOM: Coming, Mother. (*He bows slightly and withdraws, reappearing a few moments later in his place at the table.*)
AMANDA (*to her son*): Honey, don't *push* with your *fingers*. If you have to push with something, the thing to push with is a crust of bread. And chew—chew! Animals have sections in their stomachs which enable them to digest food without mastication, but human beings are supposed to chew their food before they swallow it down. Eat food leisurely, son, and really enjoy it. A well-cooked meal has lots of delicate flavors that have to be held in the mouth for appreciation. So chew your food and give your salivary glands a chance to function!

"Où sont les neiges": "Où sont les neiges d'antan?" ("Where are the snows of yesteryear?") is a line from a poem by fifteenth-century French poet François Villon.

(*Tom deliberately lays his imaginary fork down and pushes his chair back from the table.*)

TOM: I haven't enjoyed one bite of this dinner because of your constant directions on how to eat it. It's you that makes me rush through meals with your hawk-like attention to every bite I take. Sickening—spoils my appetite—all this discussion of animals' secretion—salivary glands—mastication!

AMANDA (*lightly*): Temperament like a Metropolitan° star! (*He rises and crosses downstage.*) You're not excused from the table.

TOM: I'm getting a cigarette.

AMANDA: You smoke too much.

(*Laura rises.*)

LAURA: I'll bring in the blancmange.

(*He remains standing with his cigarette by the portieres during the following.*)

AMANDA (*rising*): No, sister, no, sister—you be the lady this time and I'll be the darky.

LAURA: I'm already up.

AMANDA: Resume your seat, little sister—I want you to stay fresh and pretty—for gentlemen callers!

LAURA: I'm not expecting any gentlemen callers.

AMANDA (*crossing out to kitchenette. Airily*): Sometimes they come when they are least expected! Why, I remember one Sunday afternoon in Blue Mountain—(*Enters kitchenette.*)

TOM: I know what's coming!

LAURA: Yes. But let her tell it.

TOM: Again?

LAURA: She loves to tell it.

(*Amanda returns with bowl of dessert.*)

AMANDA: One Sunday afternoon in Blue Mountain—your mother received—*seventeen!*—gentlemen callers! Why, sometimes there weren't chairs enough to accommodate them all. We had to send the nigger over to bring in folding chairs from the parish house.

TOM (*remaining at portieres*): How did you entertain those gentlemen callers?

AMANDA: I understood the art of conversation!

TOM: I bet you could talk.

AMANDA: Girls in those days *knew* how to talk, I can tell you.

TOM: Yes?

Metropolitan: Metropolitan Opera.

(*Image: Amanda as a girl on a porch greeting callers.*)

AMANDA: They knew how to entertain their gentlemen callers. It wasn't
enough for a girl to be possessed of a pretty face and a graceful
figure—although I wasn't slighted in either respect. She also needed
to have a nimble wit and a tongue to meet all occasions.

TOM: What did you talk about?

AMANDA: Things of importance going on in the world! Never anything
coarse or common or vulgar. (*She addresses Tom as though he were seated
in the vacant chair at the table though he remains by portieres. He plays this
scene as though he held the book.*) My callers were gentlemen—all!
Among my callers were some of the most prominent young planters of
the Mississippi Delta—planters and sons of planters!

(*Tom motions for music and a spot of light on Amanda.*)
(*Her eyes lift, her face glows, her voice becomes rich and elegiac.*)
(*Screen legend: "Où Sont les Neiges."*)

There was young Champ Laughlin who later became vice-president of
the Delta Planters Bank. Hadley Stevenson who was drowned in Moon
Lake and left his widow one hundred and fifty thousand in Government
bonds. There were the Cutrere brothers, Wesley and Bates. Bates was
one of my bright particular beaux! He got in a quarrel with that wild
Wainright boy. They shot it out on the floor of Moon Lake Casino. Bates
was shot through the stomach. Died in the ambulance on his way to
Memphis. His widow was also well-provided for, came into eight or ten
thousand acres, that's all. She married him on the rebound—never
loved her—carried my picture on him the night he died! And there was
that boy that every girl in the Delta had set her cap for! That beautiful,
brilliant young Fitzhugh boy from Greene County!

TOM: What did he leave his widow?

AMANDA: He never married! Gracious, you talk as though all of my old
admirers had turned up their toes to the daisies!

TOM: Isn't this the first you mentioned that still survives?

AMANDA: That Fitzhugh boy went North and made a fortune—came to
be known as the Wolf of Wall Street! He had the Midas touch, whatever he touched turned to gold! And I could have been Mrs. Duncan J.
Fitzhugh, mind you! But—I picked your *father!*

LAURA (*rising*): Mother, let me clear the table.

AMANDA: No, dear, you go in front and study your typewriter chart. Or
practice your shorthand a little. Stay fresh and pretty!—It's almost
time for our gentlemen callers to start arriving. (*She flounces girlishly
toward the kitchenette.*) How many do you suppose we're going to entertain this afternoon?

(*Tom throws down the paper and jumps up with a groan.*)

LAURA (*alone in the dining room*): I don't believe we're going to receive any, Mother.

AMANDA (*reappearing, airily*): What? No one—not one? You must be joking! (*Laura nervously echoes her laugh. She slips in a fugitive manner through the half-open portieres and draws them gently behind her. A shaft of very clear light is thrown on her face against the faded tapestry of the curtains. Music: "The Glass Menagerie" under faintly. Lightly.*) Not one gentleman caller? It can't be true! There must be a flood, there must have been a tornado!

LAURA: It isn't a flood, it's not a tornado, Mother. I'm just not popular like you were in Blue Mountain. . . . (*Tom utters another groan. Laura glances at him with a faint, apologetic smile. Her voice catching a little.*) Mother's afraid I'm going to be an old maid.

(*The scene dims out with "Glass Menagerie" music.*)

SCENE 2

(*"Laura, Haven't You Ever Liked Some Boy?"*)

(*On the dark stage the screen is lighted with the image of blue roses.*)

(*Gradually Laura's figure becomes apparent and the screen goes out.*)

(*The music subsides.*)

(*Laura is seated in the delicate ivory chair at the small clawfoot table.*)

(*She wears a dress of soft violet material for a kimono—her hair tied back from her forehead with a ribbon.*)

(*She is washing and polishing her collection of glass.*)

(*Amanda appears on the fire escape steps. At the sound of her ascent, Laura catches her breath, thrusts the bowl of ornaments away and seats herself stiffly before the diagram of the typewriter keyboard as though it held her spellbound. Something has happened to Amanda. It is written in her face as she climbs to the landing: a look that is grim and hopeless and a little absurd.*)

(*She has on one of those cheap or imitation velvety-looking cloth coats with imitation fur collar. Her hat is five or six years old, one of those dreadful cloche hats that were worn in the late twenties, and she is clasping an enormous black patent-leather pocketbook with nickel clasp and initials. This is her full-dress outfit, the one she usually wears to the D.A.R.°*)

(*Before entering she looks through the door.*)

D.A.R.: Daughters of the American Revolution is a patriotic organization for women whose ancestors were part of the American War of Independence.

(*She purses her lips, opens her eyes wide, rolls them upward and shakes her head.*)

(*Then she slowly lets herself in the door. Seeing her mother's expression Laura touches her lips with a nervous gesture.*)

LAURA: Hello, Mother, I was—(*She makes a nervous gesture toward the chart on the wall. Amanda leans against the shut door and stares at Laura with a martyred look.*)

AMANDA: Deception? Deception? (*She slowly removes her hat and gloves, continuing the swift suffering stare. She lets the hat and gloves fall on the floor—a bit of acting.*)

LAURA (*shakily*): How was the D.A.R. meeting? (*Amanda slowly opens her purse and removes a dainty white handkerchief which she shakes out delicately and delicately touches to her lips and nostrils.*) Didn't you go to the D.A.R. meeting, Mother?

AMANDA (*faintly, almost inaudibly*):—No.—No. (*Then more forcibly*). I did not have the strength—to go to the D.A.R. In fact, I did not have the courage! I wanted to find a hole in the ground and hide myself in it forever! (*She crosses slowly to the wall and removes the diagram of the typewriter keyboard. She holds it in front of her for a second, staring at it sweetly and sorrowfully—then bites her lips and tears it in two pieces.*)

LAURA (*faintly*): Why did you do that, Mother? (*Amanda repeats the same procedure with the chart of the Gregg Alphabet.*) Why are you—

AMANDA: Why? Why? How old are you, Laura?

LAURA: Mother, you know my age.

AMANDA: I thought that you were an adult; it seems that I was mistaken. (*She crosses slowly to the sofa and sinks down and stares at Laura.*)

LAURA: Please don't stare at me, Mother.

(*Amanda closes her eyes and lowers her head. Count ten.*)

AMANDA: What are we going to do, what is going to become of us, what is the future?

(*Count ten.*)

LAURA: Has something happened, Mother? (*Amanda draws a long breath and takes out the handkerchief again. Dabbing process.*) Mother, has—something happened?

AMANDA: I'll be all right in a minute. I'm just bewildered—(*Count five.*)—by life. . . .

LAURA: Mother, I wish that you would tell me what's happened.

AMANDA: As you know, I was supposed to be inducted into my office at the D.A.R. this afternoon. (*Image: a swarm of typewriters.*) But I stopped off at Rubicam's Business College to speak to your teachers about your

having a cold and ask them what progress they thought you were making down there.

LAURA: Oh. . . .

AMANDA: I went to the typing instructor and introduced myself as your
mother. She didn't know who you were. Wingfield, she said. We don't
have any such student enrolled at the school! I assured her she did,
that you had been going to classes since early in January. "I wonder,"
she said, "if you could be talking about that terribly shy little girl who
dropped out of school after only a few days' attendance?" "No," I said,
"Laura, my daughter, has been going to school every day for the past
six weeks!" "Excuse me," she said. She took the attendance book out
and there was your name, unmistakably printed, and all the dates you
were absent until they decided that you had dropped out of school. I
still said, "No, there must have been some mistake! There must have
been some mix-up in the records!" And she said, "No—I remember
her perfectly now. Her hands shook so that she couldn't hit the right
keys! The first time we gave a speed test, she broke down completely—
was sick at the stomach and almost had to be carried into the washroom! After that morning she never showed up any more. We phoned
the house but never got any answer"—while I was working at Famous
and Barr, I suppose, demonstrating those—Oh! I felt so weak I could
barely keep on my feet. I had to sit down while they got me a glass of
water! Fifty dollars' tuition, all of our plans—my hopes and ambitions
for you—just gone up the spout, just gone up the spout like that.
(*Laura draws a long breath and gets awkwardly to her feet. She crosses to the
victrola and winds it up.*) What are you doing?

LAURA: Oh! (*She releases the handle and returns to her seat.*)

AMANDA: Laura, where have you been going when you've gone out pretending that you were going to business college?

LAURA: I've just been going out walking.

AMANDA: That's not true.

LAURA: It is. I just went walking.

AMANDA: Walking? Walking? In winter? Deliberately courting pneumonia in that light coat? Where did you walk to, Laura?

LAURA: All sorts of places—mostly in the park.

AMANDA: Even after you'd started catching that cold?

LAURA: It was the lesser of two evils, Mother. (*Image: winter scene in park.*)
I couldn't go back up. I—threw up—on the floor!

AMANDA: From half past seven till after five every day you mean to tell
me you walked around in the park, because you wanted to make me
think that you were still going to Rubicam's Business College?

LAURA: It wasn't as bad as it sounds. I went inside places to get warmed up.

AMANDA: Inside where?
LAURA: I went in the art museum and the bird houses at the Zoo. I vis-
ited the penguins every day! Sometimes I did without lunch and went
to the movies. Lately I've been spending most of my afternoons in the
Jewel-box, that big glass house where they raise the tropical flowers.
AMANDA: You did all this to deceive me, just for the deception? (*Laura
looks down.*) Why?
LAURA: Mother, when you're disappointed, you get that awful suffering
look on your face, like the picture of Jesus' mother in the museum!
AMANDA: Hush!
LAURA: I couldn't face it.

(*Pause. A whisper of strings.*)
(*Legend: "The Crust of Humility."*)

AMANDA (*hopelessly fingering the huge pocketbook*): So what are we going to
do the rest of our lives? Stay home and watch the parades go by?
Amuse ourselves with the glass menagerie, darling? Eternally play
those worn-out phonograph records your father left as a painful
reminder of him? We won't have a business career—we've given that
up because it gave us nervous indigestion! (*Laughs wearily.*) What is
there left but dependency all our lives? I know so well what becomes of
unmarried women who aren't prepared to occupy a position. I've seen
such pitiful cases in the South—barely tolerated spinsters living upon
the grudging patronage of sister's husband or brother's wife!—stuck
away in some little mousetrap of a room—encouraged by one in-law to
visit another—little birdlike women without any nest—eating the
crust of humility all their life! Is that the future that we've mapped out
for ourselves? I swear it's the only alternative I can think of! It isn't a
very pleasant alternative, is it? Of course—some girls do *marry*. (*Laura
twists her hands nervously.*) Haven't you ever liked some boy?
LAURA: Yes. I liked one once. (*Rises.*) I came across his picture a while ago.
AMANDA (*with some interest*): He gave you his picture?
LAURA: No, it's in the yearbook.
AMANDA (*disappointed*): Oh—a high-school boy.

(*Screen image: Jim as high school hero bearing a silver cup.*)

LAURA: Yes. His name was Jim. (*Laura lifts the heavy annual from the clawfoot table.*) Here he is in *The Pirates of Penzance.*
AMANDA (*absently*): The what?
LAURA: The operetta the senior class put on. He had a wonderful voice
and we sat across the aisle from each other Mondays, Wednesdays,
and Fridays in the Aud. Here he is with the silver cup for debating! See
his grin?

AMANDA (*absently*): He must have had a jolly disposition.
LAURA: He used to call me — Blue Roses.

(*Image: blue roses.*)

AMANDA: Why did he call you such a name as that?
LAURA: When I had that attack of pleurosis — he asked me what was the
  matter when I came back. I said pleurosis — he thought that I said
  Blue Roses! So that's what he always called me after that. Whenever
  he saw me, he'd holler, "Hello, Blue Roses!" I didn't care for the girl
  that he went out with. Emily Meisenbach. Emily was the best-dressed
  girl at Soldan. She never struck me, though, as being sincere . . . It
  says in the Personal Section — they're engaged. That's — six years ago!
  They must be married by now.
AMANDA: Girls that aren't cut out for business careers usually wind up
  married to some nice man. (*Gets up with a spark of revival.*) Sister, that's
  what you'll do!

(*Laura utters a startled, doubtful laugh. She reaches quickly for a piece of glass.*)

LAURA: But, Mother —
AMANDA: Yes? (*Crossing to photograph.*)
LAURA (*in a tone of frightened apology*): I'm — crippled!

(*Image: screen.*)

AMANDA: Nonsense! Laura, I've told you never, never to use that word.
  Why, you're not crippled, you just have a little defect — hardly noticeable, even! When people have some slight disadvantage like that, they
  cultivate other things to make up for it — develop charm — and vivacity — and — *charm!* That's all you have to do! (*She turns again to the photograph.*) One thing your father had *plenty of* — was *charm!*

(*Tom motions to the fiddle in the wings.*)
(*The scene fades out with music.*)

SCENE 3

(*Legend on screen: "After the Fiasco —"*)
(*Tom speaks from the fire escape landing.*)

TOM: After the fiasco at Rubicam's Business College, the idea of getting a
  gentleman caller for Laura began to play a more important part in
  Mother's calculations. It became an obsession. Like some archetype of
  the universal unconscious, the image of the gentleman caller haunted

our small apartment. . . . (*Image: young man at door with flowers.*) An evening at home rarely passed without some allusion to this image, this specter, this hope. . . . Even when he wasn't mentioned, his presence hung in Mother's preoccupied look and in my sister's frightened, apologetic manner—hung like a sentence passed upon the Wingfields! Mother was a woman of action as well as words. She began to take logical steps in the planned direction. Late that winter and in the early spring—realizing that extra money would be needed to properly feather the nest and plume the bird—she conducted a vigorous campaign on the telephone, roping in subscribers to one of those magazines for matrons called *The Home-maker's Companion,* the type of journal that features the serialized sublimations of ladies of letters who think in terms of delicate cuplike breasts, slim, tapering waists, rich, creamy thighs, eyes like wood smoke in autumn, fingers that soothe and caress like strains of music, bodies as powerful as Etruscan sculpture.

(*Screen image: glamor magazine cover.*)
   (*Amanda enters with phone on long extension cord. She is spotted in the dim stage.*)

AMANDA: Ida Scott? This is Amanda Wingfield! We *missed* you at the D.A.R. last Monday! I said to myself: She's probably suffering with that sinus condition! How is that sinus condition? Horrors! Heaven have mercy!—You're a Christian martyr, yes, that's what you are, a Christian martyr! Well I just now happened to notice that your subscription to the *Companion's* about to expire! Yes, it expires with the next issue, honey!—just when that wonderful new serial by Bessie Mae Hopper is getting off to such an exciting start. Oh, honey, it's something that you can't miss! You remember how *Gone with the Wind* took everybody by storm? You simply couldn't go out if you hadn't read it. All everybody *talked* was Scarlett O'Hara. Well, this is a book that critics already compare to *Gone with the Wind.* It's the *Gone with the Wind* of the post–World War generation!—What?—Burning?—Oh, honey, don't let them burn, go take a look in the oven and I'll hold the wire! Heavens—I think she's hung up!

(*Dim out.*)
   (*Legend on screen: "You Think I'm in Love with Continental Shoemakers?"*)
   (*Before the stage is lighted, the violent voices of Tom and Amanda are heard.*)
   (*They are quarreling behind the portieres. In front of them stands Laura with clenched hands and panicky expression.*)
   (*A clear pool of light on her figure throughout this scene.*)

TOM: What in Christ's name am I—
AMANDA (*shrilly*): Don't you use that—

Toм: Supposed to do!

AMANDA: Expression! Not in my—

Toм: Ohhh!

AMANDA: Presence! Have you gone out of your senses?

Toм: I have, that's true, *driven* out!

AMANDA: What is the matter with you, you—big—big—IDIOT!

Toм: Look—I've got *no thing*, no single thing—

AMANDA: Lower your voice!

Toм: In my life here that I can call my OWN! Everything is—

AMANDA: Stop that shouting!

Toм: Yesterday you confiscated my books! You had the nerve to—

AMANDA: I took that horrible novel back to the library—yes! That hideous book by that insane Mr. Lawrence. (*Tom laughs wildly.*) I cannot control the output of diseased minds or people who cater to them—(*Tom laughs still more wildly.*) BUT I WON'T ALLOW SUCH FILTH BROUGHT INTO MY HOUSE! No, no, no, no, no!

Toм: House, house! Who pays rent on it, who makes a slave of himself to—

AMANDA (*fairly screeching*): Don't you DARE to—

Toм: No, no, *I* mustn't say things! *I've* got to just—

AMANDA: Let me tell you—

Toм: I don't want to hear any more! (*He tears the portieres open. The upstage area is lit with a turgid smoky red glow.*)

(*Amanda's hair is in metal curlers and she wears a very old bathrobe, much too large for her slight figure, a relic of the faithless Mr. Wingfield.*)

   (*An upright typewriter and a wild disarray of manuscripts are on the dropleaf table. The quarrel was probably precipitated by Amanda's interruption of his creative labor. A chair lying overthrown on the floor.*)

   (*Their gesticulating shadows are cast on the ceiling by the fiery glow.*)

AMANDA: You *will* hear more, you—

Toм: No, I won't hear more, I'm going out!

AMANDA: You come right back in—

Toм: Out, out out! Because I'm—

AMANDA: Come back here, Tom Wingfield! I'm not through talking to you!

Toм: Oh, go—

LAURA (*desperately*): Tom!

AMANDA: You're going to listen, and no more insolence from you! I'm at the end of my patience! (*He comes back toward her.*)

Toм: What do you think I'm at? Aren't I supposed to have any patience to reach the end of, Mother? I know, I know. It seems unimportant to you, what I'm *doing*—what I *want* to do—having a little *difference* between them! You don't think that—

AMANDA: I think you've been doing things that you're ashamed of. That's why you act like this. I don't believe that you go every night to the movies. Nobody goes to the movies night after night. Nobody in their right minds goes to the movies as often as you pretend to. People don't go to the movies at nearly midnight, and movies don't let out at two A.M. Come in stumbling. Muttering to yourself like a maniac! You get three hours' sleep and then go to work. Oh, I can picture the way you're doing down there. Moping, doping, because you're in no condition.

TOM (*wildly*): No, I'm in no condition!

AMANDA: What right have you got to jeopardize your job? Jeopardize the security of us all? How do you think we'd manage if you were—

TOM: Listen! You think I'm crazy *about* the *warehouse*? (*He bends fiercely toward her slight figure.*) You think I'm in love with the Continental Shoemakers? You think I want to spend fifty-five *years* down there in that—*celotex interior!* with—*fluorescent*—*tubes!* Look! I'd rather somebody picked up a crowbar and battered out my brains—than go back mornings! I *go!* Every time you come in yelling that God damn *"Rise and Shine!" "Rise and Shine!"* I say to myself, *"How lucky dead people are!"* But I get up. I *go!* For sixty-five dollars a month I give up all that I dream of doing and being *ever!* And you say self—*self's* all I ever think of. Why, listen, if self is what I thought of, Mother, I'd be where he is—GONE! (*Pointing to father's picture.*) As far as the system of transportation reaches! (*He starts past her. She grabs his arm.*) Don't grab at me, Mother!

AMANDA: Where are you going?

TOM: I'm going to the *movies!*

AMANDA: I don't believe that lie!

TOM (*Crouching toward her, overtowering her tiny figure. She backs away, gasping.*): I'm going to opium dens! Yes, opium dens, dens of vice and criminals' hangouts, Mother. I've joined the Hogan gang, I'm a hired assassin, I carry a tommy-gun in a violin case! I run a string of cathouses in the Valley! They call me Killer, Killer Wingfield, I'm leading a double life, a simple, honest warehouse worker by day, by night, a dynamic *czar* of the *underworld, Mother.* I go to gambling casinos, I spin away fortunes on the roulette table! I wear a patch over one eye and a false mustache, sometimes I put on green whiskers. On those occasions they call me—*El Diablo!* Oh, I could tell you things to make you sleepless! My enemies plan to dynamite this place. They're going to blow us all skyhigh some night! I'll be glad, very happy, and so will you! You'll go up, up on a broomstick, over Blue Mountain with seventeen gentlemen callers! You ugly—babbling old—*witch*. . . . (*He goes through a series of violent, clumsy movements, seizing his overcoat, lunging to the door, pulling it fiercely open. The women watch him, aghast. His arm catches in the sleeve of the coat as he struggles to pull it on. For a moment he is pinioned by the bulky garment. With an outraged groan he tears the coat off again, splitting the shoulders of it, and hurls it across the room. It strikes against the shelf of Laura's glass collection, there is a tinkle of shattering glass. Laura cries out as if wounded.)*

(Music legend: "The Glass Menagerie.")

LAURA *(shrilly)*: My glass!—menagerie. . . . *(She covers her face and turns away.)*

(But Amanda is still stunned and stupefied by the "ugly witch" so that she barely notices this occurrence. Now she recovers her speech.)

AMANDA *(in an awful voice)*: I won't speak to you—until you apologize!
(She crosses through portieres and draws them together behind her. Tom is left with Laura. Laura clings weakly to the mantel with her face averted. Tom stares at her stupidly for a moment. Then he crosses to shelf. Drops awkwardly to his knees to collect the fallen glass, glancing at Laura as if he would speak but couldn't.)

("The Glass Menagerie" steals in as the scene dims out.)

SCENE 4

(The interior is dark. Faint light in the alley.)
(A deep-voiced bell in a church is tolling the hour of five as the scene commences.)
(Tom appears at the top of the alley. After each solemn boom of the bell in the tower, he shakes a little noisemaker or rattle as if to express the tiny spasm of man in contrast to the sustained power and dignity of the Almighty. This and the unsteadiness of his advance make it evident that he has been drinking.)
(As he climbs the few steps to the fire escape landing light steals up inside. Laura appears in nightdress, observing Tom's empty bed in the front room.)
(Tom fishes in his pockets for the door key, removing a motley assortment of articles in the search, including a perfect shower of movie ticket stubs and an empty bottle. At last he finds the key, but just as he is about to insert it, it slips from his fingers. He strikes a match and crouches below the door.)

TOM *(bitterly)*: One crack—and it falls through!

(Laura opens the door.)

LAURA: Tom! Tom, what are you doing?

TOM: Looking for a door key.

LAURA: Where have you been all this time?

TOM: I have been to the movies.

LAURA: All this time at the movies?

TOM: There was a very long program. There was a Garbo picture and a Mickey Mouse and a travelogue and a newsreel and a preview of coming attractions. And there was an organ solo and a collection for the milk fund—simultaneously—which ended up in a terrible fight between a fat lady and an usher!

LAURA (*innocently*): Did you have to stay through everything?

TOM: Of course! And, oh, I forgot! There was a big stage show! The headliner on this stage show was Malvolio the Magician. He performed wonderful tricks, many of them, such as pouring water back and forth between pitchers. First it turned to wine and then it turned to beer and then it turned to whiskey. I know it was whiskey it finally turned into because he needed somebody to come up out of the audience to help him, and I came up—both shows! It was Kentucky Straight Bourbon. A very generous fellow, he gave souvenirs. (*He pulls from his back pocket a shimmering rainbow-colored scarf.*) He gave me this. This is his magic scarf. You can have it, Laura. You wave it over a canary cage and you get a bowl of goldfish. You wave it over the goldfish bowl and they fly away canaries. . . . But the wonderfullest trick of all was the coffin trick. We nailed him into a coffin and he got out of the coffin without removing one nail. (*He has come inside.*) There is a trick that would come in handy for me—get me out of this 2 by 4 situation! (*Flops onto bed and starts removing shoes.*)

LAURA: Tom—Shhh!

TOM: What you shushing me for?

LAURA: You'll wake up Mother.

TOM: Goody, goody! Pay 'er back for all those "Rise an' Shines." (*Lies down, groaning.*) You know it don't take much intelligence to get yourself into a nailed-up coffin, Laura. But who in hell ever got himself out of one without removing one nail?

(*As if in answer, the father's grinning photograph lights up.*)
(*Scene dims out.*)
(*Immediately following: The church bell is heard striking six. At the sixth stroke the alarm clock goes off in Amanda's room, and after a few moments we hear her calling: "Rise and Shine! Rise and Shine! Laura, go tell your brother to rise and shine!"*)

TOM (*sitting up slowly*): I'll rise—but I won't shine.

(*The light increases.*)

AMANDA: Laura, tell your brother his coffee is ready.

(*Laura slips into front room.*)

LAURA: Tom! it's nearly seven. Don't make Mother nervous. (*He stares at her stupidly. Beseechingly.*) Tom, speak to Mother this morning. Make up with her, apologize, speak to her!

TOM: She won't to me. It's her that started not speaking.

LAURA: If you just say you're sorry she'll start speaking.

TOM: Her not speaking—is that such a tragedy?

LAURA: Please—please!

AMANDA (*calling from kitchenette*): Laura, are you going to do what I asked you to do, or do I have to get dressed and go out myself?

LAURA: Going, going—soon as I get on my coat! (*She pulls on a shapeless felt hat with nervous, jerky movement, pleadingly glancing at Tom. Rushes awkwardly for coat. The coat is one of Amanda's, inaccurately made over, the sleeves too short for Laura.*) Butter and what else?

AMANDA (*entering upstage*): Just butter. Tell them to charge it.

LAURA: Mother, they make such faces when I do that.

AMANDA: Sticks and stones may break my bones, but the expression on Mr. Garfinkel's face won't harm us! Tell your brother his coffee is getting cold.

LAURA (*at door*): Do what I asked you, will you, will you, Tom?

(*He looks sullenly away.*)

AMANDA: Laura, go now or just don't go at all!

LAURA (*rushing out*): Going—going! (*A second later she cries out. Tom springs up and crosses to the door. Amanda rushes anxiously in. Tom opens the door.*)

TOM: Laura?

LAURA: I'm all right. I slipped, but I'm all right.

AMANDA (*peering anxiously after her*): If anyone breaks a leg on those fire escape steps, the landlord ought to be sued for every cent he possesses! (*She shuts door. Remembers she isn't speaking and returns to other room.*)

(*As Tom enters listlessly for his coffee, she turns her back to him and stands rigidly facing the window on the gloomy gray vault of the areaway. Its light on her face with its aged but childish features is cruelly sharp, satirical as a Daumier print.*)

(*Music under: "Ave Maria."*)

(*Tom glances sheepishly but sullenly at her averted figure and slumps at the table. The coffee is scalding hot; he sips it and gasps and spits it back in the cup. At his gasp, Amanda catches her breath and half turns. Then catches herself and turns back to window.*)

(*Tom blows on his coffee, glancing sidewise at his mother. She clears her throat. Tom clears his. He starts to rise. Sinks back down again, scratches his*) *head, clears his throat again. Amanda coughs. Tom raises his cup in both hands to blow on it, his eyes staring over the rim of it at his mother for several moments. Then he slowly sets the cup down and awkwardly and hesitantly rises from the chair.*)

Tom (*hoarsely*): Mother. I—I apologize. Mother. (*Amanda draws a quick, shuddering breath. Her face works grotesquely. She breaks into childlike tears.*) I'm sorry for what I said, for everything that I said, I didn't mean it.

AMANDA (*sobbingly*): My devotion has made me a witch and so I make myself hateful to my children!

Tom: *No*, you *don't*.

AMANDA: I worry so much, don't sleep, it makes me nervous!

Tom (*gently*): I understand that.

AMANDA: I've had to put up a solitary battle all these years. But you're my right-hand bower! Don't fall down, don't fail!

Tom (*gently*): I try, Mother.

AMANDA (*with great enthusiasm*): Try and you will SUCCEED! (*The notion makes her breathless.*) Why, you—you're just *full* of natural endowments! Both of my children—they're *unusual* children! Don't you think I know it? I'm so—*proud*! Happy and—feel I've—so much to be thankful for but—Promise me one thing, son!

Tom: What, Mother?

AMANDA: Promise, son, you'll—never be a drunkard!

Tom (*turns to her grinning*): I will never be a drunkard, Mother.

AMANDA: That's what frightened me so, that you'd be drinking! Eat a bowl of Purina!

Tom: Just coffee, Mother.

AMANDA: Shredded wheat biscuit?

Tom: No, no, Mother, just coffee.

AMANDA: You can't put in a day's work on an empty stomach. You've got ten minutes—don't gulp! Drinking too-hot liquids makes cancer of the stomach. . . . Put cream in.

Tom: No, thank you.

AMANDA: To cool it.

Tom: No! No, thank you, I want it black.

AMANDA: I know, but it's not good for you. We have to do all that we can to build ourselves up. In these trying times we live in, all that we have to cling to is—each other. . . . That's why it's so important to—Tom, I—I sent out your sister so I could discuss something with you. If you hadn't spoken I would have spoken to you. (*Sits down.*)

Tom (*gently*): What is it, Mother, that you want to discuss?

AMANDA: *Laura!*

(*Tom puts his cup down slowly.*)
  (*Legend on screen: "Laura."*)
  (*Music: "The Glass Menagerie."*)

TOM: —Oh.—Laura . . .

AMANDA (*touching his sleeve*): You know how Laura is. So quiet but—still water runs deep! She notices things and I think she—broods about them. (*Tom looks up.*) A few days ago I came in and she was crying.

TOM: What about?

AMANDA: You.

TOM: Me?

AMANDA: She has an idea that you're not happy here.

TOM: What gave her that idea?

AMANDA: What gives her any idea? However, you do act strangely. I—I'm not criticizing, understand *that!* I know your ambitions do not lie in the warehouse, that like everybody in the whole wide world—you've had to—make sacrifices, but—Tom—Tom—life's not easy, it calls for—Spartan endurance! There's so many things in my heart that I cannot describe to you! I've never told you but I—*loved your father.* . . .

TOM (*gently*): I know that, Mother.

AMANDA: And you—when I see you taking after his ways! Staying out late—and—well, you *had* been drinking the night you were in that—terrifying condition! Laura says that you hate the apartment and that you go out nights to get away from it! Is that true, Tom?

TOM: No. You say there's so much in your heart that you can't describe to me. That's true of me, too. There's so much in my heart that I can't describe to *you!* So let's respect each other's—

AMANDA: But, why—*why*, Tom—are you always so *restless*? Where do you go to, nights?

TOM: I—go to the movies.

AMANDA: Why do you go to the movies so much, Tom?

TOM: I go to the movies because—I like adventure. Adventure is something I don't have much of at work, so I go to the movies.

AMANDA: But, Tom, you go to the movies *entirely* too *much!*

TOM: I like a lot of adventure.

(*Amanda looks baffled, then hurt. As the familiar inquisition resumes he becomes hard and impatient again. Amanda slips back into her querulous attitude toward him.*)
  (*Image on screen: sailing vessel with Jolly Roger.°*)

Jolly Roger: A black flag with a white skull and crossbones formerly used by pirates.

AMANDA: Most young men find adventure in their careers.

TOM: Then most young men are not employed in a warehouse.

AMANDA: The world is full of young men employed in warehouses and offices and factories.

TOM: Do all of them find adventure in their careers?

AMANDA: They do or they do without it! Not everybody has a craze for adventure.

TOM: Man is by instinct a lover, a hunter, a fighter, and none of those instincts are given much play at the warehouse!

AMANDA: Man is by instinct! Don't quote instinct to me! Instinct is something that people have got away from! It belongs to animals! Christian adults don't want it!

TOM: What do Christian adults want, then, Mother?

AMANDA: Superior things! Things of the mind and the spirit! Only animals have to satisfy instincts! Surely your aims are somewhat higher than theirs! Than monkeys — pigs —

TOM: I reckon they're not.

AMANDA: You're joking. However, that isn't what I wanted to discuss.

TOM (*rising*): I haven't much time.

AMANDA (*pushing his shoulders*): Sit down.

TOM: You want me to punch in red at the warehouse, Mother?

AMANDA: You have five minutes. I want to talk about Laura.

(*Legend: "Plans and Provisions."*)

TOM: All right! What about Laura?

AMANDA: We have to be making plans and provisions for her. She's older than you, two years, and nothing has happened. She just drifts along doing nothing. It frightens me terribly how she just drifts along.

TOM: I guess she's the type that people call home girls.

AMANDA: There's no such type, and if there is, it's a pity! That is unless the home is hers, with a husband!

TOM: What?

AMANDA: Oh, I can see the handwriting on the wall as plain as I see the nose in front of my face! It's terrifying! More and more you remind me of your father! He was out all hours without explanation—Then *left!* *Good-bye!* And me with a bag to hold. I saw that letter you got from the Merchant Marine. I know what you're dreaming of. I'm not standing here blindfolded. Very well, then. Then *do* it! But not till there's somebody to take your place.

TOM: What do you mean?

AMANDA: I mean that as soon as Laura has got somebody to take care of her, married, a home of her own, independent—why, then you'll be free to go wherever you please, on land, on sea, whichever way the wind blows you! But until that time you've got to look out for your sister. I don't say me because I'm old and don't matter! I say for your sister because she's young and dependent. I put her in business college—a dismal failure! Frightened her so it made her sick to her stomach. I took her over to the Young People's League at the church. Another fiasco. She spoke to nobody, nobody spoke to her. Now all she does is fool with those pieces of glass and play those worn-out records. What kind of a life is that for a girl to lead!

Tom: What can I do about it?

Amanda: Overcome selfishness! Self, self, self is all that you ever think of! (*Tom springs up and crosses to get his coat. It is ugly and bulky. He pulls on a cap with earmuffs.*) Where is your muffler? Put your wool muffler on! (*He snatches it angrily from the closet and tosses it around his neck and pulls both ends tight.*) Tom! I haven't said what I had in mind to ask you.

Tom: I'm too late to—

Amanda (*Catching his arms—very importunately. Then shyly*): Down at the warehouse, aren't there some—nice young men?

Tom: No!

Amanda: There *must* be—*some* . . .

Tom: Mother—

(*Gesture.*)

Amanda: Find out one that's clean-living—doesn't drink and—ask him out for sister!

Tom: What?

Amanda: For *sister!* To *meet!* Get *acquainted!*

Tom (*stamping to door*): Oh, my *go-osh!*

Amanda: Will you? (*He opens door. Imploringly.*) Will you? (*He starts down.*) Will you? *Will* you, dear?

Tom (*calling back*): YES!

(*Amanda closes the door hesitantly and with a troubled but faintly hopeful expression.*)

(*Screen image: glamor magazine cover.*)

(*Spot° Amanda at phone.*)

Amanda: Ella Cartwright? This is Amanda Wingfield! How are you, honey? How is that kidney condition? (*Count five.*) Horrors! (*Count five.*) You're a Christian martyr, yes, honey, that's what you are, a Christian martyr! Well, I just happened to notice in my little red book

___

Spot: Spotlight.

that your subscription to the *Companion* has just run out! I knew that you wouldn't want to miss out on the wonderful serial starting in this new issue. It's by Bessie Mae Hopper, the first thing she's written since *Honeymoon for Three*. Wasn't that a strange and interesting story? Well, this one is even lovelier, I believe. It has a sophisticated society background. It's all about the horsey set on Long Island!

(*Fade out.*)

SCENE 5

(*Legend on screen "Annunciation." Fade with music.*)

(*It is early dusk of a spring evening. Supper has just been finished in the Wingfield apartment. Amanda and Laura in light colored dresses are removing dishes from the table, in the upstage area, which is shadowy, their movements formalized almost as a dance or ritual, their moving forms as pale and silent as moths.*)

(*Tom, in white shirt and trousers, rises from the table and crosses toward the fire escape.*)

AMANDA (*as he passes her*): Son, will you do me a favor?

TOM: What?

AMANDA: Comb your hair! You look so pretty when your hair is combed! (*Tom slouches on sofa with evening paper. Enormous caption "Franco Triumphs."*) There is only one respect in which I would like you to emulate your father.

TOM: What respect is that?

AMANDA: The care he always took of his appearance. He never allowed himself to look untidy. (*He throws down the paper and crosses to fire escape.*) Where are you going?

TOM: I'm going out to smoke.

AMANDA: You smoke too much. A pack a day at fifteen cents a pack. How much would that amount to in a month? Thirty times fifteen is how much, Tom? Figure it out and you will be astounded at what you could save. Enough to give you a night school course in accounting at Washington U! Just think what a wonderful thing that would be for you, son!

(*Tom is unmoved by the thought.*)

TOM: I'd rather smoke. (*He steps out on landing, letting the screen door slam.*)

AMANDA (*sharply*): I know! That's the tragedy of it. . . . (*Alone, she turns to look at her husband's picture.*)

(*Dance music: "All the World is Waiting for the Sunrise!"*)

TOM (*to the audience*): Across the alley from us was the Paradise Dance Hall. On evenings in spring the windows and doors were open and the music came outdoors. Sometimes the lights were turned out except for a large glass sphere that hung from the ceiling. It would turn slowly about and filter the dusk with delicate rainbow colors. Then the orchestra played a waltz or a tango, something that had a slow and sensuous rhythm. Couples would come outside, to the relative privacy of the alley. You could see them kissing behind ash-pits and telephone poles. This was the compensation for lives that passed like mine, without any change or adventure. Adventure and change were imminent in this year. They were waiting around the corner for all these kids. Suspended in the mist over Berchtesgaden, caught in the folds of Chamberlain's umbrella—In Spain there was Guernica!° But here there was only hot swing music and liquor, dance halls, bars, and movies, and sex that hung in the gloom like a chandelier and flooded the world with brief, deceptive rainbows. . . . All the world was waiting for bombardments!

(*Amanda turns from the picture and comes outside.*)

AMANDA (*sighing*): A fire escape landing's a poor excuse for a porch. (*She spreads a newspaper on a step and sits down, gracefully and demurely as if she were settling into a swing on a Mississippi veranda.*) What are you looking at?
TOM: The moon.
AMANDA: Is there a moon this evening?
TOM: It's rising over Garfinkel's Delicatessen.
AMANDA: So it is! A little silver slipper of a moon. Have you made a wish on it yet?
TOM: Um-hum.
AMANDA: What did you wish for?
TOM: That's a secret.
AMANDA: A secret, huh? Well, I won't tell mine either. I will be just as mysterious as you.
TOM: I bet I can guess what yours is.
AMANDA: Is my head so transparent?

Berchtesgaden . . . Chamberlain's . . . Guernica: All World War II references. Berchtesgaden was Hitler's summer home. Neville Chamberlain was a British prime minister who tried to avoid war with Hitler through the Munich Pact. Guernica was a Spanish town bombed by Germany during the Spanish Civil War.

Tom: You're not a sphinx.

Amanda: No, I don't have secrets. I'll tell you what I wished for on the moon. Success and happiness for my precious children! I wish for that whenever there's a moon, and when there isn't a moon, I wish for it, too.

Tom: I thought perhaps you wished for a gentleman caller.

Amanda: Why do you say that?

Tom: Don't you remember asking me to fetch one?

Amanda: I remember suggesting that it would be nice for your sister if you brought home some nice young man from the warehouse. I think I've made that suggestion more than once.

Tom: Yes, you have made it repeatedly.

Amanda: Well?

Tom: We are going to have one.

Amanda: *What?*

Tom: A gentleman caller!

(*The annunciation is celebrated with music.*)
   (*Amanda rises.*)
   (*Image on screen: caller with bouquet.*)

Amanda: You mean you have asked some nice young man to come over?

Tom: Yep. I've asked him to dinner.

Amanda: You really did?

Tom: I did!

Amanda: You did, and did he —*accept*?

Tom: He did!

Amanda: Well, well —well, well! That's —lovely!

Tom: I thought that you would be pleased.

Amanda: It's definite, then?

Tom: Very definite.

Amanda: Soon?

Tom: Very soon.

Amanda: For heaven's sake, stop putting on and tell me some things, will you?

Tom: What things do you want me to tell you?

Amanda: *Naturally* I would like to know when he's *coming!*

Tom: He's coming tomorrow.

Amanda: *Tomorrow?*

Tom: Yep. Tomorrow.

Amanda: But, Tom!

Tom: Yes, Mother?

Amanda: Tomorrow gives me no time!

Tom: Time for what?

AMANDA: Preparations! Why didn't you phone me at once, as soon as you asked him, the minute that he accepted? Then, don't you see, I could have been getting ready!

Tom: You don't have to make any fuss.

AMANDA: Oh, Tom, Tom, Tom, of course I have to make a fuss! I want things nice, not sloppy! Not thrown together. I'll certainly have to do some fast thinking, won't I?

Tom: I don't see why you have to think at all.

AMANDA: You just don't know. We can't have a gentleman caller in a pigsty! All my wedding silver has to be polished, the monogrammed table linen ought to be laundered! The windows have to be washed and fresh curtains put up. And how about clothes? We have to *wear* something, don't we?

Tom: Mother, this boy is no one to make a fuss over!

AMANDA: Do you realize he's the first young man we've introduced to your sister? It's terrible, dreadful, disgraceful that poor little sister has never received a single gentleman caller! Tom, come inside! (*She opens the screen door.*)

Tom: What for?

AMANDA: I want to ask you some things.

Tom: If you're going to make such a fuss, I'll call it off, I'll tell him not to come.

AMANDA: You certainly won't do anything of the kind. Nothing offends people worse than broken engagements. It simply means I'll have to work like a Turk! We won't be brilliant, but we'll pass inspection. Come on inside. (*Tom follows, groaning.*) Sit down.

Tom: Any particular place you would like me to sit?

AMANDA: Thank heavens I've got that new sofa! I'm also making payments on a floor lamp I'll have sent out! And put the chintz covers on, they'll brighten things up! Of course I'd hoped to have these walls repapered. . . . What is the young man's name?

Tom: His name is O'Connor.

AMANDA: That, of course, means fish—tomorrow is Friday!° I'll have that salmon loaf—with Durkee's dressing! What does he do? He works at the warehouse?

Tom: Of course! How else would I—

AMANDA: Tom, he—doesn't drink?

Tom: Why do you ask me that?

---

fish . . . Friday: Reference to the religious doctrine that prohibited Catholics from eating meat on Fridays.

AMANDA: Your father *did!*

TOM: Don't get started on that!

AMANDA: He *does* drink, then?

TOM: Not that I know of!

AMANDA: Make sure, be certain! The last thing I want for my daughter's a boy who drinks!

TOM: Aren't you being a little premature? Mr. O'Connor has not yet appeared on the scene!

AMANDA: But will tomorrow. To meet your sister, and what do I know about his character? Nothing! Old maids are better off than wives of drunkards!

TOM: Oh, my God!

AMANDA: Be still!

TOM (*leaning forward to whisper*): Lots of fellows meet girls whom they don't marry!

AMANDA: Oh, talk sensibly, Tom — and don't be sarcastic! (*She has gotten a hairbrush.*)

TOM: What are you doing?

AMANDA: I'm brushing that cowlick down! What is this young man's position at the warehouse?

TOM (*submitting grimly to the brush and the interrogation*): This young man's position is that of a shipping clerk, Mother.

AMANDA: Sounds to me like a fairly responsible job, the sort of a job *you* would be in if you just had more *get-up*. What is his salary? Have you got any idea.

TOM: I would judge it to be approximately eighty-five dollars a month.

AMANDA: Well — not princely, but —

TOM: Twenty more than I make.

AMANDA: Yes, how well I know! But for a family man, eighty-five dollars a month is not much more than you can just get by on. . . .

TOM: Yes, but Mr. O'Connor is not a family man.

AMANDA: He might be, mightn't he? Some time in the future?

TOM: I see. Plans and provisions.

AMANDA: You are the only young man that I know of who ignores the fact that the future becomes the present, the present the past, and the past turns into everlasting regret if you don't plan for it!

TOM: I will think that over and see what I can make of it.

AMANDA: Don't be supercilious with your mother! Tell me some more about this — what do you call him?

TOM: James D. O'Connor. The D. is for Delaney.

AMANDA: Irish on *both* sides! *Gracious!* And doesn't drink?

TOM: Shall I call him up and ask him right this minute?

AMANDA: The only way to find out about those things is to make discreet inquiries at the proper moment. When I was a girl in Blue Mountain and it was suspected that a young man drank, the girl whose attentions he had been receiving, if any girl *was,* would sometimes speak to the minister of his church, or rather her father would if her father was living, and sort of feel him out on the young man's character. That is the way such things are discreetly handled to keep a young woman from making a tragic mistake!

TOM: Then how did you happen to make a tragic mistake?

AMANDA: That innocent look of your father's had everyone fooled! He *smiled*—the world was *enchanted!* No girl can do worse than put herself at the mercy of a handsome appearance! I hope that Mr. O'Connor is not too good-looking.

TOM: No, he's not too good-looking. He's covered with freckles and hasn't too much of a nose.

AMANDA: He's not right-down homely, though?

TOM: Not right-down homely. Just medium homely, I'd say.

AMANDA: Character's what to look for in a man.

TOM: That's what I've always said, Mother.

AMANDA: You've never said anything of the kind and I suspect you would never give it a thought.

TOM: Don't be suspicious of me.

AMANDA: At least I hope he's the type that's up and coming.

TOM: I think he really goes in for self-improvement.

AMANDA: What reason have you to think so?

TOM: He goes to night school.

AMANDA (*beaming*): Splendid! What does he do, I mean study?

TOM: Radio engineering and public speaking!

AMANDA: Then he has visions of being advanced in the world! Any young man who studies public speaking is aiming to have an executive job some day! And radio engineering? A thing for the future! Both of these facts are very illuminating. Those are the sort of things that a mother should know concerning any young man who comes to call on her daughter. Seriously or—not.

TOM: One little warning. He doesn't know about Laura. I didn't let on that we had dark ulterior motives. I just said, why don't you come have dinner with us? He said okay and that was the whole conversation.

AMANDA: I bet it was! You're eloquent as an oyster. However, he'll know about Laura when he gets here. When he sees how lovely and sweet and pretty she is, he'll thank his lucky stars he was asked to dinner.

TOM: Mother, you mustn't expect too much of Laura.

AMANDA: What do you mean?

TOM: Laura seems all those things to you and me because she's ours and we love her. We don't even notice she's crippled anymore.

AMANDA: Don't say crippled! You know that I never allow that word to be used!

TOM: But face facts, Mother. She is and—that's not all—

AMANDA: What do you mean not all?

TOM: Laura is very different from other girls.

AMANDA: I think the difference is all to her advantage.

TOM: Not quite all—in the eyes of others—strangers—she's terribly shy and lives in a world of her own and those things make her seem a little peculiar to people outside the house.

AMANDA: Don't say peculiar.

TOM: Face the facts. She is.

(*The dance-hall music changes to a tango that has a minor and somewhat ominous tone.*)

AMANDA: In what way is she peculiar—may I ask?

TOM (*gently*): She lives in a world of her own—a world of—little glass ornaments, Mother. . . . (*Gets up. Amanda remains holding brush, looking at him, troubled.*) She plays old phonograph records and—that's about all—(*He glances at himself in the mirror and crosses to door.*)

AMANDA (*sharply*): Where are you going?

TOM: I'm going to the movies. (*Out screen door.*)

AMANDA: Not to the movies, every night to the movies! (*Follows quickly to screen door.*) I don't believe you always go to the movies! (*He is gone. Amanda looks worriedly after him for a moment. Then vitality and optimism return and she turns from the door. Crossing to portieres.*) Laura! Laura! (*Laura answers from kitchenette.*)

LAURA: Yes, Mother.

AMANDA: Let those dishes go and come in front! (*Laura appears with dish towel. Gaily.*) Laura, come here and make a wish on the moon!

LAURA (*entering*): Moon—moon?

AMANDA: A little silver slipper of a moon. Look over your left shoulder, Laura, and make a wish! (*Laura looks faintly puzzled as if called out of sleep. Amanda seizes her shoulders and turns her at an angle by the door.*) Now! Now, darling, *wish!*

LAURA: What shall I wish for, Mother?

AMANDA (*her voice trembling and her eyes suddenly filling with tears*): Happiness! Good Fortune!

(*The violin rises and the stage dims out.*)

SCENE 6

(*Image: high school hero.*)

TOM: And so the following evening I brought Jim home to dinner. I had known Jim slightly in high school. In high school Jim was a hero. He had tremendous Irish good nature and vitality with the scrubbed and polished look of white chinaware. He seemed to move in a continual spotlight. He was a star in basketball, captain of the debating club, president of the senior class and the glee club and he sang the male lead in the annual light operas. He was always running or bounding, never just walking. He seemed always at the point of defeating the law of gravity. He was shooting with such velocity through his adolescence that you would logically expect him to arrive at nothing short of the White House by the time he was thirty. But Jim apparently ran into more interference after his graduation from Soldan. His speed had definitely slowed. Six years after he left high school he was holding a job that wasn't much better than mine.

(*Image: clerk.*)

He was the only one at the warehouse with whom I was on friendly terms. I was valuable to him as someone who could remember his former glory, who had seen him win basketball games and the silver cup in debating. He knew of my secret practice of retiring to a cabinet of the washroom to work on poems when business was slack in the warehouse. He called me Shakespeare. And while the other boys in the warehouse regarded me with suspicious hostility, Jim took a humorous attitude toward me. Gradually his attitude affected the others, their hostility wore off and they also began to smile at me as people smile at an oddly fashioned dog who trots across their path at some distance.

I knew that Jim and Laura had known each other at Soldan, and I had heard Laura speak admiringly of his voice. I didn't know if Jim remembered her or not. In high school Laura had been as unobtrusive as Jim had been astonishing. If he did remember Laura, it was not as my sister, for when I asked him to dinner, he grinned and said, "You know, Shakespeare, I never thought of you as having folks!"

He was about to discover that I did. . . .

(*Light up stage.*)
(*Legend on screen: "The Accent of a Coming Foot."*)
(*Friday evening. It is about five o'clock of a late spring evening which comes "scattering poems in the sky."*)
(*A delicate lemony light is in the Wingfield apartment.*)

(*Amanda has worked like a Turk in preparation for the gentleman caller. The results are astonishing. The new floor lamp with its rose-silk shade is in place, a colored paper lantern conceals the broken light fixture in the ceiling, new billowing white curtains are at the windows, chintz covers are on chairs and sofa, a pair of new sofa pillows make their initial appearance.*)

(*Open boxes and tissue paper are scattered on the floor.*)

(*Laura stands in the middle with lifted arms while Amanda crouches before her, adjusting the hem of the new dress, devout and ritualistic. The dress is colored and designed by memory. The arrangement of Laura's hair is changed; it is softer and more becoming. A fragile, unearthly prettiness has come out in Laura: she is like a piece of translucent glass touched by light, given a momentary radiance, not actual, not lasting.*)

AMANDA (*impatiently*): Why are you trembling?

LAURA: Mother, you've made me so nervous!

AMANDA: How have I made you nervous?

LAURA: By all this fuss! You make it seem so important!

AMANDA: I don't understand you, Laura. You couldn't be satisfied with just sitting home, and yet whenever I try to arrange something for you, you seem to resist it. (*She gets up.*) Now take a look at yourself. No, wait! Wait just a moment—I have an idea!

LAURA: What is it now?

(*Amanda produces two powder puffs which she wraps in handkerchiefs and stuffs in Laura's bosom.*)

LAURA: Mother, what are you doing?

AMANDA: They call them "Gay Deceivers"!

LAURA: I won't wear them!

AMANDA: You will!

LAURA: Why should I?

AMANDA: Because, to be painfully honest, your chest is flat.

LAURA: You make it seem like we were setting a trap.

AMANDA: All pretty girls are a trap, a pretty trap, and men expect them to be. (*Legend: "A Pretty Trap."*) Now look at yourself, young lady. This is the prettiest you will ever be! I've got to fix myself now! You're going to be surprised by your mother's appearance! (*She crosses through portieres, humming gaily.*)

(*Laura moves slowly to the long mirror and stares solemnly at herself.*)

(*A wind blows the white curtains inward in a slow, graceful motion and with a faint, sorrowful sighing.*)

AMANDA (*offstage*): It isn't dark enough yet. (*She turns slowly before the mirror with a troubled look.*)

(*Legend on screen: "This Is My Sister: Celebrate Her with Strings!" Music.*)

AMANDA (*laughing, off*): I'm going to show you something. I'm going to make a spectacular appearance!

LAURA: What is it, Mother?

AMANDA: Possess your soul in patience—you will see! Something I've resurrected from that old trunk! Styles haven't changed so terribly much after all. . . . (*She parts the portieres.*) Now just look at your mother! (*She wears a girlish frock of yellowed voile with a blue silk sash. She carries a bunch of jonquils—the legend of her youth is nearly revived. Feverishly.*) This is the dress in which I led the cotillion. Won the cakewalk twice at Sunset Hill, wore one spring to the Governor's ball in Jackson! See how I sashayed around the ballroom, Laura? (*She raises her skirt and does a mincing step around the room.*) I wore it on Sundays for my gentlemen callers! I had it on the day I met your father—I had malaria fever all that spring. The change of climate from East Tennessee to the Delta—weakened resistance—I had a little temperature all the time—not enough to be serious—just enough to make me restless and giddy! Invitations poured in—parties all over the Delta!—"Stay in bed," said Mother, "you have fever!"—but I just wouldn't.—I took quinine but kept on going, going!—Evenings, dances!—Afternoons, long, long rides! Picnics—lovely!—So lovely, that country in May,—All lacy with dogwood, literally flooded with jonquils!—That was the spring I had the craze for jonquils. Jonquils became an absolute obsession. Mother said, "Honey, there's no more room for jonquils." And still I kept on bringing in more jonquils. Whenever, wherever I saw them, I'd say, "Stop! Stop! I see jonquils!" I made the young men help me gather the jonquils! It was a joke, Amanda and her jonquils! Finally there were no more vases to hold them, every available space was filled with jonquils. No vases to hold them? All right, I'll hold them myself! And then I— (*She stops in front of the picture. Music.*) met your father! Malaria fever and jonquils and then—this—boy. . . . (*She switches on the rose-colored lamp.*) I hope they get here before it starts to rain. (*She crosses upstage and places the jonquils in bowl on table.*) I gave your brother a little extra change so he and Mr. O'Connor could take the service car home.

LAURA (*with altered look*): What did you say his name was?

AMANDA: O'Connor.

LAURA: What is his first name?

AMANDA: I don't remember. Oh, yes, I do. It was—Jim!

(*Laura sways slightly and catches hold of a chair.*)
   (*Legend on screen: "Not Jim!"*)

LAURA (*faintly*): Not—Jim!

AMANDA: Yes, that was it, it was Jim! I've never known a Jim that wasn't nice!

(*Music: ominous.*)

LAURA: Are you sure his name is Jim O'Connor?

AMANDA: Yes. Why?

LAURA: Is he the one that Tom used to know in high school?

AMANDA: He didn't say so. I think he just got to know him at the warehouse.

LAURA: There was a Jim O'Connor we both knew in high school—(*Then, with effort.*) If that is the one that Tom is bringing to dinner—you'll have to excuse me, I won't come to the table.

AMANDA: What sort of nonsense is this?

LAURA: You asked me once if I'd ever liked a boy. Don't you remember I showed you this boy's picture?

AMANDA: You mean the boy you showed me in the yearbook?

LAURA: Yes, that boy.

AMANDA: Laura, Laura, were you in love with that boy?

LAURA: I don't know, Mother. All I know is I couldn't sit at the table if it was him!

AMANDA: It won't be him! It isn't the least bit likely. But whether it is or not, you will come to the table. You will not be excused.

LAURA: I'll have to be, Mother.

AMANDA: I don't intend to humor your silliness, Laura. I've had too much from you and your brother, both! So just sit down and compose yourself till they come. Tom has forgotten his key so you'll have to let them in, when they arrive.

LAURA (*panicky*): Oh, Mother—*you* answer the door!

AMANDA (*lightly*): I'll be in the kitchen—busy!

LAURA: Oh, Mother, please answer the door, don't make me do it!

AMANDA (*crossing into kitchenette*): I've got to fix the dressing for the salmon. Fuss, fuss—silliness!—over a gentleman caller!

(*Door swings shut. Laura is left alone.*)

  (*Legend: "Terror!"*)

  (*She utters a low moan and turns off the lamp—sits stiffly on the edge of the sofa, knotting her fingers together.*)

  (*Legend on screen: "The Opening of a Door!"*)

  (*Tom and Jim appear on the fire escape steps and climb to landing. Hearing their approach, Laura rises with a panicky gesture. She retreats to the portieres.*)

  (*The doorbell. Laura catches her breath and touches her throat. Low drums.*)

AMANDA (*calling*): Laura, sweetheart! The door!

(*Laura stares at it without moving.*)

JIM: I think we just beat the rain.

Tom: Uh-huh. (*He rings again, nervously. Jim whistles and fishes for a cigarette.*)

Amanda (*very, very gaily*): Laura, that is your brother and Mr. O'Connor! Will you let them in, darling?

(*Laura crosses toward kitchenette door.*)

Laura (*breathlessly*): Mother—you go to the door!

(*Amanda steps out of kitchenette and stares furiously at Laura. She points imperiously at the door.*)

Laura: Please, please!

Amanda (*in a fierce whisper*): What is the matter with you, you silly thing?

Laura (*desperately*): Please, you answer it, *please!*

Amanda: I told you I wasn't going to humor you, Laura. Why have you chosen this moment to lose your mind?

Laura: Please, please, please, you go!

Amanda: You'll have to go to the door because I can't!

Laura (*despairingly*): I can't either!

Amanda: *Why?*

Laura: I'm *sick!*

Amanda: I'm sick, too—of your nonsense! Why can't you and your brother be normal people? Fantastic whims and behavior! (*Tom gives a long ring.*) Preposterous goings on! Can you give me one reason— (*Calls out lyrically.*) Coming! Just one second!—why should you be afraid to open a door? Now you answer it, Laura!

Laura: Oh, oh, oh . . . (*She returns through the portieres. Darts to the victrola and winds it frantically and turns it on.*)

Amanda: Laura Wingfield, you march right to that door!

Laura: Yes—yes, Mother!

(*A faraway, scratchy rendition of "Dardanella" softens the air and gives her strength to move through it. She slips to the door and draws it cautiously open.*)
(*Tom enters with the caller, Jim O'Connor.*)

Tom: Laura, this is Jim. Jim, this is my sister, Laura.

Jim (*stepping inside*): I didn't know that Shakespeare had a sister!

Laura (*retreating stiff and trembling from the door*): How—how do you do?

Jim (*heartily extending his hand*): Okay!

(*Laura touches it hesitantly with hers.*)

Jim: Your hand's *cold*, Laura!

Laura: Yes, well—I've been playing the victrola. . . .

Jim: Must have been playing classical music on it! You ought to play a little hot swing music to warm you up!

LAURA: Excuse me—I haven't finished playing the victrola. . . .

(*She turns awkwardly and hurries into the front room. She pauses a second by the victrola. Then catches her breath and darts through the portieres like a frightened deer.*)

JIM (*grinning*): What was the matter?

TOM: Oh—with Laura? Laura is—terribly shy.

JIM: Shy, huh? It's unusual to meet a shy girl nowadays. I don't believe you ever mentioned you had a sister.

TOM: Well, now you know. I have one. Here is the *Post Dispatch*. You want a piece of it?

JIM: Uh-huh.

TOM: What piece? The comics?

JIM: Sports! (*Glances at it.*) Ole Dizzy Dean is on his bad behavior.

TOM (*disinterest*): Yeah? (*Lights cigarette and crosses back to fire escape door.*)

JIM: Where are *you* going?

TOM: I'm going out on the terrace.

JIM (*goes after him*): You know, Shakespeare—I'm going to sell you a bill of goods!

TOM: What goods?

JIM: A course I'm taking.

TOM: Huh?

JIM: In public speaking! You and me, we're not the warehouse type.

TOM: Thanks—that's good news. But what has public speaking got to do with it?

JIM: It fits you for—executive positions!

TOM: Awww.

JIM: I tell you it's done a helluva lot for me.

(*Image: executive at desk.*)

TOM: In what respect?

JIM: In every! Ask yourself what is the difference between you an' me and men in the office down front? Brains?—No!—Ability?—No! Then what? Just one little thing—

TOM: What is that one little thing?

JIM: Primarily it amounts to—social poise! Being able to square up to people and hold your own on any social level!

AMANDA (*offstage*): Tom?

TOM: Yes, Mother?

AMANDA: Is that you and Mr. O'Connor?

TOM: Yes, Mother.

AMANDA: Well, you just make yourselves comfortable in there.

TOM: Yes, Mother.

AMANDA: Ask Mr. O'Connor if he would like to wash his hands.

JIM: Aw,—no—no—thank you—I took care of that at the warehouse. Tom—

TOM: Yes?

JIM: Mr. Mendoza was speaking to me about you.

TOM: Favorably?

JIM: What do you think?

TOM: Well—

JIM: You're going to be out of a job if you don't wake up.

TOM: I am waking up—

JIM: You show no signs.

TOM: The signs are interior.

(*Image on screen: the sailing vessel with Jolly Roger again.*)

TOM: I'm planning to change. (*He leans over the rail speaking with quiet exhilaration. The incandescent marquees and signs of the first-run movie houses light his face from across the alley. He looks like a voyager.*) I'm right at the point of committing myself to a future that doesn't include the warehouse and Mr. Mendoza or even a night school course in public speaking.

JIM: What are you gassing about?

TOM: I'm tired of the movies.

JIM: Movies!

TOM: Yes, movies! Look at them—(*A wave toward the marvels of Grand Avenue.*) All of those glamorous people—having adventures—hogging it all, gobbling the whole thing up! You know what happens? People go to the *movies* instead of *moving!* Hollywood characters are supposed to have all the adventures for everybody in America, while everybody in America sits in a dark room and watches them have them! Yes, until there's a war. That's when adventure becomes available to the masses! *Everyone's* dish, not only Gable's! Then the people in the dark room come out of the dark room to have some adventures themselves—Goody, goody!—It's our turn now, to go to the South Sea Island—to make a safari—to be exotic, far-off!—But I'm not patient. I don't want to wait till then. I'm tired of the *movies* and I am *about* to *move!*

JIM (*incredulously*): Move?

TOM: Yes.

JIM: When?

TOM: Soon!

JIM: Where? Where?

(Theme three music seems to answer the question, while Tom thinks it over. He searches among his pockets.)

TOM: I'm starting to boil inside. I know I seem dreamy, but inside— well, I'm boiling! Whenever I pick up a shoe, I shudder a little thinking how short life is and what I am doing!—Whatever that means. I know it doesn't mean shoes—except as something to wear on a traveler's feet! *(Finds paper.)* Look—

JIM: What?

TOM: I'm a member.

JIM *(reading):* The Union of Merchant Seamen.

TOM: I paid my dues this month, instead of the light bill.

JIM: You will regret it when they turn the lights off.

TOM: I won't be here.

JIM: How about your mother?

TOM: I'm like my father. The bastard son of a bastard! See how he grins? And he's been absent going on sixteen years!

JIM: You're just talking, you drip. How does your mother feel about it?

TOM: Shhh!—Here comes Mother! Mother is not acquainted with my plans!

AMANDA *(enters portieres):* Where are you all?

TOM: On the terrace, Mother.

(They start inside. She advances to them. Tom is distinctly shocked at her appearance. Even Jim blinks a little. He is making his first contact with girlish Southern vivacity and in spite of the night school course in public speaking is somewhat thrown off the beam by the unexpected outlay of social charm.)

(Certain responses are attempted by Jim but are swept aside by Amanda's gay laughter and chatter. Tom is embarrassed but after the first shock Jim reacts very warmly. Grins and chuckles, is altogether won over.)

(Image: Amanda as a girl.)

AMANDA *(coyly smiling, shaking her girlish ringlets):* Well, well, well, so this is Mr. O'Connor. Introductions entirely unnecessary. I've heard so much about you from my boy. I finally said to him, Tom—good gra- cious!—why don't you bring this paragon to supper? I'd like to meet this nice young man at the warehouse!—Instead of just hearing him sing your praises so much! I don't know why my son is so standoffish— that's not Southern behavior! Let's sit down and—I think we could stand a little more air in here! Tom, leave the door open. I felt a nice fresh breeze a moment ago. Where has it gone to? Mmm, so warm already! And not quite summer, even. We're going to burn up when summer really gets started. However, we're having—we're having a very light supper. I think light things are better fo' this time of year. The same as light clothes are. Light clothes an' light food are what warm weather calls fo'. You know our blood gets so thick during th' winter—it takes a while fo' us to *adjust* ou'selves!—when the season changes . . . It's come so quick this year. I wasn't prepared. All of a sudden—heavens! Already summer!—I ran to the trunk an' pulled out this light dress—Terribly old! Historical almost! But feels so good—so good an' co-ol, y'know. . . .

TOM: Mother—

AMANDA: Yes, honey?

TOM: How about—supper?

AMANDA: Honey, you go ask Sister if supper is ready! You know that Sister is in full charge of supper! Tell her you hungry boys are waiting for it. (*To Jim.*) Have you met Laura?

JIM: She—

AMANDA: Let you in? Oh, good, you've met already! It's rare for a girl as sweet an' pretty as Laura to be domestic! But Laura is, thank heavens, not only pretty but also very domestic. I'm not at all. I never was a bit. I never could make a thing but angel food cake. Well, in the South we had so many servants. Gone, gone, gone. All vestiges of gracious living! Gone completely! I wasn't prepared for what the future brought me. All of my gentlemen callers were sons of planters and so of course I assumed that I would be married to one and raise my family on a large piece of land with plenty of servants. But man proposes—and woman accepts the proposal!—To vary that old, old saying a little bit—I married no planter! I married a man who worked for the telephone company!—That gallantly smiling gentleman over there! (*Points to the picture.*) A telephone man who—fell in love with long distance!—Now he travels and I don't even know where!—But what am I going on for about my—tribulations! Tell me yours—I hope you don't have any! Tom?

TOM (*returning*): Yes, Mother?

AMANDA: Is supper nearly ready?

TOM: It looks to me like supper is on the table.

AMANDA: Let me look—(*She rises prettily and looks through portieres.*) Oh, lovely!—But where is Sister?

TOM: Laura is not feeling well and she says that she thinks she'd better not come to the table.

AMANDA: What?—Nonsense!—Laura? Oh, Laura!

LAURA (*offstage, faintly*): Yes, Mother.

AMANDA: You really must come to the table! We won't be seated until you come to the table! Come in, Mr. O'Connor. You sit over there, and I'll—Laura? Laura Wingfield! You're keeping us waiting, honey! We can't say grace until you come to the table!

(The back door is pushed weakly open and Laura comes in. She is obviously quite faint, her lips trembling, her eyes wide and staring. She moves unsteadily toward the table.)
   (Legend: "Terror!")
   (Outside a summer storm is coming abruptly. The white curtains billow inward at the windows and there is a sorrowful murmur and deep blue dusk.)
   (Laura suddenly stumbles—she catches at a chair with a faint moan.)

TOM: Laura!

AMANDA: Laura! *(There is a clap of thunder.) (Legend: "Ah!") (Despairingly.)*
   Why, Laura, you *are* sick, darling! Tom, help your sister into the living room, dear! Sit in the living room, Laura—rest on the sofa. Well! *(To the gentleman caller.)* Standing over the hot stove made her ill!—I told her that it was just too warm this evening, but—*(Tom comes back in. Laura is on the sofa.)* Is Laura all right now?

TOM: Yes.

AMANDA: What *is* that? Rain? A nice cool rain has come up! *(She gives the gentleman caller a frightened look.)* I think we may—have grace—now . . . *(Tom looks at her stupidly.)* Tom, honey—you say grace!

TOM: Oh . . . "For these and all thy mercies—" *(They bow their heads, Amanda stealing a nervous glance at Jim. In the living room Laura, stretched on the sofa, clenches her hand to her lips, to hold back a shuddering sob.)* God's Holy Name be praised—

(The scene dims out.)

SCENE 7

(A Souvenir)
   (Half an hour later. Dinner is just being finished in the upstage area which is concealed by the drawn portieres.)
   (As the curtain rises Laura is still huddled upon the sofa, her feet drawn under her, her head resting on a pale blue pillow, her eyes wide and mysteriously watchful. The new floor lamp with its shade of rose-colored silk gives a soft, becoming light to her face, bringing out the fragile, unearthly prettiness which usually escapes attention. There is a steady murmur of rain, but it is slackening and stops soon after the scene begins; the air outside becomes pale and luminous as the moon breaks out.)
   (A moment after the curtain rises, the lights in both rooms flicker and go out.)

JIM: Hey, there, Mr. Light Bulb!

(Amanda laughs nervously.)
   (Legend: "Suspension of a Public Service.")

AMANDA: Where was Moses when the lights went out? Ha-ha. Do you know the answer to that one, Mr. O'Connor?

JIM: No, Ma'am, what's the answer?

AMANDA: In the dark! (*Jim laughs appreciably.*) Everybody sit still. I'll light the candles. Isn't it lucky we have them on the table? Where's a match? Which of you gentlemen can provide a match?

JIM: Here.

AMANDA: Thank you, sir.

JIM: Not at all, Ma'am!

AMANDA: I guess the fuse has burnt out. Mr. O'Connor, can you tell a burnt-out fuse? I know I can't and Tom is a total loss when it comes to mechanics. (*Sound: getting up: voices recede a little to kitchenette.*) Oh, be careful you don't bump into something. We don't want our gentleman caller to break his neck. Now wouldn't that be a fine howdy-do?

JIM: Ha-ha! Where is the fuse box?

AMANDA: Right here next to the stove. Can you see anything?

JIM: Just a minute.

AMANDA: Isn't electricity a mysterious thing? Wasn't it Benjamin Franklin who tied a key to a kite? We live in such a mysterious universe, don't we? Some people say that science clears up all the mysteries for us. In my opinion it only creates more! Have you found it yet?

JIM: No, Ma'am. All these fuses look okay to me.

AMANDA: Tom!

TOM: Yes, Mother?

AMANDA: That light bill I gave you several days ago. The one I told you we got the notices about?

TOM: Oh. — Yeah.

(*Legend: "Ha!"*)

AMANDA: You didn't neglect to pay it by any chance?

TOM: Why, I —

AMANDA: Didn't! I might have known it!

JIM: Shakespeare probably wrote a poem on that light bill, Mrs. Wingfield.

AMANDA: I might have known better than to trust him with it! There's such a high price for negligence in this world!

JIM: Maybe the poem will win a ten-dollar prize.

AMANDA: We'll just have to spend the remainder of the evening in the nineteenth century, before Mr. Edison made the Mazda lamp!

JIM: Candlelight is my favorite kind of light.

AMANDA: That shows you're romantic! But that's no excuse for Tom. Well, we got through dinner. Very considerate of them to let us get through dinner before they plunged us into everlasting darkness, wasn't it, Mr. O'Connor?

JIM: Ha-ha!

AMANDA: Tom, as a penalty for your carelessness you can help me with the dishes.

JIM: Let me give you a hand.

AMANDA: Indeed you will not!

JIM: I ought to be good for something.

AMANDA: Good for something? (*Her tone is rhapsodic.*) You? Why, Mr. O'Connor, nobody, *nobody's* given me this much entertainment in years—as you have!

JIM: Aw, now, Mrs. Wingfield!

AMANDA: I'm not exaggerating, not one bit! But Sister is all by her lonesome. You go keep her company in the parlor! I'll give you this lovely old candelabrum that used to be on the altar at the church of the Heavenly Rest. It was melted a little out of shape when the church burnt down. Lightning struck it one spring. Gypsy Jones was holding a revival at the time and he intimated that the church was destroyed because the Episcopalians gave card parties.

JIM: Ha-ha.

AMANDA: And how about coaxing Sister to drink a little wine? I think it would be good for her! Can you carry both at once?

JIM: Sure. I'm Superman!

AMANDA: Now, Thomas, get into this apron!

(*The door of kitchenette swings closed on Amanda's gay laughter; the flickering light approaches the portieres.*)

(*Laura sits up nervously as he enters. Her speech at first is low and breathless from the almost intolerable strain of being alone with a stranger.*)

(*The legend: "I Don't Suppose You Remember Me at All!"*)

(*In her first speeches in this scene, before Jim's warmth overcomes her paralyzing shyness, Laura's voice is thin and breathless as though she has just run up a steep flight of stairs.*)

(*Jim's attitude is gently humorous. In playing this scene it should be stressed that while the incident is apparently unimportant, it is to Laura the climax of her secret life.*)

JIM: Hello, there, Laura.

LAURA (*faintly*): Hello. (*She clears her throat.*)

JIM: How are you feeling now? Better?

LAURA: Yes. Yes, thank you.

JIM: This is for you. A little dandelion wine. (*He extends it toward her with extravagant gallantry.*)

LAURA: Thank you.

JIM: Drink it—but don't get drunk! (*He laughs heartily. Laura takes the glass uncertainly; laughs shyly.*) Where shall I set the candles?

LAURA: Oh—oh, anywhere . . .

JIM: How about here on the floor? Any objections?

LAURA: No.

JIM: I'll spread a newspaper under to catch the drippings. I like to sit on the floor. Mind if I do?

LAURA: Oh, no.

JIM: Give me a pillow?

LAURA: What?

JIM: A pillow!

LAURA: Oh . . . (*Hands him one quickly.*)

JIM: How about you? Don't you like to sit on the floor?

LAURA: Oh—yes.

JIM: Why don't you, then?

LAURA: I—will.

JIM: Take a pillow! (*Laura does. Sits on the other side of the candelabrum. Jim crosses his legs and smiles engagingly at her.*) I can't hardly see you sitting way over there.

LAURA: I can—see you.

JIM: I know, but that's not fair, I'm in the limelight. (*Laura moves her pillow closer.*) Good! Now I can see you! Comfortable?

LAURA: Yes.

JIM: So am I. Comfortable as a cow. Will you have some gum?

LAURA: No, thank you.

JIM: I think that I will indulge, with your permission. (*Musingly unwraps it and holds it up.*) Think of the fortune made by the guy that invented the first piece of chewing gum. Amazing, huh? The Wrigley Building is one of the sights of Chicago.—I saw it summer before last when I went up to the Century of Progress. Did you take in the Century of Progress?

LAURA: No, I didn't.

JIM: Well, it was quite a wonderful exposition. What impressed me most was the Hall of Science. Gives you an idea of what the future will be in America, even more wonderful than the present time is! (*Pause. Smiling at her.*) Your brother tells me you're shy. Is that right, Laura?

LAURA: I—don't know.

JIM: I judge you to be an old-fashioned type of girl. Well, I think that's a pretty good type to be. Hope you don't think I'm being too personal— do you?

LAURA (*hastily, out of embarrassment*): I believe I *will* take a piece of gum, if you—don't mind. (*Clearing her throat.*) Mr. O'Connor, have you— kept up with your singing?

JIM: Singing? Me?

LAURA: Yes. I remember what a beautiful voice you had.

JIM: When did you hear me sing?

(*Voice offstage in the pause.*)

VOICE (*offstage*): O blow, ye winds, heigh-ho,
  A-roving I will go!
    I'm off to my love
    With a boxing glove—
  Ten thousand miles away!

JIM: You say you've heard me sing?

LAURA: Oh, yes! Yes, very often . . . I—don't suppose you remember me—
at all?

JIM (*smiling doubtfully*): You know I have an idea I've seen you before. I
had that idea soon as you opened the door. It seemed almost like I was
about to remember your name. But the name that I started to call
you—wasn't a name! And so I stopped myself before I said it.

LAURA: Wasn't it—Blue Roses?

JIM (*Springs up. Grinning.*): Blue Roses! My gosh, yes—Blue Roses! That's
what I had on my tongue when you opened the door! Isn't it funny what
tricks your memory plays? I didn't connect you with the high school
somehow or other. But that's where it was; it was high school. I didn't
even know you were Shakespeare's sister! Gosh, I'm sorry.

LAURA: I didn't expect you to. You—barely knew me!

JIM: But we did have a speaking acquaintance, huh?

LAURA: Yes, we—spoke to each other.

JIM: When did you recognize me?

LAURA: Oh, right away!

JIM: Soon as I came in the door?

LAURA: When I heard your name I thought it was probably you. I knew
that Tom used to know you a little in high school. So when you came
in the door—Well, then I was—sure.

JIM: Why didn't you *say* something, then?

LAURA (*breathlessly*): I didn't know what to say, I was—too surprised!

JIM: For goodness' sakes! You know, this sure is funny!

LAURA: Yes! Yes, isn't it, though . . .

JIM: Didn't we have a class in something together?

LAURA: Yes, we did.

JIM: What class was that?

LAURA: It was—singing—Chorus!

JIM: Aw!

LAURA: I sat across the aisle from you in the Aud.

JIM: Aw.

LAURA: Mondays, Wednesdays, and Fridays.

JIM: Now I remember—you always came in late.

LAURA: Yes, it was so hard for me, getting upstairs. I had that brace on my leg—it clumped so loud!

JIM: I never heard any clumping.

LAURA (*wincing at the recollection*): To me it sounded like—thunder!

JIM: Well, well, well, I never even noticed.

LAURA: And everybody was seated before I came in. I had to walk in front of all those people. My seat was in the back row. I had to go clumping all the way up the aisle with everyone watching!

JIM: You shouldn't have been self-conscious.

LAURA: I know, but I was. It was always such a relief when the singing started.

JIM: Aw, yes, I've placed you now! I used to call you Blue Roses. How was it that I got started calling you that?

LAURA: I was out of school a little while with pleurosis. When I came back you asked me what was the matter. I said I had pleurosis—you thought I said Blue Roses. That's what you always called me after that!

JIM: I hope you didn't mind.

LAURA: Oh, no—I liked it. You see, I wasn't acquainted with many—people . . .

JIM: As I remember you sort of stuck by yourself.

LAURA: I—I—never had much luck at—making friends.

JIM: I don't see why you wouldn't.

LAURA: Well, I—started out badly.

JIM: You mean being—

LAURA: Yes, it sort of—stood between me—

JIM: You shouldn't have let it!

LAURA: I know, but it did, and—

JIM: You were shy with people!

LAURA: I tried not to be but never could—

JIM: Overcome it?

LAURA: No, I—I never could!

JIM: I guess being shy is something you have to work out of kind of gradually.

LAURA (*sorrowfully*): Yes—I guess it—

JIM: Takes time!

LAURA: Yes—

JIM: People are not so dreadful when you know them. That's what you have to remember! And everybody has problems, not just you, but practically everybody has got some problems. You think of yourself as having the only problems, as being the only one who is disappointed. But just look around you and you will see lots of people as disappointed as you are. For instance, I hoped when I was going to high school that I would be further along at this time, six years later, than I am now—You remember that wonderful write-up I had in *The Torch*?

LAURA: Yes! (*She rises and crosses to table.*)

JIM: It said I was bound to succeed in anything I went into! (*Laura returns with the annual.*) Holy Jeez! *The Torch*! (*He accepts it reverently. They smile across it with mutual wonder. Laura crouches beside him and they begin to turn through it. Laura's shyness is dissolving in his warmth.*)

LAURA: Here you are in *Pirates of Penzance*!

JIM (*wistfully*): I sang the baritone lead in that operetta.

LAURA (*rapidly*): So—*beautifully*!

JIM (*protesting*): Aw—

LAURA: Yes, yes—beautifully—beautifully!

JIM: You heard me?

LAURA: All three times!

JIM: No!

LAURA: Yes!

JIM: All three performances?

LAURA (*looking down*): Yes.

JIM: Why?

LAURA: I—wanted to ask you to—autograph my program.

JIM: Why didn't you ask me to?

LAURA: You were always surrounded by your own friends so much that I never had a chance to.

JIM: You should have just—

LAURA: Well, I—thought you might think I was—

JIM: Thought I might think you was—what?

LAURA: Oh—

JIM (*with reflective relish*): I was beleaguered by females in those days.

LAURA: You were terribly popular!

JIM: Yeah—

LAURA: You had such a—friendly way—

JIM: I was spoiled in high school.

LAURA: Everybody—liked you!

JIM: Including you?

LAURA: I—yes, I—I did, too—(*She gently closes the book in her lap.*)

JIM: Well, well, well!—Give me that program, Laura. (*She hands it to him. He signs it with a flourish.*) There you are—better late than never!

LAURA: Oh, I—what a—surprise!

JIM: My signature isn't worth very much right now. But some day—maybe—it will increase in value! Being disappointed is one thing and being discouraged is something else. I am disappointed but I am not discouraged. I'm twenty-three years old. How old are you?

LAURA: I'll be twenty-four in June.

JIM: That's not old age!

LAURA: No, but—

JIM: You finished high school?

LAURA (*with difficulty*): I didn't go back.

JIM: You mean you dropped out?

LAURA: I made bad grades in my final examinations. (*She rises and replaces the book and the program. Her voice strained.*) How is—Emily Meisenbach getting along?

JIM: Oh, that kraut-head!

LAURA: Why do you call her that?

JIM: That's what she was.

LAURA: You're not still—going with her?

JIM: I never see her.

LAURA: It said in the Personal Section that you were—engaged!

JIM: I know, but I wasn't impressed by that—propaganda!

LAURA: It wasn't—the truth?

JIM: Only in Emily's optimistic opinion!

LAURA: Oh—

(*Legend: "What Have You Done since High School?"*)

(*Jim lights a cigarette and leans indolently back on his elbows smiling at Laura with a warmth and charm which lights her inwardly with altar candles. She remains by the table and turns in her hands a piece of glass to cover her tumult.*)

JIM (*after several reflective puffs on a cigarette*): What have you done since high school? (*She seems not to hear him.*) Huh? (*Laura looks up.*) I said what have you done since high school, Laura?

LAURA: Nothing much.

JIM: You must have been doing something these six long years.

LAURA: Yes.

JIM: Well, then, such as what?

LAURA: I took a business course at business college—

JIM: How did that work out?

LAURA: Well, not very—well—I had to drop out, it gave me—indigestion—

(*Jim laughs gently.*)

JIM: What are you doing now?

LAURA: I don't do anything—much. Oh, please don't think I sit around doing nothing! My glass collection takes up a good deal of my time. Glass is something you have to take good care of.

JIM: What did you say—about glass?

LAURA: Collection I said—I have one—(*She clears her throat and turns away again, acutely shy.*)

JIM (*abruptly*): You know what I judge to be the trouble with you? Inferiority complex! Know what that is? That's what they call it when someone low-rates himself! I understand it because I had it, too. Although my case was not so aggravated as yours seems to be. I had it until I took up public speaking, developed my voice, and learned that I had an aptitude for science. Before that time I never thought of myself as being outstanding in any way whatsoever! Now I've never made a regular study of it, but I have a friend who says I can analyze people better than doctors that make a profession of it. I don't claim that to be necessarily true, but I can sure guess a person's psychology, Laura! (*Takes out his gum.*) Excuse me, Laura. I always take it out when the flavor is gone. I'll use this scrap of paper to wrap it in. I know how it is to get it stuck on a shoe. Yep—that's what I judge to be your principal trouble. A lack of confidence in yourself as a person. You don't have the proper amount of faith in yourself. I'm basing that fact on a number of your remarks and also on certain observations I've made. For instance that clumping you thought was so awful in high school. You say that you even dreaded to walk into class. You see what you did? You dropped out of school, you gave up an education because of a clump, which as far as I know was practically nonexistent! A little physical defect is what you have. Hardly noticeable even! Magnified thousands of times by imagination! You know what my strong advice to you is? Think of yourself as *superior* in some way!

LAURA: In what way would I think?

JIM: Why, man alive, Laura! Just look about you a little. What do you see? A world full of common people! All of 'em born and all of 'em going to die! Which of them has one-tenth of your good points! Or mine! Or anyone else's, as far as that goes—Gosh! Everybody excels in some one thing. Some in many! (*Unconsciously glances at himself in the mirror.*) All you've got to do is discover in what! Take me, for instance. (*He adjusts his tie at the mirror.*) My interest happens to lie in electrodynamics. I'm taking a course in radio engineering at night school, Laura, on top of a fairly responsible job at the warehouse. I'm taking that course and studying public speaking.

LAURA: Ohhhh.

JIM: Because I believe in the future of television! (*Turning back to her.*) I wish to be ready to go up right along with it. Therefore I'm planning to get in on the ground floor. In fact, I've already made the right connections and all that remains is for the industry itself to get under way! Full steam—(*His eyes are starry.*) *Knowledge*—Zzzzzp! *Money*—

Zzzzzzp!—*Power!* That's the cycle democracy is built on! (*His attitude is convincingly dynamic. Laura stares at him, even her shyness eclipsed in her absolute wonder. He suddenly grins.*) I guess you think I think a lot of myself!

LAURA: No—o-o-o, I—

JIM: Now how about you? Isn't there something you take more interest in than anything else?

LAURA: Well, I do—as I said—have my—glass collection—

(*A peal of girlish laughter from the kitchen.*)

JIM: I'm not right sure I know what you're talking about. What kind of glass is it?

LAURA: Little articles of it, they're ornaments mostly! Most of them are little animals made out of glass, the tiniest little animals in the world. Mother calls them a glass menagerie! Here's an example of one, if you'd like to see it! This one is one of the oldest. It's nearly thirteen. (*He stretches out his hand.*) (*Music: "The Glass Menagerie."*) Oh, be careful—if you breathe, it breaks!

JIM: I'd better not take it. I'm pretty clumsy with things.

LAURA: Go on, I trust you with him! (*Places it in his palm.*) There now—you're holding him gently! Hold him over the light, he loves the light! You see how the light shines through him?

JIM: It sure does shine!

LAURA: I shouldn't be partial, but he is my favorite one.

JIM: What kind of a thing is this one supposed to be?

LAURA: Haven't you noticed the single horn on his forehead?

JIM: A unicorn, huh?

LAURA: Mmm-hmmm!

JIM: Unicorns, aren't they extinct in the modern world?

LAURA: I know!

JIM: Poor little fellow, he must feel sort of lonesome.

LAURA (*smiling*): Well, if he does he doesn't complain about it. He stays on a shelf with some horses that don't have horns and all of them seem to get along nicely together.

JIM: How do you know?

LAURA (*lightly*): I haven't heard any arguments among them!

JIM (*grinning*): No arguments, huh? Well, that's a pretty good sign! Where shall I set him?

LAURA: Put him on the table. They all like a change of scenery once in a while!

JIM (*stretching*): Well, well, well, well—Look how big my shadow is when I stretch!

LAURA: Oh, oh, yes—it stretches across the ceiling!

JIM (*crossing to door*): I think it's stopped raining. (*Opens fire escape door.*) Where does the music come from?

LAURA: From the Paradise Dance Hall across the alley.

JIM: How about cutting the rug a little, Miss Wingfield?

LAURA: Oh, I—

JIM: Or is your program filled up? Let me have a look at it. (*Grasps imaginary card.*) Why, every dance is taken! I'll just have to scratch some out. (*Waltz music: "La Golondrina."*) Ahhh, a waltz! (*He executes some sweeping turns by himself then holds his arms toward Laura.*)

LAURA (*breathlessly*): I—can't dance!

JIM: There you go, that inferiority stuff!

LAURA: I've never danced in my life!

JIM: Come on, try!

LAURA: Oh, but I'd step on you!

JIM: I'm not made out of glass.

LAURA: How—how—how do we start?

JIM: Just leave it to me. You hold your arms out a little.

LAURA: Like this?

JIM: A little bit higher. Right. Now don't tighten up, that's the main thing about it—relax.

LAURA (*laughing breathlessly*): It's hard not to.

JIM: Okay.

LAURA: I'm afraid you can't budge me.

JIM: What do you bet I can't? (*He swings her into motion.*)

LAURA: Goodness, yes, you can!

JIM: Let yourself go, now, Laura, just let yourself go.

LAURA: I'm—

JIM: Come on!

LAURA: Trying!

JIM: Not so stiff—Easy does it!

LAURA: I know but I'm—

JIM: Loosen th' backbone! There now, that's a lot better.

LAURA: Am I?

JIM: Lots, lots better! (*He moves her about the room in a clumsy waltz.*)

LAURA: Oh, my!

JIM: Ha-ha!

LAURA: Oh, my goodness!

JIM: Ha-ha-ha! (*They suddenly bump into the table. Jim stops.*) What did we hit on?

LAURA: Table.

JIM: Did something fall off it? I think—

LAURA: Yes.

JIM: I hope that it wasn't the little glass horse with the horn!

LAURA: Yes.

JIM: Aw, aw, aw. Is it broken?

LAURA: Now it is just like all the other horses.

JIM: It's lost its—

LAURA: Horn! It doesn't matter. Maybe it's a blessing in disguise.

JIM: You'll never forgive me. I bet that that was your favorite piece of glass.

LAURA: I don't have favorites much. It's no tragedy, Freckles. Glass breaks so easily. No matter how careful you are. The traffic jars the shelves and things fall off them.

JIM: Still I'm awfully sorry that I was the cause.

LAURA (*smiling*): I'll just imagine he had an operation. The horn was removed to make him feel less—freakish! (*They both laugh.*) Now he will feel more at home with the other horses, the ones that don't have horns . . .

JIM: Ha-ha, that's very funny! (*Suddenly serious.*) I'm glad to see that you have a sense of humor. You know—you're—well—very different! Surprisingly different from anyone else I know! (*His voice becomes soft and hesitant with a genuine feeling.*) Do you mind me telling you that? (*Laura is abashed beyond speech.*) I mean it in a nice way . . . (*Laura nods shyly, looking away.*) You make me feel sort of—I don't know how to put it! I'm usually pretty good at expressing things, but—This is something that I don't know how to say! (*Laura touches her throat and clears it—turns the broken unicorn in her hands.*) (*Even softer.*) Has anyone ever told you that you were pretty? (*Pause: Music.*) (*Laura looks up slowly, with wonder, and shakes her head.*) Well, you are! In a very different way from anyone else. And all the nicer because of the difference, too. (*His voice becomes low and husky. Laura turns away, nearly faint with the novelty of her emotions.*) I wish that you were my sister. I'd teach you to have some confidence in yourself. The different people are not like other people, but being different is nothing to be ashamed of. Because other people are not such wonderful people. They're one hundred times one thousand. You're one times one! They walk all over the earth. You just stay here. They're common as—weeds, but—you— well, you're—*Blue Roses!*

(*Image on screen: blue roses.*)
   (*Music changes.*)

LAURA: But blue is wrong for—roses . . .

JIM: It's right for you—You're—pretty!

LAURA: In what respect am I pretty?

JIM: In all respects—believe me! Your eyes—your hair—are pretty! Your hands are pretty! (*He catches hold of her hand.*) You think I'm

making this up because I'm invited to dinner and have to be nice. Oh, I
could do that! I could put on an act for you, Laura, and say lots of
things without being very sincere. But this time I am. I'm talking to
you sincerely. I happened to notice you had this inferiority complex
that keeps you from feeling comfortable with people. Somebody needs
to build your confidence up and make you proud instead of shy and
turning away and—blushing—Somebody ought to—Ought to—*kiss*
you, Laura! (*His hand slips slowly up her arm to her shoulder.*) (*Music
swells tumultuously.*) (*He suddenly turns her about and kisses her on
the lips. When he releases her Laura sinks on the sofa with a bright,
dazed look. Jim backs away and fishes in his pocket for a cigarette.*)
(*Legend on screen: "Souvenir."*) Stumble-john! (*He lights the cigarette,
avoiding her look. There is a peal of girlish laughter from Amanda in the
kitchen. Laura slowly raises and opens her hand. It still contains the little broken glass animal. She looks at it with a tender, bewildered expression.*)
Stumble-john! I shouldn't have done that—That was way off the
beam. You don't smoke, do you? (*She looks up, smiling, not hearing
the question. He sits beside her a little gingerly. She looks at him speech-
lessly—waiting. He coughs decorously and moves a little farther aside as he
considers the situation and senses her feelings, dimly, with perturba-
tion. Gently.*) Would you—care for a—mint? (*She doesn't seem to hear
him but her look grows brighter even.*) Peppermint—Life Saver? My
pocket's a regular drugstore—wherever I go . . . (*He pops a mint in his
mouth. Then gulps and decides to make a clean breast of it. He speaks
slowly and gingerly.*) Laura, you know, if I had a sister like you, I'd do
the same thing as Tom. I'd bring out fellows and—introduce her to
them. The right type of boys of a type to—appreciate her. Only—
well—he made a mistake about me. Maybe I've got no call to be saying this. That may not have been the idea in having me over. But what
if it was? There's nothing wrong about that. The only trouble is that in
my case—I'm not in a situation to—do the right thing. I can't take
down your number and say I'll phone. I can't call up next week and—
ask for a date. I thought I had better explain the situation in case you
misunderstood it and—hurt your feelings. . . . (*Pause. Slowly, very
slowly, Laura's look changes, her eyes returning slowly from his to the ornament in her palm.*)

(*Amanda utters another gay laugh in the kitchen.*)

LAURA (*faintly*): You—won't—call again?
JIM: No, Laura, I can't. (*He rises from the sofa.*) As I was just explaining,
 I've—got strings on me, Laura, I've—been going steady! I go out all
 the time with a girl named Betty. She's a home-girl like you, and
 Catholic, and Irish, and in a great many ways we—get along fine. I

met her last summer on a moonlight boat trip up the river to Alton, on the *Majestic*. Well—right away from the start it was—love! (*Legend: Love!*) (*Laura sways slightly forward and grips the arm of the sofa. He fails to notice, now enrapt in his own comfortable being.*) Being in love has made a new man of me! (*Leaning stiffly forward, clutching the arm of the sofa, Laura struggles visibly with her storm. But Jim is oblivious, she is a long way off.*) The power of love is really pretty tremendous! Love is something that—changes the whole world, Laura! (*The storm abates a little and Laura leans back. He notices her again.*) It happened that Betty's aunt took sick, she got a wire and had to go to Centralia. So Tom—when he asked me to dinner—I naturally just accepted the invitation, not knowing that you—that he—that I—(*He stops awkwardly.*) Huh—I'm a stumble-john! (*He flops back on the sofa. The holy candles in the altar of Laura's face have been snuffed out! There is a look of almost infinite desolation. Jim glances at her uneasily.*) I wish that you would—say something. (*She bites her lip which was trembling and then bravely smiles. She opens her hand again on the broken glass ornament. Then she gently takes his hand and raises it level with her own. She carefully places the unicorn in the palm of his hand, then pushes his fingers closed upon it.*) What are you—doing that for? You want me to have him?—Laura? (*She nods.*) What for?

LAURA: A—souvenir . . .

(*She rises unsteadily and crouches beside the victrola to wind it up.*)
(*Legend on screen: "Things Have a Way of Turning out so Badly."*)
(*Or Image: "Gentleman Caller Waving Good-bye!—Gaily."*)
(*At this moment Amanda rushes brightly back in the front room. She bears a pitcher of fruit punch in an old-fashioned cut-glass pitcher and a plate of macaroons. The plate has a gold border and poppies painted on it.*)

AMANDA: Well, well, well! Isn't the air delightful after the shower? I've made you children a little liquid refreshment. (*Turns gaily to the gentleman caller.*) Jim, do you know that song about lemonade?
    "Lemonade, lemonade
        Made in the shade and stirred with a spade—
    Good enough for any old maid!"

JIM (*uneasily*): Ha-ha! No—I never heard it.

AMANDA: Why, Laura! You look so serious!

JIM: We were having a serious conversation.

AMANDA: Good! Now you're better acquainted!

JIM (*uncertainly*): Ha-ha! Yes.

AMANDA: You modern young people are much more serious-minded than my generation. I was so gay as a girl!

JIM: You haven't changed, Mrs. Wingfield.

AMANDA: Tonight I'm rejuvenated! The gaiety of the occasion, Mr. O'Connor! (*She tosses her head with a peal of laughter. Spills lemonade.*) Oooo! I'm baptizing myself!

JIM: Here—let me—

AMANDA (*setting the pitcher down*): There now. I discovered we had some maraschino cherries. I dumped them in, juice and all!

JIM: You shouldn't have gone to that trouble, Mrs. Wingfield.

AMANDA: Trouble, trouble? Why it was loads of fun! Didn't you hear me cutting up in the kitchen? I bet your ears were burning! I told Tom how out-done with him I was for keeping you to himself so long a time! He should have brought you over much, much sooner! Well, now that you've found your way, I want you to be a very frequent caller! Not just occasional but all the time. Oh, we're going to have a lot of gay times together! I see them coming! Mmm, just breathe that air! So fresh, and the moon's so pretty! I'll skip back out—I know where my place is when young folks are having a—serious conversation!

JIM: Oh, don't go out, Mrs. Wingfield. The fact of the matter is I've got to be going.

AMANDA: Going, now? You're joking! Why, it's only the shank of the evening, Mr. O'Connor!

JIM: Well, you know how it is.

AMANDA: You mean you're a young workingman and have to keep workingmen's hours. We'll let you off early tonight. But only on the condition that next time you stay later. What's the best night for you? Isn't Saturday night the best night for you workingmen?

JIM: I have a couple of time clocks to punch, Mrs. Wingfield. One at morning, another one at night!

AMANDA: My, but you *are* ambitious! You work at night, too?

JIM: No, Ma'am, not work but—Betty! (*He crosses deliberately to pick up his hat. The band at the Paradise Dance Hall goes into a tender waltz.*)

AMANDA: Betty? Betty? Who's—Betty! (*There is an ominous cracking sound in the sky.*)

JIM: Oh, just a girl. The girl I go steady with! (*He smiles charmingly. The sky falls.*)

(*Legend: "The Sky Falls."*)

AMANDA (*a long-drawn exhalation*): Ohhhh . . . Is it a serious romance, Mr. O'Connor?

JIM: We're going to be married the second Sunday in June.

AMANDA: Ohhhh—how nice! Tom didn't mention that you were engaged to be married.

JIM: The cat's not out of the bag at the warehouse yet. You know how they are. They call you Romeo and stuff like that. (*He stops at the oval mirror to put on his hat. He carefully shapes the brim and the crown to give a discreetly dashing effect.*) It's been a wonderful evening, Mrs. Wingfield. I guess this is what they mean by Southern hospitality.

AMANDA: It really wasn't anything at all.

JIM: I hope it don't seem like I'm rushing off. But I promised Betty I'd pick her up at the Wabash depot, an' by the time I get my jalopy down there her train'll be in. Some women are pretty upset if you keep 'em waiting.

AMANDA: Yes, I know — The tyranny of women! (*Extends her hand.*) Good-bye, Mr. O'Connor. I wish you luck — and happiness — and success! All three of them, and so does Laura! — Don't you, Laura?

LAURA: Yes!

JIM (*taking her hand*): Good-bye, Laura. I'm certainly going to treasure that souvenir. And don't you forget the good advice I gave you. (*Raises his voice to a cheery shout.*) So long, Shakespeare! Thanks again, ladies — Good night!

(*He grins and ducks jauntily out.*)

(*Still bravely grimacing, Amanda closes the door on the gentleman caller. Then she turns back to the room with a puzzled expression. She and Laura don't dare to face each other. Laura crouches beside the victrola to wind it.*)

AMANDA (*faintly*): Things have a way of turning out so badly. I don't believe that I would play the victrola. Well, well — well — Our gentleman caller was engaged to be married! Tom!

TOM (*from back*): Yes, Mother?

AMANDA: Come in here a minute. I want to tell you something awfully funny.

TOM (*enters with macaroon and a glass of the lemonade*): Has the gentleman caller gotten away already?

AMANDA: The gentleman caller has made an early departure. What a wonderful joke you played on us!

TOM: How do you mean?

AMANDA: You didn't mention that he was engaged to be married.

TOM: Jim? Engaged?

AMANDA: That's what he just informed us.

TOM: I'll be jiggered! I didn't know about that.

AMANDA: That seems very peculiar.

TOM: What's peculiar about it?

AMANDA: Didn't you call him your best friend down at the warehouse?

TOM: He is, but how did I know?

AMANDA: It seems extremely peculiar that you wouldn't know your best friend was going to be married!

TOM: The warehouse is where I work, not where I know things about people!

AMANDA: You don't know things anywhere! You live in a dream; you manufacture illusions! (*He crosses to door.*) Where are you going?

TOM: I'm going to the movies.

AMANDA: That's right, now that you've had us make such fools of ourselves. The effort, the preparations, all the expense! The new floor lamp, the rug, the clothes for Laura! All for what? To entertain some other girl's fiancé! Go to the movies, go! Don't think about us, a mother deserted, an unmarried sister who's crippled and has no job! Don't let anything interfere with your selfish pleasure! Just go, go, go—to the movies!

TOM: All right, I will! The more you shout about my selfishness to me the quicker I'll go, and I won't go to the movies!

AMANDA: Go, then! Then go to the moon—you selfish dreamer!

(*Tom smashes his glass on the floor. He plunges out on the fire escape, slamming the door. Laura screams—cut by door.*)

(*Dance hall music up. Tom goes to the rail and grips it desperately, lifting his face in the chill white moonlight penetrating the narrow abyss of the alley.*)

(*Legend on screen: "And so Good-bye . . . "*)

(*Tom's closing speech is timed with the interior pantomime. The interior scene is played as though viewed through soundproof glass. Amanda appears to be making a comforting speech to Laura who is huddled upon the sofa. Now that we cannot hear the mother's speech, her silliness is gone and she has dignity and tragic beauty. Laura's dark hair hides her face until at the end of the speech she lifts it to smile at her mother. Amanda's gestures are slow and graceful, almost dancelike, as she comforts the daughter. At the end of her speech she glances a moment at the father's picture—then withdraws through the portieres. At close of Tom's speech, Laura blows out the candles, ending the play.*)

TOM: I didn't go to the moon, I went much further—for time is the longest distance between two places—Not long after that I was fired for writing a poem on the lid of a shoebox. I left Saint Louis. I descended the steps of this fire escape for a last time and followed, from then on, in my father's footsteps, attempting to find in motion what was lost in space—I traveled around a great deal. The cities swept about me like dead leaves, leaves that were brightly colored but torn away from the branches. I would have stopped, but I was pursued by something. It always came upon me unawares, taking me altogether by surprise. Perhaps it was a familiar bit of music. Perhaps it was only a piece of transparent glass—Perhaps I am walking along a street at night, in some strange city, before I have found companions. I pass the lighted window of a shop where perfume is sold. The window is filled with pieces of colored glass, tiny transparent bottles in delicate colors, like bits of a shattered rainbow. Then all at once my sister touches my shoulder. I turn around and look into her eyes . . . Oh, Laura, Laura, I tried to leave you behind me, but I am more faithful than I intended to be! I reach for a cigarette, I cross the street, I run into the movies or a bar, I buy a drink, I speak to the nearest stranger—anything that can blow your candles out! (*Laura bends over the candles.*)—for nowadays the world is lit by lightning! Blow out your candles, Laura—and so good-bye. . . .

(*She blows the candles out.*)
(*The scene dissolves.*)

[1944]

ARTHUR MILLER [b. 1915]

Death of a Salesman

Certain Private Conversations in Two Acts
and a Requiem

Characters

WILLY LOMAN
LINDA
BIFF
HAPPY
BERNARD
THE WOMAN
CHARLEY
UNCLE BEN
HOWARD WAGNER
JENNY
STANLEY
MISS FORSYTHE
LETTA

The action takes place in Willy Loman's house and yard and in various places he visits in the New York and Boston of today.

(Throughout the play, in the stage directions, left and right mean stage left and stage right.)

ACT I

(A melody is heard, played upon a flute. It is small and fine, telling of grass and trees and the horizon. The curtain rises.)

(Before us is the Salesman's house. We are aware of towering, angular shapes behind it, surrounding it on all sides. Only the blue light of the sky falls upon the house and forestage; the surrounding area shows an angry glow of orange. As more light appears, we see a solid vault of apartment houses around the small, fragile-seeming home. An air of the dream clings to the place, a dream rising out of reality. The kitchen at center seems actual enough, for there is a kitchen table

with three chairs, and a refrigerator. But no other fixtures are seen. At the back of the kitchen there is a draped entrance, which leads to the living room. To the right of the kitchen, on a level raised two feet, is a bedroom furnished only with a brass bedstead and a straight chair. On a shelf over the bed a silver athletic trophy stands. A window opens onto the apartment house at the side.)

(Behind the kitchen, on a level raised six and a half feet, is the boys' bedroom, at present barely visible. Two beds are dimly seen, and at the back of the room a dormer window. [This bedroom is above the unseen living room.] At the left a stairway curves up to it from the kitchen.)

(The entire setting is wholly or, in some places, partially transparent. The roofline of the house is one-dimensional; under and over it we see the apartment buildings. Before the house lies an apron, curving beyond the forestage into the orchestra. This forward area serves as the back yard as well as the locale of all Willy's imaginings and of his city scenes. Whenever the action is in the present the actors observe the imaginary wall-lines, entering the house only through its door at the left. But in the scenes of the past these boundaries are broken, and characters enter or leave a room by stepping "through" a wall onto the forestage.)

(From the right, Willy Loman, the Salesman, enters, carrying two large sample cases. The flute plays on. He hears but is not aware of it. He is past sixty years of age, dressed quietly. Even as he crosses the stage to the doorway of the house, his exhaustion is apparent. He unlocks the door, comes into the kitchen, and thankfully lets his burden down, feeling the soreness of his palms. A word-sigh escapes his lips—it might be "Oh, boy, oh, boy." He closes the door then carries his cases out into the living room, through the draped kitchen doorway.)

(Linda, his wife, has stirred in her bed at the right. She gets out and puts on a robe, listening. Most often jovial, she has developed an iron repression of her exceptions to Willy's behavior—she more than loves him, she admires him, as though his mercurial nature, his temper, his massive dreams and little cruelties, served her only as sharp reminders of the turbulent longings within him, longings which she shares but lacks the temperament to utter and follow to their end.)

LINDA *(hearing Willy outside the bedroom, calls with some trepidation)*: Willy!

WILLY: It's all right. I came back.

LINDA: Why? What happened? *(Slight pause.)* Did something happen, Willy?

WILLY: No, nothing happened.

LINDA: You didn't smash the car, did you?

WILLY *(with casual irritation)*: I said nothing happened. Didn't you hear me?

LINDA: Don't you feel well?

WILLY: I'm tired to the death. *(The flute has faded away. He sits on the bed beside her, a little numb.)* I couldn't make it. I just couldn't make it, Linda.

LINDA (*very carefully, delicately*): Where were you all day? You look terrible.

WILLY: I got as far as a little above Yonkers. I stopped for a cup of coffee. Maybe it was the coffee.

LINDA: What?

WILLY (*after a pause*): I suddenly couldn't drive anymore. The car kept going off onto the shoulder, y'know?

LINDA (*helpfully*): Oh. Maybe it was the steering again. I don't think Angelo knows the Studebaker.

WILLY: No, it's me, it's me. Suddenly I realize I'm goin' sixty miles an hour and I don't remember the last five minutes. I'm—I can't seem to—keep my mind to it.

LINDA: Maybe it's your glasses. You never went for your new glasses.

WILLY: No, I see everything. I came back ten miles an hour. It took me nearly four hours from Yonkers.

LINDA (*resigned*): Well, you'll just have to take a rest, Willy, you can't continue this way.

WILLY: I just got back from Florida.

LINDA: But you didn't rest your mind. Your mind is overactive, and the mind is what counts, dear.

WILLY: I'll start out in the morning. Maybe I'll feel better in the morning. (*She is taking off his shoes.*) These goddam arch supports are killing me.

LINDA: Take an aspirin. Should I get you an aspirin? It'll soothe you.

WILLY (*with wonder*): I was driving along, you understand? And I was fine. I was even observing the scenery. You can imagine, me looking at scenery, on the road every week of my life. But it's so beautiful up there, Linda, the trees are so thick, and the sun is warm. I opened the windshield and just let the warm air bathe over me. And then all of a sudden I'm goin' off the road! I'm tellin' ya, I absolutely forgot I was driving. If I'd've gone the other way over the white line I might've killed somebody. So I went on again—and five minutes later I'm dreamin' again, and I nearly—(*He presses two fingers against his eyes.*) I have such thoughts, I have such strange thoughts.

LINDA: Willy, dear. Talk to them again. There's no reason why you can't work in New York.

WILLY: They don't need me in New York. I'm the New England man. I'm vital in New England.

LINDA: But you're sixty years old. They can't expect you to keep traveling every week.

WILLY: I'll have to send a wire to Portland. I'm supposed to see Brown and Morrison tomorrow morning at ten o'clock to show the line. Goddammit, I could sell them! (*He starts putting on his jacket.*)

LINDA (*taking the jacket from him*): Why don't you go down to the place tomorrow and tell Howard you've simply got to work in New York? You're too accommodating, dear.

WILLY: If old man Wagner was alive I'd a been in charge of New York now! That man was a prince, he was a masterful man. But that boy of his, that Howard, he don't appreciate. When I went north the first time, the Wagner Company didn't know where New England was!

LINDA: Why don't you tell those things to Howard, dear?

WILLY (*encouraged*): I will, I definitely will. Is there any cheese?

LINDA: I'll make you a sandwich.

WILLY: No, go to sleep. I'll take some milk. I'll be up right away. The boys in?

LINDA: They're sleeping. Happy took Biff on a date tonight.

WILLY (*interested*): That so?

LINDA: It was so nice to see them shaving together, one behind the other, in the bathroom. And going out together. You notice? The whole house smells of shaving lotion.

WILLY: Figure it out. Work a lifetime to pay off a house. You finally own it, and there's nobody to live in it.

LINDA: Well, dear, life is a casting off. It's always that way.

WILLY: No, no, some people—some people accomplish something. Did Biff say anything after I went this morning?

LINDA: You shouldn't have criticized him, Willy, especially after he just got off the train. You mustn't lose your temper with him.

WILLY: When the hell did I lose my temper? I simply asked him if he was making any money. Is that a criticism?

LINDA: But, dear, how could he make any money?

WILLY (*worried and angered*): There's such an undercurrent in him. He became a moody man. Did he apologize when I left this morning?

LINDA: He was crestfallen, Willy. You know how he admires you. I think if he finds himself, then you'll both be happier and not fight any more.

WILLY: How can he find himself on a farm? Is that a life? A farmhand? In the beginning, when he was young, I thought, well, a young man, it's good for him to tramp around, take a lot of different jobs. But it's more than ten years now and he has yet to make thirty-five dollars a week!

LINDA: He's finding himself, Willy.

WILLY: Not finding yourself at the age of thirty-four is a disgrace!

LINDA: Shh!

WILLY: The trouble is he's lazy, goddammit!

LINDA: Willy, please!

WILLY: Biff is a lazy bum!

LINDA: They're sleeping. Get something to eat. Go on down.

WILLY: Why did he come home? I would like to know what brought him home.

LINDA: I don't know. I think he's still lost, Willy. I think he's very lost.

WILLY: Biff Loman is lost. In the greatest country in the world a young man with such—personal attractiveness, gets lost. And such a hard worker. There's one thing about Biff—he's not lazy.

LINDA: Never.

WILLY (*with pity and resolve*): I'll see him in the morning; I'll have a nice talk with him. I'll get him a job selling. He could be big in no time. My God! Remember how they used to follow him around in high school? When he smiled at one of them their faces lit up. When he walked down the street . . . (*He loses himself in reminiscences.*)

LINDA (*trying to bring him out of it*): Willy, dear, I got a new kind of American-type cheese today. It's whipped.

WILLY: Why do you get American when I like Swiss?

LINDA: I just thought you'd like a change—

WILLY: I don't want a change! I want Swiss cheese. Why am I always being contradicted?

LINDA (*with a covering laugh*): I thought it would be a surprise.

WILLY: Why don't you open a window in here, for God's sake?

LINDA (*with infinite patience*): They're all open, dear.

WILLY: The way they boxed us in here. Bricks and windows, windows and bricks.

LINDA: We should've bought the land next door.

WILLY: The street is lined with cars. There's not a breath of fresh air in the neighborhood. The grass don't grow anymore, you can't raise a carrot in the back yard. They should've had a law against apartment houses. Remember those two beautiful elm trees out there? When I and Biff hung the swing between them?

LINDA: Yeah, like being a million miles from the city.

WILLY: They should've arrested the builder for cutting those down. They massacred the neighborhood. (*Lost.*) More and more I think of those days, Linda. This time of year it was lilac and wisteria. And then the peonies would come out, and the daffodils. What fragrance in this room!

LINDA: Well, after all, people had to move somewhere.

WILLY: No, there's more people now.

LINDA: I don't think there's more people. I think—

WILLY: There's more people! That's what's ruining this country! Population is getting out of control. The competition is maddening! Smell the stink from that apartment house! And another one on the other side . . . How can they whip cheese?

(*On Willy's last line, Biff and Happy raise themselves up in their beds, listening.*)

LINDA: Go down, try it. And be quiet.

WILLY (*turning to Linda, guiltily*): You're not worried about me, are you, sweetheart?

BIFF: What's the matter?

HAPPY: Listen!

LINDA: You've got too much on the ball to worry about.

WILLY: You're my foundation and my support, Linda.

LINDA: Just try to relax, dear. You make mountains out of molehills.

WILLY: I won't fight with him any more. If he wants to go back to Texas, let him go.

LINDA: He'll find his way.

WILLY: Sure. Certain men just don't get started till later in life. Like Thomas Edison, I think. Or B. F. Goodrich. One of them was deaf. (*He starts for the bedroom doorway.*) I'll put my money on Biff.

LINDA: And Willy—if it's warm Sunday we'll drive in the country. And we'll open the windshield, and take lunch.

WILLY: No, the windshields don't open on the new cars.

LINDA: But you opened it today.

WILLY: Me? I didn't. (*He stops.*) Now isn't that peculiar! Isn't that a remarkable—(*He breaks off in amazement and fright as the flute is heard distantly.*)

LINDA: What, darling?

WILLY: That is the most remarkable thing.

LINDA: What, dear?

WILLY: I was thinking of the Chevvy. (*Slight pause.*) Nineteen twenty-eight . . . when I had that red Chevvy—(*Breaks off.*) That funny? I coulda sworn I was driving that Chevvy today.

LINDA: Well, that's nothing. Something must've reminded you.

WILLY: Remarkable. Ts. Remember those days? The way Biff used to simonize that car? The dealer refused to believe there was eighty thousand miles on it. (*He shakes his head.*) Heh! (*To Linda.*) Close your eyes, I'll be right up. (*He walks out of the bedroom.*)

HAPPY (*to Biff*): Jesus, maybe he smashed up the car again!

LINDA (*calling after Willy*): Be careful on the stairs, dear! The cheese is on the middle shelf! (*She turns, goes over to the bed, takes his jacket, and goes out of the bedroom.*)

(*Light has risen on the boys' room. Unseen, Willy is heard talking to himself, "Eighty thousand miles," and a little laugh. Biff gets out of bed, comes downstage a bit, and stands attentively. Biff is two years older than his brother Happy, well built, but in these days bears a worn air and seems less self-assured. He has succeeded less, and his dreams are stronger and less acceptable than Happy's. Happy is tall, powerfully made. Sexuality is like a visible color on him, or a scent that many women have discovered. He, like his brother, is lost, but in a different way, for he has never allowed himself to turn his face toward defeat and is thus more confused and hard-skinned, although seemingly more content.*)

HAPPY (*getting out of bed*): He's going to get his license taken away if he keeps that up. I'm getting nervous about him, y'know, Biff?

BIFF: His eyes are going.

HAPPY: No, I've driven with him. He sees all right. He just doesn't keep his mind on it. I drove into the city with him last week. He stops at a green light and then it turns red and he goes. (*He laughs.*)

BIFF: Maybe he's color-blind.

HAPPY: Pop? Why he's got the finest eye for color in the business. You know that.

BIFF (*sitting down on his bed*): I'm going to sleep.

HAPPY: You're not still sour on Dad, are you, Biff?

BIFF: He's all right, I guess.

WILLY (*underneath them, in the living room*): Yes, sir, eighty thousand miles—eighty-two thousand!

BIFF: You smoking?

HAPPY (*holding out a pack of cigarettes*): Want one?

BIFF (*taking a cigarette*): I can never sleep when I smell it.

WILLY: What a simonizing job, heh!

HAPPY (*with deep sentiment*): Funny, Biff, y'know? Us sleeping in here again? The old beds. (*He pats his bed affectionately.*) All the talk that went across those two beds, huh? Our whole lives.

BIFF: Yeah. Lotta dreams and plans.

HAPPY (*with a deep and masculine laugh*): About five hundred women would like to know what was said in this room.

(*They share a soft laugh.*)

BIFF: Remember that big Betsy something—what the hell was her name—over on Bushwick Avenue?

HAPPY (*combing his hair*): With the collie dog!

BIFF: That's the one. I got you in there, remember?

HAPPY: Yeah, that was my first time—I think. Boy, there was a pig. (*They laugh, almost crudely.*) You taught me everything I know about women. Don't forget that.

BIFF: I bet you forgot how bashful you used to be. Especially with girls.

HAPPY: Oh, I still am, Biff.

BIFF: Oh, go on.

HAPPY: I just control it, that's all. I think I got less bashful and you got more so. What happened, Biff? Where's the old humor, the old confidence? (*He shakes Biff's knee. Biff gets up and moves restlessly about the room.*) What's the matter?

BIFF: Why does Dad mock me all the time?

HAPPY: He's not mocking you, he—

BIFF: Everything I say there's a twist of mockery on his face. I can't get near him.

HAPPY: He just wants you to make good, that's all. I wanted to talk to you about Dad for a long time, Biff. Something's—happening to him. He—talks to himself.

BIFF: I noticed that this morning. But he always mumbled.

HAPPY: But not so noticeable. It got so embarrassing I sent him to Florida. And you know something? Most of the time he's talking to you.

BIFF: What's he say about me?

HAPPY: I can't make it out.

BIFF: What's he say about me?

HAPPY: I think the fact that you're not settled, that you're still kind of up in the air . . .

BIFF: There's one or two other things depressing him, Happy.

HAPPY: What do you mean?

BIFF: Never mind. Just don't lay it all to me.

HAPPY: But I think if you just got started—I mean—is there any future for you out there?

BIFF: I tell ya, Hap, I don't know what the future is. I don't know—what I'm supposed to want.

HAPPY: What do you mean?

BIFF: Well, I spent six or seven years after high school trying to work myself up. Shipping clerk, salesman, business of one kind or another. And it's a measly manner of existence. To get on that subway on the hot mornings in summer. To devote your whole life to keeping stock, or making phone calls, or selling or buying. To suffer fifty weeks of the year for the sake of a two-week vacation, when all you really desire is to be outdoors, with your shirt off. And always to have to get ahead of the next fella. And still—that's how you build a future.

HAPPY: Well, you really enjoy it on a farm? Are you content out there?

BIFF (*with rising agitation*): Hap, I've had twenty or thirty different kinds of jobs since I left home before the war, and it always turns out the same. I just realized it lately. In Nebraska when I herded cattle, and the Dakotas, and Arizona, and now in Texas. It's why I came home now, I guess, because I realized it. This farm I work on, it's spring there now, see? And they've got about fifteen new colts. There's nothing more inspiring or—beautiful than the sight of a mare and a new colt. And it's cool there now, see? Texas is cool now, and it's spring. And whenever spring comes to where I am, I suddenly get the feeling, my God, I'm not gettin' anywhere! What the hell am I doing, playing around with horses, twenty-eight dollars a week! I'm thirty-four years old, I oughta be makin' my future. That's when I come running home. And now, I get here, and I don't know what to do with myself. (*After a pause.*) I've always made a point of not wasting my life, and every time I come back here I know that all I've done is to waste my life.

HAPPY: You're a poet, you know that, Biff? You're a—you're an idealist!

BIFF: No, I'm mixed up very bad. Maybe I oughta get married. Maybe I oughta get stuck into something. Maybe that's my trouble. I'm like a boy. I'm not married, I'm not in business, I just—I'm like a boy. Are you content, Hap? You're a success, aren't you? Are you content?

HAPPY: Hell, no!

BIFF: Why? You're making money, aren't you?

HAPPY (*moving about with energy, expressiveness*): All I can do now is wait for the merchandise manager to die. And suppose I get to be merchandise manager? He's a good friend of mine, and he just built a terrific estate on Long Island. And he lived there about two months and sold it, and now he's building another one. He can't enjoy it once it's finished. And I know that's just what I would do. I don't know what the hell I'm workin' for. Sometimes I sit in my apartment—all alone. And I think of the rent I'm paying. And it's crazy. But then, it's what I always wanted. My own apartment, a car, and plenty of women. And still, goddammit, I'm lonely.

BIFF (*with enthusiasm*): Listen, why don't you come out West with me?

HAPPY: You and I, heh?

BIFF: Sure, maybe we could buy a ranch. Raise cattle, use our muscles. Men built like we are should be working out in the open.

HAPPY (*avidly*): The Loman Brothers, heh?

BIFF (*with vast affection*): Sure, we'd be known all over the counties!

HAPPY (*enthralled*): That's what I dream about, Biff. Sometimes I want to just rip my clothes off in the middle of the store and outbox that goddam merchandise manager. I mean I can outbox, outrun and outlift anybody in that store, and I have to take orders from those common, petty sons-of-bitches till I can't stand it anymore.

BIFF: I'm tellin' you, kid, if you were with me I'd be happy out there.

HAPPY (*enthused*): See, Biff, everybody around me is so false that I'm constantly lowering my ideals . . .

BIFF: Baby, together we'd stand up for one another, we'd have someone to trust.

HAPPY: If I were around you—

BIFF: Hap, the trouble is we weren't brought up to grub for money. I don't know how to do it.

HAPPY: Neither can I!

BIFF: Then let's go!

HAPPY: The only thing is—what can you make out there?

BIFF: But look at your friend. Builds an estate and then hasn't the peace of mind to live in it.

HAPPY: Yeah, but when he walks into the store the waves part in front of him. That's fifty-two thousand dollars a year coming through the revolving door, and I got more in my pinky finger than he's got in his head.

BIFF: Yeah, but you just said—

HAPPY: I gotta show some of those pompous, self-important executives over there that Hap Loman can make the grade. I want to walk into the store the way he walks in. Then I'll go with you, Biff. We'll be together yet, I swear. But take those two we had tonight. Now weren't they gorgeous creatures?

BIFF: Yeah, yeah, most gorgeous I've had in years.

HAPPY: I get that any time I want, Biff. Whenever I feel disgusted. The only trouble is, it gets like bowling or something. I just keep knockin' them over and it doesn't mean anything. You still run around a lot?

BIFF: Naa. I'd like to find a girl—steady, somebody with substance.

HAPPY: That's what I long for.

BIFF: Go on! You'd never come home.

HAPPY: I would! Somebody with character, with resistance! Like Mom, y'know? You're gonna call me a bastard when I tell you this. That girl Charlotte I was with tonight is engaged to be married in five weeks. (*He tries on his new hat.*)

BIFF: No kiddin'!

HAPPY: Sure, the guy's in line for the vice-presidency of the store. I don't know what gets into me, maybe I just have an overdeveloped sense of competition or something, but I went and ruined her, and furthermore I can't get rid of her. And he's the third executive I've done that to. Isn't that a crummy characteristic? And to top it all, I go to their weddings! (*Indignantly, but laughing.*) Like I'm not supposed to take bribes. Manufacturers offer me a hundred-dollar bill now and then to throw an order their way. You know how honest I am, but it's like this girl, see. I hate myself for it. Because I don't want the girl, and, still, I take it and—I love it!

BIFF: Let's go to sleep.

HAPPY: I guess we didn't settle anything, heh?

BIFF: I just got one idea that I think I'm going to try.

HAPPY: What's that?

BIFF: Remember Bill Oliver?

HAPPY: Sure, Oliver is very big now. You want to work for him again?

BIFF: No, but when I quit he said something to me. He put his arm on my shoulder, and he said, "Biff, if you ever need anything, come to me."

HAPPY: I remember that. That sounds good.

BIFF: I think I'll go to see him. If I could get ten thousand or even seven or eight thousand dollars I could buy a beautiful ranch.

HAPPY: I bet he'd back you. 'Cause he thought highly of you, Biff. I mean, they all do. You're well liked, Biff. That's why I say to come back here, and we both have the apartment. And I'm tellin' you, Biff, any babe you want . . .

BIFF: No, with a ranch I could do the work I like and still be something. I just wonder though. I wonder if Oliver still thinks I stole that carton of basketballs.

HAPPY: Oh, he probably forgot that long ago. It's almost ten years. You're too sensitive. Anyway, he didn't really fire you.

BIFF: Well, I think he was going to. I think that's why I quit. I was never sure whether he knew or not. I know he thought the world of me, though. I was the only one he'd let lock up the place.

WILLY (*below*): You gonna wash the engine, Biff?

HAPPY: Shh!

(*Biff looks at Happy, who is gazing down, listening. Willy is mumbling in the parlor.*)

HAPPY: You hear that?

(*They listen. Willy laughs warmly.*)

BIFF (*growing angry*): Doesn't he know Mom can hear that?

WILLY: Don't get your sweater dirty, Biff!

(*A look of pain crosses Biff's face.*)

HAPPY: Isn't that terrible? Don't leave again, will you? You'll find a job here. You gotta stick around. I don't know what to do about him, it's getting embarrassing.

WILLY: What a simonizing job!

BIFF: Mom's hearing that!

WILLY: No kiddin', Biff, you got a date? Wonderful!

HAPPY: Go on to sleep. But talk to him in the morning, will you?

BIFF (*reluctantly getting into bed*): With her in the house. Brother!

HAPPY (*getting into bed*): I wish you'd have a good talk with him.

(*The light on their room begins to fade.*)

BIFF (*to himself in bed*): That selfish, stupid . . .

HAPPY: Sh . . . Sleep, Biff.

(*Their light is out. Well before they have finished speaking, Willy's form is dimly seen below in the darkened kitchen. He opens the refrigerator, searches in there, and takes out a bottle of milk. The apartment houses are fading out, and the entire house and surroundings become covered with leaves. Music insinuates itself as the leaves appear.*)

WILLY: Just wanna be careful with those girls, Biff, that's all. Don't make any promises. No promises of any kind. Because a girl, y'know, they always believe what you tell 'em, and you're very young, Biff, you're too young to be talking seriously to girls.

(*Light rises on the kitchen. Willy, talking, shuts the refrigerator door and comes downstage to the kitchen table. He pours milk into a glass. He is totally immersed in himself, smiling faintly.*)

WILLY: Too young entirely, Biff. You want to watch your schooling first. Then when you're all set, there'll be plenty of girls for a boy like you. (*He smiles broadly at a kitchen chair.*) That so? The girls pay for you? (*He laughs.*) Boy, you must really be makin' a hit.

(*Willy is gradually addressing—physically—a point offstage, speaking through the wall of the kitchen, and his voice has been rising in volume to that of a normal conversation.*)

WILLY: I been wondering why you polish the car so careful. Ha! Don't leave the hubcaps, boys. Get the chamois to the hubcaps. Happy, use newspaper on the windows, it's the easiest thing. Show him how to do it, Biff! You see, Happy? Pad it up, use it like a pad. That's it, that's it, good work. You're doin' all right, Hap. (*He pauses, then nods in approbation for a few seconds, then looks upward.*) Biff, first thing we gotta do when we get time is clip that big branch over the house. Afraid it's gonna fall in a storm and hit the roof. Tell you what. We get a rope and sling her around, and then we climb up there with a couple of saws and take her down. Soon as you finish the car, boys, I wanna see ye. I got a surprise for you, boys.

BIFF (*offstage*): Whatta ya got, Dad?

WILLY: No, you finish first. Never leave a job till you're finished— remember that. (*Looking toward the "big trees."*) Biff, up in Albany I saw a beautiful hammock. I think I'll buy it next trip, and we'll hang it right between those two elms. Wouldn't that be something? Just swingin' there under those branches. Boy, that would be . . .

(*Young Biff and Young Happy appear from the direction Willy was addressing. Happy carries rags and a pail of water. Biff, wearing a sweater with a block "S," carries a football.*)

BIFF (*pointing in the direction of the car offstage*): How's that, Pop, professional?

WILLY: Terrific. Terrific job, boys. Good work, Biff.

HAPPY: Where's the surprise, Pop?
WILLY: In the back seat of the car.
HAPPY: Boy! (*He runs off.*)
BIFF: What is it, Dad? Tell me, what'd you buy?
WILLY (*laughing, cuffs him*): Never mind, something I want you to have.
BIFF (*turns and starts off*): What is it, Hap?
HAPPY (*offstage*): It's a punching bag!
BIFF: Oh, Pop!
WILLY: It's got Gene Tunney's signature on it!

(*Happy runs onstage with a punching bag.*)

BIFF: Gee, how'd you know we wanted a punching bag?
WILLY: Well, it's the finest thing for the timing.
HAPPY (*lies down on his back and pedals with his feet*): I'm losing weight, you notice, Pop?
WILLY (*to Happy*): Jumping rope is good too.
BIFF: Did you see the new football I got?
WILLY (*examining the ball*): Where'd you get a new ball?
BIFF: The coach told me to practice my passing.
WILLY: That so? And he gave you the ball, heh?
BIFF: Well, I borrowed it from the locker room. (*He laughs confidentially.*)
WILLY (*laughing with him at the theft*): I want you to return that.
HAPPY: I told you he wouldn't like it!
BIFF (*angrily*): Well, I'm bringing it back!
WILLY (*stopping the incipient argument, to Happy*): Sure, he's gotta practice with a regulation ball, doesn't he? (*To Biff.*) Coach'll probably congratulate you on your initiative!
BIFF: Oh, he keeps congratulating my initiative all the time, Pop.
WILLY: That's because he likes you. If somebody else took that ball there'd be an uproar. So what's the report, boys, what's the report?
BIFF: Where'd you go this time, Dad? Gee we were lonesome for you.
WILLY (*pleased, puts an arm around each boy and they come down to the apron*): Lonesome, heh?
BIFF: Missed you every minute.
WILLY: Don't say? Tell you a secret, boys. Don't breathe it to a soul. Someday I'll have my own business, and I'll never have to leave home anymore.
HAPPY: Like Uncle Charley, heh?
WILLY: Bigger than Uncle Charley! Because Charley is not — liked. He's liked, but he's not — well liked.
BIFF: Where'd you go this time, Dad?
WILLY: Well, I got on the road, and I went north to Providence. Met the Mayor.

BIFF: The Mayor of Providence!

WILLY: He was sitting in the hotel lobby.

BIFF: What'd he say?

WILLY: He said, "Morning!" And I said, "You got a fine city here, Mayor." And then he had coffee with me. And then I went to Waterbury. Waterbury is a fine city. Big clock city, the famous Waterbury clock. Sold a nice bill there. And then Boston—Boston is the cradle of the Revolution. A fine city. And a couple of other towns in Mass., and on to Portland and Bangor and straight home!

BIFF: Gee, I'd love to go with you sometime, Dad.

WILLY: Soon as summer comes.

HAPPY: Promise?

WILLY: You and Hap and I, and I'll show you all the towns. America is full of beautiful towns and fine, upstanding people. And they know me, boys, they know me up and down New England. The finest people. And when I bring you fellas up, there'll be open sesame for all of us, 'cause one thing, boys: I have friends. I can park my car in any street in New England, and the cops protect it like their own. This summer, heh?

BIFF AND HAPPY (*together*): Yeah! You bet!

WILLY: We'll take our bathing suits.

HAPPY: We'll carry your bags, Pop!

WILLY: Oh, won't that be something! Me comin' into the Boston stores with you boys carryin' my bags. What a sensation!

(*Biff is prancing around, practicing passing the ball.*)

WILLY: You nervous, Biff, about the game?

BIFF: Not if you're gonna be there.

WILLY: What do they say about you in school, now that they made you captain?

HAPPY: There's a crowd of girls behind him every time the classes change.

BIFF (*taking Willy's hand*): This Saturday, Pop, this Saturday—just for you, I'm going to break through for a touchdown.

HAPPY: You're supposed to pass.

BIFF: I'm takin' one play for Pop. You watch me, Pop, and when I take off my helmet, that means I'm breakin' out. Then you watch me crash through that line!

WILLY (*kisses Biff*): Oh, wait'll I tell this in Boston!

(*Bernard enters in knickers. He is younger than Biff, earnest and loyal, a worried boy.*)

BERNARD: Biff, where are you? You're supposed to study with me today.

WILLY: Hey, looka Bernard. What're you lookin' so anemic about, Bernard?

BERNARD: He's gotta study, Uncle Willy. He's got Regents next week.

HAPPY (*tauntingly, spinning Bernard around*): Let's box, Bernard!

BERNARD: Biff! (*He gets away from Happy.*) Listen, Biff, I heard Mr. Birnbaum say that if you don't start studyin' math he's gonna flunk you, and you won't graduate. I heard him!

WILLY: You better study with him, Biff. Go ahead now.

BERNARD: I heard him!

BIFF: Oh, Pop, you didn't see my sneakers! (*He holds up a foot for Willy to look at.*)

WILLY: Hey, that's a beautiful job of printing!

BERNARD (*wiping his glasses*): Just because he printed University of Virginia on his sneakers doesn't mean they've got to graduate him, Uncle Willy!

WILLY (*angrily*): What're you talking about? With scholarships to three universities they're gonna flunk him?

BERNARD: But I heard Mr. Birnbaum say—

WILLY: Don't be a pest, Bernard! (*To his boys.*) What an anemic!

BERNARD: Okay, I'm waiting for you in my house, Biff.

(*Bernard goes off. The Lomans laugh.*)

WILLY: Bernard is not well liked, is he?

BIFF: He's liked, but he's not well liked.

HAPPY: That's right, Pop.

WILLY: That's just what I mean. Bernard can get the best marks in school, y'understand, but when he gets out in the business world, y'understand, you are going to be five times ahead of him. That's why I thank Almighty God you're both built like Adonises. Because the man who makes an appearance in the business world, the man who creates personal interest, is the man who gets ahead. Be liked and you will never want. You take me, for instance. I never have to wait in line to see a buyer. "Willy Loman is here!" That's all they have to know, and I go right through.

BIFF: Did you knock them dead, Pop?

WILLY: Knocked 'em cold in Providence, slaughtered 'em in Boston.

HAPPY (*on his back, pedaling again*): I'm losing weight, you notice, Pop?

(*Linda enters as of old, a ribbon in her hair, carrying a basket of washing.*)

LINDA (*with youthful energy*): Hello, dear!

WILLY: Sweetheart!

LINDA: How'd the Chevvy run?

WILLY: Chevrolet, Linda, is the greatest car ever built. (*To the boys.*) Since when do you let your mother carry wash up the stairs?

BIFF: Grab hold there, boy!

HAPPY: Where to, Mom?

LINDA: Hang them up on the line. And you better go down to your friends, Biff. The cellar is full of boys. They don't know what to do with themselves.

BIFF: Ah, when Pop comes home they can wait!

WILLY (*laughs appreciatively*): You better go down and tell them what to do, Biff.

BIFF: I think I'll have them sweep out the furnace room.

WILLY: Good work, Biff.

BIFF (*goes through wall-line of kitchen to doorway at back and calls down*): Fellas! Everybody sweep out the furnace room! I'll be right down!

VOICES: All right! Okay, Biff.

BIFF: George and Sam and Frank, come out back! We're hangin' up the wash! Come on, Hap, on the double! (*He and Happy carry out the basket.*)

LINDA: The way they obey him!

WILLY: Well, that's training, the training. I'm tellin' you, I was sellin' thousands and thousands, but I had to come home.

LINDA: Oh, the whole block'll be at that game. Did you sell anything?

WILLY: I did five hundred gross in Providence and seven hundred gross in Boston.

LINDA: No! Wait a minute, I've got a pencil. (*She pulls pencil and paper out of her apron pocket.*) That makes your commission . . . Two hundred— my God! Two hundred and twelve dollars!

WILLY: Well, I didn't figure it yet, but . . .

LINDA: How much did you do?

WILLY: Well, I—I did—about a hundred and eighty gross in Providence. Well, no—it came to—roughly two hundred gross on the whole trip.

LINDA (*without hesitation*): Two hundred gross. That's . . . (*She figures.*)

WILLY: The trouble was that three of the stores were half-closed for inventory in Boston. Otherwise I woulda broke records.

LINDA: Well, it makes seventy dollars and some pennies. That's very good.

WILLY: What do we owe?

LINDA: Well, on the first there's sixteen dollars on the refrigerator—

WILLY: Why sixteen?

LINDA: Well, the fan belt broke, so it was a dollar eighty.

WILLY: But it's brand new.

LINDA: Well, the man said that's the way it is. Till they work themselves in, y'know.

(*They move through the wall-line into the kitchen.*)

WILLY: I hope we didn't get stuck on that machine.

LINDA: They got the biggest ads of any of them!

WILLY: I know, it's a fine machine. What else?

LINDA: Well, there's nine-sixty for the washing machine. And for the vacuum cleaner there's three and a half due on the fifteenth. Then the roof, you got twenty-one dollars remaining.

WILLY: It don't leak, does it?

LINDA: No, they did a wonderful job. Then you owe Frank for the carburetor.

WILLY: I'm not going to pay that man! That goddam Chevrolet, they ought to prohibit the manufacture of that car!

LINDA: Well, you owe him three and a half. And odds and ends, comes to around a hundred and twenty dollars by the fifteenth.

WILLY: A hundred and twenty dollars! My God, if business don't pick up I don't know what I'm gonna do!

LINDA: Well, next week you'll do better.

WILLY: Oh, I'll knock 'em dead next week. I'll go to Hartford. I'm very well liked in Hartford. You know, the trouble is, Linda, people don't seem to take to me.

(*They move onto the forestage.*)

LINDA: Oh, don't be foolish.

WILLY: I know it when I walk in. They seem to laugh at me.

LINDA: Why? Why would they laugh at you? Don't talk that way, Willy.

(*Willy moves to the edge of the stage. Linda goes into the kitchen and starts to darn stockings.*)

WILLY: I don't know the reason for it, but they just pass me by. I'm not noticed.

LINDA: But you're doing wonderful, dear. You're making seventy to a hundred dollars a week.

WILLY: But I gotta be at it ten, twelve hours a day. Other men—I don't know—they do it easier. I don't know why—I can't stop myself—I talk too much. A man oughta come in with a few words. One thing about Charley. He's a man of few words, and they respect him.

LINDA: You don't talk too much, you're just lively.

WILLY (*smiling*): Well, I figure, what the hell, life is short, a couple of jokes. (*To himself.*) I joke too much! (*The smile goes.*)

LINDA: Why? You're—

WILLY: I'm fat. I'm very—foolish to look at, Linda. I didn't tell you, but Christmas time I happened to be calling on F. H. Stewarts, and a salesman I know, as I was going in to see the buyer I heard him say something about—walrus. And I—I cracked him right across the face. I won't take that. I simply will not take that. But they do laugh at me. I know that.

LINDA: Darling . . .

WILLY: I gotta overcome it. I know I gotta overcome it. I'm not dressing to advantage, maybe.

LINDA: Willy, darling, you're the handsomest man in the world—

WILLY: Oh, no, Linda.

LINDA: To me you are. (*Slight pause.*) The handsomest.

(*From the darkness is heard the laughter of a woman. Willy doesn't turn to it, but it continues through Linda's lines.*)

LINDA: And the boys, Willy. Few men are idolized by their children the way you are.

(*Music is heard as behind a scrim, to the left of the house, The Woman, dimly seen, is dressing.*)

WILLY (*with great feeling*): You're the best there is, Linda, you're a pal, you know that? On the road—on the road I want to grab you sometimes and just kiss the life outa you.

(*The laughter is loud now, and he moves into a brightening area at the left, where The Woman has come from behind the scrim and is standing, putting on her hat, looking into a "mirror" and laughing.*)

WILLY: 'Cause I get so lonely—especially when business is bad and there's nobody to talk to. I get the feeling that I'll never sell anything again, that I won't make a living for you, or a business, a business for the boys. (*He talks through The Woman's subsiding laughter; The Woman primps at the "mirror."*) There's so much I want to make for—

THE WOMAN: Me? You didn't make me, Willy. I picked you.

WILLY (*pleased*): You picked me?

THE WOMAN (*who is quite proper-looking, Willy's age*): I did. I've been sitting at that desk watching all the salesmen go by, day in, day out. But you've got such a sense of humor, and we do have such a good time together, don't we?

WILLY: Sure, sure. (*He takes her in his arms.*) Why do you have to go now?

THE WOMAN: It's two o'clock . . .

WILLY: No, come on in! (*He pulls her.*)

THE WOMAN: . . . my sisters'll be scandalized. When'll you be back?

WILLY: Oh, two weeks about. Will you come up again?

THE WOMAN: Sure thing. You do make me laugh. It's good for me. (*She squeezes his arm, kisses him.*) And I think you're a wonderful man.
WILLY: You picked me, heh?
THE WOMAN: Sure. Because you're so sweet. And such a kidder.
WILLY: Well, I'll see you next time I'm in Boston.
THE WOMAN: I'll put you right through to the buyers.
WILLY (*slapping her bottom*): Right. Well, bottoms up!
THE WOMAN (*slaps him gently and laughs*): You just kill me, Willy. (*He suddenly grabs her and kisses her roughly.*) You kill me. And thanks for the stockings. I love a lot of stockings. Well, good night.
WILLY: Good night. And keep your pores open!
THE WOMAN: Oh, Willy!

(*The Woman bursts out laughing, and Linda's laughter blends in. The Woman disappears into the dark. Now the area at the kitchen table brightens. Linda is sitting where she was at the kitchen table, but now is mending a pair of her silk stockings.*)

LINDA: You are, Willy. The handsomest man. You've got no reason to feel that—
WILLY (*coming out of The Woman's dimming area and going over to Linda*): I'll make it all up to you, Linda, I'll—
LINDA: There's nothing to make up, dear. You're doing fine, better than—
WILLY (*noticing her mending*): What's that?
LINDA: Just mending my stockings. They're so expensive—
WILLY (*angrily, taking them from her*): I won't have you mending stockings in this house! Now throw them out!

(*Linda puts the stockings in her pocket.*)

BERNARD (*entering on the run*): Where is he? If he doesn't study!
WILLY (*moving to the forestage, with great agitation*): You'll give him the answers!
BERNARD: I do, but I can't on a Regents! That's a state exam! They're liable to arrest me!
WILLY: Where is he? I'll whip him, I'll whip him!
LINDA: And he'd better give back that football, Willy, it's not nice.
WILLY: Biff! Where is he? Why is he taking everything?
LINDA: He's too rough with the girls, Willy. All the mothers are afraid of him!
WILLY: I'll whip him!
BERNARD: He's driving the car without a license!

(*The Woman's laugh is heard.*)

WILLY: Shut up!

LINDA: All the mothers—
WILLY: Shut up!
BERNARD (*backing quietly away and out*): Mr. Birnbaum says he's stuck up.
WILLY: Get outa here!
BERNARD: If he doesn't buckle down he'll flunk math! (*He goes off.*)
LINDA: He's right, Willy, you've gotta—
WILLY (*exploding at her*): There's nothing the matter with him! You want
    him to be a worm like Bernard? He's got spirit, personality . . .

(*As he speaks, Linda, almost in tears, exits into the living room. Willy is alone
in the kitchen, wilting and staring. The leaves are gone. It is night again, and
the apartment houses look down from behind.*)

WILLY: Loaded with it. Loaded! What is he stealing? He's giving it back,
    isn't he? Why is he stealing? What did I tell him? I never in my life told
    him anything but decent things.

(*Happy in pajamas has come down the stairs; Willy suddenly becomes aware of
Happy's presence.*)

HAPPY: Let's go now, come on.
WILLY (*sitting down at the kitchen table*): Huh! Why did she have to wax
    the floors herself? Everytime she waxes the floors she keels over. She
    knows that!
HAPPY: Shh! Take it easy. What brought you back tonight?
WILLY: I got an awful scare. Nearly hit a kid in Yonkers. God! Why didn't
    I go to Alaska with my brother Ben that time! Ben! That man was a
    genius, that man was success incarnate! What a mistake! He begged
    me to go.
HAPPY: Well, there's no use in—
WILLY: You guys! There was a man started with the clothes on his back
    and ended up with diamond mines!
HAPPY: Boy, someday I'd like to know how he did it.
WILLY: What's the mystery? The man knew what he wanted and went
    out and got it! Walked into a jungle, and comes out, the age of twenty-
    one, and he's rich! The world is an oyster, but you don't crack it open
    on a mattress!
HAPPY: Pop, I told you I'm gonna retire you for life.
WILLY: You'll retire me for life on seventy goddam dollars a week? And
    your women and your car and your apartment, and you'll retire me for
    life! Christ's sake, I couldn't get past Yonkers today! Where are you
    guys, where are you? The woods are burning! I can't drive a car!

(*Charley has appeared in the doorway. He is a large man, slow of speech,
laconic, immovable. In all he says, despite what he says, there is pity, and, now,*

trepidation. He has a robe over pajamas, slippers on his feet. He enters the kitchen.)

CHARLEY: Everything all right?

HAPPY: Yeah, Charley, everything's . . .

WILLY: What's the matter?

CHARLEY: I heard some noise. I thought something happened. Can't we do something about the walls? You sneeze in here, and in my house hats blow off.

HAPPY: Let's go to bed, Dad. Come on.

(*Charley signals to Happy to go.*)

WILLY: You go ahead, I'm not tired at the moment.

HAPPY (*to Willy*): Take it easy, huh? (*He exits.*)

WILLY: What're you doin' up?

CHARLEY (*sitting down at the kitchen table opposite Willy*): Couldn't sleep good. I had a heartburn.

WILLY: Well, you don't know how to eat.

CHARLEY: I eat with my mouth.

WILLY: No, you're ignorant. You gotta know about vitamins and things like that.

CHARLEY: Come on, let's shoot. Tire you out a little.

WILLY (*hesitantly*): All right. You got cards?

CHARLEY (*taking a deck from his pocket*): Yeah, I got them. Someplace. What is it with those vitamins?

WILLY (*dealing*): They build up your bones. Chemistry.

CHARLEY: Yeah, but there's no bones in a heartburn.

WILLY: What are you talkin' about? Do you know the first thing about it?

CHARLEY: Don't get insulted.

WILLY: Don't talk about something you don't know anything about.

(*They are playing. Pause.*)

CHARLEY: What're you doin' home?

WILLY: A little trouble with the car.

CHARLEY: Oh. (*Pause.*) I'd like to take a trip to California.

WILLY: Don't say.

CHARLEY: You want a job?

WILLY: I got a job, I told you that. (*After a slight pause.*) What the hell are you offering me a job for?

CHARLEY: Don't get insulted.

WILLY: Don't insult me.

CHARLEY: I don't see no sense in it. You don't have to go on this way.

WILLY: I got a good job. (*Slight pause.*) What do you keep comin' in here for?

CHARLEY: You want me to go?

WILLY (*after a pause, withering*): I can't understand it. He's going back to Texas again. What the hell is that?

CHARLEY: Let him go.

WILLY: I got nothin' to give him, Charley, I'm clean, I'm clean.

CHARLEY: He won't starve. None a them starve. Forget about him.

WILLY: Then what have I got to remember?

CHARLEY: You take it too hard. To hell with it. When a deposit bottle is broken you don't get your nickel back.

WILLY: That's easy enough for you to say.

CHARLEY: That ain't easy for me to say.

WILLY: Did you see the ceiling I put up in the living room?

CHARLEY: Yeah, that's a piece of work. To put up a ceiling is a mystery to me. How do you do it?

WILLY: What's the difference?

CHARLEY: Well, talk about it.

WILLY: You gonna put up a ceiling?

CHARLEY: How could I put up a ceiling?

WILLY: Then what the hell are you bothering me for?

CHARLEY: You're insulted again.

WILLY: A man who can't handle tools is not a man. You're disgusting.

CHARLEY: Don't call me disgusting, Willy.

(*Uncle Ben, carrying a valise and an umbrella, enters the forestage from around the right corner of the house. He is a stolid man, in his sixties, with a mustache and an authoritative air. He is utterly certain of his destiny, and there is an aura of far places about him. He enters exactly as Willy speaks.*)

WILLY: I'm getting awfully tired, Ben.

(*Ben's music is heard. Ben looks around at everything.*)

CHARLEY: Good, keep playing; you'll sleep better. Did you call me Ben?

(*Ben looks at his watch.*)

WILLY: That's funny. For a second there you reminded me of my brother Ben.

BEN: I only have a few minutes. (*He strolls, inspecting the place. Willy and Charley continue playing.*)

CHARLEY: You never heard from him again, heh? Since that time?

WILLY: Didn't Linda tell you? Couple of weeks ago we got a letter from his wife in Africa. He died.

CHARLEY: That so.

BEN (*chuckling*): So this is Brooklyn, eh?

CHARLEY: Maybe you're in for some of his money.

WILLY: Naa, he had seven sons. There's just one opportunity I had with that man . . .

BEN: I must make a train, William. There are several properties I'm looking at in Alaska.

WILLY: Sure, sure! If I'd gone with him to Alaska that time, everything would've been totally different.

CHARLIE: Go on, you'd froze to death up there.

WILLY: What're you talking about?

BEN: Opportunity is tremendous in Alaska, William. Surprised you're not up there.

WILLY: Sure, tremendous.

CHARLEY: Heh?

WILLY: There was the only man I ever met who knew the answers.

CHARLEY: Who?

BEN: How are you all?

WILLY (*taking a pot, smiling*): Fine, fine.

CHARLEY: Pretty sharp tonight.

BEN: Is Mother living with you?

WILLY: No, she died a long time ago.

CHARLEY: Who?

BEN: That's too bad. Fine specimen of a lady, Mother.

WILLY (*to Charley*): Heh?

BEN: I'd hoped to see the old girl.

CHARLEY: Who died?

BEN: Heard anything from Father, have you?

WILLY (*unnerved*): What do you mean, who died?

CHARLEY (*taking a pot*): What're you talkin' about?

BEN (*looking at his watch*): William, it's half-past eight!

WILLY (*as though to dispel his confusion he angrily stops Charley's hand*): That's my build!

CHARLEY: I put the ace—

WILLY: If you don't know how to play the game I'm not gonna throw my money away on you!

CHARLEY (*rising*): It was my ace, for God's sake!

WILLY: I'm through, I'm through!

BEN: When did Mother die?

WILLY: Long ago. Since the beginning you never knew how to play cards.

CHARLEY (*picks up the cards and goes to the door*): All right! Next time I'll bring a deck with five aces.

WILLY: I don't play that kind of game!

CHARLEY (*turning to him*): You ought to be ashamed of yourself!

WILLY: Yeah?

CHARLEY: Yeah! (*He goes out.*)

WILLY (*slamming the door after him*): Ignoramus!

BEN (*as Willy comes toward him through the wall-line of the kitchen*): So you're William.

WILLY (*shaking Ben's hand*): Ben! I've been waiting for you so long! What's the answer? How did you do it?

BEN: Oh, there's a story in that.

(*Linda enters the forestage, as of old, carrying the wash basket.*)

LINDA: Is this Ben?

BEN (*gallantly*): How do you do, my dear.

LINDA: Where've you been all these years? Willy's always wondered why you—

WILLY (*pulling Ben away from her impatiently*): Where is Dad? Didn't you follow him? How did you get started?

BEN: Well, I don't know how much you remember.

WILLY: Well, I was just a baby, of course, only three or four years old—

BEN: Three years and eleven months.

WILLY: What a memory, Ben!

BEN: I have many enterprises, William, and I have never kept books.

WILLY: I remember I was sitting under the wagon in—was it Nebraska?

BEN: It was South Dakota, and I gave you a bunch of wild flowers.

WILLY: I remember you walking away down some open road.

BEN (*laughing*): I was going to find Father in Alaska.

WILLY: Where is he?

BEN: At that age I had a very faulty view of geography, William. I discovered after a few days that I was heading due south, so instead of Alaska, I ended up in Africa.

LINDA: Africa!

WILLY: The Gold Coast!

BEN: Principally diamond mines.

LINDA: Diamond mines!

BEN: Yes, my dear. But I've only a few minutes—

WILLY: No! Boys! Boys! (*Young Biff and Happy appear.*) Listen to this. This is your Uncle Ben, a great man! Tell my boys, Ben!

BEN: Why, boys, when I was seventeen I walked into the jungle, and when I was twenty-one I walked out. (*He laughs.*) And by God I was rich.

WILLY (*to the boys*): You see what I been talking about? The greatest things can happen!

BEN (*glancing at his watch*): I have an appointment in Ketchikan Tuesday week.

WILLY: No, Ben! Please tell about Dad. I want my boys to hear. I want them to know the kind of stock they spring from. All I remember is a man with a big beard, and I was in Mamma's lap, sitting around a fire, and some kind of high music.

BEN: His flute. He played the flute.

WILLY: Sure, the flute, that's right!

(*New music is heard, a high, rollicking tune.*)

BEN: Father was a very great and a very wild-hearted man. We would start in Boston, and he'd toss the whole family into the wagon, and then he'd drive the team right across the country; through Ohio, and Indiana, Michigan, Illinois, and all the Western states. And we'd stop in the towns and sell the flutes that he'd made on the way. Great inventor Father. With one gadget he made more in a week than a man like you could make in a lifetime.

WILLY: That's just the way I'm bringing them up, Ben—rugged, well liked, all-around.

BEN: Yeah? (*To Biff.*) Hit that, boy—hard as you can. (*He pounds his stomach.*)

BIFF: Oh, no, sir!

BEN (*taking boxing stance*): Come on, get to me! (*He laughs.*)

WILLY: Go to it, Biff! Go ahead, show him!

BIFF: Okay! (*He cocks his fists and starts in.*)

LINDA (*to Willy*): Why must he fight, dear?

BEN (*sparring with Biff*): Good boy! Good boy!

WILLY: How's that, Ben, heh?

HAPPY: Give him the left, Biff!

LINDA: Why are you fighting?

BEN: Good boy! (*Suddenly comes in, trips Biff, and stands over him, the point of his umbrella poised over Biff's eye.*)

LINDA: Look out, Biff!

BIFF: Gee!

BEN (*patting Biff's knee*): Never fight fair with a stranger, boy. You'll never get out of the jungle that way. (*Taking Linda's hand and bowing.*) It was an honor and a pleasure to meet you, Linda.

LINDA (*withdrawing her hand coldly, frightened*): Have a nice—trip.

BEN (*to Willy*): And good luck with your—what do you do?

WILLY: Selling.

BEN: Yes. Well . . . (*He raises his hand in farewell to all.*)

WILLY: No, Ben, I don't want you to think . . . (*He takes Ben's arm to show him.*) It's Brooklyn, I know, but we hunt too.

BEN: Really, now.

WILLY: Oh, sure, there's snakes and rabbits and—that's why I moved out here. Why, Biff can fell any one of these trees in no time! Boys! Go right over to where they're building the apartment house and get some sand. We're gonna rebuild the entire front stoop right now! Watch this, Ben!

BIFF: Yes, sir! On the double, Hap!

HAPPY (*as he and Biff run off*): I lost weight, Pop, you notice?

(*Charley enters in knickers, even before the boys are gone.*)

CHARLEY: Listen, if they steal any more from that building the watchman'll put the cops on them!

LINDA (*to Willy*): Don't let Biff . . .

(*Ben laughs lustily.*)

WILLY: You shoulda seen the lumber they brought home last week. At least a dozen six-by-tens worth all kinds a money.

CHARLEY: Listen, if that watchman—

WILLY: I gave them hell, understand. But I got a couple of fearless characters there.

CHARLEY: Willy, the jails are full of fearless characters.

BEN (*clapping Willy on the back, with a laugh at Charley*): And the stock exchange, friend!

WILLY (*joining in Ben's laughter*): Where are the rest of your pants?

CHARLEY: My wife bought them.

WILLY: Now all you need is a golf club and you can go upstairs and go to sleep. (*To Ben.*) Great athlete! Between him and his son Bernard they can't hammer a nail!

BERNARD (*rushing in*): The watchman's chasing Biff!

WILLY (*angrily*): Shut up! He's not stealing anything!

LINDA (*alarmed, hurrying off left*): Where is he? Biff, dear! (*She exits.*)

WILLY (*moving toward the left, away from Ben*): There's nothing wrong. What's the matter with you?

BEN: Nervy boy. Good!

WILLY (*laughing*): Oh, nerves of iron, that Biff!

CHARLEY: Don't know what it is. My New England man comes back and he's bleedin', they murdered him up there.

WILLY: It's contacts, Charley, I got important contacts!

CHARLEY (*sarcastically*): Glad to hear it, Willy. Come in later, we'll shoot a little casino. I'll take some of your Portland money. (*He laughs at Willy and exits.*)

WILLY (*turning to Ben*): Business is bad, it's murderous. But not for me, of course.

BEN: I'll stop by on my way back to Africa.

WILLY (*longingly*): Can't you stay a few days? You're just what I need, Ben, because I—I have a fine position here, but I—well, Dad left when I was such a baby and I never had a chance to talk to him and I still feel—kind of temporary about myself.

BEN: I'll be late for my train.

(*They are at opposite ends of the stage.*)

WILLY: Ben, my boys — can't we talk? They'd go into the jaws of hell for me, see, but I —

BEN: William, you're being first-rate with your boys. Outstanding, manly chaps!

WILLY (*hanging on to his words*): Oh, Ben, that's good to hear! Because sometimes I'm afraid that I'm not teaching them the right kind of — Ben, how should I teach them?

BEN (*giving great weight to each word, and with a certain vicious audacity*): William, when I walked into the jungle, I was seventeen. When I walked out I was twenty-one. And, by God, I was rich! (*He goes off into darkness around the right corner of the house.*)

WILLY: . . . was rich! That's just the spirit I want to imbue them with! To walk into a jungle! I was right! I was right! I was right!

(*Ben is gone, but Willy is still speaking to him as Linda, in nightgown and robe, enters the kitchen, glances around for Willy, then goes to the door of the house, looks out and sees him. Comes down to his left. He looks at her.*)

LINDA: Willy, dear? Willy?

WILLY: I was right!

LINDA: Did you have some cheese? (*He can't answer.*) It's very late, darling. Come to bed, heh?

WILLY (*looking straight up*): Gotta break your neck to see a star in this yard.

LINDA: You coming in?

WILLY: Whatever happened to that diamond watch fob? Remember? When Ben came from Africa that time? Didn't he give me a watch fob with a diamond in it?

LINDA: You pawned it, dear. Twelve, thirteen years ago. For Biff's radio correspondence course.

WILLY: Gee, that was a beautiful thing. I'll take a walk.

LINDA: But you're in your slippers.

WILLY (*starting to go around the house at the left*): I was right! I was! (*Half to Linda, as he goes, shaking his head.*) What a man! There was a man worth talking to. I was right!

LINDA (*calling after Willy*): But in your slippers, Willy!

(*Willy is almost gone when Biff, in his pajamas, comes down the stairs and enters the kitchen.*)

BIFF: What is he doing out there?

LINDA: Sh!

BIFF: God Almighty, Mom, how long has he been doing this?

LINDA: Don't, he'll hear you.

BIFF: What the hell is the matter with him?

LINDA: It'll pass by morning.

BIFF: Shouldn't we do anything?

LINDA: Oh, my dear, you should do a lot of things, but there's nothing to do, so go to sleep.

(*Happy comes down the stair and sits on the steps.*)

HAPPY: I never heard him so loud, Mom.

LINDA: Well, come around more often, you'll hear him. (*She sits down at the table and mends the lining of Willy's jacket.*)

BIFF: Why didn't you ever write me about this, Mom?

LINDA: How would I write to you? For over three months you had no address.

BIFF: I was on the move. But you know I thought of you all the time. You know that, don't you, pal?

LINDA: I know, dear, I know. But he likes to have a letter. Just to know that there's still a possibility for better things.

BIFF: He's not like this all the time, is he?

LINDA: It's when you come home he's always the worst.

BIFF: When I come home?

LINDA: When you write you're coming, he's all smiles and talks about the future, and—he's just wonderful. And then the closer you seem to come, the more shaky he gets, and then, by the time you get here, he's arguing, and he seems angry at you. I think it's just that maybe he can't bring himself to—to open up to you. Why are you so hateful to each other? Why is that?

BIFF (*evasively*): I'm not hateful, Mom.

LINDA: But you no sooner come in the door than you're fighting!

BIFF: I don't know why. I mean to change. I'm tryin', Mom, you understand?

LINDA: Are you home to stay now?

BIFF: I don't know. I want to look around, see what's goin'.

LINDA: Biff, you can't look around all your life, can you?

BIFF: I just can't take hold, Mom. I can't take hold of some kind of a life.

LINDA: Biff, a man is not a bird, to come and go with the springtime.

BIFF: Your hair . . . (*He touches her hair.*) Your hair got so gray.

LINDA: Oh, it's been gray since you were in high school. I just stopped dyeing it, that's all.

BIFF: Dye it again, will ye? I don't want my pal looking old. (*He smiles.*)

LINDA: You're such a boy! You think you can go away for a year and . . . You've got to get it into your head now that one day you'll knock on this door and there'll be strange people here—

BIFF: What are you talking about? You're not even sixty, Mom.

LINDA: But what about your father?

BIFF (*lamely*): Well, I meant him too.

HAPPY: He admires Pop.

LINDA: Biff, dear, if you don't have any feeling for him, then you can't have any feeling for me.

BIFF: Sure I can, Mom.

LINDA: No. You can't just come to see me, because I love him. (*With a threat, but only a threat, of tears.*) He's the dearest man in the world to me, and I won't have anyone making him feel unwanted and low and blue. You've got to make up your mind now, darling, there's no leeway any more. Either he's your father and you pay him that respect, or else you're not to come here. I know he's not easy to get along with—nobody knows that better than me—but . . .

WILLY (*from the left, with a laugh*): Hey, hey, Biffo!

BIFF (*starting to go out after Willy*): What the hell is the matter with him? (*Happy stops him.*)

LINDA: Don't—don't go near him!

BIFF: Stop making excuses for him! He always, always wiped the floor with you. Never had an ounce of respect for you.

HAPPY: He's always had respect for—

BIFF: What the hell do you know about it?

HAPPY (*surlily*): Just don't call him crazy!

BIFF: He's got no character—Charley wouldn't do this. Not in his own house—spewing out that vomit from his mind.

HAPPY: Charley never had to cope with what he's got to.

BIFF: People are worse off than Willy Loman. Believe me, I've seen them!

LINDA: Then make Charley your father, Biff. You can't do that, can you? I don't say he's a great man. Willy Loman never made a lot of money. His name was never in the paper. He's not the finest character that ever lived. But he's a human being, and a terrible thing is happening to him. So attention must be paid. He's not to be allowed to fall into his grave like an old dog. Attention, attention must be finally paid to such a person. You called him crazy—

BIFF: I didn't mean—

LINDA: No, a lot of people think he's lost his—balance. But you don't have to be very smart to know what his trouble is. The man is exhausted.

HAPPY: Sure!

LINDA: A small man can be just as exhausted as a great man. He works for a company thirty-six years this March, opens up unheard-of territories to their trademark, and now in his old age they take his salary away.

HAPPY (*indignantly*): I didn't know that, Mom.

LINDA: You never asked, my dear! Now that you get your spending money someplace else you don't trouble your mind with him.

HAPPY: But I gave you money last—

LINDA: Christmas time, fifty dollars! To fix the hot water it cost ninety-seven fifty! For five weeks he's been on straight commission, like a beginner, an unknown!

BIFF: Those ungrateful bastards!

LINDA: Are they any worse than his sons? When he brought them business, when he was young, they were glad to see him. But now his old friends, the old buyers that loved him so and always found some order to hand him in a pinch—they're all dead, retired. He used to be able to make six, seven calls a day in Boston. Now he takes his valises out of the car and puts them back and takes them out again and he's exhausted. Instead of walking he talks now. He drives seven hundred miles, and when he gets there no one knows him anymore, no one welcomes him. And what goes through a man's mind, driving seven hundred miles home without having earned a cent? Why shouldn't he talk to himself? Why? When he has to go to Charley and borrow fifty dollars a week and pretend to me that it's his pay? How long can that go on? How long? You see what I'm sitting here and waiting for? And you tell me he has no character? The man who never worked a day but for your benefit? When does he get the medal for that? Is this his reward—to turn around at the age of sixty-three and find his sons, who he loved better than his life, one a philandering bum—

HAPPY: Mom!

LINDA: That's all you are, my baby! (*To Biff.*) And you! What happened to the love you had for him? You were such pals! How you used to talk to him on the phone every night! How lonely he was till he could come home to you!

BIFF: All right, Mom. I'll live here in my room, and I'll get a job. I'll keep away from him, that's all.

LINDA: No, Biff. You can't stay here and fight all the time.

BIFF: He threw me out of this house, remember that.

LINDA: Why did he do that? I never knew why.

BIFF: Because I know he's a fake and he doesn't like anybody around who knows!

LINDA: Why a fake? In what way? What do you mean?

BIFF: Just don't lay it all at my feet. It's between me and him—that's all I have to say. I'll chip in from now on. He'll settle for half my pay check. He'll be all right. I'm going to bed. (*He starts for the stairs.*)

LINDA: He won't be all right.

BIFF (*turning on the stairs, furiously*): I hate this city and I'll stay here. Now what do you want?

LINDA: He's dying, Biff.

(*Happy turns quickly to her, shocked.*)

BIFF (*after a pause*): Why is he dying?

LINDA: He's been trying to kill himself.

BIFF (*with great horror*): How?

LINDA: I live from day to day.

BIFF: What're you talking about?

LINDA: Remember I wrote you that he smashed up the car again? In February?

BIFF: Well?

LINDA: The insurance inspector came. He said that they have evidence. That all these accidents in the last year—weren't—weren't—accidents.

HAPPY: How can they tell that? That's a lie.

LINDA: It seems there's a woman . . . (*She takes a breath as*)

BIFF (*sharply but contained*): ⎤   What woman?

LINDA (*simultaneously*): ⎦   . . . and this woman . . .

LINDA: What?

BIFF: Nothing. Go ahead.

LINDA: What did you say?

BIFF: Nothing. I just said what woman?

HAPPY: What about her?

LINDA: Well, it seems she was walking down the road and saw his car. She says that he wasn't driving fast at all, and that he didn't skid. She says he came to that little bridge, and then deliberately smashed into the railing, and it was only the shallowness of the water that saved him.

BIFF: Oh, no, he probably just fell asleep again.

LINDA: I don't think he fell asleep.

BIFF: Why not?

LINDA: Last month . . . (*With great difficulty.*) Oh, boys, it's so hard to say a thing like this! He's just a big stupid man to you, but I tell you there's more good in him than in many other people. (*She chokes, wipes her eyes.*) I was looking for a fuse. The lights blew out, and I went down the cellar. And behind the fuse box—it happened to fall out—was a length of rubber pipe—just short.

HAPPY: No kidding!

LINDA: There's a little attachment on the end of it. I knew right away. And sure enough, on the bottom of the water heater there's a new little nipple on the gas pipe.

HAPPY (*angrily*): That—jerk.

BIFF: Did you have it taken off?

LINDA: I'm—I'm ashamed to. How can I mention it to him? Every day I go down and take away that little rubber pipe. But, when he comes home, I put it back where it was. How can I insult him that way? I don't know what to do. I live from day to day, boys. I tell you, I know every thought in his mind. It sounds so old-fashioned and silly, but I tell you he put his whole life into you and you've turned your backs on him. (*She is bent over in the chair, weeping, her face in her hands.*) Biff, I swear to God! Biff, his life is in your hands!

HAPPY (*to Biff*): How do you like that damned fool!

BIFF (*kissing her*): All right, pal, all right. It's all settled now. I've been remiss. I know that, Mom. But now I'll stay, and I swear to you, I'll apply myself. (*Kneeling in front of her, in a fever of self-reproach.*) It's just—you see, Mom, I don't fit in business. Not that I won't try. I'll try, and I'll make good.

HAPPY: Sure you will. The trouble with you in business was you never tried to please people.

BIFF: I know, I—

HAPPY: Like when you worked for Harrison's. Bob Harrison said you were tops, and then you go and do some damn fool thing like whistling whole songs in the elevator like a comedian.

BIFF (*against Happy*): So what? I like to whistle sometimes.

HAPPY: You don't raise a guy to a responsible job who whistles in the elevator!

LINDA: Well, don't argue about it now.

HAPPY: Like when you'd go off and swim in the middle of the day instead of taking the line around.

BIFF (*his resentment rising*): Well, don't you run off? You take off sometimes, don't you? On a nice summer day?

HAPPY: Yeah, but I cover myself!

LINDA: Boys!

HAPPY: If I'm going to take a fade the boss can call any number where I'm supposed to be and they'll swear to him that I just left. I'll tell you something that I hate to say, Biff, but in the business world some of them think you're crazy.

BIFF (*angered*): Screw the business world!

HAPPY: All right, screw it! Great, but cover yourself!

LINDA: Hap, Hap!

BIFF: I don't care what they think! They've laughed at Dad for years, and you know why? Because we don't belong in this nuthouse of a city! We should be mixing cement on some open plain, or—or carpenters. A carpenter is allowed to whistle!

(*Willy walks in from the entrance of the house, at left.*)

WILLY: Even your grandfather was better than a carpenter. (*Pause. They watch him.*) You never grew up. Bernard does not whistle in the elevator, I assure you.

BIFF (*as though to laugh Willy out of it*): Yeah, but you do, Pop.

WILLY: I never in my life whistled in an elevator! And who in the business world thinks I'm crazy?

BIFF: I didn't mean it like that, Pop. Now don't make a whole thing out of it, will ye?

WILLY: Go back to the West! Be a carpenter, a cowboy, enjoy yourself!

LINDA: Willy, he was just saying—

WILLY: I heard what he said!

HAPPY (*trying to quiet Willy*): Hey, Pop, come on now . . .

WILLY (*continuing over Happy's line*): They laugh at me, heh? Go to Filene's, go to the Hub, go to Slattery's, Boston. Call out the name Willy Loman and see what happens! Big shot!

BIFF: All right, Pop.

WILLY: Big!

BIFF: All right!

WILLY: Why do you always insult me?

BIFF: I didn't say a word. (*To Linda.*) Did I say a word?

LINDA: He didn't say anything, Willy.

WILLY (*going to the doorway of the living room*): All right, good night, good night.

LINDA: Willy, dear, he just decided . . .

WILLY (*to Biff*): If you get tired hanging around tomorrow, paint the ceiling I put up in the living room.

BIFF: I'm leaving early tomorrow.

HAPPY: He's going to see Bill Oliver, Pop.

WILLY (*interestedly*): Oliver? For what?

BIFF (*with reserve, but trying, trying*): He always said he'd stake me. I'd like to go into business, so maybe I can take him up on it.

LINDA: Isn't that wonderful?

WILLY: Don't interrupt. What's wonderful about it? There's fifty men in the City of New York who'd stake him. (*To Biff.*) Sporting goods?

BIFF: I guess so. I know something about it and—

WILLY: He knows something about it! You know sporting goods better than Spalding, for God's sake! How much is he giving you?

BIFF: I don't know, I didn't even see him yet, but—

WILLY: Then what're you talkin' about?

BIFF (*getting angry*): Well, all I said was I'm gonna see him, that's all!

WILLY (*turning away*): Ah, you're counting your chickens again.

BIFF (*starting left for the stairs*): Oh, Jesus, I'm going to sleep!

WILLY (*calling after him*): Don't curse in this house!

BIFF (*turning*): Since when did you get so clean?

HAPPY (*trying to stop them*): Wait a . . .

WILLY: Don't use that language to me! I won't have it!

HAPPY (*grabbing Biff, shouts*): Wait a minute! I got an idea. I got a feasible idea. Come here, Biff, let's talk this over now, let's talk some sense here. When I was down in Florida last time, I thought of a great idea to sell sporting goods. It just came back to me. You and I, Biff—we have a line, the Loman Line. We train a couple of weeks, and put on a couple of exhibitions, see?

WILLY: That's an idea!

HAPPY: Wait! We form two basketball teams, see? Two water polo teams. We play each other. It's a million dollars' worth of publicity. Two brothers, see? The Loman Brothers. Displays in the Royal Palms—all the hotels. And banners over the ring and the basketball court: "Loman Brothers." Baby, we could sell sporting goods!

WILLY: That is a one-million-dollar idea!

LINDA: Marvelous!

BIFF: I'm in great shape as far as that's concerned.

HAPPY: And the beauty of it is, Biff, it wouldn't be like a business. We'd be out playin' ball again . . .

BIFF (*enthused*): Yeah, that's . . .

WILLY: Million-dollar . . .

HAPPY: And you wouldn't get fed up with it, Biff. It'd be the family again. There'd be the old honor, and comradeship, and if you wanted to go off for a swim or somethin'—well, you'd do it! Without some smart cooky gettin' up ahead of you!

WILLY: Lick the world! You guys together could absolutely lick the civilized world.

BIFF: I'll see Oliver tomorrow. Hap, if we could work that out . . .

LINDA: Maybe things are beginning to—

WILLY (*wildly enthused, to Linda*): Stop interrupting! (*To Biff.*) But don't wear sport jacket and slacks when you see Oliver.

BIFF: No, I'll—

WILLY: A business suit, and talk as little as possible, and don't crack any jokes.

BIFF: He did like me. Always liked me.

LINDA: He loved you!

WILLY (*to Linda*): Will you stop! (*To Biff.*) Walk in very serious. You are not applying for a boy's job. Money is to pass. Be quiet, fine, and serious. Everybody likes a kidder, but nobody lends him money.

HAPPY: I'll try to get some myself, Biff. I'm sure I can.

WILLY: I see great things for you kids, I think your troubles are over. But remember, start big and you'll end big. Ask for fifteen. How much you gonna ask for?

BIFF: Gee, I don't know—

WILLY: And don't say "Gee." "Gee" is a boy's word. A man walking in for fifteen thousand dollars does not say "Gee!"

BIFF: Ten, I think, would be top though.

WILLY: Don't be so modest. You always started too low. Walk in with a big laugh. Don't look worried. Start off with a couple of your good stories to lighten things up. It's not what you say, it's how you say it— because personality always wins the day.

LINDA: Oliver always thought the highest of him—

WILLY: Will you let me talk?

BIFF: Don't yell at her, Pop, will ye?

WILLY (*angrily*): I was talking, wasn't I?

BIFF: I don't like you yelling at her all the time, and I'm tellin' you, that's all.

WILLY: What're you, takin' over this house?

LINDA: Willy—

WILLY (*turning to her*): Don't take his side all the time, goddammit!

BIFF (*furiously*): Stop yelling at her!

WILLY (*suddenly pulling on his cheek, beaten down, guilt ridden*): Give my best to Bill Oliver—he may remember me. (*He exits through the living room doorway.*)

LINDA (*her voice subdued*): What'd you have to start that for? (*Biff turns away.*) You see how sweet he was as soon as you talked hopefully? (*She goes over to Biff.*) Come up and say good night to him. Don't let him go to bed that way.

HAPPY: Come on, Biff, let's buck him up.

LINDA: Please, dear. Just say good night. It takes so little to make him happy. Come. (*She goes through the living room doorway, calling upstairs from within the living room.*) Your pajamas are hanging in the bathroom, Willy!

HAPPY (*looking toward where Linda went out*): What a woman! They broke the mold when they made her. You know that, Biff?

BIFF: He's off salary. My God, working on commission!

HAPPY: Well, let's face it: he's no hot-shot selling man. Except that sometimes, you have to admit, he's a sweet personality.

BIFF (*deciding*): Lend me ten bucks, will ye? I want to buy some new ties.

HAPPY: I'll take you to a place I know. Beautiful stuff. Wear one of my striped shirts tomorrow.

BIFF: She got gray. Mom got awful old. Gee, I'm gonna go in to Oliver tomorrow and knock him for a—

HAPPY: Come on up. Tell that to Dad. Let's give him a whirl. Come on.

BIFF (*steamed up*): You know, with ten thousand bucks, boy!

HAPPY (*as they go into the living room*): That's the talk, Biff, that's the first time I've heard the old confidence out of you! (*From within the living room, fading off.*) You're gonna live with me, kid, and any babe you want just say the word . . . (*The last lines are hardly heard. They are mounting the stairs to their parents' bedroom.*)

LINDA (*entering her bedroom and addressing Willy, who is in the bathroom. She is straightening the bed for him.*): Can you do anything about the shower? It drips.

WILLY (*from the bathroom*): All of a sudden everything falls to pieces. Goddam plumbing, oughta be sued, those people. I hardly finished putting it in and the thing . . . (*His words rumble off.*)

LINDA: I'm just wondering if Oliver will remember him. You think he might?

WILLY (*coming out of the bathroom in his pajamas*): Remember him? What's the matter with you, you crazy? If he'd've stayed with Oliver he'd be on top by now! Wait'll Oliver gets a look at him. You don't know the average caliber any more. The average young man today— (*he is getting into bed*)—is got a caliber of zero. Greatest thing in the world for him was to bum around.

(*Biff and Happy enter the bedroom. Slight pause.*)

WILLY (*stops short, looking at Biff*): Glad to hear it, boy.

HAPPY: He wanted to say good night to you, sport.

WILLY (*to Biff*): Yeah. Knock him dead, boy. What'd you want to tell me?

BIFF: Just take it easy, Pop. Good night. (*He turns to go.*)

WILLY (*unable to resist*): And if anything falls off the desk while you're talking to him—like a package or something—don't you pick it up. They have office boys for that.

LINDA: I'll make a big breakfast—

WILLY: Will you let me finish? (*To Biff.*) Tell him you were in the business in the West. Not farm work.

BIFF: All right, Dad.

LINDA: I think everything—

WILLY (*going right through her speech*): And don't undersell yourself. No less than fifteen thousand dollars.

BIFF (*unable to bear him*): Okay. Good night, Mom. (*He starts moving.*)

WILLY: Because you got a greatness in you, Biff, remember that. You got all kinds of greatness . . . (*He lies back, exhausted. Biff walks out.*)

LINDA (*calling after Biff*): Sleep well, darling!

HAPPY: I'm gonna get married, Mom. I wanted to tell you.

LINDA: Go to sleep, dear.

HAPPY (*going*): I just wanted to tell you.

WILLY: Keep up the good work. (*Happy exits.*) God . . . remember that Ebbets Field game? The championship of the city?

LINDA: Just rest. Should I sing to you?

WILLY: Yeah. Sing to me. (*Linda hums a soft lullaby.*) When that team came out—he was the tallest, remember?
LINDA: Oh, yes. And in gold.

(*Biff enters the darkened kitchen, takes a cigarette, and leaves the house. He comes downstage into a golden pool of light. He smokes, staring at the night.*)

WILLY: Like a young god. Hercules—something like that. And the sun, the sun all around him. Remember how he waved to me? Right up from the field, with the representatives of three colleges standing by? And the buyers I brought, and the cheers when he came out—Loman, Loman, Loman! God Almighty, he'll be great yet. A star like that, magnificent, can never really fade away!

(*The light on Willy is fading. The gas heater begins to glow through the kitchen wall, near the stairs, a blue flame beneath red coils.*)

LINDA (*timidly*): Willy dear, what has he got against you?
WILLY: I'm so tired. Don't talk anymore.

(*Biff slowly returns to the kitchen. He stops, stares toward the heater.*)

LINDA: Will you ask Howard to let you work in New York?
WILLY: First thing in the morning. Everything'll be all right.

(*Biff reaches behind the heater and draws out a length of rubber tubing. He is horrified and turns his head toward Willy's room, still dimly lit, from which the strains of Linda's desperate but monotonous humming rise.*)

WILLY (*staring through the window into the moonlight*): Gee, look at the moon moving between the buildings!

(*Biff wraps the tubing around his hand and quickly goes up the stairs.*)

ACT II

(*Music is heard, gay and bright. The curtain rises as the music fades away. Willy, in shirt sleeves is sitting at the kitchen table, sipping coffee, his hat in his lap. Linda is filling his cup when she can.*)

WILLY: Wonderful coffee. Meal in itself.
LINDA: Can I make you some eggs?
WILLY: No. Take a breath.
LINDA: You look so rested, dear.
WILLY: I slept like a dead one. First time in months. Imagine, sleeping till ten on a Tuesday morning. Boys left nice and early, heh?
LINDA: They were out of here by eight o'clock.
WILLY: Good work!

LINDA: It was so thrilling to see them leaving together. I can't get over the shaving lotion in this house!

WILLY (*smiling*): Mmm —

LINDA: Biff was very changed this morning. His whole attitude seemed to be hopeful. He couldn't wait to get downtown to see Oliver.

WILLY: He's heading for a change. There's no question, there simply are certain men that take longer to get — solidified. How did he dress?

LINDA: His blue suit. He's so handsome in that suit. He could be a — anything in that suit!

(*Willy gets up from the table. Linda holds his jacket for him.*)

WILLY: There's no question, no question at all. Gee, on the way home tonight I'd like to buy some seeds.

LINDA (*laughing*): That'd be wonderful. But not enough sun gets back there. Nothing'll grow any more.

WILLY: You wait, kid, before it's all over we're gonna get a little place out in the country, and I'll raise some vegetables, a couple of chickens . . .

LINDA: You'll do it yet, dear.

(*Willy walks out of his jacket. Linda follows him.*)

WILLY: And they'll get married, and come for a weekend. I'd build a little guest house. 'Cause I got so many fine tools, all I'd need would be a little lumber and some peace of mind.

LINDA (*joyfully*): I sewed the lining . . .

WILLY: I could build two guest houses, so they'd both come. Did he decide how much he's going to ask Oliver for?

LINDA (*getting him into the jacket*): He didn't mention it, but I imagine ten or fifteen thousand. You going to talk to Howard today?

WILLY: Yeah. I'll put it to him straight and simple. He'll just have to take me off the road.

LINDA: And Willy, don't forget to ask for a little advance, because we've got the insurance premium. It's the grace period now.

WILLY: That's a hundred . . . ?

LINDA: A hundred and eight, sixty-eight. Because we're a little short again.

WILLY: Why are we short?

LINDA: Well, you had the motor job on the car . . .

WILLY: That goddam Studebaker!

LINDA: And you got one more payment on the refrigerator . . .

WILLY: But it just broke again!

LINDA: Well, it's old, dear.

WILLY: I told you we should've bought a well-advertised machine. Charley bought a General Electric and it's twenty years old and it's still good, that son-of-a-bitch.

LINDA: But, Willy—

WILLY: Whoever heard of a Hastings refrigerator? Once in my life I would like to own something outright before it's broken! I'm always in a race with the junkyard! I just finished paying for the car and it's on its last legs. The refrigerator consumes belts like a goddamn maniac. They time those things. They time them so when you finally paid for them, they're used up.

LINDA (*buttoning up his jacket as he unbuttons it*): All told, about two hundred dollars would carry us, dear. But that includes the last payment on the mortgage. After this payment, Willy, the house belongs to us.

WILLY: It's twenty-five years!

LINDA: Biff was nine years old when we bought it.

WILLY: Well, that's a great thing. To weather a twenty-five year mortgage is—

LINDA: It's an accomplishment.

WILLY: All the cement, the lumber, the reconstruction I put in this house! There ain't a crack to be found in it anymore.

LINDA: Well, it served its purpose.

WILLY: What purpose? Some stranger'll come along, move in, and that's that. If only Biff would take this house, and raise a family . . . (*He starts to go.*) Good-by, I'm late.

LINDA (*suddenly remembering*): Oh, I forgot! You're supposed to meet them for dinner.

WILLY: Me?

LINDA: At Frank's Chop House on Forty-eighth near Sixth Avenue.

WILLY: Is that so! How about you?

LINDA: No, just the three of you. They're gonna blow you to a big meal!

WILLY: Don't say! Who thought of that?

LINDA: Biff came to me this morning, Willy, and he said, "Tell Dad, we want to blow him to a big meal." Be there six o'clock. You and your two boys are going to have dinner.

WILLY: Gee whiz! That's really somethin'. I'm gonna knock Howard for a loop, kid. I'll get an advance, and I'll come home with a New York job. Goddammit, now I'm gonna do it!

LINDA: Oh, that's the spirit, Willy!

WILLY: I will never get behind a wheel the rest of my life!

LINDA: It's changing, Willy, I can feel it changing!

WILLY: Beyond a question. G'by, I'm late. (*He starts to go again.*)

LINDA (*calling after him as she runs to the kitchen table for a handkerchief*): You got your glasses?

WILLY (*feels for them, then comes back in*): Yeah, yeah, got my glasses.

LINDA (*giving him the handkerchief*): And a handkerchief.

WILLY: Yeah, handkerchief.

LINDA: And your saccharine?
WILLY: Yeah, my saccharine.
LINDA: Be careful on the subway stairs.

(*She kisses him, and a silk stocking is seen hanging from her hand. Willy notices it.*)

WILLY: Will you stop mending stockings? At least while I'm in the house. It gets me nervous. I can't tell you. Please.

(*Linda hides the stocking in her hand as she follows Willy across the forestage in front of the house.*)

LINDA: Remember, Frank's Chop House.
WILLY (*passing the apron*): Maybe beets would grow out there.
LINDA (*laughing*): But you tried so many times.
WILLY: Yeah. Well, don't work hard today. (*He disappears around the right corner of the house.*)
LINDA: Be careful!

(*As Willy vanishes, Linda waves to him. Suddenly the phone rings. She runs across the stage and into the kitchen and lifts it.*)

LINDA: Hello? Oh, Biff! I'm so glad you called, I just . . . Yes, sure, I just told him. Yes, he'll be there for dinner at six o'clock, I didn't forget. Listen, I was just dying to tell you. You know that little rubber pipe I told you about? That he connected to the gas heater? I finally decided to go down the cellar this morning and take it away and destroy it. But it's gone! Imagine? He took it away himself, it isn't there! (*She listens.*) When? Oh, then you took it. Oh—nothing, it's just that I'd hoped he'd taken it away himself. Oh, I'm not worried, darling, because this morning he left in such high spirits, it was like the old days! I'm not afraid any more. Did Mr. Oliver see you? . . . Well, you wait there then. And make a nice impression on him, darling. Just don't perspire too much before you see him. And have a nice time with Dad. He may have big news too! . . . That's right, a New York job. And be sweet to him tonight, dear. Be loving to him. Because he's only a little boat looking for a harbor. (*She is trembling with sorrow and joy.*) Oh, that's wonderful, Biff, you'll save his life. Thanks, darling. Just put your arm around him when he comes into the restaurant. Give him a smile. That's the boy . . . Good-by, dear. . . . You got your comb? . . . That's fine. Good-by, Biff dear.

(*In the middle of her speech, Howard Wagner, thirty-six, wheels in a small typewriter table on which is a wire-recording machine and proceeds to plug it in. This is on the left forestage. Light slowly fades on Linda as it rises on Howard. Howard is intent on threading the machine and only glances over his shoulder as Willy appears.*)

WILLY: Pst! Pst!

HOWARD: Hello, Willy, come in.

WILLY: Like to have a little talk with you, Howard.

HOWARD: Sorry to keep you waiting. I'll be with you in a minute.

WILLY: What's that, Howard?

HOWARD: Didn't you ever see one of these? Wire recorder.

WILLY: Oh. Can we talk a minute?

HOWARD: Records things. Just got delivery yesterday. Been driving me crazy, the most terrific machine I ever saw in my life. I was up all night with it.

WILLY: What do you do with it?

HOWARD: I bought it for dictation, but you can do anything with it. Listen to this. I had it home last night. Listen to what I picked up. The first one is my daughter. Get this. (*He flicks the switch and "Roll out the Barrel" is heard being whistled.*) Listen to that kid whistle.

WILLY: That is lifelike, isn't it?

HOWARD: Seven years old. Get that tone.

WILLY: Ts, ts. Like to ask a little favor if you . . .

(*The whistling breaks off, and the voice of Howard's daughter is heard.*)

HIS DAUGHTER: Now you, Daddy.

HOWARD: She's crazy for me! (*Again the same song is whistled.*) That's me! Ha! (*He winks.*)

WILLY: You're very good!

(*The whistling breaks off again. The machine runs silent for a moment.*)

HOWARD: Sh! Get this now, this is my son.

HIS SON: "The capital of Alabama is Montgomery; the capital of Arizona is Phoenix; the capital of Arkansas is Little Rock; the capital of California is Sacramento . . ." (*and on, and on.*)

HOWARD (*holding up five fingers*): Five years old, Willy!

WILLY: He'll make an announcer some day!

HIS SON (*continuing*): "The capita . . ."

HOWARD: Get that—alphabetical order! (*The machine breaks off suddenly.*) Wait a minute. The maid kicked the plug out.

WILLY: It certainly is a—

HOWARD: Sh, for God's sake!

HIS SON: "It's nine o'clock, Bulova watch time. So I have to go to sleep."

WILLY: That really is—

HOWARD: Wait a minute! The next is my wife.

(*They wait.*)

HOWARD'S VOICE: "Go on, say something." (*Pause.*) "Well, you gonna talk?"

HIS WIFE: "I can't think of anything."

HOWARD'S VOICE: "Well, talk—it's turning."

HIS WIFE (*shyly, beaten*): "Hello." (*Silence.*) "Oh, Howard, I can't talk into this . . ."

HOWARD (*snapping the machine off*): That was my wife.

WILLY: That is a wonderful machine. Can we—

HOWARD: I tell you, Willy, I'm gonna take my camera, and my bandsaw, and all my hobbies, and out they go. This is the most fascinating relaxation I ever found.

WILLY: I think I'll get one myself.

HOWARD: Sure, they're only a hundred and a half. You can't do without it. Supposing you wanna hear Jack Benny, see? But you can't be at home at that hour. So you tell the maid to turn the radio on when Jack Benny comes on, and this automatically goes on with the radio . . .

WILLY: And when you come home you . . .

HOWARD: You can come home twelve o'clock, one o'clock, any time you like, and you get yourself a Coke and sit yourself down, throw the switch, and there's Jack Benny's program in the middle of the night!

WILLY: I'm definitely going to get one. Because lots of times I'm on the road, and I think to myself, what I must be missing on the radio!

HOWARD: Don't you have a radio in the car?

WILLY: Well, yeah, but who ever thinks of turning it on?

HOWARD: Say, aren't you supposed to be in Boston?

WILLY: That's what I want to talk to you about, Howard. You got a minute? (*He draws a chair in from the wing.*)

HOWARD: What happened? What're you doing here?

WILLY: Well . . .

HOWARD: You didn't crack up again, did you?

WILLY: Oh, no. No . . .

HOWARD: Geez, you had me worried there for a minute. What's the trouble?

WILLY: Well, tell you the truth, Howard. I've come to the decision that I'd rather not travel anymore.

HOWARD: Not travel! Well, what'll you do?

WILLY: Remember, Christmas time, when you had the party here? You said you'd try to think of some spot for me here in town.

HOWARD: With us?

WILLY: Well, sure.

HOWARD: Oh, yeah, yeah. I remember. Well, I couldn't think of anything for you, Willy.

WILLY: I tell ya, Howard. The kids are all grown up, y'know. I don't need much anymore. If I could take home—well, sixty-five dollars a week, I could swing it.

HOWARD: Yeah, but Willy, see I—

WILLY: I tell ya why, Howard. Speaking frankly and between the two of us, y'know—I'm just a little tired.

HOWARD: Oh, I could understand that, Willy. But you're a road man, Willy, and we do a road business. We've only got a half-dozen salesmen on the floor here.

WILLY: God knows, Howard, I never asked a favor of any man. But I was with the firm when your father used to carry you in here in his arms.

HOWARD: I know that, Willy, but—

WILLY: Your father came to me the day you were born and asked me what I thought of the name Howard, may he rest in peace.

HOWARD: I appreciate that, Willy, but there just is no spot here for you. If I had a spot I'd slam you right in, but I just don't have a single solitary spot.

(*He looks for his lighter. Willy has picked it up and gives it to him. Pause.*)

WILLY (*with increasing anger*): Howard, all I need to set my table is fifty dollars a week.

HOWARD: But where am I going to put you, kid?

WILLY: Look, it isn't a question of whether I can sell merchandise, is it?

HOWARD: No, but it's business, kid, and everybody's gotta pull his own weight.

WILLY (*desperately*): Just let me tell you a story, Howard—

HOWARD: 'Cause you gotta admit, business is business.

WILLY (*angrily*): Business is definitely business, but just listen for a minute. You don't understand this. When I was a boy—eighteen, nineteen—I was already on the road. And there was a question in my mind as to whether selling had a future for me. Because in those days I had a yearning to go to Alaska. See, there were three gold strikes in one month in Alaska, and I felt like going out. Just for the ride, you might say.

HOWARD (*barely interested*): Don't say.

WILLY: Oh, yeah, my father lived many years in Alaska. He was an adventurous man. We've got quite a little streak of self-reliance in our family. I thought I'd go out with my older brother and try to locate him, and maybe settle in the North with the old man. And I was almost decided to go, when I met a salesman in the Parker House. His name was Dave Singleman. And he was eighty-four years old, and he'd drummed merchandise in thirty-one states. And old Dave, he'd go up to his room, y'understand, put on his green velvet slippers—I'll never forget—and pick up his phone and call the buyers, and without ever leaving his room, at the age of eighty-four, he made his living. And when I saw that, I realized that selling was the greatest career a man could want. 'Cause what could be more satisfying than to be able to go, at the age of eighty-four, into twenty or thirty different cities, and pick up a phone, and be remembered and loved and helped by so many different people? Do you know? When he died—and by the way he died the death of a salesman, in his green velvet slippers in the smoker of the New York, New Haven and Hartford, going into Boston—when he died, hundreds of salesmen and buyers were at his funeral. Things were sad on a lotta trains for months after that. (*He stands up. Howard has not looked at him.*) In those days there was personality in it, Howard. There was respect and comradeship, and gratitude in it. Today, it's all cut and dried, and there's no chance for bringing friendship to bear—or personality. You see what I mean? They don't know me any more.

HOWARD (*moving away, to the right*): That's just the thing, Willy.

WILLY: If I had forty dollars a week—that's all I'd need. Forty dollars, Howard.

HOWARD: Kid, I can't take blood from a stone, I—

WILLY (*desperation is on him now*): Howard, the year Al Smith was nominated, your father came to me and—

HOWARD (*starting to go off*): I've got to see some people, kid.

WILLY (*stopping him*): I'm talking about your father! There were promises made across this desk! You mustn't tell me you've got people to see—I put thirty-four years into this firm, Howard, and now I can't pay my insurance! You can't eat the orange and throw the peel away—a man is not a piece of fruit! (*After a pause.*) Now pay attention. Your father—in 1928 I had a big year. I averaged a hundred and seventy dollars a week in commissions.

HOWARD (*impatiently*): Now, Willy, you never averaged—

WILLY (*banging his hand on the desk*): I averaged a hundred and seventy dollars a week in the year of 1928! And your father came to me—or rather I was in the office here—it was right over this desk—and he put his hand on my shoulder—

HOWARD (*getting up*): You'll have to excuse me, Willy, I gotta see some people. Pull yourself together. (*Going out.*) I'll be back in a little while.

(*On Howard's exit, the light on his chair grows very bright and strange.*)

WILLY: Pull myself together! What the hell did I say to him? My God, I was yelling at him! How could I? (*Willy breaks off, staring at the light, which occupies the chair, animating it. He approaches this chair, standing across the desk from it.*) Frank, Frank, don't you remember what you told me that time? How you put your hand on my shoulder, and Frank . . . (*He leans on the desk and as he speaks the dead man's name he accidentally switches on the recorder, and instantly*)

HOWARD'S SON: "... of New York is Albany. The capital of Ohio is Cincinnati, the capital of Rhode Island is ..." (*The recitation continues.*)
WILLY (*leaping away with fright, shouting*): Ha! Howard! Howard! Howard!
HOWARD (*rushing in*): What happened?
WILLY (*pointing at the machine, which continues nasally, childishly, with the capital cities*): Shut it off! Shut it off!
HOWARD (*pulling the plug out*): Look, Willy ...
WILLY (*pressing his hands to his eyes*): I gotta get myself some coffee. I'll get some coffee ...

(*Willy starts to walk out. Howard stops him.*)

HOWARD (*rolling up the cord*): Willy, look ...
WILLY: I'll go to Boston.
HOWARD: Willy, you can't go to Boston for us.
WILLY: Why can't I go?
HOWARD: I don't want you to represent us. I've been meaning to tell you for a long time now.
WILLY: Howard, are you firing me?
HOWARD: I think you need a good long rest, Willy.
WILLY: Howard—
HOWARD: And when you feel better, come back, and we'll see if we can work something out.
WILLY: But I gotta earn money, Howard. I'm in no position to—
HOWARD: Where are your sons? Why don't your sons give you a hand?
WILLY: They're working on a very big deal.
HOWARD: This is no time for false pride, Willy. You go to your sons and you tell them that you're tired. You've got two great boys, haven't you?
WILLY: Oh, no question, no question, but in the meantime ...
HOWARD: Then that's that, heh?
WILLY: All right, I'll go to Boston tomorrow.
HOWARD: No, no.
WILLY: I can't throw myself on my sons. I'm not a cripple!
HOWARD: Look, kid, I'm busy this morning.
WILLY (*grasping Howard's arm*): Howard, you've got to let me go to Boston!
HOWARD (*hard, keeping himself under control*): I've got a line of people to see this morning. Sit down, take five minutes, and pull yourself together, and then go home, will ya? I need the office, Willy. (*He starts to go, turns, remembering the recorder, starts to push off the table holding the recorder.*) Oh, yeah. Whenever you can this week, stop by and drop off the samples. You'll feel better, Willy, and then come back and we'll talk. Pull yourself together, kid, there's people outside.

(*Howard exits, pushing the table off left. Willy stares into space, exhausted. Now the music is heard—Ben's music—first distantly, then closer, closer. As Willy speaks, Ben enters from the right. He carries valise and umbrella.*)

WILLY: Oh, Ben, how did you do it? What is the answer? Did you wind up the Alaska deal already?

BEN: Doesn't take much time if you know what you're doing. Just a short business trip. Boarding ship in an hour. Wanted to say good-by.

WILLY: Ben, I've got to talk to you.

BEN (*glancing at his watch*): Haven't the time, William.

WILLY (*crossing the apron to Ben*): Ben, nothing's working out. I don't know what to do.

BEN: Now, look here, William. I've bought timberland in Alaska and I need a man to look after things for me.

WILLY: God, timberland! Me and my boys in those grand outdoors!

BEN: You've a new continent at your doorstep, William. Get out of these cities, they're full of talk and time payments and courts of law. Screw on your fists and you can fight for a fortune up there.

WILLY: Yes, yes! Linda, Linda!

(*Linda enters as of old, with the wash.*)

LINDA: Oh, you're back?

BEN: I haven't much time.

WILLY: No, wait! Linda, he's got a proposition for me in Alaska.

LINDA: But you've got—(*To Ben.*) He's got a beautiful job here.

WILLY: But in Alaska, kid, I could—

LINDA: You're doing well enough, Willy!

BEN (*to Linda*): Enough for what, my dear?

LINDA (*frightened of Ben and angry at him*): Don't say those things to him! Enough to be happy right here, right now. (*To Willy, while Ben laughs.*) Why must everybody conquer the world? You're well liked, and the boys love you, and someday—(*To Ben*)—why, old man Wagner told him just the other day that if he keeps it up he'll be a member of the firm, didn't he, Willy?

WILLY: Sure, sure. I am building something with this firm, Ben, and if a man is building something he must be on the right track, mustn't he?

BEN: What are you building? Lay your hand on it. Where is it?

WILLY (*hesitantly*): That's true, Linda, there's nothing.

LINDA: Why? (*To Ben.*) There's a man eighty-four years old—

WILLY: That's right, Ben, that's right. When I look at that man I say, what is there to worry about?

BEN: Bah!

WILLY: It's true, Ben. All he has to do is go into any city, pick up the phone, and he's making his living and you know why?

BEN (*picking up his valise*): I've got to go.
WILLY (*holding Ben back*): Look at this boy!

(*Biff, in his high school sweater, enters carrying suitcase. Happy carries Biff's shoulder guards, gold helmet, and football pants.*)

WILLY: Without a penny to his name, three great universities are begging for him, and from there the sky's the limit, because it's not what you do, Ben. It's who you know and the smile on your face! It's contacts, Ben, contacts! The whole wealth of Alaska passes over the lunch table at the Commodore Hotel, and that's the wonder, the wonder of this country, that a man can end with diamonds here on the basis of being liked! (*He turns to Biff.*) And that's why when you get out on that field today it's important. Because thousands of people will be rooting for you and loving you. (*To Ben, who has again begun to leave.*) And Ben! when he walks into a business office his name will sound out like a bell and all the doors will open to him! I've seen it, Ben, I've seen it a thousand times! You can't feel it with your hand like timber, but it's there!
BEN: Good-by, William.
WILLY: Ben, am I right? Don't you think I'm right? I value your advice.
BEN: There's a new continent at your doorstep, William. You could walk out rich. Rich! (*He is gone.*)
WILLY: We'll do it here, Ben! You hear me? We're gonna do it here!

(*Young Bernard rushes in. The gay music of the Boys is heard.*)

BERNARD: Oh, gee, I was afraid you left already!
WILLY: Why? What time is it?
BERNARD: It's half-past one!
WILLY: Well, come on, everybody! Ebbets Field next stop! Where's the pennants? (*He rushes through the wall-line of the kitchen and out into the living room.*)
LINDA (*to Biff*): Did you pack fresh underwear?
BIFF (*who has been limbering up*): I want to go!
BERNARD: Biff, I'm carrying your helmet, ain't I?
HAPPY: No, I'm carrying the helmet.
BERNARD: Oh, Biff, you promised me.
HAPPY: I'm carrying the helmet.
BERNARD: How am I going to get in the locker room?
LINDA: Let him carry the shoulder guards. (*She puts her coat and hat on in the kitchen.*)
BERNARD: Can I, Biff? 'Cause I told everybody I'm going to be in the locker room.
HAPPY: In Ebbets Field it's the clubhouse.
BERNARD: I meant the clubhouse. Biff!

HAPPY: Biff!

BIFF (*grandly, after a slight pause*): Let him carry the shoulder guards.

HAPPY (*as he gives Bernard the shoulder guards*): Stay close to us now.

(*Willy rushes in with the pennants.*)

WILLY (*handing them out*): Everybody wave when Biff comes out on the field. (*Happy and Bernard run off.*) You set now, boy?

(*The music has died away.*)

BIFF: Ready to go, Pop. Every muscle is ready.

WILLY (*at the edge of the apron*): You realize what this means?

BIFF: That's right, Pop.

WILLY (*feeling Biff's muscles*): You're comin' home this afternoon captain of the All-Scholastic Championship Team of the City of New York.

BIFF: I got it, Pop. And remember, pal, when I take off my helmet, that touchdown is for you.

WILLY: Let's go! (*He is starting out, with his arm around Biff, when Charley enters, as of old, in knickers.*) I got no room for you, Charley.

CHARLEY: Room? For what?

WILLY: In the car.

CHARLEY: You goin' for a ride? I wanted to shoot some casino.

WILLY (*furiously*): Casino! (*Incredulously.*) Don't you realize what today is?

LINDA: Oh, he knows, Willy. He's just kidding you.

WILLY: That's nothing to kid about!

CHARLEY: No, Linda, what's goin' on?

LINDA: He's playing in Ebbets Field.

CHARLEY: Baseball in this weather?

WILLY: Don't talk to him. Come on, come on! (*He is pushing them out.*)

CHARLEY: Wait a minute, didn't you hear the news?

WILLY: What?

CHARLEY: Don't you listen to the radio? Ebbets Field just blew up.

WILLY: You go to hell! (*Charley laughs. Pushing them out.*) Come on, come on! We're late.

CHARLEY (*as they go*): Knock a homer, Biff, knock a homer!

WILLY (*the last to leave, turning to Charley*): I don't think that was funny, Charley. This is the greatest day of his life.

CHARLEY: Willy, when are you going to grow up?

WILLY: Yeah, heh? When this game is over, Charley, you'll be laughing out of the other side of your face. They'll be calling him another Red Grange. Twenty-five thousand a year.

CHARLEY (*kidding*): Is that so?

WILLY: Yeah, that's so.

CHARLEY: Well, then, I'm sorry, Willy. But tell me something.

WILLY: What?
CHARLEY: Who is Red Grange?
WILLY: Put up your hands. Goddam you, put up your hands!

(*Charley, chuckling, shakes his head and walks away, around the left corner of the stage. Willy follows him. The music rises to a mocking frenzy.*)

WILLY: Who the hell do you think you are, better than everybody else? You don't know everything, you big, ignorant, stupid . . . Put up your hands!

(*Light rises, on the right side of the forestage, on a small table in the reception room of Charley's office. Traffic sounds are heard. Bernard, now mature, sits whistling to himself. A pair of tennis rackets and an overnight bag are on the floor beside him.*)

WILLY (*offstage*): What are you walking away for? Don't walk away! If you're going to say something say it to my face! I know you laugh at me behind my back. You'll laugh out of the other side of your goddam face after this game. Touchdown! Touchdown! Eighty thousand people! Touchdown! Right between the goal posts.

(*Bernard is a quiet, earnest, but self-assured young man. Willy's voice is coming from right upstage now. Bernard lowers his feet off the table and listens. Jenny, his father's secretary, enters.*)

JENNY (*distressed*): Say, Bernard, will you go out in the hall?
BERNARD: What is that noise? Who is it?
JENNY: Mr. Loman. He just got off the elevator.
BERNARD (*getting up*): Who's he arguing with?
JENNY: Nobody. There's nobody with him. I can't deal with him anymore, and your father gets all upset everytime he comes. I've got a lot of typing to do, and your father's waiting to sign it. Will you see him?
WILLY (*entering*): Touchdown! Touch—(*He sees Jenny.*) Jenny, Jenny, good to see you. How're ya? Workin'? Or still honest?
JENNY: Fine. How've you been feeling?
WILLY: Not much any more, Jenny. Ha, ha! (*He is surprised to see the rackets.*)
BERNARD: Hello, Uncle Willy.
WILLY (*almost shocked*): Bernard! Well, look who's here! (*He comes quickly, guiltily, to Bernard and warmly shakes his hand.*)
BERNARD: How are you? Good to see you.
WILLY: What are you doing here?
BERNARD: Oh, just stopped by to see Pop. Get off my feet till my train leaves. I'm going to Washington in a few minutes.
WILLY: Is he in?

BERNARD: Yes, he's in his office with the accountant. Sit down.

WILLY (*sitting down*): What're you going to do in Washington?

BERNARD: Oh, just a case I've got there, Willy.

WILLY: That so? (*Indicating the rackets.*) You going to play tennis there?

BERNARD: I'm staying with a friend who's got a court.

WILLY: Don't say. His own tennis court. Must be fine people, I bet.

BERNARD: They are, very nice. Dad tells me Biff's in town.

WILLY (*with a big smile*): Yeah, Biff's in. Working on a very big deal, Bernard.

BERNARD: What's Biff doing?

WILLY: Well, he's been doing very big things in the West. But he decided to establish himself here. Very big. We're having dinner. Did I hear your wife had a boy?

BERNARD: That's right. Our second.

WILLY: Two boys! What do you know!

BERNARD: What kind of a deal has Biff got?

WILLY: Well, Bill Oliver—very big sporting-goods man—he wants Biff very badly. Called him in from the West. Long distance, carte blanche, special deliveries. Your friends have their own private tennis court?

BERNARD: You still with the old firm, Willy?

WILLY (*after a pause*): I'm—I'm overjoyed to see how you made the grade, Bernard, overjoyed. It's an encouraging thing to see a young man really—really—Looks very good for Biff—very—(*He breaks off, then.*) Bernard—(*He is so full of emotion, he breaks off again.*)

BERNARD: What is it, Willy?

WILLY (*small and alone*): What—what's the secret?

BERNARD: What secret?

WILLY: How—how did you? Why didn't he ever catch on?

BERNARD: I wouldn't know that, Willy.

WILLY (*confidentially, desperately*): You were his friend, his boyhood friend. There's something I don't understand about it. His life ended after that Ebbets Field game. From the age of seventeen nothing good ever happened to him.

BERNARD: He never trained himself for anything.

WILLY: But he did, he did. After high school he took so many correspondence courses. Radio mechanics; television; God knows what, and never made the slightest mark.

BERNARD (*taking off his glasses*): Willy, do you want to talk candidly?

WILLY (*rising, faces Bernard*): I regard you as a very brilliant man, Bernard. I value your advice.

BERNARD: Oh, the hell with the advice, Willy. I couldn't advise you. There's just one thing I've always wanted to ask you. When he was supposed to graduate, and the math teacher flunked him—

WILLY: Oh, that son-of-a-bitch ruined his life.

BERNARD: Yeah, but, Willy, all he had to do was go to summer school and make up that subject.

WILLY: That's right, that's right.

BERNARD: Did you tell him not to go to summer school?

WILLY: Me? I begged him to go. I ordered him to go!

BERNARD: Then why wouldn't he go?

WILLY: Why? Why! Bernard, that question has been trailing me like a ghost for the last fifteen years. He flunked the subject, and laid down and died like a hammer hit him!

BERNARD: Take it easy, kid.

WILLY: Let me talk to you—I got nobody to talk to. Bernard, Bernard, was it my fault? Y'see? It keeps going around in my mind, maybe I did something to him. I got nothing to give him.

BERNARD: Don't take it so hard.

WILLY: Why did he lay down? What is the story there? You were his friend!

BERNARD: Willy, I remember, it was June, and our grades came out. And he'd flunked math.

WILLY: That son-of-a-bitch!

BERNARD: No, it wasn't right then. Biff just got very angry, I remember, and he was ready to enroll in summer school.

WILLY (*surprised*): He was?

BERNARD: He wasn't beaten by it at all. But then, Willy, he disappeared from the block for almost a month. And I got the idea that he'd gone up to New England to see you. Did he have a talk with you then?

(*Willy stares in silence.*)

BERNARD: Willy?

WILLY (*with a strong edge of resentment in his voice*): Yeah, he came to Boston. What about it?

BERNARD: Well, just that when he came back—I'll never forget this, it always mystifies me. Because I'd thought so well of Biff, even though he'd always taken advantage of me. I loved him, Willy, y'know? And he came back after that month and took his sneakers—remember those sneakers with "University of Virginia" printed on them? He was so proud of those, wore them every day. And he took them down in the cellar, and burned them up in the furnace. We had a fist fight. It lasted at least half an hour. Just the two of us, punching each other down the cellar, and crying right through it. I've often thought of how strange it was that I knew he'd given up his life. What happened in Boston, Willy?

(*Willy looks at him as at an intruder.*)

BERNARD: I just bring it up because you asked me.

WILLY (*angrily*): Nothing. What do you mean, "What happened?" What's that got to do with anything?

BERNARD: Well, don't get sore.

WILLY: What are you trying to do, blame it on me? If a boy lays down is that my fault?

BERNARD: Now, Willy, don't get —

WILLY: Well, don't — don't talk to me that way! What does that mean, "What happened?"

(*Charley enters. He is in his vest, and he carries a bottle of bourbon.*)

CHARLEY: Hey, you're going to miss that train. (*He waves the bottle.*)

BERNARD: Yeah, I'm going. (*He takes the bottle.*) Thanks, Pop. (*He picks up his rackets and bag.*) Good-by, Willy, and don't worry about it. You know, "If at first you don't succeed . . ."

WILLY: Yes, I believe in that.

BERNARD: But sometimes, Willy, it's better for a man just to walk away.

WILLY: Walk away?

BERNARD: That's right.

WILLY: But if you can't walk away?

BERNARD (*after a slight pause*): I guess that's when it's tough. (*Extending his hand.*) Good-by, Willy.

WILLY (*shaking Bernard's hand*): Good-by, boy.

CHARLEY (*an arm on Bernard's shoulder*): How do you like this kid? Gonna argue a case in front of the Supreme Court.

BERNARD (*protesting*): Pop!

WILLY (*genuinely shocked, pained, and happy*): No! The Supreme Court!

BERNARD: I gotta run. 'By, Dad!

CHARLEY: Knock 'em dead, Bernard!

(*Bernard goes off.*)

WILLY (*as Charley takes out his wallet*): The Supreme Court! And he didn't even mention it!

CHARLEY (*counting out money on the desk*): He don't have to — he's gonna do it.

WILLY: And you never told him what to do, did you? You never took any interest in him.

CHARLEY: My salvation is that I never took any interest in anything. There's some money — fifty dollars. I got an accountant inside.

WILLY: Charley, look . . . (*With difficulty.*) I got my insurance to pay. If you can manage it — I need a hundred and ten dollars.

(*Charley doesn't reply for a moment; merely stops moving.*)

WILLY: I'd draw it from my bank but Linda would know, and I . . .

CHARLEY: Sit down, Willy.

WILLY (*moving toward the chair*): I'm keeping an account of everything, remember. I'll pay every penny back. (*He sits.*)

CHARLEY: Now listen to me, Willy.

WILLY: I want you to know I appreciate . . .

CHARLEY (*sitting down on the table*): Willy, what're you doin'? What the hell is goin' on in your head?

WILLY: Why? I'm simply . . .

CHARLEY: I offered you a job. You make fifty dollars a week. And I won't send you on the road.

WILLY: I've got a job.

CHARLEY: Without pay? What kind of a job is a job without pay? (*He rises.*) Now, look, kid, enough is enough. I'm no genius but I know when I'm being insulted.

WILLY: Insulted!

CHARLEY: Why don't you want to work for me?

WILLY: What's the matter with you? I've got a job.

CHARLEY: Then what're you walkin' in here every week for?

WILLY (*getting up*): Well, if you don't want me to walk in here—

CHARLEY: I'm offering you a job.

WILLY: I don't want your goddam job!

CHARLEY: When the hell are you going to grow up?

WILLY (*furiously*): You big ignoramus, if you say that to me again I'll rap you one! I don't care how big you are! (*He's ready to fight.*)

(*Pause.*)

CHARLEY (*kindly, going to him*): How much do you need, Willy?

WILLY: Charley, I'm strapped. I'm strapped. I don't know what to do. I was just fired.

CHARLEY: Howard fired you?

WILLY: That snotnose. Imagine that? I named him. I named him Howard.

CHARLEY: Willy, when're you gonna realize that them things don't mean anything? You named him Howard, but you can't sell that. The only thing you got in this world is what you can sell. And the funny thing is that you're a salesman, and you don't know that.

WILLY: I've always tried to think otherwise, I guess. I always felt that if a man was impressive, and well liked, that nothing—

CHARLEY: Why must everybody like you? Who liked J. P. Morgan?° Was he impressive? In a Turkish bath he'd look like a butcher. But with his

---

J. P. Morgan: (1837–1913), a wealthy American businessman who made his money primarily from investments in banking, railroads, and steel and who collected art.

pockets on he was very well liked. Now listen, Willy, I know you don't like me, and nobody can say I'm in love with you, but I'll give you a job because—just for the hell of it, put it that way. Now what do you say?

WILLY: I—I just can't work for you, Charley.

CHARLEY: What're you, jealous of me?

WILLY: I can't work for you, that's all, don't ask me why.

CHARLEY (*angered, takes out more bills*): You been jealous of me all your life, you dammed fool! Here, pay your insurance. (*He puts the money in Willy's hand.*)

WILLY: I'm keeping strict accounts.

CHARLEY: I've got some work to do. Take care of yourself. And pay your insurance.

WILLY (*moving to the right*): Funny, y'know? After all the highways, and the trains, and the appointments, and the years, you end up worth more dead than alive.

CHARLEY: Willy, nobody's worth nothin' dead. (*After a slight pause.*) Did you hear what I said?

(*Willy stands still, dreaming.*)

CHARLEY: Willy!

WILLY: Apologize to Bernard for me when you see him. I didn't mean to argue with him. He's a fine boy. They're all fine boys, and they'll end up big—all of them. Someday they'll all play tennis together. Wish me luck, Charley. He saw Bill Oliver today.

CHARLEY: Good luck.

WILLY (*on the verge of tears*): Charley, you're the only friend I got. Isn't that a remarkable thing? (*He goes out.*)

CHARLEY: Jesus!

(*Charley stares after him a moment and follows. All light blacks out. Suddenly raucous music is heard, and a red glow rises behind the screen at right. Stanley, a young waiter, appears, carrying a table, followed by Happy, who is carrying two chairs.*)

STANLEY (*putting the table down*): That's all right, Mr. Loman, I can handle it myself. (*He turns and takes the chairs from Happy and places them at the table.*)

HAPPY (*glancing around*): Oh, this is better.

STANLEY: Sure, in the front there you're in the middle of all kinds of noise. Whenever you got a party, Mr. Loman, you just tell me and I'll put you back here. Y'know, there's a lotta people they don't like it private, because when they go out they like to see a lotta action around them because they're sick and tired to stay in the house by theirself. But I know you, you ain't from Hackensack. You know what I mean?

HAPPY (*sitting down*): So how's it coming, Stanley?

STANLEY: Ah, it's a dog life. I only wish during the war they'd a took me in the Army. I coulda been dead by now.

HAPPY: My brother's back, Stanley.

STANLEY: Oh, he come back, heh? From the Far West.

HAPPY: Yeah, big cattle man, my brother, so treat him right. And my father's coming too.

STANLEY: Oh, your father too!

HAPPY: You got a couple of nice lobsters?

STANLEY: Hundred percent, big.

HAPPY: I want them with the claws.

STANLEY: Don't worry, I don't give you no mice. (*Happy laughs.*) How about some wine? It'll put a head on the meal.

HAPPY: No. You remember, Stanley, that recipe I brought you from overseas? With the champagne in it?

STANLEY: Oh, yeah, sure. I still got it tacked up yet in the kitchen. But that'll have to cost a buck apiece anyways.

HAPPY: That's all right.

STANLEY: What'd you, hit a number or somethin'?

HAPPY: No, it's a little celebration. My brother is—I think he pulled off a big deal today. I think we're going into business together.

STANLEY: Great! That's the best for you. Because a family business, you know what I mean?—that's the best.

HAPPY: That's what I think.

STANLEY: 'Cause what's the difference? Somebody steals? It's in the family. Know what I mean? (*Sotto voce.°*) Like this bartender here. The boss is goin' crazy what kinda leak he's got in the cash register. You put it in but it don't come out.

HAPPY (*raising his head*): Sh!

STANLEY: What?

HAPPY: You notice I wasn't lookin' right or left, was I?

STANLEY: No.

HAPPY: And my eyes are closed.

STANLEY: So what's the—?

HAPPY: Strudel's comin'.

STANLEY (*catching on, looks around*): Ah, no, there's no—

(*He breaks off as a furred, lavishly dressed girl enters and sits at the next table. Both follow her with their eyes.*)

STANLEY: Geez, how'd ya know?

HAPPY: I got radar or something. (*Staring directly at her profile.*) Ooooooooo . . . Stanley.

Sotto voce: "In a soft voice," i.e., stage whisper.

STANLEY: I think that's for you, Mr. Loman.

HAPPY: Look at that mouth. Oh, God. And the binoculars.

STANLEY: Geez, you got a life, Mr. Loman.

HAPPY: Wait on her.

STANLEY (*going to the girl's table*): Would you like a menu, ma'am?

GIRL: I'm expecting someone, but I'd like a—

HAPPY: Why don't you bring her—excuse me, miss, do you mind? I sell champagne, and I'd like you to try my brand. Bring her a champagne, Stanley.

GIRL: That's awfully nice of you.

HAPPY: Don't mention it. It's all company money. (*He laughs.*)

GIRL: That's a charming product to be selling, isn't it?

HAPPY: Oh, gets to be like everything else. Selling is selling, y'know.

GIRL: I suppose.

HAPPY: You don't happen to sell, do you?

GIRL: No, I don't sell.

HAPPY: Would you object to a compliment from a stranger? You ought to be on a magazine cover.

GIRL (*looking at him a little archly*): I have been.

(*Stanley comes in with a glass of champagne.*)

HAPPY: What'd I say before, Stanley? You see? She's a cover girl.

STANLEY: Oh, I could see, I could see.

HAPPY (*to the Girl*): What magazine?

GIRL: Oh, a lot of them. (*She takes the drink.*) Thank you.

HAPPY: You know what they say in France, don't you? "Champagne is the drink of the complexion"—Hya, Biff!

(*Biff has entered and sits with Happy.*)

BIFF: Hello, kid. Sorry I'm late.

HAPPY: I just got here. Uh, Miss—?

GIRL: Forsythe.

HAPPY: Miss Forsythe, this is my brother.

BIFF: Is Dad here?

HAPPY: His name is Biff. You might've heard of him. Great football player.

GIRL: Really? What team?

HAPPY: Are you familiar with football?

GIRL: No, I'm afraid I'm not.

HAPPY: Biff is quarterback with the New York Giants.

GIRL: Well, that is nice, isn't it? (*She drinks.*)

HAPPY: Good health.

GIRL: I'm happy to meet you.

HAPPY: That's my name. Hap. It's really Harold, but at West Point they called me Happy.

GIRL (*now really impressed*): Oh, I see. How do you do? (*She turns her profile.*)

BIFF: Isn't Dad coming?

HAPPY: You want her?

BIFF: Oh, I could never make that.

HAPPY: I remember the time that idea would never come into your head. Where's the old confidence, Biff?

BIFF: I just saw Oliver—

HAPPY: Wait a minute. I've got to see that old confidence again. Do you want her? She's on call.

BIFF: Oh, no. (*He turns to look at the Girl.*)

HAPPY: I'm telling you. Watch this. (*Turning to the Girl*): Honey? (*She turns to him.*) Are you busy?

GIRL: Well, I am . . . but I could make a phone call.

HAPPY: Do that, will you, honey? And see if you can get a friend. We'll be here for a while. Biff is one of the greatest football players in the country.

GIRL (*standing up*): Well, I'm certainly happy to meet you.

HAPPY: Come back soon.

GIRL: I'll try.

HAPPY: Don't try, honey, try hard.

(*The Girl exits. Stanley follows, shaking his head in bewildered admiration.*)

HAPPY: Isn't that a shame now? A beautiful girl like that? That's why I can't get married. There's not a good woman in a thousand. New York is loaded with them, kid!

BIFF: Hap, look—

HAPPY: I told you she was on call!

BIFF (*strangely unnerved*): Cut it out, will ya? I want to say something to you.

HAPPY: Did you see Oliver?

BIFF: I saw him all right. Now look, I want to tell Dad a couple of things and I want you to help me.

HAPPY: What? Is he going to back you?

BIFF: Are you crazy? You're out of your goddam head, you know that?

HAPPY: Why? What happened?

BIFF (*breathlessly*): I did a terrible thing today, Hap. It's been the strangest day I ever went through. I'm all numb, I swear.

HAPPY: You mean he wouldn't see you?

BIFF: Well, I waited six hours for him, see? All day. Kept sending my name in. Even tried to date his secretary so she'd get me to him, but no soap.

HAPPY: Because you're not showin' the old confidence Biff. He remembered you, didn't he?

BIFF (*stopping Happy with a gesture*): Finally, about five o'clock, he comes out. Didn't remember who I was or anything. I felt like such an idiot, Hap.

HAPPY: Did you tell him my Florida idea?

BIFF: He walked away. I saw him for one minute. I got so mad I could've torn the walls down! How the hell did I ever get the idea I was a salesman there? I even believed myself that I'd been a salesman for him! And then he gave me one look and—I realized what a ridiculous lie my whole life has been! We've been talking in a dream for fifteen years. I was a shipping clerk.

HAPPY: What'd you do?

BIFF (*with great tension and wonder*): Well, he left, see. And the secretary went out. I was all alone in the waiting room. I don't know what came over me, Hap. The next thing I know I'm in his office—paneled walls, everything. I can't explain it. I—Hap, I took his fountain pen.

HAPPY: Geez, did he catch you?

BIFF: I ran out. I ran down all eleven flights. I ran and ran and ran.

HAPPY: That was an awful dumb—what'd you do that for?

BIFF (*agonized*): I don't know, I just—wanted to take something, I don't know. You gotta help me, Hap. I'm gonna tell Pop.

HAPPY: You crazy? What for?

BIFF: Hap, he's got to understand that I'm not the man somebody lends that kind of money to. He thinks I've been spiting him all these years and it's eating him up.

HAPPY: That's just it. You tell him something nice.

BIFF: I can't.

HAPPY: Say you got a lunch date with Oliver tomorrow.

BIFF: So what do I do tomorrow?

HAPPY: You leave the house tomorrow and come back at night and say Oliver is thinking it over. And he thinks it over for a couple of weeks, and gradually it fades away and nobody's the worse.

BIFF: But it'll go on forever!

HAPPY: Dad is never so happy as when he's looking forward to something!

(*Willy enters.*)

HAPPY: Hello, scout!

WILLY: Gee, I haven't been here in years!

(*Stanley has followed Willy in and sets a chair for him. Stanley starts off but Happy stops him.*)

HAPPY: Stanley!

(*Stanley stands by, waiting for an order.*)

BIFF (*going to Willy with guilt, as to an invalid*): Sit down, Pop. You want a drink?

WILLY: Sure, I don't mind.

BIFF: Let's get a load on.

WILLY: You look worried.

BIFF: N-no. (*To Stanley.*) Scotch all around. Make it doubles.

STANLEY: Doubles, right. (*He goes.*)

WILLY: You had a couple already, didn't you?

BIFF: Just a couple, yeah.

WILLY: Well, what happened, boy? (*Nodding affirmatively, with a smile.*) Everything go all right?

BIFF (*takes a breath, then reaches out and grasps Willy's hand*): Pal . . . (*He is smiling bravely, and Willy is smiling too.*) I had an experience today.

HAPPY: Terrific, Pop.

WILLY: That so? What happened?

BIFF (*high, slightly alcoholic, above the earth*): I'm going to tell you everything from first to last. It's been a strange day. (*Silence. He looks around, composes himself as best he can, but his breath keeps breaking the rhythm of his voice.*) I had to wait quite a while for him, and—

WILLY: Oliver?

BIFF: Yeah, Oliver. All day, as a matter of cold fact. And a lot of—instances—facts, Pop, facts about my life came back to me. Who was it, Pop? Who ever said I was a salesman with Oliver?

WILLY: Well, you were.

BIFF: No, Dad, I was a shipping clerk.

WILLY: But you were practically—

BIFF (*with determination*): Dad, I don't know who said it first, but I was never a salesman for Bill Oliver.

WILLY: What're you talking about?

BIFF: Let's hold on to the facts tonight, Pop. We're not going to get anywhere bullin' around. I was a shipping clerk.

WILLY (*angrily*): All right, now listen to me—

BIFF: Why don't you let me finish?

WILLY: I'm not interested in stories about the past or any crap of that kind because the woods are burning, boys, you understand? There's a big blaze going on all around. I was fired today.

BIFF (*shocked*): How could you be?

WILLY: I was fired, and I'm looking for a little good news to tell your mother, because the woman has waited and the woman has suffered. The gist of it is that I haven't got a story left in my head, Biff. So don't give me a lecture about facts and aspects. I am not interested. Now what've you got to say to me?

(*Stanley enters with three drinks. They wait until he leaves.*)

WILLY: Did you see Oliver?

BIFF: Jesus, Dad!

WILLY: You mean you didn't go up there?

HAPPY: Sure he went up there.

BIFF: I did. I—saw him. How could they fire you?

WILLY (*on the edge of his chair*): What kind of a welcome did he give you?

BIFF: He won't even let you work on commission?

WILLY: I'm out! (*Driving.*) So tell me, he gave you a warm welcome?

HAPPY: Sure, Pop, sure!

BIFF (*driven*): Well, it was kind of—

WILLY: I was wondering if he'd remember you. (*To Happy.*) Imagine, man doesn't see him for ten, twelve years and gives him that kind of a welcome!

HAPPY: Damn right!

BIFF (*trying to return to the offensive*): Pop, look—

WILLY: You know why he remembered you, don't you? Because you impressed him in those days.

BIFF: Let's talk quietly and get this down to the facts, huh?

WILLY (*as though Biff had been interrupting*): Well, what happened? It's great news, Biff. Did he take you into his office or'd you talk in the waiting room?

BIFF: Well, he came in, see, and—

WILLY (*with a big smile*): What'd he say? Betcha he threw his arm around you.

BIFF: Well, he kinda—

WILLY: He's a fine man. (*To Happy.*) Very hard man to see, y'know.

HAPPY (*agreeing*): Oh, I know.

WILLY (*to Biff*): Is that where you had the drinks?

BIFF: Yeah, he gave me a couple of—no, no!

HAPPY (*cutting in*): He told him my Florida idea.

WILLY: Don't interrupt. (*To Biff.*) How'd he react to the Florida idea?

BIFF: Dad, will you give me a minute to explain?

WILLY: I've been waiting for you to explain since I sat down here! What happened? He took you into his office and what?

BIFF: Well—I talked. And—and he listened, see.

WILLY: Famous for the way he listens, y'know. What was his answer?

BIFF: His answer was—(*He breaks off, suddenly angry.*) Dad, you're not letting me tell you what I want to tell you!

WILLY (*accusing, angered*): You didn't see him, did you?

BIFF: I did see him!

WILLY: What'd you insult him or something? You insulted him, didn't you?

BIFF: Listen, will you let me out of it, will you just let me out of it!
HAPPY: What the hell!
WILLY: Tell me what happened!
BIFF (*to Happy*): I can't talk to him!

(*A single trumpet note jars the ear. The light of green leaves stains the house, which holds the air of night and a dream. Young Bernard enters and knocks on the door of the house.*)

YOUNG BERNARD (*frantically*): Mrs. Loman, Mrs. Loman!
HAPPY: Tell him what happened!
BIFF (*to Happy*): Shut up and leave me alone!
WILLY: No, no! You had to go and flunk math!
BIFF: What math? What're you talking about?
YOUNG BERNARD: Mrs. Loman, Mrs. Loman!

(*Linda appears in the house, as of old.*)

WILLY (*wildly*): Math, math, math!
BIFF: Take it easy, Pop!
YOUNG BERNARD: Mrs. Loman!
WILLY (*furiously*): If you hadn't flunked you'd've been set by now!
BIFF: Now, look, I'm gonna tell you what happened, and you're going to listen to me.
YOUNG BERNARD: Mrs. Loman!
BIFF: I waited six hours—
HAPPY: What the hell are you saying?
BIFF: I kept sending in my name but he wouldn't see me. So finally he . . . (*He continues unheard as light fades low on the restaurant.*)
YOUNG BERNARD: Biff flunked math!
LINDA: No!
YOUNG BERNARD: Birnbaum flunked him! They won't graduate him!
LINDA: But they have to. He's gotta go to the university. Where is he? Biff! Biff!
YOUNG BERNARD: No, he left. He went to Grand Central.
LINDA: Grand—You mean he went to Boston!
YOUNG BERNARD: Is Uncle Willy in Boston?
LINDA: Oh, maybe Willy can talk to the teacher. Oh, the poor, poor boy!

(*Light on house area snaps out.*)

BIFF (*at the table, now audible, holding up a gold fountain pen*): . . . so I'm washed up with Oliver, you understand? Are you listening to me?
WILLY (*at a loss*): Yeah, sure. If you hadn't flunked—
BIFF: Flunked what? What're you talking about?
WILLY: Don't blame everything on me! I didn't flunk math—you did! What pen?

HAPPY: That was awful dumb, Biff, a pen like that is worth—

WILLY (*seeing the pen for the first time*): You took Oliver's pen?

BIFF (*weakening*): Dad, I just explained it to you.

WILLY: You stole Bill Oliver's fountain pen!

BIFF: I didn't exactly steal it! That's just what I've been explaining to you!

HAPPY: He had it in his hand and just then Oliver walked in, so he got nervous and stuck it in his pocket!

WILLY: My God, Biff!

BIFF: I never intended to do it, Dad!

OPERATOR'S VOICE: Standish Arms, good evening!

WILLY (*shouting*): I'm not in my room!

BIFF (*frightened*): Dad, what's the matter? (*He and Happy stand up.*)

OPERATOR: Ringing Mr. Loman for you!

WILLY: I'm not there, stop it!

BIFF (*horrified, gets down on one knee before Willy*): Dad, I'll make good, I'll make good. (*Willy tries to get to his feet. Biff holds him down.*) Sit down now.

WILLY: No, you're no good, you're no good for anything.

BIFF: I am, Dad, I'll find something else, you understand? Now don't worry about anything. (*He holds up Willy's face.*) Talk to me, Dad.

OPERATOR: Mr. Loman does not answer. Shall I page him?

WILLY (*attempting to stand, as though to rush and silence the Operator*): No, no, no!

HAPPY: He'll strike something, Pop.

WILLY: No, no . . .

BIFF (*desperately, standing over Willy*): Pop, listen! Listen to me! I'm telling you something good. Oliver talked to his partner about the Florida idea. You listening? He—he talked to his partner, and he came to me . . . I'm going to be all right, you hear? Dad, listen to me, he said it was just a question of the amount!

WILLY: Then you . . . got it?

HAPPY: He's gonna be terrific, Pop!

WILLY (*trying to stand*): Then you got it, haven't you? You got it! You got it!

BIFF (*agonized, holds Willy down*): No, no. Look, Pop. I'm supposed to have lunch with them tomorrow. I'm just telling you this so you'll know that I can still make an impression, Pop. And I'll make good somewhere, but I can't go tomorrow, see?

WILLY: Why not? You simply—

BIFF: But the pen, Pop!

WILLY: You give it to him and tell him it was an oversight!

HAPPY: Sure, have lunch tomorrow!

BIFF: I can't say that—

WILLY: You were doing a crossword puzzle and accidentally used his pen!

BIFF: Listen, kid, I took those balls years ago, now I walk in with his fountain pen? That clinches it, don't you see? I can't face him like that! I'll try elsewhere.

PAGE'S VOICE: Paging Mr. Loman!

WILLY: Don't you want to be anything?

BIFF: Pop, how can I go back?

WILLY: You don't want to be anything, is that what's behind it?

BIFF (*now angry at Willy for not crediting his sympathy*): Don't take it that way! You think it was easy walking into that office after what I'd done to him? A team of horses couldn't have dragged me back to Bill Oliver!

WILLY: Then why'd you go?

BIFF: Why did I go? Why did I go! Look at you! Look at what's become of you!

(*Off left, The Woman laughs.*)

WILLY: Biff, you're going to go to that lunch tomorrow, or—

BIFF: I can't go. I've got no appointment!

HAPPY: Biff, for . . . !

WILLY: Are you spiting me?

BIFF: Don't take it that way! Goddammit!

WILLY (*strikes Biff and falters away from the table*): You rotten little louse! Are you spiting me?

THE WOMAN: Someone's at the door, Willy!

BIFF: I'm no good, can't you see what I am?

HAPPY (*separating them*): Hey, you're in a restaurant! Now cut it out, both of you! (*The girls enter.*) Hello, girls, sit down.

(*The Woman laughs, off left.*)

MISS FORSYTHE: I guess we might as well. This is Letta.

THE WOMAN: Willy, are you going to wake up?

BIFF (*ignoring Willy*): How're ya, miss, sit down. What do you drink?

MISS FORSYTHE: Letta might not be able to stay long.

LETTA: I gotta get up very early tomorrow. I got jury duty. I'm so excited! Were you fellows ever on a jury?

BIFF: No, but I been in front of them! (*The girls laugh.*) This is my father.

LETTA: Isn't he cute? Sit down with us, Pop.

HAPPY: Sit him down, Biff!

BIFF (*going to him*): Come on, slugger, drink us under the table. To hell with it! Come on, sit down, pal.

(*On Biff's last insistence, Willy is about to sit.*)

THE WOMAN (*now urgently*): Willy, are you going to answer the door!

(*The Woman's call pulls Willy back. He starts right, befuddled.*)

BIFF: Hey, where are you going?
WILLY: Open the door.
BIFF: The door?
WILLY: The washroom . . . the door . . . where's the door?
BIFF (*leading Willy to the left*): Just go straight down.

(*Willy moves left.*)

THE WOMAN: Willy, Willy, are you going to get up, get up, get up, get up?

(*Willy exits left.*)

LETTA: I think it's sweet you bring your daddy along.
MISS FORSYTHE: Oh, he isn't really your father!
BIFF (*at left, turning to her resentfully*): Miss Forsythe, you've just seen a prince walk by. A fine, troubled prince. A hard-working, unappreciated prince. A pal, you understand? A good companion. Always for his boys.
LETTA: That's so sweet.
HAPPY: Well, girls, what's the program? We're wasting time. Come on, Biff. Gather round. Where would you like to go?
BIFF: Why don't you do something for him?
HAPPY: Me!
BIFF: Don't you give a damn for him, Hap?
HAPPY: What're you talking about? I'm the one who —
BIFF: I sense it, you don't give a good goddam about him. (*He takes the rolled-up hose from his pocket and puts it on the table in front of Happy.*) Look what I found in the cellar, for Christ's sake. How can you bear to let it go on?
HAPPY: Me? Who goes away? Who runs off and —
BIFF: Yeah, but he doesn't mean anything to you. You could help him — I can't! Don't you understand what I'm talking about? He's going to kill himself, don't you know that?
HAPPY: Don't I know it! Me!
BIFF: Hap, help him! Jesus . . . help him . . . Help me, help me, I can't bear to look at his face! (*Ready to weep, he hurries out, up right.*)
HAPPY (*starting after him*): Where are you going?
MISS FORSYTHE: What's he so mad about?
HAPPY: Come on, girls, we'll catch up with him.
MISS FORSYTHE (*as Happy pushes her out*): Say, I don't like that temper of his!
HAPPY: He's just a little overstrung, he'll be all right!
WILLY (*off left, as The Woman laughs*): Don't answer! Don't answer!
LETTA: Don't you want to tell your father —

HAPPY: No, that's not my father. He's just a guy. Come on, we'll catch Biff, and, honey, we're going to paint this town! Stanley, where's the check! Hey, Stanley!

(*They exit. Stanley looks toward left.*)

STANLEY (*calling to Happy indignantly*): Mr. Loman! Mr. Loman!

(*Stanley picks up a chair and follows them off. Knocking is heard off left. The Woman enters, laughing. Willy follows her. She is in a black slip; he is buttoning his shirt. Raw, sensuous music accompanies their speech.*)

WILLY: Will you stop laughing? Will you stop?

THE WOMAN: Aren't you going to answer the door? He'll wake the whole hotel.

WILLY: I'm not expecting anybody.

THE WOMAN: Whyn't you have another drink, honey, and stop being so damn self-centered?

WILLY: I'm so lonely.

THE WOMAN: You know you ruined me, Willy? From now on, whenever you come to the office, I'll see that you go right through to the buyers. No waiting at my desk anymore, Willy. You ruined me.

WILLY: That's nice of you to say that.

THE WOMAN: Gee, you are self-centered! Why so sad? You are the saddest, self-centeredest soul I ever did see-saw. (*She laughs. He kisses her.*) Come on inside, drummer boy. It's silly to be dressing in the middle of the night. (*As knocking is heard.*) Aren't you going to answer the door?

WILLY: They're knocking on the wrong door.

THE WOMAN: But I felt the knocking. And he heard us talking in here. Maybe the hotel's on fire!

WILLY (*his terror rising*): It's a mistake.

THE WOMAN: Then tell him to go away!

WILLY: There's nobody there.

THE WOMAN: It's getting on my nerves, Willy. There's somebody standing out there and it's getting on my nerves!

WILLY (*pushing her away from him*): All right, stay in the bathroom here, and don't come out. I think there's a law in Massachusetts about it, so don't come out. It may be that new room clerk. He looked very mean. So don't come out. It's a mistake, there's no fire.

(*The knocking is heard again. He takes a few steps away from her, and she vanishes into the wing. The light follows him, and now he is facing Young Biff, who carries a suitcase. Biff steps toward him. The music is gone.*)

BIFF: Why didn't you answer?

WILLY: Biff! What are you doing in Boston?

BIFF: Why didn't you answer? I've been knocking for five minutes, I called you on the phone—

WILLY: I just heard you. I was in the bathroom and had the door shut. Did anything happen home?

BIFF: Dad—I let you down.

WILLY: What do you mean?

BIFF: Dad . . .

WILLY: Biffo, what's this about? (*Putting his arm around Biff.*) Come on, let's go downstairs and get you a malted.

BIFF: Dad, I flunked math.

WILLY: Not for the term?

BIFF: The term. I haven't got enough credits to graduate.

WILLY: You mean to say Bernard wouldn't give you the answers?

BIFF: He did, he tried, but I only got a sixty-one.

WILLY: And they wouldn't give you four points?

BIFF: Birnbaum refused absolutely. I begged him, Pop, but he won't give me those points. You gotta talk to him before they close the school. Because if he saw the kind of man you are, and you just talked to him in your way, I'm sure he'd come through for me. The class came right before practice, see, and I didn't go enough. Would you talk to him? He'd like you, Pop. You know the way you could talk.

WILLY: You're on. We'll drive right back.

BIFF: Oh, Dad, good work! I'm sure he'll change it for you!

WILLY: Go downstairs and tell the clerk I'm checkin' out. Go right down.

BIFF: Yes, sir! See, the reason he hates me, Pop—one day he was late for class so I got up at the blackboard and imitated him. I crossed my eyes and talked with a lithp.

WILLY (*laughing*): You did? The kids like it?

BIFF: They nearly died laughing!

WILLY: Yeah? What'd you do?

BIFF: The thquare root of thixthy twee is . . . (*Willy bursts out laughing; Biff joins.*) And in the middle of it he walked in!

(*Willy laughs and The Woman joins in offstage.*)

WILLY (*without hesitation*): Hurry downstairs and—

BIFF: Somebody in there?

WILLY: No, that was next door.

(*The Woman laughs offstage.*)

BIFF: Somebody got in your bathroom!

WILLY: No, it's the next room, there's a party—

THE WOMAN (*enters, laughing. She lisps this.*): Can I come in? There's something in the bathtub, Willy, and it's moving!

(*Willy looks at Biff, who is staring open-mouthed and horrified at The Woman.*)

WILLY: Ah—you better go back to your room. They must be finished painting by now. They're painting her room so I let her take a shower here. Go back, go back . . . (*He pushes her.*)

THE WOMAN (*resisting*): But I've got to get dressed, Willy, I can't—

WILLY: Get out of here! Go back, go back . . . (*Suddenly striving for the ordinary.*) This is Miss Francis, Biff, she's a buyer. They're painting her room. Go back, Miss Francis, go back . . .

THE WOMAN: But my clothes, I can't go out naked in the hall!

WILLY (*pushing her offstage*): Get outa here! Go back, go back!

(*Biff slowly sits down on his suitcase as the argument continues offstage.*)

THE WOMAN: Where's my stockings? You promised me stockings, Willy!

WILLY: I have no stockings here!

THE WOMAN: You had two boxes of size nine sheers for me, and I want them!

WILLY: Here, for God's sake, will you get outa here!

THE WOMAN (*enters holding a box of stockings*): I just hope there's nobody in the hall. That's all I hope. (*To Biff.*) Are you football or baseball?

BIFF: Football.

THE WOMAN (*angry, humiliated*): That's me too. G'night. (*She snatches her clothes from Willy, and walks out.*)

WILLY (*after a pause*): Well, better get going. I want to get to the school first thing in the morning. Get my suits out of the closet. I'll get my valise. (*Biff doesn't move.*) What's the matter! (*Biff remains motionless, tears falling.*) She's a buyer. Buys for J. H. Simmons. She lives down the hall—they're painting. You don't imagine—(*He breaks off. After a pause.*) Now listen, pal, she's just a buyer. She sees merchandise in her room and they have to keep it looking just so . . . (*Pause. Assuming command.*) All right, get my suits. (*Biff doesn't move.*) Now stop crying and do as I say. I gave you an order. Biff, I gave you an order! Is that what you do when I give you an order? How dare you cry! (*Putting his arm around Biff.*) Now look, Biff, when you grow up you'll understand about these things. You mustn't—you mustn't overemphasize a thing like this. I'll see Birnbaum first thing in the morning.

BIFF: Never mind.

WILLY (*getting down beside Biff*): Never mind! He's going to give you those points. I'll see to it.

BIFF: He wouldn't listen to you.

WILLY: He certainly will listen to me. You need those points for the U. of Virginia.

BIFF: I'm not going there.

WILLY: Heh? If I can't get him to change that mark you'll make it up in summer school. You've got all summer to—

BIFF (*his weeping breaking from him*): Dad . . .

WILLY (*infected by it*): Oh, my boy . . .

BIFF: Dad . . .

WILLY: She's nothing to me, Biff. I was lonely, I was terribly lonely.

BIFF: You—you gave her Mama's stockings! (*His tears break through and he rises to go.*)

WILLY (*grabbing for Biff*): I gave you an order!

BIFF: Don't touch me, you—liar!

WILLY: Apologize for that!

BIFF: You fake! You phony little fake! You fake! (*Overcome, he turns quickly and weeping fully goes out with his suitcase. Willy is left on the floor on his knees.*)

WILLY: I gave you an order! Biff, come back here or I'll beat you! Come back here! I'll whip you!

(*Stanley comes quickly in from the right and stands in front of Willy.*)

WILLY (*shouts at Stanley*): I gave you an order . . .

STANLEY: Hey, let's pick it up, pick it up, Mr. Loman. (*He helps Willy to his feet.*) Your boys left with the chippies. They said they'll see you home.

(*A second waiter watches some distance away.*)

WILLY: But we were supposed to have dinner together.

(*Music is heard, Willy's theme.*)

STANLEY: Can you make it?

WILLY: I'll—sure, I can make it. (*Suddenly concerned about his clothes.*) Do I—I look all right?

STANLEY: Sure, you look all right. (*He flicks a speck off Willy's lapel.*)

WILLY: Here—here's a dollar.

STANLEY: Oh, your son paid me. It's all right.

WILLY (*putting it in Stanley's hand*): No, take it. You're a good boy.

STANLEY: Oh, no, you don't have to . . .

WILLY: Here—here's some more, I don't need it anymore. (*After a slight pause.*) Tell me—is there a seed store in the neighborhood?

STANLEY: Seeds? You mean like to plant?

(*As Willy turns, Stanley slips the money back into his jacket pocket.*)

WILLY: Yes. Carrots, peas . . .

STANLEY: Well, there's hardware stores on Sixth Avenue, but it may be too late now.

WILLY (*anxiously*): Oh, I'd better hurry. I've got to get some seeds. (*He starts off to the right.*) I've got to get some seeds, right away. Nothing's planted. I don't have a thing in the ground.

(*Willy hurries out as the light goes down. Stanley moves over to the right after him, watches him off. The other waiter has been staring at Willy.*)

STANLEY (*to the waiter*): Well, whatta you looking at?

(*The waiter picks up the chairs and moves off right. Stanley takes the table and follows him. The light fades on this area. There is a long pause, the sound of the flute coming over. The light gradually rises on the kitchen, which is empty. Happy appears at the door of the house, followed by Biff. Happy is carrying a large bunch of long-stemmed roses. He enters the kitchen, looks around for Linda. Not seeing her, he turns to Biff, who is just outside the house door, and makes a gesture with his hands, indicating "Not here, I guess." He looks into the living room and freezes. Inside, Linda, unseen, is seated, Willy's coat on her lap. She rises ominously and quietly and moves toward Happy, who backs up into the kitchen, afraid.*)

HAPPY: Hey, what're you doing up? (*Linda says nothing but moves toward him implacably.*) Where's Pop? (*He keeps backing to the right, and now Linda is in full view in the doorway to the living room.*) Is he sleeping?

LINDA: Where were you?

HAPPY (*trying to laugh it off*): We met two girls, Mom, very fine types. Here, we brought you some flowers. (*Offering them to her.*) Put them in your room, Ma.

(*She knocks them to the floor at Biff's feet. He has now come inside and closed the door behind him. She stares at Biff, silent.*)

HAPPY: Now what'd you do that for? Mom, I want you to have some flowers—

LINDA (*cutting Happy off, violently to Biff*): Don't you care whether he lives or dies?

HAPPY (*going to the stairs*): Come upstairs, Biff.

BIFF (*with a flare of disgust, to Happy*): Go away from me! (*To Linda.*) What do you mean, lives or dies? Nobody's dying around here, pal.

LINDA: Get out of my sight! Get out of here!

BIFF: I wanna see the boss.

LINDA: You're not going near him!

BIFF: Where is he? (*He moves into the living room and Linda follows.*)

LINDA (*shouting after Biff*): You invite him for dinner. He looks forward to it all day—(*Biff appears in his parents' bedroom, looks around, and exits*)—and then you desert him there. There's no stranger you'd do that to!

HAPPY: Why? He had a swell time with us. Listen, when I—(*Linda comes back into the kitchen*)—desert him I hope I don't outlive the day!

LINDA: Get out of here!

HAPPY: Now look, Mom . . .

LINDA: Did you have to go to women tonight? You and your lousy rotten whores!

(*Biff reenters the kitchen.*)

HAPPY: Mom, all we did was follow Biff around trying to cheer him up! (*To Biff.*) Boy, what a night you gave me!

LINDA: Get out of here, both of you, and don't come back! I don't want you tormenting him any more. Go on now, get your things together! (*To Biff.*) You can sleep in his apartment. (*She starts to pick up the flowers and stops herself.*) Pick up this stuff, I'm not your maid anymore. Pick it up, you bum, you!

(*Happy turns his back to her in refusal. Biff slowly moves over and gets down on his knees, picking up the flowers.*)

LINDA: You're a pair of animals! Not one, not another living soul would have had the cruelty to walk out on that man in a restaurant!

BIFF (*not looking at her*): Is that what he said?

LINDA: He didn't have to say anything. He was so humiliated he nearly limped when he came in.

HAPPY: But, Mom, he had a great time with us —

BIFF (*cutting him off violently*): Shut up!

(*Without another word, Happy goes upstairs.*)

LINDA: You! You didn't even go in to see if he was all right!

BIFF (*still on the floor in front of Linda, the flowers in his hand; with self-loathing*): No. Didn't. Didn't do a damned thing. How do you like that, heh? Left him babbling in a toilet.

LINDA: You louse. You . . .

BIFF: Now you hit it on the nose! (*He gets up, throws the flowers in the wastebasket.*) The scum of the earth, and you're looking at him!

LINDA: Get out of here!

BIFF: I gotta talk to the boss, Mom. Where is he?

LINDA: You're not going near him. Get out of this house!

BIFF (*with absolute assurance, determination*): No. We're gonna have an abrupt conversation, him and me.

LINDA: You're not talking to him.

(*Hammering is heard from outside the house, off right. Biff turns toward the noise.*)

LINDA (*suddenly pleading*): Will you please leave him alone?

BIFF: What's he doing out there?

LINDA: He's planting the garden!

BIFF (*quietly*): Now? Oh, my God!

(*Biff moves outside, Linda following. The light dies down on them and comes up on the center of the apron as Willy walks into it. He is carrying a flashlight, a hoe, and a handful of seed packets. He raps the top of the hoe sharply to fix it firmly, and then moves to the left, measuring off the distance with his foot. He holds the flashlight to look at the seed packets, reading off the instructions. He is in the blue of night.)*

WILLY: Carrots ... quarter-inch apart. Rows ... one-foot rows. (*He measures it off.*) One foot. (*He puts down a package and measures off.*) Beets. (*He puts down another package and measures again.*) Lettuce. (*He reads the package, puts it down.*) One foot—(*He breaks off as Ben appears at the right and moves slowly down to him.*) What a proposition, ts, ts. Terrific, terrific. 'Cause she's suffered, Ben, the woman has suffered. You understand me? A man can't go out the way he came in, Ben, a man has got to add up to something. You can't, you can't—(*Ben moves toward him as though to interrupt.*) You gotta consider, now. Don't answer so quick. Remember, it's a guaranteed twenty-thousand-dollar proposition. Now look, Ben, I want you to go through the ins and outs of this thing with me. I've got nobody to talk to, Ben, and the woman has suffered, you hear me?

BEN (*standing still, considering*): What's the proposition?

WILLY: It's twenty thousand dollars on the barrelhead. Guaranteed, gilt-edged, you understand?

BEN: You don't want to make a fool of yourself. They might not honor the policy.

WILLY: How can they dare refuse? Didn't I work like a coolie to meet every premium on the nose? And now they don't pay off? Impossible!

BEN: It's called a cowardly thing, William.

WILLY: Why? Does it take more guts to stand here the rest of my life ringing up a zero?

BEN (*yielding*): That's a point, William. (*He moves, thinking, turns.*) And twenty thousand—that is something one can feel with the hand, it is there.

WILLY (*now assured, with rising power*): Oh, Ben, that's the whole beauty of it! I see it like a diamond, shining in the dark, hard and rough, that I can pick up and touch in my hand. Not like—like an appointment! This would not be another damned-fool appointment, Ben, and it changes all the aspects. Because he thinks I'm nothing, see, and so he spites me. But the funeral—(*Straightening up.*) Ben, that funeral will be massive! They'll come from Maine, Massachusetts, Vermont, New Hampshire! All the old-timers with the strange license plates—that boy will be thunderstruck, Ben, because he never realized—I am known! Rhode Island, New York, New Jersey—I am known, Ben and he'll see it with his eyes once and for all. He'll see what I am, Ben! He's in for a shock, that boy!

BEN (*coming down to the edge of the garden*): He'll call you a coward.

WILLY (*suddenly fearful*): No, that would be terrible.

BEN: Yes. And a damned fool.

WILLY: No, no, he mustn't, I won't have that! (*He is broken and desperate.*)

BEN: He'll hate you, William.

(*The gay music of the Boys is heard.*)

WILLY: Oh, Ben, how do we get back to all the great times? Used to be so full of light, and comradeship, the sleigh-riding in winter, and the ruddiness on his cheeks. And always some kind of good news coming up, always something nice coming up ahead. And never even let me carry the valises in the house, and simonizing, simonizing that little red car! Why, why can't I give him something and not have him hate me?

BEN: Let me think about it. (*He glances at his watch.*) I still have a little time. Remarkable proposition, but you've got to be sure you're not making a fool of yourself.

(*Ben drifts off upstage and goes out of sight. Biff comes down from the left.*)

WILLY (*suddenly conscious of Biff, turns and looks up at him, then begins picking up the packages of seeds in confusion*): Where the hell is that seed? (*Indignantly.*) You can't see nothing out here! They boxed in the whole goddam neighborhood!

BIFF: There are people all around here. Don't you realize that?

WILLY: I'm busy. Don't bother me.

BIFF (*taking the hoe from Willy*): I'm saying good-by to you, Pop. (*Willy looks at him, silent, unable to move.*) I'm not coming back any more.

WILLY: You're not going to see Oliver tomorrow?

BIFF: I've got no appointment, Dad.

WILLY: He put his arm around you, and you've got no appointment?

BIFF: Pop, get this now, will you? Everytime I've left it's been a fight that sent me out of here. Today I realized something about myself and I tried to explain it to you and I—I think I'm just not smart enough to make any sense out of it for you. To hell with whose fault it is or anything like that. (*He takes Willy's arm.*) Let's just wrap it up, heh? Come on in, we'll tell Mom. (*He gently tries to pull Willy to left.*)

WILLY (*frozen, immobile, with guilt in his voice*): No, I don't want to see her.

BIFF: Come on! (*He pulls again, and Willy tries to pull away.*)

WILLY (*highly nervous*): No, no, I don't want to see her.

BIFF (*tries to look into Willy's face, as if to find the answer there*): Why don't you want to see her?

WILLY (*more harshly now*): Don't bother me, will you?

BIFF: What do you mean, you don't want to see her? You don't want them calling you yellow, do you? This isn't your fault; it's me, I'm a bum. Now come inside! (*Willy strains to get away.*) Did you hear what I said to you?

(*Willy pulls away and quickly goes by himself into the house. Biff follows.*)

LINDA (*to Willy*): Did you plant, dear?

BIFF (*at the door, to Linda*): All right, we had it out. I'm going and I'm not writing any more.

LINDA (*going to Willy in the kitchen*): I think that's the best way, dear. 'Cause there's no use drawing it out, you'll just never get along.

(*Willy doesn't respond.*)

BIFF: People ask where I am and what I'm doing, you don't know, and you don't care. That way it'll be off your mind and you can start brightening up again. All right? That clears it, doesn't it? (*Willy is silent, and Biff goes to him.*) You gonna wish me luck, scout? (*He extends his hand.*) What do you say?

LINDA: Shake his hand, Willy.

WILLY (*turning to her, seething with hurt*): There's no necessity to mention the pen at all, y'know.

BIFF (*gently*): I've got no appointment, Dad.

WILLY (*erupting fiercely*): He put his arm around . . . ?

BIFF: Dad, you're never going to see what I am, so what's the use of arguing? If I strike oil I'll send you a check. Meantime forget I'm alive.

WILLY (*to Linda*): Spite, see?

BIFF: Shake hands, Dad.

WILLY: Not my hand.

BIFF: I was hoping not to go this way.

WILLY: Well, this is the way you're going. Good-by.

(*Biff looks at him a moment, then turns sharply and goes to the stairs.*)

WILLY (*stops him with*): May you rot in hell if you leave this house!

BIFF (*turning*): Exactly what is it that you want from me?

WILLY: I want you to know, on the train, in the mountains, in the valleys, wherever you go, that you cut down your life for spite!

BIFF: No, no.

WILLY: Spite, spite, is the word of your undoing! And when you're down and out, remember what did it. When you're rotting somewhere beside the railroad tracks, remember, and don't you dare blame it on me!

BIFF: I'm not blaming it on you!

WILLY: I won't take the rap for this, you hear?

(*Happy comes down the stairs and stands on the bottom step, watching.*)

BIFF: That's just what I'm telling you!

WILLY (*sinking into a chair at a table, with full accusation*): You're trying to put a knife in me—don't think I don't know what you're doing!

BIFF: All right, phony! Then let's lay it on the line. (*He whips the rubber tube out of his pocket and puts it on the table.*)

HAPPY: You crazy . . .

LINDA: Biff! (*She moves to grab the hose, but Biff holds it down with his hand.*)

BIFF: Leave it there! Don't move it!

WILLY (*not looking at it*): What is that?

BIFF: You know goddam well what that is.

WILLY (*caged, wanting to escape*): I never saw that.

BIFF: You saw it. The mice didn't bring it into the cellar! What is this supposed to do, make a hero out of you? This supposed to make me sorry for you?

WILLY: Never heard of it.

BIFF: There'll be no pity for you, you hear it? No pity!

WILLY (*to Linda*): You hear the spite!

BIFF: No, you're going to hear the truth—what you are and what I am!

LINDA: Stop it!

WILLY: Spite!

HAPPY (*coming down toward Biff*): You cut it now!

BIFF (*to Happy*): The man don't know who we are! The man is gonna know! (*To Willy.*) We never told the truth for ten minutes in this house!

HAPPY: We always told the truth!

BIFF (*turning on him*): You big blow, are you the assistant buyer? You're one of the two assistants to the assistant, aren't you?

HAPPY: Well, I'm practically . . .

BIFF: You're practically full of it! We all are! and I'm through with it. (*To Willy.*) Now hear this, Willy, this is me.

WILLY: I know you!

BIFF: You know why I had no address for three months? I stole a suit in Kansas City and I was in jail. (*To Linda, who is sobbing.*) Stop crying. I'm through with it.

(*Linda turns away from them, her hands covering her face.*)

WILLY: I suppose that's my fault!

BIFF: I stole myself out of every good job since high school!

WILLY: And whose fault is that?

BIFF: And I never got anywhere because you blew me so full of hot air I could never stand taking orders from anybody! That's whose fault it is!

WILLY: I hear that!

LINDA: Don't, Biff!

BIFF: It's goddam time you heard that! I had to be boss big shot in two weeks, and I'm through with it!

WILLY: Then hang yourself! For spite, hang yourself!

BIFF: No! Nobody's hanging himself, Willy! I ran down eleven flights
with a pen in my hand today. And suddenly I stopped, you hear me?
And in the middle of that office building, do you hear this? I stopped in
the middle of that building and I saw—the sky. I saw the things that I
love in this world. The work and the food and time to sit and smoke.
And I looked at the pen and said to myself, what the hell am I grabbing
this for? Why am I trying to become what I don't want to be? What am
I doing in an office, making a contemptuous begging fool of myself,
when all I want is out there, waiting for me the minute I say I know
who I am! Why can't I say that, Willy? (*He tries to make Willy face him,
but Willy pulls away and moves to the left.*)

WILLY (*with hatred, threateningly*): The door of your life is wide open!

BIFF: Pop! I'm a dime a dozen, and so are you!

WILLY (*turning on him now in an uncontrolled outburst*): I am not a dime a
dozen! I am Willy Loman, and you are Biff Loman!

(*Biff starts for Willy, but is blocked by Happy. In his fury, Biff seems on the
verge of attacking his father.*)

BIFF: I am not a leader of men, Willy, and neither are you. You were
never anything but a hard-working drummer who landed in the ash
can like all the rest of them! I'm one dollar an hour, Willy! I tried seven
states and couldn't raise it. A buck an hour! Do you gather my meaning? I'm not bringing home any prizes any more, and you're going to
stop waiting for me to bring them home!

WILLY (*directly to Biff*): You vengeful, spiteful mutt!

(*Biff breaks from Happy. Willy, in fright, starts up the stairs. Biff grabs him.*)

BIFF (*at the peak of his fury*): Pop, I'm nothing! I'm nothing, Pop. Can't
you understand that? There's no spite in it any more. I'm just what I
am, that's all.

(*Biff's fury has spent itself and he breaks down, sobbing, holding on to Willy,
who dumbly fumbles for Biff's face.*)

WILLY (*astonished*): What're you doing? What're you doing? (*To Linda.*)
Why is he crying?

BIFF (*crying, broken*): Will you let me go, for Christ's sake? Will you take
that phony dream and burn it before something happens? (*Struggling
to contain himself he pulls away and moves to the stairs.*) I'll go in the
morning. Put him—put him to bed. (*Exhausted, Biff moves up the stairs
to his room.*)

WILLY (*after a long pause, astonished, elevated*): Isn't that—isn't that
remarkable? Biff—he likes me!

LINDA: He loves you, Willy!

HAPPY (*deeply moved*): Always did, Pop.

WILLY: Oh, Biff! (*Staring wildly.*) He cried! Cried to me. (*He is choking with his love, and now cries out his promise.*) That boy—that boy is going to be magnificent!

(*Ben appears in the light just outside the kitchen.*)

BEN: Yes, outstanding, with twenty thousand behind him.

LINDA (*sensing the racing of his mind, fearfully, carefully*): Now come to bed, Willy. It's all settled now.

WILLY (*finding it difficult not to rush out of the house*): Yes, we'll sleep. Come on. Go to sleep, Hap.

BEN: And it does take a great kind of a man to crack the jungle.

(*In accents of dread, Ben's idyllic music starts up.*)

HAPPY (*his arm around Linda*): I'm getting married, Pop, don't forget it. I'm changing everything. I'm gonna run that department before the year is up. You'll see, Mom. (*He kisses her.*)

BEN: The jungle is dark but full of diamonds, Willy.

(*Willy turns, moves, listening to Ben.*)

LINDA: Be good. You're both good boys, just act that way, that's all.

HAPPY: 'Night, Pop. (*He goes upstairs.*)

LINDA (*to Willy*): Come, dear.

BEN (*with greater force*): One must go in to fetch a diamond out.

WILLY (*to Linda, as he moves slowly along the edge of kitchen, toward the door*): I just want to get settled down, Linda. Let me sit alone for a little.

LINDA (*almost uttering her fear*): I want you upstairs.

WILLY (*taking her in his arms*): In a few minutes, Linda. I couldn't sleep right now. Go on, you look awful tired. (*He kisses her.*)

BEN: Not like an appointment at all. A diamond is rough and hard to the touch.

WILLY: Go on now. I'll be right up.

LINDA: I think this is the only way, Willy.

WILLY: Sure, it's the best thing.

BEN: Best thing!

WILLY: The only way. Everything is gonna be—go on, kid, get to bed. You look so tired.

LINDA: Come right up.

WILLY: Two minutes.

(*Linda goes into the living room, then reappears in her bedroom. Willy moves just outside the kitchen door.*)

WILLY: Loves me. (*Wonderingly.*) Always loved me. Isn't that a remarkable thing? Ben, he'll worship me for it!

BEN (*with promise*): It's dark there, but full of diamonds.

WILLY: Can you imagine that magnificence with twenty thousand dollars in his pocket?

LINDA (*calling from her room*): Willy! Come up!

WILLY (*calling into the kitchen*): Yes! yes. Coming! It's very smart, you realize that, don't you, sweetheart? Even Ben sees it. I gotta go, baby. 'By! 'By! (*Going over to Ben, almost dancing.*) Imagine? When the mail comes he'll be ahead of Bernard again!

BEN: A perfect proposition all around.

WILLY: Did you see how he cried to me? Oh, if I could kiss him, Ben!

BEN: Time, William, time!

WILLY: Oh, Ben, I always knew one way or another we were gonna make it, Biff and I!

BEN (*looking at his watch*): The boat. We'll be late. (*He moves slowly off into the darkness.*)

WILLY (*elegiacally, turning to the house*): Now when you kick off, boy, I want a seventy-yard boot, and get right down the field under the ball, and when you hit, hit low and hit hard, because it's important, boy. (*He swings around and faces the audience.*) There's all kinds of important people in the stands, and the first thing you know . . . (*Suddenly realizing he is alone.*) Ben! Ben, where do I . . . ? (*He makes a sudden movement of search.*) Ben, how do I . . . ?

LINDA (*calling*): Willy, you coming up?

WILLY (*uttering a gasp of fear, whirling about as if to quiet her*): Sh! (*He turns around as if to find his way; sounds, faces, voices, seem to be swarming in upon him and he flicks at them, crying, Sh! Sh! Suddenly music, faint and high, stops him. It rises in intensity, almost to an unbearable scream. He goes up and down on his toes, and rushes off around the house.*) Shhh!

LINDA: Willy?

(*There is no answer. Linda waits. Biff gets up off his bed. He is still in his clothes. Happy sits up. Biff stands listening.*)

LINDA (*with real fear*): Willy, answer me! Willy!

(*There is the sound of a car starting and moving away at full speed.*)

LINDA: No!

BIFF (*rushing down the stairs*): Pop!

(*As the car speeds off, the music crashes down in a frenzy of sound, which becomes the soft pulsation of a single cello string. Biff slowly returns to his bedroom. He and Happy gravely don their jackets. Linda slowly walks out of her room. The music has developed into a dead march. The leaves of day are appearing over everything. Charley and Bernard, somberly dressed, appear and knock on the kitchen door. Biff and Happy slowly descend the stairs to the kitchen as Charley and Bernard enter. All stop a moment when Linda, in clothes of mourning, bearing a little bunch of roses, comes through the draped doorway into the kitchen. She goes to Charley and takes his arm. Now all move toward the audience, through the wall-line of the kitchen. At the limit of the apron, Linda lays down the flowers, kneels, and sits back on her heels. All stare down at the grave.)*

REQUIEM

CHARLEY: It's getting dark, Linda.

(Linda doesn't react. She stares at the grave.)

BIFF: How about it, Mom? Better get some rest, heh? They'll be closing the gate soon.

(Linda makes no move. Pause.)

HAPPY *(deeply angered)*: He had no right to do that. There was no necessity for it. We would've helped him.

CHARLEY *(grunting)*: Hmmm.

BIFF: Come along, Mom.

LINDA: Why didn't anybody come?

CHARLEY: It was a very nice funeral.

LINDA: But where are all the people he knew? Maybe they blame him.

CHARLEY: Naa. It's a rough world, Linda. They wouldn't blame him.

LINDA: I can't understand it. At this time especially. First time in thirty-five years we were just about free and clear. He only needed a little salary. He was even finished with the dentist.

CHARLEY: No man only needs a little salary.

LINDA: I can't understand it.

BIFF: There were a lot of nice days. When he'd come home from a trip; or on Sundays, making the stoop; finishing the cellar; putting on the new porch; when he built the extra bathroom; and put up the garage. You know something, Charley, there's more of him in that front stoop than in all the sales he ever made.

CHARLEY: Yeah. He was a happy man with a batch of cement.

LINDA: He was so wonderful with his hands.

BIFF: He had the wrong dreams. All, all, wrong.

HAPPY *(almost ready to fight Biff)*: Don't say that!

BIFF: He never knew who he was.

CHARLEY (*stopping Happy's movement and reply. To Biff*): Nobody dast blame this man. You don't understand: Willy was a salesman. And for a salesman, there is no rock bottom to the life. He don't put a bolt to a nut, he don't tell you the law or give you medicine. He's a man way out there in the blue, riding on a smile and a shoeshine. And when they start not smiling back—that's an earthquake. And then you get yourself a couple of spots on your hat, and you're finished. Nobody dast blame this man. A salesman is got to dream, boy. It comes with the territory.

BIFF: Charley, the man didn't know who he was.

HAPPY (*infuriated*): Don't say that!

BIFF: Why don't you come with me, Happy?

HAPPY: I'm not licked that easily. I'm staying right in this city, and I'm gonna beat this racket! (*He looks at Biff, his chin set.*) The Loman Brothers!

BIFF: I know who I am, kid.

HAPPY: All right, boy. I'm gonna show you and everybody else that Willy Loman did not die in vain. He had a good dream. It's the only dream you can have—to come out number-one man. He fought it out here, and this is where I'm gonna win it for him.

BIFF (*with a hopeless glance at Happy, bends toward his mother*): Let's go, Mom.

LINDA: I'll be with you in a minute. Go on, Charley. (*He hesitates.*) I want to, just for a minute. I never had a chance to say good-by.

(*Charley moves away, followed by Happy. Biff remains a slight distance up and left of Linda. She sits there, summoning herself. The flute begins, not far away, playing behind her speech.*)

LINDA: Forgive me, dear. I can't cry. I don't know what it is, but I can't cry. I don't understand it. Why did you ever do that? Help me, Willy, I can't cry. It seems to me that you're just on another trip. I keep expecting you. Willy, dear, I can't cry. Why did you do it? I search and search and I search, and I can't understand it, Willy. I made the last payment on the house today. Today, dear. And there'll be nobody home. (*A sob rises in her throat.*) We're free and clear. (*Sobbing more fully, released.*) We're free. (*Biff comes slowly toward her.*) We're free . . . We're free . . .

(*Biff lifts her to her feet and moves out up right with her in his arms. Linda sobs quietly. Bernard and Charley come together and follow them, followed by Happy. Only the music of the flute is left on the darkening stage as over the house the hard towers of the apartment buildings rise into sharp focus, and the curtain falls.*)

[1949]

CARYL CHURCHILL [b. 1938]

Top Girls

Characters
MARLENE
WAITRESS/KIT/SHONA
ISABELLA BIRD/JOYCE/MRS. KIDD
LADY NIJO/WIN
DULL GRET/ANGIE
POPE JOAN/LOUISE
PATIENT GRISELDA/NELL/JEANINE

Act I
Scene I: *A Restaurant.*
Scene II: *Top Girls' Employment Agency, London.*
Scene III: *Joyce's backyard in Suffolk.*

Act II
Scene I: *Top Girls' Employment Agency.*
Scene II: *A Year Earlier. Joyce's kitchen.*

Production Note: *The seating order for Act I, Scene I, in the original production at the Royal Court Theatre was (from right) Gret, Nijo, Marlene, Joan, Griselda, Isabella.*

The Characters
ISABELLA BIRD (1831–1904): *Lived in Edinburgh, traveled extensively between the ages of forty and seventy.*
LADY NIJO (B. 1258): *Japanese, was an Emperor's courtesan and later a Buddhist nun who traveled on foot through Japan.*
DULL GRET: *Is the subject of the Brueghel painting* DULLE GRIET, *in which a woman in an apron and armor leads a crowd of women charging through hell and fighting the devils.*
POPE JOAN: *Disguised as a man, is thought to have been pope between 854 and 856.*
PATIENT GRISELDA: *Is the obedient wife whose story is told by Chaucer in "The Clerk's Tale" of* THE CANTERBURY TALES.

The Layout: *A speech usually follows the one immediately before it but: (1) When one character starts speaking before the other has finished, the point of interruption is marked /. E.g.,*

1091

ISABELLA: This is the Emperor of Japan? / I once met the Emperor of Morocco.

NIJO: In fact he was the ex-Emperor.

(2) *A character sometimes continues speaking right through another's speech. E.g.,*

ISABELLA: When I was forty I thought my life was over. / Oh I was pitiful. I was

NIJO: I didn't say I felt it for twenty years. Not every minute.

ISABELLA: sent on a cruise for my health and felt even worse. Pains in my bones, pins and needles . . . etc.

(3) *Sometimes a speech follows on from a speech earlier than the one immediately before it, and continuity is marked*. E.g.,*

GRISELDA: I'd seen him riding by, we all had. And he'd seen me in the fields with the sheep.*

ISABELLA: I would have been well suited to minding sheep.

NIJO: And Mr. Nugent went riding by.

ISABELLA: Of course not, Nijo, I mean a healthy life in the open air.

JOAN: *He just rode up while you were minding the sheep and asked you to marry him?

where "in the fields with the sheep" is the cue to both "I would have been" and "He just rode up."

ACT I   *Scene I*

(*Restaurant. Saturday night. There is a table with a white cloth set for dinner with six places. The lights come up on Marlene and the Waitress.*)

MARLENE: Excellent, yes, table for six. One of them's going to be late but we won't wait. I'd like a bottle of Frascati straight away if you've got one really cold. (*The Waitress goes. Isabella Bird arrives.*) Here we are. Isabella.

ISABELLA: Congratulations, my dear.

MARLENE: Well, it's a step. It makes for a party. I haven't time for a holiday. I'd like to go somewhere exotic like you but I can't get away. I don't know how you could bear to leave Hawaii. / I'd like to lie

ISABELLA: I did think of settling.

MARLENE: in the sun forever, except of course I can't bear sitting still.

ISABELLA: I sent for my sister Hennie to come and join me. I said, Hennie we'll live here forever and help the natives. You can buy two sirloins of beef for what a pound of chops cost in Edinburgh. And

Hennie wrote back, the dear, that yes, she would come to Hawaii if I wished, but I said she had far better stay where she was. Hennie was suited to life in Tobermory.

MARLENE: Poor Hennie.

ISABELLA: Do you have a sister?

MARLENE: Yes in fact.

ISABELLA: Hennie was happy. She was good. I did miss its face, my own pet. But I couldn't stay in Scotland. I loathed the constant murk.

(*Lady Nijo arrives.*)

MARLENE (*seeing her*): Ah! Nijo! (*The Waitress enters with the wine.*)

NIJO: Marlene! (*To Isabella.*) So excited when Marlene told me / you were coming.

ISABELLA: I'm delighted / to meet you.

MARLENE: I think a drink while we wait for the others. I think a drink anyway. What a week. (*Marlene seats Nijo. The Waitress pours the wine.*)

NIJO: It was always the men who used to get so drunk. I'd be one of the maidens, passing the sake.

ISABELLA: I've had sake. Small hot drink. Quite fortifying after a day in the wet.

NIJO: One night my father proposed three rounds of three cups, which was normal, and then the Emperor should have said three rounds of three cups, but he said three rounds of nine cups, so you can imagine. Then the Emperor passed his sake cup to my father and said, "Let the wild goose come to me this spring."

MARLENE: Let the what?

NIJO: It's a literary allusion to a tenth-century epic, / His Majesty was very cultured.

ISABELLA: This is the Emperor of Japan? / I once met the Emperor of Morocco.

NIJO: In fact he was the ex-Emperor.

MARLENE: But he wasn't old? / Did you, Isabella?

NIJO: Twenty-nine.

ISABELLA: Oh it's a long story.

MARLENE: Twenty-nine's an excellent age.

NIJO: Well I was only fourteen and I knew he meant something but I didn't know what. He sent me an eight-layered gown and I sent it back. So when the time came I did nothing but cry. My thin gowns were badly ripped. But even that morning when he left / he'd a green

MARLENE: Are you saying he raped you?

NIJO: robe with a scarlet lining and very heavily embroidered trousers, I already felt different about him. It made me uneasy. No, of course not, Marlene, I belonged to him, it was what I was brought up for from a baby. I soon found I was sad if he stayed away. It was depressing day after day not knowing when he would come. I never enjoyed taking other women to him.

ISABELLA: I certainly never saw my father drunk. He was a clergyman. / And I didn't get married till I was fifty. (*The Waitress brings the menus.*)

NIJO: Oh, my father was a very religious man. Just before he died he said to me, "Serve His Majesty, be respectful, if you lose his favor enter holy orders."

MARLENE: But he meant stay in a convent, not go wandering round the country.

NIJO: Priests were often vagrants, so why not a nun? You think I shouldn't? / I still did what my father wanted.

MARLENE: No no, I think you should. / I think it was wonderful.

(*Dull Gret arrives.*)

ISABELLA: I tried to do what my father wanted.

MARLENE: Gret, good. Nijo. Gret / I know Griselda's going to be late, but should we wait for Joan? / Let's get you a drink.

ISABELLA: Hello, Gret! (*She continues to Nijo.*) I tried to be a clergyman's daughter. Needlework, music, charitable schemes. I had a tumor removed from my spine and spent a great deal of time on the sofa. I studied the metaphysical poets and hymnology. / I thought I enjoyed intellectual pursuits.

NIJO: Ah, you like poetry. I come of a line of eight generations of poets. Father had a poem / in the anthology.

ISABELLA: My father taught me Latin although I was a girl. / But really I was

MARLENE: They didn't have Latin at my school.

ISABELLA: more suited to manual work. Cooking, washing, mending, riding horses. / Better than reading

NIJO: Oh but I'm sure you're very clever.

ISABELLA: books, eh Gret? A rough life in the open air.

NIJO: I can't say I enjoyed my rough life. What I enjoyed most was being the Emperor's favorite / and wearing thin silk.

ISABELLA: Did you have any horses, Gret?

GRET: Pig.

(*Pope Joan arrives.*)

MARLENE: Oh Joan, thank God, we can order. Do you know everyone? We were just talking about learning Latin and being clever girls. Joan was by way of an infant prodigy. Of course you were. What excited you when you were ten?

JOAN: Because angels are without matter they are not individuals. Every angel is a species.

MARLENE: There you are. (*They laugh. They look at the menus.*)

ISABELLA: Yes, I forgot all my Latin. But my father was the mainspring of my life and when he died I was so grieved. I'll have the chicken, please, / and the soup.

NIJO: Of course you were grieved. My father was saying his prayers and he dozed off in the sun. So I touched his knee to rouse him. "I wonder what will happen," he said, and then he was dead before he finished the sentence. / If he'd

MARLENE: What a shock.

NIJO: died saying his prayers he would have gone straight to heaven. / Waldorf salad.

JOAN: Death is the return of all creatures to God.

NIJO: I shouldn't have woken him.

JOAN: Damnation only means ignorance of the truth. I was always attracted by the teachings of John the Scot, though he was inclined to confuse / God and the world.

ISABELLA: Grief always overwhelmed me at the time.

MARLENE: What I fancy is a rare steak. Gret?

ISABELLA: I am of course a member of the / Church of England.

MARLENE: Gret?

GRET: Potatoes.

MARLENE: I haven't been to church for years. / I like Christmas carols.

ISABELLA: Good works matter more than church attendance.

MARLENE: Make that two steaks and a lot of potatoes. Rare. But I don't do good works either.

JOAN: Canelloni, please, / and a salad.

ISABELLA: Well, I tried, but oh dear. Hennie did good works.

NIJO: The first half of my life was all sin and the second / all repentance.*

MARLENE: Oh what about starters?

GRET: Soup.

JOAN: *And which did you like best?

MARLENE: Were your travels just a penance? Avocado vinaigrette. Didn't you / enjoy yourself?

JOAN: Nothing to start with for me, thank you.

NIJO: Yes, but I was very unhappy. / It hurt to remember the past.

MARLENE: And the wine list.

NIJO: I think that was repentance.

MARLENE: Well I wonder.

NIJO: I might have just been homesick.

MARLENE: Or angry.

NIJO: Not angry, no, / why angry?

GRET: Can we have some more bread?

MARLENE: Don't you get angry? I get angry.

NIJO: But what about?

MARLENE: Yes let's have two more Frascati. And some more bread, please. (*The Waitress exits.*)

ISABELLA: I tried to understand Buddhism when I was in Japan but all this birth and death succeeding each other through eternities just filled me with the most profound melancholy. I do like something more active.

NIJO: You couldn't say I was inactive. I walked every day for twenty years.

ISABELLA: I don't mean walking. / I mean in the head.

NIJO: I vowed to copy five Mahayana sutras.° / Do you know how long they are?

MARLENE: I don't think religious beliefs are something we have in common. Activity yes. (*Gret empties the bread basket into her apron.*)

NIJO: My head was active. / My head ached.

JOAN: It's no good being active in heresy.

ISABELLA: What heresy? She's calling the Church of England / a heresy.

JOAN: There are some very attractive / heresies.

NIJO: I had never heard of Christianity. Never / heard of it. Barbarians.

MARLENE: Well I'm not a Christian. / And I'm not a Buddhist.

ISABELLA: You have heard of it?

MARLENE: We don't all have to believe the same.

ISABELLA: I knew coming to dinner with a Pope we should keep off religion.

JOAN: I always enjoy a theological argument. But I won't try to convert you, I'm not a missionary. Anyway I'm a heresy myself.

ISABELLA: There are some barbaric practices in the east.

NIJO: Barbaric?

ISABELLA: Among the lower classes.

NIJO: I wouldn't know.

ISABELLA: Well theology always made my head ache.

MARLENE: Oh good, some food. (*The Waitress brings the first course, serves it during the following, then exits.*)

NIJO: How else could I have left the court if I wasn't a nun? When father died I had only His Majesty. So when I fell out of favor I had nothing. Religion is a kind of nothing / and I dedicated what was left of me to nothing.

ISABELLA: That's what I mean about Buddhism. It doesn't brace.

MARLENE: Come on, Nijo, have some wine.

NIJO: Haven't you ever felt like that? You've all felt / like that. Nothing will ever happen again. I am dead already.

Mahayana sutras: Buddhist scriptures.

ISABELLA: You thought your life was over but it wasn't.

JOAN: You wish it was over.

GRET: Sad.

MARLENE: Yes, when I first came to London I sometimes . . . and when I got back from America I did. But only for a few hours. Not twenty years.

ISABELLA: When I was forty I thought my life was over. / Oh I was pitiful. I was sent

NIJO: I didn't say I felt it for twenty years. Not every minute.

ISABELLA: on a cruise for my health and I felt even worse. Pains in my bones, pins and needles in my hands, swelling behind the ears, and— oh, stupidity. I shook all over, indefinable terror. And Australia seemed to me a hideous country, the acacias stank like drains. / I

NIJO: You were homesick. (*Gret steals a bottle of wine.*)

ISABELLA: had a photograph taken for Hennie but I told her I wouldn't send it, my hair had fallen out and my clothes were crooked, I looked completely insane and suicidal.

NIJO: So did I, exactly, dressed as a nun. / I was wearing walking shoes for the first time.

ISABELLA: I longed to go home, / but home to what? Houses are so perfectly dismal.*

NIJO: I longed to go back ten years.

MARLENE: *I thought traveling cheered you both up.

ISABELLA: Oh it did / of course. It was on

NIJO: I'm not a cheerful person, Marlene. I just laugh a lot.

ISABELLA: the trip from Australia to the Sandwich Isles, I fell in love with the sea. There were rats in the cabin and ants in the food but suddenly it was like a new world. I woke up every morning happy, knowing there would be nothing to annoy me. No nervousness. No dressing.

NIJO: Don't you like getting dressed? I adored my clothes. / When I was chosen

MARLENE: You had prettier colors than Isabella.

NIJO: to give sake to His Majesty's brother, the Emperor Kameyana, on his formal visit, I wore raw silk pleated trousers and a seven-layered gown in shades of red, and two outer garments, / yellow lined with green

MARLENE: Yes, all that silk must have been very—(*The Waitress enters, clears the first course and exits.*)

JOAN: I dressed as a boy when I left home.*

NIJO: and a light green jacket. Lady Betto had a five-layered gown in shades of green and purple.

ISABELLA: *You dressed as a boy?

MARLENE: Of course, / for safety.

JOAN: It was easy, I was only twelve. / Also women weren't allowed in the library. We wanted to study in Athens.

MARLENE: You ran away alone?

JOAN: No, not alone, I went with my friend. / He was

NIJO: Ah, an elopement.

JOAN: sixteen but I thought I knew more science than he did and almost as much philosophy.

ISABELLA: Well I always traveled as a lady and I repudiated strongly any suggestion in the press that I was other than feminine.

MARLENE: I don't wear trousers in the office. / I could but I don't.

ISABELLA: There was no great danger to a woman of my age and appearance.

MARLENE: And you got away with it, Joan?

JOAN: I did then. (*The Waitress brings in the main course.*)

MARLENE: And nobody noticed anything?

JOAN: They noticed I was a very clever boy. / And

MARLENE: I couldn't have kept pretending for so long.

JOAN: when I shared a bed with my friend, that was ordinary—two poor students in a lodging house. I think I forgot I was pretending.

ISABELLA: Rocky Mountain Jim, Mr. Nugent, showed me no disrespect. He found it interesting, I think, that I could make scones and also lasso cattle. Indeed he declared his love for me, which was most distressing.

NIJO: What did he say? / We always sent poems first.

MARLENE: What did you say?

ISABELLA: I urged him to give up whiskey, / but he said it was too late.

MARLENE: Oh Isabella.

ISABELLA: He had lived alone in the mountains for many years.

MARLENE: But did you—? (*The Waitress goes.*)

ISABELLA: Mr. Nugent was a man that any woman might love but none could marry. I came back to England.

NIJO: Did you write him a poem when you left? / Snow on the mountains. My sleeves

MARLENE: Did you never see him again?

ISABELLA: No, never.

NIJO: are wet with tears. In England no tears, no snow.

ISABELLA: Well, I say never. One morning very early in Switzerland, it was a year later, I had a vision of him as I last saw him / in his trapper's clothes with his

NIJO: A ghost!

ISABELLA: hair round his face, and that was the day, / I learned later, he died with a

NIJO: Ah!

ISABELLA: bullet in his brain. / He just bowed to me and vanished.

MARLENE: Oh Isabella.

NIJO: When your lover dies — One of my lovers died. / The priest Ariake.

JOAN: My friend died. Have we all got dead lovers?

MARLENE: Not me, sorry.

NIJO (*to Isabella*): I wasn't a nun, I was still at court, but he was a priest, and when he came to me he dedicated his whole life to hell. / He knew that when he died he would fall into one of the three lower realms. And he died, he did die.

JOAN (*to Marlene*): I'd quarreled with him over the teachings of John the Scot,° who held that our ignorance of God is the same as his ignorance of himself. He only knows what he creates because he creates everything he knows but he himself is above being — do you follow?

MARLENE: No, but go on.

NIJO: I couldn't bear to think / in what shape would he be reborn.*

JOAN: St. Augustine maintained that the Neo-Platonic Ideas are indivisible

ISABELLA: *Buddhism is really most uncomfortable.

JOAN: from God, but I agreed with John that the created world is essences derived from Ideas which derived from God. As Denys the Areopagite° said — the pseudo-Denys — first we give God a name, then deny it, / then reconcile the contradiction

NIJO: In what shape would he return?

JOAN: by looking beyond / those terms —

MARLENE: Sorry, what? Denys said what?

JOAN: Well we disagreed about it, we quarreled. And next day he was ill, / I was so annoyed with him

NIJO: Misery in this life and worse in the next, all because of me.

JOAN: all the time I was nursing him I kept going over the arguments in my mind. Matter is not a means of knowing the essence. The source of the species is the Idea. But then I realized he'd never understand my arguments again, and that night he died. John the Scot held that the individual disintegrates / and there is no personal immortality.

ISABELLA: I wouldn't have you think I was in love with Jim Nugent. It was yearning to save him that I felt.

MARLENE (*to Joan*): So what did you do?

JOAN: First I decided to stay a man. I was used to it. And I wanted to devote my life to learning. Do you know why I went to Rome? Italian men didn't have beards.

ISABELLA: The loves of my life were Hennie, my own pet, and my dear husband the doctor, who nursed Hennie in her last illness. I knew it

---

John the Scot: Controversial ninth-century Irish religious philosopher.
Denys the Areopagite: First-century Greek religious philosopher.

would be terrible when Hennie died but I didn't know how terrible. I felt half of myself had gone. How could I go on my travels without that sweet soul waiting at home for my letters? It was Doctor Bishop's devotion to her in her last illness that made me decide to marry him. He and Hennie had the same sweet character. I had not.

NIJO: I thought His Majesty had sweet character because when he found out about Ariake he was so kind. But really it was because he no longer cared for me. One night he even sent me out to a man who had been pursuing me. / He lay awake on the other side of the screens and listened.

ISABELLA: I did wish marriage had seemed more of a step. I tried very hard to cope with the ordinary drudgery of life. I was ill again with carbuncles on the spine and nervous prostration. I ordered a tricycle, that was my idea of adventure then. And John himself fell ill, with erysipelas and anemia. I began to love him with my whole heart but it was too late. He was a skeleton with transparent white hands. I wheeled him on various seafronts in a bathchair. And he faded and left me. There was nothing in my life. The doctors said I had gout / and my heart was much affected.

NIJO: There was nothing in my life, nothing, without the Emperor's favor. The Empress had always been my enemy, Marlene, she said I had no right to wear three-layered gowns. / But I was the adopted daughter of my grandfather the Prime Minister. I had been publicly granted permission to wear thin silk.

JOAN: There was nothing in my life except my studies. I was obsessed with pursuit of the truth. I taught at the Greek School in Rome, which St. Augustine had made famous. I was poor, I worked hard, I spoke apparently brilliantly, I was still very young, I was a stranger, suddenly I was quite famous, I was everyone's favorite. Huge crowds came to hear me. The day after they made me cardinal I fell ill and lay two weeks without speaking, full of terror and regret. / But then I got up determined to

MARLENE: Yes, success is very . . .

JOAN: go on. I was seized again / with a desperate longing for the absolute.

ISABELLA: Yes, yes, to go on. I sat in Tobermory among Hennie's flowers and sewed a complete outfit in Jaeger flannel. / I was fifty-six years old.

NIJO: Out of favor but I didn't die. I left on foot, nobody saw me go. For the next twenty years I walked through Japan.

GRET: Walking is good. (*Meanwhile, the Waitress enters, pours lots of wine, then shows Marlene the empty bottle.*)

JOAN: Pope Leo died and I was chosen. All right then. I would be Pope. I would know God. I would know everything.

ISABELLA: I determined to leave my grief behind and set off for Tibet.

MARLENE: Magnificent all of you. We need some more wine, please, two bottles I think, Griselda isn't even here yet, and I want to drink a toast to you all. (*The Waitress exits.*)

ISABELLA: To yourself surely, / we're here to celebrate your success.

NIJO: Yes, Marlene.

JOAN: Yes, what is it exactly, Marlene?

MARLENE: Well it's not Pope but it is managing director.*

JOAN: And you find work for people.

MARLENE: Yes, an employment agency.

NIJO: *Over all the women you work with. And the men.

ISABELLA: And very well deserved too. I'm sure it's just the beginning of something extraordinary.

MARLENE: Well it's worth a party.

ISABELLA: To Marlene.*

MARLENE: And all of us.

JOAN: *Marlene.

NIJO: Marlene.

GRET: Marlene.

MARLENE: We've all come a long way. To our courage and the way we changed our lives and our extraordinary achievements. (*They laugh and drink a toast.*)

ISABELLA: Such adventures. We were crossing a mountain pass at seven thousand feet, the cook was all to pieces, the muleteers suffered fever and snow blindness. But even though my spine was agony I managed very well.*

MARLENE: Wonderful.

NIJO: *Once I was ill for four months lying alone at an inn. Nobody to offer a horse to Buddha. I had to live for myself, and I did live.

ISABELLA: Of course you did. It was far worse returning to Tobermory. I always felt dull when I was stationary. / That's why I could never stay anywhere.

NIJO: Yes, that's it exactly. New sights. The shrine by the beach, the moon shining on the sea. The goddess had vowed to save all living things. / She would even save the fishes. I was full of hope.

JOAN: I had thought the Pope would know everything. I thought God would speak to me directly. But of course he knew I was a woman.

MARLENE: But nobody else even suspected? (*The Waitress brings more wine and then exits.*)

JOAN: In the end I did take a lover again.*

ISABELLA: In the Vatican?

GRET: *Keep you warm.

NIJO: *Ah, lover.

MARLENE: *Good for you.

JOAN: He was one of my chamberlains. There are such a lot of servants when you're Pope. The food's very good. And I realized I did know the truth. Because whatever the Pope says, that's true.

NIJO: What was he like, the chamberlain?*

GRET: Big cock.

ISABELLA: Oh, Gret.

MARLENE: *Did he fancy you when he thought you were a fella?

NIJO: What was he like?

JOAN: He could keep a secret.

MARLENE: So you did know everything.

JOAN: Yes, I enjoyed being Pope. I consecrated bishops and let people kiss my feet. I received the King of England when he came to submit to the church. Unfortunately there were earthquakes, and some village reported it had rained blood, and in France there was a plague of giant grasshoppers, but I don't think that can have been my fault, do you?* (*Laughter.*) The grasshoppers fell on the English Channel / and were washed up on shore

NIJO: I once went to sea. It was very lonely. I realized it made very little difference where I went.

JOAN: and their bodies rotted and poisoned the air and everyone in those parts died. (*Laughter.*)

ISABELLA: *Such superstition! I was nearly murdered in China by a howling mob. They thought the barbarians ate babies and put them under railway sleepers to make the tracks steady, and ground up their eyes to make the lenses of cameras. / So they were shouting,

MARLENE: And you had a camera!

ISABELLA: "Child-eater, child-eater." Some people tried to sell girl babies to Europeans for cameras or stew! (*Laughter.*)

MARLENE: So apart from the grasshoppers it was a great success.

JOAN: Yes, if it hadn't been for the baby I expect I'd have lived to an old age like Theodora of Alexandria, who lived as a monk. She was accused by a girl / who fell in love with her of being the father of her child and—

NIJO: But tell us what happened to your baby. I had some babies.

MARLENE: Didn't you think of getting rid of it?

JOAN: Wouldn't that be a worse sin than having it? / But a Pope with a child was about as bad as possible.

MARLENE: I don't know, you're the Pope.

JOAN: But I wouldn't have known how to get rid of it.

MARLENE: Other Popes had children, surely.

JOAN: They didn't give birth to them.

NIJO: Well you were a woman.

JOAN: Exactly and I shouldn't have been a woman. Woman, children, and lunatics can't be Pope.

MARLENE: So the only thing to do / was to get rid of it somehow.

NIJO: You had to have it adopted secretly.

JOAN: But I didn't know what was happening. I thought I was getting fatter, but then I was eating more and sitting about, the life of a Pope is quite luxurious. I don't think I'd spoken to a woman since I was twelve. The chamberlain was the one who realized.

MARLENE: And by then it was too late.

JOAN: Oh I didn't want to pay attention. It was easier to do nothing.

NIJO: But you had to plan for having it. You had to say you were ill and go away.

JOAN: That's what I should have done I suppose.

MARLENE: Did you want them to find out?

NIJO: I too was often in embarrassing situations, there's no need for a scandal. My first child was His Majesty's, which unfortunately died, but my second was Akebono's. I was seventeen. He was in love with me when I was thirteen, he was very upset when I had to go the Emperor, it was very romantic, a lot of poems. Now His Majesty hadn't been near me for two months so he thought I was four months pregnant when I was really six, so when I reached the ninth month / I announced I was seriously ill,

JOAN: I never knew what month it was.

NIJO: and Akebono announced he had gone on a religious retreat. He held me round the waist and lifted me up as the baby was born. He cut the cord with a short sword, wrapped the baby in white and took it away. It was only a girl but I was sorry to lose it. Then I told the Emperor that the baby had miscarried because of my illness, and there you are. The danger was past.

JOAN: But, Nijo, I wasn't used to having a woman's body.

ISABELLA: So what happened?

JOAN: I didn't know of course that it was near the time. It was Rogation Day, there was always a procession. I was on the horse dressed in my robes and a cross was carried in front of me, and all the cardinals were following, and all the clergy of Rome, and a huge crowd of people. / We set off from St. Peter's to go

MARLENE: Total Pope. (*Gret pours the wine and steals the bottle.*)

JOAN: to St. John's. I had felt a slight pain earlier, I thought it was something I'd eaten, and then it came back, and came back more often. I thought when this is over I'll go to bed. There were still long gaps when I felt perfectly all right and I didn't want to attract attention to myself and spoil the ceremony. Then I suddenly realized what it must be. I had to last out till I could get home and hide. Then something changed, my breath started to catch, I couldn't plan things properly anymore. We were in a little street that goes between St. Clement's and the Colosseum, and I just had to get off the horse and sit down for a minute. Great waves of pressure were going through my body, I heard sounds like a cow lowing, they came out of my mouth. Far away I heard people screaming, "The Pope is ill, the Pope is dying." And the baby just slid out onto the road.*

MARLENE: The cardinals / won't have known where to put themselves.

NIJO: Oh dear, Joan, what a thing to do! In the street!

ISABELLA: *How embarrassing.

GRET: In a field, yah. (*They are laughing.*)

JOAN: One of the cardinals said, "The Antichrist!" and fell over in a faint. (*They all laugh.*)

MARLENE: So what did they do? They weren't best pleased.

JOAN: They took me by the feet and dragged me out of town and stoned me to death. (*They stop laughing.*)

MARLENE: Joan, how horrible.

JOAN: I don't really remember.

NIJO: And the child died too?

JOAN: Oh yes, I think so, yes. (*The Waitress enters to clear the plates. Pause. They start talking very quietly.*)

ISABELLA (*to Joan*): I never had any children. I was very fond of horses.

NIJO (*to Marlene*): I saw my daughter once. She was three years old. She wore a plum-red / small sleeved gown. Akebono's wife

ISABELLA: Birdie was my favorite. A little Indian bay mare I rode in the Rocky Mountains.

NIJO: had taken the child because her own died. Everyone thought I was just a visitor. She was being brought up carefully so she could be sent to the palace like I was. (*Gret steals her empty plate.*)

ISABELLA: Legs of iron and always cheerful, and such a pretty face. If a stranger led her she reared up like a bronco.

NIJO: I never saw my third child after he was born, the son of Ariake the priest. Ariake held him on his lap the day he was born and talked to him as if he could understand, and cried. My fourth child was Ariake's too. Ariake died before he was born. I didn't want to see anyone, I stayed alone in the hills. It was a boy again, my third son. But oddly enough I felt nothing for him.

MARLENE: How many children did you have, Gret?

GRET: Ten.

ISABELLA: Whenever I came back to England I felt I had so much to atone for. Hennie and John were so good. I did no good in my life. I spent years in self-gratification. So I hurled myself into committees, I nursed the people of Tobermory in the epidemic of influenza, I lectured the Young Women's Christian Association on Thrift. I talked and talked explaining how the East was corrupt and vicious. My travels must do good to someone besides myself. I wore myself out with good causes.

MARLENE (*pause*): Oh God, why are we all so miserable?

JOAN (*pause*): The procession never went down that street again.

MARLENE: They rerouted it specially?

JOAN: Yes they had to go all round to avoid it. And they introduced a pierced chair.

MARLENE: A pierced chair?

JOAN: Yes, a chair made out of solid marble with a hole in the seat / and it was

MARLENE: You're not serious.

JOAN: in the Chapel of the Savior, and after he was elected the Pope had to sit in it.

MARLENE: And someone looked up his skirts? / Not really!

ISABELLA: What an extraordinary thing.

JOAN: Two of the clergy / made sure he was a man.

NIJO: On their hands and knees!

MARLENE: A pierced chair!

GRET: Balls!

(*Griselda arrives unnoticed.*)

NIJO: Why couldn't he just pull up his robe?

JOAN: He had to sit there and look dignified.

MARLENE: You could have made all your chamberlains sit in it.*

GRET: Big one. Small one.

NIJO: Very useful chair at court.

ISABELLA: *Or the Laird of Tobermory in his kilt.

(*They are quite drunk. They get the giggles. Marlene notices Griselda and gets up to welcome her. The others go on talking and laughing. Gret crosses to Joan and Isabella and pours them wine from her stolen bottles. The Waitress gives out the menus.*)

MARLENE: Griselda! / There you are. Do you want to eat?

GRISELDA: I'm sorry I'm so late. No, no, don't bother.

MARLENE: Of course it's no bother. / Have you eaten?

GRISELDA: No really, I'm not hungry.

MARLENE: Well have some pudding.

GRISELDA: I never eat pudding.

MARLENE: Griselda, I hope you're not anorexic. We're having pudding, I am, and getting nice and fat.

GRISELDA: Oh if everyone is. I don't mind.

MARLENE: Now who do you know? This is Joan who was Pope in the ninth century, and Isabella Bird, the Victorian traveler, and Lady Nijo from Japan, Emperor's concubine and Buddhist nun, thirteenth century, nearer your own time, and Gret who was painted by Brueghel. Griselda's in Boccaccio and Petrarch and Chaucer because of her extraordinary marriage. I'd like profiteroles because they're disgusting.

JOAN: Zabaglione, please.

ISABELLA: Apple pie / and cream.

NIJO: What's this?

MARLENE: Zabaglione, it's Italian, it's what Joan's having, / it's delicious.

NIJO: A Roman Catholic / dessert? Yes please.

MARLENE: Gret?

GRET: Cake.

GRISELDA: Just cheese and biscuits, thank you. (*The Waitress exits.*)

MARLENE: Yes, Griselda's life is like a fairy story, except it starts with marrying the prince.

GRISELDA: He's only a marquis, Marlene.

MARLENE: Well everyone for miles around is his liege and he's absolute lord of life and death and you were the poor but beautiful peasant girl and he whisked you off. / Near enough a prince.

NIJO: How old were you?

GRISELDA: Fifteen.

NIJO: I was brought up in court circles and it was still a shock. Had you ever seen him before?

GRISELDA: I'd seen him riding by, we all had. And he'd seen me in the fields with the sheep.*

ISABELLA: I would have been well suited to minding sheep.

NIJO: And Mr. Nugent riding by.

ISABELLA: Of course not, Nijo, I mean a healthy life in the open air.

JOAN: *He just rode up while you were minding the sheep and asked you to marry him?

GRISELDA: No, no, it was on the wedding day. I was waiting outside the door to see the procession. Everyone wanted him to get married so there'd be an heir to look after us when he died, / and at last he

MARLENE: I don't think Walter wanted to get married. It is Walter? Yes.

GRISELDA: announced a day for the wedding but nobody knew who the bride was, we thought it must be a foreign princess, we were longing to see her. Then the carriage stopped outside our cottage and we couldn't see the bride anywhere. And he came and spoke to my father.

NIJO: And your father told you to serve the Prince.

GRISELDA: My father could hardly speak. The Marquis said it wasn't an order, I could say no, but if I said yes I must always obey him in everything.

MARLENE: That's when you should have suspected.

GRISELDA: But of course a wife must obey her husband. / And of course I must obey the Marquis.*

ISABELLA: I swore to obey dear John, of course, but it didn't seem to arise. Naturally I wouldn't have wanted to go abroad while I was married.

MARLENE: *Then why bother to mention it at all? He'd got a thing about it, that's why.

GRISELDA: I'd rather obey the Marquis than a boy from the village.

MARLENE: Yes, that's a point.

JOAN: I never obeyed anyone. They all obeyed me.

NIJO: And what did you wear? He didn't make you get married in your own clothes? That would be perverse.*

MARLENE: Oh, you wait.

GRISELDA: *He had ladies with him who undressed me and they had a white silk dress and jewels for my hair.

MARLENE: And at first he seemed perfectly normal?

GRISELDA: Marlene, you're always so critical of him. / Of course he was normal, he was very kind.

MARLENE: But, Griselda, come on, he took your baby.

GRISELDA: Walter found it hard to believe I loved him. He couldn't believe I would always obey him. He had to prove it.

MARLENE: I don't think Walter likes women.

GRISELDA: I'm sure he loved me, Marlene, all the time.

MARLENE: He just had a funny way / of showing it.

GRISELDA: It was hard for him too.

JOAN: How do you mean he took away your baby?

NIJO: Was it a boy?

GRISELDA: No, the first one was a girl.

NIJO: Even so it's hard when they take it away. Did you see it at all?

GRISELDA: Oh yes, she was six weeks old.

NIJO: Much better to do it straight away.

ISABELLA: But why did your husband take the child?

GRISELDA: He said all the people hated me because I was just one of them. And now I had a child they were restless. So he had to get rid of the child to keep them quiet. But he said he wouldn't snatch her, I had to agree and obey and give her up. So when I was feeding her a man came in and took her away. I thought he was going to kill her even before he was out of the room.

MARLENE: But you let him take her? You didn't struggle?

GRISELDA: I asked him to give her back so I could kiss her. And I asked him to bury her where no animals could dig her up. / It was Walter's child to do what he

ISABELLA: Oh, my dear.
GRISELDA: liked with.*
MARLENE: Walter was bonkers.
GRET: Bastard.
ISABELLA: *But surely, murder.
GRISELDA: I had promised.
MARLENE: I can't stand this. I'm going for a pee.

(*Marlene goes out. The Waitress brings the dessert, serves it during the follow-ing, then exits.*)

NIJO: No, I understand. Of course you had to, he was your life. And were you in favor after that?
GRISELDA: Oh yes, we were very happy together. We never spoke about what had happened.
ISABELLA: I can see you were doing what you thought was your duty. But didn't it make you ill?
GRISELDA: No, I was very well, thank you.
NIJO: And you had another child?
GRISELDA: Not for four years, but then I did, yes, a boy.
NIJO: Ah a boy. / So it all ended happily.
GRISELDA: Yes he was pleased. I kept my son till he was two years old. A peasant's grandson. It made the people angry. Walter explained.
ISABELLA: But surely he wouldn't kill his children / just because—
GRISELDA: Oh it wasn't true. Walter would never give in to the people. He wanted to see if I loved him enough.
JOAN: He killed his children / to see if you loved him enough?
NIJO: Was it easier the second time or harder?
GRISELDA: It was always easy because I always knew I would do what he said. (*Pause. They start to eat.*)
ISABELLA: I hope you didn't have any more children.
GRISELDA: Oh no, no more. It was twelve years till he tested me again.
ISABELLA: So whatever did he do this time? / My poor John, I never loved him enough, and he would never have dreamt . . .
GRISELDA: He sent me away. He said the people wanted him to marry someone else who'd give him an heir and he'd got special permis-sion from the Pope. So I said I'd go home to my father. I came with nothing / so I went with nothing. I took
NIJO: Better to leave if your master doesn't want you.
GRISELDA: off my clothes. He let me keep a slip so he wouldn't be shamed. And I walked home barefoot. My father came out in tears. Everyone was crying except me.
NIJO: At least your father wasn't dead. / I had nobody.

ISABELLA: Well it can be a relief to come home. I loved to see Hennie's sweet face again.

GRISELDA: Oh yes, I was perfectly content. And quite soon he sent for me again.

JOAN: I don't think I would have gone.

GRISELDA: But he told me to come. I had to obey him. He wanted me to help prepare his wedding. He was getting married to a young girl from France / and nobody except me knew how to arrange things the way he liked them.

NIJO: It's always hard taking him another woman. (*Marlene comes back.*)

JOAN: I didn't live a woman's life. I don't understand it.

GRISELDA: The girl was sixteen and far more beautiful than me. I could see why he loved her. / She had her younger brother with her as a page. (*The Waitress enters.*)

MARLENE: Oh God, I can't bear it. I want some coffee. Six coffees. Six brandies. / Double brandies. Straightaway. (*The Waitress exits.*)

GRISELDA: They all went into the feast I'd prepared. And he stayed behind and put his arms round me and kissed me. / I felt half asleep with the shock.

NIJO: Oh, like a dream.

MARLENE. And he said, "This is your daughter and your son."

GRISELDA: Yes.

JOAN: What?

NIJO: Oh. Oh I see. You got them back.

ISABELLA: I did think it was remarkably barbaric to kill them but you learn not to say anything. / So he had them brought up secretly I suppose.

MARLENE: Walter's a monster. Weren't you angry? What did you do?

GRISELDA: Well I fainted. Then I cried and kissed the children. / Everyone was making a fuss of me.

NIJO: But did you feel anything for them?

GRISELDA: What?

NIJO: Did you feel anything for the children?

GRISELDA: Of course, I loved them.

JOAN: So you forgave him and lived with him?

GRISELDA: He suffered so much all those years.

ISABELLA: Hennie had the same sweet nature.

NIJO: So they dressed you again?

GRISELDA: Cloth of gold.

JOAN: I can't forgive anything.

MARLENE: You really are exceptional, Griselda.

NIJO: Nobody gave me back my children. (*She cries.*)

(*The Waitress brings the brandies and then exits. During the following, Joan goes to Nijo.*)

ISABELLA: I can never be like Hennie. I was always so busy in England, a kind of business I detested. The very presence of people exhausted my emotional reserves. I could not be like Hennie however I tried. I tried and was as ill as could be. The doctor suggested a steel net to support my head, the weight of my own head was too much for my diseased spine. It is dangerous to put oneself in depressing circumstances. Why should I do it?

JOAN (*to Nijo*): Don't cry.

NIJO: My father and the Emperor both died in the autumn. So much pain.

JOAN: Yes, but don't cry.

NIJO: They wouldn't let me into the palace when he was dying. I hid in the room with his coffin, then I couldn't find where I'd left my shoes, I ran after the funeral procession in bare feet, I couldn't keep up. When I got there it was over, a few wisps of smoke in the sky, that's all that was left of him. What I want to know is, if I'd still been at court, would I have been allowed to wear full mourning?

MARLENE: I'm sure you would.

NIJO: Why do you say that? You don't know anything about it. Would I have been allowed to wear full mourning?

ISABELLA: How can people live in this dim pale island and wear our hideous clothes? I cannot and will not live the life of a lady.

NIJO: I'll tell you something that made me angry. I was eighteen, at the Full Moon Ceremony. They make a special rice gruel and stir it with their sticks, and then they beat their women across the loins so they'll have sons and not daughters. So the Emperor beat us all / very hard as

MARLENE: What a sod. (*The Waitress enters with the coffees.*)

NIJO: usual—that's not it, Marlene, that's normal, what made us angry he told his attendants they could beat us too. Well they had a wonderful time. / So Lady Genki and I made a plan, and the ladies

MARLENE: I'd like another brandy, please. Better make it six. (*The Waitress exits.*)

NIJO: all hid in his rooms, and Lady Mashimizu stood guard with a stick at the door, and when His Majesty came in Genki seized him and I beat him till he cried out and promised he would never order anyone to hit us again. Afterward there was a terrible fuss. The nobles were horrified. "We wouldn't even dream of stepping on Your Majesty's shadow." And I had hit him with a stick. Yes, I hit him with a stick.

(*The Waitress brings the brandy bottle and tops up the glasses. Joan crosses in front of the table and back to her place while drunkenly reciting:*)

JOAN: Suave, mari magno turantibus aequora ventis,
  e terra magnum alterius spectare laborem;
  non quia vexari quemquamst iucunda voluptas,
  sed quibus ipse malis careas quia cernere suave est.
  Suave etiam belli certamina magna tueri
  per campos instructa tua sine parse pericli.
  Sed nil dulcius est, bene quam munita tenere
  edita doctrine sapientum temple serena, /
  despicere uncle queas alios passimque videre
  errare atque viam palantis quaerere vitae,°
GRISELDA: I do think — I do wonder — it would have been nicer if Walter
  hadn't had to.
ISABELLA: Why should I? Why should I?
MARLENE: Of course not.
NIJO: I hit him with a stick.
JOAN: certare ingenio, contendere nobilitate,
  noctes atque dies niti praestante labore
  ad summas emergere opes rerumque potiri.
  O miseras hominum mentis, / o pectora caeca!*
ISABELLA: O miseras!
NIJO: *Pectora caeca!
JOAN: qualibus in tenebris vitae quantisque periclis
  degitur hoc aevi quodcumquest! / none videre
  nil aliud sibi naturam latrare, nisi utqui
  corpore seiunctus dolor absit, mente fruatur . . . (*She subsides.*)
GRET: We come to hell through a big mouth. Hell's black and red. / It's
MARLENE (*to Joan*): Shut up, pet.
GRISELDA: Hush, please.
ISABELLA: Listen, she's been to hell.
GRET: like the village where I come from. There's a river and a bridge
  and houses. There's places on fire like when the soldiers come. There's
  a big devil sat on a roof with a big hole in his arse and he's scooping
  stuff out of it with a big ladle and it's falling down on us, and it's
  money, so a lot of the women stop and get some. But most of us is
  fighting the devils. There's lots of little devils, our size, and we get
  them down all right and give them a beating. There's lots of funny
  creatures round your feet, you don't like to look, like rats and lizards,

---

Suave, mari . . . quaerere vitae: Here and in her next several speeches, Joan
quotes from the philosophical poem *De rerum natura* (*On the Nature of Things*) by
first-century B.C.E. Roman philosopher Lucretius. The passage considers differences between the active and the contemplative life. As Joan becomes drunk, her
recitation grows more fragmentary and error-ridden.

and nasty things, a bum with a face, and fish with legs, and faces on things that don't have faces on. But they don't hurt, you just keep going. Well we'd had worse, you see, we'd had the Spanish. We'd all had family killed. My big son die on a wheel. Birds eat him. My baby, a soldier run her through with a sword. I'd had enough, I was mad, I hate the bastards. I come out of my front door that morning and shout till my neighbors come out and I said, "Come on, we're going where the evil come from and pay the bastards out." And they all come out just as they was / from baking or

NIJO: All the ladies come.

GRET: washing in their aprons, and we push down the street and the ground opens up and we go through a big mouth into a street just like ours but in hell. I've got a sword in my hand from somewhere and I fill a basket with gold cups they drink out of down there. You just keep running on and fighting, / you didn't stop for nothing. Oh we give them devils such a beating.*

NIJO: Take that, take that.

JOAN: *Something something something mortisque timores
tum vacuum pectus—damn.
Quod si ridicula—
something something on and on and on
and something splendorem purpureai.

ISABELLA: I thought I would have a last jaunt up the west river in China. Why not? But the doctors were so very grave I just went to Morocco. The sea was so wild I had to be landed by ship's crane in a coal bucket. / My horse was a terror to me, a powerful black charger.

GRET: Coal bucket good.

JOAN: nos in luce timemus
something
terrorem

(*Nijo is laughing and crying. Joan gets up and is sick. Griselda looks after her.*)

GRISELDA: Can I have some water, please? (*The Waitress exits.*)

ISABELLA: So off I went to visit the Berber sheikhs in full blue trousers and great brass spurs. I was the only European woman ever to have seen the Emperor of Morocco. I was (*the Waitress brings the water*) seventy years old. What lengths to go to for a last chance of joy. I knew my return of vigor was only temporary, but how marvelous while it lasted.

Scene II

(*"Top Girls" Employment Agency. Monday morning. The lights come up on Marlene and Jeanine.*)

MARLENE: Right, Jeanine, you are Jeanine aren't you? Let's have a look. O's and A's.° / No A's, all those

JEANINE: Six O's.

MARLENE: O's you probably could have got an A. / Speeds, not brilliant, not too bad.

JEANINE: I wanted to go to work.

MARLENE: Well, Jeanine, what's your present job like?

JEANINE: I'm a secretary.

MARLENE: Secretary or typist?

JEANINE: I did start as a typist but the last six months I've been a secretary.

MARLENE: To?

JEANINE: To three of them, really, they share me. There's Mr. Ashford, he's the office manager, and Mr. Philly / is sales, and—

MARLENE: Quite a small place?

JEANINE: A bit small.

MARLENE: Friendly?

JEANINE: Oh it's friendly enough.

MARLENE: Prospects?

JEANINE: I don't think so, that's the trouble. Miss Lewis is secretary to the managing director and she's been there forever, and Mrs. Bradford / is—

MARLENE: So you want a job with better prospects?

JEANINE: I want a change.

MARLENE: So you'll take anything comparable?

JEANINE: No, I do want prospects. I want more money.

MARLENE: You're getting—?

JEANINE: Hundred.

MARLENE: It's not bad you know. You're what? Twenty?

JEANINE: I'm saving to get married.

MARLENE: Does that mean you don't want a long-term job, Jeanine?

JEANINE: I might do.

MARLENE: Because where do the prospects come in? No kids for a bit?

JEANINE: Oh no, not kids, not yet.

MARLENE: So you won't tell them you're getting married?

JEANINE: Had I better not?

MARLENE: It would probably help.

O's and A's: O-levels and A-levels (for Ordinary and Advanced), academic achievement exams usually taken by British students at ages sixteen and eighteen.

JEANINE: I'm not wearing a ring. We thought we wouldn't spend on a ring.

MARLENE: Saves taking it off.

JEANINE: I wouldn't take it off.

MARLENE: There's no need to mention it when you go for an interview. / Now, Jeanine, do you have a feel

JEANINE: But what if they ask?

MARLENE: for any particular kind of company?

JEANINE: I thought advertising.

MARLENE: People often do think advertising. I have got a few vacancies but I think they're looking for something glossier.

JEANINE: You mean how I dress? / I can

MARLENE: I mean experience.

JEANINE: dress different. I dress like this on purpose for where I am now.

MARLENE: I have a marketing department here of a knitwear manufacturer. / Marketing is near enough

JEANINE: Knitwear?

MARLENE: advertising. Secretary to the marketing manager, he's thirty-five, married, I've sent him a girl before and she was happy, left to have a baby, you won't want to mention marriage there. He's very fair I think, good at his job, you won't have to nurse him along. Hundred and ten, so that's better than you're doing now.

JEANINE: I don't know.

MARLENE: I've a fairly small concern here, father and two sons, you'd have more say potentially, secretarial and reception duties, only a hundred but the job's going to grow with the concern and then you'll be in at the top with new girls coming in underneath you.

JEANINE: What is it they do?

MARLENE: Lampshades. / This would be my first choice for you.

JEANINE: Just lampshades?

MARLENE: There's plenty of different kinds of lampshade. So we'll send you there, shall we, and the knitwear second choice. Are you free to go for an interview any day they call you?

JEANINE: I'd like to travel.

MARLENE: We don't have any foreign clients. You'd have to go elsewhere.

JEANINE: Yes I know. I don't really . . . I just mean . . .

MARLENE: Does your fiancé want to travel?

JEANINE: I'd like a job where I was here in London and with him and everything but now and then— I expect it's silly. Are there jobs like that?

MARLENE: There's personal assistant to a top executive in a multi-national. If that's the idea you need to be planning ahead. Is that where you want to be in ten years?

JEANINE: I might not be alive in ten years.

MARLENE: Yes but you will be. You'll have children.

JEANINE: I can't think about ten years.

MARLENE: You haven't got the speeds anyway. So I'll send you to these two shall I? You haven't been to any other agency? Just so we don't get crossed wires. Now, Jeanine, I want you to get one of these jobs, all right? If I send you that means I'm putting myself on the line for you. Your presentation's OK, you look fine, just be confident and go in there convinced that this is the best job for you and you're the best person for the job. If you don't believe it they won't believe it.

JEANINE: Do you believe it?

MARLENE: I think you could make me believe it if you put your mind to it.

JEANINE: Yes, all right.

Scene III

(*Joyce's back yard. Sunday afternoon. The house with a back door is upstage. Downstage is a shelter made of junk, made by children. The lights come up on two girls, Angie and Kit, who are squashed together in the shelter. Angie is sixteen, Kit is twelve. They cannot be seen from the house.*)

JOYCE (*off, calling from the house*): Angie. Angie, are you out there?

(*Silence. They keep still and wait. When nothing else happens they relax.*)

ANGIE: Wish she was dead.

KIT: Wanna watch *The Exterminator*?

ANGIE: You're sitting on my leg.

KIT: There's nothing on telly. We can have an ice cream. Angie?

ANGIE: Shall I tell you something?

KIT: Do you wanna watch *The Exterminator*?

ANGIE: It's X, innit?

KIT: I can get into Xs.

ANGIE: Shall I tell you something?

KIT: We'll go to something else. We'll go to Ipswich. What's on the Odeon?

ANGIE: She won't let me, will she.

KIT: Don't tell her.

ANGIE: I've no money.

KIT: I'll pay.

ANGIE: She'll moan though, won't she.

KIT: I'll ask her for you if you like.

ANGIE: I've no money, I don't want you to pay.

KIT: I'll ask her.

ANGIE: She don't like you.

KIT: I still got three pounds birthday money. Did she say she don't like me? I'll go by myself then.

ANGIE: Your mum don't let you. I got to take you.

KIT: She won't know.

ANGIE: You'd be scared who'd sit next to you.

KIT: No I wouldn't. She does like me anyway. Tell me then.

ANGIE: Tell you what?

KIT: It's you she doesn't like.

ANGIE: Well I don't like her so tough shit.

JOYCE (*off*): Angie. Angie. Angie. I know you're out there. I'm not coming out after you. You come in here. (*Silence. Nothing happens.*)

ANGIE: Last night when I was in bed. I been thinking yesterday could I make things move. You know, make things move by thinking about them without touching them. Last night I was in bed and suddenly a picture fell down off the wall.

KIT: What picture?

ANGIE: My gran, that picture. Not the poster. The photograph in the frame.

KIT: Had you done something to make it fall down?

ANGIE: I must have done.

KIT: But were you thinking about it?

ANGIE: Not about it, but about something.

KIT: I don't think that's very good.

ANGIE: You know the kitten?

KIT: Which one?

ANGIE: There only is one. The dead one.

KIT: What about it?

ANGIE: I heard it last night.

KIT: Where?

ANGIE: Out here. In the dark. What if I left you here in the dark all night?

KIT: You couldn't. I'd go home.

ANGIE: You couldn't.

KIT: I'd / go home.

ANGIE: No you couldn't, not if I said.

KIT: I could.

ANGIE: Then you wouldn't see anything. You'd just be ignorant.

KIT: I can see in the daytime.

ANGIE: No you can't. You can't hear it in the daytime.

KIT: I don't want to hear it.

ANGIE: You're scared that's all.

KIT: I'm not scared of anything.

ANGIE: You're scared of blood.

KIT: It's not the same kitten anyway. You just heard an old cat, / you just heard some old cat.

ANGIE: You don't know what I heard. Or what I saw. You don't know nothing because you're a baby.

KIT: You're sitting on me.

ANGIE: Mind my hair / you silly cunt.

KIT: Stupid fucking cow, I hate you.

ANGIE: I don't care if you do.

KIT: You're horrible.

ANGIE: I'm going to kill my mother and you're going to watch.

KIT: I'm not playing.

ANGIE: You're scared of blood. (*Kit puts her hand under dress, brings it out with blood on her finger.*)

KIT: There, see, I got my own blood, so. (*Angie takes Kit's hand and licks her finger.*)

ANGIE: Now I'm a cannibal. I might turn into a vampire now.

KIT: That picture wasn't nailed up right.

ANGIE: You'll have to do that when I get mine.

KIT: I don't have to.

ANGIE: You're scared.

KIT: I'll do it, I might do it. I don't have to just because you say. I'll be sick on you.

ANGIE: I don't care if you are sick on me, I don't mind sick. I don't mind blood. If I don't get away from here I'm going to die.

KIT: I'm going home.

ANGIE: You can't go through the house. She'll see you.

KIT: I won't tell her.

ANGIE: Oh great, fine.

KIT: I'll say I was by myself. I'll tell her you're at my house and I'm going there to get you.

ANGIE: She knows I'm here, stupid.

KIT: Then why can't I go through the house?

ANGIE: Because I said not.

KIT: My mum don't like you anyway.

ANGIE: I don't want her to like me. She's a slag.

KIT: She is not.

ANGIE: She does it with everyone.

KIT: She does not.

ANGIE: You don't even know what it is.

KIT: Yes I do.

ANGIE: Tell me then.

KIT: We get it all at school, cleverclogs. It's on television. You haven't done it.
ANGIE: How do you know?
KIT: Because I know you haven't.
ANGIE: You know wrong then because I have.
KIT: Who with?
ANGIE: I'm not telling you / who with.
KIT: You haven't anyway.
ANGIE: How do you know?
KIT: Who with?
ANGIE: I'm not telling you.
KIT: You said you told me everything.
ANGIE: I was lying wasn't I.
KIT: Who with? You can't tell me who with because / you never—
ANGIE: Sh.

(*Joyce has come out of the house. She stops halfway across the yard and listens. They listen.*)

JOYCE: You there Angie? Kit? You there Kitty? Want a cup of tea? I've got some chocolate biscuits. Come on now I'll put the kettle on. Want a choccy biccy, Angie? (*They all listen and wait.*) Fucking rotten little cunt. You can stay there and die. I'll lock the door.

(*They all wait. Joyce goes back to the house. Angie and Kit sit in silence for a while.*)

KIT: When there's a war, where's the safest place?
ANGIE: Nowhere.
KIT: New Zealand is, my mum said. Your skin's burned right off. Shall we go to New Zealand?
ANGIE: I'm not staying here.
KIT: Shall we go to New Zealand?
ANGIE: You're not old enough.
KIT: You're not old enough.
ANGIE: I'm old enough to get married.
KIT: You don't want to get married.
ANGIE: No but I'm old enough.
KIT: I'd find out where they were going to drop it and stand right in the place.
ANGIE: You couldn't find out.
KIT: Better than walking round with your skin dragging on the ground. Eugh. / Would you like walking round with your skin dragging on the ground?

ANGIE: You couldn't find out, stupid, it's a secret.

KIT: Where are you going?

ANGIE: I'm not telling you.

KIT: Why?

ANGIE: It's a secret.

KIT: But you tell me all your secrets.

ANGIE: Not the true secrets.

KIT: Yes you do.

ANGIE: No I don't.

KIT: I want to go somewhere away from the war.

ANGIE: Just forget the war.

KIT: I can't.

ANGIE: You have to. It's so boring.

KIT: I'll remember it at night.

ANGIE: I'm going to do something else anyway.

KIT: What? Angie, come on. Angie.

ANGIE: It's a true secret.

KIT: It can't be worse than the kitten. And killing your mother. And the war.

ANGIE: Well I'm not telling you so you can die for all I care.

KIT: My mother says there's something wrong with you playing with someone my age. She says why haven't you got friends your own age. People your own age know there's something funny about you. She says you're a bad influence. She says she's going to speak to your mother. (*Angie twists Kit's arm till she cries out.*)

ANGIE: Say you're a liar.

KIT: She said it not me.

ANGIE: Say you eat shit.

KIT: You can't make me. (*Angie lets go.*)

ANGIE: I don't care anyway. I'm leaving.

KIT: Go on then.

ANGIE: You'll all wake up one morning and find I've gone.

KIT: Go on then.

ANGIE: You'll wake up one morning and find I've gone.

KIT: Good.

ANGIE: I'm not telling you when.

KIT: Go on then.

ANGIE: I'm sorry I hurt you.

KIT: I'm tired.

ANGIE: Do you like me?

KIT: I don't know.

ANGIE: You do like me.

KIT: I'm going home. (*She gets up.*)

ANGIE: No you're not.

KIT: I'm tired.

ANGIE: She'll see you.

KIT: She'll give me a chocolate biscuit.

ANGIE: Kitty.

KIT: Tell me where you're going.

ANGIE: Sit down.

KIT (*sitting down again*): Go on then.

ANGIE: Swear?

KIT: Swear.

ANGIE: I'm going to London. To see my aunt.

KIT: And what?

ANGIE: That's it.

KIT: I see my aunt all the time.

ANGIE: I don't see my aunt.

KIT: What's so special?

ANGIE: It is special. She's special.

KIT: Why?

ANGIE: She is.

KIT: Why?

ANGIE: She is.

KIT: Why?

ANGIE: My mother hates her.

KIT: Why?

ANGIE: Because she does.

KIT: Perhaps she's not very nice.

ANGIE: She is nice.

KIT: How do you know?

ANGIE: Because I know her.

KIT: You said you never see her.

ANGIE: I saw her last year. You saw her.

KIT: Did I?

ANGIE: Never mind.

KIT: I remember her. That aunt. What's so special?

ANGIE: She gets people jobs.

KIT: What's so special?

ANGIE: I think I'm my aunt's child. I think my mother's really my aunt.

KIT: Why?

ANGIE: Because she goes to America, now shut up.

KIT: I've been to London.

ANGIE: Now give us a cuddle and shut up because I'm sick.

KIT: You're sitting on my arm.

(*They curl up in each other's arms. Silence. Joyce comes out of the house and comes up to them quietly.*)

JOYCE: Come on.
KIT: Oh hello.
JOYCE: Time you went home.
KIT: We want to go to the Odeon.
JOYCE: What time?
KIT: Don't know.
JOYCE: What's on?
KIT: Don't know.
JOYCE: Don't know much do you?
KIT: That all right then?
JOYCE: Angie's got to clean her room first.
ANGIE: No I don't.
JOYCE: Yes you do, it's a pigsty.
ANGIE: Well I'm not.
JOYCE: Then you're not going. I don't care.
ANGIE: Well I am going.
JOYCE: You've no money, have you?
ANGIE: Kit's paying anyway.
JOYCE: No she's not.
KIT: I'll help you with your room.
JOYCE: That's nice.
ANGIE: No you won't. You wait here.
KIT: Hurry then.
ANGIE: I'm not hurrying. You just wait. (*Angie goes slowly into the house. Silence.*)
JOYCE: I don't know. (*Silence.*) How's school then?
KIT: All right.
JOYCE: What are you now? Third year?
KIT: Second year.
JOYCE: Your mum says you're good at English. (*Silence.*) Maybe Angie should've stayed on.
KIT: She didn't like it.
JOYCE: I didn't like it. And look at me. If your face fits at school it's going to fit other places too. It wouldn't make no difference to Angie. She's not going to get a job when jobs are hard to get. I'd be sorry for anyone in charge of her. She'd better get married. I don't know who'd have her, mind. She's one of those girls might never leave home. What do you want to be when you grow up, Kit?
KIT: Physicist.
JOYCE: What?

KIT: Nuclear physicist.

JOYCE: Whatever for?

KIT: I could, I'm clever.

JOYCE: I know you're clever, pet. (*Silence.*) I'll make a cup of tea. (*Silence.*)
Looks like it's going to rain. (*Silence.*) Don't you have friends your own
age?

KIT: Yes.

JOYCE: Well then.

KIT: I'm old for my age.

JOYCE: And Angie's simple is she? She's not simple.

KIT: I love Angie.

JOYCE: She's clever in her own way.

KIT: You can't stop me.

JOYCE: I don't want to.

KIT: You can't, so.

JOYCE: Don't be cheeky, Kitty. She's always kind to little children.

KIT: She's coming so you better leave me alone.

(*Angie comes out. She has changed into an old best dress, slightly small for
her.*)

JOYCE: What you put that on for? Have you done your room? You can't
clean your room in that.

ANGIE: I looked in the cupboard and it was there.

JOYCE: Of course it was there, it's meant to be there. Is that why it was a
surprise, finding something in the right place? I should think she's surprised, wouldn't you, Kit, to find something in her room in the right
place.

ANGIE: I decided to wear it.

JOYCE: Not today, why? To clean your room? You're not going to the pictures till you've done your room. You can put your dress on after if you
like. (*Angie picks up a brick.*) Have you done your room? You're not getting out of it, you know.

KIT: Angie, let's go.

JOYCE: She's not going till she's done her room.

KIT: It's starting to rain.

JOYCE: Come on, come on then. Hurry and do your room, Angie, and
then you can go to the cinema with Kit. Oh it's wet, come on. We'll
look up the time in the paper. Does your mother know, Kit, it's going to
be a late night for you, isn't it? Hurry up, Angie. You'll spoil your dress.
You make me sick. (*Joyce and Kit run into the house. Angie stays where she
is. There is the sound of rain. Kit comes out of the house.*)

KIT (*shouting*): Angie. Angie, come on, you'll get wet. (*She comes back to
Angie.*)

ANGIE: I put on this dress to kill my mother.
KIT: I suppose you thought you'd do it with a brick.
ANGIE: You can kill people with a brick. (*She puts the brick down.*)
KIT: Well you didn't, so.

ACT II   *Scene I*

(*"Top Girls" Employment Agency. Monday morning. There are three desks in the main office and a separate small interviewing area. The lights come up in the main office on Win and Nell who have just arrived for work.*)

NELL: Coffee coffee coffee coffee / coffee.
WIN: The roses were smashing. / Mermaid.
NELL: Ohhh.
WIN: Iceberg. He taught me all their names. (*Nell has some coffee now.*)
NELL: Ah. Now then.
WIN: He has one of the finest rose gardens in West Sussex. He exhibits.
NELL: He what?
WIN: His wife was visiting her mother. It was like living together.
NELL: Crafty, you never said.
WIN: He rang on Saturday morning.
NELL: Lucky you were free.
WIN: That's what I told him.
NELL: Did you hell.
WIN: Have you ever seen a really beautiful rose garden?
NELL: I don't like flowers. / I like swimming pools.
WIN: Marilyn. Esther's Baby. They're all called after birds.°
NELL: Our friend's late. Celebrating all weekend I bet you.
WIN: I'd call a rose Elvis. Or John Conteh.°
NELL: Is Howard in yet?
WIN: If he is he'll be bleeping us with a problem.
NELL: Howard can just hang on to himself.
WIN: Howard's really cut up.
NELL: Howard thinks because he's a fella the job was his as of right. Our
   Marlene's got far more balls than Howard and that's that.
WIN: Poor little bugger.
NELL: He'll live.
WIN: He'll move on.
NELL: I wouldn't mind a change of air myself.

birds: Women (slang).
John Conteh: British boxing champion turned actor.

WIN: Serious?

NELL: I've never been a staying-put lady. Pastures new.

WIN: So who's the pirate?

NELL: There's nothing definite.

WIN: Inquiries?

NELL: There's always inquiries. I'd think I'd got bad breath if there stopped being inquiries. Most of them can't afford me. Or you.

WIN: I'm all right for the time being. Unless I go to Australia.

NELL: There's not a lot of room upward.

WIN: Marlene's filled it up.

NELL: Good luck to her. Unless there's some prospects moneywise.

WIN: You can but ask.

NELL: Can always but ask.

WIN: So what have we got? I've got a Mr. Holden I saw last week.

NELL: Any use?

WIN: Pushy. Bit of a cowboy.

NELL: Goodlooker?

WIN: Good dresser.

NELL: High flyer?

WIN: That's his general idea certainly but I'm not sure he's got it up there.

NELL: Prestel wants six flyers and I've only seen two and a half.

WIN: He's making a bomb on the road but he thinks it's time for an office. I sent him to IBM but he didn't get it.

NELL: Prestel's on the road.

WIN: He's not overbright.

NELL: Can he handle an office?

WIN: Provided his secretary can punctuate he should go far.

NELL: Bear Prestel in mind then, I might put my head round the door. I've got that poor little nerd I should never had said I could help. Tender heart me.

WIN: Tender like old boots. How old?

NELL: Yes well forty-five.

WIN: Say no more.

NELL: He knows his place, he's not after calling himself a manager, he's just a poor little bod wants a better commission and a bit of sunshine.

WIN: Don't we all.

NELL: He's just got to relocate. He's got a bungalow in Dymchurch.

WIN: And his wife says.

NELL: The lady wife wouldn't care to relocate. She's going through the change.

WIN: It's his funeral, don't waste your time.

NELL: I don't waste a lot.

WIN: Good weekend you?

NELL: You could say.

WIN: Which one?

NELL: One Friday, one Saturday.

WIN: Aye—aye.

NELL: Sunday night I watched telly.

WIN: Which of them do you like best really?

NELL: Sunday was best, I like the Ovaltine.

WIN: Holden, Barker, Gardner, Duke.

NELL: I've a lady here thinks she can sell.

WIN: Taking her on?

NELL: She's had some jobs.

WIN: Services?

NELL: No, quite heavy stuff, electric.

WIN: Tough bird like us.

NELL: We could do with a few more here.

WIN: There's nothing going here.

NELL: No but I always want the tough ones when I see them. Hang on to them.

WIN: I think we're plenty.

NELL: Derek asked me to marry him again.

WIN: He doesn't know when he's beaten.

NELL: I told him I'm not going to play house, not even in Ascot.

WIN: Mind you, you could play house.

NELL: If I chose to play house I would play house ace.

WIN: You could marry him and go on working.

NELL: I could go on working and not marry him.

(*Marlene arrives.*)

MARLENE: Morning ladies. (*Win and Nell cheer and whistle.*) Mind my head.

NELL: Coffee coffee coffee.

WIN: We're tactfully not mentioning you're late.

MARLENE: Fucking tube.°

WIN: We've heard that one.

NELL: We've used that one.

WIN: It's the top executive doesn't come in as early as the poor working girl.

MARLENE: Pass the sugar and shut your face, pet.

WIN: Well I'm delighted.

tube: London underground train system.

NELL: Howard's looking sick.

WIN: Howard is sick. He's got ulcers and heart. He told me.

NELL: He'll have to stop then, won't he?

WIN: Stop what?

NELL: Smoking, drinking, shouting. Working.

WIN: Well, working.

NELL: We're just looking through the day.

MARLENE: I'm doing some of Pam's ladies. They've been piling up while she's away.

NELL: Half a dozen little girls and an arts graduate who can't type.

WIN: I spent the whole weekend at his place in Sussex.

NELL: She fancies his rose garden.

WIN: I had to lie down in the back of the car so the neighbors wouldn't see me go in.

NELL: You're kidding.

WIN: It was funny.

NELL: Fuck that for a joke.

WIN: It was funny.

MARLENE: Anyway they'd see you in the garden.

WIN: The garden has extremely high walls.

NELL: I think I'll tell the wife.

WIN: Like hell.

NELL: She might leave him and you could have the rose garden.

WIN: The minute it's not a secret I'm out on my ear.

NELL: Don't know why you bother.

WIN: Bit of fun.

NELL: I think it's time you went to Australia.

WIN: I think it's pushy Mr. Holden time.

NELL: If you've any really pretty bastards, Marlene, I want some for Prestel.

MARLENE: I might have one this afternoon. This morning it's all Pam's secretarial.

NELL: Not long now and you'll be upstairs watching over us all.

MARLENE: Do you feel bad about it?

NELL: I don't like coming second.

MARLENE: Who does?

WIN: We'd rather it was you than Howard. We're glad for you, aren't we, Nell?

NELL: Oh yes. Aces.

(Louise enters the interviewing area. The lights crossfade to Win and Louise in the interviewing area. Nell exits.)

WIN: Now, Louise, hello, I have your details here. You've been very loyal
    to the one job I see.
LOUISE: Yes I have.
WIN: Twenty-one years is a long time in one place.
LOUISE: I feel it is. I feel it's time to move on.
WIN: And you are what age now?
LOUISE: I'm in my early forties.
WIN: Exactly?
LOUISE: Forty-six.
WIN: It's not necessarily a handicap, well it is of course we have to face
    that, but it's not necessarily a disabling handicap, experience does
    count for something.
LOUISE: I hope so.
WIN: Now between ourselves is there any trouble, any reason why
    you're leaving that wouldn't appear on the form?
LOUISE: Nothing like that.
WIN: Like what?
LOUISE: Nothing at all.
WIN: No long-term understandings come to a sudden end, making for
    an insupportable atmosphere?
LOUISE: I've always completely avoided anything like that at all.
WIN: No personality clashes with your immediate superiors or inferiors?
LOUISE: I've always taken care to get on very well with everyone.
WIN: I only ask because it can affect the reference and it also affects
    your motivation, I want to be quite clear why you're moving on. So I
    take it the job itself no longer satisfies you. Is it the money?
LOUISE: It's partly the money. It's not so much the money.
WIN: Nine thousand is very respectable. Have you dependents?
LOUISE: No, no dependents. My mother died.
WIN: So why are you making a change?
LOUISE: Other people make changes.
WIN: But why are you, now, after spending most of your life in the one
    place?
LOUISE: There you are, I've lived for that company, I've given my life
    really you could say because I haven't had a great deal of social life,
    I've worked in the evenings. I haven't had office entanglements for the
    very reason you just mentioned and if you are committed to your work
    you don't move in many other circles. I had management status from
    the age of twenty-seven and you'll appreciate what that means. I've
    built up a department. And there it is, it works extremely well, and
    I feel I'm stuck there. I've spent twenty years in middle manage-
    ment. I've seen young men who I trained go on, in my own company

or elsewhere, to higher things. Nobody notices me, I don't expect it, I don't attract attention by making mistakes, everybody takes it for granted that my work is perfect. They will notice me when I go, they will be sorry I think to lose me, they will offer me more money of course, I will refuse. They will see when I've gone what I was doing for them.

WIN: If they offer you more money you won't stay?

LOUISE: No I won't.

WIN: Are you the only woman?

LOUISE: Apart from the girls of course, yes. There was one, she was my assistant, it was the only time I took on a young woman assistant, I always had my doubts. I don't care greatly for working with women, I think I pass as a man at work. But I did take on this young woman, her qualifications were excellent, and she did well, she got a department of her own, and left the company for a competitor where she's now on the board and good luck to her. She has a different style, she's a new kind of attractive well dressed—I don't mean I don't dress properly. But there is a kind of woman who is thirty now who grew up in a different climate. They are not so careful. They take themselves for granted. I have had to justify my existence every minute, and I have done so, I have proved—well.

WIN: Let's face it, vacancies are ones where you'll be in competition with younger men. And there are companies that will value your experience enough that you'll be in with a chance. There are also fields that are easier for a woman, there is a cosmetic company here where your experience might be relevant. It's eight and a half, I don't know if that appeals.

LOUISE: I've proved I can earn money. It's more important to get away. I feel it's now or never. I sometimes / think—

WIN: You shouldn't talk too much at an interview.

LOUISE: I don't. I don't normally talk about myself. I know very well how to handle myself in an office situation. I only talk to you because it seems to me this is different, it's your job to understand me, surely. You asked the questions.

WIN: I think I understand you sufficiently.

LOUISE: Well good, that's good.

WIN: Do you drink?

LOUISE: Certainly not. I'm not a teetotaler, I think that's very suspect, it's seen as being an alcoholic if you're teetotal. What do you mean? I don't drink. Why?

WIN: I drink.

LOUISE: I don't.

WIN: Good for you.

(*The lights crossfade to the main office with Marlene sitting at her desk. Win and Louise exit. Angie arrives in the main office.*)

ANGIE: Hello.

MARLENE: Have you an appointment?

ANGIE: It's me. I've come.

MARLENE: What? It's not Angie?

ANGIE: It was hard to find this place. I got lost.

MARLENE: How did you get past the receptionist? The girl on the desk, didn't she try to stop you?

ANGIE: What desk?

MARLENE: Never mind.

ANGIE: I just walked in. I was looking for you.

MARLENE: Well you found me.

ANGIE: Yes.

MARLENE: So where's your mum? Are you up in town for the day?

ANGIE: Not really.

MARLENE: Sit down. Do you feel all right?

ANGIE: Yes thank you.

MARLENE: So where's Joyce?

ANGIE: She's at home.

MARLENE: Did you come up on a school trip then?

ANGIE: I've left school.

MARLENE: Did you come up with a friend?

ANGIE: No. There's just me.

MARLENE: You came up by yourself, that's fun. What have you been doing? Shopping? Tower of London?

ANGIE: No, I just come here. I come to you.

MARLENE: That's very nice of you to think of paying your aunty a visit. There's not many nieces make that the first port of call. Would you like a cup of coffee?

ANGIE: No thank you.

MARLENE: Tea, orange?

ANGIE: No thank you.

MARLENE: Do you feel all right?

ANGIE: Yes thank you.

MARLENE: Are you tired from the journey?

ANGIE: Yes, I'm tired from the journey.

MARLENE: You sit there for a bit then. How's Joyce?

ANGIE: She's all right.

MARLENE: Same as ever.

ANGIE: Oh yes.

MARLENE: Unfortunately you've picked a day when I'm rather busy, if there's ever a day when I'm not, or I'd take you out to lunch and we'd go to Madame Tussaud's.° We could go shopping. What time do you have to be back? Have you got a day return?

ANGIE: No.

MARLENE: So what train are you going back on?

ANGIE: I came on the bus.

MARLENE: So what bus are you going back on? Are you staying the night?

ANGIE: Yes.

MARLENE: Who are you staying with? Do you want me to put you up for the night, is that it?

ANGIE: Yes please.

MARLENE: I haven't got a spare bed.

ANGIE: I can sleep on the floor.

MARLENE: You can sleep on the sofa.

ANGIE: Yes please.

MARLENE: I do think Joyce might have phoned me. It's like her.

ANGIE: This is where you work is it?

MARLENE: It's where I have been working the last two years but I'm going to move into another office.

ANGIE: It's lovely.

MARLENE: My new office is nicer than this. There's just the one big desk in it for me.

ANGIE: Can I see it?

MARLENE: Not now, no, there's someone else in it now. But he's leaving at the end of next week and I'm going to do his job.

ANGIE: Is that good?

MARLENE: Yes, it's very good.

ANGIE: Are you going to be in charge?

MARLENE: Yes I am.

ANGIE: I knew you would be.

MARLENE: How did you know?

ANGIE: I knew you'd be in charge of everything.

MARLENE: Not quite everything.

ANGIE: You will be.

MARLENE: Well we'll see.

ANGIE: Can I see it next week then?

MARLENE: Will you still be here next week?

ANGIE: Yes.

Madame Tussaud's: Wax museum; a popular London tourist attraction.

MARLENE: Don't you have to go home?
ANGIE: No.
MARLENE: Why not?
ANGIE: It's all right.
MARLENE: Is it all right?
ANGIE: Yes, don't worry about it.
MARLENE: Does Joyce know where you are?
ANGIE: Yes of course she does.
MARLENE: Well does she?
ANGIE: Don't worry about it.
MARLENE: How long are you planning to stay with me then?
ANGIE: You know when you came to see us last year?
MARLENE: Yes, that was nice wasn't it.
ANGIE: That was the best day of my whole life.
MARLENE: So how long are you planning to stay?
ANGIE: Don't you want me?
MARLENE: Yes yes, I just wondered.
ANGIE: I won't stay if you don't want me.
MARLENE: No, of course you can stay.
ANGIE: I'll sleep on the floor. I won't be any bother.
MARLENE: Don't get upset.
ANGIE: I'm not, I'm not. Don't worry about it.

(*Mrs. Kidd comes in.*)

MRS. KIDD: Excuse me.
MARLENE: Yes.
MRS. KIDD: Excuse me.
MARLENE: Can I help you?
MRS. KIDD: Excuse me bursting in on you like this but I have to talk to you.
MARLENE: I am engaged at the moment. / If you could go to reception—
MRS. KIDD: I'm Rosemary Kidd, Howard's wife, you don't recognize me
    but we did meet, I remember you of course / but you wouldn't—
MARLENE: Yes of course, Mrs. Kidd, I'm sorry, we did meet. Howard's
    about somewhere I expect, have you looked in his office?
MRS. KIDD: Howard's not about, no. I'm afraid it's you I've come to see if
    I could have a minute or two.
MARLENE: I do have an appointment in five minutes.
MRS. KIDD: This won't take five minutes. I'm very sorry. It is a matter of
    some urgency.
MARLENE: Well of course. What can I do for you?
MRS. KIDD: I just wanted a chat, an informal chat. It's not something I
    can simply—I'm sorry if I'm interrupting your work. I know office
    work isn't like housework / which is all interruptions.

MARLENE: No no, this is my niece. Angie. Mrs. Kidd.

MRS. KIDD: Very pleased to meet you.

ANGIE: Very well thank you.

MRS. KIDD: Howard's not in today.

MARLENE: Isn't he?

MRS. KIDD: He's feeling poorly.

MARLENE: I didn't know. I'm sorry to hear that.

MRS. KIDD: The fact is he's in a state of shock. About what's happened.

MARLENE: What has happened?

MRS. KIDD: You should know if anyone. I'm referring to you being appointed managing director instead of Howard. He hasn't been at all well all weekend. He hasn't slept for three nights. I haven't slept.

MARLENE: I'm sorry to hear that, Mrs. Kidd. Has he thought of taking sleeping pills?

MRS. KIDD: It's very hard when someone has worked all these years.

MARLENE: Business life is full of little setbacks. I'm sure Howard knows that. He'll bounce back in a day or two. We all bounce back.

MRS. KIDD: If you could see him you'd know what I'm talking about. What's it going to do to him working for a woman? I think if it was a man he'd get over it as something normal.

MARLENE: I think he's going to have to get over it.

MRS. KIDD: It's me that bears the brunt. I'm not the one that's been promoted. I put him first every inch of the way. And now what do I get? You women this, you women that. It's not my fault. You're going to have to be very careful how you handle him. He's very hurt.

MARLENE: Naturally I'll be tactful and pleasant to him, you don't start pushing someone around. I'll consult him over any decisions affecting his department. But that's no different, Mrs. Kidd, from any of my other colleagues.

MRS. KIDD: I think it is different, because he's a man.

MARLENE: I'm not quite sure why you came to see me.

MRS. KIDD: I had to do something.

MARLENE: Well you've done it, you've seen me. I think that's probably all we've time for. I'm sorry he's been taking it out on you. He really is a shit, Howard.

MRS. KIDD: But he's got a family to support. He's got three children. It's only fair.

MARLENE: Are you suggesting I give up the job to him then?

MRS. KIDD: It had crossed my mind if you were unavailable after all for some reason, he would be the natural second choice I think, don't you? I'm not asking.

MARLENE: Good.

MRS. KIDD: You mustn't tell him I came. He's very proud.

MARLENE: If he doesn't like what's happening here he can go and work somewhere else.

MRS. KIDD: Is that a threat?

MARLENE: I'm sorry but I do have some work to do.

MRS. KIDD: It's not that easy, a man of Howard's age. You don't care. I thought he was going too far but he's right. You're one of these ball-breakers, / that's what you

MARLENE: I'm sorry but I do have some work to do.

MRS. KIDD: are. You'll end up miserable and lonely. You're not natural.

MARLENE: Could you please piss off?

MRS. KIDD: I thought if I saw you at least I'd be doing something. (*Mrs. Kidd goes.*)

MARLENE: I've got to go and do some work now. Will you come back later?

ANGIE: I think you were wonderful.

MARLENE: I've got to go and do some work now.

ANGIE: You told her to piss off.

MARLENE: Will you come back later?

ANGIE: Can't I stay here?

MARLENE: Don't you want to go sightseeing?

ANGIE: I'd rather stay here.

MARLENE: You can stay here I suppose, if it's not boring.

ANGIE: It's where I most want to be in the world.

MARLENE: I'll see you later then.

(*Marlene goes. Shona and Nell enter the interviewing area. Angie sits at Win's desk. The lights crossfade to Nell and Shona in the interviewing area.*)

NELL: Is this right? You are Shona?

SHONA: Yeh.

NELL: It says here you're twenty-nine.

SHONA: Yeh.

NELL: Too many late nights, me. So you've been where you are for four years, Shona, you're earning six basic and three commission. So what's the problem?

SHONA: No problem.

NELL: Why do you want a change?

SHONA: Just a change.

NELL: Change of product, change of area?

SHONA: Both.

NELL: But you're happy on the road?

SHONA: I like driving.

NELL: You're not after management status?

SHONA: I would like management status.

NELL: You'd be interested in titular management status but not come off the road?

SHONA: I want to be on the road, yeh.

NELL: So how many calls have you been making a day?

SHONA: Six.

NELL: And what proportion of those are successful?

SHONA: Six.

NELL: That's hard to believe.

SHONA: Four.

NELL: You find it easy to get the initial interest do you?

SHONA: Oh yeh, I get plenty of initial interest.

NELL: And what about closing?

SHONA: I close, don't I?

NELL: Because that's what an employer is going to have doubts about with a lady as I needn't tell you, whether she's got the guts to push through to a closing situation. They think we're too nice. They think we listen to the buyer's doubts. They think we consider his needs and his feelings.

SHONA: I never consider people's feelings.

NELL: I was selling for six years, I can sell anything, I've sold in three continents, and I'm jolly as they come but I'm not very nice.

SHONA: I'm not very nice.

NELL: What sort of time do you have on the road with the other reps? Get on all right? Handle the chat?

SHONA: I get on. Keep myself to myself.

NELL: Fairly much of a loner are you?

SHONA: Sometimes.

NELL: So what field are you interested in?

SHONA: Computers.

NELL: That's a top field as you know and you'll be up against some very slick fellas there, there's some very pretty boys in computers, it's an American-style field.

SHONA: That's why I want to do it.

NELL: Video systems appeal? That's a high-flying situation.

SHONA: Video systems appeal OK.

NELL: Because Prestel have half a dozen vacancies I'm looking to fill at the moment. We're talking in the area of ten to fifteen thousand here and upwards.

SHONA: Sounds OK.

NELL: I've half a mind to go for it myself. But it's good money here if you've got the top clients. Could you fancy it do you think?

SHONA: Work here?

NELL: I'm not in a position to offer, there's nothing officially going just now, but we're always on the lookout. There's not that many of us. We could keep in touch.

SHONA: I like driving.

NELL: So the Prestel appeals.

SHONA: Yeh.

NELL: What about ties?

SHONA: No ties.

NELL: So relocation wouldn't be a problem.

SHONA: No problem.

NELL: So just fill me in a bit more could you about what you've been doing.

SHONA: What I've been doing. It's all down there.

NELL: The bare facts are down here but I've got to present you to an employer.

SHONA: I'm twenty-nine years old.

NELL: So it says here.

SHONA: We look young. Youngness runs in the family in our family.

NELL: So just describe your present job for me.

SHONA: My present job at present. I have a car. I have a Porsche. I go up the M1° a lot. Burn up the M1 a lot. Straight up the M1 in the fast lane to where the clients are, Staffordshire, Yorkshire, I do a lot in Yorkshire. I'm selling electric things. Like dishwashers, washing machines, stainless steel tubs are a feature and the reliability of the program. After sales service, we offer a very good after sales service, spare parts, plenty of spare parts. And fridges, I sell a lot of fridges specially in the summer. People want to buy fridges in the summer because of the heat melting the butter and you get fed up standing the milk in a basin of cold water with a cloth over, stands to reason people don't want to do that in this day and age. So I sell a lot of them. Big ones with big freezers. Big freezers. And I stay in hotels at night when I'm away from home. On my expense account. I stay in various hotels. They know me, the ones I go to. I check in, have a bath, have a shower. Then I go down to the bar, have a gin and tonic, have a chat. Then I go into the dining room and have dinner. I usually have fillet steak and mushrooms, I like mushrooms. I like smoked salmon very much. I like having a salad on the side. Green salad. I don't like tomatoes.

NELL: Christ what a waste of time.

SHONA: Beg your pardon?

NELL: Not a word of this is true, is it?

SHONA: How do you mean?

M1: The main north-south expressway connecting London to Yorkshire.

NELL: You just filled in the form with a pack of lies.

SHONA: Not exactly.

NELL: How old are you?

SHONA: Twenty-nine.

NELL: Nineteen?

SHONA: Twenty-one.

NELL: And what jobs have you done? Have you done any?

SHONA: I could though, I bet you.

(*The lights crossfade to the main office with Angie sitting as before. Win comes in to the main office. Shona and Nell exit.*)

WIN: Who's sitting in my chair?

ANGIE: What? Sorry.

WIN: Who's been eating my porridge?

ANGIE: What?

WIN: It's all right, I saw Marlene. Angie, isn't it? I'm Win. And I'm not going out for lunch because I'm knackered. I'm going to set me down here and have a yogurt. Do you like yogurt?

ANGIE: No.

WIN: That's good because I've only got one. Are you hungry?

ANGIE: No.

WIN: There's a café on the corner.

ANGIE: No thank you. Do you work here?

WIN: How did you guess?

ANGIE: Because you look as if you might work here and you're sitting at the desk. Have you always worked here?

WIN: No I was headhunted. That means I was working for another outfit like this and this lot came and offered me more money. I broke my contract, there was a hell of a stink. There's not many top ladies about. Your aunty's a smashing bird.

ANGIE: Yes I know.

MARLENE: Fan are you? Fan of your aunty's?

ANGIE: Do you think I could work here?

WIN: Not at the moment.

ANGIE: How do I start?

WIN: What can you do?

ANGIE: I don't know. Nothing.

WIN: Type?

ANGIE: Not very well. The letters jump up when I do capitals. I was going to do a CSE° in commerce but I didn't.

CSE: Certificate of Secondary Education; a less prestigious exam than O-levels, generally taken in vocational rather than academic subjects.

WIN: What have you got?
ANGIE: What?
WIN: CSE's, O's.
ANGIE: Nothing, none of that. Did you do all that?
WIN: Oh yes, all that, and a science degree funnily enough. I started out doing medical research but there's no money in it. I thought I'd go abroad. Did you know they sell Coca-Cola in Russia and Pepsi-Cola in China? You don't have to be qualified as much as you might think. Men are awful bullshitters, they like to make out jobs are harder than they are. Any job I ever did I started doing it better than the rest of the crowd and they didn't like it. So I'd get unpopular and I'd have a drink to cheer myself up. I lived with a fella and supported him for four years, he couldn't get work. After that I went to California. I like the sunshine. Americans know how to live. This country's too slow. Then I went to Mexico, still in sales, but it's no country for a single lady. I came home, went bonkers for a bit, thought I was five different people, got over that all right, the psychiatrist said I was perfectly sane and highly intelligent. Got married in a moment of weakness and he's inside now, he's been inside four years, and I've not been to see him too much this last year. I like this better than sales, I'm not really that aggressive. I started thinking sales was a good job if you want to meet people, but you're meeting people that don't want to meet you. It's no good if you like being liked. Here your clients want to meet you because you're the one doing them some good. They hope. (*Angie has fallen asleep. Nell comes in.*)
NELL: You're talking to yourself, sunshine.
WIN: So what's new?
NELL: Who is this?
WIN: Marlene's little niece.
NELL: What's she got, brother, sister? She never talks about her family.
WIN: I was telling her my life story.
NELL: Violins?
WIN: No, success story.
NELL: You've heard Howard's had a heart attack?
WIN: No, when?
NELL: I heard just now. He hadn't come in, he was at home, he's gone to hospital. He's not dead. His wife was here, she rushed off in a cab.
WIN: Too much butter, too much smoke. We must send him some flowers. (*Marlene comes in.*) You've heard about Howard?
MARLENE: Poor sod.
NELL: Lucky he didn't get the job if that's what his health's like.
MARLENE: Is she asleep?
WIN: She wants to work here.

MARLENE: Packer in Tesco° more like.
WIN: She's a nice kid. Isn't she?
MARLENE: She's a bit thick. She's a bit funny.
WIN: She thinks you're wonderful.
MARLENE: She's not going to make it.

Scene II

(Joyce's kitchen. Sunday evening, a year earlier. The lights come up on Joyce, Angie, and Marlene. Marlene is taking presents out of a bright carrier bag. Angie has already opened a box of chocolates.)

MARLENE: Just a few little things. / I've
JOYCE: There's no need.
MARLENE: no memory for birthdays have I, and Christmas seems to slip by. So I think I owe Angie a few presents.
JOYCE: What do you say?
ANGIE: Thank you very much. Thank you very much, Aunty Marlene. *(She opens a present. It is the dress from Act I, new.)* Oh look, Mum, isn't it lovely?
MARLENE: I don't know if it's the right size. She's grown up since I saw her. / I knew she was always
ANGIE: Isn't it lovely?
MARLENE: tall for her age.
JOYCE: She's a big lump.
MARLENE: Hold it up, Angie, let's see.
ANGIE: I'll put it on, shall I?
MARLENE: Yes, try it on.
JOYCE: Go on to your room then, we don't want / a strip show thank you.
ANGIE: Of course I'm going to my room, what do you think. Look, Mum, here's something for you. Open it, go on. What is it? Can I open it for you?
JOYCE: Yes, you open it, pet.
ANGIE: Don't you want to open it yourself? / Go on.
JOYCE: I don't mind, you can do it.
ANGIE: It's something hard. It's—what is it? A bottle. Drink is it? No, it's what? Perfume, look. What a lot. Open it, look, let's smell it. Oh it's strong. It's lovely. Put it on me. How do you do it? Put it on me.
JOYCE: You're too young.
ANGIE: I can play wearing it like dressing up.
JOYCE: And you're too old for that. Here, give it here, I'll do it, you'll tip the whole bottle over yourself / and we'll have you smelling all summer.

Tesco: A supermarket chain.

ANGIE: Put it on you. Do I smell? Put it on Aunty too. Put it on Aunty too. Let's all smell.

MARLENE: I didn't know what you'd like.

JOYCE: There's no danger I'd have it already, / that's one thing.

ANGIE: Now we all smell the same.

MARLENE: It's a bit of nonsense.

JOYCE: It's very kind of you Marlene, you shouldn't.

ANGIE: Now I'll put on the dress and then we'll see. (*Angie goes.*)

JOYCE: You've caught me on the hop with the place in the mess. / If you'd let me

MARLENE: That doesn't matter.

JOYCE: know you was coming I'd have got something in to eat. We had our dinner dinnertime. We're just going to have a cup of tea. You could have an egg.

MARLENE: No, I'm not hungry. Tea's fine.

JOYCE: I don't expect you take sugar.

MARLENE: Why not?

JOYCE: You take care of yourself.

MARLENE: How do you mean you didn't know I was coming?

JOYCE: You could have written. I know we're not on the phone but we're not completely in the dark ages, / we do have a postman.

MARLENE: But you asked me to come.

JOYCE: How did I ask you to come?

MARLENE: Angie said when she phoned up.

JOYCE: Angie phoned up, did she.

MARLENE: Was it just Angie's idea?

JOYCE: What did she say?

MARLENE: She said you wanted me to come and see you. / It was a couple of

JOYCE: Ha.

MARLENE: weeks ago. How was I to know that's a ridiculous idea? My diary's always full a couple of weeks ahead so we fixed it for this weekend. I was meant to get here earlier but I was held up. She gave me messages from you.

JOYCE: Didn't you wonder why I didn't phone you myself?

MARLENE: She said you didn't like using the phone. You're shy on the phone and can't use it. I don't know what you're like, do I?

JOYCE: Are there people who can't use the phone?

MARLENE: I expect so.

JOYCE: I haven't met any.

MARLENE: Why should I think she was lying?

JOYCE: Because she's like what she's like.

MARLENE: How do I know / what she's like?

JOYCE: It's not my fault you don't know what she's like. You never come and see her.

MARLENE: Well I have now / and you don't seem over the moon.*

JOYCE: Good. *Well I'd have got a cake if she'd told me. (*Pause.*)

MARLENE: I did wonder why you wanted to see me.

JOYCE: I didn't want to see you.

MARLENE: Yes, I know. Shall I go?

JOYCE: I don't mind seeing you.

MARLENE: Great, I feel really welcome.

JOYCE: You can come and see Angie any time you like, I'm not stopping you. / You

MARLENE: Ta ever so.

JOYCE: know where we are. You're the one went away, not me. I'm right here where I was. And will be a few years yet I shouldn't wonder.

MARLENE: All right. All right. (*Joyce gives Marlene a cup of tea.*)

JOYCE: Tea.

MARLENE: Sugar? (*Joyce passes Marlene the sugar.*) It's very quiet down here.

JOYCE: I expect you'd notice it.

MARLENE: The air smells different too.

JOYCE: That's the scent.

MARLENE: No, I mean walking down the lane.

JOYCE: What sort of air you get in London then?

(*Angie comes in, wearing the dress. It fits.*)

MARLENE: Oh, very pretty. / You do look pretty, Angie.

JOYCE: That fits all right.

MARLENE: Do you like the color?

ANGIE: Beautiful. Beautiful.

JOYCE: You better take it off, / you'll get it dirty.

ANGIE: I want to wear it. I want to wear it.

MARLENE: It is for wearing after all. You can't just hang it up and look at it.

ANGIE: I love it.

JOYCE: Well if you must you must.

ANGIE: If someone asks me what's my favorite color I'll tell them it's this. Thank you very much Aunty Marlene.

MARLENE: You didn't tell your mum you asked me down.

ANGIE: I wanted it to be a surprise.

JOYCE: I'll give you a surprise / one of these days.

ANGIE: I thought you'd like to see her. She hasn't been here since I was nine. People do see their aunts.

MARLENE: Is it that long? Doesn't time fly.

ANGIE: I wanted to.

JOYCE: I'm not cross.

ANGIE: Are you glad?

JOYCE: I smell nicer anyhow, don't I?

(*Kit comes in without saying anything, as if she lived there.*)

MARLENE: I think it was a good idea, Angie, about time. We are sisters after all. It's a pity to let that go.

JOYCE: This is Kitty, / who lives up the road. This is Angie's Aunty Marlene.

KIT: What's that?

ANGIE: It's a present. Do you like it?

KIT: It's all right. / Are you coming out?*

MARLENE: Hello, Kitty.

ANGIE: *No.

KIT: What's that smell?

ANGIE: It's a present.

KIT: It's horrible. Come on.*

MARLENE: Have a chocolate.

ANGIE: *No, I'm busy.

KIT: Coming out later?

ANGIE: No.

KIT (*to Marlene*): Hello. (*Kit goes without a chocolate.*)

JOYCE: She's a little girl Angie sometimes plays with because she's the only child lives really close. She's like a little sister to her really. Angie's good with little children.

MARLENE: Do you want to work with children, Angie? / Be a teacher or a nursery nurse?

JOYCE: I don't think she's ever thought of it.

MARLENE: What do you want to do?

JOYCE: She hasn't an idea in her head what she wants to do. / Lucky to get anything.

MARLENE: Angie?

JOYCE: She's not clever like you. (*Pause.*)

MARLENE: I'm not clever, just pushy.

JOYCE: True enough. (*Marlene takes a bottle of whiskey out of the bag.*) I don't drink spirits.

ANGIE: You do at Christmas.

JOYCE: It's not Christmas, is it?

ANGIE: It's better than Christmas.

MARLENE: Glasses?

JOYCE: Just a small one then.

MARLENE: Do you want some, Angie?

ANGIE: I can't, can I?

JOYCE: Taste it if you want. You won't like it. (*Angie tastes it.*)

ANGIE: Mmm.

MARLENE: We got drunk together the night your grandfather died.

JOYCE: We did not get drunk.

MARLENE: I got drunk. You were just overcome with grief.

JOYCE: I still keep up the grave with flowers.

MARLENE: Do you really?

JOYCE: Why wouldn't I?

MARLENE: Have you seen Mother?

JOYCE: Of course I've seen Mother.

MARLENE: I mean lately.

JOYCE: Of course I've seen her lately, I go every Thursday.

MARLENE (*to Angie*): Do you remember your grandfather?

ANGIE: He got me out of the bath one night in a towel.

MARLENE: Did he? I don't think he ever gave me a bath. Did he give you a bath, Joyce? He probably got soft in his old age. Did you like him?

ANGIE: Yes of course.

MARLENE: Why?

ANGIE: What?

MARLENE: So what's the news? How's Mrs. Paisley? Still going crazily? / And Dorothy. What happened to Dorothy?*

ANGIE: Who's Mrs. Paisley?

JOYCE: *She went to Canada.

MARLENE: Did she? What to do?

JOYCE: I don't know. She just went to Canada.

MARLENE: Well / good for her.

ANGIE: Mr. Connolly killed his wife.

MARLENE: What, Connolly at Whitegates?

ANGIE: They found her body in the garden. / Under the cabbages.

MARLENE: He was always so proper.

JOYCE: Stuck up git,° Connolly. Best lawyer money could buy but he couldn't get out of it. She was carrying on with Matthew.

MARLENE: How old's Matthew then?

JOYCE: Twenty-one. / He's got a motorbike.

MARLENE: I think he's about six.

ANGIE: How can he be six? He's six years older than me. / If he was six I'd be nothing, I'd be just born this minute.

JOYCE: Your aunty knows that, she's just being silly. She means it's so long since she's been here she's forgotten about Matthew.

ANGIE: You were here for my birthday when I was nine. I had a pink cake. Kit was only five then, she was four, she hadn't started school

___

git: Fool.

yet. She could read already when she went to school. You remember my birthday? / You remember me?

MARLENE: Yes, I remember the cake.

ANGIE: You remember me?

MARLENE: Yes, I remember you.

ANGIE: And Mum and Dad was there, and Kit was.

MARLENE: Yes, how is your dad? Where is he tonight? Up the pub?

JOYCE: No, he's not here.

MARLENE: I can see he's not here.

JOYCE: He moved out.

MARLENE: What? When did he? / Just recently?*

ANGIE: Didn't you know that? You don't know much.

JOYCE: *No, it must be three years ago. Don't be rude, Angie.

ANGIE: I'm not, am I, Aunty? What else don't you know?

JOYCE: You was in America or somewhere. You sent a postcard.

ANGIE: I've got that in my room. It's the Grand Canyon. Do you want to see it? Shall I get it? I can get it for you.

MARLENE: Yes, all right. (*Angie goes.*)

JOYCE: You could be married with twins for all I know. You must have affairs and break up and I don't need to know about any of that so I don't see what the fuss is about.

MARLENE: What fuss? (*Angie comes back with the postcard.*)

ANGIE: "Driving across the states for a new job in L.A. It's a long way but the car goes very fast. It's very hot. Wish you were here. Love from Aunty Marlene."

JOYCE: Did you make a lot of money?

MARLENE: I spent a lot.

ANGIE: I want to go to America. Will you take me?

JOYCE: She's not going to America, she's been to America, stupid.

ANGIE: She might go again, stupid. It's not something you do once. People who go keep going all the time, back and forth on jets. They go on Concorde and Laker and get jet lag. Will you take me?

MARLENE: I'm not planning a trip.

ANGIE: Will you let me know?

JOYCE: Angie, / you're getting silly.

ANGIE: I want to be American.

JOYCE: It's time you were in bed.

ANGIE: No it's not. / I don't have to go to bed at all tonight.

JOYCE: School in the morning.

ANGIE: I'll wake up.

JOYCE: Come on now, you know how you get.

ANGIE: How do I get? / I don't get anyhow.*

JOYCE: Angie. *Are you staying the night?

MARLENE: Yes, if that's all right. / I'll see you in the morning.

ANGIE: You can have my bed. I'll sleep on the sofa.

JOYCE: You will not, you'll sleep in your bed. / Think

ANGIE: Mum.

JOYCE: I can't see through that? I can just see you going to sleep / with us
talking.

ANGIE: I would, I would go to sleep, I'd love that.

JOYCE: I'm going to get cross, Angie.

ANGIE: I want to show her something.

JOYCE: Then bed.

ANGIE: It's a secret.

JOYCE: Then I expect it's in your room so off you go. Give us a shout
when you're ready for bed and your aunty'll be up and see you.

ANGIE: Will you?

MARLENE: Yes of course. (*Angie goes. Silence.*) It's cold tonight.

JOYCE: Will you be all right on the sofa? You can / have my bed.

MARLENE: The sofa's fine.

JOYCE: Yes the forecast said rain tonight but it's held off.

MARLENE: I was going to walk down to the estuary but I've left it a bit
late. Is it just the same?

JOYCE: They cut down the hedges a few years back. Is that since you
were here?

MARLENE: But it's not changed down the end, all the mud? And the
reeds? We used to pick them up when they were bigger than us. Are
there still lapwings?

JOYCE: You get strangers walking there on a Sunday. I expect they're
looking at the mud and the lapwings, yes.

MARLENE: You could have left.

JOYCE: Who says I wanted to leave?

MARLENE: Stop getting at me then, you're really boring.

JOYCE: How could I have left?

MARLENE: Did you want to?

JOYCE: I said how, / how could I?

MARLENE: If you'd wanted to you'd have done it.

JOYCE: Christ.

MARLENE: Are we getting drunk?

JOYCE: Do you want something to eat?

MARLENE: No, I'm getting drunk.

JOYCE: Funny time to visit, Sunday evening.

MARLENE: I came this morning. I spent the day—

ANGIE (*off*): Aunty! Aunty Marlene!

MARLENE: I'd better go.

JOYCE: Go on then.

MARLENE: All right.

ANGIE (*off*): Aunty! Can you hear me? I'm ready.

(*Marlene goes. Joyce goes on sitting, clears up, sits again. Marlene comes back.*)

JOYCE: So what's the secret?

MARLENE: It's a secret.

JOYCE: I know what it is anyway.

MARLENE: I bet you don't. You always said that.

JOYCE: It's her exercise book.

MARLENE: Yes, but you don't know what's in it.

JOYCE: It's some game, some secret society she has with Kit.

MARLENE: You don't know the password. You don't know the code.

JOYCE: You're really in it, aren't you. Can you do the handshake?

MARLENE: She didn't mention a handshake.

JOYCE: I thought they'd have a special handshake. She spends hours writing that but she's useless at school. She copies things out of books about black magic, and politicians out of the paper. It's a bit childish.

MARLENE: I think it's a plot to take over the world.

JOYCE: She's been in the remedial class the last two years.

MARLENE: I came up this morning and spent the day in Ipswich. I went to see Mother.

JOYCE: Did she recognize you?

MARLENE: Are you trying to be funny?

JOYCE: No, she does wander.

MARLENE: She wasn't wandering at all, she was very lucid thank you.

JOYCE: You were very lucky then.

MARLENE: Fucking awful life she's had.

JOYCE: Don't tell me.

MARLENE: Fucking waste.

JOYCE: Don't talk to me.

MARLENE: Why shouldn't I talk? Why shouldn't I talk to you? / Isn't she my mother too?

JOYCE: Look, you've left, you've gone away, / we can do without you.

MARLENE: I left home, so what, I left home. People do leave home / it is normal.

JOYCE: We understand that, we can do without you.

MARLENE: We weren't happy. Were you happy?

JOYCE: Don't come back.

MARLENE: So it's just your mother is it, your child, you never wanted me round, / you were jealous

JOYCE: Here we go.

MARLENE: of me because I was the little one and I was clever.

JOYCE: I'm not clever enough for all this psychology / if that's what it is.

MARLENE: Why can't I visit my own family / without

JOYCE: Aah.

MARLENE: all this?

JOYCE: Just don't go on about Mum's life when you haven't been to see her for how many years. / I go

MARLENE: It's up to me.

JOYCE: and see her every week.

MARLENE: Then don't go and see her every week.

JOYCE: Somebody has to.

MARLENE: No they don't. / Why do they?

JOYCE: How would I feel if I didn't go?

MARLENE: A lot better.

JOYCE: I hope you feel better.

MARLENE: It's up to me.

JOYCE: You couldn't get out of here fast enough. (*Pause.*)

MARLENE: Of course I couldn't get out of here fast enough. What was I going to do? Marry a dairyman who'd come home pissed? / Don't you fucking this

JOYCE: Christ.

MARLENE: fucking that fucking bitch fucking tell me what to fucking do fucking.

JOYCE: I don't know how you could leave your own child.

MARLENE: You were quick enough to take her.

JOYCE: What does that mean?

MARLENE: You were quick enough to take her.

JOYCE: Or what? Have her put in a home? Have some stranger / take her would you rather?

MARLENE: You couldn't have one so you took mine.

JOYCE: I didn't know that then.

MARLENE: Like hell, / married three years.

JOYCE: I didn't know that. Plenty of people / take that long.

MARLENE: Well it turned out lucky for you, didn't it?

JOYCE: Turned out all right for you by the look of you. You'd be getting a few less thousand a year.

MARLENE: Not necessarily.

JOYCE: You'd be stuck here / like you said.

MARLENE: I could have taken her with me.

JOYCE: You didn't want to take her with you. It's no good coming back now, Marlene, / and saying —

MARLENE: I know a managing director who's got two children, she breast-feeds in the board room, she pays a hundred pounds a week on domestic help alone and she can afford that because she's an extremely high-powered lady earning a great deal of money.

JOYCE: So what's that got to do with you at the age of seventeen?

MARLENE: Just because you were married and had somewhere to live—

JOYCE: You could have lived at home. / Or live

MARLENE: Don't be stupid.

JOYCE: with me and Frank. / You

MARLENE: You never suggested.

JOYCE: said you weren't keeping it. You shouldn't have had it / if you wasn't

MARLENE: Here we go.

JOYCE: going to keep it. You was the most stupid, / for someone so clever you was the most stupid, get yourself pregnant, not go to the doctor, not tell.

MARLENE: You wanted it, you said you were glad, I remember the day, you said I'm glad you never got rid of it, I'll look after it, you said that down by the river. So what are you saying, sunshine, you don't want her?

JOYCE: Course I'm not saying that.

MARLENE: Because I'll take her, / wake her up and pack now.

JOYCE: You wouldn't know how to begin to look after her.

MARLENE: Don't you want her?

JOYCE: Course I do, she's my child.

MARLENE: Then what are you going on about / why did I have her?

JOYCE: You said I got her off you / when you didn't—

MARLENE: I said you were lucky / the way it—

JOYCE: Have a child now if you want one. You're not old.

MARLENE: I might do.

JOYCE: Good. (*Pause.*)

MARLENE: I've been on the pill so long / I'm probably sterile.

JOYCE: Listen when Angie was six months I did get pregnant and I lost it because I was so tired looking after your fucking baby / because she cried so

MARLENE: You never told me.

JOYCE: much—yes I did tell you— / and the doctor

MARLENE: Well I forgot.

JOYCE: said if I'd sat down all day with my feet up I'd've kept it / and that's the only chance I ever had because after that—

MARLENE: I've had two abortions, are you interested? Shall I tell you about them? Well I won't, it's boring, it wasn't a problem. I don't like messy talk about blood / and what a bad time we all had. I

JOYCE: If I hadn't had your baby. The doctor said.

MARLENE: don't want a baby. I don't want to talk about gynecology.

JOYCE: Then stop trying to get Angie off of me.

MARLENE: I come down here after six years. All night you've been saying I don't come often enough. If I don't come for another six years she'll be twenty-one, will that be OK?

JOYCE: That'll be fine, yes, six years would suit me fine. (*Pause.*)

MARLENE: I was afraid of this. I only came because I thought you wanted . . . I just want . . . (*She cries.*)

JOYCE: Don't grizzle,° Marlene, for God's sake. Marly? Come on, pet. Love you really. Fucking stop it, will you? (*She goes to Marlene.*)

MARLENE: No, let me cry. I like it. (*They laugh, Marlene begins to stop crying.*) I knew I'd cry if I wasn't careful.

JOYCE: Everyone's always crying in this house. Nobody takes any notice.

MARLENE: You've been wonderful looking after Angie.

JOYCE: Don't get carried away.

MARLENE: I can't write letters but I do think of you.

JOYCE: You're getting drunk. I'm going to make some tea.

MARLENE: Love you. (*Joyce goes to make tea.*)

JOYCE: I can see why you'd want to leave. It's a dump here.

MARLENE: So what's this about you and Frank?

JOYCE: He was always carrying on, wasn't he. And if I wanted to go out in the evening he'd go mad, even if it was nothing, a class, I was going to go to an evening class. So he had this girlfriend, only twenty-two poor cow, and I said go on, off you go, hoppit. I don't think he even likes her.

MARLENE: So what about money?

JOYCE: I've always said I don't want your money.

MARLENE: No, does he send you money?

JOYCE: I've got four different cleaning jobs. Adds up. There's not a lot round here.

MARLENE: Does Angie miss him?

JOYCE: She doesn't say.

MARLENE: Does she see him?

JOYCE: He was never that fond of her to be honest.

MARLENE: He tried to kiss me once. When you were engaged.

JOYCE: Did you fancy him?

MARLENE: No, he looked like a fish.

JOYCE: He was lovely then.

MARLENE: Ugh.

JOYCE: Well I fancied him. For about three years.

MARLENE: Have you got someone else?

JOYCE: There's not a lot round here. Mind you, the minute you're on your own, you'd be amazed how your friends' husbands drop by. I'd sooner do without.

MARLENE: I don't see why you couldn't take my money.

JOYCE: I do, so don't bother about it.

grizzle: Whimper.

MARLENE: Only got to ask.

JOYCE: So what about you? Good job?

MARLENE: Good for a laugh. / Got back

JOYCE: Good for more than a laugh I should think.

MARLENE: from the US of A a bit wiped out and slotted into this speedy employment agency and still there.

JOYCE: You can always find yourself work then?

MARLENE: That's right.

JOYCE: And men?

MARLENE: Oh there's always men.

JOYCE: No one special?

MARLENE: There's fellas who like to be seen with a high-flying lady. Shows they've got something really good in their pants. But they can't take the day to day. They're waiting for me to turn into the little woman. Or maybe I'm just horrible of course.

JOYCE: Who needs them.

MARLENE: Who needs them. Well I do. But I need adventures more. So on on into the sunset. I think the eighties are going to be stupendous.

JOYCE: Who for?

MARLENE: For me. / I think I'm going up up up.

JOYCE: Oh for you. Yes, I'm sure they will.

MARLENE: And for the country, come to that. Get the economy back on its feet and whoosh. She's a tough lady, Maggie.° I'd give her a job. / She just needs to hang

JOYCE: You voted for them, did you?

MARLENE: in there. This country needs to stop whining. / Monetarism is not

JOYCE: Drink your tea and shut up, pet.

MARLENE: stupid. It takes time, determination. No more slop. / And

JOYCE: Well I think they're filthy bastards.

MARLENE: who's got to drive it on? First woman prime minister. Terrifico. Aces. Right on. / You must admit. Certainly gets my vote.

JOYCE: What good's first woman if it's her? I suppose you'd have liked Hitler if he was a woman. Ms. Hitler. Got a lot done, Hitlerina. / Great adventures.

MARLENE: Bosses still walking on the worker's faces? Still dadda's little parrot? Haven't you learned to think for yourself? I believe in the individual. Look at me.

JOYCE: I am looking at you.

MARLENE: Come on, Joyce, we're not going to quarrel over politics.

Maggie: Margaret Thatcher, conservative British prime minister from 1979 to 1991.

JOYCE: We are though.

MARLENE: Forget I mentioned it. Not a word about the slimy unions will cross my lips. (*Pause.*)

JOYCE: You say Mother had a wasted life.

MARLENE: Yes I do. Married to that bastard.

JOYCE: What sort of life did he have? /

MARLENE: Violent life?

JOYCE: Working in the fields like an animal. / Why

MARLENE: Come off it.

JOYCE: wouldn't he want a drink? You want a drink. He couldn't afford whiskey.

MARLENE: I don't want to talk about him.

JOYCE: You started, I was talking about her. She had a rotten life because she had nothing. She went hungry.

MARLENE: She was hungry because he drank the money. / He used to hit her.

JOYCE: It's not all down to him / Their

MARLENE: She didn't hit him.

JOYCE: lives were rubbish. They were treated like rubbish. He's dead and she'll die soon and what sort of life / did they have?

MARLENE: I saw him one night. I came down.

JOYCE: Do you think I didn't? / They

MARLENE: I still have dreams.

JOYCE: didn't get to America and drive across it in a fast car. / Bad nights, they had bad days.

MARLENE: America, America, you're jealous. / I had to get out, I knew when I

JOYCE: Jealous?

MARLENE: was thirteen, out of their house, out of them, never let that happen to me, / never let him, make my own way, out.

JOYCE: Jealous of what you've done, you'd be ashamed of me if I came to your office, your smart friends, wouldn't you, I'm ashamed of you, think of nothing but yourself, you've got on, nothing's changed for most people, / has it?

MARLENE: I hate the working class / which is what

JOYCE: Yes you do.

MARLENE: you're going to go on about now, it doesn't exist any more, it means lazy and stupid. / I don't

JOYCE: Come on, now we're getting it.

MARLENE: like the way they talk. I don't like beer guts and football vomit and saucy tits / and brothers and sisters—

JOYCE: I spit when I see a Rolls Royce, scratch it with my ring / Mercedes it was.

MARLENE: Oh very mature—

JOYCE: I hate the cows I work for / and their dirty dishes with blanquette of fucking veau.

MARLENE: and I will not be pulled down to their level by a flying picket and I won't be sent to Siberia / or a loony bin just because I'm original. And I support

JOYCE: No, you'll be on a yacht, you'll be head of Coca-Cola and you wait, the eighties is going to be stupendous all right because we'll get you lot off our backs—

MARLENE: Reagan even if he is a lousy movie star because the reds are swarming up his map and I want to be free in a free world—

JOYCE: What? / What?

MARLENE: I know what I mean / by that—not shut up here.

JOYCE: So don't be round here when it happens because if someone's kicking you I'll just laugh. (*Silence.*)

MARLENE: I don't mean anything personal. I don't believe in class. Anyone can do anything if they've got what it takes.

JOYCE: And if they haven't?

MARLENE: If they're stupid or lazy or frightened, I'm not going to help them get a job, why should I?

JOYCE: What about Angie?

MARLENE: What about Angie?

JOYCE: She's stupid, lazy, and frightened, so what about her?

MARLENE: You run her down too much. She'll be all right.

JOYCE: I don't expect so, no. I expect her children will say what a wasted life she had. If she has children. Because nothing's changed and it won't with them in.

MARLENE: Them, them. / Us and them?

JOYCE: And you're one of them.

MARLENE: And you're us, wonderful us, and Angie's us / and Mum and Dad's us.

JOYCE: Yes, that's right, and you're them.

MARLENE: Come on, Joyce, what a night. You've got what it takes.

JOYCE: I know I have.

MARLENE: I didn't really mean all that.

JOYCE: I did.

MARLENE: But we're friends anyway.

JOYCE: I don't think so, no.

MARLENE: Well it's lovely to be out in the country. I really must make the effort to come more often. I want to go to sleep. I want to go to sleep. (*Joyce gets blankets for the sofa.*)

JOYCE: Goodnight then. I hope you'll be warm enough.

MARLENE: Goodnight. Joyce—

JOYCE: No, pet. Sorry. (*Joyce goes. Marlene sits wrapped in a blanket and has another drink. Angie comes in.*)
ANGIE: Mum?
MARLENE: Angie? What's the matter?
ANGIE: Mum?
MARLENE: No, she's gone to bed. It's Aunty Marlene.
ANGIE: Frightening.
MARLENE: Did you have a bad dream? What happened in it? Well you're awake now, aren't you, pet?
ANGIE: Frightening.

[1982]

ATHOL FUGARD [b. 1932]

"MASTER HAROLD"
. . . and the boys

Characters
WILLIE
SAM
HALLY

(*The St. George's Park Tea Room on a wet and windy Port Elizabeth afternoon.*)

(*Tables and chairs have been cleared and are stacked on one side except for one which stands apart with a single chair. On this table a knife, fork, spoon and side plate in anticipation of a simple meal, together with a pile of comic books.*)

(*Other elements: a serving counter with a few stale cakes under glass and a not very impressive display of sweets, cigarettes and cool drinks, etc.; a few cardboard advertising handouts—Cadbury's Chocolate, Coca-Cola—and a blackboard on which an untrained hand has chalked up the prices of Tea, Coffee, Scones, Milkshakes—all flavors—and Cool Drinks; a few sad ferns in pots; a telephone; an old-style jukebox.*)

(*There is an entrance on one side and an exit into a kitchen on the other.*)

(*Leaning on the solitary table, his head cupped in one hand as he pages through one of the comic books, is Sam. A black man in his mid-forties. He wears the white coat of a waiter. Behind him on his knees, mopping down the floor with a bucket of water and a rag, is Willie. Also black and about the same age as Sam. He has his sleeves and trousers rolled up.*)

(*The year: 1950.*)

WILLIE (*singing as he works*): "She was scandalizin' my name,
  She took my money
  She called me honey
  But she was scandalizin' my name.
  Called it love but was playin' a game. . . ."

(*He gets up and moves the bucket. Stands thinking for a moment, then, raising his arms to hold an imaginary partner, he launches into an intricate ballroom dance step. Although a mildly comic figure, he reveals a reasonable degree of accomplishment.*)

1153

Hey, Sam.

(*Sam, absorbed in the comic book, does not respond.*)

Hey, Boet° Sam!

(*Sam looks up.*)

I'm getting it. The quickstep. Look now and tell me. (*He repeats the step.*) Well?

SAM (*encouragingly*): Show me again.

WILLIE: Okay, count for me.

SAM: Ready?

WILLIE: Ready.

SAM: Five, six, seven, eight. . . . (*Willie starts to dance.*) A-n-d one two three four . . . and one two three four. . . . (*Ad libbing as Willie dances.*) Your shoulders, Willie . . . your shoulders! Don't look down! Look happy, Willie! Relax, Willie!

WILLIE (*desperate but still dancing*): I am relax.

SAM: No, you're not.

WILLIE (*he falters*): Ag no man, Sam! Mustn't talk. You make me make mistakes.

SAM: But you're stiff.

WILLIE: Yesterday I'm not straight . . . today I'm too stiff!

SAM: Well, you are. You asked me and I'm telling you.

WILLIE: Where?

SAM: Everywhere. Try to glide through it.

WILLIE: Glide?

SAM: Ja, make it smooth. And give it more style. It must look like you're enjoying yourself.

WILLIE (*emphatically*): I wasn't.

SAM: Exactly.

WILLIE: How can I enjoy myself? Not straight, too stiff and now it's also glide, give it more style, make it smooth. . . . Haai! Is hard to remember all those things, Boet Sam.

SAM: That's your trouble. You're trying too hard.

WILLIE: I try hard because it *is* hard.

SAM: But don't let me see it. The secret is to make it look easy. Ballroom must look happy, Willie, not like hard work. It must. . . . Ja! . . . it must look like romance.

WILLIE: Now another one! What's romance?

SAM: Love story with happy ending. A handsome man in tails, and in his arms, smiling at him, a beautiful lady in evening dress!

Boet: Brother.

WILLIE: Fred Astaire, Ginger Rogers.

SAM: You got it. Tapdance or ballroom, it's the same. Romance. In two weeks' time when the judges look at you and Hilda, they must see a man and a woman who are dancing their way to a happy ending. What I saw was you holding her like you were frightened she was going to run away.

WILLIE: Ja! Because that is what she wants to do! I got no romance left for Hilda anymore, Boet Sam.

SAM: Then pretend. When you put your arms around Hilda, imagine she is Ginger Rogers.

WILLIE: With no teeth? You try.

SAM: Well, just remember, there's only two weeks left.

WILLIE: I know, I know! (*To the jukebox.*) I do it better with music. You got sixpence for Sarah Vaughan?

SAM: That's a slow foxtrot. You're practicing the quickstep.

WILLIE: I'll practice slow foxtrot.

SAM (*shaking his head*): It's your turn to put money in the jukebox.

WILLIE: I only got bus fare to go home. (*He returns disconsolately to his work.*) Love story and happy ending! She's doing it all right, Boet Sam, but is not me she's giving happy endings. Fuckin' whore! Three nights now she doesn't come practice. I wind up gramophone, I get record ready and I sit and wait. What happens? Nothing. Ten o'clock I start dancing with my pillow. You try and practice romance by yourself, Boet Sam. Struesgod, she doesn't come tonight I take back my dress and ballroom shoes and I find me new partner. Size twenty-six. Shoes size seven. And now she's also making trouble for me with the baby again. Reports me to Child Wellfed, that I'm not giving her money. She lies! Every week I am giving her money for milk. And how do I know is my baby? Only his hair looks like me. She's fucking around all the time I turn my back. Hilda Samuels is a bitch! (*Pause.*) Hey, Sam!

SAM: Ja.

WILLIE: You listening?

SAM: Ja.

WILLIE: So what you say?

SAM: About Hilda?

WILLIE: Ja.

SAM: When did you last give her a hiding?

WILLIE (*reluctantly*): Sunday night.

SAM: And today is Thursday.

WILLIE (*he knows what's coming*): Okay.

SAM: Hiding on Sunday night, then Monday, Tuesday, and Wednesday she doesn't come to practice . . . and you are asking me why?

WILLIE: I said okay, Boet Sam!

SAM: You hit her too much. One day she's going to leave you for good.

WILLIE: So? She makes me the hell-in too much.

SAM (*emphasizing his point*): *Too* much and *too* hard. You had the same trouble with Eunice.

WILLIE: Because she also make the hell-in, Boet Sam. She never got the steps right. Even the waltz.

SAM: Beating her up every time she makes a mistake in the waltz? (*Shaking his head.*) No, Willie! That takes the pleasure out of ballroom dancing.

WILLIE: Hilda is not too bad with the waltz, Boet Sam. Is the quickstep where the trouble starts.

SAM (*teasing him gently*): How's your pillow with the quickstep?

WILLIE (*ignoring the tease*): Good! And why? Because it got no legs. That's her trouble. She can't move them quick enough, Boet Sam. I start the record and before halfway Count Basie is already winning. Only time we catch up with him is when gramophone runs down. (*Sam laughs.*) Haaikona, Boet Sam, is not funny.

SAM (*snapping his fingers*): I got it! Give her a handicap.

WILLIE: What's that?

SAM: Give her a ten-second start and then let Count Basie go. Then I put my money on her. Hot favorite in the Ballroom Stakes: Hilda Samuels ridden by Willie Malopo.

WILLIE (*turning away*): I'm not talking to you no more.

SAM (*relenting*): Sorry, Willie. . . .

WILLIE: It's finish between us.

SAM: Okay, okay . . . I'll stop.

WILLIE: You can also fuck off.

SAM: Willie, listen! I want to help you!

WILLIE: No more jokes?

SAM: I promise.

WILLIE: Okay. Help me.

SAM (*his turn to hold an imaginary partner*): Look and learn. Feet together. Back straight. Body relaxed. Right hand placed gently in the small of her back and wait for the music. Don't start worrying about making mistakes or the judges or the other competitors. It's just you, Hilda and the music, and you're going to have a good time. What Count Basie do you play?

WILLIE: "You the cream in my coffee, you the salt in my stew."

SAM: Right. Give it to me in strict tempo.

WILLIE: Ready?

SAM: Ready.

WILLIE: A-n-d . . . (*Singing.*)
"You the cream in my coffee.
You the salt in my stew.

You will always be my necessity.
I'd be lost without you. . . ." (*etc.*)

(*Sam launches into the quickstep. He is obviously a much more accomplished dancer than Willie. Hally enters. A seventeen-year-old white boy. Wet raincoat and school case. He stops and watches Sam. The demonstration comes to an end with a flourish. Applause from Hally and Willie.*)

HALLY: Bravo! No question about it. First place goes to Mr. Sam Semela.

WILLIE (*in total agreement*): You was gliding with style, Boet Sam.

HALLY (*cheerfully*): How's it, chaps?

SAM: Okay, Hally.

WILLIE (*springing to attention like a soldier and saluting*): At your service, Master Harold!

HALLY: Not long to the big event, hey!

SAM: Two weeks.

HALLY: You nervous?

SAM: No.

HALLY: Think you stand a chance?

SAM: Let's just say I'm ready to go out there and dance.

HALLY: It looked like it. What about you, Willie?

(*Willie groans.*)

What's the matter?

SAM: He's got leg trouble.

HALLY (*innocently*): Oh, sorry to hear that, Willie.

WILLIE: Boet Sam! You promised. (*Willie returns to his work.*)

(*Hally deposits his school case and takes off his raincoat. His clothes are a little neglected and untidy: black blazer with school badge, gray flannel trousers in need of an ironing, khaki shirt and tie, black shoes. Sam has fetched a towel for Hally to dry his hair.*)

HALLY: God, what a lousy bloody day. It's coming down cats and dogs out there. Bad for business, chaps. . . . (*Conspiratorial whisper.*) . . . but it also means we're in for a nice quiet afternoon.

SAM: You can speak loud. Your Mom's not here.

HALLY: Out shopping?

SAM: No. The hospital.

HALLY: But it's Thursday. There's no visiting on Thursday afternoons. Is my Dad okay?

SAM: Sounds like it. In fact, I think he's going home.

HALLY (*stopped short by Sam's remark*): What do you mean?

SAM: The hospital phoned.

HALLY: To say what?

SAM: I don't know. I just heard your Mom talking.

HALLY: So what makes you say he's going home?
SAM: It sounded as if they were telling her to come and fetch him.

(*Hally thinks about what Sam has said for a few seconds.*)

HALLY: When did she leave?
SAM: About an hour ago. She said she would phone you. Want to eat?

(*Hally doesn't respond.*)

Hally, want your lunch?
HALLY: I suppose so. (*His mood has changed.*) What's on the menu? . . . as if I don't know.
SAM: Soup, followed by meat pie and gravy.
HALLY: Today's?
SAM: No.
HALLY: And the soup?
SAM: Nourishing pea soup.
HALLY: Just the soup. (*The pile of comic books on the table.*) And these?
SAM: For your Dad. Mr. Kempston brought them.
HALLY: You haven't been reading them, have you?
SAM: Just looking.
HALLY (*examining the comics*): *Jungle Jim . . . Batman and Robin . . . Tarzan* . . . God, what rubbish! Mental pollution. Take them away.

(*Sam exits waltzing into the kitchen. Hally turns to Willie.*)

HALLY: Did you hear my Mom talking on the telephone, Willie?
WILLIE: No, Master Hally. I was at the back.
HALLY: And she didn't say anything to you before she left?
WILLIE: She said I must clean the floors.
HALLY: I mean about my Dad.
WILLIE: She didn't say nothing to me about him, Master Hally.
HALLY (*with conviction*): No! It can't be. They said he needed at least another three weeks of treatment. Sam's definitely made a mistake. (*Rummages through his school case, finds a book and settles down at the table to read.*) So, Willie!
WILLIE: Yes, Master Hally! Schooling okay today?
HALLY: Yes, okay. . . . (*He thinks about it.*) . . . No, not really. Ag, what's the difference? I don't care. And Sam says you've got problems.
WILLIE: Big problems.
HALLY: Which leg is sore?

(*Willie groans.*)

Both legs.
WILLIE: There is nothing wrong with my legs. Sam is just making jokes.

HALLY: So then you *will* be in the competition.

WILLIE: Only if I can find a partner.

HALLY: But what about Hilda?

SAM (*returning with a bowl of soup*): She's the one who's got trouble with her legs.

HALLY: What sort of trouble, Willie?

SAM: From the way he describes it, I think the lady has gone a bit lame.

HALLY: Good God! Have you taken her to see a doctor?

SAM: I think a vet would be better.

HALLY: What do you mean?

SAM: What do you call it again when a racehorse goes very fast?

HALLY: Gallop?

SAM: That's it!

WILLIE: Boet Sam!

HALLY: "A gallop down the homestretch to the winning post." But what's that got to do with Hilda?

SAM: Count Basie always gets there first.

(*Willie lets fly with his slop rag. It misses Sam and hits Hally.*)

HALLY (*furious*): For Christ's sake, Willie! What the hell do you think you're doing?

WILLIE: Sorry, Master Hally, but it's him. . . .

HALLY: Act your bloody age! (*Hurls the rag back at Willie.*) Cut out the nonsense now and get on with your work. And you too, Sam. Stop fooling around.

(*Sam moves away.*)

No. Hang on. I haven't finished! Tell me exactly what my Mom said.

SAM: I have. "When Hally comes, tell him I've gone to the hospital and I'll phone him."

HALLY: She didn't say anything about taking my Dad home?

SAM: No. It's just that when she was talking on the phone. . . .

HALLY (*interrupting him*): No, Sam. They can't be discharging him. She would have said so if they were. In any case, we saw him last night and he wasn't in good shape at all. Staff nurse even said there was talk about taking more X-rays. And now suddenly today he's better? If anything, it sounds more like a bad turn to me . . . which I sincerely hope it isn't. Hang on . . . how long ago did you say she left?

SAM: Just before two . . . (*His wrist watch.*) . . . hour and a half.

HALLY: I know how to settle it. (*Behind the counter to the telephone. Talking as he dials.*) Let's give her ten minutes to get to the hospital, ten minutes to load him up, another ten, at the most, to get home, and another ten to get him inside. Forty minutes. They should have been home for at least half an hour already. (*Pause—he waits with the receiver to his ear.*) No reply, chaps. And you know why? Because she's at his bedside in hospital helping him pull through a bad turn. You definitely heard wrong.

SAM: Okay.

(*As far as Hally is concerned, the matter is settled. He returns to his table, sits down, and divides his attention between the book and his soup. Sam is at his school case and picks up a textbook.*)

Modern Graded Mathematics for Standards Nine and Ten. (*Opens it at random and laughs at something he sees.*) Who is this supposed to be?

HALLY: Old fart-face Prentice.

SAM: Teacher?

HALLY: Thinks he is. And believe me, that is not a bad likeness.

SAM: Has he seen it?

HALLY: Yes.

SAM: What did he say?

HALLY: Tried to be clever, as usual. Said I was no Leonardo da Vinci and that bad art had to be punished. So, six of the best, and his are bloody good.

SAM: On your bum?

HALLY: Where else? The days when I got them on my hands are gone forever, Sam.

SAM: With your trousers down!

HALLY: No. He's not quite that barbaric.

SAM: That's the way they do it in jail.

HALLY (*flicker of morbid interest*): Really?

SAM: Ja. When the magistrate sentences you to "strokes with a light cane."

HALLY: Go on.

SAM: They make you lie down on a bench. One policeman pulls down your trousers and holds your ankles, another one pulls your shirt over your head and holds your arms. . . .

HALLY: Thank you! That's enough.

SAM: . . . and the one that gives you the strokes talks to you gently and for a long time between each one. (*He laughs.*)

HALLY: I've heard enough, Sam! Jesus! It's a bloody awful world when you come to think of it. People can be real bastards.

SAM: That's the way it is, Hally.

HALLY: It doesn't *have* to be that way. There is something called progress, you know. We don't exactly burn people at the stake anymore.

SAM: Like Joan of Arc.

HALLY: Correct. If she was captured today, she'd be given a fair trial.

SAM: And then the death sentence.

HALLY (*a world-weary sigh*): I know, I know! I oscillate between hope and despair for this world as well, Sam. But things will change, you wait and see. One day somebody is going to get up and give history a kick up the backside and get it going again.

SAM: Like who?

HALLY (*after thought*): They're called social reformers. Every age, Sam, has got its social reformer. My history book is full of them.

SAM: So where's ours?

HALLY: Good question. And I hate to say it, but the answer is: I don't know. Maybe he hasn't even been born yet. Or is still only a babe in arms at his mother's breast. God, what a thought.

SAM: So we just go on waiting.

HALLY: Ja, looks like it. (*Back to his soup and the book.*)

SAM (*reading from the textbook*): "Introduction: In some mathematical problems only the magnitude. . . ." (*He mispronounces the word "magnitude."*)

HALLY (*correcting him without looking up*): Magnitude.

SAM: What's it mean?

HALLY: How big it is. The size of the thing.

SAM (*reading*): ". . . magnitude of the quantities is of importance. In other problems we need to know whether these quantities are negative or positive. For example, whether there is a debit or credit bank balance . . ."

HALLY: Whether you're broke or not.

SAM: ". . . whether the temperature is above or below Zero. . . ."

HALLY: Naught degrees. Cheerful state of affairs! No cash and you're freezing to death. Mathematics won't get you out of that one.

SAM: "All these quantities are called . . ." (*spelling the word*) . . . s-c-a-l. . . .

HALLY: Scalars.

SAM: Scalars! (*Shaking his head with a laugh.*) You understand all that?

HALLY (*turning a page*): No. And I don't intend to try.

SAM: So what happens when the exams come?

HALLY: Failing a math exam isn't the end of the world, Sam. How many times have I told you that examination results don't measure intelligence?

SAM: I would say about as many times as you've failed one of them.

HALLY (*mirthlessly*): Ha, ha, ha.

SAM (*simultaneously*): Ha, ha, ha.

HALLY: Just remember Winston Churchill didn't do particularly well at school.

SAM: You've also told me that one many times.

HALLY: Well, it just so happens to be the truth.

SAM (*enjoying the word*): Magnitude! Magnitude! Show me how to use it.

HALLY (*after thought*): An intrepid social reformer will not be daunted by the magnitude of the task he has undertaken.

SAM (*impressed*): Couple of jaw-breakers in there!

HALLY: I gave you three for the price of one. Intrepid, daunted, and magnitude. I did that once in an exam. Put five of the words I had to explain in one sentence. It was half a page long.

SAM: Well, I'll put my money on you in the English exam.

HALLY: Piece of cake. Eighty percent without even trying.

SAM (*another textbook from Hally's case*): And history?

HALLY: So-so. I'll scrape through. In the fifties if I'm lucky.

SAM: You didn't do too badly last year.

HALLY: Because we had World War One. That at least has some action. You try to find that in the South African Parliamentary system.

SAM (*reading from the history textbook*): "Napoleon and the principle of equality." Hey! This sounds interesting. "After concluding peace with Britain in 1802, Napoleon used a brief period of calm to in-sti-tute . . ."

HALLY: Introduce.

SAM: ". . . many reforms. Napoleon regarded all people as equal before the law and wanted them to have equal opportunities for advancement. All ves-ti-ges of the feu-dal sys-tem with its oppression of the poor were abol-ished." Vestiges, feudal system, and abolished. I'm all right on oppression.

HALLY: I'm thinking. He swept away . . . abol-ished . . . the last remains . . . vestiges . . . of the bad old days . . . feudal system.

SAM: Ha! There's the social reformer we're waiting for. He sounds like a man of some magnitude.

HALLY: I'm not so sure about that. It's a damn good title for a book, though. A man of magnitude!

SAM: He sounds pretty big to me, Hally.

HALLY: Don't confuse historical significance with greatness. But maybe I'm being a bit prejudiced. Have a look in there and you'll see he's two chapters long. And hell! . . . has he only got dates, Sam, all of which you've got to remember! This campaign and that campaign, and then, because of all the fighting, the next thing is we get Peace Treaties all over the place. And what's the end of the story? Battle of Waterloo, which he loses. Wasn't worth it. No, I don't know about him as a man of magnitude.

SAM: Then who would you say was?

HALLY: To answer that, we need a definition of greatness, and I suppose that would be somebody who . . . somebody who benefited all mankind.

SAM: Right. But like who?

HALLY (*he speaks with total conviction*):   Charles Darwin. Remember him? That big book from the library. *The Origin of the Species.*
SAM: Him?
HALLY: Yes. For his Theory of Evolution.
SAM: You didn't finish it.
HALLY: I ran out of time. I didn't finish it because my two weeks was up. But I'm going to take it out again after I've digested what I read. It's safe. I've hidden it away in the Theology section. Nobody ever goes in there. And anyway who are you to talk? You hardly even looked at it.
SAM: I tried. I looked at the chapters in the beginning and I saw one called "The Struggle for an Existence." Ah ha, I thought. At last! But what did I get? Something called the mistiltoe which needs the apple tree and there's too many seeds and all are going to die except one . . . ! No, Hally.
HALLY (*intellectually outraged*): What do you mean, No! The poor man had to start somewhere. For God's sake, Sam, he revolutionized science. Now we know.
SAM: What?
HALLY: Where we come from and what it all means.
SAM: And that's a benefit to mankind? Anyway, I still don't believe it.
HALLY: God, you're impossible. I showed it to you in black and white.
SAM: Doesn't mean I got to believe it.
HALLY: It's the likes of you that kept the Inquisition in business. It's called bigotry. Anyway, that's my man of magnitude. Charles Darwin! Who's yours?
SAM (*without hesitation*): Abraham Lincoln.
HALLY: I might have guessed as much. Don't get sentimental, Sam. You've never been a slave, you know. And anyway we freed your ancestors here in South Africa long before the Americans. But if you want to thank somebody on their behalf, do it to Mr. William Wilberforce.° Come on. Try again. I want a real genius.

(*Now enjoying himself, and so is Sam. Hally goes behind the counter and helps himself to a chocolate.*)

SAM: William Shakespeare.
HALLY (*no enthusiasm*): Oh. So you're also one of them, are you? You're basing that opinion on only one play, you know. You've only read my *Julius Caesar* and even I don't understand half of what they're talking

Mr. William Wilberforce: (1759–1833), British politician and humanitarian who campaigned for the abolition of the slave trade.

about. They should do what they did with the old Bible: bring the language up to date.

SAM: That's all you've got. It's also the only one *you've* read.

HALLY: I know. I admit it. That's why I suggest we reserve our judgment until we've checked up on a few others. I've got a feeling, though, that by the end of this year one is going to be enough for me, and I can give you the names of twenty-nine other chaps in the Standard Nine class of the Port Elizabeth Technical College who feel the same. But if you want him, you can have him. My turn now. (*Pacing.*) This is a damned good exercise, you know! It started off looking like a simple question and here it's got us really probing into the intellectual heritage of our civilization.

SAM: So who is it going to be?

HALLY: My next man . . . and he gets the title on two scores: social reform and literary genius . . . is Leo Nikolaevich Tolstoy.

SAM: That Russian.

HALLY: Correct. Remember the picture of him I showed you?

SAM: With the long beard.

HALLY (*trying to look like Tolstoy*): And those burning, visionary eyes. My God, the face of a social prophet if ever I saw one! And remember my words when I showed it to you? Here's a *man*, Sam!

SAM: Those were words, Hally.

HALLY: Not many intellectuals are prepared to shovel manure with the peasants and then go home and write a "little book" called *War and Peace*. Incidentally, Sam, he was somebody else who, to quote, ". . . did not distinguish himself scholastically."

SAM: Meaning?

HALLY: He was also no good at school.

SAM: Like you and Winston Churchill.

HALLY (*mirthlessly*): Ha, ha, ha.

SAM (*simultaneously*): Ha, ha, ha.

HALLY: Don't get clever, Sam. That man freed his serfs of his own free will.

SAM: No argument. He was a somebody, all right. I accept him.

HALLY: I'm sure Count Tolstoy will be very pleased to hear that. Your turn. Shoot. (*Another chocolate from behind the counter.*) I'm waiting, Sam.

SAM: I've got him.

HALLY: Good. Submit your candidate for examination.

SAM: Jesus.

HALLY (*stopped dead in his tracks*): Who?

SAM: Jesus Christ.

HALLY: Oh, come on, Sam!

SAM: The Messiah.

HALLY: Ja, but still . . . No, Sam. Don't let's get started on religion. We'll just spend the whole afternoon arguing again. Suppose I turn around and say Mohammed?

SAM: All right.

HALLY: You can't have them both on the same list!

SAM: Why not? You like Mohammed, I like Jesus.

HALLY: I *don't* like Mohammed. I never have. I was merely being hypothetical. As far as I'm concerned, the Koran is as bad as the Bible. No. Religion is out! I'm not going to waste my time again arguing with you about the existence of God. You know perfectly well I'm an atheist . . . and I've got homework to do.

SAM: Okay, I take him back.

HALLY: You've got time for one more name.

SAM (*after thought*): I've got one I know we'll agree on. A simple straightforward great Man of Magnitude . . . and no arguments. And *he* really *did* benefit all mankind.

HALLY: I wonder. After your last contribution I'm beginning to doubt whether anything in the way of an intellectual agreement is possible between the two of us. Who is he?

SAM: Guess.

HALLY: Socrates? Alexandre Dumas? Karl Marx? Dostoevsky? Nietzsche?

(*Sam shakes his head after each name.*)

Give me a clue.

SAM: The letter *P* is important. . . .

HALLY: Plato!

SAM: . . . and his name begins with an *F*.

HALLY: I've got it. Freud and Psychology.

SAM: No. I didn't understand him.

HALLY: That makes two of us.

SAM: Think of moldy apricot jam.

HALLY (*after a delighted laugh*): Penicillin and Sir Alexander Fleming! And the title of the book: *The Microbe Hunters*. (*Delighted.*) Splendid, Sam! Splendid. For once we are in total agreement. The major breakthrough in medical science in the Twentieth Century. If it wasn't for him, we might have lost the Second World War. It's deeply gratifying, Sam, to know that I haven't been wasting my time in talking to you. (*Strutting around proudly.*) Tolstoy may have educated his peasants, but I've educated you.

SAM: Standard Four to Standard Nine.

HALLY: Have we been at it as long as that?

SAM: Yep. And my first lesson was geography.

HALLY (*intrigued*): Really? I don't remember.

SAM: My room there at the back of the old Jubilee Boarding House. I had just started working for your Mom. Little boy in short trousers walks in one afternoon and asks me seriously: "Sam, do you want to see South Africa?" Hey man! Sure I wanted to see South Africa!

HALLY: Was that me?

SAM: . . . So the next thing I'm looking at a map you had just done for homework. It was your first one and you were very proud of yourself.

HALLY: Go on.

SAM: Then came my first lesson. "Repeat after me, Sam: Gold in the Transvaal, mealies in the Free State, sugar in Natal, and grapes in the Cape." I still know it!

HALLY: Well, I'll be buggered. So that's how it all started.

SAM: And your next map was one with all the rivers and the mountains they came from. The Orange, the Vaal, the Limpopo, the Zambezi. . . .

HALLY: You've got a phenomenal memory!

SAM: You should be grateful. That is why you started passing your exams. You tried to be better than me.

(*They laugh together. Willie is attracted by the laughter and joins them.*)

HALLY: The old Jubilee Boarding House. Sixteen rooms with board and lodging, rent in advance and one week's notice. I haven't thought about it for donkey's years . . . and I don't think that's an accident. God, was I glad when we sold it and moved out. Those years are not remembered as the happiest ones of an unhappy childhood.

WILLIE (*knocking on the table and trying to imitate a woman's voice*): "Hally, are you there?"

HALLY: Who's that supposed to be?

WILLIE: "What you doing in there, Hally? Come out at once!"

HALLY (*to Sam*): What's he talking about?

SAM: Don't you remember?

WILLIE: "Sam, Willie . . . is he in there with you boys?"

SAM: Hiding away in our room when your mother was looking for you.

HALLY (*another good laugh*): Of course! I used to crawl and hide under your bed! But finish the story, Willie. Then what used to happen? You chaps would give the game away by telling her I was in there with you. So much for friendship.

SAM: We couldn't lie to her. She knew.

HALLY: Which meant I got another rowing for hanging around the "servants' quarters." I think I spent more time in there with you chaps than anywhere else in that dump. And do you blame me? Nothing but bloody misery wherever you went. Somebody was always complaining about the food, or my mother was having a fight with Micky Nash because she'd caught her with a petty officer in her room. Maud Meiring was another one. Remember those two? They were prostitutes, you know. Soldiers and sailors from the troopships. Bottom fell out of the business when the war ended. God, the flotsam and jetsam that life washed up on our shores! No joking, if it wasn't for your room, I would have been the first certified ten-year-old in medical history. Ja, the memories are coming back now. Walking home from school and thinking: "What can I do this afternoon?" Try out a few ideas, but sooner or later I'd end up in there with you fellows. I bet you I could still find my way to your room with my eyes closed. (*He does exactly that.*) Down the corridor . . . telephone on the right, which my Mom keeps locked because somebody is using it on the sly and not paying . . . past the kitchen and unappetizing cooking smells . . . around the corner into the backyard, hold my breath again because there are more smells coming when I pass your lavatory, then into that little passageway, first door on the right and into your room. How's that?

SAM: Good. But, as usual, you forgot to knock.

HALLY: Like that time I barged in and caught you and Cynthia . . . at it. Remember? God, was I embarrassed! I didn't know what was going on at first.

SAM: Ja, that taught you a lesson.

HALLY: And about a lot more than knocking on doors, I'll have you know, and I don't mean geography either. Hell, Sam, couldn't you have waited until it was dark?

SAM: No.

HALLY: Was it that urgent?

SAM: Yes, and if you don't believe me, wait until your time comes.

HALLY: No, thank you. I am not interested in girls. (*Back to his memories. . . . Using a few chairs he re-creates the room as he lists the items.*) A gray little room with a cold cement floor. Your bed against that wall . . . and I now know why the mattress sags so much! . . . Willie's bed . . . it's propped up on bricks because one leg is broken . . . that wobbly little table with the washbasin and jug of water . . . Yes! . . . stuck to the wall above it are some pin-up pictures from magazines. Joe Louis. . . .

WILLIE: Brown Bomber. World Title. (*Boxing pose.*) Three rounds and knockout.

HALLY: Against who?

SAM: Max Schmeling.

HALLY: Correct. I can also remember Fred Astaire and Ginger Rogers, and Rita Hayworth in a bathing costume which always made me hot and bothered when I looked at it. Under Willie's bed is an old suitcase with all his clothes in a mess, which is why I never hide there. Your things are neat and tidy in a trunk next to your bed, and on it there is a picture of you and Cynthia in your ballroom clothes, your first silver cup for third place in a competition and an old radio which doesn't work anymore. Have I left out anything?

SAM: No.

HALLY: Right, so much for the stage directions. Now the characters. (*Sam and Willie move to their appropriate positions in the bedroom.*) Willie is in bed, under his blankets with his clothes on, complaining nonstop about something, but we can't make out a word of what he's saying because he's got his head under the blankets as well. You're on your bed trimming your toenails with a knife — not a very edifying sight — and as for me. . . . What am I doing?

SAM: You're sitting on the floor giving Willie a lecture about being a good loser while you get the checkerboard and pieces ready for a game. Then you go to Willie's bed, pull off the blankets and make him play with you first because you know you're going to win, and that gives you the second game with me.

HALLY: And you certainly were a bad loser, Willie!

WILLIE: Haai!

HALLY: Wasn't he, Sam? And so slow! A game with you almost took the whole afternoon. Thank God I gave up trying to teach you how to play chess.

WILLIE: You and Sam cheated.

HALLY: I never saw Sam cheat, and mine were mostly the mistakes of youth.

WILLIE: Then how is it you two was always winning?

HALLY: Have you ever considered the possibility, Willie, that it was because we were better than you?

WILLIE: Every time better?

HALLY: Not every time. There were occasions when we deliberately let you win a game so that you would stop sulking and go on playing with us. Sam used to wink at me when you weren't looking to show me it was time to let you win.

WILLIE: So then you two didn't play fair.

HALLY: It was for your benefit, Mr. Malopo, which is more than being fair. It was an act of self-sacrifice. (*To Sam.*) But you know what my best memory is, don't you?

SAM: No.

HALLY: Come on, guess. If your memory is so good, you must remember it as well.

SAM: We got up to a lot of tricks in there, Hally.

HALLY: This one was special, Sam.

SAM: I'm listening.

HALLY: It started off looking like another of those useless nothing-to-do afternoons. I'd already been down to Main Street looking for adventure, but nothing had happened. I didn't feel like climbing trees in the Donkin Park or pretending I was a private eye and following a stranger . . . so as usual: See what's cooking in Sam's room. This time it was you on the floor. You had two thin pieces of wood and you were smoothing them down with a knife. It didn't look particularly interesting, but when I asked you what you were doing, you just said, "Wait and see, Hally. Wait . . . and see". . . . in that secret sort of way of yours, so I knew there was a surprise coming. You teased me, you bugger, by being deliberately slow and not answering my questions!

(*Sam laughs.*)

And whistling while you worked away! God, it was infuriating! I could have brained you! It was only when you tied them together in a cross and put that down on the brown paper that I realized what you were doing. "Sam is making a kite?" And when I asked you and you said, "Yes". . . ! (*Shaking his head with disbelief.*) The sheer audacity of it took my breath away. I mean, seriously, what the hell does a black man know about flying a kite? I'll be honest with you, Sam, I had no hopes for it. If you think I was excited and happy, you got another guess coming. In fact, I was shit-scared that we were going to make fools of ourselves. When we left the boarding house to go up onto the hill, I was praying quietly that there wouldn't be any other kids around to laugh at us.

SAM (*enjoying the memory as much as Hally*): Ja, I could see that.

HALLY: I made it obvious, did I?

SAM: Ja. You refused to carry it.

HALLY: Do you blame me? Can you remember what the poor thing looked like? Tomato-box wood and brown paper! Flour and water for glue! Two of my mother's old stockings for a tail, and then all those bits and pieces of string you made me tie together so that we could fly it! Hell, no, that was now only asking for a miracle to happen.

SAM: Then the big argument when I told you to hold the string and run with it when I let go.

HALLY: I was prepared to run, all right, but straight back to the boarding house.

SAM (*knowing what's coming*): So what happened?

HALLY: Come on, Sam, you remember as well as I do.

SAM: I want to hear it from you.

(*Hally pauses. He wants to be as accurate as possible.*)

HALLY: You went a little distance from me down the hill, you held it up ready to let it go. . . . "This is it," I thought. "Like everything else in my life, here comes another fiasco." Then you shouted, "Go, Hally!" and I started to run. (*Another pause.*) I don't know how to describe it, Sam. Ja! The miracle happened! I was running, waiting for it to crash to the ground, but instead suddenly there was something alive behind me at the end of the string, tugging at it as if it wanted to be free. I looked back . . . (*Shakes his head.*) . . . I still can't believe my eyes. It was flying! Looping around and trying to climb even higher into the sky. You shouted to me to let it have more string. I did, until there was none left and I was just holding that piece of wood we had tied it to. You came up and joined me. You were laughing.

SAM: So were you. And shouting, "It works, Sam! We've done it!"

HALLY: And we had! I was so proud of us! It was the most splendid thing I had ever seen. I wished there were hundreds of kids around to watch us. The part that scared me, though, was when you showed me how to make it dive down to the ground and then just when it was on the point of crashing, swoop up again!

SAM: You didn't want to try yourself.

HALLY: Of course not! I would have been suicidal if anything had happened to it. Watching you do it made me nervous enough. I was quite happy just to see it up there with its tail fluttering behind it. You left me after that, didn't you? You explained how to get it down, we tied it to the bench so that I could sit and watch it, and you went away. I wanted you to stay, you know. I was a little scared of having to look after it by myself.

SAM (*quietly*): I had work to do, Hally.

HALLY: It was sort of sad bringing it down, Sam. And it looked sad again when it was lying there on the ground. Like something that had lost its soul. Just tomato-box wood, brown paper and two of my mother's old stockings! But, hell, I'll never forget that first moment when I saw it up there. I had a stiff neck the next day from looking up so much.

(*Sam laughs. Hally turns to him with a question he never thought of asking before.*)

Why did you make that kite, Sam?

SAM (*evenly*): I can't remember.

HALLY: Truly?

SAM: Too long ago, Hally.

HALLY: Ja, I suppose it was. It's time for another one, you know.

SAM: Why do you say that?

HALLY: Because it feels like that. Wouldn't be a good day to fly it, though.

SAM: No. You can't fly kites on rainy days.

HALLY (*He studies Sam. Their memories have made him conscious of the man's presence in his life.*): How old are you, Sam?

SAM: Two score and five.

HALLY: Strange, isn't it?

SAM: What?

HALLY: Me and you.

SAM: What's strange about it?

HALLY: Little white boy in short trousers and a black man old enough to be his father flying a kite. It's not every day you see that.

SAM: But why strange? Because the one is white and the other black?

HALLY: I don't know. Would have been just as strange, I suppose, if it had been me and my Dad . . . cripple man and a little boy! Nope! There's no chance of me flying a kite without it being strange. (*Simple statement of fact—no self-pity.*) There's a nice little short story there. "The Kite-Flyers." But we'd have to find a twist in the ending.

SAM: Twist?

HALLY: Yes. Something unexpected. The way it ended with us was too straightforward . . . me on the bench and you going back to work. There's no drama in that.

WILLIE: And me?

HALLY: You?

WILLIE: Yes me.

HALLY: You want to get into the story as well, do you? I got it! Change the title: "Afternoons in Sam's Room". . . . expand it and tell all the stories. It's on its way to being a novel. Our days in the old Jubilee. Sad in a way that they're over. I almost wish we were still in that little room.

SAM: We're still together.

HALLY: That's true. It's just that life felt the right size in there . . . not too big and not too small. Wasn't so hard to work up a bit of courage. It's got so bloody complicated since then.

(*The telephone rings. Sam answers it.*)

SAM: St. George's Park Tea Room . . . Hello, Madam . . . Yes, Madam, he's here. . . . Hally, it's your mother.

HALLY: Where is she phoning from?

SAM: Sounds like the hospital. It's a public telephone.

HALLY (*relieved*): You see! I told you. (*The telephone.*) Hello, Mom . . . Yes . . . Yes no fine. Everything's under control here. How's things with poor old Dad? . . . Has he had a bad turn? . . . What? . . . Oh, God! . . . Yes, Sam told me, but I was sure he'd made a mistake. But what's this all about, Mom? He didn't look at all good last night. How can he get better so quickly? . . . Then very obviously you must say no. Be firm with him. You're the boss. . . . You know what it's going to be like if he comes home. . . . Well then, don't blame me when I fail my exams at the end of the year. . . . Yes! How am I expected to be fresh for school when I spend half the night massaging his gammy leg? . . . So am

I! . . . So tell him a white lie. Say Dr. Colley wants more X-rays of his stump. Or bribe him. We'll sneak in double tots of brandy in future. . . . What? . . . Order him to get back into bed at once! If he's going to behave like a child, treat him like one. . . . All right, Mom! I was just trying to . . . I'm sorry. . . . I said I'm sorry. . . . Quick, give me your number. I'll phone you back. (*He hangs up and waits a few seconds.*) Here we go again! (*He dials.*) I'm sorry, Mom. . . . Okay. . . . But now listen to me carefully. All it needs is for you to put your foot down. Don't take no for an answer. . . . Did you hear me? And whatever you do, don't discuss it with him. . . . Because I'm frightened you'll give in to him. . . . Yes, Sam gave me lunch. . . . I ate all of it! . . . No, Mom not a soul. It's still raining here. . . . Right, I'll tell them. I'll just do some homework and then lock up. . . . But remember now, Mom. Don't listen to anything he says. And phone me back and let me know what happens. . . . Okay. Bye, Mom. (*He hangs up. The men are staring at him.*) My Mom says that when you're finished with the floors you must do the windows. (*Pause.*) Don't misunderstand me, chaps. All I want is for him to get better. And if he was, I'd be the first person to say: "Bring him home." But he's not, and we can't give him the medical care and attention he needs at home. That's what hospitals are there for. (*Brusquely.*) So don't just stand there! Get on with it!

(*Sam clears Hally's table.*)

You heard right. My Dad wants to go home.

SAM: Is he better?

HALLY (*sharply*): No! How the hell can he be better when last night he was groaning with pain? This is not an age of miracles!

SAM: Then he should stay in hospital.

HALLY (*seething with irritation and frustration*): Tell me something I don't know, Sam. What the hell do you think I was saying to my Mom? All I can say is fuck-it-all.

SAM: I'm sure he'll listen to your Mom.

HALLY: You don't know what she's up against. He's already packed his shaving kit and pajamas and is sitting on his bed with his crutches, dressed and ready to go. I know him when he gets in that mood. If she tries to reason with him, we've had it. She's no match for him when it comes to a battle of words. He'll tie her up in knots. (*Trying to hide his true feelings.*)

SAM: I suppose it gets lonely for him in there.

HALLY: With all the patients and nurses around? Regular visits from the Salvation Army? Balls! It's ten times worse for him at home. I'm at school and my mother is here in the business all day.

SAM: He's at least got you at night.

HALLY (*before he can stop himself*): And we've got him! Please! I don't want to talk about it anymore. (*Unpacks his school case, slamming down books on the table.*) Life is just a plain bloody mess, that's all. And people are fools.

SAM: Come on, Hally.

HALLY: Yes, they are! They bloody well deserve what they get.

SAM: Then don't complain.

HALLY: Don't try to be clever, Sam. It doesn't suit you. Anybody who thinks there's nothing wrong with this world needs to have his head examined. Just when things are going along all right, without fail someone or something will come along and spoil everything. Somebody should write that down as a fundamental law of the Universe. The principle of perpetual disappointment. If there is a God who created this world, he should scrap it and try again.

SAM: All right, Hally, all right. What you got for homework?

HALLY: Bullshit, as usual. (*Opens an exercise book and reads.*) "Write five hundred words describing an annual event of cultural or historical significance."

SAM: That should be easy enough for you.

HALLY: And also plain bloody boring. You know what he wants, don't you? One of their useless old ceremonies. The commemoration of the landing of the 1820 Settlers, or if it's going to be culture, Carols by Candlelight every Christmas.

SAM: It's an impressive sight. Make a good description, Hally. All those candles glowing in the dark and the people singing hymns.

HALLY: And it's called religious hysteria. (*Intense irritation.*) Please, Sam! Just leave me alone and let me get on with it. I'm not in the mood for games this afternoon. And remember my Mom's orders . . . you're to help Willie with the windows. Come on now, I don't want any more nonsense in here.

SAM: Okay, Hally, okay.

(*Hally settles down to his homework; determined preparations . . . pen, ruler, exercise book, dictionary, another cake . . . all of which will lead to nothing.*)

(*Sam waltzes over to Willie and starts to replace tables and chairs. He practices a ballroom step while doing so. Willie watches. When Sam is finished, Willie tries.*)

Good! But just a little bit quicker on the turn and only move in to her after she's crossed over. What about this one?

(*Another step. When Sam is finished, Willie again has a go.*)

Much better. See what happens when you just relax and enjoy yourself? Remember that in two weeks' time and you'll be all right.

WILLIE: But I haven't got partner, Boet Sam.

SAM: Maybe Hilda will turn up tonight.

WILLIE: No, Boet Sam. (*Reluctantly.*) I gave her a good hiding.

SAM: You mean a bad one.

WILLIE: Good bad one.

SAM: Then you mustn't complain either. Now you pay the price for losing your temper.

WILLIE: I also pay two pounds ten shilling entrance fee.

SAM: They'll refund you if you withdraw now.

WILLIE (*appalled*): You mean, don't dance?

SAM: Yes.

WILLIE: No! I wait too long and I practice too hard. If I find me new partner, you think I can be ready in two weeks? I ask Madam for my leave now and we practice every day.

SAM: Quickstep nonstop for two weeks. World record, Willie, but you'll be mad at the end.

WILLIE: No jokes, Boet Sam.

SAM: I'm not joking.

WILLIE: So then what?

SAM: Find Hilda. Say you're sorry and promise you won't beat her again.

WILLIE: No.

SAM: Then withdraw. Try again next year.

WILLIE: No.

SAM: Then I give up.

WILLIE: Haaikona, Boet Sam, you can't.

SAM: What do you mean, I can't? I'm telling you: I give up.

WILLIE (*adamant*): No! (*Accusingly.*) It was you who start me ballroom dancing.

SAM: So?

WILLIE: Before that I use to be happy. And is you and Miriam who bring me to Hilda and say here's partner for you.

SAM: What are you saying, Willie?

WILLIE: You!

SAM: But me what? To blame?

WILLIE: Yes.

SAM: Willie . . . ? (*Bursts into laughter.*)

WILLIE: And now all you do is make jokes at me. You wait. When Miriam leaves you is my turn to laugh. Ha! Ha! Ha!

SAM (*he can't take Willie seriously any longer*): She can leave me tonight! I know what to do. (*Bowing before an imaginary partner.*) May I have the pleasure? (*He dances and sings.*)

"Just a fellow with his pillow . . .

Dancin' like a willow . . .

In an autumn breeze. . . ."

WILLIE: There you go again!

(*Sam goes on dancing and singing.*)

Boet Sam!

SAM: There's the answer to your problem! Judges' announcement in two weeks' time: "Ladies and gentlemen, the winner in the open section . . . Mr. Willie Malopo and his pillow!"

(*This is too much for a now really angry Willie. He goes for Sam, but the latter is too quick for him and puts Hally's table between the two of them.*)

HALLY (*exploding*): For Christ's sake, you two!

WILLIE (*still trying to get at Sam*): I donner you, Sam! Struesgod!

SAM (*still laughing*): Sorry, Willie . . . Sorry. . . .

HALLY: Sam! Willie! (*Grabs his ruler and gives Willie a vicious whack on the bum.*) How the hell am I supposed to concentrate with the two of you behaving like bloody children!

WILLIE: Hit him too!

HALLY: Shut up, Willie.

WILLIE: He started jokes again.

HALLY: Get back to your work. You too, Sam. (*His ruler.*) Do you want another one, Willie?

(*Sam and Willie return to their work. Hally uses the opportunity to escape from his unsuccessful attempt at homework. He struts around like a little despot, ruler in hand, giving vent to his anger and frustration.*)

Suppose a customer had walked in then? Or the Park Superintendent. And seen the two of you behaving like a pair of hooligans. That would have been the end of my mother's license, you know. And your jobs? Well, this is the end of it. From now on there will be no more of your ballroom nonsense in here. This is a business establishment, not a bloody New Brighton dancing school. I've been far too lenient with the two of you. (*Behind the counter for a green cool drink and a dollop of ice cream. He keeps up his tirade as he prepares it.*) But what really makes me bitter is that I allow you chaps a little freedom in here when business is bad and what do you do with it? The foxtrot! Specially you, Sam. There's more to life than trotting around a dance floor and I thought at least you knew it.

SAM: It's a harmless pleasure, Hally. It doesn't hurt anybody.

HALLY: It's also a rather simple one, you know.

SAM: You reckon so? Have you ever tried?

HALLY: Of course not.

SAM: Why don't you? Now.

HALLY: What do you mean? Me dance?

SAM: Yes. I'll show you a simple step—the waltz—then you try it.

HALLY: What will that prove?

SAM: That it might not be as easy as you think.

HALLY: I didn't say it was easy. I said it was simple—like in simple-minded, meaning mentally retarded. You can't exactly say it challenges the intellect.

SAM: It does other things.

HALLY: Such as?

SAM: Make people happy.

HALLY (*the glass in his hand*): So do American cream sodas with ice cream. For God's sake, Sam, you're not asking me to take ballroom dancing serious, are you?

SAM: Yes.

HALLY (*sigh of defeat*): Oh, well, so much for trying to give you a decent education. I've obviously achieved nothing.

SAM: You still haven't told me what's wrong with admiring something that's beautiful and then trying to do it yourself.

HALLY: Nothing. But we happen to be talking about a foxtrot, not a thing of beauty.

SAM: But that is just what I'm saying. If you were to see two champions doing, two masters of the art . . . !

HALLY: Oh God, I give up. So now it's also art!

SAM: Ja.

HALLY: There's a limit, Sam. Don't confuse art and entertainment.

SAM: So then what is art?

HALLY: You want a definition?

SAM: Ja.

HALLY (*He realizes he has got to be careful. He gives the matter a lot of thought before answering.*): Philosophers have been trying to do that for centuries. What is Art? What is Life? But basically I suppose it's . . . the giving of meaning to matter.

SAM: Nothing to do with beautiful?

HALLY: It goes beyond that. It's the giving of form to the formless.

SAM: Ja, well, maybe it's not art, then. But I still say it's beautiful.

HALLY: I'm sure the word you mean to use is entertaining.

SAM (*adamant*): No. Beautiful. And if you want proof come along to the Centenary Hall in New Brighton in two weeks' time.

(*The mention of the Centenary Hall draws Willie over to them.*)

HALLY: What for? I've seen the two of you prancing around in here often enough.

SAM (*he laughs*): This isn't the real thing, Hally. We're just playing around in here.

HALLY: So? I can use my imagination.

SAM: And what do you get?

HALLY: A lot of people dancing around and having a so-called good time.

SAM: That all?

HALLY: Well, basically it is that, surely.

SAM: No, it isn't. Your imagination hasn't helped you at all. There's a lot more to it than that. We're getting ready for the championships, Hally, not just another dance. There's going to be a lot of people, all right, and they're going to have a good time, but they'll only be spectators, sitting around and watching. It's just the competitors out there on the dance floor. Party decorations and fancy lights all around the walls! The ladies in beautiful evening dresses!

HALLY: My mother's got one of those, Sam, and, quite frankly, it's an embarrassment every time she wears it.

SAM (*undeterred*): Your imagination left out the excitement.

(*Hally scoffs.*)

Oh, yes. The finalists are not going to be out there just to have a good time. One of those couples will be the 1950 Eastern Province Champions. And your imagination left out the music.

WILLIE: Mr. Elijah Gladman Guzana and his Orchestral Jazzonions.

SAM: The sound of the big band, Hally. Trombone, trumpet, tenor and alto sax. And then, finally, your imagination also left out the climax of the evening when the dancing is finished, the judges have stopped whispering among themselves and the Master of Ceremonies collects their scorecards and goes up onto the stage to announce the winners.

HALLY: All right. So you make it sound like a bit of a do. It's an occasion. Satisfied?

SAM (*victory*): So you admit that!

HALLY: Emotionally yes, intellectually no.

SAM: Well, I don't know what you mean by that, all I'm telling you is that it is going to be *the* event of the year in New Brighton. It's been sold out for two weeks already. There's only standing room left. We've got competitors coming from Kingwilliamstown, East London, Port Alfred.

(*Hally starts pacing thoughtfully.*)

HALLY: Tell me a bit more.

SAM: I thought you weren't interested . . . intellectually.

HALLY (*mysteriously*): I've got my reasons.

SAM: What do you want to know?

HALLY: It takes place every year?

SAM: Yes. But only every third year in New Brighton. It's East London's turn to have the championships next year.

HALLY: Which, I suppose, makes it an even more significant event.

SAM: Ah ha! We're getting somewhere. Our "occasion" is now a "significant event."

HALLY: I wonder.

SAM: What?

HALLY: I wonder if I would get away with it.

SAM: But what?

HALLY (*to the table and his exercise book*): "Write five hundred words describing an annual event of cultural or historical significance." Would I be stretching poetic license a little too far if I called your ballroom championships a cultural event?

SAM: You mean . . . ?

HALLY: You think we could get five hundred words out of it, Sam?

SAM: Victor Sylvester has written a whole book on ballroom dancing.

WILLIE: You going to write about it, Master Hally?

HALLY: Yes, gentlemen, that is precisely what I am considering doing. Old Doc Bromely—he's my English teacher—is going to argue with me, of course. He doesn't like natives. But I'll point out to him that in strict anthropological terms the culture of a primitive black society includes its dancing and singing. To put my thesis in a nutshell: The war-dance has been replaced by the waltz. But it still amounts to the same thing: the release of primitive emotions through movement. Shall we give it a go?

SAM: I'm ready.

WILLIE: Me also.

HALLY: Ha! This will teach the old bugger a lesson. (*Decision taken.*) Right. Let's get ourselves organized. (*This means another cake on the table. He sits.*) I think you've given me enough general atmosphere, Sam, but to build the tension and suspense I need facts. (*Pencil poised.*)

WILLIE: Give him facts, Boet Sam.

HALLY: What you called the climax . . . how many finalists?

SAM: Six couples.

HALLY (*making notes*): Go on. Give me the picture.

SAM: Spectators seated right around the hall. (*Willie becomes a spectator.*)

HALLY: . . . and it's a full house.

SAM: At one end, on the stage, Gladman and his Orchestral Jazzonions. At the other end is a long table with the three judges. The six finalists go onto the dance floor and take up their positions. When they are ready and the spectators have settled down, the Master of Ceremonies goes to the microphone. To start with, he makes some jokes to get people laughing. . . .

HALLY: Good touch. (*As he writes.*) ". . . creating a relaxed atmosphere which will change to one of tension and drama as the climax is approached."

SAM (*onto a chair to act out the M.C.*): "Ladies and gentlemen, we come now to the great moment you have all been waiting for this evening. . . . The finals of the 1950 Eastern Province Open Ballroom Dancing Championships. But first let me introduce the finalists! Mr. and Mrs. Welcome Tchabalala from Kingwilliamstown . . ."

WILLIE (*he applauds after every name*): Is when the people clap their hands and whistle and make a lot of noise, Master Hally.

SAM: "Mr. Mulligan Njikelane and Miss Nomhle Nkonyeni of Grahamstown; Mr. and Mrs. Norman Nchinga from Port Alfred; Mr. Fats Bokolane and Miss Dina Plaatjies from East London; Mr. Sipho Dugu and Mrs. Mable Magada from Peddie; and from New Brighton our very own Mr. Willie Malopo and Miss Hilda Samuels."

(*Willie can't believe his ears. He abandons his role as spectator and scrambles into position as a finalist.*)

WILLIE: Relaxed and ready to romance!

SAM: The applause dies down. When everybody is silent, Gladman lifts up his sax, nods at the Orchestral Jazzonions. . . .

WILLIE: Play the jukebox please, Boet Sam!

SAM: I also only got bus fare, Willie.

HALLY: Hold it, everybody. (*Heads for the cash register behind the counter.*) How much is in the till, Sam?

SAM: Three shillings. Hally . . . Your Mom counted it before she left.

(*Hally hesitates.*)

HALLY: Sorry, Willie. You know how she carried on the last time I did it. We'll just have to pool our combined imaginations and hope for the best. (*Returns to the table.*) Back to work. How are the points scored, Sam?

SAM: Maximum of ten points each for individual style, deportment, rhythm, and general appearance.

WILLIE: Must I start?

HALLY: Hold it for a second, Willie. And penalties?

SAM: For what?

HALLY: For doing something wrong. Say you stumble or bump into somebody . . . do they take off any points?

SAM (*aghast*): Hally . . . !

HALLY: When you're dancing. If you and your partner collide into another couple.

(*Hally can get no further. Sam has collapsed with laughter. He explains to Willie.*)

SAM: If me and Miriam bump into you and Hilda. . . .

(*Willie joins him in another good laugh.*)

Hally, Hally . . . !

HALLY (*perplexed*): Why? What did I say?

SAM: There's no collisions out there, Hally. Nobody trips or stumbles or bumps into anybody else. That's what that moment is all about. To be one of those finalists on that dance floor is like . . . like being in a dream about a world in which accidents don't happen.

HALLY (*genuinely moved by Sam's image*): Jesus, Sam! That's beautiful!

WILLIE (*can endure waiting no longer*): I'm starting!

(*Willie dances while Sam talks.*)

SAM: Of course it is. That's what I've been trying to say to you all afternoon. And it's beautiful because that is what we want life to be like. But instead, like you said, Hally, we're bumping into each other all the time. Look at the three of us this afternoon: I've bumped into Willie, the two of us have bumped into you, you've bumped into your mother, she bumping into your Dad. . . . None of us knows the steps and there's no music playing. And it doesn't stop with us. The whole world is doing it all the time. Open a newspaper and what do you read? America has bumped into Russia, England is bumping into India, rich man bumps into poor man. Those are big collisions, Hally. They make for a lot of bruises. People get hurt in all that bumping, and we're sick and tired of it now. It's been going on for too long. Are we never going to get it right? . . . Learn to dance life like champions instead of always being just a bunch of beginners at it?

HALLY (*deep and sincere admiration of the man*): You've got a vision, Sam!

SAM: Not just me. What I'm saying to you is that everybody's got it. That's why there's only standing room left for the Centenary Hall in two weeks' time. For as long as the music lasts, we are going to see six couples get it right, the way we want life to be.

HALLY: But is that the best we can do, Sam . . . watch six finalists dreaming about the way it should be?

SAM: I don't know. But it starts with that. Without the dream we won't know what we're going for. And anyway I reckon there are a few people who have got past just dreaming about it and are trying for something real. Remember that thing we read once in the paper about the Mahatma Gandhi? Going without food to stop those riots in India?

HALLY: You're right. He certainly was trying to teach people to get the steps right.

SAM: And the Pope.

HALLY: Yes, he's another one. Our old General Smuts° as well, you know. He's also out there dancing. You know, Sam, when you come to think

---

General Smuts: (1870–1950), South African statesman who helped create the Union of South Africa and the United Nations. Smuts was also a soldier in the Boer War against the British.

of it, that's what the United Nations boils down to . . . a dancing school for politicians!

SAM: And let's hope they learn.

HALLY (*a little surge of hope*): You're right. We mustn't despair. Maybe there's some hope for mankind after all. Keep it up, Willie. (*Back to his table with determination.*) This is a lot bigger than I thought. So what have we got? Yes, our title: "A World Without Collisions."

SAM: That sounds good! "A World Without Collisions."

HALLY: Subtitle: "Global Politics on the Dance Floor." No. A bit too heavy, hey? What about "Ballroom Dancing as a Political Vision"?

(*The telephone rings. Sam answers it.*)

SAM: St. George's Park Tea Room . . . Yes, Madam . . . Hally, it's your Mom.

HALLY (*back to reality*): Oh, God, yes! I'd forgotten all about that. Shit! Remember my words, Sam? Just when you're enjoying yourself, someone or something will come along and wreck everything.

SAM: You haven't heard what she's got to say yet.

HALLY: Public telephone?

SAM: No.

HALLY: Does she sound happy or unhappy?

SAM: I couldn't tell. (*Pause.*) She's waiting, Hally.

HALLY (*to the telephone*): Hello, Mom . . . No, everything is okay here. Just doing my homework. . . . What's your news? . . . You've what? . . . (*Pause. He takes the receiver away from his ear for a few seconds. In the course of Hally's telephone conversation, Sam and Willie discreetly position the stacked tables and chairs. Hally places the receiver back to his ear.*) Yes, I'm still here. Oh, well, I give up now. Why did you do it, Mom? . . . Well, I just hope you know what you've let us in for. . . . (*Loudly.*) I said I hope you know what you've let us in for! It's the end of the peace and quiet we've been having. (*Softly.*) Where is he? (*Normal voice.*) He can't hear us from in there. But for God's sake, Mom, what happened? I told you to be firm with him. . . . Then you and the nurses should have held him down, taken his crutches away. . . . I know only too well he's my father! . . . I'm not being disrespectful, but I'm sick and tired of emptying stinking chamber pots full of phlegm and piss. . . . Yes, I do! When you're not there, he asks *me* to do it. . . . If you really want to know the truth, that's why I've got no appetite for my food. . . . Yes! There's a lot of things you don't know about. For your information, I still haven't got that science textbook I need. And you know why? He borrowed the money you gave me for it. . . . Because I didn't want to start another fight between you two. . . . He says that every time. . . . All right, Mom! (*Viciously.*) Then just remember to start hiding your bag away again, because he'll be at your purse before long for money for booze. And when he's well enough to come down here, you better keep an eye on the till as well, because that is also going to develop a leak. . . . Then don't complain to me when he starts his old tricks. . . . Yes, you do. I get it from you on one side and from him on the other, and it makes life hell for me. I'm not going to be the peacemaker anymore. I'm warning you now: when the two of you start fighting again, I'm leaving home. . . . Mom, if you start crying, I'm going to put down the receiver. . . . Okay. . . . (*Lowering his voice to a vicious whisper.*) Okay, Mom. I heard you. (*Desperate.*) No. . . . Because I don't want to. I'll see him when I get home! Mom! . . . (*Pause. When he speaks again, his tone changes completely. It is not simply pretense. We sense a genuine emotional conflict.*) Welcome home, chum! . . . What's that? . . . Don't be silly, Dad. You being home is just about the best news in the world. . . . I bet you are. Bloody depressing there with everybody going on about their ailments, hey! . . . How you feeling? . . . Good. . . . Here as well, pal. Coming down cats and dogs. . . . That's right. Just the day for a kip and a toss in your old Uncle Ned. . . . Everything's just hunky-dory on my side, Dad. . . . Well, to start with, there's a nice pile of comics for you on the counter. . . . Yes, old Kemple brought them in. *Batman and Robin, Submariner* . . . just your cup of tea. . . . I will. . . . Yes, we'll spin a few yarns tonight. . . . Okay, chum, see you in a little while. . . . No, I promise. I'll come straight home. . . . (*Pause—his mother comes back on the phone.*) Mom? Okay. I'll lock up now. . . . What? . . . Oh, the brandy . . . Yes, I'll remember! . . . I'll put it in my suitcase now, for God's sake. I know well enough what will happen if he doesn't get it. . . . (*Places a bottle of brandy on the counter.*) I *was* kind to him, Mom. I didn't say anything nasty! . . . All right. Bye. (*End of telephone conversation. A desolate Hally doesn't move. A strained silence.*)

SAM (*quietly*): That sounded like a bad bump, Hally.

HALLY (*Having a hard time controlling his emotions. He speaks carefully.*): Mind your own business, Sam.

SAM: Sorry. I wasn't trying to interfere. Shall we carry on? Hally? (*He indicates the exercise book. No response from Hally.*)

WILLIE (*also trying*): Tell him about when they give out the cups, Boet Sam.

SAM: Ja! That's another big moment. The presentation of the cups after the winners have been announced. You've got to put that in.

(*Still no response from Hally.*)

WILLIE: A big silver one, Master Hally, called floating trophy for the champions.

SAM: We always invite some big-shot personality to hand them over. Guest of honor this year is going to be His Holiness Bishop Jabulani of the All African Free Zionist Church.

(*Hally gets up abruptly, goes to his table, and tears up the page he was writing on.*)

HALLY: So much for a bloody world without collisions.

SAM: Too bad. It was on its way to being a good composition.

HALLY: Let's stop bullshitting ourselves, Sam.

SAM: Have we been doing that?

HALLY: Yes! That's what all our talk about a decent world has been . . . just so much bullshit.

SAM: We did say it was still only a dream.

HALLY: And a bloody useless one at that. Life's a fuckup and it's never going to change.

SAM: Ja, maybe that's true.

HALLY: There's no maybe about it. It's a blunt and brutal fact. All we've done this afternoon is waste our time.

SAM: Not if we'd got your homework done.

HALLY: I don't give a shit about my homework, so, for Christ's sake, just shut up about it. (*Slamming books viciously into his school case.*) Hurry up now and finish your work. I want to lock up and get out of here. (*Pause.*) And then go where? Home-sweet-fucking-home. Jesus, I hate that word.

(*Hally goes to the counter to put the brandy bottle and comics in his school case. After a moment's hesitation, he smashes the bottle of brandy. He abandons all further attempts to hide his feelings. Sam and Willie work away as unobtrusively as possible.*)

Do you want to know what is really wrong with your lovely little dream, Sam? It's not just that we are all bad dancers. That does happen to be perfectly true, but there's more to it than just that. You left out the cripples.

SAM: Hally!

HALLY (*now totally reckless*): Ja! Can't leave them out, Sam. That's why we always end up on our backsides on the dance floor. They're also out there dancing . . . like a bunch of broken spiders trying to do the quickstep! (*An ugly attempt at laughter.*) When you come to think of it, it's a bloody comical sight. I mean, it's bad enough on two legs . . . but one and a pair of crutches! Hell, no, Sam. That's guaranteed to turn that dance floor into a shambles. Why you shaking your head? Picture it, man. For once this afternoon let's use our imaginations sensibly.

SAM: Be careful, Hally.

HALLY: Of what? The truth? I seem to be the only one around here who is prepared to face it. We've had the pretty dream, it's time now to wake up and have a good long look at the way things really are. Nobody knows the steps, there's no music, the cripples are also out there tripping up everybody and trying to get into the act, and it's all called the All-Comers-How-to-Make-a-Fuckup-of-Life Championships. (*Another ugly laugh.*) Hang on, Sam! The best bit is still coming. Do you know what the winner's trophy is? A beautiful big chamber pot with roses on the side, and it's full to the brim with piss. And guess who I think is going to be this year's winner.

SAM (*almost shouting*): Stop now!

HALLY (*suddenly appalled by how far he has gone*): Why?

SAM: Hally? It's your father you're talking about.

HALLY: So?

SAM: Do you know what you've been saying?

(*Hally can't answer. He is rigid with shame. Sam speaks to him sternly.*)

No, Hally, you mustn't do it. Take back those words and ask for forgiveness! It's a terrible sin for a son to mock his father with jokes like that. You'll be punished if you carry on. Your father is your father, even if he is a . . . cripple man.

WILLIE: Yes, Master Hally. Is true what Sam say.

SAM: I understand how you are feeling, Hally, but even so. . . .

HALLY: No, you don't!

SAM: I think I do.

HALLY: And I'm telling you you don't. Nobody does. (*Speaking carefully as his shame turns to rage at Sam.*) It's your turn to be careful, Sam. Very careful! You're treading on dangerous ground. Leave me and my father alone.

SAM: I'm not the one who's been saying things about him.

HALLY: What goes on between me and my Dad is none of your business!

SAM: Then don't tell me about it. If that's all you've got to say about him, I don't want to hear.

(*For a moment Hally is at loss for a response.*)

HALLY: Just get on with your bloody work and shut up.

SAM: Swearing at me won't help you.

HALLY: Yes, it does! Mind your own fucking business and shut up!

SAM: Okay. If that's the way you want it, I'll stop trying.

(*He turns away. This infuriates Hally even more.*)

HALLY: Good. Because what you've been trying to do is meddle in something you know nothing about. All that concerns you in here, Sam, is to try and do what you get paid for—keep the place clean and serve the customers. In plain words, just get on with your job. My mother is right. She's always warning me about allowing you to get too familiar. Well, this time you've gone too far. It's going to stop right now.

(*No response from Sam.*)

You're only a servant in here, and don't forget it.

(*Still no response. Hally is trying hard to get one.*)

And as far as my father is concerned, all you need to remember is that he is your boss.

SAM (*needled at last*): No, he isn't. I get paid by your mother.

HALLY: Don't argue with me, Sam!

SAM: Then don't say he's my boss.

HALLY: He's a white man and that's good enough for you.

SAM: I'll try to forget you said that.

HALLY: Don't! Because you won't be doing me a favor if you do. I'm telling you to remember it.

(*A pause. Sam pulls himself together and makes one last effort.*)

SAM: Hally, Hally . . . ! Come on now. Let's stop before it's too late. You're right. We *are* on dangerous ground. If we're not careful, somebody is going to get hurt.

HALLY: It won't be me.

SAM: Don't be so sure.

HALLY: I don't know what you're talking about, Sam.

SAM: Yes, you do.

HALLY (*furious*): Jesus, I wish you would stop trying to tell me what I do and what I don't know.

(*Sam gives up. He turns to Willie.*)

SAM: Let's finish up.

HALLY: Don't turn your back on me! I haven't finished talking.

(*He grabs Sam by the arm and tries to make him turn around. Sam reacts with a flash of anger.*)

SAM: Don't do that, Hally! (*Facing the boy.*) All right, I'm listening. Well? What do you want to say to me?

HALLY (*pause as Hally looks for something to say*): To begin with, why don't you also start calling me Master Harold, like Willie.

SAM: Do you mean that?

HALLY: Why the hell do you think I said it?

SAM: And if I don't?

HALLY: You might just lose your job.

SAM (*quietly and very carefully*): If you make me say it once, I'll never call you anything else again.

HALLY: So? (*The boy confronts the man.*) Is that meant to be a threat?

SAM: Just telling you what will happen if you make me do that. You must decide what it means to you.

HALLY: Well, I have. It's good news. Because that is exactly what Master Harold wants from now on. Think of it as a little lesson in respect, Sam, that's long overdue, and I hope you remember it as well as you do your geography. I can tell you now that somebody who will be glad to hear I've finally given it to you will be my Dad. Yes! He agrees with my Mom. He's always going on about it as well. "You must teach the boys to show you more respect, my son."

SAM: So now you can stop complaining about going home. Everybody is going to be happy tonight.

HALLY: That's perfectly correct. You see, you mustn't get the wrong idea about me and my Dad, Sam. We also have our good times together. Some bloody good laughs. He's got a marvelous sense of humor. Want to know what our favorite joke is? He gives out a big groan, you see, and says: "It's not fair, is it, Hally?" Then I have to ask: "What, chum?" And then he says: "A nigger's arse". . . and we both have a good laugh.

(*The men stare at him with disbelief.*)

What's the matter, Willie? Don't you catch the joke? You always were a bit slow on the uptake. It's what is called a pun. You see, fair means both light in color and to be just and decent. (*He turns to Sam.*) I thought *you* would catch it, Sam.

SAM: Oh ja, I catch it all right.

HALLY: But it doesn't appeal to your sense of humor.

SAM: Do you really laugh?

HALLY: Of course.

SAM: To please him? Make him feel good?

HALLY: No, for heavens sake! I laugh because I think it's a bloody good joke.

SAM: You're really trying hard to be ugly, aren't you? And why drag poor old Willie into it? He's done nothing to you except show you the respect you want so badly. That's also not being fair, you know . . . and *I* mean just or decent.

WILLIE: It's all right, Sam. Leave it now.

SAM: It's me you're after. You should just have said "Sam's arse". . . because that's the one you're trying to kick. Anyway, how do you know it's not fair? You've never seen it. Do you want to? (*He drops his trousers and underpants and presents his backside for Hally's inspection.*) Have a

good look. A real Basuto arse . . . which is about as nigger as they can
come. Satisfied? (*Trousers up.*) Now you can make your Dad even happier when you go home tonight. Tell him I showed you my arse and he
is quite right. It's not fair. And if it will give him an even better laugh
next time, I'll also let *him* have a look. Come, Willie, let's finish up and
go.

(*Sam and Willie start to tidy up the tea room. Hally doesn't move. He waits for
a moment when Sam passes him.*)

HALLY (*quietly*): Sam . . .

(*Sam stops and looks expectantly at the boy. Hally spits in his face. A long and
heartfelt groan from Willie. For a few seconds Sam doesn't move.*)

SAM (*taking out a handkerchief and wiping his face*): It's all right, Willie.

(*To Hally.*)

Ja, well, you've done it . . . Master Harold. Yes, I'll start calling you
that from now on. It won't be difficult anymore. You've hurt yourself,
Master Harold. I saw it coming. I warned you, but you wouldn't listen.
You've just hurt yourself *bad.* And you're a coward, Master Harold.
The face you should be spitting in is your father's . . . but you used
mine, because you think you're safe inside your fair skin . . . and this
time I don't mean just or decent. (*Pause, then moving violently toward
Hally.*) Should I hit him, Willie?

WILLIE (*stopping Sam*): No, Boet Sam.

SAM (*violently*): Why not?

WILLIE: It won't help, Boet Sam.

SAM: I don't want to help! I want to hurt him.

WILLIE: You also hurt yourself.

SAM: And if he had done it to you, Willie?

WILLIE: Me? Spit at me like I was a dog? (*A thought that had not occurred
to him before. He looks at Hally.*) Ja. Then I want to hit him. I want to hit
him hard!

(*A dangerous few seconds as the men stand staring at the boy. Willie turns
away, shaking his head.*)

But maybe all I do is go cry at the back. He's little boy, Boet Sam. Little
white boy. Long trousers now, but he's still little boy.

SAM (*his violence ebbing away into defeat as quickly as it flooded*): You're
right. So go on, then: groan again, Willie. You do it better than me. (*To
Hally.*) You don't know all of what you've just done . . . Master Harold.
It's not just that you've made me feel dirtier than I've ever been in my
life . . . I mean, how do I wash off yours and your father's filth? . . . I've

also failed. A long time ago I promised myself I was going to try and do something, but you've just shown me . . . Master Harold . . . that I've failed. (*Pause.*) I've also got a memory of a little white boy when he was still wearing short trousers and a black man, but they're not flying a kite. It was the old Jubilee days, after dinner one night. I was in my room. You came in and just stood against the wall, looking down at the ground, and only after I'd asked you what you wanted, what was wrong, I don't know how many times, did you speak and even then so softly I almost didn't hear you. "Sam, please help me to go and fetch my Dad." Remember? He was dead drunk on the floor of the Central Hotel Bar. They'd phoned for your Mom, but you were the only one at home. And do you remember how we did it? You went in first by yourself to ask permission for me to go into the bar. Then I loaded him onto my back like a baby and carried him back to the boarding house with you following behind carrying his crutches. (*Shaking his head as he remembers.*) A crowded Main Street with all the people watching a little white boy following his drunk father on a nigger's back! I felt for that little boy . . . Master Harold. I felt for him. After that we still had to clean him up, remember? He'd messed in his trousers, so we had to clean him up and get him into bed.

HALLY (*great pain*): I love him, Sam.

SAM: I know you do. That's why I tried to stop you from saying these things about him. It would have been so simple if you could have just despised him for being a weak man. But he's your father. You love him and you're ashamed of him. You're ashamed of so much! . . . And now that's going to include yourself. That was the promise I made to myself: to try and stop that happening. (*Pause.*) After we got him to bed you came back with me to my room and sat in a corner and carried on just looking down at the ground. And for days after that! You hadn't done anything wrong, but you went around as if you owed the world an apology for being alive. I didn't like seeing that! That's not the way a boy grows up to be a man! . . . But the one person who should have been teaching you what that means was the cause of your shame. If you really want to know, that's why I made you that kite. I wanted you to look up, be proud of something, of yourself . . . (*bitter smile at the memory*) . . . and you certainly were that when I left you with it up there on the hill. Oh, ja . . . something else! . . . If you ever do write it as a short story, there *was* a twist in our ending. I couldn't sit down there and stay with you. It was a "Whites Only" bench. You were too young, too excited to notice then. But not anymore. If you're not careful . . . Master Harold . . . you're going to be sitting up there by yourself for a long time to come, and there won't be a kite in the sky. (*Sam has got nothing more to say. He exits into the kitchen, taking off his waiter's jacket.*)

WILLIE: Is bad. Is all bad in here now.

HALLY (*books into his school case, raincoat on*): Willie . . . (*It is difficult to speak.*) Will you lock up for me and look after the keys?

WILLIE: Okay.

(*Sam returns. Hally goes behind the counter and collects the few coins in the cash register. As he starts to leave. . . .*)

SAM: Don't forget the comic books.

(*Hally returns to the counter and puts them in his case. He starts to leave again.*)

SAM (*to the retreating back of the boy*): Stop . . . Hally. . . .

(*Hally stops, but doesn't turn to face him.*)

Hally . . . I've got no right to tell you what being a man means if I don't behave like one myself, and I'm not doing so well at that this afternoon. Should we try again, Hally?

HALLY: Try what?

SAM: Fly another kite, I suppose. It worked once, and this time I need it as much as you do.

HALLY: It's still raining, Sam. You can't fly kites on rainy days, remember.

SAM: So what do we do? Hope for better weather tomorrow?

HALLY (*helpless gesture*): I don't know. I don't know anything anymore.

SAM: You sure of that, Hally? Because it would be pretty hopeless if that was true. It would mean nothing has been learnt in here this afternoon, and there was a hell of a lot of teaching going on . . . one way or the other. But anyway, I don't believe you. I reckon there's one thing you know. You don't *have* to sit up there by yourself. You know what that bench means now, and you can leave it any time you choose. All you've got to do is stand up and walk away from it.

(*Hally leaves. Willie goes up quietly to Sam.*)

WILLIE: Is okay, Boet Sam. You see. Is . . . (*he can't find any better words*) . . . is going to be okay tomorrow. (*Changing his tone.*) Hey, Boet Sam! (*He is trying hard.*) You right. I think about it and you right. Tonight I find Hilda and say sorry. And make promise I won't beat her no more. You hear me, Boet Sam?

SAM: I hear you, Willie.

WILLIE: And when we practice I relax and romance with her from beginning to end. Nonstop! You watch! Two weeks' time: "First prize for promising newcomers: Mr. Willie Malopo and Miss Hilda Samuels." (*Sudden impulse.*) To hell with it! I walk home. (*He goes to the jukebox, puts in a coin and selects a record. The machine comes to life in the gray twilight, blushing its way through a spectrum of soft, romantic colors.*) **How did you say it, Boet Sam? Let's dream.** (*Willie sways with the music and gestures for Sam to dance.*)

(*Sarah Vaughan sings.*)

"Little man you're crying,
I know why you're blue,
Someone took your kiddy car away;
Better go to sleep now,
Little man you've had a busy day." (*etc., etc.*)
You lead. I follow.

(*The men dance together.*)

"Johnny won your marbles,
Tell you what we'll do;
Dad will get you new ones right away;
Better go to sleep now,
Little man you've had a busy day."

[1982]

AUGUST WILSON [b. 1945]

The Piano Lesson

Gin my cotton
Sell my seed
Buy my baby
Everything she need
— SKIP JAMES

Characters

DOAKER
BOY WILLIE
LYMON
BERNIECE
MARETHA
AVERY
WINING BOY
GRACE

The Setting: *The action of the play takes place in the kitchen and parlor of the house where Doaker Charles lives with his niece, Berniece, and her eleven-year-old daughter, Maretha. The house is sparsely furnished, and although there is evidence of a woman's touch, there is a lack of warmth and vigor. Berniece and Maretha occupy the upstairs rooms. Doaker's room is prominent and opens onto the kitchen. Dominating the parlor is an old upright piano. On the legs of the piano, carved in the manner of African sculpture, are mask-like figures resembling totems. The carvings are rendered with a grace and power of invention that lifts them out of the realm of craftsmanship and into the realm of art. At left is a staircase leading to the upstairs.*

ACT 1   Scene 1

(The lights come up on the Charles household. It is five o'clock in the morning. The dawn is beginning to announce itself, but there is something in the air that belongs to the night. A stillness that is a portent, a gathering, a coming together of something akin to a storm. There is a loud knock at the door.)

1191

BOY WILLIE (*offstage, calling*): Hey, Doaker . . . Doaker!

(*He knocks again and calls.*)

Hey, Doaker! Hey, Berniece! Berniece!

(*Doaker enters from his room. He is a tall, thin man of forty-seven, with severe features, who has for all intents and purposes retired from the world though he works full-time as a railroad cook.*)

DOAKER: Who is it?

BOY WILLIE: Open the door, nigger! It's me . . . Boy Willie!

DOAKER: Who?

BOY WILLIE: Boy Willie! Open the door!

(*Doaker opens the door and Boy Willie and Lymon enter. Boy Willie is thirty years old. He has an infectious grin and a boyishness that is apt for his name. He is brash and impulsive, talkative and somewhat crude in speech and manner. Lymon is twenty-nine. Boy Willie's partner, he talks little, and then with a straightforwardness that is often disarming.*)

DOAKER: What you doing up here?

BOY WILLIE: I told you, Lymon. Lymon talking about you might be sleep. This is Lymon. You remember Lymon Jackson from down home? This my Uncle Doaker.

DOAKER: What you doing up here? I couldn't figure out who that was. I thought you was still down in Mississippi.

BOY WILLIE: Me and Lymon selling watermelons. We got a truck out there. Got a whole truckload of watermelons. We brought them up here to sell. Where's Berniece?

(*Calls.*)

Hey, Berniece!

DOAKER: Berniece up there sleep.

BOY WILLIE: Well, let her get up.

(*Calls.*)

Hey, Berniece!

DOAKER: She got to go to work in the morning.

BOY WILLIE: Well she can get up and say hi. It's been three years since I seen her.

(*Calls.*)

Hey, Berniece! It's me . . . Boy Willie.

DOAKER: Berniece don't like all that hollering now. She got to work in the morning.

BOY WILLIE: She can go on back to bed. Me and Lymon been riding two
 days in that truck . . . the least she can do is get up and say hi.
DOAKER (*looking out the window*): Where you all get that truck from?
BOY WILLIE: It's Lymon's. I told him let's get a load of watermelons and
 bring them up here.
LYMON: Boy Willie say he going back, but I'm gonna stay. See what it's
 like up here.
BOY WILLIE: You gonna carry me down there first.
LYMON: I told you I ain't going back down there and take a chance on
 that truck breaking down again. You can take the train. Hey, tell him
 Doaker, he can take the train back. After we sell them watermelons he
 have enough money he can buy him a whole railroad car.
DOAKER: You got all them watermelons stacked up there no wonder the
 truck broke down. I'm surprised you made it this far with a load like
 that. Where you break down at?
BOY WILLIE: We broke down three times! It took us two and a half days
 to get here. It's a good thing we picked them watermelons fresh.
LYMON: We broke down twice in West Virginia. The first time was just as
 soon as we got out of Sunflower. About forty miles out she broke
 down. We got it going and got all the way to West Virginia before she
 broke down again.
BOY WILLIE: We had to walk about five miles for some water.
LYMON: It got a hole in the radiator but it runs pretty good. You have to
 pump the brakes sometime before they catch. Boy Willie have his door
 open and be ready to jump when that happens.
BOY WILLIE: Lymon think that's funny. I told the nigger I give him ten
 dollars to get the brakes fixed. But he thinks that funny.
LYMON: They don't need fixing. All you got to do is pump them till they
 catch.

(*Berniece enters on the stairs. Thirty-five years old, with an eleven-year-old
daughter, she is still in mourning for her husband after three years.*)

BERNIECE: What you doing all that hollering for?
BOY WILLIE: Hey, Berniece. Doaker said you was sleep. I said at least you
 could get up and say hi.
BERNIECE: It's five o'clock in the morning and you come in here with all
 this noise. You can't come like normal folks. You got to bring all that
 noise with you.
BOY WILLIE: Hell, I ain't done nothing but come in and say hi. I ain't got
 in the house good.
BERNIECE: That's what I'm talking about. You start all that hollering and
 carry on as soon as you hit the door.

BOY WILLIE: Aw hell, woman, I was glad to see Doaker. You ain't had to come down if you didn't want to. I come eighteen hundred miles to see my sister I figure she might want to get up and say hi. Other than that you can go back upstairs. What you got, Doaker? Where your bottle? Me and Lymon want a drink.

(*To Berniece.*)

This is Lymon. You remember Lymon Jackson from down home.

LYMON: How you doing, Berniece. You look just like I thought you looked.

BERNIECE: Why you all got to come in hollering and carrying on? Waking the neighbors with all that noise.

BOY WILLIE: They can come over and join the party. We fixing to have a party. Doaker, where your bottle? Me and Lymon celebrating. The Ghosts of the Yellow Dog got Sutter.

BERNIECE: Say what?

BOY WILLIE: Ask Lymon, they found him the next morning. Say he drowned in his well.

DOAKER: When this happen, Boy Willie?

BOY WILLIE: About three weeks ago. Me and Lymon was over in Stoner County when we heard about it. We laughed. We thought it was funny. A great big old three-hundred-and-forty-pound man gonna fall down his well.

LYMON: It remind me of Humpty Dumpty.

BOY WILLIE: Everybody say the Ghosts of the Yellow Dog pushed him.

BERNIECE: I don't want to hear that nonsense. Somebody down there pushing them people in their wells.

DOAKER: What was you and Lymon doing over in Stoner County?

BOY WILLIE: We was down there working. Lymon got some people down there.

LYMON: My cousin got some land down there. We was helping him.

BOY WILLIE: Got near about a hundred acres. He got it set up real nice. Me and Lymon was down there chopping down trees. We was using Lymon's truck to haul the wood. Me and Lymon used to haul wood all around them parts.

(*To Berniece.*)

Me and Lymon got a truckload of watermelons out there.

(*Berniece crosses to the window to the parlor.*)

Doaker, where your bottle? I know you got a bottle stuck up in your room. Come on, me and Lymon want a drink.

(*Doaker exits into his room.*)

BERNIECE: Where you all get that truck from?

BOY WILLIE: I told you it's Lymon's.

BERNIECE: Where you get the truck from, Lymon?

LYMON: I bought it.

BERNIECE: Where he get that truck from, Boy Willie?

BOY WILLIE: He told you he bought it. Bought it for a hundred and twenty dollars. I can't say where he got that hundred and twenty dollars from . . . but he bought that old piece of truck from Henry Porter. (*To Lymon.*) Where you get that hundred and twenty dollars from, nigger?

LYMON: I got it like you get yours. I know how to take care of money.

(*Doaker brings a bottle and sets it on the table.*)

BOY WILLIE: Aw hell, Doaker got some of that good whiskey. Don't give Lymon none of that. He ain't used to good whiskey. He liable to get sick.

LYMON: I done had good whiskey before.

BOY WILLIE: Lymon bought that truck so he have him a place to sleep. He down there wasn't doing no work or nothing. Sheriff looking for him. He bought that truck to keep away from the sheriff. Got Stovall looking for him too. He down there sleeping in that truck ducking and dodging both of them. I told him come on let's go up and see my sister.

BERNIECE: What the sheriff looking for you for, Lymon?

BOY WILLIE: The man don't want you to know all his business. He's my company. He ain't asking you no questions.

LYMON: It wasn't nothing. It was just a misunderstanding.

BERNIECE: He in my house. You say the sheriff looking for him, I wanna know what he looking for him for. Otherwise you all can go back out there and be where nobody don't have to ask you nothing.

LYMON: It was just a misunderstanding. Sometimes me and the sheriff we don't think alike. So we just got crossed on each other.

BERNIECE: Might be looking for him about that truck. He might have stole that truck.

BOY WILLIE: We ain't stole no truck, woman. I told you Lymon bought it.

DOAKER: Boy Willie and Lymon got more sense than to ride all the way up here in a stolen truck with a load of watermelons. Now they might have stole them watermelons, but I don't believe they stole that truck.

BOY WILLIE: You don't even know the man good and you calling him a thief. And we ain't stole them watermelons either. Them old man Pitterford's watermelons. He give me and Lymon all we could load for ten dollars.

DOAKER: No wonder you got them stacked up out there. You must have five hundred watermelons stacked up out there.

BERNIECE: Boy Willie, when you and Lymon planning on going back?

BOY WILLIE: Lymon say he staying. As soon as we sell them watermelons I'm going on back.

BERNIECE (*starts to exit up the stairs*): That's what you need to do. And you need to do it quick. Come in here disrupting the house. I don't want all that loud carrying on around here. I'm surprised you ain't woke Maretha up.

BOY WILLIE: I was fixing to get her now.

(*Calls.*)

Hey, Maretha!

DOAKER: Berniece don't like all that hollering now.

BERNIECE: Don't you wake that child up!

BOY WILLIE: You going up there . . . wake her up and tell her her uncle's here. I ain't seen her in three years. Wake her up and send her down here. She can go back to bed.

BERNIECE: I ain't waking that child up . . . and don't you be making all that noise. You and Lymon need to sell them watermelons and go on back.

(*Berniece exits up the stairs.*)

BOY WILLIE: I see Berniece still try to be stuck up.

DOAKER: Berniece alright. She don't want you making all that noise. Maretha up there sleep. Let her sleep until she get up. She can see you then.

BOY WILLIE: I ain't thinking about Berniece. You hear from Wining Boy? You know Cleotha died?

DOAKER: Yeah, I heard that. He come by here about a year ago. Had a whole sack of money. He stayed here about two weeks. Ain't offered nothing. Berniece asked him for three dollars to buy some food and he got mad and left.

LYMON: Who's Wining Boy?

BOY WILLIE: That's my uncle. That's Doaker's brother. You heard me talk about Wining Boy. He play piano. He done made some records and everything. He still doing that, Doaker?

DOAKER: He made one or two records a long time ago. That's the only ones I ever known him to make. If you let him tell it he a big recording star.

BOY WILLIE: He stopped down home about two years ago. That's what I hear. I don't know. Me and Lymon was up on Parchman Farm doing them three years.

DOAKER: He don't never stay in one place. Now, he been here about eight months ago. Back in the winter. Now, you subject not to see him for another two years. It's liable to be that long before he stop by.

BOY WILLIE: If he had a whole sack of money you liable never to see him. You ain't gonna see him until he get broke. Just as soon as that sack of money is gone you look up and he be on your doorstep.

LYMON (*noticing the piano*): Is that the piano?

BOY WILLIE: Yeah . . . look here, Lymon. See how it's carved up real nice and polished and everything? You never find you another piano like that.

LYMON: Yeah, that look real nice.

BOY WILLIE: I told you. See how it's polished? My mama used to polish it every day. See all them pictures carved on it? That's what I was talking about. You can get a nice price for that piano.

LYMON: That's all Boy Willie talked about the whole trip up here. I got tired of hearing him talk about the piano.

BOY WILLIE: All you want to talk about is women. You ought to hear this nigger, Doaker. Talking about all the women he gonna get when he get up here. He ain't had none down there but he gonna get a hundred when he get up here.

DOAKER: How your people doing down there, Lymon?

LYMON: They alright. They still there. I come up here to see what it's like up here. Boy Willie trying to get me to go back and farm with him.

BOY WILLIE: Sutter's brother selling the land. He say he gonna sell it to me. That's why I come up here. I got one part of it. Sell them watermelons and get me another part. Get Berniece to sell that piano and I'll have the third part.

DOAKER: Berniece ain't gonna sell that piano.

BOY WILLIE: I'm gonna talk to her. When she see I got a chance to get Sutter's land she'll come around.

DOAKER: You can put that thought out your mind. Berniece ain't gonna sell that piano.

BOY WILLIE: I'm gonna talk to her. She been playing on it?

DOAKER: You know she won't touch that piano. I ain't never known her to touch it since Mama Ola died. That's over seven years now. She say it got blood on it. She got Maretha playing on it though. Say Maretha can go on and do everything she can't do. Got her in an extra school down at the Irene Kaufman Settlement House. She want Maretha to grow up and be a schoolteacher. Say she good enough she can teach on the piano.

BOY WILLIE: Maretha don't need to be playing on no piano. She can play on the guitar.

DOAKER: How much land Sutter got left?

BOY WILLIE: Got a hundred acres. Good land. He done sold it piece by piece, he kept the good part for himself. Now he got to give that up. His brother come down from Chicago for the funeral . . . he up there in Chicago got some kind of business with soda fountain equipment. He anxious to sell the land, Doaker. He don't want to be bothered with it. He called me to him and said cause of how long our families done known each other and how we been good friends and all, say he wanted to sell the land to me. Say he'd rather see me with it than Jim Stovall. Told me he'd let me have it for two thousand dollars cash money. He don't know I found out the most Stovall would give him for it was fifteen hundred dollars. He trying to get that extra five hundred out of me telling me he doing me a favor. I thanked him just as nice. Told him what a good man Sutter was and how he had my sympathy and all. Told him to give me two weeks. He said he'd wait on me. That's why I come up here. Sell them watermelons. Get Berniece to sell that piano. Put them two parts with the part I done saved. Walk in there. Tip my hat. Lay my money down on the table. Get my deed and walk on out. This time I get to keep all the cotton. Hire me some men to work it for me. Gin my cotton. Get my seed. And I'll see you again next year. Might even plant some tobacco or some oats.

DOAKER: You gonna have a hard time trying to get Berniece to sell that piano. You know Avery Brown from down there don't you? He up here now. He followed Berniece up here trying to get her to marry him after Crawley got killed. He been up here about two years. He call himself a preacher now.

BOY WILLIE: I know Avery. I know him from when he used to work on the Willshaw place. Lymon know him too.

DOAKER: He after Berniece to marry him. She keep telling him no but he won't give up. He keep pressing her on it.

BOY WILLIE: Avery think all white men is bigshots. He don't know there some white men ain't got as much as he got.

DOAKER: He supposed to come past here this morning. Berniece going down to the bank with him to see if he can get a loan to start his church. That's why I know Berniece ain't gonna sell that piano. He tried to get her to sell it to help him start his church. Sent the man around and everything.

BOY WILLIE: What man?

DOAKER: Some white fellow was going around to all the colored people's houses looking to buy up musical instruments. He'd buy anything. Drums. Guitars. Harmonicas. Pianos. Avery sent him past here. He looked at the piano and got excited. Offered her a nice price. She turned him down and got on Avery for sending him past. The man kept on her about two weeks. He seen where she wasn't gonna sell it, he gave her his number and told her if she ever wanted to sell it to call him first. Say he'd go one better than what anybody else would give her for it.

BOY WILLIE: How much he offer her for it?

DOAKER: Now you know me. She didn't say and I didn't ask. I just know it was a nice price.

LYMON: All you got to do is find out who he is and tell him somebody else wanna buy it from you. Tell him you can't make up your mind who to sell it to, and if he like Doaker say, he'll give you anything you want for it.

BOY WILLIE: That's what I'm gonna do. I'm gonna find out who he is from Avery.

DOAKER: It ain't gonna do you no good. Berniece ain't gonna sell that piano.

BOY WILLIE: She ain't got to sell it. I'm gonna sell it. I own just as much of it as she does.

BERNIECE (offstage, hollers): Doaker! Go on get away. Doaker!

DOAKER (calling): Berniece?

(Doaker and Boy Willie rush to the stairs, Boy Willie runs up the stairs, passing Berniece as she enters, running.)

DOAKER: Berniece, what's the matter? You alright? What's the matter?

(Berniece tries to catch her breath. She is unable to speak.)

DOAKER: That's alright. Take your time. You alright. What's the matter?

(He calls.)

Hey, Boy Willie?

BOY WILLIE (offstage): Ain't nobody up here.

BERNIECE: Sutter . . . Sutter's standing at the top of the steps.

DOAKER (calls): Boy Willie!

(Lymon crosses to the stairs and looks up. Boy Willie enters from the stairs.)

BOY WILLIE: Hey Doaker, what's wrong with her? Berniece, what's wrong? Who was you talking to?

DOAKER: She say she seen Sutter's ghost standing at the top of the stairs.

BOY WILLIE: Seen what? Sutter? She ain't seen no Sutter.

BERNIECE: He was standing right up there.

BOY WILLIE (entering on the stairs): That's all in Berniece's head. Ain't nobody up there. Go on up there, Doaker.

DOAKER: I'll take your word for it. Berniece talking about what she seen. She say Sutter's ghost standing at the top of the steps. She ain't just make all that up.

BOY WILLIE: She up there dreaming. She ain't seen no ghost.

LYMON: You want a glass of water, Berniece? Get her a glass of water, Boy Willie.

BOY WILLIE: She don't need no water. She ain't seen nothing. Go on up there and look. Ain't nobody up there but Maretha.

DOAKER: Let Berniece tell it.

BOY WILLIE: I ain't stopping her from telling it.

DOAKER: What happened, Berniece?

BERNIECE: I come out my room to come back down here and Sutter was standing there in the hall.

BOY WILLIE: What he look like?

BERNIECE: He look like Sutter. He look like he always look.

BOY WILLIE: Sutter couldn't find his way from Big Sandy to Little Sandy. How he gonna find his way all the way up here to Pittsburgh? Sutter ain't never even heard of Pittsburgh.

DOAKER: Go on, Berniece.

BERNIECE: Just standing there with the blue suit on.

BOY WILLIE: The man ain't never left Marlin County when he was living . . . and he's gonna come all the way up here now that he's dead?

DOAKER: Let her finish. I want to hear what she got to say.

BOY WILLIE: I'll tell you this. If Berniece had seen him like she think she seen him she'd still be running.

DOAKER: Go on, Berniece. Don't pay Boy Willie no mind.

BERNIECE: He was standing there . . . had his hand on top of his head. Look like he might have thought if he took his hand down his head might have fallen off.

LYMON: Did he have on a hat?

BERNIECE: Just had on that blue suit . . . I told him to go away and he just stood there looking at me . . . calling Boy Willie's name.

BOY WILLIE: What he calling my name for?

BERNIECE: I believe you pushed him in the well.

BOY WILLIE: Now what kind of sense that make? You telling me I'm gonna go out there and hide in the weeds with all them dogs and things he got around there . . . I'm gonna hide and wait till I catch him looking down his well just right . . . then I'm gonna run over and push him in. A great big old three-hundred-and-forty-pound man.

BERNIECE: Well, what he calling your name for?

BOY WILLIE: He bending over looking down his well, woman . . . how he know who pushed him? It could have been anybody. Where was you when Sutter fell in his well? Where was Doaker? Me and Lymon was over in Stoner County. Tell her, Lymon. The Ghosts of the Yellow Dog got Sutter. That's what happened to him.

BERNIECE: You can talk all that Ghosts of the Yellow Dog stuff if you want. I know better.

LYMON: The Ghosts of the Yellow Dog pushed him. That's what the people say. They found him in his well and all the people say it must be the Ghosts of the Yellow Dog. Just like all them other men.

BOY WILLIE: Come talking about he looking for me. What he come all the way up here for? If he looking for me all he got to do is wait. He could have saved himself a trip if he looking for me. That ain't nothing but in Berniece's head. Ain't no telling what she liable to come up with next.

BERNIECE: Boy Willie, I want you and Lymon to go ahead and leave my house. Just go on somewhere. You don't do nothing but bring trouble with you everywhere you go. If it wasn't for you Crawley would still be alive.

BOY WILLIE: Crawley what? I ain't had nothing to do with Crawley getting killed. Crawley three time seven. He had his own mind.

BERNIECE: Just go on and leave. Let Sutter go somewhere else looking for you.

BOY WILLIE: I'm leaving. Soon as we sell them watermelons. Other than that I ain't going nowhere. Hell, I just got here. Talking about Sutter looking for me. Sutter was looking for that piano. That's what he was looking for. He had to die to find out where that piano was at . . . If I was you I'd get rid of it. That's the way to get rid of Sutter's ghost. Get rid of that piano.

BERNIECE: I want you and Lymon to go on and take all this confusion out of my house!

BOY WILLIE: Hey, tell her, Doaker. What kind of sense that make? I told you, Lymon, as soon as Berniece see me she was gonna start something. Didn't I tell you that? Now she done made up that story about Sutter just so she could tell me to leave her house. Well, hell, I ain't going nowhere till I sell them watermelons.

BERNIECE: Well why don't you go out there and sell them! Sell them and go on back!

BOY WILLIE: We waiting till the people get up.

LYMON: Boy Willie say if you get out there too early and wake the people up they get mad at you and won't buy nothing from you.

DOAKER: You won't be waiting long. You done let the sun catch up with you. This the time everybody be getting up around here.

BERNIECE: Come on, Doaker, walk up here with me. Let me get Maretha up and get her started. I got to get ready myself. Boy Willie, just go on out there and sell them watermelons and you and Lymon leave my house.

(Berniece and Doaker exit up the stairs.)

BOY WILLIE *(calling after them)*: If you see Sutter up there . . . tell him I'm down here waiting on him.

LYMON: What if she see him again?

BOY WILLIE: That's all in her head. There ain't no ghost up there.

(Calls.)

   Hey, Doaker . . . I told you ain't nothing up there.

LYMON: I'm glad he didn't say he was looking for me.

BOY WILLIE: I wish I would see Sutter's ghost. Give me a chance to put a whupping on him.

LYMON: You ought to stay up here with me. You be down there working his land . . . he might come looking for you all the time.

BOY WILLIE: I ain't thinking about Sutter. And I ain't thinking about staying up here. You stay up here. I'm going back and get Sutter's land. You think you ain't got to work up here. You think this the land of milk and honey. But I ain't scared of work. I'm going back and farm every acre of that land.

(*Doaker enters from the stairs.*)

I told you there ain't nothing up there, Doaker. Berniece dreaming all that.

DOAKER: I believe Berniece seen something. Berniece levelheaded. She ain't just made all that up. She say Sutter had on a suit. I don't believe she ever seen Sutter in a suit. I believe that's what he was buried in, and that's what Berniece saw.

BOY WILLIE: Well, let her keep on seeing him then. As long as he don't mess with me.

(*Doaker starts to cook his breakfast.*)

I heard about you, Doaker. They say you got all the women looking out for you down home. They be looking to see you coming. Say you got a different one every two weeks. Say they be fighting one another for you to stay with them.

(*To Lymon.*)

Look at him, Lymon. He know it's true.

DOAKER: I ain't thinking about no women. They never get me tied up with them. After Coreen I ain't got no use for them. I stay up on Jack Slattery's place when I be down there. All them women want is somebody with a steady payday.

BOY WILLIE: That ain't what I hear. I hear every two weeks the women all put on their dresses and line up at the railroad station.

DOAKER: I don't get down there but once a month. I used to go down there every two weeks but they keep switching me around. They keep switching all the fellows around.

BOY WILLIE: Doaker can't turn that railroad loose. He was working the railroad when I was walking around crying for sugartit. My mama used to brag on him.

DOAKER: I'm cooking now, but I used to line track. I pieced together the Yellow Dog stitch by stitch. Rail by rail. Line track all up around there. I lined track all up around Sunflower and Clarksdale. Wining Boy worked with me. He helped put in some of that track. He'd work it for six months and quit. Go back to playing piano and gambling.

BOY WILLIE: How long you been with the railroad now?

DOAKER: Twenty-seven years. Now, I'll tell you something about the railroad. What I done learned after twenty-seven years. See, you got North. You got West. You look over here you got South. Over there you got East. Now, you can start from anywhere. Don't care where you at. You got to go one of them four ways. And whichever way you decide to go they got a railroad that will take you there. Now, that's something simple. You think anybody would be able to understand that. But you'd be surprised how many people trying to go North get on a train going West. They think the train's supposed to go where they going rather than where it's going.

Now, why people going? Their sister's sick. They leaving before they kill somebody . . . and they sitting across from somebody who's leaving to keep from getting killed. They leaving cause they can't get satisfied. They going to meet someone. I wish I had a dollar for every time that someone wasn't at the station to meet them. I done seen that a lot. In between the time they sent the telegram and the time the person get there . . . they done forgot all about them.

They got so many trains out there they have a hard time keeping them from running into each other. Got trains going every whichaway. Got people on all of them. Somebody going where somebody just left. If everybody stay in one place I believe this would be a better world. Now what I done learned after twenty-seven years of railroading is this . . . if the train stays on the track . . . it's going to get where it's going. It might not be where you going. If it ain't, then all you got to do is sit and wait cause the train's coming back to get you. The train don't never stop. It'll come back every time. Now I'll tell you another thing . . .

BOY WILLIE: What you cooking over there, Doaker? Me and Lymon's hungry.

DOAKER: Go on down there to Wylie and Kirkpatrick to Eddie's restaurant. Coffee cost a nickel and you can get two eggs, sausage, and grits for fifteen cents. He even give you a biscuit with it.

BOY WILLIE: That look good what you got. Give me a little piece of that grilled bread.

DOAKER: Here . . . go on take the whole piece.

BOY WILLIE: Here you go, Lymon . . . you want a piece?

(*He gives Lymon a piece of toast. Maretha enters from the stairs.*)

BOY WILLIE: Hey, sugar. Come here and give me a hug. Come on give Uncle Boy Willie a hug. Don't be shy. Look at her, Doaker. She done got bigger. Ain't she got big?

DOAKER: Yeah, she getting up there.

BOY WILLIE: How you doing, sugar?

MARETHA: Fine.

BOY WILLIE: You was just a little old thing last time I seen you. You
   remember me, don't you? This your Uncle Boy Willie from down
   South. That there's Lymon. He my friend. We come up here to sell
   watermelons. You like watermelons?

(Maretha nods.)

   We got a whole truckload out front. You can have as many as you
   want. What you been doing?

MARETHA: Nothing.

BOY WILLIE: Don't be shy now. Look at you getting all big. How old is you?

MARETHA: Eleven. I'm gonna be twelve soon.

BOY WILLIE: You like it up here? You like the North?

MARETHA: It's alright.

BOY WILLIE: That there's Lymon. Did you say hi to Lymon?

MARETHA: Hi.

LYMON: How you doing? You look just like your mama. I remember you
   when you was wearing diapers.

BOY WILLIE: You gonna come down South and see me? Uncle Boy Willie
   gonna get him a farm. Gonna get a great big old farm. Come down
   there and I'll teach you how to ride a mule. Teach you how to kill a
   chicken, too.

MARETHA: I seen my mama do that.

BOY WILLIE: Ain't nothing to it. You just grab him by his neck and twist
   it. Get you a real good grip and then you just wring his neck and throw
   him in the pot. Cook him up. Then you got some good eating. What
   you like to eat? What kind of food you like?

MARETHA: I like everything . . . except I don't like no black-eyed peas.

BOY WILLIE: Uncle Doaker tell me your mama got you playing that
   piano. Come on play something for me.

(Boy Willie crosses over to the piano followed by Maretha.)

   Show me what you can do. Come on now. Here . . . Uncle Boy Willie
   give you a dime . . . show me what you can do. Don't be bashful now.
   That dime say you can't be bashful.

(Maretha plays. It is something any beginner first learns.)

   Here, let me show you something.

(Boy Willie sits and plays a simple boogie-woogie.)

   See that? See what I'm doing? That's what you call the boogie-woogie.
   See now . . . you can get up and dance to that. That's how good it

sound. It sound like you wanna dance. You can dance to that. It'll hold you up. Whatever kind of dance you wanna do you can dance to that right there. See that? See how it go? Ain't nothing to it. Go on you do it.

MARETHA: I got to read it on the paper.

BOY WILLIE: You don't need no paper. Go on. Do just like that there.

BERNIECE: Maretha! You get up here and get ready to go so you be on time. Ain't no need you trying to take advantage of company.

MARETHA: I got to go.

BOY WILLIE: Uncle Boy Willie gonna get you a guitar. Let Uncle Doaker teach you how to play that. You don't need to read no paper to play the guitar. Your mama told you about that piano? You know how them pictures got on there?

MARETHA: She say it just always been like that since she got it.

BOY WILLIE: You hear that, Doaker? And you sitting up here in the house with Berniece.

DOAKER: I ain't got nothing to do with that. I don't get in the way of Berniece's raising her.

BOY WILLIE: You tell your mama to tell you about that piano. You ask her how them pictures got on there. If she don't tell you I'll tell you.

BERNIECE: Maretha!

MARETHA: I got to get ready to go.

BOY WILLIE: She getting big, Doaker. You remember her, Lymon?

LYMON: She used to be real little.

(*There is a knock on the door. Doaker goes to answer it. Avery enters. Thirty-eight years old, honest and ambitious, he has taken to the city like a fish to water, finding in it opportunities for growth and advancement that did not exist for him in the rural South. He is dressed in a suit and tie with a gold cross around his neck. He carries a small Bible.*)

DOAKER: Hey, Avery, come on in. Berniece upstairs.

BOY WILLIE: Look at him . . . look at him . . . he don't know what to say. He wasn't expecting to see me.

AVERY: Hey, Boy Willie. What you doing up here?

BOY WILLIE: Look at him, Lymon.

AVERY: Is that Lymon? Lymon Jackson?

BOY WILLIE: Yeah, you know Lymon.

DOAKER: Berniece be ready in a minute, Avery.

BOY WILLIE: Doaker say you a preacher now. What . . . we supposed to call you Reverend? You used to be plain old Avery. When you get to be a preacher, nigger?

LYMON: Avery say he gonna be a preacher so he don't have to work.

BOY WILLIE: I remember when you was down there on the Willshaw place planting cotton. You wasn't thinking about no Reverend then.

AVERY: That must be your truck out there. I saw that truck with them watermelons, I was trying to figure out what it was doing in front of the house.

BOY WILLIE: Yeah, me and Lymon selling watermelons. That's Lymon's truck.

DOAKER: Berniece say you all going down to the bank.

AVERY: Yeah, they give me a half day off work. I got an appointment to talk to the bank about getting a loan to start my church.

BOY WILLIE: Lymon say preachers don't have to work. Where you working at, nigger?

DOAKER: Avery got him one of them good jobs. He working at one of them skyscrapers downtown.

AVERY: I'm working down there at the Gulf Building running an elevator. Got a pension and everything. They even give you a turkey on Thanksgiving.

LYMON: How you know the rope ain't gonna break? Ain't you scared the rope's gonna break?

AVERY: That's steel. They got steel cables hold it up. It take a whole lot of breaking to break that steel. Naw, I ain't worried about nothing like that. It ain't nothing but a little old elevator. Now, I wouldn't get in none of them airplanes. You couldn't pay me to do nothing like that.

LYMON: That be fun. I'd rather do that than ride in one of them elevators.

BOY WILLIE: How many of them watermelons you wanna buy?

AVERY: I thought you was gonna give me one seeing as how you got a whole truck full.

BOY WILLIE: You can get one, get two. I'll give you two for a dollar.

AVERY: I can't eat but one. How much are they?

BOY WILLIE: Aw, nigger, you know I'll give you a watermelon. Go on, take as many as you want. Just leave some for me and Lymon to sell.

AVERY: I don't want but one.

BOY WILLIE: How you get to be a preacher, Avery? I might want to be a preacher one day. Have everybody call me Reverend Boy Willie.

AVERY: It come to me in a dream. God called me and told me he wanted me to be a shepherd for his flock. That's what I'm gonna call my church . . . The Good Shepherd Church of God in Christ.

DOAKER: Tell him what you told me. Tell him about the three hobos.

AVERY: Boy Willie don't want to hear all that.

LYMON: I do. Lots a people say your dreams can come true.

AVERY: Naw. You don't want to hear all that.

DOAKER: Go on. I told him you was a preacher. He didn't want to believe me. Tell him about the three hobos.

AVERY: Well, it come to me in a dream. See . . . I was sitting out in this railroad yard watching the trains go by. The train stopped and these three hobos got off. They told me they had come from Nazareth and was on their way to Jerusalem. They had three candles. They gave me one and told me to light it . . . but to be careful that it didn't go out. Next thing I knew I was standing in front of this house. Something told me to go knock on the door. This old woman opened the door and said they had been waiting on me. Then she led me into this room. It was a big room and it was full of all kinds of different people. They looked like anybody else except they all had sheep heads and was making noise like sheep make. I heard somebody call my name. I looked around and there was these same three hobos. They told me to take off my clothes and they give me a blue robe with gold thread. They washed my feet and combed my hair. Then they showed me these three doors and told me to pick one.

I went through one of them doors and that flame leapt off that candle and it seemed like my whole head caught fire. I looked around and there was four or five other men standing there with these same blue robes on. Then we heard a voice tell us to look out across this valley. We looked out and saw the valley was full of wolves. The voice told us that these sheep people that I had seen in the other room had to go over to the other side of this valley and somebody had to take them. Then I heard another voice say, "Who shall I send?" Next thing I knew I said, "Here I am. Send me." That's when I met Jesus. He say, "If you go, I'll go with you." Something told me to say, "Come on. Let's go." That's when I woke up. My head still felt like it was on fire . . . but I had a peace about myself that was hard to explain. I knew right then that I had been filled with the Holy Ghost and called to be a servant of the Lord. It took me a while before I could accept that. But then a lot of little ways God showed me that it was true. So I became a preacher.

LYMON: I see why you gonna call it the Good Shepherd Church. You dreaming about them sheep people. I can see that easy.

BOY WILLIE: Doaker say you sent some white man past the house to look at that piano. Say he was going around to all the colored people's houses looking to buy up musical instruments.

AVERY: Yeah, but Berniece didn't want to sell that piano. After she told me about it . . . I could see why she didn't want to sell it.

BOY WILLIE: What's this man's name?

AVERY: Oh, that's a while back now. I done forgot his name. He give Berniece a card with his name and telephone number on it, but I believe she throwed it away.

(*Berniece and Maretha enter from the stairs.*)

BERNIECE: Maretha, run back upstairs and get my pocketbook. And wipe that hair grease off your forehead. Go ahead, hurry up.

(*Maretha exits up the stairs.*)

How you doing, Avery? You done got all dressed up. You look nice. Boy Willie, I thought you and Lymon was going to sell them watermelons.

BOY WILLIE: Lymon done got sleepy. We liable to get some sleep first.

LYMON: I ain't sleepy.

DOAKER: As many watermelons as you got stacked up on that truck out there, you ought to have been gone.

BOY WILLIE: We gonna go in a minute. We going.

BERNIECE: Doaker. I'm gonna stop down there on Logan Street. You want anything?

DOAKER: You can pick up some ham hocks if you going down there. See if you can get the smoked ones. If they ain't got that get the fresh ones. Don't get the ones that got all that fat under the skin. Look for the long ones. They nice and lean.

(*He gives her a dollar.*)

Don't get the short ones lessen they smoked. If you got to get the fresh ones make sure that they the long ones. If they ain't got them smoked then go ahead and get the short ones.

(*Pause.*)

You may as well get some turnip greens while you down there. I got some buttermilk . . . if you pick up some cornmeal I'll make me some cornbread and cook up them turnip greens.

(*Maretha enters from the stairs.*)

MARETHA: We gonna take the streetcar?

BERNIECE: Me and Avery gonna drop you off at the settlement house. You mind them people down there. Don't be going down there showing your color. Boy Willie, I done told you what to do. I'll see you later, Doaker.

AVERY: I'll be seeing you again, Boy Willie.

BOY WILLIE: Hey, Berniece . . . what's the name of that man Avery sent past say he want to buy the piano?

BERNIECE: I knew it. I knew it when I first seen you. I knew you was up to something.

BOY WILLIE: Sutter's brother say he selling the land to me. He waiting on me now. Told me he'd give me two weeks. I got one part. Sell them watermelons get me another part. Then we can sell that piano and I'll have the third part.

BERNIECE: I ain't selling that piano, Boy Willie. If that's why you come up here you can just forget about it.

(*To Doaker.*)

Doaker, I'll see you later. Boy Willie ain't nothing but a whole lot of mouth. I ain't paying him no mind. If he come up here thinking he gonna sell that piano then he done come up here for nothing.

(*Berniece, Avery, and Maretha exit the front door.*)

BOY WILLIE: Hey, Lymon! You ready to go sell these watermelons.

(*Boy Willie and Lymon start to exit. At the door Boy Willie turns to Doaker.*)

Hey, Doaker . . . if Berniece don't want to sell that piano . . . I'm gonna cut it in half and go on and sell my half.

(*Boy Willie and Lymon exit.*)

(*The lights go down on the scene.*)

Scene 2

(*The lights come up on the kitchen. It is three days later. Wining Boy sits at the kitchen table. There is a half-empty pint bottle on the table. Doaker busies himself washing pots. Wining Boy is fifty-six years old. Doaker's older brother, he tries to present the image of a successful musician and gambler, but his music, his clothes, and even his manner of presentation are old. He is a man who looking back over his life continues to live it with an odd mixture of zest and sorrow.*)

WINING BOY: So the Ghosts of the Yellow Dog got Sutter. That just go to show you I believe I always lived right. They say every dog gonna have his day and time it go around it sure come back to you. I done seen that a thousand times. I know the truth of that. But I'll tell you out-right . . . if I see Sutter's ghost I'll be on the first thing I find that got wheels on it.

(*Doaker enters from his room.*)

DOAKER: Wining Boy!

WINING BOY: And I'll tell you another thing . . . Berniece ain't gonna sell that piano.

DOAKER: That's what she told him. He say he gonna cut it in half and go on and sell his half. They been around here three days trying to sell them watermelons. They trying to get out to where the white folks live but the truck keep breaking down. They go a block or two and it break down again. They trying to get out to Squirrel Hill and can't get around the corner. He say soon as he can get that truck empty to where he can set the piano up in there he gonna take it out of here and go sell it.

WINING BOY: What about them boys Sutter got? How come they ain't farming that land?

DOAKER: One of them going to school. He left down there and come North to school. The other one ain't got as much sense as that frying pan over yonder. That is the dumbest white man I ever seen. He'd stand in the river and watch it rise till it drown him.

WINING BOY: Other than seeing Sutter's ghost how's Berniece doing?

DOAKER: She doing alright. She still got Crawley on her mind. He been dead three years but she still holding on to him. She need to go out here and let one of these fellows grab a whole handful of whatever she got. She act like it done got precious.

WINING BOY: They always told me any fish will bite if you got good bait.

DOAKER: She stuck up on it. She think it's better than she is. I believe she messing around with Avery. They got something going. He a preacher now. If you let him tell it the Holy Ghost sat on his head and heaven opened up with thunder and lightning and God was calling his name. Told him to go out and preach and tend to his flock. That's what he gonna call his church. The Good Shepherd Church.

WINING BOY: They had that joker down in Spear walking around talking about he Jesus Christ. He gonna live the life of Christ. Went through the Last Supper and everything. Rented him a mule on Palm Sunday and rode through the town. Did everything . . . talking about he Christ. He did everything until they got up to that crucifixion part. Got up to that part and told everybody to go home and quit pretending. He got up to the crucifixion part and changed his mind. Had a whole bunch of folks come down there to see him get nailed to the cross. I don't know who's the worse fool. Him or them. Had all them folks come down there . . . even carried the cross up this little hill. People standing around waiting to see him get nailed to the cross and he stop everything and preach a little sermon and told everybody to go home. Had enough nerve to tell them to come to church on Easter Sunday to celebrate his resurrection.

DOAKER: I'm surprised Avery ain't thought about that. He trying every little thing to get him a congregation together. They meeting over at his house till he get him a church.

WINING BOY: Ain't nothing wrong with being a preacher. You got the preacher on one hand and the gambler on the other. Sometimes there ain't too much difference in them.

DOAKER: How long you been in Kansas City?

WINING BOY: Since I left here. I got tied up with some old gal down there.

(Pause.)

You know Cleotha died.

DOAKER: Yeah, I heard that last time I was down there. I was sorry to hear that.

WINING BOY: One of her friends wrote and told me. I got the letter right here.

(*He takes the letter out of his pocket.*)

I was down in Kansas City and she wrote and told me Cleotha had died. Name of Willa Bryant. She say she know cousin Rupert.

(*He opens the letter and reads.*)

Dear Wining Boy: I am writing this letter to let you know Miss Cleotha Holman passed on Saturday the first of May she departed this world in the loving arms of her sister Miss Alberta Samuels. I know you would want to know this and am writing as a friend of Cleotha. There have been many hardships since last you seen her but she survived them all and to the end was a good woman whom I hope have God's grace and is in His Paradise. Your cousin Rupert Bates is my friend also and he give me your address and I pray this reaches you about Cleotha. Miss Willa Bryant. A friend.

(*He folds the letter and returns it to his pocket.*)

They was nailing her coffin shut by the time I heard about it. I never knew she was sick. I believe it was that yellow jaundice. That's what killed her mama.

DOAKER: Cleotha wasn't but forty-some.

WINING BOY: She was forty-six. I got ten years on her. I met her when she was sixteen. You remember I used to run around there. Couldn't nothing keep me still. Much as I loved Cleotha I loved to ramble. Couldn't nothing keep me still. We got married and we used to fight about it all the time. Then one day she asked me to leave. Told me she loved me before I left. Told me, Wining Boy, you got a home as long as I got mine. And I believe in my heart I always felt that and that kept me safe.

DOAKER: Cleotha always did have a nice way about her.

WINING BOY: Man that woman was something. I used to thank the Lord. Many a night I sat up and looked out over my life. Said, well, I had Cleotha. When it didn't look like there was nothing else for me, I said, thank God, at least I had that. If ever I go anywhere in this life I done known a good woman. And that used to hold me till the next morning.

(*Pause.*)

What you got? Give me a little nip. I know you got something stuck up in your room.

DOAKER: I ain't seen you walk in here and put nothing on the table. You
    done sat there and drank up your whiskey. Now you talking about
    what you got.
WINING BOY: I got plenty money. Give me a little nip.

(*Doaker carries a glass into his room and returns with it half-filled. He sets it on
the table in front of Wining Boy.*)

WINING BOY: You hear from Coreen?
DOAKER: She up in New York. I let her go from my mind.
WINING BOY: She was something back then. She wasn't too pretty but
    she had a way of looking at you made you know there was a whole lot
    of woman there. You got married and snatched her out from under us
    and we all got mad at you.
DOAKER: She up in New York City. That's what I hear.

(*The door opens and Boy Willie and Lymon enter.*)

BOY WILLIE: Aw hell . . . look here! We was just talking about you.
    Doaker say you left out of here with a whole sack of money. I told him
    we wasn't going see you till you got broke.
WINING BOY: What you mean broke? I got a whole pocketful of money.
DOAKER: Did you all get that truck fixed?
BOY WILLIE: We got it running and got halfway out there on Centre and
    it broke down again. Lymon went out there and messed it up some
    more. Fellow told us we got to wait till tomorrow to get it fixed. Say he
    have it running like new. Lymon going back down there and sleep in
    the truck so the people don't take the watermelons.
LYMON: Lymon nothing. You go down there and sleep in it.
BOY WILLIE: You was sleeping in it down home, nigger! I don't know
    nothing about sleeping in no truck.
LYMON: I ain't sleeping in no truck.
BOY WILLIE: They can take all the watermelons. I don't care. Wining Boy,
    where you coming from? Where you been?
WINING BOY: I been down in Kansas City.
BOY WILLIE: You remember Lymon? Lymon Jackson.
WINING BOY: Yeah, I used to know his daddy.
BOY WILLIE: Doaker say you don't never leave no address with nobody.
    Say he got to depend on your whim. See when it strike you to pay a
    visit.
WINING BOY: I got four or five addresses.
BOY WILLIE: Doaker say Berniece asked you for three dollars and you
    got mad and left.
WINING BOY: Berniece try and rule over you too much for me. That's
    why I left. It wasn't about no three dollars.

BOY WILLIE: Where you getting all these sacks of money from? I need to be with you. Doaker say you had a whole sack of money . . . turn some of it loose.

WINING BOY: I was just fixing to ask you for five dollars.

BOY WILLIE: I ain't got no money. I'm trying to get some. Doaker tell you about Sutter? The Ghosts of the Yellow Dog got him about three weeks ago. Berniece done seen his ghost and everything. He right upstairs.

(Calls.)

Hey Sutter! Wining Boy's here. Come on, get a drink!

WINING BOY: How many that make the Ghosts of the Yellow Dog done got?

BOY WILLIE: Must be about nine or ten, eleven or twelve. I don't know.

DOAKER: You got Ed Saunders. Howard Peterson. Charlie Webb.

WINING BOY: Robert Smith. That fellow that shot Becky's boy . . . say he was stealing peaches . . .

DOAKER: You talking about Bob Mallory.

BOY WILLIE: Berniece say she don't believe all that about the Ghosts of the Yellow Dog.

WINING BOY: She ain't got to believe. You go ask them white folks in Sunflower County if they believe. You go ask Sutter if he believe. I don't care if Berniece believe or not. I done been to where the Southern cross the Yellow Dog and called out their names. They talk back to you, too.

LYMON: What they sound like? The wind or something?

BOY WILLIE: You done been there for real, Wining Boy?

WINING BOY: Nineteen thirty. July of nineteen thirty I stood right there on that spot. It didn't look like nothing was going right in my life. I said everything can't go wrong all the time . . . let me go down there and call on the Ghosts of the Yellow Dog, see if they can help me. I went down there and right there where them two railroads cross each other . . . I stood right there on that spot and called out their names. They talk back to you, too.

LYMON: People say you can ask them questions. They talk to you like that?

WINING BOY: A lot of things you got to find out on your own. I can't say how they talked to nobody else. But to me it just filled me up in a strange sort of way to be standing there on that spot. I didn't want to leave. It felt like the longer I stood there the bigger I got. I seen the train coming and it seem like I was bigger than the train. I started not to move. But something told me to go ahead and get on out the way. The train passed and I started to go back up there and stand some more. But something told me not to do it. I walked away from there feeling like a king. Went on and had a stroke of luck that run on for three years. So I don't care if Berniece believe or not. Berniece ain't got to believe. I know cause I been there. Now Doaker'll tell you about the Ghosts of the Yellow Dog.

DOAKER: I don't try and talk that stuff with Berniece. Avery got her all tied up in that church. She just think it's a whole lot of nonsense.

BOY WILLIE: Berniece don't believe in nothing. She just think she believe. She believe in anything if it's convenient for her to believe. But when that convenience run out then she ain't got nothing to stand on.

WINING BOY: Let's not get on Berniece now. Doaker tell me you talking about selling that piano.

BOY WILLIE: Yeah . . . hey, Doaker, I got the name of that man Avery was talking about. The man what's fixing the truck gave me his name. Everybody know him. Say he buy up anything you can make music with. I got his name and his telephone number. Hey, Wining Boy, Sutter's brother say he selling the land to me. I got one part. Sell them watermelons get me the second part. Then . . . soon as I get them watermelons out that truck I'm gonna take and sell that piano and get the third part.

DOAKER: That land ain't worth nothing no more. The smart white man's up here in these cities. He cut the land loose and step back and watch you and the dumb white man argue over it.

WINING BOY: How you know Sutter's brother ain't sold it already? You talking about selling the piano and the man's liable to sold the land two or three times.

BOY WILLIE: He say he waiting on me. He say he give me two weeks. That's two weeks from Friday. Say if I ain't back by then he might gonna sell it to somebody else. He say he wanna see me with it.

WINING BOY: You know as well as I know the man gonna sell the land to the first one walk up and hand him the money.

BOY WILLIE: That's just who I'm gonna be. Look, you ain't gotta know he waiting on me. I know. Okay. I know what the man told me. Stovall already done tried to buy the land from him and he told him no. The man say he waiting on me . . . he waiting on me. Hey, Doaker . . . give me a drink. I see Wining Boy got his glass.

(*Doaker exits into his room.*)

Wining Boy, what you doing in Kansas City? What they got down there?

LYMON: I hear they got some nice-looking women in Kansas City. I sure like to go down there and find out.

WINING BOY: Man, the women down there is something else.

(*Doaker enters with a bottle of whiskey. He sets it on the table with some glasses.*)

DOAKER: You wanna sit up here and drink up my whiskey, leave a dollar on the table when you get up.

BOY WILLIE: You ain't doing nothing but showing your hospitality. I know we ain't got to pay for your hospitality.

WINING BOY: Doaker say they had you and Lymon down on the Parchman Farm. Had you on my old stomping grounds.

BOY WILLIE: Me and Lymon was down there hauling wood for Jim Miller and keeping us a little bit to sell. Some white fellows tried to run us off of it. That's when Crawley got killed. They put me and Lymon in the penitentiary.

LYMON: They ambushed us right there where that road dip down and around that bend in the creek. Crawley tried to fight them. Me and Boy Willie got away but the sheriff got us. Say we was stealing wood. They shot me in my stomach.

BOY WILLIE: They looking for Lymon down there now. They rounded him up and put him in jail for not working.

LYMON: Fined me a hundred dollars. Mr. Stovall come and paid my hundred dollars and the judge say I got to work for him to pay him back his hundred dollars. I told them I'd rather take my thirty days but they wouldn't let me do that.

BOY WILLIE: As soon as Stovall turned his back, Lymon was gone. He down there living in that truck dodging the sheriff and Stovall. He got both of them looking for him. So I brought him up here.

LYMON: I told Boy Willie I'm gonna stay up here. I ain't going back with him.

BOY WILLIE: Ain't nobody twisting your arm to make you go back. You can do what you want to do.

WINING BOY: I'll go back with you. I'm on my way down there. You gonna take the train? I'm gonna take the train.

LYMON: They treat you better up here.

BOY WILLIE: I ain't worried about nobody mistreating me. They treat you like you let them treat you. They mistreat me I mistreat them right back. Ain't no difference in me and the white man.

WINING BOY: Ain't no difference as far as how somebody supposed to treat you. I agree with that. But I'll tell you the difference between the colored man and the white man. Alright. Now you take and eat some berries. They taste real good to you. So you say I'm gonna go out and get me a whole pot of these berries and cook them up to make a pie or whatever. But you ain't looked to see them berries is sitting in the white fellow's yard. Ain't got no fence around them. You figure anybody want something they'd fence it in. Alright. Now the white man come along and say that's my land. Therefore everything that grow on it belong to me. He tell the sheriff, "I want you to put this nigger in jail as a warning to all the other niggers. Otherwise first thing you know these niggers have everything that belong to us."

BOY WILLIE: I'd come back at night and haul off his whole patch while he was sleep.

WINING BOY: Alright. Now Mr. So and So, he sell the land to you. And he come to you and say, "John, you own the land. It's all yours now. But them is my berries. And come time to pick them I'm gonna send my boys over. You got the land . . . but them berries, I'm gonna keep them. They mine." And he go and fix it with the law that them is his berries. Now that's the difference between the colored man and the white man. The colored man can't fix nothing with the law.

BOY WILLIE: I don't go by what the law say. The law's liable to say anything. I go by if it's right or not. It don't matter to me what the law say. I take and look at it for myself.

LYMON: That's why you gonna end up back down there on the Parchman Farm.

BOY WILLIE: I ain't thinking about no Parchman Farm. You liable to go back before me.

LYMON: They work you too hard down there. All that weeding and hoeing and chopping down trees. I didn't like all that.

WINING BOY: You ain't got to like your job on Parchman. Hey, tell him, Doaker, the only one got to like his job is the waterboy.

DOAKER: If he don't like his job he need to set that bucket down.

BOY WILLIE: That's what they told Lymon. They had Lymon on water and everybody got mad at him cause he was lazy.

LYMON: That water was heavy.

BOY WILLIE: They had Lymon down there singing:

(*Sings.*)

> O Lord Berta Berta O Lord gal oh-ah
> O Lord Berta Berta O Lord gal well

(*Lymon and Wining Boy join in.*)

> Go 'head marry don't you wait on me oh-ah
> Go 'head marry don't you wait on me well
> Might not want you when I go free oh-ah
> Might not want you when I go free well

BOY WILLIE: Come on, Doaker. Doaker know this one.

(*As Doaker joins in the men stamp and clap to keep time. They sing in harmony with great fervor and style.*)

> O Lord Berta Berta O Lord gal oh-ah
> O Lord Berta Berta O Lord gal well

Raise them up higher, let them drop on down oh-ah
Raise them up higher, let them drop on down well
Don't know the difference when the sun go down oh-ah
Don't know the difference when the sun go down well

Berta in Meridan and she living at ease oh-ah
Berta in Meridan and she living at ease well
I'm on old Parchman, got to work or leave oh-ah
I'm on old Parchman, got to work or leave well

O Alberta, Berta, O Lord gal oh-ah
O Alberta, Berta, O Lord gal well

When you marry, don't marry no farming man oh-ah
When you marry, don't marry no farming man well
Everyday Monday, hoe handle in your hand oh-ah
Everyday Monday, hoe handle in your hand well

When you marry, marry a railroad man, oh-ah
When you marry, marry a railroad man, well
Everyday Sunday, dollar in your hand oh-ah
Everyday Sunday, dollar in your hand well

O Alberta, Berta, O Lord gal oh-ah
O Alberta, Berta, O Lord gal well

BOY WILLIE: Doaker like that part. He like that railroad part.
LYMON: Doaker sound like Tangleye. He can't sing a lick.
BOY WILLIE: Hey, Doaker, they still talk about you down on Parchman.
They ask me, "You Doaker Boy's nephew?" I say, "Yeah, me and him is
family." They treated me alright soon as I told them that. Say, "Yeah,
he my uncle."
DOAKER: I don't never want to see none of them niggers no more.
BOY WILLIE: I don't want to see them either. Hey, Wining Boy, come on
play some piano. You a piano player, play some piano. Lymon wanna
hear you.
WINING BOY: I give that piano up. That was the best thing that ever happened to me, getting rid of that piano. That piano got so big and I'm
carrying it around on my back. I don't wish that on nobody. See, you
think it's all fun being a recording star. Got to carrying that piano
around and man did I get slow. Got just like molasses. The world just
slipping by me and I'm walking around with that piano. Alright. Now,
there ain't but so many places you can go. Only so many road wide
enough for you and that piano. And that piano get heavier and heavier.
Go to a place and they find out you play piano, the first thing they
want to do is give you a drink, find you a piano, and sit you right

down. And that's where you gonna be for the next eight hours. They
ain't gonna let you get up! Now, the first three or four years of that is
fun. You can't get enough whiskey and you can't get enough women
and you don't never get tired of playing that piano. But that only last
so long. You look up one day and you hate the whiskey, and you hate
the women, and you hate the piano. But that's all you got. You can't do
nothing else. All you know how to do is play that piano. Now, who am
I? Am I me? Or am I the piano player? Sometime it seem like the only
thing to do is shoot the piano player cause he the cause of all the trouble
I'm having.

DOAKER: What you gonna do when your troubles get like mine?

LYMON: If I knew how to play it, I'd play it. That's a nice piano.

BOY WILLIE: Whoever playing better play quick. Sutter's brother say he
waiting on me. I sell them watermelons. Get Berniece to sell that
piano. Put them two parts with the part I done saved . . .

WINING BOY: Berniece ain't gonna sell that piano. I don't see why you
don't know that.

BOY WILLIE: What she gonna do with it? She ain't doing nothing but letting it sit up there and rot. That piano ain't doing nobody no good.

LYMON: That's a nice piano. If I had it I'd sell it. Unless I knew how to
play like Wining Boy. You can get a nice price for that piano.

DOAKER: Now I'm gonna tell you something, Lymon don't know
this . . . but I'm gonna tell you why me and Wining Boy say Berniece
ain't gonna sell that piano.

BOY WILLIE: She ain't got to sell it! I'm gonna sell it! Berniece ain't got no
more rights to that piano than I do.

DOAKER: I'm talking to the man . . . let me talk to the man. See,
now . . . to understand why we say that . . . to understand about that
piano . . . you got to go back to slavery time. See, our family was
owned by a fellow named Robert Sutter. That was Sutter's grandfather.
Alright. The piano was owned by a fellow named Joel Nolander. He
was one of the Nolander brothers from down in Georgia. It was coming up on Sutter's wedding anniversary and he was looking to buy his
wife . . . Miss Ophelia was her name . . . he was looking to buy her an
anniversary present. Only thing with him . . . he ain't had no money.
But he had some niggers. So he asked Mr. Nolander to see if maybe he
could trade off some of his niggers for that piano. Told him he would
give him one and a half niggers for it. That's the way he told him. Say
he could have one full grown and one half grown. Mr. Nolander agreed
only he say he had to pick them. He didn't want Sutter to give him just
any old nigger. He say he wanted to have the pick of the litter. So
Sutter lined up his niggers and Mr. Nolander looked them over and
out of the whole bunch he picked my grandmother . . . her name was

Berniece . . . same like Berniece . . . and he picked my daddy when he wasn't nothing but a little boy nine years old. They made the trade-off and Miss Ophelia was so happy with that piano that it got to be just about all she would do was play on that piano.

WINING BOY: Just get up in the morning, get all dressed up and sit down and play on that piano.

DOAKER: Alright. Time go along. Time go along. Miss Ophelia got to missing my grandmother . . . the way she would cook and clean the house and talk to her and what not. And she missed having my daddy around the house to fetch things for her. So she asked to see if maybe she could trade back that piano and get her niggers back. Mr. Nolander said no. Said a deal was a deal. Him and Sutter had a big falling out about it and Miss Ophelia took sick to the bed. Wouldn't get out of the bed in the morning. She just lay there. The doctor said she was wasting away.

WINING BOY: That's when Sutter called our granddaddy up to the house.

DOAKER: Now, our granddaddy's name was Boy Willie. That's who Boy Willie's named after . . . only they called him Willie Boy. Now, he was a worker of wood. He could make you anything you wanted out of wood. He'd make you a desk. A table. A lamp. Anything you wanted. Them white fellows around there used to come up to Mr. Sutter and get him to make all kinds of things for them. Then they'd pay Mr. Sutter a nice price. See, everything my granddaddy made Mr. Sutter owned cause he owned him. That's why when Mr. Nolander offered to buy him to keep the family together Mr. Sutter wouldn't sell him. Told Mr. Nolander he didn't have enough money to buy him. Now . . . am I telling it right, Wining Boy?

WINING BOY: You telling it.

DOAKER: Sutter called him up to the house and told him to carve my grandmother and my daddy's picture on the piano for Miss Ophelia. And he took and carved this . . .

(Doaker crosses over to the piano.)

See that right there? That's my grandmother, Berniece. She looked just like that. And he put a picture of my daddy when he wasn't nothing but a little boy the way he remembered him. He made them up out of his memory. Only thing . . . he didn't stop there. He carved all this. He got a picture of his mama . . . Mama Esther . . . and his daddy, Boy Charles.

WINING BOY: That was the first Boy Charles.

DOAKER: Then he put on the side here all kinds of things. See that? That's when him and Mama Berniece got married. They called it jumping the broom. That's how you got married in them days. Then he got here when my daddy was born . . . and here he got Mama Esther's funeral . . . and down here he got Mr. Nolander taking Mama Berniece and my daddy away down to his place in Georgia. He got all kinds of things what happened with our family. When Mr. Sutter seen the piano with all them carvings on it he got mad. He didn't ask for all that. But see . . . there wasn't nothing he could do about it. When Miss Ophelia seen it . . . she got excited. Now she had her piano and her niggers too. She took back to playing it and played on it right up till the day she died. Alright . . . now see, our brother Boy Charles . . . that's Berniece and Boy Willie's daddy . . . he was the oldest of us three boys. He's dead now. But he would have been fifty-seven if he had lived. He died in 1911 when he was thirty-one years old. Boy Charles used to talk about that piano all the time. He never could get it off his mind. Two or three months go by and he be talking about it again. He be talking about taking it out of Sutter's house. Say it was the story of our whole family and as long as Sutter had it . . . he had us. Say we was still in slavery. Me and Wining Boy tried to talk him out of it but it wouldn't do any good. Soon as he quiet down about it he'd start up again. We seen where he wasn't gonna get it off his mind . . . so, on the Fourth of July, 1911 . . . when Sutter was at the picnic what the county give every year . . . me and Wining Boy went on down there with him and took that piano out of Sutter's house. We put it on a wagon and me and Wining Boy carried it over into the next county with Mama Ola's people. Boy Charles decided to stay around there and wait until Sutter got home to make it look like business as usual.

Now, I don't know what happened when Sutter came home and found that piano gone. But somebody went up to Boy Charles's house and set it on fire. But he wasn't in there. He must have seen them coming cause he went down and caught the 3:57 Yellow Dog. He didn't know they was gonna come down and stop the train. Stopped the train and found Boy Charles in the boxcar with four of them hobos. Must have got mad when they couldn't find the piano cause they set the boxcar afire and killed everybody. Now, nobody know who done that. Some people say it was Sutter cause it was his piano. Some people say it was Sheriff Carter. Some people say it was Robert Smith and Ed Saunders. But don't nobody know for sure. It was about two months after that that Ed Saunders fell down his well. Just upped and fell down his well for no reason. People say it was the ghost of them men who burned up in the boxcar that pushed him in his well. They started calling them the Ghosts of the Yellow Dog. Now, that's how all that got started and that why we say Berniece ain't gonna sell that piano. Cause her daddy died over it.

BOY WILLIE: All that's in the past. If my daddy had seen where he could have traded that piano in for some land of his own, it wouldn't be sitting up here now. He spent his whole life farming on somebody else's land. I ain't gonna do that. See, he couldn't do no better. When he come along he ain't had nothing he could build on. His daddy ain't had nothing to give him. The only thing my daddy had to give me was that piano. And he died over giving me that. I ain't gonna let it sit up there and rot without trying to do something with it. If Berniece can't see that, then I'm gonna go ahead and sell my half. And you and Wining Boy know I'm right.

DOAKER: Ain't nobody said nothing about who's right and who's wrong. I was just telling the man about the piano. I was telling him why we say Berniece ain't gonna sell it.

LYMON: Yeah, I can see why you say that now. I told Boy Willie he ought to stay up here with me.

BOY WILLIE: You stay! I'm going back! That's what I'm gonna do with my life! Why I got to come up here and learn to do something I don't know how to do when I already know how to farm? You stay up here and make your own way if that's what you want to do. I'm going back and live my life the way I want to live it.

(*Wining Boy gets up and crosses to the piano.*)

WINING BOY: Let's see what we got here. I ain't played on this thing for a while.

DOAKER: You can stop telling that. You was playing on it the last time you was through here. We couldn't get you off of it. Go on and play something.

(*Wining Boy sits down at the piano and plays and sings. The song is one which has put many dimes and quarters in his pocket, long ago, in dimly remembered towns and way stations. He plays badly, without hesitation, and sings in a forceful voice.*)

WINING BOY: (*Singing.*)
I am a rambling gambling man
I gambled in many towns
I rambled this wide world over
I rambled this world around
I had my ups and downs in life
And bitter times I saw
But I never knew what misery was
Till I lit on old Arkansas.

I started out one morning
to meet that early train

He said, "You better work for me
I have some land to drain.
I'll give you fifty cents a day,
Your washing, board and all
And you shall be a different man
In the state of Arkansas."

I worked six months for the rascal
Joe Herrin was his name
He fed me old corn dodgers
They was hard as any rock
My tooth is all got loosened
And my knees begin to knock
That was the kind of hash I got
In the state of Arkansas.

Traveling man
I've traveled all around this world
Traveling man
I've traveled from land to land
Traveling man
I've traveled all around this world
Well it ain't no use
writing no news
I'm a traveling man.

(*The door opens and Berniece enters with Maretha.*)

BERNIECE: Is that . . . Lord, I know that ain't Wining Boy sitting there.

WINING BOY: Hey, Berniece.

BERNIECE: You all had this planned. You and Boy Willie had this planned.

WINING BOY: I didn't know he was gonna be here. I'm on my way down home. I stopped by to see you and Doaker first.

DOAKER: I told the nigger he left out of here with that sack of money, we thought we might never see him again. Boy Willie say he wasn't gonna see him till he got broke. I looked up and seen him sitting on the doorstep asking for two dollars. Look at him laughing. He know it's the truth.

BERNIECE: Boy Willie, I didn't see that truck out there. I thought you was out selling watermelons.

BOY WILLIE: We done sold them all. Sold the truck too.

BERNIECE: I don't want to go through none of your stuff. I done told you to go back where you belong.

BOY WILLIE: I was just teasing you, woman. You can't take no teasing?

BERNIECE: Wining Boy, when you get here?

WINING BOY: A little while ago. I took the train from Kansas City.

BERNIECE: Let me go upstairs and change and then I'll cook you something to eat.

BOY WILLIE: You ain't cooked me nothing when I come.

BERNIECE: Boy Willie, go on and leave me alone. Come on, Maretha, get up here and change your clothes before you get them dirty.

(*Berniece exits up the stairs, followed by Maretha.*)

WINING BOY: Maretha sure getting big, ain't she, Doaker. And just as pretty as she want to be. I didn't know Crawley had it in him.

(*Boy Willie crosses to the piano.*)

BOY WILLIE: Hey, Lymon . . . get up on the other side of this piano and let me see something.

WINING BOY: Boy Willie, what is you doing?

BOY WILLIE: I'm seeing how heavy this piano is. Get up over there, Lymon.

WINING BOY: Go on and leave that piano alone. You ain't taking that piano out of here and selling it.

BOY WILLIE: Just as soon as I get them watermelons out that truck.

WINING BOY: Well, I got something to say about that.

BOY WILLIE: This my daddy's piano.

WINING BOY: He ain't took it by himself. Me and Doaker helped him.

BOY WILLIE: He died by himself. Where was you and Doaker at then? Don't come telling me nothing about this piano. This is me and Berniece's piano. Am I right, Doaker?

DOAKER: Yeah, you right.

BOY WILLIE: Let's see if we can lift it up, Lymon. Get a good grip on it and pick it up on your end. Ready? Lift!

(*As they start to move the piano, the sound of Sutter's Ghost is heard. Doaker is the only one to hear it. With difficulty they move the piano a little bit so it is out of place.*)

BOY WILLIE: What you think?

LYMON: It's heavy . . . but you can move it. Only it ain't gonna be easy.

BOY WILLIE: It wasn't that heavy to me. Okay, let's put it back.

(*The sound of Sutter's Ghost is heard again. They all hear it as Berniece enters on the stairs.*)

BERNIECE: Boy Willie . . . you gonna play around with me one too many times. And then God's gonna bless you and West is gonna dress you. Now set that piano back over there. I done told you a hundred times I ain't selling that piano.

BOY WILLIE: I'm trying to get me some land, woman. I need that piano to get me some money so I can buy Sutter's land.

BERNIECE: Money can't buy what that piano cost. You can't sell your soul for money. It won't go with the buyer. It'll shrivel and shrink to know that you ain't taken on to it. But it won't go with the buyer.

BOY WILLIE: I ain't talking about all that, woman. I ain't talking about selling my soul. I'm talking about trading that piece of wood for some land. Get something under your feet. Land the only thing God ain't making no more of. You can always get you another piano. I'm talking about some land. What you get something out the ground from. That's what I'm talking about. You can't do nothing with that piano but sit up there and look at it.

BERNIECE: That's just what I'm gonna do. Wining Boy, you want me to fry you some pork chops?

BOY WILLIE: Now, I'm gonna tell you the way I see it. The only thing that make that piano worth something is them carvings Papa Willie Boy put on there. That's what make it worth something. That was my great-granddaddy. Papa Boy Charles brought that piano into the house. Now, I'm supposed to build on what they left me. You can't do nothing with that piano sitting up here in the house. That's just like if I let them watermelons sit out there and rot. I'd be a fool. Alright now, if you say to me, Boy Willie, I'm using that piano. I give out lessons on it and that help me make my rent or whatever. Then that be something else. I'd have to go on and say, well, Berniece using that piano. She building on it. Let her go on and use it. I got to find another way to get Sutter's land. But Doaker say you ain't touched that piano the whole time it's been up here. So why you wanna stand in my way? See, you just looking at the sentimental value. See, that's good. That's alright. I take my hat off whenever somebody say my daddy's name. But I ain't gonna be no fool about no sentimental value. You can sit up here and look at the piano for the next hundred years and it's just gonna be a piano. You can't make more than that. Now I want to get Sutter's land with that piano. I get Sutter's land and I can go down and cash in the crop and get my seed. As long as I got the land and the seed then I'm alright. I can always get me a little something else. Cause that land give back to you. I can make me another crop and cash that in. I still got the land and the seed. But that piano don't put out nothing else. You ain't got nothing working for you. Now, the kind of man my daddy was he would have understood that. I'm sorry you can't see it that way. But that's why I'm gonna take that piano out of here and sell it.

BERNIECE: You ain't taking that piano out of my house.

(*She crosses to the piano.*)

Look at this piano. Look at it. Mama Ola polished this piano with her tears for seventeen years. For seventeen years she rubbed on it till her hands bled. Then she rubbed the blood in . . . mixed it up with the rest of the blood on it. Every day that God breathed life into her body she rubbed and cleaned and polished and prayed over it. "Play something for me, Berniece. Play something for me, Berniece." Every day. "I cleaned it up for you, play something for me, Berniece." You always talking about your daddy but you ain't never stopped to look at what his foolishness cost your mama. Seventeen years' worth of cold nights and an empty bed. For what? For a piano? For a piece of wood? To get even with somebody? I look at you and you're all the same. You, Papa Boy Charles, Wining Boy, Doaker, Crawley . . . you're all alike. All this thieving and killing and thieving and killing. And what it ever lead to? More killing and more thieving. I ain't never seen it come to nothing. People getting burned up. People getting shot. People falling down their wells. It don't never stop.

DOAKER: Come on now, Berniece, ain't no need in getting upset.

BOY WILLIE: I done a little bit of stealing here and there, but I ain't never killed nobody. I can't be speaking for nobody else. You all got to speak for yourself, but I ain't never killed nobody.

BERNIECE: You killed Crawley just as sure as if you pulled the trigger.

BOY WILLIE: See, that's ignorant. That's downright foolish for you to say something like that. You ain't doing nothing but showing your ignorance. If the nigger was here I'd whup his ass for getting me and Lymon shot at.

BERNIECE: Crawley ain't knew about the wood.

BOY WILLIE: We told the man about the wood. Ask Lymon. He knew all about the wood. He seen we was sneaking it. Why else we gonna be out there at night? Don't come telling me Crawley ain't knew about the wood. Them fellows come up on us and Crawley tried to bully them. Me and Lymon seen the sheriff with them and give in. Wasn't no sense in getting killed over fifty dollars' worth of wood.

BERNIECE: Crawley ain't knew you stole that wood.

BOY WILLIE: We ain't stole no wood. Me and Lymon was hauling wood for Jim Miller and keeping us a little bit on the side. We dumped our little bit down there by the creek till we had enough to make a load. Some fellows seen us and we figured we better get it before they did. We come up there and got Crawley to help us load it. Figured we'd cut him in. Crawley trying to keep the wolf from his door . . . we was trying to help him.

LYMON: Me and Boy Willie told him about the wood. We told him some fellows might be trying to beat us to it. He say let me go back and get my thirty-eight. That's what caused all the trouble.

BOY WILLIE: If Crawley ain't had the gun he'd be alive today.

LYMON: We had it about half loaded when they come up on us. We seen the sheriff with them and we tried to get away. We ducked around near the bend in the creek . . . but they was down there too. Boy Willie say let's give in. But Crawley pulled out his gun and started shooting. That's when they started shooting back.

BERNIECE: All I know is Crawley would be alive if you hadn't come up there and got him.

BOY WILLIE: I ain't had nothing to do with Crawley getting killed. That was his own fault.

BERNIECE: Crawley's dead and in the ground and you still walking around here eating. That's all I know. He went off to load some wood with you and ain't never come back.

BOY WILLIE: I told you, woman . . . I ain't had nothing to do with . . .

BERNIECE: He ain't here, is he? He ain't here!

(*Berniece hits Boy Willie.*)

I said he ain't here. Is he?

(*Berniece continues to hit Boy Willie, who doesn't move to defend himself, other than back up and turning his head so that most of the blows fall on his chest and arms.*)

DOAKER (*grabbing Berniece*): Come on, Berniece . . . let it go, it ain't his fault.

BERNIECE: He ain't here, is he? Is he?

BOY WILLIE: I told you I ain't responsible for Crawley.

BERNIECE: He ain't here.

BOY WILLIE: Come on now, Berniece . . . don't do this now. Doaker get her. I ain't had nothing to do with Crawley . . .

BERNIECE: You come up there and got him!

BOY WILLIE: I done told you now. Doaker, get her. I ain't playing.

DOAKER: Come on. Berniece.

(*Maretha is heard screaming upstairs. It is a scream of stark terror.*)

MARETHA: Mama! . . . Mama!

(*The lights go down to black. End of Act One.*)

ACT 2   Scene 1

(*The lights come up on the kitchen. It is the following morning. Doaker is ironing the pants to his uniform. He has a pot cooking on the stove at the same time. He is singing a song. The song provides him with the rhythm for his work and he moves about the kitchen with the ease born of many years as a railroad cook.*)

DOAKER:
 Gonna leave Jackson Mississippi
 and go to Memphis
 and double back to Jackson

Come on down to Hattiesburg
Change cars on the Y. D.
coming through the territory to
Meridian
and Meridian to Greenville
and Greenville to Memphis
I'm on my way and I know where

Change cars on the Katy
Leaving Jackson
and going through Clarksdale
Hello Winona!
Courtland!
Bateville!
Como!
Senitobia!
Lewisberg!
Sunflower!
Glendora!
Sharkey!
And double back to Jackson
Hello Greenwood
I'm on my way Memphis
Clarksdale
Moorhead
Indianola
Can a highball pass through?
Highball on through sir
Grand Carson!
Thirty First Street Depot
Fourth Street Depot
Memphis!

(*Wining Boy enters carrying a suit of clothes.*)

DOAKER: I thought you took that suit to the pawnshop?
WINING BOY: I went down there and the man tell me the suit is too old.
Look at this suit. This is one hundred percent silk! How a silk suit
gonna get too old? I know what it was he just didn't want to give me
five dollars for it. Best he wanna give me is three dollars. I figure a silk
suit is worth five dollars all over the world. I wasn't gonna part with it
for no three dollars so I brought it back.
DOAKER: They got another pawnshop up on Wylie.

WINING BOY: I carried it up there. He say he don't take no clothes. Only thing he take is guns and radios. Maybe a guitar or two. Where's Berniece?

DOAKER: Berniece still at work. Boy Willie went down there to meet Lymon this morning. I guess they got that truck fixed, they been out there all day and ain't come back yet. Maretha scared to sleep up there now. Berniece don't know, but I seen Sutter before she did.

WINING BOY: Say what?

DOAKER: About three weeks ago. I had just come back from down there. Sutter couldn't have been dead more than three days. He was sitting over there at the piano. I come out to go to work . . . and he was sitting right there. Had his hand on top of his head just like Berniece said. I believe he broke his neck when he fell in the well. I kept quiet about it. I didn't see no reason to upset Berniece.

WINING BOY: Did he say anything? Did he say he was looking for Boy Willie?

DOAKER: He was just sitting there. He ain't said nothing. I went on out the door and left him sitting there. I figure as long as he was on the other side of the room everything be alright. I don't know what I would have done if he had started walking toward me.

WINING BOY: Berniece say he was calling Boy Willie's name.

DOAKER: I ain't heard him say nothing. He was just sitting there when I seen him. But I don't believe Boy Willie pushed him in the well. Sutter here cause of that piano. I heard him playing on it one time. I thought it was Berniece but then she don't play that kind of music. I come out here and ain't seen nobody, but them piano keys was moving a mile a minute. Berniece need to go on and get rid of it. It ain't done nothing but cause trouble.

WINING BOY: I agree with Berniece. Boy Charles ain't took it to give it back. He took it cause he figure he had more right to it than Sutter did. If Sutter can't understand that . . . then that's just the way that go. Sutter dead and in the ground . . . don't care where his ghost is. He can hover around and play on the piano all he want. I want to see him carry it out the house. That's what I want to see. What time Berniece get home? I don't see how I let her get away from me this morning.

DOAKER: You up there sleep. Berniece leave out of here early in the morning. She out there in Squirrel Hill cleaning house for some bigshot down there at the steel mill. They don't like you to come late. You come late they won't give you your carfare. What kind of business you got with Berniece?

WINING BOY: My business. I ain't asked you what kind of business you got.

DOAKER: Berniece ain't got no money. If that's why you was trying to catch her. She having a hard enough time trying to get by as it is. If she go ahead and marry Avery . . . he working every day . . . she go ahead and marry him they could do alright for themselves. But as it stands she ain't got no money.

WINING BOY: Well, let me have five dollars.

DOAKER: I just give you a dollar before you left out of here. You ain't gonna take my five dollars out there and gamble and drink it up.

WINING BOY: Aw, nigger, give me five dollars. I'll give it back to you.

DOAKER: You wasn't looking to give me five dollars when you had that sack of money. You wasn't looking to throw nothing my way. Now you wanna come in here and borrow five dollars. If you going back with Boy Willie you need to be trying to figure out how you gonna get train fare.

WINING BOY: That's why I need the five dollars. If I had five dollars I could get me some money.

(*Doaker goes into his pocket.*)

Make it seven.

DOAKER: You take this five dollars . . . and you bring my money back here too.

(*Boy Willie and Lymon enter. They are happy and excited. They have money in all of their pockets and are anxious to count it.*)

DOAKER: How'd you do out there?

BOY WILLIE: They was lining up for them.

LYMON: Me and Boy Willie couldn't sell them fast enough. Time we got one sold we'd sell another.

BOY WILLIE: I seen what was happening and told Lymon to up the price on them.

LYMON: Boy Willie say charge them a quarter more. They didn't care. A couple of people give me a dollar and told me to keep the change.

BOY WILLIE: One fellow bought five. I say now what he gonna do with five watermelons? He can't eat them all. I sold him the five and asked him did he want to buy five more.

LYMON: I ain't never seen nobody snatch a dollar fast as Boy Willie.

BOY WILLIE: One lady asked me say, "Is they sweet?" I told her say, "Lady, where we grow these watermelons we put sugar in the ground." You know, she believed me. Talking about she had never heard of that before. Lymon was laughing his head off. I told her, "Oh, yeah, we put the sugar right in the ground with the seed." She say, "Well, give me another one." Them white folks is something else . . . ain't they, Lymon?

LYMON: Soon as you holler watermelons they come right out their door. Then they go and get their neighbors. Look like they having a contest to see who can buy the most.

WINING BOY: I got something for Lymon.

(*Wining Boy goes to get his suit. Boy Willie and Lymon continue to count their money.*)

BOY WILLIE: I know you got more than that. You ain't sold all them watermelons for that little bit of money.

LYMON: I'm still looking. That ain't all you got either. Where's all them quarters?

BOY WILLIE: You let me worry about the quarters. Just put the money on the table.

WINING BOY (*entering with his suit*): Look here, Lymon . . . see this? Look at his eyes getting big. He ain't never seen a suit like this. This is one hundred percent silk. Go ahead . . . put it on. See if it fit you.

(*Lymon tries the suit coat on.*)

Look at that. Feel it. That's one hundred percent genuine silk. I got that in Chicago. You can't get clothes like that nowhere but New York and Chicago. You can't get clothes like that in Pittsburgh. These folks in Pittsburgh ain't never seen clothes like that.

LYMON: This is nice, feel real nice and smooth.

WINING BOY: That's a fifty-five-dollar suit. That's the kind of suit the bigshots wear. You need a pistol and a pocketful of money to wear that suit. I'll let you have it for three dollars. The women will fall out their windows they see you in a suit like that. Give me three dollars and go on and wear it down the street and get you a woman.

BOY WILLIE: That looks nice, Lymon. Put the pants on. Let me see it with the pants.

(*Lymon begins to try on the pants.*)

WINING BOY: Look at that . . . see how it fits you? Give me three dollars and go on and take it. Look at that, Doaker . . . don't he look nice?

DOAKER: Yeah . . . that's a nice suit.

WINING BOY: Got a shirt to go with it. Cost you an extra dollar. Four dollars you got the whole deal.

LYMON: How this look, Boy Willie?

BOY WILLIE: That look nice . . . if you like that kind of thing. I don't like them dress-up kind of clothes. If you like it, look real nice.

WINING BOY: That's the kind of suit you need for up here in the North.

LYMON: Four dollars for everything? The suit and the shirt?

WINING BOY: That's cheap. I should be charging you twenty dollars. I give you a break cause you a homeboy. That's the only way I let you have it for four dollars.

LYMON (*going into his pocket*): Okay . . . here go the four dollars.

WINING BOY: You got some shoes? What size you wear?

LYMON: Size nine.

WINING BOY: That's what size I got! Size nine. I let you have them for three dollars.

LYMON: Where they at? Let me see them.

WINING BOY: They real nice shoes, too. Got a nice tip to them. Got pointy toe just like you want.

(*Wining Boy goes to get his shoes.*)

LYMON: Come on, Boy Willie, let's go out tonight. I wanna see what it looks like up here. Maybe we go to a picture show. Hey, Doaker, they got picture shows up here?

DOAKER: The Rhumba Theater. Right down there on Fullerton Street. Can't miss it. Got the speakers outside on the sidewalk. You can hear it a block away. Boy Willie know where it's at.

(*Doaker exits into his room.*)

LYMON: Let's go to the picture show, Boy Willie. Let's go find some women.

BOY WILLIE: Hey, Lymon, how many of them watermelons would you say we got left? We got just under a half a load . . . right?

LYMON: About that much. Maybe a little more.

BOY WILLIE: You think that piano will fit up in there?

LYMON: If we stack them watermelons you can sit it up in the front there.

BOY WILLIE: I'm gonna call that man tomorrow.

WINING BOY (*returns with his shoes*): Here you go . . . size nine. Put them on. Cost you three dollars. That's a Florsheim shoe. That's the kind Staggerlee wore.

LYMON (*trying on the shoes*): You sure these size nine?

WINING BOY: You can look at my feet and see we wear the same size. Man, you put on that suit and them shoes and you got something there. You ready for whatever's out there. But is they ready for you? With them shoes on you be the King of the Walk. Have everybody stop to look at your shoes. Wishing they had a pair. I'll give you a break. Go on and take them for two dollars.

(*Lymon pays Wining Boy two dollars.*)

LYMON: Come on, Boy Willie . . . let's go find some women. I'm gonna go upstairs and get ready. I'll be ready to go in a minute. Ain't you gonna get dressed?

BOY WILLIE: I'm gonna wear what I got on. I ain't dressing up for these city niggers.

(*Lymon exits up the stairs.*)

That's all Lymon think about is women.

WINING BOY: His daddy was the same way. I used to run around with him. I know his mama too. Two strokes back and I would have been his daddy! His daddy's dead now . . . but I got the nigger out of jail one time. They was fixing to name him Daniel and walk him through the Lion's Den. He got in a tussle with one of them white fellows and the sheriff lit on him like white on rice. That's how the whole thing come about between me and Lymon's mama. She knew me and his daddy used to run together and he got in jail and she went down there and took the sheriff a hundred dollars. Don't get me to lying about where she got it from. I don't know. The sheriff looked at that hundred dollars and turned his nose up. Told her, say, "That ain't gonna do him no good. You got to put another hundred on top of that." She come up there and got me where I was playing at this saloon . . . said she had all but fifty dollars and asked me if I could help. Now the way I figured it . . . without that fifty dollars the sheriff was gonna turn him over to Parchman. The sheriff turn him over to Parchman it be three years before anybody see him again. Now I'm gonna say it right . . . I will give anybody fifty dollars to keep them out of jail for three years. I give her the fifty dollars and she told me to come over to the house. I ain't asked her. I figure if she was nice enough to invite me I ought to go. I ain't had to say a word. She invited me over just as nice. Say, "Why don't you come over to the house?" She ain't had to say nothing else. Them words rolled off her tongue just as nice. I went on down there and sat about three hours. Started to leave and changed my mind. She grabbed hold to me and say, "Baby, it's all night long." That was one of the shortest nights I have ever spent on this earth! I could have used another eight hours. Lymon's daddy didn't even say nothing to me when he got out. He just looked at me funny. He had a good notion something had happened between me an' her. L. D. Jackson. That was one bad-luck nigger. Got killed at some dance. Fellow walked in and shot him thinking he was somebody else.

(*Doaker enters from his room.*)

Hey, Doaker, you remember L. D. Jackson?

DOAKER: That's Lymon's daddy. That was one bad-luck nigger.

BOY WILLIE: Look like you ready to railroad some.

DOAKER: Yeah, I got to make that run.

(*Lymon enters from the stairs. He is dressed in his new suit and shoes, to which he has added a cheap straw hat.*)

LYMON: How I look?

WINING BOY: You look like a million dollars. Don't he look good, Doaker? Come on, let's play some cards. You wanna play some cards?

BOY WILLIE: We ain't gonna play no cards with you. Me and Lymon gonna find some women. Hey, Lymon, don't play no cards with Wining Boy. He'll take all your money.

WINING BOY (*to Lymon*): You got a magic suit there. You can get you a woman easy with that suit . . . but you got to know the magic words. You know the magic words to get you a woman?

LYMON: I just talk to them to see if I like them and they like me.

WINING BOY: You just walk right up to them and say, "If you got the harbor I got the ship." If that don't work ask them if you can put them in your pocket. The first thing they gonna say is, "It's too small." That's when you look them dead in the eye and say, "Baby, ain't nothing small about me." If that don't work then you move on to another one. Am I telling him right, Doaker?

DOAKER: That man don't need you to tell him nothing about no women. These women these days ain't gonna fall for that kind of stuff. You got to buy them a present. That's what they looking for these days.

BOY WILLIE: Come on, I'm ready. You ready, Lymon? Come on, let's go find some women.

WINING BOY: Here, let me walk out with you. I wanna see the women fall out their window when they see Lymon.

(*They all exit and the lights go down on the scene.*)

Scene 2

(*The lights come up on the kitchen. It is late evening of the same day. Berniece has set a tub for her bath in the kitchen. She is heating up water on the stove. There is a knock at the door.*)

BERNIECE: Who is it?

AVERY: It's me, Avery.

(*Berniece opens the door and lets him in.*)

BERNIECE: Avery, come on in. I was just fixing to take my bath.

AVERY: Where Boy Willie? I see that truck out there almost empty. They done sold almost all them watermelons.

BERNIECE: They was gone when I come home. I don't know where they went off to. Boy Willie around here about to drive me crazy.

AVERY: They sell them watermelons . . . he'll be gone soon.

BERNIECE: What Mr. Cohen say about letting you have the place?

AVERY: He say he'll let me have it for thirty dollars a month. I talked him out of thirty-five and he say he'll let me have it for thirty.

BERNIECE: That's a nice spot next to Benny Diamond's store.

AVERY: Berniece . . . I be at home and I get to thinking you up here an' I'm down there. I get to thinking how that look to have a preacher that ain't married. It makes for a better congregation if the preacher was settled down and married.

BERNIECE: Avery . . . not now. I was fixing to take my bath.

AVERY: You know how I feel about you, Berniece. Now . . . I done got the place from Mr. Cohen. I get the money from the bank and I can fix it up real nice. They give me a ten cents a hour raise down there on the job . . . now Berniece, I ain't got much in the way of comforts. I got a hole in my pockets near about as far as money is concerned. I ain't never found no way through life to a woman I care about like I care about you. I need that. I need somebody on my bond side. I need a woman that fits in my hand.

BERNIECE: Avery, I ain't ready to get married now.

AVERY: You too young a woman to close up, Berniece.

BERNIECE: I ain't said nothing about closing up. I got a lot of woman left in me.

AVERY: Where's it at? When's the last time you looked at it?

BERNIECE (*stunned by his remark*): That's a nasty thing to say. And you call yourself a preacher.

AVERY: Anytime I get anywhere near you . . . you push me away.

BERNIECE: I got enough on my hands with Maretha. I got enough people to love and take care of.

AVERY: Who you got to love you? Can't nobody get close enough to you. Doaker can't half say nothing to you. You jump all over Boy Willie. Who you got to love you, Berniece?

BERNIECE: You trying to tell me a woman can't be nothing without a man. But you alright, huh? You can just walk out of here without me—without a woman—and still be a man. That's alright. Ain't nobody gonna ask you, "Avery, who you got to love you?" That's alright for you. But everybody gonna be worried about Berniece. "How Berniece gonna take care of herself? How she gonna raise that child without a man? Wonder what she do with herself. How she gonna live like that?" Everybody got all kinds of questions for Berniece. Everybody telling me I can't be a woman unless I got a man. Well, you tell me, Avery—you know—how much woman am I?

AVERY: It wasn't me, Berniece. You can't blame me for nobody else. I'll own up to my own shortcomings. But you can't blame me for Crawley or nobody else.

BERNIECE: I ain't blaming nobody for nothing. I'm just stating the facts.

AVERY: How long you gonna carry Crawley with you, Berniece? It's been over three years. At some point you got to let go and go on. Life's got

all kinds of twists and turns. That don't mean you stop living. That
don't mean you cut yourself off from life. You can't go through life carrying Crawley's ghost with you. Crawley's been dead three years. Three
years, Berniece.

BERNIECE: I know how long Crawley's been dead. You ain't got to tell me
that. I just ain't ready to get married right now.

AVERY: What is you ready for, Berniece? You just gonna drift along from
day to day. Life is more than making it from one day to another. You
gonna look up one day and it's all gonna be past you. Life's gonna be
gone out of your hands—there won't be enough to make nothing with.
I'm standing here now, Berniece—but I don't know how much longer
I'm gonna be standing here waiting on you.

BERNIECE: Avery, I told you . . . when you get your church we'll sit down
and talk about this. I got too many other things to deal with right now.
Boy Willie and the piano . . . and Sutter's ghost. I thought I might have
been seeing things, but Maretha done seen Sutter's ghost, too.

AVERY: When this happen, Berniece?

BERNIECE: Right after I came home yesterday. Me and Boy Willie was
arguing about the piano and Sutter's ghost was standing at the top of
the stairs. Maretha scared to sleep up there now. Maybe if you bless
the house he'll go away.

AVERY: I don't know, Berniece. I don't know if I should fool around with
something like that.

BERNIECE: I can't have Maretha scared to go to sleep up there. Seem like
if you bless the house he would go away.

AVERY: You might have to be a special kind of preacher to do something
like that.

BERNIECE: I keep telling myself when Boy Willie leave he'll go on and
leave with him. I believe Boy Willie pushed him in the well.

AVERY: That's been going on down there a long time. The Ghosts of the
Yellow Dog been pushing people in their wells long before Boy Willie
got grown.

BERNIECE: Somebody down there pushing them people in their wells.
They ain't just upped and fell. Ain't no wind pushed nobody in their
well.

AVERY: Oh, I don't know. God works in mysterious ways.

BERNIECE: He ain't pushed nobody in their wells.

AVERY: He caused it to happen. God is the Great Causer. He can do anything. He parted the Red Sea. He say I will smite my enemies.
Reverend Thompson used to preach on the Ghosts of the Yellow Dog
as the hand of God.

BERNIECE: I don't care who preached what. Somebody down there pushing them people in their wells. Somebody like Boy Willie. I can see

him doing something like that. You ain't gonna tell me that Sutter just upped and fell in his well. I believe Boy Willie pushed him so he could get his land.

AVERY: What Doaker say about Boy Willie selling the piano?

BERNIECE: Doaker don't want no part of that piano. He ain't never wanted no part of it. He blames himself for not staying behind with Papa Boy Charles. He washed his hands of that piano a long time ago. He didn't want me to bring it up here—but I wasn't gonna leave it down there.

AVERY: Well, it seems to me somebody ought to be able to talk to Boy Willie.

BERNIECE: You can't talk to Boy Willie. He been that way all his life. Mama Ola had her hands full trying to talk to him. He don't listen to nobody. He just like my daddy. He get his mind fixed on something and can't nobody turn him from it.

AVERY: You ought to start a choir at the church. Maybe if he seen you was doing something with it—if you told him you was gonna put it in my church—maybe he'd see it different. You ought to put it down in the church and start a choir. The Bible say "Make a joyful noise unto the Lord." Maybe if Boy Willie see you was doing something with it he'd see it different.

BERNIECE: I done told you I don't play on that piano. Ain't no need in you to keep talking this choir stuff. When my mama died I shut the top on that piano and I ain't never opened it since. I was only playing it for her. When my daddy died seem like all her life went into that piano. She used to have me playing on it . . . had Miss Eula come in and teach me . . . say when I played it she could hear my daddy talking to her. I used to think them pictures came alive and walked through the house. Sometime late at night I could hear my mama talking to them. I said that wasn't gonna happen to me. I don't play that piano cause I don't want to wake them spirits. They never be walking around in this house.

AVERY: You got to put all that behind you, Berniece.

BERNIECE: I got Maretha playing on it. She don't know nothing about it. Let her go on and be a schoolteacher or something. She don't have to carry all of that with her. She got a chance I didn't have. I ain't gonna burden her with that piano.

AVERY: You got to put all of that behind you, Berniece. That's the same thing like Crawley. Everybody got stones in their passway. You got to step over them or walk around them. You picking them up and carrying them with you. All you got to do is set them down by the side of the road. You ain't got to carry them with you. You can walk over there right now and play that piano. You can walk over there right now and

God will walk over there with you. Right now you can set that sack of stones down by the side of the road and walk away from it. You don't have to carry it with you. You can do it right now.

(*Avery crosses over to the piano and raises the lid.*)

Come on, Berniece . . . set it down and walk away from it. Come on, play "Old Ship of Zion." Walk over here and claim it as an instrument of the Lord. You can walk over here right now and make it into a celebration.

(*Berniece moves toward the piano.*)

BERNIECE: Avery . . . I done told you I don't want to play that piano. Now or no other time.

AVERY: The Bible say, "The Lord is my refuge . . . and my strength!" With the strength of God you can put the past behind you, Berniece. With the strength of God you can do anything! God got a bright tomorrow. God don't ask what you done . . . God ask what you gonna do. The strength of God can move mountains! God's got a bright tomorrow for you . . . all you got to do is walk over here and claim it.

BERNIECE: Avery, just go on and let me finish my bath. I'll see you tomorrow.

AVERY: Okay, Berniece. I'm gonna go home. I'm gonna go home and read up on my Bible. And tomorrow . . . if the good Lord give me strength tomorrow . . . I'm gonna come by and bless the house . . . and show you the power of the Lord.

(*Avery crosses to the door.*)

It's gonna be alright, Berniece. God say he will soothe the troubled waters. I'll come by tomorrow and bless the house.

(*The lights go down to black.*)

Scene 3

(*Several hours later. The house is dark. Berniece has retired for the night. Boy Willie enters the darkened house with Grace.*)

BOY WILLIE: Come on in. This my sister's house. My sister live here. Come on, I ain't gonna bite you.

GRACE: Put some light on. I can't see.

BOY WILLIE: You don't need to see nothing, baby. This here is all you need to see. All you need to do is see me. If you can't see me you can feel me in the dark. How's that, sugar?

(*He attempts to kiss her.*)

GRACE: Go on now . . . wait!

BOY WILLIE: Just give me one little old kiss.

GRACE (*pushing him away*): Come on, now. Where I'm gonna sleep at?

BOY WILLIE: We got to sleep out here on the couch. Come on, my sister
    don't mind. Lymon come back he just got to sleep on the floor. He run
    off with Dolly somewhere he better stay there. Come on, sugar.

GRACE: Wait now . . . you ain't told me nothing about no couch. I
    thought you had a bed. Both of us can't sleep on that little old couch.

BOY WILLIE: It don't make no difference. We can sleep on the floor. Let
    Lymon sleep on the couch.

GRACE: You ain't told me nothing about no couch.

BOY WILLIE: What difference it make? You just wanna be with me.

GRACE: I don't want to be with you on no couch. Ain't you got no bed?

BOY WILLIE: You don't need no bed, woman. My granddaddy used to
    take women on the backs of horses. What you need a bed for? You just
    want to be with me.

GRACE: You sure is country. I didn't know you was this country.

BOY WILLIE: There's a lot of things you don't know about me. Come on,
    let me show you what this country boy can do.

GRACE: Let's go to my place. I got a room with a bed if Leroy don't come
    back there.

BOY WILLIE: Who's Leroy? You ain't said nothing about no Leroy.

GRACE: He used to be my man. He ain't coming back. He gone off with
    some other gal.

BOY WILLIE: You let him have your key?

GRACE: He ain't coming back.

BOY WILLIE: Did you let him have your key?

GRACE: He got a key but he ain't coming back. He took off with some
    other gal.

BOY WILLIE: I don't wanna go nowhere he might come. Let's stay here.
    Come on, sugar.

(*He pulls her over to the couch.*)

Let me heist your hood and check your oil. See if your battery needs
charged.

(*He pulls her to him. They kiss and tug at each other's clothing. In their anxiety
they knock over a lamp.*)

BERNIECE: Who's that . . . Wining Boy?

BOY WILLIE: It's me . . . Boy Willie. Go on back to sleep. Everything's
    alright.

(*To Grace.*)

That's my sister. Everything's alright, Berniece. Go on back to sleep.

BERNIECE: What you doing down there? What you done knocked over?

BOY WILLIE: It wasn't nothing. Everything's alright. Go on back to sleep.

(*To Grace.*)

That's my sister. We alright. She gone back to sleep.

(*They begin to kiss. Berniece enters from the stairs dressed in a nightgown. She cuts on the light.*)

BERNIECE: Boy Willie, what you doing down here?

BOY WILLIE: It was just that there lamp. It ain't broke. It's okay. Everything's alright. Go on back to bed.

BERNIECE: Boy Willie, I don't allow that in my house. You gonna have to take your company someplace else.

BOY WILLIE: It's alright. We ain't doing nothing. We just sitting here talking. This here is Grace. That's my sister Berniece.

BERNIECE: You know I don't allow that kind of stuff in my house.

BOY WILLIE: Allow what? We just sitting here talking.

BERNIECE: Well, your company gonna have to leave. Come back and talk in the morning.

BOY WILLIE: Go on back upstairs now.

BERNIECE: I got an eleven-year-old girl upstairs. I can't allow that around here.

BOY WILLIE: Ain't nobody said nothing about that. I told you we just talking.

GRACE: Come on . . . let's go to my place. Ain't nobody got to tell me to leave but once.

BOY WILLIE: You ain't got to be like that, Berniece.

BERNIECE: I'm sorry, Miss. But he know I don't allow that in here.

GRACE: You ain't got to tell me but once. I don't stay nowhere I ain't wanted.

BOY WILLIE: I don't know why you want to embarrass me in front of my company.

GRACE: Come on, take me home.

BERNIECE: Go on, Boy Willie. Just go on with your company.

(*Boy Willie and Grace exit. Berniece puts the light on in the kitchen and puts on the teakettle. Presently there is a knock at the door. Berniece goes to answer it. Berniece opens the door. Lymon enters.*)

LYMON: How you doing, Berniece? I thought you'd be asleep. Boy Willie been back here?

BERNIECE: He just left out of here a minute ago.

LYMON: I went out to see a picture show and never got there. We always end up doing something else. I was with this woman she just wanted

to drink up all my money. So I left her there and came back looking for
Boy Willie.

BERNIECE: You just missed him. He just left out of here.

LYMON: They got some nice-looking women in this city. I'm gonna like it
up here real good. I like seeing them with their dresses on. Got them
high heels. I like that. Make them look like they real precious. Boy
Willie met a real nice one today. I wish I had met her before he did.

BERNIECE: He come by here with some woman a little while ago. I told
him to go on and take all that out of my house.

LYMON: What she look like, the woman he was with? Was she a brown-
skinned woman about this high? Nice and healthy? Got nice hips on her?

BERNIECE: She had on a red dress.

LYMON: That's her! That's Grace. She real nice. Laugh a lot. Lot of fun to
be with. She don't be trying to put on. Some of these woman act like
they the Queen of Sheba. I don't like them kind. Grace ain't like that.
She real nice with herself.

BERNIECE: I don't know what she was like. He come in here all drunk
knocking over the lamp, and making all kind of noise. I told them to
take that somewhere else. I can't really say what she was like.

LYMON: She real nice. I seen her before he did. I was trying not to act like
I seen her. I wanted to look at her a while before I said something. She
seen me when I come into the saloon. I tried to act like I didn't see her.
Time I looked around Boy Willie was talking to her. She was talking to
him kept looking at me. That's when her friend Dolly came. I asked her
if she wanted to go to the picture show. She told me to buy her a drink
while she thought about it. Next thing I knew she done had three
drinks talking about she too tired to go. I bought her another drink,
then I left. Boy Willie was gone and I thought he might have come
back here. Doaker gone, huh? He say he had to make a trip.

BERNIECE: Yeah, he gone on his trip. This is when I can usually get me
some peace and quiet, Maretha asleep.

LYMON: She look just like you. Got them big eyes. I remember her when
she was in diapers.

BERNIECE: Time just keep on. It go on with or without you. She going on
twelve.

LYMON: She sure is pretty. I like kids.

BERNIECE: Boy Willie say you staying . . . what you gonna do up here in
this big city? You thought about that?

LYMON: They never get me back down there. The sheriff looking for me.
All because they gonna try and make me work for somebody when I
don't want to. They gonna try and make me work for Stovall when
he don't pay nothing. It ain't like that up here. Up here you more or
less do what you want to. I figure I find me a job and try to get set up

and then see what the year brings. I tried to do that two or three times down there . . . but it never would work out. I was always in the wrong place.

BERNIECE: This ain't a bad city once you get to know your way around.

LYMON: Up here is different. I'm gonna get me a job unloading boxcars or something. One fellow told me say he know a place. I'm gonna go over there with him next week. Me and Boy Willie finish selling them watermelons I'll have enough money to hold me for a while. But I'm gonna go over there and see what kind of jobs they have.

BERNIECE: You shouldn't have too much trouble finding a job. It's all in how you present yourself. See now, Boy Willie couldn't get no job up here. Somebody hire him they got a pack of trouble on their hands. Soon as they find that out they fire him. He don't want to do nothing unless he do it his way.

LYMON: I know. I told him let's go to the picture show first and see if there was any women down there. They might get tired of sitting at home and walk down to the picture show. He say he wanna look around first. We never did get down there. We tried a couple of places and then we went to this saloon where he met Grace. I tried to meet her before he did but he beat me to her. We left Wining Boy sitting down there running his mouth. He told me if I wear this suit I'd find me a woman. He was almost right.

BERNIECE: You don't need to be out there in them saloons. Ain't no telling what you liable to run into out there. This one liable to cut you as quick as that one shoot you. You don't need to be out there. You start out that fast life you can't keep it up. It makes you old quick. I don't know what them women out there be thinking about.

LYMON: Mostly they be lonely and looking for somebody to spend the night with them. Sometimes it matters who it is and sometimes it don't. I used to be the same way. Now it got to matter. That's why I'm here now. Dolly liable not to even recognize me if she sees me again. I don't like women like that. I like my women to be with me in a nice and easy way. That way we can both enjoy ourselves. The way I see it we the only two people like us in the world. We got to see how we fit together. A woman that don't want to take the time to do that I don't bother with. Used to. Used to bother with all of them. Then I woke up one time with this woman and I didn't know who she was. She was the prettiest woman I had ever seen in my life. I spent the whole night with her and didn't even know it. I had never taken the time to look at her. I guess she kinda knew I ain't never really looked at her. She must have known that cause she ain't wanted to see me no more. If she had wanted to see me I believe we might have got married. How come you ain't married? It seem like to me you would be married. I remember

Avery from down home. I used to call him plain old Avery. Now he
Reverend Avery. That's kinda funny about him becoming a preacher. I
like when he told about how that come to him in a dream about them
sheep people and them hobos. Nothing ever come to me in a dream
like that. I just dream about women. Can't never seem to find the right
one.

BERNIECE: She out there somewhere. You just got to get yourself ready
to meet her. That's what I'm trying to do. Avery's alright. I ain't really
got nobody in mind.

LYMON: I get me a job and a little place and get set up to where I can
make a woman comfortable I might get married. Avery's nice. You
ought to go ahead and get married. You be a preacher's wife you won't
have to work. I hate living by myself. I didn't want to be no strain on
my mama so I left home when I was about sixteen. Everything I tried
seem like it just didn't work out. Now I'm trying this.

BERNIECE: You keep trying it'll work out for you.

LYMON: You ever go down there to the picture show?

BERNIECE: I don't go in for all that.

LYMON: Ain't nothing wrong with it. It ain't like gambling and sinning. I
went to one down in Jackson once. It was fun.

BERNIECE: I just stay home most of the time. Take care of Maretha.

LYMON: It's getting kind of late. I don't know where Boy Willie went off
to. He's liable not to come back. I'm gonna take off these shoes. My
feet hurt. Was you in bed? I don't mean to be keeping you up.

BERNIECE: You ain't keeping me up. I couldn't sleep after that Boy Willie
woke me up.

LYMON: You got on that nightgown. I likes women when they wear them
fancy nightclothes and all. It makes their skin look real pretty.

BERNIECE: I got this at the five-and-ten-cents store. It ain't so fancy.

LYMON: I don't too often get to see a woman dressed like that.

(*There is a long pause. Lymon takes off his suit coat.*)

Well, I'm gonna sleep here on the couch. I'm supposed to sleep on the
floor but I don't reckon Boy Willie's coming back tonight. Wining Boy
sold me this suit. Told me it was a magic suit. I'm gonna put it on
again tomorrow. Maybe it bring me a woman like he say.

(*He goes into his coat pocket and takes out a small bottle of perfume.*)

I almost forgot I had this. Some man sold me this for a dollar. Say it
come from Paris. This is the same kind of perfume the Queen of
France wear. That's what he told me. I don't know if it's true or not. I
smelled it. It smelled good to me. Here . . . smell it see if you like it.
I was gonna give it to Dolly. But I didn't like her too much.

BERNIECE (*takes the bottle*): It smells nice.

LYMON: I was gonna give it to Dolly if she had went to the picture with me. Go on, you take it.

BERNIECE: I can't take it. Here . . . go on you keep it. You'll find somebody to give it to.

LYMON: I wanna give it to you. Make you smell nice.

(*He takes the bottle and puts perfume behind Berniece's ear.*)

They tell me you supposed to put it right here behind your ear. Say if you put it there you smell nice all day.

(*Berniece stiffens at his touch. Lymon bends down to smell her.*)

There . . . you smell real good now.

(*He kisses her neck.*)

You smell real good for Lymon.

(*He kisses her again. Berniece returns the kiss, then breaks the embrace and crosses to the stairs. She turns and they look silently at each other. Lymon hands her the bottle of perfume. Berniece exits up the stairs. Lymon picks up his suit coat and strokes it lovingly with the full knowledge that it is indeed a magic suit. The lights go down on the scene.*)

Scene 4

(*It is late the next morning. The lights come up on the parlor. Lymon is asleep on the sofa. Boy Willie enters the front door.*)

BOY WILLIE: Hey, Lymon! Lymon, come on get up.

LYMON: Leave me alone.

BOY WILLIE: Come on, get up, nigger! Wake up, Lymon.

LYMON: What you want?

BOY WILLIE: Come on, let's go. I done called the man about the piano.

LYMON: What piano?

BOY WILLIE (*dumps Lymon on the floor*): Come on, get up!

LYMON: Why you leave, I looked around and you was gone.

BOY WILLIE: I come back here with Grace, then I went looking for you. I figured you'd be with Dolly.

LYMON: She just want to drink and spend up your money. I come on back here looking for you to see if you wanted to go to the picture show.

BOY WILLIE: I been up at Grace's house. Some nigger named Leroy come by but I had a chair up against the door. He got mad when he couldn't get in. He went off somewhere and I got out of there before he could come back. Berniece got mad when we came here.

LYMON: She say you was knocking over the lamp busting up the place.

BOY WILLIE: That was Grace doing all that.

LYMON: Wining Boy seen Sutter's ghost last night.

BOY WILLIE: Wining Boy's liable to see anything. I'm surprised he found the right house. Come on, I done called the man about the piano.

LYMON: What he say?

BOY WILLIE: He say to bring it on out. I told him I was calling for my sister, Miss Berniece Charles. I told him some man wanted to buy it for eleven hundred dollars and asked him if he would go any better. He said yeah, he would give me eleven hundred and fifty dollars for it if it was the same piano. I described it to him again and he told me to bring it out.

LYMON: Why didn't you tell him to come and pick it up?

BOY WILLIE: I didn't want to have no problem with Berniece. This way we just take it on out there and it be out the way. He want to charge twenty-five dollars to pick it up.

LYMON: You should have told him the man was gonna give you twelve hundred for it.

BOY WILLIE: I figure I was taking a chance with that eleven hundred. If I had told him twelve hundred he might have run off. Now I wish I had told him twelve-fifty. It's hard to figure out white folks sometimes.

LYMON: You might have been able to tell him anything. White folks got a lot of money.

BOY WILLIE: Come on, let's get it loaded before Berniece come back. Get that end over there. All you got to do is pick it up on that side. Don't worry about this side. You wanna stretch you' back for a minute?

LYMON: I'm ready.

BOY WILLIE: Get a real good grip on it now.

(*The sound of Sutter's Ghost is heard. They do not hear it.*)

LYMON: I got this end. You get that end.

BOY WILLIE: Wait till I say ready now. Alright. You got it good? You got a grip on it?

LYMON: Yeah, I got it. You lift up on that end.

BOY WILLIE: Ready? Lift!

(*The piano will not budge.*)

LYMON: Man, this piano is heavy! It's gonna take more than me and you to move this piano.

BOY WILLIE: We can do it. Come on—we did it before.

LYMON: Nigger—you crazy! That piano weighs five hundred pounds!

BOY WILLIE: I got three hundred pounds of it! I know you can carry two hundred pounds! You be lifting them cotton sacks! Come on lift this piano!

(*They try to move the piano again without success.*)

LYMON: It's stuck. Something holding it.

BOY WILLIE: How the piano gonna be stuck? We just moved it. Slide you' end out.

LYMON: Naw—we gonna need two or three more people. How this big old piano get in the house?

BOY WILLIE: I don't know how it got in the house. I know how it's going out though! You get on this end. I'll carry three hundred and fifty pounds of it. All you got to do is slide your end out. Ready?

(*They switch sides and try again without success. Doaker enters from his room as they try to push and shove it.*)

LYMON: Hey, Doaker . . . how this piano get in the house?

DOAKER: Boy Willie, what you doing?

BOY WILLIE: I'm carrying this piano out the house. What it look like I'm doing? Come on, Lymon, let's try again.

DOAKER: Go on let the piano sit there till Berniece come home.

BOY WILLIE: You ain't got nothing to do with this, Doaker. This my business.

DOAKER: This is my house, nigger! I ain't gonna let you or nobody else carry nothing out of it. You ain't gonna carry nothing out of here without my permission!

BOY WILLIE: This is my piano. I don't need your permission to carry my belongings out of your house. This is mine. This ain't got nothing to do with you.

DOAKER: I say leave it over there till Berniece come home. She got part of it too. Leave it set there till you see what she say.

BOY WILLIE: I don't care what Berniece say. Come on, Lymon. I got this side.

DOAKER: Go on and cut it half in two if you want to. Just leave Berniece's half sitting over there. I can't tell you what to do with your piano. But I can't let you take her half out of here.

BOY WILLIE: Go on, Doaker. You ain't got nothing to do with this. I don't want you starting nothing now. Just go on and leave me alone. Come on, Lymon. I got this end.

(*Doaker goes into his room. Boy Willie and Lymon prepare to move the piano.*)

LYMON: How we gonna get it in the truck?

BOY WILLIE: Don't worry about how we gonna get it on the truck. You got to get it out the house first.

LYMON: It's gonna take more than me and you to move this piano.

BOY WILLIE: Just lift up on that end, nigger!

(*Doaker comes to the doorway of his room and stands.*)

DOAKER (*quietly with authority*): Leave that piano set over there till Berniece come back. I don't care what you do with it then. But you gonna leave it sit over there right now.

BOY WILLIE: Alright . . . I'm gonna tell you this, Doaker. I'm going out of here . . . I'm gonna get me some rope . . . find me a plank and some wheels . . . and I'm coming back. Then I'm gonna carry that piano out of here . . . sell it and give Berniece half the money. See . . . now that's what I'm gonna do. And you . . . or nobody else is gonna stop me. Come on, Lymon . . . let's go get some rope and stuff. I'll be back, Doaker.

(*Boy Willie and Lymon exit. The lights go down on the scene.*)

Scene 5

(*The lights come up. Boy Willie sits on the sofa, screwing casters on a wooden plank. Maretha is sitting on the piano stool. Doaker sits at the table playing solitaire.*)

BOY WILLIE (*to Maretha*): Then after that them white folks down around there started falling down their wells. You ever seen a well? A well got a wall around it. It's hard to fall down a well. You got to be leaning way over. Couldn't nobody figure out too much what was making these fellows fall down their well . . . so everybody says the Ghosts of the Yellow Dog must have pushed them. That's what everybody called them four men what got burned up in the boxcar.

MARETHA: Why they call them that?

BOY WILLIE: Cause the Yazoo Delta railroad got yellow boxcars. Sometime the way the whistle blow sound like an old dog howling so the people call it the Yellow Dog.

MARETHA: Anybody ever see the Ghosts?

BOY WILLIE: I told you they like the wind. Can you see the wind?

MARETHA: No.

BOY WILLIE: They like the wind you can't see them. But sometimes you be in trouble they might be around to help you. They say if you go where the Southern cross the Yellow Dog . . . you go to where them two railroads cross each other . . . and call out their names . . . they say they talk back to you. I don't know, I ain't never done that. But Uncle Wining Boy he say he been down there and talked to them. You have to ask him about that part.

(*Berniece has entered from the front door.*)

BERNIECE: Maretha, you go on and get ready for me to do your hair.

(*Maretha crosses to the steps.*)

Boy Willie, I done told you to leave my house.

(*To Maretha.*)

Go on, Maretha.

(*Maretha is hesitant about going up the stairs.*)

BOY WILLIE: Don't be scared. Here, I'll go up there with you. If we see Sutter's ghost I'll put a whupping on him. Come on, Uncle Boy Willie going with you.

(*Boy Willie and Maretha exit up the stairs.*)

BERNIECE: Doaker—what is going on here?

DOAKER: I come home and him and Lymon was moving the piano. I told them to leave it over there till you got home. He went out and got that board and them wheels. He say he gonna take that piano out of here and ain't nobody gonna stop him.

BERNIECE: I ain't playing with Boy Willie. I got Crawley's gun upstairs. He don't know but I'm through with it. Where Lymon go?

DOAKER: Boy Willie sent him for some rope just before you come in.

BERNIECE: I ain't studying Boy Willie or Lymon—or the rope. Boy Willie ain't taking that piano out this house. That's all there is to it.

(*Boy Willie and Maretha enter on the stairs. Maretha carries a hot comb and a can of hair grease. Boy Willie crosses over and continues to screw the wheels on the board.*)

MARETHA: Mama, all the hair grease is gone. There ain't but this little bit left.

BERNIECE (*gives her a dollar*): Here . . . run across the street and get another can. You come straight back, too. Don't you be playing around out there. And watch the cars. Be careful when you cross the street.

(*Maretha exits out the front door.*)

Boy Willie, I done told you to leave my house.

BOY WILLIE: I ain't in you' house. I'm in Doaker's house. If he ask me to leave then I'll go on and leave. But consider me done left your part.

BERNIECE: Doaker, tell him to leave. Tell him to go on.

DOAKER: Boy Willie ain't done nothing for me to put him out of the house. I told you if you can't get along just go on and don't have nothing to do with each other.

BOY WILLIE: I ain't thinking about Berniece.

(*He gets up and draws a line across the floor with his foot.*)

There! Now I'm out of your part of the house. Consider me done left your part. Soon as Lymon come back with that rope. I'm gonna take that piano out of here and sell it.

BERNIECE: You ain't gonna touch that piano.

BOY WILLIE: Carry it out of here just as big and bold. Do like my daddy would have done come time to get Sutter's land.

BERNIECE: I got something to make you leave it over there.

BOY WILLIE: It's got to come better than this thirty-two-twenty.

DOAKER: Why don't you stop all that! Boy Willie, go on and leave her alone. You know how Berniece get. Why you wanna sit there and pick with her?

BOY WILLIE: I ain't picking with her. I told her the truth. She the one talking about what she got. I just told her what she better have.

BERNIECE: That's alright, Doaker. Leave him alone.

BOY WILLIE: She trying to scare me. Hell, I ain't scared of dying. I look around and see people dying every day. You got to die to make room for somebody else. I had a dog that died. Wasn't nothing but a puppy. I picked it up and put it in a bag and carried it up there to Reverend C. L. Thompson's church. I carried it up there and prayed and asked Jesus to make it live like he did the man in the Bible. I prayed real hard. Knelt down and everything. Say ask in Jesus' name. Well, I must have called Jesus' name two hundred times. I called his name till my mouth got sore. I got up and looked in the bag and the dog still dead. It ain't moved a muscle! I say, "Well, ain't nothing precious." And then I went out and killed me a cat. That's when I discovered the power of death. See, a nigger that ain't afraid to die is the worse kind of nigger for the white man. He can't hold that power over you. That's what I learned when I killed that cat. I got the power of death too. I can command him. I can call him up. The white man don't like to see that. He don't like for you to stand up and look him square in the eye and say, "I got it too." Then he got to deal with you square up.

BERNIECE: That's why I don't talk to him, Doaker. You try and talk to him and that's the only kind of stuff that comes out his mouth.

DOAKER: You say Avery went home to get his Bible?

BOY WILLIE: What Avery gonna do? Avery can't do nothing with me. I wish Avery would say something to me about this piano.

DOAKER: Berniece ain't said about that. Avery went home to get his Bible. He coming by to bless the house see if he can get rid of Sutter's ghost.

BOY WILLIE: Ain't nothing but a house full of ghosts down there at the church. What Avery look like chasing away somebody's ghost?

(*Maretha enters the front door.*)

BERNIECE: Light that stove and set that comb over there to get hot. Get something to put around your shoulders.

BOY WILLIE: The Bible say an eye for an eye, a tooth for a tooth, and a life for a life. Tit for tat. But you and Avery don't want to believe that.

You gonna pass up that part and pretend it ain't in there. Everything else you gonna agree with. But if you gonna agree with part of it you got to agree with all of it. You can't do nothing halfway. You gonna go at the Bible halfway. You gonna act like that part ain't in there. But you pull out the Bible and open it and see what it say. Ask Avery. He a preacher. He'll tell you it's in there. He the Good Shepherd. Unless he gonna shepherd you to heaven with half the Bible.

BERNIECE: Maretha, bring me that comb. Make sure it's hot.

(Maretha brings the comb. Berniece begins to do her hair.)

BOY WILLIE: I will say this for Avery. He done figured out a path to go through life. I don't agree with it. But he done fixed it so he can go right through it real smooth. Hell, he liable to end up with a million dollars that he done got from selling bread and wine.

MARETHA: OWWWWWW!

BERNIECE: Be still, Maretha. If you was a boy I wouldn't be going through this.

BOY WILLIE: Don't you tell that girl that. Why you wanna tell her that?

BERNIECE: You ain't got nothing to do with this child.

BOY WILLIE: Telling her you wished she was a boy. How's that gonna make her feel?

BERNIECE: Boy Willie, go on and leave me alone.

DOAKER: Why don't you leave her alone? What you got to pick with her for? Why don't you go on out and see what's out there in the streets? Have something to tell the fellows down home.

BOY WILLIE: I'm waiting on Lymon to get back with that truck. Why don't you go on out and see what's out there in the streets? You ain't got to work tomorrow. Talking about me . . . why don't you go out there? It's Friday night.

DOAKER: I got to stay around here and keep you all from killing one another.

BOY WILLIE: You ain't got to worry about me. I'm gonna be here just as long as it takes Lymon to get back here with that truck. You ought to be talking to Berniece. Sitting up there telling Maretha she wished she was a boy. What kind of thing is that to tell a child? If you want to tell her something tell her about that piano. You ain't even told her about that piano. Like that's something to be ashamed of. Like she supposed to go off and hide somewhere about that piano. You ought to mark down on the calendar the day that Papa Boy Charles brought that piano into the house. You ought to mark that day down and draw a circle around it . . . and every year when it come up throw a party. Have a celebration. If you did that she wouldn't have no problem in life. She could walk around here with her head held high. I'm talking about a big party!

Invite everybody! Mark that day down with a special meaning. That
way she know where she at in the world. You got her going out here
thinking she wrong in the world. Like there ain't no part of it belong
to her.

BERNIECE: Let me take care of my child. When you get one of your own
then you can teach it what you want to teach it.

(*Doaker exits into his room.*)

BOY WILLIE: What I want to bring a child into this world for? Why I
wanna bring somebody else into all this for? I'll tell you this . . . If I was
Rockefeller I'd have forty or fifty. I'd make one every day. Cause they
gonna start out in life with all the advantages. I ain't got no advantages
to offer nobody. Many is the time I looked at my daddy and seen him
staring off at his hands. I got a little older I know what he was thinking.
He sitting there saying, "I got these big old hands but what I'm gonna
do with them? Best I can do is make a fifty-acre crop for Mr. Stovall.
Got these big old hands capable of doing anything. I can take and build
something with these hands. But where's the tools? All I got is these
hands. Unless I go out here and kill me somebody and take what they
got . . . it's a long row to hoe for me to get something of my own. So
what I'm gonna do with these big old hands? What would you do?"

See now . . . if he had his own land he wouldn't have felt that way. If
he had something under his feet that belonged to him he could stand
up taller. That's what I'm talking about. Hell, the land is there for
everybody. All you got to do is figure out how to get you a piece. Ain't
no mystery to life. You just got to go out and meet it square on. If you
got a piece of land you'll find everything else fall right into place. You
can stand right up next to the white man and talk about the price of
cotton . . . the weather, and anything else you want to talk about. If
you teach that girl that she living at the bottom of life, she's gonna
grow up and hate you.

BERNIECE: I'm gonna teach her the truth. That's just where she living.
Only she ain't got to stay there.

(*To Maretha.*)

Turn you' head over to the other side.

BOY WILLIE: This might be your bottom but it ain't mine. I'm living at
the top of life. I ain't gonna just take my life and throw it away at the
bottom. I'm in the world like everybody else. The way I see it everybody else got to come up a little taste to be where I am.

BERNIECE: You right at the bottom with the rest of us.

BOY WILLIE: I'll tell you this . . . and ain't a living soul can put a come
back on it. If you believe that's where you at then you gonna act that

way. If you act that way then that's where you gonna be. It's as simple as that. Ain't no mystery to life. I don't know how you come to believe that stuff. Crawley didn't think like that. He wasn't living at the bottom of life. Papa Boy Charles and Mama Ola wasn't living at the bottom of life. You ain't never heard them say nothing like that. They would have taken a strap to you if they heard you say something like that.

(*Doaker enters from his room.*)

Hey, Doaker . . . Berniece say the colored folks is living at the bottom of life. I tried to tell her if she think that . . . that's where she gonna be. You think you living at the bottom of life? Is that how you see yourself?

DOAKER: I'm just living the best way I know how. I ain't thinking about no top or no bottom.

BOY WILLIE: That's what I tried to tell Berniece. I don't know where she got that from. That sound like something Avery would say. Avery think cause the white man give him a turkey for Thanksgiving that makes him better than everybody else. That's gonna raise him out of the bottom of life. I don't need nobody to give me a turkey. I can get my own turkey. All you have to do is get out my way. I'll get me two or three turkeys.

BERNIECE: You can't even get a chicken let alone two or three turkeys. Talking about get out your way. Ain't nobody in your way.

(*To Maretha.*)

Straighten your head, Maretha! Don't be bending down like that. Hold your head up!

(*To Boy Willie.*)

All you got going for you is talk. You' whole life that's all you ever had going for you.

BOY WILLIE: See now . . . I'll tell you something about me. I done strung along and strung along. Going this way and that. Whatever way would lead me to a moment of peace. That's all I want. To be as easy with everything. But I wasn't born to that. I was born to a time of fire.

The world ain't wanted no part of me. I could see that since I was about seven. The world say it's better off without me. See, Berniece accept that. She trying to come up to where she can prove something to the world. Hell, the world a better place cause of me. I don't see it like Berniece. I got a heart that beats here and it beats just as loud as the next fellow's. Don't care if he black or white. Sometime it beats louder. When it beats louder, then everybody can hear it. Some people get scared of that. Like Berniece. Some people get scared to hear a nigger's heart beating. They think you ought to lay low with that heart. Make it beat quiet and go along with everything the way it is. But my mama ain't birthed me for nothing. So what I got to do? I got to mark my passing on the road. Just like you write on a tree, "Boy Willie was here." That's all I'm trying to do with that piano. Trying to put my mark on the road. Like my daddy done. My heart say for me to sell that piano and get me some land so I can make a life for myself to live in my own way. Other than that I ain't thinking about nothing Berniece got to say.

(*There is a knock at the door. Boy Willie crosses to it and yanks it open thinking it is Lymon. Avery enters. He carries a Bible.*)

BOY WILLIE: Where you been, nigger? Aw . . . I thought you was Lymon. Hey, Berniece, look who's here.

BERNIECE: Come on in, Avery. Don't you pay Boy Willie no mind.

BOY WILLIE: Hey . . . Hey, Avery . . . tell me this . . . can you get to heaven with half the Bible?

BERNIECE: Boy Willie . . . I done told you to leave me alone.

BOY WILLIE: I just ask the man a question. He can answer. He don't need you to speak for him. Avery . . . if you only believe on half the Bible and don't want to accept the other half . . . you think God let you in heaven? Or do you got to have the whole Bible? Tell Berniece . . . if you only believe in part of it . . . when you see God he gonna ask you why you ain't believed in the other part . . . then he gonna send you straight to Hell.

AVERY: You got to be born again. Jesus say unless a man be born again he cannot come unto the Father and who so ever heareth my words and believeth them not shall be cast into a fiery pit.

BOY WILLIE: That's what I was trying to tell Berniece. You got to believe in it all. You can't go at nothing halfway. She think she going to heaven with half the Bible.

(*To Berniece.*)

You hear that . . . Jesus say you got to believe in it all.

BERNIECE: You keep messing with me.

BOY WILLIE: I ain't thinking about you.

DOAKER: Come on in, Avery, and have a seat. Don't pay neither one of them no mind. They been arguing all day.

BERNIECE: Come on in, Avery.

AVERY: How's everybody in here?

BERNIECE: Here, set this comb back over there on that stove.

(*To Avery.*)

Don't pay Boy Willie no mind. He been around here bothering me since I come home from work.

BOY WILLIE: Boy Willie ain't bothering you. Boy Willie ain't bothering nobody. I'm just waiting on Lymon to get back. I ain't thinking about you. You heard the man say I was right and you still don't want to believe it. You just wanna go and make up anythin'. Well there's Avery . . . there's the preacher . . . go on and ask him.

AVERY: Berniece believe in the Bible. She been baptized.

BOY WILLIE: What about that part that say an eye for an eye a tooth for a tooth and a life for a life? Ain't that in there?

DOAKER: What they say down there at the bank, Avery?

AVERY: Oh, they talked to me real nice. I told Berniece . . . they say maybe they let me borrow the money. They done talked to my boss down at work and everything.

DOAKER: That's what I told Berniece. You working every day you ought to be able to borrow some money.

AVERY: I'm getting more people in my congregation every day. Berniece says she gonna be the Deaconess. I get me my church I can get married and settled down. That's what I told Berniece.

DOAKER: That be nice. You all ought to go ahead and get married. Berniece don't need to be by herself. I tell her that all the time.

BERNIECE: I ain't said nothing about getting married. I said I was thinking about it.

DOAKER: Avery get him his church you all can make it nice.

(*To Avery.*)

Berniece said you was coming by to bless the house.

AVERY: Yeah, I done read up on my Bible. She asked me to come by and see if I can get rid of Sutter's ghost.

BOY WILLIE: Ain't no ghost in this house. That's all in Berniece's head. Go on up there and see if you see him. I'll give you a hundred dollars if you see him. That's all in her imagination.

DOAKER: Well, let her find that out then. If Avery blessing the house is gonna make her feel better . . . what you got to do with it?

AVERY: Berniece say Maretha seen him too. I don't know, but I found a part in the Bible to bless the house. If he is here then that ought to make him go.

BOY WILLIE: You worse than Berniece believing all that stuff. Talking about . . . if he here. Go on up there and find out. I been up there I ain't seen him. If you reading from that Bible gonna make him leave out of Berniece imagination, well, you might be right. But if you talking about . . .

DOAKER: Boy Willie, why don't you just be quiet? Getting all up in the man's business. This ain't got nothing to do with you. Let him go ahead and do what he gonna do.

BOY WILLIE: I ain't stopping him. Avery ain't got no power to do nothing.
AVERY: Oh, I ain't got no power. God got the power! God got power over
everything in His creation. God can do anything. God say, "As I com-
mandeth so it shall be." God said, "Let there be light," and there was
light. He made the world in six days and rested on the seventh. God's
got a wonderful power. He got power over life and death. Jesus raised
Lazareth from the dead. They was getting ready to bury him and Jesus
told him say, "Rise up and walk." He got up and walked and the people
made great rejoicing at the power of God. I ain't worried about him
chasing away a little old ghost!

(*There is a knock at the door. Boy Willie goes to answer it. Lymon enters carrying a coil of rope.*)

BOY WILLIE: Where you been? I been waiting on you and you run off
somewhere.
LYMON: I ran into Grace. I stopped and bought her drink. She say she
gonna go to the picture show with me.
BOY WILLIE: I ain't thinking about no Grace nothing.
LYMON: Hi, Berniece.
BOY WILLIE: Give me that rope and get up on this side of the piano.
DOAKER: Boy Willie, don't start nothing now. Leave the piano alone.
BOY WILLIE: Get that board there, Lymon. Stay out of this, Doaker.

(*Berniece exits up the stairs.*)

DOAKER: You just can't take the piano. How you gonna take the piano?
Berniece ain't said nothing about selling that piano.
BOY WILLIE: She ain't got to say nothing. Come on, Lymon. We got to lift
one end at a time up on the board. You got to watch so that the board
don't slide up under there.
LYMON: What we gonna do with the rope?
BOY WILLIE: Let me worry about the rope. You just get up on this side
over here with me.

(*Berniece enters from the stairs. She has her hand in her pocket where she has
Crawley's gun.*)

AVERY: Boy Willie . . . Berniece . . . why don't you all sit down and talk
this out now?
BERNIECE: Ain't nothing to talk out.
BOY WILLIE: I'm through talking to Berniece. You can talk to Berniece
till you get blue in the face, and it don't make no difference. Get up on
that side, Lymon. Throw that rope around there and tie it to the leg.
LYMON: Wait a minute . . . wait a minute, Boy Willie. Berniece got to say.
Hey, Berniece . . . did you tell Boy Willie he could take this piano?

BERNIECE: Boy Willie ain't taking nothing out of my house but himself. Now you let him go ahead and try.

BOY WILLIE: Come on, Lymon, get up on this side with me.

(*Lymon stands undecided.*)

Come on, nigger! What you standing there for?

LYMON: Maybe Berniece is right, Boy Willie. Maybe you shouldn't sell it.

AVERY: You all ought to sit down and talk it out. See if you can come to an agreement.

DOAKER: That's what I been trying to tell them. Seem like one of them ought to respect the other one's wishes.

BERNIECE: I wish Boy Willie would go on and leave my house. That's what I wish. Now, he can respect that. Cause he's leaving here one way or another.

BOY WILLIE: What you mean one way or another? What's that supposed to mean? I ain't scared of no gun.

DOAKER: Come on, Berniece, leave him alone with that.

BOY WILLIE: I don't care what Berniece say. I'm selling my half. I can't help it if her half got to go along with it. It ain't like I'm trying to cheat her out of her half. Come on, Lymon.

LYMON: Berniece . . . I got to do this . . . Boy Willie say he gonna give you half of the money . . . say he want to get Sutter's land.

BERNIECE: Go on, Lymon. Just go on . . . I done told Boy Willie what to do.

BOY WILLIE: Here, Lymon . . . put that rope up over there.

LYMON: Boy Willie, you sure you want to do this? The way I figure it . . . I might be wrong . . . but I figure she gonna shoot you first.

BOY WILLIE: She just gonna have to shoot me.

BERNIECE: Maretha, get on out the way. Get her out the way, Doaker.

DOAKER: Go on, do what your mama told you.

BERNIECE: Put her in your room.

(*Maretha exits to Doaker's room. Boy Willie and Lymon try to lift the piano. The door opens and Wining Boy enters. He has been drinking.*)

WINING BOY: Man, these niggers around here! I stopped down there at Seefus. . . . These folks standing around talking about Patchneck Red's coming. They jumping back and getting off the sidewalk talking about Patchneck Red this and Patchneck Red that. Come to find out . . . you know who they was talking about? Old John D. from up around Tyler! Used to run around with Otis Smith. He got everybody scared of him. Calling him Patchneck Red. They don't know I whupped the nigger's head in one time.

BOY WILLIE: Just make sure that board don't slide, Lymon.

LYMON: I got this side. You watch that side.

WINING BOY: Hey, Boy Willie, what you got? I know you got a pint stuck up in your coat.

BOY WILLIE: Wining Boy, get out the way!

WINING BOY: Hey, Doaker. What you got? Gimme a drink. I want a drink.

DOAKER: It look like you had enough of whatever it was. Come talking about "What you got?" You ought to be trying to find somewhere to lay down.

WINING BOY: I ain't worried about no place to lay down. I can always find me a place to lay down in Berniece's house. Ain't that right, Berniece?

BERNIECE: Wining Boy, sit down somewhere. You been out there drinking all day. Come in here smelling like an old polecat. Sit on down there, you don't need nothing to drink.

DOAKER: You know Berniece don't like all that drinking.

WINING BOY: I ain't disrespecting Berniece. Berniece, am I disrespecting you? I'm just trying to be nice. I been with strangers all day and they treated me like family. I come in here to family and you treat me like a stranger. I don't need your whiskey. I can buy my own. I wanted your company, not your whiskey.

DOAKER: Nigger, why don't you go upstairs and lay down? You don't need nothing to drink.

WINING BOY: I ain't thinking about no laying down. Me and Boy Willie fixing to party. Ain't that right, Boy Willie? Tell him. I'm fixing to play me some piano. Watch this.

(*Wining Boy sits down at the piano.*)

BOY WILLIE: Come on, Wining Boy! Me and Lymon fixing to move the piano.

WINING BOY: Wait a minute . . . wait a minute. This a song I wrote for Cleotha. I wrote this song in memory of Cleotha.

(*He begins to play and sing.*)

Hey little woman what's the matter with you now
Had a storm last night and blowed the line all down

Tell me how long
Is I got to wait
Can I get it now
Or must I hesitate

It takes a hesitating stocking in her hesitating shoe
It takes a hesitating woman wanna sing the blues

> Tell me how long
> Is I got to wait
> Can I kiss you now
> Or must I hesitate.

BOY WILLIE: Come on, Wining Boy, get up! Get up, Wining Boy! Me and Lymon's fixing to move the piano.

WINING BOY: Naw . . . Naw . . . you ain't gonna move this piano!

BOY WILLIE: Get out the way, Wining Boy.

(*Wining Boy, his back to the piano, spreads his arms out over the piano.*)

WINING BOY: You ain't taking this piano out the house. You got to take me with it!

BOY WILLIE: Get on out the way, Wining Boy! Doaker get him!

(*There is a knock on the door.*)

BERNIECE: I got him, Doaker. Come on, Wining Boy. I done told Boy Willie he ain't taking the piano.

(*Berniece tries to take Wining Boy away from the piano.*)

WINING BOY: He got to take me with it!

(*Doaker goes to answer the door. Grace enters.*)

GRACE: Is Lymon here?

DOAKER: Lymon.

WINING BOY: He ain't taking that piano.

BERNIECE: I ain't gonna let him take it.

GRACE: I thought you was coming back. I ain't gonna sit in that truck all day.

LYMON: I told you I was coming back.

GRACE: (*Sees Boy Willie.*) Oh, hi, Boy Willie. Lymon told me you was gone back down South.

LYMON: I said he was going back. I didn't say he had left already.

GRACE: That's what you told me.

BERNIECE: Lymon, you got to take your company someplace else.

LYMON: Berniece, this is Grace. That there is Berniece. That's Boy Willie's sister.

GRACE: Nice to meet you.

(*To Lymon.*)

> I ain't gonna sit out in that truck all day. You told me you was gonna take me to the movie.

LYMON: I told you I had something to do first. You supposed to wait on me.

BERNIECE: Lymon, just go on and leave. Take Grace or whoever with you. Just go on get out my house.

BOY WILLIE: You gonna help me move this piano first, nigger!

LYMON: (*To Grace.*) I got to help Boy Willie move the piano first.

(*Everybody but Grace suddenly senses Sutter's presence.*)

GRACE: I ain't waiting on you. Told me you was coming right back. Now you got to move a piano. You just like all the other men.

(*Grace now senses something.*)

Something ain't right here. I knew I shouldn't have come back up in this house.

(*Grace exits.*)

LYMON: Hey, Grace! I'll be right back, Boy Willie.

BOY WILLIE: Where you going, nigger?

LYMON: I'll be back. I got to take Grace home.

BOY WILLIE: Come on, let's move the piano first!

LYMON: I got to take Grace home. I told you I'll be back.

(*Lymon exits. Boy Willie exits and calls after him.*)

BOY WILLIE: Come on, Lymon! Hey . . . Lymon! Lymon . . . come on!

(*Again, the presence of Sutter is felt.*)

WINING BOY: Hey, Doaker, did you feel that? Hey, Berniece . . . did you get cold? Hey, Doaker . . .

DOAKER: What you calling me for?

WINING BOY: I believe that's Sutter.

DOAKER: Well, let him stay up there. As long as he don't mess with me.

BERNIECE: Avery, go on and bless the house.

DOAKER: You need to bless that piano. That's what you need to bless. It ain't done nothing but cause trouble. If you gonna bless anything go on and bless that.

WINING BOY: Hey, Doaker, if he gonna bless something let him bless everything. The kitchen . . . the upstairs. Go on and bless it all.

BOY WILLIE: Ain't no ghost in this house. He need to bless Berniece's head. That's what he need to bless.

AVERY: Seem like that piano's causing all the trouble. I can bless that. Berniece, put me some water in that bottle.

(*Avery takes a small bottle from his pocket and hands it to Berniece, who goes into the kitchen to get water. Avery takes a candle from his pocket and lights it. He gives it to Berniece as she gives him the water.*)

Hold this candle. Whatever you do make sure it don't go out.

O Holy Father we gather here this evening in the Holy Name to cast out the spirit of one James Sutter. May this vial of water be empowered with thy spirit. May each drop of it be a weapon and a shield against the presence of all evil and may it be a cleansing and blessing of this humble abode.

Just as Our Father taught us how to pray so He say, "I will prepare a table for you in the midst of mine enemies," and in His hands we place ourselves to come unto his presence. Where there is Good so shall it cause Evil to scatter to the Four Winds.

(*He throws water at the piano at each commandment.*)

AVERY: Get thee behind me, Satan! Get thee behind the face of Righteousness as we Glorify His Holy Name! Get thee behind the Hammer of Truth that breaketh down the Wall of Falsehood! Father. Father. Praise. Praise. We ask in Jesus' name and call forth the power of the Holy Spirit as it is written . . .

(*He opens the Bible and reads from it.*)

I will sprinkle clean water upon thee and ye shall be clean.

BOY WILLIE: All this old preaching stuff. Hell, just tell him to leave.

(*Avery continues reading throughout Boy Willie's outburst.*)

AVERY: I will sprinkle clean water upon you and you shall be clean: from all your uncleanliness, and from all your idols, will I cleanse you. A new heart also will I give you, and a new spirit will I put within you: and I will take out of your flesh the heart of stone, and I will give you a heart of flesh. And I will put my spirit within you, and cause you to walk in my statutes, and ye shall keep my judgments, and do them.

(*Boy Willie grabs a pot of water from the stove and begins to fling it around the room.*)

BOY WILLIE: Hey Sutter! Sutter! Get your ass out this house! Sutter! Come on and get some of this water! You done drowned in the well, come on and get some more of this water!

(*Boy Willie is working himself into a frenzy as he runs around the room throwing water and calling Sutter's name. Avery continues reading.*)

BOY WILLIE: Come on, Sutter!

(*He starts up the stairs.*)

Come on, get some water! Come on, Sutter!

(*The sound of Sutter's Ghost is heard. As Boy Willie approaches the steps he is suddenly thrown back by the unseen force, which is choking him. As he struggles he frees himself, then dashes up the stairs.*)

BOY WILLIE: Come on, Sutter!

AVERY (*continuing*): A new heart also will I give you and a new spirit will I put within you: and I will take out of your flesh the heart of stone, and I will give you a heart of flesh. And I will put my spirit within you, and cause you to walk in my statutes, and ye shall keep my judgments, and do them.

(*There are loud sounds heard from upstairs as Boy Willie begins to wrestle with Sutter's Ghost. It is a life-and-death struggle fraught with perils and faultless terror. Boy Willie is thrown down the stairs. Avery is stunned into silence. Boy Willie picks himself up and dashes back upstairs.*)

AVERY: Berniece, I can't do it.

(*There are more sounds heard from upstairs. Doaker and Wining Boy stare at one another in stunned disbelief. It is in this moment, from somewhere old, that Berniece realizes what she must do. She crosses to the piano. She begins to play. The song is found piece by piece. It is an old urge to song that is both a commandment and a plea. With each repetition it gains in strength. It is intended as an exorcism and a dressing for battle. A rustle of wind blowing across two continents.*)

BERNIECE (*singing*):
    I want you to help me
    I want you to help me
    I want you to help me
    I want you to help me
    I want you to help me
    I want you to help me
    Mama Berniece
    I want you to help me
    Mama Esther
    I want you to help me
    Papa Boy Charles
    I want you to help me
    Mama Ola
    I want you to help me

    I want you to help me
    I want you to help me
    I want you to help me
    I want you to help me
    I want you to help me
    I want you to help me
    I want you to help me
    I want you to help me

(*The sound of a train approaching is heard. The noise upstairs subsides.*)

BOY WILLIE: Come on, Sutter! Come back, Sutter!

(*Berniece begins to chant:*)

BERNIECE:
Thank you.
Thank you.
Thank you.

(*A calm comes over the house. Maretha enters from Doaker's room. Boy Willie enters on the stairs. He pauses a moment to watch Berniece at the piano.*)

BERNIECE:
Thank you.
Thank you.
BOY WILLIE: Wining Boy, you ready to go back down home? Hey, Doaker, what time the train leave?
DOAKER: You still got time to make it.

(*Maretha crosses and embraces Boy Willie.*)

BOY WILLIE: Hey Berniece . . . if you and Maretha don't keep playing on that piano . . . ain't no telling . . . me and Sutter both liable to be back.

(*He exits.*)

BERNIECE: Thank you.

(*The lights go down to black.*)

[1987]

Writing about Literature

Writing about Literature

Some students really enjoy reading imaginative literature and writing papers about it, while others find the task intimidating, frustrating, or just plain dull. If you're in the first group, you're lucky; your literature class will be fun and interesting for you, and—not incidentally—you'll probably do good work in the course. If you've never been fond of reading and writing about literature, though, you might spend a little time thinking about why some of your classmates enjoy this sort of work as well as what you might do to increase your own enjoyment of literature and investment in the writing process. You'll be happier and write better papers if you can put aside any previous negative experiences with literature and writing you may have had and approach your task with a positive mindset.

So let's take a moment to reflect on why we read and write about literature. Of course, there is no single or simple answer. People read to be informed, to be entertained, to be exposed to new ideas, or to have familiar concepts reinforced. Often, people read just to enjoy a good story or to get a glimpse of how other people think and feel. But literature does much more than give us a compelling plot or a look into an author's thoughts and emotions—although at its best it does these things as well. Literature reflects not only the mind of its author but also the larger world and the ways in which people interact with that world and with one another. So even when what we read is entirely fictional, we nevertheless learn about real life. And, indeed, by affecting our thoughts and feelings, literature can indirectly affect our actions as well. Thus literature not only reflects but even helps to shape our world.

Writing about literature also has real-world usefulness. By forcing us to organize our thoughts and state clearly what we think, writing an essay helps us to clarify what we know and believe. It gives us a chance to affect the thinking of our readers. Even more important, we actually learn as we write. In the process of writing, we often make new discoveries and forge new connections between ideas. We find and work through contradictions in our thinking, and we create whole new lines of thought as we work to make linear sense out of an often chaotic jumble of impressions. So, while *reading* literature can teach us much about the world, *writing* about literature often teaches us about ourselves.

CHAPTER 1

The Role of Good Reading

Writing about literature begins, of course, with reading, so it stands to reason that good reading is the first step toward successful writing. But what exactly is "good reading"? Good reading is, generally speaking, not fast reading. In fact, often the best advice a student can receive about reading is to *slow down*. Reading well is all about paying attention, and you can't pay attention if you're racing to get through an assignment and move on to "more important" things. If you make a point of giving yourself plenty of time and minimizing your distractions, you'll get more out of your reading and probably enjoy it more as well.

A second important thing to remember is that the best reading is often rereading. Some students believe that good readers, especially teachers and those students who often make valuable contributions to class discussions, are somehow able to absorb and understand a complex literary text after reading through it only once. In truth, the best readers are those who are willing to go back and reread a piece of literature again and again. It is not uncommon for professional literary critics—who are, after all, some of the most skilled readers—to read a particular poem, story, or play literally dozens of times before they feel equipped to write about it. And well-written literature rewards this willingness to reread, allowing readers to continue seeing new things with each reading. Realistically, of course, you will not have the time to read every assigned piece many times before discussing it in class or preparing to write about it, but you should not give up or feel frustrated if you fail to "get" a piece of literature on the first reading. Be prepared to go back and reread key sections, or even a whole work, if doing so could help with your understanding.

What we are trying to encourage is what is sometimes called "active reading" or "critical reading," though *critical* here does not imply fault-finding but rather thoughtful consideration. Much of the reading we do in everyday life is passive and noncritical. We glance at street signs to see where we are; we check the sports section to find out how our favorite team is doing in the standings; we read packages for information about the products we use. And in general, we take in all this information passively, without questioning it or looking for deeper meaning. For many kinds of reading, this is perfectly appropriate. It would hardly make sense to ask, "*Why* is this Pine Street?" or "What do they *mean* when they say there are 12 ounces of soda in this can?" There is, however, another type of reading, one that involves asking critical questions and probing more deeply into the meaning of what we read, and this is the kind of reading most appropriate to imaginative literature (especially if we intend to discuss or write about that literature later).

There is a persistent myth in literature classes that the purpose of reading is to scour a text for "hidden meaning." Do not be taken in by this myth. In fact, many instructors dislike the phrase *hidden meaning*, which has unpleasant and inaccurate connotations. First, it suggests a sort of willful subterfuge on the part of the author, a deliberate attempt to make his or her work difficult to understand or to exclude the reader. Second, it makes the process of reading sound like digging for buried treasure rather than a systematic intellectual process. Finally, the phrase implies that there is a single, true meaning to a text and that communication and understanding move in one direction only: from the crafty author to the searching reader.

In truth, the meanings in literary texts are not hidden, and your job as a reader is not to root around for them. Rather, if a text is not immediately accessible to you, it is because you need to read more actively, and meaning will then emerge in a collaborative effort as you work *with* the text to create a consistent interpretation. Obviously, this requires effort. If you find this sort of reading hard, take that as a good sign. It means you're paying the sort of attention that a well-crafted poem, story, or play requires of a reader. You also should not assume that English teachers have a key that allows them to unlock the one secret truth of a text. If, as is often the case, your instructor sees more or different meanings in a piece of literature than you do, this is because he or she is trained to read actively and has probably spent much more time than you have with literature in general and more time with the particular text assigned to you.

ACTIVE READING: ANNOTATING, NOTE TAKING, JOURNAL KEEPING

If the first suggestions for active reading are to slow down and to know that a second (or even a third) reading is in order, the next suggestion is to read with a pen or pencil in hand in order to annotate your text and take notes. If you look inside a literature textbook belonging to your instructor or to an advanced literature student, chances are you'll see something of a mess — words and passages circled or underlined, comments and questions scrawled in the margins (technically called *marginalia*) or even between the lines (called *interlinear*), and unexplained punctuation marks or other symbols decorating the pages. You should not interpret this as disrespect for the text or author or as a sign of a disordered mind. Indeed, it is quite the opposite of both these things. It is simply textual annotation, and it means that someone has been engaged in active reading. (The poet and critic Samuel Taylor Coleridge was famous for annotating not only his own books but those he borrowed from friends — a habit unlikely to secure a friendship — and his marginalia actually makes up one entire volume of his collected works.)

If you are not accustomed to textual annotation, it may be hard to know where to begin. There is no single, widely used system of annotation, and you will almost certainly begin to develop your own techniques as you practice active reading. Here, however, are a few tips to get you started:

- **Underline, circle, or otherwise highlight passages that strike you as particularly important.** These may be anything from single words to whole paragraphs, but stick to those points in the text that really stand out, the briefer and more specific, the better. Don't worry that you need to find *the* most crucial parts of a poem, play, or story. Everyone sees things a little differently, so just note what makes an impression on *you*.

- **Make notes in the margins as to *why* certain points strike you.** Don't just underline; jot down at least a word or two in the margin to remind yourself what you were thinking when you chose to highlight a particular point. It may seem obvious to you at the moment, but when you return to the text in two weeks to write your paper, you may not remember.

- **Ask questions of the text.** Perhaps the most important aspect of active reading is the practice of asking critical questions of a text. Nobody — not even the most experienced literary critic — understands everything about a literary text immediately, and noting where you are confused or doubtful is an important first step toward resolving any confusion. We discuss types of questions a little later in this chapter, but for now just remember that any point of confusion is fair game, from character **motivation** (*"Why would she do that?"*), to cultural or historical references (*"Where is Xanadu?"*), to the definitions of individual words (*"Meaning?"*). Most likely, you will eventually want to propose some possible answers, but on a first reading of the text, it's enough to note that you have questions.

- **Talk back to the text.** Occasionally, something in a literary text may strike you as suspicious, offensive, or just plain wrong. Just because a story, poem, or play appears in a textbook does not make its author above criticism. Try to keep an open mind and realize that there may be an explanation that would satisfy your criticism, but if you think an author has made a misstep, don't be afraid to make note of your opinion.

- **Look for unusual features of language.** In creating a mood and making a point, literary works rely much more heavily than do purely informational texts on features of language such as style and imagery. As a reader of literature, then, you need to heighten your awareness of style. Look for patterns of images, repeated words or phrases, and any other unusual stylistic features — right down to idiosyncratic grammar or punctuation — and make note of them in your marginalia.

- **Develop your own system of shorthand.** Annotating a text, while it obviously takes time, shouldn't become a burden or slow your reading too much, so keep your notes and questions short and to the point. Sometimes all you need is an exclamation point to indicate an important passage. An underlined term combined with a question mark in the margin can remind you that you didn't immediately understand what a word meant. Be creative, but try also to be consistent, so you'll know later what you meant by a particular symbol or comment.

Annotating your text is a big step in active reading and in improving your understanding and enjoyment of literature, but there are some cases when it's not quite enough. You may also need to take different sorts of notes or even keep a reading journal. It's a good idea, especially if you are reading a difficult text or one about which you expect to be writing, to keep a notebook handy as you read, a place to make notes that would be too long or complex to fit in the margins. You might even want to use the same notebook you keep with you in class, so you can make quick reference to your class notes while reading at home and bring the insights from your reading to your class discussions.

You may be assigned to keep a reading journal for your class. Of course, you should follow your instructor's guidelines, but if you aren't sure what to write in a reading journal, think of it as a place to go a step further than you do in your annotations and notes. Try out possible answers, preferably several different ones, to the questions you have raised. Expand your ideas from single phrases and sentences into entire paragraphs, and see how they hold up under this deeper probing. Although a reading journal is substantially different from a personal journal or diary, it can at times contain reflections on any connections you make between a piece of literature and your own life and ideas. Some journal writers like to use a sort of double-entry system, with questions and direct references to the text on one side of a page and original ideas or free associations on the other. Even if your instructor doesn't require a journal for your class, many students find it a useful tool for getting more out of their reading, not to mention a wealth of material to draw from when they sit down to write a paper.

One final and very important tool of active reading is the dictionary. Many students are reluctant to use the dictionary while reading, thinking they should be able to figure out the meanings of words from their context and not wanting to interrupt their reading. But the simple truth is that not all words are definable from context alone, and you'll get much more out of your reading if you are willing to make the small effort involved in looking up unknown words. If you are reading John Donne's "A Valediction: Forbidding Mourning" and you don't know what the word *valediction* means, you obviously start at a big disadvantage. A quick look at a dictionary would tell you that a *valediction* is a speech given at a time of parting (like the one a *valedict*orian gives at a graduation ceremony). Armed with that simple piece of information, you begin your reading of Donne's poem already knowing that it is about leaving someone or something, and understanding the poem becomes much simpler.

ASKING CRITICAL QUESTIONS OF LITERATURE

As mentioned, one important part of active, critical reading is asking questions. If you are reading well, your textual annotations and notes will probably be full of questions. Some of these might be simple inquiries of fact, the sort of thing that can be answered by asking your instructor or by doing some quick research. But ideally, many of your questions will be more complex and meaty than that, the sort of probing queries that may have multiple, complex, or even contradictory answers. These are the questions that will provoke you and your classmates to think still more critically about the literature you read. You need not worry—at least not at first—about finding answers to all of your questions. As you work more with the text, discussing it with your instructor and classmates, writing about it, and reading other related stories, poems, and plays, you will begin to respond to the most important of the issues you've raised. And even if you never form a satisfactory answer to some questions, they will have served their purpose if they have made you think.

Questions about literature fall into one of four categories—those about the text, the author, the reader, and the cultural contexts of the work. Queries regarding the text can sometimes, though not always, be answered with a deeper examination of the story, poem, or play at hand. Answering those in the other categories, however, often requires some additional research, discussion, or reading.

Some suggestions follow about the specific types of questions that can lead you toward more active reading, and eventually toward good, critical writing. First take a look at Ben Jonson's poem "On My First Son," in which a grieving father bids goodbye to his dead child. In the sections that follow, you will see the questions one active reader asked upon first reading this poem. Though they by no means represent a complete list of what an attentive reader might ask, they should give you a sense of how even a relatively short piece of literature can generate many topics for discussion and writing.

BEN JONSON   [1572–1637]

On My First Son

Farewell, thou child of my right hand, and joy;
My sin was too much hope of thee, loved boy:
Seven years thou wert lent to me, and I thee pay,
Exacted by thy fate, on the just day.
O could I lose all father now! For why   5
Will man lament the state he should envy,
To have so soon 'scaped world's and flesh's rage,
And, if no other misery, yet age?
Rest in soft peace, and asked, say, "Here doth lie
Ben Jonson his best piece of poetry."   10
For whose sake henceforth all his vows be such
As what he loves may never like too much.

[1616]

Questions about the Text

Questions about a text are those that focus on issues such as genre, structure, language, and style. You might ask about the presence of certain images—or about their absence, if you have reason to expect them and find that they are not there. Sometimes authors juxtapose images or language in startling or unexpected ways, and you might ask about the purpose and effect of such **juxtaposition**. You might wonder about the meanings of specific words in the context of the work. (This is especially true with older works of literature, as meanings evolve and change over time, and a word you know today might have had a very different definition in the past.) When looking at a poem, you might inquire about the purpose and effect of sound, rhythm, rhyme, and so forth.

Your previous experiences are a big help here, including both your experiences of reading literature and your experiences in everyday life. You know from personal experience how you expect people to think and act in certain situations, and you can compare these expectations to the literature. What might motivate the characters or persons to think and act as they do? Your previous reading has likewise set up expectations for you. How does the text fulfill or frustrate these expectations? What other literature does this remind you of? What images seem arresting or unexpected? Where do the words seem particularly powerful, strange, or otherwise noteworthy?

Here are several questions one reader asked upon first reading Jonson's "On My First Son."

- Why is hope for his child a "sin"? Isn't it natural?
- Why the words *lent* and *pay*, as if the son is a bank transaction? Borrowed from and paid to whom? (God? Jonson also mentions *fate.*)
- The word *just* has two meanings: exact and fair. Which does the poet mean? Both? How can a child's death be fair?
- What does he mean by "O could I lose all father now"? (Confusing.)
- Is the Ben Jonson in line 8 the father or the son? Both?

Questions about the Author

When thinking about the connection between authors and the works they produce, two contradictory impulses come into play. One is the desire to ignore the biography of the author entirely and focus solely on the work at hand, and the other is to look closely at an author's life to see what might have led him or her to write a particular poem, story, or play. It is easy to understand the first impulse. After all, we are not likely to be able to ask an author what is meant by a certain line in a play or whether an image in a story is supposed to be read symbolically. The work of literature is what we have before us, and it should stand or fall on its own merits. This was, in fact, one of the principal tenets of the so-called New Critics, who dominated literary criticism for much of the twentieth century.

We cannot deny, however, that a writer's life does affect that writer's expression. An author's age, gender, religious beliefs, family structure, and many other factors have an impact on everything from topic choice to word choice. It is, therefore, appropriate sometimes to ask questions about an author as we try to come to a better understanding of a piece of literature. It is crucial, however, that we remember that not everything an author writes is to be taken at surface value. If, for instance, the narrator or principal character of a story is beaten or neglected by his parents, we should not jump to the conclusion that the author was an abused child. And if this character then goes on to justify his own actions by pointing to the abuse, we should also not assume that the author endorses this justification. In other words we must distinguish between narrative voice and the actual author as well as between what is written and what is meant.

This separation of biography and narrative is relatively easy to effect with stories and plays that we know to be fiction; just because a character says something doesn't necessarily mean the author believes it. Poetry is a little trickier though because it has the reputation of being straight from the heart. Not all poetry, however, is an accurate representation of its author's thoughts or beliefs. To give just two examples, T. S. Eliot's "The Love Song of J. Alfred Prufrock" voices the thoughts of the fictional Prufrock, not of Eliot himself, and many of the poems of Robert Browning are "dramatic monologues," delivered by speakers very different from Browning himself, including murderous noblemen and corrupt clergy.

To demonstrate the tension between focusing on or ignoring an author's biography, let us try a small thought experiment. Suppose you were to discover that Ben Jonson's eldest son did not die in childhood, or that Jonson was a lifelong bachelor who had no children. How would that change your interpretation of this poem? Neither is true: young Ben was Jonson's real child, and he really did die on his seventh birthday. But if this fanciful speculation were true, the poem would no longer be a sincere expression of a father's mourning. It would be more like a character study, an attempt on the part of the poet (who was also an accomplished playwright, adept at creating characters) to get inside the mind of a man in mourning. Would this make it a worse poem? Not necessarily. But chances are that most readers would experience it as a very different kind of poem. Knowing something about an author's life, then, can help us understand how to read a work of literature.

Here are some questions about Jonson's life and its connection to his poem.

- How old was Jonson when his son died?
- Did he have other children? Other boys? ("First Son" suggests he did.)

- Did he lose any other children?
- How long after his son's death did Jonson write the poem?
- What religion was Jonson? How pious was he?
- Did he really stop loving his family after his son's death, as the last line suggests?

Questions about the Cultural Context

Just as events in an author's life affect his or her writing, so too do events in the wider social and cultural context. We are all creatures of a particular time and place, and nobody, no matter how unique and iconoclastic, is immune to the subtle and pervasive force of social history. Many appropriate questions about literature, then, involve the cultural context of the work. What was going on in history at the time a piece of literature was written? Were there wars or other forms of social disruption? What was the standard of living for most people in the author's society? What was day-to-day life like? What were the typical religious beliefs and traditions? How was society organized in terms of power relations, work expectations, and educational possibilities? How about typical family structure? Did extended families live together? What were the expected gender roles inside (and outside) the family? All of these issues, and many more besides, have an impact on how authors see the world and how they respond to it in their writing.

As you read and ask questions of literature, you have another cultural context to be concerned with: your own. How does being a resident of twenty-first century America affect your reading and understanding? We are every bit as influenced by issues of history, culture, and lifestyle as were authors and readers of the past, but it is harder for us to see this, since the dominant way of living tends to seem "natural" or even "universal." Indeed, one of the great benefits of reading literature is that it teaches us about history and helps us to understand and appreciate diverse cultures, not the least of which is our own.

In asking and answering the following questions about Ben Jonson's culture (seventeenth-century England), an attentive reader of "On My First Son" will also note features of our own present-day society, in which childhood death is relatively rare, family roles may be different, and religious attitudes and beliefs are considerably more diverse.

- How common was childhood death in the seventeenth century? What was the life expectancy?
- Typically, how involved were fathers in young children's lives at the time?
- Is the quotation in the poem (lines 9–10) the boy's epitaph?

- How difficult was life then? What exactly does Jonson mean by the "world's and flesh's rage"?
- How common was poetry on this topic? How "original" was Jonson's poem?
- What attitudes about God and heaven were common then? What was the conception of sin?

Questions about the Reader

Except in the case of private diaries, all writing is intended to be read by somebody, and an intended audience can have a big influence on the composition of the writing in question. Think about the differences in tone and structure between an e-mail you send to a friend and a paper you write for a course, and you'll get some idea of the impact of intended audience on a piece of writing. It is therefore worth considering a work's originally intended readers as you seek to understand a piece more fully. Who were these intended readers? Were they actually the people who read the literature when it was first published? How are readers' expectations fulfilled or disappointed by the structure and content of the literature? How did the original readers react? Was the work widely popular, or did only certain readers enjoy it? Did it have detractors as well? Was there any controversy over the work?

Of course, in addition to the original readers of any work of literature, there are also contemporary readers, including yourself. It is often said that great literature stands the test of time and can cross cultures to speak to many different sorts of people, but your reaction to a work may be very different from that of its original audience, especially if you are far removed from the work by time or culture. In earlier centuries in Europe and America, nearly all educated people were very familiar with the Bible and with stories and myths from Greek and Roman antiquity. Writers, therefore, could assume such knowledge on the part of their readers and make liberal reference in their work to stories and characters from these sources. Today many readers are less familiar with these sources, and we often need the help of footnotes or other study aids to understand such references. So what might have been enjoyable and enlightening for the original readers of a work might sometimes be tedious or frustrating for later readers. If we are to read a work critically, we must keep both past and present audiences in mind.

The first three questions following deal with the original audience of "On My First Son," while the final two compare this audience and a contemporary one.

- If childhood death was common in the seventeenth century, would many of Jonson's readers have related to the subject of his poem?

- People who actually knew the boy (and the father) would have a strong response to the boy's death. Did Jonson write this for wide circulation, or was it meant just for family and friends?
- Where was it first published, and who was likely to read it?
- Do readers with children of their own read it differently? Would I?
- Now that childhood death is fairly uncommon, do we take this poem more seriously than past readers? Or less seriously?

Looking over all these groups of questions about Jonson's poem — about the text, the author, the cultural context, and the reader — you will note that there are many differences among them. Some can be answered with a simple yes or no (*Is the quotation the boy's epitaph?*), while others require much more complex responses (*What was the conception of sin in Jonson's time?*). Some are matters of fact (*Did Jonson have other children?*), while others are matters of conjecture, opinion, or interpretation (*Do contemporary readers take this poem more seriously?*). Some can be answered simply by rereading and considering (*How can a child's death ever be considered fair?*), while others require discussion (*Do readers with children respond to the poem differently?*) or research (*Where was the poem first published?*).

Some inquiries you may have tentative answers for, as did the reader who asked these questions when she proposed both God and fate as potential candidates for who "lent" the child to the father. Others you won't be able to answer at first. If you are genuinely curious about any of them, do a little informal research to begin formulating answers. Some basic information can be found in the brief biographies or notes about authors that appear in most textbooks. There you could learn, for instance, the dates of Jonson's birth and death and some basic facts about his life and family. A quick look at a reputable reference work or Web site could provide still more valuable background information, like the fact that Jonson also lost his first daughter and that he wrote a poem about her death as well.

Having simply formulated some questions, you've already gone a long way toward understanding and interpreting a poem. If you bring such a list of questions with you to class, you will be more than ready to contribute to any discussion of the poem, and when the time comes to write an essay, you will find you have a rich mine of source material from which to draw.

CHAPTER 2

The Writing Process

CHOOSING A TOPIC

Obviously, your choice of a topic for your paper is of key importance, since everything else follows from that first decision. Your instructor may assign a specific topic (see "Some Common Writing Assignments" on pages 1302–17 for examples of the kinds of assignments you might encounter), or the choice may be left to you. Instructors know that some students love to be given a free choice of writing topics whereas others hate it. Free choice can be liberating and fun, but it can also be daunting, leaving you wondering where to begin.

The most important piece of advice we can give for choosing a topic is to write about something you genuinely care about. Students sometimes spend a lot of energy attempting to second-guess their instructors, trying to figure out what these instructors would like to see in a paper. This is almost always a bad idea. First off, you may be wrong about what your instructor wants to see. Second, you may end up writing a paper very similar to that of many other students who have made the same, possibly erroneous, assumption. If your instructor gives your class a choice, chances are he or she really wants to see a variety of topics and approaches and expects you to find a topic that works for *you*. You'll write a better paper if your topic is something of genuine interest to you. A bored or uncertain writer usually writes a boring or unconvincing paper. On the other hand, if you care about your topic, your enthusiasm will show in the writing, and the paper will be far more successful.

Even if your instructor assigns a fairly specific topic, you still need to spend a little time thinking about and working with it. You want your paper to stand out from the rest, and you should do whatever you can to make the assignment your own. Melanie Smith, who wrote the paper in the "Writing about Stories" section (pp. 1318–24), was assigned to compare and contrast two short stories, Charlotte Perkins Gilman's "The

Yellow Wallpaper" and Kate Chopin's "The Story of an Hour" and to draw some conclusions about women's roles in late–nineteenth century America. At first glance, it might not seem as though there was much room for students to bring their own ideas and interests to bear on the assignment. In reality, though, there are a number of ways to approach such a topic, and students in the class ended up writing very different papers. Melanie's essay, as you will see, focuses primarily on the stories' male characters, the husbands of the female **protagonists**. One student in the class, a nursing major, chose to write about the apparent cultural assumption that women were inherently sickly and frail, while another student wrote about images of confinement and freedom in both stories. When you receive an assignment, give some thought as to how it might relate to your own interests and how you might call upon your background and knowledge to approach the topic in fresh and interesting ways.

Finally, if you've put in some thought and effort but still don't know what to write about, remember that you do not need to go it alone. Seek out guidance and help. Talk with other students in your class and see what they have decided to write about; though of course you don't want simply to copy someone else's topic, hearing what others think can often spark a fresh idea. And don't forget your instructor. Most teachers are more than happy to spend a little time helping you come up with a topic and approach that will help you write a good paper.

DEVELOPING A THESIS

With the possible exception of a summary (see "Some Common Writing Assignments" pp. 1302–17), all writing about literature is to some degree a form of argument. Before proceeding, though, let's dispel some of the negative connotations of the word *argument*. In everyday usage, this term can connote a heated verbal fight, and it suggests two (or more) people growing angry and, often, becoming less articulate and more abusive as time passes. It suggests combat and implies that the other party in the process is an opponent. In this sort of argument, there are winners and losers.

Clearly this is not what we have in mind when we say you will be writing argumentatively about literature. Used in a different, more traditional sense, *argument* refers to a writer or speaker's attempt to establish the validity of a given position. In other words, when you write a paper you work to convince your reader that what you are saying is true. The reader is not the enemy, not someone whose ideas are to be crushed and refuted, but rather a person whose thoughts and feelings you have a chance to affect. You are not arguing *against* your reader; rather, you are using your argumentative abilities to *help* your reader see the logic and value of your position.

To begin writing a literary argument, then, you must take a position and have a point to make. This principal point will be the *thesis* of your paper. It is important to distinguish between a topic and a thesis: Your topic is the issue or area upon which you will focus your attention, and your thesis is a statement *about* this topic. It might help to phrase your thesis as a complete sentence in which the topic is the subject, followed by a verb that makes a firm statement or claim regarding your topic. This is your thesis statement, and it will probably appear toward the beginning of your paper. The foremost purpose of a paper, then, is to explain, defend, and ultimately prove the truth of its thesis.

When asked to state the thesis of their papers, students will sometimes simply identify their chosen topic or focus. Melanie Smith, author of the paper beginning on page 1322, for instance, came to her professor saying she was having trouble getting started on the assignment. When asked to articulate her tentative thesis, she said it was "the husbands in the two stories." Granted, these men are interesting characters, and their roles in the stories are worth examining, but a character is not a thesis. The professor prompted, "What about the husbands?" to which Melanie replied, "People in class were really hard on them, but I didn't think they were so bad, considering when they lived." This was better, suggesting as it did which aspect of the men's stories interested Melanie, but it still was not a thesis. After a bit more discussion with her professor, Melanie ended up with a tentative thesis that read "Although they are in part to blame for their wives' oppression, the men in 'The Yellow Wallpaper' and 'The Story of an Hour' are victims of their time, just as their wives are." While her thesis was still not perfectly refined, and it would evolve as she worked through the writing process, now she was getting somewhere. This version of the thesis was a complete sentence that both identified the topic and made a claim about it. Melanie left the meeting ready to start writing because she now had a clear goal—to prove that the two men in the stories were not as much to blame as her classmates had insisted.

Keep the following guidelines in mind as you think about a tentative thesis for your paper.

- **Your thesis should be both clear and specific.** The purpose of a thesis is to serve as a guide to both the reader and the writer, so it needs to be understandable and to point clearly to the specific aspects of the literature that you will discuss. This does not mean it will stand alone or need no further development or explanation— after all that's what the rest of the paper is for. But a reader who is familiar with the story, poem, or play you are writing about (and it is fair to assume a basic familiarity) should have a good sense of what your thesis means and how it relates to the literature.

- **Your thesis should be relevant.** The claim you make should not only interest you as a writer but also give your reader a reason to keep reading by sparking his or her interest and desire to know more. Not every paper is going to change lives or minds, of course, but you should at least state your thesis in such a way that your reader won't have the most dreaded of responses: "Who cares?"

- **Your thesis should be debatable.** Since the purpose of an argumentative paper is to convince a reader that your thesis is correct (or at least that it has merit), it cannot simply be an irrefutable fact. A good thesis will be something that a reasonable person, having read the literature, might disagree with or might not have considered at all. It should give you something to prove.

- **Your thesis should be original.** Again, originality does not imply that every thesis you write must be a brilliant gem that nobody but you could have discovered. But it should be something you have thought about independently, it should avoid clichés, contain something of you, and do more than parrot back something said in your class or written in your textbook.

- **You should be able to state your thesis as a complete sentence.** This sentence, generally referred to as the *thesis statement,* should first identify your topic and then make a claim about it. (Occasionally, especially for longer papers with more complex ideas behind them, you will need more than one sentence to state your thesis clearly. Even in these cases, though, the complete thesis must both identify the topic and make a claim about it.)

- **Your thesis should be appropriate to the assignment.** This may seem obvious, but as we work with literature, taking notes, asking questions, and beginning to think about topics and theses, it is possible to lose sight of the assignment as it was presented. After you have come up with a tentative thesis, it's a good idea to go back and review the assignment as your instructor gave it, making sure your paper will fulfill its requirements.

You will note that in this discussion, the phrase *tentative thesis* has come up a number of times. The word *tentative* is important. As you start to gather support and to write your paper, your thesis will help you focus clearly on your task and sort out which of your ideas, observations, and questions are relevant to the project at hand. But you should keep an open mind as well, realizing that your thesis is likely to evolve as you write. You are likely to change the focus in subtle or not so subtle ways, and it's even possible that you will change your mind completely as you write and therefore need to create a new thesis from scratch. If this happens, don't regard it as a failure. On the contrary, it means you have succeeded in learning something genuine from the experience of writing, and that is what a literature class is all about.

GATHERING AND ORGANIZING SUPPORT FOR YOUR THESIS

Once you have crafted a tentative thesis, it is time to think about the evidence or support you will need to convince your reader of the claim's validity. But what exactly counts as support? What can you include in your paper as evidence that your thesis is true? Essentially, all support comes from one of three sources:

- **The text itself is the most obvious source of support.** It is not enough to *say* that a certain piece of literature says or means a certain thing. You will need to *show* this by summarizing, paraphrasing, or quoting the literature itself. Advice on how to quote literature effectively can be found on pages 1296–1300.

- **Other people's ideas are a good source of support.** Chances are you will find a lot of useful material for your paper if you pay attention to easily available sources of ideas from other readers. These include the notes and biographical information in your textbooks, research conducted online or in the library, lectures and discussions in class, and even informal conversations about the literature with your friends and classmates.

- **Your own thoughts are your most important source of support.** Remember that although you may want to integrate ideas and information from a variety of sources, your paper is yours and as such should reflect *your* thinking. The most indispensable source of material for your paper is your own mind; your own thoughts and words should always carry the heaviest weight in any paper you write.

To begin gathering support for your thesis, return to your annotated texts, your reading notes and class notes, and your questions. Most likely, you will have noted many things that are not especially relevant to your thesis. Let them go for now, no matter how interesting they are. In one paper you can't say everything about a piece of literature, and you shouldn't try. If you include every clever idea, every interesting quotation, your paper will end up unfocused and cluttered. Your job now is to zero in on the pertinent evidence that will support your thesis. At this point, you'll also want to reread the primary texts with your thesis in mind, taking note of any new ideas that strike you in light of your tentative focus. Chances are some new and interesting evidence will strike you in this more focused reading.

Once you've determined what evidence to use, it is time to begin sorting and organizing it. The organizing principle for any paper is the sequence of paragraphs, so at this stage you should be thinking at the level of paragraph content. Remember that each paragraph should contain one main idea and sufficient evidence and explanation to support that idea. When added together, these paragraph-level ideas lead a reader to your paper's ultimate point—your thesis. So the first stage of organizing the content of your essay is to cluster together similar ideas in order to begin shaping the substance of individual paragraphs. The second stage is to determine the order in which these paragraphs will appear.

Your paper's organization may end up following the structure of a story, poem, or play about which you write, but this organizational strategy is less common in literary argument than you might think, and you should keep your mind open to other organizing principles as well. You might isolate individual characters, images, and so forth, analyzing each in a separate paragraph. Your paper might move from cause to effect, from your weakest to your strongest argument, from simple to complex, or along many other developmental lines. Often one organizational strategy seems to make the most sense for a particular project, but usually any of several different strategies might work for any given paper, and you will need to assess which will work best for your purposes. Indeed, your thesis itself may provide a guide to you by suggesting a certain organizational logic.

You may have encountered the concept of essay structure sometimes characterized by the instructions: "Tell them what you're going to tell them, tell them, then tell them what you told them." Using this method, you start your introduction with a broad, sweeping claim and then narrow down to your thesis statement at the end of the first paragraph. The thesis statement itself provides an overview of the upcoming paragraphs. Each subsequent paragraph begins with a topic sentence, a sort of mini thesis statement for the paragraph, which is followed by explanation and supporting evidence. Finally, the concluding paragraph restates the thesis (preferably in different words) and then broadens out to a more general statement that serves to leave the reader with a sense of the paper's wider significance. (Sometimes this is called the five-paragraph essay because of the myth that an essay should include exactly three body paragraphs plus an introduction and a conclusion. In reality, though, there is no "correct" number of paragraphs for an essay; topic, essay length, and internal logic should always determine how many paragraphs your paper has.)

There is, however, a certain attractive logic to the structure just described. It gives both writer and reader a clear sense of direction and helps keep an essay from wandering off on tangents or getting bogged down too much on any one idea. Indeed, at the stage of planning, it can be a good idea to keep this structure in the back of your mind as a very rough guide, especially if it has worked well for you in the past. But, if followed too closely, any one approach can lead to a less than stimulating paper, both for you and for your reader. It suggests that one form is appropriate for all types of content, as if it were a container into which you pour your thoughts, and your thoughts had better conform to the mold rather than the other way around. You need to keep an open mind about structure and organization, or your paper could well begin to sound more like a lab report than a literary exploration.

As you write and revise your paper, you may have different ideas about how to structure it. You may want to put the topic sentence somewhere other than at the beginning of a paragraph, or perhaps the topic is so clear that no specific topic sentence is even needed. You may devise a more interesting way to structure your introduction or conclusion. (Some additional, more specific thoughts for those tricky introductory and concluding paragraphs follow, on pages 1293–95.) Unless your instructor has specified the form in which your paper is to be organized, you should feel free to experiment a bit. You may end up using some parts of the structure described above while rejecting others. Look, for instance, at the introduction to the research paper by Jarrad Nunes on page 1365. Jarrad begins not with a sweeping generalization or a philosophical statement but rather with a specific observation and a quotation about Emily Dickinson's beliefs and styles. He does, however, conclude the opening paragraph with a thesis statement suggesting to readers the content, scope, and argument of his paper.

For most writers, creating some version of an outline is the best way to approach the task of organizing evidence into a logical sequence for a paper. In the past you may have been asked to write a formal outline, complete with roman numerals and capital letters. If this technique has been helpful in organizing your thoughts, by all means continue to use it. For many writers, however, an informal outline works just as well and is less cumbersome. To construct an informal outline, simply jot down a heading that summarizes the topic of each paragraph you intend to write. Then cluster your gathered evidence — quotations or paraphrases from the literature, ideas for analysis, and so on — into groups under the headings.

Patrick McCorkle wrote the paper about Shakespeare's Sonnet 116 that begins on page 1329. He wanted his essay to demonstrate how the balance of positive and negative language in the poem makes for a more interesting definition of love than he had seen in other love poems. He gathered his ideas and evidence about the poem into an informal outline.

Introduction

    Two kinds of typical love poems: happy and sad

    Sonnet 116 is more complex and interesting

    <u>Tentative thesis:</u> By including both negative and positive images and language, this sonnet gives a complex and realistic definition of love.

Vivid images in poem

    <u>Positive/expected:</u> "star," "ever-fixèd mark," "rosy lips and cheeks"

    <u>Negative/unexpected:</u> "sickle" (deathlike), "wandering bark" (lost boat), "tempests"

Negative language

    <u>words/phrases:</u> "Let me not," "Love is not," "never," "nor," "no," etc.

    <u>abstractions:</u> "alteration," "impediments," "error"

Conclusion

    Love never changes

    Shakespeare's definition still works some 400 years later

This is not, obviously, a formal outline. It does, however, group similar items and ideas together, and it gives the writer a basic structure to follow as he continues with the composing process. If you compare this outline to Patrick's actual paper, you will find substantial differences, including a refined thesis, the addition of several more short quotations, and additional paragraphs of analysis. The final paper is stronger and more thorough than this outline suggests, because Patrick knew to use his informal outline as a starting point only, allowing the paper to take shape and evolve as he proceeded with writing and revision.

DRAFTING, REVISING, AND EDITING

You have a topic. You have a tentative thesis. You have gathered evidence. You have an outline or tentative structure in mind for this evidence. It is time to begin writing your first draft. Every writer has his or her own slightly different process for getting the words down on paper.

Some begin at the beginning of the paper, or with the first body paragraph, and work straight through to the end in a clear, organized fashion. Others write bits and pieces of the paper out of order and allow the
overall structure to emerge at a later time.

You no doubt have developed your own work habits during your years
of schooling, and if you have found a method that works for you, then by
all means stick with it. The exception to this rule is if you have been a
procrastinator in the past. Some writers claim that they work better at
the last minute and focus better under the pressure of a looming dead-
line. This, however, is almost always a justification for sloppy work
habits, and procrastination rarely if ever really results in a superior
paper. When habitual procrastinators change their working methods
and give themselves more time on a project, they are frequently surprised to discover that the process is more enjoyable and the final product of their efforts better than what they have produced in the past. Start
early and work steadily—it will prove more than worth it.

A well-written essay often gives the impression that its structure and
language are inevitable, that it makes its point in the only reasonable
way. This sense of inevitability might suggest that a skilled writer sits
down with a good idea, starts at the first sentence, and writes straight
through to the end, maybe taking a moment to proofread or put a few
finishing touches on the essay. This is almost never the case. Nearly all
writers write in fits and starts, change their minds as they write, and go
back frequently to rework passages or even restructure an entire written
work. One of the biggest differences between beginning writers and
more experienced, highly skilled writers is that the more experienced
ones tend not to worry about getting the first draft "right," trusting that
they will be able to improve on the draft in revision.

The process of writing breaks down roughly into prewriting, drafting,
revising, and finally, editing and proofreading. One writing instructor
compares writing to baking. Prewriting—brainstorming, choosing a
topic, developing a tentative thesis, and considering possible support—
is like gathering together the ingredients to make a rich, delicious cake.
Writing the first draft is the equivalent of mixing the batter. You don't
expect batter to look, feel, or taste like the cake itself. To make a good
batter—just like a good draft—you need to mix in the best ingredients
you can. Revision is the equivalent of baking the cake; this is the stage
where it takes shape, firms up, and becomes something worthy of serving to your guests. Final editing and proofreading, getting all the details
just right, are like frosting and decorating the cake, making it look as
good as it can.

So, with this analogy in mind, try to write your first draft fairly
quickly. You don't need to get every sentence just right—that's what the

revision phase of writing is for. What you want now is just to get as much good raw material as possible into the mix and see what works. Don't worry too much yet about style, transitions, grammar, and so forth. In fact, you don't even need to start at the beginning or work right through to the end. If you get stuck on one part, move on. You can always come back and fill in the gaps later. Introductions can be especially tricky, particularly since you haven't yet finished the essay and don't really know what it is you're introducing. Some writers find it easier to just start with the body of the essay, or to write a short, sloppy introduction as a placeholder. You can go back and work on the real introduction when the draft is complete. (Some advice on how to do this can be found on page 1295.)

Once you have a complete, or near complete, draft, it's time to begin thinking about revision. Try to avoid the common pitfall of thinking of revision as locating and fixing mistakes. Revision is far more than this. Looking at the parts of the word, you can see that *re-vision* means seeing again, and indeed the revision stage of the writing process is your chance to see your draft anew and make real and substantial improvements to every facet of it, from its organization to its tone to your word choices. Most successful writers will tell you that it is in the revision stage that the real work gets done, where the writing takes shape and begins to emerge in its final form. Don't skimp on this part of the process or try to race through it. We suggest a three-phase process, consisting of global, or large-scale, revisions; local, or small-scale, revisions; and a final editing and proofreading. If you haven't done so before, revising your paper three times may seem like a lot of work, but bear in mind that most professional writers revise their work many more times than that, and revision is the real key to writing the best paper you can.

It is a good idea not to start a major revision the minute a draft is complete. Take a break. Exercise, have a meal, do something completely different to clear your mind. If possible, put the draft aside for at least a day so that when you return to it you'll have a fresh perspective and can begin truly re-seeing it. Print out your draft. Attempting serious revision on-screen is generally a bad idea—we see differently, and we usually see more, when we read off a printed page. Read with a pen in your hand and annotate your text just the way you would a piece of literature, looking for the strengths and weaknesses of your argument.

On a first pass at revision—the large-scale, global part of the process—don't worry too much about details like word choice, punctuation, and so forth. Too many students focus so much on these issues that they miss the big picture. The details are important, but you will deal with them in depth later. You wouldn't want to spend your time getting the wording of a sentence just right only to decide later that the paragraph it is in weakens your argument and needs to be deleted. So at first, look at the overall picture—the argument, organization, and tone of the paper as a whole. While there's nothing wrong with making a few small improvements as you read, nothing smaller than a paragraph should concern you at this point. Here are some possibilities for how you might revise your paper globally.

- **You might refine or develop your focus and thesis.** Now that you've finished a draft, ask yourself how convincing your argument is. Can you make your thesis clearer or more specific? How has your thinking about the issues evolved as you have written? At this stage, remember, it is not about tinkering with word choice to make your *thesis statement* sound better. Rather, it is about reconsidering your focus and thesis as a whole and assessing the degree to which you can revise, refine, or clarify your point.

- **You might reorganize your paper.** Does the order of the ideas and paragraphs make immediate sense to you, or does some alternate structure suggest itself? The cut-and-paste feature on your word processor makes it easy to try out different organizational strategies, though of course some additional rewriting will likely be necessary if you change the structure, especially at the transitions between paragraphs.

- **You might expand your paper with new paragraphs or with new evidence within existing paragraphs.** Often, fresh ideas occur to us as we read, which might require that you add to existing paragraphs or write new ones. It may also necessitate returning to the literary text or other external sources and seeking out more quotations or other evidence to bolster your argument.

- **You might eliminate any unnecessary, contradictory, or distracting passages.** For some writers, this is the hardest thing to do, as it is easy to get attached to what we write. Cutting something seems like a waste of our previous efforts. However, it is best to develop a thick skin about this. If an image, a piece of evidence, a sentence, or even a whole paragraph or more doesn't serve to strengthen your paper, then it is at best a distraction for your readers and at worst a contradiction that weakens your argument. Cut it.

- **You might clarify any difficult passages with more specific explanations or evidence.** As you read over your draft, try to be especially sensitive to any areas where readers might need a little additional help in order to follow your point. Is it clear how each paragraph supports your thesis? If anything seems unclear, you can refine your analysis and explanation, gather further evidence from the literature or another source, or both.

- **You might change the overall tone of the paper.** Spend a little time thinking about the general tone or style of your paper. Is it serious or lighthearted? Do you come across as an expert sharing your knowledge, or do you seem to be probing and exploring ideas? Is the vocabulary elevated and "academic" or simple and to the point? Is your tone funny? Sad? Sarcastic? How *consistent* is the tone? How appropriate is it to the point you are trying to make? An overall tune-up may be in order, making many small changes in word choice and so on to fashion a more suitable tone.

Once you have completed your first, large-scale revision, chances are you will feel more confident about the content and structure of your paper. The thesis and focus are strong, the evidence is lined up, the major points are clear. Print out the new version, take another break if you can, and prepare to move on to the second phase of revision, the one that takes place at the local level of words, phrases, and sentences. The focus here is on style and clarity. The types of changes you will make in this stage are, essentially, small-scale versions of the changes you made in the first round of revision: adding, cutting, reorganizing, and clarifying. Are you sure about the meanings of any difficult or unusual words you have used? Is there enough variety in sentence style to keep your writing interesting? Do the same words or phrases appear again and again? Are the images vivid? Are the verbs strong? One way to assess the effectiveness of a paper's style is to read it aloud and hear how it sounds. You may feel a little foolish doing this, but many people find it very helpful.

Once you have revised your essay a second time and achieved both content and a style that pleases you, it's time for final editing. This is where you make it "correct." Make sure all words are spelled correctly. (Should it be *their* or *there*? *It's* or *its*?) Check punctuation, looking especially at things that have caused you trouble in the past. (Should you use a comma or a semicolon? Does the period go inside or outside of the quotation marks?) If you are writing a research paper, make sure all the references are in the correct format and the bibliographic style is perfect (or as close to perfect as you can manage). Double-check that the manuscript format and layout are as they should be. Nobody expects you to know all the rules on your own, but you should know where to look for them. If you are unsure about any of these things, look them up in this book or in a good dictionary, grammar handbook, or other reference. Make any final, necessary corrections and then print out your final paper and proofread it one last time.

It's tempting to skimp on this final phase of editing and proofreading. After all, you've already spent hours reading, writing, and revising, and you've probably read the paper so many times that you no longer see it well. But the harder you've worked on the paper, the more important the editing is. Any errors will distract readers and undercut your authority and professionalism. If you can't be bothered to edit and proofread, how will the reader know if your quotations and facts are accurate? Why should a reader trust your ideas and opinions? Even the smartest idea loses some of its power when it is presented in a forest of errors. Don't diminish the hours of work you've already put into your paper by short-changing this last step of the process.

PEER EDITING AND WORKSHOPS

One final word of advice as you revise your paper: ask for help. Doing so is neither cheating nor is it an admission of defeat. In fact, professional writers do it all the time. Despite the persistent image of writers toiling in isolation, most successful writers seek advice at various stages. More important, they are willing to listen to that advice and to rethink what they have written if it seems not to be communicating what they had intended.

Some instructors give class time for draft workshops, sometimes called peer editing, in which you work with your fellow students, trying to help one another improve your work-in-progress. Such workshops can benefit you in two ways. First, your classmates can offer you critiques and advice on what you might have missed in your own rereading. Second, reading and discussing papers other than your own will help you to grow as a writer, showing you a variety of ways in which a topic can be approached. If you really like something about a peer's paper—say, a vivid introduction or the effective use of humor—make note of how it works within the paper and consider integrating something similar into a future paper of your own. We are not, of course, advocating copying your classmates; rather, we are pointing out that other people's writing has much to teach us.

Some students are uncomfortable with such workshops. They may feel they don't know enough about writing to give valid advice to others, or they may doubt whether advice from their peers is particularly valuable. But you don't need to be a great literary critic, much less an expert on style or grammar, in order to give genuinely useful advice to a fellow writer. Whatever your skills or limitations as a writer, you have something invaluable to give: the thoughts and impressions of a real reader working through a paper. It is only when we see how a reader responds to what we've written that we know if a paper is communicating its intended message. If you are given an opportunity to engage in peer workshops, make the most of them.

Your instructor may give you guidelines regarding what to look for in others' drafts, or you may be left more or less on your own. In either case, keep these general guidelines in mind.

- **Be respectful of one another's work.** You should, of course, treat your peers' work with the same respect and seriousness that you'd want for your own. Keep your criticism constructive and avoid personal attacks, even if you disagree strongly with an opinion. You can help your fellow writers by expressing a contrary opinion in a civilized and thoughtful manner.

- **Be honest.** This means giving real, constructive criticism when it is due. Don't try to spare your workshop partner's feelings by saying "That's great" or "It's fine," when it really isn't. When asked what went badly in a peer workshop, students most commonly respond *not* that their peers were too harsh on their work but that they were not harsh enough. Wouldn't you rather hear about a problem with your work from a peer in a draft workshop than from your professor after you have already handed in the final draft? So would your classmates.

- **Look for the good as well as the bad in a draft.** No paper, no matter how rough or problematic, is completely without merit. And no paper, no matter how clever or well-written, couldn't be improved. By pointing out both what works and what doesn't, you will help your classmates grow as writers.

- **Keep an eye on the time.** It's easy to get wrapped up in a discussion of an interesting paper and not allow adequate time to another. Say you're given half an hour to work with your draft and that of one classmate. When you reach the 15-minute mark, move on, no matter how interesting your discussion is. Fair is fair. On the other hand, don't stop short of the allotted time. If you are really reading carefully and thinking hard about one another's drafts, it should be impossible to finish early.

- **Take notes, on your draft itself or on a separate sheet.** You may be certain that you will remember what was said in a workshop, but you would be amazed how often people forget the good advice they heard and intended to follow. Better safe than sorry—take careful notes.

- **Ask questions.** Asking questions about portions of a draft you don't understand or find problematic can help its writer see what needs to be clarified, expanded, or reworked. Useful questions can range from the large scale (*What is the purpose of this paragraph?*) to the small (*Is this a quote? Who said it?*).

- **Don't assume that explaining yourself to your workshop partner can replace revision.** Sometimes your workshop partners will ask a question, and when you answer it for them they will say, "Oh, right, that makes sense," leaving you with the impression that everything is clear now. But remember, your classmates didn't understand it from the writing alone and you won't be there to explain it to your teacher.

- **Be specific in your comments.** Vague comments like "The introduction is good" or "It's sort of confusing here" are not much help. Aim for something more like "The introduction was funny and really made me want to read on" or "This paragraph confused me because it seems to contradict what you said in the previous one." With comments like these, a writer will have a much better sense of where to focus his or her revision energies.

- **Try to focus on the big picture.** It's tempting when reading a draft to zero in on distracting little mistakes in spelling, punctuation, or word choice. While it's generally fine to point out or circle such surface matters as you go along, a draft workshop is not about correcting mistakes. It's about helping one another to re-see and rethink your papers on a global scale.

- **Push your partners to help you more.** If your workshop partners seem shy or reluctant to criticize, prompt them to say more by letting them know that you really want advice and that you are able to take criticism. Point out to them what you perceive as the trouble spots in the essay, and ask if they have any ideas to help you out. It feels good, of course, to hear that someone likes your paper and cannot imagine how to improve it. But in the long run it is even better to get real, useful advice that will lead to a better paper. If your classmates are not helping you enough, it's your responsibility to ask for more.

Even if your class does not include workshop time, this in no way prevents you from using the many resources available to you on campus. Find one or two other members of your class and make time to have your own peer workshop, reading and critiquing one another's drafts. Be sure to arrange such a meeting far enough in advance of the due date so that you will have ample time to implement any good revision advice you receive. Many campuses also have writing or tutoring centers, and the workers in these centers, often advanced students who are skilled writers, can offer a good deal of help. Remember, again, that you should make an appointment to see a tutor well in advance of the paper's due date, and you should *not* expect a tutor to revise or "fix" your paper for you. That is, ultimately, your job. And, of course, you can also approach your instructor at any phase of the writing process and ask for advice and help.

But remember, no matter where you turn for advice, the final responsibility for your paper is yours. Any advice and help you receive from classmates, tutors, friends—or even your instructor—is just that: advice and help. It is *your* paper, and *you* must be the one to make the decisions about which advice to follow, which to ignore, and how to implement changes to improve your paper. The key is to keep an open mind, seek help from all available sources, and give yourself plenty of time to turn your first draft into a final paper that makes you truly proud.

TROUBLE SPOTS: INTRODUCTIONS, CONCLUSIONS, AND TRANSITIONS

Ideally, of course, your entire paper will be equally compelling and polished, but there are certain points in a paper that most often cause trouble for writers and readers, and these points may require a little additional attention on your part. The most typical trouble spots are introductory and concluding paragraphs and the transitional sentences that connect paragraphs. Although there is no one formula to help you to navigate these waters, as each writing situation and each paper is different, there are some general guidelines that can help you think through the problems that might arise in these areas.

As we mentioned earlier, many writers find it easier to write an introduction *after* drafting their essay. At that point, you have a clear sense of where you are going, the essay's overall tone, and so forth; you really know at that point what it is your introduction should be introducing. Essentially, an introduction accomplishes two things. First, it gives a sense of both your topic and your approach to that topic, which is why it is common to make your thesis statement a part of the introduction. Second, an introduction compels your readers' interest and makes them want to read on and find out what your paper has to say. Some common strategies used in effective introductions are to begin with a probing rhetorical question, a vivid description, or an intriguing quotation. Weak introductions tend to speak in generalities or in philosophical ideas that are only tangentially related to the real topic of your paper. Don't spin your wheels: get specific and get to the point right away.

Concluding paragraphs are another sore spot for some writers. By the time you finally make it to the conclusion, you may have said all you feel is necessary, and you don't want to drag your feet or repeat yourself, leaving the reader bored or restless. While it is not a bad idea to include a quick summary of a sentence or two, reminding a reader of your paper's principal claims or reasserting your thesis (in different words, of course), your conclusion should do more than this. It should give your reader something new to think about, a reason not to just forget your essay. Some writers like to use the conclusion to return to an idea, a quotation, or an image first raised in the introduction, creating a satisfying feeling of completeness and self-containment. Note how Sarah Johnson, in her paper about Susan Glaspell's *Trifles* beginning on page 1335, poses a philosophical question at the very beginning of the paper and then offers a tentative answer in her conclusion. Some writers use the conclusion to show the implications of their claims or the connections between the literature and real life. This is your chance to make a good final impression, so don't waste it with simple summary and restatement.

The transitional sentences that begin and end paragraphs are another persistent source of grief for students. Many writers have been told that they need to provide stronger transitions, and some have even learned lists of "transitional words and phrases." In fact, though, transitions are not puzzles to be solved with a bag of "trick" words. Each paragraph is built around a different idea, and the job of the transitions is to show how these separate ideas are related to one another, to make the juxtaposition of two paragraphs seem as logical to a reader as it is to the writer. When you fear a transition isn't working effectively, the first question you should ask yourself is *why* does one paragraph follow another in this particular order? Would it make more sense to change the placement of some paragraphs, or is this really the best organizational strategy for this portion of the paper? Once you know why your paper is structured as it is, transitions become much easier to write, simply making apparent to your audience the connections you already know to be there. As you begin each new paragraph, give some consideration to the links between it and the previous paragraph, and try to make those links explicit in the opening sentence.

As with any other aspect of your writing, if you've had trouble in the past with introductions, conclusions, or transitions, one of your best sources of help is to be an attentive reader of others' writing. Pay special attention to these potential trouble spots in the writing you admire, whether by a classmate or a professional author, and see how he or she navigates them. Don't stick with the writing methods that have caused you headaches in the past. Be willing to try out different strategies, seeing which ones work best for you. In time you'll find you have a whole array of ways to approach these trouble spots, and you'll be able to find a successful response to each particular writing situation.

TIPS FOR WRITING ABOUT LITERATURE

Each genre of literature—fiction, poetry, and drama—poses its own, slightly different set of assumptions and problems for writers, which are covered in more detail in the sections that follow. However, there are certain general principles that can help you as you write about any form of literature.

- **Don't assume that your readers will remember (or consider important) the same ideas or incidents in the literature that you do.** You should assume that your readers have *read* the literature but not necessarily that they have reacted to it the same way you have. Therefore, whenever possible, use specific examples and evidence in the form of quotations and summaries to back up your claims.

- **Do not retell the plot or text at length.** Some writers are tempted to begin with a plot summary or even to include the text of a short poem at the beginning of a paper. However, this strategy can backfire by delaying the real substance of your paper. Be discriminating when you summarize — keep quotations short and get to the *point* you want to make as quickly as possible.

- **Do not assume that quotations or summaries are self-sufficient and prove your point automatically.** Summaries and quotations are a starting point; you need to *analyze* them thoroughly in your own words, explaining why they are important. As a general rule, each quotation or summary should be followed by at least several sentences of analysis.

- **It is customary to use the present tense when writing about literature,** even if the events discussed take place in the distant past. Example:

When she sees that Romeo is dead, Juliet kills herself with his knife.

- **The first time you mention an author, use his or her full name.** For subsequent references, the last name is sufficient. (Do not use first names only; it sounds as if you know an author personally.)

- **Titles of poems, stories, and essays should be put in quotation marks. Titles of books, plays, and periodicals (magazines, newspapers, etc.) should be underlined or italicized.** In titles and in all quotations, follow spelling, capitalization, and punctuation *exactly* as it occurs in the work itself.

- **Give your paper a title.** A title doesn't need to be elaborate or super clever, but it should give some clue as to what the paper is about and begin setting up expectations for your reader. Simply restating the assignment, such as "Essay #2" or "Comparison and Contrast Paper," is of little help to a reader and might even suggest intellectual laziness on the part of the writer. For the same reason, avoid giving your paper the same title as the work of literature you are writing about; unless you're Shakespeare or Hemingway, don't title your paper *Hamlet* or "A Clean, Well-Lighted Place."

- **Above all, use common sense and *be consistent*.**

USING QUOTATIONS EFFECTIVELY

At some point, you will want to quote the literature you are writing about, and you might also want to quote some secondary research sources as well. Be selective, though, in your use of quotations so that the dominant voice of the paper is your own, not a patchwork of the words of others. Because they are laid out differently on the page, stories, poems, and plays each present slightly different formal issues of quotation, and these are dealt with later, in the separate sections devoted to each genre (pages 1318, 1325, and 1331). For now, here is general advice to help you integrate quotations effectively into your essays.

Try to avoid floating quotations. Sometimes writers simply lift a sentence out of the original, put quotation marks around it, and identify the source (if at all) in a subsequent sentence.

"I met a traveler from an antique land." This is how Shelley's poem "Ozymandias" begins.

Doing so can create confusion for a reader, who is momentarily left to ponder where the quotation comes from and why have you quoted it. In addition to potentially causing confusion, such quoting can read as awkward and choppy, as there is no transition between another writer's words and yours.

Use at least an attributed quotation; that is, one that names the source *within* the sentence containing the quotation, usually in a lead-in phrase.

Shelley begins his poem "Ozymandias" with the words, "I met a traveler from an antique land."

This way the reader knows right away who originally wrote or said the quoted material and knows (or at least expects) that your commentary will follow. It also provides a smoother transition between your words and the quotation.

Whenever possible, use an integrated quotation. To do this, you make the quotation a part of your own sentence.

When the narrator of "Ozymandias" begins by saying that he "met a traveler from an antique land," we are immediately thrust into a mysterious world.

This is the hardest sort of quoting to do since it requires that you make the quoted material fit in grammatically with your own sentence, but the payoff in clarity and sharp prose is usually well worth the extra time spent on sentence revision.

Sometimes, especially when you are using integrated quotations effectively, you will find that you need to slightly alter the words you are quoting. You should, of course, keep quotations exact whenever possible, but occasionally the disparity between the tense, point of view, or grammar of your sentence and that of the quoted material will necessitate some alterations. Other difficulties can arise when you quote a passage that already contains a quotation or when you need to combine quotation marks with other punctuation marks. When any of these situations arise, the following guidelines should prove useful. The examples of quoted text that follow are all drawn from this original passage from *Hamlet*, in which Hamlet and his friend Horatio are watching a gravedigger unearth old skulls in a cemetery:

> HAMLET: That skull had a tongue in it, and could sing once. How the knave jowls it to the ground, as if 'twere Cain's jaw-bone, that did the first murder! This might be the pate of a politician, which this ass now o'erreaches, one that would circumvent God, might it not?
> HORATIO: It might, my lord.
> HAMLET: Or of a courtier, which could say "Good morrow, sweet lord! How dost thou, sweet lord?" This might be my Lord Such-a-one, that praised my Lord Such-a-one's horse when 'a meant to beg it, might it not?

Adding to or Altering a Quotation

If you ever alter anything in a quotation or add words to it in order to make it clear and grammatically consistent with your own writing, you need to signal to your readers what you have added or changed. This is done by enclosing your words within square brackets in order to distinguish them from those in the source. If, for instance, you feel Hamlet's reference to the gravedigger as "this ass" is unclear, you could clarify it either by substituting your own words, as in the first example here, or by adding the identifying phrase to the original quote, as in the second example:

> Hamlet wonders if it is "the pate of a politician, which [the gravedigger] now o'erreaches."

> Hamlet wonders if it is "the pate of a politician, which this ass [the gravedigger] now o'erreaches."

Omitting Words from a Quotation

In order to keep a quotation focused and to the point, you will some-times want to omit words, phrases, or even whole sentences that do not contribute to your point. Any omission is signaled by ellipses, or three spaced periods, with square brackets around them. (The brackets are required to distinguish your own ellipses from any that might occur in the original source.)

> Hamlet wonders if the skull "might be the pate of a politician [. . .] that would circumvent God."

It is usually not necessary to use ellipses at the beginning or end of a quotation, since a reader assumes you are quoting only a relevant por-tion of text.

Quotations within Quotations

If you are quoting material that itself contains a quotation, the internal quotation is set off with single quotation marks rather than the standard double quotation marks that will enclose the entire quotation.

> Hamlet wonders if he might be looking at the skull "of a courtier, which could say 'Good morrow, sweet lord! How dost thou, sweet lord?'"

When the text you're quoting contains *only* material already in quotation marks in the original, the standard double quotation marks are all you need.

> Hamlet wonders if the courtier once said "Good morrow, sweet lord! How dost thou, sweet lord?"

Quotation Marks with Other Punctuation

When a period or a comma comes at the end of a quotation, it should always be placed inside the closing quotation marks, whether or not this punctuation was in the original source. In the first example that follows, note that the period following "horse" is within the quotation marks, even though there is no period there in the original. In the second exam-ple, the comma following "once" is also within the quotation marks, even though in Shakespeare's original "once" is followed by a period.

> Hamlet muses that the skull might have belonged to "my Lord Such-a-one, that praised my Lord Such-a-one's horse."

> "That skull had a tongue in it, and could sing once," muses Hamlet.

Other marks of punctuation (semicolons, question marks, etc.), are placed inside quotation marks if they are part of the original quotation and outside of the marks if they are part of your own sentence but not of the passage you are quoting. In the first example, the question is Hamlet's, and so the question mark must be placed within the quotation marks; in the second example, the question is the essay writer's, and so the question mark is placed outside of the quotation marks.

> Hamlet asks Horatio if the skull "might be my Lord Such-a-one, that praised my Lord Such-a-one's horse when 'a meant to beg it, might it not?"

> Why is Hamlet so disturbed that this skull "might be the pate of a politician"?

These sorts of punctuation details are notoriously hard to remember, so you should not feel discouraged if you begin forgetting such highly specialized rules moments after reading them. At least know where you can look them up and do so when you proofread your paper. A willingness to attend to detail is what distinguishes serious students and gives writing a polished, professional appearance. Also, the more you work with quotations, the easier it will be to remember the rules.

A Checklist for Quotations

- **Double-check the wording, spelling, and punctuation of every quotation you use.** Even if something seems "wrong" in the original source—a nonstandard spelling, a strange mark of punctuation, or even a factual error—resist the urge to correct it. When you put quotation marks around something, you indicate that you are reproducing it exactly as it first appeared. If you feel the need to clarify that an error or inconsistency is not yours, you may follow it by the word *sic* (Latin for *thus*), not italicized, in square brackets. Example:

  The mother in the anonymous poem "Lord Randal" asks her son "wha [sic] met ye there?"

- **Use the shortest quotation you can while still making your point.** Remember, the focus should always be on your own ideas, and the dominant voice should be yours. Don't quote a paragraph from a source when a single sentence contains the heart of what you need. Don't quote a whole sentence when you can simply integrate a few words into one of your own sentences.

- **Never assume a quotation is self-explanatory.** Each time you include a quotation, analyze it and explain why you have quoted it. Remember that your reader may have a different reaction to the quotation than you did.
- **If you are quoting a *character* in a story, play, or poem, be sure to distinguish that character from the *author*.** Hamlet says "To be or not to be," not Shakespeare, and you should make that distinction clear.
- **Take care not to distort the meaning of a quotation.** It is intellectually dishonest to quote an author or speaker out of context or to use ellipses or additions in such a way as to change the meaning or integrity of source material. Treat your sources with the same respect you would want if you were to be quoted in a newspaper or magazine.

MANUSCRIPT FORM

If your instructor gives you directions about what your paper should look like, follow them exactly. If not, the following basic guidelines on manuscript form, recommended by the Modern Language Association of America (MLA), will work well in most instances. (You will be hearing more about MLA format in the section dealing with research papers, on pages 1349–64.) Each of the four student papers presented in this book demonstrate the MLA form. The guiding principle here is readability—you want the look of your paper to distract as little as possible from the content.

- **Use plain white paper, black ink, and a standard, easy-to-read font.** To make your paper stand out from the masses, it might seem like a nice touch to use visual design elements like colored or decorated paper, fancy fonts, and so forth. However, your instructor has a lot of reading to do, and anything that distracts or slows that reading down is a minus, not a plus, for your paper. For the same reason, avoid illustrations unless they are needed to clarify a point. Distinguish your paper through content and style, not flashy design.
- **No separate cover page is needed.** Also, don't waste your time and money on report covers or folders unless asked to do so by your instructor. Many instructors, in fact, find covers cumbersome and distracting.
- **Include vital information in the upper left corner of your first page.** This information usually consists of your name, the name of your instructor, the course number of the class, and the date you submit the paper.

- **Center your paper's title.** The title should appear in upper and lower case letters, and in the same font as the rest of your paper — not italicized, boldface, or set in quotation marks.

- **Page numbers should appear in the upper right corner of each page.** Do not include the word *page* or the abbreviation *p.* with the page numbers. If possible, use your word processing program's "header" or "running head" feature to include your last name before the page numbers. (See the sample student papers in this book for examples.)

These basic guidelines should carry you through most situations, but if you have any questions regarding format, ask your instructor for his or her preferences.

CHAPTER 3

Some Common
Writing Assignments

SUMMARY

A summary is a brief recap of the most important points—plot, character, and so on—in a work of literature. In order to demonstrate that you have understood a play or story, for instance, you may be asked to summarize its plot as homework before a class discussion. It is rare for a full essay assignment to be based on summary alone, as little argument or independent thought is involved. It is, however, a useful skill to be able to focus on the most important part of a work of literature, knowing what is most vital, and short summaries are commonly used as part of the supporting evidence in more complex papers.

EXPLICATION AND CLOSE READING

One common assignment is to perform an explication or a close reading of a poem or short prose passage. As the word implies, an *explication* takes what is implicit or subtle in a work of literature and makes it explicit and clear. Literary language tends to be densely packed with meaning, and your job as you explicate it is to unfold that meaning and lay it out for your reader. The principal technique of explication is close reading; indeed, explication and close reading are so closely related that the words are often used virtually interchangeably. When you write this sort of paper, you will examine a piece of literature very closely, paying special attention to such elements of the language as sentence structure, style, imagery, figurative language, word choice, and perhaps even grammar and punctuation. The job of an explication is twofold: to point out particular, salient elements of style, and to explain the purpose and effect of these elements within the text.

It is tempting when assigned an explication or close reading to simply walk through a text line by line, pointing out interesting features of style as they occur. A paper written in this way, though, can devolve into little more than summary or restatement of the literature in more prosaic language. A better idea is to isolate the various features of the literature on which you will focus and then deal separately with the specifics and implications of each. Notice how Patrick McCorkle, author of the close reading of Shakespeare's Sonnet 116 on page 1329, organized his paper. The paper first covers the poem's imagery, then its negative and positive language. The writer provides plenty of analysis of these features, showing how each works within the poem as a whole. Notice also how Patrick clearly connects each point he makes to the paper's thesis, that Shakespeare creates a balanced and complex definition of love.

ANALYSIS

To analyze, by definition, is to take something apart and examine how the individual parts relate to one another and function within the whole. Engineers frequently analyze complex machinery, looking for ways to improve efficiency or performance. In a similar way, you can take apart a piece of literature to study how a particular part of it functions and what that part contributes to the whole. Typical candidates for literary analysis include plot development, characterization, tone, irony, and symbols.

In the paper beginning on page 1335, Sarah Johnson analyzes the development of an individual character in Susan Glaspell's *Trifles*, from the character's moral absolutism to her more situational view of morality. Sarah isolates a single character, Mrs. Peters, and traces her speech and actions throughout the play to show how she presents herself at first, the moments of crisis and difficulty she encounters, and who she is by the end. Though other things happen in the play and other characters make important contributions, in writing her analysis Sarah keeps her focus on the one character and mentions the others only to the extent that they interact with Mrs. Peters.

COMPARISON AND CONTRAST

Another common paper assignment is the comparison and contrast essay. You might be asked to draw comparisons and contrasts within a single work of literature — say, between two characters in a story or play.

Even more common is an assignment that asks you to compare and contrast a particular element—a character, setting, style, tone, and so on—in two or more stories, poems, or plays. A *comparison* emphasizes the similarities between two or more items, while a *contrast* highlights their differences. Though some papers do both, it is typical for an essay to emphasize one or the other.

If you are allowed to choose the works of literature for a comparison and contrast paper, take care to select works that have enough in common to make such a comparison interesting and valid. Even if Henrik Ibsen's *A Doll House* and Shirley Jackson's "The Lottery" are your favorites, it is difficult to imagine a well-focused paper comparing these two, as they share virtually nothing in terms of authorship, history, theme, or style. It would make far more sense to select two seventeenth-century poems or two love stories. When Melanie Smith was assigned to write the paper that begins on page 1322, she was asked to focus on Kate Chopin's "The Story of an Hour" and Charlotte Perkins Gilman's "The Yellow Wallpaper." The stories provide many immediate points of comparison, as they were written within a few years of each other, both authors are American women, and both feature female protagonists who live in confining marriages.

There are two basic organizational strategies for comparison and contrast essays: proceeding item by item or point by point. An item-by-item organization deals first with one work under consideration and then with another, reserving the analysis and direct comparison or contrast until after both works have been presented. Melanie, for instance, first could have written about Gilman's story and then gone on to write about Chopin's. She chose, however, to do a point-by-point comparison, devoting one paragraph to how the husbands in both stories provide for their families, another to whether or not they truly love their wives, and so on, talking about both works at once. Though she acknowledges some definite contrasts between the stories and the characters, her paper is largely a comparison, showing similarities between the two marriages and thus helping to support her claim that somewhat stifling unions were common at the time.

LITERARY CRITICISM AND LITERARY THEORY

Anytime you sit down to write about literature, or even to discuss a story, play, or poem with classmates, you are acting as a literary critic. The word *criticism* is often interpreted as negative and faultfinding. But literary criticism is a discipline and includes everything from a glowing review to a scathing attack to a thoughtful and balanced interpretation. Criticism can be broken down into two broad categories: evaluative and interpretive. Evaluative criticism seeks to determine how accomplished a work is and what place it should hold in the evolving story of literary history. Book reviews are the most common form of evaluative criticism. Interpretive criticism comprises all writing that seeks to explain, analyze, clarify, or question the meaning and significance of literature. Although you may engage in a certain amount of evaluative criticism in your literature class, and while your attitude about the value of literature will likely be apparent in your writing, the criticism you write for class will consist largely of interpretation.

If you were to go to the library and find a dozen recent articles on *Hamlet* by professional critics, the variety would be staggering. One critic may say that *Hamlet* is about the psychological problems of the prince, another may say it is about the structure of political power in Elizabethan England, and a third may believe she has found connections between *Hamlet* and another popular play of a previous generation. All of them make good cases, so far as you understand them, but they seem to be speaking at cross purposes to one another. Part of the reason lies in the fact that each critic begins from a different base of literary theory. Nobody has the one key to understanding the play perfectly, but each critic and each theory adds one more piece to our knowledge and thus helps to flesh out our understanding. Think of the various types of criticism as a series of lenses through which you can look at literature—each bringing into focus a different aspect of a text.

All literary critics, including you, begin with some form of literary theory. Just as you may not have thought of yourself as a literary critic, you probably haven't thought of yourself as using literary theory. But you are doing so every time you write about literature, and it is a good idea to become familiar with some of the most prevalent types of theory. This familiarity will help you understand why so many respected literary critics seem to disagree with one another and why they write such different analyses of the same work of literature. It may also help to explain why you might disagree with your classmates, or even your instructor, in your interpretation of a particular story, poem, or play. Perhaps you are simply starting from a different theoretical base. You will be able to explain your thinking more eloquently if you understand that base.

Literary theory has the reputation of being incredibly dense and difficult. Indeed, the theories—sometimes called *schools* of criticism—discussed in the following pages are all complex, but here they are presented in their most basic, stripped-down forms. As such, these explanations are necessarily incomplete and selective. You should not feel you need to master the complexities of literary theory right now. You need only be aware of the existence of these various schools and watch for them as you read and write. Doing so will give you a better sense of what you're reading and hearing about the literature you explore, and it will make your writing more informed and articulate. There are many other schools and subschools in addition to those described here, but these are the most significant—the ones you are most likely to encounter as you continue to explore literature.

Formalism and New Criticism

For a large part of the twentieth century, literary criticism was dominated by various types of theory that can broadly be defined as **formalism** and **New Criticism**. (New Criticism is no longer new, having begun to fall out of prominence in the 1970s, but its name lives on.) Formalist critics focus their attention, unsurprisingly, on the formal elements of a literary text—things like structure, tone, characters, setting, symbols, and linguistic features. Explication and close reading (explained on pages 1302–03) are techniques of formalist criticism. While poetry, which is most self-consciously formal in its structure, lends itself most obviously to formalist types of criticism, prose fiction and drama are also frequently viewed through this lens.

Perhaps the most distinguishing feature of formalism and New Criticism is that they focus on the text itself and not on extratextual factors. Formalist critics are interested in how parts of a text relate to one another and to the whole, and they seek to create meaning by unfolding and examining these relationships. Excluded from consideration are questions about the author, the reader, history or culture, and the relationship of the literary text to other texts or artwork. Chances are you have written some formalist criticism yourself, either in high school or in college. If you have ever written a paper on symbolism, character development, or the relationship between sound patterns and sense in a poem, you have been a formalist critic.

Feminist and Gender Criticism

Have you ever had a classroom discussion of a piece of literature in which the focus was on the roles of women in the literature or the culture, or on the relationships between men and women? If so, you have engaged in feminist criticism. Some version of feminist criticism has been around for as long as readers have been interested in gender roles, but the school rose to prominence in the 1970s, at the same time as the modern feminist movement was gaining steam. Most **feminist criticism** from this time was clearly tied to raising consciousness about the patriarchy in which many women felt trapped. Some feminist critics sought to reveal how literary texts demonstrated the repression and powerlessness of women in different periods and cultures. Others had a nearly opposite agenda, showing how female literary characters—and by analogy real women—could overcome the sexist power structures that surround them and exercise real power in their worlds. Still others looked to literary history and sought to rediscover and promote writing by women whose works had been far less likely than men's to be regarded as "great" literature.

It was not long, however, before some critics began to point out that women were not alone in feeling social pressure to conform to gender roles. Over the years, men have usually been expected to be good providers, to be strong (both physically and emotionally), and to keep their problems and feelings more or less to themselves. Though the expectations are different, men are socialized no less than women to think and behave in certain ways, and these social expectations are also displayed in works of literature. Feminist criticism has expanded in recent years to become gender criticism. Any literary criticism that highlights gender roles or relationships between the sexes can be a type of gender criticism, whether or not it is driven by an overt feminist agenda. Melanie Smith's essay (p. 1322) on the role of husbands in "The Story of an Hour" and "The Yellow Wallpaper" is a good example of gender criticism with a focus on male roles and expectations.

Marxist Criticism

Just as feminist criticism came into its own because of the political agenda of certain critics, so too did **Marxist criticism**, which originally sought to use literature and criticism to forward a socialist political program. Early Marxist critics began with Karl Marx's (1818–1883) insistence that all human interactions are economically driven and that the basic model of human progress is based on a struggle for power between different social classes. For Marxist critics, then, literature was just another battleground, another venue for the ongoing quest for individual material gain. Literary characters could be divided into powerful oppressors and their powerless victims, and literary plots and themes could be examined to uncover the economic forces that drove them. According to this model, the very acts of writing and reading literature can be characterized as production and consumption, and some Marxist critics have studied the external forces that drive education, publication, and literary tastes.

The sort of Marxist criticism that ignores all forces but those that are socioeconomic is sometimes referred to as *vulgar* Marxism because, in its single-mindedness, it ignores certain complexities of individual thought and action. Its sole purpose is to expose the inequalities that underlie all societies and to thus raise the consciousness of readers and move society closer to a socialist state. Such Marxist criticism tends to be full of the language of Marxist political analysis—references to *class struggle*, to the economic *base* and *superstructure*, to the *means of production*, to worker *alienation* and *reification* (the process whereby oppressed workers lose their sense of individual humanity), and so forth.

But just as feminist criticism soon opened up into the broader and more complex school of gender criticism, so too did some Marxist criticism break free of a single-minded political agenda. You no longer have to be a committed Marxist to engage in Marxist criticism; all you need to do is acknowledge that socioeconomic forces do, in fact, affect people's lives. If you notice inequalities in power between characters in a work of literature, if you question how the class or educational background of an author affects his or her work, or if you believe that a certain type of literature—a Shakespearean sonnet, say, or a pulp Western novel— appeals more to readers of a particular social background, then you are, at least in part, engaging in Marxist criticism.

Cultural Studies

Cultural studies is the general name given to a wide variety of critical practices, some of which might seem on the surface to have little in common with one another. Perhaps the best way to understand cultural studies is to begin with the notion that certain texts are privileged in our society while others are dismissed or derided. Privileged texts are the so-called great works of literature one commonly finds in anthologies and on course syllabi. Indeed, when we hear the word *literature*, these are probably the works we imagine. All other writing—from pulp romance novels to the slogans on bumper-stickers—belong to a second category of texts, those generally overlooked by traditional literary critics.

One major trend in cultural studies is the attempt to broaden the **canon**—those texts read and taught again and again and held up as examples of the finest expressions of the human experience. Critics have pointed out that canonical authors—Shakespeare, Milton, Keats, Steinbeck—tend (with obvious exceptions) to be from a fairly narrow segment of society: they are usually middle to upper-middle class, well-educated, heterosexual, white males. Some cultural critics, therefore, have sought out and celebrated the writing of historically disadvantaged groups such as African Americans or gay and lesbian authors. One very active branch of cultural studies is **postcolonial criticism**, which focuses on writing from former British (and other) colonies around the world, where local authors often display attitudes and tastes very different from their former colonial masters. Other branches of cultural studies turn their attention to the works of various social "outsiders," like prisoners, school children, or mental patients. This attempt at broadening the canon is designed to provide students and scholars alike with a more inclusive definition of what art and literature are all about.

Cultural critics seek to blur or erase the line separating "high" from "low" art in the minds of the literary establishment. Some cultural critics believe that all texts are to some extent artistic expressions of a culture, and that any text can therefore give us vital insights into the human experience. Rather than traditional literary objects, then, a cultural critic might choose to study such things as movies and television shows, advertisements, religious tracts, graffiti, and comic books. These texts—and virtually any other visual or verbal work you can imagine—are submitted to the same rigorous scrutiny as a sonnet or a classic novel. Some cultural critics go so far as to suggest that English departments should become departments of cultural studies, in which a course on rap music would be valued as much as a course on Victorian poetry.

Historical Criticism and New Historicism

If you have ever written a research paper that involved some background reading about the life and times of an author, you have already engaged in a form of **historical criticism**. Literary scholars have long read history books and various sorts of historical documents—from newspaper articles to personal letters—to gain insights into the composition and significance of a given work. The explanatory footnotes that often appear in literary reprints and anthologies are one obvious manifestation of this type of sleuthing. Indeed, a work of literature could be virtually inexplicable if we did not understand something of the times in which it was written and first read. If you did not know that Walt Whitman's "When Lilacs Last in the Dooryard Bloom'd" was an elegy written upon the assassination of Abraham Lincoln, it would be difficult to make any sense at all of the poem, since neither the president's name nor the cause of his death actually appear in the work.

Likewise, historians have long turned to literary works and the visual arts in order to gain insights into the periods they study. While archives and contemporary documents can teach us a lot about the broad sweep of history—wars, leaders, the controversies of the day—it is often difficult to see from these documents what life was like for ordinary people, whose interior lives were not often documented. We may be able to learn from parish burial records, for example, how common childhood mortality was at a particular time in English history, but only when we read

Ben Jonson's poem "On My First Son" do we begin to understand how this mortality affected the parents who lost their children. Likewise, the few pages of James Joyce's story "Araby" may tell us more about how adolescent boys lived and thought in turn-of-the-century Dublin than several volumes of social history.

One school of historical criticism, known as **New Historicism**, takes account of both what history has to teach us about literature *and* what literature has to teach us about history. (New Historicism has been around since the 1960s, and as with New Criticism, the name of the school is no longer as accurate as it once was.) New Historicists are sometimes said to read literary and nonliterary texts *in parallel*, attempting to see how each illuminates the other. Typically, New Historicists will examine many different types of documents — government records, periodicals, private diaries, bills of sale — in order to re-create, as much as possible, the rich cultural context that surrounded both an author and that author's original audience. In doing so, they seek to give modern audiences a reading experience as rich and informed as the original readers of a literary work.

Psychological Theories

At the beginning of the twenty-first century, it is easy to underestimate the enormous influence that the theories of the psychoanalyst Sigmund Freud (1856–1939) have had on our understanding of human behavior and motivation. For many modern readers, Freud seems to have little to say; his work is too focused on sex and too thoroughly bound by the norms of the repressive Viennese society in which he lived. But if you have ever wondered what the buried significance of a dream was or whether someone had a subconscious motivation for an action, you have been affected by Freudian thinking. Freud popularized the notions that the mind can be divided into conscious and unconscious components and that we are often motivated most strongly by the unconscious. He taught us to think in terms of overt and covert desires (often referred to in Freudian language as *manifest* and *latent*) as the basis of human actions.

Like many intellectual movements of the twentieth century, psychology, and specifically Freudian psychology, has had a major influence on literary criticism. The most typical **psychological literary criticism** examines the internal mental states, the desires, and the motivations of literary characters. (In fact, Freud himself used Shakespeare's Hamlet as an example of a man whose life was ruled by what the psychiatrist called an Oedipal complex — man's unhealthy, but not uncommon, interest in his mother's sexuality.) Another subject of psychological criticism can be the author. A critic may examine the possible unconscious urges that drove an author to write a particular story or poem. Finally, a critic might examine the psychology of readers, trying to determine what draws us to or repels us from certain literary themes or forms. If any of these aspects of literature have ever interested you, you have engaged in psychological literary criticism.

Psychological critics often interpret literature as a psychologist might interpret a dream or a wish. Special attention is often paid to symbols as the manifest representation of a deeper, hidden meaning. Attention is also focused on the unstated motives and unconscious states of mind of characters, authors, or readers. Freud is not the only psychological theorist whose ideas are frequently used in literary analysis. Other important figures include Carl Jung (1875–1961), who gave us the notion of the collective unconscious and the influence of **archetypes** on our thinking, and Jacques Lacan (1901–1981), who had a special interest in the unconscious and the nature of language. You don't, however, need to be well-versed in the intricacies of psychoanalytic theory in order to be interested in the inner workings of the human mind or the ways in which they manifest themselves in literature.

Reader Response Theories

You no doubt have heard the old question: If a tree falls in the forest and nobody sees or hears it, did the tree indeed fall? Let us rephrase that question: If a book sits on a shelf and nobody reads it, does the book really exist? If you use **reader-response criticism**, your answer to that question will be a resounding no. Of course, the book exists as a physical object, a sheaf of paper bound in a cover and printed with symbols. But, say reader-response critics, as a work of art or a conduit for meaning, no text exists without a reader.

A text, according to the various theories of reader-response criticism, is not a container filled with meaning by its author but rather an interaction between an author and a reader, and it can never be complete unless readers bring to it their own unique insights. These insights come from a number of sources, including the reader's life experience as well as his or her beliefs, values, state of mind at the time of the reading, and, of course, previous reading experience. Reading is not a passive attempt to understand what lies within a text but an act of creation, no less so than the writing itself. Reader-response critics try to understand the process by which we make meaning out of words on a page. If you have ever wondered why a classmate or friend saw something entirely different than you did in a story or poem, then you have been a reader-response critic.

Two key terms associated with reader-response criticisms are *gaps* and *process*. Gaps are those things that a text doesn't tell us, that we need to fill in and work out for ourselves. Let us say, for instance, that you read a story told from the perspective of a child, but the author never explicitly mentions the child's age. How, then, do you imagine the narrator as you read? You pay attention to his or her actions and thoughts, and you compare this to your experience of real children you have known and others whose stories you have read. In doing so, you fill in a *gap* in the text and help solidify the text's meaning. Imagine, though, that as the story continues, new clues emerge and you need to adjust your assumptions about the child's age. This highlights the idea that reading is a *process*, that the meaning of the text is not fixed and complete but rather evolving as the text unfolds in the time it takes to read.

Some reader-response critics focus on the ways that meanings of a text change over time. To illustrate this idea, let us look at a specific example. Contemporary readers of Kate Chopin's short novel *The Awakening*, first published in 1899, tend to find the book's treatment of the heroine's sexuality subtle or even invisible. Such readers are often shocked or amused to learn that the book was widely condemned at the time of its publication as tasteless and overly explicit. Expectations and tastes change over time and place, and we can tell a lot about a society by examining how it responds to works of art. Reader-response critics, therefore, sometimes ask us to look at our own reactions to literature and to ask how, if at all, they match up with those of earlier readers. When we look at reactions to *The Awakening* at the end of the nineteenth century and then at the beginning of the twenty-first, we learn not only about Chopin's culture but also about our own.

Structuralism

Structuralism, as the name implies, is concerned with the structures that help us to understand and interpret literary texts. This may sound like a return to formalism, which, as we saw earlier, examines the formal and linguistic elements of a text. But the elements scrutinized by structuralist critics are of a different order entirely, being the structures that order our thinking rather than the interior architecture of poems, stories, and plays. Structuralist criticism actually derives from the work of anthropologists, linguists, and philosophers of the mid-twentieth century who sought to understand how humans thought and communicated. The basic insight at the heart of the movement is the realization that we understand nothing in isolation but rather that every piece of our knowledge is part of a network of associations. Take, for instance, the question, "Is Jim a good father?" In order to form a simple yes or no answer to this question, we must consider, among other things, the spectrum of "good" and "bad," the expectations our culture holds for fathers, and all we know of Jim's relationship with his children.

For a structuralist literary critic, questions about literature are answered with the same sort of attention to context. Two different types of context are especially salient—the cultural and the literary. Cultural context refers to an understanding of all aspects of an author's (and a reader's) culture, including but not limited to the organizing structures of history, politics, religion, education, work, and family. Literary context refers to all related texts, literary and nonliterary, that affect our ability to interpret a text. What had the author read that might have affected the creation of the text? What have we read that might affect our interpretation? What are the norms of the textual genre, and how does this piece of literature conform to or break from those norms?

According to structuralist critics, then, we can only understand a text by placing it within the broader contexts of culture (that of both the reader and the author) and other texts (literary and nonliterary). To fully understand one of Shakespeare's love sonnets to the mysterious "dark lady," for example, we would need to understand the conventions of romantic love, the conceptions of dark versus fair women in culturally accepted standards of beauty, and the acceptable interactions between men and women in Shakespeare's England. We would also need to relate the sonnet to the history of love poems generally, to the development of the sonnet form specifically, and to the other works in Shakespeare's cycle of 154 sonnets.

Poststructuralism and Deconstruction

Poststructuralism, it will come as no surprise, begins with the insights of structuralism but carries them one step further. If, as the structuralists insist, we can understand things only in terms of other things, then perhaps there is no center point of understanding but only an endlessly interconnected web of ideas leading to other ideas leading to still other ideas. This is the starting point of poststructuralist criticism, which posits that no text has a fixed or real meaning because no meaning exists outside of the network of other meanings to which it is connected. Meaning, then, including literary meaning, is forever shifting and altering as our understanding of the world changes. The best-known version of poststructuralism is **deconstruction**, a school of philosophy and literary criticism that first gained prominence in France and that seeks to overturn the very basis of Western philosophy by undermining the notion that reality has any stable existence.

At its worst, of course, this school of thought leads to the most slippery sort of relativism. What does it matter what I think of this poem or this play? I think what I want, you think what you want. Perhaps next week I will think something different. Who cares? Every interpretation is of equal value, and none has any real value at all. At its best, though, poststructuralist criticism can lead toward truly valuable insights into literature. It reminds us that meaning within a text is contingent on all sorts of exterior understandings; it allows for several interpretations, even contradictory interpretations, to exist simultaneously; and, by insisting that no text and no meaning is absolute, it allows for a playful approach to even the most "serious" of literary objects. Indeed, one of the recurrent themes of deconstructionist criticism is the French term *jouissance*, often translated as *bliss*, which refers to a free-spirited, almost sexual enjoyment of literary language.

Having thus briefly described deconstruction, we would do well to dispel a common misconception about the word. In recent years, many people, both within and outside of academia, have begun to use *deconstruct* as a synonym for *analyze*. You might hear, for instance, "We completely deconstructed that poem in class—I understand it much better now," or "The defense attorney deconstructed the prosecutor's argument." In both these cases, what the speaker likely means has little if anything to do with the literary critical practice of deconstruction. When we take apart a text or an argument and closely examine the parts, we are engaging not in deconstruction but in analysis.

By now you may be wondering what sort of literary critic you are. You may feel that you have been a formalist one day and a psychological critic the next. This is not surprising, and it should cause you no worry, as virtually none of these schools are mutually exclusive. Indeed, most professional critics mix and match the various schools in whatever way best suits their immediate needs. The close reading techniques of the New Critics, for instance, are frequently adopted by those who would fervently reject the New Critical stance that social and political context be excluded from consideration. If you wished to write about the social decline of Mme. Loisel in Guy de Maupassant's story "The Necklace," you might well find yourself in the position of a Marxist-feminist-New Historicist critic. That's fine. Writing with the knowledge that you are drawing from Marxism, feminism, and New Historicism, you will almost certainly write a better-organized, better-informed, and more thorough paper than you would have had you begun with no conscious basis in literary theory.

TAKING ESSAY EXAMS

The key to getting through the potentially stressful situation of an essay exam is to be prepared and to know what will be expected of you.

Preparation takes two forms: knowing the material and anticipating the questions. Knowing the material starts with keeping up with all reading and homework assignments throughout the term. You can't possibly read several weeks' or months' worth of material the night before the test and hope to remember it all. The days before the test should be used not for catching up but for review—revisiting the readings, skimming or rereading key passages, and studying your class notes. It's best to break up study sessions into manageable blocks if possible. Reviewing for two hours a night for three nights before the exam will be far more effective than a single six-hour cram session on the eve of the test.

Anticipating the questions that might be on the exam is a bit trickier, but it can be done. What themes and issues have come up again and again in class lectures or discussions? What patterns do you see in your class notes? What points did your instructor stress? These are the topics most likely to appear on the exam. Despite what it might seem like, it is very rare that an instructor poses intentionally obscure exam questions in an attempt to trip students up or expose their ignorance. Most often, the instructor is providing you with an opportunity to demonstrate what you know, and you should be ready to take that opportunity. You can't, of course, second-guess your instructor perfectly and know for sure what will be on the test, but you can spend some time in advance thinking about what sorts of questions you are likely to encounter and how you would answer them.

Your exam may be open-book or closed-book; find out in advance which it will be, so you can plan and study accordingly. In an open-book test, you are allowed to use your textbook during the exam. This is a big advantage, obviously, as it allows you access to specific evidence, including quotations, to support your points. If you know the exam is going to be open-book, you might also jot down any important notes in the book itself, where you can find them readily if you need them. Use your textbook sparingly, though—just enough to find the evidence you know to be there. Don't waste time browsing the literature hoping to find inspiration or ideas. For a closed-book exam, you have to rely on your memory alone. But you should still try to be as specific as possible in your references to the literature, using character names, recalling plot elements, and so forth.

When you sit down to take the exam, you may have the urge to start writing right away, since your time is limited. Suppress that urge and read through the entire exam first, paying special attention to the instruction portion. Often there will be choices to make, such as "Answer two of the following three questions" or "Select a single poem as the basis of your answer." If you miss such cues, you may find yourself racing to write three essays and running out of time or discussing several poems shallowly instead of one in depth. Once you are certain what is expected of you, take a few more minutes to plan your answers before you start writing. A few jotted notes or an informal outline may take a moment, but it will likely save you time as you write. If you will be writing more than one essay, take care not to repeat yourself or to write more than one essay about any one piece of literature. The idea is to show your instructor your mastery of the course, and to do so effectively you should demonstrate breadth of knowledge.

When you do begin writing, bear in mind that instructors have different expectations for exam answers than they do for essays written outside of class. They know that in timed exams you have no time for research or extensive revisions. Clarity and conciseness are the keys; elegant prose style is not expected (though, of course, it will come as a pleasant surprise if you can manage it). Effective essay answers are often more formulaic than other sorts of effective writing, relying on the schematic of a straightforward introduction, simple body paragraphs, and a brief conclusion.

Your introduction should be simple and to the point. A couple of sentences is generally all that is needed, and these should avoid rhetorical flourishes or digressions. Often the best strategy is to parrot back the instructions as an opening statement. Imagine, for instance, you were asked to choose from among several options, including, "Select two poems by different poets, each of which deals with the theme of time, and compare how the authors present this theme." A possible beginning might be:

> Shakespeare's Sonnet 73 (That time of year thou mayst in me behold) and Herrick's "To the Virgins, to Make Much of Time" both deal with the theme of time. Though there are important differences in their focus and style, both poems end up urging their readers to love well and make the most of the time they have left.

Although this is not shatteringly original, and the prose style is blunt and not particularly memorable, this introduction does its job. It lets the reader know which question the student is answering, which poems will be examined, and what the general point of the essay will be.

Body paragraphs for essay answers should also be simple, and will often, though not always, be briefer than they would be in an essay you worked on at home. They should still be as specific as possible, making reference to and perhaps even quoting the literature to illustrate your points. Just as in a more fully developed essay, try to avoid dwelling in generalities; use specific examples and evidence. Following the introduction above, for instance, you might expect one paragraph discussing the theme of time in Shakespeare's poem, another paragraph doing the same for Herrick's, and perhaps a third making explicit the connections between the two. Conclusions for essay exams are usually brief, just a sentence or two of summary.

Finally, take a watch with you on exam day and keep a close eye on the time. Use all the time you are given and budget it carefully. If you have an hour to write two answers, don't spend forty-five minutes on the first. Even though you will likely be pressed for time, save a few minutes at the end to proofread your answers. Make any corrections as neatly and legibly as possible. Watch the time, but try not to watch your classmates' progress. Keep focused on your own process. Just because someone else is using his or her book a lot, you shouldn't feel you need to do the same. If someone finishes early and leaves, don't take this as a sign that you are running behind or that you are less efficient or smart than that person. Students who don't make full use of the exam time are often underprepared; they tend to write vague and underdeveloped answers and should not be your role models.

CHAPTER 4
Writing about Stories

Fiction has long been broken down and discussed in terms of specific elements common to all stories, and chances are you will be focusing on one or more of these when you write an essay about a story.

ELEMENTS OF FICTION

The **elements of fiction** most commonly identified are **plot, character, point of view, setting, theme, symbol,** and **style.** If you find yourself wondering what to write about a story, a good place to begin is isolating these elements and seeing how they work on a reader and how they combine to create the unique artifact that is a particular story.

While on some level we all read stories to find out what happens next, in truth **plot** is usually the least interesting of the elements of fiction. Students who have little experience writing about fiction tend to spend too much time retelling the plot. You can avoid this by bearing in mind that your readers will also have read the literature in question and don't need a thorough replay of what happened. In general, all readers need are small reminders of the key points of plot about which you will write, and these should not be self-standing but rather should serve as springboards into analysis and discussion. Still, there are times when writing about the plot makes sense, especially when the plot surprises your expectations by, for instance, rearranging the chronology of events or otherwise presenting things in nonrealistic ways. When this happens in a story, the plot may indeed prove fertile ground for analysis and may be the basis of an interesting paper.

Many interesting essays analyze the actions, motivations, and development of individual **characters.** How does the author reveal a character to the reader? How does a character grow and develop over the course of a story? These questions can be fertile ground for analysis. Although the most obvious character to write about is usually the **protagonist**, don't let your imagination stop there. Often the **antagonist** or even a minor character can be an interesting object of study. Usually less has been said and written about less prominent characters, so you will be more free to create your own interpretations. (Playwright Tom Stoppard wrote a very successful full-length play entitled *Rosencrantz and Guildenstern Are Dead* about two of the least developed characters in *Hamlet.*)

Related to character is the issue of **point of view**. The perspective from which a story is told can make a big difference in how we perceive it. Sometimes a story is told in the *first person,* from the point of view of one of the characters. Whether this is a major or a minor character, we must always remember that **first-person narrators** can be unreliable, as they do not have access to all vital information, and their own agendas can often skew the way they see events. The **narrator** of Edgar Allen Poe's "The Cask of Amontillado" seeks to gain sympathy for a hideous act of revenge, giving us a glimpse into a deeply disturbed mind. A **third-person narrator** may be **omniscient**, knowing everything pertinent to a story; or limited, knowing, for instance, the thoughts and motives of the protagonist but not of any of the other characters. As you read a story, ask yourself what the point of view contributes and why the author may have chosen to present the story from a particular perspective.

Sometimes a **setting** is merely the backdrop for a story, but often place plays an important role in our understanding of a work. John Updike chooses a small, conservative New England town as the setting of his story "A & P." It is the perfect milieu for an exploration of values and class interaction, and the story would have a very different feel and meaning if it had been set, say, in New York City. Ask yourself as you read how significant a setting is and what it adds to the meaning of a story. Remember that setting refers to time as well as place. "A & P" is about three young women walking into a small-town grocery store wearing only bathing suits, an action more shocking when the story was written in 1961 than it would be now (although it would doubtless still raise eyebrows in many places).

All **short stories** have at least one **theme**—an abstract concept such as *love, war, friendship, revenge, art,* and so forth—brought to life and made real through the plot, characters, and so on. Identifying a theme or themes is one of the first keys to understanding a story, but it is not the end point. Pay some attention to how the theme is developed. Is it blatant or subtle? What actions, events, or symbols make the theme apparent to you? Generally, the driving force of a story is the author's desire to convey something *about* a particular theme, to make readers think and feel in a certain way. First ask yourself what the author seems to be saying about love or war or whatever themes you have noted; second, whether you agree with the author's perceptions; and finally, why or why not.

Some students get frustrated when their instructors or their classmates begin to talk about **symbolism**. How do we know that an author intended a symbolic reading? Maybe that flower is just a real flower, not a stand-in for youth or for life and regeneration as some readers insist. And even if it is a symbol, how do we know we are reading it correctly? "Sometimes," as Freud said, "a cigar is just a cigar." But careful writers choose their words and images for maximum impact, filling them with as much meaning as possible and inviting their readers to interpret them. The more prominent an image in a story, the more likely it is meant to be read symbolically. When Sarah Orne Jewett entitles her story "A White Heron," we would do well to ask if the heron is really just a bird or if we are being asked to look for a greater significance.

The final element of fiction we will isolate here is **style**, sometimes spoken of under the heading of tone or language. It is often fairly easy to identify the dominant tone of a story. A text will instantly strike you as sad or lighthearted, formal or casual, and so on. It may make you feel nostalgic, or it may make your heart race with excitement. Somewhat more difficult, though, is isolating the elements of language that contribute to a particular tone or effect. Look for characteristic stylistic elements that make up the language. Is the vocabulary elevated and difficult, or ordinary and simple? Are the sentences long and complex, or short and to the point? Is there dialogue? If so, how do the characters who speak this dialogue come across? Does the style stay consistent throughout the story, or does it change? Paying close attention to linguistic matters like these will take you far in your understanding of how a particular story achieves its effect.

QUOTING FROM STORIES

The guidelines that follow should be used not only when you quote from stories but also when you quote from any prose work, be it fiction or nonfiction. For further specifics about using quotations, see pages 1296–1300.

Short Quotations

For short quotations of fewer than four lines, run the quotation in with your own text, using quotation marks to signal the beginning and end of the quotation.

Young Goodman Brown notices that the branches touched by his companion "became strangely withered and dried up, as with a week's sunshine."

Long Quotations

When a quotation is longer than four lines in your text, set it off from your essay by beginning a new line and indenting it one inch from the left margin only, as shown here. This is called a block quotation:

Young Goodman Brown then notices something strange about his companion:

As they went, he plucked a branch of maple to serve for a walking stick, and began to strip it of the twigs and little boughs, which were wet with evening dew. The moment his fingers touched them they became strangely withered and dried up, as with a week's sunshine.

Note that no quotation marks are used with block quotations. The indentation is sufficient to signal to your readers that this is a quotation.

SAMPLE PAPER

Melanie Smith was given the assignment to compare and contrast an element of her choosing in two stories, Kate Chopin's "The Story of an Hour" (p. 66) and Charlotte Perkins Gilman's "The Yellow Wallpaper," (p. 82) and to draw some conclusions about gender roles in the nineteenth century. Rather than examining the female protagonists, Melanie chose to focus on the minor male characters in the stories. She wrote a point-by-point comparison designed to demonstrate that these men, despite the opinions of them that she heard expressed in class, were not bad people. Rather, they were led by their social training to behave in ways that were perfectly acceptable in their day, even if they now strike readers as oppressive.

Melanie Smith
English 109
Professor Hallet
18 May 2003

Good Husbands in Bad Marriages

When twenty-first-century readers first encounter literature of earlier times, it is easy for us to apply our own standards of conduct to the characters and situations. Kate Chopin's "The Story of an Hour" and Charlotte Perkins Gilman's "The Yellow Wallpaper" offer two good examples of this. Both written by American women in the last decade of the nineteenth century, the stories give us a look into the lives, and especially the marriages, of middle-class women of the time. By modern standards, the husbands of the two protagonists, particularly John in "The Yellow Wallpaper," seem almost unbearably controlling of their wives. From the vantage point of the late nineteenth century, however, their behavior looks quite different. Both men are essentially well meaning and try to be good husbands. Their only real crime is that they adhere too closely to the conventional Victorian wisdom about marriage.

To begin with, both men are well respected in their communities. John in "The Yellow Wallpaper" is described as "a physician of high standing" who has "an intense horror of superstition, and he scoffs openly at any talk of things not to be felt and seen and put down in figures." These are just the qualities that we might expect to find in a respectable doctor, even today. It is less clear what Brently Mallard in "The Story of an Hour" does for a living. (In fact, Chopin's story is so short that we learn fairly little about any of the characters.) But the couple seems to live in a comfortable house, and they are surrounded by family and friends, suggesting a secure, well-connected lifestyle. In the nineteenth century, a man's most important job was to take care of his wife and family, and both men in these stories seem to be performing this job very well.

In addition to providing a comfortable life for them, it also seems that both men love their wives. When she believes her husband has died, Mrs. Mallard thinks of his "kind, tender hands folded in death; the face that had never looked save with love upon her." Her own love for him is less certain, which may be why she feels "free" when he dies, but his for her seems gen-uine. The case of John in "The Yellow Wallpaper" is a bit more complicated. To a modern reader, it seems that he treats his wife more like a child than a grown woman. He puts serious restraints on her actions, and at one point he even calls her "little girl." But he also calls her "my darling" and "dear," and she does say, "He loves me very dearly." When he has to leave her alone, he even has his sister come to look after her, which is a kind gesture, even if it seems a bit like he doesn't trust his wife. If the narrator, who is in a position to know, doesn't doubt her husband's love, what gives us the right to judge it?

To a certain extent, we must admit that both husbands do oppress their wives by being overprotective. Part of the point of both stories is to show how even acceptable, supposedly good marriages of the day could be overly confining to women. This is especially obvious when we see how much John restricts his wife—forbidding her even to visit her cousins or to write let-ters—and how everyone expects her to agree to his demands. Though Mrs. Mallard isn't literally confined to a house or a room the way the narrator of "The Yellow Wallpaper" is, she stays inside the house and is looking out the window longingly when she realizes she wants to be free. But it is important for a reader not to blame the husbands, because they really don't intend to be oppressive.

In fact, it is true that both of the wives are in somewhat frail health. Mrs. Mallard is "afflicted with a heart trouble," and the narrator of "The Yellow Wallpaper" seems to have many physical and mental problems, so it is not surprising that their husbands worry about them. It is not evil intent that leads the men to act as they do, it is simply ignorance. John seems less inno-cent then Brently because he is so patronizing and he puts such restrictions on his wife's behavior and movement, but that kind of attitude was normal for the day, and as a doctor, John seems really to be doing what he thinks is best.

All the other characters in the stories see both men as good and loving husbands, which suggests that society would have approved of their behav-ior. Even the wives themselves, who are the victims of these oppressive mar-riages, don't blame the men at all. The narrator of "The Yellow Wallpaper" even thinks she is "ungrateful" when she doesn't appreciate John's loving care more. Once we understand this, readers should not be too quick to blame the men either. The real blame falls to the society that gave these men the idea that women are frail and need protection from the world. The men may be the immediate cause of the women's suffering, but the real cause is much deeper and has to do with cultural attitudes and how the men were brought up to protect and provide for women.

Most people who live in a society don't see the flaws in that society's conventional ways of thinking and living. We now know that women are capable and independent and that protecting them as if they were children ultimately does more harm than good. But in the late Victorian era, such an idea would have seemed either silly or dangerously radical to most people, men and women alike. Stories like these, however, could have helped their original readers begin to think about how confining these supposedly good marriages were. Fortunately, authors such as Chopin and Gilman come along from time to time and show us the problems in our conventional thinking, so society can move forward and we can begin to see how even the most well-meaning actions should sometimes be questioned.

CHAPTER 5
Writing about Poems

As with stories, there are certain elements you should be aware of as you prepare to write about poetry. Sometimes these elements are the same as for fiction. A **narrative poem**, for instance, will have a **plot**, **setting**, and **characters**, and all poems speak from a particular point of view. To the extent that any of the elements of fiction help you to understand a poem, by all means use them in your analysis. Poetry, however, does present a special set of concerns for a reader, and elements of poetry frequently provide rich ground for analysis.

ELEMENTS OF POETRY

First, consider the speaker of the poem. Imagine that someone is saying the words of this poem aloud. Who is speaking, where is this speaker, and what is his or her state of mind? Sometimes the voice is that of the poet him- or herself, but frequently a poem speaks from a different perspective, just as a short story might be from a point of view very different from the author's. It's not always apparent when this is the case, but some poets will signal who the **narrator** is in a title, as Christopher Marlowe does in "The Passionate Shepherd to His Love" or T. S. Eliot in "The Love Song of J. Alfred Prufrock." Be alert to signals that will help you recognize the speaker, and remember that some poems have more than one speaker.

Be attentive also to any other persons in the poem, particularly an implied listener. Is there a "you" to whom the poem is addressed? If the poem is being spoken aloud, who is supposed to hear it? When, early in his poem "Dover Beach," Mathew Arnold writes, "Come to the window, sweet is the night-air!" he gives us an important clue as to how to read the poem. We should imagine both the speaker and the implied listener together in a room, with a window open to the night. As we read on, we can look for further clues as to who these two people are and why they are together on this night.

Just as you should be open to the idea that there are frequently symbols in stories, you should pay special attention to the **images** in poems. Although poems are often about such grand themes as love or death, they rarely dwell long in these abstractions. Rather, the best poetry seeks to make the abstraction concrete by creating vivid images appealing directly to the senses. A well-written poem will provide the mind of an attentive reader with sights, sounds, tastes, scents, and sensations. Since poems tend to be short and densely packed with meaning, every word and image is there for a reason. Isolate these images and give some thought to what they make you think and how they make you feel. Are they typical or unexpected? You might expect a love poem to be full of sunshine and flowers, but when John Donne describes a drafting compass, for instance, in "A Valediction: Forbidding Mourning," it comes as something of a surprise. By examining the images in a poem, their placement, juxtaposition, and effect, you will have gone a long way toward understanding the poem as a whole.

Of all the genres, poetry is the one that most self-consciously highlights language, so it is necessary to pay special attention to style and sound. In fact, it is always a good idea to read a poem aloud, giving yourself opportunity to experience the role that **rhyme**, **rhythm**, and sound play in the poem's meaning. Look especially for *patterns* of sound. A repeated rhyme scheme, for instance, helps to set up a series of expectations in the reader, expectations that the poet may choose to fulfill or to betray. A repeated *s* sound might give the effect of hissing or whispering. If you are attentive to such details, you will get more out of your reading of poetry, and you will be more specific and convincing in your writing.

There is a highly developed and somewhat complex language used specifically to describe the linguistic elements of poetry—terms like *ballad stanza, villanelle, iamb, trochee, tetrameter, Alexandrine, enjambment, consonance,* and *feminine rhyme,* among hundreds of others. Each has a very precise meaning. (*Enjambment,* for instance, refers to the practice of continuing the grammatical structure and sense of one line of poetry into the following line.) The terminology of poetic language can be quite daunting for a student, but don't let this worry you. You will probably learn some new terms as you study poetry in your class, and as you become comfortable with them, you may want to integrate them into your writing. If you don't know the technical term for something, though, you can still refer to it in your paper; just describe what you see or hear as clearly and concisely as you can, and go on to explain the effect it had on your reading and understanding.

QUOTING FROM POEMS

Short Quotations

For quotations of up to three lines, run the text right into your own, using quotation marks just as you would with a prose quotation. However, since the placement of line endings can be significant in a poem, you need to indicate where they occur. This is done by including a slash mark, with a single space on each side, where the line breaks occur. (Some students find this awkward looking at first, but you will quickly get used to it. Your instructor will expect you to honor the poet's choices regarding line breaks.)

> In "Sailing to Byzantium," Yeats describes an old man as "a paltry
> thing, / A tattered coat upon a stick."

Long Quotations

For quotations of four lines or more, "block" the material, setting it off one inch from the left margin, duplicating all line breaks of the original. Do not use quotation marks with block quotations.

> In "Sailing to Byzantium," Yeats describes both the ravages of age and
> the possibility of renewal in the poem's second stanza:
>> An aged man is but a paltry thing,
>> A tattered coat upon a stick, unless
>> Soul clap its hands and sing, and louder sing
>> For every tatter in its mortal dress,
>> Nor is there singing school but studying
>> Monuments of its own magnificence;

SAMPLE PAPER

Patrick McCorkle, the author of the following paper, was given the assignment to perform a close reading of one of Shakespeare's sonnets. He needed first to pick a poem and then to choose specific features of its language to isolate and analyze. After a class discussion about how several poets dealt with the theme of love, he chose Shakespeare's Sonnet 116 (p. 380) because it seemed to him to offer an interesting and balanced definition of this subject. After rereading the poem, he became interested in several unexpectedly negative, even unsettling images that seemed out of place in a poem about the positive emotion of love. This was a good start, and it allowed him to write a draft of the paper. When he was finished, however, the essay was a little shorter than he had hoped it would be. During a peer workshop in class, he discussed the sonnet and his draft with two classmates, and together they noticed how many negative words appeared in the poem as well. That was the insight Patrick needed to fill out his essay and feel satisfied with the results.

Patrick McCorkle
Professor Bobrick
English 102
10 January 2003

Shakespeare Defines Love

From the earliest written rhymes to the latest top-40 radio hit, love is among the eternal themes for poetry. Most love poetry seems to fall into one of two categories. Either the poet sings the praises of the beloved and the unending joys of love in overly exaggerated terms, or the poet laments the loss of love with such bitterness and distress that it seems like the end of life. Anyone who has been in love, though, can tell you that both of these views are limited and incomplete and that real love is neither entirely joyous nor entirely sad. In Sonnet 116, "Let me not to the marriage of true minds," Shakespeare creates a more realistic image of love. By balancing negative with positive images and language, this sonnet does a far better job than thousands of songs and poems before and since, defining love in all its complexities and contradictions.

Like many poems, Sonnet 116 relies on a series of visual images to paint vivid pictures for a reader, but not all of these images are what we might expect in a poem celebrating the pleasures of lasting love. A reader can easily picture "an ever-fixèd mark," a "tempest," a "star," a "wandering bark" (meaning a boat lost at sea), "rosy lips and cheeks," and a "bending sickle." Some of these, like stars and rosy lips, are just the sort of sunny, positive images we typically find in love poems of the joyous variety. Others, though, are more unexpected. Flowers and images of springtime, for instance, are standard issue in happy love poetry, but a sickle is associated with autumn and the death of the year, and metaphorically with death itself in the form of the grim reaper. Likewise, a boat tossed in a raging tempest is not exactly the typical poetic depiction of happy love.

Such pictures would hardly seem to provide an upbeat image of what love is all about, and in fact they might be more at home in one of the sad poems about the loss of love. But these tempests and sickles are more realistic than the hearts and flowers of so many lesser love poems. In fact, they show that the poet recognizes the bad times that occur in all relationships, even those strong enough to inspire love sonnets. And the negative images are tempered because of the contexts in which they occur. The "wandering bark" for instance might represent trouble and loss, but love itself is seen as the star that will lead the boat safely back to calm waters. Meanwhile, the beloved's "rosy lips and cheeks" may fade, but real love outlives even the stroke of death's sickle, lasting "to the edge of doom."

Just as positive and negative images are juxtaposed, so are positive and negative language. The first four lines of Sonnet 116 are made up of two sentences, both negatives, beginning with the words "Let me not" and "Love is not." The negatives of the first few lines continue in phrases like "Whose worth's unknown" and "Love's not time's fool." From here, the poem goes on to dwell in abstract ideas such as "alteration," "impediments," and "error." None of this is what readers of love poems have been led to expect in their previous reading, and we might even wonder if the poet finds this love thing worth the trouble. This strange and unexpected language continues on through the last line of the poem, which contains no fewer than three negative words: "never," "nor," and "no."

Where, a reader might ask, are the expected positive descriptions of love? Where are the summer skies, the smiles and laughter? Clearly, Shakespeare doesn't mean to sweep his readers up in rosy images of a lover's bliss. Ultimately, though, even with the preponderance of negative images and words, the poem strikes a hopeful tone. The hedging about what love isn't and what it can't do are balanced with positive words and phrases, saying clearly what love is: "it is an ever-fixèd mark" and "it is the star." Love, it would seem, does not make our lives perfect, but it gives us the strength, stability, and direction to survive the bad times.

Though more than 400 years have passed since Shakespeare wrote his sonnets, some things never change, and among these is the nature of complex human emotions. In a mere fourteen lines, Shakespeare succeeds where many others have failed through the years, providing a much more satisfying definition of love than one normally sees in one-dimensional, strictly happy or sad poetry. The love he describes is the sort that not everyone is lucky enough to find — a "marriage of true minds" — complicated, unsettling, and very real.

CHAPTER 6

Writing about Plays

Perhaps the earliest literary critic in the Western tradition was Aristotle, who, in the fifth century B.C.E., set about explaining the power of the genre of **tragedy** by identifying the six **elements of drama** and analyzing the contribution each of these elements makes to the functioning of a play as a whole. The elements Aristotle identified as common to all dramas were **plot, characterization, theme, diction, melody,** and **spectacle.** Some of these are the same as or very similar to the basic components of prose fiction and poetry, but others are slightly different when it comes to drama.

ELEMENTS OF DRAMA

The words *plot, character,* and *theme* mean basically the same thing in drama as they do in fiction, though there is a difference in how they are presented. A story *tells* you about a series of events, whereas a play *shows* you these events happening in real time. The information that might be conveyed in descriptive passages in prose fiction must be conveyed in a play through **dialogue** (and to a lesser extent through **stage directions** and the **set** and character descriptions that sometimes occur at the start of a play). This means that as a reader you must be especially attentive to nuances of language in a play, which often means imagining what might be happening onstage during a particular passage of speech. Using your imagination in this way—in effect, staging the play in your mind—will help you with some of the difficulties inherent in play reading.

When Aristotle speaks of **diction,** he means the specific words that a playwright chooses to put into the mouth of a character. In a well-written play, different characters will have different ways of speaking, and these will tell us a good deal about their character and personality. Does one character sound very formal and well educated? Does another speak in slang or dialect? Does someone hesitate or speak in fits and starts, perhaps indicating distraction or nervousness? Practice paying attention to these nuances. And keep in mind that just because a character says something, that doesn't make it true. As in real life, some characters might be hiding the truth or even telling outright lies.

When Aristotle writes of **melody**, he is referring to the fact that Greek drama was written in verse and was chanted or sung onstage. Melody is much less significant in drama today, though some plays do contain songs, of course, and the rhythm of spoken words can be important in a play, just as it is in a poem. **Spectacle** refers to what we actually see onstage when we go to a play—the costumes, the actors' movements, the sets, the lights, and so forth. In reading a play, it is important to remember that it was not written to be read only, but rather so that it would be seen onstage in the communal setting of a theater. Reading with this in mind and trying to imagine the spectacle of a real production will increase your enjoyment of plays immensely.

Setting, which Aristotle ignores completely, is just as important in drama as it is in fiction. But again, in drama it must be either displayed onstage or alluded to through the characters' words rather than being described as it might in a story or a poem. Modern plays often (though not always) begin with elaborate descriptions of the stage, furniture, major props, and so forth, which can be very useful in helping you to picture a production. These tend to be absent in older plays, so in some cases you will have to use your imagination. In act 4 of *Hamlet*, the characters are in a castle one moment and on a windswept plain the next. The words and actions of characters at times sufficiently signal a change of locale.

QUOTING FROM PLAYS

Short Single-Speaker Passages

When you quote a short passage of drama with a single speaker, treat the quoted text just as you would prose fiction:

> Nora's first words in *A Doll House* are "Hide the tree well, Helene. The children mustn't get a glimpse till this evening, after it's trimmed."

Longer or More Complex Passages

For a longer quotation, or a quotation of any length involving more than one character, you will need to block off the quotation. Begin each separate piece of dialogue indented one inch from the left margin with the character's name, typed in all capital letters, followed by a period. Subsequent lines of the character's speech should be indented an additional quarter inch. (Your word processor's "hanging indent" function is useful for achieving this effect without having to indent each separate line.) As with fiction or poetry, do not use quotation marks for block quotations.

> We see the tension between Nora and her husband in their very first confrontation:
>> NORA. Oh, but Torvald, this year we really should let
>>> ourselves go a bit. It's the first Christmas we
>>> haven't had to economize.
>>
>> HELMER. But you know we can't go squandering.
>>
>> NORA. Oh yes, Torvald, we can squander a little now.
>>> Can't we?

Verse Drama

Many older plays, including classical Greek drama and much of the work of Shakespeare and his contemporaries, are written at least partly in poetic verse. When you quote a verse drama, you must respect the line endings, just as you do in quoting poetry. The first example here shows a short quotation with slash marks that indicate line endings; the second shows a longer, block quotation in verse form.

> Hamlet's most famous soliloquy begins, "To be, or not to be, that is the question: / Whether 'tis nobler in the mind to suffer / The slings and arrows of outrageous fortune."

> Hamlet then begins his most famous soliloquy:
>> To be, or not to be, that is the question:
>> Whether 'tis nobler in the mind to suffer
>> The slings and arrows of outrageous fortune,
>> Or to take arms against a sea of troubles,
>> And by opposing end them.

SAMPLE PAPER

Sarah Johnson was free to choose the topic and focus of her paper. In the same semester as her literature class, she was enrolled in a philosophy course on ethics where she was introduced to the idea of situational ethics, the notion that exterior pressures often cause people to act in ways they might normally deem unethical, often to prevent or allay a worse evil. This philosophical concept was on Sarah's mind when she read *Trifles* (p. 944), and she noticed that the character of Mrs. Peters does indeed end up behaving in a way she would probably never have imagined for herself. This seemed an interesting concept to pursue, so Sarah decided to trace the development of Mrs. Peters's journey away from her original moral certainty.

Sarah Johnson
English 253
Professor Riley
24 October 2002

Moral Ambiguity and Character Development
in Trifles

What is the relationship between legality and morality? Susan Glaspell's short play Trifles asks us to ponder this question, but it provides no clear answers. Part murder mystery, part battle of the sexes, the play makes its readers confront and question many issues about laws, morals, and human relationships. In the person of Mrs. Peters, a sheriff's wife, the play chronicles one woman's moral journey from a certain, unambiguous belief in the law to a more situational view of ethics. Before it is over, this once legally minded woman is even willing to cover up the truth and let someone get away with murder.

At the beginning of the play, Mrs. Peters believes that law, truth, and morality are one and the same. Though never unkind about the accused, Mrs. Wright, Mrs. Peters is at first firm in her belief that the men will find the truth and crime will be punished as it should be. Mrs. Hale feels the men are "kind of sneaking" as they look about Mrs. Wright's abandoned house for evidence against her, but Mrs. Peters assures her that "the law is the law." It is not that Mrs. Peters is less sympathetic toward women than her companion, but she is even more sympathetic toward the lawmen, because her version of morality is so absolute. When the men deride the women's interest in so-called trifles, like sewing and housework, Mrs. Hale takes offense. But Mrs. Peters, convinced that the law must prevail, defends them, saying, "It's no more than their duty," and later, "They've got awful important things on their minds."

As she attempts to comply with the requirements of the law, Mrs. Peters is described in a stage direction as "businesslike," and she tries to maintain a skeptical attitude as she waits for the truth to emerge. Asked if she thinks Mrs. Wright killed her husband, she says "Oh, I don't know." She seems to be trying to convince herself that the accused is innocent until proven guilty, though she admits that her husband thinks it "looks bad for her." She seems to have absorbed her husband's attitudes and values and to be keeping a sort of legalistic distance from her feelings about the case.

Mrs. Hale is less convinced of the rightness of the men or the law. Even before the two women discover a possible motive for the murder, Mrs. Hale is already tampering with evidence, tearing out the erratic sewing stitches that suggest Mrs. Wright was agitated. Mrs. Peters says "I don't think we ought to touch things," but she doesn't make any stronger move to stop Mrs. Hale, who continues to fix the sewing. At this point, we see her first beginning to waver from her previously firm stance on right and wrong.

It is not that Mrs. Peters is unsympathetic to the hard life that Mrs. Wright has led. She worries with Mrs. Hale about the accused woman's frozen jars of preserves, her half-done bread, and her unfinished quilt. But she tries to think, like the men, that these things are "trifles" and that what matters is the legal truth. But when she sees a bird with a wrung neck, things begin to change in a major way. She remembers the boy who killed her kitten when she was a child, and the sympathy she has felt for Mrs. Wright begins to turn to empathy. The empathy is enough to cause her first lie to the men. When the county attorney spies the empty bird cage, she corroborates Mrs. Hale's story about a cat getting the bird, even though she knows there was no cat in the house.

Even after she has reached that point of empathy, Mrs. Peters tries hard to maintain her old way of thinking and of being. Alone again with Mrs. Hale, she says firmly, "We don't know who killed the bird," even though convincing evidence points to John Wright. More importantly, she says of Wright himself, "We don't know who killed him. We don't _know_." But her repetition and her "rising voice," described in a stage direction, show how agitated she has become. As a believer in the law, she should feel certain that everyone is innocent until proven guilty, but she thinks she knows the truth, and, perhaps for the first time in her life, legal truth does not square with moral truth. Her empathy deepens further still when she thinks about the stillness of the house in which Mrs. Wright was forced to live after the death of her beloved pet, who brought song to an otherwise grim life. She knows Mrs.

Wright is childless, and she now remembers not just the death of her childhood kitten but also the terrible quiet in her own house after her first child
died. She reaches a moment of crisis between her two ways of thinking when
she says "I know what stillness is. (Pulling herself back.) The law has got
to punish crimes, Mrs. Hale." This is perhaps the most important line in the
chronicle of her growth as a character. First she expresses her newfound
empathy with the woman she believes to be a murderer; then, as the stage
directions say, she tries to pull herself back and return to the comfortable
moral certainty that she felt just a short time before. It is too late for that,
though.

In the end, Mrs. Peters gives in to what she believes to be emotionally
right rather than what is legally permissible. She collaborates with Mrs. Hale
to cover up evidence of the motive and hide the dead canary. Though very
little time has gone by, she has undergone a major transformation. She may
be, as the county attorney says, "married to the law," but she is also divorced
from her old ideals. When she tries to cover up the evidence, a stage direction
says she "goes to pieces," and Mrs. Hale has to help her. By the time she pulls
herself together, the new woman she is will be a very different person from
the old one. She, along with the reader, is now in a world where the relationship between legality and morality are far more complex than she had ever
suspected.

CHAPTER 7

Writing a Literary Research Paper

Writing a research paper is generally a more complex and longer-term project than writing other sorts of essays, but you should not regard it as an entirely different process. In fact, writing a literary research paper draws on the same set of skills as writing any other paper—choosing a topic, developing a thesis, gathering and organizing support, and so on. The main difference between research writing and other sorts of writing lies in the number and types of sources from which one's support comes. All writing about literature begins with a primary source—the poem, story, or play on which the writing is based. Research papers also incorporate secondary sources, such as biographical, historical, and critical essays.

The most important thing to remember as you begin the process of research writing is that you are writing a critical argument. Your paper should not end up reading like a book report or a catalog of what others have said about the literature. Rather, it should begin and end by making an original point based on your own ideas, and like any other paper, it needs a clear, sharply focused thesis. The sources, both primary and secondary, are there to support your thesis, not to take over the paper.

Until quite recently, students were usually instructed to conduct their research by keeping notes and bibliographic information on index cards and then organizing these cards and transcribing the notes as they wrote. If this is something you have done before, and if it has helped you complete your project, then you should certainly continue doing so. Most writers these days, though, keep electronic files and update these continually as they work through the writing process. Use whatever method or combination of methods that works best for you. But don't cling to familiar approaches if they have not produced good results for you in the past or if research has not been a pleasant and intellectually stimulating experience.

1338

The method laid out below seems very linear and straightforward: find and evaluate sources for your paper, read them and take notes, and then write a paper integrating material from these sources. In reality, the process is rarely, if ever, this neat. As you read and write, you will discover gaps in your knowledge or you will ask yourself new questions that will demand more research. Be flexible. Keep in mind that the process of research is recursive, requiring a writer to move back and forth between various stages. Naturally, this means that for research writing, even more than for other kinds of writing, you should start early and give yourself plenty of time to complete the project.

FINDING AND EVALUATING SOURCES

For many students, research is more or less synonymous with the Internet. There is a widely held perception that all the information anybody could ever want is available online, readily and easily accessible. But when it comes to literary research, this is not the case at all. True, there are plenty of Web sites and newsgroups devoted to literary figures, but the type of information available on these sites tends to be limited to a narrow range—basic biographies of authors, plot summaries, and so forth—and the quality of information is highly variable. Though serious literary scholarship does exist online, it is still relatively rare. Print books and journals are still the better sources for you in most cases.

The place to begin your search, then, is with your college or university library's catalog. (Other libraries, no matter how well-run, seldom carry the scholarly journals and other sorts of specialized sources needed for college-level research.) Start by looking for one or two good books on your topic. Books tend to be more general in their scope than journal articles, and they can be especially useful at the early stages of your research to help you focus and refine your thinking. If you have given yourself sufficient time for the process, take a book or two home and skim them to determine which parts would be most useful for you. When you return to the library to perform more research, you will have a clearer sense of what you are looking for and will be therefore more efficient at completing the rest of your search.

Next, look at periodicals. At this point, you should be aware of the distinction between magazines, which are directed at a general readership, and scholarly journals, which are written by and for specialists in various academic fields. *Scientific American,* for instance, is a well-respected magazine available on newsstands, whereas *The Journal of Physical Chemistry* is a scholarly journal, generally available only by subscription and read more or less exclusively by chemists and chemistry students. In the field of literary studies there are literally hundreds of journals, ranging from publications covering a general period or topic *(American Literary Realism, Modern Drama)* to those devoted to specific authors *(Walt Whitman Review, Melville Society Extracts).*

While magazines are sometimes appropriate research sources, and you certainly should not rule them out, the highest quality and most sophisticated literary criticism tends to appear in journals. If you are uncertain whether you are looking at a scholarly journal, look for the following typical characteristics:

- Scholarly journal articles tend to be longer than magazine articles, ranging anywhere from five to more than fifty pages.
- Journal articles are written by specialists for researchers, professors, and college students. The author's professional credentials and institutional affiliation are often listed.
- Journal articles tend to be written in a given profession's special language and can be difficult for nonspecialists to understand. Articles in literary journals use the specialized language of literary theory and criticism.
- Journal articles are usually peer-reviewed or refereed, meaning that other specialists have read them and determined that they make a significant contribution to the field. Peer referees are often listed as an editorial board on the journal's masthead page.
- Journal articles usually include footnotes or endnotes and an often substantial references, bibliography, or works cited section.

Your college library is likely to subscribe to a number of services that index journal and magazine articles in order to help researchers find what they are looking for. Some of the most useful indexes for literary research are the *MLA International Bibliography,* the *Humanities Index* (published by H. W. Wilson), and the *Expanded Academic ASAP* (from InfoTRAC). If you do not know how to access these sources, ask the reference librarian on duty at your college library. Helping students find what they need is this person's principal job, and you will likely learn a lot from him or her. Both your librarian and your instructor can also suggest additional indexes to point you toward good secondary sources.

Although print versions exist for many indexes, most researchers find they get better and more efficient results using electronic versions of these databases. When you begin searching, be prepared with fairly specific search terms to help the database focus on what you really need and to filter out irrelevant material. Let's say you are researching the nature of love in Shakespeare's sonnets. If you perform a search on the keyword or topic *Shakespeare,* you will get thousands of hits, many of them about topics unrelated to yours. Searching on both *Shakespeare* and *sonnet*, however, will get you closer to what you want, while searching on *Shakespeare, sonnet,* and *love* will yield far fewer and far better, targeted results. If your search nets you fewer results than you expected, try again with different terms (substitute *romance* for *love,* for example). Be patient, and don't be afraid to ask your instructor or librarian for help if you are experiencing difficulty.

Once you have a screen full of results, you will be able to access a text, an abstract, or a citation. Some results will give you a link to the complete text of an article; just click on the link and you can read the article on-screen, print it out, or e-mail it to yourself. Frequently, a link is provided to an abstract of the article, a brief summary (generally just a few sentences) that overviews the content of the full article. Reading an abstract is a very good way of finding out whether it is worth tracking down the whole article for your paper. A citation gives only the most basic information about an article—its title, author, the date of publication, and its page numbers, and it is up to you to then find and read the whole article.

It may be tempting to settle on only those articles available immediately in full-text versions. Don't fall into this trap. As we mentioned earlier, many of the best sources of literary research are available only in print, and the only way to get to these is to follow the citation's lead and locate the journal in the library stacks. If a title or abstract looks promising, go and retrieve the article. If you think getting up and tracking down a journal is frustrating or time-consuming, imagine how frustrating and time-consuming it will be to attempt writing a research paper without great sources.

If you find a promising lead but discover your library doesn't have a particular book or has no subscription to the needed periodical, you still may be in luck. Nearly all libraries offer interlibrary loan services, which can track down books and articles from a large network of other libraries and send them to your home institution, generally free of charge. Of course, this process takes time—usually, a couple of days to a couple of weeks—and this is yet another reason to get started as early as possible on your research.

Lastly, if your quest for books and periodicals has not yielded all the results you want, search the World Wide Web. As with a search of a specialized index, you will do better and filter out a lot of the low-quality sources if you come up with some well-focused search terms in advance. Many students find it better to perform a directory search rather than simply entering a term or terms into a search engine. Most search engines (Yahoo!, AltaVista, Excite, Google, etc.) have a function that organizes the Web into categories—home, arts, news, etc.—and allows searchers to narrow their topics through a series of increasingly more specialized menus. If, for instance, you are writing about the poetry of Alfred, Lord Tennyson and using the Yahoo! search engine, you would follow the path Arts/Humanities/Literature/Authors/T/Tennyson, clicking successively on each link until you arrive at a list of sites dedicated to the poet. Though these are not guaranteed to be top-quality sites, they have at least been through some sort of screening process before being added to Yahoo!'s list. If you use the Web for your research, look especially for scholarly sites, written by professors or researchers and maintained by colleges and universities. Also potentially useful are the online equivalents of scholarly journals, as well as discussion groups or newsgroups dedicated to particular authors, literary schools, or periods.

As you locate research sources, you should engage in a continual process of evaluation to determine both the reliability of the potential source and its appropriateness to your particular topic and needs. Keep the following questions in mind to help you evaluate both print and electronic sources.

- **Who is the author, and what are his or her credentials?** If this information is not readily available, you might ask yourself why not. Is the author or publisher trying to hide something?

- **What is the medium of publication?** Books, journals, magazines, newspapers, and electronic publications all have something to offer a researcher, but they do not all offer the same thing. A good researcher will usually seek out a variety of sources.

- **How respectable is the publisher?** Not all publishers are created equal, and some have a much better reputation than others for reliability. Just because something is published, that doesn't make it accurate — think of all those supermarket tabloids publishing articles about alien autopsies. In general, your best sources are books from university presses and major, well-established publishers; scholarly journal articles; and articles from well-regarded magazines and newspapers such as the *Atlantic Monthly* or the *New York Times*. If you are not sure how respectable or reliable a particular publisher or source might be, ask your instructor or librarian.

- **If it's an online publication, who is hosting the site?** Though commercial sites (whose Web addresses end in *.com*) should not be ruled out, keep in mind that these sites are often driven by profit as much as a desire to educate the public. Sites hosted by educational institutions, nonprofit organizations, or the government (*.edu*, *.org*, and *.gov*, respectively) tend to be more purely educational.

- **How recent is the publication?** While there are many instances in which older publications are appropriate — you may be doing historical research or you may want to refer to a classic in a certain field—newer ones are preferable, all other things being equal. Newer publications take advantage of more recent ideas and theories, and they often summarize or incorporate older sources.

- **How appropriate is the source to your specific project?** Even the highest quality scholarly journal or a book by the top expert in a given field will be appropriate only for a very limited number of research projects. Let your topic, your tentative thesis, and your common sense be your guides.

How do you know when you have enough sources? Many instructors specify a minimum number of sources for research papers, and many students find exactly that number of sources and then look no further. Your best bet is to stop looking for sources when you really believe you have enough material to write a top-quality paper. Indeed, it is far better to gather up too many sources and not end up using them all than to get too few and find yourself wanting more information as you write. And remember that any "extra" research beyond what you actually cite in your paper isn't really wasted effort—every piece of information you read contributes to your background knowledge and overall understanding of your topic, making your final paper sound smarter and better informed.

TAKING NOTES: QUOTING, SUMMARIZING, PARAPHRASING, AND COMMENTING

You now have a stack of books, articles, and perhaps printouts of electronic sources. How do you work through these to get the support you need for your paper? First, sort the various sources by expected relevance, with those you think will be most informative and useful to you on the top of the list. Then, skim or read through everything quickly, highlighting or making note of the parts that seem most directly applicable to your paper. (Obviously, you should not mark up or otherwise deface library materials—take notes on a separate page.) Then slow down and reread the important passages again, this time taking careful notes. Keep yourself scrupulously well organized at this point, making sure that you always know which of your notes refers to which source. If you are taking notes by hand, it's a good idea to start a separate page for each source. If you are using a computer to take notes, start a separate file or section for each new source you read.

Notes will generally fall into one of four categories: quotations, paraphrases, summaries, and commentaries. While quotations are useful, and you will almost certainly incorporate several into your paper, resist the urge to transcribe large portions of text from your sources. Papers that rely too heavily on quotations can be unpleasant reading, with a cluttered or choppy style that comes from moving back and forth between your prose and that of the various authors you quote. Reserve direct quoting for those passages that are especially relevant and that you simply can't imagine phrasing as clearly or elegantly yourself. When you do make note of a quotation, be sure also to note the pages on which it appears in the source material so that later you will be able to cite it accurately.

Most often, you should take notes in the form of paraphrase or summary. To paraphrase, simply put an idea or opinion drawn from a source into your own words. Generally, a paraphrase will be about equal in length to the passage being paraphrased, while a summary will be much shorter, capturing the overall point of a passage while leaving out supporting details. Paraphrasing and summarizing are usually superior to quoting for two reasons. First, if you can summarize or paraphrase with confidence, then you know you have really understood what you have read. Second, a summary or paraphrase will be more easily transferred from your notes to your paper and will fit in well with your individual prose style. Just as with quotations, make a note of the page numbers in the source material from which your summaries and paraphrases are drawn.

Finally, some of your notes can be written as commentaries. When something you read strikes you as interesting, you can record your reaction to it. Do you agree or disagree strongly? Why? What exactly is the connection between the source material and your topic or tentative thesis? Making copious commentaries will help you to keep your own ideas in the forefront and will keep your paper from devolving into a shopping list of other writers' priorities. Be sure to note carefully when you are commenting rather than summarizing or paraphrasing. When you are drafting your paper, you will want to distinguish carefully between which ideas are your own and which are borrowed from others.

As you take notes on the substance of your reading, it is also essential that you record the source's author, title, and publication information for later use in compiling your works cited list, or bibliography. Nothing is more frustrating than having to return to the library or retrace your research steps on a computer just to get a page reference or the full title of a source. Most accomplished researchers actually put together their works cited list as they go along rather than waiting until the essay is drafted. Such a strategy will ensure you have all the information you need, and it will save you from the painstaking (and potentially tedious) task of having to create the list all at once at the end of your process.

The specific information you will need to create an entry in your works cited list varies by type of source—books, journal articles, interviews, Internet resources, etc. In general, the information you should take down includes the full name of the author or authors; the title, including any subtitles; names of editors or translators (if any); publication information, including the publisher's name, date and place of publication, page numbers, etc.; and, in the case of electronic publications, the URL or electronic pathway followed to reach the source. Details about what to include from each type of source are explained in "Preparing Your Works Cited List" (p. 1354). It would be a good idea to keep this information handy as your research proceeds, so you can resolve any uncertainty and keep your records clear.

WRITING THE PAPER: INTEGRATING SOURCES

After what may seem like a long time spent gathering and working with your sources, you are now ready to begin the actual writing of your paper. Start by looking again at your tentative thesis. Now that you have read a lot and know much more about your topic, does your proposed thesis still seem compelling and appropriate? Is it a little too obvious, something that other writers have already said or have taken for granted? Do you perhaps need to refine or modify it in order to take into account the information you have learned and opinions you have encountered? If necessary—and it usually is—refine or revise your tentative thesis so it can help you stay focused as you write.

Next you will need, just as with any other essay, to organize the supporting evidence of your thesis. Follow whatever process for organization you have used successfully in writing other papers, while bearing in mind that this time you will likely have more, and more complex, evidence to deal with. You likely will need an outline—formal or informal—to help you put your materials in a coherent and sensible order. But, once again, flexibility is the key here. If, as you begin to work your way through the outline, some different organizational strategy begins to make sense to you, revise your outline rather than forcing your ideas into a preconceived format.

The actual drafting of the research paper is probably the part you will find most similar to writing other papers. Try to write fairly quickly and fluently, knowing you can and will add examples, fill in explanations, eliminate redundancies, and work on style during the revision phase. As with your other papers, you may want to write straight through from beginning to end, or you may want to save difficult passages like the introduction for last. Interestingly, many writers find that the process of drafting a research paper actually goes a bit more quickly than does drafting other papers, largely because their considerable research work has left them so well versed in the topic that they have a wealth of ideas for writing.

What might slow you down as you draft your research papers are the citations, which you provide so that a reader knows which ideas are your own and which come from outside sources. Before you begin drafting, familiarize yourself with the conventions for MLA in-text citations, explained on pages 1351–54. Each time you incorporate a quotation, paraphrase, or summary into your essay, you will need to cite the author's name and the relevant page numbers from the source material. Do not, however, get hung up at this stage trying to remember how to punctuate citations and so forth. There will be time to hammer out these details later, and it is important as you write to keep your focus on the big picture.

As you go through the revision process, you should do so with an eye toward full integration of your source material. Are all connections between quotations, paraphrases, or summaries and your thesis clear? Do you include sufficient commentary explaining the inclusion of all source material? Is it absolutely clear which ideas come from which research source? Most important, is the paper still a well-focused argument, meant to convince an audience of the validity of your original thesis? Bearing these questions in mind, you will be ready to make the same sorts of global revision decisions that you would for any other paper — what to add, what to cut, how to reorganize, and so forth.

During the final editing and proofreading stage, include one editorial pass just for checking quotations and documentation format. Make sure each quotation is accurate and exact. Ensure that each reference to a source has an appropriate in-text citation and that your list of works cited (bibliography) is complete and correct. Double-check manuscript format and punctuation issues with the guidelines included in this book or with another appropriate resource. After putting so much time and effort into researching and writing your paper, it would be a shame to have its effectiveness diminished by small inaccuracies or errors.

UNDERSTANDING AND AVOIDING PLAGIARISM

Everyone knows that plagiarism is wrong. Buying or borrowing someone else's work, downloading all or part of a paper from the Web, and similar practices are beyond reprehensible. Most colleges and universities have codes of academic honesty forbidding such practices and imposing severe penalties — including expulsion from the institution in some cases—on students who are caught breaking them. Many educators feel these penalties are, if anything, not severe enough. Instructors tend to be not only angered but also baffled by students who plagiarize. In addition to the obvious wrongs of cheating and lying (nobody likes being lied to), students who plagiarize are losing out on a learning opportunity, a waste of the student's time as well as the instructor's.

Not everyone, though, is altogether clear on what plagiarism entails, and a good deal of plagiarism can actually be unintentional on the part of the student. A working definition of plagiarism will help to clarify what plagiarism is:

- presenting someone else's ideas as your own;
- using information from any print or electronic source without fully citing the source;
- buying or "borrowing" a paper from any source;
- submitting work that someone else has written, in whole or in part;
- having your work edited to the point that it is no longer your work;
- submitting the same paper for more than one class without the express permission of the instructors involved.

Some of this is obvious. You know it is cheating to have a friend do your homework or to download a paper from the Web and submit it as your own. But the first and last items on the list are not as clear-cut or self-explanatory. What exactly does it mean to present someone else's ideas as your own? Many students mistakenly believe that as long as they rephrase an idea into their own words, they have done their part to avoid plagiarism. This, however, is not true. Readers assume, and reasonably so, that everything in your paper is a product of your own thinking, not just your own phrasing, unless you share credit with another by documenting your source. No matter how it is phrased, an original idea belongs to the person who first thought of it and wrote it down; in fact the notion of possession in this context is so strong that the term applied to such ownership is *intellectual property.*

As an analogy, imagine you invented a revolutionary product, patented it, and put it up for sale. The next week, you find that your neighbor has produced the same product, painted it a different color, changed the name, and is doing a booming business selling the product. Is your neighbor any less guilty of stealing your idea just because he or she is using a new name and color for the product? Of course not. Your intellectual property, the idea behind the product, has been stolen. And you are no less guilty of plagiarism if you glean a piece of information, an opinion, or even an abstract concept from another person, put it into your own words, and "sell" it in your paper without giving proper credit.

Let us say, for example, that you find this passage about William Butler Yeats in the biographical notes at the back of your textbook:

> Religious by temperament but unable to accept orthodox Christianity, Yeats throughout his life explored esoteric philosophies in search of a tradition that would substitute for a lost religion. He became a member of the Theosophical Society and the Order of the Golden Dawn, two groups interested in Eastern occultism, and later developed a private system of symbols and mystical ideas.

Drawing from this passage, you write:

> Yeats rejected the Christianity of his native Ireland, but he became interested in occultism and Eastern philosophy. From these sources, he developed his own system of mystical symbols which he used in his poetry.

Clearly the words of this new passage are your own, and some elements of the original have been streamlined while other information has been added. However, the essential line of reasoning and the central point of both passages is largely the same. If this second passage appears in your paper without an acknowledgment of the original source, *this is plagiarism.*

Finally, let's look at the last item on the list: submitting the same paper for more than one class without the express permission of the instructors involved. Sometimes, you will find substantial overlap in the subject matter of two or more of your classes. A literature class, for instance, has elements of history, psychology, sociology, and other disciplines, and once in a while you might find yourself working on writing projects in courses that share common features. You might be tempted to let your research and writing in such a case do double duty, and there is not necessarily anything wrong with that. However, if you wish to write a paper on a single topic for more than one class, clear these plans with both instructors first. And, of course, even if you use the same research sources for both assignments, you will almost certainly need to write two separate essays, tailoring each to meet the specifications of individual classes and disciplines.

WHAT TO DOCUMENT AND WHAT NOT TO DOCUMENT

Everything borrowed from another source needs to be documented. Obviously, you should document every direct quotation of any length from primary or secondary sources. Equally important is the documentation of all your paraphrases and summaries of ideas, information, and opinions, citing authors and page numbers as explained in "In-Text Citations" on pages 1351–54. The rule of thumb is that if you didn't make it up yourself, you should probably document it.

The word *probably* in the previous sentence suggests that there are exceptions, and indeed there are. You do not need to document proverbial sayings ("Live and let live") or very familiar quotations ("I have a dream"), though in the case of the latter you may want to allude to the speaker in your text. You also do not need to document any information that can be considered common knowledge. Common knowledge here refers not only to information that you would expect nearly every adult to know immediately (that Shakespeare wrote *Hamlet*, for instance, or that George Washington was the first president of the United States). Common knowledge also encompasses undisputed information that you could look up in a general or specialized reference work. The average person on the street probably couldn't tell you that T. S. Eliot was born in 1888, but you don't need to say where that piece of information comes from, as it is widely available to anyone who wishes to find it.

Use both your common sense and your sense of fairness to make any necessary decisions about whether or not to document something. When in doubt, ask your Instructor, and remember, it's better to document something unnecessarily than to be guilty of plagiarism.

DOCUMENTING SOURCES: MLA FORMAT

Some students seem to believe that English teachers find footnotes and bibliographies and textual citations fun and interesting. In truth, few people know better than those who have to teach it how tedious format and documentation can be for a writer. Chances are your instructor will insist on your getting it right because he or she knows that it is important for at least three reasons. First, a sense of fair play requires that we give proper credit to those whose ideas benefit us. Second, by documenting your sources, you make it possible for your readers to find the sources themselves and follow up if they become interested in something in your paper. Third, documenting your sources, and doing it accurately, enhances your credibility as a writer by highlighting your professionalism and thoroughness.

As you read the following pages, and as you work on documenting sources in your own papers, don't say that you don't get it or that you can't learn this. If you learned the difficult and abstract skills of reading and writing, you can certainly learn something as concrete as documentation. Actually, documentation is the easy part of research writing, since there is only one right way to do it. The hard part is the creative work of discovering and presenting your original ideas and integrating them fluently with the work of others. And, of course, there is no need to actually memorize the specifics of format. Nobody does. When you need to know how to cite an anonymous newspaper article or what to include in a bibliographic entry for a radio broadcast, for instance, you can look it up. That's what professional writers do all the time.

There are many different forms and formulas for documenting sources—the APA (American Psychological Association) format commonly used in the social sciences, the CBE (Council of Biology Editors) format used in the life sciences, the *Chicago (Chicago Manual of Style)* format used in history, and so on. Each system highlights the type of information most relevant to experts in a particular field. If you have received contradictory instructions about documentation format for research projects in the past—include dates in your in-text references or don't, use footnotes or use endnotes—chances are you were working in different documentation systems. The format most often used in the humanities is MLA, the system developed by the Modern Language Association.

MLA format breaks down into two main elements: in-text citations and a works cited list (bibliography). In-text citations are parenthetical references that follow each quotation, paraphrase, or summary and give the briefest possible information about the source, usually the author's last name and a page number. The works cited list, which comes at the end of the paper, gives more detailed information about all sources used. The idea is that a reader coming across a parenthetical reference in your text can easily turn to the works cited list and get full details about the type of publication from which the material comes, the date of publication, etc. (Some writers make use of a third element of MLA style, content endnotes, which come between the end of the paper and the works cited list and contain extra information not readily integrated into the paper. Although you may use endnotes if you wish, they are not necessary.)

The following pages describe the major types of sources you are likely to encounter and how to reference those sources both in the text of your research paper and in your works cited list. The information here, however, is not exhaustive. If you want to cite a source not covered here, or if you would like more information about MLA style and citation format, turn to:

Gibaldi, Joseph. *The MLA Handbook for Writers of Research Papers.* 6th ed. New York: Modern Language Association of America, 2003.

In-Text Citations

The purpose of an in-text citation is to give a very brief acknowledgement of a source within the body of your essay. In MLA format, in-text citations take the form of brief parenthetical interruptions directly following each quotation, paraphrase, or summary. Some students find these interruptions a bit distracting at first, but you will quickly find that you grow accustomed to them and that soon they will not slow your reading or comprehension. The explanations and examples of in-text citations that follow should cover most instances you will encounter.

Citing Author and Page Number in Parentheses

Typically, a citation will contain the last name of the author being cited and a page number. The first example here shows a direct quotation, the second a paraphrase.

> One reviewer referred to Top Girls as, "among other things, a critique of bourgeois feminism" (Munk 33).

> When English wool was in demand, the fens were rich, but for many years now they have been among the poorest regions in England (Chamberlain 13).

Coming across these references in your text, your readers will know that they can turn to your works cited list and find out the full names of Munk and Chamberlain, the titles of what they have written, and where and when the works were published.

Please note:

- **In-text references contain no extraneous words or punctuation.** There is no comma between the name and the page number. The word *page* or the abbreviation *p.* do not precede the number. There are no extra spaces, just the name and the number.
- **Quotation marks close *before* the citation.** The in-text citation is not part of a direct quotation, so it does not belong inside the quotation marks.
- **The period that ends the sentence is placed *after* the citation.** Probably the most common error students make in MLA in-text citation is to put the period (or other closing quotation mark) at the end of the quotation or paraphrase and then give the reference in parentheses. Doing so, however, makes the citation the beginning of the next sentence rather than the end of the one being cited.

Citing the Author in Body Text and Only the Page Number in Parentheses

If you have already named the author in your own text, for instance in a lead-in phrase, you do not need to repeat the name in parentheses, as your reader will already know which author to look for in your works cited. In this case, the parenthetical reference need only contain the page numbers. The two examples already given could be rewritten as follows:

> Reviewer Erika Munk referred to Top Girls as, "among other things, a critique of bourgeois feminism" (33).

> Martha Chamberlain writes that when English wool was in demand, the fens were rich, but for many years now they have been among the poorest regions in England (13).

Citing Multiple Pages in a Source

You may find yourself wanting to make a brief summary of an extended passage, in which case you might need to cite the inclusive pages of the summarized material.

> John McGrath's Scottish theater company was destroyed by the end of government subsidies, as Elizabeth MacLennan chronicles in her book, The Moon Belongs to Everyone (137-99).

Citing Multiple Sources at Once

Sometimes several different sources say roughly the same thing, or at least there is substantial overlap in the parts you want to cite. Following are two ways of handling this situation; use whichever one you find most clear.

> This particular passage in the play has been the source of much critical speculation, especially by Freudian critics (Anders 19; Olsen 116; Smith 83-84; Watson 412).

> A number of Freudian critics have commented on this passage, including Anders (19), Olsen (116), Smith (83-84), and Watson (412).

Citing Two or More Sources by the Same Author

It is common for one author to write multiple books or articles on the same general topic, and you might want to use more than one of them in your paper. In this case, a shortened version of the title must appear in the parenthetical reference, to show which work by the author is being quoted or cited. In citations for an article and a book about playwright Caryl Churchill, both by the author Geraldine Cousin, one would give the first word of the work's title (other than *the* or *a*, etc.). As seen here, *Common* and *Churchill* are the first words in the title of the article and the book, respectively.

> Churchill claims that this sentiment was really expressed to her by one of the gangmasters she encountered in the fens (Cousin, "Common" 6).

> Churchill's notebooks from her visit to the fens record her seeing baby prams parked around the fields in which the women worked (Cousin, Churchill 47).

Note the comma between the author's name and the title. Note that these shortened titles are punctuated (with underscoring or quotation marks) just as they would be in the works cited list or elsewhere in your writing, in quotation marks for an article and in italics or underscored for an article.

   If the author is named in a signal phrase, only the shortened title and page number are needed in the parenthetical reference.

> "Violence," says Ruby Cohn, "is the only recourse in these brutalized lives on the Fen" (Retreats 139).

Citing a Quotation or Source within a Source

On page 58 of his book about Margaret Thatcher, Charles Moser writes:

> In a speech to Parliament in June of 1983, Thatcher said, "A return to Victorian values will encourage personal responsibility, personal initiative, self-respect, and respect for others and their property."

Let us say you do not have the text of Thatcher's original speech and that Moser doesn't make reference to a primary source that you can track down. But Moser is a reliable author, so you believe the Thatcher quotation is accurate and want to use a portion of it in your paper. This is done by giving the original speaker's name (in this case Margaret

Thatcher) in your text and using the abbreviation *qtd. in* and the author from whom you got the quote (in this case Charles Moser) in the parenthetical citation.

> These "Victorian values," Thatcher claimed, would "encourage personal responsibility, personal initiative, self-respect, and respect for others" (qtd. in Moser 58).

PREPARING YOUR WORKS CITED LIST

It is a good idea to begin preparing your list of works cited during the research process, adding new entries each time you find a source that might be useful to you. That way, when the time comes to finalize your paper, you can just edit the list you already have, making sure it contains all the necessary entries and no extraneous ones, and checking each for accuracy and format. If you wait until the end to create your works cited list, you will have to compile the whole list from scratch at a time when you are most tired and therefore least able to focus your attention on this necessary, detailed work.

General Guidelines

- **Begin your list of works cited on a new page.** Continue paginating as you have throughout the paper, with your last name and the page number appearing in the upper right corner.
- **Center the heading Works Cited at the top of the page** in capitals and lowercase letters; do not use italics, boldface print, or quotation marks.
- **Arrange sources alphabetically, by the last name of the source's author** (or by title, in the case of anonymous works), regardless of the order in which the sources are cited in your paper.
- **Begin each entry flush with the left margin.** When an entry takes up more than one line, all lines after the first are indented one-half inch. (For an example, see the works cited list in the research paper by Jarrad Nunes, on p. 1365.) This is called a hanging indent, and all major word processing programs can be set to format your entries this way.
- **Double-space the entire list.**
- **Do not put extra line spaces between entries.**
- **As always, carefully follow any additional or contrary instructions provided by your instructor.**

Citing Books

To list books in your works cited, include as much of the following information as is available and appropriate, in the following order and format. Each bulleted element here should be separated by a period. If no other formatting (quotation marks, underlining, etc.) is specified, then none should be added.

- **The name of the author or editor,** last name first for the first author or editor listed. Names of additional authors or others listed, anywhere in the entry, should appear in the regular order (first name first). (Multiple authors or editors should be listed in the order in which they appear on the book's title page. Use initials or middle names, just as they appear. You need not include titles, affiliations, and any academic degrees that precede or follow names.)

- **Title of a part of a book,** in quotation marks. Needed only if you cite a chapter, introduction, or other part of a book written by someone other than the principal author or editor listed on the title page. See "A work in an anthology or a compilation," "An article in a reference work," or "An introduction, preface, foreword, or afterword" on the following pages.

- **The title of the book,** underlined or italicized. If there is a subtitle, put a colon after the main title, and follow this with the full subtitle. This is the standard format for a works cited entry, even if there is no colon on the book's title page. (If the main title ends in a question mark, an exclamation point, or a dash, however, do not add a colon between the main title and subtitle.)

- **Name of the editor** (for books with both an author and an editor), **translator,** or **compiler,** if different from the primary author(s), with the abbreviation Ed., Trans., or Comp., as appropriate.

- **Edition used,** if other than the first.

- **Volume used,** if a multivolume work.

- **Series name,** if the book is part of a series.

- **City or place of publication,** followed by a colon (if more than one city is listed on the title page, use only the first one); **name of the publisher,** followed by a comma; **year of publication** (if multiple copyright dates are listed, use the most recent one).

- **Page numbers.** Needed only if you cite a chapter, introduction, or other part of a book written by someone other than the principal author or editor listed on the title page. See "A Work in an Anthology or a Compilation," "An Article in a Reference Work," or "An Introduction, Preface, Foreword, or Afterword" on the following pages.

Copy your entries directly from the book's title page, which provides more complete and accurate information than a cover or another bibliography. The following examples cover most of the sorts of books you are likely to encounter.

A Book by a Single Author

The simplest entry is a single-volume book by a single author, not part of a series, and without additional editors, translators, etc. (Note the colon before the subtitle.)

> Goldhagen, Daniel Jonah. Hitler's Willing Executioners: Ordinary Germans and the Holocaust. New York: Vintage-Random, 1996.

If a book has an editor, translator, or compiler in addition to an author, identify this person by role and by name, between the book's title and the place of publication.

> Sebald, W. G. The Rings of Saturn. Trans. Michael Hulse. New York: New Directions, 1998.

The following example cites a second edition book by a single author.

> Richter, David H. The Critical Tradition: Classic Texts and Contemporary Trends. 2nd ed. Boston: Bedford, 1998.

A Book by Two or Three Authors

Note that in the following example only the first author's name appears in reverse order. Note also the series title, Oxford Shakespeare Topics, included when citing a book in a series. UP (with no periods) is the abbreviation for University Press.

> Gurr, Andrew, and Mariko Ichikawa. Staging in Shakespeare's Theaters. Oxford Shakespeare Topics. Oxford: Oxford UP, 2000.

A Book by Four or More Authors

If there are four or more authors or editors listed on a book's title page, give only the name of the first, followed by *et al* (Latin for "and others").

> Gardner, Janet E., et al, eds. Literature: A Portable Anthology. Boston: Bedford/St. Martin's, 2004.

A Book by an Unknown or Anonymous Author

> Bhagavad-Gita: Krishna's Counsel in Time of War. Trans. Barbara Stoler
>
> Miller. New York: Bantam, 1986.

A Book by a Corporate Author

Corporate authorship refers to a book that lists an organization rather than an individual as its author. This is especially common with publications from government and nonprofit organizations. GPO stands for the Government Printing Office, which publishes most U.S. federal documents.

> Bureau of the Census. Historical Statistics of the United States, 1789-
>
> 1945: A Supplement to the Statistical Abstract of the United States.
>
> Washington: GPO, 1945.

Two or More Books by the Same Author

If you cite more than one work by a single author, alphabetize the entries by title. For the second and all subsequent entries by the same author, replace the author's name with three hyphens.

> Bloom, Harold. Hamlet: Poem Unlimited. New York: Riverhead-Penguin,
>
> 2003.

> ---. Shakespeare's Poems and Sonnets. Bloom's Major Poets. Broomall,
>
> PA: Chelsea House, 1999.

A Work in an Anthology or Compilation

The first example that follows is a citation from a literature anthology; the second is from a scholarly work in which each chapter is written by a different author. The title of the work or chapter being cited is usually enclosed in quotation marks. However, if the piece is a play or novel, you should underline its title instead.

> Baldwin, James. "Sonny's Blues." Literature: A Portable Anthology.
>
> Ed. Janet E. Gardner, et al. Boston: Bedford/St. Martin's, 2004.
>
> 220-47.

Keyishian, Harry. "Shakespeare and the Movie Genre: The Case of Hamlet." The Cambridge Companion to Shakespeare on Film. Ed. Russell Jackson. Cambridge: Cambridge UP, 2000. 72-81.

Two or More Works in a Single Anthology or Compilation

If you cite two or more works from a single anthology or collection, you can create a cross-reference, citing the full publication information for the collection as a whole and cross-referencing the individual pieces using only the name of the editor and page numbers of the particular work within the anthology or compilation.

Chopin, Kate. "The Story of an Hour." Gardner, et al. 66-68.

Gardner, Janet E., et al, eds. Literature: A Portable Anthology. Boston: Bedford/St. Martin's, 2004.

Gilman, Charlotte Perkins. "The Yellow Wallpaper." Gardner, et al. 82-96.

An Article in a Reference Work

The format for citing material from dictionaries, encyclopedias, or other specialized reference works is similar to that for a work in an anthology, but the name of the reference work's editor is omitted. Often, such reference articles are anonymous anyway. The first example is for a signed article in a print book, the second for an anonymous entry in an electronic encyclopedia.

Brown, Andrew. "Sophocles." The Cambridge Guide to Theatre. Cambridge: Cambridge UP, 1988. 899-900.

"Browning, Elizabeth Barrett." 1998 World Book Multimedia Encyclopedia. CD-ROM. Redmond, WA: World Book, 1998.

An Introduction, Preface, Foreword, or Afterword

After the author's name, give the name of the part of the book being cited, capitalized but neither underlined nor in quotation marks, followed by the title of the book and all relevant publication information.

Bode, Carl. Introduction. The Portable Thoreau. By Henry David Thoreau.
Ed. Carl Bode. Revised ed. The Viking Portable Library. Harmonds-
worth, Eng.: Penguin, 1977. 1-27.

Periodicals

An Article in a Scholarly Journal

Most scholarly journals publish several issues in each annual volume
and paginate continuously throughout the entire volume. (In other
words, if one issue ends on page 230, the next will begin with page 231.)
Your works cited entry should list the author, article title, journal title,
volume number (in arabic numerals, even if it appears in roman
numeral form on the journal cover), the year (in parentheses), and page
numbers. Follow the punctuation shown here exactly.

Miller, Greg. "The Bottom of Desire in Suzan-Lori Parks's Venus." Modern
Drama 4 (2002): 125-37.

If the journal you are citing paginates each issue separately, you must
also include the issue number. Add a period after the volume number, no
space, and then the issue number.

Orban, Clara. "Antonioni's Women, Lost in the City." Modern Language
Studies 31.2 (2001): 11-27.

An Article in a Magazine

For an article in a magazine, omit the volume and issue numbers (if
given) and include the date of publication. The first example here shows
the format for a monthly, bimonthly, or quarterly magazine; the second,
which includes the date as well as the month, is appropriate for weekly
and biweekly magazines.

McChesney, Robert W., and John Nichols. "Holding the Line at the FCC."
The Progressive Apr. 2003: 26-29.

Welch, Jilly. "Campaign Spells Out Concern for Literacy." People
Management 18 Apr. 1996: 6-7.

An Article in a Newspaper

When a newspaper is separated into sections, note the letter or number designating the section as a part of the page reference. Newspapers and some magazines frequently place articles on nonconsecutive pages. When this happens, give the number of the first page only, followed by the plus sign. For locally published newspapers, state the city of the publication if not included in the paper's name. Do this by adding the city in square brackets after the newspaper's name: Argus Leader [Sioux Falls]. If the masthead notes a specific edition, add a comma after the date and list the edition (for example, natl. ed., late ed.). Different editions of the same issue of a newspaper contain different material, so it's important to note which edition you are using.

> Mahren, Elizabeth. "University's 'Leap of Faith' Becomes Lesson in Community." Los Angeles Times 16 Mar. 2003: A1+.

A Review

To cite a review, you must include the title and author of the work being reviewed between the review title and the periodical title. The first entry that follows is for a book review in a magazine. The second is an untitled review in a scholarly journal that includes the name of an adaptor as well as the place and date of the play's production.

> Ilan Stavans. "Familia Faces." Rev. of Caramelo, by Sandra Cisneros. The Nation 10 Feb. 2003. 30-34.

> Sofer, Andrew. Rev. of Lysistrata, by Aristophanes. Adapted by Robert Brustein. American Repertory Theater, Cambridge, MA, 28 May 2002. Theater Journal 55 (2003): 137-38.

Electronic Sources

Sometimes online sources do not list all the information required for a complete citation. They are, for instance, frequently anonymous, and they do not always record the dates when they were written or updated. Give as much of the information as you can find, using the formats that follow. Note that entries for online sources generally contain two dates. The first is the date when the document was posted or updated; the second is the date the researcher accessed the document. Online addresses are enclosed in angle brackets. (Remember to turn off the function that your word processing program uses to turn Web addresses into hyperlinks.)

A CD-ROM

An entry for a CD-ROM resembles a book entry, with the addition of the acronym *CD-ROM* inserted between the work's title and the publication information.

> Shakespeare: His Life, Times, Works, and Sources. CD-ROM. Princeton, NJ:
> Films for the Humanities and Sciences, 1995.

An Online Scholarly Project or Database

A full entry for an online scholarly project or database includes the title of the project, underlined; the editor's name; publication information, including the version number (if other than the first), the date of the project's most recent update, and the name of the sponsoring organization or institution; the date that you accessed the project; and the online address.

> Walt Whitman Archive. Ed. Ed Folsom and Keneth M. Price. 14 Feb. 2003.
> University of Virginia. 14 Mar. 2003. <http://jefferson.village.
> virginia.edu/whitman/introduction/>.

An Online Journal or Magazine

The first entry that follows is from an online scholarly journal that publishes by volume number, the second from the online version of a popular magazine.

> Fukuda, Tatsuaki. "Faulknerian Topography." The Faulkner Journal of
> Japan 4 (Sept. 2002). 20 Mar. 2003 <http://www.senshu-u.ac.jp/
> ~thb0559/No4/Fukuda.htm>.

> Zoglin, Richard, and Kate Novak. "Fighting the War of Words." Time
> 28 Apr. 2003. 30 Apr. 2003 <http://www.time.com/time/magazine/
> article/0,9171,1101030428-444975,00.html>.

A Professional or Personal Web Page

Include as much of the following information as appropriate and available: the author of the document or site; the document title, in quotation marks (if the site is divided into separate documents); the name of the site, underlined; the date of creation or most recent update; the sponsoring organization or institution; your date of access and the online address or the specific document or full site (as appropriate). If the site has no official title, provide a brief identifying phrase, neither underlined nor in quotation marks, as in the second example below.

> Werner, Liz. "A Brief History of the Dickinson Homestead." The Dickinson
> Homestead: Home of Emily Dickinson. 2001. Amherst College.
> 12 June 2003 <http://www.dickinsonhomestead.org/hist.html>.

> Olinesis, John. Home page. 12 Apr. 2003. 5 May 2003 <http://guinness.
> cs.stevens-tech.edu/~oliensis/>.

A Posting to a Discussion List or Newsgroup

Give the author's name, the title of the document (in quotation marks) taken from the subject line, the identifying phrase *Online posting*, the date of posting, the name of the forum (no special formatting), your date of access, and the online address. If the Internet site is not known, the e-mail address of the list's supervisor can be listed instead.

> Arnove, Anthony. "Query Regarding Arthur Miller." Online posting.
> 28 Jan. 2000. Campaign Against Sanctions on Iraq. 20 Apr. 2003
> <http://www.casi.org.uk/discuss/2000/msg00061.html>.

Other Miscellaneous Sources

A Television or Radio Program

Begin with the name of the author or another individual (director, narrator, etc.), only if you refer primarily to the work of a particular individual. Otherwise, begin with the title of a segment or episode (if appropriate), in quotation marks; the title of the program, underlined; the title of the series (if applicable), underlined; the name of the network; the call letters and city of the local station (if applicable), and the date of broadcast. The first entry that follows is a citation of a segment of a radio broadcast, the second is of an episode of a television program.

> Alison, Jay. "For Sale." This American Life. Public Radio International.
> WCAI, Woods Hole, MA. 11 Oct. 2002.

> "Tales from the Public Domain." The Simpsons. WFXT, Boston. 17 Mar.
> 2002.

A Film, Video, or DVD

Film citations begin with the film title (underlined), followed by *Dir.* and the director's name, the year the film was originally released, the medium (videocassette, DVD, etc.), the distributor, and the year of release in the stated medium.

> <u>Hamlet</u>. Dir. Laurence Olivier. 1948. DVD. Home Vision Entertainment,
>
> 2000.

An Interview

Begin with the name of the person interviewed. For a published interview, give the title, if any, in quotation marks (if there is no title, simply use the designation *Interview,* neither in quotation marks nor italicized), followed by the name of the interviewer and publication information. The first example that follows is for an interview published in a magazine. The second example is of an interview conducted personally by the author of the research paper and gives the name of the person interviewed.

> Shields, David. "The Only Way Out Is Deeper In." Interview with Andrew
>
> C. Gottlieb. <u>Poets & Writers</u> July/Aug. 2002: 27-31.

> Scipione, Stephen. Personal interview. 20 Mar. 2002.

A Lecture or Speech

To cite a speech or lecture that you've attended, use the following format, listing the speaker's name; the title of the presentation, in quotation marks (if announced or published, otherwise use a descriptive label such as *Address* or *Lecture*); the meeting or sponsoring organization; the location; and the date. The first example given here is for a speech with an announced title. The second is for an untitled address.

> Cohen, Amy R. "Sharing the Orchestra: How Modern Productions Reveal
>
> Ancient Conventions." Sixth National Symposium on Theater in Aca-
>
> deme. Washington and Lee University, Lexington, VA. 15 Mar. 2003.

> Nader, Ralph. Address. University of Massachusetts Dartmouth, N. Dart-
>
> mouth. 24 Mar. 2003.

To cite a lecture, speech, or address you've seen in a film or TV broadcast or heard on the radio, use the appropriate format for the medium of transmission. Generally speaking, you do not need to cite a class lecture; to quote or otherwise refer to something an instructor says in class, you may do so simply by crediting the instructor in the text of your essay.

A Letter or E-mail

There are three kinds of letters: published, unpublished (in archives), and personal. A published letter includes the writer's name, the recipient's name (in quotation marks), the date of the letter, the number of the letter (if assigned by the editor), and publication information for the book or periodical in which it appears.

> Thomas, Dylan. "To Donald Taylor." 28 Oct. 1944. Dylan Thomas: The
> Collected Letters. Ed. Paul Ferris. New York: Macmillan, 1985.
> 529-30.

In citing an unpublished letter, give the writer's name, the title or a description of the material (for example, Letter to Havelock Ellis), the date, and any identifying number assigned to it. Include the name and location of the library or institution housing the material.

> Sanger, Margaret. Letter to Havelock Ellis. 14 July 1924. Margaret Sanger
> Papers. Sophia Smith Collection. Smith College, Northampton, MA.

To cite a letter or e-mail you received personally, include the author, the designation Letter (or E-mail) to the author, and the date posted.

> Green, Barclay. Letter to the author. 1 Sept. 2002.

> Kapadia, Parmita. E-mail to the author. 12 Mar. 2003.

SAMPLE RESEARCH PAPER

When choosing a research paper topic, Jarrad Nunes recalled how interesting he had found Emily Dickinson's poem "Because I could not stop for Death," which seemed to defy his expectations of literature about death and dying. Jarrad decided to see what professional literary critics had to say on the subject and how closely their ideas matched his own. His paper, which follows, is a type of reader-response criticism, because it attends to reader expectations and how Dickinson manipulates these, and it combines a close reading of the primary literary text with research from a variety of secondary sources.

Jarrad S. Nunes
English 204
Professor Gardner
2 April 2003

Emily Dickinson's "Because I could
not stop for Death":
Challenging Readers' Expectations

With a keen eye for detail and a steadfast "resilience not to be overcome
by mysteries that eluded religion, science, and the law" (Eberwein 42), Emily
Dickinson's poetry records the abstractions of human life so matter-of-factly
that her readers often take her technical skill for granted. Take, for example,
the six-stanza poem "Because I could not stop for Death"—a detached, but
never completely dispassionate, recollection of a human's journey to its final
conclusion. The verse is crafted so succinctly and with such precision that its
complex and vivid images are made even more extraordinary and meaningful.
We might expect literature on the theme of death to invoke religious imagery,
stillness, and a sense of dread or foreboding, but none of this is the case.
Instead, the poem challenges the preconceptions Dickinson's contemporaries
had about death, and in doing so it makes us challenge ours as well.

From the start, Dickinson infuses this often-grim topic with a palpable
humanity, beginning with her personification of death as the courteous, careful carriage driver bearing the narrator's body to rest. Literary critic Harold
Bloom asserts, "The image here of a woman and her escort, Death, meditating
on the prospect of eternity, is neither one of despair nor loss nor outrage, but
of resignation" (37). This "resignation," though, does not come across as the
predictable acceptance of God's will. In fact, any mention of God or the soul
is remarkably absent from this poem about death and eternity. This suggests
the uneasy relationship Dickinson had with the strict religious beliefs of her
society and her family. "Raised during the period of New England Revivalism,"
writes David Yezzi, "Dickinson declined to make the public confession of faith
that would admit her to the church (her father made his twice) and by the
age of thirty she left off attending services altogether." Clearly at odds with
familial and social expectations, Dickinson nonetheless fearlessly expresses

her religious "doubt, which her poems later absorbed as ambiguity and con-tradiction" (Yezzi).

Dickinson's narrator does not fear death, perhaps because death is asso-ciated here not so much with endings or divine judgment but instead with a very human journey. The driver seems affable, "kindly stopp[ing]" and driving slowly. In stanza two, the narrator puts her work away to observe the driver calmly (490). It may seem unlikely that she would be trusting of so ominous a character, but as Thomas Johnson explains it:

> Emily Dickinson envisions Death as a person she knew and trusted, or
> believed that she could trust. He might be any Amherst gentleman, a
> William Howland or an Elbridge Bowdoin, or any of the lawyers or teach-
> ers or ministers whom she remembered from her youth, with whom she
> had exchanged valentines, and who at one time or another had acted as
> her squire. (222)

Indeed, the fact that the carriage driver has stopped for the narrator on a day when she was too busy to do the same emphasizes his courtesy and thought-fulness as a character. This is an original and deeply humanistic perception of death, in which the personified entity is neither a black-cloaked grim reaper nor a stern servant of God.

Along with its deep humanity, Dickinson's image of Death has a fluidity and graceful movement that is, at first, juxtaposed against our more frighten-ing preconceptions of the idea. This tangible sense of motion is perhaps best illustrated in the poem's perfectly constructed third stanza. Here, a series of images metaphorically re-creates a natural progression—childish play gives way to growing grain, and, eventually, to the setting of the sun (490). At least one critic has pointed out how these three images might represent childhood, maturity, and old age (Shaw 20). The very fact that the narrator views these scenes from a slowly rolling carriage lends the passage a clear sense of movement and an unexpected vitality. The absurdity of this mean-dering vessel passing "the Setting Sun" perhaps suggests a sense of quick-ening as death draws near, or it may even signal the dissolution of temporal reality altogether. Regardless, the steady progression of this section is undeniable.

The strong sense of motion is continued in the fourth stanza, though with some differences. Here, the movement is less concrete, as the narrator herself moves from a life marked by careful self-control into a position in which she all but succumbs to outside forces. As "the Dews drew quivering and chill" (490), the narrator has lost the ability to keep herself warm. Her earthly garments do not provide adequate protection. From her philosophical viewpoint, however, these difficulties, like death itself, are to be calmly accepted rather than feared. Indeed, up to this point, there is not a single truly fearful image in this remarkable poem about death.

As the poem moves into its fifth stanza, the momentum is halted temporarily and a more traditional death image is finally introduced with the line "We paused before a House that seemed / A Swelling of the Ground" (490). At this point, the character of Death seems to bid his passenger a rather unceremonial goodbye at the foot of her earthen grave. As the resting place is described, he retreats, returning to the world of the living to repeat his duty with another passenger. While the sparse but vivid description of the grave should invoke a paralyzing loneliness, Dickinson again thwarts our expectations, tempering the reader's fear by having her narrator merely pause at the sight, as if staying for a short while at a hotel or a friend's house. Once again, a usual symbol of finality is given a transitive purpose.

The final stanza seemingly places the narrator at a new destination, Eternity. While this would certainly be the logical end of her journey, Dickinson's exquisite use of language suggests that the entire account may simply be a daydream—a mental dress rehearsal for the real death to come. Consider this account of the poem's final stanza:

> All of this poetically elapsed time "Feels shorter than the Day," the day of death brought to an end by the setting sun of the third stanza. [. . .] "Surmised," carefully placed near the conclusion, is all the warranty one needs for reading this journey as one that has taken place entirely in her mind [. . .] the poem returns to the very day, even the same instant, when it started. (Anderson 245)

Thus even the most basic facts about death—its finality and permanence—are brought into question.

Finally, "Because I could not stop for Death" indicates both Dickinson's precise and vivid style and her unwillingness to settle for the ordinary interpretation. Death no longer conforms to the readers' preconceptions, as religion, stillness, and finality give way to humanist philosophy, motion, and continuity. The poet observes, experiences, and recounts her perceptions in metaphor. She opens up many questions about the nature of death, yet she provides no easy answers to her readers. Instead, we are provided with an account of death that weaves in and out of time, finally looping back on its own structure to provide a stunningly dramatic conclusion. In six short stanzas, Dickinson cleverly exposes what she saw as fundamental flaws in the traditional conception of death, burial, and the eternal afterlife, and in doing so, she opens up new pathways of thought for us all.

Nunes 5

Works Cited

Anderson, Charles R. Emily Dickinson's Poetry: Stairway of Surprise. New York: Holt, Rinehart and Winston, 1960.

Bloom, Harold. Emily Dickinson. Bloom's Major Poets. New York: Chelsea House, 1999.

Dickinson, Emily. "Because I could not stop for Death." Literature: A Portable Anthology. Ed. Janet E. Gardner, et al. Boston: Bedford/St. Martin's, 2004. 490.

Eberwein, Jane Donahue. "Dickinson's Local, Global, and Cosmic Perspectives." The Emily Dickinson Handbook. Ed. Gudrun Grabher. Amherst: U of Massachusetts P, 1998. 27-43.

Johnson, Thomas. Emily Dickinson: An Interpretive Biography. Cambridge: Harvard UP, 1955.

Shaw, Mary Neff. "Dickinson's 'Because I could not stop for Death'." Explicator 50 (1991): 20-21.

Yezzi, David. "Straying Close to Home." Commonweal 9 Oct. 1998. FindArticles. 2000. Gale Group. 22 Mar. 2003 <http://findarticles.com/cf_0/m1252/n17_v125/21227668/p1/article.jhtml>

Biographical Notes on the Authors

[Albert] Chinua[Iumogu] Achebe (b. 1930) was born and raised in Ogidi, in eastern Nigeria. A member of the Igbo tribe, Achebe spoke only Igbo, his tribal language, until he was eight, when he began to learn English. He studied at the Government College at Umuahia and the University College of Ibadan, from which he was graduated in 1953. The same year he received a B.A. from London University and, in 1956, studied broadcasting at the British Broadcasting Corporation in London. In 1967, during the Biafran war and following the secession of Eastern Nigeria, Achebe left his post as director of external broadcasting in Nigeria and joined the Biafran Ministry of Information. After the civil war, he was named senior research fellow at the University of Nigeria, Nsukka, and was invited to lecture in the United States and elsewhere. Achebe, who long held the view that Africa had been largely misrepresented by non-African writers, encouraged and published native writers. In 1990 an automobile accident left him paralyzed from the waist down. His literary works include *Girls at War and Other Stories* (1973) and the novels *Things Fall Apart* (1958, translated into nearly fifty languages), *Arrow of God* (1964), and *Anthills of the Savannah* (1988).

Self-described as one-half Japanese, one-eighth Choctaw, one-fourth black, and one-sixteenth Irish, Ai (b. 1947) was born Florence Anthony in Albany, Texas, and grew up in Tucson, Arizona. She legally changed her name to "Ai," which means "love" in Japanese. She received a B.A. in Japanese from the University of Arizona and an M.F.A. from the University of California at Irvine. She is the author of half a dozen books of poetry, among them *Vice* (1999), which won the National Book Award for poetry. She has taught at Wayne State University, George Mason University, and the University of Kentucky, and she currently teaches at Oklahoma State University and lives in Stillwater, Oklahoma.

Of Spokane/Coeur d'Alene Native American descent, Sherman Alexie (b. 1966) was born on the Spokane Indian Reservation in Wellpinit, Washington. He earned his B.A. from Washington State University in Pullman. He has published eight books of poetry and several novels and collections of short fiction, including *The Lone Ranger and Tonto Fistfight in Heaven* (1993). He based the script for the film *Smoke Signals* on one of his short stories. "Postcards to Columbus" reflects Alexie's concern for the devaluation of his native culture.

Agha Shahid Ali (1949–2001) was born in New Delhi and grew up Muslim in Kashmir. He was educated at the University of Kashmir, Srinagar, and at the University of Delhi. He earned a Ph.D. from Pennsylvania State University in

1984 and an M.F.A. from the University of Arizona in 1985. He was a poet (author of eight books of poetry), critic (author of *T. S. Eliot as Editor*, 1986), translator (*The Rebel's Silhouette: Selected Poems by Faiz Ahmed Faiz*, 1992), and editor (*Ravishing Disunities: Real Ghazals in English*, 2000). He held teaching positions at the University of Delhi and at several colleges and universities in the United States. In "I Dream It Is Afternoon When I Return to Delhi" Ali uses Western formal cultural principles in a work that focuses on his own cultural background.

Tom Andrews (1961–2001) was born in and grew up in West Virginia. He graduated from Hope College and earned an M.F.A. at the University of Virginia. He published three books of poems and a memoir, *Codeine Diary* (1998), about coming to terms with his hemophilia and his determined refusal to let it circumscribe his life. He edited collections of essays on WILLIAM STAFFORD and CHARLES WRIGHT. "The Hemophiliac's Motorcycle" is a poem written as a single sentence and displays the same spirit of celebration one finds in CHRISTOPHER SMART's *Jubilate Agno*.

Matthew Arnold (1822–1888) was born in the small English village of Laleham and raised at Rugby School, where his father was headmaster. He attended Oxford University and, in 1857, was elected professor of poetry at Oxford, a position he held for ten years, writing mostly literary criticism. He also worked for thirty-five years as an inspector of schools and made two lecture tours of the United States.

John Ashbery (b. 1927) grew up on a farm near Rochester, New York. He attended Harvard University and later Columbia University. He studied in France for two years and then stayed on, writing art criticism. Returning to New York, he taught, edited *Art News*, and wrote for *Newsweek*. He is the author of twenty books of poetry, including *Some Trees* (1956), selected by W. H. AUDEN for the Yale Series of Younger Poets, and *Self-Portrait in a Convex Mirror* (1975), which received the Pulitzer Prize for poetry, the National Book Critics Circle Award, and the National Book Award. Ashbery has also published literary criticism, a book of art criticism, a collection of plays, and a novel. In "One Coat of Paint" one sees Ashbery's use of varied syntactical devices and the unpredictable outcome of his lines.

Born in the city of Ottawa, in Ontario, Canada, **Margaret Atwood** (b. 1939) studied at the University of Toronto, Radcliffe College, and Harvard University. A predominant figure in Canadian letters who has written more than thirty books, Atwood is widely known for her concern for the survival of vitality and humane awareness in a dangerous and exploitive world. Her poetry collections include *The Circle Game* (1964; rev. ed. 1966), which won the 1966 Governor-General's Award in Canada; *The Animals in That Country* (1968), *Procedures for Underground* (1970); *Two-Headed Poems* (1981), *Interlunar* (1984), and the two-volume *Selected Poems* (1976, 1988). Her novels include *The Edible Woman* (1969), *Surfacing* (1972), *Lady Oracle* (1976), *Life Before Man* (1979), *Bodily Harm* (1981), *The Handmaid's Tale* (1985), also made into a film, *Cat's Eye* (1988), *The Robber Bride* (1993), and *Alias Grace* (1996). Among her story collections are *Dancing Girls* (1977), *Bluebeard's Egg* (1983), *Murder in the Dark* (1983), and *Wilderness Tips* (1991).

W. H. [Wystan Hugh] Auden (1907–1973) was born in York, England. He attended private school and later Oxford University, where he began to write poetry. He supported himself by teaching and publishing, writing books based on his travels to Iceland, Spain, and China. He also wrote (with Chester Kallman) several librettos, including the one in Igor Stravinsky's *The Rake's Progress* (1951). He lived in the United States from 1939 until his death, having become a U.S. citizen in 1946. His work combines lively intelligence, quick wit, careful craftsmanship, and social concern.

Jimmy Santiago Baca (b. 1952) was born in Sante Fe, New Mexico, of Chicano and Apache heritage. Abandoned by his parents at the age of two, he lived with one of his grandparents for several years before being placed in an orphanage. He lived on the streets as a youth and was imprisoned for six years for drug possession. In prison, he taught himself to read and write and began to compose poetry. A fellow inmate convinced him to submit some of his poems for publication. He has since published seven books of poetry, a memoir, a collection of stories and essays, a play, and a screenplay. He lives outside Albuquerque in a hundred-year-old adobe house.

Born in New York City, the son of a revivalist minister, **James Baldwin** (1924–1987) was raised in poverty in Harlem where, at the age of fourteen, he became a preacher in the Fireside Pentecostal Church. After completing high school he decided to become a writer and, with the help of the black American expatriate writer Richard Wright, won a grant that enabled him to move to Paris, where he lived for most of his remaining years. There he wrote the critically acclaimed *Go Tell It on the Mountain* (1953), a novel about the religious awakening of a fourteen-year-old black youth. Subsequent works, focusing on the intellectual and spiritual trials of black men in a white, racist society, included the novels *Giovanni's Room* (1956), *Another Country* (1962)—both famous at the time for their homosexual themes—*Tell Me How Long the Train's Been Gone* (1968), *If Beale Street Could Talk* (1974), *Just Above My Head* (1979), and *Harlem Quartet* (1987); the play *Blues for Mister Charlie* (1964); and the powerful nonfiction commentaries *Notes of a Native Son* (1955), *Nobody Knows My Name* (1961), and *The Fire Next Time* (1963). Baldwin's short stories are collected in *Going to Meet the Man* (1965).

Born in New York City and raised in Harlem, **Toni Cade Bambara** (1939–1995) attended Queens College, where she wrote stories, poems, scripts, and other works and was part of the staff of the literary magazine. She continued writing stories as she studied for an M.A. at City College. After her story collection *Gorilla, My Love* (1972) was published, her sense of herself as a black writer gradually clarified and deepened. Her other story collections include *The Black Woman* (1970), *Tales and Stories for Black Folks* (1971), and *The Sea Birds Are Still Alive* (1977). Her two novels are *The Salt Eaters* (1980) and *If Blessing Comes* (1987). *Deep Sightings and Rescue Missions*, a collection of fiction and nonfiction, appeared posthumously, in 1996.

Jim Barnes (b. 1933) was born in Oklahoma of Choctaw and Welsh heritage and worked for ten years as a lumberjack. He studied at Southeastern

Oklahoma State University and received his Ph.D. from the University of Arkansas. Author of several books of poetry, he often uses formalist techniques to comment on the difficulties faced by Native Americans. Currently professor of comparative literature at Northeast Missouri State University, he is the founder and editor of the *Chariton Review*.

Aphra Behn (1640–1689) was born in East Kent, England, of middle-class parents and in her early twenties traveled to Suriname, on the northern coast of South America. When she returned home, she married a London merchant who died, probably of the plague, the following year. In financial difficulty, Behn worked as a spy in Antwerp for King Charles II; when she was not paid, she turned to writing. She first wrote plays as well as verse and later wrote in the emerging genre of prose fiction, for which she is best known for *Oroonoko*, set in Suriname.

John Berryman (1914–1972) was born John Smith in McAlester, Oklahoma; he took the name of his stepfather after his father committed suicide. He attended a private school in Connecticut, then Columbia College and Clare College, Cambridge. He taught at Wayne State University, Harvard University, Princeton University, and the University of Minnesota. His early work was traditional, highly crafted, and admired; then in his forties, Berryman wrote poetry that was boldly original and innovative. *77 Dream Songs*, published in 1964 and awarded a Pulitzer Prize, unveiled the alter egos "Henry" and "Mr. Bones" in a sequence of sonnet-like poems whose unusual diction, difficult syntax, leaps in language and tone, and mixture of lyricism and comedy

reached poignant depths of the human spirit and psyche. He added to the sequence in the following years until it totaled nearly four hundred verses collected in *The Dream Songs* (1969). Berryman, who suffered throughout his life from mental and emotional difficulties, committed suicide himself by jumping off a bridge in Minneapolis.

Born in Worcester, Massachusetts, **Elizabeth Bishop** (1911–1979) was raised in Nova Scotia by her grandparents after her father died and her mother was committed to an asylum. She attended Vassar College intending to study medicine but was encouraged by MARIANNE MOORE to be a poet. From 1935 to 1937 she traveled in France, Spain, northern Africa, Ireland, and Italy. She settled in Key West, Florida, for four years and then in Rio de Janeiro for almost twenty. She wrote slowly and carefully, producing a small body of technically sophisticated, formally varied, witty, and thoughtful poetry, revealing in precise, true-to-life images her impressions of the physical world. She served as Consultant in Poetry at the Library of Congress from 1949 to 1950.[1]

William Blake (1757–1827) was born and raised in London. His only formal schooling was in art—he studied for a year at the Royal Academy and was apprenticed to an engraver. He later worked as a professional engraver,

---

[1]The first appointment of a Consultant in Poetry at the Library of Congress was made in 1937. The title was changed to Poet Laureate Consultant in Poetry in 1986. Appointments are made for one year, beginning in September, and sometimes have been renewed for a second year.

doing commissions and illustrations, assisted by his wife, Catherine Boucher. Blake, who had started writing poetry at the age of eleven, later engraved and handprinted his own poems, in very small batches, with his own illustrations. His early work was possessed of a strong social conscience, and his mature work turned increasingly mythic and prophetic.

Born in Madison, Minnesota, **Robert Bly** (b. 1926) served in the navy during World War II. Upon his return, he studied at St. Olaf College for a year before going to Harvard University. He lived in New York for a few years, then earned an M.A. from the University of Iowa Writers' Workshop. He received a Fulbright grant in 1956 to travel to Norway and began to translate Norwegian poetry into English. In 1966 he founded (with David Ray) American Writers Against the Vietnam War. He has published more than thirty books of poetry, many books of translations, and a number of nonfiction books, and he has edited numerous collections of poetry. A best-selling author—his controversial 1990 best-seller *Iron John* was a key book in the "men's movement"—Bly is also a challenging critic of contemporary consumerist culture. "Driving to Town Late to Mail a Letter" is an example of his ability to discover a moment of epiphany in the most common of situations. He now lives on a farm near the small town of Moose Lake, Minnesota.

Louise Bogan (1897–1970) was born in Maine and educated in Boston. For thirty-eight years she was the poetry editor at the *New Yorker*. Because she was reclusive and disliked talking about herself, details regarding her private life are scarce. The majority of her poetry was written in the earlier half of her life and published in the *New Republic*, the *Nation*, *Poetry*, *Scribner's*, *Atlantic Monthly*, and in several volumes of collected verse. Her poetry is notable for its simultaneous strict adherence to lyrical forms and high emotional pitch. "Women," like much of her verse, explores the perpetual disparity of heart and mind.

Eavan Boland (b. 1944) was born in Dublin and educated there as well as in London and New York. She has taught at Trinity College and University College, Dublin; Bowdoin College; and the University of Iowa; and currently is a professor of English at Stanford University. Boland is the author of eight volumes of poetry and a collection of essays, co-editor of *The Making of a Poem: A Norton Anthology of Poetic Forms* (2000), and a regular reviewer for the *Irish Times*.

Born in Northampton, England, **Anne Bradstreet** (1612–1672) was educated by tutors, reading chiefly religious writings and the Bible. In 1628 she married Simon Bradstreet, a brilliant young Puritan educated at Cambridge. They were among the earliest settlers of the Massachusetts Bay Colony, in 1630, and her father and husband were leading figures in its governance. She wrote regularly in both prose and verse throughout her busy and difficult years in Massachusetts.

Emily Brontë (1818–1848) was the fifth of six children, three of whom (herself, Charlotte, and Anne) became famous novelists. Like her siblings she was brought up by her aunt at Haworth in Yorkshire, where her father was a clergyman. Emily was educated at home and spent the rest of her life there, near the wild Yorkshire moors she loved. Charlotte sent some of the sisters' poetry to be published, under pseudonyms, in 1846, but the venture was not successful; the Brontës then turned to writing novels. Emily is best known for the novel *Wuthering Heights*.

Born in Topeka, Kansas, **Gwendolyn Brooks** (1917–2000) was raised in Chicago and wrote her first poems at age seven. She began studying poetry at the Southside Community Art Center. Her second collection of poems, *Annie Allen* (1949), earned the first Pulitzer Prize given to an African American poet. She served as Consultant in Poetry at the Library of Congress from 1985 to 1986 and worked in community programs and poetry workshops in Chicago to encourage young African American writers.

Sterling A. Brown (1901–1989) was born in Washington, D.C., and educated at Dunbar High School, Williams College, and Harvard University. He taught for more than fifty years at Howard University. Like many other black poets of the period, he expressed his concerns about race relations in America. His first book of poems, *Southern Road* (1932), was well-received by critics, and Brown became part of the artistic tradition of the Harlem Renaissance. Brown was deeply interested in African American music and dialect and became one of the great innovators in developing poetry related to jazz. His work is known for its frank, unsentimental portraits of black people and their experiences and for its successful incorporation of African American folklore and contemporary idiom.

Born in Durham, England, **Elizabeth Barrett Browning** (1806–1861) studied with her brother's tutor. Her first book of poetry was published when she was thirteen, and she soon became the most famous female poet up until that time in English history. A riding accident at the age of sixteen left her a semi-invalid in the home of her possessive father, who forbade any of his eleven children to marry. At age thirty-nine, Elizabeth eloped with ROBERT BROWNING; the couple lived in Florence, Italy, where Elizabeth died fifteen years later. Her best-known book of poems is *Sonnets from the Portuguese*, a sequence of forty-four sonnets recording the growth of her love for her husband.

Robert Browning (1812–1889) was the son of a bank clerk in Camberwell, then a suburb of London. As an aspiring poet in 1844, Browning admired ELIZABETH BARRETT's poetry and began a correspondence with her that led to one of the world's most famous romances. He and Elizabeth's courtship lasted until 1846, when they were secretly wed and ran off to Italy, where they lived until Elizabeth's death in 1861. The years in Florence were among the happiest for both of them. To her he dedicated *Men and Women*, which contains his best poetry. Although she was the more popular poet during their time together, his reputation grew upon his return to London, after her death, assisted somewhat by public sympathy for him. The late 1860s were the peak of his career: he and TENNYSON were mentioned together as the foremost poets of the age.

Born in Andernach, Germany, **Charles Bukowski** (1920–1994) came to the United States at age three and grew up in poverty in Los Angeles. He drifted extensively, and then for much of his life made his home in San Pedro, working for many years for the U.S. Postal Service. He was familiar with the people of the streets, hustlers, and other transients. He began writing in childhood and published his first story at age twenty-four and his first poetry when he was thirty-five. He published many books of poetry in addition to novels and short stories reminiscent of Ernest Hemingway. His work is very popular in Europe. His style, which exhibits a strong immediacy and a refusal to embrace standard formal structure, was influenced by the Beat movement.

Robert Burns (1759–1796) was born in Ayrshire in southwestern Scotland, the son of a poor farming family. His formal education lasted only to about his ninth year, when he was needed to work on the farm, but he read widely and voraciously whenever he could find time. His first book of poems, published in 1785, sold out within a month. Despite living in poverty, Burns poured out a flood of his finest poems in the early 1790s. He is regarded as Scotland's national bard for his ability to depict with loving accuracy the life of his fellow rural Scots. His use of dialect brought a stimulating, much-needed freshness and raciness into English poetry, but his greatness extends beyond the limits of dialect: his poems are written about Scots, but, in tune with the rising humanitarianism of his day, they apply to a multitude of universal problems.

Born in London, **Thomas Campion** (1572–1631) was educated at Cambridge University. After studying law at Gray's Inn and medicine at the University of Caen, he set up a medical practice in London. His first book was a collection of poems in Latin, *Thomae*

Campiani Poemata (1595), and his love of quantitative versification (see quantitative verse in the Glossary) carried over to his English poems. He published a book of prosody, *Observations in the Art of English Poesy*, in 1602, defending quantitative verse against the accentual, rhymed verse characteristic of English poetry. He was a composer as well as a poet and one of the great writers of song in English. In 1601, he contributed twenty-one songs and a brief treatise on song to Philip Rosseter's *Book of Ayres* and went on to publish four books of airs himself, the last in 1617. He also wrote a number of masques for performance at King James's court. He died in London, probably of the plague.

Hayden Carruth (b. 1921) was born in Waterbury, Connecticut, and educated at the University of North Carolina at Chapel Hill and the University of Chicago. For many years he lived in northern Vermont. He now lives in upstate New York, where until recently he taught in the graduate creative writing program at Syracuse University. He has been editor of *Poetry*, poetry editor of *Harper's*, and, for twenty years, an advisory editor of the *Hudson Review*. Noted for the breadth of his linguistic and formal resources, influenced by jazz and the blues, Carruth has published twenty-nine books, chiefly poetry but also a novel, four books of criticism, and two anthologies. Many of his best-known poems are about the people and places of northern Vermont as well as about rural poverty and hardship, and reflect his political radicalism and sense of cultural responsibility.

Anne Carson (b. 1950) was born to a banker's family and raised in various Ontario towns. A scholar trained in the classics (Ph.D., University of Toronto), Carson has developed an independent voice as a poet and an essayist. Her work challenges preconceived notions of poetry, fusing classical topics with a unique and thoroughly modern style and sensibility. She has taught at a number of colleges and universities, following a pattern of teaching one semester in Canada and at least one semester in the United States.

Born in Clatskanie, Oregon, **Raymond Carver** (1938–1988) lived in Port Angeles, Washington, until his death. Among the honors accorded this short story writer and poet during his lifetime were a 1979 Guggenheim fellowship, two grants from the National Endowment for the Arts, and election to the American Academy of Arts and Letters. Carver's writing, known for its spare, stark depiction of contemporary existence, has been translated into more than twenty languages. His story collections are *Will You Please Be Quiet, Please?* (1976), nominated for a National Book Award; *Furious Seasons* (1977); *What We Talk About When We Talk About Love* (1981); *Cathedral* (1983), nominated for the Pulitzer Prize; and *Where I'm Calling From* (1988).

Lorna Dee Cervantes (b. 1954) was born in San Francisco and grew up in San Jose. There she studied at San Jose City College and San Jose State University. She has been a member of the Chicana Theatre Group, has worked at the Centro Cultural de la Gente, and founded Mango Publications, a small press that prints Chicano and other books as well as a literary journal. She is co-editor of *Red Dirt*, a cross-cultural poetry journal. Cervantes, who considers herself "a Chicana writer, a feminist writer, a political writer," lives in

Colorado and is a professor at the University of Colorado at Boulder.

Born the son of a grocer and the grandson of a serf in Taganrog, a seacoast town in southern Russia, **Anton Chekhov** (1860–1904) began writing humorous tales to support himself while studying medicine at Moscow University. In 1884 he received his medical degree and published his first collection of short stories, *Tales of Melpomene*. Other early collections are *Motley Tales* (1886), *At Twilight* (1887), and *Stones* (1888). Besides being a masterful writer of short stories, Chekhov is probably Russia's most esteemed playwright. In 1898 the Moscow Art Theatre produced his play *The Seagull*, followed by *Uncle Vanya* in 1899, *The Three Sisters* in 1901, and *The Cherry Orchard* in 1904. Chekhov, known for his sad and subtle exploration of people's inability to communicate as well as for his humanitarian activities, died at age 44 of tuberculosis, which he had contracted in his student days.

A first-generation Chinese American, **Marilyn Chin** (b. 1955) was born in Hong Kong and raised in Portland, Oregon. In addition to publishing several books of poetry, Chin has co-edited *Dissident Song: A Contemporary Asian American Anthology* (1991) and co-translated *The Selected Poems of Ai Qing* (1985). An activist who sees herself as pitted against the dominant culture in which she lives, Chin writes poetry that reflects the difficulty of bridging two cultures and that conveys a sense of exile and loss. She teaches at San Diego State University.

Born Katherine O'Flaherty, the daughter of a French Creole mother and a prosperous St. Louis businessman who died when she was four, **Kate Chopin** (1851–1904) was raised by her mother and a great-grandmother who sent her to Catholic school and trained her for a place in St. Louis society. At the age of eighteen she married Oscar Chopin and accompanied him to New Orleans, where he became a cotton broker. When her husband's business failed, the family moved to a plantation in northern Louisiana and opened a general store, which Kate managed for a year after her husband's death in 1883. She then returned to St. Louis with her six children and began a career as a writer of realistic fiction. Among her works are the story collections *Bayou Folk* (1894) and *A Night in Acadie* (1897) as well as the novel *The Awakening* (1899), shocking in its time for its frank portrayal of adultery but widely praised today for its sensitive portrayal of a woman's need for independence and sensual fulfillment.

Caryl Churchill (b. 1938) was born in England and moved with her family to Canada during World War II. She returned to England to attend Oxford University and there began writing plays for student production. After college she pursued her writing in a low-key fashion, penning short works, mostly for radio, while staying at home to raise children. By the mid-1970s, she began to produce full-length works for the London stage, chiefly at the Royal Court Theatre, a venue known for its support of promising new writers. As she became established among Britain's leading playwrights, the strength and audacity of her voice continued to grow, and by the mid-1980s she had begun to experiment with form, music, and choreography in many of her works. Churchill's range as an author can be seen in some of her best-known

plays: *Cloud Nine* (1979) explores sexuality and sexual politics, *Top Girls* (1982) critiques a newly emerging definition of success for women, *Fen* (1983) examines the lives of the rural poor, *Serious Money* (1987) offers a biting critique of free-market capitalist ideology, and *The Skriker* (1994) combines a modern fable with elements of ancient British folklore.

Born in a Hispanic neighborhood in Chicago, **Sandra Cisneros** (b. 1954) spoke Spanish at home with her Mexican father, Chicana mother, and six brothers. At ten she began writing poetry, and soon experimented with other forms. In 1977, when she was studying in the M.F.A. program at the University of Iowa Writers' Workshop, she came to see herself as a Chicana writer. Cisneros has published three books of poems; a book of interrelated narratives, *The House on Mango Street* (1983); and a fiction collection, *Woman Hollering Creek and Other Stories* (1991).

Lucille Clifton (b. 1936) was born in Depew, New York, and studied at Howard University. In addition to many books of poetry, she has published a memoir and more than sixteen books for children. She has taught at several colleges, worked in the Office of Education in Washington, D.C., served as poet laureate for the State of Maryland, and is currently Distinguished Professor of Humanities at St. Mary's College of Maryland. Her poems typically reflect her ethnic pride, womanist principles, and race and gender consciousness.

Judith Ortiz Cofer (b. 1952) was born in Puerto Rico and raised in New Jersey. A writer of poetry, prose, and fiction, Ortiz often includes different genres in the same collection. Her poetry and prose reflect her rich cultural and linguistic background. She currently lives in Georgia, where she is a professor at the University of Georgia.

Samuel Taylor Coleridge (1772–1834) was born in Devonshire and sent to school in London after his father's death. He went to Jesus College, Cambridge, in 1791, and dropped out twice without a degree. In 1798 Coleridge and WILLIAM WORDSWORTH published *Lyrical Ballads*, which initiated the Romantic movement in English poetry and established both poets' reputations. After 1802 Coleridge became addicted to opium, which he used to treat physical discomfort and seizures. He and his wife were separated, his friendship with Wordsworth ended, and he stopped producing poetry. From 1816 until his death, Coleridge lived under constant medical supervision and yet still published a journal and wrote several plays, pieces of criticism, and philosophical and religious treatises.

Born and raised in New York City, **Billy Collins** (b. 1941?) is the author of several collections of poems. Perhaps no poet since ROBERT FROST has managed to combine high critical acclaim with such broad popular appeal. The typical Collins poem opens on a clear and hospitable note but soon takes an unexpected turn; poems that begin in irony may end in a moment of lyric surprise. Collins sees his poetry as "a form of travel writing" and considers humor "a door into the serious." Collins is Distinguished Professor of Literature at Lehman College of the City University of New York and a writer-in-residence at Sarah Lawrence College. He was appointed Poet Laureate Consultant in Poetry at the Library of Congress from 2001 to 2002.

Born in Arizona, **Jayne Cortez** (b. 1936) grew up in the Watts section of Los Angeles and now lives in New York City. A poet and performance artist, she has published several collections of poetry and made a number of recordings, often performing her poetry with the jazz group the Firespitters. Her poems have been translated into twenty-eight languages. In 1964 she founded the Watts Repertory Company, and in 1972 she formed her own publishing company, Bola Press.

Born in Garrettsville, Ohio, **Hart Crane** (1899–1932) began writing verse in his early teenage years. Though he never attended college, he read widely on his own. An admirer of T. S. ELIOT, Crane combined the influences of European literature and traditional versification with a particularly American sensibility derived from WALT WHITMAN. Crane's major work, the book-length poem *The Bridge* (1930), expresses in ecstatic terms a vision of the historical and spiritual significance of America. Like Eliot, Crane used the landscape of the modern, industrialized city to create a powerful new symbolic literature. He committed suicide in 1932, at the age of thirty-three, by jumping from the deck of a steamship headed to New York from Mexico.

Born in Newark, New Jersey, **Stephen Crane** (1871–1900) was the fourteenth and youngest child of a Methodist minister. He started to write stories at the age of eight and at sixteen was writing feature articles for the *New York Tribune*. After attending Lafayette College and Syracuse University, he returned to New York where he lived in poverty as a freelance writer and journalist. His experience in the Bowery slums supplied detail for his first, self-published novel, *Maggie: A Girl of the Streets*

(1893), a pioneer work of the naturalistic movement. His most famous novel, *The Red Badge of Courage,* a realistic depiction of the Civil War from the point of view of an ordinary soldier published in 1895, was a resounding success. His achievements as a novelist won him assignments as a special newspaper correspondent and enabled him to travel widely, reporting on the Spanish-American and Graeco-Turkish wars. In addition to several volumes of essays and short stories, Crane published two collections of poems, *The Black Riders* (1895) and *War Is Kind* (1899). He settled briefly in England and died from tuberculosis in Badenweiler, Germany, a few months before his twenty-ninth birthday.

Born in Arlington, Massachusetts, **Robert Creeley** (b. 1926) attended Harvard University, then lived in France and Spain before joining the faculty at Black Mountain College (an experimental arts college in North Carolina) in 1954, where he edited the *Black Mountain Review.* His influence helped define an emerging countertradition to the literary establishment. He has published more than sixty books of poetry in the United States and abroad. Since 1989 he has been Samuel P. Capen Professor of Poetry and Humanities at the State University of New York, Buffalo. His poem "Time" illustrates his technique of fracturing lines to convey tension, anxiety, and the fragmentation of the psyche.

Born in Aguas Buenas, Puerto Rico, **Victor Hernandez Cruz** (b. 1949) moved to New York City with his family at the age of five. His first book of poetry was published when he was seventeen. A year later, he moved to California's Bay Area and published his second book. In 1971 Cruz visited

Puerto Rico and reconnected with his ancestral heritage; eighteen years later, he returned to Puerto Rico to live. He now divides his time between Puerto Rico and New York. In much of his work he explores the relation between the English language and his native Spanish, playing with grammatical and syntactical conventions within both languages to create his own bilingual idiom.

Countee Cullen (1903–1946) was born either in Louisville, Kentucky; Baltimore, Maryland; or, as he himself claimed, New York City. He was adopted by the Reverend Frederick A. Cullen and his wife and grew up, as he put it, "in the conservative atmosphere of a Methodist parsonage." He studied at New York University and Harvard University. A forerunner of the Harlem Renaissance movement, he was, in the 1920s, the most popular black literary figure in America. From the 1930s until his death, he wrote less while working as a junior high school French teacher. Cullen's reputation was eclipsed by that of other Harlem Renaissance writers, particularly LANGSTON HUGHES and Zora Neale Hurston, for many years; recently, however, there has been a resurgence of interest in Cullen's life and work.

e. e. cummings (1894–1962) was born in Cambridge, Massachusetts, where his father was a Unitarian minister and a sociology lecturer at Harvard University. He graduated from Harvard and then served as an ambulance driver during World War I. *The Enormous Room* (1922) is an account of his confinement in a French prison camp during the war. After the war, he lived in rural Connecticut and Greenwich Village, with frequent visits to Paris. In his work, Cummings experimented radically with form, punctuation, spelling, and syntax, abandoning traditional techniques and structures to create a new, highly idiosyncratic means of poetic expression. At the time of his death in 1962, he was the second most widely read poet in the United States after ROBERT FROST.

Jim Daniels (b. 1956) was born in Detroit, where he, his brothers, his father, and his grandfather all have worked in the auto industry. He graduated with a B.A. from Alma College in Michigan and earned his M.F.A. from Bowling Green University. He presently lives in Pittsburgh, where he teaches at Carnegie Mellon University. Daniels's poems often reflect and honor the lives of the working class.

Born and raised in Detroit, **Toi Derricotte** (b. 1941) earned a B.A. in special education from Wayne State University. She is the author of several collections of poetry as well as a memoir, *The Black Notebooks* (1997). With poet CORNELIUS EADY, she co-founded Cave Canem, which offers workshops and retreats for African American poets. Among the many honors she has received is the Distinguished Pioneering of the Arts Award from United Black Artists. Derricotte teaches creative writing at the University of Pittsburgh.

Emily Dickinson (1830–1886) was born in Amherst, Massachusetts, and lived there her entire life, leaving only rarely. She briefly attended a woman's seminary but became homesick and left before a year was out. Dickinson never married and became reclusive later in life, forgoing even the village routines and revelries she once had enjoyed. She published very few of the more than 1,700 poems she wrote; most were written for herself or for inclusion in her many letters. It was not until 1955 that a complete edition of the verses, attempting to present them as they were originally written, appeared.

Born in London to a prosperous Catholic family (through his mother he was related to statesman and author Sir Thomas More and the playwright John Heywood), **John Donne** (1572–1631) studied at Oxford University for several years but did not take a degree. He fought with Sir Walter Raleigh in two naval strikes against Spain. In 1601 Donne's promising political career was permanently derailed by his precipitate marriage to Anne More without her father's consent. He was briefly imprisoned, lost a very promising position with Sir Thomas Egerton, and spent years seeking political employment before finally being persuaded by King James in 1615 to become a priest of the Church of England. His life was described by Isaac Walton later in the century as having been divided into two parts. In Phase I he was "Jack Donne" of Lincoln's Inn: when young, Donne employed a sophisticated urban wit that lent a sort of jaded tone to his earlier poetry. "The Flea" presumably appeared during this stage of his life and is a typical metaphysical poem. In Phase II he was John Donne, dean of St. Paul's: after Donne took holy orders in 1615 his poetry became markedly less amorous and more religious in tone. His Holy Sonnets, of which "Batter my heart, three-personed God" is one, are as dense and complex as his earlier work but directed toward an exploration of his relationship with God.

H. D. [Hilda Doolittle] (1886–1961) was born in Bethlehem, Pennsylvania. She went to private schools in Philadelphia and then dropped out of Bryn

Mawr after a year because of ill health. She moved to England, where an old friend (and fiancé, for a time), EZRA POUND, encouraged her to write and sent some of her poetry to a journal. H. D. became a leader of Pound's Imagist group but eventually moved away from it. From 1933 to 1934 she visited Freud as a patient and later wrote *Tribute to Freud* (1956). Besides poetry, she wrote novels and translated Greek.

Mark Doty (b. 1953) is the author of six collections of poetry and two memoirs—*Heaven's Coast* (1996), about the loss of his partner, Wally Roberts, and *Firebird* (1999), a gay coming-of-age story, a chronicle of a gradual process of finding in art a place of personal belonging. He has taught at Brandeis University, Sarah Lawrence College, Vermont College, and the University of Iowa Writers' Workshop. He now lives in Provincetown, Massachusetts, and Houston, Texas, where he teaches at the University of Houston.

Rita Dove (b. 1952) was born in Akron, Ohio; her father was the first research chemist to break the race barrier in the tire industry. She graduated from Miami University in Oxford, Ohio, with a degree in English; after a year at Tübingen University in Germany on a Fulbright fellowship, she enrolled in the University of Iowa Writers' Workshop, where she earned her M.F.A. in 1977. She has taught at Tuskegee Institute and Arizona State University and now is on the faculty of the University of Virginia. In 1993 she was appointed Poet Laureate Consultant in Poetry at the Library of Congress, making her the youngest person—and the first African American—to receive this highest official honor in American letters. She was awarded the Pulitzer Prize in

1987 for *Thomas and Beulah*, a book-length sequence loosely based on the lives of her grandparents. "The Satisfaction Coal Company" is from that book ("he" is Thomas; "they" are Thomas and Beulah); it reflects Dove's respect for workaday lives and her celebration of their worth and dignity.

Born a year before Shakespeare and in the same county, Warwickshire, England, **Michael Drayton** (1563–1631) wrote sonnets, pastorals, odes, verse epistles, satires, and historical epics. His masterpiece is a topographical work on England titled *Poly-Olbion*, a poem celebrating all the counties of England and Wales. He was an influential writer of religious poetry as well. "Since there's no help, come let us kiss and part" is the sixty-first in a sequence of sonnets addressed to "Idea," the embodiment of the Platonic ideas of virtue and beauty.

Paul Laurence Dunbar (1872–1906) was the first African American to gain national eminence as a poet. Born and raised in Dayton, Ohio, the son of former slaves, he was an outstanding student. The only African American in his class, he was both class president and class poet. Although he lived to be only thirty-three years old, Dunbar was prolific, writing short stories, novels, librettos, plays, songs, and essays as well as the poetry for which he became well-known. Popular with both black and white readers of his day, Dunbar's style encompasses two distinct voices—the standard English of the classical poet and the evocative dialect of the turn-of-the-century black community in America.

Born in Oakland, California, **Robert Duncan** (1919–1988) was raised by adoptive parents who were devout theosophists and who instilled in him a lifelong interest in occult spirituality. He entered the University of California at Berkeley in 1936 and was drawn to leftist politics and a bohemian lifestyle. Drafted in 1941, he was discharged after declaring his homosexuality. His 1944 essay "The Homosexual in Society" compared the situation faced by homosexuals in modern society to that of blacks and Jews. Influenced by a variety of poets, Duncan credited his long correspondence with DENISE LEVERTOV with helping him find a new poetics— a magical, mystical blend of the experimental and the traditional. His first book, *Heavenly City, Earthly City*, was published in 1947, the same year he met Charles Olson, whose literary theories helped shape Duncan's "grand collage" concept of verse. He returned to San Francisco in 1948, becoming part of the San Francisco Renaissance and cultivating the role of a guru, discoursing on literature, spiritualism, and sexual diversity. He became affiliated with Olson's Black Mountain movement and taught at Black Mountain College in 1956. His reputation as a poet was established by three major collections: *The Opening of the Field* (1960), *Roots and Branches* (1964), and *Bending the Bow* (1968). He was awarded the Harriet Monroe Memorial Prize in 1961, a Guggenheim fellowship in 1963, the Levinson Prize in 1964, and the National Poetry Award in 1985.

Born and raised in Rochester, New York, **Cornelius Eady** (b. 1954) attended Monroe Community College and Empire State College. He began writing as a teenager. His poems are his biography, their subjects ranging from blues musicians to Eady's witnessing his father's death. He has published six volumes of poetry. With poet TOI DER-

RICOTTE, he co-founded Cave Canem, which offers workshops and retreats for African American poets, and with composer Diedre Murray he has collaborated on two highly acclaimed music-dramas. Formerly the director of the Poetry Center at the State University of New York, Stony Brook, he is currently Distinguished Writer-in-Residence at the City College of New York.

Born and raised in St. Louis, **T. S. [Thomas Stearns] Eliot** (1888–1965) went to prep school in Massachusetts and then to Harvard University, where he earned an M.A. in philosophy in 1910 and started his doctoral dissertation. He studied at the Sorbonne, in Paris, and then in Marburg, Germany, in 1914, when the war forced him to leave. Relocating to Oxford, he abandoned philosophy for poetry, and he married. After teaching and working in a bank, he became an editor at Faber and Faber and editor of the journal *Criterion* and was the dominant force in English poetry for several decades. He became a British citizen and a member of the Church of England in 1927. He won the Nobel Prize in literature in 1948. He also wrote plays and essays as well as a series of poems on cats that became the basis of a musical by Andrew Lloyd Weber. The Eliot poems included in this anthology show the poet's use of collage techniques to relate the fragmentation he saw in the culture and individual psyches of his day.

Elizabeth I (1533–1603) was queen of England from 1558 to 1603. In addition to being well educated and a skillful politician and ruler, she wrote extensively, mostly speeches and translations but also a few original poems in the forms and manner typical of her time. Though the attribution of "When I was fair and young" has been questioned, it is credited to Queen Elizabeth I in the most recent collection of her works.

Ralph Ellison (1914–1994) was born in Oklahoma City. His father, an ice and coal vendor, died when Ralph was three; his mother supported herself and her son with domestic work. After studying music at the Tuskegee Institute, in 1936 Ellison went to New York City, where, encouraged by the novelist Richard Wright, he became associated with the Federal Writers' Project. His first novel, *Invisible Man* (1952), received a 1953 National Book Award and became a classic in American fiction. Ellison taught literature and writing at Bard College, the University of Chicago, Rutgers University, and New York University. His other works include the collections of essays *Shadow and Act* (1964) and *Going to the Territory* (1986), and three posthumous works prepared by John F. Callahan: *The Collected Essays of Ralph Ellison* (1995); *Flying Home and Other Stories* (1996), a short story collection; and *Juneteenth* (1999), a novel shaped and edited by Callahan from manuscripts left unfinished when Ellison died.

Born in Long Beach, California, of Yaqui and European ancestry, **Anita Endrezze** (b. 1952) earned her M.A. from Eastern Washington University. She is a poet, writer, storyteller, teacher, and painter (in watercolor and acrylics) who also works in fiber and creates handmade books. She is a member of Atlatl, a Native American arts service organization. In addition to poetry, she has published a children's novel, *The Mountain and the Guardian Spirit*, in Danish, as well as other novels, short

stories, and nonfiction. Currently, she lives in Everett, Washington.

Of German and Chippewa Indian descent, **Louise Erdrich** (b. 1954) was born in Little Falls, Minnesota, and grew up near a Sioux Indian reservation in Wahpeton, North Dakota, where her parents taught at a Bureau of Indian Affairs boarding school. She was educated at Dartmouth College and Johns Hopkins University. At Dartmouth she met Michael Dorris, an anthropologist whom she married in 1981. Her first novel, *Love Medicine* (1984), won the National Book Critics Circle Award for fiction. Her other novels include *The Beet Queen* (1986); *Tracks* (1988); *The Crown of Columbus* (1991), written in collaboration with her husband, who has since died; *The Bingo Palace* (1994); *Tales of Burning Love* (1996); and *The Antelope Wife* (1998).

Born in Brooklyn, New York, **Martín Espada** (b. 1957) has an eclectic résumé: radio journalist in Nicaragua, welfare-rights paralegal, advocate for the mentally ill, night desk clerk in a transient hotel, attendant in a primate nursery, groundskeeper at a minor league ballpark, bindery worker in a printing plant, bouncer in a bar, and practicing lawyer in Chelsea, Massachusetts. Author of five books of poetry, he is regarded as one of the leading poets of Puerto Rican heritage in the United States. He presently teaches at the University of Massachusetts, Amherst.

Born in New Albany, Mississippi, **William Faulkner** (1897–1962) moved as a young boy to Oxford, Mississippi, the place he was to call home for the rest of his life. He completed two years of high school and a little more than one year at the University of Mississippi. After a brief stint in the Royal Air Force in Canada during World War I, he worked at various jobs before becoming a writer. His first book, *The Marble Faun* (1924), was a collection of poems. Encouraged by the writer Sherwood Anderson, whom he met in New Orleans in 1925, Faulkner wrote his first novel, *Soldier's Pay* (1926), a work that was favorably reviewed. His third novel, *Sartoris* (1929), was the first set in Yoknapatawpha County, a fictional re-creation of the area around Oxford whose setting appeared throughout his later fiction. Over three decades Faulkner published nineteen novels, more than eighty short stories, and collections of poems and essays; he also wrote several film scripts to supplement his income. Collections of his short fiction include *Go Down, Moses* (1942); *Collected Stones* (1950), which won a National Book Award; and *Big Woods* (1955). Among his best-known novels are *The Sound and the Fury* (1929), *As I Lay Dying* (1930), *Sanctuary* (1931), *Light in August* (1932), and *Absalom, Absalom!* (1936). Faulkner was awarded the Nobel Prize in literature in 1949; *A Fable* (1954) and *The Reivers* (1962) each won the Pulitzer Prize for fiction.

Born to an aristocratic family, **Anne Finch, Countess of Winchilsea** [Anne Kingsmill] (1661–1720) went to the court of Charles II at age twenty-three as a maid of honor (attendant) to the duchess of York. She married one of the Gentlemen of the Bedchamber, with whom she was forcibly retired when James II was deposed. Two years later, her husband inherited a title and an estate in the Kentish countryside. From the safety of a private country home, Finch published a volume of poetry despite the social taboo against an aristocratic woman doing so. The Finch poem included in this anthology is the introduction to that volume, a vigorous protest against the neglect and subordination of women.

Born in Detroit, **Carolyn Forché** (b. 1950) attended Michigan State University and earned an M.F.A. from Bowling Green State University. She achieved immediate success as a writer, winning the Yale Younger Poets prize in 1976. Her work underwent a remarkable change following a year spent in El Salvador on a Guggenheim fellowship, when she worked with human rights activist Archbishop Oscar Humberto Romero and with Amnesty International. After seeing countless atrocities committed in Central America, Forché began writing what she calls "poetry of witness." The volume *The Country Between Us* (1981) stirred immediate controversy because of its overtly political topics and themes. "The Colonel," a prose poem in which the speaker conveys a horrific story with chilling flatness, is probably the most disturbing and memorable poem in the collection. Over the years Forché's quest to understand the individual's struggle with social upheaval and political turmoil has taken her from El Salvador to the occupied West Bank, to Lebanon, and to South Africa. She is currently a faculty member at George Mason University, in Virginia.

Widely regarded as the father of American literature, **Philip Freneau** (1752–1832) came from a wealthy New York family. At Princeton University, he was a roommate of James Madison. He was not only an activist, public writer, and the "poet of the Revolution" but also a private romantic poet who spent two years in the West Indies writing of the beauties of nature and learning navigation, after which he took to sea as a ship's captain. Some of his best poems, including "The Indian Burying Ground" and the beautiful lyric "The Wild Honey Suckle," which established him as an important American precursor of the Romantics, were written in stolen moments during the hectic 1780s. In 1801 he retired to a farm, worked on his poems, and wrote essays attacking the greed and selfishness of corrupt politicians.

Robert Frost (1847–1963) was born in San Francisco and lived there until he was eleven. When his father died, the family moved to Massachusetts, where Robert did well in school, especially in the classics, but later dropped out of both Dartmouth College and Harvard University. He went unrecognized as a poet until 1913, when he was first published in England, where he had moved with his wife and four children. Upon returning to the States, Frost quickly achieved success with more publications and became the most celebrated poet in mid-twentieth-century America. He held a teaching position at Amherst College and received many honorary degrees as well as an invitation to recite a poem at John F. Kennedy's inauguration. Although his work is principally associated with the life and landscape of New England, and although he was a poet of traditional verse forms and meters, he is also considered a quintessentially modern poet for his adherence to language as it is actually spoken, the psychological complexity of his portraits, and the degree to which his work is infused with layers of ambiguity and irony.

Athol Fugard (b. 1932) was born to an Afrikaans mother and an English father in Cape Province, South Africa, and grew up as part of a privileged white minority under the South Afri-can system of racial segregation known as apartheid. In the late 1950s, Fugard began to work as both an actor and a playwright in an integrated theater group. Because racial mixing was not permitted on stage at the time, the company encountered legal difficul-ties. Collaboration with black performers and writers, however, helped to develop the writer's talents and secure his place in the theatrical world. *The Blood Knot* (1961), which Fugard per-formed with Zakes Moake, is a contro-versial play about two brothers, one of whom is light enough to pass as white. Fugard also collaborated in improvisa-tional workshops with black actors and the writers John Kani and Win-ston Ntshona to create such plays as *Sizwe Bansi Is Dead* (1972) and *The Island* (1974). His solo writing efforts have been no less significant, including some of his best-known works—*A Lesson from Aloes* (1978), *"MASTER HAROLD" . . . and the boys* (1982), and *Valley Song* (1996, his first major post-apartheid play). Fugard's plays typically display the playwright's interest in so-cial and political issues, including the racial and social class injustices that have defined so much of South African life. But Fugard is able to make the po-litical highly personal, and it is that gift, more than his political awareness alone, that has made him a major voice in world theater.

Alice Fulton (b. 1952) was born and grew up in Troy, New York. Winner of many fellowships and awards, she is the author of five books of poetry and a collection of essays. She has taught at the University of California, Los An-geles; Ohio State University; the Uni-versity of North Carolina, Wilmington; and the University of Michigan. She was a member of the American dele-gation at the 1988 Chinese American

Writers' Conference, held in Beijing, Xian, Leshan, Wuhan, and Shanghai. Fulton currently teaches at Cornell University. "You Can't Rhumboogie in a Ball and Chain" is a **sestina** (see the Glossary). The poem's repetitive form is particularly interesting in light of the obsessive nature of its subject.

Richard Garcia (b. 1941) was born in San Francisco, a first-generation American (his mother was from Mexico, his father from Puerto Rico). While still in high school, Garcia had a poem published by City Lights in a Beat anthology. After publishing his first collection in 1972, however, he did not write poetry again for twelve years, until an unsolicited letter from Octavio Paz inspired him to resume. Since then Garcia's work has appeared widely in such literary magazines as the *Kenyon Review, Parnassus,* and the *Gettysburg Review,* as well as in two later collections, *The Flying Garcias* (1993) and *Rancho Notorious* (2001). He is also the author of the bilingual children's book *My Aunt Otilia's Spirits* (1987). Garcia has lived in Colorado, Mexico, and Israel, and now makes his home in Los Angeles, where he is poet-in-residence at Childrens Hospital.

Gabriel García Márquez (b. 1928) was born one of twelve children in a poor family in Aracataca, a small village in Colombia, and attended the University of Bogotá. He gave up studying law to pursue a career as a writer, working as a journalist and film critic for *El Espectador,* a Colombian newspaper. His first short novel, *La Hojarasca* (1955; translated as *Leaf Storm* in 1972) was followed by *One Hundred Years of Solitude* (1967), his most famous work. *The Autumn of the Patriarch* (1975) and *Love in the Time of Cholera* (1988) are

recent novels. A political activist, García Márquez moved to Mexico in 1954, to Barcelona, Spain, in 1973, and back to Mexico in the late 1970s. He was awarded the Nobel Prize in literature in 1982. The award cited him for novels and short stories "in which the fantastic and the realistic are combined in a richly composed world of imagination, reflecting a continent's life and conflicts."

Jack Gilbert (b. 1925) was born in Pittsburgh and educated there and in San Francisco. He toured fifteen countries in 1975 as a lecturer on American literature for the U.S. State Department. He has lived for extended periods in New York, San Francisco, Japan, and the Greek islands. His book *Views of Jeopardy* was the 1962 selection for the Yale Series of Younger Poets. Both it and *Monolithos* (1982) were nominated for the Pulitzer Prize. His work is characterized by a sparse, concrete, yet powerfully affecting style that the critic David St. John has called the "stoniest and most aesthetic Romanticism in American poetry." In his poetry Gilbert makes extensive use of myth, fascinated by the contemporaneity of ancient ideas and themes.

Shortly after **Charlotte Perkins Gilman** (1860–1935) was born in Hartford, Connecticut, her father left his family and provided only a small amount of support thereafter. Gilman studied at the Rhode Island School of Design and worked briefly as a commercial artist and teacher. This great-niece of Harriet Beecher Stowe became concerned at quite a young age with issues of social inequality and the circumscribed role of women. In 1884 she married Charles Stetson but left him and moved to California four years later after the birth of a child and a severe depression. Divorced, she married George Gilman, with whom she lived for thirty-five years. In 1935, afflicted by cancer, she took her own life. Charlotte Gilman wrote many influential books and articles about social problems, including *Women and Economics* (1898). From 1909 to 1917 she published her own journal. *The Yellow Wallpaper*, written about 1890, draws on her experience with mental illness and is praised for its insight and boldness.

Born in Newark, New Jersey, **Allen Ginsberg** (1926–1997) graduated from Columbia University, after a number of suspensions, in 1948. Several years later, he left for San Francisco to join other poets of the Beat movement. His poem "Howl," the most famous poem of the movement, was published in 1956 by Lawrence Ferlinghetti's City Lights Books; the publicity of the ensuing censorship trial brought the Beats to national attention. Ginsberg was co-founder with ANNE WALDMAN of the Jack Kerouac School of Disembodied Poetics at the Naropa Institute in Boulder, Colorado. In his later years he became a distinguished professor at Brooklyn College.

Born, raised, and educated in Iowa, **Susan Glaspell** (1882–1948) came to be associated with Massachusetts, where she and her husband, George Cram Cook, founded the Provincetown Players on Cape Cod. This small theater company was influential in giving a start to several serious playwrights, most notably Eugene O'Neill, and promoting realist dramas at a time when sentimental comedy and melodrama still dominated the stage. Glaspell began her writing career publishing short stories and novels, including

the critically acclaimed *Fidelity* (1915). Glaspell's first several plays, including *Trifles* (1916), were one acts, and with them she began her lifelong interest in writing about the lives and special circumstances of women. She went on to write and produce a number of full-length plays as well, among the best known being *The Inheritors* (1921) and *Alison's House* (1930), which was based loosely on the life of Emily Dickinson and won a Pulitzer Prize. Though some of Glaspell's work was lighthearted, much of it dealt with serious issues of the day. Respected in its own time, Glaspell's writing fell out of fashion until it was "rediscovered" by feminist scholars and critics in the 1960s.

Born in New York City, **Louise Glück** (b. 1943) was educated at Sarah Lawrence College and Columbia University. She has published numerous collections of poetry, including *The Triumph of Achilles* (1985), which received the National Book Critics Circle Award and the Poetry Society of America's Melville Kane Award; *Ararat* (1990), which received the Rebekah Johnson Bobbitt National Prize for Poetry; and *The Wild Iris* (1992), which received the Pulitzer Prize and the Poetry Society of America's William Carlos Williams Award. She has also published *Proofs and Theories: Essays on Poetry* (1994). Glück teaches at Williams College and lives in Cambridge, Massachusetts.

Ray González (b. 1952) received his M.F.A. in creative writing from Southwest Texas State University. He has published five books of poetry, including *The Heat of Arrivals* (winner of the 1997 Josephine Miles Book Award) and *Cabato Sentora* (1999). He is also the author of *Memory Fever: A Journey Beyond El Paso del Norte* (1993), a book of essays dealing with growing up in the Southwest, and the editor of twelve anthologies. He served as poetry editor for *The Bloomsbury Review* for eighteen years. In 1989 he was awarded the Colorado Governor's Award for Excellence in the Arts. He has taught at the University of Illinois, Chicago, and now teaches at the University of Minnesota.

One of the great Romantic poets, **George Gordon, Lord Byron** (1788–1824), is best known for his lighthearted and humorous verse, such as *Don Juan*. Born in London and raised in Scotland, he studied at Harrow and at Trinity College, Cambridge. He inherited the title of sixth baron Byron (with estate) at age ten. The last few years of his life were spent in Italy, but he died in Greece after joining the Greek forces in their war for independence.

Born in New York City, **Jorie Graham** (b. 1950) attended New York University as an undergraduate and received an M.F.A. from the University of Iowa Writers' Workshop. She is the author of eight collections of poetry, including *The Dream of the Unified Field: Selected Poems 1974–1994*, which won the 1996 Pulitzer Prize for poetry. She also has edited two anthologies, *Earth Took of Earth: 100 Great Poems of the English Language* (1996) and *The Best American Poetry 1990*. She has taught at the University of Iowa and is currently the Boylston Professor of Rhetoric and Oratory at Harvard University. Her combination of formal constraints and daring innovations, illustrated in "Reading Plato," has influenced many contemporary poets.

Thomas Gray (1716–1771) was born in London and educated at Eton and at Cambridge University, where he studied literature and history. When in November 1741 his father died, Gray moved with his mother and aunt to the village of Stoke Poges, in Buckinghamshire, where he wrote his first important English poems, "Ode on the Spring," "Ode on a Distant Prospect of Eton College," and "Hymn to Adversity," and began his masterpiece, "Elegy Written in a Country Churchyard," called the most famous and diversified of all graveyard poems. These poems solidified his reputation as one of the most important poets of the eighteenth century. In 1757 he was named poet laureate but refused the position. In 1762 he was rejected for the Regius Professorship of Modern History at Cambridge but was given the position in 1768 when the successful candidate was killed. A painfully shy and private person, he never delivered any lectures as a professor.

Born in New York City, **Marilyn Hacker** (b. 1942) is the author of nine books of poetry, including *Presentation Piece* (1974), the Lamont Poetry Selection of the Academy of American Poets and a National Book Award winner, and *Selected Poems, 1965–1990* (1994), which received the Poets' Prize. She was editor of the *Kenyon Review* from 1990 to 1994 and has received numerous honors and awards. She lives in New York City and Paris. Often labeled a neo-formalist, Hacker often handles traditional forms in fresh ways, as "Villanelle" illustrates.

Kimiko Hahn (b. 1955) was born in Mt. Kisco, New York, to two artists, a mother from Hawaii and a father from Wisconsin. Hahn majored in English and East Asian studies at the University of Iowa and received an M.A. in Japanese literature from Columbia University. She is the author of numerous books of poems, including *The Un-*

bearable Heart (1996), which received an American Book Award. In 1995 she wrote ten portraits of women for a two-hour HBO special titled *Ain't Nuthin' but a She-Thing*. She has taught at Parsons School of Design, the Poetry Project at St. Mark's Church, and Yale University. She lives in New York and is an associate professor in the English department at Queens College/CUNY.

Mark Halliday (b. 1949) earned his Ph.D. in English from Brandeis University. He has taught at Wellesley College, the University of Pennsylvania, Western Michigan University, Indiana University, and, since 1996, at Ohio University. He has published three books of poetry—*Little Star* (1987), which received a National Poetry Series Award; *Tasker Street* (1992), which won the Juniper Prize; and *Selfwolf* (1999); as well as two works of criticism. He often combines humor with serious matters. "Functional Poem" is a good example of his conveying irony in an offhanded tone.

Thomas Hardy (1840–1928) was born in a cottage in Higher Bockhampton, Dorset, near the regional market town of Dorchester in southwestern England. Apprenticed at age sixteen to an architect, he spent most of the next twenty years restoring old churches. Having always had an interest in literature, he started writing novels in his thirties, publishing more than a dozen, including *Tess of the D'Urbervilles* (1891) and *Jude the Obscure* (1895). In 1896 Hardy gave up prose and turned to poetry, writing verse until his death at age eighty-eight. He had a consistently bleak, even pessimistic, outlook on life. Many of his works stress the dark effects of "hap" (happenstance, coincidence) in the world, a central motif in "The Convergence of the Twain."

Born in Tulsa, Oklahoma, to a mother of Cherokee-French descent and a Creek father, **Joy Harjo** (b. 1951) moved to the Southwest and began writing poetry in her early twenties. She earned her B.A. from the University of New Mexico and her M.F.A. from the University of Iowa Writers' Workshop. Harjo has published several volumes of poetry, including *In Mad Love and War* (1990), which received an American Book Award and the Delmore Schwartz Memorial Award. She performs her poetry and plays saxophone with her band, Poetic Justice. She is professor of English at the University of New Mexico, Albuquerque. Of "She Had Some Horses" Harjo has said, "This is the poem I'm asked most about and the one I have the least to say about. I don't know where it came from."

Michael S. Harper (b. 1938) was born in Brooklyn and grew up surrounded by jazz. When his family moved to Los Angeles, he worked in several sectors ranging from the U.S. Postal Service to professional football. He attended the City College of Los Angeles; California State University, Los Angeles; and the University of Iowa Writers' Workshop. He has written more than ten books of poetry, including *Dear John, Dear Coltrane* (1970), nominated for the National Book Award, and edited or co-edited several collections of African American poetry. He is University Professor and professor of English at Brown University, where he has taught since 1970. He lives in Barrington, Rhode Island.

Robert Hass (b. 1941) was born in San Francisco. His books of poetry include *Field Guide* (1973), which was selected by STANLEY KUNITZ for the Yale Series of Younger Poets. He has also translated with Czeslaw Milosz several volumes of Milosz's poetry, including *Facing the River* (1995) and *Treatise on Poetry* (2001). He is the author or editor of several other collections of essays and translations, including *The Essential Haiku: Versions of Basho, Buson, and Issa* (1994) and *Twentieth Century Pleasures: Prose on Poetry* (1984). He served as Poet Laureate Consultant in Poetry at the Library of Congress from 1995 to 1997. He lives in California and teaches at the University of California, Berkeley. "Late Spring" shows Hass's quiet, penetrating way of looking at and responding to the outside world and its effects on the inner world of the observer.

Born in Salem, Massachusetts, into a family descended from the New England Puritans, **Nathaniel Hawthorne** (1804–1864) graduated from Bowdoin College, Maine, in 1825. For the next twelve years he lived in Salem in relative seclusion, reading, observing the New England landscape and people, and writing his first novel, *Fanshawe* (published anonymously in 1828), and the first series of *Twice-Told Tales* (1837). (The second series, published in 1842, was reviewed by Edgar Allan Poe and won some notice.) To support himself Hawthorne took a job in the Boston customhouse, resigning in 1841 to live at Brook Farm, a utopian community. The following year he left Brook Farm, married Sophia Peabody, and moved to Concord, Massachusetts, where his neighbors included Ralph Waldo Emerson and Henry David Thoreau. There he wrote the stories collected in *Mosses from an Old Manse* (1846). Returning to Salem, he took a position as a customs inspector and began full-time work on what was to become his most celebrated novel, *The*

Scarlet Letter (1850). The novels *The House of the Seven Gables* (1851) and *The Blithedale Romance* (1852), based on his Brook Farm experience, quickly followed. Also in 1852, he wrote a campaign biography of Franklin Pierce, a former college friend who, on becoming president, appointed Hawthorne U.S. consul at Liverpool. Hawthorne's subsequent travels in Europe contributed to the novel *The Marble Faun* (1860), his last major work.

Raised in a poor neighborhood in Detroit, **Robert Hayden** (1913–1980) had an emotionally tumultuous childhood. Because of impaired vision, he was unable to participate in sports and spent his time reading instead. He graduated from high school in 1932 and attended Detroit City College (later Wayne State University). His first book of poems, *Heart-Shape in the Dust*, was published in 1940. After working for newspapers and on other projects, he studied under W. H. AUDEN in the graduate creative writing program at the University of Michigan, later teaching at Fisk University and the University of Michigan. His poetry gained international recognition in the 1960s; he was awarded the grand prize for poetry at the First World Festival of Negro Arts in Dakar, Senegal, in 1966 for his book *Ballad of Remembrance*. In 1976 he became the first black American to be appointed as Consultant in Poetry at the Library of Congress.

Of Lebanese and Syrian heritage, **Samuel Hazo** (b. 1928) is a highly influential Arab American writer of verse, educator, and advocate on behalf of poetry. He is the author of numerous collections of poetry, fiction, and essays. He is founder, director, and president of the International Poetry Forum in Pittsburgh and McAnulty Distinguished Professor of English Emeritus at Duquesne University. A recipient of the 1986 Hazlett Memorial Award for Excellence in the Arts, in 1993 Hazo was chosen to be the first state poet of the Commonwealth of Pennsylvania, a position he still holds.

Raised on a small farm near Castledawson, County Derry, Northern Ireland, **Seamus Heaney** (b. 1939) was educated at St. Columb's College, a Catholic boarding school situated in the city of Derry, and then at Queen's University, Belfast. As a young English teacher in Belfast in the early 1960s, he joined a poetry workshop and began writing verse, subsequently becoming a major force in contemporary Irish literature. The author of many volumes of poetry and essays as well as at least one play, he is well-known at present for his best-selling verse translation of *Beowulf* (2000). He held the chair of professor of poetry at Oxford University from 1989 to 1994. A resident of Dublin since 1976, since 1981 Heaney has spent part of each year teaching at Harvard University. He was awarded the Nobel Prize in literature in 1995.

A poet, essayist, and translator, **Lyn Hejinian** (b. 1941) was born in the San Francisco Bay area and lives in Berkeley, California. She was educated at Harvard University and has traveled and lectured extensively in Russia and Europe. Author or coauthor of fourteen books of poetry, she is one of the leading **L-A-N-G-U-A-G-E Poets** (see the Glossary). She has also published autobiographical writing and, more recently, translations from the Russian of the works of Arkadii Dragomoschenko. From 1976 to 1984, Hejinian was editor of Tuumba Press, and since 1981

she has been the coeditor of *Poetics Journal.* She is also the codirector of Atelos, a literary project commissioning and publishing cross-genre works by poets. "A Mask of Anger" shows her interest in the potential language has for shaping consciousness.

Born in Oak Park, Illinois, **Ernest Hemingway** (1899–1961) led an active, vigorous life from childhood, summering in the wilds of northern Michigan with his physician father and boxing and playing football at school. His first job as a writer was as a reporter for the Kansas City *Star.* During World War I he served as an ambulance driver in Italy; severely wounded before he had turned nineteen, he was decorated by the Italian government. Later, while working in Paris as a correspondent for the Toronto *Star,* he met Gertrude Stein, Ezra Pound, F. Scott Fitzgerald, and other artists and writers who had a significant influence on his work. Hemingway's first book, *Three Stories and Ten Poems* (1923), was followed by the well-known story collection *In Our Time* (1924; rev. and enl. ed., 1925). His novel *The Sun Also Rises* (1926) brought acclaim as well as recognition of Hemingway as the spokesman for the "lost generation." *A Farewell to Arms* (1929), based on his wartime experiences in Italy, and *For Whom the Bell Tolls* (1940), drawn from his time as a correspondent during the civil war in Spain, established his enduring reputation. In World War II he served as a correspondent and received a Bronze Star. His frequent travels took him to Spain for the bullfights, on fishing trips to the Caribbean, and on big-game expeditions to the American West and to Africa. In his later years he suffered from declining physical health and severe depression, which led to his suicide at his home in Ketcham, Idaho. The fullest collection of his short stories, the Finca-Vigia edition, came out in 1991. Hemingway was awarded the Nobel Prize in literature in 1954.

The fifth son of an ancient and wealthy Welsh family, **George Herbert** (1593–1633) studied at Cambridge, graduating with honors, and was elected public orator of the university. He served in Parliament for two years, but after falling out of political favor he became rector of Bemerton, near Salisbury. Herbert was a model Anglican priest and an inspiring preacher. All his poetry, religious in nature, was published posthumously in 1633. "Easter-wings" is among the earliest of **concrete poems** (see the Glossary), and "The Pulley" is a fine example of **metaphysical wit** (see the Glossary).

Mary [Sidney] Herbert, Countess of Pembroke (1562–1621), was an important literary patron and writer of the Elizabethan period. In addition to doing editorial work and translations, she wrote a number of original poems. She also contributed 107 poetic renderings of psalms to a series of 150 begun by her brother Sir Philip Sidney, each written in a different stanzaic and metrical pattern. "Psalm 100 *Jubilate Deo*" is taken from that collection.

The son of a well-to-do London goldsmith, **Robert Herrick** (1591–1674) was apprenticed to his uncle (also a goldsmith), studied at Cambridge University, then lived for nine years in London, where he hobnobbed with a group of poets that included BEN JONSON. Under familial pressure to do something more "worthwhile," Herrick became an Anglican priest. He was given the parish of Dean Prior, Devonshire—a rural area that he hated at

first—and there he quietly wrote poems about imagined mistresses and pagan rites (as in his well-known "Corinna's Going A-Maying") and deft but devout religious verse. When he returned to London in 1648, having been ejected from his pulpit by the Puritan revolution, he published his poetry in a volume with two titles, *Hesperides* for the secular poems and *Noble Numbers* for those with sacred subjects. Probably his most famous poem is "To the Virgins, to Make Much of Time," a short lyric on the traditional **carpe diem** theme (see the Glossary).

Raised in Michigan, **Conrad Hilberry** (b. 1928) earned his B.A. at Oberlin College and his M.A. and Ph.D. at the University of Wisconsin. He taught at Kalamazoo College until his recent retirement. Hilberry has published several collections of poetry and has been poetry editor of *Passages North* and of the anthology *Poems from the Third Coast* (1976). He has been praised for his mastery of tone, through which he achieves subtleties of implication, as is evidenced in "Player Piano."

Geoffrey Hill (1932–1999) is a major presence in contemporary British poetry. Born in Bromsgrove, Worcestershire, he attended the local grammar school there before going on to study English language and literature at Keble College, Oxford. He taught at Leeds University from 1954 to 1980, when he moved to Emmanuel College, Cambridge. In 1988 he became University Professor and a professor of literature and religion at Boston University.

Jane Hirshfield (b. 1953) is the author of five books of poetry, editor and co-translator of two anthologies of poetry by women, and author of the collection of essays *Nine Gates: Entering the*

Mind of Poetry (1997). A graduate of Princeton University, she studied Soto Zen from 1974 to 1982, including three years of monastic practice, the influence of which is apparent in her work. "For me, poetry, like Zen practice, is a path toward deeper and more life. There are ways to wake up into the actual texture of one's own existence, to widen it, to deepen and broaden it, and poetry is one of the things that does that." Hirshfield teaches at Bennington College and lives in the San Francisco Bay area.

A poet, novelist, essayist, playwright, and activist widely considered to be one of the most influential and provocative Native American figures in the contemporary American literary landscape, **Linda Hogan** (b. 1947) was born in Denver. Her father, of the Chickasaw Nation, was in the army and was transferred frequently; Hogan spent her childhood in various locations but considers Oklahoma to be her true home. In her late twenties, while working with orthopedically handicapped children, she began writing during her lunch hours, although she had no previous experience as a writer and little experience reading literature. She pursued her writing, commuting to the University of Colorado, Colorado Springs, for her undergraduate degree, and earned an M.A. in English and creative writing at the University of Colorado, Boulder, in 1978. Hogan has published more than a dozen books and received numerous awards for her work. She teaches creative writing at the University of Colorado.

Born in Volcano, Hawaii, **Garrett Kaoru Hongo** (b. 1951) grew up on Oahu and in Los Angeles, and did graduate work in Japanese language and literature at the University of Michigan. Hongo has published several books of poetry, including *The River of Heaven* (1988), the Lamont Poetry Selection of the Academy of American Poets and a finalist for the Pulitzer Prize. He has also written *Volcano: A Memoir of Hawai'i* (1995) and edited collections of Asian American verse. He currently teaches at the University of Oregon, Eugene, where he directed the creative writing program from 1989 to 1993. His work often comments through rich textures and sensuous detail on conditions endured by Japanese Americans during World War II and thereafter.

Born in London, **Gerard Manley Hopkins** (1844–1889) was the eldest of eight children. His father was a ship insurer who also wrote a book of poetry. Hopkins studied at Balliol College, Oxford, and, after converting to Catholicism, taught in a school in Birmingham. In 1868 he became a Jesuit and burned all of his early poetry, considering it "secular" and worthless. He worked as a priest and teacher in working-class London, Glasgow, and Merseyside, and later as a professor of classics at University College, Dublin. Hopkins went on to write many poems on spiritual themes but published little during his lifetime. His poems, which convey a spiritual sensuality, celebrating the wonder of nature both in their language and in their rhythms, which Hopkins called "sprung rhythm" (see **accentual meter** in the Glossary), were not widely known until they were published by his friend Robert Bridges in 1918.

A. E. Housman (1859–1936) was born in Fockbury, Worcestershire. A promising student at Oxford University, he failed his final exams (because of emotional turmoil, possibly caused by his suppressed homosexual love for a fellow student) and spent the next ten years feverishly studying and writing scholarly articles while working as a clerk at the patent office. Housman was rewarded with the chair of Latin at University College, London, and later at Cambridge University. His poetry like his scholarship was meticulous, impersonal in tone, and limited in output, consisting of two slender volumes—*A Shropshire Lad* (1896) and *Last Poems* (1922)—published during his lifetime and a small book titled *More Poems* (1936) that appeared after his death. His poems often take up the theme of doomed youths acting out their brief lives in the context of agricultural communities and activities, especially the English countryside and traditions that the poet loved.

Born in Boston to Irish American parents, **Susan Howe** (b. 1937) studied painting at the School of the Museum of Fine Arts, Boston. Her painting moved toward collage and then toward performance art, which eventually led her to poetry. She has been an actor and a stage manager at Dublin's Gate Theatre. She is the author of several books of poems, including *Pierce-Arrow* (1999), and two volumes of criticism: *My Emily Dickinson* (1985) and *The Birth-Mark: Unsettling the Wilderness in American Literary History* (1993), named an International Book of the Year by the *Times Literary Supplement*. Since 1989 she has been a professor of English at the State University of New York, Buffalo. She lives in Guilford, Connecticut.

Born in Joplin, Missouri, **Langston Hughes** (1902–1967) grew up in Lincoln, Illinois, and Cleveland, Ohio. He began writing poetry during his high school years. After attending Columbia University for one year, he held odd jobs as an assistant cook, a launderer, and a busboy and traveled to Africa and Europe working as a seaman. In 1924 he moved to Harlem. Hughes's first book of poetry, *The Weary Blues*, was published in 1926. He finished his college education at Lincoln University in Pennsylvania three years later. He wrote novels, short stories, plays, songs, children's books, essays, and memoirs as well as poetry, and is also known for his engagement with the world of jazz and the influence it had on his writing. His life and work were enormously important in shaping the artistic contributions of the Harlem Renaissance of the 1920s.

Henrik Ibsen (1828–1906) was born and raised in Skien, Norway, and he is still principally associated with that country, though he also lived for an extended period in Italy, where he did much of his writing. His earliest literary successes were the poetic plays *Brand* (1865) and *Peer Gynt* (1867), which were intended as closet dramas, though both eventually were performed on stage. His real breakthrough, though, came in the late 1870s, when he began to write realistic dramas that are sometimes called *problem plays* because they explore social issues and problems. Some of the problems Ibsen chose to depict, however, were too controversial for the theater of his day—the subjugation of women in marriage in *A Doll House* (1879), venereal disease and incest in *Ghosts* (1881), and the will of an individual against social and political pressure in *An Enemy of the People* (1882). Their subject matter led some critics in Norway and elsewhere to protest against public performances of these works. But despite their controversial nature, or perhaps because of it, these plays secured Ibsen's reputation as one of the most influential playwrights of the late nineteenth century. Important later works by Ibsen include *The Wild Duck* (1884), *Hedda Gabler* (1890), and *The Master Builder* (1892). Although many of his dramas resemble the tightly structured, plot-driven theatrical entity known as the well-made play, Ibsen's work contains subtleties of characterization and theme that raise it above commonplace theatrical experience.

Born in San Francisco, California, and raised in Rochester, New York, **Shirley Jackson** (1919–1965) was educated at the University of Rochester and Syracuse University, where she founded and edited the campus literary magazine. After graduation she married the author and literary critic Stanley Edgar Hyman and settled in North Bennington, Vermont. She is best known for her stories and novels of Gothic horror and the occult. Among her novels are *Hangasman* (1949), *The Bird's Nest* (1954), *The Haunting of Hill House* (1959), and *We Have Always Lived in the Castle* (1962). Her short stories are collected in *The Lottery* (1949), *The Magic of Shirley Jackson* (1966), and *Come Along with Me* (1968). In 1997, *Just an Ordinary Day: The Uncollected Stories of Shirley Jackson* was published.

Born in Nashville, Tennessee, **Randall Jarrell** (1914–1965) earned his B.A. and M.A. at Vanderbilt University. From 1937 to 1939 he taught at Kenyon College, where he met JOHN CROWE RANSOM and ROBERT LOWELL, and afterward taught at the University of Texas. He served in the air force during World War II. Jarrell's reputation as a poet was established in 1945 with the publication of his second book, *Little Friend, Little Friend*, which documents the in-

tense fears and moral struggles of young soldiers. Other volumes followed, all characterized by great technical skill, empathy, and deep sensitivity. Following the war, Jarrell began teaching at the University of North Carolina, Greensboro, and remained there, except for occasional leaves of absence to teach elsewhere, until his death. Besides poetry, he wrote a satirical novel, several children's books, numerous poetry reviews — collected in *Poetry and the Age* (1953) — and a translation of Goethe's *Faust*.

Robinson Jeffers (1887–1962) was born in Pittsburgh, where his father was a professor of Old Testament literature and biblical history at Western Theology Seminary. He began to learn Greek from his father at the age of five, and his early lessons were followed by travel in Europe, which included schooling in Zurich, Leipzig, and Geneva. He moved with his family to southern California in 1903. After graduating from Occidental College in 1906 and pursuing graduate studies in medicine and forestry, Jeffers decided to concentrate on poetry. In 1914 he settled in Carmel, California, and built a stone cottage and a forty-foot stone tower on land overlooking Carmel Bay and facing Point Lobos, where he lived the rest of his life (Tor House and Hawk Tower are open to the public — see www.torhouse.org). Much of Jeffers's verse celebrates the awesome beauty of the Carmel–Big Sur region, often contrasting the intense, rugged beauty of the landscape with the degraded and introverted condition of modern man.

Born in South Berwick, Maine, **Sarah Orne Jewett** (1849–1909) often accompanied her father, a physician, on his medical visits, where she learned much about the people of rural Maine, the subjects of her stories. She also read widely. When she was eighteen, she published her first story; at twenty a story of hers was accepted by *Atlantic Monthly*. Two of her most praised works are *A White Heron and Other Stories* (1886) and *The Country of the Pointed Firs* (1896), a series of related episodes about a young woman's visit to a Maine seacoast town.

Richard Jones (b. 1953) was born in London, where his father was serving in the U.S. Air Force, and studied at the University of Virginia. Jones is the author of several books of poems, including *The Blessing: New and Selected Poems*, which received the Midland Authors Award for Poetry for 2000. His most recent publication, *Body and Soul*, on compact disc, discusses the art of poetry. He has also published two critical anthologies and has been the editor of the literary journal *Poetry East* since 1979. He has taught at Piedmont College and the University of Virginia and currently is professor of English and director of the creative writing program at DePaul University in Chicago.

Born in London, **Ben Jonson** (1572–1637) was the stepson of a bricklayer (his father died before he was born). He attended Westminster School and then joined the army. Jonson later worked as an actor and was the author of such comedies as *Everyman in His Humor* (in which SHAKESPEARE acted the lead), *Volpone*, and *The Alchemist*. He wrote clear, elegant, "classical" poetry that contrasted with the intricate, subtle, "metaphysical" poetry of his contemporaries JOHN DONNE and GEORGE HERBERT. He was named poet laureate and was the idol of a generation of English writers, who dubbed themselves the Sons of Ben.

Born in London to Caribbean parents, **Allison Joseph** (b. 1967) grew up in Toronto and the Bronx. She earned her B.A. from Kenyon College and her M.F.A. from Indiana University. She is the author of three collections of poetry: *What Keeps Us Here* (winner of Ampersand Press's 1992 Women Poets Series Competition and the John C. Zacharis First Book Award), *Soul Train* (1997), and *In Every Seam* (1997). Her poems are often attuned to the experiences of women and minorities. She formerly taught at the University of Arkansas and currently is an associate professor at Southern Illinois University, Carbondale, where she is editor of the *Crab Orchard Review*.

Born in Dublin, Ireland, **James Joyce** (1882–1941) was educated at Jesuit schools in preparation for the priesthood. But at an early age he abandoned Catholicism and in 1904 left Dublin for what he felt would be the broader horizons of continental Europe. Living in Paris, Zurich, and Trieste over the next twenty-five years, he tried to support himself and his family by teaching languages and singing. In 1912 he returned to Dublin briefly to arrange for the publication of his short stories. Because of the printers' fear of censorship or libel suits, the edition was burned, and *Dubliners* did not appear until 1914 in England. During World War I Joyce lived in Zurich, where he wrote *Portrait of the Artist As a Young Man* (1916), a partly autobiographical account of his adolescent years that introduced some of the experimental techniques found in his later novels. About this time Joyce fell victim to glaucoma; for the rest of his life he suffered periods of intense pain and near blindness. His masterpiece, the novel *Ulysses* (1922), known for its "stream of consciousness" style, was written and published in periodicals between 1914 and 1921. Book publication was delayed because of obscenity charges. *Ulysses* finally was issued by Shakespeare & Company, a Paris bookstore owned and operated by Sylvia Beach, an American expatriate; U.S. publication was banned until 1933. *Finnegans Wake* (1939), an equally experimental novel, took seventeen years to write. Because of the controversy surrounding his work, Joyce earned little in royalties and often had to rely on friends for support. He died after surgery for a perforated ulcer in Zurich.

Born in Prague and raised in Bohemia the son of middle-class German-Jewish parents, **Franz Kafka** (1883–1924) studied law at the German University of Prague. After winning his degree in 1906, he was employed in the workmen's compensation division of the Austrian government. Because he wrote very slowly, he could not earn a living as a writer. At the time of his death he had published little and asked his friend Max Brod to burn his incomplete manuscripts. Brod ignored this request and arranged posthumous publication of Kafka's major long works, *The Trial* (1925), *The Castle* (1926), and *Amerika* (1927), as well as of a large number of his stories. Important stories published during his lifetime include "The Judgment" (1913), "The Metamorphosis" (1915), and "A Hunger Artist" (1924). Kafka's fiction is known for its gripping portrayals of individual helplessness before political, judicial, and paternal authority and power.

John Keats (1795–1821) was born in London. His father, a worker at a livery stable who married his employer's daughter and inherited the business, was killed by a fall from a horse when Keats was eight. When his mother died of tuberculosis six years later, Keats

and his siblings were entrusted to the care of a guardian, a practical-minded man who took Keats out of school at fifteen and apprenticed him to a doctor. But as soon as he qualified for medical practice, in 1815, Keats abandoned medicine for poetry, which he had begun writing two years earlier. In 1818, the year he himself contracted tuberculosis, he also fell madly in love with a pretty, vivacious young woman named Fanny Brawne whom he could not marry because of his poverty, illness, and devotion to poetry. In the midst of such stress and emotional turmoil, his masterpieces poured out, between January and September 1819: the great odes, a number of sonnets, and several longer lyric poems. In February 1820, his health failed rapidly; he went to Italy in the autumn, in the hope that the warmer climate would improve his health, and died there on February 23, 1821. His poems are rich with sensuous, lyrical beauty and emotional resonance, reflecting both his delight in life as well as his awareness of life's brevity and difficulty.

Born in Ann Arbor, Michigan, **Jane Kenyon** (1947–1995) grew up in the Midwest. She earned her B.A. and M.A. from the University of Michigan. During her lifetime Kenyon published four books of poetry and also translated the work of Anna Akhmatova. Two additional volumes of Kenyon's work have been published posthumously. A few months before her death in April 1995 from leukemia, she was named poet laureate of New Hampshire.

Born in St. Johns, Antigua, and raised by devoted parents, **Jamaica Kincaid** (b. 1949) entered college in the United States but withdrew to write. After her stories appeared in notable publications, she took a staff position on *The*

New Yorker. Her first book, a story collection entitled *At the Bottom of the River* (1984), won a major award from the American Academy and Institute of Arts and Letters. *Annie John* (1985), an interrelated collection, further explored life in the British West Indies as experienced by a young girl. Kincaid now lives in the United States and continues to write about her homeland in works including *A Small Place* (1988), *Lucy* (1990), *Autobiography of My Mother* (1996), and *My Brother* (1997).

Born in Providence, Rhode Island, **Galway Kinnell** (b. 1927) attended Princeton University and the University of Rochester. He served in the U.S. Navy and then visited Paris on a Fulbright fellowship. Returning to the United States he worked for the Congress on Racial Equality and then traveled widely in the Middle East and Europe. He has taught in France, Australia, and Iran as well as at numerous colleges and universities in the United States. He has published many books of poetry, including *Selected Poems* (1980), for which he received both the Pulitzer Prize and the National Book Award. He has also published translations of works by Yves Bonnefoy, Yvanne Goll, François Villon, and Rainer Maria Rilke. He divides his time between Vermont and New York City, where he is the Erich Maria Remarque Professor of Creative Writing at New York University.

Etheridge Knight (1931–1991) was born in Corinth, Mississippi. He dropped out of school at age sixteen and served in the U.S. Army in Korea from 1947 to 1951, returning with a shrapnel wound that caused him to fall deeper into a drug addiction that had begun during his service. In 1960 he was arrested for robbery and sentenced to eight years in an Indiana state prison. During this time he began writing poetry. His first book, *Poems from Prison* (1968), was published one year before his release. The book was a success, and Knight joined other poets in what came to be called the Black Arts Movement, the aesthetic and spiritual sister of the Black Power concept. He went on to write several more books of poetry and receive many prestigious honors and awards. In 1990 he earned a B.A. in American poetry and criminal justice from Martin Center University in Indianapolis.

Born in Cincinnati, after service in World War II **Kenneth Koch** (1925–2002) received his B.A. from Harvard University and his Ph.D. from Columbia University. As a young poet, Koch was known for his association with the New York School of poetry, a cosmopolitan movement influenced by the Beats, French surrealism, and European avant-gardism in general. In addition to many books of poetry, including *One Train* and *On the Great Atlantic Rainway: Selected Poems, 1950–1988* (both 1994), which together won the Bollingen Prize in 1995, and *New Addresses* (2000), a finalist for the National Book Award, Koch wrote plays, a novel, a libretto, criticism, and several influential books on teaching creative writing to children, including *Wishes, Lies, and Dreams* (1970) and *Rose, Where Did You Get That Red?* (1973). He lived in New York City, where he was professor of English at Columbia University.

Born and raised in Bogalusa, Louisiana, **Yusef Komunyakaa** (b. 1947) earned degrees at the University of Colorado, Colorado State University, and the University of California, Irvine. His numerous books of poems include *Neon Vernacular: New and Selected Poems, 1977–1989* (1994), for which he received the Pulitzer Prize and the Kingsley Tufts Poetry Award, and *Thieves of Paradise* (1998), which was a finalist for the National Book Critics Circle Award. Other publications include *Blues Notes: Essays, Interviews & Commentaries* (2000), *The Jazz Poetry Anthology* (co-edited with J. A. Sascha Feinstein, 1991), and *The Insomnia of Fire* by Nguyen Quang Thieu (co-translated with Martha Collins, 1995). He is a professor in the Council of Humanities and the creative writing program at Princeton University. He lives in New York City.

Born in Philadelphia, **Maxine Kumin** (b. 1925) received her B.A. and M.A. from Radcliffe College. She has published several books of poetry, including *Up Country: Poems of New England* (1972), for which she received the Pulitzer Prize. She is also the author of a memoir, *Inside the Halo and Beyond: The Anatomy of a Recovery* (2000); four novels; a collection of short stories; more than twenty children's books; and four books of essays. She has taught at the University of Massachusetts, Columbia University, Brandeis University, and Princeton University. She has served as Consultant in Poetry to the Library of Congress and as poet laureate of New Hampshire, where she lives.

Born in Worcester, Massachusetts, **Stanley Kunitz** (b. 1905) earned his B.A. and M.A. at Harvard University. His first two books of poetry attracted little attention, but after service in World War II he continued to write and achieved great success and recognition. Among his many books of poetry are *Selected Poems, 1928–1958*, which won the Pulitzer Prize for 1959,

and *Passing Through: The Later Poems, New and Selected* (1995), which won the National Book Award. In addition to publishing several translations, he edited the Yale Series of Younger Poets from 1969 to 1977 and is editor of *The Essential Blake* (1987) and *Poems of John Keats* (1964). (Kunitz' work has been called a contemporary extension of the vision of JOHN KEATS.) In 2000 he was named Poet Laureate Consultant in Poetry at the Library of Congress. He taught for many years in the graduate writing program at Columbia University. He lives in New York City and Provincetown, Massachusetts.

Born into a working-class family in Coventry, England, **Philip Larkin** (1922–1985) received a scholarship to attend Oxford University. With his second volume of poetry, *The Less Deceived* (1955), Larkin became the preeminent poet of his generation and a leading voice of what came to be called "The Movement," a group of young English writers who rejected the prevailing fashion for neo-Romantic writing exemplified by W. B. YEATS and DYLAN THOMAS. Like THOMAS HARDY, a major influence on his work, Larkin focused on intense personal emotion but strictly avoided sentimentality or self-pity. In addition to being a poet, Larkin was a highly respected jazz critic. He worked as a librarian in the provincial city of Hull, where he died in 1985.

Born David Herbert Lawrence in Nottinghamshire, England, the son of a coal miner and a mother who had high ambitions for her son, **D. H. Lawrence** (1885–1930) spent his early years in poverty. After graduating from University College in Nottingham, he worked as a schoolmaster in a London suburb and wrote fiction and poetry that introduced the themes of nature and the unconscious that pervaded his later work. His short stories began to be published in 1909. After his first novel, *The White Peacock* (1911), was published with the help of the writer Ford Madox Ford, Lawrence was forced by illness to return to Nottingham, where he fell in love with Frieda von Richthofen Weekley, the German wife of a professor at the college. The two eloped to continental Europe and subsequently married. They then spent the years of World War I in England where, because of Frieda's German origins and opposition to the war, they were suspected of being spies. They traveled widely and lived in Ceylon, Australia, the United States, Italy, Tahiti, Mexico, and France. In London in 1929 police raided an exhibition of Lawrence's paintings; pronouncing them obscene, authorities confiscated many of them. Three of Lawrence's novels were also suppressed. The most famous of these was *Lady Chatterley's Lover* (1928), privately printed in Italy and banned, because of its explicit depiction of loving sexuality, until 1959 in the United States and until 1960 in England. A victim of tuberculosis for many years, Lawrence succumbed to that disease at the age of forty-four. Among his other well-known novels are *Sons and Lovers* (1913), *The Rainbow* (1915), and *Women in Love* (1921). Lawrence is also widely acclaimed for his short stories, poetry, travel writing, and literary commentary.

Li-Young Lee (b. 1957) was born in Jakarta, Indonesia, to Chinese parents. His father, who had been personal physician to Mao Tse-tung, relocated his family to Indonesia, where he helped found Gamaliel University. But in 1959 the Lee family fled that country to escape anti-Chinese sentiment, settling in the United States in 1964. Lee studied at the University of Pittsburgh, the University of Arizona, and the Brockport campus of the State University of New York. He has taught at several universities, including Northwestern University and the University of Iowa. In addition to several books of poetry, he has published a prose memoir, *The Winged Seed* (1995). In his poems one often senses a profound sense of exile, the influence of his father's presence, and a rich, spiritual sensuality.

Denise Levertov (1923–1997) was born in Ilford, Essex. Her mother was Welsh and her father was a Russian Jew who had become an Anglican priest. Educated at home, Levertov said she decided to become a writer at the age of five. Her first book, *The Double Image* (1946), brought her recognition as one of a group of poets dubbed the "New Romantics"—her poems often blend objective observation with the sensibility of a spiritual searcher. Having moved to the United States after marrying the American writer Mitchell Goodman, she turned to free-verse poetry and with her first American book, *Here and Now* (1956), became an important voice in the American avant-garde. In the 1960s, she became involved in the movement protesting the Vietnam War. Levertov went on to publish more than twenty collections of poetry, four books of prose, and three volumes of poetry in translation. From 1982 to 1993, she taught at Stanford University. She spent the last decade of her life in Seattle.

Born in Detroit, **Philip Levine** (b. 1928) received his degrees from Wayne State University and the University of Iowa.

He is the author of many books of poetry, including *The Simple Truth* (1994), which won the Pulitzer Prize. He has also published a collection of essays, edited *The Essential Keats* (1987), and co-edited and translated two books of poetry by the Spanish poet Gloria Fuertes and the Mexican poet Jamie Sabines. He lives in New York City and Fresno, California, and teaches at New York University.

Raised on a farm near Fresno, California, **Larry Levis** (1946–1996) earned his B.A. from Fresno State College (now California State University), an M.A. from Syracuse University, and a Ph.D. from the University of Iowa. He published six collections of poetry—several of which received major awards—and a collection of short fiction. He taught at the University of Missouri, the University of Utah, and Virginia Commonwealth University. Levis died of a heart attack at the age of forty-nine. PHILIP LEVINE wrote that he had years earlier recognized Levis as "the most gifted and determined young poet I have ever had the good fortune to have in one of my classes."

Timothy Liu (b. 1965) was born in San Jose, California, to parents who had emigrated from the Chinese mainland. He studied at Brigham Young University, the University of Houston, and the University of Massachusetts, Amherst. He is the author of several books of poetry, including *Vox Angelica*, winner of the 1992 Norma Farber First Book Award from the Poetry Society of America, and the editor of *Word of Mouth: An Anthology of Gay American Poetry* (2000). He is an assistant professor at William Paterson University and lives in Hoboken, New Jersey.

Born in New York City to West Indian parents, **Audre Lorde** (1934–1992) grew up in Manhattan and attended Roman Catholic schools. While she was still in high school, her first poem appeared in *Seventeen* magazine. She earned her B.A. from Hunter College in New York City and her M.A. in library science from Columbia University. In 1968 she left her job as head librarian at the University of New York to become a lecturer and creative writer. She accepted a poet-in-residence position at Tougaloo College in Mississippi, where she discovered a love of teaching, published her first volume of poetry, *The First Cities* (1968), and met her long-term partner, Frances Clayton. Many volumes of poetry followed, several winning major awards. She also published four volumes of prose, among them *The Cancer Journals* (1980), which chronicled her struggles with cancer, and *A Burst of Light* (1988), which won a National Book Award. In the 1980s, Lorde and writer Barbara Smith founded Kitchen Table: Women of Color Press. She was also a founding member of Sisters in Support of Sisters in South Africa, an organization that worked to raise awareness about women under apartheid. She was the poet laureate of New York from 1991 to 1992.

Born into a prominent family in Kent, England, **Richard Lovelace** (1618–1658) went to Oxford, where his dashing appearance and wit made him a social and literary favorite. He fought in the English civil war on the Royalist side and was imprisoned and then exiled. Later he fought in France against the Spanish and was again imprisoned on his return to England. After his release he spent ten years in poverty and isolation before his death. He was a leader of the "Cavalier poets," followers of King Charles I who were soldiers and courtiers but who also wrote well-crafted, light-hearted lyric poetry. "To Lucasta, Going to the Wars" is an excellent example of the type.

Born in Boston into a prominent New England family, **Robert Lowell** (1917–1977) attended Harvard University and then Kenyon College, where he studied under JOHN CROWE RANSOM. At Louisiana State University he studied with Robert Penn Warren and Cleanth Brooks as well as Allen Tate. He was always politically active—a conscientious objector during World War II and a Vietnam War protestor—and suffered from manic depression. Lowell's reputation was established early: his second book, *Lord Weary's Castle*, was awarded the Pulitzer Prize for poetry in 1947. In the mid-1950s he began to write more directly from personal experience and loosened his adherence to traditional meter and form. The result was a watershed collection of the "confessional" school, *Life Studies* (1959), which changed the landscape of modern poetry, much as T. S. ELIOT'S *The Waste Land* had done three decades earlier. He died suddenly from a heart attack at age sixty.

Christopher Marlowe (1564–1593) was born in Canterbury the same year as WILLIAM SHAKESPEARE. The son of a shoemaker, he needed the help of scholarships to attend King's School, Canterbury, and Corpus Christi College, Cambridge. He was involved in secret political missions for the government. He was one of the most brilliant writers of his generation in narrative poetry, lyric poetry, and drama (his best-known play is *Doctor Faustus*). He died after being stabbed in a bar fight, reportedly over his bill, at the age of twenty-nine. "The Passionate Shepherd to His Love" is among the most famous of Elizabethan songs.

Born in Hull, Yorkshire, **Andrew Marvell** (1621–1678) was educated at Trinity College, Cambridge. After traveling in Europe, he worked as a tutor and in a government office (as assistant to JOHN MILTON) and later became a member of Parliament for Hull. Marvell was known in his lifetime as a writer of rough satires in verse and prose. His "serious" poetry, like "To His Coy Mistress," a famous exploration of the **carpe diem** theme, was not published until after his death.

Born in Normandy, France, **Guy de Maupassant** (1850–1893) experienced trouble at home, particularly with his stockbroker father, and at school. After serving in the army during the Franco-Prussian War (1870–1871), he studied with Gustave Flaubert for seven years and made writing his career. Although he also wrote poems, travel books, and several novel-length stories, Maupassant is primarily remembered for his more than 300 short stories, written in slightly more than ten years. His naturalistic and ironic treatment of human weaknesses in tightly structured stories won him a lasting place in literature. Maupassant died of syphilis at age forty-three.

Heather McHugh (b. 1948) was born to Canadian parents in San Diego and grew up in Virginia. She is a graduate of Radcliffe College and the University of Denver. McHugh has published numerous books of poetry, a book of prose, and four books of translations. She teaches as a core faculty member in the M.F.A. Program for Writers at Warren Wilson College and as Milliman Writer-in-Residence at the University of Washington, Seattle. She has been a visiting professor at the University of Iowa Writers' Workshop and has held chairs at the University of California, Berkeley; the University of Alabama; and the University of Cincinnati.

The son of poor farm workers, **Claude McKay** (1890–1948) was born in Sunny Ville, Jamaica. He was educated by his older brother, who possessed a library of English novels, poetry, and scientific texts. At age twenty, McKay published a book of verse called *Songs of Jamaica*, recording his impressions of black life in Jamaica in dialect. In 1912 he traveled to the United States to attend Tuskegee Institute. He soon left to study agriculture at Kansas State University. In 1914 he moved to Harlem and became an influential member of the Harlem Renaissance. After committing himself to communism and traveling to Moscow in 1922, he lived for some time in Europe and Morocco, writing fiction. McKay later repudiated communism, converted to Roman Catholicism, and returned to the United States. He published several books of poetry as well as an autobiography, *A Long Way from Home* (1937). He wrote a number of sonnets protesting the injustices of black life in the United States, "America" among them, which are of interest for the way they use the most Anglo of forms to contain and intensify what the poem's language is saying.

Born in New York City, the second son of well-established, affluent parents,

Herman Melville (1819–1891) lived comfortably until he was eleven, when his father went bankrupt and moved the family to Albany. After his father's death in 1832, Melville left school to work. In 1839 he sailed as a merchant seaman to Liverpool, and in 1841 as a whaleman to the South Pacific. On his return to the United States in 1844, he began immediately to write about his sea adventures. He wrote at an extraordinary pace, producing seven novels in six years, beginning with *Typee* (1846) and *Omoo* (1847), about the South Seas, and including *Moby-Dick* (1851) and *Pierre* (1852). The early novels were well-received, but *Moby-Dick*, now recognized as a masterpiece, was misunderstood and *Pierre* was considered a total failure. During this period Melville had married Elizabeth Shaw, daughter of the chief justice of Massachusetts; in 1850 the couple bought a farm near Pittsfield, Massachusetts, where the writer became close friends with Nathaniel Hawthorne. Despite serious financial problems and a slight nervous breakdown, Melville published stories and sketches in magazines— several of the best, including "Bartleby, the Scrivener" and "Benito Cereno," were collected in *The Piazza Tales* (1856)—as well as the novels *Israel Potter* (1855) and *The Confidence Man* (1857) before turning almost exclusively to poetry for thirty years. Needing money, he sold the farm and worked as a customs inspector in New York City for twenty years; when his wife received a small inheritance he was able to retire. In his final years he wrote the novella *Billy Budd*, which was not published until 1924, thirty-three years after he died in poverty and obscurity. Many of his unpublished stories and journals were also published posthumously.

Born in New York City, **James Merrill** (1926–1995) was the son of Charles Merrill, co-founder of Merrill Lynch. At the age of eight, James was already writing poems, and at age sixteen, while in prep school, his father had a collection of them privately printed under the title *Jim's Book*. James received his B.A. from Amherst College, after service in World War II interrupted his education. He taught for a year at Bard College and spent two and a half years traveling in Europe. In 1955 he moved to the small coastal town of Stonington, Connecticut, with his companion David Jackson. He published a memoir and two novels in addition to more than two dozen books of poetry, for which he won numerous prestigious awards, including the Pulitzer Prize for *Divine Comedies* (1976), which was composed with the help of a Ouija board. Merrill is recognized as one of the most complex and erudite of modern poets.

Born in New York City, **W. S. Merwin** (b. 1927) lived in New Jersey and Pennsylvania during his pre-college years. He studied creative writing and foreign languages at Princeton University and became a translator, living mostly in England and France until 1968, when he returned to the United States. He is the author of many books of poetry, including *A Mask for Janus* (1952), selected by W. H. AUDEN for the Yale Series of Younger Poets, and *Carrier of Ladders* (1970), which received the Pulitzer Prize. He has also published nearly twenty books of translation, including *Dante's Purgatorio* (2000); numerous plays; and four books of prose, including *The Lost Upland* (1992), his memoir of life in the south of France. He lives in Hawaii and is active in environmental movements.

Born in Rockland, Maine, **Edna St. Vincent Millay** (1892–1950) was encouraged to write from an early age by her mother. In 1912, at her mother's urging, Millay entered her poem "Renascence" into a contest; she won fourth place, publication in *The Lyric Year*, and a scholarship to Vassar. She spent the Roaring Twenties in Greenwich Village acting, writing plays and prize-winning poetry, and living a bohemian lifestyle. In 1923 her book *The Harp Weaver* was awarded the Pulitzer Prize. Millay continued to write and take an active part in political affairs for several decades thereafter, despite a diminished literary reputation.

Born and raised in New York and educated at the University of Michigan, **Arthur Miller** (b. 1915) is recognized as one of the most important American dramatists. This reputation rests largely on plays written relatively early in his career, including *All My Sons* (1947, winner of the New York Drama Critics Circle Award), *Death of a Salesman* (1949, winner of both the Drama Critics Circle Award and the Pulitzer Prize), *The Crucible* (1953), and *A View from the Bridge* (1955). Though he continued to write after the mid-1950s, his output slowed somewhat, and his later works proved less popular with both critics and the public. Miller's writing shows clearly his social and political commitments. *Death of a Salesman*, for instance, uses a story about the decline and ultimate death of a salesman, Willy Loman, to reveal the emptiness underlying the code of bourgeois American values to which Willy doggedly adheres. Indeed, Miller's best work never fails to combine this sort of social commentary with the believable characters and compelling stories that make for powerful theater. In addition to the plays,

Miller's essays on the theater, particularly on the nature of modern tragedy, are a rich source for students and devotees of drama.

The son of a well-off London businessman, **John Milton** (1608–1674) was educated at St. Paul's School and at home with private tutors. After graduating with an M.A. from Christ's College, Cambridge, he spent the next six years reading at home. Having written verse since his university days, Milton began to write prose tracts in favor of Oliver Cromwell, in whose government he was later employed as head of a department. The strain of long hours of reading and writing for the revolutionary cause aggravated a genetic weakness and resulted in his total blindness around 1651. He wrote his most famous works, *Paradise Lost* (1667), *Paradise Regained* (1671), and *Samson Agonistes* (1671), by dictating them to his daughter and other amanuenses.

Marianne Moore (1887–1972) was born near St. Louis and grew up in Carlisle, Pennsylvania. After studying at Bryn Mawr College and Carlisle Commercial College, she taught at a government Native American school in Carlisle. She moved to Brooklyn, where she became an assistant at the New York Public Library. She loved baseball and spent a good deal of time watching her beloved Brooklyn Dodgers. She began to write Imagist poetry and to contribute to the *Dial*, a prestigious literary magazine. From 1925 to 1929 she served as acting editor of *Dial* and then as editor for four years. Moore was widely recognized for her work, receiving among other honors the Bollingen Prize, the National Book Award, and the Pulitzer Prize.

Robert Morgan (b. 1944) is a native of the North Carolina mountains. Raised on land settled by his Welsh ancestors, he became an accomplished poet, novelist, and short story writer. His four historical novels, two collections of short fiction, and nine volumes of poetry impart an indelible sense of place and address themes that matter to all people: birth and death, love and loss, joy and sorrow, and the necessity for remembrance and the inevitability of forgetting. He was educated at the University of North Carolina, Chapel Hill, and earned an M.F.A. from the University of North Carolina, Greensboro. In 1971 Morgan began teaching at Cornell University, where, since 1992, he has been the Kappa Alpha Professor of English.

Born in Cleveland, Ohio, **Thylias Moss** (b. 1954) attended Syracuse University and received her B.A. from Oberlin College and M.F.A. from the University of New Hampshire. She is the author of numerous books of poetry; a memoir, *Tale of a Sky-Blue Dress* (1998); two children's books; and two plays, *Talking to Myself* (1984) and *The Dolls in the Basement* (1984). She lives in Ann Arbor, where she is a professor of English at the University of Michigan.

Born in Calcutta, India, **Bharati Mukherjee** (b. 1940) spent her childhood in London with her mother and sisters, returning to India in 1951 for university study in Calcutta and Baroda. In 1963, while pursuing a doctorate at the University of Iowa, she married Clark Blaise, a novelist, and moved to Canada. During her stay there, she published two novels, *The Tiger's Daughter* (1972) and *Wife* (1975). She returned to India with her husband for a year, collaborating on a journal, *Days and*

Nights in Calcutta (1977), that records their very different impressions of Indian culture. She settled in the United States in 1980, taught at the University of Iowa, and published her well-known collection *The Middleman and Other Stories* (1988). Other works exploring immigrant experience followed: *Jasmine* (1989), *The Holder of the World* (1993), and *Leave It to Me* (1997).

A third-generation Japanese American, **David Mura** (b. 1952) was born in Great Lakes, Illinois, and graduated from Grinnell College in Iowa; he did graduate work at the University of Minnesota and Vermont College. Mura is a poet, creative nonfiction writer, critic, playwright, and performance artist. He is the author of numerous books of poetry, including *After We Lost Our Way* (1989), which was selected by GERALD STERN as a National Poetry Series winner, and two memoirs, *Turning Japanese: Memoirs of a Sansei* (1991), which was a New York Times Notable Book of the Year, and *Where the Body Meets Memory: An Odyssey of Race, Sexuality & Identity* (1996). Mura is the artistic director of Asian-American Renaissance, an arts organization in Minnesota.

Born in Muskegon, Michigan, **John Frederick Nims** (1913–1999) studied at DePaul University, the University of Notre Dame, and the University of Chicago, where he received his Ph.D. in 1945. By that time, he had already distinguished himself as a poet and critic. He went on to teach at numerous colleges and universities, including Harvard University, the University of Florence, the University of Toronto, the Bread Loaf School of English, Williams College, and the University of Missouri. Editor of *Poetry* magazine from 1978 to 1984, Nims was the author of many books of poetry and translations as well as several critical works and a widely used textbook, *Western Wind: An Introduction to Poetry* (1983).

Born in St. Louis of a Palestinian father and an American mother, **Naomi Shihab Nye** (b. 1952) grew up in both the United States and Jerusalem. She received her B.A. from Trinity University in San Antonio, Texas, where she still resides with her family. The author of many books of poems, she has also written short stories and books for children and has edited anthologies, several of which focus on the lives of children and represent work from around the world. She is also a singer-songwriter and on several occasions has traveled to the Middle East and Asia for the U.S. Information Agency, promoting international goodwill through the arts. Nye's work often attests to a universal sense of exile—from place, home, love, and one's self—and looks at the ways the human spirit confronts it.

Born in Lockport, New York, **Joyce Carol Oates** (b. 1938) is a graduate of Syracuse University and the University of Wisconsin. Astoundingly prolific, she is the author of numerous novels, volumes of poetry, and collections of short stories, many of which deal with destructive forces and sudden violence. She is also a literary theorist. Among her many novels are the trilogy *A Garden of Earthly Delights* (1967); *Expensive People* (1968); and *them* (1969), which won a National Book Award; *Son of the Morning* (1978); *Bellefleur* (1980); *Angel of Light* (1981); *Mysteries of Winterthurn* (1984); *Solstice* (1985); *Marya: A Life* (1986); *American Appetites* (1989); *Black Water* (1992); *First Love: A Gothic Tale* (1996); *Man Crazy* (1997); *My Heart*

Laid Bare (1998); *Broke Heart Blues* (1999); and *Blonde* (2000). Her many story collections include *The Wheel of Love* (1970), *Marriages and Infidelities* (1972), *Crossing the Border* (1976), *Night-Side* (1977), *A Sentimental Education* (1981), *Last Days* (1984), *The Assignation* (1989), and *The Collector of Hearts: New Tales of the Grotesque* (1998).

Born in Austin, Minnesota, **Tim O'Brien** (b. 1946) studied at Macalester College and Harvard University. During the Vietnam War he was drafted into the army, promoted to the rank of sergeant, and decorated with a Purple Heart. Many of his novels and stories draw on his experiences during the war. His novels are *If I Die in a Combat Zone, Box Me Up and Ship Me Home* (1973); *Northern Lights* (1975); *Going after Cacciato* (1978), winner of the National Book Award; *The Nuclear Age* (1985); and *In the Lake of the Woods* (1994). His short story collection is entitled *The Things They Carried* (1990).

Born in Savannah, Georgia, and raised on a farm in Milledgeville, Georgia, **Flannery O'Connor** (1925–1964) graduated from Georgia State College for Women in 1945 and attended the Writers' Workshop at the University of Iowa, from which she received a master's degree in 1947. From Iowa she moved to New York City to begin her writing career but, after little more than two years, was forced by illness to return to her mother's Georgia farm. Confined as an invalid by the degenerative disease lupus, O'Connor spent her remaining fourteen years raising peacocks and writing fiction set in rural Georgia. Her works are distinguished by irreverent humor, often grotesque characters, and intense, almost mystical affirma-

tion of the challenges of religious belief. Her work includes two novels, *Wise Blood* (1952) and *The Violent Bear It Away* (1960), and two short story collections, *A Good Man Is Hard to Find* (1955) and *Everything That Rises Must Converge* (1965). After her death at the age of thirty-nine, a selection of occasional prose, *Mystery and Manners* (1969) was edited by her friends Sally and Robert Fitzgerald, and a collection of letters, *The Habit of Being* (1979), was edited by Sally Fitzgerald. *The Complete Stories* (1971) received the National Book Award.

Born in Baltimore and raised in Massachusetts, **Frank [Francis Russell] O'Hara** (1926–1966) studied piano at the New England Conservatory in Boston from 1941 to 1944 and served in the South Pacific and Japan during World War II. He majored in English at Harvard, then received his M.A. in English at the University of Michigan in 1951. He moved to New York, where he worked at the Museum of Modern Art and began writing poetry seriously as well as composing essays and reviews on painting and sculpture. His first volume of poems, *A City in Winter,* thirteen poems with two drawings by the artist Larry Rivers, was published in 1952. Other collaborations with artists followed. His first major collection of poetry was *Meditations in an Emergency* (1957). His poetry is often casual, relaxed in diction, and full of specific detail, seeking to convey the immediacy of life. He described his work as "I do this I do that" poetry because his poems often read like entries in a diary, as in the opening lines of "The Day Lady Died." He was killed at forty when he was struck by a sand buggy while vacationing on Fire Island, New York.

Sharon Olds (b. 1942) was born in San Francisco and educated at Stanford and Columbia Universities. She has written eight books of poetry and received numerous important prizes and awards. In the words of Elizabeth Frank, "[Olds] and her work are about nothing less than the joy of making— of making love, making babies, making poems, making sense of love, memory, death, the feel—the actual bodily texture, of life." Named New York State Poet in 1998, Olds teaches poetry workshops in New York University's graduate creative writing program along with workshops at Goldwater Hospital in New York, a public facility for physically disabled persons.

Mary Oliver (b. 1935) was born in Cleveland and educated at Ohio State University and Vassar College. She is the author of ten volumes of poetry, including *American Primitive* (1983), for which she won the Pulitzer Prize, and three books of prose. She holds the Catharine Osgood Foster Chair for Distinguished Teaching at Bennington College and lives in Provincetown, Massachusetts, and Bennington, Vermont. Oliver is one of the most respected of poets concerned with the natural world.

Born in New Rochelle, New York, **George Oppen** (1908–1984) was the son of George August Oppenheimer, a diamond merchant, and Elsie Rothfeld. He described his schooling as "minimal." In 1927 he married Mary Colby. The couple rejected the comfortable world of Oppen's parents and chose a life of independence. He was a leading figure among the "Objectivists," a group of poets who shared the conviction that the poet must be faithful to the world of facts ("The Forms of Love" is

an example of the philosophy of Objectivism). His first book of poems, *Discrete Series*, was published in 1934 by the Objectivist Press, after which he stopped writing poetry for nearly twenty-five years in favor of political activism, even living as an exile in Mexico during the McCarthy era. After returning to poetry, he received the 1969 Pulitzer Prize for *Of Being Numerous* (1968).

Simon J. Ortiz (b. 1941) was born and raised in the Acoma Pueblo Community in Albuquerque, New Mexico. He received his early education from the Bureau of Indian Affairs school on the Acoma reservation, later attending the University of New Mexico and completing his M.F.A. at the University of Iowa, where he was a part of the International Writing Program. Unlike most contemporary Native American writers, Ortiz is a full-blooded Native American, and his first language was Keresan. By learning English, he found a way to communicate with those outside his immediate culture. His poetry explores the significance of individual origins and journeys, which he sees as forming a vital link in the continuity of life. His many writing accomplishments include poems, short stories, essays, and children's books. Ortiz has taught Native American literature and creative writing at San Diego State University, Navajo Community College, Marin College, the Institute for the Arts of the American Indian, and the University of New Mexico. He is currently a faculty member at the University of Toronto.

Born in Oswestry, Shropshire, **Wilfred Owen** (1893–1918) attended Birkenhead Institute and Shrewsbury Technical School. When forced to withdraw from London University for financial reasons, Owen became a vicar's assistant in Dunsden, Oxfordshire. There he grew disaffected with the church and left to teach in France. He enlisted in 1915 and six months later was hospitalized in Edinburgh, where he met Siegfried Sassoon, whose war poems had just been published. Sent back to the front, Owen was killed one week before the armistice. He is the most widely recognized of the "war poets," a group of World War I writers who brought the realism of war to poetry.

Born in New York City, the youngest daughter of immigrant parents, **Grace Paley** (b. 1922) spoke Yiddish and Russian at home as a child. She attended Hunter College and New York University and wrote mostly poetry until the 1950s. Her first book of short stories, *The Little Disturbances of Man* (1959), was highly praised. Later story collections are *Enormous Changes at the Last Minute* (1974), *Later the Same Day* (1985), and *The Collected Stories of Grace Paley* (1994). She taught for many years at City University and Sarah Lawrence College and has widely lectured and read from her work. Paley's love of stories is matched by her social activism. She has been a dedicated participant in antiwar, antinuclear, and feminist causes. In 1988, by an act of the state legislature, Paley was named the first official New York State Author.

Born in New York City, **Linda Pastan** (b. 1932) graduated from Radcliffe College and earned an M.A. from Brandeis University. She has published many books of poetry and received numerous awards for them, including a Dylan Thomas Award. Her deeply emotional poetry often has grief at its center. Her work is referred to as "spare, plainspoken" poetry, a kind of plainsong.

Pastan served as poet laureate of Maryland from 1991 to 1994. She presently lives in Potomac, Maryland.

Born in working-class Detroit, **Marge Piercy** (b. 1936) studied at the University of Michigan and Northwestern University. She has published fourteen books of poetry, fifteen novels, and a collection of essays on poetry, *Parti-Colored Blocks for a Quilt* (1982). Much of her work deals with both the subtle and the blatant forms of oppression of women.

Wang Ping (b. 1957) received her B.A. from Beijing University and came to the United States in 1985. She earned a Ph.D. at New York University. Ping writes not only poetry but also short stories, novels, essays, and nonfiction, and she has served as an anthology editor and translator. Her work often reveals how living in two different languages can create very different experiences of the world.

Robert Pinsky (b. 1940) was born in Long Branch, New Jersey. He is the author of six books of poetry, including *The Figured Wheel: New and Collected Poems, 1966–1996* (1996), which won the 1997 Lenore Marshall Poetry Prize and was a Pulitzer Prize nominee. He has also published four books of criticism, two books of translation, and the novella, *Mindwheel,* used as the basis for a computer game. In 1999 he co-edited with Maggie Dietz *Americans' Favorite Poems: The Favorite Poem Project Anthology.* He is currently poetry editor of the weekly Internet magazine *Slate.* He teaches in the graduate writing program at Boston University, and in 1997 he was named Poet Laureate Consultant in Poetry at the Library of Congress. He lives in Newton Corner, Massachusetts.

Raised in a middle-class family in Boston, **Sylvia Plath** (1932–1963) showed early promise as a writer, having stories and poems published in magazines such as *Seventeen* while she was in high school. As a student at Smith College, she was selected for an internship at *Mademoiselle* magazine and spent a month working in New York in the summer of 1953. Upon her return home, she suffered a serious breakdown, attempted suicide, and was institutionalized. She returned to Smith College for her senior year in 1954 and received a Fulbright fellowship to study at Cambridge University in England, where she met the poet Ted Hughes. They were married in 1956. They lived in the United States as well as England, and Plath studied under ROBERT LOWELL at Boston University. Her marriage broke up in 1962, and from her letters and poems it appears that she was approaching another breakdown at that time. On February 11, 1963, she committed suicide. Four books of poetry appeared during her lifetime, and her *Selected Poems* was published in 1985. The powerful, psychologically intense poetry for which she is best known (including "Daddy") was written after 1960, influenced by the "confessional" style of LOWELL (see **confessional poetry** in the Glossary).

Born in Boston, Massachusetts, **Edgar Allan Poe** (1809–1849), the son of itinerant actors, was abandoned at one year of age by his father; his mother died soon after. The baby became the ward of John Allan of Richmond, Virginia, whose surname became Poe's middle name. When the family fortunes declined, the Allans moved to England. Poe was educated there and at the new University of Virginia upon his return to Richmond. Although an ex-cellent student, Poe drank and gambled heavily, causing Allan to withdraw him from the university after one year. Poe made his way to Boston, enlisted in the army, and eventually, with Allan's help, took an appointment at West Point. After further dissipation ended his military career, Poe set out to support himself by writing. Three volumes of poetry brought in little money, and in 1835 Poe took a position as an assistant editor of the *Southern Literary Messenger,* the first of many positions he lost because of drinking. He began to publish short stories. In 1836 he married his thirteen-year-old cousin, Virginia Clemm, and took on the support of her mother as well, increasing his financial difficulties. They went to New York City, where Poe published *The Narrative of Arthur Gordon Pym* (1838) and assembled the best stories he had published in magazines in *Tales of the Grotesque and Arabesque* (1840), his first story collection. At that time he also began to write detective stories, virtually inventing the genre. Already respected as a critic, Poe won fame as a poet with *The Raven and Other Poems* (1845). In 1847, after the death of his wife, Poe became engaged to the poet Sarah Helen Whitman, a wealthy widow six years his senior, who ultimately resisted marriage because of Poe's drinking problem. In 1849 Poe met a childhood sweetheart, Elmira Royster Shelton, now a widow, who agreed to marry him. After celebrating his apparent reversal of fortune with friends in Baltimore, he was found unconscious in the street and died shortly thereafter. Always admired in Europe, Poe's major stories of horror and detection, his major poems, and his major critical pieces on the craft of writing are considered American classics.

Born in London to a successful textile merchant, **Alexander Pope** (1688–1744) spent his childhood in the country, stunted by tuberculosis of the spine (his height never exceeded four and a half feet). Pope was also limited by his Catholicism, which prevented him from going to university, voting, or holding public office. He turned to writing and gained considerable fame for his satire *The Rape of the Lock* and for his translations of Homer. Fame also brought ridicule and vehement attacks from critics holding different political views, and Pope struck back with nasty satires of his detractors. Later in his career, he wrote a good deal of ethical and philosophical verse.

Born in Indian Creek, Texas, **Katherine Anne Porter** (1890–1980) was educated at convent and private schools in Louisiana and Texas. She held a variety of jobs, as freelance journalist, newspaper reporter, ghost writer, editor, critic, and book reviewer. Her first story was published in 1922. Although the quantity of her work is small, she is acknowledged as a master of the short story form. Her first collection of stories, *Flowering Judas and Other Stories* (1930), brought her immediate critical acclaim and public recognition, and she solidified her reputation with *The Leaning Tower and Other Stories* (1944) and *Pale Horse, Pale Rider: Three Short Novels* (1939). Her novel *Ship of Fools* (1962) was a best-seller. *The Collected Short Stories* (1965) won the National Book Award and the 1966 Pulitzer Prize for fiction.

Ezra Pound (1885–1972) was born in Idaho but grew up outside Philadelphia; he attended the University of Pennsylvania for two years and graduated from Hamilton College. He taught for two years at Wabash College, then left for Europe, living for the next few years in London, where he edited *Little Review* and founded several literary movements—including the Imagists and the Vorticists. After moving to Italy, he began his major work, the *Cantos*, and became involved in fascist politics. During World War II he did radio broadcasts from Italy in support of Mussolini, for which he was indicted for treason in the United States. Judged mentally unfit for trial, he remained in an asylum in Washington, D.C., until 1958, when the charges were dropped. Pound spent his last years in Italy. He is generally considered the poet most responsible for defining and promoting a modernist aesthetic in poetry.

Dudley Randall (b. 1914) was born in Washington, D.C., and lived most of his life in Detroit. His first published poem appeared in the *Detroit Free Press* when he was thirteen. He worked for Ford Motor Company and then for the U.S. Postal Service and served in the South Pacific during World War II. He graduated from Wayne State University in 1949 and then from the library school at the University of Michigan. In 1965 Randall established the Broadside Press, one of the most important publishers of modern black poetry. "Ballad of Birmingham," written in response to the 1963 bombing of a church in which four girls were killed, has been set to music and recorded. It became an anthem for many in the civil rights movement.

Born in Pulaski, Tennessee, **John Crowe Ransom** (1888–1974) was the son of a preacher. He studied at Vanderbilt University and then at Christ Church College, Oxford, on a Rhodes scholarship. After service in World

War I, he taught first at Vanderbilt and later at Kenyon College, where he edited the *Kenyon Review*. He published three volumes of highly acclaimed poetry, but after 1927 principally devoted himself to critical writing. He was a guiding member of the Fugitives, a group of writers who sought to preserve a traditional aesthetic ideal that was firmly rooted in classical values and forms. As a critic, he promulgated the highly influential New Criticism, which focused attention on texts as self-sufficient entities to be analyzed through rigorous methodologies intended to reveal their depth, subtleties, and intricacies of technique and theme.

Born in Birmingham, Warwickshire, **Henry Reed** (1914–1986) was educated at the University of Birmingham, where his circle of friends included W. H. AUDEN and Louis MacNiece. His service in the British army during World War II provided the basis for his famous *Lessons of the War* (three related poems, of which "Naming of Parts" is the first). In addition to his one early volume of poetry, he is well known in Britain for his many radio plays; he also published translations and a book on the novel.

Born in Baltimore, **Adrienne Rich** (b. 1929) was the elder daughter of a forceful Jewish intellectual who encouraged and critiqued her writing. While she was at Radcliffe College in 1951, W. H. AUDEN selected her book *A Change of World* for the Yale Younger Poets Award. She became involved in radical politics, especially in the opposition to the Vietnam War, and taught inner-city minority youth. Having modeled her early poetry on that of male writers, in the 1970s Rich became a feminist, freeing herself from her old models and becoming an influential figure in contemporary American literature. She is the author of nearly twenty volumes of poetry and several books of nonfiction prose. In 1999 Rich received the Lifetime Achievement Award from the Lannan Foundation. Since 1984 she has lived in California.

Alberto Ríos (b. 1952) was born to a Guatemalan father and an English mother in Nogales, Arizona, on the Mexican border. He earned a B.A. in English, a B.A. in psychology, and an M.F.A. at the University of Arizona. In addition to seven books of poetry, he has published two collections of short stories. His work often fuses realism, surrealism, and magical realism, as exemplified by "Nani." Since 1994 he has been Regents Professor of English at Arizona State University, where he has taught since 1982. He lives in Chandler, Arizona.

Born in Head Tide, Maine, **Edwin Arlington Robinson** (1869–1935) grew up in the equally provincial Maine town of Gardiner, the setting for much of his poetry. He was forced to leave Harvard University after two years because of his family's financial difficulties. He published his first two books of poetry in 1896 and 1897 ("Richard Cory" appeared in the latter). For the next quarter-century Robinson chose to live in poverty and write his poetry, relying on temporary jobs and charity from friends. President Theodore Roosevelt, at the urging of his son Kermit, used his influence to get Robinson a sinecure job in the New York Custom House in 1905, giving him time to write. He published numerous books of mediocre poetry in the next decade. The tide turned for him with *The Man Against the Sky* (1916); the numerous volumes that followed received high praise and sold well. He was awarded three Pulitzer Prizes: for *Collected Poems* in 1921, *The Man Who Died Twice* in 1924, and *Tristram* in 1927. Robinson was the first major American poet of the twentieth century, unique in that he devoted his life to poetry and willingly paid the price in poverty and obscurity.

Theodore Roethke (1908–1963) was the son of a commercial greenhouse operator in Saginaw, Michigan. As a child he spent much time in greenhouses, and the impressions of nature he formed there later influenced the subjects and imagery of his verse. Roethke graduated from the University of Michigan and studied at Harvard University. His eight books of poetry were held in high regard by critics, some of whom considered Roethke among the best poets of his generation. *The Waking* was awarded the Pulitzer Prize in 1954; *Words for the Wind* (1958) received the Bollingen Prize and the National Book Award. He taught at many colleges and universities, his career interrupted several times by serious mental breakdowns, and gained a reputation as an exceptional teacher of poetry writing.

Born in London into a literary family (her brother Dante Gabriel Rossetti was one of the Pre-Raphaelite group), **Christina Rossetti** (1830–1894) began writing poetry at an early age. Ill health saved her from a career as a governess; instead she nursed her ailing father and worked at the St. Mary Magdalen Home for Fallen Women. Rossetti's strong Anglican religiosity led her to give up theater and opera and turn down two offers of marriage. She wrote six collections of poetry as well as short stories, nursery rhymes, and religious essays.

Sonia Sanchez (b. 1934) was born Wilsonia Driver in Birmingham, Alabama. In 1943 she moved to Harlem with her sister to live with their father and his third wife. She earned a B.A. in political science from Hunter College in 1955 and studied poetry writing with LOUISE BOGAN at New York University. In the 1960s she became actively involved in the social movements of the times, and she has continued to be a voice for social change. She has published more than a dozen books of poetry, many plays, and several books for children, and she has edited two anthologies of literature. She began teaching in the San Francisco area in 1965 and was a pioneer in developing black studies courses at what is now San Francisco State University. She was the first Presidential Fellow at Temple University, where she began teaching in 1977, and held the Laura Carnell Chair in English there until her retirement in 1999. She lives in Philadelphia.

Born in Newton, Massachusetts, **Anne Sexton** (1928–1974) dropped out of Garland Junior College to get married. After suffering nervous breakdowns following the births of her two children, she was encouraged to enroll in a writing program. Studying under ROBERT LOWELL at Boston University, she was a fellow student with SYLVIA PLATH. Like the work of other "confessional" poets, Sexton's poetry is an intimate view of her life and emotions. She made the experience of being a woman a central issue in her poetry, bringing to it such subjects as menstruation and abortion as well as drug addiction. She published at least a dozen books of poetry—*Live or Die* was awarded the Pulitzer Prize for poetry in 1966—as well as four children's books co-authored with MAXINE KUMIN. Sexton's emotional problems continued, along with a growing addiction to alcohol and sedatives, and she committed suicide in 1974.

William Shakespeare (1564–1616) was born in Stratford-upon-Avon, England, where his father was a glovemaker and bailiff, and he presumably went to grammar school there. He married Anne Hathaway in 1582 and sometime before 1592 left for London to work as a playwright and actor. Shakespeare joined the Lord Chamberlain's Men (later the King's Men), an acting company for which he wrote thirty-seven plays—comedies, tragedies, histories, and romances—upon which his reputation as the finest dramatist in the English language is based. He was also arguably the finest lyric poet of his day, as exemplified by songs scattered throughout his plays, two early nondramatic poems (*Venus and Adonis* and *The Rape of Lucrece*), and the sonnet sequence expected of all noteworthy writers in the Elizabethan age. Shakespeare's sonnets were probably written in the 1590s, although they were not published until 1609. Shakespeare retired to Stratford around 1612, and by the time he died at the age of fifty-two, he was acknowledged as a leading light of the Elizabethan stage and had become successful enough to have purchased a coat of arms for his family home.

Born into a wealthy aristocratic family in Sussex County, England, **Percy Bysshe Shelley** (1792–1822) was educated at Eton and then went on to Oxford University, where he was expelled after six months for writing a defense of atheism, the first price he would pay

for his nonconformity and radical (for his time) commitment to social justice. The following year he eloped with Harriet Westbrook, daughter of a tavern keeper, despite his belief that marriage was a tyrannical and degrading social institution (she was sixteen, he eighteen). He became a disciple of the radical social philosopher William Godwin, fell in love with Godwin's daughter, Mary Wollstonecraft Godwin (the author, later, of *Frankenstein*), and went to live with her in France. Two years later, after Harriet had committed suicide, the two married and moved to Italy, where they shifted about restlessly and Shelley was generally short on money and in poor health. In such trying circumstances he wrote his greatest works. He died at age thirty, when the boat he was in was overturned by a sudden storm.

Born into an important aristocratic family in Elizabethan England, **Sir Philip Sidney** (1554–1584) attended Shrewsbury School and Oxford University, although he left without a degree and completed his education through extended travel on the Continent. He was the epitome of the well-rounded courtier idealized in his era, excelling as a soldier, writer, literary patron, and diplomat. He was the author of an important work of prose fiction (*Arcadia*), a landmark essay in literary criticism (*The Defense of Poesy*), and an important sonnet cycle (*Astrophil and Stella*, which includes "Loving in truth, and fain in verse my love to show"). His poetry has been labeled "news from the heart."

Born in Albuquerque of mixed Pueblo, Mexican, and white ancestry, **Leslie Marmon Silko** (b. 1948) grew up on the Laguna Pueblo reservation in New

Mexico. She earned her B.A. (with honors) from the University of New Mexico. In a long and productive writing career (she was already writing stories in elementary school), Silko has published poetry, novels, short stories, essays, letters, and film scripts. She taught creative writing first at the University of New Mexico and later at the University of Arizona. She has been named a Living Cultural Treasure by the New Mexico Humanities Council and has received the Native Writers' Circle of the Americas Lifetime Achievement Award. Her work is a graphic telling of the life of native peoples, maintaining its rich spiritual heritage while exposing the terrible consequences of European domination. Silko lives today on a ranch in the mountains a few miles northwest of Tucson, Arizona.

Charles Simic (b. 1938) was born in Belgrade, Yugoslavia. In 1953 he, his mother, and his brother joined his father in Chicago, where Charles continued to live until 1958. His first poems were published when he was twenty-one. In 1961 he was drafted into the U.S. Army, and in 1966 he earned his B.A. from New York University. His first book of poems, *What the Grass Says*, was published in 1967. Since then he has published more than sixty books of poetry, translations, and essays, including *The World Doesn't End: Prose Poems* (1990), for which he received the Pulitzer Prize for poetry. Since 1973 he has lived in New Hampshire, where he is a professor of English at the University of New Hampshire.

Born into an aristocratic and literary family in late Victorian England, **Edith Sitwell** (1887–1964) both shocked and amused people by her writing, eccentric behavior, and dramatic Elizabethan dress. Influenced by Baudelaire and the symbolists, T. S. ELIOT's poetry, Stravinsky's music, and abstract art, Sitwell introduced verbal and rhythmic innovations in her poetry that contrasted sharply with then-current verse.

Born in Shipbourne, Kent, **Christopher Smart** (1722–1771) attended the Durham School and was later educated at Pembroke College, Cambridge, where he won prizes for his poetry. After college, Smart lived in London, editing and writing copy for periodicals and composing songs for the popular theater. In 1752 he published his first collection, *Poems on Several Occasions*. In the 1750s Smart developed a form of religious mania that compelled him to continuous prayer. From 1756 on he was confined, with one brief intermission, until 1763 in St. Luke's Hospital and then in Mr. Potter's Madhouse in Bethnal Green. During his confinement, he wrote what many see as his most original and lasting works—*A Song to David* and *Jubilate Agno*, with its well-known homage to his cat, Jeoffry. Smart ranks as one of the most respected and influential religious poets in English literature.

Gary Snyder (b. 1930) was born in San Francisco and grew up in Oregon and Washington. He studied anthropology at Reed College and Oriental languages at the University of California, Berkeley, where he became associated with the Beat movement; however, his poetry often deals with nature rather than the urban interests more typical of Beat poetry. He has published sixteen books of poetry and prose, including *Turtle Island* (1974), which won the Pulitzer Prize for poetry. Snyder is active in the environmental movement and spent a number of years in Japan practicing Zen Buddhism. He teaches at the University of California, Davis.

Born in Hawaii and raised in the small town of Wahiawa on Oahu, **Cathy Song** (b. 1955) left Hawaii for the East Coast, studying at Wellesley College and then at Boston University. Her first book, *Picture Bride*, was chosen by Richard Hugo for the Yale Series of Younger Poets in 1982. Since then she has published three other books of poetry. She lives in Honolulu and teaches at the University of Hawaii at Manoa.

Sophocles (c. 496–c. 406 B.C.E.) was not the first important voice to emerge in drama, but as a representative of classical Greek tragedy, it is hard to imagine a more important figure. Indeed, his works were considered such models of the craft that Aristotle based much of his *Poetics* on an analysis of *Oedipus Rex*. Sophocles was born to a wealthy Athenian family and became active in many aspects of civic life as a soldier, a priest, and a statesman. Today, however, he is remembered principally for his achievements as a playwright. During a long and distinguished career, he won first prize in Greek drama competitions more often than any other writer. Though there is evidence that he wrote more than 120 plays, only seven have survived in their entirety, along with fragments of many others. In his plays, Sophocles wrestled with some of the most important issues of his time and indeed of all time — the conflict between fate and free will; between public and private morality; and between duty to one's family, the state, and the gods — giving his work enduring appeal. *Oedipus Rex* (*Oedipus the King*, first performed in 430 B.C.E.) is one of Sophocles' three Theban plays, the others being *Antigone* (441 B.C.E.) and *Oedipus at Colonus* (401 B.C.E., first performed posthumously).

Raised in Fresno, California, **Gary Soto** (b. 1952) earned his B.A. from California State University, Fresno, and an M.F.A. from the University of California, Irvine. He worked his way through college doing such jobs as picking grapes and chopping beets. Much of his poetry comes out of and reflects his working background, that of migrant workers and tenant farmers in the fields of southern California, and provides glimpses into the lives of families in the barrio. Soto's language comes from gritty, raw, everyday American speech. His first book, *The Elements of San Joaquin*, won the 1976 United States Award from the International Poetry Forum. He has published ten collections of poetry, two novels, four essay collections, and numerous young adult and children's books and has edited three anthologies. He lives in Berkeley, California.

A contemporary of WILLIAM SHAKESPEARE, **Edmund Spenser** (1552–1599) was the greatest English nondramatic poet of his time. Best known for his romantic and national epic *The Faerie Queene*, Spenser wrote poems of a number of other types as well and was important as an innovator in metric and form (as in his development of the special form of sonnet that bears his name — the Spenserian sonnet) "One day I wrote her name upon the strand" is number 75 in *Amoretti*, a sequence of sonnets about a courtship addressed to a woman named Elizabeth, probably Elizabeth Boyle, who became Spencer's second wife.

Born in Hutchinson, Kansas, **William Stafford** (1914–1995) studied at the University of Kansas and then at the University of Iowa Writers' Workshop. In between, he was a conscientious objector during World War II and worked in labor camps. In 1948 Stafford moved to Oregon, where he taught at Lewis and Clark College until he retired in 1980. His first major collection of poems, *Traveling through the Dark*, was published when Stafford was forty-eight. It won the National Book Award in 1963. He went on to publish more than sixty-five volumes of poetry and prose and came to be known as a very influential teacher of poetry. From 1970 to 1971 he was Consultant in Poetry at the Library of Congress.

Gertrude Stein (1874–1946) was born in Allegheny, Pennsylvania. After attending Radcliffe College, Harvard University, and Johns Hopkins Medical School, she moved to France in 1903 and became a central figure in the Parisian art world. An advocate of the avant-garde, her salon became a gathering place for the "new moderns." What Henri Matisse and Pablo Picasso achieved in the visual arts, Stein attempted in her writing. Her first published book, *Three Lives* (1909), the stories of three working-class women, has been called a minor masterpiece. A number of other books followed, including *The Autobiography of Alice B. Toklas* (1933), actually Stein's own autobiography.

Born in Salinas, California, **John Steinbeck** (1902–1968) was introduced to literature by his mother, a former school teacher who encouraged him to read widely. After studying at Stanford University for a while, he left for New York to become a writer. He stayed there for a short time, working as a reporter and a bricklayer. In 1927 he returned to California, where he took a variety of odd jobs, became involved in the plight of migrant workers, and completed his first novel, *A Cup of Gold* (1929). His fourth novel, *Tortilla Flat* (1935), attracted critical attention and acclaim. Succeeding novels, *In Dubious Battle* (1936), *Of Mice and Men* (1937), and his masterpiece, *The Grapes of Wrath* (1939; awarded the Pulitzer Prize), were both critical and popular successes. During World War II he served as a war correspondent for the New York *Herald Tribune,* covering the action in Italy and Africa. In addition to his novels, Steinbeck published several works of nonfiction and collections of short stories, including *The Long Valley* (1938), and wrote screenplays for motion pictures. The novels *East of Eden* (1952) and *The Winter of Our Discontent* (1961) followed. In 1962 Steinbeck received the Nobel Prize in literature.

Born in Pittsburgh, **Gerald Stern** (b. 1925) studied at the University of Pittsburgh and Columbia University. Stern came late to poetry: he was forty-six when he published his first book. Since then he has published more than ten collections of poems. Stern has often been compared to WALT WHITMAN and JOHN KEATS for his exploration of the self and the sometimes ecstatic exuberance of his verse. He taught at Columbia University, New York University, Sarah Lawrence College, the University of Pittsburgh, and the University of Iowa Writers' Workshop as well as other schools until his retirement in 1995. He now lives in Easton, Pennsylvania, and New York City.

Born in Reading, Pennsylvania, **Wallace Stevens** (1879–1955) attended Harvard University for three years. He tried journalism and then attended New York University Law School, after which he worked as a legal consultant. He spent most of his life working as an executive for the Hartford Accident and Indemnity Company, spending his evenings writing some of the most imaginative and influential poetry of his time. Although now considered one of the major American poets of the century, he did not receive widespread recognition until the publication of his *Collected Poems* just a year before his death.

Born in Havana, Cuba, **Virgil Suárez** (b. 1962) was eight years old when he left with his parents for Spain, where they lived until they came to the United States in 1974. He is the author of several collections of poetry, several novels, and a volume of short stories and is the editor of several best-selling anthologies. His work often reflects the impact of the diaspora on the everyday life of Cuban and other exiles. He is professor of creative writing at Florida State University.

Sekou Sundiata (b. 1948) was born and raised in Harlem. His work is deeply influenced by the music, poetry, and oral traditions of African American culture. A self-proclaimed radical in the 1970s, for the past several decades he has used poetry to comment on the life and times of our culture. His work, which encompasses print, performance, music, and theater, has received praise for its fusion of soul, jazz, and hiphop grooves with political insight, humor, and rhythmic speech. He regularly records and performs on tour with artists such as Craig Harris and Vernon Reid.

Born in Ireland of English parents, **Jonathan Swift** (1667–1745) was educated at Kilkenny College and Trinity College, Dublin. He worked in England for a decade as a private secretary and for four years as a political writer but spent the rest of his life in Ireland, as dean of St. Patrick's Cathedral in Dublin. Although he is best known for his satires in prose (such as *Gulliver's Travels* and "A Modest Proposal"), Swift's original ambition was to be a poet, and he wrote occasional verse throughout his life.

Born in Oakland, California, and raised to become a neurosurgeon and a concert pianist by parents who had emigrated from China to the United States two and a half years before her birth, **Amy Tan** (b. 1952) first became a consultant to programs for disabled children and then a professional writer. In 1987 she visited China for the first time and found it just as her mother had described it: "As soon as my feet touched China, I became Chinese," she has said. Her widely acclaimed novel *The Joy Luck Club* (1989) contrasts the lives of four women in pre-1949 China with those of their American-born daughters in California. Her other work includes *The Kitchen God's Wife* (1991); a children's book, *The Moon Lady* (1992); and *The Hundred Secret Senses* (1995).

A native of Kansas City, Missouri, **James Tate** (b. 1943) studied at the University of Missouri and Kansas State College during his undergraduate years. He then earned his M.F.A. at the University of Iowa Writers' Workshop in 1967, the same year his first poetry collection, *The Lost Pilot*, was published (selected by Dudley Fitts for the Yale Series of Younger Poets). Tate is the author of numerous books of poetry, including *Selected Poems* (1991), which won the Pulitzer Prize and the William Carlos Williams Award. Tate's poems often include highly unusual juxtapositions of imagery, tone, and context, as is evident in "The Wheelchair Butterfly." Tate has taught at the University of Iowa, the University of California, Berkeley, and Columbia University and now teaches at the University of Massachusetts, Amherst.

Born in England, **Edward Taylor** (1642–1729) immigrated to the colonies, where he became a clergyman in Westfield, a frontier village in what is now Massachusetts. Taylor regarded his poems as sacramental acts of private devotion and asked that they never be published. When he died, his manuscripts were placed in the Yale University library; two centuries passed before his work was discovered. The selection of his poems published in 1939 established him as a writer of genuine power, perhaps unsurpassed in America until William Cullen Bryant appeared a century and a half later.

Born in Somersby, Lincolnshire, **Alfred, Lord Tennyson** (1809–1892), grew up in the tense atmosphere of his unhappy father's rectory. He went to Trinity College, Cambridge, but when he was forced to leave because of family and financial problems, he returned home to study and practice the craft of poetry. His early volumes, published in 1830 and 1832, received bad reviews, but his *In Memoriam* (1850), an elegy on his close friend Arthur Hallam, who died of a brain seizure, won acclaim. He was unquestionably the most popular poet of his time (the "poet of the people") and arguably the greatest of the Victorian poets. He succeeded

WILLIAM WORDSWORTH as poet laureate, a position he held from 1850 until his death.

Dylan Thomas (1914–1953) was born in Swansea, Wales, and after grammar school became a journalist. He worked as a writer for the rest of his life. His first book of poetry, *Eighteen Poems*, appeared in 1934 and was followed by *Twenty-five Poems* (1936), *Deaths and Entrances* (1946), and *Collected Poems* (1952). His poems are often rich in textured rhythms and images. He also wrote prose, chiefly short stories collectively appearing as *Portrait of the Artist as a Young Dog* (1940), and a number of film scripts and radio plays. His most famous work, *Under Milk Wood*, written as a play for voices, was first performed in New York on May 14, 1953. Thomas's radio broadcasts and his lecture tours and poetry readings in the United States brought him fame and popularity. Alcoholism contributed to his early death in 1953.

Jean Toomer (1894–1967) was born in Washington, D.C., of mixed French, Dutch, Welsh, Negro, German, Jewish, and Indian blood (according to him). Although he passed for white during certain periods of his life, he was raised in a predominantly black community and attended black high schools. He began college at the University of Wisconsin but transferred to the College of the City of New York. He spent several years publishing poems and stories in small magazines. In 1921 he took a teaching job in Georgia and remained there for only four months; the experience inspired *Cane* (1923), a book of prose poetry describing the Georgian people and landscape that became a central work of the Harlem Renaissance. He later experimented in communal living and both studied and tried to promulgate the ideas of Quakerism and the Russian mystic George Gurdjieff. From 1950 on he published very little, writing mostly for himself.

Born in New York City, **Quincy Troupe** (b. 1943) grew up in East St. Louis, Illinois. He is a poet, biographer, journalist, editor, and teacher. In addition to poetry, he has written *Miles: The Autobiography* (1989), which received an American Book Award; *James Baldwin: The Legacy* (1989); and *Miles and Me: A Memoir of Miles Davis* (2000). He also edited *Giant Talk: An Anthology of Third World Writing* (1975) and is a founding editor of *Confrontation: A Journal of Third World Literature and American Rag*. He taught creative writing for the Watts Writers' Movement from 1966 to 1968 and served as director of the Malcolm X Center in Los Angeles during the summers of 1969 and 1970. He has developed many other programs to bring the arts to a wider public, from workshops in prisons and public schools to events that invite collaboration among artists in all the art forms.

Born an only child in Shillington, Pennsylvania, to a mother who was a writer and a father who taught high school, **John Updike** (b. 1932) studied at Harvard University and the Ruskin School of Drawing and Fine Art at Oxford, England. On his return to the United States he joined the staff of the *New Yorker*, where he worked from 1955 to 1957. Since 1957 he has lived and worked near Ipswich, Massachusetts. In addition to numerous volumes of poetry, books of essays and speeches, and a play, Updike has published some twenty novels and some ten collections of short fiction noteworthy for their in-cisive presentation of the quandaries of contemporary personal and social life. Among his novels are *Rabbit, Run* (1960), *The Centaur* (1963; National Book Award), *Couples* (1968), *Rabbit Redux* (1971), *Rabbit Is Rich* (1981; Pulitzer Prize), *The Witches of Eastwick* (1984), *Rabbit at Rest* (1990), and *In the Beauty of the Lilies* (1996). His story collections include *The Same Door* (1959), *Pigeon Feathers* (1962), *Olinger Stories* (1964), *The Music School* (1966), *Museums and Women* (1972), *Too Far to Go: The Maples Stories* (1979), *Bech Is Back* (1982), *Trust Me* (1987), and *The Afterlife and Other Stories* (1994).

Born in Chicago and raised in New York and Boston, **Jean Valentine** (b. 1934) is a graduate of Radcliffe College. Her first book, *Dream Barker*, was selected for a Yale Younger Poets Award in 1965. Since then she has published eight books of poetry. She teaches at Sarah Lawrence College and New York University and lives in New York City.

Born in Danville, Virginia, **Ellen Bryant Voigt** (b. 1943) studied at Converse College, the University of South Carolina, and the University of Iowa, where she earned an M.F.A. in music and literature. She is a pianist as well as a writer; her highly tuned musical ear is evident in the rich textures of sound in her poetry. She is the author of six collections of poetry and *The Flexible Lyric* (1999), a collection of essays on craft. She has taught at Goddard College, where she founded the writing program, and at M.I.T., and now teaches at Warren Wilson College in North Carolina, where she is the founding director of the writing program. She lives in Marshfield, Vermont, and is currently the Vermont State Poet.

Born on the eastern Caribbean island of St. Lucia, **Derek Walcott** (b. 1930) moves in his work between the African heritage of his family and the English cultural heritage of his reading and education. Both of his parents were educators immersed in the arts. His early training was in painting, which like his poetry was influenced by his Methodist religious training. He attended St. Mary's College and the University of the West Indies in Jamaica. His first book, *Twenty-Five Poems* (1948), appeared when he was eighteen, and he has published prolifically since then: nearly twenty books of poetry, more than twenty-five plays, and nonfiction. His work, which explores both the isolation of the artist and regional identity, is known for blending Caribbean, English, and African traditions. He was awarded the Nobel Prize for literature in 1992, the academy citing him for "a poetic oeuvre of great luminosity, sustained by a historical vision, the outcome of a multicultural achievement." He teaches creative writing at Boston University every fall and lives the rest of the year in St. Lucia.

Anne Waldman (b. 1945) was born in Millville, New Jersey, and grew up in Greenwich Village. She is associated with the bohemian poetics of the Lower East Side in New York City and with "Beat poetics." She attended Bennington College, co-founded the literary magazine *Angel Hair*, and for ten years directed the St. Mark's Church Poetry Project in New York City. She became a Buddhist, guided by the Tibetan Chogyam Trungpa Rinpoche, who would also become ALLEN GINSBERG's guru. She and Ginsberg worked together to create the Jack Kerouac School of Disembodied Poetics, at Trungpa's Naropa Institute in Boulder, Colorado. Both an author and a performance artist, Waldman has published more than forty books and gives exuberant, highly physical readings of her own work. She lives in Boulder and New York City.

Born in Eatonton, Georgia, **Alice Walker** (b. 1944) was educated at Spelman College and Sarah Lawrence College and now lives in San Francisco. Her reputation was initially based on her depiction of the lives of Southern blacks. Among her published work are the story collections *In Love & Trouble: Stories of Black Women* (1973) and *You Can't Keep a Good Woman Down* (1981); the volumes of poetry *Once* (1968), *Revolutionary Petunias* (1973), *Goodnight, Willie Lee . . .* (1979), and *Horses Make a Landscape Look More Beautiful* (1984); the novels *The Third Life of Grange Copeland* (1970), *Meridian* (1976), *The Color Purple* (1982), and *The Temple of My Familiar* (1989); and a biography of Langston Hughes for children (1973). She is also the editor of *I Love Myself When I'm Laughing . . . : A Zora Neale Hurston Reader* (1979) and *In Search of Our Mothers' Gardens: Womanist Prose* (1983). *The Color Purple* won an American Book Award and a Pulitzer Prize in 1983 and was made into a successful film in 1985. More recent work includes *Possessing the Secret of Joy* (1992) and *Anything We Love Can Be Saved: A Writer's Activism* (1997).

Born into a wealthy English family, **Edmund Waller** (1607–1687) attended Eton College and Cambridge University. He was elected to Parliament and married a rich woman who died soon thereafter. He was later exiled for involvement in a Royalist plot. Waller's poems, first published while the poet was in exile, enjoyed great popularity; Waller pioneered the smooth, balanced, antithetical **pentameter couplets** that became the staple of English poetry in the late seventeenth century and most of the eighteenth. After the restoration of the monarchy in 1660, he again joined Parliament, where he remained for many years.

James Welch (b. 1940) was born in Browning, Montana. His father was a member of the Blackfoot tribe, his mother of the Gros Ventre tribe. He attended schools on the Blackfoot and Fort Belknap reservations and took a degree from the University of Montana, where he studied under Richard Hugo. Welch has published many books of poetry, fiction, and nonfiction. His hard, spare poems often evoke the bleakest side of contemporary Native American life. He received a Lifetime Achievement Award for literature from the Native Writers' Circle in 1997. He makes his home on a farm outside Missoula, Montana.

Eudora Welty (1909–2001) was born in Jackson, Mississippi, and graduated from the University of Wisconsin. She is admired for her fine photographic studies of people—*One Time, One Place* (1972) collects her photos of Mississippi in the 1930s—as well as for her fiction, which also depicts the inhabitants of rural Mississippi. Among her seven volumes of short stories, which explore the mysteries of individuals' "separateness," are *A Curtain of Green* (1941), *The Wide Net* (1943), *The Golden Apples* (1949), *The Bride of Innisfallen* (1955), and *The Collected Stories* (1980). Her novels include *Delta Wedding* (1946), *The Ponder Heart* (1954), and *The Optimist's Daughter* (1972), which won a Pulitzer Prize. Welty also wrote many reviews, articles, and books of literary criticism.

Born in rural Long Island, **Walt Whitman** (1819–1892) was the son of a farmer and carpenter. He attended grammar school in Brooklyn and took his first job as a printer's devil for the *Long Island Patriot*. Attending the opera, dabbling in politics, participating in street life, and gaining experience as a student, printer, reporter, writer, carpenter, farmer, seashore observer, and a teacher provided the bedrock for his future poetic vision of an ideal society based on the realization of self. Although Whitman liked to portray himself as uncultured, he read widely in the King James Bible as well as SHAKESPEARE, Homer, Dante, Aeschylus, and Sophocles. He worked for many years in the newspaper business and began writing poetry only in 1847. In 1855, at his own expense, he published the first edition of *Leaves of Grass*, a thin volume of twelve long untitled poems. Written in a highly original and innovative free verse, influenced significantly by music, and with a wide-ranging subject matter, the work seemed strange to most of the poet's contemporaries—although some did recognize its value: Ralph Waldo Emerson wrote to the poet shortly after Whitman sent him a copy, saying, "I greet you at the beginning of a great career." He spent much of the remainder of his life revising and expanding this book. Today *Leaves of Grass* is considered a masterpiece of world literature, marking the beginning of modern American poetry, and Whitman is widely regarded as America's national poet.

Richard Wilbur (b. 1921) was born in New York City and grew up in rural New Jersey. He attended Amherst College and began writing poetry during World War II while fighting in Italy and France. After the war, he studied at Harvard University and then taught there and at Wellesley College, Wesleyan University, and Smith College. He has published many books of poetry, including *Things of This World* (1956), for which he received the Pulitzer Prize for poetry and the National Book Award, and *New and Collected Poems* (1988), which also won a Pulitzer. He has always been respected as a master of formal constraints, comparing them to the bottle that contains the genie, a restraint that stimulates the imagination to achieve results unlikely to be reached without it. Wilbur has also published numerous translations of French plays, two books for children, a collection of prose pieces, and editions of WILLIAM SHAKESPEARE and EDGAR ALLAN POE. In 1987 he was appointed Poet Laureate Consultant in Poetry at the Library of Congress. He lives in Cummington, Massachusetts.

Raised in Ann Arbor, Michigan, **Nancy Willard** (b. 1936) was educated at the University of Michigan and Stanford University. She is a noted writer of books for children. *A Visit to William Blake's Inn: Poems for Innocent and Experienced Travelers* (1981) was the first book of poetry to win the prestigious Newbery Medal, which recognizes the most distinguished American children's book published in a given year. Willard is also an excellent essayist and novelist. Her work in all genres frequently leads to a most uncommon experience of the common. She teaches at Vassar College and lives in Poughkeepsie, New York.

Born Thomas Lanier Williams in Columbia, Mississippi, as a child **Tennessee Williams** (1911–1983) moved with his family to St. Louis. His childhood was not easy: his parents were ill-matched, the family had little money, and both he and his beloved sister, Rose, suffered from depression and medical problems. It took Williams three attempts at college before he finished, finally earning a degree in playwriting from the University of Iowa at the age of twenty-four. His earliest efforts at writing were unsuccessful, but in 1944 *The Glass Menagerie* opened in Chicago and later began a very successful run in New York, winning the prestigious Drama Critics Circle Award. Other successes followed, including *A Streetcar Named Desire* (1947, which won a Pulitzer Prize and helped launch the career of its young star, Marlon Brando), *Cat on a Hot Tin Roof* (1955), and *Suddenly Last Summer* (1958). The American stage in the 1940s and 1950s was not yet ready to accept overt homosexuality, so Williams transformed his own tortured searching for sexual and emotional fulfillment into plays with remarkably frank heterosexual themes. This frankness and dreamy, poetic language are key elements of his style. In his later years, Williams suffered from drug and alcohol problems and was occasionally institutionalized for these and the crippling depressions that continued to plague him. Though his later work never achieved the popular success of his early plays, Williams's reputation in the American theater is secure.

William Carlos Williams (1883–1963) was born in Rutherford, New Jersey; his father was an English emigrant and his mother was of mixed Basque descent from Puerto Rico. He decided to be both a writer and a doctor while in high school in New York City. He graduated from the medical school at the University of Pennsylvania, where he was a friend of EZRA POUND and HILDA DOOLITTLE. After completing an internship in New York, writing poems between seeing patients, Williams practiced general medicine in Rutherford (he was ALLEN GINSBERG's pediatrician). His first book of poems was published in 1909, and he subsequently published poems, novels, short stories, plays, criticism, and essays. Initially one of the principal poets of the **Imagist** movement (see the Glossary), Williams sought later to invent an entirely fresh—and distinctly American—poetic whose subject matter was centered on the everyday circumstances of life and the lives of common people. Williams, like WALLACE STEVENS, became one of the major poets of the twentieth century and exerted great influence upon poets of his own and later generations.

Born and raised in the Hill District, an African American section of Pittsburgh that provides the backdrop to many of his plays, **August Wilson** (b. 1945) has come to be seen as one of the most important voices on the contemporary American stage. The son of a mixed-race marriage, his white father was not in the household when he was growing up. He dropped out of high school but continued to read widely, beginning his serious writing with poetry, the rhythms of which can be heard in his plays. In the 1960s, he became involved in the Black Power movement and also began to turn his writing talents to the stage. His best-known work is his cycle of historical plays examining important elements of African American experience, consisting of one play for each decade of the twentieth century. Among these are *Ma Rainey's Black Bottom* (1985), *Fences* (1987), *Joe Turner's Come and Gone* (1988), *The Piano Lesson* (1990), and *Seven Guitars* (1996). Each of these plays won the New York Drama Critics Circle Award, and *Fences* and *The Piano Lesson* each also earned Wilson the Pulitzer Prize.

Nellie Wong (b. 1940) was born and raised in Oakland, California's Chinatown during the 1940s. Since she began writing in the 1970s, she has spoken out against the oppression of all people, in particular workers, women, minorities, and immigrants, and has worked steadily with community-based and international organizations to achieve racial justice. She is known as both a poet and a feminist human rights activist. She is the author of three poetry volumes and the co-editor of an anthology of political essays, *Voices of Color* (1999). She has taught creative writing at several colleges in the Bay area. Until her retirement, she worked as senior analyst in the Office of Affirmative Action/Equal Opportunity at the University of San Francisco. She lives in San Francisco and continues to speak at conferences nationwide on issues of race, gender, class, literature, labor, and community organizing.

William Wordsworth (1770–1850) was born and raised in the Lake District of England. Both his parents died by the time he was thirteen. He studied at Cambridge, toured Europe on foot, and lived in France for a year during the first part of the French Revolution. He returned to England, leaving behind a lover, Annette Vallon, and their daughter, Caroline, from whom he was soon cut off by war between England

and France. He met SAMUEL TAYLOR COLERIDGE, and in 1798 they published *Lyrical Ballads*, the first great work of the English Romantic movement. He changed poetry forever by his decision to use common language in his poetry instead of heightened **poetic diction** (see the Glossary). In 1799 he and his sister Dorothy moved to Grasmere, in the Lake District, where he married Mary Hutchinson, a childhood friend. His greatest works were produced between 1797 and 1808. He continued to write for the next forty years but his work never regained the heights of his earlier verse. In 1843 he was named poet laureate, a position he held until his death in 1850.

Charles Wright (b. 1935) was born in Pickwick Dam, Tennessee, and grew up in Tennessee and North Carolina. He studied at Davidson College, served a four-year stint in Italy as a captain in the U.S. Army Intelligence Corps, and then continued his education at the University of Iowa Writers' Workshop and at the University of Rome on a Fulbright fellowship. He has published many books of poetry—including *Black Zodiac*, which won the Pulitzer Prize for poetry in 1997—two volumes of criticism, and a translation of Eugenio Montale's poetry. Wright's poems have been labeled impressionistic, combining images from the natural world, Catholicism, and the rural South. He taught at the University of California, Irvine, for almost twenty years and now is Souder Family Professor of English at the University of Virginia.

Raised in Martin's Ferry, Ohio, **James Wright** (1927–1980) attended Kenyon College, where the influence of JOHN CROWE RANSOM sent his early poetry in a formalist direction. After spending a year in Austria on a Fulbright fellowship, he returned to the United States and earned an M.A. and a Ph.D. at the University of Washington, studying under THEODORE ROETHKE and STANLEY KUNITZ. He went on to teach at the University of Minnesota, Macalester College, and Hunter College. His working-class background and the poverty that he witnessed during the Depression stirred in him a sympathy for the poor and for "outsiders" of various sorts that shaped the tone and content of his poetry. He published numerous books of poetry; his *Collected Poems* received the Pulitzer Prize in 1972.

The niece of SIR PHILIP SIDNEY and MARY SIDNEY HERBERT, **Lady Mary Wroth** (1587?–1651?) was one of the best and most prolific women writers of the English Renaissance and an important literary patron. Her husband's early death left her deeply in debt. She wrote *Pamphilia to Amphilanthus*, the only known English sonnet sequence on love themes by a woman; seventy-four poems that appeared in *Urania* (the first full-length work of prose fiction by a woman); and several other pieces. BEN JONSON said that reading her sonnets had made him "a better lover and a much better poet."

Born in Kent, **Sir Thomas Wyatt** (1503–1542) was educated at St. John's College, Cambridge. He spent most of his life as a courtier and diplomat, serving King Henry VIII as ambassador to Spain and as a member of several missions to Italy and France. In his travels Wyatt discovered the Italian writers of the High Renaissance, whose work he translated, thus introducing the sonnet form into English. He was arrested twice and charged with treason, sent to the Tower of London, and acquitted in

1541. Aristocratic poets at the time rarely published their poems themselves: works circulated in manuscript and in published collections ("miscellanies") gathered by printers. The most important of these is a volume published by Richard Tottel in 1557 titled *Songs and Sonnets,* but more commonly known as *Tottel's Miscellany,* which includes ninety-seven of Wyatt's sonnets and delightful lyrics.

Born in Lynn, Massachusetts, a year after his parents had emigrated from China, **John Yau** (b. 1950) received a B.A. from Bard College and an M.F.A. from Brooklyn College, where he studied with JOHN ASHBERY. He has published several books of poetry and two books of criticism, edited a fiction anthology, organized a retrospective of Ed Moses's paintings and drawings, and written a long essay on ROBERT CREELEY's poetry and poetics. Yau lives in Manhattan and teaches at the Maryland Institute College of Art.

William Butler Yeats (1865–1939) was born in Sandymount, Dublin, to an Anglo-Irish family. On leaving high school in 1883 he decided to be an artist, like his father, and attended art school, but soon gave it up to concentrate on poetry. His first poems were published in 1885 in the *Dublin University Review.* Religious by temperament but unable to accept orthodox Christianity, Yeats throughout his life explored esoteric philosophies in search of a tradition that would substitute for a lost religion. He became a member of the Theosophical Society and the Order of the Golden Dawn, two groups interested in Eastern occultism, and later developed a private system of symbols and mystical ideas. Through the influence of Lady Gregory, a writer

and promoter of literature, he became interested in Irish nationalist art, helping to found the Irish National Theatre and the famous Abbey Theatre. He was actively involved in Irish politics, especially after the Easter Rising of 1916. He continued to write and to revise earlier poems, leaving behind a body of verse that, in its variety and power, placed him among the greatest twentieth-century poets of the English language. He was awarded the Nobel Prize for literature in 1923.

Born at Ocean Springs, Mississippi, **Al Young** (b. 1939) lived for a decade in the South, then moved to Detroit. He attended the University of Michigan and the University of California, Berkeley. Young has been a professional guitarist and singer, a disk jockey, a medical photographer, and a warehouseman; he has written six books of poetry, five novels, several memoirs, essays, and film scripts. He also has edited a number of books, including *Yardbird Lives!* (1978) and *African American Literature: A Brief Introduction and Anthology* (1995). In the 1970s and '80s, Young co-founded the journals *Yardbird Reader* and *Quilt* with poet-novelist Ishmael Reed. He lives in Palo Alto, California.

Born in Davenport, Iowa, **David Young** (b. 1936) earned a B.A. from Carleton College and an M.A. and Ph.D. from Yale University. He is the author of nine books of poetry and several volumes of translations and has published five volumes of criticism and prose, among them studies of WILLIAM SHAKESPEARE and WILLIAM BUTLER YEATS and *Seasoning: A Poet's Year, with Seasonal Recipes* (1999). He has edited several anthologies, including *Models of the Universe: An Anthology of the Prose*

Poem (1995, with Stuart Friebert), and is co-editor of the literary magazine *Field*, the *Field* Translation Series, and the *Field* Contemporary Poetry Series. He lives in Oberlin, Ohio, where he is Longman Professor of English and Creative Writing at Oberlin College.

Ray A. Young Bear (b. 1950) was born and raised in the Mesquakie Tribal Settlement near Tama, Iowa. His poetry has been influenced by his maternal grandmother, Ada Kapayou Old Bear, and his wife, Stella L. Young Bear. He attended Claremont College in California as well as Grinnell College, the University of Iowa, Iowa State University, and Northern Iowa University. He has been a visiting faculty member at Eastern Washington University and the University of Iowa. Young Bear and his wife co-founded the Woodland Song and Dance Troupe of Arts Midwest in 1983. Young Bear's group has performed traditional Mesquakie music in the United States and the Netherlands. A writer of poetry, fiction, and nonfiction, he has contributed to contemporary Native American poetry and the study of it for nearly three decades.

Born in Canton, Ohio, **Paul Zimmer** (b. 1934) was educated at Kent State University. He is the author of more than a dozen poetry collections, including *The Great Bird of Love*, selected for the National Poetry Series in 1998. He has become well-known for his many poems in the voice of the persona "Zimmer," a kind of Buster Keaton everyman. Paul Zimmer has directed the university presses at the University of Georgia, the University of Iowa, and the University of Pittsburgh and was instrumental in the foundation of an influential poetry series at each.

The son of immigrant Russian Jews, **Louis Zukofsky** (1904–1978) grew up on the Lower East Side of Manhattan. His "Poem Beginning 'The'" brought him to the attention of EZRA POUND, at whose behest he was invited to edit a special issue of *Poetry* magazine, in which he coined the term "Objectivist poetry." He became a leading member of the Objectivist group, together with WILLIAM CARLOS WILLIAMS, Charles Reznikoff, GEORGE OPPEN, and Carl Rakosi. Widely considered an important forerunner of contemporary avant-garde writing, Zukofsky was an accomplished writer of fiction, a ceaseless experimenter in poetry and theory, and one of the most influential poets and critics of his era.

Glossary of Critical and Literary Terms

This glossary provides definitions for important literary terms used in this anthology. Words and phrases highlighted in **boldface** in individual entries are defined elsewhere in the glossary.

Abstract language Any language that employs intangible, nonspecific concepts. *Love*, *truth*, and *beauty* are abstractions. Abstract language is the opposite of concrete language. Both types have different effects and are important features of an author's style.

Absurd, theater of the Theatrical style prominent in the mid-twentieth century that seeks to dramatize the absurdity of modern life. **Conventions** of the style include disjointed or elliptical plot lines, disaffected characters, non-**naturalistic** dialogue, and, often, **black comedy**. Proponents include Eugene Ionesco and Samuel Beckett.

Accent The stress, or greater emphasis, given to some syllables of words relative to that received by adjacent syllables.

Accentual meter A metrical system in which the number of accented, or stressed, syllables per line is regular—all lines have the same number, or the corresponding lines of different stanzas have the same number—while the number of unstressed syllables in lines varies randomly. Accentual meter consisting of two accented syllables in each half-line linked by a system of alliteration was the hallmark of Old English poetry (up to the eleventh cen-

tury), and some modern poets, such as W. H. Auden, have sought to revive it. Gerard Manley Hopkins developed a unique variety of accentual verse he called *sprung rhythm* (see pp. 493–95).

Accentual-syllabic verse Verse whose meter takes into account both the number of syllables per line and the pattern of accented and unaccented syllables. The great majority of metrical poems in English are accentual-syllabic. Cf. **quantitative verse.**

Act One of the principal divisions of a full-length play. Plays of the Renaissance are commonly divided into five acts. Although four acts enjoyed a brief period of popularity in the nineteenth century, two or three acts are more typical of modern and contemporary dramas.

Agon The central conflict in a play. In Greek drama, the agon is a formal structural component, often a debate between two characters or parts of the **chorus**.

Alexandrine A poetic line with six iambic feet (iambic hexameter).

Allegory (1) An extended **metaphor** in which characters, events, objects, settings, and actions stand not only for themselves but also for abstract concepts, such as death or knowledge. Allegorical plays, often religious, were popular in medieval times; a famous example is *Everyman.* (2) A form or manner, usually narrative, in which objects, persons, and actions make coherent sense on a literal level but also are equated in a sustained and obvious way with (usually) abstract meanings that lie outside the story. A classic example in prose is John Bunyan's *The Pilgrim's Progress;* in narrative poetry, Edmund Spenser's *The Faerie Queene.* Edward Taylor's "Housewifery" (p. 399), though not narrative, is allegorical in its approach.

Alliteration The repetition of identical consonant sounds in the stressed syllables of words relatively near to each other (in the same line or adjacent lines, usually). Alliteration is most common at the beginnings of words ("as the grass was green") but can involve consonants within words ("green and carefree, famous among the barns"). Alliteration applies to sounds, not spelling: "And honoured among foxes and pheasants" is an example. (Lines excerpted from Dylan Thomas's "Fern Hill," p. 555.) Cf. **consonance**.

Allusion A figure of speech that echoes or makes brief reference to a literary or artistic work or a historical figure, event, or object, as, for example, the references to Lazarus and Hamlet in "The Love Song of J. Alfred Prufrock" (p. 525). It is usually a way of placing one's poem within or alongside a context that is evoked in a very economical fashion. See also **intertextuality**.

Alternative theater Any theater— most often political or experimental— that sets itself up in opposition to the **conventions** of the mainstream theater of its time.

Ambiguity In expository prose, an undesirable doubtfulness or uncertainty of meaning or intention resulting from imprecision in the use of one's words or the construction of one's sentences. In poetry, the desirable condition of admitting more than one possible meaning resulting from the capacity of language to function on levels other than the literal. Related terms sometimes employed are *ambivalence* and *polysemy.*

Anagnorisis A significant recognition or discovery by a character, usually the **protagonist**, that moves the **plot** forward by changing the circumstances of a play.

Anapest A metrical foot consisting of three syllables, with two unaccented syllables followed by an accented one (˘˘´). In *anapestic meter,* anapests are the predominant foot in a line or poem. The following line from William Cowper's "The Poplar Field" is in anapestic meter: "Aňd thě whís | pěriňg soúnd | ǒf thě coól | cǒlǒnnáde."

Anaphora Repetition of the same word or words at the beginning of two or more lines, clauses, or sentences. For examples, see the portion of Christopher Smart's *Jubilate Agno* included in the anthology (p. 416); Walt Whitman employs anaphora extensively in "Song of Myself" (p. 467) and "When Lilacs Last in the Dooryard Bloom'd" (p. 479).

Antagonist The character (or, less often, the force) that opposes the **protagonist**.

Anticlimax In drama, a disappointingly trivial occurrence where a **climax** would usually happen. An anticlimax can achieve comic effect or disrupt audience expectations of dramatic structure. In poetry, an anticlimax is an arrangement of details such that one of lesser importance follows one or ones of greater importance, where something of greater significance is expected; for example, "Not louder shrieks by dames to heaven are cast, / When husbands die, or lapdogs breathe their last" (Alexander Pope's, "The Rape of the Lock," p. 402).

Antihero   A character playing a hero's part but lacking the grandeur typically associated with a **hero**. Such a character may be comic or may exist to force the audience to reconsider its notions of heroism.

Antistrophe   The second part of a choral **ode** in Greek drama. The antistrophe was traditionally sung as the **chorus** moved from **stage right** to **stage left**.

Antithesis   A figure of speech in which contrasting words, sentences, or ideas are expressed in balanced, parallel grammatical structures; "She had some horses she loved. / She had some horses she hated," from Joy Harjo's "She Had Some Horses" (p. 674), illustrates antithesis.

Apostrophe   A figure of speech in which an absent person, an abstract quality, or a nonhuman entity is addressed as though present. It is a particular type of personification. See for example Ben Jonson's "On My First Son" (p. 385) and John Keats's "Ode on a Grecian Urn" (p. 454).

Approximate rhyme   See **slant rhyme**.

Archetype   An image, symbol, character type, or plot line that occurs frequently enough in literature, religion, myths, folktales, and fairy tales to be recognizable as an element of universal experience and which evokes a deep emotional response. In "Spring and Fall" (p. 495), Gerard Manley Hopkins develops the archetypes in his title, those of spring (archetype for birth and youth) and fall (archetype for old age and the approach of death).

Aside   A brief bit of dialogue spoken by a character to the audience or to him- or herself and assumed to be unheard by other characters onstage.

Assonance   The repetition of identical or similar vowel sounds in words relatively near to one another (usually within a line or in adjacent lines) whose consonant sounds differ. It can be initial ("*a*pple . . . *a*nd h*a*ppy *a*s") or, more commonly, internal ("gr*ee*n and car*ee*fr*ee*," "Time h*e*ld m*e* gr*ee*n and dying"). (Examples taken from Dylan Thomas's "Fern Hill," p. 555).

Aubade   A dawn song, ordinarily expressing two lovers' regret that day has come and they must separate.

Ballad   A poem that tells a story and was meant to be recited or sung; originally, a folk art transmitted orally, from person to person and from generation to generation. Many of the popular ballads were not written down and published until the eighteenth century, though their origins may have been centuries earlier. "Sir Patrick Spens" and "Lord Randal" (pp. 371 and 372) are popular Scottish ballads.

Ballad stanza   A quatrain in iambic meter rhyming *abcb* with (usually) four feet in the first and third lines, three in the second and fourth. See, for example, Robert Burns's "A Red, Red Rose" (p. 422).

Black comedy   A type of comedy in which the traditional material of tragedy (that is, suffering, or even death) is staged to provoke laughter.

Blank verse   Lines of unrhymed **iambic pentameter**. Blank verse is the most widely used verse form of poetry in English because it is closest to the natural rhythms of English speech. Shakespeare's plays, as well as Milton's *Paradise Lost* and *Paradise Regained*, and countless other long poems were composed in blank verse because it is well suited to narrative, dialogue, and reflection. William Wordsworth's "Lines Composed a Few Miles above Tintern Abbey" (p. 423) is in blank verse.

Blocking   The process of determining the stage positions, movement, and groupings of actors. Blocking generally is proposed in rehearsal by the director and may be negotiated and reworked by the actors themselves.

Cacophony   A harsh or unpleasant combination of sounds, as in lines 368–69 in Alexander Pope's "An Essay on Criticism": "But when loud surges lash the sounding shore, / The hoarse, rough verse should like the torrent roar." Cf. **euphony**.

Caesura   A pause or break within a line of verse, usually signaled by a mark of punctuation.

Canon   The group of literary works that form the backbone of a cultural tradition.

Carpe diem   A Latin phrase meaning "seize the day" from an ode by Horace. It became the label for a theme common in literature, especially in sixteenth- and seventeenth-century English love poetry, that life is short and fleeting and that therefore one must make the most of present pleasures. See Robert Herrick's "To the Virgins, to Make Much of Time" (p. 386) and Andrew Marvell's "To His Coy Mistress" (p. 397).

Catastrophe   The final movement of a **tragedy**, which brings about the fall or death of the **protagonist**. In plays other than classical tragedy, a **denouement** takes the place of a catastrophe.

Catharsis   A purging of the emotions of pity and fear. Aristotle argued in *Poetics* that catharsis is the natural, and beneficial, outcome of viewing a **tragedy**.

Characters,   Characterization Broadly speaking, characters are usually the people of a work of literature— although characters may be animals or some other beings. In fiction, characterization means the development of a character or characters throughout a story. Characterization includes the narrator's description of what characters look like and what they think, say, and do (these are sometimes very dissimilar). Their own actions and views of themselves, and other characters' views of and behavior toward them, are also means of characterization. Characters may be minor, like Goody Cloyse, or major, like Goodman Brown, both of Hawthorne's "Young Goodman Brown." Depending on the depth of characterization, a character may be simple or complex, flat or round. Character is one of the six **elements of drama** identified by Aristotle, and characterization is the process by which writers and actors make a character distinct and believable to an audience.

Chaucerian stanza A seven-line iambic stanza rhyming *ababbcc,* sometimes having an alexandrine (hexameter) closing line. See, for example, Sir Thomas Wyatt's "They flee from me" (p. 374).

Chorus In classical Greek theater, a group of actors who perform in the **orchestra** and whose functions might include providing **exposition,** confronting or questioning the **protagonist,** and commenting on the action of the play. Much of the **spectacle** of Greek drama lay in the chorus's singing and dancing. In theater of other times and places, particularly that of the Renaissance, the functions of the Greek chorus are sometimes given to a single character identified as "Chorus."

Climax In drama, the turning point at which a play switches from **rising action** to **falling action.** In fiction, the moment of greatest intensity and conflict in the action of a story. In Hawthorne's "Young Goodman Brown," events reach their climax when Brown and his wife stand together in the forest, at the point of conversion.

Closed form Any structural pattern or repetition of meter, rhyme, or stanza. Cf. **open form.**

Closet drama A play intended to be read rather than performed.

Comedy Originally, any play that ended with the characters in a better condition than when the play began, though the term is now used more frequently to describe a play intended to be funny. Traditional comedy is generally distinguished by low or ordinary characters (as opposed to the great men and women of tragedy), a humble style, a series of events or role reversals that create chaos and upheaval, and a conclusion or **denouement** that marks a return to normalcy and often a reintegration into society (such as with a wedding or other formal celebration).

Comic relief A funny scene or character appearing in an otherwise serious play, intended to provide the audience with a momentary break from the heavier themes of tragedy.

Commedia dell'arte Semi-improvised comedy relying heavily on **stock characters** and **stage business,** performed originally by traveling Italian players in the sixteenth and seventeenth centuries.

Complication One of the traditional elements of **plot.** Complication occurs when someone or something opposes the **protagonist.**

Compression The dropping of a syllable to make a line fit the meter, sometimes marked with an apostrophe (e.g., in line 16 of John Keats's "The Eve of St. Agnes" [p. 442]: "praying in dumb orat'ries"). Another common device is elision, the dropping of a vowel at the beginning or end of a word (e.g., in lines 7 and 28 of John Donne's "A Valediction: Forbidding Mourning" [p. 382]: " 'Twere profanation of our joys" and "To move, but doth, if th' other do").

Conceit A figure of speech that establishes a striking or far-fetched analogy between seemingly very dissimilar things, either the exaggerated, unrealistic comparisons found in love poems (such as those in Shakespeare's Sonnet 18 [p. 379] and parodied in Sonnet 130 [p. 380]) or the complex analogies of metaphysical wit (as in John Donne's "The Flea," p. 383).

Concrete language   Any specific, physical language that appeals to one or more of the senses—sight, hearing, taste, smell, or touch. *Stones, chairs,* and *hands* are concrete words. Concrete language is the opposite of abstract language. Both types are important features of an author's style.

Concrete poem   A poem shaped in the form of the object the poem describes or discusses. See, for example, George Herbert's "Easter-wings" (p. 387).

Confessional poetry   Poetry about personal, private issues in which a poet usually speaks directly, without the use of a persona. See, for example, Robert Lowell's "Skunk Hour" (p. 560) and Sylvia Plath's "Daddy" (p. 602).

Confidant   A character, major or minor, to whom another character confides secrets so that the audience can "overhear" the transaction and be apprised of unseen events.

Conflict   Antagonism between characters, ideas, or lines of action; between a character and the outside world; or between different aspects of a character's nature. Conflict is essential in a traditional plot, as in the conflict between Montressor and Fortunato in Poe's "The Cask of Amontillado" (p. 14). Shakespeare's Hamlet is in conflict both with his stepfather Claudius for killing his father and with himself as he tries to decide a course of action.

Connotation   The range of emotional implications and associations a word may carry outside of its dictionary definitions. Cf. **denotation**.

Consonance   The repetition of consonant sounds in words whose vowels are different. In perfect consonance, all consonants are the same—*live, love; chitter, chatter; reader, rider;* words in which all consonants following the main vowels are identical also are considered consonant—*dive, love; swatter, chitter; sound, bond; gate, mat; set, pit.*

Convention   An unstated rule, code, practice, or characteristic established by usage. In drama, tacit acceptance of theatrical conventions prevents the audience from being distracted by unrealistic features that are necessarily part of any theater experience. Greek audiences, for instance, accepted the convention of the **chorus**, while today's audiences readily accept the convention of the **fourth wall** in realistic drama and of songs in musical comedy.

Couplet   Two consecutive lines of poetry with the same end-rhyme. English (Shakespearean) sonnets end with a couplet; for an entire poem in tetrameter couplets, see Andrew Marvell's "To His Coy Mistress" (p. 397). See also **heroic couplets**.

Cruelty, theater of   Term coined by Antonin Artaud in the early twentieth century to describe a type of theater using light, sound, **spectacle**, and other primarily nonverbal forms of communication to create images of cruelty and destruction intended to shock audiences out of complacency.

Cultural studies   A general name given to a wide variety of critical practices that examine and challenge why certain texts are privileged in our society while others are dismissed or derided. Rather than focusing on traditional literary objects, Cultural Studies critics might choose to study movies, television shows, advertisements, graffiti, or comic books, often in conjunction with **canonical** works of literature.

Dactyl A metrical foot consisting of three syllables, an accented one followed by two unaccented ones (ˊˇˇ). In "dactylic meter," dactyls are the predominant foot of a line or poem. The following lines from Thomas Hardy's "The Voice" are in dactylic meter: "Wŏmăn mŭch | mĭssed, hŏw yŏu | call tŏ mĕ, | cáll tŏ mĕ, / Sáyĭng thăt | nów yŏu ărĕ | nót ăs yŏu | wére."

Deconstruction A variety of **poststructuralism**, deconstruction derives from the efforts of Jacques Derrida to undermine the foundations of Western philosophy, but as a literary critical practice it often emerges as a kind of close reading that reveals irreconcilable linguistic contradictions in a text that prevents the text from having a single stable meaning or message.

Denotation The basic meaning of a word; its dictionary definition(s).

Denouement Literally, "unknotting." The end of a play or other literary work, in which all elements of the **plot** are brought to their conclusion.

Description Language that presents specific features of a character, object, or setting; or the details of an action or event. The first paragraph of Kafka's "The Metamorphosis" describes Gregor's startling new appearance.

Deus ex machina Literally, "god out of the machine," referring to the mechanized system used to lower an actor playing a god onto the stage in classical Greek drama. Today the term is generally used disparagingly to indicate careless plotting and an unbelievable **resolution** in a play.

Dialogue Words spoken by characters, often in the form of a conversation between two or more characters. In stories and other forms of prose, dialogue is commonly enclosed between quotation marks. Dialogue is an important element in characterization and plot: much of the characterization and action in Hemingway's "A Clean, Well-Lighted Place" (p. 176) is presented through its characters' dialogue.

Diction A writer's selection of words; the kind of words, phrases, and figurative language used to make up a work of literature. In fiction, particular patterns or arrangements of words in sentences and paragraphs constitute prose style. Hemingway's diction is said to be precise, concrete, and economical. Aristotle identified diction as one of the six **elements of drama**. See also **poetic diction**.

Dimeter A line of verse consisting of two metrical feet.

Double rhyme A rhyme in which an accented, rhyming syllable is followed by one or more identical, unstressed syllables: *thrilling* and *killing*, *marry* and *tarry*. Formerly known as "feminine rhyme."

Downstage The part of the stage closest to the audience.

Dramatic irony A situation in which a reader or an audience knows more than the speakers or characters, about either the outcome of events or a discrepancy between a meaning intended by a speaker or character and that recognized by the reader or audience.

Dramatic monologue A poem with only one speaker, overheard in a dramatic moment (usually addressing another character or characters who do not speak), whose words reveal what is going on in the scene and expose significant depths of the speaker's temperament, attitudes, and values. See Robert Browning's "My Last Duchess" (p. 464) and T. S. Eliot's "The Love Song of J. Alfred Prufrock" (p. 525).

Elegy In Greek and Roman literature, a serious, meditative poem written in "elegiac meter" (alternating hexameter and pentameter lines); since the 1600s, a sustained and formal poem lamenting the death of a particular person, usually ending with a consolation, or one setting forth meditations on death or another solemn theme. See Thomas Gray's "Elegy Written in a Country Churchyard" (p. 412), John Milton's pastoral elegy "Lycidas" (p. 389), and Walt Whitman's "When Lilacs Last in the Dooryard Bloom'd" (p. 479). The adjective *elegiac* is also used to describe a general tone of sadness or a worldview that emphasizes suffering and loss. It is most often applied to Anglo-Saxon poems like *Beowulf* or *The Seafarer* but can also be used for modern poems as, for example, A. E. Housman's in *A Shropshire Lad*.

Elements of drama The six features identified by Aristotle in *Poetics* as descriptive of and necessary to drama. They are, in order of the importance assigned to them by Aristotle, **plot, characterization, theme, diction, melody**, and **spectacle**.

Elements of fiction Major elements of fiction are **plot, characters, setting, point of view, style**, and **theme**. Skillful employment of these entities is essential in effective novels and stories. From beginning to end, each element is active and relates to the others dynamically.

Elements of poetry Verbal, aural, and structural features of poetry, including **diction, tone, images, figures of speech, symbols, rhythm, rhyme**, and poetic form, which are combined to create poems.

Elision See **compression**.

Empathy The ability of the audience to relate to, even experience, the emotions of characters onstage or in a text.

End-rhyme Rhyme occurring at the ends of lines in a poem.

End-stopped line A line of poetry whose grammatical structure and thought reach completion by its end. Cf. **run-on line**.

English sonnet A sonnet consisting of three quatrains (three four-line units, typically rhyming *abab cdcd efef*) and a couplet (two rhyming lines). Usually, the subject is introduced in the first quatrain, expanded in the second, and expanded still further in the third; the couplet adds a logical, pithy conclusion or introduces a surprising twist. Also called the Shakespearean sonnet. Cf. **Spenserian sonnet**.

Enjambment See **run-on line**.

Epic A long narrative poem that celebrates the achievements of great heroes and heroines, often determining the fate of a tribe or nation, written in formal language and an elevated style. Examples include Homer's *Iliad* and *Odyssey*, Virgil's *Aeneid*, and John Milton's *Paradise Lost*.

Epic theater The name given by Bertold Brecht to a theatrical style emphasizing the relationship between form and ideology. It is characterized by brief scenes, narrative breaks, political and historical themes, an analytical (rather than emotional) tone, and characters with whom it is difficult to feel **empathy**. Though considered **alternative theater** when it was new, many of its **conventions** have since been adopted by mainstream dramatists.

Epigram Originally, an inscription, especially an epitaph; in modern usage a short poem, usually polished and witty with a surprising twist at the end. (Its other dictionary definition, "any terse, witty, pointed statement," generally does not apply in poetry.)

Epigraph In literature, a quotation at the beginning of a poem or on the title page or the beginning of a chapter in a book. See the epigraph at the beginning of T. S. Eliot's "The Love Song of J. Alfred Prufrock" (p. 525), which are lines from Dante's *Inferno*.

Epilogue A final speech or scene occurring after the main action of the play has ended. An epilogue generally sums up or comments on the meaning of the play.

Epiphany An appearance or manifestation, especially of a divine being; in literature, since James Joyce adapted the term to secular use in 1944, a sudden sense of radiance and revelation one may feel while perceiving a commonplace object; a moment or event in which the essential nature of a person, a situation, or an object is suddenly perceived. The term is more common in narrative than in lyric poetry. William Wordsworth writes about epiphanies in "Ode: Intimations of Immortality" (p. 428), although the poem itself does not depict them; Robert Bly depicts one in "Driving to Town Late to Mail a Letter" (p. 580).

Episode In Greek drama, the scenes of dialogue that occur between the choral **odes**. Now the term is used to mean any small unit of drama that has its own completeness and internal unity.

Euphony Language that strikes the ear as smooth, musical, and agreeable. An example can be found in Alexander Pope's "An Essay on Criticism," lines 366–67: "Soft is the strain when Zephyr gently blows, / And the smooth stream in smoother numbers flows." Cf. **cacophony**.

Exact rhyme Rhyme in which all sounds following the vowel sound are the same: *spite* and *night, art* and *heart, ache* and *fake, card* and *barred.*

Exaggeration See **hyperbole**.

Exposition A means of filling in the audience on events that occurred offstage or before the play's beginning. Clumsily handled exposition, in which characters talk at length about things they normally would not, is characteristic of much bad drama.

Expressionism Nonrealistic playmaking style using exaggerated or otherwise unreal gestures, light, and sound. Expressionistic techniques are often used to convey a sense of memory, dream, or fantasy.

Extension Pronunciation that adds a syllable for the sake of the meter. See, for example, the ninth line of John Donne's sonnet "Batter my heart, three-personed God" (p. 384): "and would be lovèd fain."

Falling action The action after the **climax** in a traditionally structured play whereby the tension lessens and the play moves toward the **catastrophe** or **denouement**.

Falling meter   Meter using a foot (usually a trochee or a dactyl) in which the first syllable is accented and those that follow are unaccented, giving a sense of stepping down. Cf. **rising meter**.

Farce   Comedy that relies on exaggerated characters, extreme situations, fast and accelerating pacing, and, often, sexual innuendo.

Feminine rhyme   See **double rhyme**.

Feminist criticism   A school of literary criticism that examines the roles of women in literature and culture as well as the relationships between men and women. Contemporary feminist criticism rose to prominence in the 1970s, when the modern feminist movement began to explore the patriarchal structures in which many women felt trapped. Some feminist critics seek to show the ways in which literary texts demonstrate the repression and powerlessness of women—or, alternately, to show how female literary characters could overcome sexist power structures. Still others seek to rediscover and promote writing by women whose works have been excluded from the mostly male **canon** of "great" literature.

Feminist theater   Any play or theater whose primary object is to shine light on the issues of women's rights and sexism.

Fiction   Generally speaking, any imaginative, usually prose, work of literature. More narrowly, narratives— **short stories**, **novellas**, or **novels**— whose plots, characters, and settings are constructions of its writer's imagination, which draws on the writer's experiences and reflections.

Figurative language   Uses of language—employing **metaphor** or **simile** or other figures of speech—that depart from standard or literal usage in order to achieve a special effect or meaning. Figurative language is often employed in poetry; although less often seen in plays and stories, it can be used powerfully in those forms. Steinbeck's short story "The Chrysanthemums" (p. 180) opens with a figurative description of the Salinas Valley in winter.

First-person narrator   In a story told by one person, the "I" who tells the story. Sometimes the first-person narrator is purely an observer; more often he or she is directly or indirectly involved in the action of the story. Montresor is the first-person narrator of, and one of two characters in, Edgar Allan Poe's "The Cask of Amontillado" (p. 14). As a first-person narrator, he reveals much about his own emotions and motivations.

Fixed form   Poetry written in definite, repeating patterns of line, rhyme scheme, or stanza.

Flashback   A writer's way of introducing important earlier material. As a narrator tells a story, he or she may stop the flow of events and direct the reader to an earlier time. Sometimes the narrator may return to the present, sometimes remain in the past. The thoughts of Granny Weatherall in Porter's "The Jilting of Granny Weatherall" (p. 153) include reminiscences that seem to occur in the present.

Foil   A character who exists chiefly to set off or display, usually by opposition, the important character traits of the **protagonist** or another important person.

Foot The basic unit in metrical verse, comprising (usually) one stressed and one or more unstressed syllables. See also **anapest, dactyl, iamb, spondee,** and **trochee.**

Foreshadowing Words, gestures, or other actions that suggest future events or outcomes. The opening of Hawthorne's "Young Goodman Brown" foreshadows serious trouble ahead when Faith, Brown's wife, begs him to stay home with her "this night, dear husband, of all nights in the year."

Form (1) Genre or literary type (e.g., the lyric form); (2) patterns of meter, lines, and rhymes (stanzaic form); (3) the organization of the parts of a literary work in relation to its total effect (e.g., "The form [structure] of this poem is very effective").

Formalism A broad term for the various types of literary theory that advocate focusing attention on the text itself and not on extratextual factors. Formalist critics are interested in the formal elements of a literary text— structure, tone, characters, setting, symbols, linguistic features—and seek to create meaning by examining the relationships between these different parts of a text.

Fourth wall The theatrical convention, dating from the nineteenth century, whereby an audience seems to be looking and listening through an invisible fourth wall, usually into a room in a private residence. The fourth wall is primarily associated with **realism** and domestic dramas.

Free verse See **open form.**

Gender criticism A broad term for literary criticism that highlights gender roles or relationships between the sexes. In this expansive sense, **feminist criticism** is a kind of gender criticism, although the latter term is most often applied to gay and lesbian approaches to literature that explore the construction of sexual identity.

Genre A type or form of literature. While the major literary genres are fiction, drama, poetry, and exposition, many other subcategories of genres are recognized, including **comedy, tragedy, tragicomedy, romance, melodrama,** epic, lyric, pastoral, novel, short story, and so on.

Haiku A lyric form, originating in Japan, of seventeen syllables in three lines, the first and third having five syllables and the second seven, presenting an image of a natural object or scene that expresses a distinct emotion or spiritual insight. Gary Snyder incorporates haiku into "Hitch Haiku" (p. 596).

Half rhyme See **slant rhyme.**

Hamartia Sometimes translated as "tragic flaw" but more properly understood as an error or general character trait that leads to the downfall of a character in **tragedy.**

Heptameter A poetic line with seven metrical feet.

Hero, heroine Sometimes used to refer to any **protagonist,** the term more properly applies only to a great figure from legend or history or to a character who performs in a remarkably honorable and selfless manner.

Heroic couplets   Couplets in iambic pentameter that usually end in a period. See Alexander Pope's "The Rape of the Lock" (p. 402). Also called "closed couplets."

Hexameter   A poetic line with six metrical feet. See also **alexandrine**.

Historical Criticism   A kind of literary criticism based on the notion that history and literature are often interrelated. For example, literary critics might read history books and various sorts of historical documents in order to gain insights into the composition and significance of a literary work.

Hubris   An arrogance or inflated sense of self that can lead to a character's downfall. The **protagonists** of **tragedy** often suffer from hubris.

Hyperbole   Exaggeration; a figure of speech in which something is stated more strongly than is logically warranted. Hyperbole is often used to make a point emphatically, as when Hamlet protests that he loves Ophelia much more than her brother does: "Forty thousand brothers / Could not with all their quantity of love / Make up my sum" (5.1.272–74). See also Robert Burns's "A Red, Red Rose" (p. 422).

Iamb   A metrical foot consisting of two syllables, an unaccented one followed by an accented one (˘ ´). In iambic meter (the most widely used of English metrical forms), iambs are the predominant foot in a line or poem. The following line from Thomas Gray's "Elegy Written in a Country Churchyard" (p. 412) is in iambic meter: "The cúr | fĕw tólls | thĕ knéll | ŏf párt | ĭng dáy."

Image   (1) Sometimes called a "word-picture," an image is a word or group of words that refers to a sensory experience or to an object that can be known by one or more of the senses. **Imagery** signifies all such language in a poem or other literary work collectively and can involve any of the senses; see, for example, the images of cold in the first stanza of John Keats's "The Eve of St. Agnes" (p. 442) or note the image of a fire evoked by Steinbeck's description of the willow scrub in "The Chrysanthemums": it "flamed with sharp and positive yellow leaves." See also **synesthesia**. (2) A metaphor or other comparison. **Imagery** in this sense refers to the characteristic that several images in a poem may have in common, as for example, the military imagery in the first part of Donne's sonnet "Batter my heart, three personed God" and the erotic imagery at the end (p. 384).

Imagist poetry   Poetry that relies on sharp, concrete images and is written in a highly concentrated style that is suggestive rather than discursive. See, for example, H. D.'s "Garden" (p. 520).

Imitation   Since Aristotle, drama has been differentiated from fiction because it is said to rely on an imitation (in Greek, *mimesis*) of human actions rather than on a narration of them.

Implied metaphor   Metaphor in which the *to be* verb is omitted and one aspect of the comparison is implied rather than stated directly. Whereas "a car thief is a dirty dog" is a direct metaphor, "some dirty dog stole my car" contains an implied metaphor. Examples from John Frederick Nims's "Love Poem" (p. 551) are "whose hands *shipwreck* vases," "A *wrench* in clocks and the solar system," and "In *traffic* of wit expertly manoeuvre."

Interlude   A brief, usually comic, performance inserted between the **acts** of a play or between courses at a formal banquet. Interludes were most popular during the Renaissance.

Internal rhyme   Rhyme that occurs with words within a line, words within lines near each other, or a word within a line and one at the end of the same or a nearby line. Edgar Allan Poe's "Annabel Lee" (p. 458) offers many examples: "chilling / And killing," "Can ever dissever," "And the stars never rise but I see the bright eyes."

Intertextuality   The implied presence of previous texts within a literary work or as context, usually conveyed through allusion or choice of genre. An intertextual approach assumes that interpretation of a text is incomplete until the relation of the work to its predecessors — response, opposition, and development — has been considered.

Irony   A feeling, tone, mood, or attitude arising from the awareness that what *is* (reality) is opposite from, and usually worse than, what *seems* to be (appearance). What a person says may be ironic (see **verbal irony**), and a discrepancy between what a character knows or means and what a reader or an audience knows can be ironic (see **dramatic irony**). A general situation also can be seen as ironic (**situational irony**). Irony should not be confused with mere coincidence. See also **Socratic irony**.

Italian sonnet   Generally speaking, a sonnet composed of an octave

(an eight-line unit), rhyming *abbaabba*, and a sestet (a six-line unit), often rhyming *cdecde* or *cdcdcd*. The octave usually develops an idea, question, or problem; then the poem pauses, or "turns," and the sestet completes the idea, answers the question, or resolves the difficulty. Sometimes called a Petrarchan sonnet. See Gerard Manley Hopkins's "God's Grandeur" (p. 494).

Juxtaposition   Placement of things side by side or close together for comparison or contrast, or to create something new from the union. See Alexander Pope's "The Rape of the Lock" (p. 402), 1. 72: "Dost sometimes counsel take — and sometimes tea."

Language poetry   Poetry evincing skepticism regarding the ability of written language to record, represent, communicate, or express anything other than its own linguistic apparatus. See Lyn Hejinian's "A Mask of Anger" (p. 638).

Line   A sequence of words printed as a separate entity on a page; the basic structural unit in poetry (except in prose poems).

Literal   In accordance with the primary or strict meaning of a word or words; not figurative or metaphorical.

Litotes   See **understatement**.

Lyric   Originally, a poem sung to the accompaniment of a lyre; now a short poem expressing the personal emotion and ideas of a single speaker.

Marxist criticism   Deriving from Karl Marx's theories of economics and class struggle, Marxist criticism sees literature as a material product of work, one that reflects or contests the ideologies that generated its production and consumption.

Masculine rhyme See **single rhyme**.

Melodrama A type of play employing broadly drawn heroes and villains, suspenseful plots, music, and a triumph of good over evil. Melodrama thrived throughout the nineteenth century and remained popular into the twentieth.

Melody One of the six **elements of drama** identified by Aristotle. Since the Greek **chorus** communicated through song and dance, melody was an important part of even the most serious play, though it is now largely confined to musical comedy.

Metaphor A figure of speech in which two things usually thought to be dissimilar are treated as if they were alike and have characteristics in common. "Whose *palms are bulls* in china" (John Frederick Nims's "Love Poem," p. 551). See also **implied metaphor**.

Metaphysical poetry The work of a number of seventeenth-century poets that was characterized by philosophical subtlety and intellectual rigor; subtle, often outrageous logic; an imitation of actual speech sometimes resulting in a "rough" meter and style; and far-fetched analogies. John Donne's "A Valediction: Forbidding Mourning" and "The Flea" (pp. 382 and 383) exemplify the type. See also **conceit**.

Meter A steady beat, or measured pulse, created by a repeating pattern of accents or syllables, or both.

Metonymy A figure of speech in which the name of one thing is substi-

tuted for something closely associated with it, as in "The *White House* announced today...," a phrase in which the name of a building is substituted for the president or the staff members who issued the announcement; "He's got *a Constable* on his wall"; "The *trains* are on strike"; or "*Wall Street* is in a panic." In the last line of John Frederick Nims's "Love Poem" (p. 551), "All the toys of the world would break," *toys* is substituted for "things that give happiness" (as toys do to a child). See also **synecdoche**.

Mock epic A literary form that imitates the grand style and conventions of the epic genre—the opening statement of a theme, an address to the muse, long formal speeches, and epic similes—but applies them to a subject unworthy of such exalted treatment. In "The Rape of the Lock" (p. 402), Alexander Pope uses the form for comic effect and at the same time treats seriously the great epic themes concerning human destiny and mortality. Also called "mock heroic." See also **epic**.

Monometer A poetic line with one metrical foot.

Motivation What drives a character to act in a particular way. To be convincing to an audience, an actor must understand and make clear to the audience the character's motivation.

Narrative A story in prose or verse; an account of events involving characters and a sequence of events told by a storyteller (narrator). Usually, the characters can be analyzed and generally understood, the events unfold in a cause-and-effect sequence, some unity can be found among the characters, plot, point of view, style, and theme. Novels as well as stories are most often narratives, and journalism commonly employs narrative form.

Narrator   The storyteller, usually an observer who is narrating from a third-person point of view or a participant in the story's action speaking in the first person. Style and tone are important clues to the nature of a narrator and the validity and objectivity of the story he or she is telling. Montresor, the narrator of "The Cask of Amontillado" (p. 14), creates his own self-portrait as he relates what has happened.

Naturalism, naturalistic   A style of writing or acting meant to mimic closely the patterns of ordinary life.

Near rhyme   See **slant rhyme**.

New comedy   An ancient form of **comedy** that told of initially forbidden but ultimately successful love and that employed **stock characters**. New comedy is particularly associated with the Greek playwright Menander (342–292 B.C.E.).

New Criticism   A kind of **formalism** that dominated Anglo-American literary criticism in the middle decades of the twentieth century. It emphasized **close reading**, particularly of poetry, to discover how a work of literature functioned as a self-contained, self-referential aesthetic object.

New Historicism   A school of **historical criticism** that takes account of both what history has to teach us about literature *and* what literature has to teach us about history. New Historicists will examine many different types of texts—government records,

periodicals, private diaries, bills of sale—in order to re-create, as much as possible, the rich cultural context that surrounded both an author and that author's original audience.

Novel   An extended prose narrative or work of prose fiction, usually published alone. Hawthorne's *The Scarlet Letter* is a fairly short novel, Melville's *Moby-Dick, or, the Whale* a very long one. The length of a novel enables its author to develop characters, plot, and settings in greater detail than a short-story writer can. Ellison's story "Battle Royal" (p. 196) is taken from his novel *Invisible Man* (1948), Tan's story "Two Kinds" (p. 348) from her novel *The Joy Luck Club* (1989).

Novella   Between the short story and the novel in size and complexity. Like them, the novella is a work of prose fiction. Sometimes it is called a long short story. Melville's "Bartleby, the Scrivener" and Kafka's "The Metamorphosis" are novellas.

Octameter   A poetic line with eight metrical feet.

Octave   The first eight lines of an Italian sonnet.

Ode   (1) A multipart song sung by the **chorus** of Greek drama. A classical ode consists of a **strophe** followed by an **antistrophe** and sometimes by a final section called the *epode*. (2) A long lyric poem, serious (often intellectual) in tone, elevated and dignified in style, dealing with a single theme. The ode is generally more complicated in form than other lyric poems. Some odes retain a formal division into strophe, antistrophe, and epode, which reflects the form's origins in Greek tragedy. See William Wordsworth's "Ode: Intimations of Immortality" (p. 428), Percy Bysshe Shelley's "Ode to the West Wind" (p. 438), and John Keats's "Ode on a Grecian Urn" (p. 454).

Old comedy   Comedy, such as that of Aristophanes, employing raucous (sometimes coarse) humor, elements of **satire** and **farce**, and often a critique of contemporary persons or political and social norms.

Omniscient narrator   A narrator who seems to know everything about a story's events and characters, even their inner feelings. Usually, an omniscient narrator maintains emotional distance from the characters. The narrator of Maupassant's "The Necklace" is omniscient.

One act   A short play that is complete in one **act**.

Onomatopoeia   The use of words whose sounds supposedly resemble the sounds they denote (such as *thump, rattle, growl, hiss*), or a group of words whose sounds help to convey what is being described; for example, Emily Dickinson's "I heard a Fly buzz—when I died" (p. 489).

Open form   A form free of any predetermined metrical and stanzaic patterns. Cf. **closed form**.

Orchestra   In Greek theater, the area in front of the stage proper where the chorus performed its songs and dances. Later, a pit for musicians in front of the stage.

Ottava rima   An eight-line stanza in iambic pentameter rhyming *abababcc*. See William Butler Yeats's "Among School Children" (p. 501).

Overstatement   See **hyperbole**.

Oxymoron   A figure of speech combining in one phrase (usually an adjective and a noun) two seemingly contradictory elements, such as "loving hate" or "feather of lead, bright smoke, cold fire, sick health" (from Shakespeare's *Romeo and Juliet* 1.1.176–80). Oxymoron is a type of **paradox**.

Pantoum   A poem composed of quatrains rhyming *abab* in which the second and fourth lines of each stanza serve as the first and third lines of the next, continuing through the last stanza, which repeats the first and third lines of the first stanza in reverse order. See Nellie Wong's "Grandmother's Song" (p. 628).

Paradox   A figure of speech in which a statement initially seeming self-contradictory or absurd turns out, seen in another light, to make good sense. The closing lines of John Donne's sonnet "Batter my heart, three-personed God" (p. 384) are paradoxical: "for I, / Except you enthrall me, never shall be free, / Nor ever chaste, except you ravish me." See also **oxymoron**.

Parallelism   (1) A verbal arrangement in which elements of equal weight within phrases, sentences, or paragraphs are expressed in a similar grammatical order and structure. It can appear within a line or pair of lines ("And he was always quietly arrayed, / And he was always human when he talked"—Edwin Arlington Robinson, "Richard Cory" [p. 505]) or, more noticeably, as a series of parallel items, as found in Langston Hughes's "Harlem" (p. 539). (2) A principle of poetic structure in which consecutive lines in open form are related by a line's repeating, expanding on, or contrasting with the idea of the line or lines before it, as in the poems of Walt Whitman (pp. 467–486).

Parody   Now, a humorous or satirical imitation of a serious piece of literature or writing. In the sixteenth and seventeenth centuries, poets such as George Herbert practiced "sacred parody" by adapting secular lyrics to devotional themes.

Partial rhyme   See **slant rhyme**.

Pastoral   A poem (also called an "eclogue," a "bucolic," or an "idyll") that expresses a city poet's nostalgic image of the simple, peaceful life of shepherds and other country folk in an idealized natural setting. Christopher Marlowe's "The Passionate Shepherd to His Love" (p. 378) uses some pastoral conventions, as do certain elegies (including John Milton's "Lycidas," p. 389).

Pause   See **caesura**.

Pentameter   A poetic line with five metrical feet.

Performance art   Loose term for a variety of performances that defy traditional categories of play, monologue, musical act, and so on. The term arose in the late twentieth century as a catchall to name the growing number of nontraditional performances, many of which addressed controversial subjects and themes.

Peripeteia   A reversal or change of fortune for a character, for better or worse.

Persona   Literally, the mask through which actors spoke in Greek plays. In some critical approaches of recent decades, *persona* refers to the "character" projected by an author, the "I" of a narrative poem or novel, or the speaker whose voice is heard in a lyric poem. In this view, a poem is an artificial construct distanced from a poet's autobiographical self. Cf. **voice**.

Personification   A figure of speech in which something nonhuman is treated as if it had human characteristics or performed human actions. Sometimes it involves abstractions, as in Thomas Gray's phrase "Fair Science frowned" ("Elegy Written in a Country Churchyard," p. 412); science cannot literally frown. In other cases concrete things are given human characteristics, as in the phrase "Wearing white for Eastertide" from A. E. Housman's "Loveliest of trees, the cherry now" (p. 495). Cherry trees do not actually wear clothes — but here they are being given, briefly, a human attribute. Difficulty can arise when personification is incorrectly defined as treating something nonhuman in terms of anything alive rather than what is specifically human; "the mouth of time," for instance, in Nancy Willard's "Questions My Son Asked Me, Answers I Never Gave Him" (p. 617) is metaphor, not personification, since animals as well as humans have mouths. See also **apostrophe**.

Petrarchan sonnet   See **Italian sonnet**.

Plot   (1) The sequence of major events in a story, usually related by cause and effect. Plot and character are intimately related, since characters carry out the plot's action. Plots may be described as simple or complex, depending on their degree of complication. "Traditional" writers, such as Poe and Maupassant, usually plot their stories tightly; modernist writers such as Joyce and Paley employ looser, often ambiguous plots. (2) The action that takes place within the play. Of the six **elements of drama**, Aristotle considered plot to be the most important. Typical elements of plot include a **prologue** or **exposition**, **rising action**, **complication**, **climax**, **falling action**, and **catastrophe** or **denouement**.

Poem   A term whose meaning exceeds all attempts at definition. Here is a slightly modified version of the definition of William Harmon and C. Hugh Holman in *A Handbook to Literature* (1996): A poem is a literary composition, written or oral, typically characterized by imagination, emotion, sense impressions, and concrete language that invites attention to its own physical features, such as sound or appearance on the page.

Poetic diction   In general, specialized language used in or considered appropriate to poetry. In the late seventeenth and the eighteenth centuries, a refined use of language that excluded "common" speech from poetry as indecorous and substituted elevated circumlocutions, archaic synonyms, or such forms as *ope* and *e'er*.

Point of view   One of the elements of fiction, point of view is the perspective, or angle of vision, from which a narrator presents a story. Point of view tells us about the narrator as well as about the characters, setting, and theme of a story. Two common points of view are *first-person narration* and *third-person narration*. If a narrator speaks of himself or herself as "I," the narration is in the first person; if the narrator's self is not apparent and the story is told about others from some distance, using "he," "she," "it," and "they," then third-person narration is likely in force. The point of view may be omniscient (all-knowing) or limited, objective or subjective. When determining a story's point of view, it is helpful to decide whether the narrator is reporting events as they are happening or as they happened in the past; is observing or participating in the action; and is or is not emotionally involved. Welty's "A Worn Path" is told from the third-person objective point of view, since its narrator observes what the character is doing, thinking, and feeling, yet seems emotionally distant. Poe's "The Cask of Amontillado" and Joyce's "Araby" are told in the first-person subjective and limited point of view, since their narrators are very much involved in the action. In Porter's "The Jilting of Granny Weatherall," shifting points of view enable us to see the dying old woman from the outside, as her children and doctors do (third-person objective), learn about her most private reminiscences and secrets (third-person subjective), and hear her thoughts directly as if we were inside her mind (first-person subjective).

Poststructuralism   Positing that no text can have a fixed or real meaning because no meaning can exist outside of the network of other meanings to which it is connected, poststructuralism carries the insights of **structuralism** one step further. If, as structuralists claim, we can understand things only in terms of other things, then perhaps there is no center point of understanding, but only an endlessly interconnected web of ideas leading to other ideas leading to still other ideas. Meaning, then, is forever shifting and altering as our understanding of the world changes.

Prologue   A speech or scene that occurs before the beginning of the **plot** proper.

Properties, props Any movable objects, beyond scenery and costumes, used in the performance of a play. Early drama was performed with few props, but as theater moved toward **realism**, props took on greater importance.

Proscenium arch An arch across the front of a stage, sometimes with a curtain. The proscenium frames the action and provides a degree of separation between the actors and the audience.

Prose poem A poem printed as prose, with lines wrapping at the right margin rather than being divided through predetermined line breaks. See Carolyn Forché's "The Colonel" (p. 669).

Prosody The principles of versification, especially of meter, rhythm, rhyme, and stanza forms.

Protagonist The lead character of a play, though not necessarily a hero in the classic sense.

Psychological criticism A broad term for the various types of literary theory that focus on the inner workings of the human psyche and the ways in which they manifest themselves in literature. Psychological critics often interpret literature as a psychologist might interpret a dream or a wish, often paying special attention to unstated motives and to the unconscious states of mind in characters, authors, or readers.

Pun A play on words based on the similarity in sound between two words having very different meanings. Also called "paronomasia." See the puns on "heart" and "kindly" in Sir Thomas Wyatt's "They flee from me" (p. 374).

Quantitative verse Verse whose meter is based on the length of syllables. (Phonetic length was a distinguishing feature of ancient Greek and Latin, whereas English is an accentual language.) Classical poetry exhibits a great variety of meters, and some English poets in the late 1500s attempted to fashion English verse on this principle. In *Evangeline*, Henry Wadsworth Longfellow used dactylic hexameter in imitation of Virgil's *Aeneid*, but defined it by accent, not quantity. Cf. **accentual-syllabic verse**.

Quatrain A stanza of four lines or other four-line unit within a larger form, such as a sonnet.

Reader-response criticism The various theories of reader-response criticism hold that a text is an interaction between author and reader, and a text can never be complete unless readers bring to it their own unique insights. Reading, then, is not a passive attempt to understand a text but is itself an act of creation, no less than writing.

Realism Any drama (or other art) that seeks to closely mimic real life. Realism more specifically refers to a sort of drama that rose in opposition to **melodrama** in the late nineteenth and early twentieth century and that attempted to avoid some of the more artificial **conventions** of theater and present the problems of ordinary people living their everyday lives.

Recognition See **anagnorsis**.

Refrain One or more identical or deliberately similar lines repeated throughout a poem, such as the final line of a stanza or a block of lines between stanzas or sections.

Resolution A satisfying outcome that effectively ends the conflict of a play.

Rhyme The repetition of the accented vowel sound of a word and all succeeding consonant sounds. See also **exact rhyme; slant rhyme.**

Rhyme royal An alternative term for **Chaucerian stanza** coined by King James I of Scotland in his poem *The Kingis Quair* ("The King's Book"), written about 1424.

Rhyme scheme The pattern of end rhymes in a poem or stanza usually represented by a letter assigned to each word-sound, the same word-sounds having the same letter (e.g., a quatrain's rhyme scheme might be described as *abcb*).

Rhythm The patterned "movement" of language created by the choice of words and their arrangement, usually described through such metaphors as fast or slow, smooth or halting, graceful or rough, deliberate or frenzied, syncopated or disjointed. Rhythm in poetry is affected by, in addition to meter, such factors as line length; line endings; pauses (or lack of them) within lines; spaces within, at the beginning or end of, or between lines; word choice; and combinations of sounds.

Rising action The increasingly tense and complicated action leading up to the **climax** in a traditionally structured play.

Rising meter A foot (usually an iamb or an anapest) in which the final, accented syllable is preceded by one or two unaccented syllables, thus giving a sense of stepping up. Cf. **falling meter.**

Romance A play neither wholly comic nor wholly tragic, often containing elements of the supernatural. The best-known examples are Shakespeare's late plays, such as *The Winter's Tale* and *The Tempest*, which have a generally comic structure but are more ruminative in theme and spirit than traditional **comedy.**

Run-on line A line whose sense and grammatical structure continue into the next line. In the following lines by William Stafford ("Traveling through the Dark," p. 554), the first line is run-on, the second end-stopped: "Traveling through the dark I found a deer / dead on the edge of the Wilson River road." Also called "enjambment." Cf. **end-stopped line.**

Sarcasm A harsh and cutting form of verbal irony, often involving apparent praise that is obviously not meant: "Oh, no, these are fine. I *prefer* my eggs thoroughly charred."

Satire A work, or manner within a work, employing **comedy** and irony to mock a particular human characteristic or social institution. Generally, a satirist wants the audience not only to laugh but also to change its opinions or actions. Alexander Pope's "The Rape of the Lock" (p. 402), for example, satirizes the values and attitudes of members of the wealthy, indolent upper classes of the poet's day.

Scansion The division of metrical verse into feet in order to determine and label its meter. Scanning a poem involves marking its stressed syllables with an accent mark ['] and its unstressed syllables with a curved line [˘], and using a vertical line to indicate the way a line divides into feet (or labeling).

The type of foot used most often and the line length—that is, the number of feet in each line—are then identified. See also **foot** and **line**.

Scene One of the secondary divisions within an **act** of a play.

Sestet The last six lines of an Italian sonnet.

Sestina A lyric poem consisting of six six-line stanzas and a three-line concluding stanza (or "envoy"). The last words of the line of the first stanza must be used as the last words of the lines of the other five stanzas in a specified pattern (the first line ends with the last word of the last line of the previous stanza, the second line with that of the first line of the previous stanza, the third line with that of the previous fifth line, the fourth line with that of the previous second line, the fifth line with that of the previous fourth line, the sixth line with that of the previous third line). The three-line envoy must use the end-words of lines five, three, and one from the first stanza, in that order, as its last words and must include the first stanza's other three end-words within its lines. See Alice Fulton's "You Can't Rhumboogie in a Ball and Chain" (p. 681).

Set The stage dressing for a play, consisting of backdrops, furniture, and similar large items.

Setting One of the elements of fiction, setting is the context for the action: the time, place, culture, and atmosphere in which it occurs. A work may have several settings; the relation among them may be significant to the meaning of the work. In Hawthorne's "Young Goodman Brown," for example, the larger setting is seventeenth-century Puritan Salem, Massachusetts, but Brown's mysterious journey is set in a forest, and its prelude and melancholy aftermath are set in the village.

Shakespearean sonnet See **English sonnet**.

Shaped poem See **concrete poem**.

Short story A short work of narrative fiction whose plot, characters, settings, point of view, style, and theme reinforce each other, often in subtle ways, creating an overall unity.

Simile Expression of a direct similarity, using such words as *like, as,* or *than,* between two things usually regarded as dissimilar, as in "Shrinking from far *headlights pale as a dime*" (John Frederick Nims's "Love Poem," p. 551). It is important to distinguish *simile* from *comparison,* in which the two things joined by "like" or "as" are *not* dissimilar.

Single rhyme A rhyme in which the stressed, rhyming syllable is the final syllable: *west* and *vest, away* and *today.* Formerly called "masculine rhyme."

Situational irony The mood evoked when an action intended to have a certain effect turns out to have a different and more sinister effect. See Thomas Hardy's "The Convergence of the Twain" (p. 491).

Slant rhyme Consonance at the ends of lines; for example, *Room* and *Storm, firm* and *Room,* and *be* and *Fly* in Emily Dickinson's "I heard a Fly buzz—when I died" (p. 489). It can also be internal, if repeated enough to form a discernible pattern.

Socratic irony A pose of self-deprecation, or of belittling oneself, in order to tease the reader into deeper insight.

Soliloquy A speech delivered by a character who is alone on stage or otherwise out of hearing of the other characters. Since the character is effectively speaking to him- or herself, a soliloquy often serves as a window into the character's mind and heart.

Sonnet A fourteen-line poem usually written in iambic pentameter; originally lyrical love poems, sonnets came to be used also for meditations on religious themes, death, and nature, and are now open to all subjects. Some variations in form have been tried: Sir Philip Sidney's "Loving in truth, and fain in verse my love to show" (p. 376) is written in hexameters; George Meredith wrote sixteen-line sonnets; John Milton's "On the New Forcers of Conscience under the Long Parliament" is a "caudate" (tailed) sonnet with a six-line coda appended; and Gerard Manley Hopkins designed "Pied Beauty" (p. 494) as a "curtal" (abbreviated) sonnet (six lines in place of the octave, then four lines, and a half-line ending in place of a sestet). See **English sonnet** and **Italian sonnet**.

Sonnet sequence A group of sonnets so arranged as to imply a narrative progression in the speaker's experience or attitudes; used especially in the sixteenth century. Also called a sonnet cycle.

Spectacle The purely visual elements of a play, including the **sets**, costumes, **props**, lighting, and special effects. Of the six **elements of drama** he identified, Aristotle considered spectacle to be the least important.

Spenserian sonnet A variation of the English sonnet that employs the structure of three quatrains followed by a couplet but joins the quatrains by linking rhymes: *abab bcbc cdcd ee*.

Spenserian stanza A stanza of nine iambic lines, the first eight in pentameter and the ninth in hexameter, rhyming *ababbcbcc* (see John Keats's "The Eve of St. Agnes," p. 442).

Spondee A metrical foot made up of two stressed syllables (´´), with no unstressed syllables. Spondees could not, of course, be the predominant foot in a poem; they are usually substituted for iambic or trochaic feet as a way of increasing emphasis, as in this line from John Donne's "Batter my heart, three-personed God," (p. 384): "As yet | but knock, | breathe, shine, | and seek | to mend."

Sprung rhythm See **accentual meter**.

Stage business Minor physical activity performed by actors on stage, often involving **props**, intended to strengthen **characterization** or modulate tension in a play.

Stage directions Written instructions in the script telling actors how to move on the stage or how to deliver a particular line. To facilitate the reading of scripts and to distinguish them from simple dialogue, stage directions are interspersed throughout the text, typically placed in parentheses and set in italics.

Stage left, stage right Areas of the stage seen from the point of view of an actor facing an audience. Stage left, therefore, is on the audience's right-hand side, and vice versa.

Stanza   A grouping of poetic lines into a section, either according to form—each section having the same number of lines and the same prosody (see Percy Bysshe Shelley's "Ode to the West Wind," p. 438)—or according to thought, creating irregular units comparable to paragraphs in prose (see William Wordsworth's "Ode: Intimations of Immortality," p. 428).

Stichomythia   Short lines of dialogue quickly alternating between two characters.

Stock character   Any of a number of traditional characters easily identified by a single, stereotypical characteristic. Stock characters include innocent young women, rakish young men, clever servants, and so forth.

Stress   See **accent**.

Strophe   The first part of a choral **ode** in Greek drama. The strophe was traditionally sung as the **chorus** moved from **stage left** to **stage right**.

Structuralism   Based on the work of anthropologists, linguists, and philosophers of the mid-twentieth century who sought to understand how humans think and communicate, structuralism is concerned with the cognitive and cultural structures that help us to understand and interpret literary texts. The basic insight at the heart of the movement is the realization that we understand nothing in isolation, but rather every piece of knowledge is part of a network of associations.

Structure   (1) The framework—the general plan, outline, or organizational pattern—of a literary work; (2) narrower patterns within the overall framework. Cf. **form**.

Style   One of the elements of fiction, style refers to the diction (choice of words), syntax (arrangement of words), and other linguistic features of a literary work. Just as no two people have identical fingerprints or voices, so no two writers use words in exactly the same way. Style distinguishes one writer's language from another's. Faulkner and Hemingway, two major modern writers, had very different styles, as the opening paragraphs of their stories show: Two noticeable differences have to do with interior or exterior focus and sentence length. Faulkner (p. 161) writes a long, complex second sentence to represent the thinking of the boy; Hemingway (p. 176) writes a series of short, almost telegraphic, sentences about an old man sitting and drinking in the shadow of a tree at a café late at night, with two waiters watching him.

Subplot   A secondary **plot** that exists in addition to the main plot and involves the minor characters. In **tragedy**, particularly, a subplot might provide **comic relief**.

Substitution   The use of a different kind of foot in place of the one normally demanded by the predominant meter of a poem, as a way of adding variety, emphasizing the dominant foot by deviating from it, speeding up or slowing down the pace, or signaling a switch in meaning.

Subtext   The unspoken meaning, sense, or **motivation** of a scene or character.

Surrealism   An artistic movement that attempted to portray or interpret the workings of the unconscious mind, especially as realized in dreams, by an irrational, noncontextual choice and arrangement of images or objects. Now more often used to refer to anything defying the normal sense of reality.

Syllabic verse A metrical pattern in which all lines in a poem have the same number of syllables (as in Sylvia Plath's "Metaphors," p. 602) or all the first lines of its stanzas have the same number, all second lines the same, and so on (see Dylan Thomas's "Fern Hill," p. 555)—while the stressed syllables are random in number and placement.

Symbol Something that is itself and also stands for something else; a literary symbol is a prominent or repeated image or action that is present in a poem (or story or play) and can be seen, touched, smelled, heard, tasted, or experienced imaginatively but also conveys a cluster of abstract meanings beyond itself. An **archetype**, or archetypal symbol, is a symbol whose associations are said to be universal, that is, they extend beyond the locale of a particular nation or culture. Religious symbols, such as the cross, are of this kind. The wallpaper in Gilman's "The Yellow Wallpaper" and the tiger in Blake's "The Tyger" are symbols. In literature, **symbolism** refers to an author's use of symbols.

Symbolism A device whereby an object or event suggests meaning beyond its immediate, physical presence. Symbolism exists in all genres of literature, but in drama it might include visual or sound elements as well as language.

Synecdoche A special kind of **metonymy** in which a part of a thing is substituted for the whole, as in the commonly used phrases "give me a hand," "lend me your ears," or "many mouths to feed." See, for example, "whose *hands* shipwreck vases" and

"For should your *hands* drop white and empty" (John Frederick Nims's "Love Poem," p. 551).

Synesthesia Description of one kind of sense experience in relation to another, such as attribution of color to sounds ("blue notes") and vice versa ("a loud tie") or of taste to sounds ("sweet music"). See, for example, "With   Blue—uncertain   stumbling Buzz—" (Emily Dickinson's "I heard a Fly buzz—when I died," p. 489).

Tercet A stanza of three lines, each usually ending with the same rhyme; but see **terza rima**. Cf. **triplet**.

Terza rima A poetic form consisting of three-line stanzas (tercets) with interlinked rhymes, *aba bcb cdc ded efe*, etc., made famous by Dante's use of it in *The Divine Comedy*. Terza rima is used in Percy Bysshe Shelley's "Ode to the West Wind" (p. 438).

Tetrameter A poetic line with four metrical feet. Robert Frost's line "The woods are lovely, dark, and deep" ("Stopping by Woods on a Snowy Evening," p. 511) is an example of iambic tetrameter.

Text Traditionally, a piece of writing. In recent reader-response criticism, "text" has come to mean the words with which the reader interacts; in this view, a poem is not an object, not a shape on the page or a spoken performance, but what is completed in the reader's mind.

Theater in the round A circular stage completely surrounded by seating for the audience.

Theater of the absurd/of cruelty See **Absurd, theater of the; Cruelty, theater of.**

Theme   The central idea embodied by or explored in a literary work; the general concept, explicit or implied, that the work incorporates and makes persuasive to the reader. Other literary elements, including characters, plot, settings, point of view, figurative language, symbols, and style, contribute to a theme's development.

Third-person narrator   The type of narration being used if a storyteller is not identified, does not speak of himself or herself with the pronoun "I," asserts no connection between the narrator and the characters in the story, and tells the story with some objectivity and distance, using the pronouns *he, she, it,* and *they*—but not *I.* Hemingway and Welty chose third-person narration to tell the moving stories of the old man in "A Clean, Well-Lighted Place" (p. 176) and of Old Phoenix in "A Worn Path" (p. 189), respectively, because as writers they wanted distance.

Title   The name attached to a work of literature. For poetry, a title in some cases is an integral part of a poem and needs to be considered in interpreting it; see, for example, George Herbert's "The Pulley" (p. 387). In other cases a title has been added as a means of identifying a poem and is not integral to its interpretation. Sometimes a poem is untitled and the first line is used as a convenient way of referring to it, but should not be thought of as a title and does not follow the capitalization rules for titles.

Tone   The implied attitude, or "stance," toward the subject and toward the reader or audience in a literary work; the "tone of voice" it seems to project (serious or playful; exaggerated or understated; formal or informal; ironic or straightforward; or a complex mixture of more than one of these). For example, the tone of Bambara's "The Lesson" is streetwise and tough, the voice of its first-person narrator.

Tragedy   A play in which the **plot** moves from relative stability to death or other serious sorrow for the **protagonist**. A traditional tragedy is written in a grand style and shows a **hero** of high social stature brought down by **peripeteia** or by events beyond his or her control.

Tragicomedy   A play in which **tragedy** and **comedy** are mingled in roughly equal proportion.

Transferred epithet   A figure of speech in which a modifier that ought, strictly, to apply to one word is transferred to another word that it does not strictly fit. In "The drunk clambering on his undulant floor" (in John Frederick Nims's "Love Poem," p. 551), the drunk's perception, not the floor, is undulating.

Trimeter   A poetic line with three metrical feet.

Triplet   A group of three consecutive lines with the same rhyme, often used for variation in a long sequence of couplets. Cf. **tercet.**

Trochee   A metrical foot consisting of two syllables, an accented one followed by an unaccented one (˜). In trochaic meter, trochees are the predominant foot in a line or poem. The following lines from William Blake's introduction to *Songs of Innocence* are in trochaic meter (each line lacking the final unaccented syllable): "Piping | down the | valleys | wild, / Piping | Songs of | pleasant | glee, / On a | cloud I | saw a | child, / And he | laughing | said to | me."

Understatement   A figure of speech expressing something in an unexpectedly restrained way. Paradoxically, understatement can be a way of emphasizing something, of making people think "there must be more to it than that." When Mercutio in *Romeo and Juliet*, after being stabbed by Tybalt, calls his wound "a scratch, a scratch" (3.1.92), he is understating, for the wound is serious—he calls for a doctor in the next line, and he dies a few minutes later.

Unities   The elements of a play that help an audience to understand the play as a unified whole. Aristotle commented on the unities of time (the action of a play usually takes place within approximately one day) and action (the play should have a single, principal plot line). Renaissance critics added a third unity—unity of place (the play has only one main setting). Though Aristotle intended these merely as observations about the most successful dramas he had seen, some later playwrights took them as inflexible laws of drama.

Unity   The oneness of a short story. Generally, each of a story's elements has a unity of its own, and all reinforce one another to create an overall unity. Although a story's unity may be evident on first reading, more often discovering the unity requires rereading, reflection, and analysis. Readers who engage in these actions experience the pleasure of seeing a story come to life.

Upstage   As an adjective, the part of the stage farthest from the audience, at the back of the playing area. As a verb, to draw the audience's attention away from another actor on stage.

Verbal irony   A figure of speech in which what is said is nearly the opposite of what is meant (such as saying "Lovely day out" when the weather actually is miserable). See Stephen Crane's "Do not weep, maiden, for war is kind" (p. 506).

Villanelle   A nineteen-line lyric poem divided into five tercets and a final four-line stanza, rhyming *aba aba aba aba aba abaa*. Line 1 is repeated to form lines 6, 12, and 18; line 3 is repeated to form lines 9, 15, and 19. See Elizabeth Bishop's "One Art" (p. 550), and Dylan Thomas's "Do not go gentle into that good night" (p. 556).

Voice   The supposed authorial presence in poems that do not obviously employ persona as a distancing device.

Well-made play   A type of play that rose to prominence in the nineteenth century and that relied for its effect on clever, causal plotting and a series of startling discoveries or revelations rather than on subtleties of character or language.

1457

Jane Hirshfield, "The Stone of Heaven" from *The October Palace.* Copyright © 1994 by Jane Hirshfield. Reprinted by permission of HarperCollins Publishers Inc.

Linda Hogan, "The History of Red" from *The Book of Medicines.* Copyright © 1993 by Linda Hogan. Reprinted with the permission of Coffee House Press, Minneapolis, Minnesota.

Garrett Kaoru Hongo, "Yellow Light" from *Yellow Light.* Copyright © 1982 by Garrett Kaoru Hongo. Reprinted by permission of Wesleyan University Press.

Susan Howe, excerpt from "Speeches at the Barriers" from *Europe of Trusts.* Copyright © 1990 by Susan Howe. Reprinted by permission of New Directions Publishing Corp.

Langston Hughes, "Harlem" and "The Negro Speaks of Rivers" from *The Collected Poems of Langston Hughes.* Copyright © 1994 by The Estate of Langston Hughes. Used by permission of Alfred A. Knopf, a division of Random House, Inc.

Henrik Ibsen, "A Doll House" from *The Complete Major Prose Plays of Henrik Ibsen,* translated by Rolf Fjelde. Translation copyright © 1965, 1970, 1978 by Rolf Fjelde. Used by permission of Dutton Signet, a division of Penguin Group (USA) Inc.

Shirley Jackson, "The Lottery" from *The Lottery.* Copyright © 1948, 1949 by Shirley Jackson and renewed 1976, 1977 by Laurence Hyman, Barry Hyman, Mrs. Sarah Webster, and Mrs. Joanne Schnurer. Reprinted by permission of Farrar, Straus and Giroux, LLC.

Randall Jarrell, "The Woman at the Washington Zoo" from *The Complete Poems.* Copyright © 1969 and renewed 1997 by Mary von S. Jarrell. Reprinted by permission of Farrar, Straus and Giroux, LLC.

Robinson Jeffers, "Hurt Hawks." Copyright © 1928 and renewed 1956 by Robinson Jeffers. From *The Selected Poetry of Robinson Jeffers.* Used by permission of Random House, Inc.

Richard Jones, "Cathedral" from *The Blessing: New and Selected Poems.* Copyright © 2000 by Richard Jones. Reprinted with the permission of Copper Canyon Press, P.O. Box 271, Port Townsend, WA 98368-0271.

Allison Joseph, "On Being Told I Don't Speak Like a Black Person." Copyright © 1999 by Allison Joseph. First appeared in *Many Mountains Moving.* Reprinted in *Imitation of Life,* Carnegie Mellon University Press, 2003. Reprinted by permission of the author.

James Joyce, "Araby" from *Dubliners.* Copyright © 1916 by B. W. Heubsch. Definitive text copyright © 1967 by the Estate of James Joyce. Used by permission of Viking Penguin, a division of Penguin Group (USA) Inc.

Franz Kafka, "The Metamorphosis" from *Franz Kafka: The Complete Stories,* edited by Nahum N. Glatzer, translated by Willa and Edwin Muir. Copyright 1946, 1947, 1948, 1949, 1954, 1958, 1971 by Schocken Books. Used by permission of Schocken Books, a division of Random House, Inc.

Jane Kenyon, "From Room to Room" from *From Room to Room.* Copyright © 1978 by Jane Kenyon. Reprinted with the permission of Alice James Books.

Jamaica Kincaid, "Girl" from *At the Bottom of the River.* Copyright © 1983 by Jamaica Kincaid. Reprinted by permission of Farrar, Straus and Giroux, LLC.

Galway Kinnell, "The Bear" from *Body Rags.* Copyright © 1965, 1966, 1967 by Galway Kinnell. Reprinted by permission of Houghton Mifflin Company. All rights reserved.

Etheridge Knight, "Hard Rock Returns to Prison from the Hospital for the Criminal Insane" from *The Essential Etheridge Knight.* Copyright © 1986. Reprinted by permission of the University of Pittsburgh Press.

Kenneth Koch, "The History of Jazz." Copyright © 1962 by Kenneth Koch. Reprinted with permission of the Kenneth Koch Literary Estate.

Yusef Komunyakaa, "Facing It" from *Neon Vernacular.* Copyright © 1993 by Yusef Komunyakaa. Reprinted by permission of Wesleyan University Press.

Maxine Kumin, "The Excrement Poem." Copyright © 1978 by Maxine Kumin. From *Selected Poems 1960–1990.* Used by permission of W. W. Norton & Company, Inc.

Stanley Kunitz, "Father and Son" from *The Collected Poems.* Copyright © 2000 by Stanley Kunitz. Used by permission of W. W. Norton & Company, Inc.

Philip Larkin, "High Windows" from *Collected Poems.* Copyright © 1988, 1989 by the Estate of Philip Larkin. Reprinted by permission of Farrar, Straus and Giroux, LLC and Faber & Faber.

D. H. Lawrence, "The Rocking-Horse Winner." Copyright © 1933 by the Estate of D. H. Lawrence and renewed © 1961 by Angelo Ravagli and C. M. Weekley, Executors of the Estate of Frieda Lawrence. From *The Complete Short Stories of D. H. Lawrence.* Used by permission of Viking Penguin, a division of Penguin Group (USA) Inc.

Li-Young Lee, "Eating Alone" from *Rose.* Copyright © 1986 by Li-Young Lee. Reprinted with the permission of BOA Editions, Ltd.

Denise Levertov, "February Evening in New York" from *Collected Earlier Poems, 1940–1960.* Copyright © 1960, 1979 by Denise Levertov. Reprinted by permission of New Directions Publishing Corp.

Philip Levine, "What Work Is" from *What Work Is.* Copyright © 1992 by Philip Levine. Used by permission of Alfred A. Knopf, a division of Random House, Inc.

Larry Levis, "The Poem You Asked For" from *Wrecking Crew.* Copyright © 1972. Reprinted by permission of the University of Pittsburgh Press.

Timothy Liu, "Thoreau" from *Burnt Offerings.* Copyright © 1995 by Timothy Liu. Reprinted with the permission of Copper Canyon Press, P.O. Box 271, Port Townsend, WA 98368-0271.

Audre Lorde, "Coal" from *Undersong: Chosen Poems Old and New.* Copyright © 1973, 1970, 1968 by Audre Lorde. Used by permission of W. W. Norton & Company, Inc.

Robert Lowell, "Skunk Hour" from *Selected Poems.* Copyright © 1976 by Robert Lowell. Reprinted by permission of Farrar, Straus and Giroux, LLC.

Heather McHugh, "What He Thought" from *Hinge & Sign: Poems, 1968–1993.* Copyright © 1994 by Heather McHugh. Reprinted by permission of Wesleyan University Press.

James Merrill, "The Pier: Under Pisces" from *Collected Poems,* edited by J. D. McClatchy and Stephen Yenser. Copyright © 2001 by the Literary Estate of James Merrill at Washington University. Used by permission of Alfred A. Knopf, a division of Random House, Inc.

W. S. Merwin, "Yesterday" from *Opening the Hand.* Copyright © 1983 by W. S. Merwin. Reprinted with permission of The Wylie Agency, Inc.

Arthur Miller, *Death of a Salesman.* Copyright © 1949 and renewed © 1977 by Arthur Miller. Used by permission of Viking Penguin, a division of Penguin Group (USA) Inc.

Robert Morgan, "Mountain Bride" from *Groundwork.* Copyright © 1979. Reprinted by permission of Gnomon Press.

Thylias Moss, "Tornados" from *Rainbow Remnants in Rock Bottom Ghetto Sky.* Copyright © 1993 by Thylias Moss. Reprinted by permission of Persea Books, Inc., New York.

Bharati Mukherjee, "The Management of Grief" from *The Middleman and Other Stories.* Copyright © 1988 by Bharati Mukherjee. Used by permission of Grove/Atlantic, Inc. and Penguin Group (Canada).

David Mura, "Grandfather-in-Law" from *After We Lost Our Way.* Copyright © 1989 by David Mura. Reprinted by permission of the author.

Henry Reed, "Lessons of War (1. Naming of Parts)" from *Henry Reed: Collected Poems*, edited by Jon Stallworthy. Copyright © 1991 by the Executor of Henry Reed's Estate. Reprinted by permission of Oxford University Press.

Adrienne Rich, "Diving into the Wreck." Copyright © 2002 by Adrienne Rich and copyright © 1973 by W. W. Norton & Company, Inc. From *The Fact of a Doorframe: Selected Poems, 1950–2001*. Used by permission of the author and W. W. Norton & Company, Inc.

Alberto Ríos, "Nani" from *Whispering to Fool the Wind*. Copyright © 1982 by Alberto Ríos. Reprinted by permission of the author.

Theodore Roethke, "My Papa's Waltz." Copyright © 1942 by Hearst Magazines, Inc. From *Collected Poems of Theodore Roethke*. Used by permission of Doubleday, a division of Random House, Inc.

Sonia Sanchez, "An Anthem" from *Under a Soprano Sky*. Copyright © 1987 by Sonia Sanchez. Reprinted with the permission of Africa World Press, Trenton, New Jersey.

Anne Sexton, "Cinderella" from *Transformations*. Copyright © 1971 by Anne Sexton. Reprinted by permission of Houghton Mifflin Company. All rights reserved.

William Shakespeare, *Hamlet, Prince of Denmark*. Footnotes from *Hamlet* from *The Complete Works of Shakespeare*, Fourth Edition, by David Bevington. Copyright © 1992 by HarperCollins Publishers. Reprinted by permission of Pearson Education, Inc.

Leslie Marmon Silko, "Prayer to the Pacific" from *Storyteller*. Copyright © 1981 by Leslie Marmon Silko. Published by Seaver Books, New York, New York. Reprinted by permission of the publisher.

Charles Simic, "Begotten of the Spleen" from *Charles Simic: Selected Early Poems*. Copyright © 1999 by Charles Simic. Reprinted by permission of George Braziller, Inc.

Edith Sitwell, "Lullaby" from *The Collected Poems of Edith Sitwell*. Copyright © 1968 by Edith Sitwell. Reprinted by permission of David Higham Associates.

Gary Snyder, "Hitch Haiku" from *The Back Country*. Copyright © 1968 by Gary Snyder. Reprinted by permission of New Directions Publishing Corp.

Cathy Song, "Girl Powdering Her Neck" from *Picture Bride*. Copyright © 1983 by Yale University Press. Reprinted by permission of Yale University Press.

Sophocles, *The Oedipus Rex of Sophocles: An English Version* by Dudley Fitts and Robert Fitzgerald. Copyright 1949 by Harcourt, Inc. and renewed 1977 by Cornelia Fitts and Robert Fitzgerald. Reprinted by permission of the publisher. CAUTION: All rights, including professional, amateur, motion picture, recitation, lecturing, performance, public reading, radio broadcasting, and television are strictly reserved. Inquiries on all rights should be addressed to Harcourt, Inc., Permissions Department, Orlando, FL 32887-6777.

Gary Soto, "The Elements of San Joaquin" from *New and Selected Poems*. Copyright © 1995. Used with permission of Chronicle Books LLC, San Francisco. Visit <www.chroniclebooks.com>.

William Stafford, "Traveling Through the Dark" from *The Way It Is: New & Selected Poems*. Copyright © 1962, 1998 by the Estate of William Stafford. Reprinted with the permission of Graywolf Press, Saint Paul, Minnesota.

John Steinbeck, "The Chrysanthemums." Copyright 1937 and renewed © 1965 by John Steinbeck. From *The Long Valley*. Used by permission of Viking Penguin, a division of Penguin Group (USA) Inc.

Gerald Stern, "Cow Worship" from *This Time: New and Selected Poems*. Copyright © 1998 by Gerald Stern. Used by permission of W. W. Norton & Company, Inc.

Wallace Stevens, "Disillusionment of Ten O'Clock," "The Emperor of Ice Cream," and "Sunday Morning" from *The Collected Poems of Wallace Stevens*. Copyright 1954 by

Wallace Stevens and renewed 1982 by Holly Stevens. Used by permission of Alfred A. Knopf, a division of Random House, Inc.

Virgil Suárez, "The Ways of Guilt" from *Spared Angola: Memories of a Cuban-American Childhood.* Copyright © 1997 by Arte Público Press, University of Houston. Reprinted with permission from the publisher.

Sekou Sundiata, "Blink Your Eyes." Copyright © 1995 by Sekou Sundiata. Reprinted by permission of the author.

Amy Tan, "Two Kinds" from *The Joy Luck Club.* Copyright © 1989 by Amy Tan. Used by permission of G.P. Putnam's Sons, a division of Penguin Group (USA) Inc.

James Tate, "The Wheelchair Butterfly" from *Selected Poems.* Copyright © 1991 by James Tate. Reprinted by permission of the author.

Dylan Thomas, "Do not go gentle into that good night" and "Fern Hill" from *The Poems of Dylan Thomas.* Copyright © 1952 by Dylan Thomas. Reprinted by permission of New Directions Publishing Corp. and David Higham Associates Limited.

Jean Toomer, "Reapers" from *Cane.* Copyright 1923 by Boni & Liveright and renewed 1951 by Jean Toomer. Used by permission of Liveright Publishing Corporation.

Quincy Troupe, "Snake-Back Solo 2" from *Avalanche.* Copyright © 1996 by Quincy Troupe. Reprinted by permission of the author.

John Updike, "A & P" from *Pigeon Feathers and Other Stories.* Copyright © 1962 and renewed 1990 by John Updike. Used by permission of Alfred A. Knopf, a division of Random House, Inc.

Jean Valentine, "December 21st" from *The Messenger.* Copyright © 1979 by Jean Valentine. Reprinted by permission of the author.

Ellen Bryant Voigt, "Woman Who Weeps" from *Two Trees.* Copyright © 1992 by Ellen Bryant Voigt. Used by permission of W. W. Norton & Company, Inc.

Derek Walcott, "Sea Grapes" from *Collected Poems, 1948–1984.* Copyright © 1986 by Derek Walcott. Reprinted by permission of Farrar, Straus and Giroux, LLC.

Anne Waldman, "Makeup on Empty Space" from *Helping the Dreamer: New and Selected Poems, 1966–1988.* Copyright © 1989 by Anne Waldman. Reprinted with the permission of Coffee House Press.

Alice Walker, "Everyday Use" from *In Love and Trouble: Stories of Black Women.* Copyright © 1973 by Alice Walker. Reprinted by permission of Harcourt, Inc.

James Welch, "Christmas Comes to Moccasin Flat" from *Riding the Earthboy 40.* Copyright © 1971 by James Welch. Reprinted by permission of the Elaine Markson Literary Agency, Inc.

Eudora Welty, "A Worn Path" from *A Curtain of Green and Other Stories.* Copyright 1941 and renewed 1969 by Eudora Welty. Reprinted by permission of Harcourt, Inc.

Richard Wilbur, "Love Calls Us to the Things of This World" from *Things of This World.* Copyright © 1956 and renewed 1984 by Richard Wilbur. Reprinted by permission of Harcourt, Inc.

Nancy Willard, "Questions My Son Asked Me, Answers I Never Gave Him" from *Household Tales of Moon and Water.* Copyright © 1978 by Nancy Willard. Reprinted by permission of Harcourt, Inc.

Tennessee Williams, *The Glass Menagerie.* Copyright 1945 by Tennesse Williams and Edwina D. Williams and renewed 1973 by Tennessee Williams. Used by permission of Random House, Inc.

William Carlos Williams, "Spring and All, Section I" "The Red Wheelbarrow," and "This Is Just to Say" from *Collected Poems: 1909–1939, Volume I.* Copyright © 1938 by New Directions Publishing Corp. Reprinted by New Directions Publishing Corp.

August Wilson, *The Piano Lesson.* Copyright © 1988, 1990 by August Wilson. Used by permission of Dutton Signet, a division of Penguin Group (USA) Inc.

Nellie Wong, "Grandmother's Song" from *Dreams in Harrison Railroad Park*. Copyright © 1977 by Nellie Wong. Reprinted by permission of the author.

Charles Wright, "March Journal" from *The World of Ten Thousand Things: Poems, 1980–1990*. Copyright © 1990 by Charles Wright. Reprinted by permission of Farrar, Straus and Giroux, LLC.

James Wright, "A Blessing" from *The Branch Will Not Break*. Copyright © 1961 by James Wright. Reprinted by permission of Wesleyan University Press.

John Yau, "Chinese Villanelle" from *Radiant Silhouette: New and Selected Work, 1974–1988*. Copyright © 1989 by John Yau. Reprinted by permission of the author.

William Butler Yeats, "The Second Coming." Copyright © 1924 by The Macmillan Company and renewed © 1952 by Bertha Georgie Yeats. "Among School Children," "Leda and the Swan," and "Sailing to Byzantium." Copyright © 1928 by The Macmillan Company and renewed © 1956 by Bertha Georgie Yeats. All poems from *The Collected Poems of W. B. Yeats, Volume 1: The Poems, Revised*, edited by Richard J. Finneran. Reprinted with the permission of Scribner, an imprint of Simon & Schuster Adult Publishing Group.

Al Young, "A Dance for Ma Rainey." Copyright © 1969, 1992 by Al Young. Reprinted with permission of the author.

David Young, "The Portable Earth-Lamp" from *The Planet on the Desk: Selected and New Poems, 1960–1990*. Copyright © 1991 by David Young. Reprinted by permission of Wesleyan University Press.

Ray A. Young Bear, "From the Spotted Night" from *The Invisible Musician*. Copyright © 1990 by Ray A. Young Bear. Reprinted by permission of Holy Cow! Press.

Paul Zimmer, "Zimmer Imagines Heaven" from *Family Reunion: Selected and New Poems*. Copyright © 1983. Reprinted by permission of the University of Pittsburgh Press.

Louis Zukofsky, excerpt from "A." Copyright © 1993 by Louis Zukofsky. Reprinted with permission of The Johns Hopkins University Press.

Index of Authors, Titles, and First Lines